THE OXFORD HANDBOOK OF

DANISH POLITICS

THE OXFORD HANDBOOK OF

DANISH POLITICS

Edited by

PETER MUNK CHRISTIANSEN, JØRGEN ELKLIT,

and

PETER NEDERGAARD

OXFORD

UNIVERSITY PRESS

UNIVERSITY PRESS

Great Clarendon Street, Oxford, OX2 6DP,
United Kingdom

Oxford University Press is a department of the University of Oxford.
It furthers the University's objective of excellence in research, scholarship,
and education by publishing worldwide. Oxford is a registered trade mark of
Oxford University Press in the UK and in certain other countries

Published in the United States of America by Oxford University Press
198 Madison Avenue, New York, NY 10016, United States of America

British Library Cataloguing in Publication Data

Data available

Library of Congress Control Number: 2020937356

ISBN 978-0-19-883359-8

Printed and bound by
CPI Group (UK) Ltd, Croydon, CR0 4YY

Contents

PART II. POLITICS
SECTION EDITOR: PETER MUNK CHRISTIANSEN

PART III. POLICIES

Section Editor: Peter Nedergaard

PART IV. POSTSCRIPT

List of Contributors

Kaare Aagaard Senior Researcher, Department of Political Science, Aarhus University

Peder Andersen Professor Emeritus, Department of Food and Resource Economics, University of Copenhagen

Torben M. Andersen Professor, Department of Economics and Business Economics, Aarhus University

Derek Beach Professor, Department of Political Science, Aarhus University

Anne Skorkjær Binderkrantz Professor, Department of Political Science, Aarhus University

Jens Peter Christensen Supreme Court Justice

Flemming Juul Christiansen Associate Professor, Department of Social Sciences and Business, Roskilde University

Peter Munk Christiansen Professor, Department of Political Science, Aarhus University

Carsten Daugbjerg Professor, Department of Food and Resource Economics, University of Copenhagen

Peter Thisted Dinesen Professor, Department of Political Science, University of Copenhagen

Niels Ejersbo Deputy Director, University College Copenhagen

Jørgen Elklit Professor Emeritus, Department of Political Science, Aarhus University

Christina Fiig Associate Professor, School of Culture and Society, Aarhus University

Ulrik Pram Gad Associate Professor, Department of Culture and Learning, Aalborg University

Christoffer Green-Pedersen Professor, Department of Political Science, Aarhus University

Caroline Howard Grøn Associate Professor, Department of Political Science, Aarhus University

Henning Otte Hansen Senior Adviser, Department of Food and Resource Economics, University of Copenhagen

Kasper M. Hansen Professor, Department of Political Science, University of Copenhagen

Martin Ejnar Hansen Senior Lecturer, Department of Social and Political Sciences, Brunel University London

Gitte Sommer Harrits Vice Rector Academic, VIA University College

Laust Høgedahl Associate Professor, Department of Politics and Society, Aalborg University

Kurt Houlberg Professor, The Danish Center for Social Science Research

Brian H. Jacobsen Associate Professor, Department of Food and Resource Economics, University of Copenhagen

Mads Dagnis Jensen Associate Professor, Department of International Economics, Government and Business, Copenhagen Business School

Mette Frisk Jensen Senior Advisor, School of Culture and Society, Aarhus University

Anne Mette Kjær Professor, Department of Political Science, Aarhus University

Ulrik Kjær Professor, Department of Political Science and Public Management, University of Southern Denmark

Ann-Kristin Kölln Associate Professor, Department of Political Science, Aarhus University

Karina Kosiara-Pedersen Associate Professor, Department of Political Science, University of Copenhagen

Henrik Larsen Professor, Department of Political Science, University of Copenhagen

Lars Thorup Larsen Associate Professor, Department of Political Science, Aarhus University

Rasmus Mariager Associate Professor, The SAXO-Institute, University of Copenhagen

Niels Mejlgaard Professor, Department of Political Science, Aarhus University

Jes Fabricius Møller Associate Professor, The SAXO-Institute, University of Copenhagen

Peter Nedergaard Professor, Department of Political Science, University of Copenhagen

Niels Wium Olesen Associate Professor, Department of History and Classical Studies, Aarhus University

Thomas Olesen Professor, Department of Political Science, Aarhus University

Helene Helboe Pedersen Professor, Department of Political Science, Aarhus University

Klaus Petersen Professor, Danish Centre for Welfare Studies & Danish Institute of Advanced Studies, University of Southern Denmark

Heidi Houlberg Salomonsen Associate Professor, Department of Management, Aarhus University

Henrik Bech Seeberg Associate Professor, Department of Political Science, Aarhus University

Birte Siim Professor Emeritus, Department of Politics and Society, Aalborg University

Kristina Bakkær Simonsen Associate Professor, Department of Political Science, Aarhus University

Asbjørn Skjæveland Associate Professor, Department of Political Science, Aarhus University

Rune Slothuus Professor, Department of Political Science, Aarhus University

Peter Birch Sørensen Professor, Department of Economics, University of Copenhagen

Rune Stubager Professor, Department of Political Science, Aarhus University

Gert Tinggaard Svendsen Professor, Department of Political Science, Aarhus University

Susanne Wiborg Reader, Institute of Education, University College London

Anders Wivel Professor, Department of Political Science, University of Copenhagen

PREFACE

FOR a considerable while, there has been a need for an up-to-date English-language book on Danish politics and Danish political institutions. Such a book should aim at meeting the needs of both established researchers and students abroad—and in Denmark—and hopefully also the general public.

A project to this effect materialized when Peter Nedergaard in 2017 suggested to Peter Munk Christiansen that the time was ripe for a Handbook of Danish Politics. Jørgen Elklit joined the editorial team subsequent to that.

Oxford University Press immediately responded very positively to our book proposal, and the reviewers' comments were very encouraging. We would like to thank Dominic Byatt from Oxford University Press for his speedy and constructive handling of our project from beginning to end.

The book idea also met positive responses when we approached potential authors. We even had requests from well-qualified academics to be part of the book project when the rumours about our plans spread in the relevant circles. We accepted a few of these requests. We thank all authors for their contributions and for productive deliberations during the editorial process.

Many of the early chapter drafts were reviewed and debated at the Annual Meeting of the Danish Political Science Association at Hotel Vejlefjord in October 2018. We thank the organizers for making room for us at the meeting. Several of the chapters benefitted substantially from this early presentation and discussion.

Many of the authors have also received various kinds of help and advice from colleagues, civil servants in the ministries, the Danish Parliament, from organisations, and so on. This is much appreciated, and the book has certainly benefitted from such help and advice.

In the final scrutiny of chapter manuscripts, Natasha Elizabeth Perera and Mette Aagaard, Department of Political Science, Aarhus University, were instrumental in ensuring that manuscripts were completed in a satisfactory way. This involved improvement of authors' written English, general sub-editing, control of references, and indexing. We are grateful as well as very impressed by Natasha's and Mette's professionalism and efficiency. We would also like to thank Rob Wilkinson for copy-editing the entire book.

We are also grateful for the funding and support for language editing, and so on, from the departments of political science at the University of Copenhagen and Aarhus University.

We hope that *The Oxford Handbook on Danish Politics* has become what we from the outset intended it to be—namely a scholarly book about most aspects of Danish politics that is also accessible to the general public.

Peter Munk Christiansen, Jørgen Elklit, and Peter Nedergaard

LIST OF FIGURES

LIST OF TABLES

CHAPTER 1

....

WHY A BOOK ON
DANISH POLITICS?

....

PETER MUNK CHRISTIANSEN, JØRGEN ELKLIT,
AND PETER NEDERGAARD

THE purpose of this handbook is to take stock of what we in the social science community know about Danish politics in recent years. We have invited authors with a track record of fine publications in relevant areas on Danish politics in order to thoroughly and critically scrutinize a large number of aspects of Danish politics. In terms of disciplinary coverage, political science is obviously well represented among the authors. However, a project of this kind must also take into account contributions from other disciplines and fields, and we have invited contributors from economics, law, history, and educational science, as well as from disciplines close to mainstream political science such as political economy and political sociology.

Why a handbook on Danish politics? On the one hand, Denmark shares important features with other smaller—Denmark has 5.8 million inhabitants—countries in North-Western Europe such as having a parliamentarian democracy, a PR electoral system, a multiparty system, a high level of public spending, a relatively stable party system, relatively strong interest groups, and a monarch with nothing but ceremonial functions. Denmark is also an EU and NATO member. Like most other countries in this group, Denmark runs a quite well-functioning welfare state, and the standard of living is high, as documented in all international comparisons.

In particular, Denmark shares characteristics with the two other Scandinavian countries, Norway and Sweden, such as a relatively strong Social Democratic party, a generous and universal welfare state, a long and strong corporatist heritage, and high levels of general and political trust.

On the other hand, Denmark also turns out to be different in some aspects, i.e. to deviate on some dimensions when compared to comparable countries like Norway, Sweden, Iceland, Finland, the Netherlands, Belgium, Austria, and Switzerland—and sometimes even Germany, the United Kingdom, New Zealand, and Canada.

We shortly discuss some of these features below: a world record in minority governments and yet a stable political system; a party system that in some aspects deviate from that of similar countries; continued reservations towards the EU despite close to 50 years of EC/EU membership; a remarkable balance between tolerance and liberalism on the one hand and what is sometimes perceived as xenophobic policies on the other; a high degree of flexibility on the labour market as far as hiring and firing is concerned, which is even supported by both employers and trade unions; an activist foreign policy—including military means—taking place in both peace-keeping and active warfare; equality of the sexes through early female employment and generous day care on the one hand and lack of a proactive gender policy on the other; and finally, the largest local and regional government sector in the world.

Generally, the authors have tried to cover both when they—through their scholarly glasses—see that something is rotten in the state of Denmark (William Shakespeare in *Hamlet*) and when Denmark is punching above its weight (Barack Obama during a visit from the Danish PM in 2011).

Denmark has been characterized by extreme minority parliamentarism since the 1950s and actually holds a world record in minority governments. Denmark has not had a majority party in Parliament since 1909, and since 1960, it has only had majority (coalition) governments in 1968–71 and 1993–4. This implies that the political parties have developed ways of creating legislative majorities and avoiding parliamentary majorities willing to terminate the lives of the incumbent governments. Negative parliamentarism, i.e. that the government must not have a majority against it in parliament (but it does not need an explicit majority), is one instrument that has proved useful on many occasions. Another instrument is the use of settlements on policy issues between the incumbent government and different and changing sets of opposition parties. The number of parties in Parliament—oftentimes more than six, and no less that ten after the 2019 general election—which to some degree is caused by the electoral system being a system of proportional representation with a low effective threshold, does not create obstacles for the development of a well-functioning polity in the short term. However, long-term perspectives are sometimes lost, and it is not always easy to raise accountability issues in relation to individual political parties or governments' policy outputs. Several of the chapters deal with these issues.

At the June 2019 election, parties established before 1960 received 72.2 per cent of all votes. While this hints towards stability, the Danish party system has also shown remarkable changes. An anti-establishment, populist party, the Progress Party (*Fremskridtspartiet*), entered Parliament as early as 1973 with 15.9 per cent of the vote. It developed into an anti-immigrant party. In 2001, a splinter from the party, the more centre-oriented Danish People's Party (*Dansk Folkeparti*), became a permanent support party for centre-right governments during 2001–11 and 2015–19, mainly on an anti-immigrant platform. While most European countries have experienced anti-establishment and anti-immigrant parties in recent years, Denmark deviates by experiencing this early on and through an early integration of the Danish People's Party into mainstream politics. The Danish party system also deviates from most other European countries by the absence of a Green party, but environmental issues were soon adopted by other parties.

Denmark's membership of the European Union also differs from that of other member states. Denmark became a member of the then European Community as of 1 January 1973 after a clear majority for entry at the referendum on 2 October 1972. EC membership opponents continued to voice their views on membership and EC/EU policies, and it is only more recently that a broad political acceptance of membership has prevailed. This is partly to be explained by the Danish opt-outs concerning the euro, home and justice affairs, and defence policy, which were formulated as a response to the 1992 rejection of the Maastricht Treaty in a popular referendum. The electorate has confirmed on two later occasions (2000 and 2015) that the opt-outs are to remain part and parcel of the Danish relation to the European Union. Danish citizens generally remain enthusiastic about EU membership as well as the opt-outs.

Denmark is—or used to be—known as a tolerant and liberal country. Almost all Danish Jews were saved during the Second World War due to popular, civil society, and political agency. Denmark was the first country in the world to free literate pornography (1967) and pictorial pornography (1969), and Denmark was the first country to legally accept same-sex relations in registered partnerships (1989). After the turn of the century, however, Denmark has also been associated with anti-tolerance and anti-liberal policies, particularly towards immigrants. Does this express political responses to popular opinion, or is it the result of other political dynamics?

Denmark is in the world's absolute top league when it comes to taxation, and it runs one of the biggest publicly financed service sectors in the world, which might be due to minority governments' never-ending quests for support on legislative proposals. In the late 1970s and early 1980s, the Danish economy was at the 'brink of the abyss' as expressed by a former Social Democratic minister of finance. The economy recovered during the 1980s and 1990s due to fiscal austerity and promotion of flexibility on the Danish labour market.

There may be many reasons to study Danish politics. We have mentioned some. We encourage readers to delve further into the book on their own to discover other findings in the various chapters.

STRUCTURE OF THE HANDBOOK

The Handbook of Danish Politics thus aims at providing overviews and analyses of a number of topics, patterns, and developments which together form what we term Danish politics, its background, and actual content. The thirty-nine substantial chapters, i.e. excluding this opening chapter and its concluding sister at the end of the volume, in the three sections all contain a reflection of state-of-the-art research on their respective topics, but they also present new arguments and insights, making contributions in their own right.

The three sections are:

I.   *Polity* (Chapters 2–13): how is Denmark structured as a state (e.g. political institutions, constitutional order, and power division)?

II. *Politics* (Chapters 14–27): what are the main elements of Danish politics (e.g. the role of political parties, the electorate, interest groups, and the media)?

III. *Policies* (Chapters 28–40): what are the most distinctive policies in Denmark (e.g. social policy, economic policy, labour market policy, immigration policy, and foreign policy)?

The section on polity contains chapters dealing with the political and administrative organization (or structuring) of the state. It thus provides a chapter on the Constitution (Chapter 2), and supplementing chapters on the special relationship between the three parts of the realm, Denmark, Greenland, and the Faroe Islands (Chapter 3), and the monarch (Chapter 4). The following two chapters deal with the electoral system (Chapter 5) and election turnout (Chapter 6). Then follow five chapters on important political institutions: the Parliament (Chapter 7); the government and the prime minister (Chapter 8); the central administration (Chapter 9); local and regional government (Chapter 10); and corporatism (Chapter 11). The last part of the polity section deals with corruption (Chapter 12) and the system for coordinating Danish politics with that of the EU (Chapter 13).

The section on politics includes chapters on the key actors and key policy processes in Danish politics. The first chapter gives an overview of the Danish party system (Chapter 14) followed by three chapters on different aspects of Danish political life: a chapter on minority governments (Chapter 15) followed by chapters on the role of classes (Chapter 16) and voters' public opinion in a longitudinal perspective (Chapter 17). The following four chapters are on four political parties to each of which we have decided to devote a full chapter: the Social Democratic Party (Chapter 18) and the Liberal Party (Chapter 19)—the biggest parties on each of the main political blocs—and the Danish People's Party (Chapter 20) and the Red-Green Alliance (Chapter 21). Then follows a chapter on voting behaviour (Chapter 22) and one on the role of gender in Danish politics (Chapter 23). Local elections (Chapter 24) and referendums (Chapter 25) are treated in separate chapters. The last two chapters in this section are on two other types of actors with important political roles, namely the media (Chapter 26) and interest organizations (Chapter 27).

The section on policies presents a series of chapters on important policy areas in Denmark. The first three chapters are devoted to Denmark's international relations: defence policy (Chapter 28), foreign policy (Chapter 29), Danish policies towards the EU (Chapter 30), and development policy (Chapter 31). Economic policy (Chapter 32) is a core policy in any country. As a member of the Scandinavian welfare state group, a chapter on the universal Danish welfare state (Chapter 33) is also a must. Labour market policy (Chapter 34) also shares traits with the other Scandinavian countries with its reliance on labour market flexibility as well as social security (i.e. flexicurity). The following two chapters deal with two core policy areas of the universal welfare state: education (Chapter 35) and health policies (Chapter 36). The remaining chapters in this section deal with different sectoral policies: immigration policy (Chapter 37), agricultural and fisheries policy (Chapter 38), policies on the environment, energy, and climate (Chapter 39), and research policy (Chapter 40).

The chapters in the three sections aim at reflecting the state-of-the-art research of the many different topics at the same time as they make new contributions in their own right, i.e. have a substantial argument and suggest future lines of research. As not everything can be covered in each chapter, readers might appreciate the cross-references between chapters.

The volume concludes with a chapter (41) where the editors try to assess critically what the state of Denmark is at this point in time after the general elections of June 2019 and at the beginning of the third decade of the twenty-first century.

PART I

POLITY

SECTION EDITOR: JØRGEN ELKLIT

CHAPTER 2

··

THE CONSTITUTION

··

JENS PETER CHRISTENSEN

THE CONSTITUTIONAL ACT AS THE FRAMEWORK FOR DANISH DEMOCRACY

THE constitutions of western democracies often begin with the mention of the fundamental principles on which the country's form of government relies. The Swedish Constitution, for instance, starts out by stating that all public authority stems from the people and that Swedish democracy is based on the free formation of public opinion and the common and equal right to vote. The second paragraph of the Norwegian Constitution states that the purpose of the Constitution is to safeguard democracy, the constitutional state, and human rights.

The Constitutional Act of Denmark might well have had a similar introductory passage, yet it does not. The Danish Constitutional Act has no such distinct paragraph about the fundamental principles for the country's form of government. Section 2 of the Danish Constitutional Act simply notes that 'the form of government is limited monarchy'. Nowhere in the Danish Constitutional Act does the word 'democracy' appear.

One reason for this is that many of the constitutional provisions in the current Constitutional Act appear almost entirely unchanged from when they were first written as part of Denmark's original Constitutional Act of 1849. During subsequent amendments, the most recent of which is the constitutional amendment of 1953, the choice has been to elaborate on the existing wording of the Constitutional Act without any comprehensive changes to the language.

The Constitutional Act is the result of a range of political compromises and reflects a number of historical strata in the constitutional evolution. For that reason, the Constitutional Act does not represent an unambiguous set of values or any singular ideology. However, we can still say that the Constitutional Act rests on at least two fundamental principles that serve as the backbone of Danish democracy and the Danish constitutional state.

The first principle is that power derives from the people and that the power vested in authorities must be exercised within the limits of the law. This principle finds expression in the Constitutional Act's provisions about how voters elect members of the *Folketinget* (the Danish Parliament) in general, secret, and direct elections. Together with the government, the *Folketinget* holds legislative power and can, by virtue of the constitutional rule about parliamentarism, at any point express its lack of confidence in the government, resulting in the government stepping down or calling for a new parliamentary election. Independent courts are responsible for ensuring that power is exercised within the bounds of the law and the Constitution.

The second fundamental principle is that citizens are guaranteed a certain minimum number of rights. In particular, the Constitution points to two types of rights. One type refers to political rights: freedom of speech, freedom of assembly, and freedom of association. The primary purpose of these rights is to ensure the proper functioning of democracy since the constitutional rules about parliamentary elections would be rendered rather useless without citizens' right to discuss political issues, form political parties and organizations, and assemble in groups. The second type of rights pertains to rules about personal freedoms and to the inviolability of property and the home. These rights are primarily designed to protect the individual against acts of random intervention by the state.

The Constitution's provisions are an expression of the fact that certain important and fundamental societal questions have been legally regulated in a way that renders them out of the realm of the common majority's political consideration and decision-making. In this way, the Constitution serves as a point of intersection between law and politics. The Constitution provides a framework for constitutional life, but it is important to note that the Constitution is only a framework and not the entire picture.

Below is a brief introduction to the provisions in the Danish Constitution about the highest state authorities and their competence as well as its provisions about constitutional rights, with continuous attention to the social and political reality to which these provisions pertain. The chapter builds in large part on Christensen et al. (2016). The Constitutional Act can be found in English with accompanying explanations at www. FT.dk (Folketinget n.d.).

THE HISTORY OF THE
CONSTITUTIONAL ACT

Denmark's current Constitution dates back to 1953. As already mentioned, many of the clauses in the current Constitutional Act remain virtually unchanged from Denmark's original Constitutional Act of 1849. That original constitution represented a break with the constitution of absolute monarchy, the King's Law (*Lex Regia*) of 1665.

The Constitution of 1849 introduced a strangely broad and democratically attuned form of government for the time with its introduction of common voting rights in parliamentary elections, which consisted of two chambers at the time, namely the *Folketinget* and the *Landstinget*. However, in accordance with the period's existing customs and beliefs, this right was limited to reputable Danish men above the age of 30 with the exception of servants without their own household, recipients of social welfare, and those lacking legal capacity.

While all power during the absolute monarchy had unambiguously been in the hands of the king, Section 2 of the Constitutional Act of 1849 introduced a tripartition of power. This meant that the legislative power was shared between the king (the government) and the parliament, the executive power belonged to the king (government), and the judicial power resided with the courts. This clause can also be found in the current Constitutional Act under Section 3.

Aside from a number of amendments during the first 15 years after the Constitution of 1849 was written (as a result of specific issues pertaining to the duchies of Schleswig-Holstein and Lauenborg occasioned by Denmark's loss in the 1864 war against Prussia and Austria), the Constitution has only been amended four times since 1849, namely in 1866, 1915, 1920, and 1953.

The amendment of 1866 was necessitated by Denmark's defeat to Prussia, which led to the loss of the above-mentioned duchies. This reduced the kingdom's territory by 40 per cent and led to the loss of approximately one million of its three million citizens. Moreover, the 1866 amendment was sustained by a sense that the Constitutional Act of 1849 had gone too far in the direction of a democratically conceived constitution. The amendment of 1866 led to the abolition of equal voting rights for the Upper House, *Landstinget*. It introduced privileged voting rights so that voters with substantial incomes or high tax payments were granted a greater level of influence on the distribution of seats in Parliament, particularly in rural districts where those individuals served directly as electors. At the same time, the king (the government) was granted the authority to appoint 12 of the *Landstinget*'s 66 members. This laid the groundwork for the constitutional battle between the *Folketinget* and *Landstinget* which lasted from 1872 until the introduction of parliamentarism as political practice in 1901 when the party holding the majority in Parliament (the Liberals) formed a new government.

The constitutional amendment of 1915 broke with the 1866 Constitution's privileged voting rights status for the wealthy and a rejection of the system whereby the king (government) appointed a certain number of members of the *Landstinget*. Furthermore, it afforded voting rights to women. In an effort to inhibit comprehensive future amendments, the 1915 Constitution introduced a rule that makes it very difficult to amend the Constitutional Act. The rule can be found in Section 88 of the current 1953 Constitution, according to which constitutional amendments require approval in the *Folketinget* and a subsequent parliamentary election. The proposed amendment has to then be approved without any changes by the new *Folketinget*. Finally, it has to be put up for a referendum and be approved by a 40 per cent majority of all voters (prior to 1953, this was 45 per cent).

As part of the agreement of European peace at the conclusion of the First World War , the minor constitutional amendment of 1920 was necessitated by the desire to regain control of the southern part of the country bordering Germany as a constitutionally integrated part of the Kingdom of Denmark following special referendums about where to draw the border.

The current Constitutional Act of 1953 barely survived the challenging amendment process. The reason that it eventually found approval had to do with the fact that it was lumped in with an amendment to the Act of Succession. In accordance with the Constitution of 1920, the law of succession only pertained to men. However, King Frederik IX, who became king in 1947, only had daughters, and in order for his eldest daughter Princess Margrethe to inherit the throne, the Act of Succession would have to be amended. Because such an amendment was very popular among the public, politicians chose to pair it with the constitutional amendment, presuming the amendment to the Act of Succession would be so popular among the Danes that it would secure approval for the entire constitutional amendment along with it.

This is exactly what happened. The proposed amendment to the Constitution was approved in the referendum with the needed support, but only barely. Despite the popular amendment to the Act of Succession, the proposed amendment only found support by 45.76 per cent of registered voters. If 19,000 of those who voted in favour had stayed home, the constitutional amendment would have been rejected. Only 12.3 per cent of voters voted against the amendment.

Other significant constitutional amendments to the 1953 Constitution were the transition from the two-chamber system to a unicameral system, a lowering of the voting age from 25 to 23, and the constitutional consolidation of parliamentarism. Most important, perhaps, was the provision to make it possible to delegate sovereignty (in the form of legislative, executive, and judicial power) to international authorities without a constitutional amendment (Section 20). That change has been hugely significant with regard to Denmark joining the EC in 1972 (now the EU), as well as Denmark's support for subsequent changes to the EU treaty.

The constitutional amendment of 1953 resulted in the following wording of Section 1 (Folketinget n.d.: 2): 'This Constitutional Act shall apply to all parts of the Kingdom of Denmark.' This means that the Constitution applies to Denmark, the Faroe Islands, and Greenland. Within the scope of the Constitution, the Faroe Islands and Greenland have their own individual home-rule agreements. Constitutionally, these agreements have the status of laws, but their political status makes it inconceivable that they could be repealed or amended in any substantial way by the Danish legislative body without the participation and support of the Faroe Islands and Greenland.

THE KING AND THE MONARCHY

As already mentioned, Section 2 of the present 1953 Constitution (Folketinget n.d.: 2) states: 'The form of government shall be that of a constitutional monarchy.' The wording hints at the autocratic rule before 1849 and confirms that while Denmark is a monarchy whose monarch is head of state (currently Queen Margrethe II), the monarch's authority is subject to the limitations inherent in the constitutional system established by the other constitutional provisions.

These limitations are far-reaching and mean that the constitutional role of the monarch is merely symbolic and ceremonial. The monarch is not granted any competence to act in state affairs independently of the government and ministers. This arrangement is not a result of a new interpretation of the Constitution. The legal literature had already established 150 years ago that independent competence for the monarch would require 'an abandonment of the entire constitutional system'. However, in practical terms, for several decades after 1849, the transition away from absolute monarchy was characterized by the king's ability to influence the government and ministers.

The monarch's lack of competence to act independently of the government and ministers in state affairs is laid out in Sections 12, 13, and 14 of the Constitution. The central tenet of these sections is that the ministers alone are liable and that the monarch is exempt from liability. The monarch's signature is required for a number of decisions regarding legislation and administrative decisions, as well as for certain decisions made in regard to particular constitutional provisions such as the appointment and dismissal of ministers (Section 14), decisions about foreign policy (Section 19), and the decision to call a general election (Section 32, Subsection 2). However, the monarch does not have the freedom to withhold his or her signature, and thus, is not entitled to veto decisions. If a monarch refuses to follow a recommendation introduced by a minister, the monarch is constitutionally obligated to comply. If the monarch is unwilling to do so, he or she is forced to abdicate.

The monarch's private dispositions fall outside the rules about the monarch's signature being accompanied by that of a minister. The grey area between private dispositions and acts of the state contains decisions about the appointment of royal court officials and awarding royal orders and decorations. In accordance with tradition, these decisions are made without the countersignature of ministers.

In addition to the aforementioned decisions regarding legislation, etc., the monarch's participation in state affairs primarily takes the form of very concrete actions. An example would be the monarch's official visit to other nations and official state visits in Denmark, participation in a number of official events, and delivering speeches at historical commemoration ceremonies or the annual New Year's speech on national television. In such instances, the principle about the monarch's exemption from liability and the liability of ministers requires the monarch to secure a minister's approval, typically from the prime minister. However, in cases when the statements are not political in nature, or in the case of representative functions not perceived to carry any political judgment, the monarch typically acts without the prior approval of a minister.

Overall, the general rule is that the monarch should be kept free of political involvement even when acting in the context of official state affairs. As such, the government should not misappropriate the monarch for the purposes of delivering partisan political viewpoints. In practical terms, the monarch stays away from politically controversial subjects by referencing only what falls within broad political consensus. The monarch is meant to represent a uniting, not a dividing, role in state affairs. It is generally agreed upon that Denmark's current monarch Queen Margrethe II has mastered this task.

Queen Margrethe II took the throne in January 1972 following the death of her father King Frederik IX. The accession of the new queen was a result of the amendment to the Act of Succession included in the constitutional amendment of 1953 which introduced female royal succession. A subsequent amendment to the Act of Succession in 2009 introduced full equality between men and women. Queen Margrethe II's oldest son Crown Prince Frederik is next in line for the throne.

THE *FOLKETINGET*

In his textbook on constitutional law from 1959, Danish Professor of Constitutional Law Alf Ross wrote that the *Folketinget* is 'the central wheelhouse of the state machine' (Ross 1959: 216, own translation). Political scientists know that a lot more can be said about this point. In any case, it remains a fact that the *Folketinget* is given a prominent position in the Danish Constitution.

By virtue of parliamentarism, the *Folketinget* is in charge of the government. The *Folketinget* has the power to dismiss the government or its individual ministers at any given time. And because of Section 6 in the Constitution, the *Folketinget* shares legislative power with the government. As the only constitutionally established state body, the *Folketinget* represents a direct popular mandate, and on that basis, it can be said to be the most significant democratic function.

The *Folketinget* consists of a 179-member assembly. Members are elected for a period of four years although the prime minister can call a general election at any point, leading to the annulment of the parliamentary mandates once the election takes place.

Section 29 of the Constitution outlines a number of preconditions for an individual's eligibility in relation to the *Folketinget*. Positive requirements include Danish citizenship, permanent domicile in the country, and being of voting age. Negative requirements include not having been declared incapable of conducting his or her own affairs (i.e. having lost legal capacity) and not having lost the right to vote due to prior convictions or the receiving of welfare benefits. However, there is no longer any law pertaining to these two final requirements.

The legal voting age is not directly established in the Constitution but is based on the Parliamentary Election Act. In accordance with Section 29 of the Constitution, changes to the legal voting age require not only that this change be signed into law but also that this law is sent to a referendum. In 1953 when the Constitutional Act was first written, the voting age was 23. Today, it is 18.

Anyone who is eligible to vote in parliamentary elections is also electable to the *Folketinget* unless the person has been convicted of an act that makes him unworthy to be a member of the *Folketinget* in the eyes of the public, cf. Section 30 of the Constitutional Act. In accordance with Section 33 of the Constitutional Act, the *Folketinget* singlehandedly determines questions of electability. Since 1953, there have been five instances when the *Folketinget* has denied electability status to one of its members.

The Constitutional Act's provisions about elections to the *Folketinget* can be found in Section 31, whereas the rules are established in more detail in the Parliamentary Election Act. According to the Constitution, elections to the *Folketinget* must be 'general, direct, and secret' (Folketinget n.d.: 16). The term 'general' implies that the authorities are expected to conduct elections in such a way that the right to vote will be available to the greatest possible number of citizens. 'Direct' elections means that the votes cast by citizens directly decide which parties and candidates are elected to the *Folketinget*. 'Secret' elections are defined in opposition to the open voting practiced before 1901; it entails that voters cast their ballots in a closed voting booth and that their ballot cannot subsequently be identified.

Section 31 outlines the general requirements of the electoral system to ensure that the views of voters—which in practical terms mean the parties—are given equal representation in the *Folketinget*. The Constitution does not pinpoint a particular model of proportional representation. This is established in the Parliamentary Election Act.

The electoral system combines 135 constituency seats and 40 compensatory seats. The latter are distributed among parties whose constituency seats have not granted them the number of seats to which they are entitled under proportional representation. The Parliamentary Election Act contains an electoral threshold which means that as a general rule, parties with less than 2 per cent of the total vote are unable to obtain compensatory seats. The purpose of this threshold is to prevent unnecessary division of the *Folketinget* into small parties that might complicate the formation of sustainable governments and effective legislation (see also Elklit 2020).

The Constitutional Act does not make explicit reference to political parties, but in practical terms, the work of the *Folketinget* is organized around party groups. According to Section 56, members of the *Folketinget* are bound solely by their own consciences, meaning that members are not legally obligated to adhere to the party line when it comes to voting in Parliament. However, there tends to be a high level of party discipline, and members of the different party groups most often vote in unison. Party discipline is further solidified by the fact that it is extremely difficult to become elected to the *Folketinget* as an independent candidate. It has only happened once during the current 1953 Constitution.

THE LEGISLATIVE PROCESS

The normal legislative process is only regulated by a very few constitutional provisions. Any member of the *Folketinget* is entitled to introduce a bill (Section 41), as are the government's ministers (Section 21). In reality, most bills are introduced by ministers. Once a bill has been introduced to Parliament, the Constitutional Act contains only one single provision about the *Folketinget*'s normal handling of the bill, which is that it has to be read three times in Parliament before it can be passed. The Standing Orders of the *Folketinget*, on the other hand, contain detailed rules on how to deal with a bill proposal, including its assignment for study to a committee. Section 48 of the Constitutional Act establishes that the Standing Orders are decided by the *Folketinget*, but the Constitution does not specify any requirements about the content of the Standing Orders. With respect to the passing of bills, the Constitution requires that more than half of the 179 members of the *Folketinget* be present and take part in voting (Section 50). In order for a bill to become law once it has been passed, a minister and the monarch must ratify it with their signatures.

In certain cases, the normal legislative process can or must be dispensed with in accordance with particular constitutional provisions, granting the parliamentary minority the opportunity to have their views considered.

First, the Constitution in Section 41 gives 2/5 of the members of the *Folketinget* the right to demand that the third reading of a bill be postponed until at least twelve working days after the bill's second reading. The purpose of this is to allow for a more thorough reading and to create public debate about the bill's content and fate. This provision has been employed quite a few times.

Second, according to Section 42, a minority of 1/3 of members of the *Folketinget* (60 MPs) can demand a referendum on a bill that has been passed. This provision was added to the Constitution in 1953. The most exciting aspect of this provision is that it has only been used once, in 1963, when the conservative opposition requested that four bills concerning the public regulation of land ownership were submitted for a referendum. A large majority of the voters rejected all four bills. Despite this success, no other parliamentary minority has made use of the provision since then. A deceased former Danish foreign minister—and a big proponent of referendums—explained this by arguing that a parliamentary minority loses one of its trump cards in the next election campaign if it has already pushed through its policies in a referendum. In some case, the mere threat of a referendum might also do the trick.

Third, it is required that the normal legislative process be dispensed with when constitutional amendments are introduced (Section 88), when delegating sovereignty to international organizations (Section 20), and in proposed amendments to the voting age (Section 29). In each of these cases, the Constitution calls for a referendum, though only in cases about delegating sovereignty if the bill does not find support from a 5/6 parliamentary majority.

As for the fourth and final provision, the Constitution contains a special minority clause concerning laws about expropriation (Section 73). In such cases, one third of the members of the *Folketinget* can request the postponement of the ratification of a passed bill until after a parliamentary election and the bill's subsequent passing by the new parliament. This provision has been used a few times.

In addition to the aforementioned provisions about referendums, the Constitution allows a parliamentary majority to call a consultative referendum. This option was used in 1986 when a consultative referendum was held about Denmark's support for the Single European Act which introduced the European single market. The government was in support of Denmark's inclusion, but a majority in Parliament was opposed. The voters said yes and the parliamentary majority complied with the voting majority.

Thus, the minority government managed to successfully use the referendum as a weapon to defeat the parliamentary majority.

CONSTITUTIONAL PROVISIONS ON PARLIAMENTARISM

The structure outlined in the Constitutional Act for political parliamentary activities is simple, and it is defined by two unambiguous constitutional provisions. First is Section 15, Subsection 2, which establishes the Parliament's right to make a motion of no confidence against the prime minister at any time. According to the Constitution, such a motion means that the government must step down or that the prime minister must call for a parliamentary election. The second provision is Section 32, Subsection 2, which establishes the prime minister's authority to call for a parliamentary election at any time.

These very simple provisions do not leave any doubt as to where to draw the line between law and politics. This in itself is an important quality about provisions that have been designed to regulate a subject as complicated and conflict-riddled as the collaboration between government and parliament. These provisions have managed to create a framework for highly changeable parliamentary situations. This became particularly clear in the 1980s when Conservative Prime Minister Poul Schlüter headed a number of minority governments.

Back in 1982, it was still possible (and rightfully so) to state in a political science textbook that a government would never accept defeat in a vote on a significant issue. 'Thus, we can say,' the author writes, 'that any vote held in Denmark represents a vote of confidence' (Worre 1982: 102, own translation). However, the ink was barely dry when parliamentary developments put the claim to shame. On a great number of issues, primarily relating to national security policies, the government was in the minority in Parliament without it resulting in the government stepping down. The same thing happened in votes on energy, environmental, and legal policies. During the period 1982–88, the government lost 1 in 12 votes in Parliament (Damgaard 1990: 28). In total, in the ten years 1982–92, the government lost more than 100 votes.

This period in the 1980s has been described as a period of 'reverse parliamentarianism' (Christensen 1993: 4). The term refers to the fact that the government almost played the role of the opposition on a number of issues, whereas the opposition played the role of government. An extended period of reverse parliamentarism of this kind has not existed since then, though there have continued to be instances where the government's proposals have been voted down without it resulting in a change of government.

There are different views on the expedience of this kind of parliamentarism, but in terms of constitutional law, there is no disagreement. If it is not possible to create a parliamentary majority in favour of a vote of no confidence, then the government stays and accepts, as it did in the 1980s, in order to figure out how to administer the policies of the opposition.

The Constitutional Act's Section 15, Subsection 2, establishing the government's obligation to step down or the prime minister's obligation to call an election if the *Folketinget* wins a vote of no confidence is supplemented by Section 15, Subsection 1, which allows the *Folketinget* to adopt a vote of no confidence against an individual minister. In such cases, the minister must resign. The Danish *Folketinget* has never made such a motion against a minister. This does not mean that this aspect of the political ministerial accountability is not effective. In fact, we might say that what happens in practice is that a minister makes sure to resign 'voluntarily' before he or she is forced to do so. Thus, this constitutional provision proves effective by virtue of its very existence.

Since the introduction of parliamentarism in 1901, the *Folketinget* has only passed a vote of no confidence against a prime minister on three occasions. The first time was in 1909, the second time in 1947, and the third and most recent as far back as 1975. However, a government might run into enough resistance that it gives up without a fight and without calling an election. This happened when Social Democratic Prime Minister Anker Jørgensen stepped down in 1982 and handed over power to Conservative Poul Schlüter. Alternatively, the government might resign because it risks otherwise being served a vote of no confidence, thus pre-empting the lack of confidence. This was part of the reason that Prime Minister Poul Schlüter stepped down in 1993 following the publication of a highly critical report about a wide-ranging political scandal (the Tamil Case).

FORMING A GOVERNMENT

Much like the constitutional provisions that concern parliamentarism, the provisions dealing with the process of forming a government are exceedingly simple. The framework for forming a government is made up by Sections 14 and 15 of the Constitutional Act. Section 14 states that the king (i.e. the prime minister) is responsible for appointing the prime minister and other ministers, while Section 15 concerns parliamentarism and entails that no government can be appointed that is presumed to be opposed by the majority in the *Folketinget*.

In cases when a government calls an election and subsequently wins the election, backed by the same parliamentary majority as before the election, the government is allowed to continue uninterrupted. The situation gets more complicated if the government loses the majority in the election, and there is no obvious majority for a new government—a scenario that has occurred frequently. In such cases, party leaders begin negotiations to determine the different possibilities for forming a government.

Over the course of the past 100 years, it has become a tradition for party leaders to inform the monarch—currently Queen Margrethe II—of their choice for prime minister. This is referred to as 'The Queen's Round of Consultations' (Christensen 2017: 34). However, this term is a bit misleading. The party leaders' negotiations do not take place in the presence of the queen. The entire procedure of forming a government is the responsibility of the sitting prime minister who makes all decisions about the process.

Political and strategic games have often been a characteristic feature of the process of forming a government. However, the legal basis for forming a government is straightforward and can be summed up in three simple constitutional rules of constitutional law:

1) The entire procedure of forming a government is the responsibility of the sitting prime minister.
2) No one who is presumed to be met by a vote of no confidence in Parliament may be nominated as a candidate for prime minister.
3) The new prime minister nominates himself (or herself), and thus, is responsible for ensuring that he or she is not opposed by a majority in Parliament.

During the process of forming a government, the simplicity of these provisions do not prevent frequent and competing claims in the press and in the political debate about the existence of other constitutional provisions. These claims, however, are not valid. Like elsewhere, the Constitution only provides a framework for the political situation, not the entire picture.

PARLIAMENTARY OVERSIGHT OF GOVERNMENT AND MINISTERS

The constitutional provisions in Section 15 regarding parliamentarism according to which a majority in the *Folketinget* can declare their lack of confidence in both individual ministers as well as the prime minister establish the *Folketinget's* ultimate authority and oversight over the government. As already mentioned, this weapon is generally not employed in practice but is effective by virtue of its very existence.

On a day-to-day basis, parliamentary oversight of the government plays out through questions addressed to the ministers, consultations with standing committees, and parliamentary interpellations. Only the latter form of oversight is constitutionally regulated as Section 53 states that any member of Parliament, with the consent of Parliament, may submit for discussion any matter of public interest and request a statement thereon from the relevant minister who is obligated to answer truthfully.

In accordance with the Standing Orders of the *Folketinget* in Section 20, any member of Parliament can address questions to the ministers, and though the ministers are not legally obligated to respond, they generally do. Ministers are also obligated to respond truthfully. In accordance with similar provisions, the committee of the *Folketinget* can address questions to the ministers, and many committee questions lead to consultations with the ministers, allowing the committee the opportunity to use further questioning to seek a more in-depth explanation.

There has been a significant increase in the *Folketinget's* use of these oversight mechanisms. Since the mid-2000s, the number of annual requests has been around 40–50.

From 2015 to 2016, the number of Section 20 questions from individual members of Parliament was approximately 1,500, and the number of committee-generated questions in the past decade has oscillated between 9,000 and 16,000 a year (White Paper 1571/2018: 66–7).

According to Section 15 in the Constitutional Act regarding parliamentarism, ministers are politically accountable to the *Folketinget*. This entails that the *Folketinget*, as the ultimate authority, can express its lack of confidence in a minister at any point. As a less drastic and more relevant response, the *Folketinget*, or a parliamentary committee, can advance different degrees of criticism of the minister. This criticism may be raised in the context of an upcoming consultation if the committee believes that the minister has not provided satisfactory answers, or if the committee believes that questions have surfaced about the minister's administration of his or her duties that is deserving of criticism.

In advancing such criticism or in the context of passing an actual vote of no confidence, the *Folketinget* is not legally bound by any rules except the majority rule. Thus, the minister does not have to have taken any legally reproachable action and disagreement with his or her policies or discomfort about his or her personality is sufficient grounds. In terms of constitutional law, the political responsibility of ministers is not defined in legal terms.

Legally, however, ministers are responsible for the conduct of the government as defined in Section 13 of the Constitution, which states that this responsibility is outlined in more detail by the law. Section 16 of the Constitution establishes that both the government and the *Folketinget* can indict ministers in cases of maladministration of office. Historically, the *Folketinget* has always been in charge of the indictment of ministers.

Individual ministerial legal responsibility is further determined in the Responsibilities of Ministers Act of 1964. The central provision of the law is Section 5 which establishes when a minister can be criminally charged in the context of administering his or her office. Subsection 1 of the provision states that a minister will be criminally charged if they deliberately or by gross negligence abandon the duties placed upon them by the Constitution, the law, and their office. Moreover, Section 5, Subsection 2, establishes that a minister can be penalized if he or she provides false or misleading information to the *Folketinget* or fails to disclose information during a parliamentary proceeding that would be of significance to Parliament's judgment of the case.

In accordance with the Constitutional Act's Section 16, criminal proceedings against ministers are decided by the High Court of the Realm. Section 59 of the Constitutional Act establishes that the High Court of the Realm consists of 15 Supreme Court justices and 15 members elected by Parliament from outside the Parliament.

Since 1849, only five cases have come before the High Court of the Realm. The last two cases are from 1910 and 1995. In the most recent case—the so-called 'Tamil Case' regarding the Justice Department's illegal order not to process a number of Tamil family reunification cases—the Justice Minister, who was also a former speaker, was sentenced to four months in prison. However, with age and health issues taken into consideration, the conviction was suspended.

The law about a minister's legal responsibility functions—not unlike the vote of no confidence concerning a minister's political responsibility—more by virtue of its existence than through practical application. Additionally, the reality of the legal ministerial responsibility is that it will often add extra liability to a minister's case if he is said to have broken the law and not only acted politically objectionably. In recent decades, this form of legally based criticism of ministers has frequently resulted in wide-ranging investigations carried out by an Inquiry Commission under the chairmanship of a judge. In a number of cases, the final report from such inquiry commissions has served as the basis for the Parliament, or subsections of Parliament, to politically criticize the involved minister. In the Tamil Case, this kind of report led to the decision by a majority in Parliament to put the former justice minister before the High Court of the Realm.

The widespread use of inquiry commissions led by judges is a testament to the fact that the political responsibility of ministers is often framed in legal terms, meaning that the Parliament's political criticism of a minister is significantly bolstered by arguments that are legal in nature. This is not all that strange since political criticism of a minister will appear more valid to the public if not merely advanced on the basis of political disagreement but also on the basis of unlawful actions by the minister in question.

DENMARK'S INTERNATIONAL RELATIONS AND DELEGATION OF SOVEREIGNTY

The king 'wages war and declares peace'. This was the brief and terse formulation of Denmark's relationship to the world around it in the Constitutional Act of 1849, Section 23. Today, this relationship is vastly more complicated and so is the Constitution.

The Constitutional Act contains two provisions about Denmark's international affairs. The first one (Section 19) primarily addresses international cooperation in the form of international agreements, or so-called treaties. Denmark has entered into hundreds of such treaties, spanning everything from trivialities to some of the most significant agreements regarding Denmark's position in the world, for example, treaties about Danish membership of the UN and NATO.

The second provision (Section 20) pertains to a particular kind of treaty, namely treaties in which Denmark delegates so-called sovereignty to an international entity. Section 20 does not use the word sovereignty but speaks of 'powers vested in the authorities of the Realm under this Constitutional Act' (Folketinget n.d.: 9). Such powers refer mainly to legislative, executive, and judicial authorities. The most significant example of this kind of treaty is the one that establishes Denmark's membership of the EU.

The distinction between the two different kinds of treaties is extremely important since the Constitutional Act makes it very easy to enter into Section 19 treaties and very difficult to enter into Section 20 treaties.

According to Section 19 of the Constitution, it is the responsibility of the government to conduct foreign policy. However, the *Folketinget* keeps the government on a short leash since any treaty of real significance requires parliamentary approval in the form of a common majority vote. That leash has become shorter over time, both legally and politically, as evidenced by Section 19, Subsection 3, of the Constitution and its provision about pre-emptive parliamentary oversight of the government's foreign policy. The government is required to consult with the Foreign Policy Committee ahead of any major decisions on foreign policy. The Committee is elected by parliament and consists of 17 members of Parliament. The provision about the Foreign Policy Committee was added to the Constitutional Act in 1953.

The government's obligation to ensure advance consultation with the Foreign Policy Committee is a legal obligation, meaning that if the government fails to do so, it could, in principle, lead to impeachment proceedings and criminal liability. On the contrary, the government is not legally obligated to follow the advice of the Foreign Policy Committee. However, an intelligent government will, at least if it wants to remain in power.

The provision from the old 1849 Constitution about the king's ability to 'wage war and declare peace' has also been curbed. Section 19, Subsection 2, of the Constitutional Act of 1953 establishes that the government cannot use military force against any foreign state without the consent of the *Folketinget*. In March 2010 in a case about the Iraq war (U 2010.1547 H), the Supreme Court ruled that it is the government and the *Folketinget* who make decisions about the use of military force in accordance with the Constitution, and that international law, including the UN treaty, does not constitutionally limit that authority.

As already mentioned, Section 20 of the Constitution concerns the specific type of treaties in which Denmark delegates legislative, executive, or judicial power to an international entity such as in the case of Denmark's membership of the EU. This provision was added to the Constitution in 1953 with the aim of making it easier to join this kind of supranational collaboration. Without Section 20, this would require a constitutional amendment.

Despite the fact that Section 20 has made this process less complicated, it is still quite challenging to enter into Section 20 treaties. According to Section 20, Subsection 2, a 5/6 parliamentary majority—i.e. at least 150 members of Parliament—are required to vote in favour of a bill that surrenders authority to an international entity. If the bill only receives a common parliamentary majority, it must be submitted to the electorate in a referendum. The bill is rejected if a majority of the electorate, consisting of a minimum of 30 per cent of eligible voters, votes no.

Danish voters have often expressed significant scepticism about the idea of expanding EU collaboration. In 1992 in a referendum on the Maastricht Treaty, a majority of 41.7 per cent of eligible voters voted against the bill, while 40.5 per cent voted in favour. In 2000, in a referendum on Denmark's participation in the euro monetary system, a majority of 46.1 per cent of eligible voters voted against the bill, while 40.5 per cent voted in favour. Similarly, in a referendum in 2015 on whether to maintain Denmark's opt-out concerning Justice and Home Affairs or replace it with an opt-in model, a majority of 37.5 per cent voted against any change, while only 33.1 per cent voted yes to the changes.

At other times, the majority of voters have voted yes such as in 1972 when Denmark voted to become a member of EU, in 1993 in a referendum on the Maastricht Treaty supplemented by the so-called Edinburgh Agreement, and again in 1998 when the Danes voted in favour of the Amsterdam Treaty. A referendum in 2014 on Denmark's participation in the Unified Patent Court also generated a majority of yes votes.

Section 20, Subsection 1, of the Constitution limits the delegation of power to an international organization to 'such an extent as shall be provided by statute'. In the Maastricht Treaty case from 1998 (U 1998.800 H), the Supreme Court ruled that the words 'as shall be provided by statute' are to be interpreted to mean that a positive delimitation must be made of the powers delegated, partly as regards the fields of responsibility and partly as regards the nature of the powers. Delimitation must enable an assessment to be made of the extent of the delegation of sovereignty. In other words, the government cannot simply write a blank cheque to the international authorities.

On the other hand, according to the Supreme Court, the formulation 'as shall be provided by statute' cannot be interpreted to mean that the powers vested in the Danish state 'can only be delegated to an international organization to a limited (lesser) degree'. However, the Supreme Court notes that it must be considered to be assumed in the Constitution that no transfer of powers can take place to such an extent that 'Denmark can no longer be considered an independent state'.

The question of where to draw the legal line for when 'Denmark can no longer be considered an independent state' is not an easy matter and quickly devolves into a political question rather than a legal one. Thus, the Supreme Court's ruling established that determining the line has to 'primarily be based on political considerations'.

The reality is that the Constitution's protections against wide-ranging surrender of authority rely primarily on the requirements of having a 5/6 majority in Parliament and having to call a referendum if a bill can only gain a regular parliamentary majority.

THE COURTS

The provision in the Danish Constitutional Act about the separation of powers (Section 3) states that the *Folketinget* and the government share legislative power, the government holds executive power, and the courts have judicial power. Together with a number of specific constitutional provisions about the courts, this provision marks the fact that Denmark is not only a democracy but also a constitutional state.

Traditionally, the central core of the concept of judicial power is the ruling in criminal cases and in legal disputes between citizens. In addition to this are cases about the legality of administrative decisions and cases concerning the constitutionality of legislation. Unlike many continental European countries, Denmark does not have special administrative courts or a special constitutional court. These types of cases are handled by the regular courts.

One word can be used to sum up the responsibility placed on the courts by the Constitution: independence. The Constitution specifically ensures this independence through a provision in Section 64 about how judges shall be governed solely by the law and cannot accept orders from the executive power. This provision also guarantees the judge's personal impartiality since a judge—according to the principal rule—can neither be dismissed nor transferred. Unless it is part of a more comprehensive reorganization of the courts, a judge can only be dismissed through a court ruling.

The Constitution does not mention the process of nominating judges. In 1999, a bill was passed that established a Judicial Appointments Council, which makes recommendations to the justice minister about nominations for judicial appointments. Applicants for a judicial position send their application to the Judicial Appointments Council who nominates one, and only one, candidate for each appointment. The law presupposes that the justice minister follows the recommendations of the Council, but in exceptional cases in which the minister does not want to accept the recommendation of the Council, the Parliamentary Legal Affairs Committee must be notified. The Judicial Appointments Council has six members: a Supreme Court justice who is chairperson, a high court judge, a district court judge, an attorney, and two public representatives. The Judicial Appointments Council guarantees that the courts will have the final say on judicial appointments.

The Constitutional Act does not contain an explicit provision about the courts' power to adjudicate the constitutionality of acts, and their competence in such matters refer back to supreme court practices from around 1920. Today, this kind of constitutional testing is done frequently, with only a single case in 1999 resulting in the direct denial of a legal provision (U 1999.841 H). In that particular case (known as the Tvind Case), the *Folketinget* and the government had passed a bill that denied a number of schools the possibility of receiving government funding. The Supreme Court ruled that this was in violation of Section 3 of the Constitutional Act about the separation of power since the Parliament and government had in effect given a court ruling.

The Supreme Court's judicial review of specific legislation has traditionally been quite cautious, since in order for a law to be overturned by the Supreme Court, its variance with the Constitution has to be of significant certainty. This is undoubtedly still true of a number of constitutional provisions; however, it is just as important to note that specific legislation will only be deemed unconstitutional on rare occasions as the Constitutional Act only places minimal restrictions on the competence of the legislative power.

It should also be mentioned that the Supreme Court's review of the constitutionality of acts of Parliament is characterized by the fact that the Supreme Court, unlike some constitutional courts in other countries, has not engaged in dynamic and creative interpretations of the Constitution. The Danish Supreme Court has instead kept its feet on the ground and focused on common legal principles of interpretation based on the wording in the Constitutional Act and the meanings that can be presumed to be behind the formulations. This has prevented the politicization of judicial appointments in Denmark.

CONSTITUTIONAL RIGHTS

As mentioned at the beginning of this chapter, the Danish Constitution is organized around two types of constitutional rights. These are the political rights of freedom of speech, freedom of assembly, and freedom of association; and the personal rights concerning provisions about personal freedom and the inviolability of home and property rights. In addition, one finds provisions about freedom of religion, the right to public assistance, and free education in public schools. These provisions are all based on the first Constitutional Act from 1849 and have only been expanded slightly in the various constitutional amendments.

In this way, Denmark stands out among most European countries, including the Nordic countries, whose catalogues of constitutional rights are much more wide-ranging. The reason for this is partly that most of these countries have amended their constitutions over the past few decades, during which there has been a great deal of focus on and interest in many different kinds of constitutional rights. The Danish Constitution is very difficult to change, remaining unchanged since 1953 as a result, and so this 'constitutional wave' has not affected the Danish Constitutional Act.

The constitutional provision about freedom of speech contains an absolute prohibition on censorship, whereas the protection of the content of speech is relegated to the fact that responsibility for speech can be placed by means of a court ruling. In the same way, the provision about freedom of association establishes that associations cannot be annulled by the government but generally require a court ruling. The freedom of assembly is even more far reaching since citizens have a constitutional right to assemble unarmed.

The Constitution protects personal freedom in particular by guaranteeing that an individual must come before a judge who will determine whether he or she will remain imprisoned within twenty-four hours of being arrested. The objective of this provision was and is to prevent government misuse of the criminal justice system.

Likewise, in principle, house searches, seizure and examination of private documents, etc. have to be preapproved by a judge. However, legislation can and often does make exceptions, for instance, when it comes to attempts by the authorities to ensure compliance with tax laws, food laws, and the like. Property rights are specifically protected in such a way that in the case of expropriation of property, it is ultimately left up to the courts to decide whether or not the owner has received complete compensation.

In an international context, Denmark has joined a number of human rights treaties since the end of the Second World War. Some of the most significant are the European Convention on Human Rights and the UN's two human rights conventions about political rights and economic and social rights. By signing treaties about human rights, the Danish state has committed itself to live up to these treaties. Generally, Danish citizens cannot rely directly on these treaties. However, if someone ends up in trial, they will get relatively close since the courts will refer to the fact that Danish laws have to be understood to the greatest extent possible in accordance with the treaties that Denmark has joined. This is different for the European Convention on Human Rights since this treaty was introduced and approved as a bill in 1992, and thus, it functions as direct law.

The law on the European Convention on Human Rights regulates a number of issues that are not regulated by the Constitution, as well as a number of the same issues such as freedom of speech, freedom of association, and freedom of assembly. However, as a law, it only has the status of a law and cannot be interpreted into the Constitution.

Imagine, for instance, if the Supreme Court interpreted Section 77 in the Constitutional Act in accordance with Article 10 of the Human Rights Convention which also deals with freedom of speech but in a much broader scope. In doing so, the judges would suddenly change the content of the Danish Constitutional Act without adhering to the complicated procedures for amending the Constitution as outlined in Section 88 of the Constitutional Act. Moreover, the judges at the European Court of Human Rights in Strasbourg regularly interpret new content into the provisions of the Convention based on something called 'dynamic' interpretation but which, in a Danish context, has been referred to in less generous terms as 'legal free-hand drawing'. In other words, if the Supreme Court interpreted the Constitution in accordance with the Human Rights Convention, it would mean that Denmark would delegate constitutional power to the judges of the Human Rights Courts in Strasbourg. Therefore, the Danish Supreme Court has never reinterpreted the Constitution in the light of convention provisions, but it has instead maintained a clear distinction between the Constitution and the treaties.

The Constitution that Never Changes

The Danish Constitutional Act has been referred to as the 'constitution that never changes' (Christensen 2002: 99). This is not entirely accurate given that the Constitution has been amended a few times. However, it is true that such amendments have been rare, and there are no expectations for additional amendments in the near future. There are two reasons for this.

The first reason is the complicated amendment procedure outlined in Section 88 of the Constitution. The practical implications of this section are that it requires very broad support in both the *Folketinget* and among voters. The second reason is that in terms of practical politics, constitutional politics are politics of necessity. Historically, the only time the Constitution has been amended has been when it blocked policies considered necessary by a substantial parliamentary majority.

Currently, there are no pressing matters requiring a constitutional amendment. As mentioned, the constitutional framework outlined in the Danish Constitutional Act for political life in Denmark is simple and has allowed ample opportunity for practical parliamentary practices to unfold in accordance with the changing times and without any constitutional crises. In some cases, the constitutional provisions about personal and political rights and freedoms are a bit flimsy, but in practice, this does not prove to be a problem. The legal system is stock full of statutory rights, and national rules are supplemented across the board by EU provisions and the European Convention on Human Rights.

There is no reason to expect a constitutional amendment in the foreseeable future. The major parties have no desire to open up the Pandora's Box that an amendment process could very well turn out to be. Political life presents many challenges on a daily basis, but the Danish Constitution is not one of them.

REFERENCES

Christensen, Jens Peter (1993). 'Debatten om grundlovsændring i forfatningsretlig belysning', *Ugeskrift for Retsvæsen*, 127/1: 1–12.

Christensen, Jens Peter (2002). 'Norm og praksis under grundloven som aldrig ændres', in Eivind Smith, ed., *Grundlagens makt. Konstitutionen som politiskt redskap och som rättslig norm*. Stockholm: SNS Förlag, 99–115.

Christensen, Jens Peter (2017). *Grundloven. Atten fortællinger*, 3rd ed. Copenhagen: Gyldendal.

Christensen, Jens Peter, Jørgen A. Jensen, and Michael H. Jensen (2016). *Dansk Statsret*, 2nd ed. Copenhagen: Jurist- og Økonomforbundets Forlag.

Damgaard, Erik (1990) (ed.). *Parlamentarisk Forandring i Norden*. Oslo: Oslo University Press.

Elklit, Jørgen (2020). 'The electoral system. Fair and well-functioning', in Peter M. Christiansen, Jørgen Elklit, and Peter Nedergaard, eds, *The Oxford Handbook of Danish Politics*. Oxford: Oxford University Press, 56–75.

Folketinget (n.d.). 'My Constitutional Act', https://www.thedanishparliament.dk/~/media/pdf/publikationer/english/my_constitutional_act_with_explanations.ashx (accessed 21 January 2019).

Ross, Alf (1959). *Dansk Statsforfatningsret I*. Copenhagen: Nyt Nordisk Forlag.

U 1998.800 H. Ugeskrift for Retsvæsen, 1998, 800–71.

U 1999.841 H. Ugeskrift for Retsvæsen, 1999, 841–51.

U 2010.1547 H. Ugeskrift for Retsvæsen, 2010, 1547–75.

White Paper (1571/2018). *Betænkning afgivet af Udvalget om undersøgelseskommissioner. Undersøgelseskommissioner og parlamentariske undersøgelsesformer*. Copenhagen: Ministry of Justice, http://www.justitsministeriet.dk/sites/default/files/media/Pressemeddelelser/pdf/2018/251018_-_betaenkning_1571_2018.pdf

Worre, Torben (1982). *Det politiske system i Danmark*, 4th ed. Copenhagen: Akademisk Forlag.

CHAPTER 3

GREENLAND, THE FAROE ISLANDS, AND DENMARK

Unity or Community?

ULRIK PRAM GAD

FROM MARGINS TO CENTRE STAGE

ALL nationalisms involve not only collective memories but also forgetting (Renan 1882/1992). The Danish nation state has largely forgotten its past and presence as a 'conglomerate state' (Bregnsbo 2004), and scholarship is complicit. Review articles covering the Nordic region often relegate autonomous territories and even sovereign Iceland to a footnote. In schoolbook maps, little boxes with the Faroe Islands and a downscaled Greenland appear, inserted in the margins without explanation. However, if mapping the world in polar projection (Figure 3.1)—which became urgent to military strategists with the advent of the nuclear age—it becomes obvious that the Kingdom of Denmark is not (only) a tiny plug in the Baltic bottleneck. Recently, the 'scramble for the Arctic' (Nuttall and Dodds 2016) set in motion by changes in global balances of climate, power, and economy has made its way to the Danish public, sparking renewed attention towards long-forgotten complications as to just what 'Denmark' is.

This chapter identifies the most important characteristics and dynamics of the Danish 'Community of the Realm', *Rigsfællesskabet*, with *Kalaallit Nunaat* (Greenland) and *Føroyar* (the Faroe Islands). The main message is that every time Danish actions, reactions, or passivity can be taken to imply that Denmark tries to keep the Realm for itself, the existence of the Community is put at stake. The chapter is structured as three narratives of the Community in terms of constitutional status, sociological aspirations, and geopolitical context. The first section sets the stage by introducing the constitutional status of Greenland and the Faroes, the struggles that produced and contest it, and the linguistic games played to keep it together. The second section identifies three phases—analytically distinct but historically entangled—in the quest for equality among the

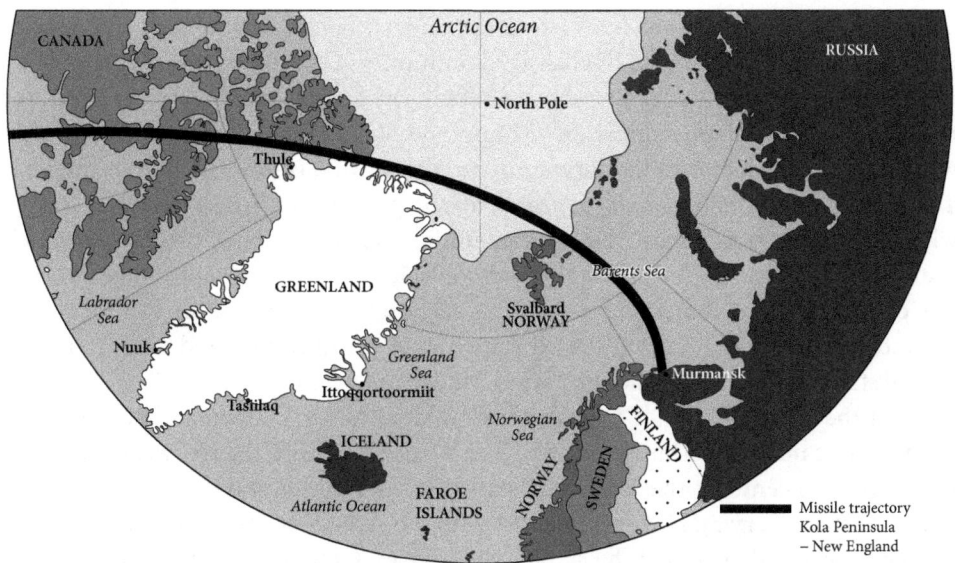

FIGURE 3.1 When seeing Greenland and the Faroe Islands between North America, Scandinavia, and Eurasia in polar projection, Denmark disappears (map adapted from geology.com).

three parties of the Community of the Realm and present examples of how they failed. The third section identifies a series of diplomatic games played: first, games played by Denmark to uphold sovereignty under difficult geopolitical conditions, and later, games played by Greenland, the Faroes, and Denmark more or less in concert to allow the two small polities independent international agency. The conclusion draws together a prognosis for how these games are likely to cross what has so far served as domestic boundaries into uncharted territory, even if international conditions are increasingly difficult.

A Constitutional Oxymoron

During the preparations for revised arrangements for the Faroe Islands and Greenland in the wake of the Second World War, the government asked the country's preeminent legal mind Alf Ross for advice. He took the opportunity to describe *Rigsfællesskabet*—the commonly used label for the fact that the Kingdom of Denmark also includes islands, small and large, in the North Atlantic—as a legal nullity (cf. Harhoff 1993: 73) since 'Community [*fællesskab*] exists among parties of equal status; unity [*enhed*] exists among parts and totality' (quoted in Spiermann 2007: 11, own translation). Official legal text long avoided using the label, and the website of the Danish Prime Minister's Office still insists on the 'Unity of the Realm' in its English version (Prime Minister's Office n.d.).

Nevertheless, *Rigsfællesskabet* remains the conceptual framework for popular imaginations and practical arrangements as well as for legal struggles and political debate over the connections between Greenlanders, Faroes, and Danes. Literally, the Danish version translates into English as 'Community of the Realm' like the Faroese *ríkisfelagsskapur*, with *felagsskapur* connoting solidarity and companionship in contrast to the alternative translation *samveldið* ('commonwealth' or community of states), which was chosen to characterize the early incarnations of what is now the European Union. The Greenlandic version, *naalagaaffeqatigiinneq*, goes even further: *naalagaq* (the one who decides) is *qatigiinneq*, that is, something you do together with someone else (Lennert 2006: 1, n. 2). The ambiguity and polyvalency of the concept appears to facilitate convivance. The remaining part of this section will introduce the historical background for the current constitutional state of the (comm)unity and characterize the formal status of Greenland and the Faroe Islands.

From the point of view of Danish constitutional history, Greenland and the Faroe Islands came under the Danish crown when it was fused with the Norwegian crown in the fourteenth century. The Norse had settled in both places and trade was conducted out of Western Norway. However, contact with the settlers in Greenland died out—and it later appeared that so had the settlers themselves. Greenland was recolonized from 1721, when Norwegian Hans Egede was sent by the King to save the souls of the Norse who had had no chance to hear about the Reformation. Since no Norse were to be found, Egede took upon himself to christen the *Inuit* who had migrated to the island. When Norway proper was lost to Sweden as part of the settlement after the Napoleonic wars, trade with and administration of Greenland and the Faroe Islands were transferred to Copenhagen. As discussed in detail below, the Faroe Islands were granted autonomy under the label 'home rule' in 1946, whereas Greenland was first decolonized by integration with the 1953 constitutional reform and achieved 'home rule' in 1979, a status that was transformed to 'self-rule' in 2009. Meanwhile, each community retains two members of the Danish Parliament (*Folketinget*) with equal status to other MPs and full voting rights in all matters (Pedersen 2020; Elklit 2020).

Official interpretations of Danish constitutional law have insisted on treating the two autonomies separately but similarly as powers devolved from a sovereign centre (Christensen 2020). In contrast, the constitutional statuses of both Greenland and the Faroe Islands have been contested in slightly different ways referring to the distinct historical trajectories of submission to Copenhagen. Some Faroese historians and lawyers have argued that the Faroese constitute a distinct nation that never accepted transfer of sovereignty from the Norwegian to the Danish crown (Spiermann 2007: 47, fn.62). Greenlandic critique has centred on whether the procedure culminating in the formal integration of Greenland in 1953 lived up to UN standards prescribing free and informed consent. Objections have particularly been directed to the fact that the alternatives to integration discussed in the UN decolonization processes—independence and free association—were not presented to the Greenlanders (Kleist 2019). Activist legal scholarship (Harhoff 1993; Spiermann 2007) argues that by now, the home and self-rule arrangements are not just irrevocable for pragmatic political reasons (Christensen 2020) but that they have a constitutional status which protects them against unilateral Danish intervention. In other words, traditional legal interpretation would categorize the Greenlandic and Faroese governments as devolved, whereas activist legal scholarship and political and diplomatic practice would point towards a categorization of Denmark's involvement with the islands as a federacy (Stepan 2013: 244; Justinussen 2019). Since the 2009 law on self-rule includes a procedure for how Greenland may declare independence, contestations have concentrated on competencies in foreign and security politics. In continuation, activist legal scholarship (Spiermann 2007: 120–3) supports increased independent international agency for Greenland and the Faroe Islands by reference to their independent status as peoples under international law, against claims from the Danish government of a constitutionally protected prerogative over external affairs.

Competencies Reaching into Core State Functions

The autonomies' spheres of competence are wide compared to the arrangements between other overseas territories and their metropole states. Greenlandic and Faroese authorities have 'taken over' (as Danish law wants it; Greenlanders and Faroese prefer 'taken home') almost all domains of domestic affairs. Most remaining affairs are listed as eligible for takeover, including core state functions such as police, prosecution, courts, the penal system, passports, aliens, and border control. In the face of each Greenlandic and Faroese demand for increased autonomy, the official Danish position has been that it would violate the Danish Constitution—until one day, the government changed its position and taking home minerals extraction and police was suddenly possible as was involvement in foreign affairs and formal recognition of Greenlandic self-government under international law. Legal scholars debate whether official Danish interpretation of constitutional law has indeed constituted consistent limits (Danielsen 2011) or whether it is all down to politics (Larsen 2011). Only 'Constitution; Citizenship; Supreme Court; Foreign, security and defence policy; Foreign exchange and monetary policy' are explicitly exempted from takeover. Even within foreign policy, advanced procedures for independent agency and involvement have been codified. The governments of Greenland and the Faroe Islands may 'on behalf of the Realm' conclude agreements with foreign states and international organizations within the 'fields of responsibility taken over'. However, Denmark takes over the steering wheel if Denmark (proper) is also involved in the matter, if both Greenland *and* the Faroe Islands are involved, or if Denmark is a member of the international organization in question. In such matters— and other foreign affairs conducted by the Danish government on behalf of the islands— intensive consultations are prescribed. Indeed, a precedence has evolved that would make it inconvenient for a Danish minister of foreign affairs to discuss Arctic affairs with a foreign colleague without a Greenlandic counterpart present (Gad 2017a: 18).

The asymmetries of what is in effect a Danish federacy, as well as the contestations that produced the asymmetries and the games which keep the federacy going, are products of two underlying factors: the quest for equality shaped by and into nationalism, and particularly for Greenland, a unique combination of geographical position and territorial and population size.

Seeking Equality in Asymmetrical Relations

Building a 'Community' only became necessary when a 'Realm' ceased to be legitimate on its own terms, i.e. with the advent of notions of popular sovereignty. Even then, hierarchies of race, civilization, and size pre-empted the need for equality among the constituent parties of the Realm. Originally, Greenlanders were considered racially different, perhaps masters of their particular ecology but unfit for civilization, and hence, in need of Danish protection (Marquardt 2009). The Faroese language was once considered an uncivilized dialect unfit for instruction (Gaini 2011). Reminiscences of both ideas live on in prejudice (sometimes internalized) claiming that Greenlanders are not really fit to show up at work every morning at 8 o' clock as they are programmed by a culture orienting life towards nature (Brochmann and Hamann 1990: 68–71), or in the way the Danish authorities may present themselves as guardians protecting the less-than-civilized Faroese customs like the *Grindadráp* harvest of pilot whales (Adler-Nissen 2014). However, the Faroese and Greenlanders have learned from their Danish overlords that the ideal way to achieve equality in a diverse world is to be a culturally homogenous nation in possession of its own state (Gad 2017a: 41–7). The last hierarchy standing concerns size; counting only some 50,000 inhabitants, some Faroese and Greenlanders join many Danes in deeming their nations too small to independently run a modern state (Breum 2019). Table 3.1 offers an overview of the asymmetries of the Community of the Realm.

No Turning Back after the Second World War

The Second World War cut off Iceland, the Faroe Islands, and Greenland, governed by local authorities while in UK and US custody, from metropole Denmark under

Table 3.1. Basic Asymmetries of the Community of the Realm 2017

Polity	Territory (km²)	Population	GDP (mDKK)	GDP/cap. (tDKK)	Block grant (mDKK)	Block grant/ budget	Block grant/ GDP
Faroe Islands	1,396	50,498	18,900	377	642	14%	3,5%
Greenland	2,166,086 Ice free: 410,449	55,860	15,309	326	3,722	59%	25%
Denmark	42,933	5,806,015	2,096,000	361	−4,364	−4%	−0,2%

Note: The annual lump sum transfers from the Danish state to the governments of the Faroe Islands and Greenland are known as 'block grants'. GDP are PPP figures based on preliminary estimates from *Danmarks Nationalbank*, Statistics Greenland, and Hágstova Føroyar.

German occupation. When reconnected, there was no turning back to established hierarchies; only programmes for further equality made sense. Globally, the war delegitimized racial hierarchies as the basis for formalized political subjugation, and integral to the formation of the United Nations was the imperative to decolonize all non-self-governing territories. However, all three North Atlantic polities ended up taking steps towards different kinds of equality. Since 1918, Iceland had been a formally sovereign state; the treaty establishing a personal union with Denmark left only foreign affairs and the coast guard to Copenhagen. Occupied, Denmark could not take part in the evaluation that the treaty stipulated for 1940, and in 1944, Iceland declared itself an independent republic, emerging as a formally, fully equal member of the international community of states.

The Faroe Islands briefly reached for the same kind of equality when a narrow plurality in a 1946 low-turnout referendum voted for secession; the speaker of the Faroese consultative assembly, *Lögting*, declared the establishment of 'The Faroese Realm', and a visiting warship seemed to signal British recognition by flying the Faroese *Merkið* flag rather than the Danish *Dannebrog* as courtesy ensign while docked in Tórshavn (Harhoff 1993: 60–1). Danish authorities intervened by dispatching its own warship, dissolving the *Lögting* (upon the request of a majority of its members), and calling a general election which (again) returned a majority *against* secession. When the dust settled in 1948, the Danish *Folketinget* passed the Faroe Islands Home Rule Act, transferring extensive legislative and executive powers in domestic affairs to Tórshavn. The Act also declared the Faroe Islands 'a self-governing community of people [*folkesamfund*] within the Danish Realm', a somewhat archaic-sounding novelty connoting something less than a people under international law but also something more distinct than the populations of other Danish islands.

The process cemented Faroese politics in a party system distributing parties along two dimensions: one traditional left/right and one union/independence. Four parties still dominate, each occupying a quadrant in the formative matrix (Adler-Nissen and Gad 2014). Hence, the status of the islands remains contested. While secessionists have instigated a series of preparatory measures when part of coalition governments, electoral and parliamentary majorities have so far stopped the process from culminating in (another) declaration of independence, particularly when confronted with Danish counter-demands. In 2001, the Danish prime minister responded to a Faroese plan for a referendum on independence with the threat of terminating Danish subsidies on only one year's notice. Another Danish prime minister used the same threat to splinter a coalition of pro-independence and con-independence parties that had agreed to formulate a Faroese constitution without proper reference to the Danish Constitution (Gad 2017a: 114).

Regarding Greenland, the Danish reaction to developments after the Second World War was to decolonize by integrating the island and its population under the 1953 Constitutional Act as an equal part of Denmark. Greenlanders did not participate in the constitutional referendum. Substantially, the integration was followed by intensified modernization drives, following demands from the Greenlandic elite, but substantially devised in and implemented by the Ministry for Greenland and its two Copenhagen-based executive arms, the Royal Greenlandic Trade (KGH) and the Greenland Technical Organization (GTO). Results were dramatic, complex, and contentious. On the one hand, the average life expectancy almost doubled (Iburg et al. 2001) due to better health services, social service, and housing quality, and the number of Greenlanders pursuing education beyond primary school rose. On the other hand, what was formally decolonization felt like neocolonialism; the physical infrastructure framing the new welfare was built by Danish entrepreneurs and builders, more Danes were recruited to man the welfare institutions, and both infrastructure and institutions were largely built on Danish blueprints (Dahl 1986). The road to equality as Danish citizens was paved with inequality. Particularly offending was the 'birth place criterion' (Janussen 2017) introduced to protect the (less productive) Greenlandic labour market from adjusting to (higher) Danish salaries; people born in Greenland were paid less than colleagues with identical education and function recruited from Denmark. These experiences of discrimination and government from far away were instrumental in spurring demands for different kinds of equality.

Finding Inspiration for New Equalities

The Faroes had been looking to Iceland, and now the obvious place to look for inspiration for Greenlandic equality was the Faroe Islands. The 1979 Greenland Home Rule Act upgraded the consultative *Landsrådet* to a legislative *Landstinget* and established the executive *Landsstyre*. To substantiate the formal transfer of powers, the monolithic KGH and GTO organizations were divided functionally (Skydsbjerg 1999), their personnel were transferred to Nuuk (or substituted with new recruits), and ambitious reforms were instigated, particularly of the all-decisive fishing industry (decentralizing production and decision making to cities and settlements along the coast) and the educational sector (prioritizing the Greenlandic language) (Gad 2017c). Already by 1992, much earlier than anyone had imagined (Skydsbjerg 1999), the home rule government had built a brand new bureaucracy from scratch in Nuuk and taken home not only political responsibility but also the practical organization of major services from hospitals and helicopters to grocery stores in next to 100 isolated settlements and a world-leading shrimp export business.

However, the feeling of being equal again proved evasive. The new positions in Nuuk under Greenlandic political control were still overwhelmingly filled with Danes sporting degrees rather than Greenlanders lacking degrees but familiar with 'Greenlandic conditions' (Binderkrantz 2008). Infrastructure, business connections, and consumer demands kept pointing traffic and commerce towards Denmark (Gad 2017a: 117) and reinforcing existing ethnic hierarchies (Gad 2017b: 220). Danish paradigms, blueprints, and education kept informing regulation, organization, and solutions to Greenlandic problems (Jakobsen 2008)—often in surprisingly automatic ways. One example is the way in which the 2007 Danish fusion of municipalities (Houlberg and Ejersbo 2020) was imitated in 2009 where eighteen Greenlandic municipalities were merged to just four. One was named *Sermersooq*, literally 'over the ice', since it fuses the capital Nuuk with the East Coast (where people speak a different language). Another named *Qaasuitsup*, spanning 1,600 kilometres of coast, was proudly declared to be the largest municipality in the world (Qaasuitsup Kommunia 2014: 8), only to be split in two as early as 2018 following popular demand and a referendum.

Apart from continued Danish dominance in import of expertise and manpower, lack of revenue under home rule was a severe barrier felt to be hindering Greenland from achieving equality as self-governing: Greenland relies on a Danish lump sum subsidy. Crucially, Greenland's rich subsoil resources, including both well-documented onshore mineral deposits and potentially immense offshore oil, remained state property under the 1979 Home Rule Act. Finally, the lack of recognition as a people eligible for self-government under international law kept rankling. In 2009, a reformed version of home rule dubbed 'self-rule' reprioritized these barriers to Greenlandic equality. First, the list of domains which Nuuk may take home was extended (as detailed above) to include even core state functions which official jurisprudence had ruled out of question in 1979. However, financially, the tables were turned; since 1979, every takeover had been accompanied by an expansion of the Danish subsidies to Greenland, but after 2009, Greenland has to finance new expenses on its own. Second, to make it possible to even imagine substantial self-funded takeovers, Greenland was allowed to take home regulation, administration, and possible revenues from extractive industries. The Greenlandic government confidently touted oils and minerals as the means to build a self-supporting economy (Gad et al. 2018), and hence, achieve financial equality.

Eligible for Equal Sovereignty?

Finally, the 2009 act staged two forms of equality between Denmark and Greenland. Symbolically, the act simulated a present equality. Even though the law was passed by the Danish Parliament, it included a preamble—highly unusual in a Danish tradition—explicitly '[r]ecognising that the people of Greenland is a people pursuant to international law with the right of self-determination' and explaining that '[a]ccordingly, the Act is based on an agreement between *Naalakkersuisut* [using the Greenlandic name of the Government of Greenland] and the Danish Government as equal partners'. However, in between these two sentences, the preamble postponed equality, intimating the motivation for the act to be 'a wish to *foster* equality and mutual respect in the partnership between Denmark and Greenland' (italics inserted). The end of the act follows up on the initial reference to international law by explicating that 'Decision[s] regarding Greenland's independence shall be taken by the people of Greenland' and drawing up a roadmap for secession. Formally, then, the Danish and Greenlandic peoples are *presently* equal as *eligible* for sovereignty; however, equality *as* sovereign is postponed for the future. Even with this temporal staggering of equality, the preamble seems to place

Greenland one step ahead of the Faroe Islands in terms of equality as the Faroes never got Denmark to issue a similar recognition of a foundation of future Faroese independence in international law (Prime Minister 2018).

Legal formalities and material substance aside, most Danish politicians have learned from the debates leading up to and following 2009 to explicitly deny hierarchy whenever mentioning the Community of the Realm. However, they tend to have more difficulties explaining just what equality among unequal partners may specifically mean (Gad 2017a: 42–44, 116). Against this background, most Greenlandic political parties and parliamentarians remain committed to equality as sovereignty; what organizes the party system is rather how fast one wants to progress with formal sovereignty and what substantial developments need to be tended to before sovereignty can be sustainable (Gad 2014).

Geopolitical and Paradiplomatic Sovereignty Games

In these negotiations of how to get to sovereign equality, diversifying dependence beyond Denmark has been central. Playing games with Denmark's sovereignty has been key to upholding it at all (Gad 2017a: 67–72). I employ the 'games' metaphor here neither as the stylized games of rational choice game theory, nor to convey the impression that actions were playful much less that the consequences were entertaining. Rather, as developed in Adler-Nissen and Gad (2014), 'sovereignty games' are linguistic and practical games constitutive of human interaction (*pace* Wittgenstein) and made possible and necessary by the idea that a state needs sovereignty to exist. Geopolitical position, territorial size, and imperial history, however, have made for very different games for Greenland and the Faroe Islands.

Imperial and Cold War Sovereignty Games

Greenland is key to controlling access to the North American continent for missiles from Eurasia in general and from the Kola Peninsula in particular. The United States took over Greenland in 1941 to keep the Germans out and facilitate US participation in the war in Europe, sending provisions for the population while leaving civilian government to the Danish authorities in place. After re-establishing connections in 1945, Copenhagen expected the Americans to leave, but the development of weapons technology made the northernmost part of Greenland essential to US nuclear strategy, both defensive and offensive. The result was the 1951 Defense of Greenland Agreement (Lidegaard 1999: 179–88, 334–5; Wivel 2020) which '[w]ithout prejudice to the sovereignty of the Kingdom of Denmark' over Greenland, allowed the US military to do whatever it wanted. The fact that Danish acceptance of US priorities extended to the storage and transportation of nuclear weapons, which the Danish government explicitly forbids in Denmark 'proper', became apparent in 1968 when a B-52 crashed into the ice-covered fiord by Thule Air Base, and finally clear in 1995 when a 1957 letter from the Danish Prime Minister to the US embassy in Copenhagen discussing the matter was declassified (DUPI 1997).

In comparison, the Faroe Islands had less negative effects from both the Second World War and the Cold War. UK troops arrived in Tórshavn as the Germans occupied Denmark, and in 1945, they left behind the island's first airport and a community that had experienced five years of locally based government as well as commercial relations beyond the realm. During the Cold War, the position occupied by the islands in the 'GIUK' gap (the straits between Greenland–Iceland–UK) made for technical installations vital to NATO's defence against Russian nuclear bombers, submarines, and missiles. Personnel were limited and mostly Danish, but the military character of some of the installations and the exact role of the Americans dispatched were kept secret from the Faroese public and Parliament, causing some local uproar when facts were uncovered (Jensen 2014; Nielsen 2017).

In contrast to the Faroese experience, the Greenland Defense Agreement stipulated that 'every effort will be made to avoid any contact between United States personnel and the local population'. This provision was in line with Danish narratives legitimizing colonization, namely that the Inuit natives needed protection from outside interference and that Denmark provided a uniquely gentle and benevolent stewardship of the modernization process. Nevertheless, Denmark's efforts to uphold sovereignty over Greenland vis-à-vis competing powers have, in certain instances, involved harsh interference in the lives of groups of Greenlanders (Gad 2017a: 69–70, 2017b). In 1925, 70 Greenlanders were transferred some 800 km north from Tasiilaq to what would be known as Ittoqqortoormiit. Like in Arctic Canada (Salter 2019), transfers were promoted to the Greenlanders as a way to reach better hunting grounds, but the decisions were actually made to secure sovereignty: North East Greenland was claimed by Norway. Ultimately, the exercise proved helpful when the International Court of Justice in The Hague ruled in favour of Denmark in 1935.

Decades later, the UN decolonization process and US military strategy conspired to push Denmark to a similar population transfer. In early 1953, the US found it necessary to protect Thule Air Base by building a tactical nuclear missile silo right in the middle of a neighbouring Inuit settlement (and the Danish authorities found the 'contact between United States personnel and the local population' unfolding in less than dignified ways). Since the revision of the Danish Constitution was due to expand civil liberties to Greenlanders from June 1953—as a reply to UN demands for decolonization of non-self-governing territories—the Danish authorities found themselves in a hurry. Hence, in the late spring, the Greenlanders were told to vacate the premises within days and pack their belongings on their dog sleds. Replacement housing at the abandoned summer campground Qaanaaq 100 km to the north was only established during the following winter. No sooner than in 1999, a high court decision established that the removal of the hunters and their families had been forced rather than voluntary as claimed by the authorities.

The number of US facilities across Greenland has gradually shrunk to one (Thule), and a series of procedures have been introduced to enhance Danish and Greenlandic involvement and insight into US military activities (Ministry of Foreign Affairs 2008). The steady stream of scandals emerging from Thule has continuously embarrassed Denmark's image as a particularly benevolent protector of its Greenlandic subjects. Hence, the 2003 *Itilleq* agreement guaranteed Greenland insight and involvement in the foreign and security policy conducted by the Danish government on behalf of the island and its population. Most spectacularly, the Government of Greenland got to co-sign the 2004 *Igaliku* agreement amending the defence agreement alongside the United States and Denmark in exchange for acceptance of US plans to revamp the Thule radars for the national missile defence system (Kristensen 2005). Denmark symbolically upholds sovereignty by flying *Dannebrog* over Thule, by dispatching the *Sirius* dogs-led patrol across uninhabited North East Greenland, and by patrolling Greenlandic waters with a handful of vessels conducting fisheries control. But all planning for war places the defence of Greenland in US hands. In parallel, Greenland now flies its flag *Erfalasorput* at Thule, but its government has not prioritized its sparse resources to dispatch an official representative at the base, and ideas for Greenlandic involvement in Danish military activities in Greenland remain jottings so detached from reality that only recently, someone thought of adding *Erfalasorput* to *Dannebrog* on the stanchions of the *Sirius* sleds (High Commissioner 2020: 10). In that sense, the games played around military affairs allow the representatives of a tiny people a certain insight while legitimizing Danish formal sovereignty and US military sovereignty over a huge territory.

European Sovereignty Games

In other parts of the foreign policy of the Community of the Realm, the benefits of playing games with sovereignty fall more decidedly to the islands. Relations with the European Union provide instructive examples (Adler-Nissen and Gad 2014), particularly since the games played in relation to the Faroe Islands and Greenland take different forms. When Denmark voted to join the European Communities in 1972, the Faroese votes under home rule were counted separately. Since a majority voted against, the Faroes were exempted from Danish membership. In contrast, Greenland's majority against accession was inconsequential; integrated as an 'equal' part, Greenland followed Denmark into the EC. The prospects of sovereignty over fisheries, vital to Greenland's economy and development plans, moving further South from Copenhagen to Brussels were decisive for the demands for a home rule status equal to the Faroes' (Rebhan 2016; Beach 2020). Aiming to replicate the Faroese example, home rule was introduced in 1979, and a second referendum in 1982 showed a majority for *leave*. However, when

Greenland did leave the EC in 1985, it ended up in a radically different position than the Faroes. The two positions involve very different benefits and drawbacks, inviting different games to be played with sovereignty.

The Faroes remain among the polities least involved in European integration. As a tiny economy outside any larger formal frameworks for cooperation and trade, it has been difficult for the islands to move themselves up the agenda of Eurocrats; only in 1991 was a trade agreement with the EU concluded (Adler-Nissen 2014). Their position outside the EU framework makes for interesting games. One example, perhaps the most intriguing to standard conceptions of international agency, played out in 2013, when herring and mackerel started moving in new patterns in the North Atlantic. Denmark has left sovereignty over fisheries to Brussels, and Tórshavn has taken home its own fisheries. The two sides could not agree on quotas, and the EU banned Faroese fishing products from the EU and Faroese vessels from EU ports (including Denmark). In return, the Faroese Ministry of Foreign Affairs advertised that it would (in Denmark's name) initiate proceedings against the EU (including Denmark) in the WTO (Lögmannsskrivstovan 2013). The dispute with the EU was settled before WTO procedures began, but in the meantime, the Faroes had redirected most of its fisheries export to Russia. More benefits from their outsider status came in 2014 when the EU introduced sanctions on Russia following the annexation of Crimea. The Faroe Islands quickly became the no. 1 exporter of fish to Russia and now works towards a free trade agreement with the Russian-led Eurasian Economic Union (Breum 2018) to protect what amounts to 29 per cent of the islands' exports.

Contrary to the Faroe Islands, Greenland left the EC only to be associated with the communities through the well-established category of Overseas Countries and Territories (OCT). The OCTs remain outside the EU *acquis,* but they enjoy free movement of people and tax-free access for exports to the Single Market. The 1985 Greenland Treaty amended the Treaty of Rome to move Greenland from Danish membership to OCT status, but tax-free status only applies on the provision that 'satisfactory' agreements on fisheries cooperation are in place. The fisheries agreements involve the EU buying fishing quotas, for decades securing annual transfers from Brussels which matched what Greenland received from regional development funds while a member (Gad 2017a: 103–4). When the European Parliament was granted oversight powers, the price paid for fishing quotas from Greenland came under pressure; counting 'paper fish' that mainly existed as potential future stocks which might conceivably one day appear in Greenlandic waters, parliamentarians found that quotas could be bought cheaper in African waters. Nevertheless, Greenland and Denmark managed to keep the amount transferred from Brussels roughly constant by convincing EU members to sign a unique Partnership Agreement aiming to support the 'sustainable development' of Greenland (Gad 2017a: 82, 104). Contrary to most OCTs, Greenland's relatively high GDP precludes eligibility for EDF funds. Particularly when contrasted to the Faroe Islands' outsider position, it is clear that the OCT status, fisheries, and partnership agreements allow Greenland uniquely independent visibility and agency in relation to the EU for a non-sovereign, non-member polity (Gad 2017a: 85–100).

Arctic Sovereignty Games

Increased attention in the wake of changes to global climate as well as economic and security balances has awarded Greenland and the Faroe Islands more possibilities to connect beyond Denmark. Both governments deploy their own diplomatic staff (with Danish diplomatic passports) to Brussels and Reykjavik, Tórshavn also sends representatives to London and Moscow, and Nuuk recently added Washington and have plans for Beijing. However, it has become increasingly clear that not all third parties are as apt as the EU at engaging in similar sovereignty games. Moreover, recent US attitudes towards the 'scramble for the Arctic' might tell Greenland that Eastern relief of economic dependence on Western countries is unacceptable.

Greenland's relations to China in particular have been complicated (Gad et al. 2018). When gearing up efforts to attract foreign investments in the extractive industries meant to finance independence, Greenlandic authorities realized that the global markets for raw materials had just plummeted with the 2007 financial crash. Soon, they began looking to China for investors driven by sufficiently long-term interests. Initially, the Chinese counterparts seemed to have some trouble deciding how to engage with this 'Tibet-size' autonomous entity; later, Greenlandic efforts—and the way they were facilitated by Danish diplomacy—appears to have persuaded Chinese organizations that it would be alright to do business with Greenland. The extension of the Chinese Belt and Road Initiative with a Polar Silk Road has possibly made a difference as well (Sørensen 2018). Recently, Chinese investors have taken steps towards realizing a couple of mining projects (Andersson et al. 2018). More controversially, Greenlandic authorities included the China Communications Construction Company (CCCC) among entrepreneurs prequalified to bid for the expansion of two airports in Greenland. However, the Danish Prime Minister unexpectedly stepped in to co-fund the economically dubious project as a way to keep Greenland out of what some in Copenhagen portrayed as a Chinese debt trap. A couple of years earlier, Denmark advertised the old US/Danish naval station at Kangilinnguit for sale only to withdraw the property from the market when a Chinese mining company showed interest in buying. Most Greenlandic politicians are content with securing Danish funds for the airports. However, particularly when seen in conjunction, the two interventions nurture suspicions that even while trying to keep up a facade of selflessly facilitating Greenland's diversification of its dependence, Denmark works to keep the dependence for itself to uphold sovereignty over Greenland.

Such Danish efforts might be made easier by a re-securitization of the wider Arctic. Russia seems to prioritize economic development of its Arctic, and to that aim, it needs Western technology and Chinese investments. Meanwhile, Russian efforts to enhance centrifugal dynamics in Europe and the West are well documented. The Faroese fisheries exports—and the Danish acquiescence—play well into both Russian strategies. Danish authorities have had trouble convincing Nuuk that the worries about Chinese involvement in Greenland originated in Washington. However, with US Secretary of State Mike Pompeo's statements at the Arctic Council Ministerial Meeting in May 2019, the Trump administration's approach to alliance politics arrived in the Arctic. While placing Russian demands to control the Northern Sea Route along its Siberian coast in 'a pattern of aggressive Russian behaviour here in the Arctic', his main worry was its inclusion in China's Polar Silk Road. Thus, he conjured up to images: First, an 'Arctic Ocean...transform[ed] into a new South China Sea, fraught with militarization and competing territorial claims'. Second, an image in which 'all nations, including non-Arctic nations,...have a right to engage peacefully in this region[...in] free and fair competition, open, by the rule of law', but since 'all the parties in the marketplace have to play by those same rules [and t]hose who violate those rules should lose their rights to participate in that marketplace, [r]espect and transparency are the price of admission' (Pompeo 2019). It was understood in whose hands admission control would best be put, as 'American leadership stands in stark contrast with the Chinese and Russian models' (Pompeo 2019).

CONCLUSION

The 'Community of the Realm' remains a constitutional oxymoron connoting both imperial hierarchy and communal bonds. Its three constituent polities share an ideal of a world of nations, each homogenous in ethnic terms, and each in command of their own state. Step by step, Denmark has met some Faroese and Greenlandic demands, but the equality aspired for proves itself elusive. Over time, the games played to protect Danish sovereignty have changed from somewhat heavy-handed, if never bloody, Danish imperialism to increasingly sophisticated and collaborative linguistic and diplomatic games. Given the nation state ideal exported from Copenhagen to its dependencies, the narratives most legitimate in the North Atlantic describe the Community as an ever-looser union. Hence, Denmark greatly enhances the viability of the Community by explicitly embracing its dissolution—in the form of Greenlandic and Faroese independence—as its ultimate goal. In contrast, whenever Danish actions, reactions, or passivity can be taken to imply that Denmark tries to keep the Realm for itself, the existence of the Community is put at stake. Looking ahead, the domestic side of these games is likely to be easier than the international side.

After initially dismissing the whole enterprise, the Danish government has changed its position, accepting that separate Faroese and Greenlandic constitutions are acceptable as long as they do not contradict the Danish Constitution, *Grundloven*. Nevertheless, after some initial confusion, the Greenlandic constitutional committee is headed towards drafting a constitution for a sovereign Greenlandic state (Schultz-Nielsen 2019). The adoption of such a text and a parallel Faroese one will formally kill off the Community of the Realm as we constitutionally know it. However, that will hardly be the end of Danish-Greenlandic-Faroese relations. Quite the contrary, a 'Community' immediately resurrected after secession, re-constituted as less of a 'Realm', is probably the most durable version. Different historical narratives producing different legal bases for demands have mostly kept Greenlandic and Faroese efforts separate. The Faroese have long looked to the 1918 Icelandic personal union (Hauge 2018), while the

Greenlanders, inspired by other decolonizing archipelagos, have fixed on 'free association' as a better fit (Kleist 2019). Increasingly, however, the specific queries and suggestions have appeared *in tandem*. The next step could be that Greenland and/or the Faroe Islands leave the Danish state, only to associate from outside. In the negotiations leading to this rearrangement, constitutional law, day-to-day foreign policy, and finances will be fought over but ultimately resolved in line with Danish pragmatism. Deal breakers will rather be either the organization of security politics or a hard choice to be made by the islanders.

The security related obstacle pertains more severely to Greenland than to the Faroes. After Secretary Pompeo at Rovaniemi had drawn up his image of a region in conflict and promised to send more naval ships, he concluded his Arctic offensive by sending a part-time diplomat to Nuuk. The traveling First Secretary presented his task as 'forging bonds between people and expanding our economic and trade bonds' (Wille and Lindstrøm 2019). However, President Trump's surprise attempt to cut through sovereignty games by simply buying Greenland might have served to explain to the Government of Greenland the bonds put on its sovereign choice of business partners by US security doctrines. This could very well start a new conversation in Greenland about its position in geopolitics. So far, geopolitics in Greenland has been discussed either as threats coming from outside in the form of US military facilities drawing attention from Russian nukes, or as opportunities to diversify dependence by engaging rising powers. Chances are, the conversation will now have to balance the risks and opportunities involved in *not* picking sides. If the resident superpower explicitly insists that it will not accept that Greenland keeps all options open, Denmark might even reappear as a convenient buffer between Greenland and the real(ist) world.

The hard choice comes from the precedence in international jurisprudence making separate citizenship the fine line deciding eligibility for independent membership of the UN and some, but far from all, other international organizations, extending from the intergovernmental organizations managing North Atlantic fish stocks to the private International Olympic Committee. Freely associated states whose citizens *also* enjoy citizenship of a metropole state are not allowed membership; those who do *not* can attend both the UN general assembly and the Olympics under their own flag (Kleist 2019). Only time will tell whether the Greenlanders and the Faroese value these flags more than access to social services in Denmark and residency and work in the European Union allowed by a Danish passport.

References

Adler-Nissen, Rebecca (2014). 'The Faroe Islands', *Cooperation & Conflict*, 49/1: 55–79.

Adler-Nissen, Rebecca, and Ulrik P. Gad (2014). 'Post-imperial sovereignty games in the Nordic region', *Cooperation & Conflict*, 49/1: 3–32.

Andersson, Patrik, Jesper Zeuthen, and Per Kalvig (2018). 'Chinese mining in Greenland: Arctic access or access to minerals?', *Arctic Yearbook 2018: Special Section: China & the Arctic*, 102–17.

Beach, Derek (2020). 'Referendums in Denmark: Influence on politics', in Peter M. Christiansen, Jørgen Elklit, and Peter Nedergaard, eds, *The Oxford Handbook of Danish Politics*. Oxford: Oxford University Press, 400–16.

Binderkrantz, Anne (2008). 'På danske hænder?', *Politica*, 40/2: 155–79.

Bregnsbo, Michael (2004). 'Fra konglomeratstat til enhedsstat', paper presented to a seminar on *The Multicultural Denmark of the long 18th century*, Hillerød, 25–26 April.

Breum, Martin (2018). 'Russian fish money keeping Faroes out of EU sanctions', EUobserver, https://euobserver.com/foreign/142847 (accessed 26 June 2019).

Breum, Martin (2019). 'Bor der virkelig mennesker nok i Grønland til at drive en stat?', djøf-bladet, https://www.djoefbladet.dk/artikler/2019/1/hvor-mange-mennesker-skal-der-til-at-drive-en-stat.aspx (accessed 26 June 2019).

Brochmann, Helene, and Bente Hamann (1990). *Forvaltning i Forandring: om kultur, rationalitet og bureaukrati i den grønlandske centraladministration*. Nuuk: Atuakkiorfik.

Christensen, Jens Peter (2020). 'The constitution', in Peter M. Christiansen, Jørgen Elklit, and Peter Nedergaard, eds, *The Oxford Handbook of Danish Politics*. Oxford: Oxford University Press, 9–27.

Dahl, Jens (1986). *Arktisk Selvstyre*. Copenhagen: Akademisk.

Danielsen, Jens (2011). 'Grønlands selvstyre og Danmarks riges Grundlov', *Juristen*, 93/1: 9–18.

DUPI (1997). *Grønland under den kolde krig: dansk og amerikansk sikkerhedspolitisk 1945–68*. Copenhagen: DUPI.

Elklit, Jørgen (2020). 'The electoral system. Fair and well-functioning', in Peter M. Christiansen, Jørgen Elklit, and Peter Nedergaard, eds, *The Oxford Handbook of Danish Politics*. Oxford: Oxford University Press, 56–75.

Gad, Ulrik P. (2014). 'Ahead of snap elections, Greenland's independence ambitions could open a window for closer co-operation with the EU', EuroPP blog, http://bit.ly/1wIzsTL (accessed 26 June 2019).

Gad, Ulrik P. (2017a). *National Identity Politics and Postcolonial Sovereignty Games: Greenland, Denmark, and the European Union*. Copenhagen: Museum Tusculanum.

Gad, Ulrik P. (2017b). 'Sex, Løgn og Landingsbaner: Thule set relationelt', *Grønland*, 65/3: 216–41.

Gad, Ulrik P. (2017c). 'What kind of nation state will Greenland be? Securitization theory as a strategy for analysing identity politics', *Politik*, 20/3: 104–20.

Gad, Ulrik P., Naja Graugaard, Anders Holgersen, Marc Jacobsen, Nina Lave, and Nikoline Schriver (2018). 'Imagining China on Greenland's road to independence', *Arctic Yearbook 2018: Special Section: China & the Arctic*, 6–28.

Gaini, Firouz (2011). 'Cultural rhapsody in shift', in Firouz Gaini, ed., *Among the Islanders of the North*. Tórshavn: Fróðskapur, 132–63.

Harhoff, Frederik (1993). *Rigsfællesskabet*. Aarhus: Klim.

Hauge, Mads (2018). 'Kongehuset og Færøerne', unpublished manuscript, https://xn—slgtogkrone-b9a.dk/wp-content/uploads/2018/05/Kongehuset-og-F%C3%A6r%C3%B8erne.pdf (accessed 26 June 2019).

High Commissioner (2020). 'Indberetning fra rigsombudsmanden i Grønland', 6 February, https://www.ft.dk/samling/20191/almdel/GRU/bilag/32/2147801.pdf (accessed 3 March 2020).

Houlberg, Kurt, and Niels Ejersbo (2020). 'Municipalities and regions. Approaching the limit of decentralization?', in Peter M. Christiansen, Jørgen Elklit, and Peter Nedergaard, eds, *The Oxford Handbook of Danish Politics*. Oxford: Oxford University Press, 141–59.

Iburg, Kim M., Henrik B. Hansen, and Peter Bjerregaard (2001). 'Health expectancy in Greenland', *Scandinavian Journal of Public Health*, 29/1: 5–12.

Jakobsen, Mads L.F. (2008). 'Et blindt fokus på Danmark?', *Politica*, 40/2: 134–54.

Janussen, Jakob (2017). *Analyse af fødestedskriteriet*. Nuuk: Forsoningskommissionen.

Jensen, Bent (2014). *Militære institutioner og anlæg på Færøerne under Den Kolde Krig*. Copenhagen: Gyldendal.

Justinussen, Jens C.S. (2019). 'Rigsfællesskabet i et føderalt perspektiv', *Politica*, 51/4: 441–68.

Kleist, Mininnguaq (2019). 'Grønlands udenrigspolitik og internationale relationer', *Politik*, 22/1: 84–101.

Kristensen, Kristian S. (2005). 'Negotiating base rights for missile defence', in Bertil Heurlin, and Steen Rynning, eds, *Missile Defense*. London: Routledge. 183–208.

Larsen, Bárður (2011). 'En håbløs søgen efter forfatningsrettens sikre fundament', *Juristen*, 93/4: 128–35.

Lennert, Karen H. (2006). 'The Danish Interests in the community with Greenland', unpublished Master's thesis, Aalborg University.

Lidegaard, Bo (1999). *I Kongens Tjeneste*. Copenhagen: Samleren.

Lögmansskrivstovan (2013). 'Faroe Islands takes the European Union to the WTO', http://www.mfa.fo/Default.aspx?ID=13626&Action=1&NewsId=5395&PID=23631 (accessed 13 March 2014).

Marquardt, Ole (2009). 'H.J. Rink', in Ole Høiris, ed., *Grønland—en refleksiv udfordring*. Aarhus: Aarhus University Press, 129–54.

Ministry of Foreign Affairs (2008). 'UGF alm. del – Svar på Spørgsmål 7', https://www.ft.dk/samling/20081/almdel/ugf/spm/7/svar/591827/629653.pdf (accessed 26 June 2019).

Nielsen, Jens P. (2017). 'Færøerne', in *Danmark under den kolde krig*, http://koldkrig-online.dk/anlaeg/faeroerne (accessed 26 June 2013).

Nuttall, Mark, and Klaus Dodds (2016). *The Scramble for the Poles*. Cambridge: Polity.

Pedersen, Helene H. (2020). 'The Parliament (*Folketinget*)', in Peter M. Christiansen, Jørgen Elklit, and Peter Nedergaard, eds, *The Oxford Handbook of Danish Politics*. Oxford: Oxford University Press, 88–106.

Pompeo, Mike (2019). 'Looking north: Sharpening America's Arctic focus', remarks to Arctic Council Ministerial Meeting, https://translations.state.gov/2019/05/06/looking-north-sharpening-americas-arctic-focus (accessed 26 June 2019).

Prime Minister (2018). 'Færøudvalget spm 8', https://www.tjodveldi.dk/spurningar/2018/4/18/frudvalget-spm-8-om-pramblen-til-den-grnlandske-selvstyrelov-forpligter-danmark-til-folkeretligt-at-respektere-grnlands-eksterne-selvbestemmelsesret-til-at-etablere-grnland-som-selvstndig-stat (accessed 5 June 2019).

Prime Minister's Office (n.d.). 'The unity of the realm', http://stm.dk/_a_2752.html (accessed 26 June 2019).

Qaasuitsup Kommunia (2014). *Kommuneplani 2014–26. Siunnersuut*. Ilulissat: Qaasuitsup Kommunia.

Rebhan, Christian (2016). *North Atlantic Euroscepticism*. Tórshavn: Froðskapur.

Renan, Ernest (1882/1992). *Qu'est-ce qu'une nation?* Paris: Presses-Pocket.

Salter, Mark (2019). 'Arctic security, territory, population', *International Political Sociology*, 13/4: 358–74.

Schultz-Nielsen, Jørgen (2019). 'Forfatningsarbejde: Omstridt punkt er skrottet', Sermitsiaq, https://sermitsiaq.ag/node/212571 (accessed 26 June 2019).

Skydsbjerg, Henrik (1999). *Grønland. 20 år med hjemmestyre*. Nuuk: Atuagkat.

Spiermann, Ole (2007). *Det danske rige i forfatningsretlig belysning*. Copenhagen: Jurist- og Økonomforbundets Forlag.

Stepan, Alfred (2013). 'A revised theory of federacy', in Joanne McEvoy, and Brendan O'Leary, eds, *Power Sharing in Deeply Divided Places*. Philadelphia, PA: University of Pennsylvania Press, 231–52.

Sørensen, Camilla T.N. (2018). 'China is in the Arctic to stay as a Great Power', *Arctic Yearbook 2018: Special Section: China & the Arctic*, 43–58.

Wille, Andreas, and Merete Lindstrøm (2019). 'Diplomaten Sung Choi skal knytte Grønland og USA tættere sammen', KNR, https://knr.gl/da/nyheder/diplomaten-sung-choi-skal-knytte-gr%C3%B8nland-og-usa-t%C3%A6ttere-sammen (accessed 26 June 2019).

Wivel, Anders (2020). 'In war and peace. Security and defence policy in a small state', in Peter M. Christiansen, Jørgen Elklit, and Peter Nedergaard, eds, *The Oxford Handbook of Danish Politics*. Oxford: Oxford University Press, 453–69.

....

CHAPTER 4

THE MONARCH

Head of State and National Symbol

....

JES FABRICIUS MØLLER

THE monarch is the head of state. According to the most recent textbook on constitutional law, the role of the monarch is 'of a purely symbolic and ceremonial character', and the monarch has no independent competencies in matters of state (Christensen et al. 2015: 59). During the twentieth century, the functions of the monarch stabilized into a predictable relation and division of labour between Parliament, government, and head of state, equal to the heads of state in the other Nordic countries.

According to the Constitution of 5 June 1849, which abolished absolute monarchy and introduced restricted monarchy, the king enjoyed a wide range of prerogatives. The role of the monarch has since changed considerably more than the wording of the Constitution, which has remained unchanged for the most part. According to Section 3, the king has executive power and shares legislative power with Parliament. According to Section 12—added in 1855—the king has 'the highest authority over all matters of the realm and executes it through his ministers', and his powers are only limited by what is stated in the Constitution itself.

Taking into consideration that Denmark today is a parliamentary democracy, the functions of the head of state are to be executed on the basis of a careful reinterpretation of the wording and the intentions of the Constitution. Although the monarch has no political power, he or she is still considered the highest-ranking person in the country, a status that is confirmed symbolically (i.e. on coins and stamps) and at official events and ceremonies. This raises the question of how the monarch fits into the system of the separation of power, according to which the organs of the state are equal and independent of each other. According to this principle, 'it is incorrect to single out one of the organs of the state as superior to the others' (Sørensen 1973: 58). The answer to this question is that all political and judicial power is divided between government, Parliament, and the courts; the monarch has neither political nor judicial power, and as such, is beyond the separation of power. The function of the monarch is to be a 'symbol of the unity of the state' (Andersen 1954: 112). The monarch does not define or incarnate but represents the state. Therefore, when the president of the Supreme Court, the speaker of Parliament, or the prime minister pays their respects to HM Queen Margrethe II, it is a sign not of subordination but of respect for the state they all serve.

The monarch is elevated above political struggle and thus liberated from the execution of power. The monarch does not vote, and neither do members of the immediate family. His or her main task is to represent the state because none of the other organs of the state can do that due to the principle of partition. It follows naturally that the monarch is obligated to avoid public discussions of a political nature and to stay neutral in any political struggle or conflict. However, this obligation is not stated explicitly in the Constitution.

HISTORY

The foundation for the present monarchy was laid in 1849 when Denmark, as one of the last countries in Europe, acquired a liberal constitution. It happened during a civil war fought over the independence of a united Schleswig-Holstein. Denmark was a composite, colonial state and an absolute monarchy, codified by the *Lex Regia* of 1665. The king was given all powers, but at the same time, he was bound by law, so his rule was absolute but not arbitrary. The government faced several challenges in the 1840s. The Oldenburg dynasty was dying out, and the union between Denmark proper and the Duchy of Holstein—a member of the German Federation—would be dissolved like the Hanoverian-British union a few years earlier if a solution to the succession crisis was not found. A constitutional reform had been halted for decades due to the composite nature of the monarchy. At the same time, nationalism as a political movement was on the rise. The conflicts converged in March 1848 when the new king, Frederik VII, gave in to pressure from the Copenhagen public to replace the government with representatives of the so-called national-liberal movement which was working towards a unification of Schleswig and Denmark proper under one constitution. This in turn triggered an uprising by supporters of a unified Schleswig-Holstein, strongly supported by public opinion in most German countries.

A constitutional assembly was formed through a combination of royal appointments and a general election in October 1848, and the assembly passed a constitution that was signed and ratified by the King on 5 June 1849. The Constitution did not replace *Lex Regia* completely; two articles concerning the house rules of the royal family are still in effect today. Known as *Danmarks Riges Grundlov*, literally 'The Founding Law of the Realm of Denmark', the Constitution had an ambiguous nature because it had strong elements of popular sovereignty, and at the same time, it was promulgated by the King and was clearly styled as such. Despite the efforts to create a unified Schleswig-Danish constitutional monarchy, the civil war ended with the *status quo ante* intact, and the Constitution was valid only for Denmark proper including the Faroe Islands, whereas the duchies—and Iceland—remained under direct monarchical rule.

At an international conference in London in 1852, the crisis of succession was solved with the election of Prince Christian of Schleswig-Holstein-Sonderburg-Glücksburg and his wife Princess Louise of Hesse-Kassel as heirs to the Danish throne, but neither the national nor the constitutional problem could be solved during the following decade. An attempt by the Danish government to pass a common constitution for Schleswig and Denmark proper in November 1863 triggered a declaration of war from the German Federation that was executed mainly by Prussian and Austrian troops. The Danish government probably had hoped that the other great powers would intervene and limit the conflict, thus providing a solution to problems that had proven politically insoluble. However, due to unfortunate circumstances, the unforeseen brilliance of Chancellor Bismarck, and a fumbled diplomacy, all three duchies Lauenburg, Holstein, and Schleswig were ceded to the enemy, and eventually, absorbed by Prussia like Hanover.

Since 1849, the Constitution has defined the form of government as limited or restricted monarchical, and the king actually appointed the governments throughout the second half of the nineteenth century. In 1872, the liberal opposition, under the label 'the Liberal Party' (*Venstre*) won an absolute majority in the second chamber of Parliament (*Folketinget*). The Liberals' main demand was that government formation should be based on the majority in *Folketinget* because it was elected by a broader electorate than the Upper House (*Landstinget*). However, King Christian IX (reg. 1863–1906) nevertheless kept appointing representatives of the landed elite as heads of conservative governments, provoking a constitutional crisis that was not solved until 1901 when the Liberal Party was eventually invited to form the government.

As a rule, no government since has been able to function with a majority in the *Folketinget* against it. This did not mean that the king ceased to have legitimate influence over government formation. In 1920, King Christian X made the mistake of sacking the government without making sure that there was a majority against it and even without the counter-signature of the prime minister himself. This was the last time a king acted on his own in political matters. It caused a severe constitutional crisis known as the Easter Crisis (*Påskekrisen*). Demonstrators in the street demanded the King's abdication and a republican constitution. Political leaders, in particular Social Democrats, negotiated a solution to the crisis and ended up supporting the monarchy. During the following years, a long-lasting and stable relationship between government and the head of state was established. For a short while during the German occupation from 1940–5, the King played an active, almost oppositional role in politics even though he stayed loyal to any government decision. Since 1920, the rule of ministerial counter-signature has ensured that the monarch never acts on his own in matters of state.

SUCCESSION

Denmark has been a hereditary monarchy since 1660. According to *Lex Regia*, succession to the throne was agnatic-cognatic. In the eighteenth and early nineteenth century, it was believed in Copenhagen that *Lex Regia* was also valid in Schleswig but that was contested, particularly by the Schleswig-Holstein independence movement that claimed that the two duchies both followed the purely male succession of most German monarchies. As part of the international agreements after the First Schleswig War 1848–50, succession was equalized in the entire Danish monarchy to become purely agnatic. The Act of Succession was revised in 1953 to give women restricted access to the throne and again in 2009 to give women equal access according to the principle of primogeniture.

The heir to the throne is considered king or queen regnant the moment their predecessor dies. Neither abdication nor usurpation has taken place since the sixteenth century. Anointment or crowning has not taken place since King Christian VIII (reg. 1839–48) ascended the throne. Neither the throne nor the regalia are in use either, and speaking of the throne or the crown is purely metaphorical. The most important ceremony when a new monarch takes up office is the proclamation performed by the prime minister from the balcony of Christiansborg Palace, which houses the Supreme Court, the Parliament, and the offices of the prime minister. The monarch must swear loyalty to the Constitution before taking office (Section 8). Usually, this oath is taken when the heir to the throne joins the Council of State (*Statsrådet*) at the age of 18. The monarch is also obliged to belong to an 'Evangelical Lutheran Church', which, in theory, could be another church than the established Church of Denmark (*folkekirken*), but it is considered self-evident that the monarch and the heirs to the throne are members of the established church. Other members of the royal family have freedom of religion. It is customary, however, that people from other denominations convert when marrying into the royal family.

Situations in which the monarch is unable to govern due to illness or absence are regulated by law (1871). If the monarch is out of the country for more than a day—officially or privately—a governor of the realm (*Rigsforstander*) is appointed so that the country is not without an acting head of state. According to the law, any person of age who is not previously convicted and is a Danish citizen of Evangelical Lutheran faith can be appointed Governor of the Realm. As a rule, members of the royal family are chosen. When the heir apparent is so appointed, his title is Regent.

THE ROYAL HOUSE

The civil list—the size of the yearly allowance and the number of buildings that are at the monarch's disposition—is decided by law with reference to Section 10 of the Constitution at the beginning of the monarch's reign. This amount is then index regulated. In 2017, the annuity for the Queen was approx. DKK 83 million. The court has a staff of 110 people, which equals 95 full-time employees (Royal House 2017). Not covered by the civil list are guards, escorts, and military parade corps or transportation on the royal yacht, which is a vessel of the navy, air force planes, and helicopters. The total public expenditure for the monarch is the object of regular press scrutiny. The royal palaces are protected by the military, and personal security of royal family members is taken care of by the Danish Security and Intelligence Service (*Politiets Efterretningstjeneste*). The cost of these services and the size of the staff are not published.

According to Section 11 of the Constitution, annuities for individual members of the royal house are allowed. 'The royal house' is not defined by law, and allowances have not followed any general rule. Both members of the immediate and extended family, within and outside of the line of succession, have received allowances. Currently, the Queen's cousin Count Ingolf of Rosenborg, who was the heir apparent until 1953, and both her sons receive an allowance. In the next generation, it is foreseen that only the eldest child of the Crown Prince will receive an allowance.

Section 21 of *Lex Regia* states that no 'prince of the blood' may marry without the consent of the monarch. This is specified in the Law of Succession. Consent is given in the Council of State (Act of Succession, Section 5), that is, by the government and the monarch collectively. An heir to the throne who marries without royal consent may lose the rights to succession and the royal title. This provision has been applied several times in the twentieth century.

Section 25 of *Lex Regia* states that 'princes and princesses of the blood' should not answer to the regular courts, only to the monarch. This is usually referred to as legal immunity, but it does not mean that members of the royal house cannot be punished. The provision dates back to when the king was actually head of the Supreme Court. The monarch herself enjoys full legal immunity (Section 13 of the Constitution). The criminal code does not contain articles on *lèse-majesté*. However, it is an aggravation if certain crimes are committed against the king or queen (Sections 112, 113, and 115).

The Court

The royal court as an institution is not defined by law. It consists of the employees who serve in the monarch's household and in the official functions of state. The court is financed by the civil list. Terms of employment equal those of public employees in general. The court is headed by the monarch. The two top officials are the Cabinet Secretary and the Lord Chamberlain. Their functions are described by the court itself as such:

> The Lord Chamberlain's office is the secretariat for The Queen. The office is in charge of all the arrangements for official functions, such as state visits at home and abroad, dinners and luncheons, and court ceremonies, including presentation of credentials by ambassadors as well as their farewell audiences. [...] The Cabinet Secretary to HM The Queen heads the Cabinet Secretariat and is the link between HM The Queen and the Government, particularly the Prime Minister's office and the Ministry of Foreign Affairs. He is the advisor and executive officer to HM The Queen in regard to her attendance at official engagements, her patronage, reception of deputations, audiences, matters pertaining to court titles and rank, and drafts of Her Majesty's speeches. The Cabinet Secretary to HM The Queen also serves as secretary to the

Chancery of the Royal Danish Orders of Chivalry, and in that capacity advises The Queen in regard to the awarding of orders and medals.   (Royal House 2019)

THE CHAPEL OF THE ROYAL ORDERS OF KNIGHTHOOD

The Chapel of Chivalry (*Ordenskapitlet*) administers the two awarded orders: the Order of the Elephant and the Order of Dannebrog. The latter is divided into six classes: Grand Commander, Grand Cross, Commander of the First and Second Degree, and Knight of the First and Second Degree. The Chapel of Chivalry serves directly under the monarch as a personal prerogative, and orders are awarded without the counter-signature of a minister. The cabinet secretary is also daily head of the Chapel of Chivalry and answers directly to the monarch. Candidates for decoration are nominated by the heads of ministerial departments. Politicians are not to exercise influence on decorations.

The exchange of decorations during state visits is coordinated with the Ministry of Foreign Affairs. Holders of the two lowest classes of the Order of Dannebrog are called knights, but it is not an aristocratic title. Neither personal nor hereditary peerages have been awarded to commoners for more than a hundred years. On occasion, members of the royal family have been elevated into the ranks of nobility when their royal title has been taken away from them, as in the case of marriage without royal consent or divorce. When Prince Joachim's first wife remarried in 2007, she was dubbed Countess of Frederiksborg. In 2008, both of the Queen's sons were given additional titles as Counts of Monpezat, thus domesticating the Prince Consort's family name as a Danish heredi-tary aristocratic title.

THE MONARCH'S FUNCTIONS

'The signature of the King to resolutions relating to legislation and government shall make such resolutions valid, provided that the signature of the King is accompanied by the signature or signatures of one or more Ministers' (Constitution, Section 14). The Queen signs government proposals and legislation. It has occurred that a law has been without validity because it had not been signed by the Queen within the given time limit of 30 days (Constitution, Section 22), but that was due to an omission by the legislative branch. The monarch's right of veto is purely theoretical.

The government's law proposals are presented in the Council of State, which convenes 5–10 times a year. The Council of State consists of all ministers of the government and the monarch, who chairs the council. When coming of age at 18, the heir apparent 'has a seat' on the Council of State (Constitution, Section 17). HM Queen Margrethe II has thus taken part in meetings on the Council of State for more than 60 years.

The Queen attends the opening meeting in the *Folketinget* every year on the first Tuesday of October. Previous monarchs occasionally gave the opening speech stating the intentions of the government, the so-called 'throne speech', but the Constitution (Section 38) now directs the prime minister to give this speech (Nielsen 2012).

The Queen has separate regular private audiences with the prime minister and the foreign minister with no other persons attending. The origin of these conversations or consultations goes back to the time when the king actually exercised influence on government affairs, but they are also valuable today because if the Queen is supposed to stay out of politics, she needs to be informed about what is on the political agenda.

One of the main tasks of the monarch is to represent Denmark when receiving ambassadors and when receiving and paying official and state visits. On official visits, the monarch is always accompanied by one or more ministers who carry the political responsibility. Other members of the royal family can make visits or receive foreign guests, but the head of state is always received by a head of state on official visits. Decorations are exchanged by prior agreement (Møller 2014).

There is clearly an increasing tendency for members of the royal family to take part in activities in support of Danish businesses when going abroad. Attempts have been made to measure the economic value of these visits, but they are not precise (Sørensen and Aksglæde 2018).

Top civil servants and military officers are formally employed by the monarch, who signs the papers of employment and promotion without having any influence on the process except when it comes to employees of her court. For historic reasons, the Queen also approves new hymn-books and altar books of the established church. She is sometimes described as head of the church, which is not correct. The monarch's role is inherited from the absolutist past since no legislation regulating the established church or defining its leadership has been passed since 1849. The church has no clear hierarchy or chain of command and is highly decentralized. As far as authority exists, it is exercised by the minister of church affairs.

The monarch as an institution is of great importance to the relationship with the Faroe Islands, Greenland, and the Community (or Commonwealth) of the Realm (*Rigsfællesskabet*) (see Gad 2020). The North Atlantic possessions were Norwegian when they came under the Danish Crown in 1380 along with Norway. Until 1721, there had been no contact with Greenland for centuries. After the Treaty of Kiel in 1814, Norway was ceded to Sweden, while Greenland, Iceland, and the Faroe Islands remained under the Danish Crown. In 1918, the sovereign Kingdom of Iceland was created in personal union with Denmark. In 1944, Iceland became a republic with overwhelming popular support. Since the Second World War, the Faroe Islands and later Greenland have gained a wide degree of autonomy in all matters other than foreign policy, defence, and justice. The situation today increasingly resembles the relationship with Iceland after 1918. Royal visits to Greenland and the Faroe Islands are relatively frequent, and the Queen never fails to mention both in her televised New Year's Eve address.

THE LEGITIMACY OF THE MONARCHY

Two main arguments are used to criticize the Danish monarchy and/or advocate for the dissolution of the monarchy. Firstly, the monarchy is expensive, and it is inappropriate for taxpayers to promote social inequality and finance royal 'lives of luxury'. Generous gifts to the royal family from businesses and other sponsors have similarly been objects of criticism (Høvsgaard 2012). Secondly, monarchical privilege based on birth defies the basic principles of democracy and meritocracy. As a recent textbook for students of law states: 'The idea that the office as head of state should be inherited by a member of a certain family is obviously out of sync with contemporary views on egalitarianism and democracy' (Christensen et al. 2016: 49).

The republican movement in Denmark, such as it is, is neither united nor strong. Only one party currently represented in Parliament, the Red-Green Alliance, is actively against the monarchy, but it does not push the agenda. Important representatives of other parties (the Alternative and the Socialist People's Party) have expressed concerns and apprehensions about some monarchical institutions. Historically, both the Social Liberals and the Social Democrats have had the abolition of the monarchy as an official policy but not any longer. However, a significant minority in both parties do still hold that opinion. More generally, members of Parliament and members of government belonging to either party, along with the Socialist People's Party and the Red-Green Alliance, do not accept decorations.

Arguments in favour of the monarchy—or legitimation strategies—can be categorized into four groups. First comes the formal or legalistic argument that the monarchy is given by the Constitution. The difficulty of changing the Constitution (see Christensen 2020) provides both *de jure* and *de facto* safeguards. As mentioned earlier, difficulties arise because the wording of the Constitution is a far cry from reality in many cases. The legal argument is related to the second argument, the democratic or popular. Since the present Constitution and Law of Succession were confirmed by a plebiscite in 1953, the monarchy can claim a considerable degree of democratic legitimacy. The Law of Succession was revised in 2009 and also confirmed by a plebiscite. Opinion polls since the late 1960s have shown that the monarchy and the monarch enjoy a high degree of popular support. Depending on the questions asked, 70-90 per cent approve of the monarchy or the monarch. Not surprisingly, political conservatives show more support for the monarchy, but left-wing support is also strong. When asked in 2013 if they agreed or disagreed with the abolition of the monarchy, 94 per cent of political conservatives disagreed, while the corresponding figure for members of the Red-Green Alliance was 66 per cent. Support or lack of support is not specific to generations: 82 per cent of 18–35-year-olds and 84 per cent of the 60+ age group disagreed (TNS Gallup 2013).

The third argument is functionalist or pragmatic. The justification of the monarchy is that it works, or at least that it does not have a negative impact on society as such. In support of this view, it is noticeable that very few members of Parliament and no present or former prime minister or ministers have spoken out against the monarchy. There have been no serious attempts to change the state form since 1920. Conversely, this functionalist approach to the monarchy also puts pressure on the monarch always to act in accordance with the expectations of politicians and the public.

Finally, the monarchy has the legitimacy of tradition. The monarchy represents stability and continuity, both of which are considered important in times of rapid change or turmoil. This is most often an expression of a more pragmatic than ideological approach. Supporters of the monarchy rarely define themselves as monarchists or anti-republican for that matter. Age and tradition are often emphasized in a more general sense, i.e. that Denmark is one of the oldest monarchies in the world (Cannadine 1983).

CONCLUSION

The role of the monarch as head of state is comparable to that of presidents and monarchs alike in the parliamentary democracies of Northern Europe. This raises the question of how this purely ceremonial and symbolic role is to be understood. There is no simple answer to that question. One element to be aware of is that ceremonies and symbols matter.

Even though HM Queen Margrethe II has no formal political authority, she is still the highest-ranking person in Denmark and attracts attention wherever she goes. The monarch and the royal house are the centre of a symbolic order that can be viewed as both egalitarian and hierarchical. On the one hand, everybody is equal in being symbolically subordinate to the monarch, but on the other, there is a clear and visible hierarchy. It has been attempted to measure citizens' place in this hierarchy by proximity to the royal house, and it gives prestige to be invited to official events. An attempt of assessing who is most influential in Denmark includes a place on the royal guest list as a relevant factor. Using Bourdieu's theory, Larsen et al. (2015: 28) thus find that businesspeople in particular are able to convert economic capital into social and (cultural) capital due to their contacts in the royal family. However, the survey does not clarify the direction of causality. Does proximity to the court generate influence, or do influential people tend to seek proximity to the court?

Twentieth-century Danish monarchs have gradually adapted to an increasingly egalitarian society. They have reached out to the general public through the media, by systematically visiting every corner of the realm, and by awarding medals of merit to loyal private and public employees with a tenure of more than 40 years. Recipients of medals and orders (1,942 medals of merit and 455 Orders of Dannebrog in 2018) are invited to public audiences. The chance that a Dane in the course of a lifetime meets a member of the royal family is not small. But the public image of the monarch and the royal family is primarily maintained by a careful media strategy, taken care of by a press secretariat in the Lord Chamberlain's office since 2004. And, as the opinion polls indicate, the strategy has been successful.

The monarch is thus not only a representative of the state but also—and perhaps more importantly—a symbol of or for the nation. This makes the monarchy as an institution dependent on public affection for the reigning monarch. The popularity of the reigning Queen is confirmed annually on her birthday, 16 April. At precisely noon, she enters the balcony of her residential palace in Copenhagen to be greeted by a crowd of thousands cheering and waving flags. When the Crown Prince turned 50 in 2018, it was announced that he would do the same on his birthday, 26 May. The palace square was even more crammed with cheering people than the month before. This was generally interpreted as an assurance that the Danish monarchy will maintain its status in the following generation as well.

References

Andersen, Poul (1954). *Dansk Statsforfatningsret*. Copenhagen: Gyldendal.

Cannadine, David (1983). 'The context, performance and meaning of ritual', in Eric J. Hobsbawm and Terence O. Ranger, eds, *The Invention of Tradition*. Cambridge: Cambridge University Press, 101–64.

Christensen, Jens Peter (2020). 'The constitution', in Peter M. Christiansen, Jørgen Elklit, and Peter Nedergaard, eds, *The Oxford Handbook of Danish Politics*. Oxford: Oxford University Press, 9–27.

Christensen, Jens Peter, Jørgen A. Jensen, and Michael H. Jensen (2015). *Grundloven med kommentarer*. Copenhagen: Jurist- og Økonomforbundets Forlag.

Christensen, Jens Peter, Jørgen A. Jensen, and Michael H. Jensen (2016). *Dansk Statsret*. Copenhagen: Jurist- og Økonomforbundets Forlag.

Gad, Ulrik P. (2020). 'Greenland, the Faroe Islands, and Denmark. Unity or community?', in Peter M. Christiansen, Jørgen Elklit, and Peter Nedergaard, eds, *The Oxford Handbook of Danish Politics*. Oxford: Oxford University Press, 28–45.

Høvsgaard, Jens (2012). *Det koster et kongerige*. Copenhagen: Rosinante.

Larsen, Anders G., Christoph Ellersgaard, and Markus Bernsen (2015). *Magteliten*. Copenhagen: Politikens Forlag.

Møller, Jes F. (2014). 'Monarkiet som Danmarks ansigt udadtil', *Økonomi og politik*, 87/4: 37–47.

Nielsen, Peter H. (2012). 'Statsministeren fik ordet. Historien om den danske åbningstale', *Økonomi og Politik*, 85/4: 87–99.

Royal House (2017). 'Årsrapport fra Kongehuset 2017', http://kongehuset.dk/aarsrapport-2017/oekonomi

Royal House (2019). 'The Court', http://kongehuset.dk/en/the-court (accessed 15 May 2019).

Sørensen, Jonas, and Jacob Aksglæde (2018). *Kongehuset og diplomatiet*. Copenhagen: Forlaget Politiske Studier.

Sørensen, Max (1973). *Statsforfatningsret,* 2nd ed. by Peter Germer. Copenhagen: Jurist- og Økonomforbundets Forlag.

TNS Gallup (2013). *Gallup om kongehuset*, 16 December 2016.

CHAPTER 5

··

THE ELECTORAL SYSTEM
Fair and Well-Functioning

··

JØRGEN ELKLIT

AREND Lijphart, the doyen of electoral systems research, has expressed his appreciation of the system used to elect the Danish Parliament (*Folketinget*) on several occasions. One example is this quote:

> Of the electoral systems analyzed in this book, I nominate the Danish system as the closest approximation to my 'ideal' model. [...] [L]et me merely highlight its main features here: list PR, an average district magnitude of about eight seats, national compensatory seats with a low 2 per cent threshold, and highly proportional allocation formulas. My one misgiving concerns the high degree of openness of the list system and the complexity of how the partly open lists work. No system is perfect! [...] Those who designed the system almost a century ago did a much better job than their contemporary counterparts [...]   (Lijphart 2005: ix)

The quote highlights some of the system's main features, which are key to understanding how it can simultaneously be both complex and simple as far as Danish voters are concerned, regardless of whether they just want to cast a vote in the elections or optimize their actual electoral power.

The system has now reached its centenary. It has developed incrementally since 1920 when it was negotiated and enacted in cooperation between the then Minister of the Interior Ove Rode and Conservative opposition MP Asger Karstensen. In 1915, Denmark had already introduced elements of proportional representation (PR) as single-member constituencies were combined with a system of compensatory seats outside the capital district of Copenhagen and Frederiksberg, which was made into a multi-member PR district (Elklit 1992; Shugart and Wattenberg 2001: 580). However, for a number of reasons, the system did not achieve an acceptable level of proportionality in the 1918 *Folketinget* elections.

It was consequently changed fundamentally in 1920 as one of several elements in the political settlement after a major constitutional crisis. This new electoral system was, in many respects, quite similar to the current system. It is indeed remarkable that the basic features of the system have survived for 100 years. The main reason is that incremental changes over this period have allowed the electoral system to adjust to social, demographic, and political changes.

Folketinget elections are generally perceived to be of a high standard when it comes to election administration and the general quality of the election processes. Other members of this top league are Finland, Norway, Iceland, Germany, the Netherlands, and Sweden; it is interesting that these countries all have PR electoral systems even though their systems vary. The quality league scoring is documented by the Electoral Integrity Project (Norris et al. 2018). It also deserves mention that Denmark adheres to the 'governmental model of electoral management' (Catt et al. 2014) as elections are organized and managed by the Ministry of Social Affairs and the Interior in close cooperation with local authorities. An English language text of the electoral law is available at the Ministry's home page (cf. below the references). Furthermore, an annotated edition of the electoral law was recently published (Miller and Elklit 2019).

This chapter deals only with the *parliamentary* electoral system, and it follows to a considerable degree the conceptualizations and notions presented in Herron et al. (2018). The electoral system used in regional and municipal elections (and European Parliament elections) is a straightforward list PR d'Hondt system allowing for *apparentement,* something not possible in *Folketinget* elections (Houlberg and Ejersbo 2020; Kjær 2020; Elklit 2016a: 48–55).

Election results are accepted by all, the electoral administration (the electoral management body, EMB), based in a small office in the Ministry, functions well and is never accused of any kind of political bias, and general trust in the system is widespread. One likely explanation for this positive state of affairs is that Denmark has not had a majority party in Parliament since 1909. All political parties have to realize that they must compromise to get legislation passed and that small parties might be necessary coalition partners. Political parties also appreciate that the electoral winners of today may be the losers of tomorrow, so the losers of today should not be treated too harshly.

The structure of the chapter is as follows. The first section presents the electoral system as it has developed since 1920. The second section describes in more detail how the system works, with all descriptions and explanations based on the outcome of the *Folketinget* elections on 5 June 2019. The third section looks at a couple of electoral law amendments to illustrate how such changes have been discussed and enacted, the purpose being to see if the political processes leading to the amendments reflect the fact that electoral laws are of a special, consensus-driven nature in Denmark. The fourth section presents a few comparisons with electoral systems elsewhere. A brief conclusion closes the chapter.

THE STRUCTURE OF THE
ELECTORAL SYSTEM

The electoral system is a straightforward, two-tier PR system where the national (upper) level is the decisive level (cf. Lijphart 1994: 32–6; Elklit and Roberts 1996), while lower level seat allocation takes place in multi-member constituencies (MMCs). This ensures that MPs have some kind of link to their constituencies. This is even more so in relation to the nomination districts (*opstillingskredse*), a sub-division of the MMCs where the local party branches nominate their candidates to stand for election. Independent candidates are allowed, but only very few stand for election; they are also linked to a nomination district even though the relevant constituency for both kinds of candidates is the MMC. The basic features of the system are described in Table 5.1, while Table 5.2 provides an overview of the development over time in the system's key features. Further details will be provided in the subsequent section where the system's actual workings are described.

Table 5.2 shows that the system has gone through seven phases since its inception in 1920. However, the picture softens if we look at the nature of the changes involved. For a general discussion of electoral system changes, see Renwick (2018).

In 1920, after the passing of the electoral law mentioned above, North Schleswig was reunited with Denmark following plebiscites in accordance with the post-First World War Versailles Settlement. The electoral system consequences were an additional MMC, North Schleswig, and a slight increase in the number of seats in the *Folketinget*.

Lijphart (1994: 13) has suggested that one should only speak of electoral system changes in two-tier systems either if the electoral formula at the decisive level is changed or if there is a change of 20 per cent or more in at least one of three important electoral systems features, namely the district size in the decisive tier, the size of the formal electoral threshold, and the assembly size.

The upper-level seat allocation formula has been the same since 1920, and the changes in the district size at the decisive (national) level—and the assembly size by implication—have not surpassed the 20 per cent criterion on any occasion. Table 5.3 shows that it is only electoral threshold changes that have generated electoral system change. The first of three changes took place in 1948, the second in connection with the constitutional amendments in 1953, and the third in 1961. Consequently, one can say that the current manifestation of the Danish electoral system comprises all twenty-one *Folketinget* elections since 1964.

In 2005, a local government reform led to a substantial reduction in the number of municipalities as well as the abolition of the counties which were replaced by five administrative regions. The counties had been used as MMCs since 1920, but having only five MMCs was not considered a good idea, so the number of MMCs was only reduced from seventeen to ten. A consequence was an increase in the average number of MMC constituency seats which is now 13.5 (i.e. considerably more than Lijphart saw as praiseworthy in the above quote). This might have entailed easier access to seats in Parliament

Table 5.1. The Overall Structure of the Danish Electoral System

Level (tier)	Central Features	Effects/Consequences
National	Seats are allocated using Hare + Largest Remainders (LR) for parties surpassing at least one of three electoral thresholds (the most important being 2 per cent of the valid vote).	High level of overall proportionality at decisive level (see Table 5.3)
	Of the 175 seats allocated in Denmark (i.e. excluding the two seats in Greenland and the two given to the Faroe Islands), 40 seats, i.e. 23 per cent, are compensatory seats.	Instrumental in reaching the high level of proportionality (cf. Taagepera and Shugart 1989: 131)
Lower (multi-member constituencies [MMCs] most often fitted to other administrative borders)	The number of seats in each multi-member constituency (MMC) is determined for a five year period based on the sum of the total population, the size of the electorate, and a factor reflecting the geographical space of the MMC in question. Seats are allocated within the MMC using a PR allocation formula. Since 2005, it has (again) been the d'Hondt formula.	Allocation of seats across the country is considered fair and reasonable. Likewise, the system of allocation of seats within the MMCs is seen as unproblematic, mainly because the allocation of compensatory seats makes up for some of the biases created by the d'Hondt formula.
Eventual (intra-party) seat allocation to individual party candidates	The MMC branches of the political parties decide on which of several available systems they will use for nominating and ordering their candidates in the MMC. This includes how the seats won eventually will be allocated to the party's candidates.	When parties organize their 'list' of candidates in an MMC, they must choose between different systems with different consequences for the eventual selection of the individual candidates. This unique feature explains to some degree the complexity of the Danish electoral system (cf. Lijphart's complaint in the quote above). It allows MMC party branches to decide which form of intra-party competition they want.
	Voters have one vote which is cast either for a party or for a specific candidate (i.e. a preferential or a personal vote). Lists are either open or various kinds of semi-open, never completely closed. In *Folketinget* elections, about 50 per cent of the voters cast a preferential vote (52 per cent in 2019).	The possibility of running on completely open lists was first available in 2019. It was used in 46 per cent of all 130 possible cases (13 parties in 10 MMCs).

Table 5.2. The Development in the Main Features of the Electoral System, 1920–2020

Period (by elections)	1920, April–1920, July	1920, Sept.–1947	1950–1953, April	1953, Sept.–1960	1964–1968	1971–2005	2007–2019
Number of elections	2	10	2	3	3	14	4
Upper level allocation formula	Hare + LR	Ditto	Ditto	Ditto	Ditto	Ditto	Ditto
Total number of seats[1]	139	148	149	175	Ditto	Ditto	Ditto
Electoral thresholds	One constituency seat or as many votes as the national votes/seats average in one of the three regions;[2] eff. electoral threshold approx.: 1.1 per cent	Ditto	Ditto	One constituency seat or 60,000 votes or as many votes as the regional votes/constituency seat average in each of the three regions;[2] eff. electoral threshold approx.: 2.6 per cent	One constituency seat or 2.0 per cent of all valid votes or as many votes as the regional average pr. constituency seats in two of the three regions;[2] eff. electoral threshold: 2.0 per cent	Ditto	Ditto, but the three regions are delineated differently
Compensatory seats	29	31	44	40	Ditto	Ditto	Ditto
Compensatory seats in per cent of total	21	Ditto	30	23	Ditto	Ditto	Ditto
Number of MMCs	22	23	Ditto	Ditto	Ditto	17	10
Periodical adjustment of allocation of seats to MMCs	No	Ditto	Yes	Ditto	Ditto	Ditto	Ditto
Average number of constituency seats in MMCs	5.0	5.1	4.6	5.9	Ditto	7.9	13.5
MMC seat allocation formula	d'Hondt	Ditto	Ditto	Modified Sainte-Laguë	Ditto	Ditto	d'Hondt
Allocation of constituency seats final?	Yes	Ditto	No	Yes	Ditto	Ditto	Ditto

[1] Excluding the Faroe Islands and Greenland.

[2] The three regions were the capital region (Copenhagen and Frederiksberg municipalities); the islands; and Jutland. This regionalization remained in use until the changes in regional delimitation in the wake of the 2005 Local Government Reform.

Table 5.3. Changes in Lijphart's Four System Change Indicators and Average Values for Gallagher Disproportionality Scores, Effective Number of Parties (N(v) and N(s)), and r

Period (by elections)	1920, April and June	1920, Sept.–1947	1950–1953, April	1953, Sept.–1960	1964–1968	1971–2005	2007–2019
Number of elections	2	10	2	3	3	14	4
Upper (decisive) level allocation formula	Hare + LR	Ditto	Ditto	Ditto	Ditto	Ditto	Ditto
Change in district size (decisive level)	NA	+ 7%	+ 1%	+ 17%	NA	NA	NA
Change in electoral threshold	NA	NA	**+ 45%**	**+ ca. 73%**	**– ca. 23%**	NA	NA
Change in assembly size	NA	+ 7%	+ 1%	+ 17%	NA	NA	NA
Gallagher's index of disproportionality	0.01	0.02	0.01	0.02	0.02	0.02	0.01
Effective number of electoral parties	3.8	3.7	4.0	3.8	4.2	5.3	5.9
Effective number of parliamentary parties	3.7	3.6	3.9	3.7	3.9	5.0	5.7
r	0.03	0.02	0.01	0.05	0.06	0.05	0.04

Note: Figures are calculated with more decimals than shown and then rounded to increase readability.

for small parties since the natural electoral threshold decreases when M, the number of seats in a constituency, increases.

However, this possibility made some fear that small parties might win a 'cheap' constituency seat in a large MMC, giving such parties access to the *Folketinget* without having won even 2 per cent of the national vote total. Consequently, the Modified Sainte-Laguë formula used in the MMCs since 1953 (Elklit 1999) was replaced by the d'Hondt formula which does not provide 'cheap' seats to small parties. So far, this safeguard aimed at avoiding unintended consequences stemming from the decrease in the number of MMCs has worked as expected. Therefore, the changes subsequent to the local government reform are best understood as an ordinary adjustment to changes in other administrative spheres and not as an electoral system change per se.

Table 5.3 also provides the information necessary to assess if the changes in electoral system features identified above have been followed by systematic changes in disproportionality scores (Gallagher 1991, 2005) or in the value of r, the relative difference between the effective number of electoral and parliamentary parties (Laakso and Taagepera 1979; Taagepera and Shugart 1989: 204, 209). Figure 5.1 illustrates the development of the effective numbers of parties since 1918. The level of disproportionality, as well as

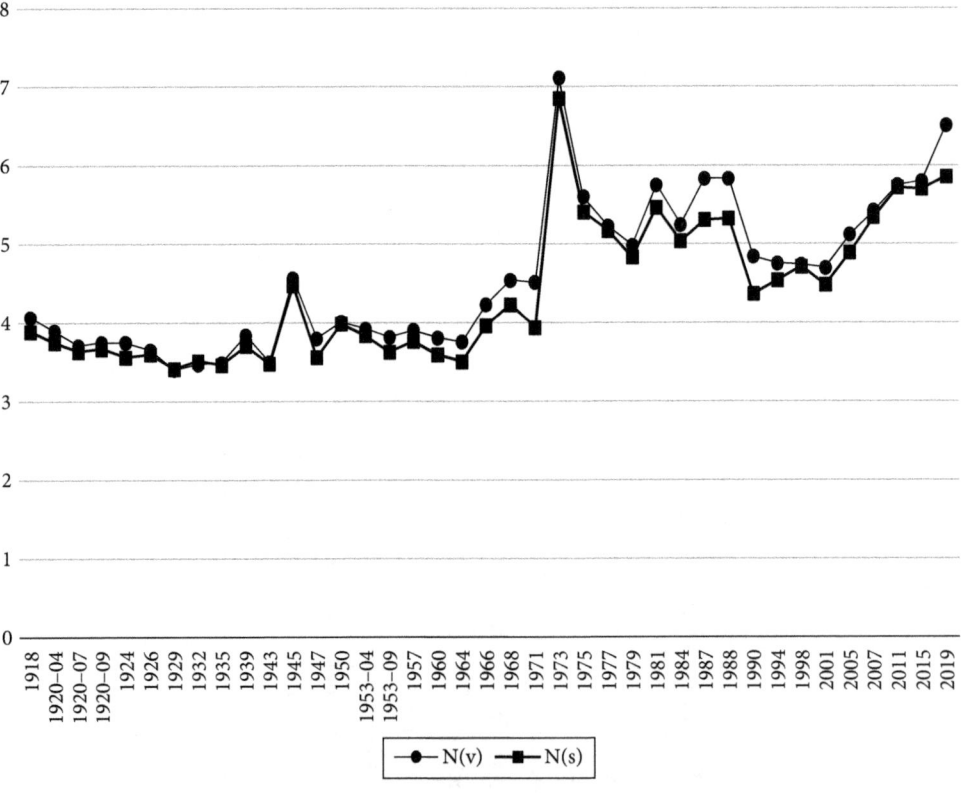

FIGURE 5.1 Effective number of parties in the electorate, N(v), and in Parliament, N(s), 1918–2019.

the relative distance between N(v) and N(s), that is r, is remarkably low—also by international comparison—which explains why the two lines are so close to each other. The disproportionality score (and r) nevertheless increased after 1953 when the Constitution was amended and the electoral law was adjusted to reflect these amendments.

The changes in the electoral threshold in 1948, 1953, and 1961 did not cause changes in the two effect variables considered here. The reason behind the increase in the r value during the 1960s, clearly visible in Figure 5.1, is the party system development between the mid-1960s and the mid-1990s where differences in party size—in the electorate and in the *Folketinget*—decreased the same time that some of the parties did not meet the 2 per cent threshold.

The number of substantial changes in key electoral system features is thus reduced to three (as indicated by the bold vertical lines in Table 5.3), a dramatic change after the 1947 elections; the amendment of the Constitution in 1953, which also entailed an amendment of the electoral law in 1953; and then an amendment in 1961 of the rules related to the electoral thresholds. The latter is discussed below as it illustrates how small parties can also sometimes have it their way.

How the Electoral System Actually Works

Political parties can participate in elections to the *Folketinget* if they fulfil one of two conditions: (1) they won representation in the previous *Folketinget* elections and still are represented in Parliament, or (2) as a new party that has registered at the Ministry of Social Affairs and the Interior and has submitted a number of supporting signatures from registered voters corresponding to at least 1/175 of the number of valid votes in the previous elections (the average 'price' of one seat). This number was 20,109 in 2019, and three new parties registered in this way. For the next elections, the corresponding number is 20,182. Ten parties fulfilled the first criterion in 2019.

A digital system for the handling of supporting signatures was implemented in 2016. The procedure is one of two steps with a period of pensiveness in between to ensure that the voter is positive that she wants to submit her signature. Two of the three new parties were in a hurry to submit the signatures, and they realized that a shortcut was possible so that the signatures could be submitted faster than prescribed by the Ministry. This created some discussion, but the Ministry decided to accept the signatures, promising that the shortcut would be closed as soon as possible. The number of required supporting signatures for new parties is considerably higher than in, for instance, Sweden and Germany, and it is seen by some as an additional electoral threshold.

Inter-party and intra-party seat allocation takes place in six sequential steps. Taken together, these steps reflect the intentions behind the electoral law as it has developed over the years: overall proportionality for parties with a minimal level of voter support, regional scattering of seats, locally rooted candidates, and voter influence not only on the political party composition of the *Folketinget* but also on the selection of the individual MPs.

The two seats allocated to Greenland and the two allocated to the Faroe Islands are allocated separately, using d'Hondt in both cases. The consequence is that the two biggest parties in each of these two parts of the realm normally win a seat each. Figure 5.2 illustrates the entire allocation process where one finds the allocation of the four North Atlantic seats just below the upper left corner. The 175 seats available for the third part of the realm (Denmark) are the sum of the 135 constituency seats allocated directly in the MMCs in the first of the six steps in the seat allocation process and the 40 compensatory seats.

Step 1

The 135 constituency seats are allocated proportionally for five-year periods to the ten MMCs based on a formula that includes population size, the size of the electorate,

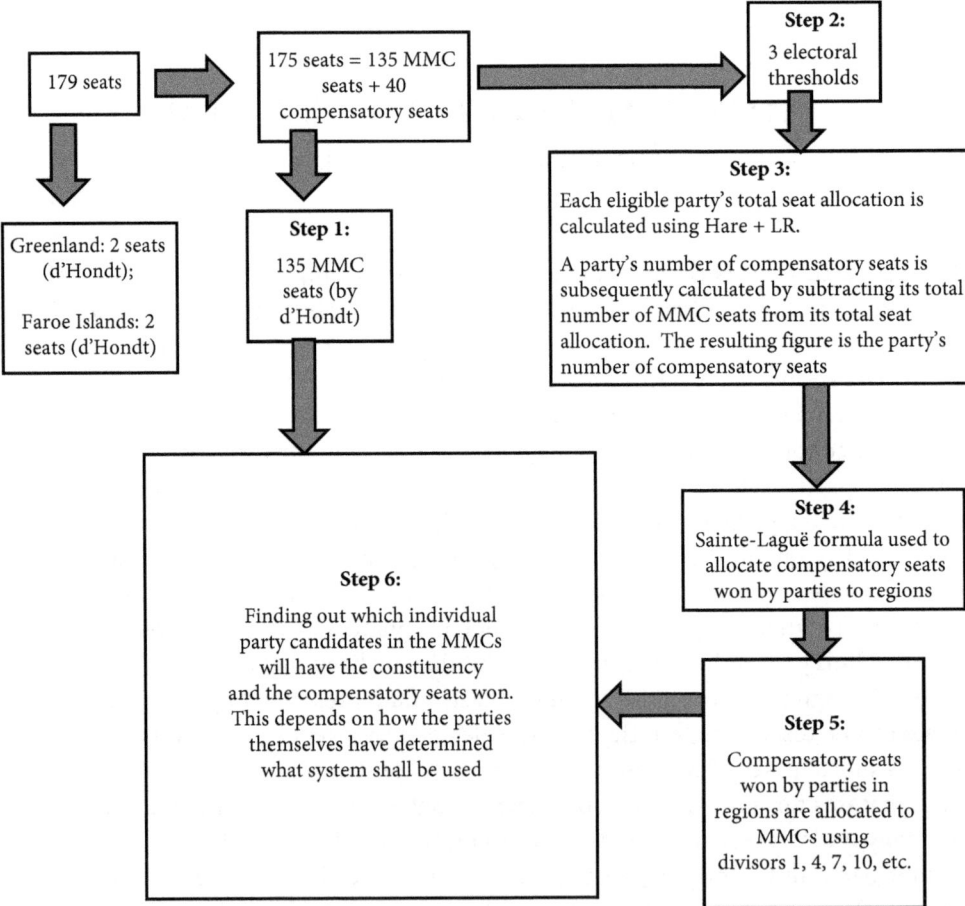

FIGURE 5.2 The six steps of seat allocation in the Danish electoral system.

and twenty times the MMC area in km² (a consideration for sparsely populated parts of the country). The number of seats in the MMCs varied in 2019 between 2 (Bornholm's MMC) and 20 (Zealand's MMC). If these calculations do not result in Bornholm, an island in the Baltic Sea, getting at least two seats, the MMC is given two seats in advance, and calculations are redone for the other nine MMCs. This ensures that the island will have at least some proportionality in its political representation in the *Folketinget*, which is not possible with only one MP.

The consideration given to geography is reminiscent of the small nineteenth-century constituencies in rural Jutland because of the peninsula's low population density, particularly in its Western part. As a result, there is now a slight tendency for parties to win marginally more seats in Jutland. However, parties with strongholds in Jutland do not get more seats in total than they would otherwise have gained as the national tier is the decisive tier.

Since the 2007 elections, the MMC constituency seats have (again) been allocated to political parties according to the d'Hondt seat allocation formula, and the Modified Sainte-Laguë formula—widely associated with Scandinavian elections—is no longer used in Denmark. This allocation is final, i.e. if a party should get more constituency seats than its overall seat entitlement, it can keep them all. The risk of that happening is, however, negligible.

Step 2

This step establishes which parties might be eligible for compensatory seats. A party must fulfil a least one of three requirements to qualify for inclusion in this allocation: (1) winning at least one constituency seat in any of the MMCs, (2) winning as many votes as the average of the regional votes/constituency seats in two of the three main electoral regions, or (3) winning at least 2 per cent of the national vote total. The latter is, for all intents and purposes, the effective electoral threshold. In 2019, where 13 parties had registered for participation in the elections, 2 per cent was equal to 70,635 votes. Five parties did not win any constituency seats, but two of them, the New Right (*Nye Borgerlige*) and the Liberal Alliance (*Liberal Alliance*), both surpassed the 70,635 vote requirement and were thus entitled to participate in the sharing of the 40 compensatory seats.

Step 3

Each party's overall seat entitlement is found by allocating all 175 seats to the eligible parties by using Hare + Largest Remainders (see Table 5.4). For instance, the Red-Green Alliance (*Enhedslisten*) was entitled to 13 of the 175 seats. They had, however, won 7 MMC seats, so they were entitled to 6 compensatory seats.

Table 5.4. The Official Result of the 2019 *Folketinget* Elections and the Computation of Compensatory Seats

	Votes	175 seats allocated proportionally based on total vote figures	175 seats allocated proportionally based on total vote figures, rounded	Constituency seats won in MMCs	Compensatory seats	Per cent of total valid vote	Per cent of all 175 seats
Total	3,375,288	175.000	175	135	40	100.0	100.0
A. Social Democrats	914,882	47.434	48	44	4	25.9	27.4
B. Social Liberals	304,714	15.799	16	12	4	8.6	9.1
C. Conservatives	233,865	12.125	12	9	3	6.6	6.9
D. New Right	83,201	4.314	4	–	4	2.4	2.3
F. Socialist People's Party	272,304	14.118	14	12	2	7.7	8.0
I. Liberal Alliance	82,270	4.265	4	–	4	2.3	2.3
O. Danish People's Party	308,513	15.996	16	11	5	8.7	9.1
V. The Liberals	826,161	42.834	43	39	4	23.4	24.6
Ø. Red-Green Alliance	245,100	12.708	13	7	6	7.0	7.4
Å. The Alternative	104,278	5.407	5	1	4	3.0	2.9
Subtotal elegible parties	3,375,288						
E. Klaus Riskær Pedersen	29,600	NA	NA	–	NA	0.8	–
K. Christian Democrats	60,944	NA	NA	–	NA	1.7	–
P. Taut Course	63,114	NA	NA	–	NA	1.8	–
13 Independent candidates	2,774	NA	NA	–	NA	0.1	–

Source: Statistics Denmark 2019: 4. The percentage distributions of votes and seats are added here.

Steps 4 and 5

These steps determine in which MMCs the parties will have their compensatory seats. Step 4 allocates each party's entitlement to one of the three main electoral regions (to ensure geographical spread). The pure Sainte-Laguë formula is used across parties and regions, and the 40 highest quotients entitle the parties in question to a compensatory seat in the region in question, provided that the party has not yet reached its full entitlement and that the region has not transgressed its previously decided share of the compensatory seats (Statistics Denmark 2019: 15–16).

In Step 5, parties have the compensatory seats allocated to regions in Step 4 further allocated to specific MMCs within the regions. The formula used is the so-called 'Danish' string of divisors (1, 4, 7, 10 . . .) which ensures geographical spread *within* the regions (because of the distance between the divisors) so that MMCs where a party is less strong also have a chance of getting a compensatory seat (Statistics Denmark 2019: 17–19). This feature was, however, more important prior to 2005 when MMCs were smaller.

Step 6

All 135 constituency seats and all 40 compensatory seats are now allocated to a particular party in a particular MMC. This final step is where it becomes clear which of each party's candidates in an MMC will eventually become members of Parliament (MPs), namely, this is the process of intra-party seat allocation. At the time of registering the candidates prior to the election, political parties and their MMC branches (and local branches in the nomination districts) have a range of options. Denmark is unique in allowing political parties the liberty of choosing between different ways of having their MPs selected from the pool (or list) of candidates. It is even the case in Denmark that a party can decide differently in different MMCs or even in different nomination districts within an MMC. The consequence is that the way voters cast their party or preference vote can have different effects when it comes to the eventual selection of the successful candidates. However, most voters probably do not understand the finer details of this part of the electoral system!

MMCs are subdivided into a number of so-called nomination districts, the idea being that party branches at this level normally choose their own candidates for Parliament, while the party's MMC branch (or the national party secretariat) will be responsible for registering the candidates with the registration authority. Some claim that the nomination districts are not particularly important these days, which might be true. But today's nomination districts are, to some degree, a continuation of the 1920 nomination districts which were the single-member constituencies used before that, and they are still a useful communication channel between voters and their representatives.

In 1920, nomination and seat allocation was simple: candidates got the votes cast for their party in their own nomination district, as well as all preference votes cast for them in all nomination districts in the MMC, including, of course, their own. This was possible because *all* candidates for *all* parties in the MMC had their names on the ballot paper and could be voted for. Candidates for a party became MPs according to their vote sums in declining order. Those not elected became substitutes, also ranked according to vote sums in declining order. This nomination option is still a possibility, even though it is only used rarely; it is called 'nomination by district' (*kredsvis opstilling*), and it decides the order in which the party's candidates are listed on the ballot paper. Each nomination district has its own distinct ballot paper, and for each party, the local candidate comes first (with the name printed in bold), followed by the other candidates in alphabetical order.

Since 1920, various other ways of nomination and intra-party seat allocation have developed, mainly as a reflection of political and social developments (including decline in party membership, increased size of the MMCs, media structure, and changing administrative borders). Space does not allow for a full account of this development; elements thereof can, however, be found elsewhere (Elklit 2005/2008, 2016a). The most recent changes were enacted in 2017, seemingly as a concession from the government to the Danish People's Party which was eager to obtain a couple of changes to the nomination and intra-party seat allocation system, *inter alia* to allow parties to list candidates on the ballot paper in the order of their own choosing. These changes took effect for the first time in 2019. Only time will show the effects of these procedures over time as they provide more options for parties than ever before.

If an MMC has, say, nine nomination districts, most parties will have a candidate in each of the nine nomination districts. All nine candidates will also be on the ballot paper in all nine nomination districts and compete against each other (as well as against all the candidates from all the other parties) since all voters in an MMC can cast a preferential vote for any of the candidates. So even though a party has a list of candidates, they are primarily a pool of equal party candidates, all interested in winning. Their chances of success in the intra-party electoral game are not decided by their place on the party's list of candidates but primarily by their party's strength in their 'own' nomination district and the number of preferential votes they get in other nomination districts. An old saying in Danish electoral politics is that it is easier to snatch a seat from a fellow party candidate than to win a seat from another party. This accurately describes the fact that electoral competition in Denmark is not only an inter-party game but also very much an intra-party affair.

The nomination and intra-party seat allocation options now available to parties in the ten MMCs and used for the first time in the 2019 elections are as follows:

1. Nomination by district as mentioned above. This option was only used very rarely in 2019.
2. Parties can decide to combine option (1) with a so-called party list where the party decides the order in which its candidates are to be elected. The list is (almost) a closed list; an extremely high number of preferential votes for a candidate can allow that candidate to break the party list even though it has only happened rarely. This option is primarily used by left-wing parties. In 2019, it

was only used by the Red-Green Alliance in the nine largest MMCs and by one of the small parties in five MMCs.

3. Parties can also opt for 'standing in parallel' (*sideordnet opstilling*), which is by far the most common option. Here, a party will nominate several candidates— normally, all its candidates in the MMC—in all nomination districts. Parties using this option can now either have their candidates listed alphabetically on the ballot paper or decide to apply some other order. In both cases, they must also decide if the list is to be open, i.e. party votes are disregarded for the intra-party allocation of seats (another novelty in 2019) or only semi-open as was formerly the most popular nomination method (Elklit 2005/2008). The semi-open option includes a distribution of the party votes in each nomination district to all candidates nominated in this way in proportion to their share of the preference votes cast for the party's candidates in a district. In a few cases, this led to candidates with fewer preference votes overall being elected instead of fellow party candidates with more preference votes overall, which was seen as grossly unfair by the latter. The solution has been to leave it to the parties to choose between the two options.

4. This means that political parties using *sideordnet opstilling* now have four options: prioritized or alphabetical, and in both of these cases, either open or semi-open. If the prioritized option is chosen, parties must consider if they want to give the top position on the ballot paper in the various nomination districts to their local candidate or not; if they then 'prioritize' other candidates in alphabetical order, they are, in effect, using the nomination system used by most parties for most elections since 1970.

If readers are confused, they are not alone! But parties and candidates are fast learners when it comes to seat allocation rules, and the 2019 elections saw no major problems caused by the recently implemented system. One reason could be that most voters are not aware of—or interested in—the reasoning behind the different ways in which the parties' candidates appear on the ballot paper, and they would also normally only see one ballot paper (in the nomination district where they cast their vote), and therefore, not detect that the ballot papers in neighbouring districts are a little different (even though they contain precisely the same candidate names). Figure 5.3 is a copy of a 2019 ballot paper from Nomination District 10 in Copenhagen MMC (*Falkoner-kredsen*).

No matter which particular option an MMC party branch has chosen, when all the votes have been counted and party votes allocated to candidates (where relevant), candidates will be listed in rank order according to the total number of votes they have won. If a party in an MMC has won three seats—whether constituency or compensatory seats— the party's three candidates with the most votes (only preference votes or preference votes + some party votes) will each obtain a seat in Parliament in declining order, while other candidates will be substitutes, also in declining order of their number of votes. With a list of substitutes available and a clear picking order, there is no need for by-elections. Constituency seats are given out first, but subsequent to that, there is no discrimination of any kind between MPs having a constituency or a compensatory seat.

Københavns Storkreds, 10. opstillingskreds

Folketingsvalget 2019

Sæt X i rubrikken til venstre for
et partinavn eller et kandidatnavn.

Sæt kun ét X på stemmesedlen.

Du må ikke udfylde rubrikken med andet end et X,
da din stemmeseddel så bliver ugyldig.

Du kan få byttet din stemmeseddel, hvis du skriver forkert.

A. Socialdemokratiet

Jørgen Merup Pedersen	Verner Sand Kirk
Yildiz Akdogan	Lone Larsen
Niels E. Bjerrum	Lars Aslan Rasmussen
Claus Hasselmann	Mette Reissmann
Sine Heltberg	Pernille Rosenkrantz-Theil
Peter Hummelgaard	Simon Simonsen

B. Radikale Venstre

Ruben Kidde	Louise Vinther Alis
Ida Auken	Rune Scharff Andreasen
Samira Nawa	Andreas Pourkamali
Mette Annelie Rasmussen	Jesper Abildgaard
Jeppe Fransson	Thomas Maare
Jens Rohde	Lartey Lawson

C. Det Konservative Folkeparti

Katarina Ammitzbøll	Marie Høgh
Lasse Vogel Andersen	Anders Johansson
Helle Bonnesen	Peter Stakemann
Nikolaj Bøgh	Caspar Stefani

D. Nye Borgerlige

Ketil Wathne Rasmussen	Cherif Tomra Ayouty
Tom Andkjær	Helle Rosenvig

E. Klaus Riskær Pedersen

Klaus Riskær Pedersen	Manja Aarslev Sørensen

F. SF – Socialistisk Folkeparti

Pia Olsen Dyhr	Louise Tuxen Romsdal
Carl Valentin	Rasmus Steenberger
Kasper Nordborg Kiær	Melissa Skovgaard Jensen
Halime Oguz	Ebbe A. Hansen
Balder Mark Andersen	Rikke Lauritsen

I. Liberal Alliance

Simon Emil Ammitzbøll-Bille	Lars Berg Andersen
Jacob Rosenberg	Martin Ancher
Danny Malkowski	David Bertelsen

K. Kristendemokraterne

Stig Grenov	Anne-Lise Wagner
Nanna Bock	Bess Serner-Pedersen
Anne Grønlund	

O. Dansk Folkeparti

Carsten Ullmann Andersen	Brian Borglund Bruun
Laila Sortland	Lars Vestergaard
Cheanne Nielsen	Paw Karslund
Peter Skaarup	Susanne Damsgaard
Søren Hald Christensen	Martin Henriksen
Julie Jacobsen	Per Brix

P. Stram Kurs

Martin Skriver	Lemmy Lundquist

V. Venstre, Danmarks Liberale Parti

Søren Sørensen	Michael Lange
Tommy Ahlers	Jens-Kristian Lütken
Martin Geertsen	Casper Pedersen
Jan E. Jørgensen	Anne Rasmussen
Kasper Kristensen	Bo Sandroos
Bjarke Kværnø	Sven Aage Schlosrich

Ø. Enhedslisten – De Rød-Grønne

Jakob Nerup	Dorthe Hecht
Pernille Skipper	Michael Naumann
Rosa Lund	David Rønne
Rune Lund	Karen Skærlund Risvig
Jette Gottlieb	Louis Jacobsen
Jonathan Simmel	Mette Bang Larsen

Å. Alternativet

Uffe Elbæk	Jonathan Ries
Carolina Magdalene Maier	Nina Svane-Mikkelsen
Kåre Traberg Smidt	Shahzad Riaz
Jan Kristoffersen	Rolf Bjerre
Asbjørn Ammitzbøll Flügge	Mette Rose Nielsen
Henrik Marstal	Kashif Ahmad

Uden for partierne

Tommy Schou Christesen	Pierre Tavares
Tom Gillesberg	John Erik Wagner
John Jørgensen	

FIGURE 5.3 2019 ballot paper from Nomination District 10 in Copenhagen MMC.

Note: The ballot paper is a long piece of white paper. It has been cut in two here to fit the page format of the book

THE NATURE OF ELECTORAL LAW AMENDMENTS

Electoral law amendments prior to 1961 have been discussed elsewhere, and for space reasons, these discussions are not repeated here (Elklit 1992, 1999, 2002). The 1961 lowering of the electoral threshold is, however, interesting and might provide some insight into the nature of electoral law change in Denmark.

The 1953 Electoral Law, which accompanied the approval of major constitutional amendments, provided for an increase in the most important electoral threshold (from approximately 1.1 per cent to about 2.6 per cent) caused by the major parties' experiences with new parties and splinter parties during previous decades. The smaller parties protested, but the Social Democrats, the Liberals, and the Conservatives got an increase enacted, even though the result in 1953 was a softer solution than first suggested. The new threshold opened three doors to parliamentary representation: a constituency seat; 60,000 votes; or that the party had won as many votes as the regional vote/constituency seat average in *all* three main regions. A new right-wing party (The Independents) did not make it in the September 1953 and 1957 elections even though they were close. The November 1960 elections saw both The Independents and the new Socialist People's Party succeed in obtaining representation, while one of the opponents of the threshold increase, the Communists, did not clear the hurdle.

The 1960 election led to a minority coalition government of Social Democrats and Social Liberals, i.e. one government partner had supported the threshold increase, while the other had been opposing it. The issue was mentioned in the government's coalition agreement as an issue to be looked into, and despite stubborn opposition from some Social Democrats, the Social Liberals managed to obtain their coalition partner's support for lowering the threshold through skilful negotiation—and because the Social Democrats wanted to remain in power. The result was a softening of two of the three different ways to obtain representation: the absolute number 60,000 was replaced with a 2 per cent requirement, and the requirement of the vote/constituency seat average was now only required to be fulfilled in two of the three regions, not all three (Ginsburg 1981). These thresholds are still in force, and there is no reason to expect a change (either way) anytime soon. The small parties—potential coalition partners for bigger parties—are very concerned about the threshold requirements, and they would react immediately if a proposal for increasing the electoral threshold was to be presented.

A pair of apparently small amendments to the electoral law were enacted in 2017 and implemented in the 2019 elections. They illustrate well the incremental development of Danish electoral legislation at the same time as they demonstrate how a party can take advantage of a particular situation in Parliament. The 2015–19 centre-right coalition minority government relied in general on the support of the Danish People's Party in the *Folketinget*. The Danish People's Party, therefore, could also on occasion expect the support of the parties in government when it wanted some legislation passed. It had been debated for decades whether an option for parties to run completely open lists should be introduced, and some of the parties—including the Danish People's Party—had put forward such a proposal as a private member's bill on a number of occasions. In 2017, the idea was again presented by members of the Danish People's Party, and suddenly, there was unanimous support for the proposal, which was subsequently employed in the 2019 elections by the parties who considered this option an improvement.

Already mentioned is the other novelty passed at the same time, namely that the alphabetical ordering of candidates when a party in an MMC runs in parallel in all nomination districts can be replaced by a candidate ordering decided by the party. The 2019 elections saw almost all local party branches use this to promote their preferred (local) top candidate or a joint candidate promoted in all the nomination districts (Statistics Denmark 2020).

Although it bears no consequences in the eventual selection of elected candidates, which is solely based on the totality of preference and party votes (if the party allows for party votes to be allocated), the order of candidates on the ballot paper matters—at least to some degree—as candidates higher up on the ballot paper are more visible to the voters and will potentially attract more preference votes than other candidates (Blom-Hansen et al. 2016).

COMPARISONS WITH OTHER ELECTORAL SYSTEMS

Electoral systems come in different forms and shapes, which forces comparativists to consider whether they should compare apples and oranges or only various apple sorts. Does it, for example, make sense to compare the disproportionality index values for majority and PR electoral systems when majority systems do not aim at achieving a low level of disproportionality? The differences in index values can still be telling, but they are obviously attributable to basic features of the two main categories of electoral systems well known from the literature.

Therefore, Table 5.5 only shows some of the differences between the three Scandinavian systems, as they all are two-tier PR systems where the national level is the decisive level. Nevertheless, one finds remarkable differences in the number of MMCs, in the effectiveness of the preferential vote, in whether snap elections can be called or not, in the formal electoral threshold, in how large the share of compensatory seats are,

Table 5.5. Selected Features of Scandinavian Electoral Systems

	Denmark	Norway	Sweden
Number of lower-level MMCs	10	19	29
Preferential voting	Of some importance	Possible but no effect	Very modest effect
When parliamentary elections can be called	At any time	Snap elections not possible	Snap elections can be called but only for the remaining part of the term
Main electoral threshold	2 per cent	4 per cent	4 per cent
Share of all seats which are compensatory seats	23 per cent	11 per cent	11 per cent
Gallagher's index of disproportionality at most recent election	0.024	0.032	0.006
Average of Gallagher's index at four most recent elections	0.011	0.030	0.018

and in the value of the disproportionality index at recent elections (Elklit 2016b). The index values not only reflect structural features of the electoral systems but also the number of parties below the relevant threshold in a particular election (*vide* the values for Denmark and Sweden).

CONCLUSION

Overall, the Danish electoral system functions very well, and the nature and functionality of the electoral system are not regarded as political issues and have not been so for decades. Whether or not it is the best electoral system in the world, as almost suggested by Lijphart, there can be no argument that it is extremely stable, well-functioning, and widely endorsed in Denmark. Since its inception 100 years ago, the electoral system has developed incrementally to accommodate changing demographic, political, and other conditions so that one hears no complaints about its workings. Even politicians from parties that do not make the electoral threshold do not argue that the threshold is unfair or that the election administration is to be blamed for them not making it into Parliament.

This—together with the high quality of the work by both central and local election administration staff—provides for a high level of electoral legitimacy. The system's legitimacy is never challenged, and there has not for many years been serious calls for simplification or greater transparency—even as regards the complexity of the seat allocation procedures created, *inter alia*, by the parties' many options with regard to the nomination of candidates, list ordering, and computation of which candidates will make it into the *Folketinget*.

This trust in the electoral system is one of several factors which explain why fundamental system changes are never suggested, and ideas of looking into the possibility of introducing some form of digital voting—even only in the form of pilot studies—were shot down immediately. As the argument goes, 'An ordinary pencil in a ballot booth cannot be hacked!'

However, it is most likely that the system for the submission of signatures in support of a new party will be redesigned before the next election so that the idea of a pensive period during the process cannot be circumvented. This is then yet another example of the incremental development of the Danish electoral system.

The 2019 parliamentary elections saw a small increase in the effective number of parties in the electorate to 6.5 and in the effective number of parties in Parliament to 5.9. The value of Gallagher's disproportionality index also rose to 0.0238 (some would say 2.38) from previous elections' 0.007 or 0.008. The reason is that three small parties did not make any of the thresholds, and therefore, did not gain any seats. Together, they had 4.3 per cent of the total vote, which meant that the other parties with 95.7 per cent of the vote could share 100 per cent of the seats, i.e. most of them got a slightly larger share of seats than of votes, which contributes to explaining the increase in the disproportionality index. The index is still low, however, compared to most other countries.

Thus, the electoral system—for the 38th consecutive time since 1920—provided Denmark with a trustworthy, fair, and unchallenged outcome to the election.

REFERENCES

Blom-Hansen, Jens, Jørgen Elklit, Søren Serritzlew, and Louise R. Villadsen (2016). 'Ballot position and election results: Evidence from a natural experiment', *Electoral Studies*, 44: 172–83.

Catt, Helena, Andrew Ellis, Michael Maley, Alan Wall, and Peter Wolf (2014). *Electoral Management Design*. Revised edition. Stockholm: International IDEA.

Elklit, Jørgen (1992). 'The best of both worlds? The Danish electoral system 1915–20 in a comparative perspective', *Electoral Studies*, 11/3: 189–205.

Elklit, Jørgen (1999). 'What was the problem if a first divisor of 1.4 was the solution?', in Erik Beukel, Kurt K. Klausen, and Poul E. Mouritzen, eds, *Elites, Parties and Democracy. Festschrift for Professor Mogens N. Pedersen*. Odense: Odense University Press, 75–101.

Elklit, Jørgen (2002). 'The politics of electoral system development and change: The Danish case', in Bernard Grofman and Arend Lijphart, eds, *The Evolution of Electoral and Party Systems in the Nordic Countries*. New York: Agathon Press, 15–66.

Elklit, Jørgen (2005/2008). 'Denmark: Simplicity embedded in complexity (or is it the other way round)?', in Michael Gallagher and Paul Mitchell, eds, *The Politics of Electoral Systems*. Oxford: Oxford University Press, 453–71.

Elklit, Jørgen (2016a). 'Valgsystemerne', in Jørgen G. Christensen and Jørgen Elklit, eds, *Det demokratiske system*. 4. ed., Copenhagen: Hans Reitzels Forlag, 30–63.

Elklit, Jørgen (2016b). 'Hvor meget styrer folket? En sammenligning af de skandinaviske lande', in Børge Dahl, Michael H. Jensen, and Søren H. Mørup, eds, *Festskrift til Jens Peter Christensen*. Copenhagen: Jurist- og Økonomforbundets Forlag, 149–66.

Elklit, Jørgen, and Nigel S. Roberts (1996). 'A category of its own? Four PR two-tier compensatory member electoral systems in 1994', *European Journal of Political Research*, 30: 217–40.

Gallagher, Michael (1991). 'Proportionality, disproportionality and electoral systems', *Electoral Studies*, 10/1: 33–51.

Gallagher, Michael (2005). 'Indices of fragmentation and disproportionality', in Michael Gallagher and Paul Mitchell, eds, *The Politics of Electoral Systems*. Oxford: Oxford University Press, 598–606.

Ginsburg, Georg (1981). 'Slaget om valglovens spærreregler', *Weekendavisen BERLINGSKE AFTEN*, 26 June–2 July: 4.

Herron, Erik S., Robert J. Pekkanen, and Matthew S. Shugart (2018). 'Terminology and basic rules of electoral systems', in Erik S. Herron, Robert J. Pekkanen, and Matthew S. Shugart, eds, *The Oxford Handbook of Electoral Systems*. New York: Oxford University Press, 1–20.

Houlberg, Kurt, and Niels Ejersbo (2020). 'Municipalities and regions. Approaching the limit of decentralization?', in Peter M. Christiansen, Jørgen Elklit, and Peter Nedergaard, eds, *The Oxford Handbook of Danish Politics*. Oxford: Oxford University Press, 141–59.

Kjær, Ulrik (2020). 'Local elections. Localized voting within a nationalized party system', in Peter M. Christiansen, Jørgen Elklit, and Peter Nedergaard, eds, *The Oxford Handbook of Danish Politics*. Oxford: Oxford University Press, 382–99.

Laakso, Markku, and Rein Taagepera (1979). '"Effective" number of parties. A measure with applications to West Europe', *Comparative Political Studies*, 12/1: 3–27.

Lijphart, Arend (1994). *Electoral Systems and Party systems. A Study of Twenty-Seven Democracies 1945–1990*. Oxford: Oxford University Press.

Lijphart, Arend (2005). 'Foreword', in Michael Gallagher and Paul Mitchell, eds, *The Politics of Electoral Systems*. Oxford: Oxford University Press, vii–x.

Miller, Nicoline N., and Jørgen Elklit (2019). *Folketingsvalgloven med kommentarer*. Copenhagen: Jurist- og Økonomforbundets Forlag.

Norris, Pippa, Thomas Wynter, and Sarah Cameron (2018). *Electoral Integrity & Campaign Media. The Electoral Integrity Project 2018 mid-year update*. Sydney: The EIP Project. www.electoral.integrityproject.com/2018midyearupdate/ (accessed 24 November 2019)

Renwick, Alan (2018). 'Electoral system change', in Erik S. Herron, Robert J. Pekkanen, and Matthew S. Shugart, eds, *The Oxford Handbook of Electoral Systems*. New York: Oxford University Press, 113–32.

Shugart, Matt S., and Martin P. Wattenberg (2001). 'Conclusion: Are mixed-member systems the best of both worlds?', in Matt S. Shugart and Martin P. Wattenberg, eds, *Mixed-Member Electoral Systems: The Best of Both Worlds?* Oxford: Oxford University Press: 571–96.

Statistics Denmark (2019). *Opgørelse af folketingsvalget den 5. juni 2019*. This is the official specification of the election result. Also available at www.dst.dk/valg/Valg1684447/other/Folketingsvalg2019.pdf (accessed 26 June 2019).

Statistics Denmark (2020). *Folketingsvalget 5. juni 2019. Danmark, Færøerne, Grønland*. Copenhagen: Danmarks Statistik. Will also be available at www.dst.dk/Publ/FolkeTingsValg (accessed 6 November 2019). This link also gives access to electoral statistics from all previous *Folketinget* elections, i.e. since 1849.

Taagepera, Rein, and Matthew S. Shugart (1989). *Seats and Votes. The Effects and Determinants of Electoral Systems*. New Haven, CT: Yale University Press.

The election-related homepage of the Ministry of Social Affairs and the Interior is available at https://valg.sim.dk; an English version is available at https://elections.sim.dk (both accessed 6 November 2019).

The *Folketinget* electoral law is available in English at https://elections.sim.dk/media/21968/folketing-parliamentary-elections-act-2019.pdf (accessed 6 November 2019).

CHAPTER 6

ELECTORAL TURNOUT

Strong Social Norms of Voting

KASPER M. HANSEN

VERY HIGH AND STABLE TURNOUT

ELECTORAL turnout is the most important health indicator for democracies with a non-compulsory voting system. Voting holds representatives accountable for their deeds and grants a mandate to rule in the next term on behalf of the people. But the act of voting is also an active expression of consent for the representative political system that provides democratic legitimacy to the system (Rousseau 1762; Beetham 1991). If turnout is low, democratic legitimacy is weak, and if turnout declines, so does democratic legitimacy, the foundation of the democratic system (Lijphart 1997; Wolfinger and Rosenstone 1980). If one defines turnout as the share of the electorate that votes, it becomes a very useful indicator of a healthy democracy that can be compared across time and space.

The four research questions that guide the chapter are: What is the turnout level in Denmark? Why is it so high comparatively? Which inequalities exist between turnout groups? And lastly, can Get-Out-The-Vote (GOTV) campaigns increase turnout equality in a high-turnout country like Denmark?

Voting is non-compulsory in Denmark, and there is a very effective automatic voter registration system based on the universal civil registration number granted by birth or residence in Denmark. This means that all eligible persons automatically receive their polling card by regular mail before the election. For national parliament elections, one is eligible to vote if one is a Danish citizen, 18 years of age, and has permanent residence in the country (Christensen 2020). For other elections, the electorate also includes EU and Nordic citizens with permanent residence. In addition, other citizens are eligible for regional and municipal elections if they have had permanent residence in Denmark for at least 3 years. Denmark has experienced high and stable turnout rates over recent decades (Figure 6.1), also compared to other countries (IDEA 2019).

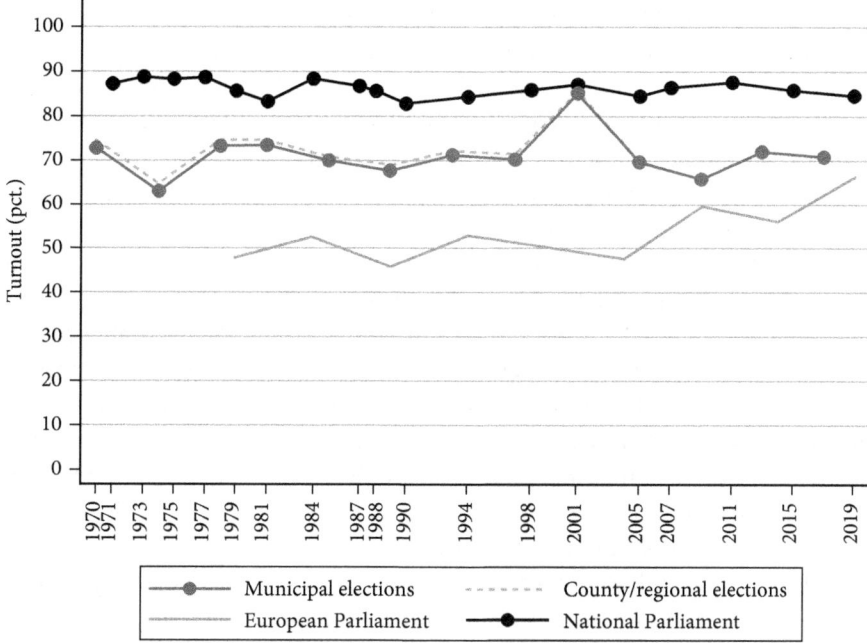

FIGURE 6.1 Turnout in Denmark 1979–2019, per cent.

The Parliament (*Folketinget*) elections in particular enjoy high and stable turnout, averaging 86 per cent since 1970. The municipality elections' average turnout is 70 per cent—if the 2001 municipality elections are excluded as they are a strong outlier due to the simultaneously held national election. To compare, the European Parliament elections' average turnout is only 53 per cent. Since the first *Folketinget* election where women had the vote (1918), the turnout rate for *Folketinget* elections has never been below 75 per cent. This is impressive, also considering that the voting age was lowered several times during the twentieth century, expanding the number of eligible voters considerably.

The high turnout level in Denmark also corresponds to a high level of satisfaction with democracy and a high level of trust in government and politicians, even though the latter has decreased over the latest decade (Bengtsson et al. 2014: 44; Stubager et al. 2019). These relationships point to high turnout at least going hand-in-hand with other more subjective measures of a well-functioning democracy. In the 2014 European Parliament elections, 55 per cent of Danish voters declared that voting for that particular election was a duty, placing Denmark in the top 5 of the 28 EU countries (Schmitt et al. 2016). This strong sense of duty is one of the key explanatory factors in trying to understand a high turnout level (Blais 2000), but quite often, it just raises the next question: where is the high sense of duty emerging from? Research points in this regard to a country's strength of democracy and social homogeneity (Galais and Blais 2017). We could add to this a strong democratic culture that is nursed in primary education and through a strong civil society. Many of the civil society organizations in Denmark still have links to the political parties and the broader public today, which contribute to a strong political awareness among the public. In addition, the mobilization of the electorate through the labour movement must not be neglected. Denmark has Europe's highest unionization rates, with close to 70 per cent of all employees being union members (ETUI 2018: 61). Even though the unions' ties to the political parties have been weakened in recent decades, the labour unions still contribute to the ongoing mobilization of the voters (Elklit and Togeby 2009; Henriksen et al. 2018).

Another factor contributing to the high turnout in Denmark is the early establishment of a popular right-wing party. It was first established in 1972 as the Progressive Party and later transformed to the Danish People's Party. This party has been able to mobilize voters on the popular right that otherwise would have been likely to abstain (Elklit and Togeby 2009). This conclusion is also supported by the fact that the party finds its base among the least educated and least interested in politics (Andersen 2017; Hansen 2007).

Another important feature that contributes to the high electoral turnout in Denmark is the strong ritual and traditions around voting (Hansen et al. 2017). Most people vote by showing up at the polling station on election day, and only few vote absentee in advance. In the 2015 and 2019 parliamentary elections, only 8.7 and 8.4 per cent of all participating voters cast an advance vote. Quite often, people vote together with fellow housemates and make it a joint social venture to go and vote. In the 2015 parliamentary election, 56 per cent of all voters in households with more than two eligible voters voted at the same time as someone else in the household (Bhatti et al. 2020).

The effective automatic voting registration, the strong feeling of citizen duty developed over previous decades, strong civic society movement, the early mobilization of the popular right, and the social aspect of voting all contribute to the explanation of the high turnout in Denmark.

Finally, it is worth mentioning that the strong public service media in Denmark, which to a large extent dominate the news coverage, cover the elections extensively and often directly encourage viewers and listeners to participate in the election.

WHO VOTES?

Not only is the level of turnout important for assessing the level of democratic legitimacy, so is the equality in turnout across groups. If certain groups have low or declining turnout, their voice is less heard in the political system, and policy developments might be less responsive to the group's wishes (Griffin and Newman 2005; Leighley and Nagler 2013). Furthermore, such groups might find it even more difficult to identify with the legislators, develop mistrust, etc. (Mansbridge 1999; Bhatti et al. 2018).

In Denmark, it has been possible to collect actual and validated turnout data since 1997. Across elections, it has been possible to merge the turnout data for almost the entire population with Statistics Denmark's several hundred socio-demographic variables, which have allowed the most fine-grained analyses of turnout in the world (e.g. Hansen 2018). These analyses have fundamentally revised our understanding of why people vote.

It has long been known that there is a general curvilinear relationship between turnout and age as the young and the elderly vote less than other age groups. But the Danish turnout data have allowed a more fine-grained analysis which has revealed the 'roller-coaster' relationship between age and turnout. First of all, the analysis has revealed a sharp decline from 18 years of age only until 21 years of age, which is not visible with sample data, self-reported turnout data, or summarized analyses with age groups collapsed (Bhatti and Hansen 2012a; Bhatti et al. 2012; Bhatti et al. 2016a, 2016b; Dahlgaard et al. 2019). The general explanation of this decline is that when the youngest leave home, their turnout declines rapidly as their social ties are disrupted. This picture is now considered universal and confirmed in the United States, Norway, Sweden, and Finland where data are available (Bhatti et al. 2012).

Figure 6.2 depicts the relationship between age and turnout in the 2015 parliamentary election and the local election in 2017. A second important observation is that the roller-coaster turnout peaks among senior citizens around the age of 72 and then declines sharply. This decline cannot be observed when survey data are used. The decline among senior citizens is partly due to deteriorating health and retirement from work, but it is also related to the social aspect of voting as more live alone in old age, especially women.

The difference in turnout between genders is also notable. Young women have a substantially higher turnout than young men. This is partly explained by lifecycle patterns as women start education, family, and the like earlier than men, but also by the fact that women on average today obtain longer educations than men. Men over 72 years have

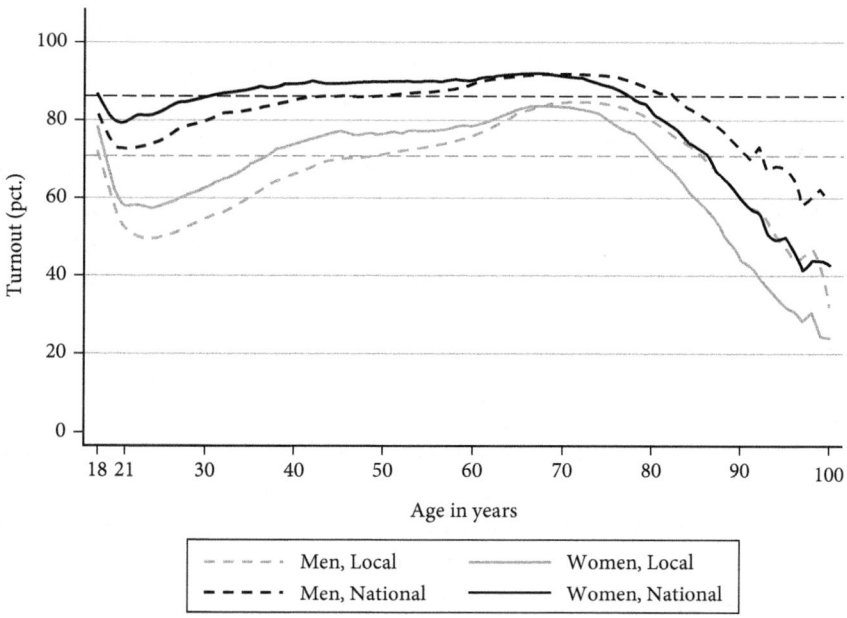

FIGURE 6.2 The rollercoaster: Turnout across age and gender in the 2015 parliamentary election and the 2017 local elections.

Note: Actual validated turnout based on administrative data; dashed horizontal lines are average turnout in the two elections

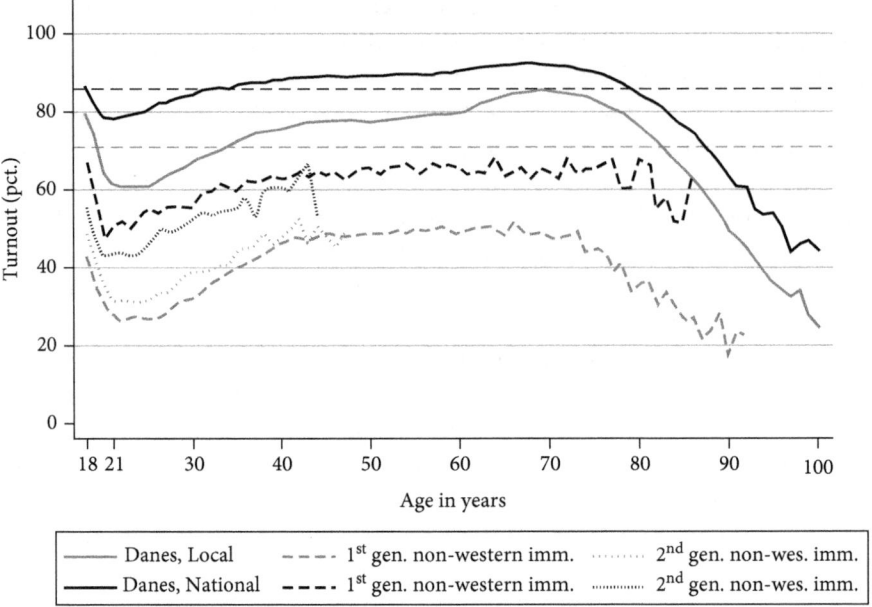

FIGURE 6.3 Turnout across ethnicity and age in the 2015 parliamentary elections and the 2017 local elections.

Note: Actual validated turnout based on administrative data; dashed horizontal lines are average turnout in the two elections

higher turnout than women, but this is explained by the fact that as women live longer and marry older men, women will also live longer alone. Adjusting for living alone makes the difference in old age across gender disappear (Bhatti and Hansen 2012b).

Another point is that the rollercoaster relationship is even steeper when we analyse less salient elections, which then confirms Tingsten's (1937) law of dispersion that stipulates that equalities in turnout across groups increase when turnout declines (Bhatti et al. 2018a). This is also clear from comparing national and local elections in Figure 6.2.

Another notable inequality in turnout is among different ethnic groups. Figure 6.3 shows the turnout across age and ethnicity.

First-generation and second-generation immigrants from non-Western countries have substantially lower turnout than Danes. The difference is somewhat larger in the local elections than in the national elections as expected according to Tingsten's law of dispersion. It is troubling from an equality standpoint that especially second-generation immigrants—who are born in Denmark—have not become active voters and are still close to the turnout level of the first-generation immigrants (i.e. their parents) as it suggests that the democracy component of integration has not succeeded. It is, therefore, a challenge to find ways to mobilize immigrants to participate actively in Danish democracy at the same level as Danes. As this group will increase in size relative to Danes in the coming years, one should expect a gradual decline in turnout.

We can analyse the turnout for specific groups in even more detail. Table 6.1 presents the turnout for particular groups in the 2015 national election and the 2017

Table 6.1. Turnout across Specific Groups, 2017 Local and 2015 National Elections

Groups	Local 2017 (pct.)	National 2015 (pct.)
60–69 years old	81.1	91.1
Long-term tertiary education	80.5	95.4
DKK 400.000–499.999 yearly income	80.5	92.9
Short and medium-term tertiary education	80.0	93.2
DKK 300.000–399.999 yearly income	75.6	90.0
50–59 years old	75.3	88.6
Danish ethnicity	75.2	87.0
Vocational education	73.3	87.5
40–49 years old	72.6	87.7
Women	72.4	86.9
Men	68.8	84.7
DKK 100.000–199.999 yearly income	67.5	82.1
Secondary education (e.g. high school)	66.7	86.1
Primary school	66.7	76.7
DKK 200.000–299.999 yearly income	65.9	82.1
30–39 years old	63.7	85.0
Less than DKK 100.000 yearly income	57.1	77.7
22–29 years old	54.9	79.1
Immigrants, Danish citizens	54.7	66.1
Early retirement	53.8	69.7
Immigrants from Iceland and Norway	47.7	82.3
Immigrants from old EU countries	46.4	82.7
Immigrants from other Western countries	46.2	76.8
Unemployment benefits	43.5	62.9
Immigrants from non-Western countries	42.0	58.6
Second-generation immigrants	40.9	53.4
First-generation immigrants, non-Danish citizens	31.8	Not eligible
First and second-gen. imm. from new EU countries	18.5	72.6

Note: Old EU countries are the first 15 member states. New EU countries are EU27–EU15, excluding Croatia. Iceland and Norway have their own category. Other Western countries are Lichtenstein, Monaco, San Marino, Andorra, Switzerland, Canada, USA, Australia, and New Zealand. Non-Western countries are all other countries. The dotted horizontal line indicates whether the groups are above or below turnout average in the particular election.

local election. It is obvious that there are substantial turnout inequalities between the groups identified in the table.

The groups with the highest turnout are the 60–69-year-olds and voters with higher education. At the bottom of the list, immigrants from new EU countries and from non-Western countries dominate. If we combine the groups' characteristics, the difference between high and low turnout becomes even more profound. For example, the group consisting of retired 60–69-year-old women with higher education and Danish citizen-ship had a turnout of 93.4 per cent in the 2017 local elections. This can be compared to the group of 22–29-year-old immigrants from new EU countries without Danish citi-zenship. The turnout in this group in the same election was only 4.8 per cent.

We can also analyse turnout inequalities by comparing core voters and permanent abstainers across the different types of elections in Denmark. If we look at voters that voted in the three consecutive elections consisting of the national parliament elections in 2015, European Parliament elections in 2014, and the local elections in 2013, we find that the group is composed of 52 per cent females, 1 per cent non-Western immigrants, and 39 per cent with higher education. If we compare this group to the group that did not vote at all in the same three elections, its composition is 47 per cent females, 12 per cent non-Western immigrants, and only 11 per cent with higher education. So there are more than 10 times as many non-Western immigrants in the permanent abstainers' group as in the group of core voters and more than 3 times as many highly educated in the core voter group compared to the permanent abstainer group (Bhatti et al. 2018a).

We can describe these two groups, i.e. core voters and permanent abstainers, as a democratic A-team dominated by highly educated females that vote in every election compared to a democratic B-team dominated by men with low levels of education and a non-Western, immigrant background. This clearly illustrates the large inequalities in the various groups' turnout even in a country like Denmark with a high general turnout.

Denmark: A European Frontrunner in Get-Out-The-Vote (GOTV)

The lower turnout in elections to the European Parliament and in local elections has cre-ated some interest in trying to mobilize voters in Denmark. There has, in particular, been an interest in the groups with low turnout such as young voters and ethnic minor-ities, but many other low-turnout groups have also been targeted in these mobilization campaigns. Some of the efforts have been conducted as large field experiments with ran-domly controlled trials building on the American tradition (Green and Gerber 2015). Various modes of delivery have been tested (postcards, letters, e-mails, digital mails, text messages on cell phones, door-to-door, and posters in hallways in social housing), the timing of mobilization (distance to election day and time of day), number of mobilization efforts, and the content of the mobilization (the Constitution, cartoons, focus on the duty of voting or the social aspect, etc.) (Bhatti et al. 2015, 2017a, 2017b, 2018b).

What can be learned from these experiments? First, it is possible to increase turnout even in a high-turnout country. Turnout among the youngest voters has actually increased more than 17 percentage points from 2009 to 2017 at local elections, which is probably a world record.

Nevertheless, only a small part of this mobilization effect can be directly contributed to the GOTV field experiments as the effect size of these experiments are similar to US GOTV experiments which are typically less than 2 or 3 percentage points (Bhatti et al. 2019; Green et al. 2013). The GOTV field experiments have also successfully identified a direct spillover effect of 30 per cent to other household members, even parents. Thus, the mobilization efforts travel not only downstream from parent to young voters but also in the opposite direction from the young voter to their parents (Bhatti et al. 2017c). Table 6.2 provides an overview of the effect size on turnout from our GOTV field experiments. It includes both the most successful experiments and the ones which did not have any mobilizing effect in order to provide a fuller picture of the experiences across local and European Parliament elections.

So even though the many field experiments have provided solid evidence of their effect using randomized controlled trials, it is also evident that the effect sizes are relatively modest compared to the structural aspect of the differences in turnout, such as the difference across age, gender, and ethnicity. Thus, GOTV undertakings are in no way a quick fix to reducing the substantial differences in turnout among the various groups of voters. Nevertheless, the experiments also have an indirect effect as they have increased the general awareness about turning out to vote from the media and public. For example, many media outlets took special initiatives to increase turnout in both 2013 and 2017 by devoting part of their election coverage to the aspect of turning out to vote.

Table 6.2. Overview of the Experiment's Total Effects

Experiment/group	Effect size in percentage points	Election and year
Posters and flyers, *Bolbro, Odense municipality* (imm.)	14.4*	Local 2013
Postcards, *Silkeborg municipality*	2.9*	Local 2013
SMS, *Ministry for CGEIS** (second-gen. immigrants)	2.9*	Local 2013
Letter and postcard, *Silkeborg municipality* (joint effect)	2.8*	Local 2013
Letter, *Silkeborg municipality*	2.8*	Local 2013
SMS, *Danish Youth Council* (before election day)	2.3*	Local 2013
SMS, *Danish Youth Council* (joint effect)	1.8*	Local 2013
Letter, *Danish Parliament* (cartoon and Constitution)	1.6*	Local 2013
SMS, *Danish Parliament* (22-29 years old)	1.3*	Local 2013
Constitution, *Danish Parliament* (joint effect)	1.1*	Local 2013
Letter, *Ministry for Eco. Affairs & Interior* (all arguments)	1.1*	Local 2013
SMS, *Council for Ethnic Minorities*	1.1**	Local 2017
SMS, *Ministry for CGEIS** (immigrants)	1.0*	Local 2013

(*continued*)

Table 6.2. Continued

Experiment/group	Effect size in percentage points	Election and year
SMS, *Danish Youth Council* (on election day only)	0.8	Local 2013
Door-to-door, *Social Democrats* (joint effect)	0.7	Local 2013
SMS, *Danish Youth Council* (joint effect)	0.7*	EU 2014
Constitution, cartoon, *Danish Parliament*	0.7**	Local 2017
SMS, *Ministry for CGEIS** (without link)	0.6*	Local 2013
Letter, *Danish Parliament* (letter and Constitution)	0.6	Local 2013
Posters in (social housing), *Council for Ethnic Mino.*	0.6	Local 2017
SMS, without name, *Danish muni.* (40+ age group)	0.5*	Local 2017
Letter, *Min. for Eco. Affairs & Interior* (joint effect)	0.4*	Local 2013
SMS, *Danish Parliament* (joint effect)	0.4	Local 2013
SMS, *Ministry for CGEIS** (joint effect)	0.3	Local 2013
Digital letter, *Silkeborg municipality*	0.3	Local 2017
Postcard, *Silkeborg municipality*	0.1	Local 2017
SMS, *Ministry for CGEIS** (with link to VAA)	0.0	Local 2013
SMS, with name, *Danish municipalities* (40+ years group)	−0.1	Local 2017
Posters and flyers, *Bolbro, Odense muni.* (joint effect)	−0.3	Local 2013
SMS, *Ministry for CGEIS** (ethnic Danes)	−0.4	Local 2013
E-mail, *DaneAge Association* (joint effect)	−0.4	Local 2013
Door-to-door, *We vote together, CPH Uni.* (joint effect)	−0.8	Local 2013
Door-to-door, *Voting on the edge, Huset Zornig***(joint eff.)	−1.9	Local 2013
Posters and flyers, *Bolbro, Odense muni.* (ethnic Danes)	−2.4	Local 2013
Door-to-door, *Local union, Randers muni.* (joint effect)	−3.8	Local 2013

Note: * $p < 0.05$, ** $p < 0.01$, one sided-test. The italic is the donor/sender of the mobilization efforts. *Ministry for Children, Gender Equality, Integration, and Social Affairs. **private consultancy, experiment conducted in Lolland municipality.

Conclusion

Turnout levels are the best health indicator for democracy as they reveal an active commitment to the functioning of representative democracy. As such, Danish democracy is strong and stable with its high and stable turnout. This goes for both national and local elections where the average turnout over the last half-century is 86 per cent and 70 per cent, respectively. The key explanations for the high and stable turnout are a strong sense of duty nursed through the education system, civil society, labour unions, and strong public service media. Furthermore, the automatic and effective voter registration system, an early mobilization of the popular right, and strong social norms of voting all contribute to the high turnout.

The register-based Danish turnout project that collects actual turnouts across elections has contributed to a new understanding of the social aspect of the decision to turn out. The analyses across elections have identified the rollercoaster relation between age and turnout, illustrating not only how 18-year-olds vote substantially more than their slighter older peers but also a steep decline in turnout in older age. The explanation is mainly social. When the young voters leave home, their social ties which nursed high turnout are disrupted. The same goes for the elderly where widowing plays a major role in understanding the steep turnout decline.

The turnout project has also identified major inequalities in turnout. Especially immigrants from non-Western countries and people on unemployment benefits have low turnout. These inequalities present a major problem as these groups seem to turn their back on democracy.

Large GOTV field experiments implemented as randomized controlled trials (RCTs) had been conducted to address turnout inequalities. The effect sizes on these experiments have been similar to GOTV experiments elsewhere. Both direct mobilizations' effect of 2–3 percentage points and spill-over effects of about 30 per cent within households have been significantly identified. But it is especially remarkable that the experiments had the largest impact among the voters least inclined to vote. GOTV experiments have thus narrowed the gap between voters most likely to vote and voters least likely to vote, thereby decreasing turnout inequalities.

References

Andersen, Jørgen G. (2017). 'Portræt af vælgernes socio-demografi', in Kasper M. Hansen and Rune Stubager, eds, *Oprør fra udkanten. Folketingsvalget 2015*. Copenhagen: Jurist- og Økonomforbundets Forlag, 41–67.

Beetham, David (1991). *The Legitimation of Power*. Basingstoke: MacMillan.

Bengtsson, Åsa, Kasper M. Hansen, Ólafur Þ. Harðarson, Hanne M. Narud, and Henrik Oscarsson (2014). *The Nordic Voter: Myths of Exceptionalism*. Colchester: ECPR Press.

Bhatti, Yosef, Jens O. Dahlgaard, Jonas H. Hansen, and Kasper M. Hansen (2015). 'Getting out the vote with evaluative thinking', *American Journal of Evaluation*, 36/3: 389–400.

Bhatti, Yosef, Jens O. Dahlgaard, Jonas H. Hansen, and Kasper M. Hansen (2016a). 'Valgdeltagelsen og vælgerne til Folketingsvalget 2015', *CVAP Working Papers Series*, 1/2016.

Bhatti, Yosef, Jens O. Dahlgaard, Jonas H. Hansen, and Kasper M. Hansen (2017a). 'How voter mobilization from short text messages travels within households and families: Evidence from two nationwide field experiments', *Electoral Studies*, 50: 39–46.

Bhatti, Yosef, Jens O. Dahlgaard, Jonas H. Hansen, and Kasper M. Hansen (2017b). 'Moving the campaign from the front door to the front pocket: Field experimental evidence on the effect of phrasing and timing of text messages on voter turnout', *Journal of Elections, Public Opinion and Parties*, 27/3: 291–310.

Bhatti, Yosef, Jens O. Dahlgaard, Jonas H. Hansen, and Kasper M. Hansen (2017c). 'How voter mobilization from short text messages travels within households and families: Evidence from two nationwide field experiments', *Electoral Studies*, 50: 39–46.

Bhatti, Yosef, Jens O. Dahlgaard, Jonas H. Hansen, and Kasper M. Hansen (2018a). 'Core and peripheral voters: Predictors of turnout across three types of elections', *Political Studies*, 67/2: 348–66.

Bhatti, Yosef, Jens O. Dahlgaard, Jonas H. Hansen, and Kasper M. Hansen (2018b). 'Can governments use get out the vote letters to solve Europe's turnout crisis? Evidence from a field experiment', *West European Politics*, 41/1: 240–60.

Bhatti, Yosef, Jens O. Dahlgaard, Jonas. H. Hansen, and Kasper M. Hansen (2019). 'Is door-to-door canvassing effective in Europe? Evidence from a meta-study across six European countries', *British Journal of Political Science*, 49/1: 279–90.

Bhatti, Yosef, Edward Fieldhouse, and Kasper M. Hansen (2020). 'It's a group thing: How voters go to the polls together', *Political Behavior*, 42/1, 1–34.

Bhatti, Yosef, and Kasper M. Hansen (2012a). 'Leaving the nest and the social act of voting: Turnout among first-time voters', *Journal of Elections, Public Opinion and Parties*, 22/4: 380–406.

Bhatti, Yosef, and Kasper M. Hansen (2012b). 'Retiring from voting: Turnout among senior voters', *Journal of Elections, Public Opinion and Parties*, 22/4: 479–500.

Bhatti, Yosef, Kasper M. Hansen, and Hanna Wass (2012). 'The relationship between age and turnout: A roller-coaster ride', *Electoral Studies*, 31/3: 588–93.

Bhatti, Yosef, Kasper M. Hansen, and Hanna Wass (2016b). 'First-time boost beats experience: The effect of past eligibility on turnout', *Electoral Studies*, 41/2: 151–8.

Blais, André (2000). *To Vote or Not to Vote? The Merits and Limits of Rational Choice Theory*. Pittsburgh, PA: University of Pittsburgh Press.

Christensen, Jens P. (2020). 'The constitution', in Peter M. Christiansen, Jørgen Elklit, and Peter Nedergaard, eds, *The Oxford Handbook of Danish Politics*. Oxford: Oxford University Press, 9–27.

Dahlgaard, Jens O., Jonas H. Hansen, Kasper M. Hansen, and Yosef Bhatti (2019). 'Bias in self-reported voting and how it distorts turnout models: Disentangling non-response bias and over-reporting among Danish voters', *Political Analysis*, 27/4: 590–8. doi:10.1017/pan.2019.9

Elklit, Jørgen, and Lise Togeby (2009). 'Where turnout holds firm: The Scandinavian exceptions', in Joan DeBardeleben and Jon H. Pammett, eds, *Activating the Citizen: Dilemmas of Citizen Participation in Europe and Canada*. New York: Macmillan, 83–105.

ETUI (2018). *Benchmarking Working Europe 2018*. ETUI: Brussels.

Galais, Carol, and André Blais (2017). 'Duty to vote and political support in Asia', *International Journal of Public Opinion Research*, 29/4: 631–56.

Green, Donald P., and Alan Gerber (2015). *Get Out the Vote: How to Increase Voter Turnout,* 3rd ed. Washington, D.C.: Brookings Institution Press.

Green, Donald P., Mary C. McGrath, and Peter M. Aronow (2013). 'Field experiments and the study of voter turnout', *Journal of Elections, Public Opinion and Parties,* 23/1: 27–48.

Griffin, John D., and Brian Newman (2005). 'Are voters better represented?', *Journal of Politics,* 67/4: 1206–27.

Hansen, Jonas, H., Kasper M. Hansen, and Klaus Levinsen (2017). 'Valgdagen som socialt ritual', in Jørgen Elklit, Christian Elmelund-Præstekjær, and Ulrik Kjær, eds, *KV13. Analyser af kommunalvalget 2013.* Odense: University Press of Southern Denmark, 133–52.

Hansen, Kasper M. (2007). 'De oplyste danskere: Hvad ved danskerne om politik og gør det en forskel?', in Jørgen G. Andersen, Johannes Andersen, Ole Borre, Kasper M. Hansen, and Hans J. Nielsen, eds, *Det nye politiske landskab. Folketingsvalget 2005 i perspektiv.* Aarhus: Academica, 257–73.

Hansen, Kasper M. (2018). 'Valgdeltagelsen ved kommunal- og regionsvalget 2017', *CVAP Working Papers Series,* 1/2018.

Henriksen, Lars S., Kristin Strømsnes, and Lars Svedberg (2018) (eds). *Civic Engagement in Scandinavia. Volunteering, Informal Help and Giving in Denmark, Norway and Sweden.* Cham: Springer. Nonprofit and Civil Society Studies.

IDEA (2019). 'Voter Turnout Database', in IDEA, ed., Stockholm: The International Institute for Democracy and Electoral Assistance (IDEA). Stockholm: IDEA.

Leighley, Jan E., and Jonathan Nagler (2013). *Who Votes Now? Demographics, Issues, Inequality, and Turnout in the United States.* Princeton, NJ: Princeton University Press.

Lijphart, Arend (1997). 'Unequal participation: democracy's unresolved dilemma', *American Political Science Review,* 91/1: 1–14.

Mansbridge, Jane (1999). 'Should Blacks represent Blacks and women represent women? A contingent "Yes"', *Journal of Politics,* 61/3: 628–57.

Rousseau, Jean-Jaques (1762). *Du contrat social ou Principes du droit politique.* Geneva: La Renaissance du Livre.

Schmitt, Hermann, Sara B. Hobolt, Sebastian A. Popa, Eftichia Teperoglou, and European Parliament, Directorate-General for Communication, Public Monitoring Unit (2016). *European Parliament Election Study 2014, Voter Study, First Post-Election Survey.* GESIS Data Archive, Cologne. ZA5160 Data file Version 4.0.0, doi:10.4232/1.12628.

Stubager, Rune, Kasper M. Hansen, Michael S. Lewis-Beck, and Richard Nadeau (2019). *The Danish Voter: Democratic Ideals and Challenges.* Michigan, IL: Michigan University Press.

Tingsten, Herbert (1937). *Political Behavior; Studies in Election Statistics.* London: P. S. King & Son.

Wolfinger, Raymond E., and Steven J. Rosenstone (1980). *Who Votes?* New Haven, CT: Yale University Press.

CHAPTER 7

THE PARLIAMENT (*FOLKETINGET*)

Powerful, Professional, and Trusted?

HELENE HELBOE PEDERSEN

THE position of parliament is constantly debated among scholars as well as politicians and political observers. In 1997, the Danish Parliament, *Folketinget*, initiated the Danish Democracy and Power Study to investigate how power was distributed and exercised in society, focusing in particular on the conditions for parliamentary control and influence. The project concluded that the *Folketing* was losing decision-making capacity due to increased EU integration and national decentralization but also that Parliament was increasingly powerful in relation to the government (Togeby et al. 2003: 134). Twenty years later, a minister and her personal advisor call upon politicians and voters to care about the 'neglected Parliament', sincerely worrying 'that the *Folketing* is becoming a 'stamping office' for the government's EU policy' (Hansen and Flindt 2018: 14, author's translation).

The position of the *Folketing*—as any legislature in democratic systems—is important because the parliament provides legitimacy to the democratic decision-making process by being directly accountable to voters and scrutinizing government on their behalf between elections. The extent to which parliament is able to provide this legitimacy depends on whether it has the institutional power and resources needed to exercise control and whether voters perceive it as a legitimate, democratic institution. This chapter, therefore, asks how powerful, professional, and trusted the Danish Parliament is.

The *Folketing* is a single-chamber legislature with 179 members. Two of these are elected in the Faroe Islands and two in Greenland. According to the Constitution (Section 56), members of Parliament (MPs) are free to follow their own conviction and not take instructions from the voters. Still, members of Parliament organize in political parties, and the parliamentary party groups are the most crucial parliamentary actors even if they are not mentioned in the Constitution (see Green-Pedersen and Kosiara-Pedersen 2020). Candidates are nominated by parties and run their campaigns under a party label. In Parliament, parties organize daily work and assign committee positions, and party unity in legislative votes is only broken in rare instances.

An important division in the study of parliaments is between the traditional, institutional studies describing the characteristics of legislatures as an institution, and the behavioural studies explaining the legislative behaviour of individual legislators. New institutionalist approaches have tried to combine these two traditions by defining the parliament as the research object while theoretically incorporating the importance of actor preferences and behaviour.

Across all legislative studies, a major concern has been to determine how powerful legislatures are (Fish and Kroenig 2009). The answer to this question is still debated. Some argue that the question is unanswerable since parliament is most often not a unitary actor but an arena in which different parliamentary actors—primarily political parties—interact (Andeweg and Nijzink 1995). These actors may be powerful but not the parliament as such. Others agree about the importance of the question but disagree about the answer. Some argue that with regard to law-making, parliaments are little more than 'rubber stamps', passing the bills that governments propose to a degree where the executive controls parliament rather than the other way around (Kreppel 2014). This claim is, however, disputed (Russell and Gover 2017). Others argue that the power of parliaments should not only be evaluated with regard to law-making but also with regard to the many other functions parliaments serve. These include scrutinizing government, legitimizing decision-making processes, and representing and aggregating citizen interests (Packenham 1970; Norton 1998; Kreppel 2014).

Dealing with this main issue of power, scholars have focused on the institutional powers vested in parliament (Sieberer 2011) as well as the resources and specialization of the parliament (Shepsle and Weingast 1987; Bowler and Farrell 1995). More recently, scholars have become increasingly concerned with the linkages between parliament and external actors such as interest groups and citizens (Norton 2002; Leston-Bandeira 2012). Such linkages are perceived as an important source for legitimacy and public trust, which is crucial for the status and impact of parliaments.

In light of these main themes, discussions, and developments in legislative studies, this chapter analyses how powerful, professional, and trusted the *Folketing* is based on existing studies of the Danish Parliament as well as new data. In the first section, the institutional power of the *Folketing* is analysed based on a principal-agent framework suggested by Sieberer (2011), but the analysis is extended by including data on parliamentary activities to bridge the divide between the institutional approach and the behavioural approach. In the second section, the institutional resources of the *Folketing* are analysed under the headline of professionalization. This is used as a conceptual umbrella for uniting research on parliamentary resources such as staff and money, on patterns of parliamentary recruitment, and on the specialization within parliaments. All of these sub-disciplines relate to the professional capacities of parliament. The third section engages with the more recent research agenda within legislative studies, analysing how trusted the *Folketing* is among Danish voters and its interaction with civil society. The chapter concludes by summarizing the findings of the analysis and suggesting an answer to how powerful, professional, and trusted the *Folketing* actually is.

A Powerful Parliament?

Power is as difficult to define and measure in legislative studies as in any other field of political science. However, scholars continuously venture into the study of power even though they know 'that measuring the powers of legislatures perfectly is a vain hope' (Fish and Kroenig 2009: 1).

With regard to the Danish case, the frequent formation of minority governments (Green-Pedersen and Skjæveland 2020) offers parties outside government more influence than systems with majority governments do (Strøm 1990a; Ganghof and Bräuninger 2006). It can thus be argued that Parliament is stronger when government is weak. However, this argument rests on a highly party-based understanding of legislatures, judging the power of legislatures based on how much legislative power parties in and out of government have. Even though political parties are crucial parliamentary actors, parliaments may offer these actors different opportunities for exercising power. As an institution, parliaments make different tools 'dispositional' for the various actors (Dowding 1996: 3-4 cited in Sieberer 2011: 735), and therefore, there is more to parliamentary power than the relative number of seats controlled by parties in and out of office.

Sieberer offers a cohesive theoretical framework to analyse the institutional powers that parliamentary actors have at their disposal. In line with a rational-choice new institutionalist perspective, the power of parliamentary actors is assumed to rest on institutional resources that allow them to influence the government to a greater or lesser extent (Sieberer 2011: 735). In parliamentary systems, the parliament is the principal vis-à-vis the government, and the relevant institutional resources are those that allow the parliament to control that the government produces policy outcomes in accordance with the preferences of the parliamentary majority. These institutions relate to: 1) legislative influence, 2) *ex ante* selection control, and 3) *ex post* oversight control.

Legislative Influence

Parliamentary actors may control policy-outcomes by limiting delegation to the government and controlling legislation on their own. The direct legislative influence of a parliament depends on the extent to which the parliament controls its own agenda, the law-making capacities of the parliamentary committees, and the influence parliament has with regard to the budget (Sieberer 2011).

According to the Danish Constitution, the Speaker has the prerogative to set the parliamentary agenda (Section 39). In practice, the chair often involves the Committee on the Rules of Procedure when planning parliamentary work, but the Parliament sets the agenda, not the government. The Rules of Procedure further specify that there must be at least 30 days between a proposal and the final vote to allow committees enough time to consider the proposal. Bills can be proposed by members of Parliament (private member bills) or by the government. The committees cannot propose bills as committee bills, but their members may, of course, propose a bill as a private member bill. In practice (as illustrated in Figure 7.1), the government makes most of the proposals, which are then assigned by Parliament to the relevant standing committee (Mattson and Strøm 2004).

During committee work, the committee may ask the minister questions related to the bill or receive input from external actors. It is only ministers that committees can compel to provide evidence (Mattson and Strøm 1995). Based on committee discussions and bill readings, the committee produces a report indicating the support for or against the bill. Compared to parliamentary committees in other countries, Danish committees have relatively high agenda setting power as the Parliament decides on the parliamentary agenda and committees decide when to finalize their reports; however, since they cannot write or split bills, their drafting authority is limited (Mattson and Strøm 1995: 299).

Even though Danish MPs have institutional resources that allow them to influence policy outcomes directly, Figure 7.1 shows clearly that the government proposes more bills than members of Parliament and that it is more likely that a government bill is passed than a private member's bill. This is the case in most parliamentary systems, and it has not changed much over the years in Denmark. Actually, the number of private member bills is slightly decreasing, whereas the government is becoming even more successful in passing proposals through Parliament.

The seeming dominance of the government does not, however, reveal the extent to which proposals have been pre-negotiated in a parliamentary majority coalition. Thus, the success rate of government proposals may indicate legislative influence rather than executive dominance. First, the formal power of MPs to propose legislation and hereby force legislation that the government does not approve of through Parliament is no idle threat. During the 1980s, an 'alternative majority' formed in Parliament, forcing the

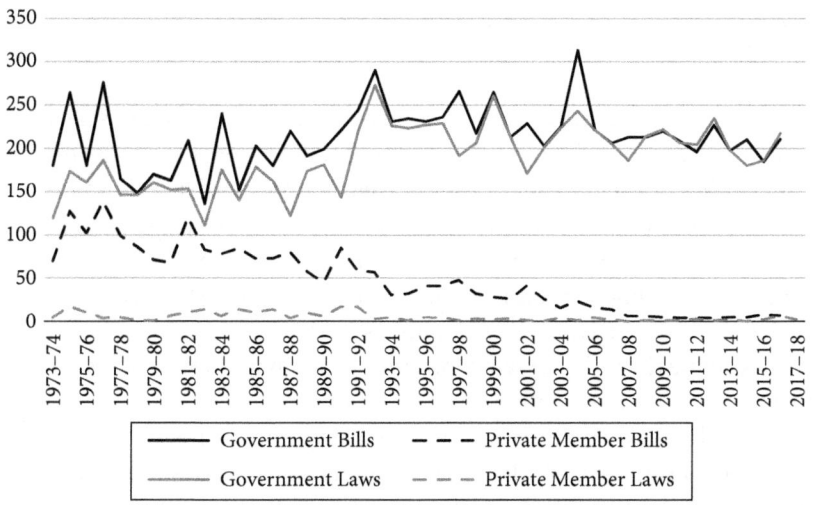

FIGURE 7.1 Number of government and Private Member Bills and laws, 1973–2018.

Note: Data provided by the Folketinget Report on the 2017–2018 parliamentary term bourgeois government to implement policies—foreign policy in particular—with which it did not agree. From 1982 to 1988, the government lost 8 per cent of the final votes in Parliament (Ganghof and Bräuninger 2006: 528–9; Damgaard 1992). Danish governments thus have incentives to negotiate with parties outside government prior to proposing legislation.

Second, informal practices for building and maintaining legislative majority coalitions have developed and institutionalized in the *Folketing*. Legislative agreements (*forlig*) oblige participating parties to act in certain prescribed ways. By entering the agreement, parties win the right to veto any change to the agreement. In exchange, they undertake to support the policy in the legislature as well as in public until the agreement is renewed or expires (Pedersen 2010: 742–3; Christiansen 2008). These legislative norms have developed gradually from the end of the nineteenth century and are still central to the legislative practice in Denmark (Pedersen 2011; Christiansen and Seeberg 2016). *Forlig* have different expiration dates, but some may run over several electoral terms, providing parties substantial policy influence even if the parliamentary majority changes. Informal institutions are rarely included in comparative studies of legislative influence, but in the *Folketing*, they offer political parties out of government significant power in blocking policy changes related to issues included in this particular kind of agreement.

Legislative rules and informal practices of the *Folketing* allow parliamentary actors to influence policy outcomes in accordance with the parliamentary majority. The main reason why governments might still dominate the legislative process is the party discipline that runs across the executive and legislative institutions (Andeweg and Nijzink 1995). Since party leadership often take office when parties move into government, they may be able to enforce discipline in government as well as in the parliamentary party group, hereby dominating the legislative process.

Ex Ante Selection Control

Another way for parliamentary actors to control policy outcomes is to select an agent—a government—that is more likely to share and enact the preferences of the parliamentary majority. According to Sieberer (2011: 738–42), elective power depends on 1) nomination rights, 2) selection requirements, and 3) selection procedures. The nomination rights determine who has the opportunity to nominate candidates and define the pool of possible agents. If Parliament nominates candidates without interference from government or other actors, the elective power resources of Parliament are stronger. Selection requirements define the terms of selection, and the main difference is between simple or qualified majority requirements. Parliament is perceived as stronger in relation to government if selection requires a qualified majority. Finally, the selection procedure is relevant for the autonomy of parliamentary actors in exercising elective power. If the vote is secret, the risk of sanctions from party or government leadership is smaller than in the case of open votes. Therefore, secret votes are categorized as a stronger power resource of parliamentary actors.

The *Folketing* must be categorized as comparatively weak with regard to elective power since there is no investiture vote. The prime minister or the cabinet are not required to win any formal vote among members of Parliament before taking office. This is a negative version of parliamentarism, in which a parliamentary majority can remove a government from office, rather than a positive version, where an explicit parliamentary majority is needed to take office. With regard to institutional elective power, negative parliamentarism is weaker than positive parliamentarism, but negative parliamentarism is also part of the reason for the frequent formation of minority governments which makes Parliament more, rather than less, powerful relative to the government. This shows how dimensions of institutional parliamentary power are not necessarily correlated since they substitute each other to some extent. If Parliament has a strong, direct influence on decision-making, it is less in need of strong elective powers because it delegates less power to the executive.

Besides the limited elective power of the *Folketing*, the government also has the opportunity to dissolve Parliament. General elections must be held at least every fourth year (see Elklit 2020), but the prime minister can call an election sooner if he wishes to renew the government mandate, finds that Parliament blocs salient legislation, or just sees an opportunity to maximize chances of retaining office. Just as Parliament can send government out of office, the prime minister can dissolve Parliament and call an election.

Ex Post Oversight Control

Finally, an important dimension of parliamentary power is the extent to which legislative institutions allow parliamentary actors to scrutinize and sanction the government and hereby discover and correct the situation if the government does not act in accordance with the preferences of the parliamentary majority. This include committees' rights to question ministers and to require documents, the availability of parliamentary questions, and rules regarding votes of no confidence.

With regard to the vote of no confidence, the *Folketing* can express no confidence to individual minsters or the prime minister. The vote does not require that Parliament agrees to support an alternative minister or government, and it only requires a simple majority to vote the government or a minister out of office. Votes of no confidence are very rare, but individual ministers do occasionally face the threat of such a vote. Usually, they anticipate the result and step down before the vote is enacted.

When it comes to committee rights, committees can ask ministers written as well as oral committee questions related to any issue within their jurisdiction. Committees can also ask for consultations with the minister (*samråd*). These consultations are open to the public if at least three committee members ask for it. Most often, they are open to the public. Besides this, members of Parliament may ask individual questions, so-called section 20 questions, referring to the relevant section in the Rules of Procedure. These questions may be oral or written, and ministers are required to respond within 6 days. A member of Parliament (or several members) may also ask for an interpellation in which the relevant minister and members of Parliament will debate the matter in plenum. The Parliament permits these interpellations and only very few are denied.

The *Folketing* has also taken new initiatives. Since 2013, a number of question times are held in Parliament. During these question times, only the prime minister answers questions, and these are not submitted in advance. In 2019, party leader debates were introduced to promote deliberation rather than government opposition confrontations. The *Folketing* thus offers its members plenty of powerful resources for scrutinizing the government.

If we turn to how these controlling resources are used by the actors, Figure 7.2 illustrates the development in section 20 and committee questions. There are three phases. From the early 1970s until the early 1990s, there is a steady but relatively modest increase in the number of section 20 questions from around 500 to about 1,500 per term. In the same period, the number of committee questions also increases steadily, but at a faster pace, from around 2,000 to 8,000 committee questions. From the mid-1990s to around 2006, the number of section 20 questions explodes, reaching 7,642 in the 2005–6 term. The number of committee questions continues to increase more gradually, with a maximum of 9,674 committee questions in the 2004–5 term. After 2006, the pattern changes as the number of section 20 questions starts decreasing, while the increase in the number of committee questions accelerates.

The increase in parliamentary questions may relate to the increasing number of bills processed through Parliament, yet the number of questions per bill increases with the same pace as the absolute number of questions. Instead, Green-Pedersen (2010) offers a party competition explanation for the increase in non-legislative activities, not only in Denmark but across Western European parliaments. Party competition has changed from primarily involving position taking and mobilization of core constituents to

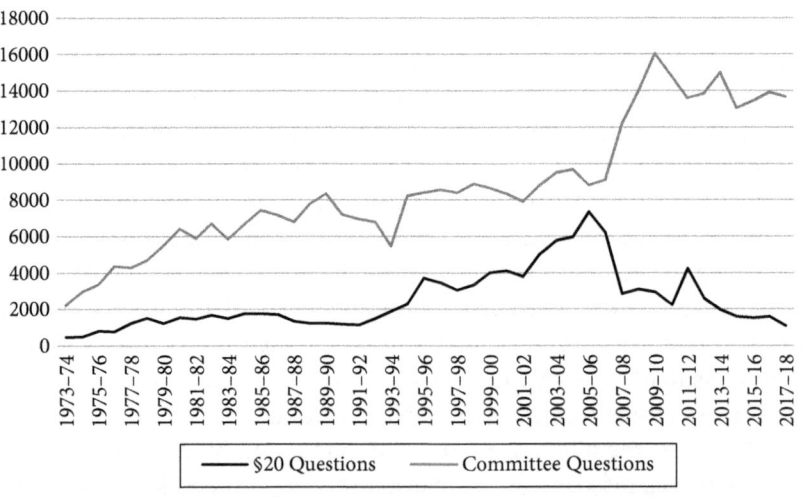

FIGURE 7.2 Number of Section 20 Questions and Committee Questions, 1973–2018.

Note: Data provided by the Folketinget Report on the 2017–2018 parliamentary term agenda-setting competition trying to push forward issues parties believe are beneficial to them. Opposition parties in particular, who lack governing parties' control over the legislative agenda, can use parliamentary questions to influence the political agenda.

In the Danish case, it is indeed primarily opposition parties that ask section 20 questions, and Green-Pedersen (2010) shows that Danish MPs especially ask questions related to issues where their party has issue-ownership. However, party competition dynamics do not explain the sudden drop in section 20 questions and increase in committee questions after 2006. This change is caused by an institutional reform. From 2007, the Rules of Procedure specify that section 20 questions should only be used for clarifying the position of the minister, whereas technical and other types of specific information should be obtained via committee questions. This led to the evident change in question practices, and to the extent that parliamentary actors adjust according to the Rules of Procedure, we may also conclude that part of the increased section 20 questioning activity prior to 2007 was, at least to some degree, due to information seeking rather than intensified issue competition.

A Parliament with Powerful Institutions

The institutional powers the *Folketing* offers parliamentary actors are substantial, both with regard to direct legislative influence and with regard to control, whereas the elective power is limited compared to other parliaments. From an institutional perspective, Danish parliamentary actors have solid opportunities to make the government act in accordance with the preferences of a majority within the legislature. Parliamentary actors—parties and individual MPs—have multiple motives (Strøm 1990b), but if their main motive is to pass legislation in accordance with their policy preferences, the Danish Parliament has the institutional power to make sure that a majority is able to enact its will even if it contradicts the preferences of the government.

A PROFESSIONAL PARLIAMENT?

It is not only the motives of parliamentary actors that decide to what extent the institutional power of parliament is used efficiently. Actors also need sufficient resources to make use of the institutional opportunities. Actors need time, expertise, and staff support to make parliaments work professionally. Under the headline of parliamentary professionalism, this section analyses the *Folketing* in relation to three major issues concerned with changes and developments in legislative institutions. The first issue is legislative institutionalization (Kornberg 1973). Institutionalization is a broad and not very clear concept (Damgaard 1977), but in empirical terms, it often narrows down to describe developments in institutional autonomy and resources. The second issue is legislative specialization, which refers to the division of labour and expertise developments in legislatures and often involves empirical analyses of parliamentary committees. Finally, the third issue is legislative professionalization, referring to how politics increasingly becomes a profession of its own, and focuses especially on changes in MP recruitment (Bovens and Wille 2017; Best and Cotta 2000; Kjær and Pedersen 2004).

Institutional Resources

The *Folketing* has a staff of about 425 employees (Folketinget 2018). This includes committee secretaries, HR personnel, library and information staff, and maintenance employees. It does not include staff in institutions associated with Parliament such as the Ombudsman or the Auditor General. There are no official accounts describing developments in the legislative staff. Damgaard (1977: 65) reports that the number of employees with college degrees in the parliamentary administration increased from 12 in 1954 to 21 in 1974. Even though the current 425 employees are not categorized into subcategories, the institutional resources in terms of parliamentary staff has clearly increased over time.

The parliamentary staff is responsible for handling practical and administrative tasks, and in this way, they support members of Parliament in focusing on their political tasks. Aside from the parliamentary staff, the parliamentary party groups are supported financially. Each parliamentary group—regardless of size and status as opposition or government party—receive one basic amount (the equivalent of about USD 63,000 per month in 2017), plus an additional amount per seat (the equivalent of about USD 10,000 per month in 2017). The purpose is to support the parliamentary work of the groups and individual members. Since 1965, the support has increased significantly (Bille 2000: 133).

Figure 7.3 shows the development over the last 15 years where the subsidy has increased gradually, with a substantial increase in 2017. In 2016, Parliament decided to increase the parliamentary group support by adding an *expertise grant*. The purpose of the grant was to strengthen the resources of Parliament relative to the government, who has privileged access to the expertise in the central administration. The figure also shows that this subsidy translates into significant staff support, amounting to 274 full-time parliamentary party group employees in 2017. Counting both parliamentary and party group staff, 4 staff workers on average support each MP to allow her to focus on the parliamentary work and make use of the available institutional powers.

Specialization and Expertise

Even with the help of staff workers, it is challenging for individual MPs to stay informed about details in the various issues and bills being discussed in Parliament. As a consequence, individual MPs may lack the sufficient knowledge to keep tabs on the government even if they have the institutional powers to do so. To address this challenge, labour is

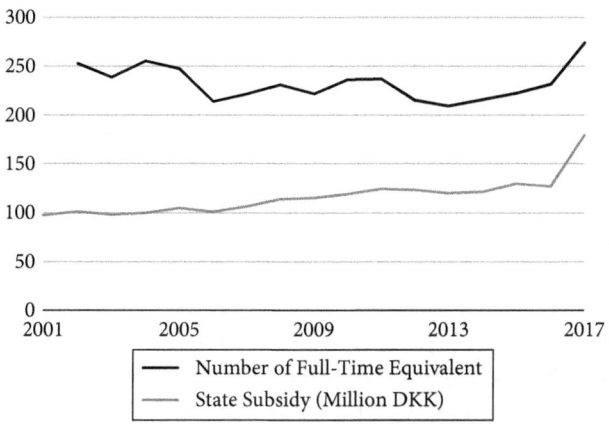

FIGURE 7.3 Parliamentary group subsidy and staff, 2001–2017.

Note: Data is collected from parliamentary party groups' yearly financial accounts, (https://www.ft.dk/da/organisation/folketingets-adminstration/folketingets-regnskaber, accessed 23 October 2018)

divided within Parliament and parliamentary party groups. Within Parliament, labour is divided between legislative committees. Within parliamentary party groups, labour is divided between party spokespersons. Through this division of labour, Parliament becomes more efficient and specialized (Mattson and Strøm 1995), which is necessary to handle the complexity of law-making and workload.

The *Folketing* is organized into 25 standing committees, mirroring the ministry structure of the government. Of these, 21 committees have 29 members, while 4 of them have fewer members. Committee members have two main tasks. Most importantly, they read and discuss bills proposed within the jurisdiction of the committee. After the first plenary reading, the bill is assigned by Parliament to a committee, and members of this committee will then scrutinize the bill and clarify the positions of the political parties in a committee report. The second task is called the *general part* and primarily involves listening to various stakeholders, experts, and citizens interested in issues related to the subject of the committee. Committees receive input via letters and deputations, and some of them also arrange expert meetings to obtain more information about an issue. MPs, therefore, obtain specialized knowledge through committee work, and the allocation of committee seats is key to promoting specialization and expertise in Parliament.

According to the Constitution (Section 52), committee seats are proportionally allocated between political parties at the beginning of each parliamentary year. Parties then decide how to distribute those seats among their MPs. The size of the party as well as MPs' interests, experience, and position within the parliamentary group are decisive factors for the intra-party allocation of committee seats. Especially in small parties, MPs will have multiple committees to attend to, while the competition is fiercer in larger parties. The seats are distributed by the parliamentary party leadership, and it may be used to discipline MPs (Martin 2014). As a result, the party leadership may offer loyal MPs seats in more important committees such as the Committee of Finance or the Committee of

Foreign Affairs. Though the instances are rare, MPs have also been stripped off all committee positions or moved to other committees after controversies with the party leadership. Committee positions may thus be used to reward as well as sanction MPs, and MPs are expected to act on behalf of their parties in their committee work (Damgaard 1995).

One way to increase expertise in legislative committees is to assign seats to members with sectoral knowledge relevant to the committee jurisdiction. According to this *sectorization* logic, teachers will be assigned to the Education Committee, trade unionists to the Labour Market Committee, and farmers to the Agriculture Committee. Over time, the sectorization of legislative committees in Denmark has decreased. In the 1970s, Damgaard found that on average, 50 per cent of committee members had sector knowledge. In the 1990s, Jensen (1995) found that the share had dropped to 40 per cent. In the 2000s, Hansen (2010) shows that no more than 20 per cent of committee members on average have sector knowledge. The share, however, varies substantially across committees. The Local Government Committee in particular is still habituated by MPs with experiences from local government (82 per cent), while very few have sector knowledge in the Environmental Committee (4 per cent) (Hansen 2010: 393). It follows from the decreasing sectorization that Danish MPs increasingly have to obtain sector knowledge through their political work rather than building on previous experience. Therefore, securing specialization by reassigning MPs to the same committees over time may be increasingly important. Unfortunately, there is no data available on the stability of committee membership.

The parliamentary division of labour is also reflected in the organization of the parliamentary party groups (Bille 2000). The party leadership not only assigns committee memberships but also party spokespersons who are responsible for monitoring and formulating party positions on specific issues such as tax, the environment, or migration. Within the parties, the spokesperson system facilitates division of labour, reduces the workload of individual MPs, and secures expertise in the party group. The spokesperson is expected to specialize and act on behalf of the party in plenary debates, in the relevant legislative committees, in communication with the press, and in negotiations with other parties. Studies on Danish parliamentary groups illustrate the importance of the relationship between spokespersons, the group, and the party leadership, which is based on expertise, loyalty, and trust (Bille 2000; Jensen 2002; Damgaard 1995).

Politics as a Profession

The decreasing sectorization in legislative committees may reflect that fewer MPs bring sector expertise into Parliament because Parliament is increasingly populated by professional politicians. 'Professional' is a broad and loosely used term (Cairney 2007). In an early study of the professionalization of politics, Sartori (1961: 596) listed four dimensions relevant for understanding professionalization: 1) the functional dimension, i.e. specialization, 2) the representative dimension, involving politicians distancing themselves from their social origin, 3) the character dimension, involving politicians' manipulation skills and possible lack of principles and opportunism, and 4) the economic dimension which is related to the existence of full-time, fully paid, elective positions where politicians have no other vocation and have to live off politics. Sartori highlights that the first and last dimensions are the most crucial, and perhaps defining, elements of professionalization (ibid.), leaving out the personal aspects of social distancing and opportunism. More recent studies focus especially on the educational and occupational background of politicians when trying to describe the degree of parliamentary professionalization (Bovens and Wille 2017; Cairney 2007; Best and Cotta 2000) because the job as an MP has become a full-time, fully paid job in most parliaments. In Denmark, a yearly salary for MPs replaced daily allowances in 1920, and the earliest account of hours MPs work from 1960 indicates that, on average, MPs work substantially more than normally expected of a full-time job (Damgaard 1977: 77–8). With regard to the economic dimension, the Danish Parliament is professionalized.

With regard to the functional dimension, more and more MPs have a university degree. Figure 7.4 shows that the share of MPs with a university degree has increased since 1953, reaching 60 per cent in the June 2019 election. At the same time, the average age of MPs has dropped, indicating that MPs enter Parliament after a shorter professional career outside politics. Many of them have experience from local government, working part time as politicians prior to entering Parliament. In 2019, 44 per cent of all elected Danish MPs had experience from city or regional councils. Furthermore, it is not only the level but also the type of education that has changed over time. Almost half (48 percent) of all MPs elected in 2019 had a social science degree (law, economics, and

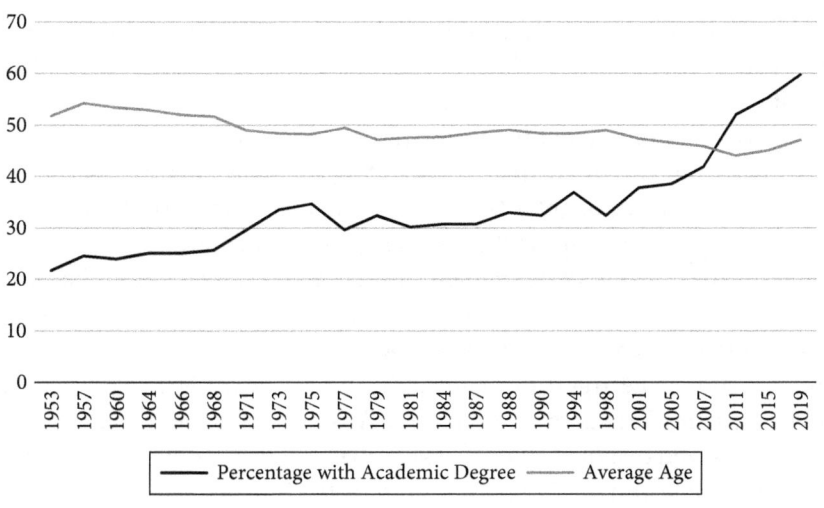

FIGURE 7.4 Age and education of Danish MPs, 1953–2019.

Note: Data on MP education from 1953 to 2005 are kindly made available by Ulrik Kjær and parts of them also published in Kjær and Pedersen (2004). These data are supplemented by data from the last three general elections. Data on the mean age of MPs are provided by *Folketinget* (https://www.ft.dk/da/folkestyret/folketinget/tal-og-fakta-om-folketinget, accessed 14 January 2019) except for the 2019 election where data are collected based on parliament and candidate websites

political science), whereas this share was below 20 per cent in 1998. This indicates that MPs are not only highly educated but increasingly educated to understand government. More Danish MPs are educated to be politicians and specialize in politics as their main career. They are, as such, functionally professional.

A Professional Parliament with Lower Specialization

The *Folketing* is professional with full-time, fully paid, and highly-educated politicians who are able to focus on their political tasks with the assistance of parliamentary and party staff. It has been questioned whether the resources of Parliament are sufficient and reasonably allocated to control government effectively, but the resources have increased over time. The *Folketing* is also organized in order to promote division of labour and specialization. Standing committees and party spokespersons make individual MPs focus on specific issues and hereby obtain detailed knowledge. However, the level of specialization is still unclear. Sectorization in committee assignment has decreased, more MPs enter politics earlier in their professional career, and there is no available data on the permanence of committee membership. The Danish Parliament may be increasingly professional but perhaps with a lower level of specialized knowledge.

A Trusted Parliament?

The notion that parliaments have multiple functions and that legitimization is one of them—and an important one—has been acknowledged for decades (Packenham 1970). The activities of parliament provide symbolic assurance that government is democratic. This is important for functional and normative reasons (Holmberg et al. 2017). If people trust that laws are passed in a democratic way, they are more likely to respect and live by these laws. Normatively, people's trust that key democratic institutions can facilitate rule by the people is crucial for the foundation of democratic rule as such. Trust is important for the position of parliament in society and in relation to the executive as legitimacy is an informal source of power. However, public trust in political actors and institutions is low and decreasing in more places.

Figure 7.5 shows the trend in Danish citizens' trust in Parliament, government, and political parties from 2008 to 2018/2019. Trust in Parliament has decreased. While 75 per cent answered that they tend to trust Parliament in 2008, only 68 per cent did the same in 2019. The lowest level of trust was recorded in 2016 (56 per cent), while more Danes indicate trusting the *Folketing* in 2018 and 2019. The downward trend may thus have stopped and even turned around over the last couple of years. The *Folketing* is relatively more trusted than the government and especially the political parties, and it is also among the most trusted parliaments in Europe. The *Folketing* is thus trusted but less so than it used to be.

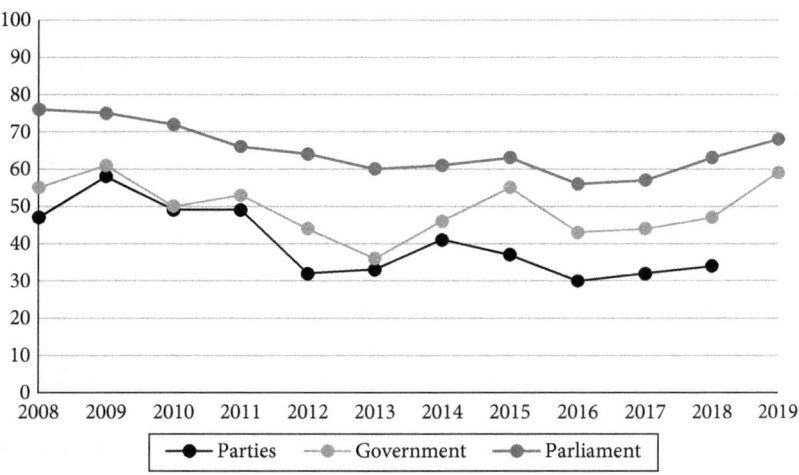

FIGURE 7.5 Trust in parliament, government, and political parties, 2008–2019 (per cent).

Note: Eurobarometer (70, 71, 73, 75, 77, 79, 81, 83, 85, 87, 89, 91). Question: I would like to ask you a question about how much trust you have in certain institutions. For each of the following institutions, please tell me if you tend to trust it or tend not to trust it. Dots show share of respondents tending to trust national political parties, government, and Parliament. Trust in parties was still not reported in the published data reports for the 2019 survey at the time of publication

The declining trust in parliaments around the world is puzzling. Norton (2017) explains how the UK Parliament is simultaneously facing the worst and best times in its history. It is the best time in relation to the executive because Parliament has become more powerful and independent. But it is the worst time in relation to the public because people have become less satisfied with and ascribe less importance to Parliament. It is as if 'the public have been more influenced by the perceptions of parliamentarians' behaviour than a results-based performance' (Norton 2017: 191). Leston-Bandeira (2012: 520) reviews developments across parliaments in various countries and concludes that 'the 2012 parliaments are definitely more open to citizens' ideas and views, and are providing information in a way never seen before. Yet overall trust in parliament has never been so low'. Parliaments are stronger, more transparent, and open, but at the same time, they are less trusted and less valued.

The *Folketing* face similar challenges. The parliamentary committees are probably among the most accessible committees to external actors such as interest groups, businesses, public institutions, and citizens because any of these actors can send letters to committees and show up in deputations without invitation and in relation to any issue they find important (Pedersen et al. 2015). During the 2017–18 parliamentary term, the parliamentary committees received 2,197 letters and welcomed 307 deputations. More committee work has become open to the public. This is the case for consultations with ministers and for meetings in the European Affairs Committee. Question times and party leader debates have been introduced to make political debates in Parliament less predictable and livelier. Besides these institutional changes, Parliament as well as parliamentarians have engaged with new media platforms. The *Folketing* has a public Facebook page informing about the agenda and happenings in Parliament. In 2016, 148 MPs (83 per cent) hosted a public Facebook page. Over the course of the year, they posted 27,695 updates and received more than 7.5 million reactions to these updates. Parliament as well as parliamentarians make great efforts to reach out to the public and be accessible to individual voters as well as interest groups. Still, trust in Parliament has declined.

The cause of declining trust and the key to changing the trend are still unidentified. Norton (2017) looks to the politicians, asking for a proactive and collective effort to change public perception. As a minimum, they should work harder to convey a sense of public service. Leston-Bandeira (2012: 522) on the other hand argues that 'it is, in fact, unlikely that parliaments' own actions have considerable impact on people's feeling of trust towards the institutions, as this is often more dependent on external factors [...]'. Rather, she calls upon researchers to refocus on symbolic representation in the relationship between parliaments and citizens to understand how citizens' sense of identification with parliament is established. Hibbing and Theiss-Morse (2002) direct attention towards voters. Their study of American voters' preferences regarding democratic decision-making suggests that politicians have indeed misunderstood what citizens are asking for by opening up and making Parliament more accessible and transparent. American voters want empathetic and non-self-interested politicians rather than responsive and accountable institutions. This is in line with Leston-Bandeira's idea that identification is perhaps more crucial to trust than involvement, but it is still an open question as to how politicians become perceived as empathetic and non-self-interested or how citizens come to identify with parliaments.

Conclusion

The answer to the question of how powerful, professional, and trusted the *Folketing* is depends on the comparisons made to reach the answer. Compared to many other parliaments, the *Folketing* is powerful, professional, and trusted. The *Folketing* provides particularly strong institutions for controlling the government and strong institutions for influencing decision-making but weak institutions for electing the government compared to many Western parliaments (Sieberer 2011). The high frequency of minority governments and strong informal institutions regarding legislative agreements further supports the decision-making power of the *Folketing*. The *Folketing* is also trusted by a majority of Danish voters. In 2018, the *Folketing* was the third most trusted national parliament among the EU member state legislatures. In relation to professionalization, the *Folketing* has reached almost the same level of highly educated MPs as other Western European parliaments (Bovens and Wille 2017: 114).

Compared to older versions of the *Folketing*, professionalization and resources have increased, which should allow MPs to make more efficient use of the institutional powers available to them. The sectorization has, however, decreased, indicating that expertise may be falling behind or have to be acquired during the political work of the incoming MPs. Moreover, the *Folketing* has become less trusted among Danish citizens over time, suggesting that the upheld legitimacy may not be everlasting.

The *Folketing* is thus a comparably strong parliament, but it also faces challenges similar to many other national legislatures of decreasing public trust, increasing pressure on the legislative process from international decision-making and the EU in particular, and difficulties in keeping tabs on the government due to information and resource asymmetries. The Parliament presidium (Speaker and 4 deputy speakers) has been occupied trying to mediate some of these challenges, holding conferences to understand the decreasing trust, initiating investigations of delegated legislation and incorporation of EU regulation to evaluate the legislative control of the *Folketing*, and establishing new forms of parliamentary debates to make the *Folketing* more deliberative and reactive to fast moving agendas. These efforts may have been successful since public trust in Parliament has started increasing slowly since 2017.

Legislative research may contribute to these efforts. For future studies of the *Folketing*, it is important to engage with the identified puzzle of decreasing trust in accessible, high-performance parliaments. Different ideas have been suggested. Some blame politicians for misbehaviour resulting in scandals damaging for public trust. Others point toward the media emphasizing the strategic elements of politics and disproportionally covering personal and political scandals. Finally, some emphasize the influence of economic developments for public trust in political institutions, implying that trust will increase as economies stabilize. Still, no clear answer or understanding of the puzzle has been provided.

It is also important for future legislative studies to bridge the divide between institutional and behavioural approaches by investigating the content of parliamentary activities, and hereby understand how and when parliamentary institutions are used by parliamentary actors. This has only been done to a limited extent in a Danish context (see e.g. Green-Pedersen 2010) but with highly informative results in other contexts (see e.g. Kirkland and Slapin 2019; Martin 2011). As legislative actors need to prioritize their tasks given the restricted time and staff resources, it is crucial to know not only what parliamentary institutions make MPs capable of doing but also what MPs actually do (Auel et al. 2015).

References

Andeweg, Rudy B., and Lia Nijzink (1995). 'Beyond the two-body image: Relations between ministers and MPs', in Herbert Döring, ed., *Parliaments and Majority Rule in Western Europe*. Frankfurt: Campus Verlag, 152–78.

Auel, Katrin, Olivier Rozenberg, and Angela Tacea (2015). 'To scrutinise or not to scrutinise? Explaining variation in EU-related activities in national parliaments', *West European Politics*, 38/2: 282–304.

Best, Heinrich, and Maurizio Cotta (2000). *Parliamentary Representatives in Europe, 1848–2000: Legislative Recruitment and Careers In Eleven European Countries*. Oxford: Oxford University Press.

Bille, Lars (2000). 'A power centre in Danish politics', in Knut Heidar and Ruud Koole, eds, *Parliamentary Party Groups in European Democracies. Political Parties Behind Closed Doors.* New York: Routledge, 130–44.

Bovens, Mark, and Anchrit Wille (2017). *Diploma Democracy: The Rise of Political Meritocracy.* Oxford: Oxford University Press.

Bowler, Shaun, and David M. Farrell (1995). 'The organizing of the European Parliament: Committees, specialization and co-ordination', *British Journal of Political Science*, 25/2: 219–43.

Cairney, Paul (2007). 'The professionalisation of MPs: Refining the 'politics-facilitating' Explanation', *Parliamentary Affairs*, 60/2: 212–33.

Christiansen, Flemming J. (2008). *Politiske forlig i Folketinget: partikonkurrence og samarbejde.* Aarhus: Politica.

Christiansen, Flemming J., and Henrik B. Seeberg (2016). 'Cooperation between counterparts in parliament from an agenda-setting perspective: Legislative coalitions as a trade of criticism and policy', *West European Politics*, 39/6: 1160–80.

Damgaard, Erik (1977). *Folketinget under forandring.* Copenhagen: Samfundsvidenskabeligt Forlag.

Damgaard, Erik (1992). 'Denmark: Experiments in parliamentary government', in Erik Damgaard and Dag Anckar, eds, *Parliamentary Change in the Nordic Countries.* Oslo: Universitetsforlaget, 18–49.

Damgaard, Erik (1995). 'How parties control committee members', in Herbert Döring, ed., *Parliaments and Majority Rule in Western Europe.* Frankfurt: Campus Verlag, 308–25.

Dowding, Keith (1996). *Power.* Buckingham: Open University Press.

Elklit, Jørgen (2020). 'The electoral system. Fair and well-functioning', in Peter M. Christiansen, Jørgen Elklit, and Peter Nedergaard, eds, *The Oxford Handbook of Danish Politics.* Oxford: Oxford University Press, 56–75.

Fish, M. Steven, and Matthew Kroenig (2009). *The Handbook of National Legislatures: A Global Survey.* Cambridge: Cambridge University Press.

Folketinget (2018). 'Administrationens arbejde', https://www.ft.dk/da/organisation/folketingets-adminstration/administrationens-arbejde accessed 22 October 2018).

Ganghof, Steffen, and Thomas Bräuninger (2006). 'Government status and legislative behaviour: Partisan veto players in Australia, Denmark, Finland and Germany', *Party Politics*, 12/4: 521–39.

Green-Pedersen, Christoffer (2010). 'Bringing parties into parliament: The development of parliamentary activities in Western Europe', *Party Politics*, 16/3: 347–69.

Green-Pedersen, Christoffer, and Karina Kosiara-Pedersen (2020). 'Party System: Open yet Stable', in Peter M. Christiansen, Jørgen Elklit, and Peter Nedergaard, eds, The Oxford Handbook of Danish Politics. Oxford: Oxford University Press, 213–29.

Green-Pedersen, Christoffer, and Asbjørn Skjæveland (2020). 'Governments in action. Consensual politics and minority governments', in Peter M. Christiansen, Jørgen Elklit, and Peter Nedergaard, eds, *The Oxford Handbook of Danish Politics.* Oxford: Oxford University Press, 230–41.

Hansen, Eva K., and Morten Flindt (2018). *Det forsømte Folketing. En opsang til folkestyret.* Copenhagen: Gyldendal.

Hansen, Martin E. (2010). 'Committee assignment politics in the Danish Folketing', *Scandinavian Political Studies*, 33/4: 381–401.

Hibbing, John R., and Elizabeth Theiss-Morse (2002). *Stealth Democracy: Americans' Beliefs about How Government Should Work.* Cambridge: Cambridge University Press.

Holmberg, Sören, Staffan Lindberg, and Richard Svensson (2017). 'Trust in parliament', *Journal of Public Affairs*, 17/1–2: e1647.

Jensen, Henrik (1995). *Arenaer eller aktører?* Copenhagen: Samfundslitteratur.

Jensen, Henrik (2002). *Partigrupperne i Folketinget.* Copenhagen: Jurist- og Økonomiforbundets Forlag.

Kirkland, Justin H., and Jonathan B. Slapin (2019). *Roll Call Rebels. Strategic Dissent in the United States and United Kingdom.* Cambridge: Cambridge University Press.

Kjær, Ulrik, and Mogens N. Pedersen (2004). *De danske folketingsmedlemmer. En parlamentarisk elite og dens rekruttering, cirkulation og transformation 1849–2001.* Aarhus: Aarhus University Press.

Kornberg, Allan (1973). *Legislatures in Comparative Perspective.* New York: D. McKay Company.

Kreppel, Amie (2014). 'Typologies and classifications', in Shane Martin, Thomas Saalfeld, and Kaare Strøm, eds, *The Oxford Handbook of Legislative Studies.* Oxford: Oxford University Press, 82–100.

Leston-Bandeira, Cristina (2012). 'Parliaments' Endless Pursuit of Trust: Re-focusing on Symbolic Representation', *The Journal of Legislative Studies*, 18/3–4: 514–26.

Martin, Shane (2011). 'Using parliamentary questions to measure constituency focus: An application to the Irish case', *Political Studies*, 59/2: 472–88.

Martin, Shane (2014). 'Why electoral systems don't always matter: The impact of "mega-seats" on legislative behaviour in Ireland', *Party Politics*, 20/3: 467–79.

Mattson, Ingvar, and Kaare Strøm (1995). 'Parliamentary committees', in Herbert Döring, ed., *Parliaments and Majority Rule in Western Europe.* Frankfurt: Campus Verlag, 249–307.

Mattson, Ingvar, and Kaare Strøm (2004). 'Committee effects on legislation', in Herbert Döring, ed., *Patterns of Parliamentary Behaviour. Passage of Legislation across Western Europe.* Aldershot: Ashgate, 91–111.

Norton, Phillip (1998). 'Nascent institutionalisation: Committees in the British parliament', *The Journal of Legislative Studies*, 4/1: 143–62.

Norton, Phillip (2002). *Parliaments and Citizens in Western Europe*, Volume 3. London: Frank Cass.

Norton, Phillip (2017). 'Speaking for parliament', *Parliamentary Affairs*, 70/2: 191–206.

Packenham, Robert A. (1970). 'Legislatures and political development', in Allan Kornberg and Lloyd D. Musolf, eds, *Legislatures in Developmental Perspective.* Durham, NC: Duke University Press, 521–82.

Pedersen, Helene H. (2010). 'How intra-party power relations affect the coalition behaviour of political parties', *Party Politics*, 16/6: 737–54.

Pedersen, Helene H. (2011). 'Etableringen af politiske forlig som parlamentarisk praksis', *Politica*, 43/1: 48–67.

Pedersen, Helene H., Darren Halpin, and Anne Rasmussen (2015). 'Who gives evidence to parliamentary committees? A comparative investigation of parliamentary committees and their constituencies', *The Journal of Legislative Studies*, 21/3: 408–27.

Russell, Meg, and Daniel Gover (2017). *Legislation at Westminster: Parliamentary Actors and Influence in the Making of British Law.* Oxford: Oxford University Press.

Sartori, Giovanni (1961). 'Parliamentarians in Italy', *International Social Science Journal*, 13/4: 583–99.

Shepsle, Kenneth A., and Barry R. Weingast (1987). 'The institutional foundations of committee power', *American Political Science Review*, 81/1: 85–104.

Sieberer, Ulrich (2011). 'The institutional power of Western European parliaments: A multidimensional analysis', *West European Politics*, 34/4: 731–54.

Strøm, Kaare (1990a). *Minority Government and Majority Rule*. Cambridge: Cambridge University Press.

Strøm, Kaare (1990b). 'A behavioral theory of competitive political parties', *American Journal of Political Science*, 34/2: 565–98.

Togeby, Lise, Jørgen G. Andersen, Peter M. Christiansen, Torben B. Jørgensen, and Signild Vallgårda (2003). *Magt og demokrati i Danmark. Hovedresultater fra magtudredningen.* Aarhus: Aarhus University Press.

....

CHAPTER 8

THE GOVERNMENT AND THE PRIME MINISTER

More than Primus Inter Pares?

....

MARTIN EJNAR HANSEN

A POPULAR CASE OF COALITIONS AND MINORITY GOVERNMENTS

....

THE Danish government and especially its formation has been of interest to political scientists and historians over the past 65 years. Political scientists have studied the formation of Danish governments (Damgaard 2000), the termination of Danish governments (Damgaard 1994, 2008), the use of coalitions in Danish politics (Damgaard 1969), and the frequent minority governments (Christiansen and Damgaard 2008; Damgaard and Svensson 1989). Coordination within the government (Christensen 1985), portfolio turnover (Mortensen and Green-Pedersen 2015), and ministerial turnover (Hansen et al. 2013) have also been topics of focus, all in a frequently comparative perspective. Historians have predominantly described cases of government formation (e.g. Kaarsted 1988) and the cabinets in general (Kaarsted 1992; Olesen 2017, 2018), or taken a more popular approach to explore the nature of Danish prime ministers (Mørch 2004), notwithstanding the number of well-researched biographies on Danish prime ministers and memoirs available.

The case of Denmark has always been popular in comparative studies of governments, not least due to its frequent use of minority coalitions and their relative stability. This is also the basis on which the topics of the government and prime minister will be explored in this chapter. In particular, the focus will be on why minority coalitions function so well in Denmark. This topic will be discussed in relation to how Danish governments are formed, how coalitions are governed and coordinate policy, what role the prime minister plays in the governance, and with regard to the selection and turnover of ministers, and design and allocation of portfolios. The chapter proceeds with a discussion of government formation and termination, including the formation of coalitions, before turning to the prime minister, followed by ministers and ministerial turnover before discussing coordination within government. The discussions are summarized and set into context in the conclusion where some avenues for further research are also discussed.

GOVERNMENT FORMATION AND TERMINATION IN DENMARK

On the evening of a general election, when the votes are counted and it is clear how many seats each party has won, it is for the most part also clear which party leader will become prime minister. If the fortunes of the incumbent government and its support parties has not declined, it can continue. Should the government and its support parties have lost seats, making it possible that a parliamentary majority can be commanded against it, it cannot continue and will resign as a government (Christensen 2019: 89). In such a case, it is necessary for either an informateur or a formateur to be selected. Each party leader advises the Queen what their party will support, and on the advice of the outgoing prime minister, a decision will be taken to appoint either an informateur, i.e. a person with a clear task to clarify the demands and objectives of potential coalition partners in terms of policy programmes and preferences over government leadership and party composition (de Winter 1995: 120), or a formateur, i.e. a person asked to start formal negotiations to form a government (de Winter 1995: 120). Damgaard (2000: 241) argues that the distinction between the two roles may be negligible for practical purposes. However, de Winter (1995: 125) finds Denmark to be one of the few countries actively using informateurs, albeit infrequently. From a legal perspective, Christensen (2019: 94-97) also distinguishes between the idea of the informateur and formateur and the limits that may be placed on either. An example where both roles were used was seen after the 1988 election where two informateurs, the Speaker of the Parliament, Svend Jakobsen, and the leader of the Social Liberals, Niels Helveg Petersen, were appointed in turn before the formateur, Poul Schlüter, was asked to form a government (Olesen 2018: 359–64). When a new government is to be formed, the outgoing government continues as an interim government until the new government can take office.

Government formation and termination come in different forms. According to Damgaard (1994), findings regarding terminations of Danish governments depend on how the concept of a government is defined. The literature has different views on when a new government is formed. For Strøm (1984), a new government is formed whenever a prime minister changes, no matter the reason. Damgaard's (1969) study of Danish coalitions use a change in party composition as an indicator for government change. Laver and Schofield (1991: 147) argue that a new government occurs after an election even when the government continues without a change in the partisan composition, as the bargaining situation changes in terms of seats and policy positions. In this chapter, a new government occurs when there is a change in the prime minister, a change in partisan composition, or after an election. The overview of all Danish governments since 1953 can be seen in Table 8.1 where the official date of entry, the formal resignation date, the government composition, and the majority status can be found.

Since 1953, Danish governments have primarily been minority governments. Only the governments serving from 1957–60, 1968–71, and 1993–4 were majority governments, and for the latter government, it is even debatable whether it commanded a majority throughout its entire existence. Coalition governments have been much more predominant, especially in the last 35 years, than single-party governments—the latter observed only in 1953–7, 1964–8, 1971–8, 1979–82, 2015–16, and then again from 2019. All of the majority governments were coalition governments, meaning that even the single-party governments needed support from one or more parties to pass any policies. This does not mean that Danish politics is chaotic and that governments secure support at random. To a large extent, Danish politics can be seen as having two blocs of parties: one centre-left and one centre-right (Green-Pedersen and Thomsen 2005), and it is within these blocs that the government secures its primary support. In modern popular vernacular, we can speak of a 'red' bloc consisting of the Social Democrats, the Socialist People's Party, the Red-Green Alliance, and for the most part, the Social Liberals, as well as the Alternative since 2015, whereas the opposite is the 'blue' bloc made up of the Liberals, the Conservatives, the Danish People's Party, and the Liberal Alliance. Only the Social Liberals have been a part of either bloc at various times over the past 65 years and served in governments led by Social Democrats and Conservatives, although the Social Liberals appear more firmly in the left bloc since 1993. The formation of two blocs also means that the traditional choice for prime minister is the leader of the largest party in the bloc with the most support.

Coalitions and Coalition Governance

Given the predominance of minority coalition governments and their relative success, it is important to study how coalitions are governed in order to understand their occurrence. The literature on coalition governance suggests distinct perspectives of how government coordinates. For instance, there is the notion of ministerial government where each minister is powerful in his or her own right to determine policy through a division of labour (Laver and Shepsle 1994: 8), or a system is setup to keep tabs on ministers from a different party either through junior ministers (Thies 2001) or parliamentary committees (Martin and Vanberg 2004). There is little evidence for Denmark to suggest coalition partners use strategic assignment of members to parliamentary committees to coordinate policy or keep tabs on each other (Hansen 2019), and junior ministers are not used in the Danish government.

Table 8.1. Government Formation in Denmark

Prime Minister	Date In	Formal Resignation	Government Composition	Majority/Minority
Hedtoft III	30.9.1953	29.1.1955	S	Minority
Hansen I	1.2.1955	14.5.1957	S	Minority
Hansen II	28.5.1957	19.2.1960	S, RV, RF	Majority
Kampmann I	21.2.1960	15.11.1960	S, RV, RF	Majority
Kampmann II	18.11.1960	3.9.1962	S, RV	Minority
Krag I	3.9.1962	22.9.1964	S, RV	Minority
Krag II	26.9.1964	22.11.1966	S	Minority
Krag III	22.11.1966	22.2.1968	S	Minority
Baunsgaard	22.2.1968	21.9.1971	RV, KF, V	Majority
Krag IV	11.10.1971	5.10.1972	S	Minority
Jørgensen I	5.10.1972	4.12.1973	S	Minority
Hartling	19.12.1973	9.1.1975	V	Minority
Jørgensen II	13.2.1975	15.2.1977	V	Minority
Jørgensen III	15.2.1977	30.8.1978	S, V	Minority
Jørgensen IV	30.8.1978	23.10.1979	S	Minority
Jørgensen V	26.10.1979	8.12.1981	S	Minority
Jørgensen VI	30.12.1981	3.9.1982	S	Minority
Schlüter I	10.9.1982	10.1.1984	KF, V, CD, KRF	Minority
Schlüter II	10.1.1984	8.9.1987	KF, V, CD, KRF	Minority
Schlüter III	10.9.1987	10.5.1988	KF, V, CD, KRF	Minority
Schlüter IV	3.6.1988	12.12.1990	KF, V, RV	Minority
Schlüter V	18.12.1990	15.1.1993	KF, V	Minority
Nyrup Rasmussen I	25.1.1993	21.9.1994	S, RV, CD, KRF	Majority
Nyrup Rasmussen II	27.9.1994	30.12.1996	S, RV, CD	Minority
Nyrup Rasmussen III	30.12.1996	11.3.1998	S, RV	Minority
Nyrup Rasmussen IV	11.3.1998	20.11.2001	S, RV	Minority
Fogh Rasmussen I	27.11.2001	8.2.2005	V, KF	Minority
Fogh Rasmussen II	18.2.2005	13.11.2007	V, KF	Minority
Fogh Rasmussen III	23.11.2007	5.4.2009	V, KF	Minority
Løkke Rasmussen I	5.4.2009	15.9.2011	V, KF	Minority
Thorning-Schmidt I	3.10.2011	3.2.2014	S, RV, SF	Minority
Thorning-Schmidt II	3.2.2014	18.6.2015	S, RV	Minority
Løkke Rasmussen II	28.6.2015	28.11.2016	V	Minority
Løkke Rasmussen III	28.11.2016	6.6.2019	V, KF, LA	Minority
Frederiksen	27.6.2019	–	S	Minority

Note: This table is based partially on Damgaard (2000: 242).

Coalitions are negotiated between parties, and besides the distribution of portfolios, the focus of the coalition is also negotiated and written down in a coalition agreement. This agreement has the dual role of signalling a coherent policy agreed on by the government as well as committing parties and ministers to a common goal. This might be a reason for enhancing the durability of minority coalitions in that the coalition partners agree what direction policy is to take in general yet still leave certain aspects open to the individual ministers. It is the case that while the coalition agreements can be specific, they far from cover every topic, allowing individual ministers some leeway on matters not specified in the agreement (Christiansen and Pedersen 2014), which might characterize the government as using a form of controlled division of labour when it comes to categorizing the Danish approach to ministerial government.

Given that the vast majority of Danish governments are minority governments, it is necessary when forming a government that it can secure support from parties outside the government, ensuring that no majority is found against it. In most cases, knowledge of which government a party is willing to support is clear. When the Liberal leader Anders Fogh Rasmussen formed a government in 2001, it was with the support of the Danish People's Party who supported his governments throughout their existence, as well as those of his successor Lars Løkke Rasmussen. The Danish People's Party did not enter government but secured much influence on the policies put forward by the government in return for their support in the government formation and the life of the governments. The presence of support parties can entail that a notional minority government can be as stable as a majority government if the pay-off provided to the support party is large enough to make the relationship stable. The negotiations with support parties mean that significant concessions are granted to these parties and that they take on a role as veto players on the policy issues where the concessions are granted (Ganghof and Bräuninger 2006). Generally speaking, the government must pay attention to the preferences of not only the supporters of their own parties but also to those of their support parties (Hobolt and Klemmensen 2005). While negotiations between support parties and the government are done at the ministry level between the minister and the support party spokespeople in the day-to-day operations, it also often results in legislative agreements (Green-Pedersen and Skjæveland 2020; Pedersen 2020). With the clear knowledge of which parties support the government, it is possible for a minority government to have the functional equivalence of a stable majority as it is also in the interest of the support parties to stay in power to increase their policy influence. This contributes to explaining the relative success of minority coalition governments in Denmark.

Government Termination

The duration between elections in Denmark is four years at most. However, it is the prerogative of the prime minister to call early elections if he so decides. Elections are also the most important reasons for governments to terminate. If the election results in the government losing enough support to make it questionable as to whether the government can command a majority with its support parties, the government will usually terminate. In 1975, the incumbent Liberal government performed well in the election and attempted to carry on, but only two weeks after the election, a motion of no confidence was passed in Parliament and the government stepped down. This is the last example of a government attempting to carry on and losing a confidence vote in Parliament. Twice, Danish governments have terminated without an election, and the new government came from the other bloc as in 1982 when the Social Democrat Anker Jørgensen's government terminated in favour of the Conservative Poul Schlüter, and in 1993 when Schlüter's government terminated, and Social Democrat Poul Nyrup Rasmussen took office. A change in coalition status outside of an election has happened four times since 1953: first, when the Liberals joined the Social Democrats in a coalition in 1978, terminating the previous single-party Social Democratic government, then in 1996 when the Centre Democrats left the coalition with the Social Democrats and Social Liberals, in 2014 when the Socialist People's Party left the coalition with the Social Democrats and Social Liberals, and finally, in 2016 when the Liberal single-party government was terminated when the party was joined in a coalition by the Conservatives and the Liberal Alliance.

A change in prime minister is also a termination event, and Danish governments have seen the death of two prime ministers while in office: Hans Hedtoft in 1955 and H. C. Hansen in 1960. Viggo Kampmann resigned in 1962 due to illness, and Jens Otto Krag stepped down voluntarily in 1972. Anders Fogh Rasmussen resigned in 2009 to take up the position of Secretary General of NATO. In all other instances, Danish governments have terminated due to elections and a resulting change in the bargaining environment. The overview of all terminations can be found in Table 8.2 below.

THE PRIME MINISTER

The prime minister is the head of government, and as such, ultimately responsible for its successes and failures. The Prime Minister's Office is responsible for a relatively small portfolio of policy areas, namely only the North Atlantic area (Greenland and the Faroe Islands), the media, government affairs (government formation, constitutional law, and portfolio distribution), and all issues concerning the Royal House and the flag. Most of the work dealt with by the Prime Minister's Office is focused directly on supporting the prime minister in his work, be it on foreign policy, the EU, or domestic policy where the prime minister takes on a coordinating role. Work relating to the European Union has obviously increased in line with the increased integration (Damgaard 2004: 120–1), but broader foreign policy has also become more important. This appears to have been the case particularly since Poul Nyrup Rasmussen took office in 1993 (Pedersen and Knudsen 2005: 162–4). Where previous prime ministers played a less active role in foreign policy, Rasmussen and his successors as prime minister have all allowed foreign policy to become more important in their job, decreasing the importance of the previously strong Minister for Foreign Affairs and allowing the Prime Minister's Office more control over foreign policy (Damgaard 2004: 120).

For most of the occupants of the post, the traditional way to become prime minister has been through the post of leader of the largest party in their bloc. The only exception

Table 8.2. Government Termination in Denmark

Prime Minister	Date In	Formal Resignation	Government Composition	Reason for Termination
Hedtoft III	30.9.1953	29.1.1955	S	Death of PM
Hansen I	1.2.1955	14.5.1957	S	Elections four months before end of term
Hansen II	28.5.1957	19.2.1960	S, RV, RF	Death of PM
Kampmann I	21.2.1960	15.11.1960	S, RV, RF	Elections six months before end of term
Kampmann II	18.11.1960	3.9.1962	S, RV	Resignation of PM due to illness
Krag I	3.9.1962	22.9.1964	S, RV	Election due to end of term
Krag II	26.9.1964	22.11.1966	S	Election called to improve government bargaining position
Krag III	22.11.1966	22.2.1968	S	Election due to parliamentary defeat
Baunsgaard	22.2.1968	21.9.1971	RV, KF, V	Election four months before end of term
Krag IV	11.10.1971	5.10.1972	S	Resignation of PM due to leaving politics
Jørgensen I	5.10.1972	4.12.1973	S	Election called due to parliamentary defeat
Hartling	19.12.1973	9.1.1975	V	Election called to improve government bargaining position; no confidence vote after elections
Jørgensen II	13.2.1975	15.2.1977	V	Election called to improve government bargaining position
Jørgensen III	15.2.1977	30.8.1978	S, V	Coalition formed
Jørgensen IV	30.8.1978	23.10.1979	S	Election called due to conflict between coalition partners
Jørgensen V	26.10.1979	8.12.1981	S	Election called due to parliamentary defeat
Jørgensen VI	30.12.1981	3.9.1982	S	Voluntary resignation of government
Schlüter I	10.9.1982	10.1.1984	KF, V, CD, KRF	Budget proposal defeated
Schlüter II	10.1.1984	8.9.1987	KF, V, CD, KRF	Election called five months before end of term
Schlüter III	10.9.1987	10.5.1988	KF, V, CD, KRF	Election called due to parliamentary defeat
Schlüter IV	3.6.1988	12.12.1990	KF, V, RV	Election called to improve government bargaining position
Schlüter V	18.12.1990	15.1.1993	KF, V	Voluntary resignation of government
Nyrup Rasmussen I	25.1.1993	21.9.1994	S, RV, CD, KRF	Election called three months before end of term
Nyrup Rasmussen II	27.9.1994	30.12.1996	S, RV, CD	Party left coalition
Nyrup Rasmussen III	30.12.1996	11.3.1998	S, RV	Election called six months before end of term
Nyrup Rasmussen IV	11.3.1998	20.11.2001	S, RV	Election called four months before end of term

(continued)

Table 8.2. Continued

Prime Minister	Date In	Formal Resignation	Government Composition	Reason for Termination
Fogh Rasmussen I	27.11.2001	8.2.2005	V, KF	Election called two months before end of term
Fogh Rasmussen II	18.2.2005	13.11.2007	V, KF	Election called to improve government bargaining position
Fogh Ramussen III	23.11.2007	5.4.2009	V, KF	Resignation of PM to become Secretary-General of NATO
Løkke Rasmussen I	5.4.2009	15.9.2011	V, KF	Election called two months before end of term
Thorning-Schmidt I	3.10.2011	3.2.2014	S, RV, SF	Party left coalition
Thorning-Schmidt II	3.2.2014	18.6.2015	S, RV	Election called four months before end of term
Løkke Rasmussen II	28.6.2015	28.11.2016	V	Coalition formed
Løkke Rasmussen III	28.11.2016	6.6.2019	V, KF, LA	Election called at end of term
Frederiksen	27.6.2019		S	

Note: Partially based on Damgaard (2000: 254–7).

to date was the 1968–71 government of the Social Liberals, the Liberals, and the Conservatives where the latter party was the largest and the post of prime minister nevertheless went to the Social Liberals, the smallest of the three parties. Where prime ministers have resigned or passed away in office, the person nominated to take over also became the party leader. Most often, there was a clear heir apparent, for example, when H. C. Hansen took over from Hans Hedtoft, when Hansen passed away and Viggo Kampmann became prime minister, and when Kampmann's health forced him to resign and Jens Otto Krag was the heir apparent. Jens Otto Krag's choice of Anker Jørgensen as his successor in 1972 was not a case of an heir apparent being chosen, but it was nevertheless accepted by the party (Olesen 2017: 22–30), and Jørgensen served several terms as prime minister. The prime ministers of the 1950s and 1960s left office predominantly due to death or illness. Krag losing the election in 1968 was the first time since 1953 that an incumbent prime minister lost an election, and since then, turnover due to electoral losses has become the norm. When Lars Løkke Rasmussen lost the 2011 election and still ran as the prime ministerial candidate at the 2015 election, it was the first time since the election of 1975 that a former prime minister ran again after having a full term away from serving as prime minister.

It was not until 2011 that Denmark had its first female prime minister when Social Democrat Helle Thorning-Schmidt became prime minister in her second election as leader of the Social Democrats. When it comes to the age profile of when prime ministers are first appointed, most of those serving since 1953 have been just under 50 when they took office. Lars Løkke Rasmussen and Helle Thorning-Schmidt were in their mid-40s when they took office, and Poul Hartling and Poul Schlüter were the eldest (59 and 53, respectively). In terms of seniority, the three latest Social Democratic prime ministers, Helle Thorning-Schmidt, Poul Nyrup Rasmussen, and Anker Jørgensen, had less than 10 years of parliamentary service when they took office (6, 5, and 8 years, respectively). However, the three latest Liberal or Conservative prime ministers were all in the double digits when it comes to years of parliamentary experience before taking office, with 15 years for Lars Løkke Rasmussen, 23 years for Anders Fogh Rasmussen, and 19 years for Poul Schlüter.

Prime ministers rarely propose legislation in Parliament due to the limited policy areas under their direct control. They are, however, required to give an opening speech each year when Parliament opens or after an election to set out the status and the agenda of the country. These speeches are seen as the authoritative presentation of the governments' goals in the coming legislative period (Hobolt and Klemmensen 2005, 2008) and can, therefore, be used to examine government policy agenda (Mortensen et al. 2011). Recently, Klüver and Zubek (2017) found that the government will put forward close to 90 per cent of the proposals laid out in the opening speech. Overall, the opening speeches are perhaps one of the best sources for examining the dynamic element of government policy priorities that must necessarily develop between elections. It also provides an annual opportunity to reassess the plans of the government and set the agenda for what negotiations its support parties can expect during the coming parliamentary year.

MINISTERS AND MINISTERIAL TURNOVER

The formal power of hiring and firing cabinet ministers lie with the prime minister. In a single-party government, the prime minister will also be the leader of his or her party, and the selection and de-selection of ministers is not subject to outside influence, bar a necessity to balance internal party divisions. In coalition governments, the prime minister will usually allow the coalition partners to choose their ministers as they please, given the constraints of which portfolios have been made available to which party.

The division of labour between ministers—otherwise known as portfolios—is provided by the prime minister. At each government formation, new ministerial departments are created and others vanish. Mortensen and Green-Pedersen (2015) studied the overall development of Danish ministries and found that the rising number of ministries was explained by the expanding issue agenda. While there mostly is a clear relationship between the number of seats a party brings to the coalition and the number of ministers they get, there is a different relationship when it comes to which portfolios each party receives.

Not all ministerial portfolios are equal, and party leaders have the first choice of which government position they would prefer. Some party leaders would prefer to increase the number of ministers they are allocated and give up portfolios seen as important. For example, at the 1993 government formation, the Social Liberals had seven parliamentary seats and took three portfolios (economic affairs, foreign affairs, and education). In contrast, the Centre Democrats had nine parliamentary seats and took four portfolios (church affairs, communication and tourism, research, and coordination), two of which were new portfolios with limited content. This example suggests that studying the number of ministries tells only part of the story. Part of the survival of minority coalitions is that the smaller coalition partners are given some, if not all, of the portfolios they desire, allowing them to concentrate their efforts on policy areas with which they have an affinity.

While the number of ministries can be stable, expand, or contract, it is also necessary to consider how much change there is in the design of the portfolios, and that is likely linked to the issue agenda. When the Liberal-Conservative government took power in 2001, the previously powerful Ministry for Environment and Energy was stripped, with energy going to the Ministry of Economics, and other issues that were higher on the agenda for the government parties formed the basis of a new ministry, namely the Ministry for Refugees, Immigrants, and Integration. Changes in portfolio design can be based on purely administrative reasons if the responsibility for an office is moved from one ministry to another. It can also be due to a name change as when the Ministry for Agriculture and Fisheries in 1997 was renamed the Ministry for Food, Agriculture, and Fisheries and at the same time was given some responsibilities previously in the domain of the Health Ministry.

There is no requirement for a minister to be a member of Parliament, and a policy has been in place at times to allow ministers to be granted leave from their parliamentary seat for the duration of their ministerial tenure. This has mostly been used by the smaller parties, although not all minor parties have taken up the possibility. It is a normal occurrence that one or two ministers are found outside Parliament, either due to particular competencies that otherwise are missing, or former MPs not getting re-elected or serving in other positions—in recent years, mostly as members of the European Parliament. Ministers selected this way normally run in the next election and attempt to secure a parliamentary seat although this is far from guaranteed to end successfully. The vast majority of ministers are selected from within the parliamentary party group, and there is a balance to be struck on gender and age profiles but also with regard to duration of previous tenure, whether anyone holds previous ministerial experience, or whether they were previously spokespersons for the party on the particular subject matter. When Helle Thorning-Schmidt formed her coalition government in 2011, only one of her Social Democratic ministers had previous ministerial experience. This is an extreme example of very little previous experience being included, whereas most other governments will have more than just one member having previously served in government.

It is rare that a government serves the entire period without changes. In the past, being a minister was a hazardous job, and most governments of the 1950 and 1960s lost at least one—if not more—members to illness and death. In recent years, it is rare that ministers step down due to illness. What is much more likely to happen is either that the prime minister decides that it is time for a change and wants to reshuffle the ministers, that a party leader changes or decides to freshen up his team to prepare for an election, that a minister steps down of their own accord to pursue a role outside of politics, or the rare event that a minister is involved in some form of scandal that obligates them to step down. There is also the theoretical possibility that a minister could be forced to resign if they lost a vote of confidence in Parliament, but in practice, no vote of confidence has been called on individual ministers as the ministers have usually resigned of their own accord or been removed by the prime minister. Lars Løkke Rasmussen's third government (2016–2019) experienced the unusual feature that it went into the 2019 election with three serving ministers not running for re-election, with one seeking election to the European Parliament and the other two deciding that three years as a minister was enough and wanting a different career, though all were kept in office after stating their intention not to run again.

The literature on ministerial turnover relies on the assumption that the prime minister delegates power to cabinet ministers (Strøm 2003). When a prime minister delegates power, delegation problems can threaten the policy efficacy of the prime minister and potentially his position within the government. At the time of the ministerial appointment, the prime minister in some cases only has limited information about a minister's ability to run a ministerial department effectively, and it may happen that a minister uses his or her portfolio in a way that is counter-productive to the prime minister's interests, for example, if ministers become too aligned with the sectoral interests associated with their department. In coalitions, there is the further danger that ministers focus on the interests of their parties and not the coalition as such (Müller and Meyer 2010). Strøm et al. (2010) argue that there are *ex ante* and *ex post* mechanisms to deal with these problems. *Ex ante*: the parties should engage in a screening of their ministerial candidates, allowing for the selection of a cohesive set of ministers. *Ex post*: the most used tool is the reshuffle either by moving ministers to portfolios more suitable to their skills or dismissal (Huber and Martinez-Gallardo 2008).

Ministerial remuneration guarantees each minister at least DKK 1,227,675 (approx. USD188,000) before tax, with the prime minister earning DKK1,534,594 (approx. USD234,695), while the foreign minister and finance minister are entitled to 1,350,443 (approx. USD206,565). If the minister is also a member of Parliament, the ministerial salary is reduced by the income from being an MP. It is expected that all other offices and positions than MP are resigned when taking office as a minister. A declaration of financial interests must also be completed by the minister, and it is expected, though not required, to also include the economic interests of the minister's partner. Ministers have the right to a severance pay depending on their tenure, regardless of how short. Six months of salary is the minimum paid after one day of tenure, with the maximum being 36 months of salary after 6 or more years of tenure. For pension rights to be earned, a tenure of one year is required, which would provide a yearly payment of DKK80,000 (approx. USD12,000). The maximum pension rights that can be earned is 8 years of service, which would provide a yearly payment of 287,000DKK (approx. 44,000USD). Ministerial pensions are payable to ministers after they have left office and their severance pay has ended and then depending on when they were appointed. For those appointed after 2017, it is payable when the minister reaches the normal retirement age. For ministers appointed from 2006–17, it is payable when early retirement is allowed, which is currently at 62 years, and for those appointed from 2000–6, it is payable when the minister turns 60. Ministers who were appointed before 2000 had the right to a ministerial pension the day after their severance pay ended. Earnings from public sector jobs will result in a deduction in pension, but jobs in the private sector will not.

Since 1998, all ministers have been allowed to hire a special advisor who is to leave at the same time as the minister (Knudsen 2011). The recruitment is done by the minister, and the result is often, but not exclusively, advisors with backgrounds in media. Some ministers, the prime minister, and in recent years, party leaders in a coalition government are allowed two special advisors. These advisors have no instructive power over the bureaucracy and are mostly there to help the minister navigate the intersection between media and policy related to the minister's performance (White Paper 1537/2013; Christiansen and Salomonsen 2018: 58). Danish ministers can only draw on their special advisors and no other politically appointed staff. This along with the limited number of advisors sets Denmark apart from the other Scandinavian countries in institutional design (see also Kolltveit 2016: 483). In turn, much of the work done by special advisors in other countries is performed by career civil servants in Denmark (Christiansen and Salomonsen 2018: 62).

COORDINATION WITHIN THE GOVERNMENT

The government ministers meet as a cabinet in two separate meetings. One is the Council of State which meets less than once a month, is chaired by the Queen, and has no political role to play but is the forum where the head of state signs the bills passed by Parliament. The other meeting is the weekly cabinet meeting which can be used for debates and ironing out any issues within the government and its coalition partners. However, with often more than twenty ministers in attendance, such meetings can be difficult forums for in-depth discussion, which is why more specialized coordination is left to a series of cabinet committees.

The general policy direction of the government is set out in the coalition agreement, but how this direction is implemented into bills presented to Parliament, apart from those which might be explicitly mentioned in the coalition agreement, are discussed in a number of cabinet committees. The two most important cabinet committees are the Coordination Committee and the Economic Committee, the former chaired by the prime minister and the latter by the finance minister. The Coordination Committee has been in place since the late 1960s and can now been viewed as the norm for policy coordination within the government (Christensen 1985:116). The composition of the committees in terms of how many and what policy areas are covered and membership in terms of ministers are set by the prime minister but is agreed as a part of the coalition formation process. The most important committees include the most important ministers, and in coalition governments, this would also be the party leaders of the coalition parties. The Coordination Committee is important for the success of the coalition government as it allows for issues between the coalition partners to be sorted out before beginning negotiations with support parties in order to pass policies. It is possible that even though agreement within the coalition is reached, the necessity for securing support from yet another party (or parties) could re-open the agreement reached within the cabinet committee. Membership of the cabinet committees also signal the power distribution within the government and could been seen as a guide for who are viable successors to the prime minister within their own party (Christensen 1985: 126–7).

The functional aspects of the cabinet committees include several aspects, the most important being policy planning for the government and mutual control in a coalition governments. Policy planning alludes to the possibility for a group of relevant ministers to have in-depth discussions about which policies to pursue and put forward and deal with issues that appear on the public agenda. While policy disagreements should be expected mostly among coalition governments, the Social Democratic governments from 1979–82 were severely troubled by policy disagreement within the party that spilled over into the public, and the cabinet committees were a tool for alleviating such disagreements (Christensen 1985: 130–1).

Where the Danish government differs from other European countries is the relatively small size of the Prime Minister's Office and the absence of a dedicated cabinet office. When Poul Nyrup Rasmussen took office in 1993, he expanded the staffing of the Prime Minister's Office though, comparatively, it is still a small entity. This also means that for the cabinet committees, the administrative support is given by either the Prime Minister's Office and their limited staff (Coordination Committee) or by the Ministry of Finance (Economic Committee), which highlights the importance of these two offices even more in all aspects of government policy work. The importance of the Ministry of Finance for nearly all policy areas has become ever more pronounced since the governments of Poul Nyrup Rasmussen, and this development has continued since (see Jensen 2008).

Despite the importance of coalition coordination and the importance of the cabinet committees, there is also comparative evidence that government decision has moved even more towards a presidential style of decision-making with the prime minister making a growing number of decisions on his or her own, which is attributed to increased internationalization, increased importance of the state, the increased import-ance of communication, and the diminishing effect of classic cleavage politics (Poguntke and Webb 2005: 13–17). The same presidentialization in Denmark can be traced back to the government change in 1993 where Poul Nyrup Rasmussen replaced Poul Schlüter as prime minister. Rasmussen increased his involvement in cabinet committees, especially those focusing on international affairs, and this was continued by his successors (Pedersen and Knudsen 2005: 163–4).

Conclusion

The frequency of minority governments, and especially minority coalitions, in Denmark means that research on government survival without an in-built majority usually includes the Danish case. Yet the Danish case was also one of the first where a Western European government was dependent for its survival on a populist right-wing party, the Danish People's Party. From 2001–11 and again from 2015–19, it is difficult to understand the survival of the Danish governments and their policies without also understanding the relationship with their primary parliamentary support party and support parties in general (see also Green-Pedersen and Skjæveland 2020). The relationships with support parties might be one of the most important factors to explain the relative success of minority coalition governments in Denmark, and it might be necessary to reconsider their importance overall. This should also be seen in connection with the now established norm of Danish governments presenting government declarations when they take office. The government declaration is the plan of which policies the government will seek to promote during its tenure, but it is also a document that is not negotiated *ex ante* with support parties. While it is generally well established that an electoral bonus might be coming for a party holding the post of prime minister, there is still precious little research on what policy benefits a prime ministerial party gets from holding the highest office of government. Recently, Green-Pedersen et al. (2018) have presented comparative research to alleviate this gap, and Becher and Christiansen (2015) have shown that the party holding the office of prime minister can threaten dissolution to enhance its policy priorities. The work by Becher and Christiansen (2015) explicitly takes into account the necessity of support parties and should, therefore, be highlighted as a starting point for those wishing to achieve a deeper understanding of the still understudied relationship between support parties and government.

Reshuffles of ministers is a common feature of most modern Danish governments, although between elections, it is predominantly a reshuffle of persons and not portfolios. The restructuring and reshaping of portfolios happen predominantly during the government formation process, creating a stability in this part of coalition governance that helps the survival of the minority coalition governments. Which parties get which government portfolios, how these are prioritized internally in the parties, and what effect it has on the policy outcomes is another area where there is still a gap in the existing research. If the belief is that it matters who gets what portfolio and how the portfolio is shaped, then it is necessary to consider these elements in the understanding of the government formation process.

There can be little doubt that the Danish prime minister is more powerful than ever internally in the government. Yet the role of the prime minister within the government has evolved from a *primus inter pares* role to a much more presidentialized role where the prime minister is involved more in detailed policies than ever before, not least in relation to international affairs. However, the importance of prime ministerial involvement in coalition bargaining and especially coalition governance is not waning, as the importance of more formalized, established support parties have increased over the last two decades. This may be one of the most important factors for the success of minority governments, and especially minority coalitions, in Danish politics.

References

Becher, Michael, and Flemming J. Christiansen (2015). 'Dissolution threats and legislative bargaining', *American Journal of Political Science*, 59/3: 641–55.

Christensen, Jens Peter (2019). 'Regeringsdannelse', *Ugeskrift for Retsvæsen*, 2019/12: 89–99.

Christensen, Jørgen G. (1985). 'In search of unity: Cabinet committees in Denmark', in Thomas T. Mackie and Brian W. Hogwood, eds, *Unlocking the Cabinet: Cabinet Structures in Comparative Perspective*. London: Sage, 114–37.

Christiansen, Flemming J., and Erik Damgaard (2008). 'Parliamentary opposition under minority parliamentarism: Scandinavia', *The Journal of Legislative Studies*, 14/1–2: 46–76.

Christiansen, Flemming J., and Helene H. Pedersen (2014). 'Regeringsgrundlag i Danmark. Hvordan benytter regeringen dem, og hvordan reagerer oppositionen?', *Politica*, 46/3: 362–85.

Christiansen, Peter M., and Heidi H. Salomonsen (2018). 'Denmark: Loyalty and the political adviser bargain', in Richard Shaw and Chris Eichbaum, eds, *Ministers, Minders and Mandarins*. Cheltenham: Edward Elgar Publishing, 53–71.

Damgaard, Erik (1969). 'The parliamentary basis of Danish governments: The patterns of coalition formation', *Scandinavian Political Studies*, 4: 30–57.

Damgaard, Erik (1994). 'Termination of Danish government coalitions: Theoretical and empirical aspects', *Scandinavian Political Studies*, 17/3: 193–211.

Damgaard, Erik (2000). 'Denmark: The life and death of government coalitions', in Wolfgang C. Müller and Kaare Strøm, eds, *Coalition Governments in Western Europe*. Oxford: Oxford University Press, 231–63.

Damgaard, Erik (2004). 'Developments in Danish parliamentary democracy: Accountability, parties and external constraints', *Scandinavian Political Studies*, 27/2: 115–31.

Damgaard, Erik (2008). 'Cabinet termination', in Kaare Strøm, Wolfgang C. Müller, and Torbjörn Bergman, eds, *Cabinets and Coalition Bargaining: The Democratic Life Cycle in Western Europe*. Oxford: Oxford University Press, 301–26.

Damgaard, Erik, and Palle Svensson (1989). 'Who governs? Parties and policies in Denmark', *European Journal of Political Research*, 17/6: 731–45.

de Winter, Lieven (1995). 'The role of parliament in government formation and resignation', in Herbert Döring, ed., *Parliaments and Majority Rule in Western Europe*. London: St Martin's Press, 115–51.

Ganghof, Steffen, and Thomas Bräuninger (2006). 'Government status and legislative behaviour: Partisan veto players in Australia, Denmark, Finland and Germany', *Party Politics*, 12/4: 521–39.

Green-Pedersen, Christoffer, Peter B. Mortensen, and Florence So (2018). 'The agenda-setting power of the prime minister party in coalition governments', *Political Research Quarterly*, 71/4: 743–56.

Green-Pedersen, Christoffer, and Asbjørn Skjæveland (2020). 'Governments in action. Consensual politics and minority governments', in Peter M. Christiansen, Jørgen Elklit, and

Peter Nedergaard, eds, *The Oxford Handbook of Danish Politics*. Oxford: Oxford University Press, 230–41.

Green-Pedersen, Christoffer, and Lisbeth H. Thomsen (2005). 'Bloc politics vs broad cooperation? The functioning of Danish minority parliamentarism', *The Journal of Legislative Studies*, 11/2: 153–69.

Hansen, Martin E. (2019). 'Distributing chairs and seats in committees: A parliamentary perspective', *Parliamentary Affairs*, 72/1: 202–22.

Hansen, Martin E., Robert Klemmensen, Sara B. Hobolt, and Hanna Bäck (2013). 'Portfolio saliency and ministerial turnover: Dynamics in Scandinavian postwar cabinets', *Scandinavian Political Studies*, 36/3: 227–48.

Hobolt, Sara B., and Robert Klemmensen (2005). 'Responsive government? Public opinion and government policy preferences in Britain and Denmark', *Political Studies*, 53/2: 379–402.

Hobolt, Sara B., and Robert Klemmensen (2008). 'Government responsiveness and political competition in comparative perspective', *Comparative Political Studies*, 41/3: 309–37.

Huber, John D., and Cecilia Martinez-Gallardo (2008). 'Replacing cabinet ministers: Patterns of ministerial stability in parliamentary democracies', *American Political Science Review*, 102/2: 169–80.

Jensen, Lotte (2008). *Væk fra afgrunden*. Odense: University Press of Southern Denmark.

Kaarsted, Tage (1988). *Regeringen, vi aldrig fik. Regeringsdannelsen 1975 og dens baggrund*. Odense: University Press of Southern Denmark.

Kaarsted, Tage (1992). *De danske ministerier 1953–72*. Copenhagen: PFA Pension.

Klüver, Heike, and Radoslaw Zubek (2017). 'Minority governments and legislative reliability: Evidence from Denmark and Sweden', *Party Politics*, 24/6: 719–30.

Knudsen, Tim (2011). 'Den politiserende embedsmand i Danmark', *Nordisk Administrativt Tidsskrift*, 88/3: 206–12.

Kolltveit, Kristoffer (2016). 'Spenninger i det politisk-administrative systemet: erfaringer fra Norge', *Politica*, 48/4: 481–96.

Laver, Michael, and Norman Schofield (1991). *Multiparty Government. The Politics of Coalition in Europe*. Oxford: Oxford University Press.

Laver, Michael, and Kenneth A. Shepsle (1994). 'Cabinet ministers and government formation in parliamentary democracies', in Michael Laver and Kenneth A. Shepsle, eds, *Cabinet Ministers and Parliamentary Government*. Cambridge: Cambridge University Press, 3–14.

Martin, Lanny W., and Georg Vanberg (2004). 'Policing the bargain: Coalition government and parliamentary scrutiny', *American Journal of Political Science*, 48/1: 13–27.

Mørch, Søren (2004). *25 statsministre: 25 fortællinger om magten i Danmark i det tyvende århundrede*. Copenhagen: Gyldendal.

Mortensen, Peter B., and Christoffer Green-Pedersen (2015). 'Institutional effects of changes in political attention: Explaining organizational changes in the top bureaucracy', *Journal of Public Administration Research and Theory*, 25/1: 165–89.

Mortensen, Peter B., Christoffer Green-Pedersen, Gerard Breeman, Laura B. Chaques, Will Jennings, Peter John, Anna Palau, and Arco Timmermans (2011). 'Comparing government agendas: Executive speeches in the Netherlands, United Kingdom and Denmark', *Comparative Political Studies*, 44/8: 973–1000.

Müller, Wolfgang C., and Thomas M. Meyer (2010). 'Meeting the challenges of representation and accountability in multi-party governments', *West European Politics*, 33/5: 1065–92.

Olesen, Niels W. (2018). *De Danske Ministerier 1972–1993: Poul Schlüters Tid 1982–1993*. Copenhagen: Gads Forlag.

Olesen, Thorsten B. (2017). *De Danske Ministerier 1972–1993: Anker Jørgensens Tid 1972–1982*. Copenhagen: Gads Forlag.

Pedersen, Helene H. (2020). 'The Parliament (*Folketinget*)', in Peter M. Christiansen, Jørgen Elklit, and Peter Nedergaard, eds, *The Oxford Handbook of Danish Politics*. Oxford: Oxford University Press, 88–106.

Pedersen, Karina, and Tim Knudsen (2005). 'Denmark: Presidentialization in a consensual democracy', in Thomas Poguntke and Paul Webb, eds, *The Presidentialization of Politics: A Comparative Study of Modern Democracies*. Oxford: Oxford University Press, 159–75.

Poguntke, Thomas, and Paul Webb (2005). 'The presidentialization of politics in democratic socities: A framework for analysis', in Thomas Poguntke and Paul Webb, eds, *The Presidentialization of Politics: A Comparative Study of Modern Democracies*. Oxford: Oxford University Press, 1–25.

Strøm, Kaare (1984). 'Minority governments in parliamentary democracies. The rationality of nonwinning Cabinet solutions', *Comparative Political Studies*, 17: 199–227.

Strøm, Kaare (2003). 'Parliamentary democracy and delegation', in Kaare Strøm, Wolfgang C. Müller, and Torbjörn Bergman, eds, *Delegation and Accountability in Parliamentary Democracies*. Oxford: Oxford University Press, 55–106.

Strøm, Kaare, Wolfgang C. Müller, and Daniel M. Smith (2010). 'parliamentary control of coalition governments', *annual Review of Political Science*, 13: 517–35.

Thies, Michael F. (2001). 'Keeping tabs on partners: The logic of delegation in coalition governments', *American Journal of Political Science*, 45/3: 580–98.

White Paper (1537/2013). *Betænkning 1537 fra Udvalget om særlige rådgivere. Ministrenes Særlige Rådgivere: Et Serviceeftersyn*. Copenhagen: Ministry of Finance, http://kb-prod-dab-01.kb.dk:8080/wayback/20151119132321/http://www.statensnet.dk/betaenkninger/1401-1600/1537-2013/1537-2013_pdf/printversion_1537-2013.pdf (accessed 18 November 2019).

CHAPTER 9

ORGANIZING CENTRAL GOVERNMENT

A Pragmatic Meritocracy?

CAROLINE HOWARD GRØN AND HEIDI HOULBERG SALOMONSEN

DENMARK has one of the best civil services in the world if we believe some of the indicators used to compare such institutions. Denmark has ranked between the 97th and the 100th percentile worldwide when it comes to Government Effectiveness, Rule of Law, and Control of Corruption every year between 2006 and 2016 according to the World Bank Governance Indicators.

Similarly, the country habitually comes out at the top of measurements like the Transparency International Corruption Perception Index (Transparency International 2018), the OECD measures of a well-functioning justice system (OECD 2017), and the UNPD Human Development Index where Denmark was 11th in the world in 2018 (UNDP 2018). What lies behind this apparent success? What are the principles guiding the behaviour of a civil service of this quality? This chapter argues that the organization and functioning of Danish central government, like much of Danish society and policies (Grøn et al. 2015; Wivel 2013), is basically a pragmatic endeavour.

The organization of central government has been debated in recent years, and particularly the question of physical relocation of government agencies to areas outside of the capital area has gained a lot of attention (Danish Government 2015, 2018). However, when we take a closer look at the way central government is organized, we find extensive variation allowing for pragmatic variations within the ministries, often based on political contingencies. Similarly, this pragmatism is reflected in the way a neutral civil service has adjusted to increasing demands for political-tactical advice. By exploring central features of Danish central government, we aim to give an introduction to one of the best functioning and performing civil services in the world, while also illustrating the very strong pragmatism which underlies its organization and function.

What Does Central Government Do?

The Danish public sector is comparatively big and constituted 51 per cent of GDP in 2017 (DKK 1,100 billion) (Ministry of Finance 2018). Central government spends approximately 25 per cent of this (Statistics Denmark 2017; see also Houlberg and Ejersbo 2020). Within the OECD, only France and Finland use a bigger share of GDP on the public sector than Denmark does (Ministry of Finance 2018: 6)

Central government serves different purposes. First, the central government performs regulation and prepares all legislative work that is later decided on in the Danish Parliament, *Folketinget*. Central government also oversees parts of its implementation just as it holds responsibilities in the transposition of EU and international law into Danish law.

Second, central government produces some services, including policing, the justice system, defence, and taxation, as well as secondary and tertiary education. Furthermore, central government is responsible for important parts of national infrastructure like highways, trains, and airports.

Third, central government has important vertical coordinating tasks across levels of government. The Ministry of Finance holds an important role in coordinating Danish economy and public spending. While municipalities have the right to collect their own taxes, spending in municipalities is heavily regulated through negotiated agreements between the Ministry of Finance and Local Government Denmark (*KL*), agreements which are supported by legislative initiatives and the budget law (Sørensen 2014). While this coordinating role was challenged by local governments for many decades, the financial crisis in 2008 and the policy initiatives taken following this left central government and especially the Ministry of Finance with much more potent tools to keep municipalities in check (Sørensen 2014). However, central government also has or takes on coordinating tasks across the other levels of government. For instance, this is the case when central government negotiates how cooperation within health policy between municipalities and regions will function and be financed (Danish Government and Danish Regions 2018).

Fourthly, central government is responsible for Danish foreign policy, including Danish EU policies and participation in the activities of the UN and other international organizations. Central government coordinates EU positions (Jensen and Nedergaard 2020) and represents Denmark in negotiations.

Who Runs Central Government?

Denmark has parliamentary governments. These governments are, however, often minority and coalition governments (Christensen 2006; Hansen 2020). This calls for intense horizontal coordination between the coalition partners within the government as well as coordination between the government and its supporting parties. In recent years, supporting parties have demonstrated less stability in their support and loyalty to the government of the day (Rhodes and Salomonsen 2018), although no guarantee for support on specific policy issues has been the case since the 1980s (Christensen 2006: 999). Danish governments are organized according to the principle of ministerial governance, with ministries formally headed by the minister who holds the ultimate formal authority. As described by Christensen (2006: 999), this means that '[a]s political executives minsters are placed on top of a hierarchy and endowed with formal authority to issue general instructions on any business within their portfolio and also to intervene personally into any decision falling within it', unless juridical regulation specifies particular exemptions where this authority is formally delegated.

As the political heads of their ministries, ministers are formally accountable to Parliament for all decisions and actions taken in the ministry. The Parliament is empowered by a number of different control mechanisms to hold ministers accountable, including different types of questions and interpellations, and holds the formal authority to remove ministers from their position. As noted by Rhodes and Salomonsen (2018):

> The principle of ministerial governance *de jure* grants substantial autonomy to the individual ministers of the Danish cabinet. However, the close alignment of the Ministry of Finance (MoF) and the Prime Minister (PM) and his office *de facto* reduces the policy autonomy formally granted to ministers individually and as cabinet members [...]   (Rhodes and Salomonsen 2018: 6, italics in original)

The autonomy, however, is also related to decisions on the organization of the ministries, generating some variation in terms of how ministries are formally organized and the distribution of tasks across the departmental and agency levels (see also Christensen 2006: 1000).

The Prime Minister's Office is comparatively small, holding a very small policy portfolio of its own (Hansen 2020). Although, according to the Danish Constitutional Act, it is the prime minister's prerogative to appoint ministers as well as decide the number and portfolios of ministries (Mortensen 2014). The decision is often rather constrained by the preferences of coalition party leaders. Another political explanation for the creation as well as elimination of Danish ministries is offered by Mortensen and Green-Pedersen (2015) who demonstrate how political attention reflected on the political agenda is not only related to the number of ministries but also to decisions on the establishment or termination of ministries.

In addition, the prime minister, along with the other party leaders of a coalition government, decides which ministers are granted a position in the central cabinet committees: the Coordination Committee (*Koordinationsudvalget* or *K-udvalget*) and the Economics Committee (*Økonomiudvalget* or *Ø-udvalget*).

In sum, this means that the relative importance of the prime minister in terms of running Danish governments is contingent upon his or her mandate and/or ability to manage coalition partners and the relationship with the supporting parties of government in Parliament, as well as the prime minister's de facto power position within his or her own party.

THE ORGANIZATION OF
CENTRAL GOVERNMENT

Ministries are typically organized in departments (*departementer*) and different types of agencies (*styrelser* and *institutioner*), some '[…] without any *legal independence* but with some managerial autonomy', and other types of agencies which are legally independent '[…] with managerial autonomy, either based on public law (2a) or private law (2b)' (van Thiel 2012: 20, italics in original), or which are 'Private or private-law based organizations established by or on behalf of the government like a foundation or corporation, company, or enterprise' (van Thiel 2012: 20).

Generally, the organization of ministerial portfolios reflects the ministerial posts. This means that when government is reorganized, so is the bureaucracy. As a consequence, certain policy areas, like housing and building regulation, are regularly moved between different ministries as the way portfolios are designed changes over time. This also means that the bureaucracy of central government is generally in a state of reorganization; not only following elections but also when government is redesigned or when individual ministers or senior civil servants see a reorganization fit. Since 1953, each government has been in office a little more than two years on average; however, these bigger reshuffles were supplemented with a number of smaller reorganizations of central government which are not comparable to more general government reshuffles.

Closest to the ministers, we find departments. Departments coordinate the work of the minister, do the most political work, and prepare cases for political acceptance or negotiations. Typically, each minister has his or her 'own' department, but in recent years, there have been a number of situations where more ministers are positioned in the same department. This has traditionally been the case in the Ministry of Foreign Affairs, which includes a minister of foreign affairs, a minister for development, and from time to time, a European minister. In the government Løkke Rasmussen III (2016), the Ministry of Foreign Affairs included the foreign minister, the minister for development cooperation, and the minister for fisheries and equal opportunities and Nordic cooperation.

Departments are typically relatively 'narrow' in the Danish system, following a general framework from the 1960s with smaller, politically oriented departments and bigger agencies that deal with less politicized tasks: developing new legislation, managing existing legislation, and ensuring implementation (Christensen et al. 2017). However, we see some variations, and in 2012, Hansen and Andersen concluded (2012: 216) that ministries have never been organized strictly according to one principle. These variations may reflect the overall size of the policy area (e.g. the Prime Minister's Office is always relatively small), but they may also reflect political priorities as when the department of the Ministry of Environment and Food was expanded as a consequence of the relocations of government agencies mentioned in the beginning of the chapter. As the Environmental Protection Agency was moved away from the capital area, certain politically important parts of it were relocated into the department rather than moved 150 km away to Odense.

Most departments have one or more agencies in direct reference. Some agencies, as indicated above, operate at arm's length of the ministerial hierarchy and are typically responsible for less politicized tasks. However, most agencies are more closely linked to the political system (being type 1 according to the van Thiel typology) compared to, for instance, Sweden (being primarily type 2) (Jacobsson et al. 2004: 75; Niklasson 2012). An increase in the number of agencies as a consequence of New Public Management (NPM) has been studied in many different countries, underlining the opportunity of making more focused organizations with a larger degree of managerial autonomy (Verhoest et al. 2012: 4). This tendency has been named 'agencification' and has been seen as challenging the coordination of government as well as the legitimacy of decisions made within agencies when these are kept outside political control. However, post-NPM has seen a reconsolidation of agencies and politicians willing to take back control of them (Verhoest et al. 2012).

In Denmark, Hansen and Andersen (2012: 213) counted 262 agencies in 2012. This count includes both agencies without legal independence from government departments (type 1), agencies which are legally independent (type 2), and private organizations which are established by the government (type 3). While the number of all types of agencies has been declining for some years (Hansen and Andersen 2012: 222), and amalgamations have been seen among both agencies and educational institutions (e.g. the case of the establishment of University Colleges), recent years have seen reverse tendencies. In 2015, the Danish Health Authority (*Sundhedsstyrelsen*) was split into three agencies following public criticism, the taxation authority (*SKAT*) was split into seven agencies in 2018, and the relocation of government agencies has similarly led to a split-up of a number of agencies into more organizational units.

While most agencies enjoy some managerial autonomy relative to their parent ministry, they have traditionally been controlled through the ministerial hierarchy as well as through input mechanisms. In addition, NPM has brought management by objectives (MBO) into the mix. As Kristiansen (2015) shows, the model of MBO has changed substantially over time but has, nevertheless, stayed on the agenda since the early 1990s.

However, some government institutions are kept outside the ministerial hierarchy, including the central bank of Denmark (*Danmarks Nationalbank*), the Competition and Consumer Authority (*Konkurrence- og Forbrugerstyrelsen*), and the courts (Christensen et al. 2017: 231), some of which are governed by independent boards. These institutions are placed outside the ministerial hierarchy to ensure their credibility and to avoid what Miller and Whitford (2016) describe as the principal's moral hazard and ensure 'credible commitment' to, for instance, a policy of fixed exchange rates as has been the case in Denmark since 1982. Furthermore, the system is also characterized by the extensive use of different forms of advisory committees (*råd, nævn, udvalg*) (see Christiansen 2020). In 2015, Christensen and Nørgaard counted 415 such committees (cited in Christensen et al. 2017: 259). While some of these included organized interests, this was far from always the case. The roles of such advisory bodies have generally been debated, especially since the Fogh Rasmussen I government took office in 2001. However, despite a decrease in their number, advisory committees still play an important role in the function of central government.

Finally, central government delivers services directly to citizens in a few areas, for example secondary education, with the state running 173 high schools across the country. While these are 'self-owned' (comparable to charter institutions), meaning they have extensive economic autonomy, they are still subdued national regulation as well as an activity-based funding system. Similarly, the Ministry of Justice runs the Danish police, which are organized in fourteen police districts. Finally, in their 2009 count, Hansen and Andersen found that the Ministry of Culture was the ministry with most of these institutions, including theatres, museums, and educational institutions (Hansen and Andersen 2012: 213).

While international trends like privatization, marketization, and downsizing of government have also been reflected in the way Danish government is organized (Hansen and Andersen 2012), it is fair to underline that some of the basic elements of the way central government is organized has remained stable since the 1960s. The changing political and organizational priorities linked to NPM have had some effect but not in the basic institutional underpinning of the way central government is organized. However, this section illustrates that within the framework established then, we find substantial variation. These variations reflect a pragmatic way of accommodating the political order or situation of the day, be it the internal power distribution between parties in a coalition government or the more macro priorities reflected in the relocation of government agencies.

How Is Central Government Coordinated?

Horizontal coordination—not least in coalition governments—is an ongoing task. This section discusses the mechanisms available to the Danish central government, including the central government committees the Coordination and the Economic Committees, as well as the coordinating roles of the Ministry of Finance and the Prime Minister's Office.

The prerogative of the prime minister to decide on the number and composition of ministries and the relative distribution of their portfolios can be considered a coordination mechanism in themselves (Mortensen 2014); however, one that is often relatively constrained due to the minority and coalition nature of Danish government.

In recent years, one has seen a second mechanism, namely government coalition agreements used to govern the relationship between the governing parties when forming a government. However, the degree to which they actually function as a coordinating mechanism and as a tool for prioritization by the prime minister vary (Mortensen 2014: 98), *inter alia*, depending on the degree to which they specify concrete and detailed goals for the ministers (Rhodes and Salomonsen 2018).

A third mechanism is a weekly cabinet meeting on Tuesday mornings. The meetings are primarily an arena where previously coordinated policies are presented to the government as a whole rather than an arena for substantial negotiation and coordination across ministries (Mortensen 2014: 99). As such, the meetings have been described by a former minister as 'complete theatre' (Rhodes and Salomonsen 2018: 8).

Fourth, there is often a biannual governmental seminar where the government discusses its present and future agenda, among other things.

The main mechanism for coordination is, however, the government committees, and in particular, the Coordination Committee chaired by the prime minister and the Economic Committee chaired by the minister of finance. Ministers appointed to those committees are described as comprising a de facto 'inner cabinet' (Mortensen 2014: 101), or 'an inner court of politics' in Danish governments (Rhodes and Salomonsen 2018). The vital coordinating role of the two committees is partly enabled by the parallel committees of permanent secretaries for the ministers in the two governmental committees called steering committees. The role of the steering committees is to prepare the meetings for the two political committees and perform the main bulk of coordination across ministries before the policies, etc. reach the political agenda. While the Coordination Committee handles issues of a strategic and planning nature, the Economic Committee handles the main part of the policy coordination (Mortensen 2014: 100; Rhodes and Salomonsen 2018: 16–17). This gives the minister of finance and the Ministry of Finance a powerful role in Danish government, requiring intense coordination with the Prime Minister's Office and its permanent secretary. The vital role performed by the minister and Ministry of Finance in policy coordination suggests that Danish governments are primarily run by a 'duopoly' where the Ministry of Finance functions as a cabinet office for the prime minister and his or her office (Rhodes and Salomonsen 2018).[2]

THE BUREAUCRACY

Danish bureaucracy is a meritocracy. It has been so since the kings in the decades after the introduction of absolutism in 1660 began electing their civil servants among the city citizenry rather than among the nobility (Knudsen 2001).

According to the Agency for Modernisation, the government employs 180,000 people (Agency for Modernisation 2019). Most of these people work in educational institutions (58 per cent), whereas only 10 per cent work in the administrative parts of central government. The last 32 per cent work in areas such as police and defence.

Central government is organized as a Weberian bureaucracy. Most people employed in central government have an academic degree, but the rank and file of the civil service also contains secretarial staff as well as people educated within the armed forces or the police.

Of senior civil servants, including permanent secretaries, agency heads, and heads of divisions, an increasing number have a political science degree compared to a law degree (Gram 2017: 50), with almost 30 per cent of top civil servants now having a political science degree. Looking at career trajectories, more than a third of senior civil servants have spent time in the Ministry of Finance, and for permanent secretaries, this was the case for 42 per cent in 2017 (Gram 2017: 55). In addition, senior civil servants with experience from the Ministry of Finance made it to their current position 5.2 years faster than senior civil servants with no previous experience from the Ministry of Finance (Gram 2017: 60). This export of managers, formalized in the vision of the Ministry of Finance which states that the ministry is to 'create the top managers of the future', is part of a trend towards a dominance of the Ministry of Finance within the government which has been debated since the 1990s (Jensen 2003; Gjertsen 2017).

Career patterns differ between branches of the civil service, for example distinguishing careers in the Foreign Service from careers within the Ministry of Justice and other parts of central government (Gram 2017: 69), despite the fact that these policy areas have become more alike over time.

While many of the changes in career patterns have not been an explicit policy, leader mobility has been promoted by the Ministry of Finance (Danish Government 2019: 17), and central government has seen increased turnover among permanent secretaries (Christensen et al. 2014), with an increasing number of permanent secretaries leaving the civil service before retirement. Similarly, managers at lower levels also experience extensive turnover. The Danish Leadership and Management Commission (2017: 30) reports that 44 per cent of managers in central government have less than 2 years of experience in their current position.

While the bureaucracy is generally characterized by classic Weberian traits, we also find that increased mobility, increasing dominance by the Ministry of Finance in delivering managers to the rest of central government, and increased turnover all contribute to a shift towards a more managerial civil service where a top management position to some extent is more akin to what we would find among senior managers in other big (private) organizations than to that of a classic bureaucrat.

THE POLITICIZATION OF THE BUREAUCRACY

The politicization of the Danish civil service can be assessed using three different types of politicization (Hustedt and Salomonsen 2014). They are: (1) the degree of formal politicization, which is the degree to which positions within the central governmental bureaucracy is filled with actors appointed on criteria other than merit; (2) the degree of functional politicization, which is the degree to which actors formally appointed on merit—and hence part of the politically neutral civil service—perform tasks that are considered political in nature, for example, providing political-tactical advice; and (3) the degree of administrative politicization, which is the extent to which the relationship between politically appointed and neutral civil servants is characterized by the former interfering in the advice provided by the latter. This can be performed either by preventing the provision of frank and fearless advice from the civil service (Mulgan 2007) when performing a gatekeeping role or by colouring the advice from the service in ways suitable to and in alignment with the minister's preferences. For all three types of politicization, their presence is assessed and compared to their relative development over time and/or to other civil service systems in other established Western democracies.

Regarding the formal politicization, Denmark is one of the least formally politicized systems among Western democracies. Before 1998, all civil servants were formally appointed based on a criterion of merit. However, since 1998, Danish ministers have been allowed to appoint one or two *special advisers* (Christiansen and Salomonsen 2018), that is, civil servants appointed on criteria other than merit. Contrary to governments in, for example, the UK and Sweden, Danish governments have not used this opportunity extensively to increase the number of special advisers in the line ministries nor in the Prime Minister's Office (Christiansen and Salomonsen 2018). However, the tasks and types of advice performed and provided by special advisers have developed over time. Where the first wave of advisers was primarily media advisers, the second wave was appointed to carry out policy advisory functions (Christiansen and Salomonsen 2018).

In contrast to how they are often portrayed in the media, the role of the special advisers has remained constrained. Contrary to their colleagues in Sweden, especially those in the core executive's offices, their role in the central coordination of (the minority and coalition) government has remained limited, leaving the crucial task of coordinating government policies and tactics a primarily bureaucratic endeavour (Hustedt and Salomonsen 2017). Special advisers are never present in the central government committee meetings (Rhodes and Salomonsen 2018),[1] and they have, in general, not taken over as the most intimate and central advisers to the minister. This is still a role performed primarily by the permanent secretaries. Instead, advisers have taken the tasks of cultivating and coordinating the minister's relations with the party, and by doing so, they are able to prevent the permanent civil service from becoming too involved in party political issues and functions (Hustedt and Salomonsen 2017; Rhodes and Salomonsen 2018)—something welcomed by the permanent civil service which is otherwise unafraid of entering the grey zone of politics and administration.

By demonstrating a willingness and ability to provide advice within this grey zone, the permanent civil service in general and the permanent secretaries in particular may be characterized as rather extensively functionally politicized. This characterization becomes evident both when comparing the degree to which permanent secretaries themselves report the extent to which they provide advice on a political-tactical nature over time (Ministry of Finance 1998, 2004, 2013) and comparing the accounts of their roles and tasks to civil servants in other countries, including Germany, Belgium, the UK, and Sweden (Hustedt and Salomonsen 2014; Christiansen et al. 2016). Thus, in 2015, permanent secretaries pointed to advice of a political-tactical nature to be the most important task they performed by far (Smith-Udvalget 2015: 139).

In relation to this discussion, it is worth mentioning that the average length of time a permanent secretary held his or her position has decreased rather dramatically since the 1970s from 18.5 years in 1970-1979 to 8.8 years in the period from 2010–14 (Smith-Udvalget 2015: 142). However, this is not being interpreted as a reflection of formal politicization 'through the back door', but rather that replacements are made based upon assessments of competencies and personal chemistry (Christensen et al. 2014: 236). Ministers increasingly demand political responsiveness and advice in terms of man-oeuvring in a complex political environment within coalition minority governments where support from Parliament is constantly to be negotiated. The increasing functional politicization demonstrates the 'resilience of the merit civil service' (Christensen et al. 2014: 236) which rests upon a pragmatic interpretation of what is appropriate behaviour for a neutral and competent civil service in contemporary governmental organizations (Hustedt and Salomonsen 2018). This pragmatic interpretation from the actors involved, i.e. the ministers and the civil servants, is, *inter alia*, facilitated by the fact that their relationship can be characterized as a pragmatic and rather informal bargain (Salomonsen and Knudsen 2011), reflecting that there are few laws and for-malized norms regulating their behaviour. In addition, this demonstrates that shifting governments and oppositions, albeit taking an interest in the civil service from time to time, have refrained until now from introducing radical changes in the organization of advice to ministers.

Finally, regarding the administrative politicization, research shows that while the degree of administrative politicization is generally experienced as low by the Danish civil service (de Visscher and Salomonsen 2013), civil servants experience a higher degree of contestability, i.e. more tensions between civil servants and politically appointed civil servants, than their Swedish colleagues (Öhberg et al. 2017).

THE ETHICS OF BUREAUCRACY

The Danish civil service can be characterized as having a rather informal, pragmatic relationship with their political principals. However, since the 1990s, the normative regula-tion has been subject to both political and public debate, subsequently leading to the development of a number of White Papers and most recently a codex that explicates, and to some extent, formalizes the normative rules. While explicit references to 'a civil service eth-ics' are relatively absent in Danish political and public debates, this process began on the backdrop of a discussion on the ethics of the civil service in the early 1990s, triggered by a scandal known as the 'Tamil case', in which the Minister of Justice was accused of illegalities in the administration of Tamil refugees. While the consequences for the Minister was a conviction at court for trial of high crimes and misdemeanours and for the government its resignation, the Permanent Secretary was suspended and subsequently demoted to a position outside the Ministry of Justice (Salomonsen and Knudsen 2011: 1028).

In the aftermath of the scandal, the apparent increasing involvement of the civil service in the provision of political-tactical advice became a central issue in public, professional, and political debates. On this background, one of the main unions organizing civil servants, the Association of Lawyers and Economists (*DJØF*) formulated the first ethical code for the civil service, *Professional Ethical Principles in Public Administration* (White Paper 1993). As argued by Salomonsen and Knudsen (2011: 1028), this code points to such political-tactical advice as '[...] an unavoidable, necessary and appropriate aspect of the advice provided by top civil servants to their respective ministers and therefore ethically valid'.

Since then, the norms regulating the advisory behaviour of the civil service have been politically discussed and explicated in a number of White Papers published on the initiative of *Folketinget* (Ministry of Finance 1998, 2004, 2013). All White Papers reflect the norms that regulate the behaviour of the permanent civil service, including professional standards, party-political neutrality, legality, and the obligation to speak the truth (Ministry of Finance 2004: 277–8), while stressing the importance of party-political neutrality at the same time. While civil servants are to assist in promoting the government of the day, it is important that they remain neutral in a party-political sense. In contrast to the UK (e.g. the Committee on Standards in Public Life), there is no organization independent of the government to protect the neutrality in the recruitment and function of the permanent civil service. Therefore, debates about the behaviour of the civil service are often triggered by the media and/or Parliament (Hustedt and Salomonsen 2018). Important to add is that the White Papers also address and explicate the norms regulating the special advisers' behaviour, and it is fair to say that such advisers' behaviour has been the main trigger for the formulation of the White Papers rather than the behaviour of the permanent civil service.

However, more recently, a number of 'scandals' have surfaced in which the civil service has been accused of acting *too* responsively and politically. While these incidents have not led to parliamentary initiatives, they once again triggered the main union of the civil service, DJØF, to take action and perform yet another empirical investigation into how the civil service perceived the norms regulating their behaviour (Smith-Udvalget 2015).

In addition, the intense discussions of the civil service resulted in the government issuing a code of conduct with the title *Seven Key Duties for Civil Servants in Central Government* (Ministry of Finance 2015). The code summarizes the duties of the civil service under seven headings: 1. Legality, 2. Truthfulness, 3. Professionalism, 4. Development and cooperation, 5. Responsibility and management, 6. Openness about errors, and 7. Party-political neutrality. The code, rather extensively, builds on the previously published White Papers. However, it points to an explicit ambition of revitalizing and institutionalizing discussions concerning the rules regulating and the limits of the advice and assistance that permanent civil servants provide to their minister (Ministry of Finance 2015: 58–9). This is an exercise the permanent secretaries themselves stress as being important 'in the light of the recent "season" of scandals' (Hustedt and Salomonsen 2018: 78).

Summing up, the description of the tendency to further explicate the norms regulating the behaviour of the civil service does not radically change the characterization of a rather pragmatic civil service regulated by norms rather than by legal rules. They still allow for a rather extensive flexibility in the way the political aspects of their assistance and advice to the government of the day are interpreted. It is maybe also worth noticing that although formal regulation regulates ministerial responsibility and the like, the behaviour of Danish ministers is not subject to any normative regulation as, for example, in the UK (cf. the ministerial code [Cabinet Office 2010]).

Keeping Central Government in Check

As in other liberal democracies, central government is kept in check by independent watchdogs. Denmark, like many other countries, has a well-established Ombudsman as well as a court of auditors. These two institutions oversee the legality and frugality of central government. The courts can, of course, address questions of legality as well, but compared to other European countries, Denmark has no tradition of legal activism (Wind 2010).

The Ombudsman (*Folketingets Ombudsmand*) controls the legality of the way public authorities act. The Ombudsman can take up cases on its own initiative, but citizens may also send complaints directly to the Ombudsman to make the institution take up cases. In recent years, the Ombudsman has received between 4,000 and 5,000 complaints a year from citizens who believe that public authorities have made a mistake (Ombudsman 2019). While the Ombudsman criticizes the way in which public authorities act, it does not fall within the institution's competency to change decisions.

The Auditors General's Office (*Rigsrevisionen*) is the other main institutional control of central government. The court of auditors performs financial audits regarding central government; however, to a larger and larger extent, the court also audits performance, focusing on ensuring an 'efficient, effective and financially sound administration'. The court prepares reports to Parliament's Public Accounts Committee, which mainly consists of parliamentarians. The court can take independent initiatives to investigate but is also asked by the Public Accounts Committee to investigate certain issues.

In recent years, both the Ombudsman and the Auditors General's Office have been subject to criticism from incumbent governments and parliamentarians (DR 2017, 2018a, 2018b). They have, in particular, criticized the Ombudsman from 1987–2012, Dr Gammeltoft-Hansen, for politicizing, whereas the Løkke Rasmusen III government decided to take a more confrontational line with the Auditors General's Office in a meeting in the Coordination Committee. Following the meeting, Minister of Defence Claus Hjort Frederiksen (DR 2018a) accused the Auditors General's Office of meddling in the political decision-making process. Both cases illustrate that while checks and balances may be deeply rooted in the way Danish central government works, recent years have seen some critical discussion about the extent to which the independent watchdogs are making life difficult for governments. However, others have argued that such criticism in itself may weaken the institutions' possibilities to perform their role as formal accountability fora (Kildegaard and Rohde 2018).

Conclusion

The chapter started out by pointing to the relative success of the Danish public sector, not least the central government. We asked which institutional underpinnings could be identified to sustain such a well-functioning civil service. Throughout the chapter, we have tried to illustrate the lack of strong formal institutions and how the relatively weak existing institutions are up for an ongoing pragmatic reinterpretation. We identify this room for interpretation when analysing the formal organization of central government, the ongoing discussions regarding the ethics of the bureaucracy, and the way politicians and civil servants work together. Indeed, this institutional flexibility—or pragmatism—may be part of the explanation of why the Danish public sector is so well functioning, and it is in line with previous analyses of the cultural characteristics of the Danish public sector at large (Hansen and Jørgensen 2009). As Hansen and Jørgensen pointed out, the Danish public sector is characterized by trust and a large extent of local autonomy allowing for local solutions. This trust-based approach (which is a general trait of Danish society; see Jensen and Svendsen 2020) could also be part of the explanation as to why central government and the regulation of the use of power are so relatively weakly institutionalized. Trust traditionally replaces control mechanisms and reduces transaction costs, increasing efficiency and flexibility.

However, in recent years, trust in government and civil servants has been decreasing (Holst 2018). Denmark might still have high trust levels, but our analysis as well as the ongoing debate about the way the civil service works (Tynell 2016; Koch and Knudsen 2014) illustrate that trust in government cannot be taken for granted. Especially in situations where politicians reinterpret the boundaries of their influence, this calls for a renewed interest in the formal institutions that keep power in check.

The literature has shown that trust is easier to build among relatively similar people (Zucker 1986). However, just as Danish society has become more heterogeneous, so has the political landscape. This development reinforces the need to consider how the strong informal norms needed to support the weak formal institutions surrounding Danish central government can be ensured.

All these trends taken together may indicate that the high trust levels and the high degree of common informal understanding of the norms underlying the relatively weak formal institutions could be in jeopardy. This is not to sound alarmist but to emphasize that the way central government is organized depends on a common agreement on basic informal norms if a system of weak formal institutions is not to become dysfunctional, allowing for the misuse of power or even corruption. The Danish public sector is still one of the best performing in the world, but this status should not be taken for granted.

To ensure this position, supporting strong, common informal norms around the use of the power in and of the civil service seems to be key in a society and a political landscape that is becoming increasingly heterogeneous. This is especially the case if pragmatism is part of the explanation as to why it has been performing so well so far.

NOTE

1. In the present single, minority government led by Mette Frederiksen from the Social Democratic Party (June 2019–present) this, however, changed in the sense that one of her special advisers is present in the two most central government committee meetings, the Coordination and the Economic Committee. This change in the positioning of special advisers were subject for quite substantial public and political debate, and was among others subject for discussion in the presidium of the Parliament (*Folketinget*).
2. The present Prime Minister, Mette Frederiksen, has established a political secretariat in the PMO, for the purpose of strengthening the strategic management of the government and to ensure policy development and implementation of the governments political agenda. This has been seen as diminishing the influence of the Ministry of Finance.

REFERENCES

Agency for Modernisation (2019). 'Statens medarbejdere', https://modst.dk/modernisering/staten-i-tal/statens-medarbejdere/ (accessed 18 November 2019).

Cabinet Office (2010). *Ministerial Code*. London: Cabinet Office UK.

Christensen, Jørgen G. (2006). 'Ministers and mandarins under Danish parliamentarism', *International Journal of Public Administration*, 29/12: 997–1019.

Christensen, Jørgen G., Peter M. Christiansen, and Marius Ibsen (2017). *Politik og forvaltning*, 4th ed. Copenhagen: Hans Reitzels Forlag.

Christensen, Jørgen G., Robert Klemmensen, and Niels Opstrup (2014). 'Politicization and replacement of top civil servants in Denmark', *Governance*, 27/2: 215–41.

Christiansen, Peter M. (2020). 'Corporatism. Exaggerated death rumours?', in Peter M. Christiansen, Jørgen Elklit, and Peter Nedergaard, eds, *The Oxford Handbook of Danish Politics*. Oxford: Oxford University Press, 160–76.

Christiansen, Peter M., Birgitta Niklasson, and Patrick Öhberg (2016). 'Does politics crowd out professional competence? The organization of ministerial advice in Denmark and Sweden', *West European Politics*, 39/6: 1230–50.

Christiansen, Peter M., and Heidi H. Salomonsen (2018). 'Denmark – Loyalty and the public advisor bargain', in Chris Eichbaum and Richard Shaw, eds, *Ministers, Minders and Mandarins. An international Study of Relationships at the Executive Summit of Parliamentary Democracies*. Cheltenham, UK and Northampton, MA: Edward Elgar, 53–71.

Danish Government (2015). 'Bedre balance – statslige arbejdspladser tættere på borgere og virksomheder', http://www.fm.dk/publikationer/2015/bedre-balance (accessed 18 November 2019).

Danish Government (2018). 'Bedre balance II - statslige arbejdspladser tættere på borgere og virksomheder', https://www.fm.dk/publikationer/2018/bedre-balance-ii (accessed 18 November 2019).

Danish Government (2019). 'En Offentlig Sektor Rustet til Fremtiden. Ledelse og kompetencer i den offentlige sektor', https://www.fm.dk/publikationer/2019/en-offentlig-sektor-rustet-til-fremtiden (accessed 15 August 2019).

Danish Government and Danish Regions (2018). 'Aftale om regionernes økonomi for 2019', https://www.regeringen.dk/media/5347/aftale-om-regionernes-oekonomi-for-2019.pdf (accessed 18 November 2019).

Danish Leadership and Management Commission (2017). 'Offentlige ledere og ledelse anno 2017. Samlet afrapportering fra Ledelseskommissionens spørgeskemaundersøgelse', https://ledelseskom.dk/files/media/documents/publikationer/offentlige_ledere_og_ledelse_anno_2017_-_samlet_afrapportering_fra_ledelseskommissionens_spoergeskemaundersoegelse_2017.pdf (accessed 15 August 2019).

de Visscher, Christian, and Heidi H. Salomonsen (2013). 'Explaining differences in ministerial ménages à trois: Multiple bargains in Belgium and Denmark', *International Review of Administrative Sciences*, 79/1: 71–90.

DR (2017, 8 February). 'ANALYSE Ballade om barnebrude svækker ombudsmanden', *DR.dk*.

DR (2018a, 14 May). 'Regeringen til angreb på Rigsrevisionen', *DR.dk*.

DR (2018b, 15 Apr.). 'Statens vagthund får kritik af regeringen: Her har den bidt ministre i haserne', *DR.dk*.

Gjertsen, Marchen N. (2017, 1 July). 'V-profil i opgør om Finansministeriet', *Jyllands-Posten*.

Gram, Hjalte (2017). 'Skolet i den røde bygning. Karrieremønstre i topembedsværket', Master thesis, Department of Political Science, University of Copenhagen.

Grøn, Caroline H., Peter Nedergaard, and Anders Wivel (2015) (eds). *The Nordic Countries and the European Union: Still the Other European Community?* London: Routledge.

Hansen, Hanne F., and Torben B. Jørgensen (2009). 'Den danske forvaltningsmodel og globaliseringens udfordringer', in Martin Marcussen and Karsten Ronit, eds, *Globaliseringens udfordringer*. Copenhagen: Hans Reitzels Forlag, 36–64.

Hansen, Martin E. (2020). 'The government and the prime minister. More than *primus inter pares*?', in Peter M. Christiansen, Jørgen Elklit, and Peter Nedergaard, eds, *The Oxford Handbook of Danish Politics*. Oxford: Oxford University Press, 107–23.

Hansen, Morten B., and Vibeke N. Andersen (2012). 'Denmark', in Koen Verhoest, Sandra van Thiel, Geert Bouckaert, and Per Lægreid, eds, *Government Agencies: Practices and Lessons from 30 Countries*. London: Palgrave Macmillan, 212–22.

Holst, Emma Q. (2018, 23 August). 'Embedsmænd og politikere helt i bund: Se de mest troværdige faggrupper', *Altinget.dk*.

Houlberg, Kurt, and Niels Ejersbo (2020). 'Municipalities and regions. Approaching the limit of decentralization?', in Peter M. Christiansen, Jørgen Elklit, and Peter Nedergaard, eds, *The Oxford Handbook of Danish Politics*. Oxford: Oxford University Press, 141–59.

Hustedt, Thurid, and Heidi H. Salomonsen (2014). 'Ensuring political responsiveness: politicisation mechanisms in ministerial bureaucracies', *International Review of Administrative Science*, 80/4: 746–65.

Hustedt, Thurid, and Heidi H. Salomonsen (2017). 'Political control of government coordination? The roles of ministerial advisers in government coordination in Denmark and Sweden', *Public Administration*, 95/2: 393–406.

Hustedt, Thurid, and Heidi H. Salomonsen (2018). 'From neutral competence to competent neutrality: Revisiting neutrality as the core normative foundation of Western bureaucracy', *Comparative Social Research*, 33: 69–88.

Jacobsson, Bengt, Per Lægreid, and Ove K. Pedersen (2004). *Europeanization and Transnational States. Comparing Nordic Central Governments*. London: Routledge.

Jensen, Lotte (2003). *Den store koordinator: Finansministeriet som moderne styringsaktør*. Copenhagen: Jurist- og Økonomforbundets forlag.

Jensen, Mads D., and Peter Nedergaard (2020). 'Coordination for the European Union. A strong and stable institution', in Peter M. Christiansen, Jørgen Elklit, and Peter Nedergaard, eds, *The Oxford Handbook of Danish Politics*. Oxford: Oxford University Press, 193–212.

Jensen, Mette F., and Gert T. Svendsen (2020). 'Corruption and bureaucratic reforms. 'Getting to Denmark'?, in Peter M. Christiansen, Jørgen Elklit, and Peter Nedergaard, eds, *The Oxford Handbook of Danish Politics*. Oxford: Oxford University Press, 177–59.

Kildegaard, Kasper, and Thomas S. Rohde (2018, 19 Dec.). 'Regeringen får hård kritik for at stække vigtige vagthunde: "De skal holde fingrene for sig selv" ', *Berlingske Tidende*.

Knudsen, Tim (2001). *Da demokrati blev til folkestyre. Dansk demokratihistorie I*. Copenhagen: Akademisk forlag.

Koch, Pernille B., and Tim Knudsen (2014). *Ansvaret der forsvandt- om magten, ministrene og embedsværket*. Frederiksberg: Samfundslitteratur.

Kristiansen, Mads B. (2015). 'Kontinuitet og forandring i statens målstyringskoncept', *Politik*, 18/1: 18–29.

Miller, Gary J., and Andrew B. Whitford (2016). *Above Politics—Bureaucratic Discretion and Credible Commitment*. New York: Cambridge University Press.

Ministry of Finance (1998). *Betænkning nr. 1354. Forholdet mellem minister og embedsmænd*. Copenhagen: Schultz.

Ministry of Finance (2004). *Betænkning nr. 1443. Embedsmænds rådgivning og bistand*. Copenhagen: Schultz.

Ministry of Finance (2013). *Betænkning nr. 1537. Ministrenes særlige rådgivere. Et Serviceeftersyn*. Copenhagen: Schultz.

Ministry of Finance (2015). 'Code VII: Seven Key Duties for Civil Servants in Central Government', Ministry of Finance, https://modst.dk/media/17483/kodex_vii_english_version.pdf (accessed 18 November 2019).

Ministry of Finance (2018). 'Udviklingen i de offentlige udgifter fra 2000 til 2017', https://www.fm.dk/oekonomi-og-tal/oekonomisk-analyse/2018/udviklingen-i-de-off-udgifter-fra-2000-til-2017 (accessed 18 November 2019).

Mortensen, Peter B. (2014). 'Statens forvaltning', in Jens Blom-Hansen, Peter M. Christiansen, Thomas Pallesen, and Søren Serritzlew, eds, *Offentlig Forvaltning—et politologisk perspektiv*. Copenhagen: Hans Reitzels Forlag, 78–106.

Mortensen, Peter. B., and Christoffer Green-Pedersen (2015). 'Institutional effects of changes in political attention: Explaining organizational changes in the top bureaucracy', *Journal of Public Administration Research and Theory*, 25: 165–89.

Mulgan, Richard (2007). 'Truth in government and the politicization of public service advice', *Public Administration*, 85/3: 569–86.

Niklasson, Birgitta (2012). 'Sweden', in Koen Verhoest, Sandra van Thiel, Geert Bouckaert, and Per Lægreid eds, *Government agencies: practices and lessons from 30 countries*. London: Palgrave Macmillan, 245–58.

OECD (2017). *Government at a glance 2017. Highlights*. OECD.

Öhberg, Patrik, Peter M. Christiansen, and Birgitta Niklasson (2017). 'Administrative politicization or contestability? How political advisers affect neutral competence in policy processes', *Public Administration*, 95/1: 269–85.

Ombudsman (2019). 'The Danish Parliamentary Ombudsman', http://en.ombudsmanden.dk/ (accessed 18 November 2019).

Rhodes, Rod, and Heidi H. Salomonsen (2018). 'Duopoly, court politics and the Danish Core Executive', presented at Seminar on 'Cabinet Government for the Twenty First Century', University of Cambridge, 17–18 September 2018.

Salomonsen, Heidi H., and Tim Knudsen (2011). 'Changes in public service bargains: Ministers and civil servants in Denmark', *Public Administration*, 89/3: 1015–35.

Smith-Udvalget, Bo (2015). *Embedsmanden i det moderne folkestyre*. Copenhagen: Jurist- og Økonomforbundets Forlag.

Sørensen, Eva M. (2014). 'Økonomisk styring af kommunerne i en krisetid', in Caroline H. Grøn, Mads B. Kristiansen, and Hanne F. Hansen, eds, *Offentlig styring: Forandringer i en krisetid*. Copenhagen: Hans Reitzels Forlag.

Statistics Denmark (2017). 'Kommuner og regioner står for trefjerdedele af det offentlige forbrug' (Corrected 7 June 2018), https://www.dst.dk/da/Statistik/bagtal/2017/2017-13-10-kommuner-og-regioner-staar-for-trefjerdedele-af-det-offentlige-forbrug (accessed 18 November 2019).

Transparency International (2018). 'Corruption perceptions index, 2017', https://www.transparency.org/news/feature/corruption_perceptions_index_2017#table (accessed 18 November 2019).

Tynell, Jesper (2016). *Mørkelygten. Embedsmænd fortæller om politisk tilskæring af tal, jura og fakta*. Frederiksberg: Samfundslitteratur.

UNDP (2018). *Human Development Indicies and Indicators. 2018 Statistical Report*. United Nations Development Program.

van Thiel, Sandra (2012). 'Comparing agencies across countries', in Koen Verhoest, Sandra van Thiel, Geert Bouckaert, and Per Lægreid, eds, *Government Agencies: Practices and Lessons from 30 Countries*. London: Palgrave MacMillan: 18–26.

Verhoest, Koen, Sandra van Thiel, Geert Bouckaert, and Per Lægreid. (2012). 'Introduction', in Koen Verhoest, Sandra van Thiel, Geert Bouckaert, and Per Lægreid, eds, *Government Agencies: Practices and Lessons from 30 Countries*. London: Palgrave Macmillan, 3–17.

White Paper (1993). *Fagligt etiske principper i offentlig administration. Betænkning afgivet af DJØF's fagligt etiske arbejdsgruppe, September*. Copenhagen: DJØF.

Wind, Marlene (2010). 'The Nordics, the EU and the reluctance towards supranational judicial review', *Journal of Common Market Studies*, 4/48: 1039–63.

Wivel, Anders (2013). 'From peacemaker to warmonger? Explaining Denmark's Great Power politics', *Swiss Political Science Review*, 19/3: 298–321.

Zucker, Lynne G. (1986). 'Production of trust: Institutional sources of economic structure, 1840–1920', *Organizational Behavior*, 8: 53–111.

....

CHAPTER 10

MUNICIPALITIES AND REGIONS

Approaching the Limit of Decentralization?

....

KURT HOULBERG AND NIELS EJERSBO

LOCAL POLITICS IN THE EYE OF DECENTRALIZATION, A BIG-BANG LOCAL GOVERNMENT REFORM, AND A TOUGHENED NATIONAL SPENDING REGIME

DENMARK is among the most decentralized countries in the world, both when it comes to fiscal decentralization (Ivanyna and Shah 2014; Rodden 2004) and local autonomy (Ladner et al. 2016). The three-tier level of government today encompasses two levels of subnational governments besides the state level: regions and municipalities. After decades of gradual consolidation and stabilization (Blom-Hansen 1999) and no dramatic changes in the Danish local government system (Elklit and Kjær 2007), the turn of the millennium marked dramatic changes. In 2007, a quick and radical local government reform was implemented (Mouritzen 2010). In 2002, the Minister of the Interior stated that the government had no plans to change the structure of the local governments, but four months later, a commission on administrative structure was formed, and after another four years, the biggest local government reform in 35 years was implemented by 1 January 2007 (Mouritzen 2010). This included the amalgamation of 271 municipalities into 98 municipalities and the replacement of 14 counties with 5 new regions as well as simultaneous transfers of functions between the three tiers. As a consequence of the mergers, the average population size of municipalities changed dramatically from approximately 20,000 inhabitants to 55,000 inhabitants (Blom-Hansen et al. 2014), and Danish municipalities are now relatively large in comparative terms (Baldersheim and

Rose 2010). At regional level, the size of the jurisdictions simultaneously increased from 340,000 to 1.1 million inhabitants.

Less than two years after the local government reform, Denmark was hit by the financial crisis, and in the wake of the crisis, the national government implemented a strengthened spending regime on all three tiers of government, including spending ceilings enforced by law for both municipalities and regions overall (Houlberg 2018; Suenson et al. 2016). This so-called 'Budget Law' has been labelled the most important public spending act ever (Suenson et al. 2016), and it has affected central-local relations, the role of Local Government Denmark (LGDK), and the Danish Regions (DR), as well as local discretion and fiscal management focus. Budget overruns usually characterized the municipalities as well as the regions at large prior to the Budget Law, whereas budget *under*runs seem to be a permanent feature after the implementation of the sanction regime (Houlberg 2018). Against this background, we ask: what are the consequences of a major local government reform followed by a national spending regime for a highly decentralized local government system?

First, the chapter briefly describes the administrative structure of Denmark after the local government reform. Second, we describe and discuss the local political system and the administrative and political structure of municipalities and regions. This is followed by a discussion of local discretion in the light of changed central regulation. We then look at local expenditures and revenues and how their distribution is influenced by the reform and by changes in central-local relations. We conclude with a discussion of the challenges and opportunities for the Danish local government system.

The Administrative Structure of Denmark

Denmark is a unitary state consisting of central government, 5 regions, and 98 municipalities. As part of the local government reform in 2007, tasks were transferred from counties to the state (e.g. youth education and larger roads) and to the municipalities (e.g. environmental regulation and specialized institutions for the disabled), and from municipalities to the state (e.g. tax assessment). Table 10.1 shows the functions of the three tiers after 2007, including the subsequent transfer of responsibility for the insured unemployed from central government to municipalities in 2009.

The local government reform was both a centralization and a decentralization reform. On the one hand, the main direction of task transfers was from regional to local level, i.e. increased decentralization. On the other hand, the main entities for local democracy and provision of public services, the municipalities, got larger, thus increasing the distance between citizens and politicians. Transfers of tasks to central level from municipal level (tax assessment) and regional level (youth education) represent other elements of centralization.

Table 10.1. Functions of Central Government, Regions, and Municipalities

Functions	Central Government	Regions	Municipalities
Service	• General planning of healthcare • Education and research—except primary and lower secondary school • The social area: national knowledge • Some cultural arrangements • Reception of asylum applicants	• Hospitals, general practitioners • Operation of services for espoused groups and groups with special needs and institutions for children and young people with social and behavioural problems that have not been taken over by the municipalities	• Childcare • Primary school, including *special education* • Eldercare • *Special education for adults* • The social area: financial, supply, and regulation. *Including responsibility for espoused groups and groups with special needs and institutions for children and young people with social and behavioural problems (some of which are operated by the regions)* • Healthcare: out-patient treatment and *joint financial responsibility* • Libraries and other cultural areas • Employment service • Integration of immigrants • Business service and promotion of tourism
Infrastructure	• Road and rail system	• Responsible for setting up regional transportation	• Part of regional collective transportation • The local road system • Supply company and emergency services
Regulation	• Police, defence, administration of justice • *Tax assessment* • General planning of nature and environment • Business economy subsidies	• Few functions in the area of environment, planning, and (business) development	• Town and district plans • Construction projects • Environment

Note: Adopted from Andersen (2010) and Ministry of Interior and Health (2005). Functions reshuffled as part of the 2007 reform are marked in *italics*.

Table 10.1 shows that the municipalities are multi-purpose units responsible for large, expensive, politically salient and important tasks. Apart from hospitals, the municipalities are responsible for all citizen-related public services and account for 50 per cent of total public expenditure. In contrast in 2007, the regions were stripped of almost all other tasks with the exception of hospitals and therefore resemble single-purpose jurisdictions today. In sum, the regional tasks account for 12 per cent of total public expenditure (Mortensen 2014: 87). Thus, the municipal level is more than ever the focal pivot for balancing between local democracy and implementing agency of the state (Blom-Hansen and Heeager 2011).

THE LOCAL POLITICAL SYSTEM
AND DEMOCRACY

The political system in the municipalities consists of three bodies: a council, a set of standing committees, and a mayor (Blom-Hansen and Heeager 2011). The political rule of the system may be termed a committee-leader rule (Mouritzen and Svara 2002: 60). The municipalities are governed by the city councils with between 9 and 31 members (except Copenhagen with 55 members) elected every four years. The mayor is elected by and among local councillors on a simple majority basis and is the formal head of the administration as well as the chair of the Financial Committee. The mayor is the only full-time politician in the municipality.

The mandatory Financial Executive Committee is responsible for and supervises the budget and other financial affairs of the municipality. The tasks of the Financial Executive Committee are determined by statute. There are fewer legal restrictions to the establishment of the standing committees; however, at least one in addition to the Financial Committee must be established. Most municipalities have between four and seven such committees. These are typically the Financial Committee, a social committee, a school and culture committee, and a technical committee responsible for public utilities, roads, and environmental regulation (Blom-Hansen 2002: 88). The members of the standing committees are also elected by and among the council members but on a proportional basis. All councillors are guaranteed at least one committee seat.

Power is dispersed between the committees, the Financial Executive Committee, and the mayor (Andersen 2010). The committees are responsible for the day-to-day administration of the various policy areas and formally elect their chairman on a simple majority basis (Blom-Hansen and Heeager 2011). In practice, however, chairmanships are often an integral part of the negotiations of the winning coalitions. Although the chairmen, in contrast to the mayor, are only part-time politicians and have few formal powers, they can be quite powerful since considerable influence is often delegated to them. A consequence of the committee rule is that one central centre in the municipalities cannot be identified. Power is dispersed between different political bodies as well as between politicians and council officials. Denmark has formally prioritized a layman rule, dispersion of power, and consensus with the consequence that the power structure between the mayor, the committees, and the administration is rather opaque (Andersen 2010; Kjær and Mouritzen 2003: 204–5).

At regional level, the counties had a political system similar to the municipalities until the 2007 reform, but important changes in the regional political system were implemented as part of the 2007 reform (Blom-Hansen and Heeager 2011). The regional council, which has 41 members, is the supreme body. In addition, there is a regional chairman holding a position comparable to the municipal mayor. However, the regions do not have a committee system. They may, but are not obliged to, leave daily administrative matters to an executive committee, but they cannot establish standing sectoral committees like the municipalities and the old counties (Blom-Hansen and Heeager 2011).

Elections for municipal and regional councils are held simultaneously every four years. The turnout has remained relatively stable and comparatively high at approximately 70 per cent (for a discussion on local elections and electoral turnout see Kjær 2020; Hansen 2020). As turnout has been stable for many years, Danish municipalities have not experienced a political crisis regarding local democratic legitimacy (Andersen 2010). However, the historically high levels of political trust and political self-efficacy at local level as well as identification with the municipality have been showing declining tendencies, not least in the municipalities amalgamated in 2007 and the first years after the 2007 reform (Hansen and Hjelmar 2015; Kjær et al. 2010; Lassen and Serritzlew 2011). Turnout, however, seems to be unaffected by the municipal amalgamations in 2007 (Olsen 2010).

The Administrative Structure of Municipalities and Regions

The administrative structure in Danish municipalities has always been subject to change (Hansen et al. 2010), and there has been considerable variation in structural arrangements (Bækgaard 2009; Ejersbo 1998).

The administration of the municipalities typically follows one of two models. About one third of the municipalities use the sector-based departmental model, while the other two thirds use either an executive board model or some mixed forms (Bækgaard 2011). The departmental model has been the traditional model for organizing the administration in the municipalities but is subject to considerable local variation. In this model, the administration is divided into a number of departments/sections representing the major welfare services, each managed by a director with responsibility for the preparation of policy decisions as well as for subsequent execution (Christensen et al. 2017). The average number of departments in municipalities has changed over time, increasing since the 2007 local government reform (Bækgaard 2009). The departmental model provides a close relationship between the political committee (and especially the chairman) and the director of the department, and potentially increases the departmentalization of the political system. In the executive board model, a number of directors form a top management team that is collectively in charge of the administration. This team prepares policy decisions and services the committee. The model is supposed to increase coordination and collaboration across the departments and committees (Bækgaard 2011) and strengthen the overall management of the municipality.

LOCAL DISCRETION IN THE LIGHT OF CHANGED CENTRAL-LOCAL RELATIONS

Within the framework of national regulation and the so-called 'budget cooperation system', the municipalities—like municipalities in other Nordic countries—have a high level of local autonomy (Ladner et al. 2016). Recent changes in central-local relations, however, have affected the level and content of local discretion.

According to the Constitution, the right of municipalities to manage their own affairs independently—under state supervision—shall be laid down by statute. The Constitution also prescribes that some of the public tasks should be allocated to the local governments and that Parliament (*Folketinget*) decides how much should be allocated. Denmark has no single local government act defining the tasks of the municipalities, but over time, Danish municipalities have been granted a wide scope of predefined tasks laid down by law in various acts and legal statutes. In addition, municipalities can perform certain tasks based on the so-called municipal authority rules (*kommunalfuldmagtsreglerne*), which is a general term for the unwritten rules (principles) of the local non-statutory duties. The precise definition of the municipal authority rules is often complex as the authority rules cover a series of inaccurate and often overlapping unwritten rules. In practice, the municipal authority rules imply that tasks the municipality wants to perform must be of some benefit to the community, must not be tasks delegated to other levels of government, and must not provide support for individuals or individual companies without specific legal cover. Municipalities are basically not allowed to engage in trade or industry. Classic examples of tasks that municipalities may carry out according to the municipal authority rules are public transportation and initiatives in leisure, culture, and sport.

Within the framework of fiscal federalism, Denmark is among the most fiscally decentralized countries in the world (Ivanyna and Shah 2014; Rodden 2004), and over the last four decades, an increasing number of tasks and responsibilities have been transferred to the municipalities (Blom-Hansen et al. 2012). Financial and budgetary reforms during this period aimed to strengthen the financial responsibility of local government as well as provide tools for assessing the total public budget by standardizing budgets and accounts (Blom-Hansen et al. 2012). A general feature of many reforms has been a decrease in conditional grants/reimbursements rates for specific municipal expenditures and a gradual conversion of these to general grants (Pedersen and Frandsen 2017). There are few formal or legal requirements regarding local economic activity. The most important constraint is that local revenues and expenditures are required to balance within some limits (Andersen 2010). Furthermore, budgets and accounts must be specified according to standards set by the Ministry of the Interior, and the local government act stipulates the procedure for setting a budget (e.g. it must be debated twice in the council and be presented and decided upon at a certain date) (Serritzlew and Blom-Hansen 2014), and relatively restricted options for loans apply (Andersen 2010). However, the economic activities of the municipalities are mainly regulated through informal procedures. The most important of these is the 'budget cooperation system'.

The high level of decentralization has made coordinating local economic activity with national economic policies increasingly important, and since the beginning of the 1980s, the 'budget cooperation system' has been institutionalized in the form of annual negotiations and agreements between the national government and the Local Government Denmark (LGDK) and the Danish Regions (DR), respectively (Andersen 2010; Blom-Hansen et al. 2012: 117–38). These annual agreements set collective guidelines for the annual general expenditure and income for the municipalities and regions.

Over the years, the agreements have changed from a few pages setting guidelines for the overall taxation and expenditures to more voluminous documents of 25–30 pages setting not only the overall guidelines but also a number of common understandings and agreements on the desired development of specific sectors or policies. The level of detail varies from merely recommending a rate of real expenditure growth to specifying that taxes cannot be raised and to setting specific growth rates for particular sectors (Juul and Kyvsgaard 2004: 242–4) and/or setting specific aims for the level of outsourcing of services or aims for efficiency gains to be achieved from more coordinated procurement of goods.

The economic agreements are agreements on the tax and expenditure level for the municipalities collectively (Blom-Hansen et al. 2012; Houlberg 2018). No frames are set for the individual municipality, and the agreement is not binding for the individual municipality (or region). In principal, each municipality is still able to set its own rates and policies—as long as the collective limits for the municipalities at large are not violated. In order to keep the collective budgets of the municipalities within the agreed level, the LGDK has an active role in coordinating the budget processes of the individual municipalities, especially since 2011 when a national sanction regime was implemented, and the coordination of the LGDK evolved into a phase-divided budget process involving an increasing frequency of meetings and consultations with all or parts of the municipal mayors, CEOs, and/or heads of finance.

Until 2010, the municipalities at large were typically overrunning the agreed levels of taxes or expenditures, often in the approved budgets and even more so in the final accounts (Serritzlew and Blom-Hansen 2014; Houlberg 2018). Until 2010, the partners, however, had an implicit common understanding that the approved budgets were the basis for evaluating whether the agreements were kept, and though the possibilities of sanctioning the local governments were articulated by the national government, the national government rarely used the parliamentary channel to sanction the violation of the agreements in practice (Houlberg 2018).

National government policy changed dramatically in the wake of the financial crisis and the historically large municipal budget overruns in 2009. In 2011, the national parliament implemented a sanction regime on the municipalities, later integrated in the so-called 'Budget Law' (Houlberg 2018; Suenson et al. 2016). The sanction regime implies that economic sanctions are enforced by law if the municipalities (and regions) are not keeping the economic agreements in both the approved budgets and the final accounts. Possible sanctions will be implemented by cuts of up to DKK 3 billion in general grants. In addition, the law stipulates that if the budgets are overrun, the sanctions will be directed by 60 per cent on the individual violating municipalities and 40 per cent collectively on all municipalities. So far, no actual sanctions have been practised; the threat of sanctions combined with an increased crisis consciousness seems to have been successful (Houlberg 2018; Suenson et al. 2016).

Budget overruns typically characterized the municipalities and regions at large prior to the sanction regime, whereas budget *under*runs seems to be a permanent feature after the implementation of the sanction regime in 2011 (Houlberg 2018). Figure 10.1 illustrates this as the grey pillars are lower than the dark pillars since 2011, and the budgets of the municipalities at large have been underrun by DKK 1–6 billion each year. As a by-product of the increased focus on keeping the budget, the economic policies of municipalities have partly moved away from performance management in favour of expenditure control (Sørensen and Foged 2015), and the political influence on agenda-setting and decision-making in the municipal councils has been redistributed from the councillors not on the Finance Committee towards members of the Finance Committee (Houlberg et al. 2018).

A similar pattern such as in Figure 10.1 applies for the regions, albeit the level of the agreed expenditures in general has been increasing as a reflection of the high policy prioritization of healthcare in Parliament. In addition to expenditure limitations, the economic agreements at regional level since 2002 have included a demand for 2 per cent yearly hospital efficiency gains. Within the same level of expenditures, the hospital has, in other words, had to produce 2 per cent more activities each year. Otherwise, activity-based state grants are not released to regions not fulfilling the demanded efficiency gains.

From 2003 to 2015, the hospitals on average increased efficiency as demanded (Højgaard et al. 2018: 172) but not without feedback consequences for the budget cooperation system. According to the DR, the continuous efficiency demand implies that hospitals are not always delivering the best possible service to citizens and that the hospital staff is too busy. In the agreements for the regions for 2018 and 2019, the efficiency demand has been suspended. In addition, a significant share of the efficiency gains has been realized by switching activities towards ambulant/outpatient treatment, and the LGDK have accused the DR of having realized efficiency gains by shifting costs to the municipalities as the costs of patient rehabilitation is a regional responsibility, whereas the costs of rehabilitation of citizens is a municipal responsibility. Thus, the

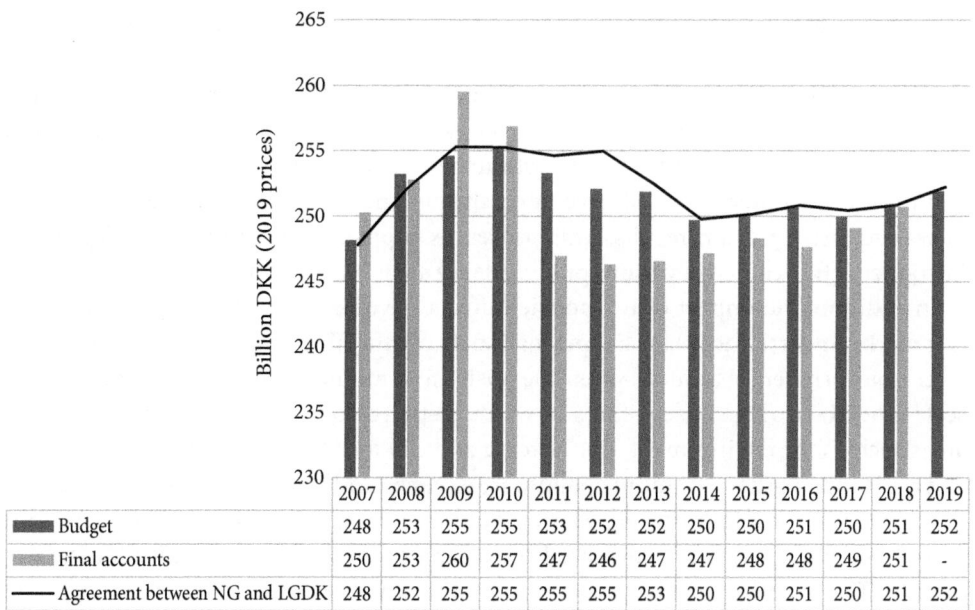

	2007	2008	2009	2010	2011	2012	2013	2014	2015	2016	2017	2018	2019
▆▆ Budget	248	253	255	255	253	252	252	250	250	251	250	251	252
▓▓ Final accounts	250	253	260	257	247	246	247	247	248	248	249	251	-
── Agreement between NG and LGDK	248	252	255	255	255	255	253	250	250	251	250	251	252

FIGURE 10.1 Municipal service expenditures, 2007–2019 (2019 price and task level).
Source: LGDK

exact functional and financial interface between regions and municipalities continues
to be challenging and disputed. Though the agreements between the national government and the LGDK and the DR are, in principle, two separate pillars of the budget
cooperation system, the agreements are chronologically synchronous, and in practice,
connected and interwoven.

A tax stop has been a core element of national tax policies since 2001, and unchanged
tax levels for municipalities and regions at large have correspondingly been an integral
part of the yearly agreements. From 2007, the regions have no right to levy taxes, and
accordingly, this element is no longer part of the regional agreements but continues to
be a core element of the municipal agreements. However, less and less municipalities are
actually changing their tax rates (Blom-Hansen et al. 2012: 129). The system thus loses
flexibility as municipalities are only allowed to raise taxes if other municipalities similarly lower the taxes, and municipalities that have the economic possibilities and the
political ambitions to lower taxes may refrain from doing so as they fear they will not
be allowed to raise taxes again if the economic situation worsens. Put in other words, the
local income taxation right, which has traditionally been considered a cornerstone
of Danish local self-government, is losing its vitality and mainly exists on paper (Blom-
Hansen et al. 2012: 129).

Besides a tighter economic steering regime in central-local relations, a setting of
tighter norms and the centralization by the national level has occurred since the mid-
1990s. Central regulation of the municipalities is increasingly a regulation of the administrative processes in the municipalities, i.e. process regulation (Andersen 2010). Process

regulation refers, *inter alia*, to regulation on user involvement, requirements to produce plans of actions, visitation and requirements on applying specific methods, follow-up actions, free choice, and applying standards of quality. Within specific sector areas such as health and basic education, the national government has interfered more, and more emphasis is put on the results achieved within these areas (Andersen 2010). Municipalities and regions document their achievements through benchmarking and the publication of waiting lists or exam results. This process is supplemented by national legislation introducing free choice in various public service areas (Andersen 2010).

In addition, the impact of EU policies affects the discretion of local government in Denmark (Andersen 2010). As a supra-national unit, the EU primarily affects the national level of government. However, given the position of municipalities in the Danish public sector, the EU also has consequences for the discretion of local government, particularly in areas such as the environment, outsourcing and call for tenders, regional development, and the labour market. The municipalities are either bound by EU regulation in these areas or responsible for administering EU regulation. In sum, the steady decentralization of tasks has, on the one hand, increased the discretion of the municipalities for the past decades. On the other hand, this decentralization has subsequently been accompanied by process regulation that restricts the discretion of the municipalities. The 'national mood' may also have changed in the sense that less emphasis is put on local diversity (Andersen 2010). However, as pointed out below, considerable diversity still exists.

Fiscal Autonomy Regarding Expenditures and Revenues

Changes in central regulation through the implementation of major reforms and changes in spending regimes may influence the level of expenditures and revenues and the variation in these between local entities. Evaluations of the economic effects of the 2007 reform show that the amalgamated municipalities—compared to the non-amalgamated ones—improved their fiscal management capacity and realized economies of scale with regard to the costs of administration and road maintenance (Hansen et al. 2014; Blom-Hansen et al. 2014; Blom-Hansen et al. 2016). Conversely, expenditures for children and young people with social/behavioural problems and for labour market activities increased relatively, and no economies of scale with regard to total expenditures were realized (Blom-Hansen et al. 2016). Below, we take a closer look at the variation and development in expenditures and revenues after the reform and the new spending regime.

Expenditures

Table 10.2 shows the distribution of municipal and regional expenditures by main functional categories. In line with the task portfolios set by the 2007 reform, healthcare is by

Table 10.2. Gross Current and Capital Expenditures of Municipalities and Regions (2019 Budget)

Municipalities	DKK billions	Percent	Regions	DKK billions	Percent
Urban and environmental affairs	17.9	4.0	Healthcare	130.9	93.3
Public utilities	9.7	2.1	Social affairs	4.3	3.0
Traffic and infrastructure	15.2	3.4	Regional development	3.4	2.4
Education and culture	79.4	17.5	Administration	1.7	1.2
Healthcare	31.8	7.0			
Social affairs and employment	253.0	55.8			
Administration	46.1	10.2			
Total	**453.1**	**100.0**	**Total**	**140.3**	**100.0**
Hereof:					
Capital expenditures (gross)	20.3	4.5		7.9	5.6
Service expenditures (net current)	251.8	55.6			
Social benefits and employment (net current)	80.9	17.9			
Co-financing of regional healthcare (net current)	22.5	5.0			

Source: Statistics Denmark.

far the most important task of the regions. Hospitals account for the majority of the health expenditures, but primary healthcare by general practitioners and the like is also included. National regulations and standards delimit the regional autonomy substantially, basically leaving the regional councils with fairly little discretion only for prioritizing and organizing within the hospital sector.

At municipal level, the most important task category is social affairs and employment. This includes a number of policy areas like daycare, eldercare, specialized services for children, youth, and adults with special needs, social benefits, and employment activities for the unemployed, as well as education accounts for a substantial part of the budget. In contrast to the regions, the municipalities are entitled to a high level of local decision-making autonomy with respect to allocating resources according to local needs and preferences. Within the framework of national legislation and the yearly economic agreement between the government and the LGDK, the municipal councils have the autonomy to decide the allocation of resources across policy areas and have a large degree of discretion in setting the standard and quality of services (Andersen 2010). This discretion is reflected in the substantial differences in the levels of expenditure among the municipalities, cf. Table 10.3.

Table 10.3. Variations in Selected Municipal Expenditure and Taxation Levels (2019 Budget)

	Mean	Minimum	Maximum	Standard deviation	Coefficient of variation
Expenditures (DKK)					
Daycare per 0–5-year-old	70,974	53,566	89,719	6,488	0.091
Schools per 6–16-year-old	80,118	69,257	109,902	8,566	0.107
Eldercare per 65+-year-old	39,711	25,078	58,906	5,846	0.147
Children and youth with special needs per 0–22-year-old	10,827	5,614	25,919	3,740	0.345
Adults with special needs per 18–64-year-old	9,457	6,508	16,478	1,715	0.181
Culture per inhabitant	1,770	894	3,089	445	0.252
Road maintenance per inhabitant	1,140	404	2,801	387	0.340
Administration per inhabitant	6,502	4,685	14,760	1,443	0.222
Selected tax rates					
Income tax rate (%)	25.3	22.5	27.8	1.0	0.039
Land tax rate, farm buildings (‰)	6.8	1.2	7.2	1.0	0.151
Land tax rate, other buildings (‰)	26.2	16.0	34.0	4.7	0.179

Source: Statistics Denmark.

The differences in expenditures at municipal level do not necessarily indicate similar differences in the quality of service. They may reflect differences in expenditure needs and municipal wealth, and for most policy areas, 50–80 per cent of the inter-municipal variations may be explained by differences in fiscal environment (Houlberg et al. 2018), indicating that the municipalities are adapting policies to local needs and preferences. However, the difference between the municipalities with the highest and lowest expenditures within a number of sector areas is considerable. Though national regulation through the budget cooperation system has been strengthened and has become more detailed, considerable variation in the levels of expenditure across the municipalities remains and reflects the autonomy and discretion entitled at municipal level.

Furthermore, some delegation of functions and financial responsibility from the municipal level to the service-producing institutions has been implemented in most municipalities since the early 1990s (Andersen 2010). We find a decentralized system not just between the state and the municipalities but also within the municipalities. Though many municipalities seem to have restricted the access of transferring budgets from one budget year to another in the wake of the Budget Law, the managers at schools, daycare centres, and eldercare centres still have a large degree of discretion with regard to finance and organization.

Revenues

Municipal and regional expenditures are financed by different income sources. The regions are not allowed to levy taxes, so state grants are by far the most important revenue source. General grants account for 75 per cent of the revenue and are distributed to the individual regions according to demographic and socioeconomic criteria. Besides these activity-independent grants, the regions are financed by activity-based co-financing from municipalities for citizens' treatment at hospitals and general practitioners and until 2018 by activity-dependent grants from the state (depending on an assessment of the 2 per cent efficiency demands).

At the municipal level, taxes are the main source of revenue (Blom-Hansen and Heeager 2011). Taxes account for nearly two thirds of the revenue of the municipalities at large (see Table 10.4). The most important tax source is local income tax. In addition, municipalities levy land taxes and corporate taxes, but these generate far less revenue. The second most important revenue source is grants from central government in the form of a general block grant and conditional grants for expenditures, mainly for income transfers to recipients of unemployment benefits, social benefits, sickness benefits, etc. Moreover, municipalities levy fees and user charges within the utility area and the social area. Finally, borrowing is generally forbidden, but exemptions are granted for a number of capital goods specified by central government regulation (Blom-Hansen and Heeager 2011).

The figures in Table 10.4, however, represent the average revenue profile, and considerable variation exists across municipalities due to variations in local fiscal environments and local policies. In some municipalities, general grants account for 35 per cent of the revenue, whereas in other municipalities, general grants account for *minus* 30 per cent of the revenue. These differences reflect the importance of the equalization scheme which aims at evening out the differences in the economic situation within the municipalities and giving the municipalities approximately the same financial basis on which to solve their tasks (Ministry for Economic Affairs and the Interior 2014).

Table 10.4. Municipal Revenue Sources (2019 Budget)

	DKK Billion	Percent
Taxes	291.2	64.3
General grants and equalization	79.1	17.5
Conditional grants	24.0	5.3
Fees and user charges	61.4	13.5
Net borrowing	−1.4	−0.3
Other	−1.1	−0.2
Total	453.1	100.0

Source: Statistics Denmark. 'Other' includes the sale of capital assets, net interest payment, and use of liquid assets.

The equalization scheme is complex and includes a set of special subsidies and equalization schemes. The main elements are a national equalization scheme covering all municipalities and an additional capital equalization scheme for the municipalities in the capital area. Based on a number of indicators for demographic and economic expenditure needs, 61 per cent of the inter-municipal differences in expenditure needs relative to local tax bases are equalized in the national equalization scheme, and an additional 27 per cent in the capital equalization scheme. The level of equalization in the national scheme was increased as part of the 2007 reform, and the new tasks were transferred to the municipalities. Combined with the subsequent redistribution of conditional grants and less flexibility in the economic agreements to adjust taxes, this has turned general grants and equalization into an important and viable part of municipal revenues.

CHALLENGES AND OPPORTUNITIES

The continuingly high level of decentralization turns local governments into important arenas for local democracy as well as important implementing agencies of the welfare state. Danish municipalities and regions thus enjoy a delicate balance between self-government and central control (Blom-Hansen and Heeager 2011), and developments, reforms, and increased decentralization have accentuated a number of challenging elements.

First, in the political rhetoric, the reshuffling of functions in the 2007 structural reform was intended to eliminate 'functional overlaps' and ambiguous vertical responsibilities between the three tiers of government. However, the reform has invoked new forms of challenges regarding the functional and financial interface between municipalities and regions, especially with regard to specialized social tasks and health (Blom-Hansen and Heeager 2011). One example is retraining and rehabilitation of patients after hospital admission. The regions are responsible for the hospitals and for financing patient-related rehabilitation, whereas the municipalities are responsible for financing citizen-related rehabilitation. Increased use of outpatient/ambulant treatment at the hospitals means that patients are increasingly discharged from hospitals right after treatment and staying in their homes in the period of rehabilitation. Consequently, municipalities and regions are continuously discussing the financial interface between patient-related rehabilitation and citizen-related rehabilitation—and thus who is responsible for financing a specific rehabilitation activity.

Second, the regions created by the 2007 reform are hybrid and crippled political institutions in the sense that they are basically single-purpose entities responsible for only hospitals, are not allowed to set up standing committees apart from the executive committees, and have no independent taxation rights (Blom-Hansen and Heeager 2011). In addition, citizens have no strong affective attachment to the regions, and their single-purpose status is likely to further decrease voter interest and democratic legitimacy. Thus, the future of the regions appears uncertain (Blom-Hansen and Heeager 2011).

Third, not all municipalities have the sufficient professional and economic capacity for handling the more complex social and educational tasks transferred to municipalities in 2007. Increased horizontal coordination may thus be needed, and/or the quality of the services will come under pressure or vary across municipalities. A number of institutional arrangements have been established in order to remedy this. Among these are mandatory agreements between the municipalities and the regions in each area involving multiple actors with potentially conflicting interests (Blom-Hansen and Heeager 2011) and a state agency supervising and overseeing the municipalities' ability to handle specialized social and educational tasks. Such institutional arrangements are complex arenas for coordination and may reduce democratic accountability as it becomes less transparent for voters whom to blame electorally if unsatisfied with the service delivered.

Fourth, the increased decentralization and the development in state-local relations since the turn of the century has challenged the budget cooperation system between the national government and local government associations. The regions rely solely on state grants and thus have strong incentives to join forces with interest organizations in the healthcare area and pressure central government for increased funding in the annual negotiations between the government and the DR (Blom-Hansen and Heeager 2011). At municipal level, a tax stop has been an integral part of the annual economic agreements between the government and the LGDK since 2001 and has contributed to reducing the system's flexibility. Although the tax stop applies to the municipalities at large, the number of individual municipalities lowering tax rates have been reduced significantly after the tax stop, and the flexibility of the budget cooperation system reduced equally as tax reduction in one municipality is a prerequisite for an increase in another municipality. This de facto freezing of tax rates rocks a core element of local self-government: the independent taxation right (Blom-Hansen et al. 2012: 129). Since 2001, the LGDK's role as coordinator has become increasingly important to ensure that the sum of the individual municipal decisions stays within the expenditure limits both in the budgets and in the final accounts. Though the expenditure limits apply to the municipalities at large, in years of zero-growth, municipalities wishing to increase service expenditures cannot do so if other municipalities are not reducing their expenditures equally. In this collective action dilemma, municipalities are reluctant to lower taxes or reduce expenditures as they are not sure they will be able to increase it again at a later stage if needs are increasing and/or political preferences for higher service levels gain ground. Thus, the flexibility of the system to adjust taxes and service levels to local needs and preferences is under continuous pressure.

Fifth, the sanction regime allows no transferals of unused budgets from one year's ceiling to another year's ceiling. Consequently, unused budgets end up in the municipal purse, and the liquid assets of the municipalities have now reached a historic height of DKK 50 billion. Another by-product is an increased tendency of 'expenditure-burning' towards the end of the budget year (Bæk et al. 2016).

Sixth, in line with the increased economic importance of the equalization scheme, the content of the scheme is increasingly being politicized both at national and local level. An increasing number of municipalities or groups of municipalities are questioning the level of equalization and/or the criteria of the equalization scheme, the relative weights of the criteria, or the measurement of the individual criteria and are calling for a more 'just' equalization scheme. However, the scheme is a zero-sum game, and what one group of municipalities argue to be more 'just', other municipalities argue to be the opposite. As stakeholders often evaluate loses higher than gains (Kahneman and Tversky 1979), any national reform of the equalization scheme is likely to produce more local opponents than proponents.

Despite these challenges, the local government system has demonstrated an impressive level of adaptability to changing conditions and externalities. Besides the adaption of policies to a strengthened national sanction regime, the municipalities at large have, for instance, reorganized eldercare to focus more on rehabilitation in the light of an ageing population and have focused services for children and young people with social/behavioural problems more on preventive and less intervening activities.

CONCLUSION

The Danish local government system is one of the most decentralized systems in Western democracies. The system has been through major changes over the past years. In 2007, a local government reform was implemented, changing the local government structure and the division of tasks among state, local, and regional government. Later, a new national spending regime put tougher limitations on the spending of local governments, backed up by law-enforced economic sanctions if the municipalities (and regions) at large do not keep spending within the expenditure limits. The question raised was: what are the consequences of a major structural reform followed by a national spending regime for a highly decentralized local government system? The main answer is that Danish local governments experience an increased level of decentralization of tasks but also witness an increasing central regulation, reducing the autonomy of local government to adjust taxes and service levels to local needs and preferences. Though the local government system experiences less autonomy, there continues to be variation in local government taxes and expenditures. However, as the flexibility of the system to adjust taxes and service has been reduced, the variations between municipalities is increasingly a reflection of past rather than present choices and preferences. In addition, local government revenues become more dependent on general grants and the functioning of the equalization scheme.

Summing up, increasing decentralization seems to be accompanied by decreasing autonomy. The Danish local government system can still be characterized as highly decentralized, but it faces significant challenges in maintaining the delicate balance between local self-government and implementing agency of the state. Besides an uncertain future for the hybrid and crippled political institutions at regional level and insufficient professional and economic capacity at municipal level for handling the most complex decentralized tasks, the challenges also include issues like complex arenas for coordination and national supervision challenging local democratic accountability, reduced flexibility to adjust taxes and service levels to local needs and preferences, pressure on the institutional framework for coordination of the local government's economic activities with overall national policies, and increasing politicization of the equalization scheme. Nevertheless, the local government system continues to demonstrate a high level of viability and capability for adapting to changing conditions and externalities.

REFERENCES

Andersen, Vibeke N. (2010). 'Changes in central-local relations. Denmark', in Michael J. Goldsmith and Edward C. Page, eds, *Changing Government Relations in Europe: From Localism to Intergovernmentalism*. London: Routledge, 47–66.

Bæk, Thomas A., Mikkel M. Q. Andersen, and Steffen K. J. Krahn (2016). *Sanktionslovgivningen og kommunernes økonomiske styring*. Copenhagen: KORA.

Bækgaard, Martin (2009). 'Organizational change in local governments: The impact of the Danish local government reform', *World Political Science Review* 5/1, article 6.

Bækgaard, Martin (2011). 'The impact of formal organizational structure on politico-administrative interaction: Evidence from a natural experiment', *Public Administration*, 89/3: 1063–80.

Baldersheim, Harald, and Lawrence E. Rose (2010). *Territorial Choice: The Politics of Boundaries and Borders*. Basingstoke: Palgrave Macmillan.

Blom-Hansen, Jens (1999). 'Avoiding the 'joint-decision trap': Lessons from intergovernmental relations in Scandinavia', *European Journal of Political Research*, 35/1: 35–67.

Blom-Hansen, Jens (2002). *Den fjerde statsmagt. Kommunernes Landsforening i Dansk Politik*. Magtudredningen. Aarhus: Aarhus University Press.

Blom-Hansen, Jens, and Anne Heeager (2011). 'Denmark: Between local democracy and implementing agency of the welfare state', in John Loughlin, Frank Hendriks, and Anders Lidström, eds, *The Oxford Handbook of Local and Regional Democracy in Europe*. Oxford: Oxford University Press, 221–41.

Blom-Hansen, Jens, Kurt Houlberg, and Søren Serritzlew (2014). 'Size, democracy, and the economic costs of running the political system', *American Journal of Political Science*, 58/4: 790–803.

Blom-Hansen, Jens, Kurt Houlberg, Søren Serritzlew, and Daniel Treisman (2016). 'Jurisdiction size and local government policy expenditure: Assessing the effect of municipal amalgamation', *American Political Science Review*, 110/4: 812–31.

Blom-Hansen, Jens, Marius Ibsen, Thorkil Juul, and Poul Erik Mouritzen (2012). *Fra sogn til velfærdsproducent. kommunestyret gennem fire årtier*. Odense: University Press of Southern Denmark.

Christensen, Jørgen G., Peter M. Christiansen, and Marius Ibsen (2017). *Politik og Forvaltning*, Copenhagen: Hans Reitzels Forlag.

Ejersbo, Niels (1998). 'Kommunale strukturer – et studie i lokal variation', *Politica*, 30/3: 285–97.

Elklit, Jørgen, and Ulrik Kjær (2007). 'The decreasing number of candidates at Danish local elections – Local democracy in crisis?', *Local Government Studies*, 33/2: 195–213.

Hansen, Kasper M. (2020). 'Electoral turnout. Strong social norms of voting', in Peter M. Christiansen, Jørgen Elklit, and Peter Nedergaard, eds, *The Oxford Handbook of Danish Politics*. Oxford: Oxford University Press, 76–87.

Hansen, Morten B., Jens T. Pedersen, and Emil Thylin (2010). 'Regeneration og strukturel forandring i de danske kommuners lederskab 1980–2008. Dokumentation af en undersøgelse baseret på kommunale årbøger', *Kommunalpolitiske Studier*, nr. 27.

Hansen, Sune W., and Ulf Hjelmar (2015). 'Når kommuner bliver større: De korte og mere langsigtede konsekvenser for lokaldemokratiet', *Politica*, 47/3: 464–84.

Hansen, Sune W., Kurt Houlberg, and Lene H. Pedersen (2014). 'Do municipal mergers improve fiscal outcomes?', *Scandinavian Political Studies*, 37/2: 196–214.

Houlberg, Kurt (2018). 'Lokale styringsvilkårs betydning for kommunernes økonomiske styring - fungerer sanktionslovgivningen som brandtæppe eller ilttelt?', *Politica*, 50/1: 45–64.

Houlberg, Kurt, Sune W. Voigt, and Lene H. Pedersen (2018). 'How is political influence redistributed in times of fiscal austerity?', *Scandinavian Political Studies*, 41/1: 98–119.

Højgaard, Betina, Jakob Kjellberg, and Mickael Bech (2018). *Den statslige styring af det regionale sundhedsområde. Analyse af centrale instrumenter*. Copenhagen: VIVE.

Ivanyna, Maksym, and Anwar Shah (2014). 'How close is your government to its people? Worldwide indicators on localization and decentralization', *Economics*, 8/3: 1.

Juul, Thorkil, and Henrik Kyvsgaard (2004). *Kommunens budget—udgifter og finansiering*. Frederiksberg: Danmarks Forvaltningshøjskoles Forlag.

Kahneman, Daniel, and Amos Tversky (1979). 'Prospect theory: An analysis of decision under risk', *Econometrica*, 47/2: 263–92.

Kjær, Ulrik (2020). 'Local elections. Localized voting within a nationalized party system', in Peter M. Christiansen, Jørgen Elklit, and Peter Nedergaard, eds, *The Oxford Handbook of Danish Politics*. Oxford: Oxford University Press, 382–99.

Kjær, Ulrik, Ulf Hjelmar, and Asmus L. Olsen (2010). 'Municipal amalgamations and the democratic functioning of local councils. The case of the Danish 2007 structural reform', *Local Government Studies*, 36/4: 569–85.

Kjær, Ulrik, and Poul Erik Mouritzen (2003) (eds). *Kommunestørrelse og lokalt demokrati*. Odense: University Press of Southern Denmark.

Ladner, Andreas, Nicolas Keuffer, and Harald Baldersheim (2016). 'Measuring local autonomy in 39 countries (1990–2014)', *Regional & Federal Studies*, 26/3: 321–57.

Lassen, David D., and Søren Serritzlew (2011). 'Jurisdiction size and local democracy: Evidence on internal political efficacy from large-scale municipal reform', *American Political Science Review*, 105/2: 238–58.

Ministry for Economic Affairs and the Interior (2014). *Municipalities and Regions—Tasks and Financing 2014*. Copenhagen: Ministry of Economic Affairs and the Interior.

Ministry of Interior and Health (2005). *The Local Government Reform—In Brief*, Copenhagen: Ministry of Interior and Health.

Mortensen, Peter B. (2014). 'Udviklingen i de offentlige udgifter', in Peter M. Christiansen, ed., *Budgetlægning og offentlige udgifter*. 2nd ed. Copenhagen: Hans Reitzel, 66–91.

Mouritzen, Poul Erik (2010). 'The Danish revolution in local government: How and why?', in Harald Baldersheim and Lawrence E. Rose, eds, *Territorial Choice: The Politics of Boundaries and Borders*. Houndmills: Palgrave, 21–41.

Mouritzen, Poul Erik, and James H. Svara (2002). *Leadership at the Apex*. Pittsburgh, PA: University of Pittsburgh Press.

Olsen, Asmus L. (2010). 'Kommunalreformens konsekvenser: kommunalpolitikernes rolle, borgernes lokaldemokratiske opfattelse og den administrative organisering', *Tidsskriftet Politik*, 13/3: 38–47.

Pedersen, Niels Jørgen M., and Maja F. Frandsen (2017). 'Decentralisation at sectoral level: Developing the role of local governments on labour market oriented social benefits', in Junghun Kim and Niels J. M. Pedersen, eds, *Decentralisation of Education, Health and Social Protection: Issues and Challenges*. The Copenhagen Workshop 2015. Copenhagen: The Korea Institute of Public Finance and the Danish Ministry for Economic Affairs and the Interior, 79–109.

Rodden, Jonathan (2004). 'Comparative federalism and decentralization: On meaning and measurement', *Comparative Politics*, 36/4: 481–500.

Serritzlew, Søren, and Jens Blom-Hansen (2014). 'Budgetlægning i kommuner og regioner', in Peter M. Christiansen, ed., *Budgetlægning og offentlige udgifter*. 2nd ed. Copenhagen: Hans Reitzel, 170–201.

Sørensen, Eva M., and Søren K. Foged (2015). 'Mål- og resultatstyring i kommunerne efter krisen', *Økonomi & Politik*, 88/1: 46–56.

Suenson, Emil L., Peter Nedergaard, and Peter M. Christiansen (2016). 'Why lash yourself to the mast? The case of the Danish "Budget Law"', *Public Budgeting and Finance*, 36/1: 3–21.

CHAPTER 11

CORPORATISM

Exaggerated Death Rumours?

PETER MUNK CHRISTIANSEN

MANY aspects of Danish politics and policies cannot be understood without reference to the role played by corporatist institutions and actors. Labour market relations, industrial policies, environmental policy, and management of public service institutions are all affected by corporatism.

Many writers have declared Danish—and other Scandinavian—corporatism to be weakened or even vanishing (e.g. Lewin 1994; Christiansen and Rommetvedt 1999; Rothstein and Bergström 1999; Blom-Hansen 2000, 2001; Lindvall and Rothstein 2006; Christiansen et al. 2010; Öberg et al. 2011), while others have pointed out that while changes definitely have taken place, there are still signs of solid corporatist structures and actors (e.g. Mailand 2009; Binderkrantz and Christiansen 2015; Christiansen et al. 2018).

This chapter asks: to what extent and in what sense has Danish corporatism changed, and why does Danish corporatism seem to be more tenacious than many scholars have predicted? The chapter proceeds with sections on the definition of corporatism and the origin of Danish corporatism. Then follows a review of the existing literature on the decline of corporatism, to be followed by, first, an analysis of new data on interest group representation in public commissions from 1972–2018, and second, a number of cases which can illustrate some of the changes in Danish corporatism. The section preceding the conclusion discusses possible explanations of the tenacious nature of Danish corporatism.

CORPORATISM DEFINED: A VARIETY OF DEMOCRACY

Corporatism is a contested concept and phenomenon and has been defined in different ways. Part of the literature is occupied with corporatism as a way of coordinating the behaviour of economic actors. This literature studies the effects of different ways of organizing industrial relations on economic parameters and policy outcomes. In this meaning, corporatism is a type of economic coordination mechanism between firms and between business and state actors, and it belongs to the study of varieties of capitalism (e.g. Hall and Soskice 2001; Hall and Gingerich 2009).

Corporatism can also be seen as a way of organizing political and administrative decision-making processes in cooperation between state actors and interest group representatives. In this view, corporatism is a way of organizing political processes with consequences for political outputs. It thus belongs to the study of varieties of democracy. In line with the Danish and Scandinavian research traditions, this chapter applies the latter view on corporatism, defined as '[…] institutionalized and privileged integration of organized interests in the preparation and/or implementation of public policies' (Christiansen et al. 2010: 27).

Institutionalized integration implies that interest groups' access to the policy process is regulated by formal rules as well as by informal norms. This again implies that interest groups have strong expectations of being involved in policy-making and implementation when relevant. In a number of cases, consultation procedures are formalized and established by law (Christiansen and Nørgaard 2003: 48).

Privileged integration means that some groups enjoy a more prominent position than others. Elected officials and civil servants cannot deliberate and negotiate with all relevant interest groups in an area on an equal basis—if for no other reason than practical ones. A privileged position is earned over some years during which a group has proved itself to be a credible and trustworthy partner in the exchange relation between groups and state actors. A privileged position will often, but not necessarily, be earned by the largest group within a sector.

THE ORIGIN OF DANISH CORPORATISM

Danish corporatism did not develop as an outcome of a grand design. Rather, it developed as a result of trial and error in response to changing societal challenges. Among the constituent issues and courses of action in the establishment of Danish corporatism are the labour question; the establishment of cooperation between social partners; the establishment of the Ghent model in unemployment insurance; the formation of strong interest groups; and finally, the role of wars and crises.

Around the end of the nineteenth and the beginning of the twentieth century, 'the labour question' was a generic term for some of the problems related to the growing urban proletariat. Child labour, long working hours, unemployment and sickness benefits, etc. entered the political agenda fuelled by fear of social unrest. In 1898, the Council for Industrial Injury Insurance (*Arbejderforsikringsrådet*) was established with representatives for the unions and the employers' organizations as members. The council is an example of an early corporatist body that played a large role for the legal regulation of the Danish labour market. Collegial bodies with state representatives and representatives for the involved partners proved a feasible way of settling political issues (Nørgaard 1997).

Shortly after the establishment of the Council for Industrial Injury Insurance, an important agreement was entered into by the Confederation of Trade Unions and the Confederation of Danish Employers. The 'September Compromise' became the pillar for solving disputes between employers and employees. The agreement stated the management prerogative and the employees' right to organize, and ultimately, the right to strike or lockout in the case of no settlement (Due et al. 2000). The September Agreement guided the construction of the collective bargaining system still at work. It also paved the way for strong labour market interest groups (Madsen et al. 2015).

A high unionization rate was realized in the following years. Denmark introduced the Ghent model (named after the Belgian city where it was first instituted) in 1908. The model implies that state subsidized unemployment benefits are administered by private organizations affiliated with the unions (Scruggs 2002). The Ghent system was introduced in many European countries but later abandoned in most countries. Denmark and a few other countries (Sweden, Finland, Iceland, and partly Belgium) still stick to the Ghent system today. It is an irony of history that the Ghent system was enacted by an alliance between the Conservative and the Liberal parties (Nørgaard 1997) because it produces positive feedback to the level of unionization (Scruggs 2002). Countries who stuck to the Ghent model have kept high unionization rates (Denmark 68.6 per cent, Finland 66.6 per cent, Sweden 66.8 per cent, Iceland 85.5 per cent), while countries who left the Ghent model have significantly lower rates (e.g. Germany 17.6 per cent, the Netherlands 17.7 per cent, Norway 52.5 per cent (all figures from 2015 except for Iceland which is from 2016 [stats.oecd.org]).

The unions were not the only ones who grew strong during these years. This was also the case for business organizations within agriculture and the urban industries (Hertz 1987). Many of todays' dominating organizations were established at that time (Buksti and Johansen 1979). Danish corporatism is built on a layer of strong interest groups with a large proportion of the workforce unionized and a large proportion of all firms organized in employers' or industrial branch organizations (Binderkrantz 2020). Corporatism implies a self-reinforcing dynamic that favours strong interest groups (Fisker 2015) which, again, strengthen corporatism. In some cases, corporatism even helps bring interest groups into being.

A last point to be made on the origin of Danish corporatism is the role played by wars and economic crises. Shortly after corporatist structures began to take root, the First World War broke out. Although Denmark had a neutral position during the war, the effects on trade and supplies were enormous. Many aspects of economic life had to be regulated by the state. The Extraordinary Commission (*Den Overordentlige Kommission*) and its many subcommittees marked a new level of involvement of business in policy preparation and implementation (Christiansen and Nørgaard 2003: 38–43). The economic crisis following the Wall Street Crash in 1929 further pushed for state regulation. The agricultural sector got closely involved with the state in order to deal with agricultural exports (Just 1992), and restrictions on imports were administered in close cooperation with business organizations (Christiansen and Nørgaard 2003). When the crisis finally released its hold, a new war was waiting a few years ahead with new demands for state involvement in many aspects of life.

When peace broke out after the Second World War, the institutionalized integration of privileged interest groups in policy formulation and integration had proven to be a robust, pragmatic, and efficient way to deal with many sorts of political and administrative problems. Interest groups got their say in building and administrating the country, and state actors received political the support and information necessary to target public policies. This exchange relationship was also exploited in the decades following the Second World War and economic deregulation, industrial development, and the construction of the welfare state. This chapter does not analyse the 1950s and 1960s (see Christiansen and Nørgaard 2003: ch. 4), but it suffices to say that corporatism became part and parcel of Danish politics and was so for many years. Corporatist structures entered a wide range of policy areas such as state-local government relations (Blom-Hansen 1999), environmental policy (Christiansen 1999), and the governance structure in public schools (Mailand 2016). Corporatist structures were not prevalent in all policy areas—economic policy is an example without strong interest group involvement (cf. Blom-Hansen 2001: 404–5)—but it was an integrated part of Danish political life. In a paper from 1982, Johansen and Kristensen (1982: 216) stated that the '[...] postwar period in Denmark is characterized by an ever increasing incorporation of interest groups into the apparatus of the state'.

DECLINING CORPORATISM?

Had Johansen and Kristensen (1982) written their report a few years later, the conclusion might have slightly differed. Denmark was hit hard by the oil crises in the 1970s, but unlike many countries, Denmark was reluctant to address the problems with proper reforms. In 1979, the outgoing Social Democratic Minister of Finance Knud Heinesen declared the Danish economy to be at the 'brink of the abyss' (Nannestad and Green-Pedersen 2008). The 1980s invited severe restructuring of the Danish economy, policy reforms, and stronger public expenditure control.

Other developments with possible consequences for corporatism took place from the 1970s and onwards. The 1973 general elections (Green-Pedersen and Kosiara-Pedersen 2020) implied permanent changes to the party system and bore witness to changing social structures and new political agendas, and the political role of the media changed (Binderkrantz 2020). Much hints that the traditional corporatist structures and actors entered a partly changed reality during the 1980s.

There is—unfortunately—no straightforward measure of the strength of corporatism, and further challenges are added if one wants to include a temporal perspective. Blom-Hansen (2000: 167–71) points to different data sources, interviews, official documents, and data for representations which all represent valid strategies, each, however, with their shortcomings. In the following analysis, the chapter draws on data on representation in public commissions and committees and on case studies that highlight some mechanisms involved in the transformation of Danish corporatism.

Committee Representation

The most commonly used measure of corporatism in the Scandinavian literature is interest group representation in public committees, councils, commissions, etc. (hereafter only commissions). They constitute an integration of interest groups into the state apparatus in order to participate in the preparation of new decisions, advice on political and administrative matters, and direct administration performed by such committees. These collective bodies are full-blooded corporatist structures because they represent a truly institutionalized and privileged access to decision-making arenas. Moreover, they are useful for time series since they can be established back in time. Such representation data have been collected with varying intensity in the Scandinavian countries (Johansen and Kristensen 1982; Christiansen and Rommetvedt 1999; Christiansen et al. 2010; Binderkrantz et al. 2015). Table 11.1 includes the most recent data on the stock of Danish public committees.

The table reveals a couple of developments. Firstly, the core corporatist bodies are not only a phenomenon of the past. The number of committees appears to be halved during the 1980s, only to recover somewhat during the 1990s. PM Anders Fogh Rasmussen launched a campaign against committees in 2002 ('tasting panels' as they were patronizingly called), but since 2005, there seems to be a rather stable number of commissions—a little more than 400—but a somewhat declining number with members from interest groups. Nevertheless, this part of the corporatist structure has hardly been dismantled.

The functions of committees have changed dramatically. There are few committees left with the main task of preparing decisions. The number has been declining since the 220 commissions in 1980. This is also what Christiansen et al. (2010) conclude on figures running up to 2005. However, interest group involvement in administrative tasks has only been slightly effected. In 2015, there were almost as many committees with interest group membership who performed administrative tasks as in 1980. Many are appeals committees regarding consumer protection or appeals committees for administrative decisions (Binderkrantz and Christiansen 2015).

In the following, we dig a little further into the policy preparing committees. Table 11.1 counts the stock of committees alive at each year's end. Data presented in Figures 11.1–11.3 are commission reports per year. Every year, government departments issue a number of white papers, some of which are numbered. Unlike the Norwegian (regjeringen.no/no/dokument/nou-ar/id1767/) and Swedish Official Reports (sou.gov. se), there are no clear rules about which reports get a number. The practice for numbering reports somehow changed during the 1990s; less and less reports were numbered. The data series presented below therefore contains more than the numbered reports, based on an examination of all available government departments' and agencies' outlets from

Table 11.1. Number of Commissions, Committees, etc. with Interest Group Representatives, 1975–2015

	1975	1980	1990	2000	2005	2010	2015
Total number of committees	667	715	388	513	434	436	416
Number with interest group representation	380	571	328	422	361	313	286
Hereof preparation of decisions:	156	220	65	73	41	31	10
Hereof administrative tasks:	224[1]	117	103	145	136	137	110
Hereof advisory tasks		234	160	204	184	145	166

[1] Includes advisory tasks.

Source: Christiansen and Nørgaard (2003) and own database.

1995 and onwards with the aim of establishing a data series that is as consistent and comprehensive over time as possible. The main criteria for including a report in the series is that it 1) is targeted towards digging into problems and/or solutions to political problems; 2) is written by a collegial body; 3) includes named members; 4) operates under a written mandate; and 5) is not a yearly report, an evaluation report, or an inspection report. Compared to Table 11.1, the numbers in Figures 11.1–11.3 reflect a narrower concept on representation. Almost all commissions in the latter figures are temporary, and they are all employed with policy preparation.

As shown in Figure 11.1, the number of yearly reports from 1972–2017 fluctuates somewhat, with 45 reports in 2004, 9 in 2012, and a tendency to a slight drop over the period. However, we do not see the same dramatic development in the number of yearly reports as we found for the stock of committees.

Figure 11.2 shows the share of committees with representation from at least one civil servant, one interest group representative, or one academic expert: the three dominating member types. The figure shows a fairly stable picture over the 35 years. As expected, civil servants are members of by far the most policy preparing committees. This makes sense, in so far as civil servants are supposed to control policy preparation in order to make proposals fit into the ministry's policies. It is worth noticing that there is a significant and difficult to explain drop in the proportion of committees with civil servant representation in 2017 and 2018. More interestingly, we do not find the expected drop in the proportion of committees with interest group representation. Actually, the tendency is towards a slightly higher proportion of committees with interest group representation.

There may be more than one representative of each group in policy preparing committees. Figure 11.3 shows the share of the total number of committee seats in each year for each of the three groups. Experts have taken up a slightly increasing share of committee seats since the turn of the century, but there is no clear direction in the share of interest groups' committee seats since the early 1970s. The fluctuations are considerable. In 1977, interest groups only had 19 per cent of all seats, while they had 48 per cent in 1992 and 1996, and as late as 2016, interest groups had 44 per cent of all commission seats.

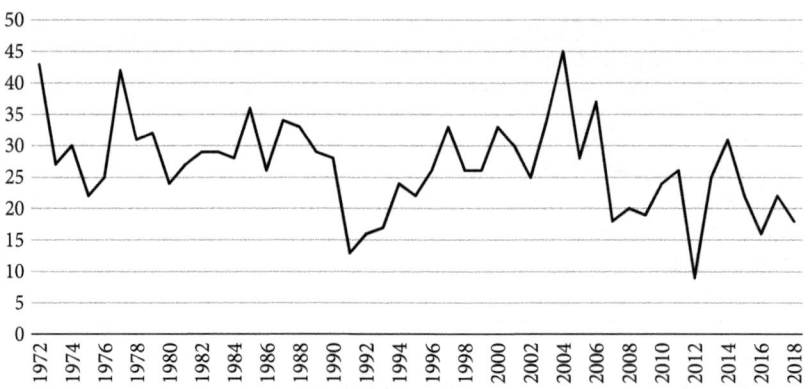

FIGURE 11.1 Yearly number of commission reports, 1972–2018.

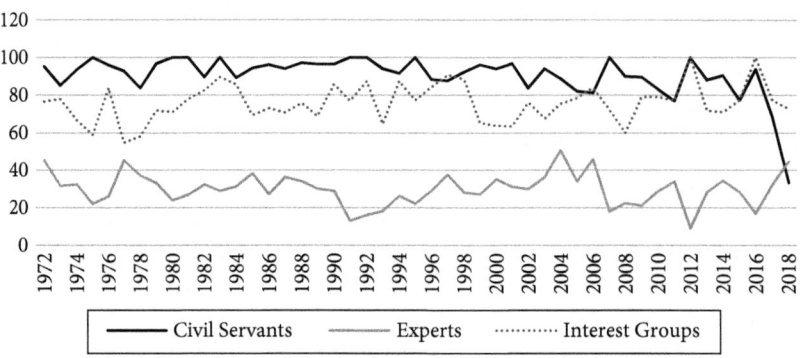

FIGURE 11.2 Share of commissions with at least one civil servant, expert, or interest group as member, 1972–2018.

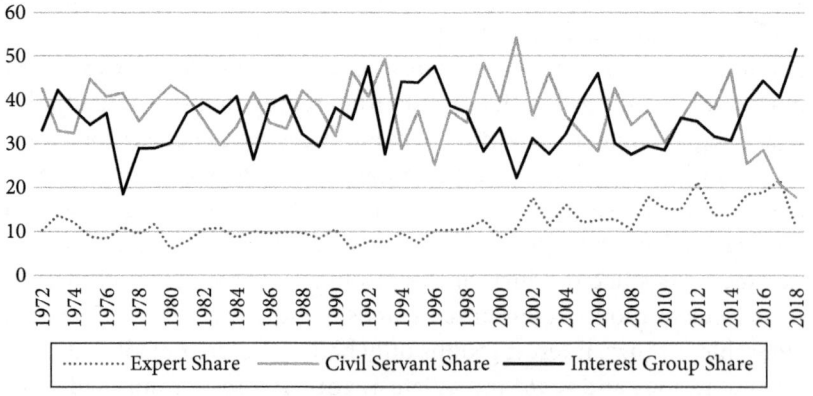

FIGURE 11.3 Experts', civil servants', and interest groups' share of commission seats, 1972–2018.

The data presented in Figures 11.1–11.3 do not show the expected downturn of corporatism in the preparation of public policies, nor do they correspond well with the data presented in Table 11.1. Since data on representation do not give us a clear picture, we turn towards a different method.

Studies of Government Reform Strategies

Corporatist policy-making proved to be a strong feature in the shaping of institutions and policies during the twentieth century. Interest groups delivered knowledge and political support in the construction of industrial policies, labour market policies, and the enormous expansion of the welfare state after 1960 (Andersen and Christiansen 1991: 28), just to mention the most important policies.

However, trees do not grow to the sky. Denmark was seriously hit by the two oil crises of the 1970s (Nannestad and Green-Pedersen 2008). A tough and exhaustive restructuring of policies and public expenditure management took place from the early 1980s, and Denmark has undergone many institutional and many policy reforms since then.

Some of these reforms fit into a cluster that affects the parameters of the political exchange logic: in cases where negative consequences of reforms are predicted to hit well-organized groups, the exchange relation is sharpened. Political principals and their closest agents may minimize or totally close negotiations and consultations from presumed reform opponents. This implies that otherwise strong and well-recognized interest groups are deprived of political exchange. Or to put it differently, if political and administrative principals do not predict a positive return from the involvement of interest groups, they calculate a strategy to pursue their goal without such involvement. This brings some benefits: 1) time and energy will not be spent on convincing groups to accept costs that they will ultimately not accept or where possible compensation for losses outweigh the estimated advantages from reform, and 2) presumed reform opponents may have less chance to mobilize broader groups for further reform opposition. On the cost side, political principals and civil servants must calculate the risk of 1) reduced reform legitimacy and 2) implementation problems if the excluded group is supposed to play a role in the implementation process.

Some examples, picked from different sectors with traditionally strong corporatist structures, may illustrate these mechanisms. They concern some major labour market reforms carried out since the early 1990s and right up to the 2010s; reforms of the regional level in Denmark in the 1990s, in the early 2000s, and in the late 2010s; and finally the reform of teachers' working hours in the early 2010s.

The first example concerns a core corporatist sector: Danish labour market policy at the end of the 2010s is very different from that of the 1980s. Rights and duties of the unemployed have changed dramatically during the last decades. Until the 1980s, the unemployment scheme was rather generous as unemployment benefits—heavily state subsidized but administered by a Ghent system with private unemployment funds closely related to the unions—had no maximum period in practice because the right for an extended period of benefits could be earned by attending vocational training or other qualifying courses (Christiansen et al. 2004: 88–117). For labour market newcomers, it was easy to earn the right to unemployment benefits. An early retirement scheme also made it attractive to withdraw from the labour market at the age of 60 (van Oorschot and Jensen 2009).

By 2020, unemployment and early retirement schemes look very different. The maximum period for obtaining unemployment benefits has been reduced to two years, and a new two-year period requires employment for another year. Demands for active job searching have been sharpened significantly and so has supervision regarding unemployment funds. The early retirement scheme has been severely reduced in coverage, and eligibility requirements have been significantly sharpened. Finally, the close relations between the unemployment funds and the unions have been weakened (cf. Scruggs 2002) through the introduction of non-union related unemployment funds. Reforms were carried out in subsequent reforms. Klitgaard and Nørgaard (2014: 410) count ten significant reforms from 1980 through 2008 carried out by centre-left as well as centre-right governments, and a handful of reforms have come into being after 2008.

The unemployment and early retirement schemes are the lifeblood of the labour unions, and they have resisted almost every piece of reform. They have, nevertheless, lost every single time. Where unions and employers took part in and endorsed most labour market reforms prior to 1980, the picture is different for post-1980 reforms. During the 1980s, reforms—mostly simple cuts in entitlements—under centre-right governments were carried out under vocal protests from the unions, whereas the unions were more accommodating and accommodated during the 1990s reforms under centre-left governments (Christiansen et al. 2004: 88–117), even if the bonds between the unions and the Social Democrats were loosening during the 1990s (Allern et al. 2007). An exception to the relatively peaceful relations between the unions and the Social Democrats was a severe cut in the early retirement scheme in 1998, where neither the unions nor the employers were even informed about the proposal when the government entered a settlement with the largest opposition party (Elmelund-Præstekær et al. 2015).

The 2000s proved to be much tougher. In 2002, the Liberal-Conservative government paved the way for cross-trade unemployment funds with the possible consequence of impairing the close relations between unemployment funds and unions so central to the Ghent model and a high level of unionization (Klitgaard and Nørgaard 2014; Scruggs 2002). In 2010, the eligibility period for unemployment benefits was halved from four to two years and the period for earning a new two-year period was doubled to 12 months. The proposal was never discussed in public, nor were there any consultations with the social partners until the proposal was part of a political settlement. More labour market examples could be mentioned. However, it is clear that earlier times' strong unions—topped by the Confederation of Trade Unions—have lost their privileged position in the formulation and implementation of part of the labour market policies. They have lost part of their value as partners with whom changing governments can enter into political exchange.

Nevertheless, during the same years, other important labour market policies were carried out under the deployment of traditional corporatist instruments. The 1991 pension reform—admired in many countries for its creation of a sustainable pension system—was the outcome of a tripartite commission that delivered the complicated framework for the pension reform to enter the collective wage agreements from 1991 (Kangas et al. 2010; Ministry of Labour 1988). Another example is a 2006 tripartite agreement on vocational training and lifelong learning based on commission work from 2004–6. Mailand (2011) counts eight major tripartite agreements between 1980 and 2011, six of which were reached during centre-right governments: corporatist policy-making old style.

The second example regards a sector with a much younger but nevertheless a strong corporatist heritage: the political and administrative organization of the regional level. A major amalgamation reform of municipalities and counties took place in 1970. Subsequent reorganization of the responsibilities for a broad range of public services and administrative tasks fostered one of the most decentralized Western states in terms of the distribution of tasks and autonomy (Blom-Hansen and Heeager 2011). Metropolitan Copenhagen was not part of the amalgamation reform, and the organization of the Greater Copenhagen Area continued to be a problem. In the mid-1990s, a commission report (White Paper 1307/1995) set up a number of solutions. Long public and political deliberations ended in a deadlock, and a reform was set aside (Christiansen and Klitgaard 2008: 46).

In 2001, the issue was raised again, but now with a much broader scope. A new commission with representatives from the civil service, the regional and municipal associations, and a number of experts were to consider how a wide range of public sector tasks could be distributed on different levels and how these levels should be put together. The commission's report (White Paper 1434/2004) prompted a wide debate in early 2004. When the government released its proposal in April 2004, it was received with surprise. The proposal had no resemblance to any of the commission report's models. Instead, it implied that the 14 counties were to be replaced by 5 regions that should only take care of health and have no right to levy taxes. A narrow political settlement on the biggest administrative reform ever in Denmark was reached in June 2004 (Christiansen and Klitgaard 2009).

Between January 2004—when the commission report was released—and April 2004, the following negotiations took place. While county and municipal Denmark was deliberating the commission's models, the Liberal-Conservative government negotiated a totally different model in secret with its support party, the Danish People's Party, and the association of municipalities, Local Government Denmark (LGDK). The Association of Danish Counties—traditionally a close partner for any government—was kept in the cold, not even aware of the ongoing negotiations. The government's reform strategy was simple and effective. The opposition parties and the counties' association were kept out of the negotiations in order to avoid reform opponents from mobilizing (Blom-Hansen et al. 2012). However, the government did not get all its reform proposals through during negotiations with the opposition parties in May and early June 2004 in order to seek a broad settlement—traditionally valued in Danish politics. A settlement was never reached, but the government stuck to the (small) concessions given to the opposition parties before the negotiations fell through (Christiansen and Klitgaard 2008: 130).

In 2019, the centre-right government proposed a new reorganization of the Danish public health sector, implying further weakening the regions by transferring some health tasks to the municipalities and by replacing the democratically elected Regional Councils with professional boards. Again, the proposal was not negotiated with any of the relevant interest groups, and in particular, not with the Danish Regions, the association of the regions.

Alongside these battles with the counties and later the regions, the counties'/regions' association cooperated closely with shifting governments and with government departments, just like in the old days of corporatist policy-making. A number of commission reports were produced, the government and the Danish Regions entered into their yearly agreements on next year's economy, and many smaller and larger adjustments in health policy were negotiated between the Danish Regions and government civil servants: corporatist policy-making old style.

The final example of a reform breaking with corporatist policy-making regards the teachers' working hours and school principals' room for leadership. The case is different from the two previous cases because it mixes corporatist policy-making with collective agreements. The core content of the case is the municipal association's (LGDK) dissatisfaction with the collective agreement for teachers. In the association's opinion, the agreement left too little leadership room for school principals, and during the 2000s, the association was looking for ways to change the collective agreement. Like the tango, it takes two to change collective agreements, and the Union of Teachers did not want to dance on this issue. Attempts for a renewal of the collective agreement in 2008 and 2011 were unsuccessful.

The LGDK became impatient. The agreement between the Ministry of Finance and LGDK for 2013 (Agreement 2012: 15, own translation) stated that '[…] the government and Local Government Denmark agree that there is a need for more teaching time within the present level of resources'. The renewal of the collective agreements for teachers also took place in 2013. The employers demanded the wording on working time reduced to a few lines and a winding up of all local agreements on work hours. Without results, the employers decided to lockout the teachers—a never before seen move from a public sector employer without a prior strike warning. After a three-and-a-half week lockout of school teachers, the government and a majority in Parliament intervened by law. For all practical purposes, the law mirrored the demands of LGDK. In an unusual way, the old collective agreements between LGDK and the teachers' union was replaced by a law that clearly favoured the employers' interests (Mailand 2016). A broadly accepted construction—particularly among the teachers—was that the LGDK used its close collaboration with the state (the Ministry of Finance in particular) to run the teachers' union over, and in this way, jeopardized the collective agreement system (Mailand 2016; Mathiasen 2017). The issue was unsettled after the negotiations on collective agreements in 2018, but a commission with members from the teachers' union, the municipal employers, experts, and a Supreme Court judge was set up in order to settle the issue—again, a well-proven corporatist instrument.

The three cases illustrate that in the same sector, corporatist policy-making can co-exist with policy-making that bypasses and neglects corporatist traditions and structures. When state actors presume that they are unable to reach their policy preferences through the integration of strong interest groups in the decision-making process, they may bypass these groups without compliance with traditional corporatist norms in order to overcome interest group resistance. Danish governments have increasingly adhered to strategic exclusion of reform resistant interest groups. 'Resources count, but votes decide' to contradict Stein Rokkan's (1966: 106) famous claim that 'votes count, but resources decide'. This implies a sharpening of the political exchange relation between decision-makers and interest groups in which interest groups have to bring something to the negotiation table even when they risk ending up as losers. Interest group access to decision-making arenas comes at a price. However, interest groups suffering from strategic exclusion in some cases can be involved in continued corporatist policy-making in the same sector and with the same state actors. Corporatist deliberations and negotiations are well suited for linear changes of existing policies, not for radical changes with costs for a corporatist actor.

Why Is Corporatism so Tenacious?

While the three reforms are examples of changes in corporatism, one should note that there are also stable elements of corporatism as documented by the numbers in Table 11.1 and Figures 11.1–11.3. Administrative corporatism is still strong, and at least in some cases of policy formation, interest groups are still integrated into the political and administrative decision-making machine. There are (at least) two reasons why political exchange relations still take place within a corporatist set-up to a considerable extent.

The first reason is that Denmark has strong interest groups, and they are partly created as a consequence of many years of corporatist policy-making. With unionization at a level only shared with few other countries, Denmark has comparatively strong and wealthy unions. The business sector is also well organized. Strong agricultural groups attest to a strong ability to create and sustain a still important business sector. Almost all Danish firms with more than a couple of employees are members of one or more central organizations—such as the Confederation of Danish Industries or the Danish Chamber of Commerce—or one of the almost 250 branch organizations in Danish industry. Denmark also has strong identity groups (such as students or the elderly), leisure groups (such as umbrella organizations for sports organizations), and public interest groups (such as environmental groups) (Binderkrantz and Christiansen 2015).

Strong interest groups are to some extent a construction of corporatism. Universities Denmark—organizing all Danish universities—is partly created out of the demand for the Ministry of Higher Education and Science to have only one organization to negotiate with instead of having to negotiate with each university. The Danish Society for Nature Conservation has an informal privileged status among the almost 50 green interest groups in Denmark.

Strong interest groups tend to sustain corporatism. Few and strong interest groups are better at aggregating and expressing the interests of different parts of society towards decision-makers than many small groups each representing a smaller part of society. Strong interest groups also shape some of society's institutions in ways that sustain corporatism. The unions have incentives to fight for sticking to the Ghent system for unemployment insurance—and they do. The agricultural sector has been successful in upholding some of their tax-financed support schemes. The social partners at the labour market—the Danish Employer's Confederation and the Danish Trade Union Confederation—guard the governance structure of the technical colleges where they both have representatives at every single school. Part of the surplus from the state-owned Danish Gambling Authority is distributed to support sport activities, non-profit social work, cultural activities, etc. The distribution takes place in cooperation with umbrella organizations within these areas.

The second reason that Danish corporatism does not wither away is that government actors also need civil society and social partners with whom they can deliberate and negotiate. Ministers and civil servants still benefit from political exchange in many cases. The case for the abolition of committees launched by PM Anders Fogh Rasmussen in 2002 is illustrative of this. The campaign did result in the closure of a number of committees. However, as witnessed by Table 11.1, more than 400 committees were still in existence in 2005 after three years of campaigning, and still in 2015, more than 400 committees were alive even though the number with interest group representatives had gone down to 286. The interpretation is straightforward: committees are a useful means in the hands of ministers and civil servants.

Conclusion

Corporatist actors and structures played a central role in the creation of present-day Denmark. A well-organized and flexible labour market, a comparatively low level of income inequality, a large universal welfare system, and probably also a high level of generalized trust and consensus (see Jensen and Svendsen 2020) are to some extent the outcomes of the inclusion of strong and privileged interest groups in the political and administrative decision-making processes. Corporatism is conducive to the invention and expansion of programmes where there are possible gains for all involved actors and where all actors may come out as winners if not always as equal winners. Corporatism also goes well with linear policy changes and reforms, i.e. policy changes that are within the zone of acceptance of all actors participating in the policy process.

Traditional corporatism, however, did not survive when economic crises, fiscal austerity, and reforms demanded tough concessions and losses to be accepted by traditional corporatist actors. The state increasingly turned towards new ways of organizing policy-making in order to increase the chances for realizing political goals. Stricter control with the process of decision preparation, stricter control of information on possible outcomes, and strategic exclusion of interest groups has increasingly characterized policy processes in classic corporatist sectors as well as other venues in the Danish decision-making system. Surprisingly, these new types of policy preparation coexist with traditional corporatist policy-making in the very same sector and sometimes also involving the very same actors. Despite significant changes in the role of interest groups in the policy process, corporatism has historically paved the way for strong interest groups that can still deliver in political exchanges today. In many cases, ministers and civil servants still rely on and demand inclusion and advice from interest groups—even the groups that in some cases have been left out in the cold where they were not believed to deliver on political exchange. There is still a positive return in the political exchange between state actors and interest groups but not always and not under all circumstances.

The Danish case illustrates that political agency has played and still plays an important role in the Danish political and administrative decision-making system. Even strong and vested interests can be overcome when enough is at stake. Conservatism bolstered by a strong corporatist tradition may be challenged and overcome by political entrepreneurs in pursuit of political goals outside of the comfort zone of the corporatist usual suspects. This places Denmark as a country with a strong capacity to carry through even tough and controversial reforms. It comes, however, at the price of inclusion and consensus.

The alternative to corporatism is not pluralism as some have suggested (e.g. Christiansen and Rommetvedt 1999). Rather, in a country like Denmark with strong interest groups and a long corporatist heritage, the alternative is stronger ministerial and bureaucratic control with information and decision-making processes, and thus, more closed and less open decisions such as witnessed by the three reform examples presented above. If corporatism is correlated with closed decision-making arenas, its Danish alternative is even fewer open arenas.

References

Agreement (2012). *Aftale om kommunernes økonomi for 2013*. Copenhagen: Ministry of Finance and Local Government Denmark, https://www.fm.dk/~/media/files/nyheder/pressemeddelelser/2012/06/kl-aftale/aftale_kommunernes-oekonomi-for-2013.ashx?la=da (accessed 19 November 2019).

Allern, Elin H., Nicholas Aylott, and Flemming J. Christiansen (2007). 'Democrats and trade unions in Scandinavia: The decline and persistence of institutional relationships', *European Journal of Political Research*, 46/5: 607–35.

Andersen, Jørgen G., and Peter M. Christiansen (1991). *Skatter uden velfærd. De offentlige udgifter i international belysning*. Copenhagen: Jurist- og Økonomforbundets Forlag.

Binderkrantz, Anne S. (2020). 'Interest groups. A democratic necessity and a necessary evil', in Peter M. Christiansen, Jørgen Elklit, and Peter Nedergaard, eds, *The Oxford Handbook of Danish Politics*. Oxford: Oxford University Press, 433–449.

Binderkrantz, Anne S., and Peter M. Christiansen (2015). 'From classic to modern corporatism. Interest group representation in Danish public committees in 1975 and 2010', *Journal of European Public Policy*, 22/7: 1022–39.

Binderkrantz, Anne S., Peter M. Christiansen, and Helene H. Pedersen (2015). 'Interest group access to the bureaucracy, parliament and the media', *Governance*, 28/1: 95–112.

Blom-Hansen, Jens (1999). 'Policy-making in central-local government relations: Balancing local autonomy, macroeconomic control, and sectoral policy goals', *Journal of Public Policy*, 19/3: 237–64.

Blom-Hansen, Jens (2000). 'Still corporatism in Scandinavia? A survey of recent empirical findings', *Scandinavian Political Studies*, 23/2: 157–81.

Blom-Hansen, Jens (2001). 'Organized interests and the state: A disintegrating relationship? Evidence from Denmark', *European Journal of Political Research*, 39/3: 391–416.

Blom-Hansen, Jens, Peter M. Christiansen, Anne Lise Fimreite, and Per Selle (2012). 'Reform strategies matter: Explaining the perplexing results of regional government reforms in Norway and Denmark', *Local Government Studies*, 38/1: 70–90.

Blom-Hansen, Jens, and Anne Heeager (2011). 'Denmark: Between local democracy and implementing agency of the welfare state', in Frank Hendriks, Anders Lidström, and John Loughlin, eds, *The Oxford Handbook of Local and Regional Democracy in Europe*. Oxford: Oxford University Press, 221–41.

Buksti, Jacob, and Lars N. Johansen (1979). 'Variations in organizational participation in government: The case of Denmark', *Scandinavian Political Studies*, 2/3: 197–220.

Christiansen, Peter M. (1999). 'Miljøpolitik og interesseorganisationer: Mellem anarki og integration', in Jens Blom-Hansen, and Carsten Daugbjerg, eds, *Magtens organisering: Stat og interesseorganisationer i Danmark*. Aarhus: Systime, 146–62.

Christiansen, Peter M., and Michael B. Klitgaard (2008). *Den utænkelige reform. Strukturreformens tilblivelse 2002-2005*. Odense: University Press of Southern Denmark.

Christiansen, Peter M., and Michael B. Klitgaard (2009). 'Behind the veil of vagueness: Success and failure in institutional reform', *Journal of Public Policy*, 30/2: 183–200.

Christiansen, Peter M., André Mach, and Frédéric Varone (2018). 'How corporatist institutions shape the access of citizen groups to policy makers: Evidence from Denmark and Switzerland', *Journal of European Public Policy*, 25/4: 526–45.

Christiansen, Peter M., and Asbjørn S. Nørgaard (2003). *Faste forhold—flygtige forbindelser. Stat og interesseorganisationer i det 20. århundrede*. Aarhus: Aarhus University Press.

Christiansen, Peter M., Asbjørn S. Nørgaard, and Niels C. Sidenius (2004). *Hvem skriver lovene? Interesseorganisationer og politiske beslutninger*. Aarhus: Aarhus University Press.

Christiansen, Peter M., Asbjørn S. Nørgaard, Hilmar Rommetvedt, Torsten Svensson, Gunnar Thesen, and PerOla Öberg (2010). 'Varieties of democracy: Interest groups and corporatist committees in Scandinavian policy making', *Voluntas—International Journal of Voluntary and Nonprofit Organizations*, 21/1: 22–40.

Christiansen, Peter M., and Hilmar Rommetvedt (1999). 'From corporatism to lobbyism? Parliaments, executives, and organized interest in Denmark and Norway', *Scandinavian Political Studies*, 22/3: 195–220.

Due, Jesper, Jørgen S. Madsen, and Carsten Jensen (2000). 'The "September compromise": A strategic choice by Danish employers in 1899', *Historical Studies in Industrial Relations*, 10: 43–70.

Elmelund-Præstekær, Christian, Michael B. Klitgaard, and Gijs Schumacher (2015). 'What wins public support? Communicating or obfuscating welfare state retrenchment', *European Political Science Review*, 7/3: 427–50.

Fisker, Helene (2015). 'Dead or alive? Explaining the long-term survival chances of interest groups', *West European Politics*, 38/3: 709–29.

Green-Pedersen, Christoffer, and Karina Kosiara-Pedersen (2020). 'Party system. Open yet stable', in Peter M. Christiansen, Jørgen Elklit, and Peter Nedergaard, eds, *The Oxford Handbook of Danish Politics*. Oxford: Oxford University Press, 213–229.

Hall, Peter A., and Daniel W. Gingerich (2009). 'Varieties of capitalism and institutional complementarities in the political economy: An empirical analysis', *British Journal of Political Science*, 39/3: 449–82.

Hall, Peter A., and David Soskice (2001). *Varieties of Capitalism: The Institutional Foundations of Comparative Advantage*. Oxford: Oxford University Press.

Hertz, Michael (1987). 'Handelsministeriet, organisationerne og næringslovgivningen 1908–1931. Et samspil fæstner sig', in Birgit N. Thomsen, ed., *Samspillet mellem organisationer og stat*. Copenhagen: Rigsarkivet/G.E.C.GAD, 157–232.

Jensen, Mette F., and Gert T. Svendsen (2020). 'Corruption and bureaucratic reforms. "Getting to Denmark"?', in Peter M. Christiansen, Jørgen Elklit, and Peter Nedergaard, eds, *The Oxford Handbook of Danish Politics*. Oxford: Oxford University Press, 177–192.

Johansen, Lars N., and Ole P. Kristensen (1982). 'Corporatist traits in Denmark 1946–76', in Gerhart Lehmbruch and Philippe Schmitter, eds, *Consequences of Corporatist Policy-Making*. London: Sage, 189–218.

Just, Flemming (1992). *Landbruget, staten og eksporten 1930–1950*. Esbjerg: University Press of Southern Denmark.

Kangas, Olli, Urban Lundberg, and Niels Ploug (2010). 'Three routes to pension reform: Politics and institutions in reforming pensions in Denmark, Finland and Sweden', *Social Policy & Administration*, 44/3: 265–84.

Klitgaard, Michael B., and Asbjørn S. Nørgaard (2014). 'Structural stress or deliberate decision? How governments have disempowered unions in Denmark', *European Journal of Political Research*, 53/2: 404–21.

Lewin, Leif (1994). 'The rise and decline of corporatism: The case of Sweden', *European Journal of Political Research*, 26/1: 59–79.

Lindvall, Jonas, and Bo Rothstein (2006). 'The fall of the strong state', *Scandinavian Political Studies*, 29/1: 47–63.

Madsen, Jørgen S., Jesper Due, and Søren K. Andersen (2015). 'Employment relations in Denmark', in Greg J. Bamber, Russell D. Lansbury, Nick Wail, and Chris F. Wright, eds, *International and Comparative Employment Relations. National Regulation, Global Changes*. London: Sage, 224–51.

Mailand, Mikkel (2009). 'Perspektiven des skandinavischen Korporatismus – Dänemark und Norwegen im Vergleich', *WSI Mitteiligungen*, 1/2009: 17–24.

Mailand, Mikkel (2011). *Trepartssamarbejdet gennem tiderne—hvordan, hvornår og hvilke udfordringer?* Copenhagen: FAOS. University of Copenhagen.

Mailand, Mikkel (2016). 'Proactive employers and teachers' working time regulation: Public sector industrial conflicts in Denmark and Norway', *Economic and Industrial Democracy* 40/3, doi: 10.1177/0143831X16657414.

Mathiasen, Anders-Peter (2017). *Søren og Mette i benlås. En kritisk krønike om folkeskolen, lærerlockouten og new public management*. Copenhagen: Politikens Forlag.

Ministry of Labour (1988). Redegørelse fra Arbejdsmarkedspensionsudvalget [Report from the Committee on Labour Market Pensions], Copenhagen: Arbejdsmarkedspensionsudvalget.

Nannestad, Peter, and Christoffer Green-Pedersen (2008). 'Keeping the bumblebee flying. Economic policy in the welfare state of Denmark, 1973–99', in Erik Albæk, Leslie C. Eliason,

Asbjørn S. Nørgaard, and Herman M. Schwartz, eds, *Crisis, Miracles, and Beyond. Negotiated Adaptation of the Danish Welfare State*. Aarhus: Aarhus University Press, 33–74.

Nørgaard, Asbjørn S. (1997). *The Politics of Institutional Control: Corporatism in Danish Occupational Safety and Health Regulation and Unemployment Insurance, 1870–1995*. Aarhus: Politica.

Öberg, PerOla, Torsten Svensson, Peter M. Christiansen, Asbjørn S. Nørgaard, Hilmar Rommetvedt, and Gunnar Thesen (2011). 'Disrupted exchange and declining corporatism: Government authority and interest group capability in Scandinavia', *Government and Opposition*, 46/3: 365–91.

van Oorschot, Wim, and Per H. Jensen (2009). 'Early retirement differences between Denmark and The Netherlands: A cross-national comparison of push and pull factors in two small European welfare states', *Journal of Aging Studies*, 23/4: 267–78.

Rokkan, Stein (1966). 'Norway: Numerical democracy and corporate pluralism', in Robert A. Dahl, ed., *Political Opposition in Western Democracies*. New Haven, CT: Yale University Press, 70–115.

Rothstein, Bo, and Jonas Bergström (1999). *Korporativismens fall och den svenske models krise*. Stockholm: SNS Förlag.

Scruggs, Lyle (2002). 'The Ghent system and union membership in Europe, 1970–1996', *Political Research Quarterly*, 55/2: 275–97.

White Paper (1307/1995). *Betænkning 1307 fra Hovedstadskommissionen om hovedstadsområdets fremtidige struktur. Vurderinger og forslag*. Copenhagen: Ministry of the Interior, http://kb-prod-dab-01.kb.dk:8080/wayback/20160630145517/http://www.statensnet.dk/betaenkninger/1201-1400/1307-1995-3/1307-1995-3_pdf/searchable_1307-1995-3.pdf (accessed 19 November 2019).

White Paper (1434/2004). *Strukturkommissionens betænkning*. Copenhagen: Ministry of The Interior and Health, https://oim.dk/media/17098/strukturkommissionens-sammenfatning.pdf (accessed 19 November 2019).

....

CHAPTER 12

CORRUPTION AND BUREAUCRATIC REFORMS

'Getting to Denmark'?

....

METTE FRISK JENSEN AND
GERT TINGGAARD SVENDSEN

'GETTING TO DENMARK'

....

'GETTING to Denmark' has become a metaphoric catchphrase for the long-term goal of building well-functioning, impartial, and uncorrupted states (Pritchett and Woolcock 2008; Fukuyama 2011). Yet, it is a great puzzle as to how the historical process by which a state reaches a low level of corruption has taken place (Teorell and Rothstein 2015a, 2015b). Some scholars, including Ostrom (1990), Fukuyama (1995), and Putnam (1993), have provided ideas about the importance of historical events. If so, the historical lessons learned on how to achieve the current state of affairs may guide both poor and rich economies in their efforts to maintain and improve living conditions even further in the longer run (Gundlach and Svendsen 2019; Aidt 2019). Thus, our research question is: can historical bureaucratic reforms explain the low level of corruption in Denmark?

Below, we focus on corruption as being the independent variable in an 'institutions matter' approach (Nannestad et al. 2014). Although there are only few theories about the notion and impact of corruption, there is general agreement across academic disciplines that its core element is the misuse of public power for private gain. Broad definitions include deviant acts such as bribery, embezzlement, and nepotism. The term 'private gain' relates to receiving money or valuable assets, but it may also encompass increases in power or status (Lambsdorff 2007; Rose-Ackerman 1999).

Thus, one could hypothesize that causality runs from top-down institutional change (bureaucratic reforms) to less corruption. In this setting, institutional change means bureaucratic reforms where it no longer pays to be corrupt. In other words, the costs from being corrupt (C) must now exceed the benefits (B) so that C > B for the individual bureaucrat. Benefits could be bribes, embezzlement or nepotism, whereas costs could be risk of detection, size of punishment, loss in utility from not respecting an oath to the king, etc.

During recent years, the destructive effects of corruption have been widely documented. Corruption leads to an enormous decline in national resources and has crucial consequences for a country's affluence and growth, along with the living conditions and health of its population. There is, therefore, a presumably close connection between the degree of corruption and a country's wealth. It is hardly coincidental that Denmark is the least corrupt country in the world and simultaneously one of the wealthiest. In a global context, the low levels of corruption in Denmark and the other Nordic countries are exceptional since about 85 per cent of the world's population live in a state that can be described as corrupt; that is, they live under adverse economic and social conditions such as high transaction costs due to illegal lobbying, corrupt practices, and limited opportunities for economic progress (Méon and Sekkat 2005; Brandt and Svendsen 2016). For example, a study from 2013 showed that if the EU member states could all manage to control corruption at the Danish level, tax collection in Europe would annually bring in about EUR 323 billion more, i.e. about twice the current EU budget (Mungiu-Pippidi 2013).

If, for instance, central institutions in a country such as the courts or the police can be bribed into making decisions that do not comply with the law, it affects the population's general trust in the system. The same applies when citizens are able to pay their way out of having cases investigated and brought to court or being fined by the police, and are not equal before the law in general. Sadly, exactly this kind of abuse of office is experienced in many countries in the world which are affected by a high level of corruption, and the negative consequences it has not only affects the level of trust but also the countries' economic growth, the populations' health and quality of life, as well as political legitimacy. Internationally, a high level of absence of corruption, as in the Scandinavian countries, is indeed an exception, and corruption-ridden and thereby dysfunctional states are unfortunately common. Corruption is also described as a deviation from the standard of impartiality in public institutions, and one of the important circumstances in the Danish development is precisely how it has been possible to establish a culture among the civil servants in the country's courts and in the administration in general where impartiality is standard (Rothstein and Teorell 2008; Rothstein 2013).

The emergence of corruption networks, gangs, and mafias substituting state tasks presupposes state failure or at least political instability (Svendsen et al. 2012). The modern Danish state is characterized, in particular, by welfare state institutions. Here, the state takes the role of the supplier of social services and benefits which are predominantly financed through taxes. At the same time, it should be emphasized that according to recent studies (Teorell and Rothstein 2015a, 2015b; Jensen 2013), some critical junctures in the evolution of today's levels of corruption can be traced through early and pragmatic bureaucratic reforms that efficiently fought corruption, thus preceding the onset of the modern welfare state. Although corruption is not widespread in Denmark, it is certainly not unknown, and a number of recent cases exist. Despite the fact that Denmark ranked as the least corrupt country in the 2018 TI index, it was only with a score of 88 out of 100. In 2014, the score was 92 out of 100, demonstrating how the development is not necessarily going in the direction of less corruption; Denmark is well-functioning but certainly not perfect.

CORRUPTION AND ANTI-CORRUPTION IN DENMARK

According to the Corruption Perception Index from Transparency International, Denmark has consistently been in the top as one of the four least corrupt countries in the world since 1995. In other international measures on corruption, Denmark also performs well due to indicators such as integrity in the public administration and freedom of the press. The 2017 World Governance Indicators published by the World Bank showed how Denmark has been placed in the best end in terms of both control of corruption and rule of law for more than a decade. The general level of reported bribery is also low according to surveys of both citizens' and businesses' experiences (European Commission 2017; GRECO 2014). Paying bribes for accessing public benefits from the police, the courts, the health service, the educational system, etc. are extremely rare.

Recently, Denmark has been home to what is probably one of the world's biggest cases of money laundering. Through Danske Bank's branch in Estonia, an estimated USD 230 billion were laundered for a number of clients from Russia and Azerbaijan, among others, between 2007 and 2015 (Financial Supervisory Authority 2019). A corruption scandal of mismanagement in the Danish Tax Agency has also taken place recently, costing the Danish state close to DKK 12 billion (USD 1.8 billion). Foreign companies applied for tax refunds for fictional shareholdings over several years and were wrongly paid the large sums, despite numerous warning to the Tax Authority (Danish Tax Agency 2018).

Recently, a case of fraud was discovered in the National Board of Health and Welfare where a highly trusted employee committed embezzlement for about DKK 120 million over a period of 25 years. A large case of bribery and embezzlement within the IT Company ATEA took place in 2009–14, involving several principal employees. The company was the supplier of IT infrastructure to the public sector and provided gifts such as paid vacations and IT equipment for public employees. Close to fifty public servants were arrested and convicted by the state prosecutor for Serious Economic and International Crime (Agency for Modernisation 2018).

The penal code prohibits corruption, including fraud and embezzlement, and the laws are enforced to a large degree. Since 2007, a formal written code of conduct in the public sector has been in place to guide both the authorities and employees in some of the fundamental conditions and rules of public administration (Agency for Public Employees 2007). Some of the central principles and values are based on the rule of law, democracy, integrity, openness, and impartiality. In relation to anti-corruption, the principle of impartiality is important to secure decisions on objective grounds and avoid an employee's special personal or financial interests in a certain outcome. Also, the acceptance of minor gifts and other benefits offered to public employees is very limited and regulated in detail by both general administrative law and the criminal code (GRECO 2014).

Denmark does not have a specific anti-corruption agency; instead, a large number of public institutions with a strong practice of integrity work to prevent corruption. This holds true for the State Prosecutor for Serious Economic and International Crime (SØIK), the Auditor General's Office (Rigsrevisionen), the Parliamentary Ombudsmand, and the judicial system (the judiciary is said to be the most trusted institution in Denmark). Both the police, the prosecutors, and the courts are independent of the legislature and the executive in practice, and the law enforcement institutions are thought to be strong in general (National Integrity System Study Denmark 2011).

Historical Bureaucratic Reforms and the Fight Against Corruption in Denmark

The history of anti-corruption, state-building, and the establishment of an increasingly Weberian type of bureaucracy in the centuries after 1660 has played an important role in forming today's central administration. The trajectory of curbing corruption at an early point in history has probably been a precondition for the establishment and financing of the welfare state and the creation of a basis for building trust in the administration and rule of law. By the middle of the nineteenth century, the level of corruption had been minimized and the use of bribery in the civil administration was a criminal act, unaccepted by the ruler (Jensen 2013, 2018a).

A number of what can be seen as anti-corruption mechanisms and practices were introduced after 1660. These were elements such as establishing rule of law and a strong focus on creating civil servants loyal to the king and state. These conditions were established gradually as part of the Danish process of state-building after the introduction of absolutism in 1660. Initially, these conditions developed primarily to consolidate the supremacy and power of the absolute monarchy. For this to be possible, the kings needed loyal civil servants to exercise their will as head of the state as well as of the Lutheran Church. A conscious attempt by the country's rulers came to create a reliable and devoted administration that gradually transformed the administration towards the Weberian ideals of the bureaucracy and to a large extent minimized the use of bribery during the eighteenth century.

By the middle of the nineteenth century, a number of legal reforms that changed civil servants' working conditions and the strong will of the rule to ensure that mal-administration was minimized—a combination that later came to be known as the Weberian model of bureaucracy—proved effective in curbing corruption in the state administration. This established a low base level for both bureaucratic and political corruption, which has on the whole been maintained since the mid-nineteenth century (Jensen 2013, 2018a).

After the introduction of absolutism, the king's government reorganized itself and its administration in a highly hierarchical manner centered on the monarch and based on the rule of law. In the kings' attempt to consolidate absolute supremacy, an essential tool was to deprive the nobility of its former political power. In the years after 1660, the distinctions of rank were minimized and all citizens were considered to be on a par under the absolute king. At the same time, the monopoly of the aristocracy on landowning and the higher offices in the king's civil administration and in the military service were abolished (Lind 2000). The first monarchs after 1660 used their right to appoint actively to change the corps of royal officials and establish an administration closely linked to the king in person. In the early years of absolute rule, receiving a royal office was still seen as an act of grace from the king to a person he wished to support. But during the regency of Frederik IV (1699–1730), the qualifications a royal servant needed to perform his duties became a prerequisite for receiving an office. This paved the way for meritocracy in the recruitment of civil servants and also for greater social equality. For the royal servants, it was made clear that the power they exercised was only a loan from the Crown and they never owned the office themselves (Jensen 1987).

To obtain an office, the royal servant had to swear an oath of fidelity and loyalty to the king in person, thereby promising to perform his duties according to the king's laws and guidelines. It was specified that the civil servant must be honest, hardworking, diligent, work for the king's best at all times, and secure the king's fortune. Within a few decades, at the end of the seventeenth century, actions such as bribery, embezzlement, and fraud were criminalized, especially for civil servants, and a large number of more and more detailed instructions on how to perform the administration were given (Jensen 1987; Lind 2000). From an anti-corruption perspective, the imposition of standards for regulating the ethics of office and the legal framework criminalizing corruption were significant. At the time the laws were passed, they were to a large extent part of the monarchs' attempts to preserve their position and power. But over the years, the legislation contributed to the establishment of an administration with a corps of civil servants who, in general, were loyal to the king and the laws of the country rather than private self-interests.

Even though absolutism as described in the King's Law (*Lex Regia*) of 1665 was the most sovereign form of absolutism in Europe, the rule cannot be characterized as a simple dictatorship but more as regulated despotism. The kings had special responsibilities as the secular leaders of the Lutheran Church after the reformation in 1536. The state was to a large extent a religious state, and the absolute rule took up the responsibility for turning the population into 'true' Christians. Starting in the late eighteenth century, the kings and their governments were inspired by the ideas of the Enlightenment, and royal power in the latter part of the period has been interpreted as an absolute monarchy guided by public opinion, where government to some extent was performed in accordance with the will of the people. The royal government worked in the interests of the people in maintaining law and order and gradually introducing to some extent reforms desired by people which the regime, *inter alia*, could follow through the use of petitions (*supplikker*). This form of communication gave the subjects of the king more than just an impression of being heard (Lind 2000).

In 1683, Denmark had followed several of the other early modern European states in setting up a system of petitions. Under the Danish law of 1683, any of the king's subjects were given the right to send in these applications or petitions. The topics brought to the attention of the king's administration in this way ranged from issues that pertained to trade, family, and legal matters such as applications for the king's pardon, a farmer's assertion that he was harassed by a landlord, general complaints from or about the royal servants, or suggestions for changes and improvements to the administrative procedures. Throughout the eighteenth century, the use of petitions increased intensely (Bregnsbo 1997). This established a formal space for communication between the king, his administration, and the people where wishes or complaints about the system and its administration could be filed.

The system of *supplikker* gave the crown a way of receiving information about maladministration by the royal servants. In more general terms, it also contributed to a rule in which the king's subjects had a chance to be heard while the monarch had an opportunity to exhibit and emphasize the legitimacy of his rule by being merciful, accessible, and able to guarantee law and justice (Bregnsbo 2011; Lind 2000).

At the University of Copenhagen, a law degree law was established in 1736, and at the same time, it was decided that no official was to achieve the office of judge without having a formal law degree. The establishment of the law school was intended to improve the officials' skills and knowledge of Danish law. The law graduates, mainly of bourgeois origin, came to occupy the offices in the administration, thereby contributing to the professionalization of the civil service. During the eighteenth century, jurists gradually took over the bureaucratic offices, starting in the central administration in Copenhagen and slowly spreading to most regional and local higher public offices. In the early nineteenth century, recruitment to the royal nominations in the administration was fundamentally meritocratic and had improved the conditions for building a state governed by the rule of law (Gøbel 2000; Feldbæk 2000).

The absolute rule was exercised under various forms during the centuries but proved remarkably durable and lasted until the introduction of a liberal constitution in 1848–9. During the early nineteenth century, a new set of reforms were introduced, bringing the administration closer to the rational working bureaucracy Weber came to describe in the beginning of the following century. Detailed control of the civil servants' accounts were set up between 1803 and 1830, separation of private and public account was fulfilled by 1841, salaries had been raised by the 1850s so that civil servants in general became a part of the well-to-do middleclass, and pensions were guaranteed in the Constitution of 1849 (Knudsen 2006; Jensen 2013).

In total, this set of legal and administrative modifications in combination with the will of the kings and their top advisors to condemn the misconducts of civil servants made it worthwhile to work according to the rules and receive a pension than to increase one's income through corrupt means. This contributed to a new—and fairly non-corrupt—overall setting for the Danish administration, which was in place around the mid-nineteenth century. Over several centuries, the absolute rule of Denmark demonstrated a will and power to fight the corruption of civil servants, both high and low in the bureaucratic hierarchy, through a fairly consistent condemnation of their wrongdoings, which is important in fighting corruption in any state administration (Jensen 2013, 2018b).

Recent studies of administrative dysfunction in Denmark, Norway, and Sweden in the nineteenth century are surprisingly similar in their findings, indicating that corruption in the administration of the Scandinavian states were addressed either before or within the span of a few decades in the mid-nineteenth century. This—in all likelihood—documents a fairly high degree of already established bureaucratic capacity and efficiency (Teige 2015; Teorell and Rothstein 2015a, 2015b; Jensen 2018b). The monarchies of Denmark, Norway (part of Denmark until 1814), and Sweden all had a common background with Lutheran state churches after the reformations in the sixteenth century. Today, the three countries are among the least corrupt countries in the world (Transparency International CPI 2018). Lutheranism might have played a durable role as a moral backbone in the Scandinavian societies.

STEPS IN THE ESTABLISHMENT OF RULE OF LAW

In anti-corruption research, independent legal institutions are seen as crucial for rule of law and the possibility to fight corruption together with transparency in public decisions and high standards for accounting (Rothstein 2013; Mungiu-Pippidi 2016; Dahlberg and Holmberg 2016). In the comprehensive 1683 Danish Law of King Christian V, a number of requirements to the country's judges and rules of court were drawn up. In the first book of the Danish Law, the fifth chapter concerns the judges' functions and activities, which are described in as much as 27 articles. One of the requirements was that the judges had to be 'men of good character', meaning that they could not be convicted or guilty of an action that was considered dishonorable in public opinion. This would disqualify them from the public trust that was necessary to hold the office.

Moreover, judges were required to deny any accusations of misconduct or accusations—also of a private nature—that concerned their honor in general. They were not allowed to discharge the judicial office until they were cleared in court of the accusations (Danske Lov 1683: 1-5-2). The law also specifically stated that the judges could not be susceptible to bribery, had to be impartial, and could not judge arbitrarily or in consideration of family. The competence requirement came into focus, and in addition to that, a number of other provisions were also intended to ensure that judges acted as reliable royal civil servants who only carried out their duties and judged according to the letter of the law. At the same time, the 1683 Danish Law contained several provisions about how civil servants should be controlled and how misconduct should be sentenced (Westrup 1983).

Apart from the Danish Law of 1683, a number of other laws were introduced that were important for both the judges and the king's civil servants more generally. In 1679, bribery was criminalized, and in 1700, the law on bribery was toughened. The sentence for this crime was loss of office and a fine of twice the value of the bribe received. As regards the legal rights, provisions were also made in the 1683 Danish Law that the judges could not delay cases unduly and that decisions should be made within a reasonable time frame. Moreover, the law contained provisions regarding how the attorney general should be the state prosecutor in cases about misconduct and treason and oversee the royal civil servants, and that the king's laws and regulations were observed.

Legal historians have discussed whether some of the most central steps in the emergence of rule of law in Denmark took place at the end of the eighteenth century or whether it was only a fact until the second half of the twentieth century. There is now more or less agreement that many important steps towards rule of law and legal rights were made in the period 1660–1849 (Johansen 1994; Dübeck 1993).

The period from the end of the eighteenth century is also described as the enlightened absolutism, where the rule to a certain extent was attentive of the population's requirements and wishes which changed in line with developments in society and the view of the state's function. Over the years, the rule slowly became characterized by a more and more well-described legislative and administrative practice and thereby regulations for the work carried out. The humanistic ideals and principles for citizens' legal rights of today were not in force, but by the standards of the time, the rule was aware of the subjects' welfare to some extent. The actual activity level in the administration also grew rapidly. If we, for example, look at the extent of published law text in the period 1683–1800, it rose from about 60 to 330 pages a year (Gøbel 2000).

AN INSTITUTIONS MATTER MODEL

The mentioned bureaucratic reforms may also have other positive side effects such as social trust. In this way, social trust can be depicted as a positive externality from fighting corruption, which is not necessarily intended (Gundlach and Svendsen 2019). Social trust is just an extra bonus resulting from that, along with less corruption. It can be defined as the broad societal assessment of how trustworthy people generally believe others to be and does not refer to specific persons. Hence, social trust reflects both a person's more or less optimistic expectations when interacting with others (Uslaner 2002) as well as the underlying understanding of how the social fabric of society works (Ostrom and Ahn 2009). A person's level of social trust thus reflects his standard estimate of an unknown other's trustworthiness (Dinesen and Sønderskov 2012). When trust is high, it is easier to cooperate in everyday life, thus creating more win-win situations among agents, and consequently, socio-economic benefits for society overall (Svendsen and Svendsen 2016).

Social trust is measured by the percentage answering yes to the question: 'In general, do you think most people can be trusted or can't you be too careful?' This question has proved a dependable and valid indicator in numerous surveys since it was introduced by Rosenberg (1956). A main finding in the literature is that low corruption correlates with high social trust. Serritzlew et al. (2014) report a correlation of 0.75 for 34 OECD countries. Denmark and the other Nordic countries score high on social trust and low on corruption in contrast to countries such as Mexico, Turkey, and Poland. Many other surveys have also found a strong correlation between social trust and absence of corruption and that they both foster economic growth. The literature also indicates that corruption has a causal effect on social trust, while the opposite effect is more uncertain. This means that a potential double dividend may be coined from fighting corruption as more social trust can enhance economic growth even further due to lower transaction costs (ibid.).

There is substantial evidence that low-trust and high-trust countries are stable over time. Consequently, many third world countries—despite large amounts of development aid—have been caged in 'social traps' characterized by inequality, low social trust, and corruption, while others (as the Scandinavian countries) have been in a good cycle for decades, characterized by equality, high trust, and low corruption (e.g. Uslaner 2009; Svendsen et al. 2012). Corruption is costly because it imposes a welfare loss on society and may as well reduce the level of social trust in the country at the same time. Furthermore, corruption can change people's mindsets and thereby affect social interaction in everyday life, thus implying socio-economic effects (Serritzlew et al. 2014).

A dominant theory about the relationship between corruption and social trust is Putnam's explanation that social trust is built *bottom-up* by ordinary citizens in voluntary civic associations, clearing a path for well-functioning and non-corrupt institutions (Putnam 1993). In recent years, however, Putnam's approach has been criticized for being one-sided (Bjørnskov 2009; Bjørnskov and Svendsen 2013). Alternative explanations and extensions of Putnam's approach refer to the impact of socialization (Dohmen et al. 2008), culture (Uslaner 2002, 2009), religion (Weber 2009), types of networking, including bridging, bonding, and linking, and the quality of state institutions (Rothstein 2009). The state's role in promoting social trust is also a subject eagerly discussed (Herreros and Criado 2009).

Bottom-up explanations have given way to *top-down* explanations with the concomitant belief that state policies and institutions can change society radically and within a reasonable time horizon. In such an 'institutions matter' context, the beneficial effects of non-corrupt welfare state institutions have been stressed. For example, Rothstein and others have argued that the invention of the universal welfare state in the Nordic countries is conducive to high levels of social trust (Rothstein 2009; Jensen and Svendsen 2011). Advocating this top-down approach, Kumlin and Rothstein (2005) have criticized Putnam's civic society approach, turning the 'institutions matter' argument into the policy recommendation that when investing in social trust, governments should increase 'the quality of political institutions' rather than support voluntary civic associations (Kumlin and Rothstein 2005: 362). This argumentation does not necessarily nullify the Putnamian civic society argument as formal and informal institutions may interact in an ongoing feedback effect process (Putnam 1993).

Thus, in the course of history, informal institutions tend to be formalized into specific rules of the game, which serve to maintain and perhaps further accumulate social trust, or in case of institutional breakdowns and political anomie, ruin social trust. Overall, the direction of causality between corruption and social trust is disputed in the literature (Serritzlew et al. 2014; Graeff and Svendsen 2013; Uslaner 2009). However, there is consensus that the two concepts are strongly correlated. The move from ingrained systems of patrimonialism to a Weberian-type state—its timing, causes, and everyday manifestations—can be grasped more easily through historical and contextual analyses of longitudinal data (Fritzen et al. 2014; Teorell and Rothstein 2015a, 2015b; Jensen 2018b). Such a cocktail of low corruption and high social trust may thus be part of answering the question of how states 'get to Denmark' and how socio-economic benefits are coined.

This leads us to the 'institutions matter' model in Figure 12.1. Here, a change in institutional setup (Δ) for more efficient anti-corruption efforts will curb corruption and have a positive effect on social trust. Last, but not least, absence of corruption, together with social trust, enhances the socio-economic benefits for overall society even further.

FIGURE 12.1 An 'institutions matter' model.

CONCLUSION

The research question in this chapter was: can historical bureaucratic reforms explain the low level of corruption in Denmark? To answer this question, we investigated the institutionalization process and bureaucratic reforms in Denmark from 1660 to 1866, and we looked at the roots of efficient anti-corruption measures that initiated a good path, culminating in the contemporary Scandinavian universal welfare states. Table 12.1 summarizes eleven central bureaucratic reforms in Denmark, 1660–1866, and how these reforms increased the costs of being corrupt among civil servants.

Table 12.1. Bureaucratic Reforms, 1660–1866

Time	Bureaucratic Reforms	Increased Costs of Being Corrupt
1660–1700	**1. Comprehensive Reorganization of the Administration** The administration of the Danish king was reorganized in a highly hierarchical manner with strong focus on creating an administration loyal to the rule.	The hierarchy of offices was defined to a much larger extent than previously, increasing professionalization and loyalty and thereby the utility from being non-corrupt.
After 1660	**2. An Oath of Office** The requirements for the royal servants were specified in an oath of office. The royal servant had to swear an oath of fidelity and loyalty to the king in person and hereby promise to perform his duties according to the king's laws and guidelines. It was specified that the civil servant must be honest, hardworking, work for the king's best interest at all times, and secure the king's fortune.	Regulated and set clearer standards for civil servants' allowed behaviour, and in general, increased the ethics and utility of office.
1676–1690	**3. The Criminalization of Corruption** Bribery, fraud, and embezzlement by the civil servants was criminalized in new laws. Imposed punishments of life imprisonment and loss of office for the crimes of corruption.	Set new laws for civil servants' behaviour and the ethics of office with severe punishments for being corrupt.
1700–1800	**4. The Appointment of Civil Servants** The procedures for recruitment came to be based on formal qualifications and merit.	Contributed to the development of a state governed by law and by civil servants deriving utility from being loyal to the king in person, and later, to the state.
1736–1821	**5. Formal Qualifications in Law** Introduction of a university examination in law at the University of Copenhagen in 1736. During the eighteenth century, jurists gradually took over the bureaucratic offices.	By the beginning of the nineteenth century, recruitment to the royal nominations in the administration was meritocratic. Such new jurists face the risk of losing such a prestigious and honorable position and the utility from being loyal.
1803–1830	**6. New Procedures for Closer Monitoring** Initiatives were taken to strengthen control over the local and regional administration to ensure that practice was conducted according to the law and the instructions given to civil servants.	The likelihood of civil servants' maladministration being discovered increased considerably.

(continued)

Table 12.1. Continued

Time	Bureaucratic Reforms	Increased Costs of Being Corrupt
1840	**7. New Penal Code** A penal code was introduced which included the crimes of embezzlement, fraud, and bribery which were described in far greater detail than in the laws of the late seventeenth century, and new standards for meting out penalties were introduced.	The new penal code defines even clearer standards for crimes, punishments and ethics of office.
1841	**8. New Procedures for Accounting and Audits** A new law for the administration of public accounts introduced a more detailed keeping of accounts, separate account books for separate offices, and a considerable intensification of audits.	The law abolished civil servants' right to borrow from public funds and stipulated a clear demarcation between civil servants' private and public funds.
The Danish Constitution of 1849	**9. Retirement Pensions** Stated the right of civil servants to receive a retirement pension at the age of 70 or in case of illness. The detailed rules of the retirement reform were specified further in an act in 1851 which also stated that the right to a pension could be lost in the event of misconduct in office.	Contributed to the establishment of an increasingly Weberian and professionalized bureaucracy. Risk of losing retirement pension if caught being corrupt.
1861	**10. The Salaries** New law on the salary system for the state's civil service was passed which abolished the former fee system and granted fixed salaries to all categories of officials.	Contributed to the establishment of an increasingly Weberian and professionalized bureaucracy. A bureaucrat will lose this future fixed salary if fired due to corrupt behaviour.
1866	**11. New Penal Code** The 1840 penal code was changed in 1866 to include a separate chapter specifying the forms of misconduct by public servants in greater detail.	Clearer standards for the formal rules of the game and the ethics of office.

In this way, Weberian bureaucracy, and to a large extent also rule of law, was de facto established around the middle of the nineteenth century. This is before Weber actually described his model for the ideal bureaucracy in the early twentieth century, i.e. Weber before Weber. The Weberian institutional framework proved to be the case in both Denmark and Sweden where the bureaucratic reforms were an integral part of the state-building process (Bågenholm 2018; Jensen 2018b). In the Lutheran monarchies of Denmark, Norway, and Sweden, corruption was already curbed and showed to be limited around the middle of the nineteenth century.

In Denmark, this institutional framework and integrity system also led to other positive externalities. There is, for example, ample evidence for the link between the amount of social trust and the amount of corruption in a country. In recent years, Denmark has taken the place as the country in the world with the lowest level of corruption, and at the same time, highest level of social trust. Today, a measurable and strong connection is seen between low levels of corruption and high levels of trust, and in Denmark, these two features probably make up some of the very central components behind the possibility of creating the modern Danish welfare state. The process of establishing the constitutional state in Denmark over the last centuries, including a reliable and impartial application of the law with competent employees in legal institutions and the authorities in general, has played a crucial role here. This combination of low corruption and high social trust is thus instrumental for a relatively well-functioning and rich country.

Overall, we argued that institutional change caused a relatively low level of corruption which again had a positive effect on the level of social trust and socio-economic benefits. This 'institutions matter' model could help explaining 'Getting to Denmark'.

References

Aidt, Toke S. (2019). 'Corruption', in Roger D. Congleton, Bernard Grofman, and Stefan Voigt, eds, *Oxford Handbook of Public Choice*. Oxford: Oxford University Press.

Agency for Modernisation (2018). 'Konsekvenser af Atea-dommen', https://modst.dk/nyheder/ nyhedsarkiv/2018/juni/konsekvenser-af-atea-dommen/ (accessed 29 November 2019).

Agency for Public Employees (2007). 'God adfærd i det offentlige', https://www.modst.dk/ media/16547/god_adfaerd_juni_2007.pdf (accessed 19 November 2019).

Bågenholm, Andreas (2018). 'Corruption and anticorruption in early-nineteenth-century Sweden: A snapshot of the state of the Swedish bureaucracy', in Ronald Kroeze, André Vitoria, and Guy Geltner, eds, *Anti-Corruption in History: From Antiquity to the Modern Era*. Oxford: Oxford University Press, 239–50.

Bjørnskov, Christian (2009). 'Economic growth', in Gert T. Svendsen and Gunnar L. H. Svendsen, eds, *Handbook of Social Capital: The Troika of Sociology. Political Science and Economics*. Cheltenham: Edward Elgar Publishing, 337–53.

Bjørnskov, Christian, and Gert T. Svendsen (2013). 'Does social trust determine the size of the welfare state? Evidence using historical identification', *Public Choice*, 157: 269–86.

Brandt, Urs S., and Gert T. Svendsen (2016). *The Politics of Persuasion: Should Lobbying be Regulated in the EU?* Cheltenham: Edward Elgar Publishing.

Bregnsbo, Michael (1997). *Folk skriver til kongen. Supplikkerne og deres funktion i den dansk-norske enevælde i 1700-tallet. Et kildestudie i Danske Kancellis supplikprotokoller*. Copenhagen: Selskabet for Udgivelse af Kilder til Dansk Historie.

Bregnsbo, Michael (2011). 'Struensee and the political culture of absolutism', in Pasi Ihalainen, Michael Bregnsbo, Karin Sennefelt, and Patrik Winton, eds, *Scandinavia in the Age of Revolution. Nordic Political Cultures, 1740–1820*. Farnham: Ashgate, 55–65.

Dahlberg, Stefan, and Holmberg Sören (2016). 'The importance of electoral and judicial trust for regime support', *Review of Public Administration and Management*, vol. 4, https://www. longdom.org/open-access/the-importance-of-electoral-and-judicial-trust-for-regime-support-2315-7844-1000182.pdf (accessed 19 November 2019).

Danish Tax Agency (2018). 'Status: Bankordning og aktieudlån på udbytteområde', https:// www.ft.dk/samling/20181/almdel/sau/spm/12/svar/1525118/1961812/index.htm (accessed 19 November 2019).

Danske Lov (1683). (*Kong Christian den femtis Danske Lov*) udgivet med kildehenvisninger af V.A. Secher, 2. udgave, København 1911.

Dinesen, Peter T., and Kim. M. Sønderskov (2012). 'Trust in a time of increasing diversity: On the relationship between ethnic heterogeneity and social trust in Denmark from 1979 until today', *Scandinavian Political Studies*, 35/4: 273–94.

Dohmen, Thomas, Armin Falk, David Huffman, and Uwe Sunde (2008). 'The intergenerational transmission of risk and trust attitudes', *IZA Working Paper 2380*. Bonn: Institute for the Study of Labour.

Dübeck, Inger (1993). 'Hvornår blev Danmark en retsstat?', in Helle Blomquist and Per Ingesman, eds, *Forvaltningshistorisk antologi*. Copenhagen: Jurist- og Økonomforbundets Forlag, 99–113.

European Commission (2017). Special Euroarometer 470 Report on Corruption.

Feldbæk, O. (2000). *Vækst og reformer—dansk forvaltning 1720–1814. Dansk Forvaltningshistorie. Stat, forvaltning og samfund (Vol. 1, pp. 227–340)*. Copenhagen: Jurist-og Økonomforbundets Forlag.

Financial Supervisory Authority (2019). 'Redegørelse om Finanstilsynets tilsyn med Danske Bank i forhold til Estland-sagen', https://www.finanstilsynet.dk/~/media/Nyhedscenter/2019/Redegrelse-om-Finanstilsynets-tilsyn-med-Danske-Bank-i-forhold-til-Estlandsagen-med-bilag.pdf (accessed 19 November 2019).

Fritzen, Scott A., Søren Serritzlew, and Gert T. Svendsen (2014). 'Corruption, trust and their public sector consequences', *Journal of Comparative Policy Analysis*, 16/2: 117–20.

Fukuyama, Francis (1995). *Trust: The Social Virtues and the Creation of Prosperity*. New York: The Free Press.

Fukuyama, Francis (2011). *The Origins of Political Order. From Prehuman Times to the French Revolution*. New York: Farrar, Straus and Giroux.

Gøbel, Erik (2000). *De styrede rigerne—Embedsmændene i den dansk-norske civile centraladministration 1660–1814*. Odense: University Press of Southern Denmark.

Graeff, Peter, and Gert T. Svendsen (2013). 'Trust and corruption: The influence of positive and negative social capital on the economic development in the European Union', *Quality and Quantity*, 47/5: 2829–46.

GRECO (2014). 'Evaluation report Denmark. Corruption prevention in respect of members of parliament, judges and prosecutors', Fourth Evaluation Round, March 2014.

Gundlach, Erich, and Gert T. Svendsen (2019). 'How do high and low levels of social trust affect the long-run performance of poor economies?', *Journal of International Development*, 31/1: 3–21.

Herreros, Francisco, and Henar Criado (2009). 'Social trust, social capital and perceptions of immigration', *Political Studies*, 57/2: 337–55.

Jensen, Birgit B. (1987). *Udnævnelsesretten i enevældens magtpolitiske system 1660–1703*. Copenhagen: The Danish National Archive, Gads Forlag.

Jensen, Carsten, and Gert T. Svendsen (2011). 'Giving money to strangers. European welfare states and social trust', *International Journal of Social Welfare*, 20/1: 3–9.

Jensen, Mette F. (2013). 'Korruption og embedsetik. Danske embedsmænds korruption i perioden 1800 til 1866', PhD dissertation, University of Southern Denmark.

Jensen, Mette F. (2018a). 'Statebuilding, establishing rule of law and fighting corruption in Denmark 1660–1900', in Ronald Kroeze, André Vitoria, and Guy Geltner, eds, *Anticorruption in History: From Antiquity to the Modern Era*. Oxford: Oxford University Press, 197–209.

Jensen, Mette F. (2018b). 'The building of the Scandinavian states: Establishing Weberian bureaucracy and curbing corruption from the mid-seventeenth to mid-nineteenth century', in Haldor Byrkjeflot and Frederik Engelstad, eds, *Bureaucracy and Society in Transition: Comparative Perspective vol. 33.* Bingley: Emerald Publishing Limited, 179–203.

Johansen, Jens Chr. (1994). 'Retssikkerheden før Retsstaten', *Retfærd*, årg.17–66/67: 111–23.

Knudsen, Tim (2006). *Fra enevælde til folkestyre. Dansk demokratihistorie indtil 1973.* Copenhagen: Akademisk Forlag.

Kumlin, Staffan, and Bo Rothstein (2005). 'Making and breaking social capital: The impact of welfare-state institutions', *Comparative Political Studies*, 38/4: 339–65.

Lambsdorff, Johann G. (2007). *The Institutional Economics of Corruption and Reform: Theory, Evidence and Policy.* Cambridge: Cambridge University Press.

Lind, Gunner (2000). 'Den heroiske Tid? Administrationen under den tidlige enevælde 1660–1720', in Erling L. Petersen, Grethe Ilsøe, Leon Jespersen, Tim Knudsen, Ditlev Tamm, and Jacob Ravn, eds, *Dansk Forvaltningshistorie: Stat, forvaltning og samfund, vol. 1.* Copenhagen: Jurist- og Økonomforbundets Forlag, 159–225.

Méon, Pierre-Guillaume, and Khalid Sekkat (2005). 'Does corruption grease or sand the wheels of growth?', *Public Choice*, 122: 69–97.

Mungiu-Pippidi, Alina (2013). *Volume 1: Controlling Corruption in Europe. The Anticorruption Report.* Barbara Budrich Publisher.

Mungiu-Pippidi, Alina (2016). 'The good, the bad and the ugly: Controlling corruption in the European Union', http://anticorrp.eu/publications/the-good-the-bad-and-the-ugly-controlling-corruption-in-the-european-union-3/ (accessed 19 November 2019).

Nannestad, Peter, Gert T. Svendsen, Peter T. Dinesen, and Kim M. Sønderskov (2014). 'Do Institutions or culture determine the level of social trust? The natural experiment of migration from non-western to western countries', *Journal of Ethnic and Migration Studies*, 40/4: 544–65.

National Integrity System Study, Denmark (2011). Transparency International, https://transparency.dk/wp-content/uploads/2019/05/NIS-DK-20120119.pdf (accessed 19 November 2019).

Ostrom, Elinor (1990). *Governing the Commons. The Evolution of Institutions for Collective Action.* Cambridge: Cambridge University Press.

Ostrom, Elinor, and T.K. Ahn (2009). 'The meaning of social capital and its link to collective action', in Gert T. Svendsen and Gunnar L. H. Svendsen, eds, *Handbook of Social Capital. The Troika of Sociology, Political Science and Economics.* Cheltenham: Edward Elgar Publishing, 17–35.

Pritchett, Lant, and Michael Woolcock (2008). 'Solutions when the solution is the problem: Arraying the disarray in development', *World Development*, 32/2: 191–212.

Putnam, Robert (1993). *Making Democracy Work. Civic traditions in Modern Italy.* Princeton, NJ: Princeton University Press.

Rose-Ackerman, Susan (1999). *Corruption and Government: Causes, Consequences, and Reform.* Cambridge: Cambridge University Press.

Rosenberg, Morris (1956). 'Misanthropy and political ideology', *American Sociological Review*, 21/3: 690–5.

Rothstein, Bo (2009). 'The universal welfare state', in Gert T. Svendsen and Gunnar L. H. Svendsen, eds, *Handbook of Social Capital. The Troika of Sociology, Political Science and Economics.* Cheltenham: Edward Elgar Publishing, 212–27.

Rothstein, Bo (2013). 'Corruption and social trust: Why the fish rots from the head down', *Social Research*, 80/4: 1009–32.

Rothstein, Bo, and Jan Teorell (2008). 'What is quality of government: A theory of impartial political institutions', *Governance*, 21/2: 165–90.

Serritzlew, Søren, Kim M. Sønderskov, and Gert T. Svendsen (2014). 'Do corruption and social trust affect economic growth? A review', *Journal of Comparative Policy Analysis*, 16/2: 121–39.

Svendsen, Gert T., and Gunnar L. H. Svendsen (2016). *Trust, Social Capital and the Scandinavian Welfare State: Explaining the Flight of the Bumblebee*. Cheltenham: Edward Elgar Publishing.

Svendsen, Gunnar L. H., Gert T. Svendsen, and Peter Graeff (2012). 'Explaining the emergence of social trust: Denmark and Germany', *Historical Social Research*, 37/3: 351–67.

Teige, Ola (2015). 'Korrupsjon i det norske og danske embetsverket etter 1814', in Finn-Einar Eliassen, Bård Frydenlund, Erik Opsahl, and Kai Østerberg (eds), *Den rianske vending. Festskrift i anledning professor Øystein Rians 70-årsdag 23. februar 2015*. Oslo: Novus Forlag, 193–208.

Teorell, Jan, and Bo Rothstein (2015a). 'Getting to Sweden, Part I: War and malfeasance, 1720–1850', *Scandinavian Political Studies*, 38/3: 217–37.

Teorell, Jan, and Bo Rothstein (2015b). 'Getting to Sweden, Part II: Breaking with corruption in the nineteenth century', *Scandinavian Political Studies*, 38/3: 238–54.

Transparency International CPI (2018). https://www.transparency.org/cpi2018 (accessed 19 November 2019).

Uslaner, Eric M. (2002). *The Moral Foundations of Trust*. Cambridge: Cambridge University Press.

Uslaner, Eric M. (2009). 'Corruption', in Gert T. Svendsen and Gunnar L. H. Svendsen, eds, *Handbook of Social Capital: the Troika of Sociology, Political Science and Economics*. Cheltenham: Edward Elgar Publishing, 127–42.

Weber, Ralph (2009). 'Religion-philosophical Roots', in Gert T. Svendsen and Gunnar L. H. Svendsen, eds, *Handbook of Social Capital: The Troika of Sociology, Political Science and Economics*. Cheltenham: Edward Elgar Publishing, 107–23.

Westrup, Morten (1983). 'Danske lov og kongens embedsmænd', in Ditlev Tamm, ed., *Danske og Norske Lov i 300 år*. Copenhagen: Jurist- og Økonomforbundets Forlag, 113–28.

CHAPTER 13

....

COORDINATION FOR THE EUROPEAN UNION

A Strong and Stable Institution

....

MADS DAGNIS JENSEN AND
PETER NEDERGAARD

THE COORDINATION SYSTEM FOR THE EUROPEAN UNION

....

Coordination as Orderly Aggregation of Interests

MEMBER states of the European Union (EU) are represented in the Council where they are expected to send authorized ministers to commit their government in the negotiations.[1] This follows from Article 203 in the Treaty of the European Union according to which: 'The Council shall consist of a representative of each Member State at ministerial level, authorised to commit the government of that Member State.'

There is room for the member states to decide who exactly qualifies as a 'representative at the ministerial level' as long as the person is 'authorised to commit the government' (Hayes-Renshaw et al. 2005: 14). Even though the European Parliament is involved in still more EU decision-making, the Council remains the most powerful decision-making body of the EU. To develop instructions for their ministers on the Council, all member states, including Denmark, have established an EU coordination system (Pappas 1995; Dimitrova and Toshkov 2007; Gärner et al. 2011; Jensen 2014, 2017; Kassim et al. 2000; Kassim 2003a, 2003b; Pedersen 2000; Nedergaard 1995, 2014).

Generally, coordination can be defined as ways of creating order among certain elements. In the political world, both legitimacy and efficiency considerations are involved in all kinds of coordination. In addition, organizational rivalry is an inevitable ingredient of political decision making, as some institutions will gain while others lose. Another issue is whether to use formal or more informal means of coordination; however, as far as EU coordination is concerned, both means are normally in use (Nedergaard 2014: 203).

The Danish EU coordination system is managed by the government but encompasses other actors in the political system such as the Parliament (*Folketinget*) and interest groups. Understanding the structures and processes that together constitute the Danish EU coordination system is highly important as it is the main device for aggregating Danish interests and transmitting them into the authoritative policymaking system in the Council (Wessels 1991; Hayes-Renshaw et al. 2005).

This chapter analyses the Danish EU coordination system from four different perspectives. The first is the *diachronic perspective* which maps the evolution of the Danish coordination system from the outset of European integration in the 1950s to 2019. The second is the *synchronic perspective* which outlines the organizational structures and processes that together constitute the system. The third is the *evaluative perspective* which discusses the weaknesses and strengths concerning both the historical development and present features of the coordination systems. The fourth and final is the *comparative perspective* where the features of the Danish system are contrasted with other member states' EU coordination systems. In all perspectives, both formal rules as well as informal norms are included in the analysis.

THE DIACHRONIC PERSPECTIVE: THE EVOLUTION OF THE DANISH COORDINATION SYSTEM FROM 1950–2019

Denmark was not a part of the launch of European integration in 1951 with the European Coal and Steel Community. Nevertheless, the Danish government monitored the European integration process closely because of its potential, wide-ranging consequences. However, when it became clear that Denmark's main trading partner at that time, the United Kingdom (UK), would not join, a Danish application for membership was not on the table (see also Larsen 2020 and Jensen and Nedergaard 2020).

The calculation of whether to be part of the European integration process changed radically when the six founding members agreed on the Treaty of Rome in March 1957. The Danish government estimated that the Treaty of Rome would have considerable consequences for Denmark. A tough choice had to be made between 1) becoming a part of the Treaty of Rome; 2) creating a less binding but more inclusive free-trade zone proposed by the UK; or 3) developing close cooperation between the Nordic countries. Although the Danish government preferred the second option, it decided to keep the other options open. This was used successfully to pressure the UK into accepting the inclusion of agricultural products in the free-trade zone that became known as the European Free Trade Association (EFTA). Furthermore, the Danish government managed to negotiate relatively favourable trade deals on agricultural products with Germany. Thus, it decided not to join the Treaty of Rome (Nedergaard and Jensen 2015).

The situation changed during the 1960s where Denmark followed its then main trading partner the UK in two unsuccessful attempts to join the European Community (EC), and Denmark withdrew its application when France vetoed UK membership. Countries outside the EC were especially attracted by the fact that EC countries experienced exceptionally high growth rates because of the Common Market. Different ad hoc administrative and political units were set up by Danish governments in the 1960s to handle the negotiation process in terms of a special government committee, and from 1966 on, a new market minister was appointed who received support from civil servants in the Market Secretariat of the Ministry of Foreign Affairs (MFA). The ad hoc units involved in the negotiation process shaped the subsequent formation of the coordination system when Denmark eventually joined the EC in 1973 along with the UK and Ireland (Auken et al. 1975).

During the more than decade-long negotiation process until 1973, different analyses were commissioned, and there were considerable public debates over the consequences and merits of membership (Esmark 2002). Both the analyses and the debates primarily centred on the assumed trade-off between the potential economic gains from membership versus the political losses in terms of legal transfer of sovereignty from the national level to the European institutions (Ministry of Foreign Affairs 1962, 1968). This alleged transaction between economic benefits versus sovereignty costs has remained central in Danish debates about the EC/EU after accession.

When it became clear that Denmark would join the EC, rivalry began at the administrative level over the future organization of the coordination system. As the main body responsible for the entry negotiations, the MFA was in a strong position to set the agenda by proposing a model in which it would be the hub of coordination. This, however, was met with opposition from other ministries, most notably the Ministry of Finance, and in the end, a compromise was found in which the MFA was granted responsibility for the procedural coordination, while the concerned sectoral ministries would execute the substantive scrutiny of proposals (Christensen 2003). Thus, the original coordination system combined features from the centralized French system where one unit called *Secrétariat général du Comité interministériel pour les questions de coopération économique européenne* was responsible for coordination with the features from the decentralized German system which left considerable autonomy to the sector ministries (following the *Ressortprinzip*) in the coordination process.

After the referendum on 2 October 1972 where a majority (63.4 per cent) of the participating voters supported membership, Denmark entered the EC on 1 January 1973 (Beach 2020). At the beginning of Denmark's membership of the EU, a doctrine of Danish EU coordination was formulated and put forward in the Danish Parliament by former Minister of Foreign Affairs K.B. Andersen:

> It is important to keep in mind as a central point that Danish policy positions have to be presented in negotiations against foreign partners in a coordinated fashion,

where the balance between different yet not necessarily coincident interests are found beforehand in cooperative work at the domestic level. In order to solve this task, close cooperation is not only needed between the Ministry of Foreign Affairs, other parts of government, and other bodies and institutions; it is also required that constant coordination takes place at all levels within the Ministry of Foreign Affairs.

(Translated from Danish Folketingstidende 1973–1974 Tillæg A: 986)

The key words in this doctrine are the three 'c's: coordinated, coincident, and cooperative. It is our claim that the doctrine is a constant in Danish EU coordination from 1973 through 2019.

In the period following the membership in 1973, and until the EC changed to a political union with the Maastricht Treaty, several changes took place in the Danish coordination system. Within the government, the balance of power gradually shifted from coordination centralized around the MFA to a more decentralized coordination around the sectoral ministries in which scrutiny of proposals followed existing, standard administrative procedures, according to which the responsible sectoral ministry coordinated with other affected ministries and interest groups (Christiansen 2020). This power shift came about because the sectoral ministries were gaining more experience in EU affairs as time passed (Nedergaard 2005: 391–4).

The sectoral ministries also created linkages to actors in Brussels and other member states, resulting in a somewhat decreased dependence on the MFA. These linkages are not least created through the many committees set up by the Commission (Nedergaard 2006). Three indicators underline the rise of the sectoral ministries in the coordination system. First, the number of *special committees* for European affairs increased steadily from 18 in 1972 to 27 in 1985 (Ministry of Foreign Affairs 1995). Today, the number has stabilized around 35 (the number increases and decreases due to various EU initiatives) (Nedergaard 2014: 208). Second, the number of international units in sector ministries increased from 21 to 66 from 1972–1982 (Dosenrode 1993). Third, the MFA changed the instruction procedure in 1986 so that the ministries could instruct their attachés in the working groups in Brussels directly, cf. the following (Christensen 2003: 79). However, one should not overstate the decline of the MFA in the coordination system. Despite the strong centrifugal forces, the MFA maintained a strong position because it has remained present in all parts of the coordination system and acted as a strategic partner for the sectoral ministries, mediated inter-ministerial conflicts, secured consistent positions, and determined Denmark's overall EC policy. In addition, all instructions for the Danish EU ambassador in Coreper still come from the MFA (see more below about Coreper).

An ad hoc parliamentary committee (*Markedsforhandlingsudvalg*) already established in 1961 to follow the accession negotiations was transformed into the permanent Market Committee (*Markedsudvalget*) in 1973 (Jensen 2003: 33). While first accepting the government freedom to manoeuvre in Brussels, after accession, the Market Committee made a U-turn a few months after the Danish EC membership by declaring that the government should obtain a mandate from it in all items of major significance as well as in all items of considerable importance before meetings in the Council.

This was unprecedented and made the Danish Parliament famous for its powerful role in European affairs (Raunio 2007; Jensen and Martinsen 2015).

The powerful role of the Market Committee in the coordination system was a function of a Danish tradition for minority governments in which the Parliament wanted to make sure that the government would not bind Denmark in the negotiations for something that a majority in Parliament could not support. The Single European Act from 1986 led to a significant tightening in the Danish coordination system: the Market Committee of the Parliament demanded that it should receive information from the government and at an earlier stage in the form of an explanatory memorandum, the so-called 'basic explanatory memorandum' (cf. later). Within the government, the sectoral ministries became responsible for delivering early warnings about pending proposals from the Commission (Nedergaard 2005: 410–14).

A majority of the participating Danish voters voted against the Maastricht Treaty from 1992, leading to the Edinburgh Agreement of 1993, whereby Denmark took four opt-outs that were approved by a subsequent referendum. The adaptation of the Edinburgh Agreement onwards continued the momentum for change in the Danish coordination system. Several adjustments were made in the government coordination system to accommodate the broader and more binding nature of the post-Maastricht EU. This included increased emphasis on involving interest groups in the coordination process via the special committees to improve legitimacy; the addition of new ministries to the EU coordination procedures; the setting up of a special committee to deal with issues concerning Pillar II about Common Foreign and Security Policy, and Pillar III about Police and Judicial Co-Operation in Criminal Matters; the emphasis on the need for swifter and more consistent coordination; and the enhancement of the role of the Prime Minister's Office. The stronger role of the prime minister in European affairs at the expense of the foreign minister is not something particular to Denmark, but a common trend reflecting the increased importance of the European Council in terms of solving thorny issues and setting the direction for European integration (Jensen et al. 2016).

In the Danish Parliament, the Market Committee changed its name to the European Affairs Committee (EAC) after the Maastricht Treaty, and created several new procedures in the 1990s and 2000s in order to be involved earlier in the coordination process to compel the sectoral committees to be more engaged in the scrutiny process, and to create more openness towards the public. The reason for this was the new voting procedures in the Council, with more a qualified majority voting contrary to the dominance of unanimity decision-making earlier on. Qualified majority voting means that 55 per cent of the member states in the Council representing at least 65 per cent of the EU population are necessary in order to adopt directives and regulations. In addition, the Parliament demanded that should it be better informed about cases against Denmark at the European Court of Justice due to their potential wide-ranging consequences for the Danish political system (Jensen et al. 2016).

Over time, the Danish coordination system has undergone changes, leading to the following developments:

i. Increased decentralization where the MFA has granted the sectoral ministries more autonomy.
ii. Parliamentarization where the Danish Parliament has been empowered with regard to defining the mandates of the Danish ministers in Brussels.
iii. Increased transnationalization where linkages have been made to the administrations in the EU and other member states.

Nevertheless, the doctrine of EU coordination formulated in 1973 has remained intact.

The Synchronic Perspective: The Organization of the Danish EU Coordination System

The Council is often pictured as consisting of a pyramid structure with three strata. The lowest stratum comprises 250–300 issue-specific working groups in which civil servants from the member states scrutinize the draft legislation. In the middle stratum, called *Comité des Représentants Permanents* (Coreper), high-ranking civil servants (so-called EU ambassadors) are allocated the tasks of solving problems that the working groups could not agree on and preparing meetings for the ministers. Finally, there are the ministers of the member states, who are the top stratum and responsible for handling the political parts of the draft legislation and passing them democratically. In case of agreement at the lower level, the higher level decides through a written procedure, whereas in case of disagreement at the lower level, a deliberation takes place at the higher level.

The Danish EU coordination system corresponds to the structure of the three strata of the Council in Brussels. Most of the EU coordination measured in terms of time and substantial negotiations takes place at the bottom of the system in the special committees (*specialudvalg*) managed by the sectoral ministries. The special committees are important centres of information for the external members of the committee. Especially interest organizations with strong secretariats often contribute with significant inputs to the Danish government's position on Commission proposals. Legislative proposals from the Commission is allocated by the MFA to the relevant sectoral ministry, which through its special committee will review their impact on Denmark in terms of the political, legal, and economic consequences (Nedergaard 2014: 208–9). In accordance with the doctrine on Danish EU coordination, the sectoral ministry is obliged to involve other affected ministries and interest groups in the process of illuminating the consequences for Denmark and summarizes the information in a so-called 'framework paper' (*rammenotat*). The pluralistic possibilities for interest organization participation is accepted in all relevant special committees with the aim of finding coincident interests with other actors, cf. the doctrine of Danish EU coordination.

The sectoral ministries also send Danish representatives to working group meetings in Brussels held under the auspices of the Secretariat of the Council, unless the ministries' own attachés (who are formally employed by the MFA) at the Permanent Representation in Brussels take part in these meetings. As mentioned, negotiations here are based on instructions from the relevant ministry (Nedergaard 2014: 206).

Although the duration of the special committee phase often lasts several weeks and sometimes months, an early 'basic memorandum' (*Grundnotat*) must be send to the Parliament's EAC no later than four weeks after the legislative proposal by the Commission is available in Danish. The sectoral minister and ministry are entrusted the final say as far as the proposals for a Danish governmental position are concerned. In a few incidences, a controversial or very important EU proposal is also discussed in the government's Committees for Coordination (*Koordinationsudvalg*) or Economics (*Økonomiudvalg*). As mentioned, afterwards, a so-called 'framework paper' (*rammenotat*) is prepared by the sectoral ministry based on inputs from other ministries and (when relevant) interest organizations. The framework paper establishes a detailed governmental position approximately 4 to 6 weeks after a proposal was sent to the ministry. This paper provides the guidelines for negotiations in the working groups in Brussels, and the relevant special committee always (at least tacitly) accepts it. As for the content, it corresponds to the so-called 'document with an annotated agenda' (*kommenteret dagsorden*) prepared approximately 1.5 weeks before the meeting in the Council. In this document, all items on the agenda of the meeting in the Council are discussed. The 'document with an annotated agenda' differs not least from a 'framework paper' by having a sentence stating that it is recommended that Denmark works for 'x' or endorses 'y' at the end of each point on the agenda (Nedergaard 2014: 208). This document also constitutes the basis for the minister's presentation in the meetings in the EAC.

Before the ministers meet in the EAC, there is a meeting in the EU Committee under the auspices of the MFA, with the involvement of mid-ranking to high-ranking civil servants from sectoral ministries at the level of chief consultant, head of division, or head of department. This step of coordination always takes place on Tuesdays, approximately one week before the meeting in the relevant EU Council. It is an important policing step by the MFA in accordance with the EU coordination doctrine in order to safeguard inputs from other ministries, but these inputs normally only consist of a few sentences to be included in the final document of the sectoral ministry before their minister has to meet his or her colleagues in Brussels (Jensen 2014).

It is very seldom that recommendations from the special committee are changed later in the EU coordination process in Denmark. According to investigations by Nedergaard (2005) and interviewees from the MFA, more than 95 per cent of the recommendations from the special committee in the 'document with an annotated agenda' are kept intact, around 4 per cent are changed by the EU Committee, and less than 1 per cent (normally only one or two cases per year) are changed by government ministers in the internal EU procedure of the government after the meeting in the EU Committee. One reason is that recommendations from the special committee normally represent balanced compromises. Another reason is an administrative consensus culture where conflicts are 'avoided' (Nedergaard 2014: 209). In the very few instances where there are still unsolved problems after the meeting in the EU Committee, either the permanent secretaries or the ministers will get in touch via telephone in order to find a solution to a possible disagreement.

Whereas the special committees correspond to the working groups of the Council, the EU Committee is comparable to Coreper, cf. Figure 13.1. The EU Committee is a horizontal problem-solving committee that performs four key functions. First, the EU Committee assesses the quality of the work in the special committees in form of the 'document with an annotated agenda'. Second, the EU Committee examines whether the special committee has taken a complete approach in its scrutiny that corresponds to the government's overall EU strategy and political priorities in general. In addition, in accordance with the doctrine of Danish EU coordination, the MFA also reminds the ministries to act in accordance with the parliamentary majority and to secure that there is no majority against the government's positon in the EAC. Third, the EU Committee makes it possible for all involved ministers to follow cases within other ministries' jurisdictions that might have a spillover effect. Fourth, the EU Committee functions as a

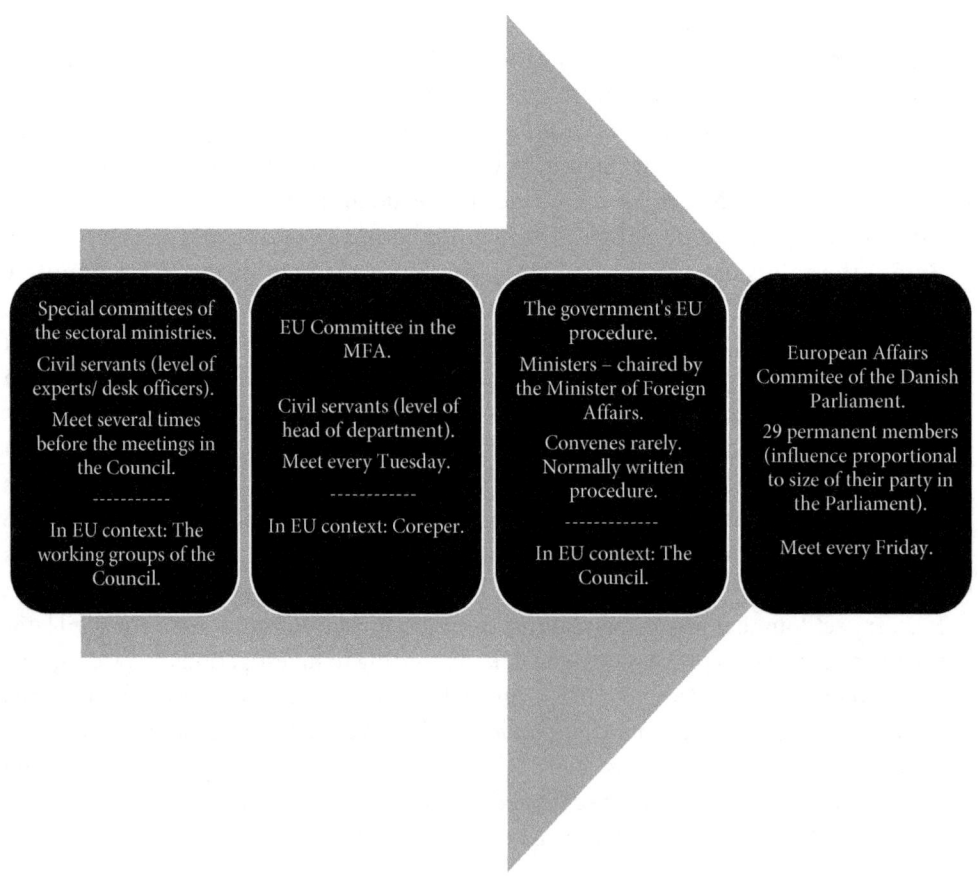

FIGURE 13.1 The system of Danish EU coordination.

problem solver concerning critical aspects that could not be resolved in the special committees. This would typically be cases where two or more sectoral ministries could not reach an agreement. In such cases, and in accordance with the EU coordination doctrine, the president of the EU Committee from the MFA will often take the role of broker to secure a compromise, and a representative from the Prime Minister's Office will also be present, which serves like a shadow of hierarchy. Generally, the Danish EU coordination system can be characterized as a 'police patrol' system, with the MFA assuming the policing role in order to ensure that the EU coordination doctrine is followed. The anticipation is that the sectoral ministries will act according to the norm of being obedient citizens. Only where they do not 'toe the line' does the MFA step in (Nedergaard 2005: 415–20; Pedersen 2000: 226).

In principle, the coordination at the level of government ministers after the EU Committee meeting in the government's internal EU procedure is executed before the meetings in the EAC of the Parliament. The government's internal EU procedure represents the highest level in the inter-ministerial EU coordination system, with the formal legitimacy to sanction the government's position before the meeting of the Council. When ministers meet in the government's internal EU procedure, they do so on Thursdays, i.e. two days after the meetings in the EU Committee and the day before the meeting of the Parliament's EAC on Friday. In practice, however, the Foreign Affairs Committee convenes only very rarely and cases are normally handled by written procedure. Through this procedure, government coalition partners can also oversee what is taking place in the ministries as far as EU coordination is concerned. Besides sanctioning the government's policy position before a meeting in the Council, there are also EU cases that are treated independently by the government's Committees for Coordination (*Koordinationsudvalget*), Economics (*Økonomiudvalget*), and Implementation (*Implementeringsudvalget*). Examples are adaption of general Danish policy guidelines for solving EU budgetary problems, reforming the CAP, planning an upcoming Danish EU Presidency, and Treaty infringement actions underway in the Commission towards Denmark (Nedergaard 2014: 210–11).

After the government's internal EU procedure, the next phase in the Danish EU coordination chain is the EAC of Parliament. The main purpose of the EAC is to conduct democratic control with the government and ensure that there is not a majority in Parliament against the government's negotiation position in Brussels. It is the MFA's task to handle all communication (also from sectoral ministries) with the Parliament's EAC. Most items on the meeting agenda in the Council are presented in the EAC, though some technical decisions may be omitted. Eight days prior to an EAC meeting, the government submits the agendas to the EAC for the upcoming meetings of the Council as well as summary memoranda on all items on the Council meeting agendas. On the Friday before the meetings in the Council, the relevant ministers will go to the EAC and orally present the negotiation position on all EU proposals on the Council agenda that the government considers to be of major significance. These are automatically considered approved if there is not a majority expressing itself against the proposal at the meeting. The EAC consists of 29 members distributed among the political parties in accordance with their respective strength in Parliament. When counting the votes in the EAC, the spokesperson of each political party carries a voting weight reflecting the party's strength in the Chamber. In principle, a government that enjoys the support of a majority in the Parliament also has the backing of a majority in the EAC (Nedergaard 2014: 211). However, when it comes to EU coordination, the support of the government's position normally comes from a group of centre-oriented political parties across the aisle between the 'red' bloc (centre-left) and 'blue' bloc (centre-right) parties. Even though ministers are only obliged to secure a mandate from the EAC on proposals of major significance before they can vote in Brussels, they will normally play it safe and seek to obtain a mandate if they are in doubt about whether it is necessary (Jensen 2014).

Meetings of the EAC may take up to five or six hours as different ministers appear before the Committee to present cases and obtain mandates. However, on average they take 2–2.5 hours. Before the presentation of the proposed negotiation position, the responsible minister or his or her officials will normally have contacted the parties supporting the EU proposal in the opposition to secure backing for the required mandates. In spite of this, things can happen at the meeting that leaves the minister without a mandate.

In most cases, however, the minister will get the proposed negotiation position approved by the EAC—sometimes with minor modifications in the Danish position. A minister fails to get approval for the negotiating position when the EAC considers itself misinformed or mistreated/not accommodated by the minister. This sometimes happens when the government's own committees have handled a case, which sometimes leaves the minister attending the EAC with very little room for flexibility. In most cases, however, the minister will have anticipated the reaction of the EAC. The negotiation positions are largely formulated so they secure considerable room for manoeuvre for the Danish minister in the Council. The flexibility of the mandate given by the Committee depends on whether a case is politicized.

In the aftermath of the Lisbon Treaty and national parliaments' new role in scrutinizing whether or not the subsidiary principle is observed by the EU institutions, the Danish Parliament has strengthened the secretarial support to the EAC and the sectoral committees of Parliament which decide to become more actively involved in EU matters. However, as long as the exclusive power of giving mandates to the government lies with the EAC, other committees of Parliament are discouraged from engaging more in EU matters (Nedergaard 2014).

The Evaluative Perspective: The Weaknesses and Strengths of the Danish EU Coordination System

In contrast to other coordination systems, the Danish one has not been subject to considerable academic debate in terms of its merits. However, based on direct information and the studies that do evaluate the Danish coordination system, it is possible to identify a range of weaknesses and strengths.

One fundamental weakness in the coordination system is its bureaucratic nature, which requires considerable coordination to establish and approve a negotiation position. This causes some major problems as outlined in the following. The comprehensive coordination along the line of the Danish EU coordination doctrine sometimes limits the possibility of realizing Danish interests due to a lack of tactical room for manoeuvring in the Council. When negotiating with the Council, it is important to give the impression that one can be convinced to vote for the proposal, as the Presidency and the Commission have an incentive to accommodate one's wishes. In contrast, if it is clear from the outset that a member state intends to vote against a proposal, it is likely that the compromise will move away from the position of that member state as qualified majority voting must be created with other member states.

In addition, there is a tendency of 'tunnel vision' in the Danish coordination process as the system is calibrated to focus on cases on the agenda of the Parliament's EAC in the nearest future, and thereby, the system tends to neglect cases further away in the time horizon (Jensen et al. 2016). The problem of 'tunnel vision' has a systemic nature because the coordination system is built around the EAC's approval of the government's negotiation positions. This is the focal point of most activities in the Danish coordination system. However, it is also important for member states to be proactive by influencing proposals before they appear on the formal agenda in Brussels to secure that the Commission proposal is as close as possible to the member states' preferred policy. The bureaucratic nature of the coordination system occupies many resources as it is estimated that the overwhelming part of all work concerning EU affairs focuses on domestic EU coordination. Had the system been less bureaucratic, some of these resources could have been used to cultivate Danish interests in Brussels or focus on long-term interests in the EU (Jensen 2014). In this respect, the EU coordination doctrine is a hindrance for other and more 'proactive' EU activities. In spite of this, Danish civil servants from all ministries do try to promote Danish interests at an early stage through the distribution of non-papers, position papers, and through the formation of alliances with 'like-minded' member states before the final decision-making on the Council (Nedergaard 2007).

Generally, the Danish EU coordination system suffers from several weaknesses concerning parliamentary coordination (Nedergaard 2005: 428–32). First, the EAC becomes overloaded because it has not delegated tasks to the other parliamentary committees. A member of the EAC must scrutinize a large number of cases which, *ceteris paribus*, limits the thoroughness with which each case can be processed, and thereby, the effect of parliamentary control (Christensen 2003: 84). Second, problems exist concerning the quantity and quality of information given by the government to the EAC. More precisely, the Committee has complained about being over-informed in some cases, whereas it is under-informed in others (Nedergaard 2014: 214). Third, the question of the timing of the Committee's involvement has been a recurring point of dispute between Parliament and the government. The EAC has argued that it is often involved too late in the Brussels negotiations, giving it no possibility to exercise influence even though so-called 'basic memorandums' are send to the committee on a regular basis (see above).

The problems, as described in the diachronic analysis, have been dealt with by changing the time and information demands of the government. Seen in a democratic perspective, one can argue that the discussion reflects a natural tension between the legislative and the executive branch in the political system. On the one hand, the Parliament has an interest in securing the greatest possible influence in the coordination process, whereas on the other hand, the government has an interest in maintaining as much room as possible for political manoeuvre for as long as possible. In short, it is an eternal tension between political legitimacy and effectiveness. However, this tension extracts resources from the coordination system that could otherwise be useful in promoting Danish interests (Nedergaard 1995), even though attempts are being increasingly taken to carry out this promotion.

The Danish EU coordination system also has several strengths. In relation to the domestic scene and following the EU coordination doctrine of 1973, the system facilitates an open and pluralistic process in which many actors are involved, helping to reduce conflicts. It is difficult to exclude interests as the system is open at the bottom through (most of) the special committees and at the top by approaching members of Parliament. The comprehensiveness of the system ensures that the Danish government has one position, and it is likely to be consistent over time and sectors.

A second advantage is that the system makes it possible to identify and solve problems in advance. One of the explanations for why Denmark is at the top concerning implementation of EU legislation is that a wide range of actors are involved before decisions are made in Brussels, facilitating support (Bursens 2002). Generally, it secures acceptance of proposals that must be implemented because all of the important actors have been involved in the prior coordination process.

Seen from an efficiency perspective, the EAC's comparatively strong role in the coordination system sometimes reduces the government's freedom to manoeuvre, thereby impeding the representation of Danish interests. However, it also ensures that Danish negotiators have a strong democratic mandate in Brussels. In some international negotiations, it can sometimes even be an advantage to have tied hands (Putnam 1988). The coordination system also forces the civil servants and the ministers to acquaint themselves with the cases on the agenda of the Council, which may rearm them as negotiators because they have in-depth knowledge of the subject.

Concerning the Council, the coordination system ensures that Denmark, in contrast to some other member states, speaks with one voice relatively early in the negotiations, which has three advantages. First, it makes it possible for Danish negotiators to exercise influence early on in the negotiation process as they put forward the Danish position. Second, the system secures that the negotiators appear to have a high degree of credibility in the eyes of other delegations as they can be sure that the position presented is the official Danish position and will not be reversed. Third, as mentioned, the Danish EU coordination system is part of the explanation for a high score when it comes to implementation of EU legislation in Denmark.

THE COMPARATIVE PERSPECTIVE: CONTRASTING EU COORDINATION IN DENMARK WITH OTHER MEMBER STATES

Having explored the Danish EU coordination diachronically, synchronically, and evaluated its weaknesses as well as strengths, the last part of the chapter examines how it compares to the systems of other member states. Traditionally, Denmark is regarded as a typical example of a member state belonging to the centralized camp, as are France, the UK, the Netherlands, Poland, Belgium, and Spain. On the other hand, member states such as Germany, Italy, Luxembourg, Ireland, Austria, Greece, and Portugal are seen as member states with a decentralized EU coordination system based on ad hoc meetings between the involved ministries (Nedergaard 2014: 204).

According to Kassim's (2003a) classical typology, Denmark has a centralized, comprehensive EU coordination system like the UK and France. Such systems are characterized by having a central coordinator responsible for the coordination process and for establishing positions on all cases under negotiation. These systems stand in contrast to decentralized systems like that of Germany where the central coordinator cannot enforce consistency across polices and to a selective system like that of Greece which only develops positions for proposals of strategic interest to the country.

Using principal component analysis and cluster analysis, Jensen (2017) classifies the Danish system as unicentric as it is characterized by a formalized coordination process, a central coordinator in terms of the MFA, a coordination ambition of developing negotiation positions on all cases, and a governmental committee system to solve problems as well as secure coherence. The classification of Denmark as a centralized or unicentric coordination system might seem to contradict the diachronic analysis which demonstrated how the balance has tipped from the MFA in favour of the sectoral ministries over time. However, a similar tendency has happened in systems like that of Germany which were decentralized from the outset, concurrent with the widening of European policy areas and the sectoral ministries learning to play the Brussels game. Thus, despite the centrifugal forces, the Danish coordination system is, in comparative terms, still centralized/unicentric due to formalized structures and processes that secure clear and consistent positions on all negotiated proposals. The EU coordination doctrine from 1973 still applies.

While the questions of how centralized the system is and how many cases it develops positions on are key, there are also other important dimensions to be considered. First, one can distinguish between systems that are proactive by trying to influence a wide set of EU institutions versus systems that are reactive by focusing on the Council. As already hinted at, Denmark belongs to the category of reactive systems (even though attempts have been made to do more promotion), which stands in contrast to the systems of France, the Netherlands, and Sweden. These last member states target several institutions at the European level and try to be pacesetting regarding shaping European integration (Jensen et al. 2016; Jensen 2017).

Another distinction can be drawn between systems where the coordination process is politicized by including actors such as ministers, parliamentarians, and lobbyists versus systems that are depoliticized where the process of developing negotiation positions mainly involves civil servants (Jensen 2017). Here, Denmark belongs to the cluster of politicized coordination systems, which is unsurprising given the considerable involvement of the Parliament and interest groups when it comes to defining national interests. In member states such as Portugal, Spain, and Sweden, the coordination process is perceived to be more bureaucratic. Third, one can try to group coordination systems according to how well they are perceived to perform. Here, Denmark is placed among the high efficacy systems as positions usually are developed on time clearly and consistently, and reflect Council negotiations as well as domestic concerns (Jensen 2017).

CONCLUSION

The purpose of this chapter has been to examine the Danish coordination system from four different perspectives. The *diachronic perspective* mapped the evolution of the Danish coordination system from the outset of European integration in the 1950s to 2019 where the system changed by becoming more decentralized, parliamentarized and transnationalized. However, the core principles 'coordinated, coincident, and cooperative' have remained intact despite significant changes. The *synchronic perspective* outlined the organizational structures in terms of a pyramid of committees mirroring the Council that constitute the system as a whole. It also illuminated a highly formalized process, in which a number of notes must be prepared on an ongoing basis, not least in order to satisfy the Parliament's EAC wish to be involved. The *evaluative perspective* discussed the weaknesses of the system in terms of constrained tactical room, tunnel vision, and parliamentary overload and strengths such as a pluralistic process, pre-emption of problems, consistency, and legitimacy. The system's *modus operandi* is a function of a natural tension between the government and the Parliament, which partially reflects the balance between efficiency versus legitimacy. The *comparative perspective* contrasted the features of the Danish coordination system with other member states, highlighting that Denmark has a unicentric system with central coordination in terms of the MFA and an ambition of developing positions on all cases, that the coordination process is politicized by involving actors from the Parliament and interest groups, and that the system is highly effective by delivering clear and consistent positions on time. By and large, the Danish EU coordination system is a reflection of the Danish political system in which it is embedded.

ACKNOWLEDGEMENT

We acknowledge the highly qualified comments we have received from experts in the MFA and from the EU secretariat of the Danish Parliament (Morten Knudsen and Iben Tybjærg Schacke-Barfoed).

NOTE

1. This chapter draws on Jensen (2011, 2014) and Nedergaard (2005, 2014), among others.

REFERENCES

Auken, Svend, Jacob Buksti, and Carsten L. Sørensen (1975). 'Denmark joins Europe: Patterns of adaption in the Danish political and administrative processes as a result of membership of the European communities', *Journal of Common Market Studies*, 14/1: 1–36.

Beach, Derek (2020). 'Referendums in Denmark. Influence on politics', in Peter M. Christiansen, Jørgen Elklit, and Peter Nedergaard, eds, *The Oxford Handbook of Danish Politics*. Oxford: Oxford University Press, 400–416.

Bursens, Peter (2002). 'State structures', in Paolo Graziano and Maarten P. Vink, eds, *Europeanization—New Research Agendas*. Basingstoke: Palgrave, 115–27.

Christensen, Jørgen G. (2003). 'Den fleksible og robuste forvaltning', in Martin Marcussen and Karsten Ronit, eds, *Internationalisering af den offentlige forvaltning i Danmark. Forandring og kontinuitet*. Aarhus: Aarhus University Press, 57–94.

Christiansen, Peter M. (2020). 'Corporatism. Exaggerated death rumours?', in Peter M. Christiansen, Jørgen Elklit, and Peter Nedergaard, eds, *The Oxford Handbook of Danish Politics*. Oxford: Oxford University Press, 160–176.

Dimitrova, Antoaneta, and Dimeter Toshkov (2007). 'The dynamics of domestic coordination of EU policy in new member states: Impossible to lock in?', *West European Politics*, 30/5: 961–85.

Dosenrode, Søren (1993). 'Danmarks administrative tilpasning til EF', *Nordisk Administrativt Tidsskrift*, 74/4: 454–65.

Esmark, Anders (2002). *At forvalte Europa: den danske centraladministrations omstilling til det europæiske samarbejde*. Copenhagen: Københavns Universitet.

Folketingstidende (n.d.). 1973–1974 Tillæg A: 986

Gärner, Laura, Julian Hörner, and Lukas Obholzer (2011). 'National coordination of EU policy: A comparative study of the twelve "new" member states', *Journal of Contemporary European Research*, 7/1: 77–100.

Hayes-Renshaw, Fiona, Wim van Aken and Helen Wallace (2005). *When and Why the Council of Ministers of the EU Votes Explicitly*. European University Institute, Florence Robert Schuman Centre for Advanced Studies.

Jensen, Henrik (2003). *Europaudvalget—et udvalg i Folketinget*. Aarhus: Aarhus University Press.

Jensen, Mads D. (2011). 'A veto players' game? Comparing and explaining domestic coordination regarding the European Union in Germany and Denmark', Doctoral dissertation, Florence: European University Institute.

Jensen, Mads D. (2014). 'Markedsdiplomatiet', in Martin Marcussen and Karsten Ronit, eds, *Dansk diplomati: Klassiske træk og nye tendenser*. Copenhagen: Hans Reitzels Forlag. Samfund i forandring, 129–46.

Jensen, Mads D. (2017). 'Exploring central governments' coordination of European Union affairs', in *Public Administration*, 95/1: 249–68.

Jensen, Mads D., Mathias Jopp, and Peter Nedergaard (2016). 'Coordination of EU Policy positions in Germany and Denmark: A politics of institutional choice approach', *Journal of Contemporary European Research*, 12/2: 634–52.

Jensen, Mads D., and Dorte S. Martinsen (2015). 'Out of time? National parliaments and early decision-making in the European Union', *Government and Opposition*, 50/2: 240–70.

Jensen, Mads D., and Peter Nedergaard (2020). 'Danish European Union Policies. Sailing Between Economic Benefits and Political Sovereignty', in Peter M. Christiansen, Jørgen Elklit, and Peter Nedergaard, eds, *The Oxford Handbook of Danish Politics*. Oxford: Oxford University Press, 487–501.

Kassim, Hussein (2003a). 'Meeting the demands of EU membership: The Europeanization of national administrative systems', in Kenneth Featherstone and Claudio M. Radaelli, eds, *The Politics of Europeanization*. Oxford: Oxford University Press, 83–111.

Kassim, Hussein (2003b). 'The European administration: Between Europeanization and Domestication', in Jack Heyward and Anand Menon, eds, *Governing Europe*. Oxford: Oxford University Press: 139–61.

Kassim, Hussein, Guy Peters, and Vincent Wright (2000). *The National Co-ordination of EU Policy: The Domestic Level*. Oxford: Oxford University Press.

Larsen, Henrik (2020). 'New Directions in a Changing World Order?' in Peter M. Christiansen, Jørgen Elklit, and Peter Nedergaard, eds, *The Oxford Handbook of Danish Politics*. Oxford: Oxford University Press, 470–486.

Ministry of Foreign Affairs (1962). *Danmark og det europæiske økonomiske fællesskab*. Copenhagen.

Ministry of Foreign Affairs (1968). *Danmark og de europæiske fællesskaber*. Copenhagen.

Ministry of Foreign Affairs (1995). *Den danske EU beslutningsprocedure*. Copenhagen.

Nedergaard, Peter (1995). 'The case of Denmark', in Spyros A. Pappas, ed., *National administrative procedures for the preparation and implementation of community decisions*. Maastricht: European Institute of Public Administration, 111–32.

Nedergaard, Peter (2005). *Organiseringen af Den Europæiske Union. Bureaukrater og Institutioner: EU-forvaltningens effektivitet og legitimitet. Et dansk perspektiv*. Copenhagen: Handelshøjskolens Forlag.

Nedergaard, Peter (2006). 'Which countries learn from which? A comparative analysis of the direction of mutual learning processes within the open method of co-ordination committees of the European Union and among the Nordic countries', *Cooperation & Conflict*, 41/4: 427–47.

Nedergaard, Peter (2007). 'Blocking minorities. Networks and meaning in the opposition against the proposal for a directive on temporary work in the Council of Ministers of the European Union', *JCMS: Journal of Common Market Studies*, 45/3: 695–717.

Nedergaard, Peter (2014). 'EU coordination processes in Denmark: Change in order to pre-serve', in Lee Miles and Anders Wivel, eds, *Denmark and the European Union*. Abingdon: Routledge, 203–16.

Nedergaard, Peter, and Mads D. Jensen (2015). 'Market integration in Europe and the Nordic Countries: The ambivalent path dependency', in Anders Wivel, Peter Nedergaard, and Caroline Grøn, eds, *The Nordic Countries and the European Union: Still the Other European Community?* Abingdon: Routledge.

Pappas, Spyros A. (1995). *National Administrative Procedures for the Preparation and Implementation of Community Decisions*. Maastricht: European Institute of Public Administration.

Pedersen, Thomas (2000). 'Denmark', in Hussein Kassim, Guy Peters, Vincent Wright, eds, *The National Co-ordination of EU Policy: The Domestic Level*. Oxford: Oxford University Press.

Putnam, Robert D. (1988). 'Diplomacy and domestic politics: The logic of two-level games', *International Organization*, 42/3: 427–60.

Raunio, Tapio (2007). 'Holding governments accountable in European Affairs: Explaining cross-national variation', in Arthur Benz and Katrin Auel, eds, *The Europeanisation of Parliamentary Democracy*. London: Routledge.

Wessels, Wolfgang (1991). 'EPC after the Single European Act: Towards a European foreign policy via treaty obligations?', in Martin Holland, ed., *The Future of European Political Cooperation*. London: Palgrave Macmillan.

PART II

POLITICS

SECTION EDITOR:
PETER MUNK CHRISTIANSEN

CHAPTER 14

THE PARTY SYSTEM

Open yet Stable

CHRISTOFFER GREEN-PEDERSEN
AND KARINA KOSIARA-PEDERSEN

THE EARTHQUAKE ELECTION AND ITS LONG-TERM AFTERMATH

ON 4 December 1973, the 'earthquake election' shocked Danish politics. The established parties lost 30–50 per cent of their seats, and three new parties entered Parliament, among them the Progress Party (*Fremskridtspartiet*), which came in second after the Social Democratic Party with 15.9 per cent of the vote (Pedersen 1988). In an international perspective, the 1973 election in Denmark was also the first sign that the world of stable and even 'frozen' party landscapes was coming to an end. From that perspective, looking at the Danish party system today, one might expect that the established parties that lost so heavily 45 years ago were long gone and that the Danish party system today is very different from what it was before 1973.

Looking at the development of the Danish party system since 1973, a lot has certainly happened as new parties have come and gone, and some new parties have established themselves as central actors in the Danish party system. However, the earthquake election in 1973 was far from the beginning of the end for the established Danish parties. During the past 45 years, they have remained the central actors in the Danish party system, and this is not likely to change fundamentally in the short run.

The purpose of this chapter it to provide the essentials on the Danish party system and parties. We first present the historical foundation and development of the Danish party system. This includes a presentation of the political parties currently represented in the Danish Parliament but not covered in chapters 18–21 of this volume. Second, we depict the parties' place on the two relevant political dimensions, and third, the size of their electoral support. The last part of the chapter is dedicated to a characterization of party organizations with a focus on party membership, intra-party democracy, and party financing.

THE DANISH PARTY SYSTEM

The core of the Danish party system was established at the beginning of the twentieth century. Due to a proportional electoral system, low threshold for representation, and manageable requirements for being eligible to stand for election, the Danish party system has been rather open and supplemented with various parties over the years as a result. Nevertheless, the core of the Danish party system has been about the same for the last 100 years.

The Four Old Parties and the Historical Cleavages in the Danish Party System

The rural-urban and employer-employee cleavages are the founding cleavages of the Danish party system (Elklit 1986; Lipset and Rokkan 1967). The rural-urban cleavage originally distinguished between the left and right of Parliament: the Liberals (established in 1870 with a name change to the current *Venstre* in 1910) represented the rural interests, and the Conservatives (established as *Højre* in 1881 with a name change in 1915) represented the urban businesses.

The rural-urban divide in its historical form is long gone from the Danish party system, and for decades, the Liberals and Conservatives have competed for the position as the major mainstream centre-right party in Denmark. This competition became more pronounced when the Liberals started clearly to distance themselves from their rural/agrarian background in the 1980s (see Christiansen 2020). In 1994, the Liberal Party got more votes than the Conservatives did. The latter won between 15 per cent and 20 per cent of the vote from 1950 and until the earthquake election in 1973 where the party only gained 9.2 per cent of the vote. This left the Conservatives in a state of crisis, including a strong internal conflict between the classical conservatives and the centrist part of the party. In the end, the latter won under the leadership of Poul Schlüter who was prime minister for more than ten years from 1982. The centrist position of the Conservatives formed the basis for electoral success in the 1980s where the party peaked at 23.4 per cent of the vote in 1984, clearly making them the biggest centre-right party. Their success, however, was short-lived. The Conservatives have lost votes at most elections since and acquired only 6.6 per cent of the vote in 2019. The electoral decline of the Conservatives has led to a more distinct centre-right profile in several cases but without much electoral success. Even if they doubled their representation in 2019, this did still not bring them back to the 2007 level. Hence, they are still far from the success of the 1980s.

The industrial revolution led to the emergence of the employer-employee cleavage. The urban working class became represented by the Social Democratic Party (*Socialdemokratiet*), established in 1871 (see Mariager and Olesen 2020). The smallholders and landless became represented by the Social-Liberal Party (*Radikale Venstre*) who emerged in 1905 as a split from the Liberals, who remained the representatives of the farmers. The profile of representing the smallholders and the landless has completely disappeared from the Social Liberals today. Over the past decades, the party has increasingly become the party of the well-educated, social-cultural professionals. This is also evident from the party's ideological profile. It has pursued a centre-right position on economic-related issues, but on 'new politics' or socio-cultural issues, the party has developed a centre-left profile, similar to the Dutch D66 and UK Liberal Democrats (Close 2019). Environmental concerns in the 1980s initiated this profile, which has been enforced by the immigration issue during the last couple of decades.

This development has had implications for the party's role in the Danish party system. Historically, it has been the only party in the Danish Parliament that has been part of both the left and the right bloc. The Social Liberals have mainly supported the left bloc, i.e. Social Democratic-led governments, but from 1968 to 1971, a Social-Liberal prime minister headed a majority coalition with the Liberals and the Conservatives, and from 1982 to 1993, the Social Liberals either supported or participated in centre-right minority governments. However, since 1993, the Social Liberals have been placed in the left bloc, and the party's left-wing position on the new politics dimension makes a move towards the centre-right bloc unlikely.

The Social Democrats, the Liberals, the Conservatives, and the Social Liberals form the core of the Danish party system. These are the traditional parties in the Danish party system known as the 'four old parties'. Prior to the Second World War, various minor parties were only shortly represented. The only party with more (but not completely) permanent representation (from 1932 and onwards) was the Communist Party (*Danmarks Kommunistiske Parti*), who, due to Soviet loyalty, remained a pariah party. After the Second World War, a number of smaller parties were shortly represented, including the Justice Party (*Retsforbundet*), a Georgist 'single tax' party.

The first significant expansion of the party system beyond the four old parties was the emergence of the Socialist People's Party (*Socialistisk Folkeparti, SF*), which split from the Communists in 1959 in the wake of the Soviet invasion of Hungary and has been represented in Parliament since 1960. The party has always been a moderate left-wing party oriented towards parliamentary influence and cooperation. Already in 1966, it closely supported a Social Democratic minority government. This led to internal disagreement in the party, and six members of the parliamentary group broke out and formed the Left Socialists (*Venstresocialisterne, VS*) in 1967. The Socialist People's Party then stabilized itself as the major left-wing party in Denmark, gaining somewhere between 3.9 per cent of the vote in 1973 and 14.6 per cent in 1987. The success of the party in the 1980s was, among other things, due to a green profile in a party system without an established Green party. The next time the party moved close to power was its participation in the Social Democratic-led government from 2011 to 2014 together with the Social-Liberal Party. The government participation was hard on the party both internally and in the electoral arena, which declined to 4.2 per cent of the vote in 2015 after a high of 13 per cent in 2007. It regained some of its strength in 2019 with 7.7 of the vote, but the Socialist People's Party's government participation has paved the way for the Red-Green Alliance (*Enhedslisten*) to become a party of equal strength on the left.

The formation and representation of these various parties indicated some rumble in the Danish party system. Still, stability was the most characteristic feature of the Danish party system by the end of the 1960s. Lipset and Rokkan's freezing thesis seemed to fit the Danish case very well (Damgaard 1974).

The Development of the Danish Party System since 1973

The earthquake election of 1973 drastically altered the party system. The number of parties in Parliament doubled, and parliamentary relations changed. The Communists and the Justice Party regained representation, and three new parties entered Parliament: the Progress Party (not represented since 2000), the Centre Democrats (*Centrum Demokraterne*, not represented since 2001), and the Christian People's Party (*Kristeligt Folkeparti*, established in 1970, renamed *Kristendemokraterne*/the Christian Democrats in 2003, and not represented since 2005). The latter two centre parties played a role in government formation in the 1980s and 1990s together with the Social Liberals. While causing a dramatic change at the time, the five newly represented parties in 1973 are almost extinct today. The only one of them running for the 2019 election was the Christian Democrats.

The most significant party emerging out of the earthquake election was the Progress Party led by its charismatic and controversial leader Mogens Glistrup. He was a highly esteemed tax-lawyer who went on TV declaring that he did not pay taxes and then formed an anti-tax party. From the outset, the party was an unpredictable force in the Danish party system. It belonged to the centre-right bloc, but the other parties struggled to trust its parliamentary support. Whether or not the party could be trusted in parliamentary politics was a recurrent theme for the centre-right minority governments from 1982 to 1993. This was not least due to internal disagreements in the Progress Party that culminated in 1995, leading to a splinter and the emergence of the Danish People's Party (*Dansk Folkeparti*) and the disappearance of the Progress Party (see Kosiara-Pedersen 2020). The focus on immigration, which became the key point of the Danish People's Party, was already evident in the Progress Party in the 1980s when Glistrup started to talk about Muslim immigration as a threat to Danish society (Green-Pedersen and Krogstrup 2008).

A number of other parties stood for election without gaining stable parliamentarian representation in the 1970s and 1980s. The Communists were represented in Parliament in 1973–7, the Left Socialists (*Venstresocialisterne*) in 1968–71 and 1975–87, the left-populist Common Course (*Fælles Kurs*) briefly in 1987–8, and the Justice Party in 1973–5 and 1977–81. A number of parties never gained representation, and some gained less than 1,000 votes. This led to a tightening of the formalities required to stand for election in 1989 (Pedersen 2004).

The lack of electoral success of the left-wing parties prompted the creation of the Red-Green Alliance (*Enhedslisten*) in 1989 (Bischoff and Kosiara-Pedersen in press 2020), a merger between the Left Socialists, Communists, and Socialist Workers' Party (*Socialistisk Arbejderparti, SAP*), and represented in Parliament since 1994 (see Kölln and Seeberg 2020).

After the Turn of the Century

Three new parties have gained parliamentary representation since the turn of the century: first, the Liberal Alliance. Its predecessor was New Alliance (*Ny Alliance*), created in 2007 by MP/MEPs from the Social Liberals and Conservatives as a reaction to the government's rightward turn on the new politics dimension, in particular immigration (Kosiara-Pedersen 2019). This centre party started out with good polls, but despite losing a substantial part during the 2007 election campaign, nevertheless managed to gain representation. In 2009, two of three party founders left the party, which was renamed Liberal Alliance and took a liberal economic rightward turn. Its main focus is economic issues, and it is the most right-wing party on the redistributive, socio-economic left-right dimension. It increased its electoral support at the first three elections in 2007–15 but had a devastating result in 2019 where it barely surpassed the electoral threshold, and the party leader was not re-elected.

Secondly, the Alternative (*Alternativet*) was created in 2013 by a former Social Liberal. The party's overall political agenda is environmental concern, and while the party wants to break up the traditional political dimensions and transform political culture, the party is nevertheless placed towards the left both on the redistributive and libertarian dimension (Kosiara-Pedersen and Kurrild-Klitgaard 2018). The party launched itself as a 'grassroots party' practicing new forms of political participation and engagement (Husted and Plesner 2017), but its formal structure is not very different from the established parties. The party entered Parliament with 4.8 per cent of the vote in 2015 but lost a third in 2019, even though climate issues were high on the political agenda.

The third addition to the Danish party system is recent, namely at the 2019 election. The New Right (*Nye Borgerlige*) was founded in 2015 by two former Conservatives. It surpassed the electoral threshold with 2.4 per cent of the vote on a platform focusing mainly on stopping immigration and integration. On the left-right dimension, its economic programme places it to the right; hence, it is a right-wing party on both dimension as the Progress Party was in the 1980s.

Compared to other European party systems, the Danish party system seems less fragmented and volatile than some countries, but the Danish party system has still seen significant change (Lisi 2019). New parties seem to be more successful when internally created, i.e. by MPs (cf. Duverger 1954), even though this is not without exceptions as externally created parties have also been successful at times (Progress Party and Red-Green Alliance) where internally created parties have not (Centre Democrats). Secondly, while the renewal of the party system in the 1970s took place both at the centre and peripheries of the left-right dimension, more recent successful newcomers place themselves towards the extremes of either of the two relevant political dimensions: the two political dimensions to which we now turn.

The Political Dimensions of the Current Danish Party System

Since the mid-1990s, electoral research has identified two political dimensions in the Danish political system. Besides the traditional economic left-right conflict, a 'new politics' dimension emerged among voters (Borre and Goul Andersen 1997). The new politics dimension has also become important at the party level, but the Danish party system has only become two-dimensional to some extent. The importance of the left and right blocs when it comes to government formation as well as cooperation patterns in Parliament show that the Danish party system is still fundamentally, one dimensionally left-right. This is also how voters place the parties (Hjorth 2017). Hence, rather than two dimensionality, a better description is probably that the meaning of left and right has been re-interpreted to include new politics issues such as immigration and the environment. However, the issues are only partly integrated, and this challenges the internal coherence of the two blocs. In addition, there is some movement away from the aligning trend.

Looking at Figure 14.1, which shows party positions based on the 2014 version of the Chapel Hill Expert Survey (Polk et al. 2017), party positions on the two dimensions generally follow each other. The centre-left parties the Red-Green Alliance, Socialist People's Party, and the Social Democrats are, for instance, to the left of the Danish People's Party, the Liberals, and the Conservatives on both dimensions. However, there are also deviations that challenge the blocs. The Danish People's Party has moved to the left on the economic dimension and is now to the left of the Social Liberals. Even though Danish People's Party has provided the parliamentary support for the Liberal-led governments from 2015 to 2019, they have cooperated with the left bloc on welfare related questions on several occasions. In 2011, the Social Liberals also passed several welfare state reforms together with the centre-right bloc. The relative centre-right position of the Social Democrats on immigration is also a constant threat to the internal cohesion of the centre-left bloc.[1]

Thus, the right and left blocs remain the basic organizing principle of the Danish party system, but both are struggling with internal cohesion. It is also worth stressing that the dynamics are quite issue specific. While, for instance, the left bloc is struggling with internal cohesion on immigration due to the centre-right position of the Social

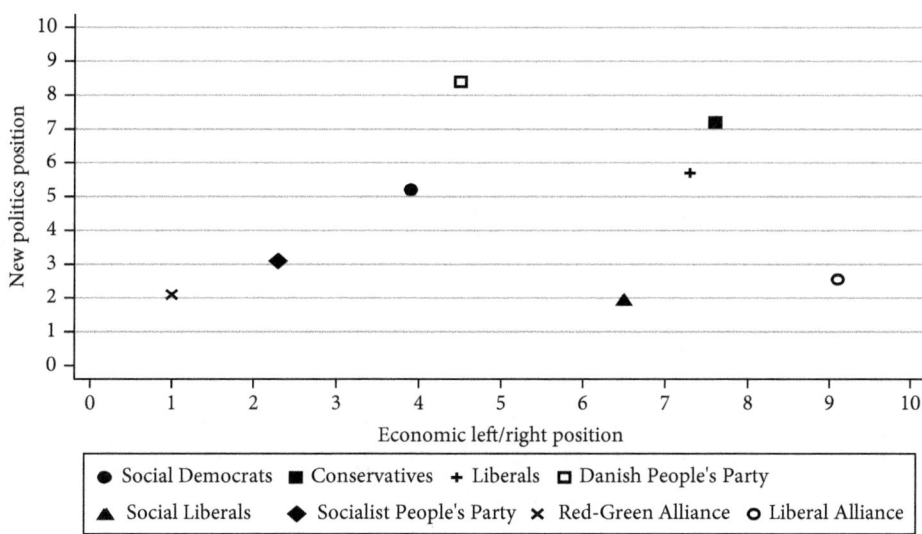

FIGURE 14.1 Party positions on the economic left-right and new politics dimensions 2014.

Note: Based on the 2014 Chapel Hill Expert Survey (Polk et al. 2017)

Democrats on this issue, the centre-left bloc is strongly united on the environment. This issue is more or less integrated with the economic left-right dimension.

European integration is an issue on its own in Danish politics. Party positions on this issue follow the U-shape identified in other countries with EU scepticism on the far left (Red Green Alliance) and the far right (Danish People's Party) (see Seeberg and Kölln 2020; Kosiara-Pedersen 2020). Thus, if a second new politics dimension distinct from the left-right dimension exists in the Danish party system, it is in reality a single-issue dimension relating to immigration. This issue, however, also plays a very central role in Danish party politics, particularly in a comparative perspective (Green-Pedersen 2014; Green-Pedersen and Otjes 2019).

ELECTORAL SUPPORT

A related aspect to the increasing internal conflicts within the blocs is the gradual weakening of the four old parties. They still make up the nucleus of the Danish party system; however, it is a shrinking nucleus. Figure 14.2 shows the electoral support of the parties represented in Parliament after the 2019 election in the 1971–2019 period.

The four old parties (the four lowest fields) were supported by 84 per cent of the voters in 1971. This decreased drastically to less than 60 per cent in the 1973 earthquake election. From then, these four old parties experienced ups and downs, with a peak (77.5 per cent) in 1994 and a downward trend from then on. Their lowest level was at just above half (54 per cent) in the 2015 election, while they regained lost ground in 2019 and acquired 64.5 per cent of the vote. The year 2019 was definitely a strengthening of the traditional

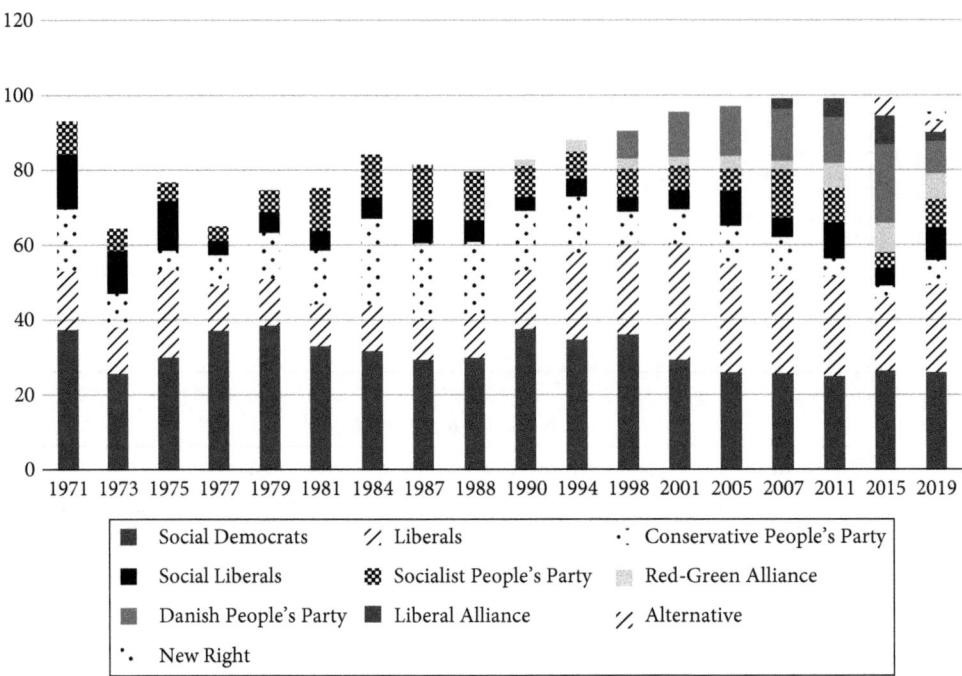

FIGURE 14.2 Electoral support of parliamentary parties as of 2019.

core of the Danish party system. The totals of Figure 14.2 indicate the extent to which the Danish party system has been renewed. While the four old parties, together with the Socialist People's Party, got 93 per cent of the vote in 1971, they lay lower at somewhere between two in three or four in five votes in the 1970s and 1980s.

The Red-Green Alliance's 1.7 per cent in 1990 did not get them any seats in Parliament. However, they were added to the system in 1994, and they have grown substantially more recently. Due to their more left-wing place on the left-right scale, they have extended the Danish political spectrum further than what is seen in other Nordic countries (Hansen and Kosiara-Pedersen 2017). The Danish People's Party was added to the system in 1998 and has been as highly successful as the other Nordic, so-called 'populist right' parties (Hansen and Kosiara-Pedersen 2017).

The effective number of parties (Laakso and Taagepera 1979) is also increasing. In the 1998–2019 period, the effective number of parties in the electoral arena—including the Parliament elected in 2019—has increased from slightly under 5 to 6.5. In the parliamentary arena, it is 5.9. The increase is partly due to new parties and partly due to the parties being more equal in size, as can be seen in Figure 14.2.

To sum up, the Danish party system today is a mix of old and new. The old is the dominance of the four old parties based on their division on the economic left-right between the centre-left bloc (the Social Democrats and the Social Liberals) and the centre-right bloc (the Liberals and the Conservatives). The new is the emergence of new parties and party positions having elements of two dimensionality. However, the new dimension is best understood as complementary to the old one rather than a replacement of it or an independent dimension.

PARTY ORGANIZATIONS

Political parties are not mentioned in the Constitution and remained unregulated until public party funding was introduced (Bille 1994). Hence, they have been free to organize within the limits set by the (proportional) electoral system and administrative system. This section briefly presents the three most important aspects of party organizations, namely party membership, intra-party democracy, and party financing.

Party Membership

There is a long and strong tradition for organizing party members in Denmark, which is one of the few countries that had well-established, democratic, membership-based parties on both sides of the left-right ideological spectrum prior to the Second World War (Scarrow 2000: 93). However, they flourished, as did other West European parties in the decades following the Second World War, where they enrolled more than a quarter of the electorate (Kosiara-Pedersen 2015). Since then, the trend has been downwards, falling drastically until 1980 and more moderately since then. Danish parties enrol around 135,000 members—less than 4 per cent of the electorate, which is just above the average across Europe (van Biezen et al. 2012; van Haute et al. 2018) yet below the figures in the other Nordic countries (Hansen and Kosiara-Pedersen 2017).

Figure 14.3 shows the trend in aggregate membership figures and member/electorate ratio, which is a meaningful depiction of the trends among the four old parties. Newer parties have not been able to make up for the membership loss of the old parties. With the exception of the Danish People's Party and the Socialist People's Party, both of whom have peaked at 15,000 members for a short while, all new parties lie below 10,000 members. Hence, when these parties experience upward and downward trends, as they have since 2000, this matters to these parties but does not affect the aggregate figures.

Tuning in on the development in parties' membership figures since 2000, Figure 14.4 shows that the trends vary across parties. The Liberals, the Social Democrats, and the Conservatives are leaking members. However, not all the other parties are. Instead, three different patterns may be identified. The Red-Green Alliance and the Danish People's Party climb upwards either at a steady pace (the latter), or first slowly and then faster (the former). The second pattern identified is that of the Liberal Alliance and the Alternative. These two parties increased membership figures when formed and then more or less remained at that level. The third pattern is the rollercoaster rides of the Social Liberals and the Socialist People's Party, peaking before or after the 2007 election as well as in 2011. In sum, besides the two largest parties (Social Democrats and the Liberals)

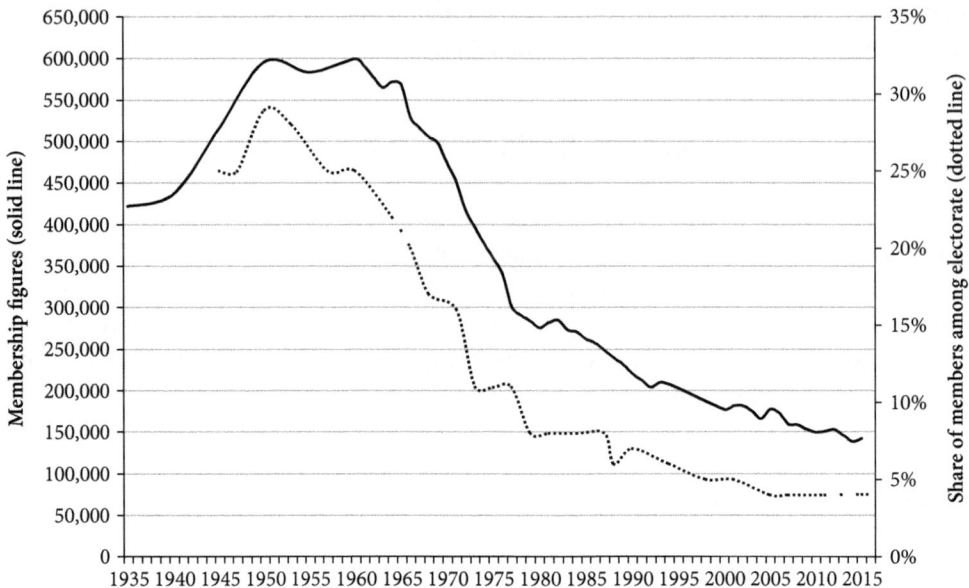

FIGURE 14.3 Danish party membership figures and member/electorate ratios.

Note: Membership figures have been collected over time by Lars Bille and Karina Kosiara-Pedersen, and they are available at www.projectmapp.eu/databases/

with 34,000 and 40,000 members, many parties have around 10,000 members, some less (Social Liberals and Liberal Alliance) and some slightly more (Danish People's Party).

Intra-Party Democracy

Danish party organizations have traits from the mass, catch-all, and cartel party types (Bille 1997). Even new parties formally tend to organize themselves similar to the established parties, including a hierarchical party organization with branches, an annual meeting as the formal highest authority, and statutes granting party members formal rights on important party decisions.

Candidate nomination lies at the heart of party democracy. It is the key task for parties, and it is, therefore, well regulated in all parties including the Danish parties (Bille 2001). Danish parties have an (almost) monopoly of getting candidates elected, and they are recruited in particular through membership organizations, as well as externally. However, it is not possible to bypass party member organizations since candidates need to be party members. In the majority of Danish parties, candidates are recruited and nominated at the level of the 92 nomination districts (see Elklit 2020), where party statutes grant party members the right to decide. Exceptions include the Liberal Alliance where candidates are nominated at the level of the ten electoral districts, and the Red-Green Alliance where the top ten candidates are chosen at the national congress. Danish parties have not introduced primaries or in other ways granted affiliated supporters or voters a say on candidate nomination. Since a maximum of a quarter of the party

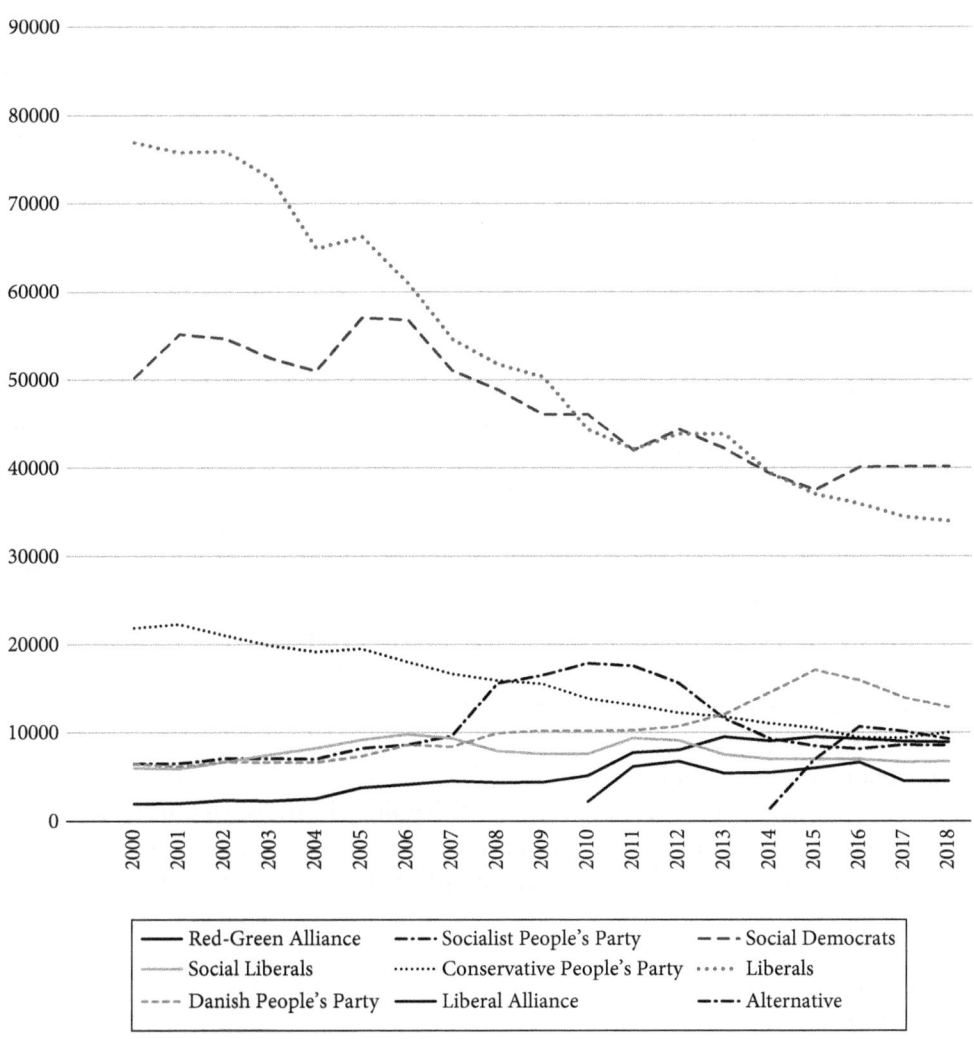

FIGURE 14.4 Danish party membership figures, 2000–2018.

Note: Membership figures are collected by Karina Kosiara-Pedersen and are available at www.projectmapp.eu/databases/

members participate in candidate nomination, this implies that no more than 1 per cent of the electorate decides on the list of candidates from which voters get to choose (Kosiara-Pedersen 2017).

While parties grant party members the formal right to provide input to the party manifesto in their statutes, and some even the right to decide at the annual national meeting/congress of the party organization, the party elites and staff de facto dominate policy development and formulation. The same largely goes for election pledges. Danish parties do not develop election manifestos as such but select a limited number of issues, and these are decided by the national party leadership.

While party members formally elect the chair of the membership organization, they do not necessarily have a say on who *the* party leader is. The most recent trend is that party members decide on the party leaders of the Socialist People's Party and the Social Democratic Party (if there is more than one candidate) through ballots. In the remaining parties, the party elite or parliamentary group decide on the party leader. The Red-Green Alliance does not have a party leader, but the parliamentary group appoints the political spokesperson who is the *de facto* party leader when compared to the other parties.

Party Financing

While the parliamentary parties have been publicly funded since 1965, public funding of party organizations came later in 1987 (Bille 1997). An amount, which drastically increased in 1995, is granted per vote at the local, regional, and national elections to the corresponding levels of the parties. Public funding for party organizations challenged the perception of parties being unregulated due to their private nature. Hence, by 1995, regulation was in place requiring both interest organizations to enable their members to opt out of (part of) their dues going to a political party, and national parties to publish their accounts. In the accounts, parties are required to name contributors who have given more than DKK 20,000 but not the amount. Since the regulation is far from watertight, this scheme does not provide transparency in party funding and is under constant discussion (White Paper 1550/2015). It was strongly criticized, for instance, by the Council of Europe in 2018 (see GRECO 2018).

The public accounts, while not including the budgets of local branches or candidates, allow for some insight into the funding of Danish political parties. Figure 14.5 shows the funding of Danish parties in 2015, which is the most recent election year for which accounts are available. First, party incomes vary from less than DKK 10 million to more

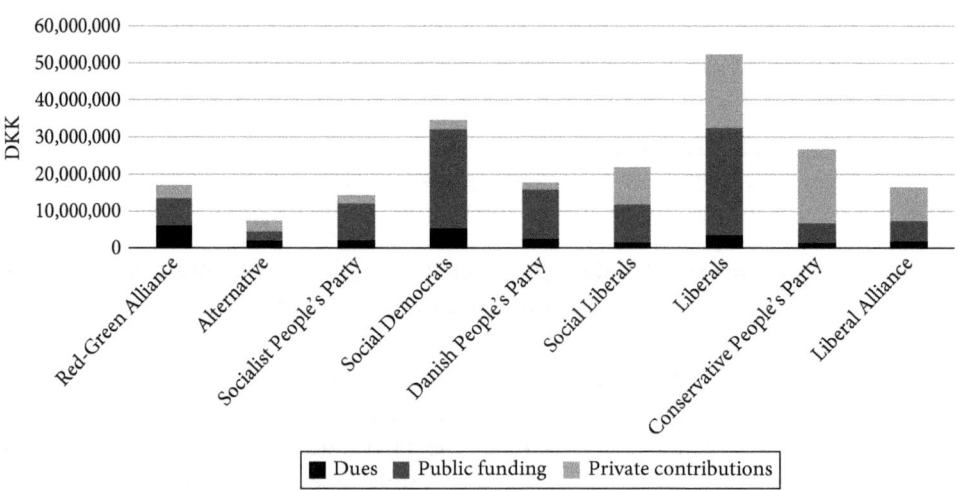

FIGURE 14.5 Danish party funding 2015.

Note: Based on parties' accounts for 2015 publicly available at www.ft.dk

than DKK 50 million. Second, parties are, to various extents, financed by party member dues, public funding, and private contributions from interest organizations and private firms. The Liberals and the Conservatives get markedly more money from private contributions (DKK 20 million), followed by the Liberal Alliance and the Social Liberals at half of that. The Social Democrats only get a little more than a tenth of the amount received by the Liberals and the Conservatives. However, the Liberals and the Social Democrats are fairly equal when it comes to public funding, receiving 29 and 27 million, respectively. The Red-Green Alliance is the only party that stands out with dues of about the same amount as public financing. In all other parties, dues make up a limited share of party income.

The composition of party income varies among parties due to their ideological foundations, historic ties, and party age. Newer parties have not been able to establish organizational and financial linkage to the same extent as that of the ties between the Social Democrats and the unions, and the Liberals and the Conservatives with the employers' organizations and businesses (Bille and Christiansen 2001). However, the old Social Liberals have never attracted this type of donors to any great extent, and the Social Democratic link to unions have faded as seen in the other Scandinavian countries (Allern et al. 2007). The Liberal Alliance was heavily funded by one private firm in their formative years.

In addition to the variation among parties, there is variation between election years and non-election years. In the former, private contributions make up a substantially larger part of party income, and the incomes are markedly higher. For example, in 2016, a non-election year, private contributions made up only 0–16 per cent of party income (except more than a third for the Conservatives). Instead, the majority of parties got most of their income from public financing. By international comparison, the means across parties in several established democracies in 2011 were 16 per cent from membership dues, 57 per cent from public funding, and 9 per cent from private sources (van Biezen and Kopecký 2017). Since these figures combine both election and non-election years, they are hard to compare. However, Danish parties are mainly publicly financed as parties elsewhere in established democracies, with the exception of centre-right parties in election years.

CONCLUSION

Political parties are the central actors in Danish politics. They structure the vote on election day, have a monopoly on getting candidates elected for national parliament, and dominate at the regional and municipal levels. They organize the work in the unicameral Danish Parliament, *Folketinget*, where party discipline is high (see Green-Pedersen and Skjæveland 2020). Knowledge about the Danish political parties and the party system is crucial for any understanding of Danish national politics.

Like many other West European countries, the current Danish party system is a mixture of old and new. The four old parties still provide the backbone of the Danish party system. For instance, Denmark is yet to see a prime minister or even a serious contender for this position not coming from any of the four old parties. The four old parties took a dip in 2015 but got almost two out of three votes in 2019. Hence, even though newer parties like the Danish People's Party and the Red-Green Alliance are now medium-sized parties in the Danish party system, the four old parties still make up the substantial core. One of the central questions for the future development of the Danish party system is how especially the Danish People's Party will behave and how this will affect the 'mechanics' of the Danish party system. Two related questions seem particularly important.

One is whether the strongly entrenched bloc structure of the Danish party system will continue. Danish political parties cooperate extensively in terms of legislative coalitions (Green-Pedersen and Skjæveland 2020), but at the same time, they are clearly entrenched in the blocs when it comes to government formation. Before the 2019 election, the Danish People's Party increasingly moved towards the centre on the economic left-right dimension. This, combined with the move to the right by the Social Democrats on issues of immigration, opened the discussion to whether the Danish People's party was becoming the pivotal player in the Danish party system with the possibility of supporting both centre-left and centre-right governments. This was something the party itself mentioned as a strategic aim. This would imply a major change in the 'mechanics' of the Danish party system. However, with the exception of the Social Democrats, the other parties in the centre-left bloc have been averse to cooperation with the Danish People's Party due to the immigration policies it pursues. The brutal defeat of the Danish People's Party at the 2019 election where it declined from 21.1 per cent of the vote to 8.7 per cent could also be seen as an indication that the electorate was not happy about this strategy.

The second question relates to government participation of new parties. Perhaps due to the rough time in government that the Socialist People's Party experienced when they entered government for the first time in 2011, the Danish People's Party has been reluctant to enter government. This was especially an issue discussed after the 2015 election where the party was the largest centre-right party. The elaborate Danish tradition for minority governments implies great flexibility in terms of coalition formation, but even in Denmark, a government like the Liberal government from 2015–16 based on less than 20 per cent of the seats has a very weak basis for having its bills passed (Green-Pedersen and Skjæveland 2020).

In terms of party organization, Danish political parties have also seen important changes. Party membership figures are in decline on the aggregate even though several parties have experienced surges. Danish parties grant their members a formal say on key party decisions; however, *de facto,* there is a high degree of centralization. While the backbone of the formal structure of Danish parties has many traits from the mass parties, Danish parties largely take on the characteristics of cartel parties: declining numbers of members primarily provide legitimacy, candidates, and limited participation, and party financing comes from the public purse. What is more remarkable is that the new and the old parties look quite alike in terms of party organization where the variance across parties has declined. For instance, centre-left parties have largely transferred power from the party on the ground to the party in Parliament.

In sum, the earthquake election in 1973 transformed the Danish party system, but the aftermath brought less dramatic changes. Party organizations have changed less, party membership is in decline, and parties are increasingly financed primarily by the public. However, parties have not opened up candidate nomination to non-members or facilitated formal affiliation through other means than party membership. While the system has adapted to current political trends, party organizations seem to lag behind.

Note

1. 'New Right' (*Nye Borgerlige*), the latest addition to the Danish party system, has not yet been included in the Chapel Hill Expert Survey.

References

Allern, Elin H., Nicholas Aylott, and Flemming J. Christiansen (2007). 'Social Democrats and trade unions in Scandinavia: The decline and persistence of institutional relationships', *European Journal of Political Research*, 46/5: 607–35.

van Biezen, Ingrid, and Petr Kopecký (2017). 'The paradox of party funding. The limited impact of state subsidies on party membership', in Susan E. Scarrow, Paul D. Webb, and Thomas Poguntke, eds, *Organizing Political Parties. Representation, Participation, and Power*. Oxford: Oxford University Press, 84–105.

van Biezen, Ingrid, Peter Mair, and Thomas Poguntke (2012). 'Going, going,… gone? The decline of party membership in contemporary Europe', *European Journal of Political Research*, 51/1: 24–56.

Bille, Lars (1994). 'Denmark: The decline of the membership party?', in Richard S. Katz and Peter Mair, eds, *How Parties Organize*. London: Sage Publications, 134–57.

Bille, Lars (1997). *Partier i forandring*. Odense: University Press of Southern Denmark.

Bille, Lars (2001). 'Democratizing a democratic procedure: Myth or reality? Candidate selection in Western European parties, 1960–1990', *Party Politics*, 7/3: 363–80.

Bille, Lars, and Flemming J. Christiansen (2001). 'Partier og Interesseorganisationer i Danmark', in Jan Sundberg, ed., *Partier och interesseorganisationer i Norden*. Copenhagen: Nordisk Ministerråd, 29–77.

Bischoff, Carina, and Karina Kosiara-Pedersen (in press). 'Denmark: A not so radical left wing party', in Fabien Escolona, Dan Keith, and Luke March, eds, *Palgrave Handbook of Radical Left Parties in Europe*. London: Palgrave Macmillan.

Borre, Ole, and Jørgen G. Andersen (1997). *Voting and Political Attitudes in Denmark: A Study of the 1994 Election*. Aarhus: Aarhus University Press.

Christiansen, Flemming J. (2020). 'The Liberal Party. From agrarian and liberal to centre-right catch-all', in Peter M. Christiansen, Jørgen Elklit, and Peter Nedergaard, eds, *The Oxford Handbook of Danish Politics*. Oxford: Oxford University Press, 296–312.

Close, Caroline (2019). 'The Liberal party family ideology: Distinct, but diverse', in Caroline Close and Emilie van Haute, eds, *Liberal Parties in Europe*. London: Routledge.

Damgaard, Erik (1974). 'Stability and change in the Danish party system over half a century', *Scandinavian Political Studies*, 9: 103–25.

Duverger, Maurice (1954). *Political Parties*. Cambridge: Cambridge University Press.

Elklit, Jørgen (1986). 'Det klassiske danske partisystem bliver til', in Jørgen Elklit and Ole Tonsgaard, eds, *Valg og Vælgeradfærd. Studier i dansk politik*, 2 ed. Aarhus: Politica, 21–38.

Elklit, Jørgen (2020). 'The electoral system. Fair and well-functioning', in Peter M. Christiansen, Jørgen Elklit, and Peter Nedergaard, eds, *The Oxford Handbook of Danish Politics*. Oxford: Oxford University Press, 56–75.

GRECO (2018). *Third Evaluation Round Sixth Interim Compliance Report on Denmark*, https://rm.coe.int/sixth-interim-compliance-report-on-denmark-incriminations-ets-173-and-/16808b07df (accessed 19 November 2019).

Green-Pedersen, Christoffer (2014). 'Party system development in Denmark. Agenda-setting dynamics and political change', in Christoffer Green-Pedersen and Stefaan Walgrave, eds, *Agenda Setting Policies, and Political Systems. A Comparative Approach*. Chicago, IL: University of Chicago Press, 69–85.

Green-Pedersen, Christoffer, and Jesper Krogstrup (2008). 'Immigration as a political issue in Denmark and Sweden: How party competition shapes political agendas', *European Journal of Political Research*, 47/5: 610–34.

Green-Pedersen, Christoffer, and Simon Otjes (2019). 'A hot topic? Immigration on the agenda in Western Europe'. *Party Politics*, 25/3: 424–34.

Green-Pedersen, Christoffer and Asbjørn Skjæveland (2020). 'Governments in action. Consensual politics and minority governments', in Peter M. Christiansen, Jørgen Elklit, and Peter Nedergaard, eds, *The Oxford Handbook of Danish Politics*. Oxford: Oxford University Press, 230–41.

Hansen, Kasper M., and Karina Kosiara-Pedersen (2017). 'Nordic voters and party systems', in Peter Nedergaard and Anders Wivel, eds, *Routledge Handbook on Scandinavian Politics*. London: Routledge, 114–23.

van Haute, Emilie, Emilien Paulis, and Vivien Sierens (2018). 'Assessing party membership figures: The MAPP Dataset', *European Political Science Review*, 17/3: 366–77.

Hjorth, Frederik (2017). 'Issue voting ved folketingsvalget 2015', in Kasper M. Hansen and Rune Stubager, eds, *Oprør fra udkanten—Folketingsvalget 2015*. Copenhagen: Jurist- og Økonomforbundets Forlag, 207–23.

Husted, Emil, and Ursula Plesner (2017). 'Spaces of open-source politics: Physical and digital conditions for political organization', *Organization*, 24/5: 648–70.

Kosiara-Pedersen, Karina (2015). 'Party membership in Denmark: Fluctuating membership figures and organizational stability', in Emilie van Haute and Anika Gauja, eds, *Party Members and Activists*. London: Routledge, 66–83.

Kosiara-Pedersen, Karina (2017). *Demokratiets ildsjæle. Partimedlemmer i Danmark*. Copenhagen: Jurist- og Økonomforbundets Forlag.

Kosiara-Pedersen, Karina (2019). 'The Danish Liberal parties', in Caroline Close and Emilie van Haute, eds, *Liberal Parties in Europe*. London: Routledge.

Kosiara-Pedersen, Karina (2020). 'The Danish People's Party. Centre oriented populists?', in Peter M. Christiansen, Jørgen Elklit, and Peter Nedergaard, eds, *The Oxford Handbook of Danish Politics*. Oxford: Oxford University Press, 313–28.

Kosiara-Pedersen, Karina, and Peter Kurrild-Klitgaard (2018). 'Change and stability in the Danish party system', in Marco Lisi, ed., *Party System Change, the European Crisis and the State of Democracy*. London: Routledge, 63–79.

Laakso, Markku, and Rein Taagepera (1979). '"Effective" number of parties: A measure with application to West Europe', *Comparative Political Studies*, 12/1: 3–27.

Lipset, Seymour M., and Stein Rokkan (1967). 'Cleavage structures, party systems, and voter alignments: An introduction', in Seymor M. Lipset and Stein Rokkan, eds, *Party Systems and Voter Alignments*. New York: Free Press.

Lisi, Marco (2019) (ed.). *Party System Change, the European Crisis and the State of Democracy*. London: Routledge.

Mariager, Rasmus, and Niels W. Olesen (2020). 'The Social Democratic Party. From exponent of societal change to pragmativ conservatism', in Peter M. Christiansen, Jørgen Elklit, and Peter Nedergaard, eds, *The Oxford Handbook of Danish Politics*. Oxford: Oxford University Press, 278–95.

Pedersen, Karina (2004). 'From aggregation to cartel?: The Danish case', in Thomas Poguntke and Kay Lawson, eds, *How Political Parties Respond: Interest Aggregation Revisited*. London: Routledge, 86–104.

Pedersen, Mogens N. (1988). 'The defeat of all parties. The Danish Folketing election 1973', in Kay Lawson and Peter Merkl, eds, *When Parties Fail*. Princeton, NJ: Princeton University Press, 257–81.

Polk, Jonathan, Jan Rovny, Ryan Bakker, Erica Edwards, Liesbet Hooghe, Seth Jolly, et al. (2017). 'Explaining the salience of anti-elitism and reducing political corruption for political parties in Europe with the 2014 Chapel Hill Expert Survey data', *Research and Politics*, 4/1: 1–9.

Scarrow, Susan (2000). 'Parties without members? Party organization in changing electoral environment', in Russell J. Dalton and Martin P. Wattenberg, eds, *Parties without Partisans. Political Change in Advanced Industrial Democracies*. Oxford: Oxford University Press, 79–101.

Seeberg, Henrik, and Ann-Kristin Kölln, (2020). 'The Red-Green Alliance. Is it red or green?', in Peter M. Christiansen, Jørgen Elklit, and Peter Nedergaard, eds, *The Oxford Handbook of Danish Politics*. Oxford: Oxford University Press, 329–46.

White Paper (1550/2015). *Betænkning om åbenhed om økonomisk støtte til politiske partier*. Copenhagen: Ministry of Justice and Ministry for Economic Affairs and the Interior.

....

CHAPTER 15

GOVERNMENTS IN ACTION

Consensual Politics and Minority Governments

....

CHRISTOFFER GREEN-PEDERSEN
AND ASBJØRN SKJÆVELAND

ONE of the most distinct aspects of Danish politics from a comparative perspective is the prevalence of minority governments. As laid out in Hansen (2020), Denmark has only seen one majority government since 1971, and this government only lasted a year and a half from 1993 to 1994. Thus, Denmark is the country of minority governments.

Minority governments are often seen as potentially problematic (cf. Strøm 1990). They are in constant risk of being toppled by the opposition, and they have no guaranteed support for their bills. However, Danish minority governments are not frequently toppled followed by a premature election. In Denmark, the PM is free to call an election any time he or she wants, but elections have to be held after four years (Section 32 of the Constitutional Act). In most cases, the PM will call an election not because the minority government has been toppled but because the PM thinks that the timing is right in light of the requirement for an election after four years. Danish minority governments are typically also successful in terms of passing legislation, including unpopular reforms, for instance, regarding the welfare state (cf. Lee et al. 2019).

Thus, one of the most striking features of Danish politics is the success of Danish minority governments in terms of both their stability and their ability to pass legislation. In addition, Danish minority governments are typically not just 'notional' minority governments in the sense that they only come into power if they have a clear deal, often in writing (cf. Bale and Bergman 2006), with support parties promising to support government bills. The Danish Constitution (see Christensen 2020) builds on negative parliamentarism. The government cannot continue with a majority against it, but it does not need a majority that actively supports its planned policies to survive or come to power.

The purpose of this chapter is to explain this apparent success of Danish minority governments. This explanation has two parts. First, a discussion of the incentives opposition parties face in terms of cooperating with minority governments. Second, a discussion of the 'institutional structure' that has developed around cooperation among Danish parties, especially the role of 'legislative agreements' (Christiansen 2008; Christiansen and Seeberg 2016). This institution facilitates the cooperation between the government and the opposition around specific legislation.

An important implication of this explanation is further that the success of Danish minority governments is not due to a unique 'consensus culture' among Danish political parties. Even the norm that so-called responsible parties should vote in favour of the budget regardless of its content has the proviso that responsible parties can use the vote on the budget to topple a government if it is unable to muster a majority (Christiansen and Skjæveland 2016). The parties cooperate because it is rational for them within the set-up of Danish minority parliamentarism. Further, the incentive for cooperation varies across time. In certain periods, Danish minority governments have struggled to generate support in Parliament for its legislation. The 1970s after the 'earthquake' election in 1973 was the period when this was most pronounced. This was also a period of frequent elections in Denmark (every second year). However, in the last decades, inability to mobilize parliamentary support for their bills has not implied that minority governments have become unstable. Rather, they have to give up passing significant legislation. As such, success in term of passing bills is by no means a given.

Party Unity

Before discussing government and opposition dynamics around legislation, one other aspect of Danish politics is worth highlighting, namely the importance of party unity. Party unity or party cohesion is very high in Denmark, and this is why government and opposition dynamics should be analysed as a question of party behaviour and not as a question of the behaviour of individual MPs. Party unity in relation to voting on bills can be measured in a number of ways. The Rice index focusing on individual votes is frequently reported. It only includes votes in favour and votes against and scores 100 if party unity is perfect and 0 if the party is completely divided. In Denmark, for final votes on bills in 2003–4 to 2007–8, the overall Rice index was 99.7 without correction for voting errors and 99.9 with corrections for reported voting errors (Skjæveland 2011). This is high, even for parliamentary democracies (Kailitz 2008). Another way of measuring party unity is through the frequency of divisions with a deviation from at least one party line. Table 15.1 presents the breach frequency session by session from 2007–8 to 2017–18 with and without corrections for reported voting errors. It shows that party unity in divisions on bills continues to be very high.

This means that the parliamentary party groups are the building blocks of legislative coalitions, not the individual MPs. Yet three perspectives provide nuances to this picture of Danish party groups as monoliths (Christiansen and Skjæveland 2016). First, party unity is not equally high on all issues. Particularly on morality issues, party unity is

Table 15.1. Party Unity in Denmark 2007/08–2017/18, Per Cent

Legislative Year	Percentage of Bills with at least One MP Deviating from Party Line Uncorrected[1]	Percentage of Bills with at least One MP Deviating from Party Line Corrected[1]	Number of Bills
2007/08	3.2	2.7	187
2008/09	2.4	1.9	212
2009/10	2.6	1.3	227
2010/11	3.8	3.4	208
2011/12	8.2	7.2	207
2012/13	4.6	2.5	237
2013/14	5.0	4.5	202
2014/15	6.7	4.4	180
2015/16	3.1	0.5	191
2016/17	3.1	0.0	224
2017/18	2.9	1.6	245
2007–2018	4.1	2.7	2320

[1] Uncorrected and corrected for voting errors based on the case summaries at the website of the Danish *Folketinget.*

lower than normal. In these votes, the party groups often let MPs decide what to vote on their own. This is in fine accordance with the fact that morality issues have not been strongly politicized in Denmark (Albæk et al. 2012). Second, Danish parties quite often split up. For instance, the Danish People's Party, which is obviously an important parliamentary player, is the result of a split from the former Progress Party (see Kosiara-Pedersen 2020). Third, in legislative negotiations, the party groups do not behave as monoliths in the sense that naturally not all party group members show up when the party group negotiates with other party groups and the ministers of the government. Generally, the party groups will be represented in negotiations by one or few MPs. Obviously, in particularly important negotiations, this will involve the party leadership, but on many slightly more mundane issues, the parties will be represented by MPs who are permanent, issue-specific party spokespersons in negotiations with the relevant minister. Thus, the negotiation process is generally atomized thanks largely to a horizontal division of labour in the party groups (Jensen 2002).

The Stability of Danish Minority Governments

The first step in understanding the success of Danish minority governments is to explain their stability. The key to doing this is to look at the 'bloc structure' of Danish party politics as laid out in Green-Pedersen and Kosiara-Pedersen (2020). Based on their placement on the left-right scale, Danish political parties group themselves into a centre-left bloc and a centre-right bloc, depending on which PM they support. Parties belonging to the centre-left bloc support a Social Democratic prime minister, while parties belonging to the centre-right bloc support a prime minister from the major centre-right party. For the last few decades, this has been the leader of the Liberals. For most parties, it is rather clear as to which bloc they belong. Of the present parties in the Danish Parliament (see Green-Pedersen and Kosiara-Pedersen 2020), only the Social Liberals have ever changed blocs. Further, they have generally made it clear before an election which bloc they support. Therefore, they have never been in a position after an election where they could choose which bloc they would support in order to maximize their political influence. The Social Liberals have supported the Social Democratic bloc since 1993.

The bloc structure implies that the question of who becomes PM is normally relatively easy to settle, especially in recent decades.[1] This is the leader of the one of the two blocs that gains the majority in Parliament.[2] This implies that the government that forms around this leader can generally rely on the support of this bloc of parties in terms of staying in power. For the wider understanding of coalition building around legislation, it is important to understand the exact dynamics around such bloc majorities. Danish governments find themselves in an equilibrium situation where a majority in Parliament prefers this government to the alternative, namely a government with a PM from the other bloc (cf. Green-Pedersen and Thomsen 2005). This equilibrium implies that the government is sure not to be toppled. The political parties belonging to the other bloc would like to topple the government, but they do not command a majority. The opposition parties belonging to the same bloc as the government can topple it but have no incentive to do so as they risk that the resulting election will lead to a majority for the other bloc.

This equilibrium situation of Danish minority governments has several important implications for their opportunities when they pursue support for legislation. First, the question of toppling the government normally plays no role in daily politics. Second, even though a minority government in Denmark is based on a bloc majority, this does not imply that the government is certain to have a majority for all bills. A majority has to be built from bill to bill. If the government cannot in any way build a majority around a specific bill, the consequence is not that the government will fall but just that the bill will not be passed. Only around the budget is the situation different, as the government has to pass a budget every year (see below). Third, for the opposition parties belonging to the same bloc as the government, this equilibrium situation significantly limits their bargaining opportunities. For instance, the Red-Green Alliance was part of the Social Democratic bloc from 2011 to 2015, and thus, part of the bloc supporting the Social Democratic-led government, which also consisted of the Social Liberals and the Socialist People's Party (until 2014). The government often chose to strike legislative deals with parties belonging to the centre-right, ignoring the Social Democratic bloc majority that kept it in power. The Red-Green Alliance complained strongly about this but could do little in reality, as a threat of toppling the government was not credible.

How Do Governments in Denmark Build Legislative Coalitions?

Given that Danish minority governments are typically not in danger of being toppled, but at the same time, have no guaranteed support for their legislation, the question is what determines their ability to pass legislation. To answer this, one needs to understand the basic incentive facing opposition parties. What the opposition parties get out of supporting legislation is primarily policy influence. Without being in government, they can influence policy content by striking a deal with the government on a particular piece of legislation. It allows the opposition to push legislation closer to its preferred policy position. A further electoral advantage of striking deals with the government is that the opposition party is able to tell voters that it is a cooperative party that takes responsibility for governing the country. However, there is also a price to be paid for opposition parties when striking legislative deals with the government. Passing legislation together with the government implies that the opposition cannot credibly criticize the government for not taking proper care of a given policy area. For instance, an opposition party that has supported a government bill on primary education cannot afterwards easily criticize government policies with regard to primary schools. Thus, there is a trade-off here for the opposition where policy influence is traded for electoral opportunities for criticizing the government (cf. Christiansen and Seeberg 2016).

There are a number of factors influencing whether or not the opposition is willing to support government bills. Some of these considerations are tied to the issue on which the bill is presented, most importantly whether the issue is one over which the opposition has issue ownership, giving it reason to believe that distinguishing itself from the government can be electorally advantageous. In this case, the opposition is less likely to strike a deal with the government. Timing can also be important; the closer to an election, the less one should expect the opposition to be willing to cooperate.

The opposition parties belonging to the same bloc as the government are likely to support government bills because the policy proposal is often closer to its preferred policy than for an opposition party from the other bloc. It may also matter how many other opposition parties need to be included. Being the only coalition partners may imply more concession from the government and a better deal. Finally, ideologically, distance between the government and the opposition party matters (Klüver and Zubek 2018). These factors all imply that for opposition parties, striking a deal with the government on a bill is based on a rational calculation of the political costs and benefits.

From the government's perspective, a decisive question is whether both its bloc majority and the real opposition parties are interested in striking a deal with the government on a bill. If both sides are interested in striking a deal with the government, the government finds itself in a favourable position with a high chance of passing a bill with limited concessions to the opposition (cf. Green-Pedersen 2001). If only one side, the bloc majority or the real opposition, is interested in striking a deal, then the government faces a de facto veto player and often needs to offer more concessions or give up on getting the bill passed.

PATTERNS OF LEGISLATIVE BEHAVIOUR

Empirically, the outcome of the bargaining situation can be studied by looking at the voting behaviour of the political parties in Denmark on bills. Table 15.2 presents the development of this voting behaviour since 1973. In the analysis, we only look at passed bills. We have excluded MPs who left their party groups and the four North Atlantic representatives. In the rare case that a party was divided, we have coded the party by the plurality line. If all voting parties voted in favour, we consider the bill passed unanimously. If no party from the opposing bloc voted in favour, we consider the bill a case of bloc politics.

Several features of legislative cooperation in Denmark are visible from Table 15.2. Typically, 30–40 per cent of legislation is passed unanimously in Parliament. Further, in 40–50 per cent of the cases, the government gains support from some parties that would rather see another government. This indicates a high level of cooperation in the Danish Parliament with some important caveats. Broad or unanimous support for bills is sometimes the result of bills being more technical in nature without much political conflict. Further, not all bills are of equal importance. Hansen and Fazekas (2015) have shown that when one takes into account the significance of the bills—measured through the length of the parliamentary debates—one finds less cooperation in the Danish Parliament. Still, cooperation or even unanimous support also often arises with regard to bills where parties have different views but are able to compromise.

In only 7–20 per cent of the cases does the government base its legislation on only those parties that keep it in power, i.e. bloc politics. As is visible in Table 15.2, the level of bloc politics varies from government to government, but it is always less frequent than broad cooperation and unanimous support. However, the opportunity of passing legislation based on its bloc majority is an important premise for Danish minority governments' ability to govern effectively (Green-Pedersen and Thomsen 2005). If the government can rely on a bloc majority that is willing to support bills from the government in most cases, the other opposition parties, i.e. those that would prefer another government, know that they most likely will not be able to block legislation. On the other hand, if the opposition parties believe that the bloc majority will not do much beyond keeping the government in power, the opposition parties wanting another government become less cooperative because they see an opportunity to display the government's political weakness.

The extent to which minority governments have been able to use its bloc majority to not only keep power but also pass legislation has varied over time as can be seen in Table 15.2. From 1973 to 1982, the bloc majority behind the primarily Social Democratic minority governments were fragile, and the level of bloc politics around bills was very

Table 15.2. Voting Patterns on Passed Bills in the Danish Parliament, 1973–2018, Per Cent

Year/Government	Unanimous	Bloc Majority	Broad Majority	Total/N
	Percent			
1973–1975, Centre-Right	32	8	60	100/117
1975–1977, Centre-Left	24	0	76	100/386
1977–1978, Centre-Left	20	2	78	100/281
1978–1979, Broad Coalition	13	0	88	100/152
1979–1981, Centre-Left	17	2	80	100/317
1981–1982, Centre-Left	16	22	62	100/157
1982–1984, Centre-Right	27	25	48	100/170
1984–1987, Centre-Right	23	19	58	100/649
1987–1988, Centre-Right	23	0	77	100/93
1988–1990, Centre-Right	30	18	51	100/415
1990–1993, Centre-Right	44	7	49	100/491
1993–1994, Centre-Left	36	25	39	100/399
1994–1998, Centre-Left	34	16	50	100/780
1998–2001, Centre-Left	30	8	62	100/776
2001–2005, Centre-Right	33	19	48	100/677
2005–2007, Centre-Right	38	14	48	100/584
2007–2011, Centre-Right	45	15	40	100/824
2011–2015, Centre-Left	38	9	53	100/812
2015–2018, Centre-Right	41	7	52	100/651

Note: We thank Tim Runck for scraping the data for 2007/8–2017/18 from the website of the Danish *Folketinget*. The data for previous years were coded by various coders.

low at 0–2 per cent. This was also a period with frequent elections and during which Danish governments struggled to pass the reforms necessary to handle the economic crisis. The following period with a right-wing minority government from 1982 to 1993 was characterized by a higher level of bloc politics (around 20 per cent), as well as much more effective governance in terms of addressing macro-economic challenges (Green-Pedersen 2001). The level of bloc politics from 1994 to 2011 has been around 15 per cent with the exception of the period from 1998 to 2001 where it was 8 per cent.[3] The level has declined since 2011, and the level of 7 per cent for the centre-right minority governments from 2015–18 is a relatively low level compared to recent decades.[4] The bloc majority behind these governments has struggled to agree on central elements, especially regarding economic and tax policy, and the opposition wanting another government has not been particularly cooperative.

To sum up, Danish minority governments are generally stable in the sense that they are not toppled, but their ability to pass legislation and govern effectively is less stable and varies over time. The bloc majority that keeps minority governments in power may not necessarily be willing to support the bills put forward by the government. The periods where the bloc majority is also supportive in terms of policymaking are also typically the periods of most effective governance, also in cooperating with the opposition parties preferring a different government. The reason for this is that the government then typically has several possible ways of securing support for its bills (Green-Pedersen 2001). If the bloc majority only keeps the government alive, the government will often find the opposition preferring another government less cooperative because it has the opportunity of displaying the political weakness of the government.

LEGISLATIVE AGREEMENTS

Legislative cooperation in Denmark is further institutionalized in the form of what is known as 'legislative agreements' (*forlig*) (Christiansen and Seeberg 2016; Christiansen 2008). This institution is not formally established in the Constitution or the standing order of Parliament, but in practice, it is well established with clear rules known and respected by the Danish political parties. The homepage of the Parliament also contains a description of the basic principles of legislative agreements.[5]

A legislative agreement is more than simply an agreement between the government and the opposition about opposition support for a specific bill or package of bills in the final vote in the third reading. A legislative agreement lasts beyond the passage of the bill(s) for a time period specified in the agreement or even for an unspecified time period. Any substantial change to the agreed policy after the initial agreement has been made requires the consent of all parties participating in the agreement, de facto giving each party a veto power. A further norm is that even though a longer time period is specified in the agreement, a party can terminate its participation in an agreement with effect from after an election if it has announced this before the election. There is also a norm that when a new government is formed, all the government parties join all existing agreements of which they are not already part. This is to avoid a situation where the party of the relevant minister is not part of a legislative agreement within the minister's portfolio. There is also a norm that the relevant minister shares important information concerning a policy problem with the parties that are part of the agreement. Thus, the parties that are part of a legislative agreement are privileged compared to the parties in Parliament that are not part of the legislative agreement (Christiansen 2008; Christiansen and Skjæveland 2016). In many ways, the parties that are part of a legislative agreement act as a majority government in relation to the specific policy problem (cf. Klemmensen 2005).

Forlig are an important tool for minority governments, and the positive role of legislative agreements is clear. They facilitate cooperation even when conflict might seem imminent because they allow parties to tie themselves credibly to agreements, thereby reducing the fear among members of the agreement that a member party may opportunistically defect at a (in)convenient moment (Christiansen 2008). Yet the darker sides of *forlig* also deserve to be mentioned. The most obvious problem is that they blur the distinction between the government and the opposition and make it harder for the voters to figure out who is responsible for the political decisions. Another possible but less obvious problem is that different opposition parties have access to different types of information. Opposition members of a legislative agreement have privileged access to information on the specific issue area covered by the legislative agreement. In other words, they have access to more information than non-members do (Christiansen and Skjæveland 2016). The parties outside the agreement are left with the ordinary means of control that were intended for holding governments accountable, not members of a legislative agreement. That may seem like a weakness, but on the other hand, only in these cases is the minister clearly legally bound to give correct and complete information.

The institution of legislative agreements goes back many years. The first registered legislative agreement was made in 1865, and the institution was developed under bicameralism where it helped the two chambers and their very often different majorities to cooperate (Arter 1991; Pedersen 2011). The number of legislative agreements has been increasing since the 1970s, and in the 2000s, they covered around 30 per cent of all bills (Christiansen 2008). Classic examples of legislative agreements are agreements on Danish defence and on the budget, but legislative agreements cover an increasing number of policy areas as well (ibid.). Legislative agreements on the budget also increasingly cover more issue areas themselves (Christiansen 2005). When one takes into account that many bills are uncontroversial, i.e. have the support of all parties in Parliament, the institution of legislative agreements plays a central role for the cooperation between the government and the opposition parties. One aspect of this development is the almost disappearance of majority governments in Denmark. Though such governments could also find legislative agreements attractive to silence the opposition, they make much less use of them than minority governments that are searching for a parliamentary majority do (see Klemmensen 2005). For a majority coalition, the coalition agreement plays a much more central role (Christiansen and Pedersen 2014). A more important reason is changes to Danish party competition (Christiansen 2008). Parallel to other countries, party competition in Denmark has been spread out to more issues (Green-Pedersen 2014, 2019), and legislative agreements are an important institution to secure cooperation on issues where parties at the same time compete intensively for votes.

CONCLUSION

The very high frequency of Danish minority governments raises two important questions: first, how can minority governments work at all; and second, how can they work effectively? The parties are the key players, and the parties—including government parties—are used to minority governments. One very important tool in the toolkit of Danish minority governments is *forlig* or legislative agreements. They help parties tie themselves to cooperation even when they compete on many issues, and conflict could be in their immediate interest. It is important to notice that *forlig* go beyond the passage of the bill(s) comprised in the legislative agreement. This includes a veto right on changes and special access to information on the topic of the bill(s). Thus, legislative agreements can work almost as issue-specific majority governments. Still, they are not actual governments, and the usage of *forlig* blurs the distinction between the government and the opposition, creating challenges for accountability. The legislative agreements that are often broad and the great number of bills that are passed with either unanimous consent or in broad cooperation provide the foundation for the description of Danish politics as consensual politics.

However, bloc politics is more important than it may seem both for the stability and for the effective functioning of Danish minority governments. For more than two decades, bloc politics has provided stability to Danish governments since majority blocs have seen governments that were acceptable to them. Furthermore, the possibility of passing bills with the bloc is the foundation for the effective functioning of Danish minority governments. While coalitions are often broad, the possibility of bloc politics is an important asset for minority governments. This is not to say that times are never difficult for Danish minority governments. Current disagreements within the two blocs bear some resemblance to the parliamentarily complicated 1970s.

The fragmentation of the Danish party system is also the strongest threat to the continued functioning of Danish minority governments. The 2019 election expanded the number of parties in Parliament further to ten parties with the entrance of the 'New Right' (cf. Green-Pedersen and Kosiara-Pedersen 2020). After the 2019 election, especially the centre-right wing bloc is struggling to agree on much more than whom they would prefer as prime minister. The centre-left wing bloc, which has taken over power after the 2019 election, is probably less fragmented but also struggles with internal disagreement, not least on immigration.

Notes

1. When identifying the majority, the four North Atlantic MPs must be counted (Skjæveland 2003).
2. After the 2015 election, the Danish People's Party was actually bigger than the Liberals in terms of seats. However, the Danish People's Party was not interested in taking office, so it was clear that the Liberals would supply the prime minister.
3. From 1993 to 1994, the government was a majority government. Such governments, of course, find themselves in a different parliamentary situation.
4. The data in Table 12.2 does not include the final parliamentary session from 2018 to 2019.
5. https://www.ft.dk/da/folkestyret/regeringen/saadan-arbejder-regeringen#F4DC47C7E46 E403F8E0749034B213B3F (accessed 19 November 2019).

References

Albæk, Erik, Christoffer Green-Pedersen, and Lars T. Larsen (2012). 'Morality issues in Denmark: Policies without politics', in Isabelle Engeli, Christoffer Green-Pedersen, and Lars T. Larsen, eds, *Morality Politics in Western Eur*ope. Basingstoke: Palgrave, 137–60.

Arter, David (1991). 'One Ting too many: The shift to unicameralism in Denmark', in Lawrence D. Longley and David M. Olson, eds, *Two Into One: The Politics and Processes of National Legislative Cameral Change*. Boulder, CO/San Francisco, CA/Oxford: Westwiew Press, 77–142.

Bale, Tim and Thorbjørn Bergman (2006). 'Captives no longer, but servants still? Contract parliamentarism and the new minority governance in Sweden and New Zealand', *Government and Opposition*, 41/3: 422–49.

Christensen, Jens Peter (2020). 'The constitution', in Peter M. Christiansen, Jørgen Elklit, and Peter Nedergaard, eds, *The Oxford Handbook of Danish Politics*. Oxford: Oxford University Press, 9–27.

Christiansen, Flemming J. (2005). 'Aftaler på tværs af sektorer i Folketinget', *Politica*, 37/4: 423–39.

Christiansen, Flemming J. (2008). *Politiske Forlig i Folketinget. Partikonkurrence og samarbejde*. Aarhus: Politica.

Christiansen, Flemming J., and Helene H. Pedersen (2014). 'Minority coalition governance in Denmark', *Party Politics*, 20/6: 940–9.

Christiansen, Flemming J., and Henrik Seeberg (2016). 'Cooperation between counterparts in parliament from an agenda-setting perspective: legislative coalitions as a trade of criticism and policy', *West European Politics*, 39/6: 1160–80.

Christiansen, Flemming J., and Asbjørn Skjæveland (2016). 'Folketinget', in Jørgen G. Christensen and Jørgen Elklit, eds, *Det Demokratiske System*, 4th ed. Copenhagen: Hans Reitzels Forlag, 94–129.

Green-Pedersen, Christoffer (2001). 'Minority governments and party politics: The political and institutional background to the "Danish miracle"', *Journal of Public Policy*, 21/1: 53–70.

Green-Pedersen, Christoffer (2014). 'Party system development in Denmark. Agenda-setting dynamics and political change', in Christoffer Green-Pedersen and Stefaan Walgrave, eds, *Agenda Setting Policies, and Political Systems. A Comparative Approach*. Chicago, IL: University of Chicago Press, 69–85.

Green-Pedersen, Christoffer (2019). *The Reshaping of West European Party Politics. Agenda Setting and Party Competition in Comparative Perspective*. Oxford: Oxford University Press.

Green-Pedersen, Christoffer, and Karina Kosiara-Pedersen (2020). 'The party system: Open yet stable', in Peter M. Christiansen, Jørgen Elklit, and Peter Nedergaard, eds, *The Oxford Handbook of Danish Politics*. Oxford: Oxford University Press, 213–29.

Green-Pedersen, Christoffer, and Lisbeth H. Thomsen (2005). 'Bloc politics vs broad cooperation. The functioning of Danish minority parliamentarism', *The Journal of Legislative Studies*, 11/2: 153–69.

Hansen, Martin E. (2020). 'The government and the prime minister: More than *primus inter pares?*', in Peter M. Christiansen, Jørgen Elklit, and Peter Nedergaard, eds, *The Oxford Handbook of Danish Politics*. Oxford: Oxford University Press, 107–23.

Hansen, Martin E., and Zoltán Fazekas (2015). 'All votes are equal? Significant legislation and party competition in the Danish Folketing', *Scandinavian Political Studies*, 38/3: 255–76.

Jensen, Henrik (2002). *Partigrupperne i Folketinget*. Copenhagen: Jurist- og Økonomforbundets Forlag.

Kailitz, Steffen (2008). 'Ein Unterschied wie Tag und Nacht? Fraktionsgeschlossenheit in Parlamentarismus und Präsidentialismus', *Zeitschrift für Politikwissenschaft*, 18/3: 291–324.

Klemmensen, Robert (2005). 'Forlig i det danske Folketing', *Politica*, 41/1: 81–91.

Klüver, Heike, and Radoslaw Zubek (2018). 'Minority governments and legislative reliability: Evidence from Denmark and Sweden', *Party Politics*, 24/6: 719–30.

Kosiara-Pedersen, Karina (2020). 'The Danish People's Party: Centre oriented populists?', in Peter M. Christiansen, Jørgen Elklit, and Peter Nedergaard, eds, *The Oxford Handbook of Danish Politics*. Oxford: Oxford University Press, 313–28.

Lee, Seonghui, Carsten Jensen, Christoph Arendt, and Georg Wenzelburger (2019). Risky Business? Welfare State Reforms and government support in Britain and Denmark', *British Journal of Political Science*, Early view.

Pedersen, Helene H. (2011). 'Etableringen af politiske forlig som parlamentarisk praksis', *Politica*, 43/1: 48–67.

Skjæveland, Asbjørn (2003). *Government Formation in Denmark 1953–1998*. Aarhus: Politica.

Skjæveland, Asbjørn (2011). 'The Effect of parliamentarism on party unity', in Thomas Persson and Matti Wiberg, eds, *Parliamentary Government in the Nordic Countries at a Crossroads: Coping with Challenges from Europeanisation and Presidentialisation*. Stockholm: Santérus Acamic Press, 113–37.

Strøm, Kaare (1990). *Minority Government and Majority Rule*. Cambridge: Cambridge University Press.

....

CHAPTER 16

CLASSES AND POLITICS

A Changing Relationship

....

GITTE SOMMER HARRITS AND RUNE STUBAGER

CLASS AND DANISH POLITICS IN A HISTORICAL PERSPECTIVE

....

THROUGHOUT most of the twentieth century, class relations have been a key foundation of Danish politics. In accordance with theories about political cleavages (Lipset and Rokkan 1967), the Danish party system stabilized early on (from the 1890s to the 1920s) on the basis of socio-economic conflicts between an urban elite and a rural class of farmers and between the growing capitalist-employer and working classes developing with industrialization (Elklit 1986).

Between 1920 and 1973 voting in Denmark was primarily structured by social class and organized by a relatively stable party system with three major parties representing the capitalist elite (the Conservative People's Party, *Konservative Folkeparti*); the farmers (the Liberal Party, *Venstre*); and the workers (the Social Democratic Party, *Socialdemokratiet*). These three parties were supplemented by smaller partiers, one representing rural workers and urban intellectual groups (the Social Liberals, *Radikale Venstre*) and two parties representing communist or socialist fractions of the working class (the Communist Party, *Danmarks Kommunistiske Parti*, and the Socialist People's Party, *Socialistisk Folkeparti*, established in 1959; see Green-Pedersen and Kosiara-Pedersen 2020). From the 1920s to 1973, these parties represented more than 80 per cent of the Danish voters (Rusk and Borre 1974).

Further, the development of the comprehensive Danish welfare state from the 1930s onwards was built on a class alliance led by a strong Social Democratic Party and including farmers and sometimes employers (Christiansen and Petersen 2001). Likewise, the Danish labour market has traditionally been regulated primarily by agreements between central organizations representing employers and workers in a strong corporatist system (Elvander 2002; see Christiansen 2020). In contrast to many other European countries, the organization of Danish politics and the labour market has thus been dominated by a class cleavage throughout the twentieth century, whereas other cleavages have been less important.

However, since 1973, the stable class foundation of Danish politics has slowly weakened. In the 1973 so-called 'Landslide Election', several new parties based on populist or one-issue agendas entered Parliament for the first time, representing 24 per cent of the voters (Rusk and Borre 1974). After the 1973 election, the stable class foundation of political cleavages slowly vanished, and in the 2011 election, the Alford Index (Alford 1963), indicating the difference between working-class and non-working-class votes for Socialist parties, was negative. Some researchers have claimed that this demonstrates the end of both classes and class politics in Danish society and the introduction of value and issue-based voting (Borre 1995; Green-Pedersen 2011). Others have suggested that Danish politics should rather be seen as building on changing cleavages and class relations, with a growing importance of education and cultural resources (Harrits et al. 2010; Stubager 2013).

The chapter argues that class relations are still an important, although no longer as dominant, foundation of Danish politics. However, in order to grasp the class dimension of Danish politics, we need to understand class as a complex and possibly multidimensional phenomenon based on the distribution of different forms of resources. We test this claim empirically using data from the Danish National Election Study (1971–2019; Hansen and Stubager 2019; see www.valgprojektet.dk). We begin the chapter by briefly presenting theories of social class and politics, followed by an analysis of the development of class relations and class identity in Denmark. Finally, we analyse class and party choice using different operationalizations of class.

THEORIES OF CLASS AND POLITICS

Sociological discussions of how to approach class analysis have been comprehensive since the 1860s and Marx's analysis of the relation between capital and labour (Marx 1867/1991, 1894/1991). In the Marxist and neo-Marxist traditions, class is typically defined by property relations, people's ownership of production assets, and the relations of exploitation that ownership and lack of ownership create. However, as the organization of production has grown more complex, other types of assets (skills and organizational authority) have come to be important for the ways in which middle classes are positioned within relations of class and exploitation (Wright 1997). Within the Weberian tradition, class has traditionally been based on commodity or labour market positions, determining people's life chances with regard to their economic or occupational interests (Weber 1922/1978). However, Weberian discussions of class have, to an increasing extent, also considered skills and organizational authority as important elements in class relations because of the ways in which these assets can enhance or even monopolize market positions and life chances (Dahrendorf 1959; Goldthorpe 1996; Parkin 1979).

Throughout the 1980s and 1990s, however, sociological theories of class were challenged by claims about individualization and the 'death of class' (Beck and Beck-Gernsheim 2002; Giddens 1991; Pakulski and Waters 1996). Nevertheless, discussions and analyses of class have carried on, not least in research by Pierre Bourdieu and scholars inspired by his work (Bennett et al. 2009; Bourdieu 1984, 1985, 1987; Savage et al. 2015). In the Bourdieusian tradition, class relations are seen as based on whatever forms of resources or assets (referred to as capital) that structure and condition people's access to further resources and life possibilities. In current societies, these resources are typically of an economic (economic capital) or cultural nature (cultural capital). Here, we define economic capital as all assets that have value on the market, and cultural capital as the knowledge and skills to process information and conduct oneself in a context-appropriate way (Bourdieu 1986; Lareau and Weininger 2003).

Moreover, whereas both Weberian and Marxist traditions see class relations as based on economic and labour market relations, with the possible addition of skills and organizational authority, the Bourdieusian tradition sees economic and cultural assets as equally important for class relations and defines class as a multi-dimensional phenomenon. It is outside the scope of this chapter to engage in a comprehensive discussion of definitions and approaches to class beyond these introductory remarks (see Harrits 2014). Here, we consider it adequate to define class as based on both economic and cultural assets. Later, we return to a discussion of what this means for the ways in which we operationalize class in the analysis.

Before moving on to the analysis, however, it is important to consider how theories of class have approached the relationship between class and politics. In the Marxist approach, class relations are inherently political since they are relations of exploitation. According to Marxist theory, this means that classes will have antagonistic interests over property relations, meaning that the realization of the interests of the exploitive class will always come at the expense of the exploited class (see also Sørensen 2000). This implies an implicit understanding of class conflict as being about different political projects for the future organization and distribution of welfare, and it follows that the working class will share interests with socialist or centre-left parties seeking societal change in the organization of property, work, welfare, and the distribution of resources.

In contrast, the Weberian tradition sees the relationship between class and politics as based on the ways in which distributions of life chances structure different preferences and interests, as well as the ways in which different forms of closure mechanisms can structure access to market positions. As explained by Goldthorpe (2000), class relations generate different constraints, opportunities, and life chances (level of income, stability in employment, and prospects for future advancement), as well as different preferences and interests regarding the development of (re)distributional welfare institutions or labour market regulation (Evans 1993). Thus, class conflicts and politics are considered more distributional than antagonistic in the Weberian approach, which implies that classes can share an interest with different (and varying) political projects and parties based on the ways in which these projects will generate rent and opportunities for each class.

Within the Bourdieusian tradition, discussions of how exactly class relations structure politics have not been widespread. Following some interpretations, Bourdieu mainly sees classes as structuring class habitus, defined as a system of cognitive, normative, aesthetic, and bodily dispositions, which then includes preferences for specific sets of political values and parties (Bourdieu 1984; Harrits et al. 2010). This interpretation, however, frames politics as a form of consumption, and it does not have much to say about the classed nature of political conflicts. One can, however, also interpret Bourdieu's class analysis in a more distributional and Weberian way, meaning that class relations create different constraints, including different opportunities for access to resources. Finally, it is also possible to derive a more antagonistic interpretation of politics in Bourdieu's understanding of class struggle as symbolic (Bourdieu 1984; Savage et al. 2005; Skeggs 2015). Here, classes are opposed because they have different opportunities and interests in symbolic struggles over which type of resources and assets are to be seen as valuable in society. Understood in this way, class politics is no longer confined to struggles over economic institutions and distribution of welfare as in the Marxist and Weberian traditions but must be understood more broadly as the struggle between different societal projects and different forms of value. Put briefly, one can say that class politics in the Bourdieusian interpretation then includes struggles over distribution, values, and recognition.

In a recent analysis of the development of French, American, and British politics after the Second World War, Thomas Piketty (2018) builds on an approach similar to that of the Bourdieusian tradition, although he theoretically frames the analysis as being about structures of inequality and political cleavages. He shows that political cleavages in the 1950s and 1960s were built on traditional economic class cleavages, with economically and educationally less privileged groups voting for centre-left parties and privileged groups voting for centre-right parties. Today, however, this has changed into what Piketty calls a 'multi-elite system', where economically privileged groups vote for centre-right parties, educationally privileged groups vote for centre-left parties, and less-privileged groups increasingly align themselves with populist parties. From a theory on multidimensional classes, these results lend support to the claim that multidimensional class relations give rise to a realignment around new and possibly broader, or even multidimensional, political conflicts (see also Harrits et al. 2010). In the following, we empirically test whether this claim holds true in the Danish context by exploring the development of the relation between different dimensions of class and party choice in Danish politics from 1971 to 2019. Before moving on to this analysis, however, let us first briefly look at the development of class relations and class identity in Danish society.

CLASS RELATIONS AND CLASS IDENTITY IN DENMARK

As is well known, Denmark is one of the most egalitarian countries in the world today when judged by income distribution and income mobility. For example, Denmark is one of the countries in the OECD with the lowest Gini coefficient (0.26 in 2015, cf. OECD 2019b) and the country with the highest income mobility, measured as the number of generations it takes to move from the lowest income group to an average income (OECD 2018a). According to Atkinson and Søgaard (2016), this current level of economic inequality is not the result of a steady decrease in income inequality over the course of the twentieth century. Rather, income inequality has decreased in specific time periods: 1870–1900, 1940–45, and during the 1970s. Also, income inequality has increased since the 1980s, although remaining at a low level by historic standards as well as compared to other OECD countries. Still, even though Denmark is comparably an economically quite egalitarian society in terms of income, it is worth mentioning that Denmark is among the countries in OECD (together with the United States and the Netherlands) with the highest wealth inequality, measured by the net wealth share held by the top 10 per cent of households (Balestra and Tonkin 2018).

Looking at education, there is no doubt that educational resources have increased, especially in the last forty years. For example, whereas around 20 per cent of Danes achieved a tertiary education in 1981, this number reached 46 per cent in 2017 (OECD 2019a). Similarly, around 1900, only about 1 per cent of Danes achieved secondary education, whereas this number reached 71 per cent in 2017 (Ministry of Education 1998; Danmarks Statistik 2018).

However, analyses of the development of inequality and mobility of education are not quite as straightforward. According to Landersø and Heckman (2017), educational mobility in Denmark is quite low and at a level comparable to the US, and as pointed out by Skaksen (2018), only around 4 per cent of children whose parents had the lowest level of education achieved higher education at the MA level themselves. Compared to this, MA-level education was achieved by around 48 per cent of children with at least one parent with education at the MA level. According to analyses from the OECD, however, Denmark fares average or well with regard to educational mobility compared to other OECD countries, both when measured as the percentage of adults (26 years or older) who report a higher educational attainment than their parents, and when measured as the relative likelihood of attaining a tertiary education when one's parents have or do not have an education (OECD 2018b). Furthermore, the results by Landersø and Heckman have been contested in recent analyses (Andrade and Thomsen 2018).

More broadly, though, results seem to converge with respect to the overall reproduction of both cultural and economic resources. Karlson and Jæger (2011) conclude that cultural, economic, and social resources are intertwined but that all forms of resources are reproduced from generation to generation. Further, Prieur and co-authors (Faber et al. 2012; Prieur et al. 2008) have shown how lifestyles in Denmark are structured by both cultural and economic capital, even though class is not necessarily salient as a cultural identity in their studies. In these studies, Denmark seems quite similar to other European countries, such as Norway (Flemmen et al. 2018) and Britain (Bennett et al. 2009; Prieur and Savage 2011). Similarly, Harrits (2011, 2013) demonstrates how both cultural and economic capital structure political resources, political efficacy, and participation—again without class being salient in the way people think about themselves when talking about political participation.

However, more recent analyses focusing directly on class identity point toward class as a meaningful identity in current Danish society. In a unique combination of historical and recent survey data, Stubager (2017) shows that levels of class consciousness (i.e. the way people think about classes) in Denmark are similar in 1954 and 2015, whereas the level of class identification (i.e. the extent to which Danes identify with a class) has decreased from 65 per cent in 1954 to 56 per cent in 2015 (see also Robison and Stubager 2017; Stubager et al. 2018). These results are supported by qualitative focus group analyses of class identity where people tend to spontaneously describe Danish society using classed categories and hierarchies and referring primarily to economic and cultural resources (Harrits and Pedersen 2018, 2019).

As seen in Figure 16.1, analysis of election data from 1971 to 2019 confirms these results. The figure shows the distribution of responses to a sequence of questions where respondents are first asked whether they feel that they belong to a particular class. Those providing a positive answer can then select from the working and middle class. Those providing a negative response (or 'don't know') are asked to state whether they feel closer to the working or middle class. Responses to the two questions are combined in the figure where the 'Total Class Identity' line denotes the proportion that choose an identity in either the first or the second question (the data is weighted to conform to the population distribution on gender, age, education, and party choice). Overall, the figure shows that class identity is quite stable from 1971 to 2019. As can also be seen, however,

FIGURE 16.1 Development of class identification (including 'leaners').

Note: See text for variable definitions

the proportion identifying as working class decreases over this period, whereas the proportion identifying as middle class increases slightly. This suggests that class relations are changing rather than disappearing altogether. Recent analysis also shows that although class labels may be used somewhat differently, with the working class label being more frequently used by Britons, the structure and use of class categories is quite similar in Denmark and Great Britain (Stubager et al. 2018).

In summary, even though Danish society today is indeed quite egalitarian judged by historical standards and compared to other countries, inequalities (such as in wealth and education) do exist. Furthermore, even though income mobility is high, economic, cultural, and social resources are reproduced from generation to generation, and both cultural and economic resources structure different and distinct lifestyles. Also, class does still exist as a meaningful and salient category and identity that Danes use when describing others and themselves. Below, we therefore move on to the question of whether class is still structuring political conflicts and party choice in Denmark.

The Development of Class-Based Party Choice

As explained above, we test the hypothesis that class has not disappeared but rather changed as an influence on Danish voter politics. More specifically, we analyse the development of how different dimensions of class influence the tendency to choose a centre-left party using survey data from the Danish National Election Study from 1971 to 2019. We are, however, somewhat limited by the available data which means that we can conduct only a somewhat simplified analysis.

We operationalize class in three ways. First, occupational class is based on an adapted EGP scheme (Erikson and Goldthorpe 1992) with four categories: self-employed, salariat, non-manual routine labour, and workers (the variables are coded on the basis of open-ended questions about occupation; initially coded based on the ISCO88 classification system). Second, as many Danish employees are working in the public sector, we also include a sector variable with two categories: public sector and private sector (including the self-employed). In traditional Marxist class analysis, public employees have a somewhat contradictory role in relations of exploitation, and within both Weberian and Bourdieusian analyses, it can be argued that public employees have market positions with specific privileges, and thus, possibly specific interests.

And third, to facilitate an analysis of the economic and cultural dimensions of class, we include both income and education. Income is measured in quartiles, resulting in four categories: 1st to 4th quartile. Education is measured by a simple measure containing only two categories: university degree and no university degree. This choice was made to manage the changing educational structure and classifications in the data throughout this long time period (unfortunately, this information is not available in the surveys for the 1973–1981 period). As seen from the definition of cultural capital above, education is only a crude measure of cultural capital since additional forms of cultural capital indeed exist, just as income is only a crude measure of economic capital since other forms of economic capital, such as wealth, exist. With these crude measures of capital as dimensions of class, however, we can get an indication of the structuring effects of class on party choice.

In order to present a simplified analysis, we further choose to reduce the complexity of party choice in the multidimensional and changing Danish party system. We focus on the choice of a centre-left party, which includes the Social Democratic Party, the Social Liberals, and the Socialist People's Party, as well as a varying group of small socialist and/ or communist parties. The choice to include the Social Liberals can be debated since this party does not necessarily represent a stable classed party choice in all years. In some years (1982–90), the Social Liberals have been in alliance with centre-right parties, but in most years, their alliance has clearly been with the Social Democratic Party and the centre-left. Today, the Social Liberals represent a clear liberal choice on the cultural dimension, with a pro-globalization agenda, mobilizing mainly people privileged with regard to cultural capital. The inclusion of the Social Liberals as a centre-left party should thus be seen as a consequence of our broad operationalization of class politics. It should be noted that this classification of the Social Liberals means that our scores for the Alford Index (cf. below) are not directly comparable with those of most previous analyses in which the party is classified as belonging to the right bloc of parties.

The analyses presented below will summarize the development of how the different dimensions of class structure party choice. In some analyses, we present the predicted probability of choosing a centre-left party for different groups. Here, we include controls for gender and generation since these are the only relevant variables antecedent to the ones included in the analyses (we include the following generations: 1) born before 1930, 2) born between 1930 and 1944, 3) born between 1945 and 1959, 4) born between 1960 and 1974, and 5) born after 1974; in addition, the data is weighted as described above). In other analyses, we display the development of the traditional class-based Alford Index, i.e. the difference between working-class and non-working-class votes for centre-left parties, along with a similar index based on education, i.e. displaying the difference between the shares of university-graduate votes and non-university-graduate votes for centre-left parties (cf. Piketty 2018). Finally, we show a model displaying the development of the predictive power of all class variables where the controls are also included.

We begin by analysing the class structuring of the choice of a centre-left party by varying dimensions of class. Looking first at occupational class (Figure 16.2), we can see that the predicted probability of working-class members voting for a centre-left party steadily decreases over the period—although it rebounds somewhat from 2015 to 2019 as part of a general swing to the left by the entire electorate—whereas the predicted probability of other classes voting for a centre-left party is more stable. It is also clear that the difference between classes decreases markedly from 1971 to 2015. Looking at occupational sector (Figure 16.3), we observe that the predicted probability of voting for a centre-left party is somewhat more stable for both public and private employees although we can

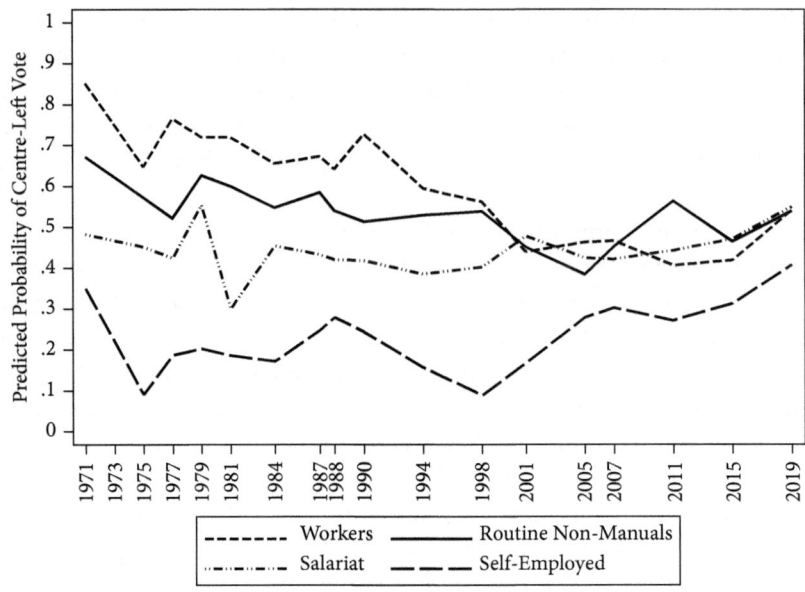

FIGURE 16.2 Occupational class and support for centre-left parties.

Note: See text for variable definitions

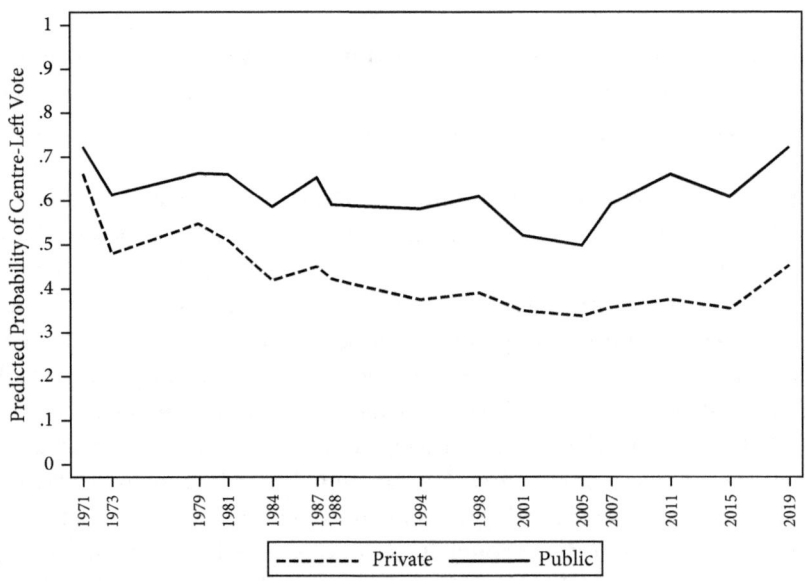

FIGURE 16.3 Sector and support for centre-left parties.

Note: See text for variable definitions

also note a clear downward trend for the privately employed except in 2019. As a result, the difference between public and private employees, which is negligible at the beginning of the 1970s, increases—especially so after 2005.

Overall, the analysis of occupational class seems to support earlier claims about the weakening of class conflict and class politics in Denmark although there is still some difference between classes even in 2019. Further, the increasing difference between private and public employees suggests that class relations understood as differences in market position might be of increasing importance. Based on our analysis, however, it is difficult to say whether differences in party choice between sectors is driven primarily by privileges. It could also be the case that the public sector in Denmark has more employees from professions within education, health, and care and that these professions have specific values which then drive differences in political attitudes and party choice.

Looking more directly at the economic and cultural dimensions of class, operationalized here as income (Figure 16.4) and education (Figure 16.5), and the tendency to support a centre-left party, we see slightly different developments than in the analyses based on occupational class. Differences between income groups are quite stable throughout the period, and they are about the same size as, or a little smaller than, the differences between classes in 2019. Differences between educational groups, however, display an interesting trend. In the 1970s, fewer people with higher education tended to support centre-left parties compared to all other groups. This is reversed from the end of the twentieth century, and in 2019, more people with higher education tend to support centre-left parties. Additionally, the difference between educational groups increases

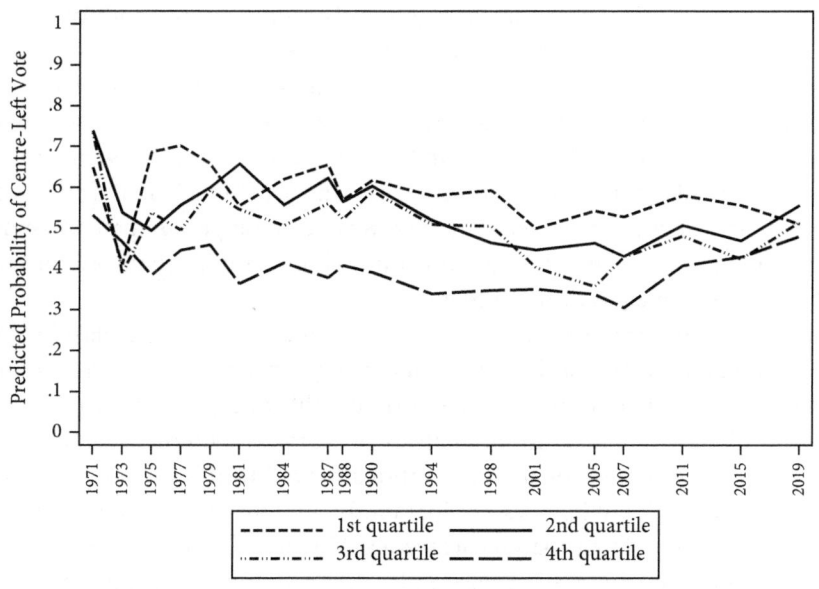

FIGURE 16.4 Income and support for centre-left parties.

Note: See text for variable definitions

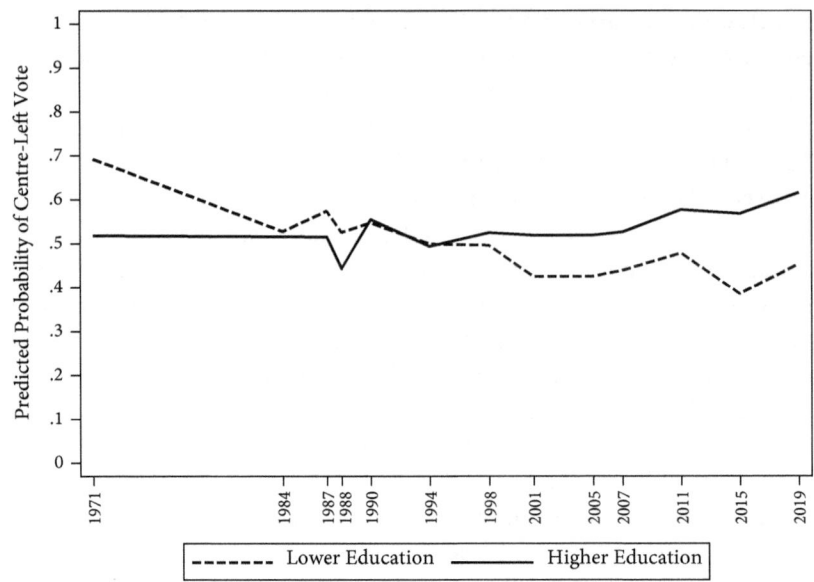

FIGURE 16.5 Education and support for centre-left parties (Higher Education vs others).
Note: See text for variable definitions

steadily from 1998 onwards so that the difference is clearly larger in 2019 than the difference between occupational classes and income groups.

Overall, the analyses of income and education suggest a more nuanced conclusion than the analyses based solely on occupational class. These analyses thus seem to support the claim that class relations are changing and becoming more multidimensional.

Taken together, the structuring effect of class can be estimated using the overall predictive power of the different class measures (including controls for gender and generation; Figure 16.6). Here, it becomes evident that class structuring of support for centre-left parties has indeed decreased in the last thirty years of the twentieth century. However, almost all of this decrease took place in the 1970s, and from the mid-1980s, the predictive power of class has hovered in the 5–8 per cent range, compared to more than 20 per cent in 1971. This suggests that class politics is not as important as it once was but that it has not completely vanished either.

Based on other existing analyses, the decreasing predictive power of class in Denmark seems to be quite similar to the development in many other countries (Jansen et al. 2013). However, not many analyses include measures capable of capturing the possibly changing nature of class relations. In an analysis of Norway, Flemmen demonstrates the importance of multidimensional class relations for political behaviour in Norway in 2009 (Flemmen 2014), but he does not include an analysis of the development of class and politics. Moreover, in an analysis of Sweden, Vestin and Oskarson (2017) document how both a traditional measure of class and a new one show a decrease in the importance of class. In this analysis, however, the new measure of class is not constructed to include cultural dimensions of class relations but rather to include different work logics

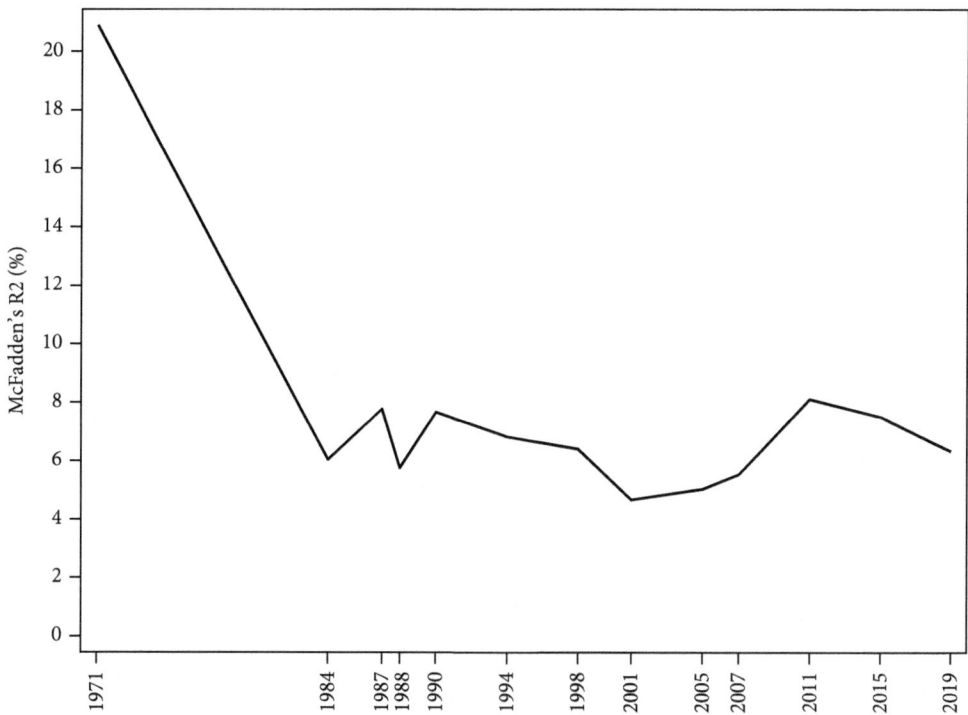

FIGURE 16.6 Predictive power of class variables on support for centre-left parties.

Note: Model includes gender, generation, income, occupation, sector, and education (higher education vs. others)

(Oesch 2008). All in all, based on existing analyses, it is difficult to say whether or not the Danish development is similar to or different from that found in other European countries.

As mentioned above, however, Thomas Piketty (2018) recently presented an analysis of French, British, and American politics which includes an examination of the development of an education-based version of the Alford Index, i.e. an analysis of the difference between university-graduates' and non-university-graduates' voting for centre-left parties. Piketty shows how an education-based cleavage has grown in all three countries, with index levels (i.e. differences between groups) increasing steadily from 1945 to 2018. Moreover, index levels have become positive in all three countries in 2018, reaching more than 10 per cent in France and the United States and more than 5 per cent in Great Britain.

Looking at Denmark, Figure 16.7 displays both the traditional Alford Index based on the difference between working-class and non-working-class votes for centre-left parties, and the education Alford Index based on the difference between university-graduates and non-university-graduates voting for centre-left parties (recall that the Social Liberals are included among centre-left parties). Thus, this figure sums up the development in the changing class structuring of Danish politics quite nicely. As can be seen, the traditional class structuring of Danish politics, i.e. the conflict between the working

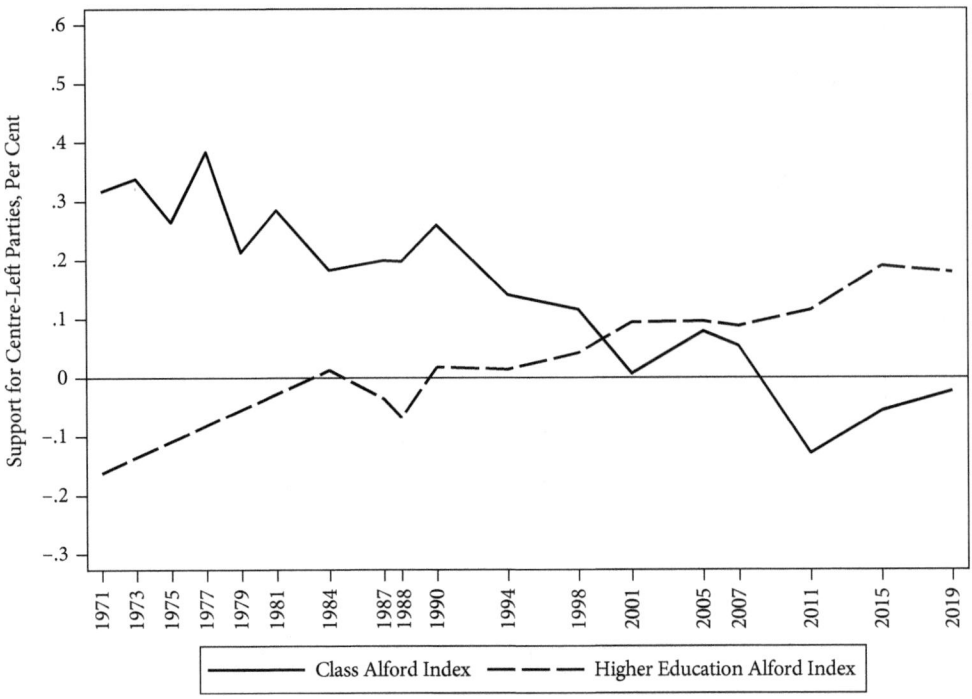

FIGURE 16.7 Class and education, Alford Index Values.

Note: See text for variable definitions

class and other classes, decreases in importance, and as already mentioned, the class Alford Index becomes negative in 2011. However, throughout the same period, the conflict between university graduates and other groups have changed. In the 1970s, university graduates tended not to support centre-left parties, but this has changed since the early 1990s where the education Alford Index in Denmark turned positive; and with a value of 17.3 in 2019, it is at a higher level than in the UK, France, and the United States.

CONCLUSION

In summary, our analysis shows both an overall decline of the structuring effects of class on party choice and a possible impact of changing class relations. In other words, our results suggest that class is no longer as dominant for political conflicts as it once was, nor has it completely vanished. Rather, class relations are changing, and the multiple dimensions of economic and cultural class may be realigning political cleavages and politics. In terms of the structure of class relations and political conflicts, our analysis suggests that the development of class and politics in Denmark is similar to the development in other European countries where it seems as if centre-left parties today are supported especially by educationally privileged groups (Piketty 2018). Piketty interprets this pattern as an emerging multi-elite system, but we prefer to approach the analysis using a vocabulary of changing class relations since this vocabulary underlines the continuing relationship between the control over societal resources and conflicts over the development of society, including the distribution and definition of values and recognition.

Here, we follow recent theoretical and empirical analyses that show how the economic and cultural aspects of politics and social relations may be deeply intertwined. In an analysis of American politics, for example, Hochschild (2016) demonstrates how conflicts between left and right, liberals and conservatives, transcend the distinction between economic interest, values, and national identity, and how these conflicts thus connect what we here call different dimensions of class. Similar suggestions are made by Mckenzie (2017) in an analysis of the British vote over Brexit. More recently, Jackson and Grusky (2018) have suggested reframing and broadening our understanding of class relations and stratification to include groups differentiated by resources as well as by ascriptive identities such as gender and ethnicity because all these aspects of stratification contribute to the legitimation of some groups' acquisition and other groups' loss. This is an approach even more 'radical' than what we have suggested with a multidimensional conception of class, but it points to a similar way of thinking when it comes to understanding how control over resources and political conflicts may become intertwined in new ways, and thus, how new structurally based cleavages may be forming. However, further work needs to be done to comprehend these developments in theoretically stringent ways.

Furthermore, the analysis included in this chapter is built on quite simple measures of both class and party choice, primarily due to the limited available data. Thus, we can only show a tendency towards changing class relations. New empirical analyses using more nuanced measures and possibly new types of data will be needed if we are to provide more elaborate answers about the nature of changing class relations and class conflicts. Such analyses can also include the focus on 'supply side' factors (i.e. parties' positioning on relevant policy dimensions) which are emerging as an important explanation for developments such as those presented in this chapter (cf. Evans and Tilley 2017). At the very least, our analysis clearly suggests that such new investigations are needed.

References

Alford, Robert R. (1963). *Party and Society*. Chicago, IL: Rand McNally.

Andrade, Stefan B., and Jens-Peter Thomsen (2018). 'Intergenerational educational mobility in Denmark and the United States', *Sociological Science*, 5/5: 93–113.

Atkinson, Anthony B., and Jakob E. Søgaard (2016). 'The long-run history of income inequality in Denmark', *Scandinavian Journal of Economics*, 118/2: 264–91.

Balestra, Carlotta, and Richard Tonkin (2018). 'Inequalities in household wealth across OECD countries', *OECD Working Paper*, 33: 1–69.

Beck, Ulrich, and Elisabeth Beck-Gernsheim (2002). *Individualization: Institutionalized Individualism and its Social and Political Consequences*. London: Sage.

Bennett, Tony, Mike Savage, Elizabeth B. Silva, Alan Warde, Modesto Gayo-Cal, and David Wright (2009). *Culture, Class, Distinction*. Abingdon: Routledge.

Borre, Ole (1995). 'Old and new politics in Denmark', *Scandinavian Political Studies*, 18/3: 187–205.

Bourdieu, Pierre (1984). *Distinction. A Social Critique of the Judgement of Taste*. London: Routledge.

Bourdieu, Pierre (1985). 'The social space and the genesis of groups', *Theory and Society*, 14/6: 723–44.

Bourdieu, Pierre (1986). 'The forms of capital', in John Richardson, ed., *Handbook of Theory and Research for the Sociology of Education*. New York: Greenwood, 241–58.

Bourdieu, Pierre (1987). 'What makes a social class? On the theoretical and practical existence of groups', *Berkeley Journal of Sociology*, 32: 1–17.

Christiansen, Niels F., and Klaus Petersen (2001). 'The dynamics of social solidarity: The Danish Welfare State, 1900–2000', *Scandinavian Journal of History*, 26/3: 177–96.

Christiansen, Peter M. (2020). 'Corporatism. Exaggerated death rumours?', in Peter M. Christiansen, Jørgen Elklit, and Peter Nedergaard, eds, *The Oxford Handbook of Danish Politics*. Oxford: Oxford University Press, 160–76.

Dahrendorf, Ralf (1959). *Class and Class Conflict in Industrial Society*. London: Routledge and Kegan Paul.

Danmarks Statistik (2018). 'NYT fra Danmarks Statistik, Fuldførte ungdomsuddannelser 2016/2017', København: Danmarks Statistik.

Elklit, Jørgen (1986). 'Det klassiske danske partisystem bliver til', in Jørgen Elklit and Ole Tonsgaard, eds, *Valg og vælgeradfærd. Studier i dansk politik*, 2. ed. Aarhus: Politica, 21–38.

Elvander, Nils (2002). 'The labour market regimes in the Nordic countries: A comparative analysis', *Scandinavian Political Studies*, 25/2: 117–37.

Erikson, Robert, and John H. Goldthorpe (1992). *The Constant Flux: A Study of Class Mobility in Industrial Societies*. Oxford: Oxford University Press.

Evans, Geoffrey (1993). 'Class, prospects and the life-cycle: Explaining the association between class position and political preferences', *Acta Sociologica*, 36/3: 263–76.

Evans, Geoffrey, and James Tilley (2017). *The New Politics of Class. The Political Exclusion of the British Working Class*. Oxford: Oxford University Press.

Faber, Stine T., Annick Prieur, Lennart Rosenlund, and Jakob Skjøtt-Larsen (2012). *Det skjulte klassesamfund*. Aarhus: Aarhus University Press.

Flemmen, Magne (2014). 'The politics of the service class. The homology of positions and position-takings', *European Societies*, 16/4: 543–69.

Flemmen, Magne, Vegard Jarness, and Lennart Rosenlund (2018). 'Social space and cultural class divisions: The forms of capital and contemporary lifestyle differentiation', *British Journal of Sociology*, 69/1: 124–53.

Giddens, Anthony (1991). *Modernity and Self-Identity: Self-Identity and Society in the Late Modern Age*. Cambridge: Polity Press.

Goldthorpe, John H. (1996). 'Class analysis and the reorientation of class theory: The case of persisting differentials in educational attainment', *British Journal of Sociology*, 47/3: 481–505.

Goldthorpe, John H. (2000). 'Rent, class conflict, and class structure: A commentary on Sorenson', *American Journal of Sociology*, 105/6: 1572–82.

Green-Pedersen, Christoffer (2011). *Partier i nye tider: Den politiske dagsorden i Danmark*. Aarhus: Aarhus University Press.

Green-Pedersen, Christoffer, and Karina Kosiara-Pedersen (2020). 'The party system. Open yet stable', in Peter M. Christiansen, Jørgen Elklit, and Peter Nedergaard, eds, *The Oxford Handbook of Danish Politics*. Oxford: Oxford University Press, 213–29.

Hansen, Kasper M., and Rune Stubager (2019). *Danish National Election Study Times Series Cumulative File 1971–2019*. Update 11 September 2019.

Harrits, Gitte S. (2011). 'Political power as symbolic capital and symbolic violence', *Journal of Political Power*, 4/2: 237–58.

Harrits, Gitte S. (2013). 'Class, culture and politics: On the relevance of a Bourdieusian concept of class in political sociology', *The Sociological Review*, 61/1: 172–202.

Harrits, Gitte S. (2014). *Klasse. En introduktion*. Copenhagen: Hans Reitzels Forlag.

Harrits, Gitte S., and Helene H. Pedersen (2018). 'Class categories and the subjective dimension of class: The case of Denmark', *British Journal of Sociology*, 69/1: 67–98.

Harrits, Gitte S., and Helene H. Pedersen (2019). 'Symbolic class struggles and the intersection of socioeconomic, cultural and moral categorisations', *Sociology*, 53/5: 861–78.

Harrits, Gitte S., Annick Prieur, Lennart Rosenlund, and Jakob Skjott-Larsen (2010). 'Class and politics in Denmark: Are both old and new politics structured by class?', *Scandinavian Political Studies*, 33/1: 1–27.

Hochschild, Arlie R. (2016). *Strangers in Their Own Land. Anger and Mourning on the American Right*. New York: The New Press.

Jackson, Michelle, and David B. Grusky (2018). 'A post-liberal theory of stratification', *British Journal of Sociology*, 49/4: 1096–133.

Jansen, Giedo, Geoffrey Evans, and Nan Dirk de Graaf (2013). 'Class voting and left-right party positions. A comparative study of fifteen Western democracies, 1960–2005', in Geoffrey Evans and Nan Dirk De Graff, eds, *Political Choice Matters. Explaining the Strength of Class and Religious Cleavages in Cross-National Perspective*. Oxford: Oxford University Press, 376–400.

Karlson, Kristian B., and Mads Jæger (2011). 'Kassen, kulturen og kontakterne', *Dansk Sociologi*, 22/3:61–80.

Landersø, Rasmus, and James J. Heckman (2017). 'The Scandinavian fantasy: The sources of intergenerational mobility in Denmark and the US', *Scandinavian Journal of Economics*, 119/1: 178–230.

Lareau, Annette, and Elliot B. Weininger (2003). 'Cultural capital in educational research: A critical assessment', *Theory and Society*, 32/5/6: 567–606.

Lipset, Seymor M., and Stein Rokkan (1967). 'Cleavage structures, party systems and voter alignments: An introduction', in Seymor M. Lipset and Stein Rokkan, eds, *Party Systems and Voter Alignments: Cross-National Perspectives*. New York: Free Press, 1–64.

Marx, Karl (1867/1991). *Capital. Volume I. A Critique of Political Economy*. London: Penguin Books.

Marx, Karl (1894/1991). *Capital. Volume III. The Process of Capitalist Production as a Whole*. London: Penguin Books.

Mckenzie, Lisa (2017). 'The class politics of prejudice: Brexit and the land of no-hope and glory', *British Journal of Sociology*, 68/S1: S265–80.

Ministry of Education (1998). *Uddannelsessystemet i tal gennem 150 år*. Copenhagen: Ministry of Education.

OECD (2018a). *A Broken Social Elevator? How to Promote Social Mobility*. Paris: OECD Publishing.

OECD (2018b). *Equity in Education: Breaking Down Barriers to Social Mobility*. Paris: PISA, OECD Publishing.

OECD (2019a). 'Population with tertiary education (indicator)', https://data.oecd.org/eduatt/population-with-tertiary-education.htm (accessed 19 August 2019).

OECD (2019b). 'Income inequality (indicator)', https://data.oecd.org/inequality/income-inequality.htm (accessed 19 August 2019).

Oesch, Daniel (2008). 'The changing shape of class voting', *European Societies*, 10/3: 329–55.

Pakulski, Jan, and Malcolm Waters (1996). *The Death of Class*. London: Sage.

Parkin, Frank (1979). *Marxism and Class Theory. A Bourgeois Critique*. London: Tavistock Publications.

Piketty, Thomas (2018). *Brahmin Left vs Merchant Right: Rising Inequality & the Changing Structure of Political Conflict*. WID.world Working paper series 2018/7, https://wid.world/wid-publications/ (accessed 19 November 2019).

Prieur, Annick, Lennart Rosenlund, and Jakob Skjott-Larsen (2008). 'Cultural capital today. A case study from Denmark', *Poetics*, 36/1: 45–71.

Prieur, Annick, and Mike Savage (2011). 'Updating cultural capital theory: A discussion based on studies in Denmark and in Britain', *Poetics*, 39/6: 566–80.

Robison, Joshua, and Rune Stubager (2017). 'The class pictures in citizens' minds', *British Journal of Sociology*, 69/4: 1220–47.

Rusk, Jerrold G., and Ole Borre (1974). 'The changing party space in Danish voter perceptions, 1971–1973', *European Journal of Political Research*, 2/4: 329–61.

Savage, Mike, Niall Cunningham, Fiona Devine, Sam Friedman, Daniel Laurison, Lisa McKenzie, Andrew G. Miles, Helene Snee, and Paul Wakeling (2015). *Social Class in the 21st Century*. London: Penguin Books.

Savage, Mike, Alan Warde, and Fiona Devine (2005). 'Capitals, assets, and resources: Some critical issues', *British Journal of Sociology*, 56/1: 31–47.

Skaksen, Jan R. (2018). *Afkast af uddannelse Det samfundsmæssige og individuelle rationale*. Odense: Rockwool Fondens Forskningsenhed and University Press of Sourthern Denmark.

Skeggs, Beverley (2015). 'Introduction: Stratification or exploitation, domination, dispossession and devaluation?', *Sociological Review*, 63/2: 205–22.

Stubager, Rune (2013). 'The changing basis of party competition: Education, authoritarian-libertarian values and voting', *Government and Opposition*, 48/3: 372–97.

Stubager, Rune (2017). 'Danskernes klassebevidsthed 1954 og 2015: Plus ça change, plus c'est la même chose', *Politica*, 49/2: 99–119.

Stubager, Rune, James Tilley, Geoffrey Evans, Joshua Robison, and Gitte S. Harrits (2018). 'In the eye of the beholder: What determines how people sort others into social classes?', *Social Science Research*, 76: 132–43.

Sørensen, Aage B. (2000). 'Toward a sounder basis for class analysis', *American Journal of Sociology*, 105/6: 1523–58.

Vestin, Erik, and Maria Oskarson (2017). 'Den svenska klassröstningen på reträtt – Gör ett nytt klasschema någon skillnad?', *Politica* 49/2: 179–98.

Weber, Max (1922/1978). *Economy and Society. An Outline of Interpretive Sociology*. Berkeley, CA: University of California Press.

Wright, Erik O. (1997). *Class Counts*. Cambridge: Cambridge University Press.

CHAPTER 17

DANISH PUBLIC OPINION
Stability, Change, and Polarization

PETER THISTED DINESEN, RUNE SLOTHUUS, AND RUNE STUBAGER

CITIZENS' political opinions are fundamental for understanding democratic politics. Normatively, a central feature of representative democracy is the 'continuing responsiveness of the government to the preferences of its citizens' (Dahl 1971: 1), and politicians should be able to justify if public policies deviate from citizens' preferences (Pitkin 1967: 224). Empirically, political opinions are important for whom citizens vote in elections (Borre and Andersen 1997; Stubager et al. 2020), set the stage for competition between political parties (Green-Pedersen 2019), motivate which issues the news media cover, and ultimately, influence the direction of public policy (Mortensen 2007; Soroka and Wlezien 2010). Thus, citizens' political opinions provide essential inputs to the political system and are important for understanding Danish political culture and the dynamics of Danish politics.

This chapter provides an overview of public opinion in Denmark. How do citizens view major issues in Danish politics, and how have these opinions developed over time? Our analysis of Danish public opinion first illuminates aggregate opinion on four issues—economic distribution, immigration, the environment, and the European Union—over four decades. We show that there is remarkable stability in aggregate public opinion over time. Second, we explore the extent to which this apparent stability in opinion conceals changing degrees of social polarization in opinions across four socio-demographic groups (gender, age, education, and occupation). Third, we analyse the development of possible political polarization in Danish public opinion by comparing opinions across voters of political parties over time. Finally, we put Danish public opinion in a comparative perspective by comparing opinion on the four issues to public opinion in six other European countries (Norway, Sweden, Great Britain, Germany, Poland, and Spain).

STABILITY OR CHANGE IN DANISH
PUBLIC OPINION

In V.O. Key's (1961: 14) classic definition, public opinion consists of 'those opinions held by private persons which governments find it prudent to heed. Governments may be compelled toward action or inaction by such opinion; in other instances they may ignore it, perhaps at their peril [...]'. As the definition makes plain, there is a clear link between citizens' opinions and democratic decision-making. The dynamics of public opinion can be gauged both at the *aggregate level* (which proportion of the Danish population holds a certain attitude at a given time) and at the *individual level* (how does the attitudes of a given citizen develop over time) (Sniderman et al. 2014; Togeby 2004). Our analysis focuses on public opinion at the aggregate (macro) level, illuminating levels of opinion and gross changes over time.

We focus on opinions toward four political issues which reflect core aspects of Danish politics. *Economic redistribution* in the form of redistributive welfare policies is the defining issue of the traditional left-right dimension revolving around material interests (Borre 1995). *Immigration*, on the other hand, has grown to become a key issue on the second political conflict dimension, over libertarian-authoritarian (or cultural) values, which has evolved since the 1970s and crystallized during the 1980s and 1990s in Denmark (Borre 1995; Inglehart 1977; Nielsen 2007). The *environment* has also been viewed as a manifestation of the libertarian-authoritarian dimension, although less strongly than immigration (Nielsen 2007). Finally, the *European Union/Community* (henceforth 'the EU') constitutes its own dimension in the minds of Danish voters (Nielsen 2007).

Figure 17.1 illustrates the development of public opinion toward each of the four issues over time, based on survey questions asked continuously by the Danish National Election Survey (DNES) (Hansen and Stubager 2019; see www.valgprojektet.dk). We have chosen the following questions that enable examining stability and change in the four issues over an extended period:

- *Economic Redistribution*: 'Which of these two statements comes closest to your own point of view. "(A) The differences in incomes and living standards are still too large in our country, so people with small incomes should have a faster improvement in their living standards than those with higher incomes", or "(B) The levelling of incomes has gone sufficiently far; the income differences that still exist should largely be maintained"'. Figure 17.1 illustrates the share of the population in agreement with statement A and B, respectively, from 1979 to 2019.
- *Immigration*: 'Immigration constitutes a serious threat to our national culture?' Figure 17.1 illustrates the share of the population in agreement ('completely agree' or 'mostly agree') or disagreement ('completely disagree' or 'mostly disagree') with this statement from 1987 to 2019. The item was phrased differently in 1979, 1981, and 1984, focusing on whether refugees should conform to Danish culture (1979

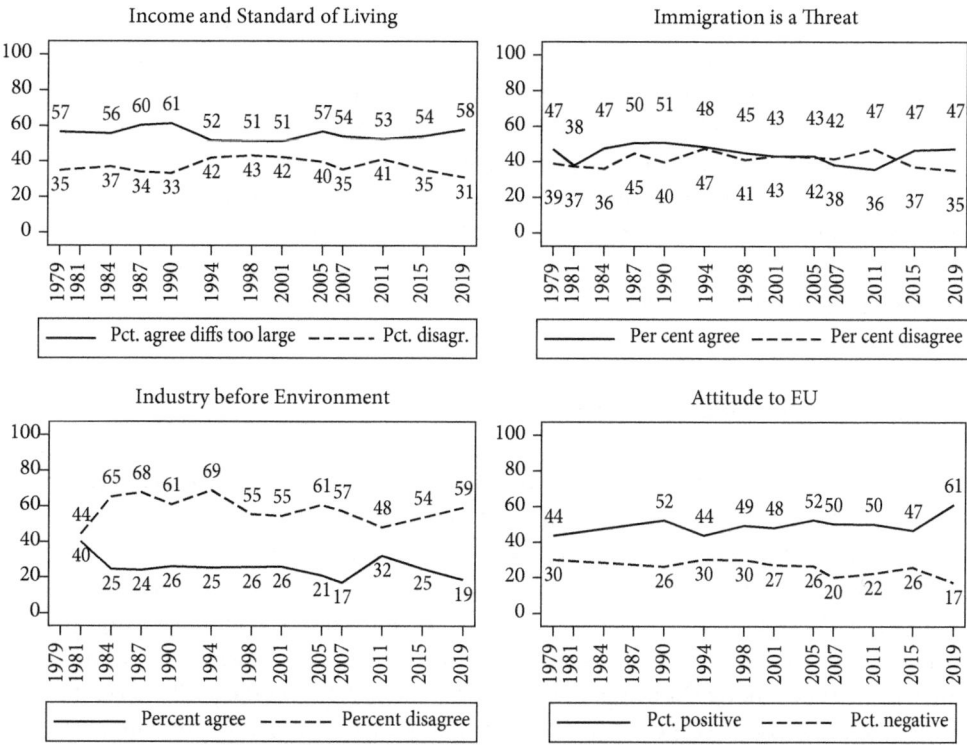

FIGURE 17.1 Development in public opinion toward economic redistribution, immigration, the environment, and the EU over time.

Note: See text for question wordings and coding. Data are weighted to be representative of the Danish voting-age population. Numbers indicate the percentage of the Danish population agreeing/positive or disagreeing/negative on a given question in a given year. The percentages do not sum to 100 per cent as 'Don't know' and/or 'Neutral/neither or' responses are excluded from the figures

and 1984) and repatriation of guest workers (1981). While differently worded, these items still tap the same underlying dimension as the main question, so we therefore also include responses to these questions in the figure.

- *The Environment*: 'Economic growth should be secured by developing the industry even though this may be in conflict with environmental interests.' Figure 17.1 illustrates the share of the population in agreement ('completely agree' or 'mostly agree') or disagreement ('completely disagree' or 'mostly disagree') with this statement from 1981 to 2019.
- *The European Union*: 'What is your general attitude toward the EEC/EU?' Figure 17.1 illustrates the share of the population indicating a positive ('very positive' or 'mostly positive') or negative ('very negative' or 'mostly negative') opinion from 1979 to 2019.

The first and perhaps most striking finding emerging from Figure 17.1 is the general stability in public opinion toward each of the four issues over the observed period.

Despite the significant societal and political changes that have occurred over the last 40 years, there is no tendency for watershed changes in opinions toward core political issues. This also implies that aggregate changes in public opinion in the Danish population cannot readily explain the changing success of various political parties over time. Instead, citizens are likely to vote differently based on their pre-existing attitudes, responding in part to real-world developments and party behaviour, for example through subtle processes such as priming (Togeby 2006). Although public opinion toward the four issues is generally stable, it does change somewhat over time—and in a meaningful fashion—as we elaborate on below.

Economic Redistribution

A stable majority of Danes agree that income differences are too large and that these should be reduced further. However, there is also a significant minority who find that redistribution has gone far enough and should be kept at its current level. Plausibly, some of these responses in reality reflect a desire for reduced redistribution. Regardless, it is evident that (further) redistribution, and the welfare state by implication, continues to be popular among Danish voters. This popularity has presumably caused the widespread support for the welfare state among Danish political parties—even those on the political right, which have historically been sceptical of it (Borre and Andersen 1997; Sniderman et al. 2014: 52–81). The most noticeable deviation from the overall state is in 1987 and 1990 where the demand for higher redistribution was especially pronounced—likely a response to the austere financial policies of the late 1980s. At the same time, the gradual reduction in benefits and transfers from 1998 onwards and rising economic inequality only seem to manifest in stronger public support for redistribution towards the very end of the time series.

Immigration

The most striking feature of this issue is the high level of disagreement in the Danish public. Across almost the entire period, Danish voters are essentially equally divided on whether they think immigration constitutes a serious threat to Danish culture or not, although we do see a slight tendency for the immigration-sceptic stance dominating by the end of the period studied (in 2015 and 2019). The divided electorate also indicates the issue's potential for taking a central position on the political agenda as an issue on which the parties disagree. Indeed, it has gained increased prominence on Danish voters' agenda since the early 1990s, peaking in the 2001 and 2015 elections where it was considered a decisive political issue (Andersen 2003; Hansen and Stubager 2017). Both elections led to a change from a Social Democratic-led government to a Liberal-led government, consistent with the widespread analysis that the right-of-centre parties benefit when the immigration issue is high on the agenda because their position on this issue has been closer to the majority of citizens' attitudes than the Social Democratic position has been (Borre and Andersen 1997: 114–59; Stubager 2010).

While this may seem counterintuitive given the equal divide in the voter population on the immigration issue, one reason may lie in the relatively hard, negative formulation of the specific question ('serious threat'). This plausibly entails that moderate immigration sceptics choose the 'non-threat' option even though they prefer a strict immigration policy. Therefore, public opinion may appear more positive toward immigration than it is in reality, where it may be closer to the immigration-sceptic stances of the right-wing parties.

The Environment

Apart from the first measurement in 1981 where they were equally divided on the issue, Danish voters are overwhelmingly pro-environment. The proportion disagreeing that industry should be developed even at the expense of the environment is generally double or triple the proportion agreeing with this statement. Apart from the first year in the time series, the most marked deviation from the overall pattern is 2011, where a notably higher proportion of voters agree with the pro-industry stance (and vice versa for the pro-environment stance). A plausible explanation for this change is the proximity to the Great Recession, which had a significant impact on the Danish economy and may, therefore, temporarily have offset environmental concerns over economic growth as support returned to the general level in 2015.

The EU

Public opinion toward the EU is remarkably stable among the Danish public from 1979 until 2015. The proportion of positive sentiments is typically between 1.5 and 2 times higher than the proportion of negative sentiments. This is perhaps somewhat surprising given the negative outcomes of various referenda on issues related to further European integration (most recently, the rejection of abandoning the Danish opt-outs in 2015) and in light of the fact that European integration has increased significantly since Denmark entered the EEC in 1973. Danes thus seem to show stable support for the EU on a general level but are more critical of specific policies furthering integration. In 2019, however, we observe a clear swing in the EU-positive direction. While it remains a conjecture, US President Donald Trump's questioning of Trans-Atlantic relations as well as the uncertainty associated with Brexit may be an explanation, leading Danes to see the EU as a counterbalance and safe harbour in times of international turmoil.

In conclusion, Danish public opinion on the four core political issues examined has been remarkably stable over the past almost 40 years, although we do see fluctuations over time that seem to reflect corresponding societal developments. Danish voters support redistribution, they strongly favour environmental concerns over industry interests, they are positively inclined toward the EU, and lastly, they are highly divided on immigration.

SOCIAL POLARIZATION OF PUBLIC
OPINION OVER TIME

The aggregate public opinion may conceal substantial differences between various social groups. By extension, the stability in Danish public opinion could potentially hide important changes in polarization across socio-demographic groups. We address the issue of social polarization in political attitudes by focusing on differences in the four attitudes over time across four salient socio-demographic categories: generation (in five categories), gender (women and men), education (compulsory versus secondary schooling) and occupation (in four categories). Figures 17.2–17.5 show the polarization over time in political attitudes across the four socio-demographic variables. To facilitate illustration and interpretation, we only report the proportion in agreement with/ who are positive towards each issue.

As a general observation, we see well-known differences in public opinion toward the four issues across the socio-demographic variables (Hansen and Stubager 2017). However,

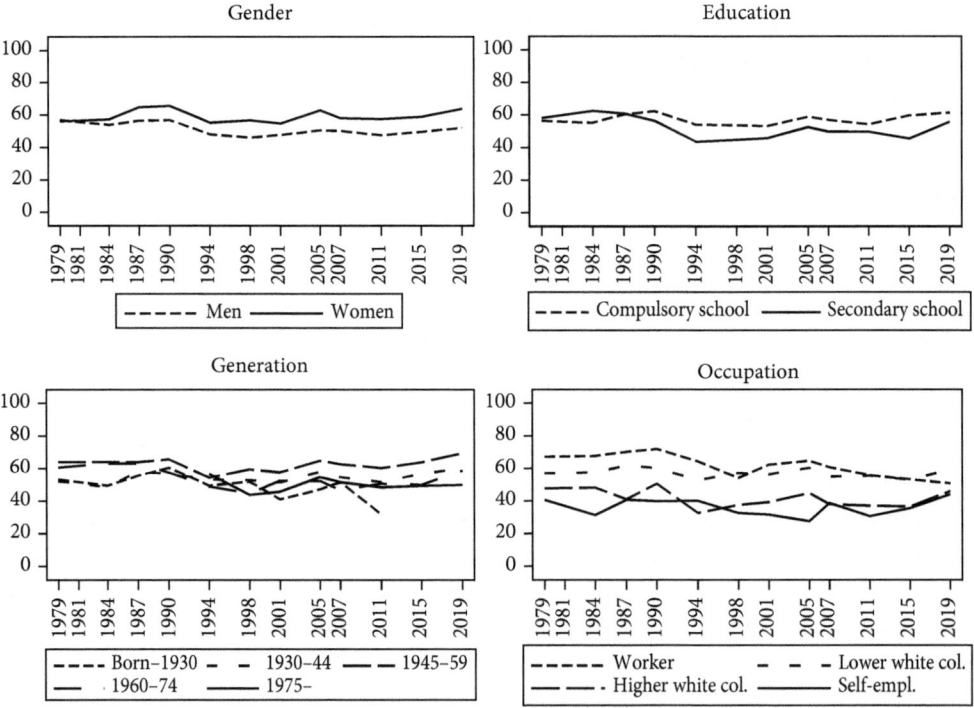

FIGURE 17.2 Socio-demographic differences in attitudes toward economic redistribution, per cent agreeing that income differences are too large.

Note: The graphs depict the percentage of respondents who agree with the statement that: 'The differences in incomes and living standards are still too large in our country, so people with small incomes should have a faster improvement of their living standards than those with higher incomes.'

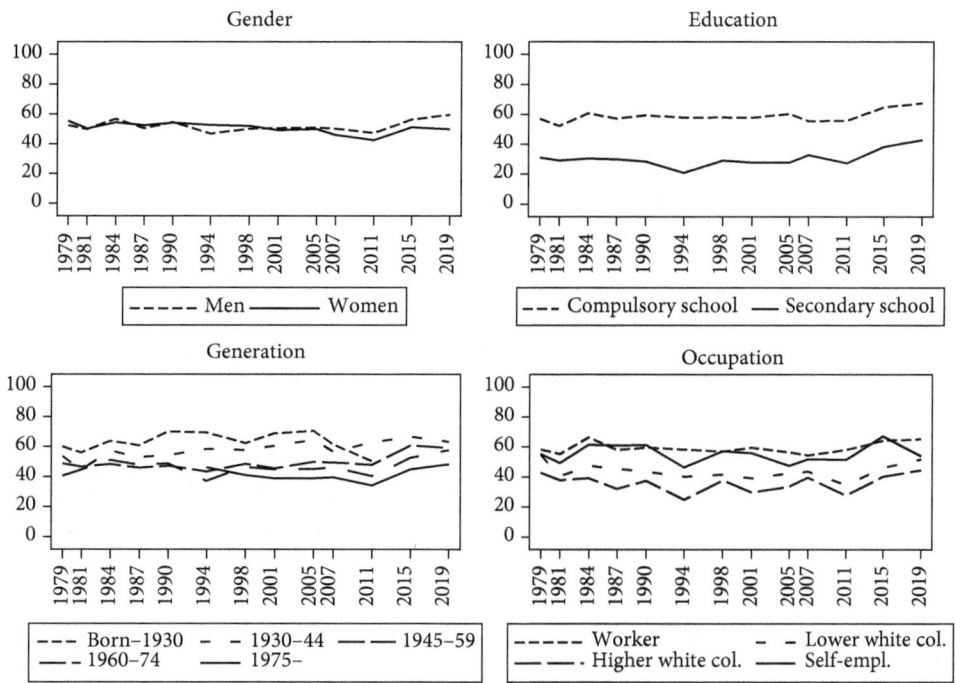

FIGURE 17.3 Socio-demographic differences in attitudes toward immigration, per cent agreeing that immigration is a threat.

Note: The graphs depict the percentage of respondents who agree with the statement that: 'Immigration constitutes a serious threat to our national culture.'

with a few notable exceptions, we do not see pronounced changes in the social gradient in opinions toward the four issues over time. Generally, there is thus little to indicate that the stability in aggregate public opinion over the past 40 years is masking a polarization among social groups. Below, we address socio-demographic polarization in opinions toward each of the four issues in more detail.

Attitudes Toward Redistribution

We observe moderate polarization in public opinion toward redistribution between different socio-demographic groups but with limited change over time. This is true for generations where we see that the oldest (born 1930 and before) and youngest cohort (born in 1975 and after) are somewhat more sceptical of redistribution than the generations born in between. In contrast to the limited generational differences, we see both gender and education cleavages emerging over time after having been essentially non-existent at the beginning of the period. In later years, women and those with lower education become more pro-redistribution, as opposed to men and better-educated individuals, which align with findings from previous international research (Jæger 2006). Lastly, we

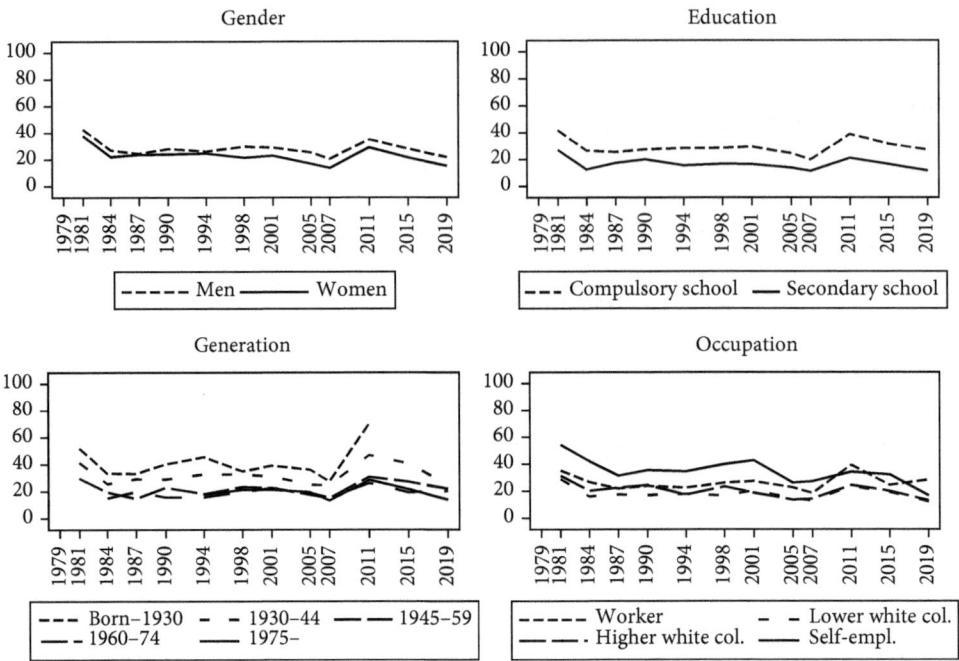

FIGURE 17.4 Socio-demographic differences in attitudes toward the environment, per cent agreeing that economic growth goes before the environment.

Note: The graphs depict the percentage of respondents who agree with the statement that: 'Economic growth should be secured by developing the industry even though this may conflict with environmental interests.'

see marked but unsurprising differences in support for redistribution between different occupations—the primary locus of redistribution preferences in traditional cleavage models (Borre and Andersen 1997: 114–59). Workers and those in lower white-collar jobs are substantially more pro-redistribution than their self-employed and higher white-collar counterparts. Interestingly, however, the gap between the occupations appears to be somewhat reduced over time, thereby indicating that the formerly primary socio-structural cleavage vis-à-vis redistribution has lost strength (Stubager 2010).

Immigration

The immigration issue arguably has the strongest socio-demographic gradient—with the notable exception of gender. The marked disagreement over this issue in the public at large ostensibly has a strong socio-structural anchoring. At the same time, however, this has only changed little over the period studied, and as such, these opinion cleavages are not a new feature of Danish politics. The various cohorts differ systematically and quite strongly in their opinions on immigration, with older generations seeing immigration as a threat to a substantially higher degree than younger generations do. Similarly, we observe highly pronounced—and stable—differences between those with secondary

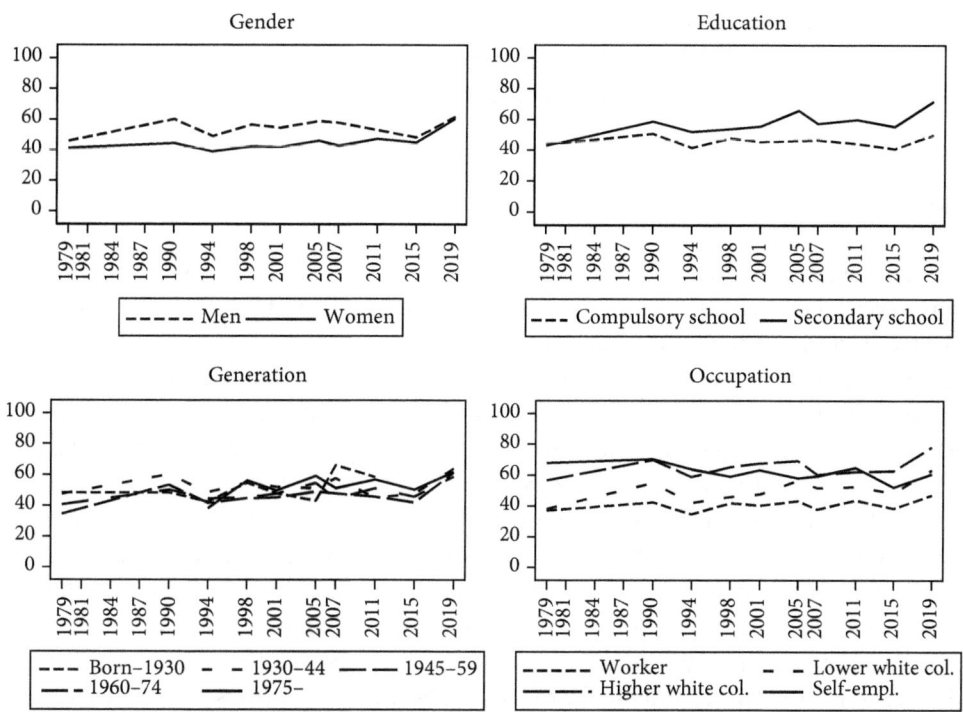

FIGURE 17.5 Socio-demographic differences in attitudes toward the EU, per cent positive.

Note: The graphs depict the percentage of respondents who have a positive attitude toward the EU

schooling (more positive) and those with lower educational attainment, as well as between those in white-collar jobs (more positive) and blue-collar workers and the self-employed. These differences correspond to findings from a broader set of European countries (Hainmüller and Hiscox 2007). Further, the strong generational, educational, and occupational differences in immigration opinions are connected to some extent; younger generations are better educated and increasingly work in white-collar professions. Lastly, we observe only minor differences between men and women in their attitudes toward immigration. This runs counter to cross-national work but matches previous findings from the Danish context (Dinesen et al. 2016).

The Environment

Although less pronounced, the socio-demographic differences (and their relative temporal stability) in public opinion toward the environment correspond to those on the immigration issue, arguably highlighting the two issues' ideological commonality. Younger generations, the better educated, and white-collar employees are substantially more sympathetic towards environmental interests relative to industry interests. The generational shift in a pro-environmental direction aligns with Inglehart's (1977) predictions about post-material values emerging in younger generations growing up under higher existential security. Lastly, since the mid-1990s, women have emerged to become slightly more supportive of environmental interests than men.

The EU

There are significant differences among different socio-demographic strata in their opinions toward the EC/EU (hereafter, just referred to as "EU"), and in the case of education, this has become more pronounced over time. The generational patterns in EU opinions are limited and by the end of the period there are virtually no differences in EU opinions across generations. We see the strongest gender differences on any of the four issues for EU attitudes. Men are generally noticeably more positively inclined toward the EU than are women, although this difference is diminished and only negligible by the end of the period. The educational differences in EU attitudes are striking. After starting out on the same level, there is a growing difference over time, with the better educated becoming substantially more positive toward the EU than the less well educated. The last two findings—regarding gender and education—also appear to have a behavioural manifestation as it matches differences in support for joining the common currency in the 2000 referendum (Buch and Hansen 2002). Finally, for the occupational sector, we observe relatively stable differences between higher white-collar employees and the self-employed who are more EU positive and workers and lower white-collar employees who are more sceptical. Yet, the latter seem to be moving in the positive direction towards the end of the period.

In conclusion, there are marked socio-demographic differences in public opinion toward the four issues studied, but they generally tend to be stable over time. Overall, generation, education, and occupation are the more important socio-structural cleavages, while gender is less important. The largest and most persistent gradient is that of education for immigration attitudes, which resonates with research showing that education is an increasingly important cleavage in Danish politics, especially in relation to cultural issues—of which immigration is the cardinal indicator—that are increasingly important for party choice (Nielsen 2007; Stubager 2010; Stubager et al. 2020).

PARTISAN POLARIZATION OF PUBLIC OPINION OVER TIME

The aggregate stability of Danish public opinion on the four issues analysed could also conceal significant differences in party political polarization and disagreement over time. Obviously, differences in opinions across partisan groups could be driven by citizens voting for the political parties sharing their policy positions (Stubager 2010; Stubager et al. 2020). However, partisan polarization of opinions could also be elite driven, as political parties to some degree shape the opinions of their supporters (Bisgaard and Slothuus 2018; Slothuus 2010; Slothuus and de Vreese 2010).

Figure 17.6 illuminates partisan polarization over time by analysing the same four opinion questions as in the preceding sections, now broken down by citizens' vote choice among the major political parties—that is, parties consistently represented in Parliament. 'Far Left' is the Red-Green Alliance (*Enhedslisten*) from 1990 onward and a mix of minor left-wing parties before then, whereas the 'Danish People's Party' (*Dansk Folkeparti*) includes only voters of the Progress Party (*Fremskridtspartiet*) until 1994 and

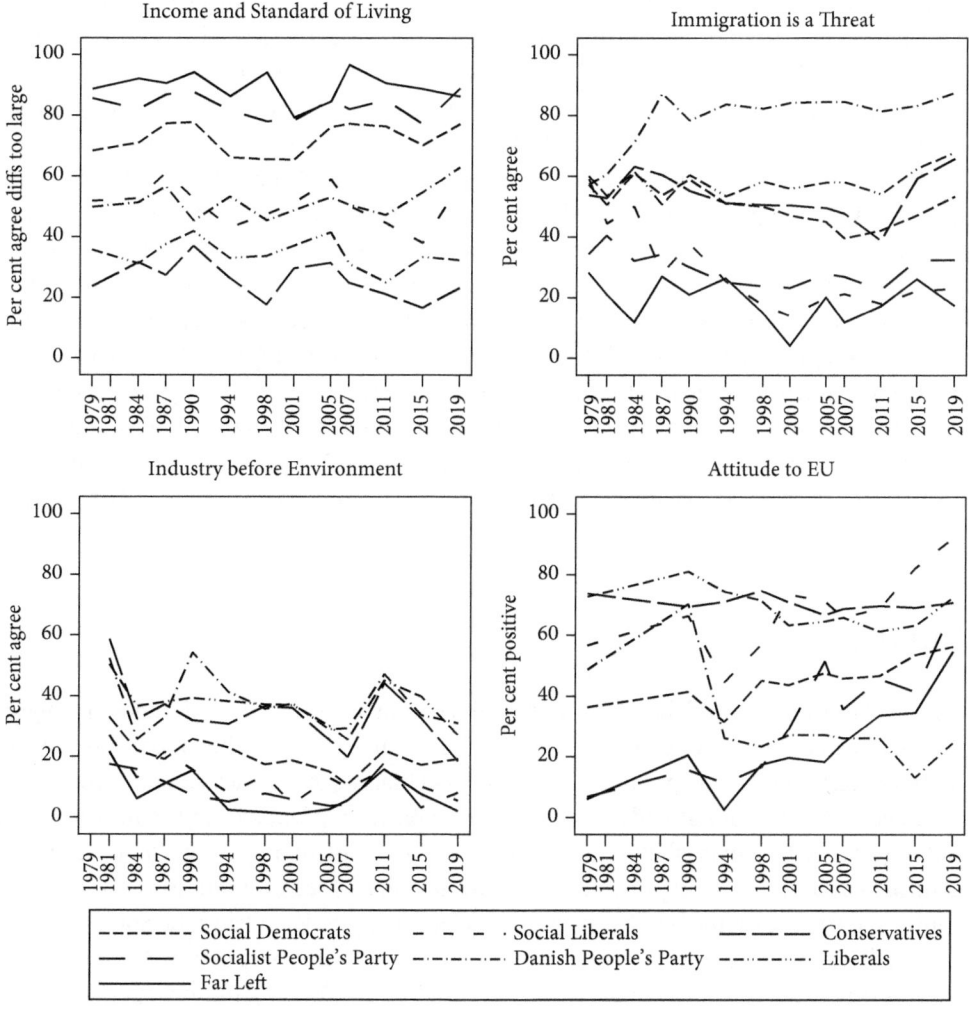

FIGURE 17.6 Development in opinions on economic redistribution, immigration, the environment, and the EU over time by partisan groups.

Note: See text and note to Figure 17.1 for question wordings, coding, and weighting. Partisan groups are voters. 'Danish People's Party' includes voters of the Progress Party

both parties until 2005 where the Progress Party stopped running. Overall, Figure 17.6 shows higher levels of partisan polarization than the social polarization analysed in the previous section and some quite interesting changes across partisan groups.

Attitudes toward Redistribution

Reflecting its status as a defining issue of the traditional left-right dimension, there is a high degree of partisan polarization over economic redistribution. Moreover, opinion differences between partisan groups are rather stable over the entire period. Voters display the pattern we would expect given the ideological positions of their parties. Thus, voters of the left-of-centre parties (Far Left and the Socialist People's Party, *Socialistisk Folkeparti*) almost universally agree that income differences are still too large in Danish society. Voters of the Social Democratic Party (*Socialdemokratiet*) are almost as supportive of this view. At the other end of the ideological continuum, voters of the Conservatives (*Konservative Folkeparti*) and the Liberals (*Venstre*) are much less favourable towards further economic redistribution; only around 30 per cent agree that income inequality should be lowered, with a slight tendency for this proportion to shrink further in the most recent years. In-between, we find the voters of the Social Liberals (*Radikale Venstre*) and the Danish People's Party where roughly 50 per cent agree that income differences are still too large, highlighting that the two parties do not distinguish themselves from each other on the economic conflict dimension. It is also worth noting that voters of the anti-tax Progress Party held virtually the same opinions as voters of the Danish People's Party, which replaced it in the mid-1990s. In sum, partisan polarization in opinions toward economic redistribution is high and stable.

Immigration

As one of the most hotly debated issues in Danish politics over the past decades, immigration has been high on the agenda during election campaigns since the 1990s (Hansen and Stubager 2017: 25). Not surprisingly then, there is a high degree of partisan polarization on the issue, with opinions already polarized across partisan groups from the mid-1980s. A stable (since 1987), overwhelming majority (80 per cent or more) of voters from the Danish People's Party (and previously, the Progress Party) see immigration as a threat. In contrast, partisans on the left (Far Left and Socialist People's Party) and the Social Liberals are much less inclined to see immigration as a threat, and this proportion declines steadily over time, falling from around 30–40 per cent in the 1980s to around 20 per cent from 2001 onwards, thereby increasing the partisan polarization on the issue. Between these extremes, supporters of the three traditionally largest parties have opinions that are more moderate. Yet there is a striking pattern. Liberal voters remain relatively sceptical towards immigration (a proportion of 50 per cent, rising to 60, see immigration as a threat). In contrast, until 2011, a still smaller proportion among Social Democrat and

Conservative voters see immigration as a threat, down from a level between 50 and 60 per cent in the 1980s to below 40 per cent in the early 2000s. However, towards the end of the time series, Social Democrat and (particularly) Conservative voters become more sceptical of immigration. This trend in partisan polarization indicates a process of sorting where anti-immigration voters increasingly vote for the Liberals, the Conservatives, and the Danish People's Party (these parties have grown in support over the period). In sum, while aggregate opinion on immigration has been rather stable during the period, partisan polarization over immigration has increased.

The Environment

While the environment has been considered part of the libertarian-authoritarian conflict dimension (Borre 1995; Stubager 2010), opinion differences between partisan groups signal more of a traditional left-right divide. Thus, voters from the Liberals, the Conservatives (except in 2019), and Danish People's Party (Progress Party) are consistently the least environmentalist and most pro-industry. Conversely, among voters supporting the Far Left, the Socialist People's Party, and the Social Liberals, only a tiny fraction (around 10 per cent) thinks that economic growth should be prioritized over environmental protection; these voters are followed by the Social Democrats' voters. Yet partisan polarization is lower on the environmental issue than on the other issues analysed. There is even a tendency towards partisan depolarization, at least until the Great Recession, leading to only a limited partisan gap in opinions in 2007, likely driven by the positive economic development in combination with more environmentalist signals from then Prime Minister Anders Fogh Rasmussen. However, the Great Recession sparked increased partisan divisions in 2011, with right-of-centre partisans changing opinions in a pro-industry direction, but already in the following elections, these parties' voters gradually returned to a more pro-environmental stance. Thus, aggregate level opinion (cf. Figure 17.1) again hides interesting partisan dynamics.

The EU

The stability in aggregate public opinion toward the EU and the stable socio-demographic patterns in these opinions are striking given the major institutional and policy changes transforming the European Community and later the European Union. Yet we see significant changes over time in partisan polarization in EU attitudes. Two changes stand out. First, as the common market was supplemented with a political union increasingly regulating the market, the traditional left-right divide has depolarized. Citizens voting for the right-of-centre parties have become somewhat less positive towards the EU. Most strikingly, the proportion among Liberal voters with positive opinions toward the EU has dropped by around 20 percentage points, from roughly 80 per cent positive in 1990 to about 60 per cent in the 2010s. Conversely, voters of the left-of-centre parties have become markedly more positive toward the European Union, from only around 10 per cent with positive attitudes until the mid-1990s to nearly 50 per cent positive by the end of the period for the Socialist People's Party and the Far Left supporters. Social Democrat voters have become somewhat more positive as well. The second notable development is that—similar to the immigration issue—the Social Liberals and the Danish People's Party's voters have come to be placed the furthest apart on the EU issue, at the positive extreme and the negative extreme, respectively. Thus, whereas opinions toward the EU have depolarized along the traditional left-right dimension, they have polarized along the libertarian-authoritarian dimension.

Danish Public Opinion in a Comparative Perspective

To put Danish public opinion in context, and thus to understand whether Danes think differently about political issues, it is useful to compare it to that of their European counterparts. More specifically, we compare Danish public opinion to equivalent attitudes in Norway, Sweden, Germany, Great Britain, Spain, and Poland to enable a broad comparison within Europe. The comparison is based on data from the European Social Survey (ESS 2016; see https://www.europeansocialsurvey.org/), a representative survey of inhabitants of European countries (aged 15 and above) collected biannually. We use data from the period 2003 to 2015. The items from the Danish Election Survey used previously are not available in the ESS. Instead, we rely on the following four items which tap into the same four underlying attitudes:

- *Economic Redistribution*: 'The government should take measures to reduce differences in income levels'. Figure 17.7 illustrates the share of the population in agreement ('Agree strongly' or 'Agree') with this statement from 2003 to 2015.
- *Immigration*: 'Would you say that [country]'s cultural life is generally undermined or enriched by people coming to live here from other countries?' Responses are measured on a scale ranging from 0 ('Cultural life undermined') to 10 ('Cultural life enriched'). Figure 17.7 illustrates the share of the population answering 0–4 on the scale (i.e. primarily considering cultural life undermined) from 2003 to 2015.
- *The Environment*: 'Please say to what extent you agree or disagree with [the following statement]: "Modern science can be relied on to solve our environmental problems"'. Figure 17.7 illustrates the share of the population in agreement ('Agree strongly' or 'Agree') with this statement from 2003 to 2011. This question taps a mix of environmental concerns and faith in science, but as it is the only available indicator on environmental attitudes going back to 2003 in the ESS, we use it, despite tapping environmental concern somewhat noisily.
- *The EU*: 'Now thinking about the European Union, some say European unification should go further. Others say it has already gone too far. Using this card,

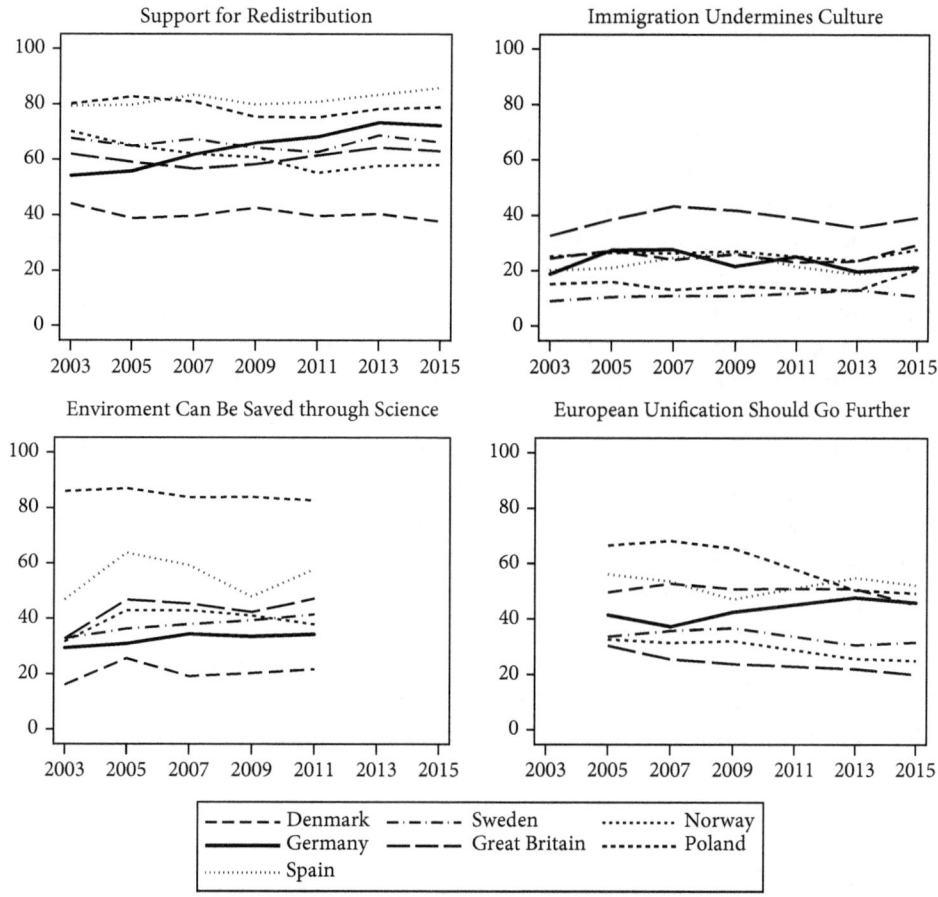

FIGURE 17.7 Public opinion on four issues in Denmark, Sweden, Norway, Germany, Great Britain, Poland, and Spain, 2003–2015, per cent in agreement.

Note: See text for question wordings and coding. Data are weighted to be representative of the population (age 15 and older) in each country. Numbers depicted indicate percentages in agreement with each opinion statement

what number on the scale best describes your position?' Responses are measured on a scale ranging from 0 ('Unification already gone too far') to 10 ('Unification should go further'). Figure 17.7 illustrates the share of the population answering 6-10 on the scale (i.e. primarily thinking that unification should go further) from 2003 to 2015.

The figures reveal significant and substantively interesting similarities and differences in public opinion between Denmark and the six other countries. Particularly interesting is that Denmark is located at one extreme on two of the four issues (redistribution and the environment). As in the previous analyses based solely on Danish data, the general insight from the comparison over time is one of relatively high levels of stability with a few notable exceptions. Below, we discuss each of the four opinions.

Economic Redistribution

Attitudes toward redistribution are relatively stable in the seven countries over the period studied (with Germany being an exception). This is interesting considering that it covers the Great Recession which could plausibly have prompted a higher demand for redistribution. Strikingly, Danes are by far the most sceptical of further redistribution among the seven countries. In Denmark, the public is essentially equally divided between desiring more government redistribution and not; an equal proportion of Danes disagree with the statement that the government should take further measures to reduce differences in income, and a significant share (around 20-25 per cent) place themselves in the neutral category. In contrast, the Spanish and Polish publics are overwhelmingly supportive of more redistribution. These differences may be taken as an indication of a thermostatic relationship between policy and attitudes (Wlezien 1995). The welfare state is more developed in Denmark and social inequalities smaller (as assessed, for example, by the Gini coefficient) than in Spain and Poland, and therefore, Danes have a more limited appetite for further redistribution. Yet the higher support for redistribution in Sweden and Norway—two countries that also have developed welfare states—indicates a more complicated story. Danes are more sceptical of redistribution than their compatriots are in the neighbouring—and in many ways comparable—Scandinavian countries. That being said, Danes are still relatively supportive of redistribution as was also reflected in the measure used in the previous analyses based on the national election study where we found somewhat stronger support.

Immigration

On balance, the publics of the seven countries do not view immigration as a threat to their national culture, at least not when phrased in starker terms ('undermine'). Using this measure, Danes are ostensibly less sceptical of a cultural threat embodied in immigration compared to the measure used in the national election survey. There is little variation within countries over time, but there is some variation between the countries, with Denmark placed roughly in the middle between Great Britain (highest threat perception) and Sweden (lowest threat perception), and largely similar to Norway. Contrary to the impression sometimes conveyed in the public debate, Danes are no more sceptical of immigration than publics in other European countries but largely on a par with them. If anything, it is neighbouring Sweden—often used as the benchmark in the Danish public debate—that stands out as perceiving immigration as less culturally threatening than in most other countries.

The Environment

There are very marked, stable differences in public opinion toward the environment between the populations in each of the seven countries examined. Noticeably, Danes have the least faith in science to solve environmental problems, which we interpret as a pro-environment stance. This mirrors the findings using a different measure in the previous analyses. It stands in sharp contrast to the Polish public, which has an overwhelming belief in science to solve environmental problems (in fact, this is the most pronounced difference on any of the four issues). More generally, the more affluent Northern European countries are more supportive of the environment than the less affluent Eastern (Poland) and Southern (Spain) European countries using this measure.

The EU

Attitudes toward the European Union are largely stable in most of the seven countries with Poland as a notable exception due to a significant drop in support. Attitudes range from primarily positive to strongly negative sentiments towards further European integration (measured as the share of positive versus negative sentiments and excluding the middle category). Danes are among the most EU-supportive publics, on a par with Germany, Spain, and Poland in later years, and more so than the neighbouring countries Sweden and Norway (the latter is, of course, not a member of the EU), and not least, Great Britain, the most EU-sceptic country. Danes are primarily pro-EU (a higher share of positive versus negative sentiments), thus confirming the findings from the national election survey.

In conclusion, comparing public opinion in Denmark to that of six other European countries reveals interesting differences and similarities. Most strikingly, Danes are the most sceptical of economic redistribution (although still relatively supportive overall) and the most supportive of the environment. In terms of immigration, Danes are essentially on a par with most of the other countries, including Norway, but in contrast to Sweden, the most positive country. Lastly, the Danish public is generally in favour of more European integration and more so than the other Northern European countries examined (except Germany).

Conclusion

This chapter has provided an overview of public opinion in Denmark on four major political issues: economic distribution, immigration, the environment, and the European Union. Aggregate public opinion on these four issues shows remarkable stability over 40 years. Danes continue to support economic redistribution, strongly favour environmental protection, are positively inclined toward the European Union, and are highly divided on immigration. Disaggregating the overall trends by socio-demographic strata, we find considerable polarization. In particular, generations are fairly divided on immigration and the environment, educational groups are highly polarized over immigration, and occupational groups polarize over economic redistribution, immigration, and the EU. Yet the degree of social polarization on these four issues has been remarkably stable during the four decades analysed.

In contrast, Danish public opinion has shown changes in partisan polarization on the four issues over time. Most strikingly, partisan groups have polarized on the immigration issue in tandem with the issue taking centre stage on the political agenda. Citizens seem to have increasingly sorted into partisan groups based on their immigration attitudes, leaving supporters of the Social Liberals and left-of-centre parties as more pro-immigration. Attitudes towards the EC/EU are another issue where the differences in opinion between partisan groups have changed dramatically over time. Voters of the three major parties occupying the Prime Minister's Office during the period have depolarized, voters of the left-of-centre parties have become much more positive toward the EU, whereas voters of the Social Liberals and the Danish People's Party are now by far the most positive and negative towards the EU, respectively. When it comes to the environment, there has been some partisan depolarization, at least until the Great Recession. Finally, partisan polarization on economic redistribution remains high and stable, indicating that the traditional left-right dimension is still highly relevant to Danish politics. Lastly, when we compare Danish public opinion to that of six other European countries, Danes turn out to be fairly representative of European public opinion in terms of their immigration sentiments, while they are the most sceptical (in relative terms) of economic redistribution and the most supportive of protecting the environment.

The conclusion is that even though public opinion in Denmark has been remarkably stable over the past four decades in the aggregate and across social groups, partisan polarization has increased on immigration, and to some extent (and with a changed character), European integration. Immigration in particular has become a highly salient issue (Hansen and Stubager 2017: 25), ostensibly leading citizens to increasingly vote based on their immigration opinions (Stubager 2010; Stubager et al. 2020). Therefore, an important key to grasping the dynamics in Danish politics is to understand how citizens' political attitudes are mobilized and to some extent even shaped by political parties and other actors. Winning public opinion is the path to political power, and in Denmark, mobilizing and polarizing attitudes toward immigration has been a strong force in determining political power at the beginning of the twenty-first century.

REFERENCES

Andersen, Jørgen G. (2003). 'Vælgernes nye politiske dagsorden', in Jørgen G. Andersen and Ole Borre, eds, *Politisk forandring. Værdipolitik og nye skillelinjer ved Folketingsvalget 2001.* Aarhus: Systime, 135–49.

Bisgaard, Martin, and Rune Slothuus (2018). 'Partisan elites as culprits? How party cues shape partisan perceptual gaps', *American Journal of Political Science*, 62/2: 456–69.

Borre, Ole (1995). 'Old and new politics in Denmark', *Scandinavian Political Studies*, 18/3: 187–205.

Borre, Ole, and Jørgen G. Andersen (1997). *Voting and Political Attitudes in Denmark.* Aarhus: Aarhus University Press.

Buch, Roger, and Kasper M. Hansen (2002). 'The Danes and Europe: From EC 1972 to Euro 2000', *Scandinavian Political Studies*, 25/1: 1–26.

Dahl, Robert A. (1971). *Polyarchy: Participation and Opposition*. New Haven, CT: Yale University Press.

Dinesen, Peter T., Robert Klemmensen, and Asbjørn S. Nørgaard (2016). 'Attitudes toward immigration: The role of personal dispositions', *Political Psychology*, 37/1: 55–72.

ESS (2016). *European Social Survey Round 1–7 Data*. Bergen: NSD—Norwegian Centre for Research Data.

Green-Pedersen, Christoffer (2019). *The Reshaping of West European Party Politics: Agenda-Setting and Party Competition in Comparative Perspective*. Oxford: Oxford University Press.

Hainmüller, Jens, and Michael J. Hiscox (2007). 'Educated preferences: Explaining individual attitudes toward immigration in Europe', *American Political Science Review*, 61/2: 399–442.

Hansen, Kasper M., and Rune Stubager (2017). *Oprør fra udkanten—Folketingsvalget 2015*. Copenhagen: Jurist- og Økonomforbundets Forlag.

Hansen, Kasper M., and Rune Stubager (2019). *Danish National Election Study Times Series Cumulative File 1971–2019*. Update 11 September 2019.

Inglehart, Ronald (1977). *The Silent Revolution. Changing Values and Political Styles Among Western Publics*. Princeton, NJ: Princeton University Press.

Jæger, Mads M. (2006). 'Welfare regimes and attitudes towards redistribution: The regime hypothesis revisited', *European Sociological Review*, 22/2: 157–70.

Key, V.O. (1961). *Public Opinion and American Democracy*. New York: Alfred A. Knopf.

Mortensen, Peter B. (2007). *The Impact of Public Opinion on Public Policy*. Aarhus: Politica.

Nielsen, Hans Jørgen (2007). 'Hvor mange dimensioner er der?', in Jørgen G. Andersen, Johannes Andersen, Ole Borre, Kasper M. Hansen, and Hans Jørgen Nielsen, eds, *Det nye politiske landskab. Folketingsvalget 2005 i perspektiv*. Aarhus: Academica, 213–32.

Pitkin, Hanna F. (1967). *The Concept of Representation*. Berkeley, CA: University of California Press.

Slothuus, Rune (2010). 'When can political parties lead public opinion? Evidence from a natural experiment', *Political Communication*, 27/2: 158–77.

Slothuus, Rune, and Claes H. de Vreese (2010). 'Political parties, motivated reasoning, and issue framing effects', *Journal of Politics*, 72/3: 630–45.

Sniderman, Paul M., Michael B. Petersen, Rune Slothuus, and Rune Stubager (2014). *Paradoxes of Liberal Democracy: Islam, Western Europe and the Danish Cartoon Crisis*. Princeton, NJ: Princeton University Press.

Soroka, Stuart N., and Christopher Wlezien (2010). *Degrees of Democracy: Politics, Public Opinion, and Policy*. New York: Cambridge University Press.

Stubager, Rune (2010). 'The development of the education cleavage: Denmark as a critical case', *West European Politics*, 33/3: 505–33.

Stubager, Rune, Kasper M. Hansen, Michael S. Lewis-Beck, and Richard Nadeau (2020). *The Danish Voter: Democratic Ideals and Challenges*. Ann Arbor, MI: University of Michigan Press.

Togeby, Lise (2004). *Man har et standpunkt . . . om stabilitet og forandring i befolkningens holdninger*. Aarhus: Aarhus University Press.

Togeby, Lise (2006). 'The context of priming', *Scandinavian Political Studies*, 30/3: 345–76.

Wlezien, Christopher (1995). 'The public as thermostat: Dynamics of preferences for spending', *American Journal of Political Science*, 39/4: 981–1000.

CHAPTER 18

THE SOCIAL DEMOCRATIC PARTY

From Exponent of Societal Change to Pragmatic Conservatism

RASMUS MARIAGER AND NIELS WIUM OLESEN

FOR the major part of its almost 150-year-long history, the Social Democratic Party (*Socialdemokratiet*) has had a strong self-perception as having a historic mission along with a strong awareness of its own past. Since the beginning of the twentieth century, the party has frequently conveyed its history in written media, films, and through works of art in order to strengthen its internal party identity and to influence the wider public with the Social Democratic view of history (Mariager 2005/2006).

Apart from the party's awareness of its own historic importance and a persistent demand for social justice and equality, it is difficult to draw a straight and continuous line in the party's ideological history. This historical overview is, therefore, divided into five time spans, each with its own distinctive character: 1) the foundation and the organizational period, 1871–1901; 2) the integration into Danish parliamentarianism, 1901–29; 3) government responsibility and defence of democracy, 1929–47; 4) the welfare state and the Cold War, 1947–89; and 5) globalization and the neoliberal turn, 1989–2020. During these five periods, the Social Democratic Party changed character several times. It started out as the Marxist party of the outcasts. Then it took on the role as a moderate government party in the troubled years of the mid-twentieth century. In the 1960s and 1970s, it headed the development of the welfare state. Finally, in the twenty-first century, the focus was primarily on protecting its major achievement, the welfare state, against the challenges of globalization.

This historical overview argues that until the end of the Cold War, the party always worked for various large-scale projects of fundamental societal change—the classless society, democratic socialism, the welfare state, and economic democracy. In contrast, recent decades are characterized by an understanding that the optimal societal form has been realized; it just needs to be conserved and maintained.

Historical Overview

The Foundation and the Organizational Period, 1871–1901

The Social Democratic Party traces its origin back to May 1871 when a Danish section of the International Workingmen's Association (the First International) was formed. From the beginning, the Danish International engaged in strikes for higher wages and better working conditions, thereby challenging the existing bourgeois and capitalist order. Consequently, the movement and its leadership was banned in 1872. However, at a conference in 1878, the Social Democratic Party was founded as an independent organization, adopting a Marxist manifesto very similar to the Gotha Programme of the German Social Democratic Party. In 1884, the Social Democratic Party had its first members elected into the Parliament (*Folketinget*) (Kristensen et al. 2007).

The Integration into Danish Parliamentarianism, 1901–1929

In 1901, parliamentarianism was introduced as the political practice, though still not inscribed in the Constitution. Soon after, the Social Democrats gained the majority in municipal elections in Copenhagen and other cities where they carried out welfare reforms, providing them with valuable experiences for later reform work at the national level. Although members still called for revolutionary change, the vast majority of the party was clearly reformist.

Denmark stayed neutral during the First World War, a stance that the Social Democrats supported. Motivated by a general sense that Denmark's security and sovereignty was vulnerable, the Social-Liberal government called for the formation of a government of national unity in 1916. The Social Democrats joined the government despite internal opposition. Some members of the minority later took part in the formation of the Danish Communist Party in 1919.

In 1924, the first Social Democratic government was formed by the skilled worker Thorvald Stauning who became prime minister. It was a minority government uncommittedly supported by the Social Liberals (*Radikale Venstre*). The government was confronted with a wide range of economic problems. Nevertheless, it tabled its usual ideological socialization proposals on greater democratic control of the means of production but had to see them rejected by the *Folketinget*. After nearly three years in office, the Social Liberals withdrew their support, and an election was called in 1926. This led to a new Liberal government. On balance, Stauning's first government was not a pronounced success; however, the party and its voters were now fully integrated into the Danish democracy (Fink-Jensen et al. 2017).

Government Responsibility and Defence of Democracy, 1929–1947

At the 1929 election, the Social Democrats received more than 42 per cent of the vote. Stauning once again formed a government, this time in coalition with the Social Liberals. The coalition won subsequent elections and held a majority in the *Folketinget* for eleven years.

The Stauning government came to power shortly before the worldwide economic crisis hit Denmark. Like in other countries, political radicalization threatened the democratic order. Among farmers, an agrarian fascist movement led to the formation of a new party challenging the Liberal Party (*Venstre*). In urban areas, Communists wooed social democratic workers to call for a revolution. Both parties achieved representation in the *Folketinget* in the 1930s. The government's response to the economic and political upheaval was state interventionist regulation of the economy and social reforms adopted by the Parliament in a number of major settlements with either the Liberals or the Conservatives (*Konservative*). The intention was not to reach socialism through a collapse of capitalism as Marx had predicted. First, the object was to save capitalism from its own shortcomings and protect the workers from social distress, and second, in due course, the party could resume the far-reaching reforms in socialist direction. In addition to economic policy, the government focused on disseminating a nationalism based on democracy, enlightenment, social equality between the classes, and joint work for the development of contemporary society. Overall, this policy was a success. Denmark fared better through the economic crisis than most other European countries, and political radicalization was curbed and held at a negligible level.

Despite the success in domestic affairs, the Stauning government was vulnerable in foreign and security policy. True to its ideals and in recognition of the fact that Denmark was without allies, the government chose a policy of adaptation towards Germany and a weakly equipped military, which gave credit to government statements that Denmark would stay neutral in case of war. This did not, however, prevent a German occupation in 1940. Danish authorities were allowed to maintain control without interference from the German side on the condition that they would secure the security of the German military on Danish soil. This scheme provided benefits, but it also constituted a dilemma for the government and the Social Democrats, especially after the government banned the Danish Communist Party and interned its leaders on the Germans' demand. Although the government maintained its commitment to Danish democracy in its appeals to the Danish population, it had now assaulted these very democratic ideals. The government stepped down in August 1943 after declining to comply with a German demand of instigating the death penalty for acts of sabotage (Olesen 2003).

Following the war, the Social Democrats presented an ambitious state interventionist election manifesto that emphasized planning and Keynesian economic policies. The programme was inspired by economic ideas in the belligerent countries and constituted a left-turn as seen in most parts of Europe in the aftermath of the war. Still, the party suffered a setback at the first post-war election in October 1945. The party lost 12 per cent of the vote while the Communists gained a similar fraction. In the following elections, in 1947 and 1950, most lost votes were regained. The outcome of the 1945 election was a Liberal minority government (Olesen 1998).

The Welfare State and the Cold War, 1947–1989

The Social Democratic Party regained government in 1947. The Cold War was emerging while Denmark's economic challenges and security problems were unresolved. To some extent, the economic problems were remedied through Denmark's participation in the Marshall Plan. After having explored the possibilities for a Scandinavian defence pact, the Social Democratic government agreed with the Liberals and the Conservatives that Denmark should follow Norway into the Atlantic Pact in 1949. From the beginning of the Cold War, the Social Democrats showed themselves to be in good understanding with US governments. They shared anti-communism, and the Americans acknowledged that the Social Democratic government and the trade unions were the most effective bulwark against communist influence in Denmark. At the same time, the Social Democrats were aware that economic cooperation with the United States contributed to a rising standard of living that made Communist agitation on a socio-economic platform more difficult, just as military cooperation with the United States gave Denmark a degree of security that it had not enjoyed since the early 1800s.

From 1953 to 1968, the Social Democrats continuously formed government. The party headed the development of the welfare state, and from 1958 onwards, they governed a country experiencing unprecedented growth rates. During this period, the welfare state replaced democratic socialism as the party's end goal. The welfare state became an ideology, a mobilization strategy, and a narrative of progress that was largely identified with the Social Democrats. The party was clearly the driving force in the development of the post-war welfare state, but since it never held a parliamentary majority of its own, it needed to engage in compromises with the centre-right parties in order to pass its reform proposals (Lidegaard 2001). Since the mid-1950s, Jens Otto Krag, PM 1962–8 and 1971–2, had harboured dreams of Danish membership of the EEC. In the Danish referendum of membership in October 1972, 63 per cent of Danes voted yes, but the Social Democratic party was divided, and only a small majority supported membership among its electorate.

At the 1973 election, centre-right discontent and high voter volatility exploded in a dramatic election. A total of 44 per cent of the voters switched party allegiances, and five extra parties were added to the existing five in the *Folketinget*. Among these was the newly formed Progress Party (*Fremskridtspartiet*) that advocated a drastic cutdown of the welfare state and claimed that tax evasion was a virtue. The Social Democrats, with their new prime minister, Anker Jørgensen, were cut drastically from 37 to 26 per cent, and the traditional centre-right parties suffered similar setbacks. The election generated a shambolic parliament, and to complicate matters further, the oil crisis of 1973 hit

Denmark simultaneously. After a year in opposition, the Social Democrats won back some of its prior strength and regained power at the beginning of 1975. During the following seven years, the Social Democrats muddled through as the governing party with ad hoc support from the parties on its right flank. Meanwhile, with rising unemployment, balance of payment deficits, budget deficits, and inflation, the economy took a turn for the worse.

The problems were further complicated by the fact that the Social Democrats' relationship with the trade unions became increasingly strained as the 1970s progressed. The Social Democratic governments were persistently calling for wage restraint. The trade unions were strongly opposed to such measures but showed willingness to compromise if wage earners were compensated through 'economic democracy'. Since the late 1960s, the Social Democrats and the trade unions had been pursuing 'economic democracy', i.e. a scheme where parts of the salaries are deposited in a central fund and invested in Danish businesses under the leadership of the trade unions. The Social Democrats, though, could not mobilize a majority in Parliament for the project. The centre-right parties were sceptical, some even against economic democracy, perceiving it as an attempt to introduce socialism through the back door, whereas the left wing considered the scheme to be too centralized. In the late 1970s and early 1980s, the government's inability to provide economic democracy in return for trade union wage restraint developed into a downright Gordian knot. In 1982, the conflict and the ever-worsening economic situation—now with a rapidly growing state budget deficit as the most pressing problem—led Anker Jørgensen and the Social Democratic government to resign without calling an election (Olesen 2017).

The Social Democrats expected that the new centre-right coalition government under the Conservative Prime Minister Poul Schlüter would be a short-lived phenomenon. Since the First World War, no Danish centre-right government had received re-election. Schlüter, however, proved to be an accomplished PM who won four elections and ruled for more than ten years. The key to his success was an alliance with the Social Liberals who had historically been an ally of the Social Democrats. The Social Democrats had difficulty in adjusting to the role of opposition party. The party was almost deprived of influence on economic policy. This led to a change in the party leadership as well as a change of strategy, and from 1987, under the new leadership of Svend Auken, the Social Democrats tended to compromise with the government on issues of economic policy.

However, already from 1982, the Social Democrats managed to hold leverage in foreign policy matters. The Social-Liberal Party, true to its tradition, chose not to support the government's NATO policy, and it had reservations against the government's European policy. A majority consisting of the Social Democrats, the Social-Liberal Party, and the political left forced the government to oppose the NATO Dual Track Decision. This majority also required Danish reservations in a number of NATO communiques, constituting a breakup of the consensus that was forged between the Social Democrats, the Conservatives, and the Liberals when Denmark joined NATO in 1949. The Social Democratic departure from the consensus was partly motivated by discussions and new views on the Cold War and security politics in the

West German and Scandinavian sister parties, and partly motivated by parliamentary tactics (Mariager 2017).

Domestic concerns also partly motivated the party's stance on European policy. When the Single European Act was to be adopted in the *Folketinget* in January 1986, the Social Democrats opposed the bill. Publicly, the decision was motivated by anxieties that the EC would prevent Denmark from pursuing progressive environmental policies, but parliamentary tactics weighed in heavily too. Without a parliamentary majority, Schlüter instead issued a referendum on SEA, which the government won (Olesen 2018).

Globalization and the Neoliberal Turn, 1989–2020?

The end of the Cold War prompted a shift in the Social Democrats' foreign policy to a more pro-European and pro-NATO position. Along with the more cooperative strategy in economic policy, this represented a more centrist line after well over half a decade dominated by hard opposition. The centrist line received accolades from potential allies, notably the Social Liberals, but general distrust in the Social Democratic leader, Auken, prevented the Social Democrats from regaining government. In a dramatic showdown in 1992, Auken's leadership was contested by the vice-chairman Poul Nyrup Rasmussen at an extraordinary conference. Nyrup Rasmussen won the vote, and in 1993, he was appointed the premiership when Prime Minister Schlüter stepped down following a political scandal in his cabinet. Nyrup Rasmussen subsequently formed a majority government.

Poul Nyrup Rasmussen was prime minister for almost nine years. He made an effort to present the Social Democrats as being highly reliable in both economic and foreign policy matters. The alternating Nyrup governments were strict in public expenditure control and privatized a number of public companies. An ambitious revival of Keynesian fiscal policy was initiated along with an active labour market policy focusing on education and training. Hereby—and with the help of an international boom—economic growth was generated after several years of stagnation, and the soaring unemployment rate was finally overcome. At the takeover of government power, 12 per cent of the workforce was registered as unemployed. When the Nyrup Rasmussen government resigned in 2001, unemployment had fallen to 5 per cent. Additionally, the government introduced an ambitious and expansionist environmental policy led by the Minister of Environment, former chairman Svend Auken. Wind energy in particular was stimulated by state subsidies, creating a huge upturn in the Danish wind turbine industry and making Denmark a world leader in this field.

While Nyrup's governments were successful in their economic policy, they faced problems on new policy areas. Dissatisfaction with the refugee and immigration policy and the alleged failed integration of citizens from the Middle East was voiced with increasing force by the centre-right. In 1995, a new party, the Danish People's Party (*Dansk Folkeparti*), was formed (cf. Seeberg and Kölln 2020). The party wooed Social Democratic voters by advocating a tougher line on immigration and improvement of welfare for especially pensioners. The Social Democrats had difficulties in responding to this threat since the party was internally split. Some Social Democrats focused on integration on the premises of the welfare system. Others advocated a softer line acknowledging multiculturalism. The internal split in the Social Democratic Party and the party's difficulties in finding a way to address the threat from the Danish People's Party was aggravated by the Social Liberals who advocated an even softer line. The consequences of these divergent lines in the government coalition was ever-shifting proposals, conflicting measures, and a communication profile that made the government extremely vulnerable in any debate on the subject (Mortensen 2006).

In the 1998 election campaign, Nyrup Rasmussen had opposed demands from the centre-right parties to put an end to a very costly scheme of early retirement, established in the late 1970s to curb youth unemployment. Instead, Nyrup promised to uphold the early retirement scheme, as he knew it was a popular programme among many middle-aged and elderly wage earners. After the election, however, the government engaged in a settlement with the Liberals on degradation of the early retirement scheme. The Social Democrats suffered a severe drop in the polls, and Nyrup Rasmussen suffered a personal loss of credibility. In combination with the problems regarding refugee and integration policy, the Social Democrats suffered a massive election defeat in November 2001. For the first time in 77 years, the Social Democratic Party was not the largest Danish political party.

Under the premiership of Anders Fogh Rasmussen, a Liberal and Conservative government stepped in, backed by the Danish People's Party. Fogh Rasmussen was personally instrumental in Denmark's decision to join the US-led invasion of Iraq in 2003. The Social Democrats were against the decision to invade Iraq but later supported the decision to send Danish stabilization forces to Iraq. Even though the Iraq War was highly controversial in Denmark, Fogh managed to neutralize the Social Democratic opposition. The Social Democrats proved bewildered and frustrated by Fogh Rasmussen's command over the political process, and in 2005, they lost yet another election when the party's backing dropped to 25 per cent (Mariager and Wivel 2019). This brought about a shift in leadership from Mogens Lykketoft, who had replaced Nyrup in 2002, to Helle Thorning-Schmidt, the first female chair of the Social Democrats.

Thorning-Schmidt also failed in tumbling Fogh Rasmussen at the election in 2007, but in 2011, the Liberals lost the election whereupon a government with the Social Democrats, the Social Liberals, and the Socialist People's Party (*Socialistisk Folkeparti*) was established. The Social Liberals held a tough stance during the negotiations leading up to the formation of the government. They demanded adherence to the two settlements on early retirement and unemployment benefits that they had reached with the bourgeois parties before the election. This was reluctantly accepted by the two other coalition parties. In return, the Social Liberals accepted the Social Democrats' demand for a continuation of the refugee policy of the former government. Most of the Social Democrats' and Socialist People's Party's proposals from before the election were scrapped. This led to recurring accusations of breach of faith with the electorate.

Through delicately controlled demand management policies, the government managed to sustain a fairly high employment rate despite the severe repercussions of the financial crisis of 2008-2009. It also passed a series of reforms of welfare benefits that were along traditional Social Democratic lines. Still, the Thorning-Schmidt government was marred by internal conflict, especially because the Socialist People's Party had difficulties stomaching the right-turn dictated by the Social Liberals. Consequently, the party left the government in 2014. In 2015, at the end of the election period, the Danish economy was quite robust. Once again, the most prominent election theme turned out to be refugee and integration policies, as it has proven to be since 2001 whenever the economy is strong. For the first time in almost 20 years, the Social Democrats gained voters at the election in 2015. The Social Liberals, however, suffered a severe setback, and the majority of the four parties that had supported the government was lost. This paved the way for a new centre-right government formed by the Liberals and the Conservatives. Thorning-Schmidt stepped down as chair of the Social Democrats, and Mette Frederiksen was elected without any rival candidate (Qvortrup 2015).

The Social Democratic assessment of the tenure in government from 2011 to 2015 is mixed. The dominating trend among the party leadership, though, is to distance itself from the period with allegations that the political line under Thorning-Schmidt was too right wing, too neoliberal, and an aberration from party tradition. At the election in 2019, the Social Democratic Party regained power and formed a one-party minority government after the collapse of the Liberal-Conservative coalition and the appearance of new extreme parties on the political right. The government is headed by Mette Frederiksen, the hitherto youngest Danish PM.

PRESENT-DAY POLICY POSITIONS AND ISSUE EMPHASIS

In the self-perception of the Social Democratic Party, it offers responsible answers to all present challenges in Denmark. Yet the present-day Social Democratic Party in general focuses on the following six policy areas: the welfare state, the private sector, education, European and foreign policies, immigration, and globalization. If one should impose two labels upon these policies, they could be 'conservative' and 'pragmatic'. It is conservative because leading Social Democratic politicians in recent years have suggested that the Social Democratic Party won the twentieth-century political struggle in Denmark. In the twenty-first century, the party will primarily have to preserve and adjust the results of this struggle to present-day challenges. It is an expression of this state of affairs that the Social Democratic Party fought its 2015 parliamentary election campaign under the slogan 'The Denmark You Know' (Social Democratic Party 2015). It is also pragmatic as the party has lately demonstrated a remarkable willingness to adapt its policies to the challenges of the new century, including the increased influence and public appeal of the Danish People's Party.

The Welfare State

According to the party mythology, the Social Democratic Party created the Danish welfare state. As noted above, this is not entirely true and fair (Petersen 1998). Still, the party has taken ownership over the welfare society, and lately, it has been a core ambition for the party to be the main determinant in defining the future of the welfare state. In 2017, the party presented its political ambitions in a new policy programme entitled 'Sharing Denmark' (*Fælles om Danmark*). According to the programme, the objective of the welfare society is to guarantee 'actual and equal' opportunities for all Danish citizens with respect to education, healthcare, childcare, and eldercare. As such, the party upholds tradition with universal welfare benefits. The party argues that equality is desirable for ideological reasons and because the Danish equality-based social model has made Denmark one of the most competitive countries in the globalized world (Social Democratic Party 2017).

An important challenge to the welfare society is the demographic development. People generally live longer, and the population expects still more public service, just as citizens overall expect continuously higher quality in public service. At the same time, fewer people will expectedly finance the future welfare benefits. Consequently, the public sector will have to deliver more and better cost-effective welfare benefits to a still more numerous and care-requiring population. This is the core challenge of the welfare society. For years, the Social Democratic answer to this task was to introduce New Public Management in order to control spending. In the 2010s, however, the party has adjusted its policies as it has been convinced that further such initiatives will not solve the problem. Consequently, the party now argues that a new approach to the public sector is needed. A core element in the new approach has been to introduce a so-called 'hands-off' reform, the goal being to improve the management of the public sector by inspiring cooperation and trust rather than competition and control. Additionally, the party will increase local influence on service delivery and public involvement (Social Democratic Party 2019a).

The Private Sector

It is a cornerstone of the Social Democratic Party's policy to provide profitable conditions for the private sector and to make it easier to do business in Denmark. Why is that? Because the precondition for an expensive Danish welfare society is a strong and competitive private sector. The party, therefore, prioritizes improving the general framework conditions so that a constantly growing private sector can generate highly specialized jobs for skilled workers and employees in a time where low-paid manual jobs are leaving the country. Thus, the Social Democratic Party is focusing on strengthening enterprises that possess assets within fields with strong international competition, especially within large-scale industry, the life science industry, the climate, and the environment. In addition, the party argues that a well-run public sector with a high educational standard, proper childcare, etc. is a precondition for a strong business community (Social Democratic Party 2019b). The Social Democratic policy towards the private sector, therefore, cannot be separated from the party's education policy, tax policy, research policy, healthcare policy, etc.

The party argues that Denmark should invest in the private sector's general framework conditions with the intention of promoting productivity within the individual companies. One particular challenge here is the educational level of workers. To that end, the party proposes upgrading the skills of blue-collar workers. Also, the party suggests creating opportunities for supplementary training and organizing parts of the supplementary training so that they meet the needs of the business community. Another ambition is to support innovation in the private sector as a precondition for competitiveness within vital export branches such as energy, biotech, the environment, and welfare technology business. In that context, the party recommends increasing tax-free allowance on research to make it more profitable for small and middle-sized enterprises to invest in technology, and increasing tax-free allowances for entrepreneurs. Finally, the party has an ambition to invest in research and to encourage investment and research in jobs that can accelerate an environmentally sustainable and greener Denmark (Social Democratic Party 2019b).

Education

The Social Democratic Party's education policy is broad and detailed, covering a wide range of subfields. Yet two subfields are of particular interest to the party: the public school system and the post-secondary education programme. In that context, the party aims to bring an end to the 2 per cent cut in public contribution to the education system that has been carried through by the centre-right government between 2015 and 2019, the so-called 'reprioritization contribution'.

The party is a strong proponent of the public elementary schools, and it sets out to make this institution the population's preferred choice of school. In 2018, however, some 20 per cent of all Danish children attended private schools. Against this, the party argues that only a maximum of 10 per cent should attend private elementary schools because of the party's goal to bring down social inequality. Consequently, the party argues that public subsidies to private schools should be reduced. As for the post-secondary education programme, the party argues that all young Danes should follow an educational programme until the age of 25. In addition, the party seeks to give priority to vocational training in order to provide the conditions for high productivity that bolster exports and a high tax base. A high educational level, whether within the context of universities or vocational training, is considered to be an important contribution to democracy and equality in the globalized world of today.

European Policy and Foreign Affairs

According to the Social Democratic Party, Denmark should be found among the US' closest allies, and in 2018, the party was one of the agents behind a new defence agreement that aims to increase the Danish defence budget with some 20 per cent between 2018 and 2023 (Ministry of Defence 2018), even if part of the increase is caused by a technical redefinition of some state expenditures. While Poul Nyrup Rasmussen was PM, Denmark was a loyal, flexible, and willing alliance partner within NATO. This became particularly clear in 1998-1999, when the government was to decide whether Denmark should support NATO and the US in the first out-of-area operation in the history of the alliance. At that time, Denmark decided to follow NATO into the intervention in Kosovo although there was no UN mandate that authorized the operation. This was a difficult decision as Denmark—as a small state—has an interest in a strong international legal system. Still, the party decided to follow NATO, thereby weakening the authority of the UN. Overall, the security policy of the present-day Social Democratic Party fits with the security policies of Nyrup Rasmussen. In the self-perception of the party, Denmark assumes a co-responsibility for international affairs in contrast to the interwar period and Cold War period where Denmark essentially conducted a cautious *lie low* policy in order not to provoke closely situated enemies, especially the Soviet Union, Poland, and East Germany. In contrast to the self-perception of the party, one could argue that the security policy of the Social Democratic Party in the post-Cold War era is just yet another example of the small state adjusting to the international situation. After the defeat to Germany in 1864, Denmark adjusted to the enemy in the south. During the Cold War era, Denmark balanced between the friends in the West and the enemies in the East. After 1989, Denmark followed Washington in what political scientists have labelled 'The American World Order'. This is also the policy of the party in 2020 (Social Democratic Party 2017; Mariager and Wivel 2019).

The Social Democratic Party is a firm supporter of the European Union (EU) as the party considers the European Union to be an important tool in handling cross-border challenges such as climate and environmental issues and international criminal conduct. Still, during recent decades, influential Social Democratic voices have critized the bureaucracy of the EU and other such problems within the EU. Yet after the 2016 UK Brexit referendum, leading Social Democratic politicians have overall abandoned critizing the EU as they seemingly do not want to share the responsibility for a potential Danish EU exit. In spite of that, the party believes that Denmark should maintain its four opt-outs from EU policies. The EU policy of the party is, however, not entirely without vision. It is an ambition of the party to ensure that the existing cooperation within the EU is capable of solving challenges on important policy areas to the benefit of the people of the EU member states. One such area is tax policies. In 2019, the Social Democratic Party posted an idea of a 'Solidarity Pact' inside the EU, which is to combat tax haven, tax evasion, prevent social dumping, and protect the European societies by agreeing on a common lower limit on corporate tax rates (Social Democratic Party 2018).

Immigration Policies

The immigration policy may be the most significant example of the above-mentioned pragmatism of the Social Democratic Party. In 2018, the party launched a new immigration policy under the caption 'Fair and Realistic. An Immigration Policy that Unites Denmark'. As stated above, the party had found itself in fierce fights with especially the centre-right parties in the 1990s and 2000s. With reference to the Danish People's Party's immigration policy, former PM Nyrup Rasmussen characterized the Danish People's Party in 1999 as 'not house-trained' (Rasmussen 1999). However, since the mid-2010s, the Social Democratic Party has changed its immigration policies considerably in the light of the demographic changes during the last generation. In order to be able to integrate new citizens, Denmark needs to reduce the influx of foreigners with a non-Western background. In 1980, only 1 per cent of Danes descended from non-Western areas. In 2019, it was around 8 per cent. Consequently, the party argues that Denmark alone should be able to decide how many non-Western foreigners are allowed to migrate to Denmark. In order to obtain that goal, the party seeks to introduce an annual ceiling. Additionally, in cooperation with other EU countries, the party seeks to set up an international centre outside the EU that is to receive refugees from non-Western countries.

On the other hand, the Social Democratic Party holds the ambition of helping a larger amount of people in troubled parts of the world than Denmark does today. To that end, the party proposes two initiatives: first, to launch a common EU-US 'Marshall Plan' in order to lift especially Africa but also parts of the Middle East and Asia out of poverty; second, and perhaps more realistically, the party plans to reform the Danish foreign aid policy (Social Democratic Party n.d.b).

Globalization

The party considers globalization to be both a challenge and an opportunity. Accordingly, the party seeks to shield Denmark against the negative effects of globalization, while it simultaneously tries to make Denmark benefit from the positive effects. On the positive side, globalization and international trade have generated economic growth and prosperity, including increased welfare for the world's poorest people. Likewise, globalization has created new jobs and growth in Denmark. As exports are an important source of income for Denmark, the party considers globalization, including free trade across borders and continents, to be a core interest of Denmark (Social Democratic Party 2017).

On the negative side, the party maintains that globalization is challenging the Danish welfare society. Specifically, the Social Democrats argue that globalization has created a highway for capitalism, and the party upholds that 'uncontrolled market forces' have obtained too much power in present-day societies as international trade and finance are only to a very small degree 'subject to political control and governance' (Social Democratic Party 2017). Moreover, the tax bases of the individual countries are eroding as nations compete with the intention of attracting enterprises by reducing corporation taxes. The Social Democratic Party finds this development injurious. The party, therefore, utilizes both national Danish legislation and the EU to limit what the party considers to be the worst effects of globalization. In particular, former PM Nyrup Rasmussen has been an active player in that respect while he was a member of the European Parliament (2004–9) and chair of the European Party of Socialists (2004–11) (Rasmussen 2007).

VOTERS

From the party's first participation in the *Folketinget* election in 1884, the Social Democratic party experienced almost constant electoral progress until 1935. Until the end of the 1930s, most of the party's gains can be attributed to structural changes in Danish society such as industrialization and urbanization. A growing number of the voters became workers, and the urban way of life focused less on tradition and hierarchies and more on egalitarian and material values in present and future times. At the election in 1884, the party received 5 per cent of the vote, and in 1903, it exceeded the 20 per cent limit. In 1920, the number had risen to one third of the vote. The 1935 election marked the highpoint with 46.4 per cent of the vote. In the interwar years and in accordance with the party's ambition to transform into a people's party, the party also mobilized agricultural workers, white-collar workers, and parts of the self-employed lower middle class.

After having held government positions for 16 years, the party experienced its first serious setback in 1945. The political and cultural disruption that followed in the wake of the Second World War resulted in only 33 per cent of the vote. Still, the first post-war election proved to be an exception. Already at the election in 1947, the Social Democrats were above 40 per cent again. This level was maintained until 1968 when the party only received 34 per cent of the vote. In 1971, the party regained 8 seats and won 37 per cent of the vote, only to experience its worst setback ever in 1973 when it lost 26 seats and received only 26 per cent of the vote. This historic setback was partly due to the split in the party's electorate regarding EC membership, but it was also the consequence of a more profound change in voting behaviour away from class-based voting and towards issue voting.

Having experienced the economic crisis after 1973, voters started gathering around the Social Democratic Party again. In the 1980s, the party suffered a loss of confidence among voters due to its failure to execute a coherent economic policy and the popularity of Schlüter's centre-right government. In the 1980s, the party's support hovered around 30 per cent. It was primarily middle-class voters that defected to the right, while some public employees and young people went to the Socialist People's Party on the left.

In 1990, the Social Democratic Party enjoyed a comeback with 37.4 per cent of the vote. The win was mainly due to the middle-class voters' waning confidence in the

Schlüter government. Nyrup Rasmussen's alternating governments could not quite maintain that level, and in the two subsequent elections, support fell to around 35 per cent. In 2001, the party experienced a severe setback with only 29 per cent of the vote. Nyrup Rasmussen's successor, Mogens Lykketoft, lost more than 3 per cent in 2005. Thus, in the two elections in 2001 and 2005, the Social Democrats lost more than 10 percentage points in total (Andersen 1996). Between 2005 and the election in 2019, the party has stabilized around 24-26 per cent of the vote. This share of the vote is definitely below the party's own expectations, but it is markedly above the European average for Social Democratic parties in the twenty-first century.

PARTY ORGANIZATION AND PARTY DEMOCRACY

The Social Democratic Party's party organization has largely been the same from the 1890s to the present, reflecting the party's identity as a member-based mass movement organized locally and from below. Party members are primarily seen as members of a local party association. In 2019, there are 245 local party associations. They are all headed by an executive committee to which there are direct elections among the party associations' members. In most municipalities, there is more than one party association; therefore, the associations' forces are gathered in a committee that is responsible for the municipal policy and the nomination of candidates for city council elections. It varies whether there are direct or indirect elections to the committee on the municipal level. There are 98 such committees in 2019.

Folketinget candidates are nominated in 92 constituencies. Like the local party associations, the constituency is led by an executive committee elected directly by the members. The local party organizations have persistently protected their prerogative to nominate *Folketinget* candidates without interference from the national level. In the country's five regions, there is also an organizational level that sets up regional candidates and is headed by a committee.

The party's highest authority is the annual national conference. The annual general meeting in both the local associations and the constituencies delegates party members to the conference. Every four years, the party leadership is elected by the conference.

Between the annual conferences, the National Executive Committee constitutes the party's highest authority. The executive committee consists of the party leadership, members elected by the regional level, members of the parliamentary group, the chairman of the national Social Democratic group in the European Parliament, a member from the party youth organization, two members from Local Government Denmark, and two from the Danish Regions. Since the early years, the Social Democratic Party and the trade unions kept a close affiliation through mutual representation in the governing bodies both on the national and the local level. This mutual representation was abolished in 1995 after more than 100 years (Christiansen 2012).

During the First World War, the Social Democratic Party had more than 50,000 party members. In the interwar years, the mobilization for new members was intense with the aim of strengthening the democratic order. In 1940, the number was 250,000, and in 1948, it was at its highest level with 306,000 citizens. From then on, the number dropped to 240,000 in 1966 and 120,000 in 1976. In 1995, party membership had fallen to 62,000. For the first time since the First World War, it was lower than the number of the Liberal Party's members. In 2019, the number had dropped to 40,000, but the party regained its status as the largest membership party.

From the party's foundation to the late 1960s, the party ethos was characterized by discipline. This ethos originated from the times when strength in numbers, solidarity, and uniformity in action were the main assets of the movement. The party chairman was worshipped and obeyed. Still, the local democracy was nourished and cherished. As a rule, the party leadership avoided interfering too bluntly in local matters. If it wanted something—for instance, the nomination of a special candidate to the *Folketinget*—it needed to go about the matter amicably and provide something in return, with no guarantee of success (Dybdahl 1969; Bertolt et al. 1955; Social Democratic Party n.d.a).

After the youth rebellion and the general weakening of authorities, the local influence on the nomination of candidates has become more pronounced. The weakening of authority also showed when Poul Nyrup Rasmussen challenged the incumbent chairman Svend Auken in 1992 and got away with it. During the last 30 years, party members have become more outspoken and critical, especially when the party has been in government. It was seen under both Nyrup Rasmussen and Thorning-Schmidt. Nevertheless, the ethos of discipline is still present. The party is famous for its 'electoral machine' based on motivated local members working for the best possible outcome.

It is a recurring question within the party whether the membership democracy regarding policy formulation has decreased over time. This mirrors similar discussions in other parties. The assertion is that the party leadership and the parliamentary group have captured the initiative and dominate the national political discourse completely, while membership participation has been eliminated to a matter of paying subscriptions and hanging up posters on lamp posts. With regard to the Social Democratic Party, this assertion fails to see that policy formulation in this party always has been an affair for the elite.

CONCLUSION

Due to the progressive industrialization and targeted political and organizational work, the Danish Social Democratic Party from its founding in 1871 developed from being the caretaker of the interests of the outcast proletariat to becoming the dominant party in the middle of the 1920s. It maintained that position until the early 1980s. During this time, the Social Democratic Party led 22 out of 26 governments.

From 1945 onwards, the party was the embodiment of the development of the Danish welfare state, for good and bad. The merits as well as the problems of the welfare state were ascribed to the Social Democratic Party, although the actual development of the socio-political legislation was the result of compromises between the Social Democratic Party and the centre-right parties in the Danish Parliament.

The party's strategy was based on integration into the Western European and North Atlantic economic and security spheres. On the one hand, the Social Democratic Party persued a policy of integration in order to obtain as many of the advantages as possible of being a member of Western society in these areas. On the other hand, the Social Democratic Party conducted a policy of screening with the aim of confirming to the Soviet Union and the Warsaw Pact that Denmark did not constitute a threat against the Eastern Bloc countries. At the same time, the Social Demoratic Party deliberately sought to create space for its own development of the Danish welfare state based on a high degree of state intervention and economic and social equality. In this perspective, the Danish welfare society during the Cold War can be seen as a Social Democratic-sponsored egalitarian society between East and West—with a considerable Western inclination.

At the turn of the millennium, the party lost its role as the dominating political party, and now, it competes with the Liberal Party (*Venstre*) and the Danish People's Party (*Dansk Folkeparti*) for the leading position regarding the political agenda as well as the government. The present-day Social Democratic Party is both 'conservative' and 'pragmatic'. It is conservative as leading Social Democrats have suggested that the Social Democratic Party won the twentieth-century political struggle in Denmark. In the twenty-first century, the party primarily endeavours to preserve and adjust the results of this struggle to present-day challenges. Whereas it is pragmatic as the party has adapted its policies to present-day challenges in the new millennium, including the increased influence and public appeal of the Danish People's Party. After almost two decades in opposition—apart from the years between 2011 and 2015—the Social Democratic Party seems to have regained its position as the dominating party in Danish politics, following the collapse of the Liberal-Conservative coalition and the appearance of new extreme parties on the political right.

REFERENCES

Andersen, Jørgen G. (1996). 'Socialdemokratiets vælgertilslutning', in Gerd Callesen, Steen Christensen, and Henning Grelle, eds, *Udfordring og omstilling. Bidrag til Socialdemokratiets historie 1971–1996*. Copenhagen: Fremad.

Bertolt, Oluf, Ernst Christiansen, and Poul Hansen (1955). *En bygning vi rejser*, vol. II. Copenhagen: Fremad.

Christiansen, Flemming J. (2012). 'Organizational de-integration of political parties and interest groups in Denmark', *Party Politics*, 18/1: 27–43.

Dybdahl, Vagn (1969). *Partier og erhverv. Studier i partioroganisationen og byerhvervenes politiske aktivitet 1880–1913*. Aarhus: Erhvervsarkivet.

Fink-Jensen, Morten, Jes F. Møller, and Niels W. Olesen (2017). *Historien om Danmark. Reformation, enevælde og demokrati.* Copenhagen: Gads Forlag.

Kristensen, Lars K., Søren Kolstrup, and Anette E. Hansen (2007). *Arbejdernes historie i Danmark 1800–2000.* Copenhagen: SFAH's Skriftserie.

Lidegaard, Bo (2001). *Jens Otto Krag 1914–1961.* Copenhagen: Gyldendal.

Mariager, Rasmus (2005/2006). 'Den brede enigheds ophør. Om baggrunden for det sikkerhedspolitiske opgør i begyndelsen af 1980erne – og noget om socialdemokratisk exceptionalisme i dansk samtidshistorie', *Historisk Tidsskrift*, 105–106/2: 553–83/646–75.

Mariager, Rasmus (2017). *Den vesttyske forbindelse. Studier i det sikkerhedspolitiske opbrud i Socialdemokratiet, dansk partipolitik og civilsamfund, ca. 1976–1988*, vol. 1–2. Copenhagen: Det Humanistiske Fakultet.

Mariager, Rasmus, and Anders Wivel (2019). *Hvorfor gik Danmark i krig?* Søborg: Rosendahls.

Ministry of Defence (2018). 'Aftale på forsvarsområdet 2018–2023', https://www.fmn.dk/temaer/forsvarsforlig/Documents/Forsvarsforlig-2018-2023.pdf (accessed 8 March 2019).

Mortensen, Hans (2006). *De fantastiske fire.* Copenhagen: Gyldendal.

Olesen, Niels W. (1998). 'Tillidskrisen. Socialdemokratisk politik mellem fortid og fremtid 1943–1947', in Henrik Dethlefsen and Henrik Lundbak, eds, *Fra mellemkrigstid til efterkrigstid.* Copenhagen: Museum Tusculanum.

Olesen, Niels W. (2003). 'Med loven – imod diktaturet! Socialdemokratiet under besættelsen', in Joachim Lund, ed., *Partier under pres.Demokratiet under besættelsen.* Copenhagen: Gyldendal.

Olesen, Niels W. (2018). *Poul Schlüters tid, 1982–1993. De danske ministerier.* Copenhagen: Gads Forlag.

Olesen, Thorsten B. (2017). *Anker Jørgensens tid, 1972–1982. De danske ministerier.* Copenhagen: Gads Forlag.

Petersen, Klaus (1998). *Legitimität und Krise. Die politische Geschichte des dänischen Wohlfahrtsstaates 1945–1973.* Berlin: Berlin Verlag.

Qvortrup, Henrik (2015). *Tre år, ni måneder og tre dage. Det utrolige drama bag kulisserne i regeringen Thorning-Schmidt.* Copenhagen: People's Press.

Rasmussen, Poul N. (1999). 'Statsminister Poul Nyrup Rasmussens replik ved åbningsdebatten i Folketinget den 7. oktober 1999', http://www.stm.dk/_p_7628.html (accessed 30 June 2019).

Rasmussen, Poul N. (2007). *I grådighedens tid—kapitalfonde og casionoøkonomi.* Copenhagen: Informations Forlag.

Seeberg, Henrik, and Ann-Kristin Kölln (2020). 'The Red-Green Alliance. Is it red or green?', in Peter M. Christiansen, Jørgen Elklit, and Peter Nedergaard, eds, *The Oxford Handbook of Danish Politics.* Oxford: Oxford University Press, 329–46.

Social Democratic Party (2015). 'Det Danmark du kender', https://www.socialdemokratiet.dk/da/nyhedsarkiv/2015/5/valggrundlag (accessed 8 March 2019).

Social Democratic Party (2017). 'Fælles om Danmark, 14, 17', https://www.socialdemokratiet.dk/da/partiet/principprogram (accessed 8 March 2019).

Social Democratic Party (2018). 'En solidaritetspagt for Europa. Debatoplæg til vedtagelse på Socialdemokratiets kongres d. 22.–23 September 2018', https://www.socialdemokratiet.dk/media/7543/solidaritetspagt.pdf (accessed 8 March 2019).

Social Democratic Party (2019a). 'Velfærd', https://www.socialdemokratiet.dk/da/politik/velfaerd/ (accessed 8 March 2019).

Social Democratic Party (2019b). 'Vækst der virker. Sådan skaber vi fremtidens arbejdspladser', https://www.socialdemokratiet.dk/media/5224/vaekst-der-virker.pdf (accessed 8 March 2019).

Social Democratic Party (n.d.a). 'Kort om Socialdemokratiets organisation', https://www.socialdemokratiet.dk/da/bliv-medlem/info-til-nye-medlemmer/kort-om-socialdemokratiets-organisation (accessed 13 March 2019).

Social Democratic Party (n.d.b). 'Retfærdig og realistisk. En udlændingepolitik der samler Danmark', https://www.socialdemokratiet.dk/media/7011/en-udlaendingepolitik-der-samler-danmark.pdf (accessed 8 March 2019).

CHAPTER 19

THE LIBERAL PARTY

*From Agrarian and Liberal to
Centre-Right Catch-All*

FLEMMING JUUL CHRISTIANSEN

THE LIBERAL PARTY

IN 2001, the Liberal Party of Denmark (*Venstre, Danmarks liberale parti*) managed to become the largest party in a general election for the first time in eighty years. It won 31.2 per cent of the vote, entered government office, and held the position of prime minister for most of the time since then (2001–11 and again 2015–19). Thereby, the party reached a key position for policy change and reform.

The success of the Liberals marked a remarkable turnaround compared with the party's situation during the 1970s and 1980s, reaching their nadir in 1987 with 10.5 per cent of the vote, which was only half the share of the Conservative People's Party. Hence, the Liberals may constitute an instance of successful ideological and/or organizational party change as a response to electoral challenges (Ware 1987; Harmel and Janda 1994; Mair 1997; Mair et al. 2004), and a transformation from a mass party towards a catch-all or electoral-professional party (Kirchheimer 1966; Panebianco 1988) pursuing office-oriented goals (cf. Strøm 1990). This is something noted in other accounts of the party (Andersen and Jensen 2001; Pedersen and Bille 2004; Kosiara-Pedersen 2019). Apparently, the Liberals had better success with such changes than the parties with agrarian roots did in the neighbouring countries of Norway and Sweden (cf. Christensen 1997; Arter 2001). An inherent challenge following a successful catch-all strategy is to maintain the high level of voters, known to be volatile. At the 2015 election, the Liberals fell back to 19.5 per cent of the vote, surpassed again by the Social Democrats and by the Danish People's Party, but the Liberals could still form a minority government. In 2019, the results reversed with the Liberal gains, winning 23.4 per cent but losing cabinet office.

Based on the above, this chapter seeks to evaluate the performance and impact of the Liberal Party of Denmark in the electorate, in particular since the 1990s, and relate it to 'adaptation' to changes and stability internally and externally. Internally, the chapter focuses on the ideological and organizational developments within the party. Externally, the chapter discusses the interaction of the Liberals with other parties in the Danish party system, with special emphasis on the Conservative People's Party, which holds very similar ideological positions. Furthermore, the chapter evaluates the impact of the Liberals on Danish politics during the 2000s and 2010s.

BRIEF HISTORICAL OUTLINE

The Liberals can trace their roots all the way back to the Society for the Friends of the Peasant that had influence on the content of the Constitution of 1849 that replaced absolutism with freedom rights and the general vote for adult men with their own household. In official party history, the Liberals' year of birth is 1870 when a number of groups in Parliament merged under the label 'United Liberals' (Lund and Pedersen 1970; cf. Bille 1997: 54). The new party demanded the introduction of parliamentary government based on the lower house where it had the majority, opposing the Conservative government appointed by the king. It took three decades of struggle with a number of Liberal groups breaking up and reuniting in various forms until the king finally appointed a government of the Liberal Reform Party in 1901. It looked like the beginning of a Liberal era in Danish politics, and a number policy reforms followed, but it soon ended. In 1905, the Social-Liberal Party (*Det Radikale Venstre*) seceded, and a huge bank scandal severely hit the Liberal leadership, dividing them even further.

In 1910, three parliamentary groups merged under the simple label of 'the Liberals' (*Venstre*). The party took part in the revision of the Constitution in 1915 that democratized the upper house and introduced general suffrage and a proportional electoral system. For the rest of the century, the Liberals only occasionally held the position of prime minister (1910–13; 1920–4; 1926–9; 1945–7; 1950–3; 1973–5). As these digits show, Liberal prime ministers were never re-elected for full four-year terms.[1] Later, the party took junior partner status in the government (1968–71; 1978–9; 1982–93).[2] After 1924, the Social Democrats became the largest party and formed most governments, usually with the Social Liberals as partners or supporters. A Liberal prime minister moved the most recent constitutional change of 1953 that abolished the upper house and made parliamentary government part of the written constitution. In 1963, the party added 'liberal' to its official name but the short form remains colloquial.[3]

THE ELECTORATE OF THE LIBERALS: DEVELOPMENT AND COMPOSITION

After the constitutional revision of 1915, the Danish party system ended up with four 'old parties' that came to dominate the electorate for the next decades in accordance with the hypothesis of 'freezing party systems' created by Lipset and Rokkan (1967). These parties primarily won votes by mobilizing distinct social groups in society, with the Liberals representing rural employers (Elklit 1988: 44). The Liberals had their largest group of voters and enjoyed their biggest support among farmers as distinct from smallholders or estate owners (Thomsen 1979; Worre 1980; Thomsen 1987; Andersen and Jensen 2001). During the nineteenth century, more than half of the population worked within this sector (Kyed 2000: 28).

The support level for the Liberals among farmers has remained steadily above 50 per cent and up to 80 per cent; a figure from the 2019 election showed 57 per cent (Thomsen 1987; Andersen and Jensen 2001: 115; Andersen and Andersen 2003; Election Study 2007; Landbrugsavisen 2019). There was only a limited de-alignment between farmers and the Liberals. Rather, the number of farmers dwindled, first due to industrialization, and later a rise in the service sector and structural changes with fewer but larger farms and mechanization, in particular after 1960 (Kyed 2000). This decline in their traditional core group of voters most likely contributed to the negative long-term trend in voter support for the Liberals that lasted until the 1980s (see Figure 19.1). This was the electoral challenge faced by the Liberals. The composition of Liberal voters was older, less educated, much more rural and independent than the rest of the population, and with various cultural habits that pointed backwards; on these grounds, the party leadership decided to modernize things (Mortensen 2008: 9–10).

Evidently, the Liberal Party managed to broaden its electoral appeal after 1990. Electoral surveys show that between 1990 and 2001, the party increased its support among workers from 7 per cent to 29 per cent, and among functionaries from 15 per cent to 31 per cent (Andersen and Andersen 2003: 210). Among independents, its share

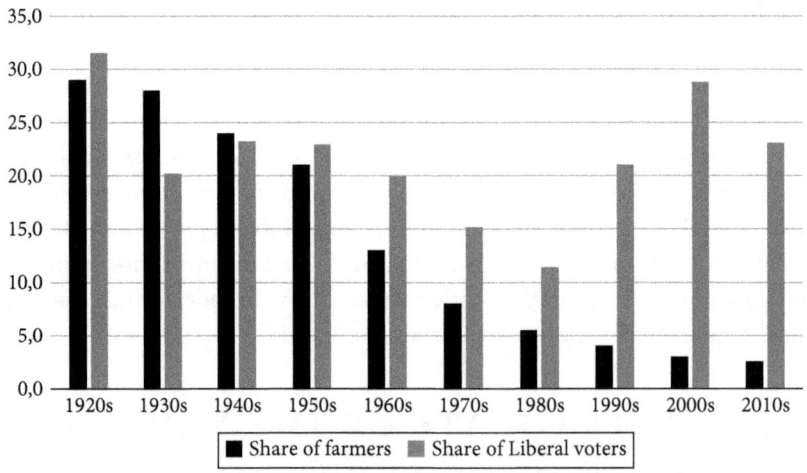

FIGURE 19.1 Share of farmers in Denmark of total labour force, and average voter support for the Liberals for each decade since the 1920s, percentages.

Sources: Kyed (2000). www.dst.dk. Kyed shows that the share of the total labour force largely resembles the share of the total population living from farming

increased just slightly. The share of farmers in its electorate fell from 25 per cent in 1987 to 7 per cent in 1998 (Andersen and Jensen 2001: 117). The party had more support from private employees as opposed to those in the public sector. On average, the Liberal voter now resembled the educational level of voters at large (Andersen and Andersen 2003: 218) but with median income a little above average. The party also enjoyed broad support among different age groups, with a slight overweight of male voters compared to women. In 2001, the negative correlation between population density and Liberal voter support remained significant but much less pronounced than previously (Hansen and Stubager 2017: 90); the party had gone 'from farmyard to city square' (Arter 2001; cf. Nielsen 1999: 40). These figures support a claim that the Liberals after the 1980s, in particular under the leaderships of Uffe Ellemann-Jensen (1984–98) and Anders Fogh Rasmussen (1998–2009, deputy 1985–98), managed to become a broad catch-all party, reaching out to centre-right voters in most social groups.

When the Liberals lost votes in the 2015 election, they did so across social groups, maintaining the basic profile described above. In 2019, the party regained some strength.

Where did the Liberal support come from? During the 1990s, the Conservative People's Party lost much support due to internal problems, allowing the Liberals to gain Conservative votes. Nielsen (1999: 44–5) shows how the Liberals won over a number of traditional Conservative and urban strongholds around Copenhagen and became the larger of the two centre-right parties. The Conservatives have never managed to reverse this development. Yet the 1998 election—lost narrowly by the centre-right—showed that the Liberal Party could not win the median voter with a pure liberalist strategy. Under a new party leader, Anders Fogh Rasmussen, the party made important changes in its appeal for voters at the 2001 election: it attained a more pro-welfare position, and it began to address the immigration issue that the Progress Party and the Danish People's Party (from 1995) had until then had for themselves (Green-Pedersen and Odmalm 2008). This was something Rasmussen's predecessor had refrained from (Mortensen 2008: 143–6). The new strategy won over former Social Democratic voters concerned with immigration, which became the most important issue in every election from the 2001 election onwards, except in 2011 during the economic crisis (Stubager et al. 2013: 26). In the 2019 elections, the Social Democrats now also promoted stricter immigration policies, and the climate issue became the most important.

The voters' evaluation of the 'competence' of the centre-right and Social Democrats changed on a number of issues (Andersen 2003: 165–7). The latter party no longer held an advantage as 'best' to achieve good conditions for the elderly and to 'balance tax and welfare'. More radically, the voters went from perceiving the Social Democrats as the best to operate a well-functioning health sector to perceiving the centre-right to be best. During this period, the Liberals persistently attacked what they considered poor performance of the health sector (Mortensen 2008: 129). The Liberals remained best in voter perception to operate the economy, whereas the Social Democrats were best to deal with unemployment and environmental matters. Since then, Social Democrats and Liberals have fought back and forth to articulate and position themselves on these and other issues (cf. Hjorth 2017: 197).

THE IDEOLOGY AND POSITIONS
OF THE LIBERALS

In international overviews, party researchers often place the Liberal Party of Denmark within the agrarian party family and the Social Liberals in the liberal family. Sometimes, the former gets the label 'agrarian-liberal' (Berglund and Lindström 1978: 17; cf. Arter 2001). Both parties belong to the ALDE group in the European Parliament and in Liberal International. So, what is the right label, and has it changed?

The Liberal Party has persistently had the interests of the farmers as a concern. For a long time, the political interests of the farmers were to achieve and maintain universal suffrage and the economic interests to promote free trade. Export interests—Danish bacon and butter—differ from more domestic market-oriented and protectionist Nordic counterparts. Yet public subsidies also became important for farming in Denmark in conflict with liberal ideals. The economic interests of farmers were a central concern when the Liberal Party strongly promoted Danish membership of the EEC, which was achieved in 1972. Since the 1990s, the Liberals have occasionally but not consistently taken positions against the interest of this sector with regard to environmental concerns (Bille 1998: 277).

The historical struggles of the Liberal Party against privilege, for the realization of the freedom rights in the Constitution, universal suffrage, and parliamentary government does place the party in a liberal tradition politically. Defence of private ownership, free enterprise, free trade, and a market economy with a limited public sector also places the party under the label of an 'economic' liberalism (cf. Salvadori 1972). The keyword throughout Liberal Party history is 'freedom' (Nevers 2013), and the term features prominently in both the programme and statutes of the Liberals (Liberal Party 2006, 2012). Broadly speaking, the Liberals adhere to a 'classic' or 'protective' version of liberal democracy rather than a 'modern', 'developmental', and 'social' liberalism (cf. Heywood 2007: 43–60; Vincent 2009: 23–55; Close 2019). Thus, the Liberals support 'negative' and not 'positive' freedom for the individual. Yet, many party supporters hold rather conservative views on issues such as defence, and law and order, and the party is divided between conservative and libertarian views on immigration and ethical matters (cf. Kosiara-Pedersen 2019: 51).

The political and religious thinker and poet N.F.S. Grundtvig (1783–1872) added a peculiar Danish perspective to the ideology of the Liberals (and the Social Liberals and was an inspiration for other parties as well). Grundtvig promoted an idea of political and national 'awakening' of the people: as they achieved freedom, they should also develop a 'free spirit'. For this purpose, he supported the establishment of 'folk high schools' self-consciously set up outside of academia (Korsgaard 2014). A high number of Liberal MPs and party activists used to attend such schools, affecting party culture (Olsen 2013: 241).

With the rise of 'neo-liberalism' during the 1980s, inspired by Reagan and Thatcher, the Liberals sought ideological revitalization and renewal. Leading party figures tried to merge Anglo-Saxon tradition with references to theorists such as Hayek and Friedman with the Danish tradition of Grundtvig (Haarder and Severinsen 1982; cf. Nevers et al. 2013: 295). The volume *From Social State to Minimal State* by the deputy chair of the party Anders Fogh Rasmussen (1993), emphasized freedom as a moral value opposite to a 'mind of slavery'. A political society called Libertas found its place in and around the Liberal Party. Political pundits mused how 'business school' replaced 'the folk high school'.

The emphasis on liberal ideology did not appeal to the median voter supporting generous, tax-financed public service and welfare schemes (Mortensen 2008: 110). Inspired by Gould's (1998) and Tony Blair's 'Third Way', the new party leader after 1998, Anders Fogh Rasmussen, the former proponent of a minimal state, introduced an ideological change from the centre-right (Mortensen 2008: 117–21; Nevers et al. 2013: 300–1). Rather than dismantling the public welfare sector, reforms and outsourcings should establish more 'freedom of choice' and efficient use of public means. This perspective integrated elements of liberal ideology with the welfare state and indicated a shift in position towards the centre.

The party leadership now suppressed any ideological debate that questioned Liberal support for the welfare state (Bille 2006: 72). Austerity policies and welfare reforms after the financial crisis of 2008–9 were passed without much reference to liberal ideology. Rather, the Liberal leader in 2019 still declared, 'The welfare state – c'est moi' (Altinget 2019). During the 2019 election campaign, the Liberals promised to increase spending on social welfare. Thus, the Liberals are no longer a beacon for ideological debate like in the 1990s.

Liberal Alliance—founded in 2007 as New Alliance—promotes economically liberal and libertarian positions to the right of the Liberals (Kosiara-Pedersen 2019: 52–3). As an office-oriented catch-all party, the Liberal Party today appears vague or internally split on a number of topics such as law and order and immigration. The party remains

Table 19.1. Positions of the Liberals and Select Other Danish Parties on Important Issue Dimensions, 2014

Issue	Liberals	Conserv. Peop. P.	Liberal Alliance	Danish Peop. P.	Social Liberals	Social Dem.
Redistribution	7	6.75	8.25	3.6	5.25	3.25
Immigration	7.7	7.1	4.1	9.7	2.6	5.5
Environment	7.2	6.7	7.75	6.9	3	4.2
EU	5.9	5.5	3.8	1.9	6.8	6
Urban/Rural	7.7	5.2	2.6	6.6	2.8	3.9
Law and order	7	7.2	5.1	8.6	3.1	5.2

Note: The variables are measured 0–10: EU position (0 con, 10 pro), Environmental policies (0 pro, 10 con), Redistribution (0 pro, 10 con), Immigration (0 not restrictive, 10 restrictive), Urban/Rural (0 urban, 10 rural), and Law and Order (0 not restrictive, 10 restrictive). Scores from 2014 except urban/rural and EU for the Social Liberals (2010).

Source: Chapel Hill expert data: Polk et al. 2017.

pro-EU but less pronounced than previously. The party also used to support decentralized solutions in relation to public sector governance, but efficiency concerns have led it to support centralization in many cases since 2001.

The CHES data set uses expert surveys to place the Liberal Party of Denmark in quantifiable terms compared with other parties (see Table 19.1). The Liberals come out as centre-right on most issues and with a stronger rural emphasis than an urban one (Polk et al. 2017). The position for 'redistribution' is 7 in 2014 (after the economic crisis), but during the 2000s, the CHES coding indicated it to be 5.9 in accordance with the perception mentioned above that the Liberals became more pro-welfare.

Party Members, Organization, and Finance

The Liberal Party in Denmark provides a case for a party that used to have many party members and a well-developed internal party democracy. According to the literature, these factors may present obstacles for the pursuit of party goals and party change (Strøm 1990; Pedersen 2010). Organizational change may be a precondition for electoral success (Harmel and Janda 1994). So, how did the Liberals manage to change while having a strong and traditional party organization?

The Liberal Party began to organize voters as members at the local level from around the 1880s and soon got the features of a mass party although it did not establish a national organization until 1929 (Bille 1997: 54). The party peaked in 1950 with 46 per cent of its voters as members, a figure higher than in the other old parties and a trait similar to other agrarian parties in the Nordic region (cf. Arter 2001). Since then, membership has been in steep decline. In 2015, the membership-to-voter ratio was 5 per cent, just slightly above the average for all parties (Kosiara-Pedersen 2017). Figure 19.2 presents the development in absolute numbers.

The Liberals still had a higher membership ratio than other parties during the 1980s when the electoral challenge became most visible. Many members had a traditional profile; in 2000, 16 per cent of their members were still independent farmers, a much higher share than in the Liberal electorate (Hermansen et al. 2003: 96). The traditional members acquiesced and accepted party change as they benefitted from it themselves. The relatively strong organization may even have been a resource, and it provided the party with a group of loyal voters on which to fall back (cf. Katz 1990). Thus, the Liberals maintained a strong presence in the governing bodies at municipality level across the country but in the rural areas in particular, as well as during the 1980s.

Despite having fewer members, the Liberals maintain a well-developed internal party democracy at the organizational level that resembles the structure of a mass party (Bille 1997). Membership is open for anyone who supports the purpose and politics of the Liberal Party, and the fee is modest. Party associations and municipality associations

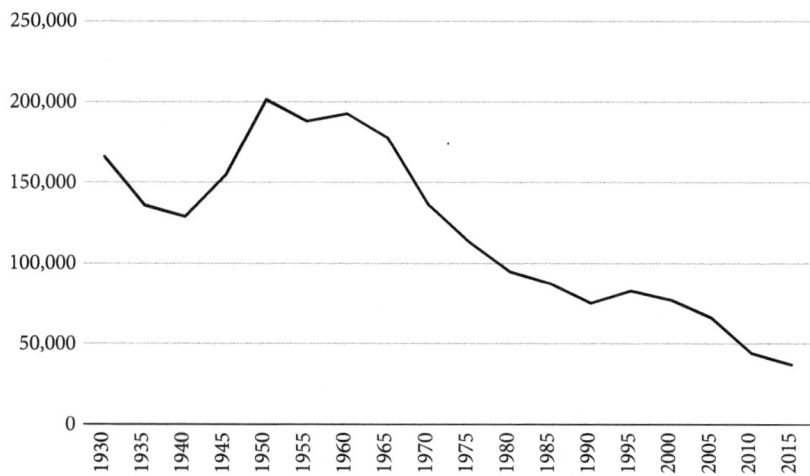

FIGURE 19.2 Liberal Party members, 1930–2015, five-year intervals.

Sources: Clausen 1979; Bille 1997; Folketingets Oplysning 2017. www.projectmapp.eu/databases/

feed into committees at the level of parliamentary districts, regions, and at national level. Almost without exception, candidates running for the party at all levels become nominated at a local or regional level. A major overhaul of party statutes in 2006 changed the structure of the Liberal Party established in 1965 and 1970 (cf. Bille 1997; Liberal Party 2012). The reform strengthened the impact of the party association at municipality level within the national committee at the expense of party associations with many members. Since some municipalities around Copenhagen only have few Liberal voters and in particular members, as opposed to some in Jutland, the reform affected the geographical balance of the Liberal Party's organization to the benefit of the 'new' members of the Liberals.

Fewer members may not mean fewer active members. In the case of the Liberal Party, a membership survey from 2000 showed that 60 per cent of the Liberal Party members were passive, a figure slightly higher than the average for other parties (Pedersen and Hansen 2003: 75). On average, Liberal Party members spent three hours per month on various party activities. In 2012, these figures were about the same (Kosiara-Pedersen 2017: 123). However, in 2012 compared with 2000, a higher share of party members were ready to run for office (Kosiara-Pedersen 2017: 139–43).

The Liberal Party's annual meeting is the highest body of the party. The local associations of the party elect one representative for every 150 members (though at least one representative for each association). A number of other representatives come from different parts of the party, both party functionaries and elected representatives.

The annual meeting elects the party chair who is also political leader. For many years, there has only been one candidate for the position. By leadership change, the party has often elected the deputy chair. An exception was the leadership election in 1984. This may be an example of a leadership change having a crucial role in a party transformation (cf. Harmel and Janda 1994). The party elected a former television journalist who was somewhat new to the party and won over the parliamentary party group chair, a farmer with appeal to the rural districts. Hence, in this case, a strong party organization did produce some resistance to change but did not prevent it. Rather, the decisive vote throughout the country for the new leader indicated that traditional members also preferred renewal to attract more electoral support at the expense of party identity.

With tenures of about ten years for each leader, the Liberals have avoided frequent shifts in its political leadership unlike its electoral rivals the Conservatives. The party leader from 2009–19 was Lars Løkke Rasmussen (PM 2009–11 and 2011–15; deputy leader from 1998). After the 2019 election, he wanted to remain in office but resigned after a few months after internal pressure and was replaced by Jakob Ellemann-Jensen, a son of the leader elected back in 1984.

While the Liberals have declined in membership at the local level, they have strengthened their central office. In 2017, the support function for the party group had 44 full-time positions compared with 28 in 1995 (Financial Affairs Office 2017: 24; Bille 1997: 270). This provides the group leadership with political, economic, and communicative analysis and skills, making the Liberal Party more of an electoral-professional party (cf. Panebianco 1988). Furthermore, the central party office spends about half as much on salaries as the party group secretariat (Folketinget 2019). This development makes it is likely that the power of the party bureaucracy and top leadership has increased.

Today, the Liberals, like the other Danish parties, get most of their income from state subsidies. Member fees made up only 12 per cent of the income in central office in 2017 (Folketinget 2019). Private contributions made up 17 per cent in 2017, although 36 per cent in the election year of 2015 (Folketinget Oplysning 2017). The Liberals receive support in particular from both urban and rural employers' associations as well as from private firms. They have a 'business club' making it possible for contributors to pool contributions and thereby remain anonymous.

Thus, the Liberals today connect with business and mostly through network (cf. Kosiara-Pedersen 2019: 57). Traditionally, there was an informal attachment between the Liberals and the farmers' associations through direct personal overlap with leaders who were often also MPs or members of the national committee, but since the 1970s, such personal overlaps have happened more and more sporadically (Christiansen 2012). Collateral associations to the Liberals retain guaranteed representation in party statutes (cf. Poguntke 2006), including the Liberal Youth and the Liberal Adult Education Association.

The parliamentary party group has traditionally had the ideal 'high to the roof and a long way to the door' which should make it possible for individual MPs to vote against the group line if announced in advance, but party cohesion is high like in other party groups (cf. Skjæveland 2001). From time to time, Liberal backbenchers complain over too much top leadership. Until the 1960s, farmers constituted half or more of the Liberal MPs, but after the 2015 election, there was only one farmer MP (out of 33) (Christiansen 2012).

Relations to Other Political Parties

Since 1973, the Danish Parliament has had between seven and eleven parties represented in Parliament, and almost every government is of the minority type (see Hansen 2020; Green-Pedersen and Skjæveland 2020). On the one hand, this means fierce electoral competition. On the other hand, it necessitates coalitions and negotiations to achieve policy results. As a central political actor, in particular since 2001, the Liberals interact with other parties both in the form of competition and cooperation. See Table 19.1 for the ideological positions of the Liberals compared to other parties.

The Liberals and the Social Democrats have been the main contenders for office for a century (cf. Pedersen and Bille 2004). Despite differing class backgrounds, both parties now have catch-all features and support centre-right and centre-left versions of market economy, combined with publically financed welfare services and Danish commitment to the EU, NATO, and the UN. The Liberals and Social Democrats usually agree on more than 80 per cent of all legislation (Christiansen 2018). With a short exception from 1978–9, and a proposal for a joint government from the Liberal leader during the 2019 electoral campaign, the two parties have never entered into a government coalition in peacetime. The two parties continue to rival for leadership of Denmark, also after the formation of a Social Democratic minority government in June 2019.

The Liberals have formed government coalitions within their own centre-right 'bloc' with the Conservative People's Party (2001–11 and 2016–19) and the Liberal Alliance (2016–19), as well as with the Danish People's Party as a support party (2001–11 and 2015–19). Between 2001 and 2011, the close cooperation between the Liberal-Conservative minority government and the Danish People's Party meant that the government was able to pass most of its coalition agreements (Christiansen and Pedersen 2014). The Liberal Party was able to operate what it labelled 'contract policy'—inspired from the Contract with America by Newt Gingrich prior to the US Congress elections in 1994. The policy encompassed strong commitment to pass and implement specific electoral pledges proposed by a singular party, as it is known from the Westminster system but much rarer in a Danish context more used to consensual style politics. Under the leadership of Lars Løkke Rasmussen, the Liberals largely resolved that this strategy with strong electoral pledges was no longer parliamentary feasible or desirable.

The Liberals' relationship with the Conservative People's Party is special because the two parties share policy positions on many items despite belonging to different ideological families. Consequently, the two parties often cooperate, yet they are also electoral rivals, and there are differences in internal party culture. A proposal by the Liberal leader in 1965 to merge the two parties did not win support among his own ranks, resulting in his resignation and effectively ending the discussion. The Conservatives apparently had the future on their side since they already appealed to the growing urban middle class. Nevertheless, for much of the twentieth century, the Liberals did manage to win slightly more votes on most occasions until the 1980s when the Conservatives temporarily got the upper hand on the centre-right before losing out during the 1990s, apparently lacking the ideological vitality, skilful conduct, and higher number of party members that characterized the Liberals. After 2001, the Conservatives became a junior partner in coalition governments with the Liberals. At the 2015 election, the Conservatives polled their worst result ever, with just 3.4 per cent of the vote but doubled its votes in 2019.

As support party after 2001, the nationalistic and EU-sceptic Danish People's Party was able to leave its status as a 'pariah' in the party system, a party ambition since it was founded in 1995. The result of the 2001 election gave the party a chance to show its reliability as a support party. It did this and is now 'mainstreamed' (Christiansen 2016; see also Kosiara-Pedersen 2020). Having won more votes than the Liberals in the 2015 election, the Danish People's Party acted much more independently towards the government it supports during the 2015–19 term than it did from 2001–11.

With the Social-Liberal Party, there have been at least two liberal parties in Danish Parliament for more than one hundred years, and three counting the recent up-comer Liberal Alliance, making Denmark one of the European democracies with the strongest presence of the liberal party family (cf. Close 2019; Kosiara-Pedersen 2019). With liberal parties both to their left and their right, the Liberals are under cross-pressure. The Social Liberals held the pivot position of the party system after most elections since the 1920s until 2001. It meant that the Liberals were only in power when the Social Liberals wanted them to be. This dependence changed after the Liberals aimed for control of the median voter.

WHAT POLICY DIFFERENCE HAVE THE LIBERALS MADE AFTER 2001?

The Liberals won office after 2001, but the party only did so after declaring acceptance for the welfare state. This raises the question as to whether the party has just become 'governmental managers' or holds an impact on public policy. Kurrild-Klitgaard (2011: 61) concludes that the Liberal-Conservative government from 2001–11 only had a limited impact on making society more centre-right—be it through policies or public opinion. Yet while in government from 2001–11 and again 2015–19, the Liberals headed a number of policy reforms with regard to welfare, taxation, immigration, and administrative reform (see Grøn and Salomonsen 2020). Since 2001, the Liberals worked with different formulas for a so-called 'tax stop'. Furthermore, tax reforms have reduced taxes, although due to higher income, the reforms have not quite reduced the 'tax burden' as a whole. It may have curbed the room for increased public expenditure but the EU-initiated Budget Bill of 2012—passed with the support of the Liberals while in opposition—may have proven more effective in this regard.

Cooperation with the Danish People's Party led to tightened immigration policies, in particular with regard to refugee status, family reunification, and citizenship (Christiansen 2017). Nevertheless, the Liberals, seconded by the employers' associations, have also promoted labour immigration.

One of the most important reforms with long-term effects passed by the Liberals was the local government and regional reform of 2007 (cf. Christiansen and Klitgaard 2009). The reform merged 275 municipalities into 98, and 14 counties into 5 regions. It combined giving more tasks to the municipalities with centralization to the state. Despite giving up rural electoral strongholds, the Liberals remained an important party at municipality level, represented in almost all municipalities, with 37 out of 98 local mayors in 2017 (down from 49 in 2013 and up from 34 in 2009).

Conclusion

The Liberal Party of Denmark provides an example of quite successful party change. The previously class-based party with a dwindling electorate managed to reach out to new voter groups and become a vote and office-oriented catch-all party that won the leading position in Danish politics in the first two decades of the twentieth century. Could changes in ideology, organization, and leadership as responses to challenges in its environment explain this success (cf. Harmel and Janda 1994)? Moreover, has the party been able to maintain its strong position?

Indeed, the Liberals developed their ideology in two steps. First, they drew upon a neo-liberal mood in the 1980s that culminated after the fall of the Berlin Wall in 1989. This helped the Liberals get an edge in the centre-right camp over the Conservatives who were in internal crisis. The weakened state of a rival party was a specific condition not directly accounted for in the party change theory. Second, the Liberals changed their policy to a more pro-welfare position and promoted the immigration issue under the influence of the Danish People's Party.

In the case of the Liberal Party in Denmark, electoral changes preceded organizational changes. It is noticeable that the Nordic parties with agrarian roots—that also used to have many members—have performed better electorally than purer liberal parties. At leadership level, the party has had leaders ready to renew the traditional stance of the party.

We could compare the response of the Liberals and of the Social Democrats to the electoral challenges posed by de-alignment and increased volatility (see Hansen and Stubager 2020; Elklit 1991: 80). For the Social Democratic Party, the main problem was de-alignment among its traditionally class-based voters in the working class. Even despite the group's decline, it maintained a size that made it electorally attractive for other parties. For the Liberal Party, the reverse was the case. Its class-based farmer voters did remain supportive of it but were dwindling. The party could have done as the Norwegian Centre Party and protected its core group of supporters through public subsidies. Yet this would not be in line with the Liberals' export-oriented free-trade ideology and the enrolment in the agricultural policies of the EU.

The Liberal Party has been an important—arguably the most important—party in Danish politics in the twenty-first century until now, but where does it stand at the threshold to the 2020s? The party maintains a position as the leading centre-right contender for government office. Its electorate resembles the social profile of the average Danish citizen, and the party is able to affect the public agenda. Yet it faces current challenges that have followed with its catch-all status. The party has to balance liberal and restrictive positions on matters of immigration and law and order. There are divergent positions among Liberal voters and loose factions inside the party. The rural/urban dimension has also resurfaced as a problem with the rural parts of the party resisting the centralization initiated to manage the public sector more efficiently and to meet the demands of the Liberals' coalition partners. Compared with the 1980s, there is less room for ideological renewal and a weaker party organization on the member side, but the party is also more professionalized. Yet after the major setback in 2015 when the Danish People's Party surpassed them in number of votes, the Liberals again emerged as the strongest centre-right and leading opposition party in the 2019 election.

NOTES

1. In 1920 and 1953, there were more elections in one year due to constitutional changes, and Liberal PMs remained in office throughout that process.
2. National coalition governments during the two World Wars excluded.
3. *Venstre* literally means 'Left', as a reference to the terms from the French Revolution and the fight against privilege, although the Danish party originates in a farmers' movement and peasant reforms of the late eighteenth century. The party does not officially translate its name into English. Nevertheless, it is common to do so in party research and is the editorial choice used in this chapter.

REFERENCES

Altinget (2019). 'Velfærdsstaten – det er mig', *Altinget 23*.

Andersen, Johannes, and Jørgen G. Andersen (2003). 'Klassernes forsvinden', in Jørgen G. Andersen and Ole Borre, eds, *Politisk Forandring: Værdipolitik og nye skillelinjer ved folketingsvalget 2001*. Aarhus: Systime Academic, 207–21.

Andersen, Jørgen G. (2003). 'Partiernes image: De borgerlige er bedst til at sikre velfærden', in Jørgen G. Andersen and Ole Borre, eds, *Politisk Forandring: Værdipolitik og nye skillelinjer ved folketingsvalget 2001*. Aarhus: Systime Academic, 151–70.

Andersen, Jørgen G., and Jan B. Jensen (2001). 'The Danish Venstre: Liberal agrarian or centrist?', in David Arter, ed., *From Farmyard To City Square? The Electoral Adaptation of the Nordic Agrarian Parties*. London: Ashgate, 96–131.

Arter, David (2001). *From Farmyard To City Square? The Electoral Adaptation of the Nordic Agrarian Parties*. London: Ashgate.

Berglund, Sten, and Ulf Lindström (1978). *The Scandinavian Party System(s): A Comparative Study*. Lund: Studentlitteratur.

Bille, Lars (1997). *Partier i forandring*. Odense: University Press of Southern Denmark.

Bille, Lars (1998). *Dansk partipolitik 1987–1998*. Copenhagen: Jurist- og Økonomforbundets Forlag.

Bille, Lars (2006). *Det nye flertal. Dansk partipolitik 2001–2005*. Copenhagen: Jurist- og Økonomforbundets Forlag.

Christensen, Dag A. (1997). 'Adaptation of agrarian parties in Norway and Sweden', *Party Politics*, 3/3: 391–406.

Christiansen, Flemming J. (2012). 'Organizational de-integration of political parties and interest groups in Denmark', *Party Politics*, 18/1: 27–43.

Christiansen, Flemming J. (2016). 'The Danish People's Party: Combining cooperation and radical positions', in Tjitske Akkerman, Sarah L. de Lange, and Matthijs Rooduijn, eds, *Radical Right-Wing Populist Parties in Western Europe: Into the Mainstream?* London: Routledge, 112–30.

Christiansen, Flemming J. (2017). 'Conflict and co-operation among the Danish mainstream as a condition for adaptation to the populist radical right', in Jonas Pontusson and Eve Hepburn, eds, *The European Mainstream and the Populist Radical Right*. London: Routledge, 49–70.

Christiansen, Flemming J. (2018). 'Strengthened opposition, yet high levels of cooperation', in Elisabetta De Giorgi and Gabriella Ilonszki, eds, *Opposition Parties in European Legislatures: Conflict Or Consensus?* London: Routledge, 17–34.

Christiansen, Flemming J., and Helene H. Pedersen (2014). 'Minority coalition governance in Denmark', *Party Politics*, 20/6: 940–9.

Christiansen, Peter M., and Michael B. Klitgaard (2009). 'Behind the veil of vagueness: Success and failure in institutional reform', *Journal of Public Policy*, 30/2: 183–200.

Clausen, H. C. (1979). '1929–1945. De første år', in Kurt Sørensen, ed., *Venstre: 50 år for folkestyret*. Holte: Forlaget Liberal, 136–69.

Close, Caroline (2019). 'The liberal party family ideology. Distinct but diverse', in Caroline Close and Emilie van Haute, eds, *Liberal Parties in Europe*. London: Routledge, 326–47.

Election Study (2007). http://www.valgprojektet.dk (accessed 16 March 2019).

Elklit, Jørgen (1988). *Fra åben til hemmelig afstemning: Aspekter af et partisystems udvikling*. Aarhus: Politica.

Elklit, Jørgen (1991). 'Faldet i medlemstal i danske politiske partier. Nogle mulige årsager', *Politica*, 23/1: 60–83.

Financial Affairs Office (2017). 'Financial accounts for party group support', https://www.ft.dk/~/media/sites/ft/pdf/organisation/folketingets-administration/folketingets-regnskaber/partierne/2017-regnskabshaefte.ashx?la=da (accessed 16 March 2019).

Folketinget (2017). Yearly Financial Account 2015', https://www.ft.dk/~/media/pdf/om_folketinget/regnskaber/partiregnskaber/partiernes-regnskab-samlet/partiregnskaber-2015.ashx (accessed 16 May 2019).

Folketinget (2019). 'Yearly Financial Account 2017', https://www.ft.dk/~/media/sites/ft/pdf/organisation/folketingets-administration/folketingets-regnskaber/partierne/2017-regnskabshaefte.ashx?la=da (accessed 20 August 2019).

Folketingets Oplysning (2017). www.projectmapp.eu/databases/

Gould, Philip (1998). *The Unfinished Revolution*. Little: Brown.

Green-Pedersen, Christoffer, and Pontus Odmalm (2008). 'Going different ways? Right-wing parties and the immigrant issue in Denmark and Sweden', *Journal of European Public Policy*, 15/3: 367–81.

Green-Pedersen, Christoffer, and Asbjørn Skjæveland (2020). 'Party system. Open yet stable', in Peter M. Christiansen, Jørgen Elklit, and Peter Nedergaard, eds, *The Oxford Handbook of Danish Politics*. Oxford: Oxford University Press, 230–41.

Grøn, Caroline H., and Heidi H. Salomonsen (2020). 'Organizing central government. A pragmatic meritocracy?', in Peter M. Christiansen, Jørgen Elklit, and Peter Nedergaard, eds, *The Oxford Handbook of Danish Politics*. Oxford: Oxford University Press, 124–40.

Haarder, Bertel, and Hanne Severinsen (1982). *Nyliberalismen og dens rødder*. Holte: Forlaget Liberal.

Hansen, Kasper M., and Rune Stubager (2017). *Oprør fra udkanten: Folketingsvalget 2015*. Copenhagen: Jurist-og Økonomforbundets Forlag.

Hansen, Kasper M., and Rune Stubager (2020). 'Dynamic stability. The anchors of voting behaviour', in Peter M. Christiansen, Jørgen Elklit, and Peter Nedergaard, eds, *The Oxford Handbook of Danish Politics*. Oxford: Oxford University Press, 347–64.

Hansen, Martin (2020). 'The government and the prime minister. More than *primus inter pares?*', in Peter M. Christiansen, Jørgen Elklit, and Peter Nedergaard, eds, *The Oxford Handbook of Danish Politics*. Oxford: Oxford University Press, 107–23.

Harmel, Robert, and Kenneth Janda (1994). 'An integrated theory of party goals and party change', *Journal of Theoretical Politics*, 6/3: 259–87.

Hermansen, Jan H., Lars Bille, Roger Buch, Jørgen Elklit, Bernhard Hansen, Karina Pedersen, and Hans J. Nielsen (2003). *Undersøgelse af medlemmerne af de danske partiorganisationer*. Aarhus: Magtudredningen.

Heywood, Andrew (2007). *Political Ideologies: An Introduction*. London: Macmillan.

Hjorth, Frederik (2017). 'Emneejerskab – hvilke partier ejer hvilke emner?', in Kasper M. Hansen and Rune Stubager, eds, *Oprør fra udkanten. Folketingsvalget 2015*. Copenhagen: Jurist-og Økonomforbundets Forlag, 193–205.

Katz, Richard S. (1990). 'Party as linkage: A vestigial function?', *European Journal of Political Research*, 18/1: 143–61.

Kirchheimer, Otto (1966). 'The transformation of the Western European party systems', in Joseph LaPalombara and Myron Weiner, eds, *Political Parties and Political Development*. Princeton, NJ: Princeton University Press, 177–200.

Korsgaard, Ove (2014). *N. F. S. Grundtvig as a Political Thinker*. Copenhagen: Jurist- og Økonomforbundets Forlag.

Kosiara-Pedersen, Karina (2017). *Demokratiets ildsjæle: Partimedlemmer i Danmark*. Copenhagen: Jurist- og Økonomforbundets Forlag.

Kosiara-Pedersen, Karina (2019). 'The Danish liberal parties', in Caroline Close and Emilie van Haute, eds, *Liberal Parties in Europe*. London: Routledge, 44–59.

Kosiara-Pedersen, Karina (2020). 'The Danish People's Party. Centre-oriented populists?', in Peter M. Christiansen, Jørgen Elklit, and Peter Nedergaard, eds, *The Oxford Handbook of Danish Politics*. Oxford: Oxford University Press, 313–28.

Kurrild-Klitgaard, Peter (2011). 'Kontraktpolitik, kulturkamp og ideologi 2001–2011', *Økonomi og Politik*, 84/3: 47–62.

Kyed, Karsten (2000). *Dansk jordbrug som erhverv i det 20. århundrede*. Copenhagen: DSR Forlag.

Landbrugsavisen (2019). 'Meningsmåling: Landmænd holder sig trofast til Venstre', 2 June 2019.

Liberal Party (2006). 'Liberal Party's policy agenda' https://www.venstre.dk/politik/principprogram (accessed 16 March 2019).

Liberal Party (2012). 'Liberal Party's by-laws' https://www.venstre.dk/_Resources/Persistent/7 1ca37e569a44e7a6e225142841229eb7f07d78a/Venstres_vedtaegter_2012.pdf (accessed 16 March 2019).

Lipset, Seymour M., and Stein Rokkan (1967). *Party Systems and Voter Alignments: Cross-National Perspectives*. New York: Free Press.

Lund, Hans, and Arne F. Pedersen (1970). *Et folk vågner. Venstre i 100 år. Bind I*. Holte: Forlaget Liberal.

Mair, Peter (1997). *Party System Change: Approaches and Interpretations*. Oxford: Oxford University Press.

Mair, Peter, Wolfgang C. Müller, and Fritz Plasser (2004). *Political Parties and Electoral Change: Party Responses to Electoral Markets*. London: Sage.

Mortensen, Hans (2008). *Tid til forvandling. Venstres vej til magten*. Copenhagen: Gyldendal.

Nevers, Jeppe (2013). 'Frihed over by og land: De liberale og liberalismen i Danmark, 1830-1940', in Jeppe Nevers, Niklas Olsen, and Casper Sylvest, eds, *Liberalisme. Danske og internationale perspektiver*. Odense: University Press of Southern Denmark, 101–25.

Nevers, Jeppe, Niklas Olsen, and Casper Sylvest (2013). 'Intermezzo: Liberalisme i Danmark siden ca. 1980', in Jeppe Nevers, Niklas Olsen, and Casper Sylvest, eds, *Liberalisme. Danske og internationale perspektiver*. Odense: University Press of Southern Denmark, 293–305.

Nielsen, Hans J. (1999). 'Rundt om i landet' in Johannes Andersen, Ole Borre, Jørgen G. Andersen, and Hans J. Nielsen, eds, *Vælgere med omtanke. En analyse af folketingsvalget 1998*. Aarhus: Systime, 39–47.

Olsen, Niklas (2013). 'Liberalismens revitalisering og afkulturalisering i Danmark, 1945-1970', in Jeppe Nevers, Niklas Olsen, and Casper Sylvest, eds, *Liberalisme. Danske og internationale perspektiver*. Odense: University Press of Southern Denmark, 221–45.

Panebianco, Angelo (1988). *Political Parties: Organization and Power*. Cambridge: Cambridge University Press.

Pedersen, Helene H. (2010). 'How intra-party power relations affect the coalition behaviour of political parties', *Party Politics*, 16/6: 737–54.

Pedersen, Karina, and Bernhard Hansen (2003). 'Partimedlemmernes aktivitet', in Lars Bille and Jørgen Elklit, eds, *Partiernes medlemmer*. Aarhus: Aarhus University Press, 73–102.

Pedersen, Karina, and Lars Bille (2004). 'Electoral fortunes and responses of the Social Democratic Party and Liberal Party in Denmark: Ups and downs', in Peter Mair, Wolfgang C. Müller, and Fritz Plasser, eds, *Political Parties and Electoral Change: Party Responses to Electoral Markets*. London: Sage, 207–33.

Poguntke, Thomas (2006). 'Political parties and other organizations', in Richars S. Katz and William Crotty, eds, *Handbook of Party Politics*. London: Sage, 396–405.

Polk, Jonathan, Jan Rovny, Ryan Bakker, Erica Edwards, Liesbet Hooghe, Seth Jolly, et al. (2017). 'Explaining the salience of anti-elitism and reducing political corruption for political parties in Europe with the 2014 Chapel Hill Expert Survey data', *Research & Politics*, 4/1: 1–9.

Rasmussen, Anders F. (1993). *Fra socialstat til minimalstat*. Copenhagen: Samleren.

Salvadori, Massimo (1972). *European Liberalism*. London: John Wiley & Sons.

Skjæveland, Asbjørn (2001). 'Party cohesion in the Danish parliament', *Journal of Legislative Studies*, 7/2: 35–56.

Strøm, Kaare (1990). 'A behavioral theory of competitive political parties', *American Journal of Political Science*, 34/2: 565–98.

Stubager, Rune, Kasper M. Hansen, and Jørgen G. Andersen (2013). *Krisevalg: Økonomien og folketingsvalget 2011*. Copenhagen: Jurist- og Økonomforbundets Forlag.

Thomsen, Niels (1979). 'Venstres vælgere: 1870–1930', in Kurt Sørensen, ed., *Venstre: 50 år for folkestyret*. Holte: Forlaget Liberal, 97–135.

Thomsen, Søren R. (1987). *Danish Elections, 1920–79: A Logit Approach to Ecological Analysis and Inference*. Aarhus: Politica.

Vincent, Andrew (2009). *Modern Political Ideologies*. London: John Wiley & Sons.

Ware, Alan (1987). *Political Parties: Electoral Change and Structural Response*. London: Blackwell.

Worre, Torben (1980). 'Class parties and class voting in the Scandinavian Countries', *Scandinavian Political Studies*, 3/4: 299–320.

CHAPTER 20

THE DANISH PEOPLE'S PARTY

Centre-Oriented Populists?

KARINA KOSIARA-PEDERSEN

'THEREFORE, I say to the Danish People's Party that no matter how much effort is made, in my eyes, you will never be housebroken' (Prime Minister's Office 1999, own translation). These are the words of then Prime Minister Poul Nyrup Rasmussen (Social Democrats) during the opening debate of the Danish Parliament, *Folketinget*, in 1999 as a reaction to the new party's rhetoric and position on immigration and integration issues. Two years later, the Danish People's Party formed the parliamentary support base of the Liberal-Conservative government, and over the course of a decade, they got policy concessions contributing to their major trademarks and furthering their political goals. In the 2015 election, they became the largest party right of the centre and the second largest in Parliament. While the Danish People's Party declined government participation, the party founder and former chair Pia Kjærsgaard could take the seat in the honourable position of Chair of Parliament—a truly remarkable journey for the Danish People's Party.

The purpose of this chapter is to characterize the Danish People's Party and show the impact of this successful party. The empirical base of the analyses is interviews, party documents, an election study, a member survey, media coverage, and social media use. The chapter is split into four parts. The first focuses briefly on party formation. Second, the size and character of their electoral support is depicted. The focus of the third part is on the character and impact of party ideology and policy, and the fourth part briefly presents the main characteristics of the party organization: party discipline, party leadership, and party resources.

A Star is Born: The Creation of the Danish People's Party

Mogens Glistrup was a tax attorney who publicly declared that he was not paying taxes, and when challenged, he went on television to show his 'zero tax form'. He was declined a nomination by the Conservative Party and instead created the Progress Party, which rocketed into Parliament with 28 seats (out of 175) at the 1973 earthquake election. While initially formed around the anti-tax issue and right-wing liberal issues, such as replacing the armed forces with an answering machine with the message 'we surrender' in Russian, the Progress Party had to develop a more comprehensive political programme. Pia Kjærsgaard stood for parliamentary election in 1979 and 1981 before being elected to the Progress Party in 1984 (Folketinget 2018). She became a political spokesperson and shared the party leadership with the leader of the parliamentary group until 1989, and from 1989–93, she was the de facto party leader on her own (Bille 1997: 386). Glistrup and Kjærsgaard represented two different strategies, and the tension between them ultimately led to the creation of the Danish People's Party. The protest line pursued by Glistrup (who was imprisoned for tax fraud in 1983–6 and expelled from the party in 1991) and his supporters focused on staunch opposition and ideological purity, while Kjærsgaard supported a more pragmatic line emphasizing the importance of collaboration and political influence.

The intra-party fragmentation culminated at the tumultuous annual meeting of the Progress Party in 1995. Pia Kjærsgaard lost the leadership fight and left the party together with three other MPs, central organizational people, and about a third of the party members (Bille 1998), all of whom were fed up with disputes and contentions within the Progress Party. Hence, in one way, the Danish People's Party is a traditional, internally created splinter party. However, it could be argued that the Danish People's Party is the successor to the Progress Party (Pedersen and Ringsmose 2005). The Progress Party stood for election in 1998 and passed the threshold due to the very popular MP Kirsten Jacobsen, who pulled two seats in the electoral district of Northern Jutland. However, all four MPs left the party in 2000, and the Progress Party ceased to exist after the 2001 election (for more on the Progress Party's deinstitutionalization, see Harmel et al. 2018). Hence, the Danish People's Party turned out to be the viable survivor.

Electoral Support

The electoral support at national elections depicts well how the Danish People's Party took over from the Progress Party, as shown in Figure 20.1. The election results of 2001–7 show slow increases from the initial 7.4 per cent at their first general election in 1998. On 20 November 2001, the Danish People's Party became the third biggest party in

Parliament (with 12 per cent of the vote), which resulted in a rise from 13 mandates to 22 out of 179. The election results of the Liberal Party, the Conservative People's Party, and the Danish People's Party together gave them a majority of the seats in Parliament. The Liberal Party leader, Anders Fogh Rasmussen, created a Liberal-Conservative minority government with the parliamentary support of the Danish People's Party.

After a small dip in 2011, their support increased drastically from 12.3 to 21.1 per cent in 2015, which was enough for the position as the largest centre-right party and the second largest party, following the Social Democrats, in Parliament. Interestingly, this was the first election with Kristian Thulesen Dahl as party chair. Hence, the Danish People's Party managed to pass the party leadership from the charismatic party founder Pia Kjærsgaard to the so-called 'crown prince' Kristian Thulesen Dahl in 2012 without being punished by the electorate. However, their electoral support declined drastically in 2019 where they lost more than half their seats, falling from 21 per cent to 8.7 per cent of the vote. This electoral slap and an electoral support not much higher than at the initial election in 1998 has resulted in a re-evaluation and some internal discussion on strategy and needed changes.

The Danish People's Party attracts voters with short formal education in particular, and hence also blue-collar workers, and they have a lower share of women and young people within their electorate (Andersen 2017; Thomsen 2017). Short formal education corresponds with the fact that voters with elementary school or vocational training are more hostile towards immigration (Thomsen 2017: 276). Initially, the Danish People's Party gained former Social Democratic voters in particular; however, more recently, they have pulled voters from the Liberals. At the 2015 election, the electoral gain of the

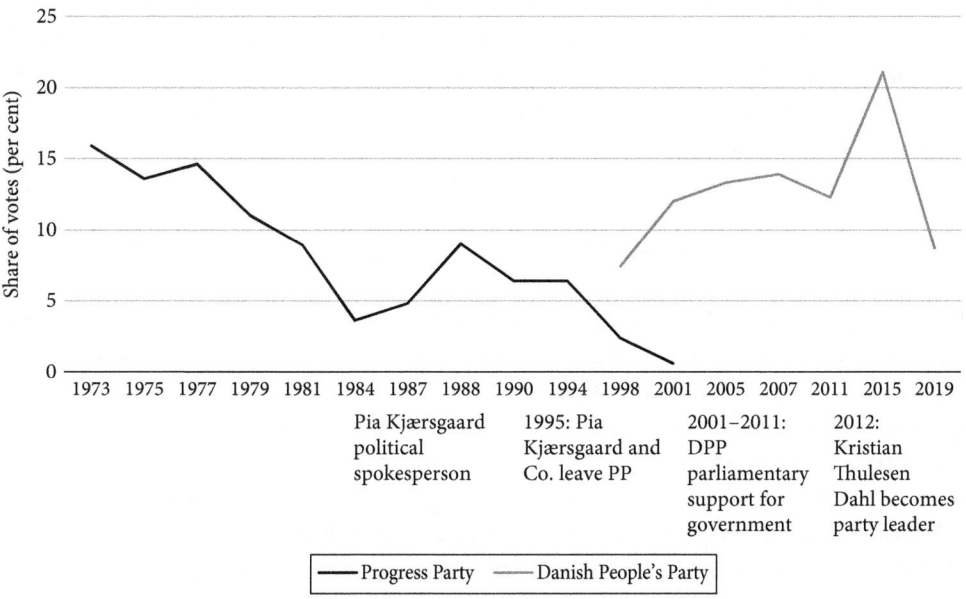

FIGURE 20.1 Electoral support of the Progress Party and the Danish People's Party, 1973–2019.

Danish People's Party coincided with the electoral loss of the Liberals (Hansen and Stubager 2017a: 37), with 4.9 per cent of voters moving from the Liberals to the Danish People's Party (Thomsen 2017), although a fair share of these seem to have gone back to the Liberals in 2019. The Danish People's Party and the Liberals had similar geographic profiles in their electoral support in 2015 (Hansen and Stubager 2017b).

Turning to the European level, the Danish People's Party has been represented in the European Parliament with 1 out of 16/14 Danish seats from 1999–2009 and 2 out of 14 from 2009–14. In 2014, the Danish People's Party became the largest party with more than a quarter of the votes and 4 out of the 13 Danish seats. This result was especially driven by MEP Morten Messerschmidt who personally acquired almost 9 per cent of all Danish votes, which is more than two-thirds of the votes cast for the party. The Danish People's Party has capitalized on being the only anti-EU party right of centre; the other anti-EU party is the left-wing Red-Green Alliance. However, Brexit and the ongoing negotiations seem to have increased Danes' support for the EU, and along with the EU funding fraud allegations against Morten Messerschmidt, this challenged the Danish People's Party in 2019 and explains why their support decreased drastically from 25 per cent to 10.8 per cent of the vote in the EP election.

The Danish People's Party catapulted into the municipal elections in 1997 just a year after the establishment of a party organization. In the first three rounds of municipal elections in 1997, 2001, and 2005, their electoral support rose only slightly from 5.1 per cent to 5.9 per cent. The increase was more marked in 2009, rising to 8.1 per cent and to 10.1 per cent in 2013. After the good results at the 2014 EP election and the general election in 2015, the Danish People's Party had high expectations at the municipal elections in 2017. However, their electoral support across the country fell to less than 9 per cent, and besides a single mayor on the small island of Læsø, they did not acquire access to any mayoral offices. In sum, the electoral support at the municipal level does not match their support at either the national or the European level. While policies are an obvious explanation for this, it is also relevant to point to the potential impact of a highly centralized and elite-focused party.

Government Participation

Pia Kjærsgaard secured the Danish People's Party political influence on their key issues when providing the various Liberal-Conservative governments with a parliamentary majority in 2001–11. Government participation was not on the table. The 2015 election left a majority for the right of centre parties with the Danish People's Party as the largest party, requiring specific reasons for not entering government. The question came up both right after the election when the Liberal government was formed, and when the other two parties in the parliamentary base of the Liberal government, the Conservatives and the Liberal Alliance, were incorporated into a minority coalition government in 2017. While the strong stance against European integration would prove a challenge for a government including the Danish People's Party, the main—and simplest—argument seems to be, in Kristian Thulesen Dahl's words, that they got more out of staying out of government. By providing the parliamentary majority for minority governments, the Danish People's Party has managed to further their key issues in particular and their political goals in general, as well as avoid the costs of government participation as, for example, seen by their Norwegian sister party. Media coverage, i.e. anecdotal evidence, suggest that at least some of their 2015 voters left them due to this decline of governmental responsibility.

Party Policy and Ideology

In order to comprehensively assess the political character and impact of the Danish People's Party, this chapter first shows where the Danish People's Party is placed along the relevant political dimensions before turning to their specific policy standpoints and priorities. Thirdly, it is discussed whether the Danish People's Party is a populist radical right party as depicted in the international literature, and fourthly, the overall impact of the Danish People's Party on the political agenda and decisions in Denmark.

Political Dimensions

When voters are asked to place themselves on a left-right dimension, the Danish People's Party's 2015 voters placed themselves right of centre on average—slightly closer to the centre than Liberal voters, with a little more distance to voters of the Liberal Alliance, and the Conservatives slightly more to the right (Hjorth 2017b: 212). They stand out as the party with the most diversion among their voters, and almost a fifth of them actually place themselves left of centre. However, the Danish political spectrum is two-dimensional and has been so since the mid-1990s (Borre and Andersen 1997). Hence, the simple left-right question should be supplemented by voters' placement of parties on specific policy questions: the economic, redistributive dimension with questions on public sector size and income inequality, and the new politics/value dimension with questions on refugees, the environment, and law and order. In such a two-dimensional space, Danish voters line up the parties from left on both to right on both, except for the Danish People's Party (Hjorth 2017b: 213). The Danish People's Party stand out as the most markedly right-wing party on the new politics dimension (against refugees and green concerns and pro law and order) and left of centre on the economic dimension.

As shown in Chapter 14 on the Danish parties and party system (Green-Pedersen and Kosiara-Pedersen 2020), experts place the parties more variedly in the two-dimensional space. Additionally, in this case, the Danish People's Party lies markedly to the right on the new dimension and in the centre on the economic dimension. This, however, has not always been the case. The Danish People's Party has, like similar parties, adopted a centrist position on the redistributive dimension (de Lange 2007) and not remained on the

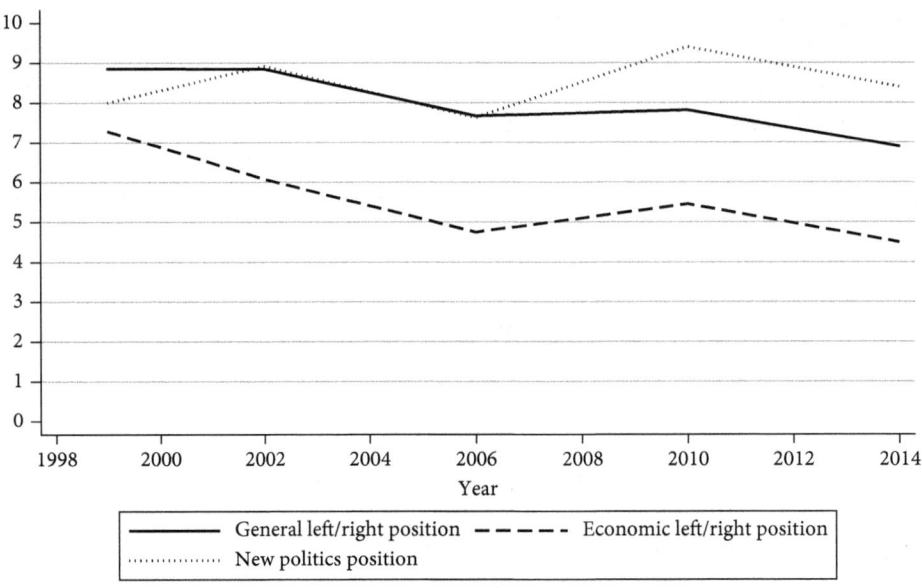

FIGURE 20.2 Left-Right placement of the Danish People's Party, 1999–2014.

Note: Chapel Hill Expert Surveys 1999, 2002, 2006, 2010, and 2014 (Polk et al. 2017). Thanks to Christoffer Green-Pedersen for providing this figure. The 0 on the Y-axis is extreme left, and 10 is extreme right

neoliberal position towards the right which Glistrup's Progress Party initially stood for and which the Norwegian Progress Party also sustains to a greater extent (Jungar and Jupskås 2014). As Figure 20.2 shows, the Danish People's Party has moved from a place on the right at 7 in 1999 to just left of centre at 4.5 in 2014. Hence, on the economic left-right dimension, the Danish People's Party has moved from the vicinity of the Liberals and the Conservatives to close to the Social Democrats. Much less has happened to their place on the new politics dimension where they oscillate between 7.5 and just above 9. This also implies that in the eyes of the country experts, the Danish People's Party is now placed further towards the area in Danish politics that have not been occupied by any parties, namely left of centre on the economic dimension and right wing on the new politics dimension—a place the Social Democrats also seem to be moving towards (see Mariager and Olesen 2020).

Policies and Issues

The specific policy preferences and issue priorities—the set of issues that they prioritize and their stance on said issues—of the Danish People's Party based on the party manifesto and their key issues when negotiating with the government are now focused upon providing a more comprehensive perspective. The Danish People's Party started out with the ideological and political luggage from the Progress Party but rather quickly found their own feet in the late 1990s. The decreasing salience of the socio-economic cleavage among the electorate left room for electoral appeal on the basis of other issues. Cleavage-based voting has been supplemented or replaced by issue voting (Borre and

Andersen 1997). The key issues promoted by the Danish People's Party previously (Christiansen 2016) as well as currently are immigration, the elderly, social, health, animal welfare, law and order, border control, and the EU (Danish People's Party 2019a).

The Danish People's Party distinguishes themselves in particular with their nativist and authoritarian attitudes on the new politics dimension. In their manifesto, the Danish People's Party emphasizes the need to protect Danish national heritage. 'The country is founded on the Danish cultural heritage and therefore, Danish culture must be preserved and strengthened' (Danish People's Party 2019b). In particular, their anti-immigration discourse was developed and promoted from the beginning in the last half of the 1990s. Multiculturalism is to be avoided. 'Denmark is not an immigrant-country and never has been. Thus we will not accept a transformation to a multi[-]ethnic society. Denmark belongs to the Danes and its citizens must be able to live in a secure community founded on the rule of law, which develops along the lines of Danish culture' (Danish People's Party 2019b).

In their combination of immigration and rule of law, the Danish People's Party combines authoritarianism and nativism. This, for instance, is seen in particular when they focus on the deportation of non-Danes convicted of crimes. Key words in their immigration policy are 'fewer arriving, more departing' (Danish People's Party 2019c). To avoid more arrivals, they want to give shelter only to refugees whose lives are endangered and to provide aid at catastrophes and in the immediate surroundings to avoid large numbers of refugees. With the so-called 'paradigm shift' of 2019, the Danish People's Party succeeded in further halting some parts of the integration measures with the aim of facilitating that foreigners are to go back to their home countries as soon as possible. If foreigners are to stay, there is a high level of requirements regarding how they must contribute to Danish society and adhere to Danish cultural norms and 'basic values such as gender equality, democracy and freedom of speech' (Danish People's Party 2019c). A political keystone for the Danish People's Party is border control with 'buildings, police and customs officers at sea, on land and in airports' (Danish People's Party 2019d). The purpose is to control who enters the country and to enable asylum applications to be processed at the border so that unwanted asylum seekers can be rejected (Danish People's Party 2019d). Contrary to similar parties, the Danish People's Party is not anti-Semitic; on the contrary, the party leadership defends Israeli interests.

The Danish People's Party is supportive of welfare for the elderly in particular. While '[h]elp should be available through an efficient social and healthcare system to all who are in need of it', they do specify that '[n]ursing and care of the elderly and the disabled is a public responsibility' (Danish People's Party 2019e). That they are able to deliver is shown on their website where they present a list with 23 initiatives implemented since 2015 (Danish People's Party 2019a); this is the only other issue than immigration which is emphasized. That the Danish People's Party takes good care of the elderly is also acknowledged by the electorate; they are by far regarded as the party best at representing the elderly (Hjorth 2017a: 201).

Hence, the Danish People's Party is pro-welfare, but social benefits should apply to nationals only. As such, they pursue welfare chauvinism. Specifically in regard to healthcare, they emphasize the free and equal access to healthcare for all citizens across the country, addressing the issue of longer response times in the rural areas (Danish People's Party 2019f). Animal welfare, in particular pet welfare, sits high on the agenda of the Danish People's Party. It has been part of the party image from the creation of the party and is also one of their eight key issues (Danish People's Party 2019g).

Authoritarianism stands strong in the Danish People's Party manifesto. The Danish People's Party supports a lower criminal age, harsher punishment for crime, especially crimes regarding personal violence, and more police and surveillance. 'Criminals should be convicted fast, hard and imprisonment must imply more punishment' (Danish People's Party 2019h). While the authoritarian law and order policies apply to all criminals, the Danish People's Party often points to the criminal acts committed by (descendants of) immigrants.

In Denmark, as elsewhere, the EU dimension is separate from the socio-economic, redistributive, and new politics value dimensions. The Danish People's Party is an anti-EU party, along with the Red-Green Alliance who sits at the most left-wing end of both political dimensions. The Danish People's Party opposes surrendering sovereignty and hence the European Union (Danish People's Party 2019i). The Danish People's Party wants European collaboration on trade, the environment, and technical collaboration, but they oppose a political union. They want Denmark to have smaller engagement but allow other countries to pursue a higher degree of integration (Danish People's Party 2019i). While Brexit seems to have halted the Danes' desire to leave the EU, this is not the case for the Danish People's Party, who staunchly supports the Brexiters, for instance, on social media. As argued above, this seems to have hurt the Danish People's Party at the EP election.

Populist Radical Right?

The field of studies of parties like the Danish People's Party has a high degree of terminological disputes. However, based on the definition that radical right parties are characterized by nativism, authoritarianism, and populism (Mudde 2004), the Danish People's Party to some extent classifies as a populist radical right party. As shown above, nativism, i.e. the combination of nationalism and xenophobia, shows clearly in their party principles and manifesto (Danish People's Party 2019a, 2019b). Denmark is supposed to be for Danes only since non-Danes threaten the homogeneous nation state. Authoritarianism, i.e. the importance of authoritative figures and emphasis on law and order, is also clear. Law and order is emphasized across the issues, and the Danish People's Party promotes a high level of punishment for crimes involving the safety of both humans and animals (Danish People's Party 2019g, 2019h).

While 'populism' is a much studied and much disputed concept, there seems to be agreement within parts of the literature that populism is a rhetoric where the pure people are positioned against the corrupt elite, that is, an anti-elite sentiment. On the one hand, the Danish People's Party does apply populist rhetoric and arguments; they pursue a populist narrative. An analysis of the Facebook sites of Danish MPs shows that Danish People's Party representatives, together with those from Red-Green Alliance, use populist rhetoric to a larger extent than other members of Parliament do, even though the variation within all parties is big (Nielsen 2018). In addition, Pia Kjærsgaard also applies her personality to the populist narrative. She has a personal background that matches the party image. She cared for the elderly from 1978–84 as a home care worker, a CV that she has used politically to indicate her base among ordinary, common people (even though her family background was not working class as her father was a shop owner). The anti-elite perspective on politics is also exhibited in the lower levels of both external and internal efficacy as well as social trust, respectively, among members and voters of the Danish People's Party when compared to those of other parties (Kosiara-Pedersen 2017: 276–80).

On the other hand, the anti-establishment narrative is challenged by the Danish People's Party's integration into the mainstream. When staying out of the ministerial offices, and hence, avoiding the 'establishment' label that inevitably would come with this, the Danish People's Party has managed to sustain the platform for a populist rhetoric to at least some extent. Nevertheless, it is challenged by the large extent to which they have legislated together with the government, having been quite decisive on some issues. Due to their involvement as the parliamentary majority of governments, the Danish People's Party is less anti-mainstream/anti-elite than, for example, the Progress Party was. This schism also comes out in the debates between the new, right-wing, economic liberal, and anti-immigration party the New Right (*Nye Borgerlige*) and the Danish People's Party in the 2019 election campaign. The New Right points to the de facto office-holding of the Danish People's Party and takes on a true anti-establishment role.

The Impact of the Danish People's Party

New parties may affect the established political system in several ways, and a distinction between the mechanics of the party system—i.e. the number of parties, political polarization, volatility, and government formation—and the policy output is applied here.

Since the Danish People's Party de facto took over from the Progress Party in 1995, the total number of parties was not affected. The Laakso and Taagepera index is rather stable around 4.5 in the 1990s (Elklit 2016). Political polarization increased on the socio-cultural dimension but not on the socio-economic dimension if assessed on the basis of the party programmes as presented in the Comparative Manifesto Data (Jupskås 2018). The creation of the Danish People's Party did not immediately make an impact on the level of electoral volatility; however, the party does contribute to the increases in both 2001 and 2015 (Hansen and Stubager 2017a) where they pull voters across the blocs in 2001 (from the Social Democrats), pull from within the blue bloc (the Liberals) in 2015, and lose to both in 2019. The Danish People's Party has left heavier footprints when it comes to government formation. The election result of 2001 gave the right of centre parties the ability to form a government without the support of the centre parties, a rarity in the Danish case. The electoral success of the Danish People's Party, and in particular, its ability to pick up votes from the Social Democrats 'across the aisle' affected government formation; even though not in government, they provided the necessary parliamentary majority for the Liberal-Conservative governments in 2001–11 and 2015–19.

Contrary to their counterparts in Sweden (*Sverigedemokraterna*) and Germany (*Alternative für Deutschland*), the Danish People's Party has been well integrated into the Danish political system from shortly after their creation. The centre-right parties did not pursue the pariah or ostracization approach launched by Poul Nyrup Rasmussen in 1999. Right of centre parties, in particular the Liberal chair Anders Fogh Rasmussen, saw the Danish People's Party as a potential ally rather than a threat early on. The opposite seems to be the case for the Social Democrats who were electorally challenged by the Danish People's Party. Anders Fogh Rasmussen based his Liberal-Conservative minority governments in the 2000s on the support of the Danish People's Party, and the latter managed to attain concessions on their key issues, immigration and the elderly in particular, in exchange for supporting the government and its policies. It was important for Pia Kjærsgaard and the Danish People's Party to show that they were a reliable and stable coalition partner, a serious and normal party. The strategic decisions of mainstream parties have largely determined how the Danish People's Party had an impact on policies.

Turning to the policy implications, the Danish People's Party has had a marked impact on both the content and priority of immigration and integration policies. The main part of the Danish party system—in particular the Liberals, the Conservatives, and the Social Democrats—has accommodated the Danish People's Party on their nativism and welfare chauvinism (Christiansen 2017). It was already on the agenda, but their more authoritarian, anti-immigration political programmes and the electoral support they received on this basis expedited the trend. While the Social Democrats were slower to adapt, they also followed suit and have converged and supported many of the radical policies, particularly in the 2015–19 election period. The reaction of a minority of parties, in particular the Red-Green Alliance and the Social Liberals, has been adversarial, creating increased polarization on the socio-cultural dimension.

During their years as the parliamentary support party for the Liberal-Conservative governments in 2001–11, the Danish People's Party also had an impact on economic policies. They exchanged their support for the government's economic policies for specific issues high on their priority list such as border gates at the Danish-German border and a check for elderly without a fortune. The extent to which the Danish People's Party has not been electorally punished for some of the welfare reductions caused by the Liberal-Conservative governments' economic reforms—in particular on the early retirement scheme and unemployment benefits—indicates that economic issues are of much less importance for their electoral support than new politics issues, particularly concerning immigration and law and order.

ONE FOR ALL, ALL FOR ONE: PARTY DISCIPLINE AND PARTY LEADERSHIP

Glistrup wanted to establish a personal party at his disposal, but he was unsuccessful, and the Progress Party took on the organizational characteristics of mainstream parties (Bille 1997; Larsen 1977). On the contrary, Pia Kjærsgaard was very deliberate in formally organizing the Danish People's Party much like the established parties but with a higher level of centralization and party discipline. The fractionalization and continuous conflicts within the Progress Party had an impact on how Pia Kjærsgaard and her colleagues decided to organize the Danish People's Party. The keywords are centralization and party discipline. The reason for the tight leadership control of the parliamentary group, party organization, and all decisions is in no doubt be found in the prattle and squabbles of the Progress Party. The Danish People's Party established a powerful leadership in order to ensure both that the 'village fools' of the Progress Party did not enrol in the Danish People's Party and that the Danish People's Party could pursue influence within Parliament. This section briefly presents the main characteristics of the organization of the Danish People's Party: party discipline, party leadership, and party resources.

Party Discipline

The Danish People's Party stands out on some characteristics due to their need for tight control and a high level of party discipline. The deliberate strategy of political impact required that Pia Kjærsgaard and the rest of the party elite kept a high level of party discipline to show that they could be entrusted with parliamentary power. This tight central control led, for example, to the expulsion of MPs in 2000. In Pia Kjærsgaard's view, the party's initial fast success meant that they had not been able to screen candidates sufficiently and had ended up with 'fortune hunters' (*lykkeridere*) and other types who did not make good and decent candidates (Kjærsgaard 2002).

In a similar vein, party discipline is upheld within the party organization. At the initial stage, all rank-and-file party members were screened by Peter Skaarup, formerly employed by the Progress Party, to ensure that the party did not accept any of the 'troublesome' members of the Progress Party. Party discipline is adhered to at all levels, and if needed, party headquarters—in particular the party secretary and organizational consultant—assists in solving local disputes, which may result in members and municipal politicians being expelled or exiting of their own volition. Members who criticize the party in public, have views that skew too right-wing, or express very extremist viewpoints such as anti-Semitism are asked to leave or expelled, as are members who in other ways may discredit the party, for instance by getting a conviction even if it is unrelated to politics. Expulsions cannot be appealed at the annual meeting of the party unlike in other

Danish parties (Danish People's Party 2019j; Kosiara-Pedersen 2015). The annual meeting is not the highest authority on this matter. The Danish People's Party leaves no stone unturned in ensuring party stability.

Pia Kjærsgaard and her colleagues decided to establish a party membership organization since 'parties are supposed to have members' (Kjærsgaard 2002). While the organizational structure in many ways formally resembles that of mainstream parties, they do have more centralizing features, and they de facto do not grant rank-and-file members much of a say on party decisions. Interestingly, the Danish People's Party members are not quite dissatisfied with intra-party democracy. On the contrary, it seems as if members enrolling in the Danish People's Party do not expect much of a say, and hence, the lack of de facto influence on party decisions is simply accepted (Kosiara-Pedersen 2014).

Party Leadership

Party leadership is central to the Danish People's Party. Since Pia Kjærsgaard left the Progress Party together with three other MPs, she was the party founder, owner, and decisive in all that the Danish People's Party decided and did. While some voters were attracted to her political messages and charisma, others were appalled by these. As mentioned above, the Danish People's Party was not electorally punished by the transition of the party leadership from Pia Kjærsgaard to Kristian Thulesen Dahl. There may be several contributing factors to this transition being smoother than what is often seen with parties led by a strong personal brand. Kristian Thulesen Dahl was one of the Progress Party MPs who left with Pia Kjærsgaard. He has a different image than Pia Kjærsgaard; an image emphasizing his political competences and knowledge in regard to economic issues in particular and less of an emphasis on immigration and integration. In the first phase, Kristian Thulesen Dahl and Pia Kjærsgaard practiced a division of labour, where the latter remained in front as spokesperson for the 'value politics'—that is, 'new politics' or 'socio-cultural politics', particularly concerning the issues of immigration and integration and law and order. When Pia Kjærsgaard became Chair of Parliament in 2015, Martin Henriksen from the next generation took over the role of prominent spokesperson on immigration. After the electoral defeat in 2019, Pia Kjærsgaard left the seat of parliamentary chair and took on the role as spokesperson on foreigners. While the party leader is above all others, it is worth mentioning that the Danish People's Party has a tight-knit leadership team that has been almost stable since their establishment.

Party Organizational Resources

The Danish People's Party created a traditional party member organization with dues-paying party members and local branches. Their dues are low at EUR 20 a year (Danish People's Party 2019k). While their electoral gains have positioned them as one of the three major parties, their membership organization has, like most new parties, never reached the size of the Social Democrats or the Liberals. From 6,500 members in 2000, their membership figures rose slowly to 10,700 members in 2012. In their years in opposition in 2012–15, their membership figures rose more markedly and peaked in 2015 with 17,000. However, there has been a decline since then. While this is (less than) half the membership figures of the Liberals and the Social Democrats, the Danish People's Party is the largest of the remaining parties (see Green-Pedersen and Kosiara-Pedersen 2020). The party members are more likely male, older, and with compulsory or vocational training; however, compared to the party voters, they are among the more representative parties (Kosiara-Pedersen 2019).

The Danish People's Party was established at a time when public party financing was well in place, and it is quite apparent when analysing their income profiles based on the annual publicly available accounts of the national party organization (Folketinget 2019). They depend heavily on public financing, which makes up 75 per cent or more of their income. Dues make up around 10 per cent. The Danish People's Party does not have strong ties with interest organizations, but they do get private contributions from some of the businesses and interest organizations that also contribute to other right of centre parties.

CONCLUSION

The Danish People's Party was the successful part of the split within the Progress Party. Pia Kjærsgaard and her supporters wanted political influence and created a party organization with party members, relying mainly on public funding, and with a high level of centralization and party discipline in order to prove parliamentarily reliable. At their second election, they became the third largest party and contributed thereby with their parliamentary support to establish and maintain a centre-right government from 2001–11 and 2015–19. During these periods, the Danish People's Party has been successful in getting policy concessions, in particular on their primary issues of less immigration and integration and more law and order. They have had a heavy influence on Danish politics in these areas. The electoral success of the Danish People's Party peaked in 2015, and government participation seemed to be an option. In sum, the Danish People's Party has been a highly successful (new) party; however, the 2019 election results—the worst since the party's first election in 1998—show that they now face certain challenges.

The leadership change from Pia Kjærsgaard to Kristian Thulesen Dahl in 2012 initially seemed electorally successful as they became the largest party right of centre in 2015. However, in 2019, their electorate seemed displeased with the strategic decisions to stay out of government and open up for collaboration with the Social Democrats. In addition, the Danish People's Party is challenged by the new party, the New Right, to the right on the new politics dimension. As an opposition party, they are able to position themselves sharply on the value dimension and pursue strict immigration and integration policies. Hence, the Danish People's Party stands a better chance of facing the challenge of the New Right than if they had been in government.

While it would have been hard to imagine that the Danish People's Party could have stayed outside government if the 2019 election had resembled the 2015 election, it remains to be seen whether the Danish People's Party will take on government responsibility if they regain their former electoral size in future elections. While it may be expected by the electorate, the Danish People's Party will be challenged by becoming integrated into government even more, where they will need to administer government compromises, implement EU policies as ministers, and become part of the establishment in general. This will challenge their populist narrative. The Danish People's Party are nativist and authoritarian like their European counterparts, and even though their populism is less pronounced than in other populist radical right parties, it is still hard to maintain their populist narrative if part of the establishment.

REFERENCES

Andersen, Jørgen G. (2017). 'Portræt af vælgernes socio-demografi', in Kasper M. Hansen and Rune Stubager, eds, *Oprør fra udkanten. Folketingsvalget 2015*. Copenhagen: Jurist- og Økonomforbundets Forlag, 41–67.

Bille, Lars (1997). *Partier i forandring*. Odense: University Press of Southern Denmark.

Bille, Lars (1998). *Dansk partipolitik 1987–1998*. Copenhagen: Jurist- og Økonomforbundets Forlag.

Borre, Ole, and Jørgen G. Andersen (1997). *Voting and Political Attitudes in Denmark: A Study of the 1994 election*. Aarhus: Aarhus University Press.

Christiansen, Flemming J. (2016). 'The Danish People's Party. Combining cooperation and radical positions', in Tjitske Akkerman, Sarah L. de Lange, and Matthijs Rooduijn, eds, *Radical Right-Wing Populist Parties in Western Europe: Into the Mainstream?* New York: Routledge, 94–112.

Christiansen, Flemming J. (2017). 'Conflict and co-operation among the Danish mainstream as a condition for adaptation to the populist radical right', in Pontus Odmalm and Eve Hepburn, eds, *The European Mainstream and the Populist Radical Right*. Abingdon: Routledge, 49–70.

Danish People's Party (2019a). 'Mærkesager', https://danskfolkeparti.dk/politik/maerkesager/ (accessed 8 March 2019).

Danish People's Party (2019b). 'The party program of the Danish People's Party', https://danskfolkeparti.dk/politik/in-another-languages-politics/1757-2/ (accessed 8 March 2019).

Danish People's Party (2019c). 'Udlændingepolitik', https://danskfolkeparti.dk/politik/maerkesager/udlaendingepolitik/ (accessed 8 March 2019).

Danish People's Party (2019d). 'Grænsekontrol', https://danskfolkeparti.dk/politik/maerkesager/graensekontrol/ (accessed 8 March 2019).

Danish People's Party (2019e). 'Tiltag på ældreområdet', https://danskfolkeparti.dk/tiltag-paa-aeldreomraadet/ (accessed 8 March 2019).

Danish People's Party (2019f). 'Sundhedspolitik', https://danskfolkeparti.dk/politik/maerkesager/sundhedspolitik/ (accessed 8 March 2019).

Danish People's Party (2019g). 'Dyrevelfærd', https://danskfolkeparti.dk/politik/maerkesager/dyrevelfaerd/ (accessed 8 March 2019).

Danish People's Party (2019h). 'Retspolitik', https://danskfolkeparti.dk/politik/maerkesager/retspolitik/ (accessed 8 March 2019).

Danish People's Party (2019i). 'EU-politik', https://danskfolkeparti.dk/politik/maerkesager/eu-politik/ (accessed 8 March 2019).

Danish People's Party (2019j). 'Vedtægter for Dansk Folkepartis landsorganisation', https://danskfolkeparti.dk/partiet/vedtaegter/ (accessed 8 March 2019).

Danish People's Party (2019k). 'Bliv medlem for 150,- kr. årligt!', https://danskfolkeparti.dk/vaer-med/bliv-dfer/ (accessed 8 March 2019).

Elklit, Jørgen (2016). 'Valgsystemerne', in Jørgen G. Christensen and Jørgen Elklit, eds, *Det demokratiske system*. 4. ed. Copenhagen: Hans Reitzels Forlag.

Folketinget (2018). 'Pia Kjærsgaard (DF)', https://www.ft.dk/da/medlemmer/folketinget smedlemmer/pia-kj%c3%a6rsgaard-(df) (accessed 8 March 2019).

Folketinget (2019). 'Gruppestøtte og regnskaber', https://www.ft.dk/partier/om-politiske-partier/gruppestoette-og-regnskaber (accessed 8 March 2019).

Green-Pedersen, Christoffer, and Karina Kosiara-Pedersen (2020). 'Party system. Open yet stable', in Peter M. Christiansen, Jørgen Elklit, and Peter Nedergaard, eds, *The Oxford Handbook of Danish Politics*. Oxford: Oxford University Press, 213–29.

Hansen, Kasper M., and Rune Stubager (2017a). 'Folketingsvalget 2015 – oprør fra udkanten', in Kasper M. Hansen and Rune Stubager, eds, *Oprør fra udkanten—Folketingsvalget 2015*. Copenhagen: Jurist- og Økonomforbundets Forlag, 21–40.

Hansen, Kasper M., and Rune Stubager (2017b). 'Stenbroen og udkantsdanmark - geografiske forskelle i partiernes tilslutning', in Kasper M. Hansen and Rune Stubager, eds, *Oprør fra udkanten. Folketingsvalget 2017*. Copenhagen: Jurist- og Økonomforbundets Forlag, 69–107.

Harmel, Robert, Lars G. Svåsand, and Hilmar Mjelde (2018). *Institutionalisation (and De-institutionalisation) of Right-Wing Protest Parties. The Progress Parties in Denmark and Norway*. London: Rowman & Littlefield.

Hjorth, Frederik (2017a). 'Emneejerskab - hvilke partier ejer hvilke emner?', in Kasper M. Hansen and Rune Stubager, eds, *Oprør fra udkanten—Folketingsvalget 2015*. Copenhagen: Jurist- og Økonomforbundets Forlag, 193–205.

Hjorth, Frederik (2017b). 'Issue voting ved folketingsvalget 2015', in Kasper M. Hansen and Rune Stubager, eds, *Oprør fra udkanten—Folketingsvalget 2015*. Copenhagen: Jurist- og Økonomforbundets Forlag, 207–23.

Jungar, Ann-Cathrine, and Anders R. Jupskås (2014). 'Populist radical right parties in the Nordic region: A new and distinct party family?', *Scandinavian Political Studies*, 37/3: 215–38.

Jupskås, Anders R. (2018). 'Shaken, but not stirred: How right-wing populist parties have changed party systems in Scandinavia', in Steven B. Wolinetz and Andrej Zaslove, eds, *Absorbing the Blow. Populist Parties and their Impact on Parties and Party Systems*. London: ECPR Press, 103–44.

Kjærsgaard, Pia (2002). Interview with Pia Kjærsgaard by the author in 2002.

Kosiara-Pedersen, Karina (2014). 'Partimedlemmernes deltagelse og syn på partidemokrati 2000-12', *Politica*, 46/3: 274–95.

Kosiara-Pedersen, Karina (2015). 'Party membership in Denmark: Fluctuating membership figures and organizational stability', in Emilie van Haute and Anika Gauja, eds, *Party Members and Activists*. London: Routledge, 66–83.

Kosiara-Pedersen, Karina (2017). *Demokratiets ildsjæle. Partimedlemmer i Danmark.* Copenhagen: Jurist- og Økonomforbundets Forlag.

Kosiara-Pedersen, Karina (2019). 'A skewed channel of participation – and even more skewed recruitment pool', in Knut Heidar and Bram Wouters, eds, *Do Parties Still Represent?: An Analysis of the Representativeness of Political Parties in Western Democracies.* London: Routledge.

de Lange, Sarah L. (2007). 'A New winning formula?: The programmatic appeal of the radical right', *Party Politics*, 13/4: 411–35.

Larsen, Bjarne V. (1977). 'En studie af Fremskridtspartiets organisation', *Politica*, 9/3–4: 59–84.

Mariager, Rasmus, and Niels W. Olesen (2020). 'The Social Democratic Party. From exponent of societal change to pragmatic conservatism', in Peter M. Christiansen, Jørgen Elklit, and Peter Nedergaard, eds, *The Oxford Handbook of Danish Politics.* Oxford: Oxford University Press, 278–95.

Mudde, Cas (2004). 'The populist Zeitgeist', *Government and Opposition*, 39/4: 541–63.

Nielsen, Christoffer M. (2018). *Populisme 2.0. En machine learning-tilgang til kortlægning af populistisk framing på Facebook.* Copenhagen: Institut for Statskundskab, University of Copenhagen.

Pedersen, Karina, and Jens Ringsmose (2005). 'Fra protest til indflydelse - organisatoriske forskelle mellem Fremskridtspartiet og Dansk Folkeparti', *Tidsskriftet Politik*, 8/3: 68–78.

Polk, Jonathan, Jan Rovny, Ryan Bakker, Erica Edwards, Liesbet Hooghe, Seth Jolly, et al. (2017). 'Explaining the salience of anti-elitism and reducing political corruption for political parties in Europe with the 2014 Chapel Hill Expert Survey data', *Research and Politics*, 4/1: 1–9.

Prime Minister's Office (1999). 'Statsminister Poul Nyrup Rasmussens replik ved åbningsdebatten i Folketinget den 7. oktober 1999', http://www.stm.dk/_p_7628.html, (accessed 8 March 2019).

Thomsen, Jens Peter F. (2017). 'Indvandring som politisk skillelinje blandt "os"', in Kasper M. Hansen and Rune Stubager, eds, *Oprør fra udkanten. Folketingsvalget 2015.* Copenhagen: Jurist- og Økonomforbundets Forlag, 265–79.

CHAPTER 21

THE RED-GREEN ALLIANCE

Is it Red or Green?

HENRIK BECH SEEBERG AND
ANN-KRISTIN KÖLLN

THE Red-Green Alliance (*Enhedslisten*; RGA) is a far-left party that has become a considerable force in the Danish Parliament in recent years with its 13 seats in Parliament (7 per cent of the 179 seats). This makes it the sixth largest party out of the ten parties in the 2019 Parliament, at a size close to the marginally larger Socialist People's Party, the Social Liberals, and the Danish People's Party, but far behind the two old mainstream parties, the Social Democratic Party and the Liberals. Despite this legislative importance, the RGA rarely attracts much scholarly attention on its own in comparison to the three larger parties. Bischoff and Kosiara-Pedersen (in press) provide the only exception, focusing on the organization and history of the party. In contrast, using multiple novel data sources, we assess the party's ideology and organization against other parties in the Danish Parliament and other Red/Green parties in Europe, thus setting the party into a broader comparative context.

As its name reveals, the RGA runs on a socialist green platform and usually takes a position on these matters to the left of the other centre-left parties in Parliament, the Socialist People's Party and the Social Democrats. In the absence of a true Green party[1] and a sizeable communist/socialist party in the Danish Parliament—the Socialist People's Party currently has 14 seats in Parliament—the RGA has considerable room to be both red and green. Yet this also raises our main research question: what is the RGA— is it more red or green? Comparative research usually does not include the RGA in the group of green parties in Western democracies (Abou-Chadi 2016; Grant and Tilley 2018), and the Comparative Manifesto Project (Volkens et al. 2018) classifies the RGA as part of the socialist party family. However, the self-proclaimed dual image is further corroborated by the party's newspaper called 'Red-Green' and the party's position in the European Parliament. One RGA member, Nikolaj Villumsen, sits in the 2019

European Parliament. In the 2014–19 term, the former RGA member Rina Ronja Kari was part of the parliamentary group Nordic Green Left, signalling a greener identification (this was not settled in the 2019 Parliament at the time of writing). While it seems that the party is consistent in its dual image, this might only be part of a rhetoric that has little to do with reality. In order to bring some empirical bearing to this question, we provide an analysis of the RGA as either predominantly 'red' or predominantly 'green'. We do that along two analytical dimensions: the party's programme and issues (ideology) and the party's organizational structure.

For both dimensions, we will investigate and determine the RGA's 'redness' and 'greenness'. While this is a straightforward task for the party's programme and ideology, there is also a sizeable old and new literature that considers party family differences in party organizations (e.g. Michels 1959; Krouwel 2012; van Biezen and Kopecký 2017; Webb and Keith 2017). Still, red and green parties are somewhat arbitrary landmarks: what does it really mean to be a 'red' or a 'green' party in terms of party programme and issue or in terms of its organizational structure? Consequently, we employ a slightly different method and compare the party with other Danish parties. This has the advantage that such an analysis resembles voters' thought processes more closely, highlighting the potential competitive advantage the party has vis-à-vis its main contenders as a result. The Socialist People's Party (SPP) serves as our yardstick for 'redness'. The SSP is more distinctly, or at least self-proclaimed, 'red' in the Danish system and of somewhat similar size. Comparisons with the SPP will show how similar the RGA is in its programme and in its organization to a socialist or 'red' party. If we observe that the RGA resembles the SPP in our analytical dimensions, we get an indication of the 'redness' of the RGA.

Our standard for evaluating the party's 'greenness' comes via the newly founded party the Alternative (*Alternativet*). After the 2019 election, the party had 5 seats in Parliament, down from nine in the 2015 election. The Alternative presents itself as a champion of environmental issues—primarily advocating sustainability (Alternative 2018)—and is also seen as such by the wider public. It means that if we observe that the RGA resembles the Alternative in our analytical dimensions, we get an indication of the 'greenness' of the RGA. To further strengthen our analyses, we compare the party to other green and left socialist parties throughout Europe.

Our results show that the RGA combines both ideologies and thus manages to straddle two political cultures. In terms of its ideology the party is definitely red, whereas its organization resembles that of other green parties more closely. This arguably plays a large part in its electoral success.

INTRODUCING THE RED-GREEN ALLIANCE

In 1989, the Red-Green Alliance was formed as a merger of three parties: the Left Socialist Party (*Venstresocialisterne*), the Communist Party of Denmark (*Danmarks Kommunistiske Parti*), and the Socialist Workers' Party (*Socialistisk Arbejderparti*).

By themselves, the three parties were unable to pass the electoral threshold, and therefore, they decided to form a common list for election—a unity list (or in Danish, *Enhedslisten*). Hence, the RGA was not considered a 'true' party at first but only a pre-election cooperation (Bille 1998: 192; Red-Green Alliance 2018a).

Based on its ideological heritage, the RGA has run on Marxist ideas to end capitalism by realizing a classless society with collective ownership of the means of production. Over time, the RGA has slowly abandoned its call for revolution, and today, it proclaims to advocate socialism and end capitalism through peaceful democratic transition (Bischoff and Kosiara-Pedersen in press; Red-Green Alliance 2018c).

Despite a natural fragmentation among the three wings of the parties, the RGA gained access to the Danish Parliament in the 1994 national election with 6 seats. Since then, it has substantially increased its vote share, sometimes suddenly as, for example, in 2011 (see Figure 21.1). In the 2019 election, the RGA won 13 seats, down from 14 in the 2015 election. While the RGA has never held office, it has been a support party to every government led by the Social Democrats since its birth (Bischoff and Kosiara-Pedersen in press; Red-Green Alliance 2018a).

Part of the RGA's recent success can be ascribed to the remarkable ideological shift of both of its main competitors on the left, the Socialist People's Party (SPP), and the Social Democrats (SD) to the right before and after the 2011 election (Hansen et al. 2011).[2] In order to form a government with the very reform-minded, centre party the Social Liberals (SL), the SPP and the SD ran on a common economic platform in 2011 to maintain the austerity policy of the centre-right incumbents in the aftermath of the financial crisis. This implied upholding retrenchment to the early retirement scheme, which was very popular among core left voters. After entering office in 2011, the SPP and the SD together with the SL cut back on entitlements to unemployment protection in order to lower corporate taxes. Moreover, the government sold a large part of its shares

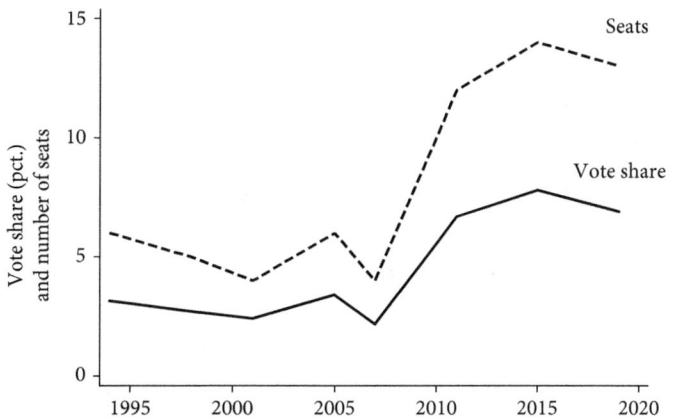

FIGURE 21.1 Vote share and seats for the Red-Green Alliance.

Note: Solid line is vote share at national elections to the Danish Parliament. Dashed line is seat share in the Danish Parliament

Source: Comparative Manifesto Project (Volkens et al. 2018)

in the Danish national energy company DONG to the American investment bank Goldman Sachs at a time when voters were still raging against the role of banks in the financial crisis.

Both decisions received a lot of media coverage, and the RGA was very vocal in its opposition to these policy changes (Bille 2011, 2012, 2013). Voters responded promptly (Seeberg et al. 2017), and the RGA picked up many disgruntled voters. In the eyes of some left-wing voters, the RGA was suddenly the only 'real' pro-welfare party of the centre-left. At the same time, it was clear from the start that the RGA lacked any black-mailing potential because it would never endorse a centre-right government.

Such vocal opposition to the Social Democrats' sale of DONG and retrenchment measures is in the DNA of the RGA—a party that stands out in the Danish Parliament as highly critical of political authorities, including the government and the EU. The RGA almost always votes against the annual government budget unlike most other parties, rarely participates in cross-party legislative agreements on large-scale legislation (Christiansen and Seeberg 2016), and 'Government operations' rank third among the topics on which the RGA issued press releases in 2004–17 according to Figure 21.4. Moreover, Figure 21.2 shows the number of questions posed to ministers per year by the RGA (solid line) as well as the average for all other parties (dashed line). The number of questions from the RGA reaches multiple times higher than average levels. Despite its relatively limited legislative size compared to the large mainstream parties, it is respon-sible for no less than 23 per cent of all questions to the ministers in the Danish Parliament from the time it entered Parliament in 1994 to 2010. Considering that it was a very small party for most of this period, this is an impressive number, and hence, scepticism towards authorities is a key characteristic of the party.

The SPP's and the SD's drastic move to the right created an ideological vacuum on the political left, which paved the way for the entry of a new party, the Alternative. This

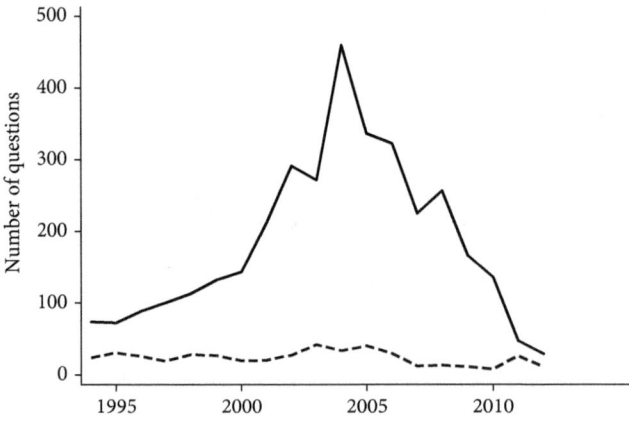

FIGURE 21.2 Number of questions to the Minister per year by parties in the Danish Parliament, 1994–2012.

Source: Comparative Agendas dataset (2018)

party was formed in 2014 as a splinter from the Social Liberals and immediately won 9 seats in 2015 (Kosiara-Pedersen 2015). After the 2019 election it is down to 5 seats. The Alternative runs on a predominantly green platform but also aims to tackle economic and social inequalities (Alternative 2018). Hence, it is an obvious rival to the RGA, and it remains to be seen if the Alternative will get in the way of the RGA.

The RGA's communist ideological heritage has also influenced its organizational structure and makeup. The RGA is assembly-based at the central level and governed through the member-elected national party board. According to party statutes (Red-Green Alliance 2018d), the members of Parliament (MPs) are required to follow the decisions of the party board, which is elected at the annual party conference, and the MPs should promote the political platform agreed upon by the board. The board is the highest authority between the annual meetings (Red-Green Alliance 2018d). Despite the prominent role of the board, the party has a flat hierarchy.

The party does not have a formal party leader or party leadership, and it has only been a recent invention to have a political spokesperson. As a further expression of its member-based organization, its candidate nomination is highly centralized and takes place at the annual meeting. The RGA uses closed party lists at elections, ensuring the opportunity to influence who gets elected. A final expression of its ambition to avoid a concentration of power is the strict rotation principle for the political and organizational posts described in its party statutes. For example, representatives cannot be nominated again when they have held office for seven years. The party strictly adheres to this principle even when it counters the party's electoral interests as the case of Johanne Schmidt Nielsen shows. After seven years in Parliament, she was not nominated again even though she was a very popular and charismatic political spokesperson, and therefore, at least in reality, the party's frontrunner during the years of steady vote share increases (Bischoff and Kosiara-Pedersen in press; Red-Green Alliance 2018b). The principle to avoid any concentration of power also resembles other green parties' organizational values.

As this brief overview shows, the RGA has managed to establish itself in the Danish Parliament. It has seemingly done so by endorsing both a red and a green image. However, the extent to which this image meets reality in terms of the party's programme and organizational structure is an empirical question to which we now turn.

IDEOLOGY

In this section, we analyse the RGA's position on socialist and environmental issues and how salient these issues are to the party in elections as well as between elections. The analysis relies on survey data about voters and on several data sources to determine the party's ideological profile, namely the Chapel Hill Expert Survey data (Polk et al. 2017) and coding of the parties' press releases and parliamentary activities based on the Comparative Agendas Project (Baumgartner et al. 2019).

We start by looking at the voters of the party based on data from the Danish National Election Study (Hansen and Stubager 2017a). We define an ideal-typical green party as primarily emphasizing the importance of ecological sustainability and environmentalist principles. This means that the party advocates environmental concerns above economic growth and industrial production (Grant and Tilley 2018). Moreover, we expect it to emphasize the environment much more than other issues. An ideal-typical socialist party advocates equality, solidarity, redistribution, and social and political rights, emphasizing these issues much more than others.

Voters of the Red-Green Alliance

In terms of demographics of RGA voters (in 2015), they are, as summarized in Table 21.1, more likely to be young, single, renting a place in the city, and employed in the public sector, and they earn less than the average voter. Hence, while few of the voters are traditional low-income workers, many of their voters (and increasingly so) are part of the

Table 21.1. Voter Demographics and Voter Opinions of the Red–Green Alliance Compared to the Other Parties in the Danish Parliament

	Red-Green Alliance	Average for other parties[1]
Demographics		
Age (average)	39.7 (16.1)	45.5 (17.1)
Single (pct.)	44.8	32.9
Lives in city 40.000+	59.6	44.5
Political interest (0 large, 4 small)	1.92 (.73)	2.2 (.86)
Income (0 low, 15 high)	4.2 (2.7)	5.4 (3.4)
House owner	37.4	58.8
Public employee	51.1	33.7
Issue saliency (most important problem)		
Unemployment & labour market policy	13.3	13.1
Social security & redistribution	18.8	12.7
EU	66.7	72.8
Environment	1.2	1.4
Attitudes		
EU (1 pro, 5 con)	3.2 (1.2)	2.9 (1.4)
Environment (1 con, 5 pro)	4.2 (0.9)	3.5 (1.0)
Foreign aid (1 less, 3 more)	2.1 (0.7)	1.7 (0.7)
Inequality (1 good, 5 bad)	4.3 (1.0)	3.4 (1.2)
More welfare rather than tax cuts (pct.)	89.9	61.3
EU identity (1 a lot, 5 little)	3.3 (1.4)	3.4 (1.3)
Left-right self-placement (1 left, 11 right)	2.6 (2.6)	5.4 (2.5)
Left-right placement of the Alliance	2.2 (3.0)	1.7 (2.4)

Note: Standard deviations in parentheses. [1]Excluding Red-Green Alliance.
Source: Danish Election Study 2015 (Hansen and Stubager 2017a).

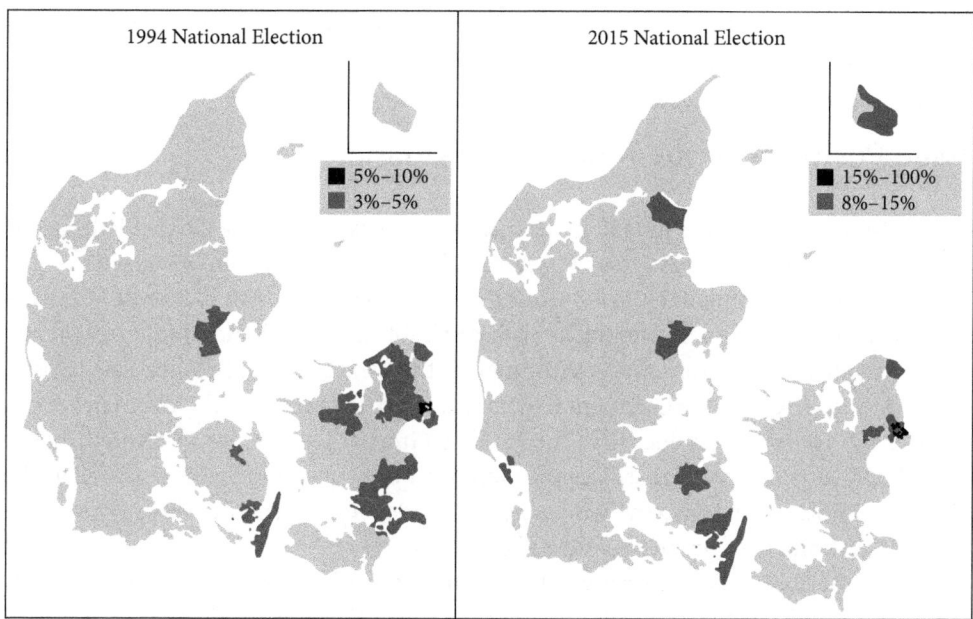

Note: 5–10 per cent (black), 3–5 per cent (dark grey), 0–3 per cent (light grey)

Note: 15+ per cent (black), 8–15 per cent (dark grey), 0–8 per cent (light grey).

FIGURE 21.3 Vote share to the Red-Green Alliance across constituencies in the Danish 1994 and 2015 national elections.

Source: Dansk Valgdata (2018)

cosmopolitan elite that de-emphasizes material interests such as home ownership and high income despite their high salaries. This characteristic of the constituency is also reflected in the maps in Figure 21.3 which shows the vote share across electoral districts in the 1994 and 2015 national elections (the most recent election with available data). The figure highlights the RGA's vote share concentration over time, as indicated by the change in measurement from 1994 to 2015. The maps show that the RGA primarily and increasingly draws its voters from the urban centres of the larger Danish cities Aalborg, Odense, Esbjerg, and Aarhus, and Copenhagen in particular. Hence, the RGA mobilizes voters on the urban side of a re-emerging rural-urban cleavage in Danish politics (Hansen and Stubager 2017b).

In terms of attitudes, the voters of the RGA place themselves on the far left of the left/right ideological continuum. They dislike inequality much more than the average voter and prefer welfare to tax cuts. They are somewhat Eurosceptic, pro-environmental, and pro-foreign aid, but not much more than the average voter (see Table 21.1). Hence, in terms of opinions vis-à-vis the electorate at large, they stand out by their red attitudes more than their green attitudes. This impression is corroborated by the issues RGA voters are concerned about. RGA voters distinguish themselves from the rest of the electorate on their much greater concern about welfare and social protection. In contrast, the electorate at large and the RGA's voters largely agree on the importance of and opinion on environmental and EU issues. Hence, judging from the positions and issue priorities of the voters vis-à-vis the electorate at large, the RGA is distinguished more by its representation of red than green voters.

Issue Positions of the Red-Green Alliance

The Red-Green Alliance is judged by Danish country experts in the Chapel Hill Expert Survey data (Polk et al. 2017) to be extremely left on redistributive questions and strongly pro-environmental. On a 0–10 scale with 10 being most right, the RGA is a 0.8 on redistribution and environment, as visible in Table 21.2, and hence, far to the left and further to the left and more pro-environmental than the Socialist People's Party (SPP). This makes the RGA as environmental in its issue position taking as the German Greens and even considerably greener than the Swedish Greens (see Table 21.2). On redistribution, the RGA is more socialist than the Greens in Germany and Sweden as well as the SPP and almost as far-left as the left parties in Sweden and Germany. This suggests that the RGA is thoroughly green and red and equally so.

Finally, the RGA takes a strong stance against the EU scoring 1.2 on a 0–10 scale (10 most pro-EU). This makes the RGA much more Eurosceptic than the SPP which scores 4.5 on the 0–10 position scale. This position is shared with the Greens in Sweden but sets itself apart from the highly pro-European Greens in Germany. This Euroscepticism is probably a legacy from the RGA's birth, seeing as it was elected to Parliament for the first time in 1994 during a turbulent time in Denmark's relationship with the EU. In 1992, Denmark voted 'No' to the Maastricht Treaty and only later voted 'Yes' to the Edinburgh Agreement in 1993 amid severe Euroscepticism from the left-wing of the Danish Parliament. At this time, the EU was a major issue in Danish politics, and the RGA's vocal EU opposition was a large part of its electoral breakthrough (Bille 1998: 192).

Table 21.2. The Position on the EU, Redistribution, and the Environment and the Issue Importance for Six Parties in Denmark, Sweden, and Germany

Country	Party	EU position	Redistribution	Environment
Sweden	Green Ecology Party	8.4	3.1	1.9
	Left Party	3.9	0.6	4.5
Denmark	Red-Green Alliance	1.2	1	0.8
	Socialist People's Party	4.5	2.4	2
Germany	Greens	2.7	3.1	0.7
	Die Linke	1.5	0.8	1.9

Note: The variables are measured 0–10: EU position (0 con, 10 pro), spend vs tax (0 spend, 10 cut tax), redistribution (pro, 10 con), left-right (0 left, 10 right), environment (0 pro, 10 con). Each saliency variable reports the expert assessment of how important each of the issues are to the party. Average scores for 1999–2014.

Source: Chapel Hill Expert Survey data (Polk et al. 2017).

Issue Priorities of the Red-Green Alliance (I): The Environment and Labour Market Policy

Figure 21.4 reports the Red-Green Alliance's everyday issue focus outside election times. The top subgraph displays the issues on which the party published press releases[3] from 2004–17, i.e. as an opposition party to the centre-right government 2004–11 and 2015–17, in between which it was a support party for a Social Democratic minority government. For comparison, the issue attention in the press releases of the Socialist People's Party (SPP) is in the subgraph below. Figure 21.5 shows how the RGA's attention to the top issues has changed over time from 2004–17. Starting with Figure 21.4, the markers form a rather steep diagonal line, revealing that the RGA's allocation of attention is very unequal across issues. It spends little time on typical right issues such as transport, business, defence, and agriculture and focuses primarily on the EU and international affairs and labour market issues. Intermediary issues include immigration, the economy, the environment, education, and crime. Hence, there are several important observations. The environment is not a defining issue for the party, and it is only rated seventh in its issue portfolio at less than 5 per cent of its attention. This is considerably less than the SPP for which the environment is most important. The environment is no more important to the RGA than crime or immigration.

Figure 21.5 indicates that its attention to the environment may even be on the decline. The average attention in its party press releases from 2004–17 is 1.3 percentage points lower after 2010 than before (but $p < 0.19$). From this perspective, green is a very weak, and probably increasingly weak, colour of the RGA. In contrast, labour market issues such as trade unions, seasonal workers, active labour market policy, and the social security scheme feature prominently in its press releases and take up about 7 per cent of its press releases from 2004–17. Although labour market issues are also a top priority of the SPP, the RGA puts greater emphasis on this issue. As Figure 21.5 shows, this is an issue the RGA has focused massively on in the aftermath of the financial crisis when unemployment rose sharply in Denmark. It emphasized this issue 1.6 percentage points more after the crisis. In this sense, the RGA is thoroughly painted in red and probably increasingly so.

Issue Priorities of the Red-Green Alliance (II): The EU and Foreign Aid

Despite its focus on labour market issues more than the environment, the RGA is no traditional socialist party because its most emphasized issues are the EU and foreign aid. Together, these two issues make up more than 10 per cent of its issue attention on average, with the EU being more important than foreign aid. This distances the RGA from the SPP, which spends about 5 per cent of its attention on the EU and international affairs (see also Green-Pedersen 2012). The RGA's attention to the EU and international

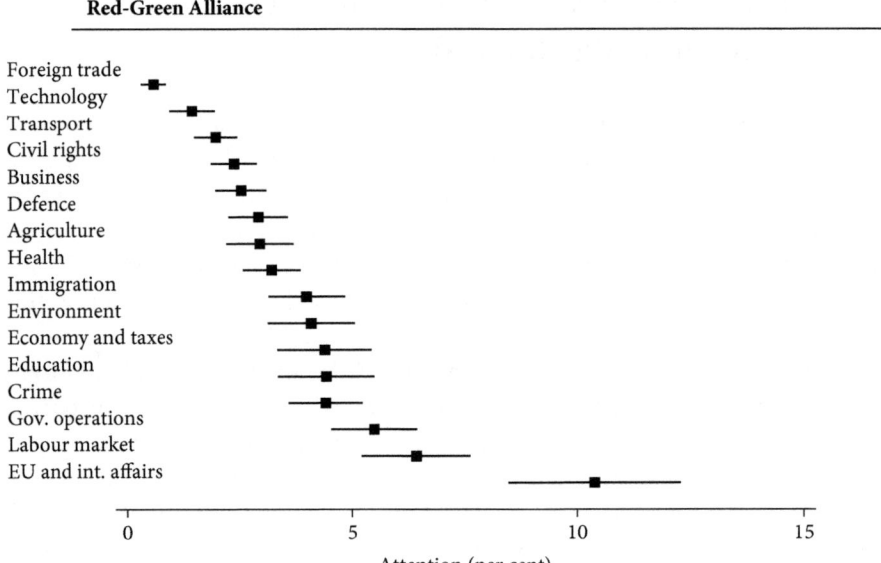

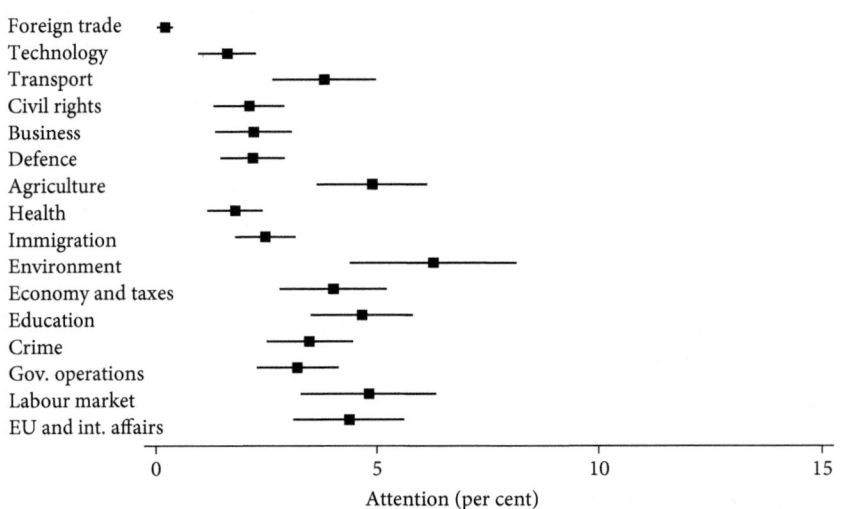

FIGURE 21.4 Average attention to issue areas in press releases for the Red-Green Alliance, Socialist People's Party, and the Social Democrats in Denmark, 2004–2017.

Source: Seeberg (2018)

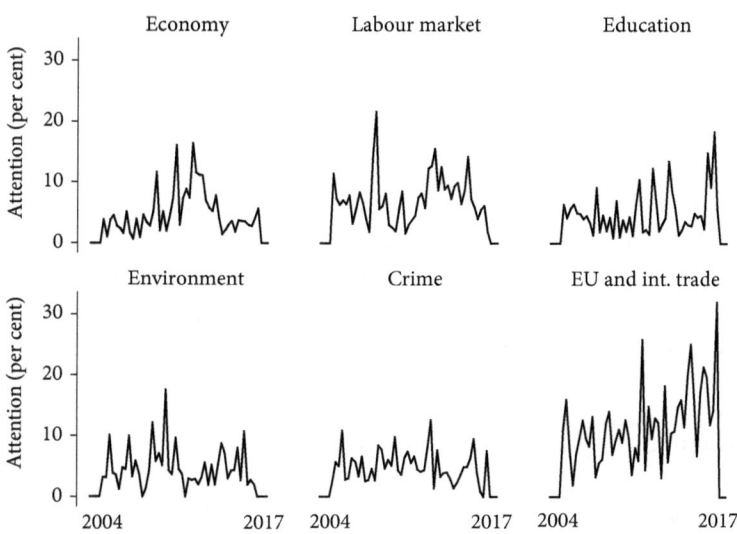

FIGURE 21.5 The Red-Green Alliance's attention to six issues in their press releases, 2004–2017.
Source: Seeberg (2018)

affairs even seems to be on the rise in Figure 21.5. A regression analysis (not reported) confirms that its attention to this issue has increased systematically by 0.66 percentage points each year from 2004–17. Hence, the EU and foreign aid might become even more defining issues for the party. These trends seem to be more than just a reflection of changes between the party's opposition and support-party-mode in the time period 2004–17.

The RGA's high Eurosceptic focus is a sign of poor representation because its voters in Table 21.1 are not particularly Eurosceptic compared to the rest of the electorate. Hence, the EU issue does not appear to be the reason why these voters support the RGA. That said, when it comes to red vs. green, the representational link between voters and the party is strong. Just like the RGA, its voters deviate more from the rest of the electorate on redistribution and equality than on the environment. In terms of assessing the colour of the RGA, the bottom line of the analysis of the party's positions and issue priorities is that it is quite thoroughly red—and, surely, more red than green.

PARTY ORGANIZATION OF THE RED-GREEN ALLIANCE

Issue positions and salience are only one part of the story of any political party's profile. The party's organization provides the backbone of the party, arranging campaigns, nominating candidates for elections, and mobilizing the electorate. As mentioned before, it is easier to analyse the 'redness' or 'greenness' of a party's ideological profile than of its organization. Yet we follow a larger literature on broader differences in how parties of different party families organize themselves (e.g. Michels 1959; Krouwel 2012; van Biezen and Kopecký 2017; Webb and Keith 2017). We study the RGA's (1) party finances, (2) party membership, and (3) intra-party democracy. All three aspects pertain to the wider concept of the party organization (e.g. see Katz and Mair 1995; Kölln 2015; Poguntke et al. 2016). Throughout, we again draw comparisons with the Socialist People's Party (SPP) and the Alternative as our relative yardsticks of 'redness' and 'green-ness', respectively. Using data from the Political Party Database (Poguntke et al. 2016), we also place the RGA in an international context and compare it with other green and left socialist parties around the world.

Party Finances of the Red-Green Alliance

We operationalize party finances through the party's income and sources of income. All data come from the party's statements of account, officially reported to and published by the Danish Parliament. We can even draw on a time series (1990–2016) going back all the way to the RGA's emergence in Parliament. Specifically, we measure both variables at the central party office (headquarters). For our variable of sources of income, we simply distinguish between the four most common categories: membership dues, state subsidies, private donations, and other (see Poguntke et al. 2016).

Figure 21.6 shows a steady growth (at a slow rate) of the RGA's annual income until making a bigger jump around 2010. The trend runs parallel to that of the SPP, albeit at a

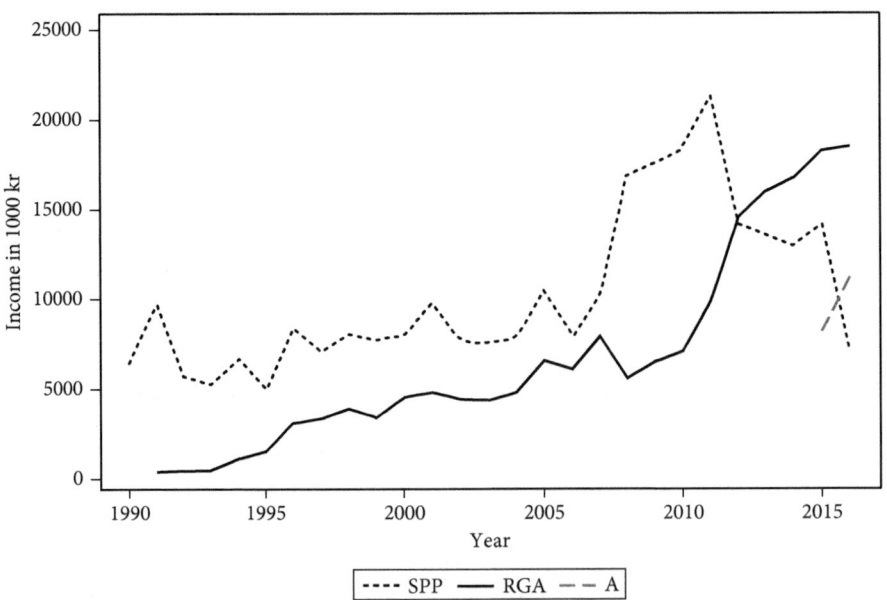

FIGURE 21.6 Annual party income (Central Office), 1990–2016.
Source: Danish Parliament

slightly lower level, up until about 2007, which is when the SPP's income increased steeply. From then onwards, the two trends seem to have little resemblance. The Alternative's income, in turn, is clearly on the rise, having recently even overtaken the SPP's. Yet its income still remains distinctively lower than the RGA's income. In 2016, the RGA reported an annual income of DKK 18.5 million, while the SPP and the Alternative's income was only DKK 7,060,083 and DKK 11,343,175, respectively.

Placing this into an international context, these resources can be compared to other green or left socialist parties around the world. According to information from the Political Party Database (Poguntke et al. 2016), the RGA's annual income in 2016 most closely resembles the green party family's mean income of national party head offices. The thirteen green parties that are part of the sample had an average mean income of EUR 5.7 million between 2010 and 2014, whereas the eleven left socialist parties had about EUR 1.5 million more to dispense on average. The RGA's converted income in 2016 of about EUR 2.5 million comes closer to the green party family's average income. Furthermore, the national pattern suggests that while the party resembled the SPP more in its income, the RGA will likely have more in common with the Alternative in this respect in the years ahead.

The total income is just one part of parties' resource base as these figures conceal where the money is coming from. The next two figures show the parties' distribution across sources of income in 2016 (Figure 21.7). Sources of income typically reveal something about the party's support base and financial dependence or independence (Hopkin 2004). Figure 21.7 shows that state subsidies provide the largest source of party income for all three parties, with the Socialist People's Party (SPP) receiving the largest share of its income from the state at approximately 65 per cent. Both the RGA and the Alternative (A) reported each having received about 45 per cent of their income from

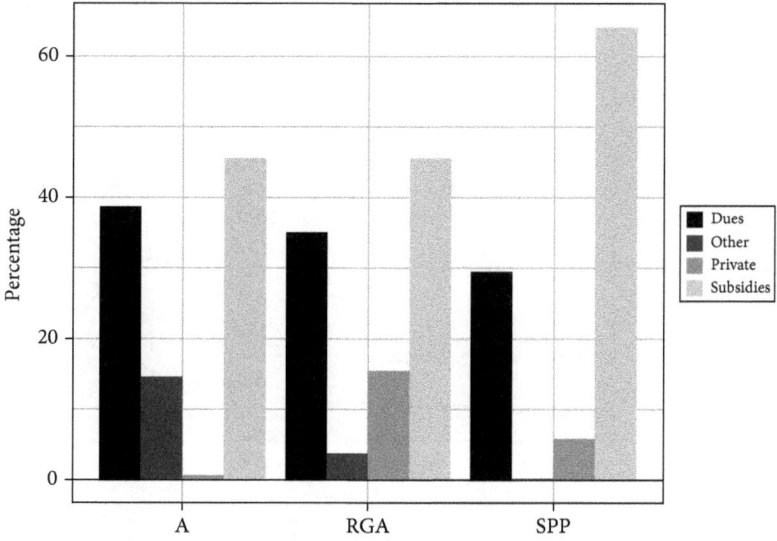

FIGURE 21.7 Distribution of sources of party income in 2016.
Source: Danish Parliament

the state, indicating a high resemblance with the Alternative. Internationally, Poguntke et al. (2016: 664) report the percentage of party income from direct public subsidies for twelve green parties (54.8 per cent) and eleven left socialist parties (60.4 per cent). These national and international comparisons suggest that the RGA resembles again, if anything, other green parties more than left socialist parties in this indicator. Additional support for this conclusion comes via the second more frequent source of income, namely membership dues, because of the similarities between the RGA and the Alternative (Figure 21.2). The two parties only differ in the shares of less important sources of income such as private donations and 'other'. Overall, this means that the RGA resembles parties belonging to the green party family more in its income and sources of income than parties belonging to the left socialist party family.

Red-Green Alliance Party Membership

For our party membership measure, we analyse the RGA's membership size as a share of the electorate (M/E ratio), which shows 'the extent to which parties provide outlets for citizen political participation' (Scarrow 2000: 87). The M/E ratio is one of the most widely used measures of a party's membership base (van Biezen et al. 2012; Kölln 2016; Scarrow 2000).

Figure 21.8 reveals that the three parties—the RGA, the SPP, and the Alternative—are all grouped very closely together in their current level of membership with little difference. All three have between 0.18 and 0.24 per cent of the electorate as members, and so no discernible differences can be observed. Also, in an international comparison, the results are rather inconclusive because the RGA held a membership base of 0.21 per cent

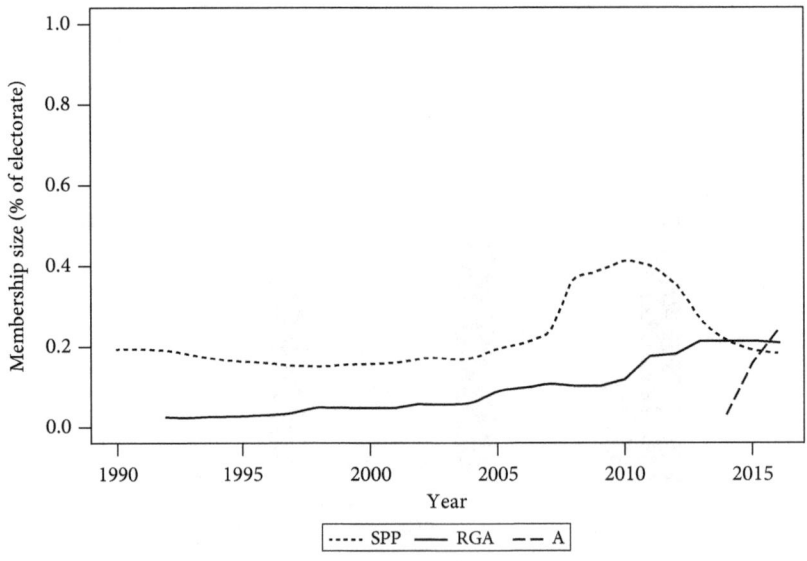

FIGURE 21.8 Membership size as share of the entire electorate, 1990–2016.

Source: Danish Parliament / International IDEA (2018)

Note: The size of the electorate in non-election years is interpolated of the Danish electorate in 2016, which lies almost half-way between the international averages reported for parties belong to the green (0.11 per cent) and left socialist (0.28 per cent) party family, respectively (Poguntke et al. 2016: 668). This suggests that the RGA's membership size as a party organizational feature provides us with little information to answer our research question.

Red-Green Alliance Intra-Party Democracy

Finally, we turn to the RGA's intra-party democracy as an organizational feature of political parties and compare, within and across party systems, the RGA's official levels of intra-party democracy. According to information from the statutes, the RGA has the highest level of intra-party democracy, followed closely by the SPP (Bolin et al. 2017: 177; see also Bischoff and Kosiara-Pedersen in press). The Alternative was, however, not part of the first round of data collection for the Political Party Database, and so it is all the more important in this case to compare the RGA internationally to parties belonging to the green or left socialist party family. Poguntke et al.'s (2016: 672) comparison of intra-party democracy indices (assembly-based and plebiscitary-based) across party families shows that the RGA has more in common with parties belonging to the green party family. The RGA scores 0.78 on the assembly-based indicator for intra-party democracy and 0.33 on the plebiscitary-based indicator, while the averages for the parties belonging to the green party family are 0.73 and 0.32, respectively. In contrast, left socialist parties in Europe seem to be less internally democratic because their averages are 0.6 and 0.12, respectively. According to its statutes, this means that the RGA's level of intra-party democracy again has more in common with parties belonging to the green party family.

All in all, we have reviewed several indicators of the RGA's party organization and placed it in comparison to the SPP's and the Alternative's organization as well as parties belonging to the green and left socialist party family around the world. The results indicate that when it comes to party finances and intra-party democracy, the RGA clearly has more in common with parties belonging to the green party family. The party's intra-party democracy is very much based on direct democratic elements and diffused power structures, which comports well with other green parties' internal makeup across the world. For the party's membership size as an organizational feature, our results are inconclusive and provide us with little information on our research question regarding the party's identity.

CONCLUSION

One of the major advantages of the Red-Green Alliance is in its name; like a chameleon, it can change colour to fit into its environment. This allows the party to darken its shades of red whenever a rival party vacates this space on the political spectrum (like they did in 2011), but also to tone greener to the extent that the Alternative becomes its main rival on the left wing (which looks unlikely from its poor performance in the 2019 election where it lost 4 of its 9 seats). Based on our analysis, we conclude from the party's positions and issue priorities that it is properly red—and more red than green. In its issue priorities, it puts greater emphasis on labour market issues than on environmental issues, and it takes a position furthest to the right of all parties on both issues as well as on the question of redistribution. The party organization, on the other hand, has more in common with the organizational setups seen in parties belonging to the green party family, especially in an international comparison. Like other green parties, the RGA runs a budget much closer in size to other green parties, and state subsidies make up a smaller share of the RGA's finances in contrast to the average across left socialist parties in Europe. Instead, an important part of the party's income is membership dues, and the party's statutes also stress a flat hierarchy and a non-leader dominated party structure much like other parties belonging to the green party family in Europe.

Insofar as the Alternative is there to stay and might regain its momentum on the centre-left wing after its weak performance in the 2019 election, it is likely that the Red-Green Alliance will come to look more like the Alternative in terms of its party organization. Despite its current colour—red more than green on its position and issue priorities—competition from the Alternative might push the Red-Green Alliance to become greener and less red. This is especially the case if the SPP has finished its venture to the right and returns to its more historic position solidly placed on the left wing.

NOTES

1. In the 1987, 1988, 1990s elections, the 'Greens' ran for election but did not pass the 2 per cent threshold. The party has never played any role in Danish politics and was dissolved in 2014.
2. Some of its success in the 2011 election can also be ascribed to voters that previously voted for the Social Liberals (Hansen et al. 2011).
3. The issue content of each press release has been categorized based on its title. The categorization uses the Comparative Agendas Codebook (Baumgartner et al. 2011; see also Seeberg 2018).

REFERENCES

Abou-Chadi, Tarik (2016). 'Niche party success and mainstream party policy shifts', *British Journal of Political Science*, 46/2: 417–36.

Alternative (2018). 'Partiprogram', https://alternativet.dk/politik/partiprogram (accessed 8 November 2018).

Baumgartner, Frank R., Christian Breunig, and Emiliano Grossman (2019). *Comparative Policy Agendas: Theory, Tools, Data*. Oxford: Oxford University Press.

Baumgartner, Frank R., Bryan Jones, and John Wilkerson (2011). 'Comparative studies of policy dynamics', *Comparative Political Studies*, 44/8: 947–72.

van Biezen, Ingrid, and Petr Kopecký (2017). 'The paradox of party funding: The limited impact of state subsidies on party membership', in Susan E. Scarrow, Paul D. Webb, and

Thomas Poguntke, eds, *Organizing Political Parties: Representation, Participation, and Power*. Oxford: Oxford University Press, 84–105.

van Biezen, Ingrid, Peter Mair, and Thomas Poguntke (2012). 'Going, going, gone...? The decline of party membership in contemporary Europe', *European Journal of Political Research*, 51/1: 24–56.

Bille, Lars (1998). *Dansk partipolitik, 1987–1998*. Copenhagen: Jurist og Økonomforbundets Forlag.

Bille, Lars (2011). 'Denmark', *European Journal of Political Research*, 50/7–8: 955–59.

Bille, Lars (2012). 'Denmark', *European Journal of Political Research Political Data Yearbook*, 51/1: 82–9.

Bille, Lars (2013). 'Denmark', *European Journal of Political Research Political Data Yearbook*, 52/1: 56–60.

Bischoff, Carina, and Karina Kosiara-Pedersen (in press). 'Radical left parties in Denmark: The Unity List (Red Green Alliance)', in *Palgrave Handbook of Radical Left Parties in Europe*.

Bolin, Niklas, Nicholas Aylott, Benjamin von dem Berge, and Thomas Poguntke (2017). 'Patterns of intra-party democracy across the world', in Susan E. Scarrow, Paul Webb, and Thomas Poguntke, eds, *Organizing Political Parties: Representation, Participation, and Power*. Oxford: Oxford University Press, 158–86.

Christiansen, Flemming, and Henrik Seeberg (2016). 'Cooperation between counterparts in parliament from an agenda-setting perspective', *West European Politics*, 39/6: 1160–80.

Grant, Zack, and James Tilley (2018). 'Fertile soil: explaining variation in the success of Green parties', *West European Politics*, doi: 10.6084/M9.FIGSHARE.7268477.V1

Green-Pedersen, Christoffer (2012). 'A Giant fast asleep? Party incentives and politicization of European integration', *Political Studies*, 60/1: 115–30.

Hansen, Kasper, and Rune Stubager (2017a). *Oprør fra udkanten*. Copenhagen: Jurist- og Økonomforbundets Forlag.

Hansen, Kasper, and Rune Stubager (2017b). 'Stenbroen og udkantsdanmark – geografiske forskelle i partiernes tilslutning', in Kasper Hansen, and Rune Stubager, eds, *Oprør fra udkanten*. Copenhagen: Jurist-og Økonomforbundets Forlag, 69–92.

Hansen, Kasper, Rune Stubager, and Jørgen Andersen (2011). *Krisevalg*. Copenhagen: Jurist-og Økonomforbundets Forlag.

Hopkin, Jonathan (2004). 'The problem with party finance: Theoretical perspectives on the funding of party politics', *Party Politics*, 10/6: 627–51.

Katz, Richard S., and Peter Mair (1995). 'Changing models of party organization and party democracy. The emergence of the cartel party', *Party Politics*, 1/1: 5–28.

Kölln, Ann-Kristin (2015). 'The effects of membership decline on party organisations in Europe', *European Journal of Political Research*, 54/4: 707–25.

Kölln, Ann-Kristin (2016). 'Party membership in Europe: Testing party-level explanations of decline', *Party Politics*, 22/4: 465–77.

Kosiara-Pedersen, Karina (2015). 'Denmark', *European Journal of Political Research Political Data Yearbook*, 54/1: 86–93.

Krouwel, André (2012). *Party Transformations in European Democracies*. New York: State University of New York Press.

Michels, Robert (1959). *Political Parties: A Sociological Study of the Oligarchical Tendencies of Modern Democracy*. New York: Dover Publications.

Poguntke, Thomas, Susan E. Scarrow, Paul D. Webb, Elin H. Allern, Nicholas Aylott, Ingrid van Biezen, et al. (2016). 'Party rules, party resources and the politics of parliamentary democracies', *Party Politics*, 22/6: 661–78.

Polk, Jonathan, Jan Rovny, Ryan Bakker, Erica Edwards, Liesbet Hooghe, Seth Jolly, et al. (2017). 'Explaining the salience of anti-elitism and reducing political corruption for political parties in Europe with the 2014 Chapel Hill Expert Survey data', *Research & Politics*, 4/1: 1–9.

Red-Green Alliance (2018a). 'Historie', https://org.enhedslisten.dk/parti/historie (accessed 8 November 2018).

Red-Green Alliance (2018b). 'Organisation', https://org.enhedslisten.dk/parti/organisation (accessed 8 November 2018).

Red-Green Alliance (2018c). 'Principprogram', https://enhedslisten.dk/programmer/ enhedslistens-principprogram (accessed 8 November 2018).

Red-Green Alliance (2018d). 'Vedtægter', https://org.enhedslisten.dk/vedtaegter/ vedtaegtsnaevnets-fortolkninger-af-enhedslistens-vedtaegter (accessed 8 November 2018).

Scarrow, Susan E. (2000). 'Parties without members? Party organization in a changing electoral environment', in Russell J. Dalton and Martin P. Wattenberg, eds, *Parties without partisans: Political change in advanced industrial democracies*. Oxford: Oxford University Press, 79–101.

Seeberg, Henrik (2018). Press releases from the nine parties in the Danish parliament. Aarhus: Data Report.

Seeberg, Henrik B., Rune Slothuus, and Rune Stubager (2017). 'Do voters learn? Evidence that voters respond accurately to changes in political parties' policy positions', *West European Politics*, 40/2: 336–56.

Volkens, Andrea, Werner Krause, Pola Lehmann, Theres Matthiess, Nicolas Merz, Sven Regel, et al. (2018). 'The manifesto data collection', Manifesto Project (MRG/CMP/MARPOR). Version 2018b. Berlin: Wissenschaftszentrum Berlin für Sozialforschung (WZB).

Webb, Paul D., and Dan Keith (2017). 'Assessing the strength of party organizational resources', in Susan E. Scarrow, Paul D. Webb, and Thomas Poguntke, eds, *Organizing Political Parties: Representation, Participation, and Power*. Oxford: Oxford University Press, 31–61.

....

CHAPTER 22

DYNAMIC STABILITY

The Anchors of Voting Behaviour

....

KASPER M. HANSEN AND RUNE STUBAGER

AT the elections for the Danish Parliament, *Folketinget*, in June 2019, 44 per cent of the voters reported having changed their vote since the previous election in June 2015. As of yet, this constitutes the culmination of a development that—although foreshadowed by the 'landslide' election of 1973 where, similarly, 44 per cent of the voters changed parties—has gained momentum from the early 1990s onwards. Furthermore, it coincides with a parallel development in the share of voters reporting that they made up their mind during the election campaign.

Not only have these changes in voter behaviour been substantial and brought Danish voters closer to the pattern exhibited by voters in other countries, such as the neighbouring Nordic countries (cf. Bengtsson et al. 2014), it also fits well with the so-called individualization thesis. The thesis claims that voter behaviour in most Western countries is becoming more and more individualized. This implies that voters are, to an increasing extent, choosing on the basis of 'idiosyncratic orientations' (Thomassen 2005: 16; cf. Dalton 2014) related to fleeting factors like the issues of the day and the parties' performance in office, rather than stable factors in the form of socio-structural and/or ideological positions. Given the more volatile nature of the issue agenda and government performance, such changes to the foundation of voter behaviour quite readily translate into increased volatility from one election to the next.

Is this the best way to understand increasing voter volatility? We think not, and the chapter is devoted to presenting the arguments as to why. The chapter begins by discussing the development in various measures of volatility in the next section. Then follows a brief discussion of the theoretical perspectives behind the central concept of 'anchor variables'. The following three sections examine the influence on the vote of both traditional and more recent socio-structural anchors as well as the two main ideological anchors—economic redistribution and cultural values—that provide the bedrock for Danish voters' behaviour before the conclusion collates the threads of the argument.

INCREASING VOTER VOLATILITY—BUT NOT AT THE BLOC LEVEL

In the 1950s and 1960s, Danish voting behaviour was most likely characterized by considerable stability. As the Danish National Election Study, on which the analyses of this chapter rely, was not started until 1971, this evaluation is based on the Pedersen Index (Pedersen 1979) of (net) volatility, i.e. seat changes from one election to the next. The scores of the index from the first election after the constitutional revision in 1953 onwards, depicted by the short dashed line in Figure 22.1, clearly show a rather low level of volatility in the years leading up to 1973. That election, on the other hand, brought a sudden eruption of vote change as evident also in the individual-level election study data available from 1971 onwards. Indeed, 1973 witnessed a doubling of the number of parties in Parliament (from five to ten), reflected in hitherto unprecedented levels of both net and gross volatility (the latter depicted by the long dashed line).

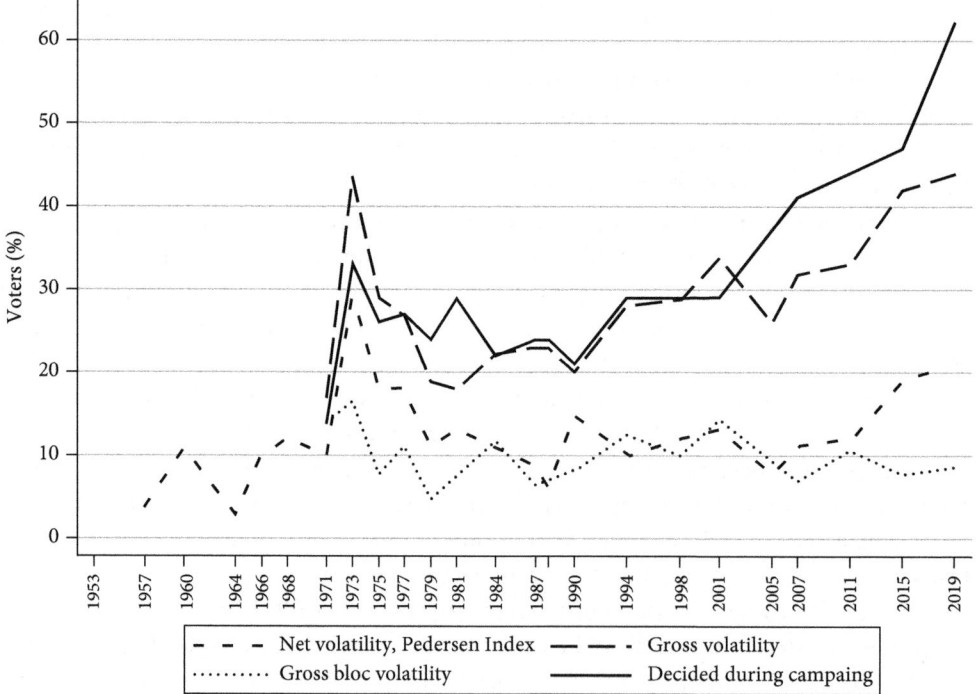

FIGURE 22.1 Electoral volatility, 1971–2019.

Note: Net volatility is measured by the Pedersen Index and calculated as the sum of seat changes divided by two. Gross volatility is the share of respondents reporting voting for different parties at two consecutive elections. Gross bloc volatility is the share of respondents reporting voting for parties in different blocs at two consecutive elections. The share of campaign deciders is assessed in the election studies

Source: Hansen, Kasper M. & Rune Stubager (2019) Danish National Election Study Times Series Cumulative File 1971–2019. V11092019

The following years show a return to more stable conditions. Thus, while the 1975 and 1977 elections can be seen as 'aftershocks' where voters recalibrated after 1973, we note how all measures of volatility revert to 1971 levels during the 1980s. From 1994, however, gross volatility trends upwards again, although at a slower pace than in 1973. The result is the same, though, in that the elections of 2015 and 2019 registered gross volatility at the 1973 level. This development is closely paralleled by another measure of volatility, namely the share of voters who report having decided whom to vote for during the (usually three-week-long) campaign as depicted by the solid line in Figure 22.1, although this share increases dramatically over the last two decades.

It is equally noticeable, however, how two other volatility measures, the Pedersen Index and gross bloc volatility, are much more stable. Thus, after the turbulent 1970s, the Pedersen Index has mostly shown trendless fluctuation and has only twice—in 2015 and 2019—gone above 15. This does not fit a situation of permanent flux although it remains to be seen whether the two last elections of the series herald a permanently higher level of net instability. Stability is—even more markedly—the most fitting description of the development in the measure of gross bloc volatility, i.e. the share of voters changing from a party in the right bloc—i.e. the Liberals (*Venstre*); the Conservatives (*Konservative Folkeparti*); the Danish People's Party (*Dansk Folkeparti*); the Liberal Alliance (*Liberal Alliance*); or the Christian Democrats (*Kristendemokraterne*)—to a party in the left bloc—i.e. the Social Democrats (*Socialdemokratiet*); the Social Liberals (*Radikale Venstre*); the Socialist People's Party (*Socialistisk Folkeparti*); the Red-Green Alliance (*Enhedslisten*); or the Alternative (*Alternativet*)—or vice versa, as depicted by the dotted line. In recent elections, this measure hovers around 10 and has shown no upward trend.

Hence, what can be observed is a situation in which voters are postponing their decisions and increasingly changing parties, but they do so primarily within the bounds of the two political blocs and with only some degree of impact on the distribution of seats, most likely because voter exchanges between the parties in many instances cancel each other out. The implication is that voters are, to considerable extent, held in place within the blocs: they are anchored. This strong bloc stability is also observed elsewhere, for example in the United States (Smidt 2017). But which anchors hold them? That is the question in focus below.

Theories about the Anchors of Voting Behaviour

Stable voter anchors come in two main varieties in the scholarly literature: socio-structural and psychological. Socio-structural anchors feature prominently in the theoretical approaches of the Columbia School (Lazarsfeld et al. 1944; Berelson et al. 1954) and the cleavage model (e.g. Lipset and Rokkan 1967). In both approaches, stable socio-structural variables such as class, religion, or place of residence are seen as the foundation on which voters base their decisions, as members of specific socio-structural groups are expected to vote for parties that represent the interests associated with the social positions of their group. And to the extent that parties maintain a relatively constant position with respect to such interests—as we shall discuss, this is an increasingly contentious assumption— we should expect the socio-structural variables to serve exactly the anchoring function in focus here, simply because voters seldom change their socio-structural positions (even if more so now than 50–60 years ago). Voters' positions in the social structure, their interests emanating from these positions, and the conflicts about such interests can keep voters in place politically. Below, we discuss exactly which social positions and conflicts are, or have been, relevant in Denmark.

Psychological anchors are usually associated with the Michigan School and its landmark study *The American Voter* (Campbell et al. 1960). Perhaps most promin- ently featured both in the study and its legacy to the field is the concept of party identifi- cation seen as 'an individual's affective orientation' to a party (Campbell et al. 1960: 121). This affective bond develops as part of childhood socialization and provides an enduring attachment of a voter to 'her' party. In the European context, the concept of party identification has been under sustained criticism (cf. e.g. Thomassen 1976) with a central argument being that it is difficult to separate party identification from actual voting behaviour. Indeed, as discussed by Stubager et al. (2020), in Denmark, 94 per cent of those providing a party identification when asked in the election studies vote for the same party with which they identify. In effect, this renders the variable useless in models of voting behaviour since it is, essentially, identical to vote choice itself.

As also discussed by Stubager et al. (2020), the main alternative to party identifica- tion as a psychological anchor invoked by many European analyses is the voters' per- ceptions of whether they are placed on the left or right. Left-right identification is also seen as developing as part of individuals' childhood and youth socialization, and hence, as an anchor tying voters to one political side, potentially for life. Over the years, the issue contents of left and right may be—and have been in the Danish case— subject to change. From the time of the formation of the Danish party system, the main issues involved were to do with the reform, or not, of society in the direction of democratic and social inclusiveness with focus gradually changing towards an emphasis on social reforms in the form of an extensive welfare state paid for by pro- gressive taxation. Over the latest decades, however, the issue of openness towards immigration and different cultures and religions has come to play a larger role for left-right identifications (e.g. Lachat 2017).

These changes notwithstanding, the core idea to retain is that individuals' sense of attachment to a political 'side' can serve to anchor them with respect to party choice. This is more so when, as has been the case for much of Danish political his- tory, the majority of parties can be seen as belonging to one of two party 'blocs', namely the left or the right bloc (cf. Green-Pedersen and Thomsen 2005). These blocs make it possible for voters to translate their ideological attachments into votes. It may be that the specific party voted for within a given bloc changes from one election to the next, but as shown in Figure 22.1, only rather few voters change blocs at any given election.

TRADITIONAL CLEAVAGE-BASED ANCHORS: PLACE OF RESIDENCE AND CLASS

The birth of the classic Danish party system is an almost prototypical case of cleavage development as theorized by Lipset and Rokkan (1967; see also Green-Pedersen and Kosiara-Pedersen 2020). Thus, the core of the system—the four 'old' parties: the Social Democrats, the Liberals, the Conservatives, and the Social Liberals—developed around the intersection of two main social conflicts: that between workers and employers, and the urban-rural conflict, which almost coincided with a centre-periphery conflict in Denmark. While the former had the distribution of surplus production value at its core, the latter involved an economic conflict over the price of food as well as a cultural layer in the form of a rebellion against state control of culture and religion. The Liberals (*Venstre*, literally meaning 'Left') developed as the representatives of independent farmers, i.e. rural employers, in opposition to the dominant urban (partly industrial) elite who, along with the nobility, were represented by the party *Højre* (literally meaning 'Right'), the forerunner of the Conservatives.

Representing urban workers, the Social Democrats rather quickly also gained a strong standing, while the Social Liberals as the representatives of rural worker interests (along with some urban intellectuals) completed the quartet. Between them, the four parties 'soaked up' most of the mobilization potential deriving from the two conflicts, thereby leading to exactly the type of 'freezing' of the party system in the years leading up to 1920 about which Lipset and Rokkan (1967) famously wrote (Elklit 1986).

These two cleavages provide the first potential anchor variables in our investigation of what may keep Danish voters anchored in place despite the increasing level of party switching documented in Figure 22.1. Figure 22.2 shows the predicted probability of a vote for a party in the left bloc for voters from different locations and classes, respectively. The data come from the Danish National Election Study, which has conducted high-quality surveys after each general election since 1971 (Hansen and Stubager 2019; see www.valgprojektet.dk). Sample sizes vary somewhat over the years but are usually around 1,000 prior to 1994 and never below 2,000 from that year onwards. The samples are probability-based random samples from the Danish population registers. The data are weighted on age, gender, education (from 1984 onwards), and party choice, just as reported estimates are controlled for variables that are causally prior (see the notes to the figures for details).

The upper panel of Figure 22.2 shows that although it has diminished somewhat since the 1970s, the urban-rural cleavage is still manifest in voter behaviour in that there is a difference of about 10 percentage points in the propensity to vote for a party in the left bloc between voters living in the cities and the countryside, respectively.

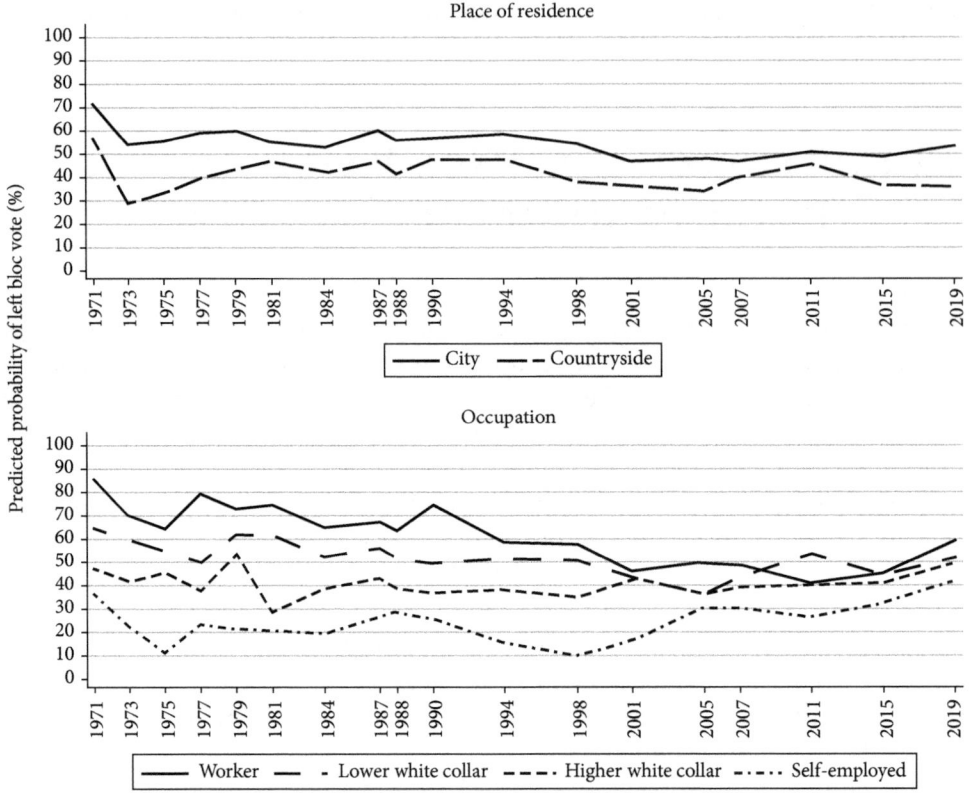

FIGURE 22.2 Support for the left bloc by place of residence and class, 1971–2019.

Note: The estimates are controlled for causally prior variables. For place of residence, these are gender, age, and education. For occupation, place of residence is also controlled

Source: Hansen, Kasper M. & Rune Stubager (2019) Danish National Election Study Times Series Cumulative File 1971–2019. V11092019

Moreover, just as from the birth of the party system, city dwellers are voting more for the left bloc. As such, the urban-rural cleavage continues to function as an anchor.

The lower panel of Figure 22.2 shows a partly different pattern. The distribution of votes at the beginning of the figure gives a precise image of what the class cleavage looked like in its heyday: the classes were clearly separated in their propensity to vote for left bloc parties, with workers and the self-employed at either end of the spectrum. Since then, however, two patterns are noteworthy. First, the working class has changed their behaviour quite significantly, shifting from a preference for left bloc parties well above 80 per cent to a level close to 50. Second, the remaining three classes have shown a much higher degree of stability, certainly when comparing the beginning and end of the figure. The combined effect of these two patterns is that the class cleavage has been clearly weakened. Thus, the working class is much less distinct in its behaviour now than it used to be. In fact, it is now almost indistinguishable from the three other classes (see also Harrits and Stubager 2020).

All in all, it is fair to say that class has been severely weakened as an anchor of vote choice; a development propelled by the working class which has abandoned its previ-ous political favourites among the left bloc parties (to the benefit, incidentally, of especially the Danish People's Party). For the two traditional anchors taken together, the magnitude of the development with respect to class overshadows the continuing existence of a geographical anchor so that the overall conclusion for the two variables taken together is that they have been weakened. That, however, is not the whole story for socio-structural anchors.

New Socio-Structural Anchors: Education and Gender

Part of the reason for the development with respect to the class cleavage—rooted as it is in the economic conflict in the labour market—is the advent of new, so-called cultural issues on the voters' agenda (e.g. Evans 2017) as discussed above. Thus, at least from the late 1980s onwards, Western Europe has seen an increase in the amount of attention devoted to issues such as immigration and law and order by both voters and parties (Kitschelt 1994; Kriesi et al. 2008). This also applies to Denmark (Stubager 2010). Cultural issues have, by now, gained an influence on vote choice that easily matches, and in some cases surpasses, that of the economic issues that previously dominated the agenda. Furthermore, voter attitudes to cultural and economic issues are not neces-sarily related. It is perfectly possible, in other words, to be to the right with respect to economic matters but to the left when it comes to immigration and other cultural issues—or vice versa.

As discussed further below, this means that the two dimensions operate as separate influences on voters' choices. It is also reflected in the fact that the socio-structural roots of cultural issues are different from the roots of economic issues. Studies in Denmark and a range of other countries (e.g. Langsæther and Stubager 2019; Stubager 2008) show that education is the most important socio-structural variable for understanding voter positions on cultural issues. Everywhere the pattern is the same: those with higher levels of education are more to the left on such issues (e.g. welcoming of immigration from other cultures and religions) than those with lower levels of education. The question lies in the extent to which this difference also translates into differences in vote choice. As Figure 22.3 shows, the answer is 'quite a bit'.

The upper panel of the figure shows the propensity to vote for parties in the left bloc for voters with only compulsory schooling and secondary schooling (grammar school or high school), respectively. This measure of education also indirectly taps respondents' further education in that secondary schooling is a prerequisite for access to university, professional colleges (for nurses or teachers, among others), etc. Thus, most respondents without secondary education have a trade-based vocational education or no education beyond compulsory school. The figure contains two distinct patterns. Up

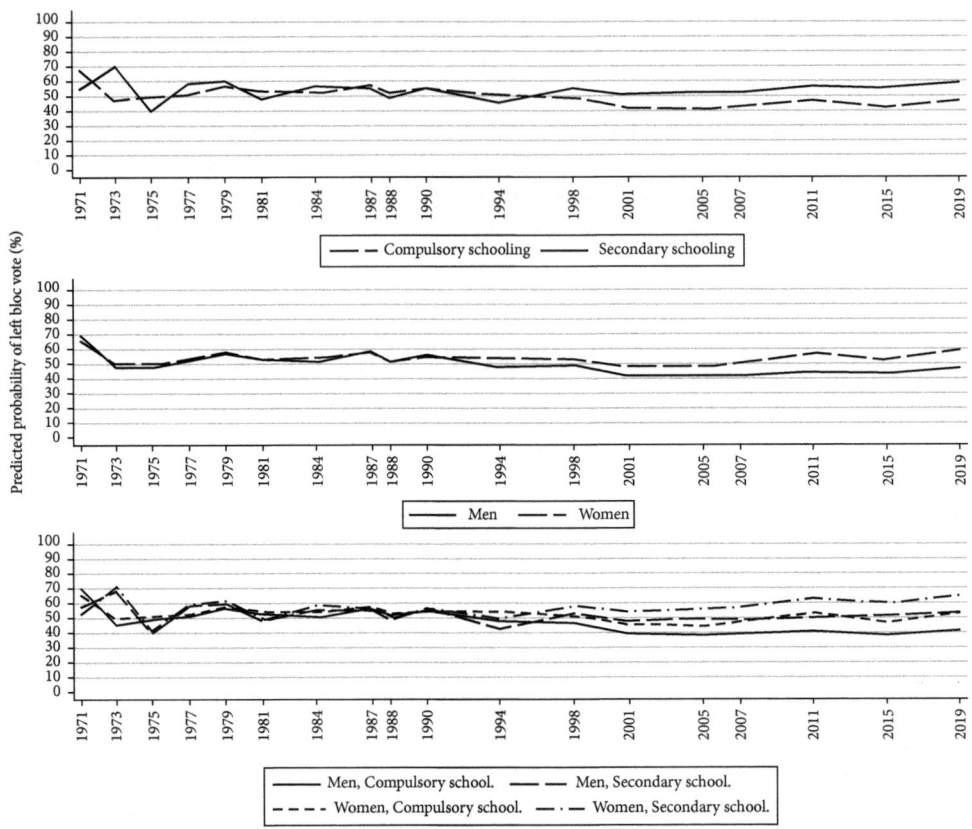

FIGURE 22.3 Support for the left bloc by education and gender, 1971–2019.

Note: For gender, the estimates are uncontrolled. For education, they are controlled for gender and age

Source: Hansen, Kasper M. & Rune Stubager (2019) Danish National Election Study Times Series Cumulative File 1971–2019. v11092019

until 1998, we see no consistent difference in vote choices between the two educational groups. From that year onwards, however, a gap seems to be developing in which voters with higher levels of education are increasingly turning towards parties in the left bloc, whereas voters with lower levels of education are turning away from that bloc. Hence, over the last two decades covered in Figure 22.3, education seems to become a stronger and stronger anchor for voters' bloc choice.

The same applies to gender, as shown in the middle panel of Figure 22.3. We observe a parallel pattern with a widening gap, although the difference between men and women starts to widen from the early 1990s. The dynamics are slightly different, though, in that men seem to change their behaviour more by turning away from the left parties while women are more stable in their bloc choices. This development is partly related to the rise of cultural issues on the political agenda, but more importantly, attitudes to the welfare state, including its generosity, seem to be at the core of the gender division of vote choice: women are clearly more in favour of generous welfare services than men are (e.g. Stubager and Andersen 2013). Gender, therefore, also seems to become a more influential anchor for voter behaviour over time.

The developments for gender and education contribute to a growing polarization of Danish voters. This is visible in the lowest panel of Figure 22.3 that shows the combined effect of gender and education on the propensity to vote for the left bloc. The effects documented for gender and education in the two upper panels of the figure compound so that we see a very large polarization between women with higher levels of education making up a left bloc pole and men with lower levels of education making up a right bloc pole. At the end of the period of investigation, the difference in the propensity to vote for left bloc parties between the two groups is more than 20 percentage points. The figure thereby illustrates how these two variables combine to provide an anchor for Danes' voting behaviour, notably, an anchor of growing importance.

This result is remarkable in its own right. Over a period of two to three decades, we see the establishment of what seems like two new cleavages—certainly structural divides—in the Danish electorate. This is not trivial phenomena. It takes on added value, however, by demonstrating how socio-structural anchors are not a thing of the past. Thus, in the wake of the reduction of the strength of class as an anchor variable, the scholarly literature (e.g. Dalton 2014; Franklin et al. 1992) as well as more journalistic accounts—not to mention politicians' rhetoric—have been replete with analyses (sometimes of a celebratory nature) claiming an end to the relationship between voters' social positions and their political behaviour. Voters were, according to this line of argument, beginning to make their own choices without the need of the cognitive 'crutches' offered by socio-structural positions. While the analyses in this section certainly show that the relationship between such positions and political choices has changed, they also show that change does not equal disappearance. To put it in the vocabulary of the research field, we seem to witness a realignment rather than a dealignment in that one set of anchors, class, is being replaced by another, gender and education. This change is directly related to the growth of cultural issues on the political agenda. The next section discusses how such issues combine to form an ideological anchor alongside the traditional, but still existing, economic left-right ideology.

A Two-Dimensional Ideological Anchor: Economic Redistribution and Cultural Values

The changes documented above for the socio-structural anchor variables are paralleled in the ideological realm. Thus, as mentioned, the advent of the cultural dimension has established a second ideological dimension in Danish politics (cf. Borre 1995; Stubager 2010), just as has been the case throughout a range of West European countries (cf. Kitschelt 1994, 1995; Kriesi et al. 2008). The electoral implications of this change for the previously one-dimensional political system have been profound. Whereas the parties' competition for votes well into the 1990s took place mostly along the single ideological dimension extended between expanding the welfare state financed by high, progressive taxation at one end and welfare retrenchment to make room for significant tax cuts at the other, it is now clearly two-dimensional. That is, and as shown below, voters continue to take their position on the economic dimension into account when forming their sense of left-right belonging and making vote choices. They also increasingly take their position on the cultural dimension into account. In addition to the immigration issue discussed above, the cultural dimension in Danish politics usually also contains voter attitudes to environmental protection and criminal justice (cf. Borre 1995). However, for comparability across time in the analysis below, focus is on the immigration issue, which is compared to the issue of taxation from the economic realm.

The first step is to show how the two-dimensionality has evolved at the ideological level; i.e. how perceptions of left-right belonging are now grounded in attitudes from both the economic and cultural dimensions. This is what Figure 22.4 shows. The figure depicts the Pearson correlation between respondents' of self-placement on a 0–10 left-right scale and their responses to two Likert-type items asking for agreement or disagreement with the statements that 'Higher incomes ought to be taxed more than

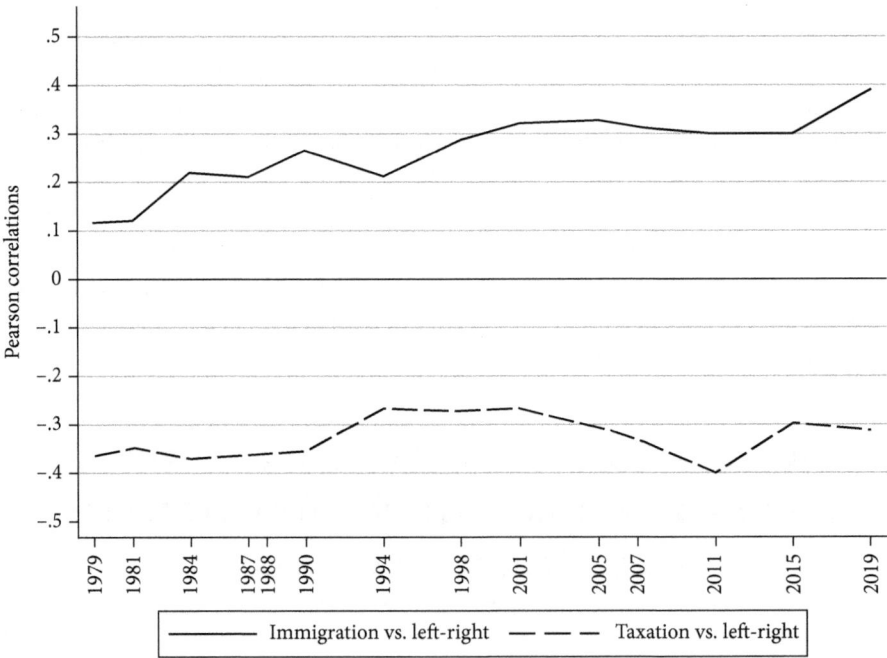

FIGURE 22.4 Correlation between economic redistribution and left-right self-placement and between cultural values and left-right self-placement, 1979–2019.

Note: The curves depict values of Pearson's *r*

Source: Hansen, Kasper M. & Rune Stubager (2019) Danish National Election Study Times Series Cumulative File 1971–2019. v11092019

is currently the case' and 'Immigration constitutes a serious threat to our national culture'. On each item, the five response categories range from completely disagree (coded 0) to completely agree (coded 100). For these two items, analyses of responses from 1979 onwards provide a good time frame for grasping the developments. It should be noted, however, that the immigration item was phrased differently in 1979, 1981, and 1984, focusing on whether refugees should conform to Danish culture (1979 and 1984) and repatriation of guest workers (1981). While differently worded, these items still tap the same underlying dimension as the main version available from 1987 onwards.

The figure shows an interesting pattern. While there is some fluctuation over time, the correlation between attitudes to taxation and left-right positioning is rather stable over time, hovering in the -0.4 to -0.3 range. For attitudes to immigration, the story is clearly different in that we observe a clear strengthening of the relationship between such attitudes and left-right positioning. This takes place in three steps: first, from 1979 to 1984, coinciding with debate about the introduction of new asylum legislation that was perceived as 'the most humane of its kind in the world' (Gaasholt and Togeby 1995: 23); second, from 1994 to 1998, coinciding with renewed attention to the consequences of immigration; and third, in 2019. The result is that at the end of the time series, the correlation is close to 0.4.

This implies that Danes' sense of left-right positioning has been based on attitudes in both the economic and cultural domains to about equal degrees from the late 1990s onwards. Not only is this interesting in and of itself by showing the breakthrough of the second dimension at the ideological level, it has implications for our search for the ideological anchors of Danish voters. Hence, it means that we have to look beyond voters' left-right positions to find the ideological anchor of the electorate. In reality, there are two such anchors: attitudes in the economic domain and attitudes in the cultural domain. Hence, the analyses below investigate how attitudes to the two issues of immigration and taxation relate to vote (or rather bloc) choice (see Dinesen et al. 2020).

The results of this investigation appear in Figure 22.5, which depicts the predicted probability of voting for a party in the left bloc for voters with different attitudes on the two issues. The upper panel looks at taxation attitudes and shows a clear and stable pattern according to which those who prefer higher taxation on high incomes show a much stronger preference for leftist parties than those who oppose such tax increases, while those neither agreeing nor disagreeing are placed in the middle. Although the difference between the two extreme categories varies somewhat over time, it is around 40 percentage points towards the end of the period and never falls below 20 percentage points. Clearly, Danes take their taxation attitudes into account when making vote choices—and they do so remarkably consistently across the period of investigation.

The second panel repeats the exercise for the immigration issue. Here, the pattern is different. From 1979 to 1998, the differences between those who agree and those who disagree that immigration is a serious threat to Danish national culture are mostly small, pointing in one direction in some years and the other direction in other years (the somewhat larger difference in 1990 may be due to the Social Democrats' success at attracting working class voters in this election, cf. also Figure 22.2). From 2001 onwards, the

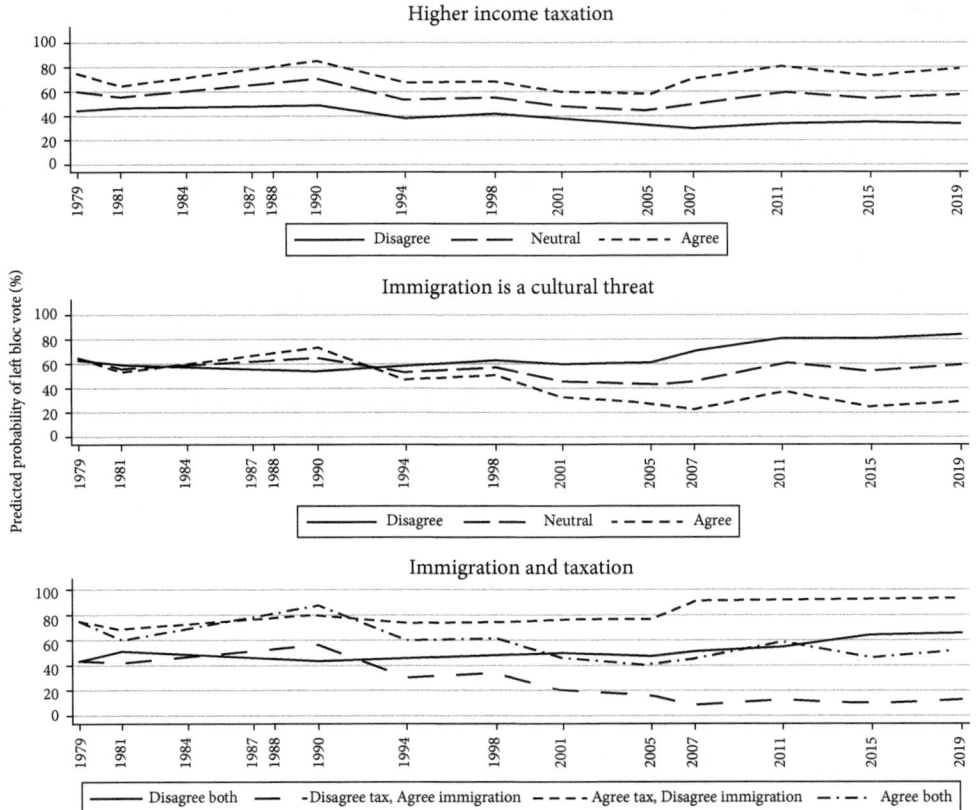

FIGURE 22.5 Support for the left bloc by taxation and immigration, 1979–2019.

Note: The estimates are controlled for gender, age, place of residence, income, education, class, and left-right self-placement and left-right self-placement squared

Source: Hansen, Kasper M. & Rune Stubager (2019) Danish National Election Study Times Series Cumulative File 1971–2019. v11092019

story is quite different in that we observe a stark polarization so that the gap in leftist voting between those who agree and those who disagree that immigration is a threat widens to more than 50 percentage points, with those disagreeing having the stronger preference for the left. This is quite likely the single most dramatic development in the recent history of Danish political behaviour. Within a time span of some 20 years, we have witnessed the breakthrough of a new political dimension with a massive polarizing capacity.

This capacity is also illustrated in the final panel of the figure which combines the two attitudes and shows leftist party preferences among four groups of voters: (1) those who disagree with both increased taxation of high incomes and immigration being a threat, (2) those who agree with both statements, (3) those who agree with increased taxation but don't think immigration is a threat, and (4) those who disagree with increased taxation but do find immigration to be culturally threatening. Unsurprisingly, the two latter groups who hold respectively leftist or rightist attitudes on both issues make up the extremes. Nevertheless, the difference between the extremes has been growing over time. From a difference of about 40 percentage points prior to 1994, those who hold straight leftist attitudes are more than 80 percentage points more likely to vote for leftist parties than those who hold straight rightist attitudes towards the end of the data series. This shows a very pronounced degree of both polarization and alignment between attitudes and votes.

Perhaps even more interestingly, the two mixed groups in the middle of Figure 22.5 show trajectories reflecting the patterns in the two upper panels. Prior to 1994, immigration attitudes mattered little to vote choice since the curves cluster based on responses to the taxation item. Beginning in 1994, however, we see a steady trend for the curves to move towards the 50 per cent mark—in other words, for the immigration issue to play a larger role. It is still too early to say with any certainty, but the trajectory of these two curves seems to be driving them closer to a pattern based on the immigration issue. If this materializes, it would reflect a stronger influence of this issue than that of taxation.

Summing up, the analyses show that the ideological anchor represented by attitudes towards taxation shows a stable influence on both left-right self-placement and vote choice. Attitudes towards immigration, however, have a dramatically increasing influence on both. In that sense, it might seem counterintuitive to see attitudes within the cultural domain, such as immigration attitudes, as an anchor of Danish voters. Certainly, the figures reveal anything but stability with respect to the influence of immigration. The latter is obviously true. However, we should maintain that cultural attitudes have anchoring qualities, not least for the future. Thus, given the strong polarizing effect of such attitudes with respect to bloc choice, it is clear that they have strong influence on voter behaviour. Since the issue of immigration is likely to remain on the political agenda for the foreseeable future, such attitudes are likely to exert a powerful influence on voters for the same foreseeable future.

A CHANGING POLITICAL SPACE: PARTY-VOTER DYNAMICS

The final step in the analysis consists of tracking the effect of the two ideological anchors on party choice. This is done in Figure 22.6 which shows the development over the 1981–2019 period of the average position of all voters as well as voters for each of the seven major parties—the Social Democrats, the Social Liberals, the Conservatives, the Socialist People's Party, the Liberals, the Danish People's Party (prior to 1998, the Progress Party), and the far left which is a combination of parties to the left of the Socialist People's Party but is mainly the Red-Green Alliance from 1990 onwards—on taxation and immigration issues. The figure takes a step beyond the bloc vote variable used in the previous figures, just as it allows tracking the changes in the attitudinal positions of the

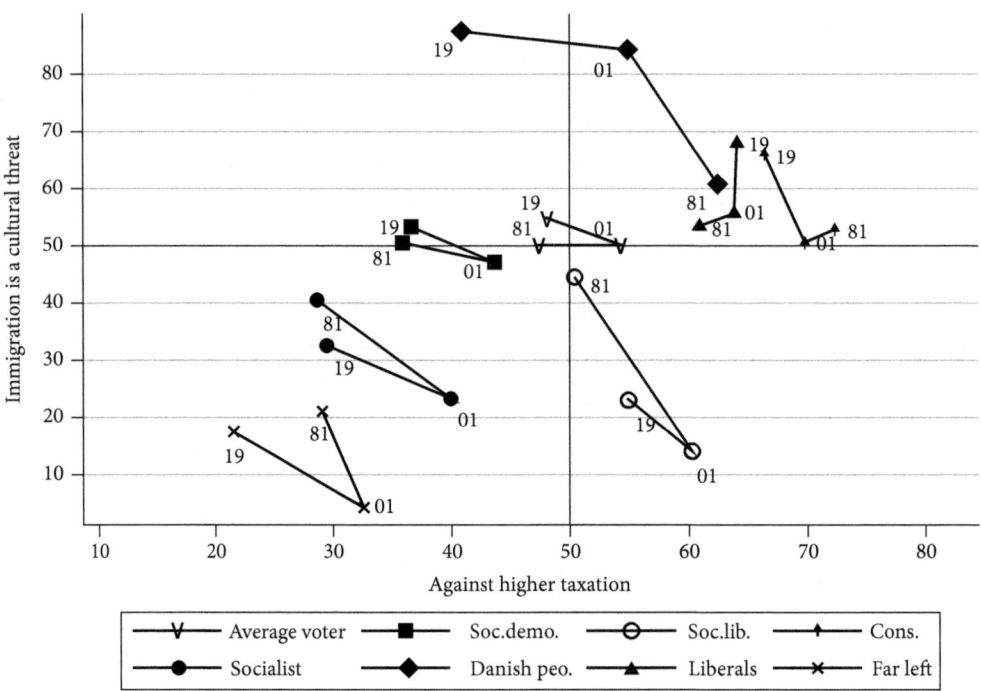

FIGURE 22.6 Parties' positions on taxation and immigration, 1981, 1990, and 2019.

Note: Markers show the parties' supporters mean self-placement on the two issues

Source: Hansen, Kasper M. & Rune Stubager (2019) Danish National Election Study Times Series Cumulative File 1971–2019. v11092019

voter groups attracted by each party. To facilitate the latter, we show positions for each party at three elections: 1981, 2001, and 2019. The election in 1981 is used to mark the beginning of the series over 1979 because the former offers more reliable estimates at the party level. The election in 2001 marks the breakthrough of the cultural dimension, whereas the election in 2019 marks the end of the series.

Figure 22.6 shows the details of the establishment of the two-dimensional structure of the Danish political space that is implied by the developments in Figure 22.5. Before delving into that, however, it is worth noting how stable the average voter position is, almost at the centre of the figure and almost completely stable on both dimensions over the nearly forty-year period covered by the figure. The considerably larger changes registered for many parties are not driven, that is, by large shifts in the position of the average voter, a point that underlines the anchoring capacity of the attitudinal dimensions.

Looking then at the changes for individual parties on the economic dimension represented by the issue of taxation, one finds both continuities and change. Thus, throughout the period covered by the figure, there is a familiar division into a group of left bloc parties, the Social Democrats, the Socialist People's Party, and the Far Left, and a group of right bloc parties, the Conservatives and the Liberals. Within these two groups, the most pronounced changes have been the back and forth shifts of voters for the left bloc parties which parallel the shift by all voters on this dimension.

The two remaining parties, the Social Liberals and the Danish People's Party, are more difficult to categorize on the economic dimension. Thus, the former tends to attract voters with centrist positions—although in some years they have tended towards the right. The Danish People's Party, for its part, has moved quite dramatically from a clearly rightist position to an equally clearly leftist one. The result is that on this dimension, the Social Liberals and the Danish People's Party have switched places. To put it more correctly, the average positions of their voters have reversed. At least on the economic dimension, the balance of power between left and right has, consequently, become more unclear with different parties controlling the pivotal vote at different times (and potentially on different issues). To the extent that this result remains stable, it constitutes a significant break with Danish political history for most of the twentieth century.

Another such break is the polarization on the cultural dimension, represented by the issue of immigration. For some parties, movements on this dimension have been even larger than the changes on the economic dimension just described. The Danish People's Party and the Social Liberals exhibit the largest shifts, and as on the economic dimension, they move in opposite directions. From positions close to the middle, voters for the former are now found on the extreme right, whereas voters for the latter are equally extreme but on the left. While the latter position was already occupied from the beginning of the period by the Far Left and is also where the Socialist People's Party's voters are found from 1990 onwards, the Danish People's Party, and its predecessor the Progress Party, broke new ground by moving to the right already around 1990 (not shown). This change, therefore, is a key contribution to the increasing polarization on this dimension already seen in Figure 22.5 since it has provided voters sceptical of immigration with an opportunity to express these attitudes at the ballot box—an opportunity that was used extensively in 2001 where the cultural dimensions made its breakthrough.

At the same time, it is remarkable how little change there has been for the three parties that have provided all Danish post-war prime ministers but one (who was a Social Liberal), namely the Social Democrats, the Conservatives, and the Liberals. Particularly the Social Democrats have, over the years, attracted voters with remarkably similar (average) preferences with respect to immigration. For the Conservatives and the Liberals, 2019 saw a slightly larger shift to the right. It is still so, however, that the polarization on the basis of immigration shown in Figure 22.5 is mostly driven by the other parties that have carved out ideological niches for themselves in the two-dimensional space spanned by the economic and cultural dimensions.

The occupation of such niches where the parties can thrive—as long as they refrain from aspiring to gain a much larger following—provides another anchoring element for the voters. Thus, because the parties are spread out across most corners of the space, they offer voters in these corners the opportunity to vote for a party representing their own political views. Given the socio-structural roots of these views, they are likely to change only slowly over time, and for many voters, maybe not much over a lifetime. Therefore, voters are likely to continue voting for parties that represent their positions on the main dimensions of political contestation. In this perspective, the spread of the parties assures that voters can act according to their socio-structurally anchored preferences, thereby providing stability at this central level of Danish democracy.

CONCLUSION

At first sight, the results presented above might seem contradictory. On the one hand, Figure 22.1 shows a pronounced increase in gross volatility and the share of late deciders. On the other hand, many of the subsequent figures have shown stable or strengthening relationships between the vote and a range of anchor variables such as gender, education, and attitudes to taxation and immigration. How can these trends be reconciled? The answer has two main components: the change to a two-dimensional structure, and partly related, the parties' behaviour.

Although rooted in stable factors such as education and longstanding values (reflected, for instance, in attitudes towards immigration), the growing importance of the cultural dimension itself has a disruptive capacity on at least two levels. First, its breakthrough has obviously entailed voter volatility in that voters have moved away from some parties such as the Social Democrats and to other parties such as the Danish People's Party. This change generates volatility during the transition phase in which the new structure is established. In other words, realignment breeds instability. Second, the existence of two ideological dimensions with an influence on vote choice may also be accompanied by permanently higher levels of volatility. This is so because the salience of the dimensions may vary from one election to the next, for example, as the result of economic crises or wars and humanitarian emergencies resulting in waves of refugees, or even more mundane factors for that matter. Since voters may not prefer the same party on both dimensions, such variations in saliency can induce volatility on a level that is likely to surpass that of the one-dimensional structure prevalent until the late 1990s.

The analyses of this chapter have focused solely on the voters. However, Lipset and Rokkan (1967) remind us that the voters are only one side of the coin. Parties and their behaviour also exert a powerful influence on the degree of electoral stability. If parties change their positions, voters with stable socio-structural and attitudinal positions may very well find that they have to change parties in order to achieve the best match between their own preferences and the policies of their chosen party. Although a full analysis falls beyond the confines of this chapter, Figure 22.6 has provided (indirect) evidence of the extent of the parties' position changes on the two ideological dimensions, and as shown by the figure, these changes are far from trivial. To some extent, the parties have moved in order to accommodate their voters' preferences, but there is also a clear strategic element to at least some of these changes in that parties jockey for the support of core voter groups, especially in light of the developments regarding the cultural dimension. The changing behaviour of working class voters in particular (cf. Figure 22.2) has given cause to (and been facilitated by) changes in the positions of the Social Democratic party, the Liberals, and the Danish People's Party, all of whom are vying for the support of these voters.

While such changes of parties and voters certainly do result in the increases in volatility depicted in Figure 22.1, we hope that the analyses and discussions above have conveyed the central message: Danish voters' changing party preferences do not first and foremost reflect a destructuration and/or individualization of voter behaviour whereby voters form decisions detached from their position in the social structure and the values and attitudes flowing from those. Rather, the increasing volatility is driven by the change from a one-dimensional to a two-dimensional political space in which voters and parties seek to find the best match between demand and supply for policies. In that sense, the development reflects a state of dynamic stability.

REFERENCES

Bengtsson, Åsa, Kasper M. Hansen, Olafur Hardarson, Hanne Marthe Narud, and Henrik Oscarsson (2014). *The Nordic Voter*. Colchester: ECPR Press.

Berelson, Bernard, Paul F. Lazarsfeld, and William McPhee (1954). *Voting*. Chicago, IL: University of Chicago Press.

Borre, Ole (1995). 'Old and New Politics in Denmark', *Scandinavian Political Studies*, 18/3: 187–205.

Campbell, Angus, Philip E. Converse, Warren E. Miller, and Donald E. Stokes (1960). *The American Voter*. Chicago, IL: University of Chicago Press.

Dalton, Russell J. (2014). *Citizen Politics. Public Opinion and Political Parties in Advanced Industrial Democracies*. Thousand Oaks, CA: CQ Press.

Dinesen, Peter T., Rune Slothuus, and Rune Stubager (2020). 'Danish public opinion. Stability, change, and polarization', in Peter M. Christiansen, Jørgen Elklit, and Peter Nedergaard, eds, *The Oxford Handbook of Danish Politics*. Oxford: Oxford University Press, 259–77.

Elklit, Jørgen (1986). 'Det klassiske danske partisystem bliver til', in Jørgen Elklit and Ole Tonsgaard, eds, *Valg og vælgeradfærd: Studier i dansk politik*. Aarhus: Politica, 21–38.

Evans, Geoffrey (2017). 'Social class and voting', in Kai Arzheimer, Jocelyn Evans, and Michael S. Lewis-Beck, eds, *The Sage Handbook of Electoral Behaviour*. Thousand Oaks, CA: Sage, 177–98.

Franklin, Mark N., Thomas T. Mackie, and Henry Valen (1992). *Electoral Change. Responses to Evolving Social and Attitudinal Structures in Western Countries*. Cambridge: Cambridge University Press.

Gaasholt, Øystein, and Lise Togeby (1995). *I syv sind. Danskernes holdninger til flygtninge og indvandrere*. Aarhus, Politica.

Green-Pedersen, Christoffer, and Karina Kosiara-Pedersen (2020). 'Party system. Open yet stable', in Peter M. Christiansen, Jørgen Elklit, and Peter Nedergaard, eds, *The Oxford Handbook of Danish Politics*. Oxford: Oxford University Press, 213–29.

Green-Pedersen, Christoffer, and Lisbeth H. Thomsen (2005). 'Bloc Politics vs Broad Cooperation', *Journal of Legislative Studies*, 11/2: 153–69.

Hansen, Kasper M., and Rune Stubager (2019). *Danish National Election Study Times Series Cumulative File 1971–2019*. Update 11 September 2019.

Harrits, Gitte S., and Rune Stubager (2020). 'Classes and politics. A changing relationship', in Peter M. Christiansen, Jørgen Elklit, and Peter Nedergaard, eds, *The Oxford Handbook of Danish Politics*. Oxford: Oxford University Press, 242–58.

Kitschelt, Herbert (1994). *The Transformation of European Social Democracy*. Cambridge: Cambridge University Press.

Kitschelt, Herbert (1995). *The Radical Right in Western Europe*. Ann Arbor, MI: University of Michigan Press.

Kriesi, Hanspeter, Edgar Grande, Romain Lachat, Martin Dolezal, Simon Bornschier, and Timotheos Frey (2008). *Western European Politics in the Age of Globalization*. Cambridge: Cambridge University Press.

Lachat, Romain (2017). 'Value cleavages', in Kai Arzheimer, Jocelyn Evans, and Michael S. Lewis-Beck, eds, *The Sage Handbook of Electoral Behavior*. Thousand Oaks, CA: Sage, 561–83.

Langsæther, Peter E., and Rune Stubager (2019). 'Old wine in new bottles? Reassessing the effects of globalization on political preferences in Western Europe', *European Journal of Political Research*, 58/4: 1213–33.

Lazarsfeld, Paul F., Bernard Berelson, and Hazel Gaudet (1944). *The People's Choice: How the Voter Makes up his Mind in a Presidential Campaign*. New York: Columbia University Press.

Lipset, Seymour M., and Stein Rokkan (1967). 'Cleavage structures, party systems, and voter alignments: An introduction', in Seymour M. Lipset and Stein Rokkan, eds, *Party Systems and Voter Alignments: Cross-National Perspectives*. New York: The Free Press, 1–64.

Pedersen, Mogens N. (1979). 'The dynamics of european party systems: Changing patterns of electoral volatility', *European Journal of Political Research*, 7/1: 1–26.

Smidt, Corwin D. (2017). 'Polarization and the decline of the American floating voter', *American Journal of Political Science*, 61/2: 365–81.

Stubager, Rune (2008). 'Education effects on authoritarian-libertarian values: A question of socialization', *The British Journal of Sociology*, 59/2: 327–50.

Stubager, Rune (2010). 'The development of the education cleavage: Denmark as a critical case', *West European Politics*, 33/3: 505–33.

Stubager, Rune, and Jørgen G. Andersen (2013). 'Godernes omfordeling: Baggrunden for vælgernes holdninger til skat og ulighed', in Rune Stubager, Kasper M. Hansen, and Jørgen G. Andersen, eds, *Krisevalg. Økonomien og folketingsvalget 2011*. Copenhagen: Jurist- og Økonomforbundets Forlag, 89–114.

Stubager, Rune, Kasper M. Hansen, Michael S. Lewis-Beck, and Richard Nadeau (2020). *The Danish Voter: Democratic Ideals and Challenges*. Ann Arbor, MI: University of Michigan Press.

Thomassen, Jacques (1976). 'Party identification as a cross-national concept: Its meaning in the Netherlands', in Ian Budge, and Dennis Farlie, eds, *Party Identification and Beyond*. London: Wiley, 63–79.

Thomassen, Jacques (2005). 'Introduction', in Jacques Thomassen, ed., *The European Voter. A Comparative Study of Modern Democracies*. Oxford: Oxford University Press, 1–21.

....

CHAPTER 23

GENDER AND POLITICS

The Limits of Equality Politics

....

CHRISTINA FIIG AND BIRTE SIIM

SETTING THE STAGE

For gender and politics scholars, it is an accepted fact that gender influences the ways we organize and think about the world and our way of knowing about the world (Celis et al. 2013: 2) and that gender (differences) characterizes the political landscape. This is also the case for Danish politics. This chapter analyses the Danish characteristics and particularities from contextual, historical, and comparative perspectives. The Danish case is contextualized by examining Nordic literature and conceptualized by the theoretical frameworks situated in gender research and political science.

One important point of departure is the introduction of women's enfranchisement in 1908 (local elections) and 1915 (parliamentary elections) and the significance of an early introduction of enfranchisement. Democratic institutions existed long before gender became an issue, but today, gender equality is an important factor in the process of democratization (Inglehart et al. 2002: 322). Denmark was among the first countries to achieve female enfranchisement and gained a leading status in terms of political gender equality, women's rights, and citizenship (Fiig 2018: 111). A 100-year history of women in politics and gender policies proves that there is no linear process leading to gender equality (Wängnerud 2015: 2). Gender gaps are significant in Danish politics, and gender equality has been, and still is, contested in politics and among the population.

A second point of departure is the interplay between the institutional perspective and the role of agency in the Danish political context. A key focus is the critical role of parliaments. It would be reasonable to believe that central political institutions such as parliaments matter for expanding or resisting gender equality, but this assumption cannot be taken for granted (Wängnerud 2015: 3). The institutional approach can be divided into three analytical levels: the role of parliaments, political parties, and individual politicians. In the past two decades, the focus on intersectionality and diversity in gender politics signals that gender equality in political science can no longer be just about 'gender' but is affected by all forms of inequalities relating, for instance, to race, ethnicity, sexuality, religion, and class (Kantola and Verloo 2018: 216).

FRAMING THE CHAPTER

Comparative Nordic research has emphasized a number of characteristics related to the universal welfare states, democracy, and citizenship that are common for Nordic gender and politics. Most researchers seem to balance similarities and diversities and settle on one Nordic model of welfare (e.g. Wivel and Nedergaard 2018: 3). One exception is Christina Bergqvist et al. (1999) who, in their study on gender-equality policy, underline the variations within and between the Nordic countries (Melby et al. 2008: 4). This chapter is framed by the Nordic characteristics with a special emphasis on Danish exceptionalism in relation to political and economic representation.

First, it is a characteristic for all the Nordic countries that women's entrance into elite politics is a post-war phenomenon that changed not only women's relationship to democracy, power, and influence but also the whole political landscape (Karvonen and Selle 1995). During the 1970s and 1980s, women in the Nordic countries became integrated into political institutions, and gender-based differences in interests and values became more and more visible and acceptable (Togeby 1994: 57, 1995). In the case of Denmark, it took almost 75 years before the representation of women reached the threshold of 30 per cent for parliamentary politics in 1988 (see also Dahlerup 1988).

Second, the Nordic countries are characterized by similarities in relation to welfare, democracy, and gender regimes, and this triangle has been important for the understanding of gender and politics. The universal welfare model, labelled by Gösta Esping-Andersen (1990), focuses on state, market, and family relations. It has formed a central point of departure for research on social policy, welfare, and gender politics. Esping-Andersen argued that the universal model, in contrast to the liberal and conservative models, was able to secure workers an acceptable standard of living through the process of 'de-commodification'. To counter the feminist scholars' critique that he neglected the gendered nature of welfare states, he later added that women's economic independence was secured through the 'defamilialization' of responsibility for providing care (cf. Siim and Borchorst 2017: 62–3; Lister 2009). Scholars have interpreted the emphasis on individual (social) rights combined with state responsibility for people's welfare through social reform and state intervention and the democratic integration of women in civil society as hallmarks of the Nordic political culture as much as women's agency is one among several factors that explain this culture (Melby et al. 2008: 5).

Today, the universal Nordic welfare and gender equality regime is usually defined by two characteristics: the dual breadwinner model, where women's labour market participation is almost the same as men's, and public responsibility for care services (Siim and

Borchorst 2017). It is generally assumed that this regime has contributed to the increase in women's political mobilization, participation, and representation.

Third, and along the same line of thought, the Nordic approach to gender politics embodies a number of similarities but also important differences. One remarkable difference of relevance for our analysis is the Danish exceptionalism as the only Nordic country that has achieved a relatively high level of gender representation in parliamentary politics without adopting a gender quota. An incremental track of a gradual development without quotas has been defined as a Danish trademark (Freidenvall et al. 2006).

As in the other Nordic countries, the Danish approach to gender equality and equal rights has generally been based on consensus policies, where conflicts have been about political means rather than about goals (Freidenvall et al. 2006: 64). Gender quotas have always been controversial in Denmark in relation to elections and in party politics as well as in relation to the labour market and public committees. Recent studies emphasize that the political representation of women (since 1998) reached nearly 40 per cent without any quota. This represents an exception to the general trend towards the rise of gender quotas in Europe (Lépinard and Rubio-Marín 2018). Gender quotas were used shortly by the Social Democratic Party and the Socialist Party but were abolished again in 1996, and since then, no gender quota exists in Danish political parties unlike in Norway and Sweden (Rolandsen Agustin et al. 2018). In addition, this result was reached at a time when the previous collective mobilization in the women's movement and momentum for gender equality policies had decreased (Christensen and Siim 2001). This development thus tends to support the dominant Danish political discourse that gender equality can be achieved without quotas (Dahlerup 2013).

The Evolution of Theoretical Debates and Key Concepts

This section provides an overview of the theoretical debates and key concepts within the literature on gender and politics. It presents some of the major concepts that have influenced the field since the 1980s, followed by two recent research paradigms: the 'institutionalist turn' (Krook and Mackay 2011) that broadens theories about women's political representation, and 'the intersectionality' approach that analyses relations between gender and multiple social inequalities (Crenshaw 1989, 1991; Mügge et al. 2018).

During the 1980s, the patriarchal models of welfare, citizenship, and democracy were the dominant feminist approaches to understanding gender politics (Pateman 1988; Siim 2000; Lister 2009). In the foundational book *The Sexual Contract* (1988), Carole Pateman presented one of the first gendered approaches to citizenship by means of analysing Mary Wollstonecraft's dilemma between the principles of equality and difference. This analysis illustrates that women in modern democracies are caught between one strategy focusing on equality and inclusion of women as 'equal citizens' that tends to deny their particularity 'as women', and another strategy focusing on the inclusion of their differences and particularities. The latter tends to reproduce inequality. Pateman's solution to this dilemma was a 'differentiated citizenship model' as a means to include women both 'as women' and as equal citizens.

At a time when most Anglo-American scholars emphasized the patriarchal character of the welfare state (Pateman 1988) and women's exclusion from politics, Scandinavian gender research analysed the potentials for achieving gender equality in the Scandinavian welfare states. Helga Hernes (1987: 15) coined the influential term 'women-friendliness', defined as a state where injustice on the basis of gender would be largely eliminated without an increase in other forms of inequality such as among groups of women. The claim that the Scandinavian model provided space for women's agency to influence politics was a paradigmatic shift in theorizing gender equality (see also Raaum 1995). Women-friendliness has been remarkably resilient as a characterization of the Nordic countries, and it is still used as a point of reference (Lister 2009). Nordic scholars have criticised the concept's lack of analytical precision and proposed to differentiate between 'women-friendly' policies and policies that promote gender equality (Borchorst and Siim 2002, 2008; Siim and Borchorst 2017: 63–5).

Hernes' optimistic approach contrasts with Yvonne Hirdman's historical study of the Swedish gender system. Hirdman (1990) offered a pessimistic diagnosis focusing on the reproduction of the system by two structural logics: segregation and hierarchy. Hernes and Hirdman both emphasized the key aspects of gender and politics in Scandinavia that were different from the dominant Anglo-American understandings, yet they gave two radically different interpretations of the capacity of the Nordic welfare states to support gender equality (Melby et al. 2008: 6). They may, however, complement each other since one focused on women's agency and the other on the unequal gender structures and both were premised on problematic assumptions about all women's common needs and interests (Siim and Borchorst 2017: 64).

Gender and politics research is inspired by contemporary European political developments (cf. Ahrens et al. 2018: 3–16). The literature on political representation distinguishes between descriptive representation, i.e. the number of women elected to parliaments who belong to the same societal group, and substantive representation, i.e. the effects of women's presence in parliaments in terms of policies (Celis and Lovenduski 2018: 150). Empirical studies show that women tend to be more active than their male colleagues in support for equality policy on the political agenda ('a shift of emphasis') (Wängnerud 2000, 2015: 4). They also find that the effect of having a high number of women elected is smaller than theoretically anticipated (Wängnerud 2015: 4). Women, when present in politics, are more likely to act for women than men are, but there is no guarantee that women will represent women since women are a heterogeneous group with different social and political interests.

The 'institutionalist turn' highlights the multiple ways in which gendered power relations of inequality are constructed, shaped, and maintained through institutional processes, practices, and rules (Krook and Mackay 2011: 4). It has recently added power struggles and women's agency to the institutional analysis in order to address the interaction between political institutions and power struggles including positional and active power (Celis and Lovenduski 2018: 149) following the strengthening of the Far Right and the growing resistance towards gender equality in Europe (Verloo 2018).

The intersectionality approach has entered European politics inspired by the need to analyse gender equality together with anti-discrimination policies in relation to race/ ethnicity, sexuality, age, and nationality (Crenshaw 1989, 1991; Collins 1990; Krizsan et al. 2012). The focus is on multiple inequalities, and it challenges the primary emphasis on gender as the main analytical category for understanding gender and politics (Mügge et al. 2018). It expands the gender approach by analysing how gender intersects with other inequality creating categories such as class, ethnicity/race, nationality, religion, and generation. The concept has a long history in black, ethnic, and gender studies centred on black women's experience in the US and on relations between feminism and racism (ibid.: 19). In Europe intersectionality is generally interpreted as a theoretical and methodological research paradigm to study the interaction of categories of difference (Siim and Mokre 2013; Siim and Borchorst 2017; Mügge et al. 2018: 19). It aims to re-conceptualize gendered and intersectional inequality in studies of power and resistance both within and outside political institutions (Mügge et. al 2018; Fiig 2019).

To sum up, the theoretical debates on gender and politics have evolved since the 1980s from a focus on women's common oppression, interests, and identities 'as women' to a focus on power struggles and resistance, taking account of the diversity of women's interests, political claims, and identities. The institutional and intersectional approaches focus on different aspects of gender politics and may complement each other, for example, in comparative studies of gender (in)equality and anti-discrimination within or outside political institutions in Europe and the Nordic countries (Siim and Borchorst 2017; Borchorst et al. 2012).

SCANDINAVIAN GENDER EQUALITY AND CITIZENSHIP

This Scandinavian citizenship (and welfare) model has been characterized by a dual focus on empowerment and mobilization from 'below' (in civil society) and representation in political institutions 'from above' (Siim 2000). This line of thinking seems to resonate with historical and empirical considerations about Scandinavia and with theoretical reflections on women's citizenship (Phillips 1995; Young 1990).

As pointed out above, Nordic women were integrated into the democratic process rather early through voluntary organizations with access to the political sphere. Civil society networks and organizations have initiated a range of political activities and have constituted an important platform for Danish women's political empowerment and mobilization, for example, in the struggle for universal enfranchisement (Fiig and

Siim 2012). The closeness and subtle boundaries between public and private, local and national, and state and civil society opened a space for women's agency in the Scandinavian countries (Melby et al. 2008: 5). This agency is an explanatory force when it comes to generating civil, political, and social rights for women in the Scandinavian welfare states (Hernes 1987; Siim 2000). Hernes' (1987) influential approach to Scandinavian citizenship combined citizens' inclusion 'from below' (through the labour and social movements) with 'state feminism' 'from above' in political institutions through 'women-friendly' gender equality and social policies.

The Nordic gender and politics literature has addressed contemporary political challenges to the Nordic/Scandinavian gender equality model (Melby et al. 2008; Siim and Borchorst 2017). One refers to the 'gender gap' in economic decision making (private industry) and women's (relative) exclusion from top positions compared to their (relative) inclusion in political institutions (Rolandsen Agustin et. al. 2018). Another refers to the 'equality gap' between majority and minority women (and men), especially in relation to the labour market and political representation (Fiig 2009; Mulinari 2008; Siim and Skjeie 2008).

The United Nation's evaluation of Denmark's eighth periodic report to CEDAW (United Nations 2015: 4–8) mirrors these concerns. The UN is concerned about the underrepresentation of women in academic institutions and in the private sector and about the low representation of women in the parliaments of Greenland and the Faroe Islands, as well as about the underrepresentation of women in municipality councils and executive boards. The UN is also concerned about intersecting forms of discrimination against migrant women and recommends targeted measures to be taken for these groups.

The Scandinavian model of gender equality and citizenship illuminates that the focus on political institutions is not sufficient; it is necessary to include political mobilization in social movements and associations to capture the range of women's political activities.

Gender and Political Mobilization, Participation, and Representation

Research has pointed at a number of factors that matter for political representation at the country level such as institutions (e.g. electoral systems and legislated gender quotas), social and economic conditions (the general level of development, women's position on the labour market, the educational system, and conditions for balancing work-life priorities), and cultural indicators (religion and general attitude towards gender equality) (see Dahlerup and Leyenaar 2013: 4 for other factors). This section first gives an overview over women's political mobilization, participation, and representation in Danish political institutions, followed by the mobilization in social movements and associations.

Denmark is a parliamentarian democracy with proportional representation. The Parliament, *Folketinget,* has 179 members, and the political parties are powerful. The courts play a modest role for gender equality compared to many other European countries (Lépinard and Rubio-Marín 2018). Gender equality is not inscribed in the Constitution and the Supreme Court is not influential in shaping policies of gender equality.

The claim for equality between men and women was introduced when women's organizations were established in the 1870s and 1880s (Melby et al. 2008: 5). Granting women the vote in 1908 and 1915 was controversial and affected fundamental power structures and male privileges in marriage, on the labour market, and in politics (Fiig and Siim 2012: 61). Historical studies point to the early transformation of the male breadwinner ideal with the Nordic marriage reforms of the 1910s and 1920s. Unlike the marriage legislation in the rest of Europe, the reforms introduced a modified male breadwinner model that recognized married women in their own right (Melby et al. 2008: 7–8).

In the early 1970s, women were virtually absent from Scandinavian political institutions, but at the end of the 1980s, their political presence became very visible (Raaum 1995: 25; also Bergqvist et al. 1999; Dahlerup 1988; Fiig 2018; Hernes 1987; Siim 2000; Skjeie 1992; Togeby 1995). The Nordic countries became the first region in the world to overcome the 30 per cent threshold of women's representation in parliamentary politics (Bergqvist et al. 1999; Dahlerup 2013: 190).[1] The pace and direction of gender equality and women's representation differ in the Nordic countries, and Denmark today has the lowest representation of women in political institutions.

The proportion of female MPs in the Danish Parliament has risen from 3 per cent in 1918, 10 per cent in 1966, and 16 per cent in 1975 to 30 per cent in 1987 and 37–39 per cent since 1998. It now seems to have stagnated at just below 40 per cent (for a discussion on stagnation see Dahlerup 2013; see also Kjær and Kosiara-Pedersen 2019). Denmark's first female prime minister headed a centre-left government between 2011 and 2015 that lost at the election in 2015. The second female prime minister took office in 2019.

At the 2019 parliamentary election, the 39 per cent female representation covers large inter-party differences. The two largest parties, the Social Democratic Party (*Socialdemokratiet*) and the Liberal Party (*Venstre*), traditionally have a low representation of female candidates and MPs. At the 2019 election, the Social Democrats got 25 per cent female MPs, and the Liberals got 35 per cent female MPs. At the other end of the scale, the left Red-Green Alliance (*Enhedslisten*) reached 45 per cent, the Social-Liberal Party (*Radikale Venstre*) 56 per cent, and the Socialist People's Party 79 per cent.

The 30 per cent threshold was only reached in Danish municipality politics in 2009, and the female representation on the municipal council is lower than in the Parliament. Moreover, women's local representation is lower than the other Nordic countries with 39 per cent in Finland, 39 per cent in Norway, 43 per cent in Sweden, and 44 per cent in Iceland (Kjær 2020), and the amount of female Danish mayors in the 98 municipalities is about 10 per cent.

Denmark has been characterized as a non-quota country (Kjær and Kosiara-Pedersen 2019) and can be further characterized as the Nordic *enfant terrible* when it comes to women's political representation. This is despite the fact that the Danish electorate is willing to vote for women, and women are more likely to be elected in parliamentarian elections than men since a higher percentage of women MPs are elected than the candidates running (about 30 per cent). The recruitment to run for Parliament continues to be highly gendered as women are systematically deselected at some of the critical junctions as they move up the ladder of recruitment (Kjær and Kosiara-Pedersen 2019: 299–317). Despite this, Kjær and Kosiara-Pedersen conclude that the strong norms on gender equality in Denmark seem to increase women's political representation on par with the quota instrument applied elsewhere (ibid.).

The institutional approach can add to the debate on political representation. It refers to the embeddedness of gender in political institutions characterized by 'stickiness' and path dependency, such as political parties and parliaments, as reasons for the lack of change (Dahlerup and Leyenaar 2013: 6; Krook and Mackay 2011). Another factor could be the lack of political mobilization and the fragmentation and diversity of women's interests.

Another aspect of gender differences in representation is women and men's parliamentary committee membership and their tenancy as committee chairs and vice-chairs. A study of a 25-year period (1990–2015) documents that significant changes have occurred but also that these changes have happened late and that segregation still exists (Fiig 2018: 121). Furthermore, the committees are relatively segregated with more than 40 per cent women in the committees on elections, housing, citizenship, ecclesiastical affairs, culture, social affairs, education and research, justice, and health throughout the period. Several committees have less than 30 per cent women throughout the period, including foreign affairs, finance, defence, agriculture, fisheries and food, taxation, and transport.

Descriptive representation raises questions about the link to substantive representation (the effects of women in parties and governments). As mentioned above, previous parliamentary studies have shown that female MPs are often more concerned with gender equality than their male colleagues are (Dahlerup 2018; Holli and Harder 2016; Wängnerud 2000, 2009). Danish political parties experience a significant gender gap in party members' attitudes towards political issues (Heidar and Pedersen 2006). Dahlerup (2018) documents a gender gap in Danish female and male MPs' active engagement in gender equality politics, with female MPs being more active than their male colleagues (ibid.: 206). It further illustrates a left-right cleavage in attitudes to the question of whether gender equality has already been achieved. Left-leaning politicians do not agree that gender equality has been achieved, whereas right-leaning politicians find that it has. However, the majority of MPs still believe that equality between women and men has not yet been realized and is worth striving for (ibid. 207). Since the 2000s, Danish parliamentarians and parties have disagreed on a number of issues such as earmarked paternity leave and binding quotas to seats in executive boards. These proposals have all been met with resistance from parties and the public.

The other dimension of women's political activities concerns the perspective of empowerment and mobilization from below with a long historical tradition in

Denmark. The mass mobilization of new social movements during the 1970s and 1980s is an illustrative example of mobilization from below based on issues related to nuclear energy, the environment, feminism, sexuality, and solidarity with the Global South (Togeby et al. 2003). These movements managed to provide their own opportunity structure by mobilizing interests, adding new resources, and trying alternative ways of organizing. All these characteristics can be ascribed to the Danish women's movement of the 1970s and early 1980s (Dahlerup 1998) which has been interpreted as a key element in transforming women's democratic citizenship (Siim 2000; Fiig 2009: 315–16).

GENDER EQUALITY POLICIES

This section presents two contested arenas for gender politics that challenge the dominant Danish self-understanding that gender equality has already been achieved and hints at limitation in the Nordic/Danish gender equality model. It asks to what extent policies have contributed to the realization of the vision of Scandinavia as gender equal countries. Research has addressed the persisting gender gap in private corporations (Rolandsen Agustin et. al. 2018) and studied new forms of inequalities and differences among groups of women (Sainsbury 2006; Siim and Skjeie 2008). These questions have been addressed by different bodies of literature and different policy arenas: one arena concerns the institutional limitations for gender equality (and anti-discrimination) politics (cf. Borchorst et al. 2012); another concerns multidimensional inequalities and that have different policy effects for various groups of women (Siim and Skjeie 2008).

The study of Danish women's underrepresentation in economic decision making is part of a broader issue of women's empowerment and independence. Women's economic citizenship (the right to work and the right to an income) is one of the most important issues in regard to women's empowerment and human dignity in the twentieth century, and it has been pivotal for women's full integration into the community of citizens (Melby et al. 2008: 12). Denmark (and the other Scandinavian countries) were for many years considered a model for European countries in terms of women's labour market participation. This contrasts with women's position in economic decision making that lags behind many European countries. In spite of this, Parliament has not been willing to agree to adopt a binding legislation on gender quotas to deal with women's underrepresentation in the economic elite (cf. Rolandsen Agustin et. al. 2018: 411–19).

Comparative studies of the unequal gender composition of elites within politics, administration, academia, and private companies suggest that it is difficult to translate the voluntary approach to gender equality from politics to the private business sector. These studies point to economic institutions as the main barriers for women in the business elite (Christiansen et al. 2002: 89). The last decade has witnessed a number of voluntary proposals to increase gender equality in economic boards but without much success.

In the mid-2000s, the Liberal-Conservative government (2001–11) introduced voluntary measures in cooperation with the business sector based on the ideas of economic advantage, increased competencies, and the unexplored female talent pool without any sanctions attached. As a result of these voluntary measures by the Danish government, some corporations adopted goals and strategies to improve the number of women on their boards, and some have adopted voluntary gender quotas.

In 2011, the newly appointed Social Democratic-headed government introduced a proposal for gender quotas in private corporations under the heading 'Gender Equality on the Boards of Private and Public Corporations'. After fierce resistance from private businesses, the proposal was replaced by a voluntary strategy. The law, adopted in 2013, obliges the 1,100 largest public and private companies to set goals for gender equality on their boards and to introduce policies stimulating the participation of women in economic decision making. This 'soft' law was labelled the 'Danish model' and perceived as an alternative to the binding measures proposed by the European Commission Directive (Rolandsen Agustin et. al. 2018: 414).

In the Danish context, 'gender balance' in private industry is still highly controversial despite the limited success of the voluntary approach in economic decision making. Compared to the struggle for quota in political representation, gender equality on company boards was not a priority issue for civil society mobilization such as women's organizations.

Studies find only a small to moderate increase in the percentage of women on boards over the last decades: the share of female board members of larger, publicly listed companies increased from 11 per cent in 2003 to 24 per cent in 2014 (Ministry for Gender Equality 2014). Statistics Denmark show that the share in listed companies with more than 250 employees increased from 11 per cent in 2005 to 19 per cent in 2015, but in all listed companies, the percentage of women on boards increased only from 10 per cent in 2009 to 13 per cent in 2013. The 2016 European Commission Database on women and men in leadership positions shows that men still outnumber women in corporate leadership, but Denmark performs above the EU average in relation to equal representation in economic decision making with a 27 per cent share of women on the boards of the largest, publicly listed companies.

Recent studies document a persistent gender gap in the power elite since white, middle-class, and middle-aged men still possess the dominant positions across the key sectors, despite a slight improvement from 20 to 25 per cent women between 2015 and 2019 (Larsen et al. 2015, 2019). Scholars question whether it is possible to break the institutional barriers to male domination in economic decision making without some kind of legal intervention (Rolandsen Agustin et. al. 2018: 420).

The second arena that can illustrate the limitations of the Nordic gender equality model concerns the new inequalities between groups of women (and men). Studies find that despite the international image of 'gender equal societies', an equality gap exists between the relative inclusion of majority women and the relative marginalization of ethnic minority women on the labour market, in politics, and in society (Sainsbury 2006; Siim and Borchorst 2017: 67–70).

The fact that the Danish approach to gender equality policies is less institutionalized than in Norway and Sweden may have negatively affected the situation of migrant women. The universal welfare state premised on wage work may have strengthened migrant women's equal social rights, but studies point to the weak tradition for affirmative action and anti-discrimination policies as barriers for overcoming low-skilled migrant women's particular problems on the labour market, in politics, and in society (Siim 2007; Borchorst et al. 2012: 73–5).

Since the 2000s, the political consensus about gender equality between Right and Left has been challenged following the Liberal-Conservative government in office between 2001 and 2011, supported by the right-wing Danish People's Party. The previous integration approach moved towards restrictive migration/integration policies targeting ethnic minority women perceived to be oppressed by their culture and religion (cf. Meret and Siim 2013). This included assimilation to 'the Danish way of life' and conforming to the dominant 'Danish' gender equality norms, dual-breadwinner model, and family values (Siim 2007; Meret and Siim 2013). Gender equality was no longer primarily a question of equal rights and social justice but became a utilitarian means to economic growth and a value-laden platform for national identity making. Studies propose that Danish (and Nordic) anti-discrimination legislation need to be strengthened in order to combat the relative marginalization of ethnic minority women on the labour market and in society (Borchorst et al. 2012; Siim and Borchorst 2017: 68).

Conclusion

The chapter has analysed the potentials and limits to gender equality in Denmark from the particular Scandinavian context. It has presented the Danish gender model, focusing on women's political mobilization, participation, and representation within political institutions and in civil society and associations. We have argued, in line with Nordic gender scholars, that political developments in crucial areas have challenged the status of Denmark and Scandinavian welfare states as gender equal models and 'laboratories of gender equality' (Fiig 2009: 323; Gomard and Krogstad 2001). This interpretation is contested since other more positive evaluations focus on the—comparatively speaking—limited gender differences (Kuhnle and Alestalo 2018: 17). Scholars tend to either focus on the comparatively positive accomplishments or evaluate gender equality against the unfulfilled promises as gender equal societies.

The chapter has pointed first at persisting gender inequalities in the economic elites and the underrepresentation of women in management and executive boards as one of the main barriers. Another important limitation is the equality gap between majority and minority women and discrimination in relation to equal rights. A third is the relative stagnation of women's political representation in political institutions with a particular focus on municipality councils.

The Danish case concerns the limitations of the voluntary approach to gender equality politics in relation to the societal power elites and to some of the political parties. Gender quotas have generally been considered a controversial political tool in relation to elections, as well as in relation to the labour market, public committees, and private corporations. The voluntary approach to gender equality thus presents an interesting exception to the general trend towards the adoption of gender quotas to increase gender balance and achieve gender equality in the political arenas (Lépinard and Rubio-Marín 2018).

It is noteworthy that the success of the voluntary Danish approach is limited mainly to political representation. The question is whether it is possible to increase women's representation in other institutional arenas such as the private sector, public administration, and academia without gender quotas. In the Danish context, gender balance in the economic elite is still contested, although gender balance—gender quota and gender parity—on company boards is on the agenda across Europe. The unequal gender gap in corporations is perceived in many countries as a democratic issue about the power to influence crucial national and transnational political and economic decisions by means of taking part in essential decision making (cf. Lépinard and Rubio-Marín 2018).

Second, the chapter has pointed to the limitations of Danish gender equality policies in relation to migrant women since 'women-friendly' social policies and the voluntary approach to gender equality have not fulfilled a more gender equal society for all women. Despite this, the equality gap between majority women and ethnic minority women is generally not seen as a political problem for gender equality policy but as an issue for migration/integration policies.

The universal approach to welfare and gender may have potentials for equal treatment, but research illustrates that it has not benefitted all groups of women equally (Sainsbury 2006). This is confirmed by our analysis of the restrictive Danish approach to migration/integration which has not succeeded in integrating ethnic minority women into the labour market and in politics on equal terms. The intersectionality approach has pointed to the need to address persistent inequalities between women from the majority and ethnic minorities of women, premised on contradictions and hierarchies between 'us and them' in Denmark and the other Scandinavian countries (Siim and Borchorst 2017).

There is still a general consensus about gender equality as a Danish and European principle although gender equality has not been among the highest political priorities. Contrary to many European countries, there has not been political resistance to issues such as gender equality, abortion, or sexual rights by right-wing political parties (cf. Siim and Fiig in press). This contrasts with the issue of migration that has been highly controversial and has divided political parties as well as the population and feminists.

Third, gender equality is still contested in politics and in the public debate. Gender equality, women's rights, and women's inclusion in the Nordic societies have long been part of the international brand of these countries. Our interpretation questions the image of this gender equality model in crucial areas. However, it is worth noticing that a 'celebratory approach to Scandinavia' is prevalent in international debates about the region (Wivel and Nedergaard 2018: 2). It remains to be seen how Nordic gender equality and intersecting inequalities fare in the coming decades.

The trend towards institutionalizing gender equality in Europe (Krizsan et al. 2012) has recently been met with political opposition across Europe. These political transformations have changed the focus away from politics as a means to achieve gender equality to a focus on the growing resistance to gender equality policies inside and outside the dominant political and economic institutions, taking account of the diversity of women's interests and identities (cf. EJPG 2018).

Gender and politics scholarship has evolved with the changing political landscape since the old theories must be reformulated in order to explain the stagnation in gender equality politics in some areas and the persistent barriers and resistance to (gender) equality in others (cf. Ahrens et. al. 2018; EJPG 2018: 3–16). Arguably, the dialogue between different bodies of literature in gender and politics needs to be strengthened, such as the one between empirical research on gender equality in political institutions, intersectional approaches to gender and multiple inequalities, and normative political theory about equality and justice for all groups of women (Kantola and Verloo 2018).

NOTE

1. For an overview of women's representation in Parliament since 1918, see http://www.ft.dk/folketinget/oplysningen/folketingsmedlemmer/kvindeprocenten.aspx (accessed 9 December 2019).

REFERENCES

Ahrens, Petra, Karen Celis, Sarah Childs, Isabelle Engeli, Elizabeth Evans, and Liza Mügge (2018). 'Politics and gender. Rocking political science and creating new horizons', *European Journal of Politics and Gender*, 1/1–2: 3–16.

Bergqvist, Christina, Anette Borchorst, Ann-Dorte Christensen, Viveca Ramstedt-Silén, Nina C. Raaum, and Audur Styrkasdóttir (1999). *Equal Democracies? Gender and Politics in the Nordic Countries*. Oslo: Scandinavian University Press.

Borchorst, Anette, Lenita Freidenvall, Johanna Kantola, Liza Reisel, and Mari Teigen (2012). 'Institutionalising intersectionality in the Nordic countries? Anti-discrimination and equality in Denmark, Finland, Norway and Sweden', in Andrea Krizsan, Hege Skjeie, and Judith Squires, eds, *Institutionalizing Intersectionality: The Changing Nature of European Equality Regimes*. Basingstoke: Palgrave Macmillan, 59–88.

Borchorst, Anette, and Birte Siim (2002). 'The women-friendly welfare state revisited', *NORA, Nordic Journal of Women's Studies*, 10/2: 90–8.

Borchorst, Anette, and Birte Siim (2008). 'Woman-friendly policies and state feminism: Theorizing Scandinavian gender equality', *Feminist Theory*, 9/2: 207–24.

Celis, Karen, Joanna Kantola, Georgina Waylen, and Laurel Weldon (2013). 'Introduction: Gender and politics. A gendered world. A gendered discipline', in Karen Celis, Joanna Kantola, Georgina Waylen, and Laurel Weldon, eds, *Oxford Handbook on Politics and Gender*. Oxford and New York: Oxford University Press, 1–26.

Celis, Karen, and Joni Lovenduski (2018). 'Power struggles: Gender equality in political representation', *European Journal of Politics and Gender*, 1/1–2: 149–66.

Christensen, Ann-Dorte, and Birte Siim (2001). *Køn, demokrati og modernitet. Mod nye politiske identiteter*. Copenhagen: Hans Reitzels Forlag.

Christiansen, Peter M., Birgit Møller, and Lise Togeby (2002). 'Køn og eliter', in Anette Borchorst, ed., *Kønsmagt under forandring*. Copenhagen: Hans Reitzels Forlag, 72–91.

Collins, Patricia H. (1990). *Black Feminist Thought: Knowledge, Consciousness, and the Politics of Empowerment*. Boston, MA: Unwin Hyman.

Crenshaw, Kimberle (1989). 'Demarginalizing the intersection of race and sex: A black feminist critique of antidiscrimination doctrine, feminist theory and antiracist politics', *The University of Chicago Legal Forum*, 1989/1: 139–67.

Crenshaw, Kimberle (1991). 'Mapping the Margins – Intersectionality, identity politics and violence against women of colour', *Stanford Law Review*, 43/6: 1241–99.

Dahlerup, Drude (1988). 'From a small to a large minority: Women in Scandinavian politics', *Scandinavian Political Studies*, 11/4: 275–98.

Dahlerup, Drude (1998). *Rødstrømperne. Den danske Rødstrømpebevægelses udvikling, nytænkning og gennemslag 1970–1985*, Vol. I, II. Copenhagen: Gyldendal.

Dahlerup, Drude (2013). 'Denmark: High representation of women without gender quota', in Drude Dahlerup and Monique Leyenaar, eds, *Breaking Male Dominance in Democracies*. Oxford: Oxford University Press, 146–71.

Dahlerup, Drude (2018). 'Gender equality as a closed case: A survey among members of the 2015 Danish Parliament', *Scandinavian Political Studies*, 41/2: 188–209.

Dahlerup, Drude, and Monique Leyenaar (2013). 'Introduction', in Drude Dahlerup and Monique Leyenaar, eds, *Breaking Male Dominance in Old Democracies*. Oxford: Oxford University Press, 1–18.

Esping-Andersen, Gösta (1990). *The Three Worlds of Welfare-Capitalism*. Oxford: Polity Press.

The European Journal of Politics and Gender (EJPG) (2018), vol. 1, Number 1–2. Issue one: Broadening the horizon of the politics and gender research area.

Fiig, Christina (2009). 'Women in Danish politics. Challenges to the notion of gender equality', in Joyce Gelb and Marian L. Palley, eds, *Women and Politics Around the World. A Comparative History and Survey*. Santa Barbara, CA: ABC-Clio, 311–27.

Fiig, Christina (2018). 'Gendered segregation in Danish standing parliamentary committees, 1990–2015', *Femina Politica*, 2: 111–25.

Fiig, Christina (2019). 'Skarpere med end uden? Kønsforskning og politologi', *Politica*, 51/1: 1–18.

Fiig, Christina, and Birte Siim (2012). 'Democratization of Denmark. The political inclusion of women', in Blanca R. Ruiz and Ruth Rubio-Marín, eds, *The Struggle for Female Suffrage in Europe. Voting to Become Citizens*. Leiden: Brill, 61–77.

Freidenvall, Lenita, Drude Dahlerup, and Hege Skjeie (2006). 'The Nordic countries. An incremental model', in Drude Dahlerup, ed., *Women, Quotas and Politics*. London: Routledge, 55–82.

Gomard, Kirsten, and Anne Krogstad (2001) (eds). *Instead of the Ideal Debate. Doing Politics and Doing Gender in Nordic Political Campain Discourse*. Aarhus: Aarhus University Press.

Hernes, Helga (1987). *Welfare State and Women Power*. Oslo: Norwegian University Press.

Heidar, Knut, and Karina Pedersen (2006). 'Party Feminism: Gender gaps within nordic political parties', *Scandinavian Political Studies*, 29/3: 192–218.

Hirdman, Yvonne (1990). 'Genussystemet', in SOU, ed., *Demokrati och Makt i Sverige. Maktutredningens huvudrapport*. Stockhold: Allmänna Förl., 73–114.

Holli, Anne Maria, and Mette Marie Harder (2016). 'Towards a Dual Approach: Comparing the Effects of Parliamentary Committees on Gender Equality in Denmark and Finland', *Parliamentary Affairs*, 69/4: 794–811.

Inglehart, Ronald, Pippa Norris, and Christian Welzel (2002). 'Gender equality and democracy', *Comparative Sociology*, 1/3–4: 321–45.

Kantola, Johanna, and Mieke Verloo (2018). 'Revisiting gender equality in times of recession: A discussion of strategies of gender and politics scholarship for dealing with equality', *European Journal of Politics and Gender*, 1/1–2: 205–22.

Karvonen, Lauri, and Per Selle (1995) (eds). *Women in Nordic Politics: Closing the Gap*. Aldershot: Dartmouth.

Kjær, Ulrik (2020). 'Local elections. Localized voting within a nationalized party system', in Peter M. Christiansen, Jørgen Elklit, and Peter Nedergaard, eds, *The Oxford Handbook on Danish Politics*. Oxford: Oxford University Press, 382–99.

Kjær, Ulrik, and Karina Kosiara-Pedersen (2019). 'The hour-glass pattern of women's representation', *Journal of Elections, Public Opinion and Parties*, 29/3: 299–317.

Krizsan, Andrea, Hege Skjeie, and Judith Squires (2012) (eds). *The Changing Nature of European Equality Regimes*. Basingstoke: Palgrave Macmillan.

Krook, Mona, and Fiona Mackay (2011). *Gender, Politics and Institutions. Towards a Feminist Institutionalism*. Basingstoke: Palgrave Macmillan.

Kuhnle, Stein, and Matti Alestalo (2018). 'The modern Scandinavian welfare state', in Peter Nedergaard, and Anders Wivel, eds, *The Routledge Handbook of Scandinavian Politics*. London: Routledge, 13–24.

Larsen, Anton G., Christoph Ellersgaard, and Markus Bernsen (2015). *Magteliten. Hvordan 423 danskere styrer landet*. Copenhagen: Politikens Forlag.

Larsen, Anton G., Christoph Ellersgaard, and Markus Bernsen (2019). *Personer forgår, Magten består. Udviklingen i magteliten over 5 år*. Copenhagen: Politikens Forlag.

Lépinard, Éléonore, and Ruth Rubio-Marín (2018) (eds). *Transforming Gender Citizenship. The Irrestistable Rise of Gender Quotas in Europe*. Cambridge: Cambridge University Press.

Lister, Ruth (2009). 'A Nordic nirvana? Gender, citizenship, and social justice in the Nordic welfare states', *Social Politics*, 16/2: 242–78.

Melby, Kari, Anna-Birte Ravn, and Christina C. Wetterberg (2008) (eds). *The Limits of Political Ambition? Gender Equality and Welfare Politics in Scandinavia*. Bristol: Policy Press.

Meret, Susi, and Birte Siim (2013). 'Gender, populism and politics of belonging: Discourses of Rightwing populist parties in Norway, Denmark and Austria', in Birte Siim, and Monika Mokre, eds, *Negotiating Gender and Diversity in an Emerging European Public Sphere*. Basingstoke: Palgrave MacMillan, 78–96.

Minister for Gender Equality (2014). *Redegørelse/Perspektiv og Handlingsplan 2014*. Copenhagen: Ministry for Gender Equality.

Mügge, Liza, Celeste Montoya, Akuungo Emejulu, and Laurel Weldon (2018). 'Intersectionality and the politics of Knowledge Production', *European Journal of Politics and Gender*, 1/1–2: 17–36.

Mulinari, Diana (2008). 'Women-friendly? Understanding gendered racism in Sweden', in Kari Melby, Anna-Birte Ravn, and Christina C. Wetterberg, eds, *Gender Equality and Welfare Politics in Scandinavia. The limits of Political Ambition*. Bristol: Policy Press, 166–82.

Pateman, Carole (1988). *The Sexual Contract*. Cambridge: Polity Press.

Phillips, Anne (1995). *The Politics of Presence*. Oxford: Clarendon Press.

Raaum, Nina C. (1995). 'Women in local democracy', in Lauri Karvonen and Per Selle, eds, *Closing the Gap. Women in Nordic Politics*. Aldershot: Dartmouth, 25–58.

Rolandsen Agustin et. al (2018). 'Gender equality without gender quotas: Dilemmas in the Danish approach to gender equality and citizenship', in Ruth Rubio-Marín and Éléonore Lépinard, eds, *Transforming Gender Citizenship*. Cambridge: Cambridge University Press, 400–23.

Sainsbury, Diana (2006). 'Immigrants social rights in comparative perspectives: Welfare Regimes, forms in immigration and immigration policy regimes', *Journal of European Social Policy*, 16/3: 229–44.

Siim, Birte (2000). *Gender and Citizenship. Politics and Agency in France, Britain and Denmark*. Cambridge: Cambridge University Press.

Siim, Birte (2007). 'The challenge of recognizing diversity from the perspective of gender equality: Dilemmas in Danish citizenship', *Critical Review of International Social and Political Philosophy*, 10/4: 491–511.

Siim, Birte, and Anette Borchorst (2017). 'Gendering European welfare states and citizenship: Revisioning inequalities', in Patricia Kennett and Noemi Lendvai-Bainton, eds, *Handbook of European Social Policy*. Cheltenham: Edward Elgar, 60–74.

Siim, Birte, and Christina Fiig (in press). 'The Populist Challenge to Gender Equality', in Gabriele Abels, Andrea Krizsan, Heather MacRae, and Anna van der vleuten, eds, *Routledge Handbook on Gender and EU Politics*. London: Routledge, chapter 27.

Siim, Birte, and Monika Mokre (2013) (eds). *Negotiating Gender and Diversity in an Emerging European Public Sphere*. Basingstoke: Palgrave Macmillan.

Siim, Birte, and Hege Skjeie (2008). 'Tracks, intersections and dead ends. Multicultural challenges to state feminism in Denmark and Norway', *Ethnicities*, 8/3: 322–44.

Skjeie, Hege (1992). *Den politiske betydningen av kjönn. En studie av norsk topppolitik*. Oslo: Institut for Samfundsforsning.

Smith, Nina (2018). 'Gender quotas on boards of directors. Gender quotas for women on boards of directors improve female share on boards but firm performance effects are mixed', IZA World of Labour 2018: 7v2 /, wol.iza.org (accessed 10 December 2019).

Togeby, Lise (1994). *Fra tilskuere til deltagere. Den kollektive politiske mobilisering af kvinder I politik, 1970–1999*. Aarhus: Politica.

Togeby, Lise (1995). 'A gender gap that vanished', in Lauri Karvonen, and Per Selle, eds, *Closing the Gap: Women in Nordic Politics*. Aldershot: Dartmouth, 313–43.

Togeby, Lise, Jørgen Goul Andersen, Peter Munck Christiansen, Torben Beck Jørgensen, and Signild Vallgårda (2003). *Power and Democracy in Denmark: Conclusion*. Århus: Magtudredningen. https://unipress.dk/media/14485/87-7934-850-5_power_and_democracy_in_denmark.pdf (accessed 10 December 2019).

United Nations (2015). 'Convention on the elimination of all forms of discrimination against women. Concluding observations on the eighth periodic report of Denmark', CEDAW /C/ DNK/CO/8. Adapted by the Committee at its 60th session (16 February–6 March 2015).

Verloo, Mieke (2018) (ed.). *Varieties of Opposition to gender Equality in Europe*. New York and London: Routledge.

Wängnerud, Lena (2000). 'Testing the politics of presence: Women's representation in the Swedish Riksdag', *Scandinavian Political Studies*, 23/1: 67–84.

Wängnerud, Lena (2009). 'Women in parliaments: Descriptive and substantive representation', *Annual Review of Political Science*, 12/1: 51–69.

Wängnerud, Lena (2015). *The Principles of Gender-Sensitive Parliaments*. New York: Routledge.

Wivel, Anders, and Peter Nedergaard (2018). 'Introduction: Scandinavian politics between myth and reality', in Peter Nedergaard and Anders Wivel, eds, *The Routledge Handbook of Scandinavian Politics*. London and New York: Routledge, 1–10.

Young, Iris M. (1990). *Justice and the Politics of Difference*. Princeton, NJ: Princeton University Press.

CHAPTER 24

LOCAL ELECTIONS

Localized Voting Within a Nationalized Party System

ULRIK KJÆR

SECOND-ORDER OR SECOND-TIER ELECTIONS?

IN all ninety-eight municipalities and five regions in Denmark, local elections were held on 21 November 2017 as they are every fourth year on the third Tuesday of November (the 2005 elections were the first within this local structure after a major amalgamation reform; see Houlberg and Ejersbo 2020). The media coverage of these local elections was as extensive as when there is a parliamentary election. From the day when the lists of candidates are filed in each municipality and region (seven weeks prior to the elections) to the local campaigns, to when the results are ready on the night of the election, and the days after when the coalitions are formed to elect a mayor among the elected councillors, the local and regional media outlets as well as the national media outlets all zoom in on the local elections. This intense focus is not that surprising to Danes since, as demonstrated in Houlberg and Ejersbo (2020), Denmark runs a very decentralized public sector, and a lot of important political decisions regarding, for instance, healthcare, public schools, eldercare, planning, and childcare are taken by the councils elected in the local elections.

Analysing local elections have often been done by treating them as 'second-order' elections (Reif and Schmitt 1980), implying that there is 'less at stake' and that voters, therefore, 'care less' about the local elections and stay home more often on election day or cast a midterm vote signalling to the national party leaderships instead of the local candidates. This approach might make sense in countries where local governments play a minor role, but it seems odd in Danish local elections to apply an analytical tool where these elections a priori are categorized as second rank. It has also been suggested to see local elections simply as a different kind of election with a smaller size of electorate and a different task portfolio (Oliver 2012), but it also seems equally odd to neglect the national political level altogether. Therefore, Kjaer and Steyvers (2019) have suggested perceiving local elections as 'second-tier' elections, acknowledging the existence of a vertical relation to the national political realm as well as some horizontal variation across local political units. Hence, the analyses in this chapter will relate the local elections to the national election for the Danish Parliament (*Folketinget*) as well as look for differences across municipalities/regions.

The analyses will be organized around five selected features of the electoral rules (Local Election Act 2018) which are important to the understanding of this political phenomenon:

1) Extended suffrage (contrary to national elections, residing EU citizens and citizens from non-EU countries who have had residency in Denmark for at least three years can vote);
2) non-concurrency (local elections are held on the same day in all municipalities and regions but not the same day as the national elections);
3) lower and higher threshold (the threshold for running is very low compared to the national election, but the natural threshold to gain representation is higher);
4) preferential votes count (after the seats are distributed between lists by the d'Hondt method with *apparantement* allowed, with each municipality/region forming one multi-member district, the preferential votes cast for each candidate are important in regard to which of the candidates gets elected since most lists opt in for an open list seat method); and
5) indirectly elected mayors (the mayor is the most important political figure, but the mayor is indirectly elected after an unregulated government formation process).

The chapter will be organized around these features with each of the next five sections devoted to one of them.

How Many Turn Out at the Local Polls?

At the municipal elections held on 21 November 2017, a total of 4,554,614 people could cast their vote—an option that 3,226,583 people used to visit one of the 1,387 polling stations scattered around the ninety-eight municipalities. This equals a turnout rate of 70.8 per cent (Statistics Denmark 2018: 26), whereas turnout at the regional elections held on the same day was 70.7 per cent.

The 70.8 per cent local turnout in Denmark is relatively high compared to other European countries where turnout is most often lower than 60 per cent. Even the other

Nordic countries have lower turnout rates with 58.9 in Finland (2017), 60.0 in Norway (2015), and 67.6 in Iceland (2018). Sweden is the only exception, but the 84.1 per cent turnout at the 2018 local elections in Sweden is likely a result of the simultaneity of local, regional, and national elections (and the 87.2 per cent turnout at the Swedish parliamentary elections). As can be seen in K.M. Hansen (2020) (Figure 6.1), the record for municipal turnout in Denmark was also observed at the only simultaneous election ever held in Denmark in 2001 where the turnout at the municipal elections reached 85.0 per cent. Figure 6.1 also shows that the municipal and regional turnout rates are significantly lower than the turnout rate at national elections. The latest elections are quite indicative for the included period with turnout at the elections for the *Folketinget* being 15 percentage points higher than at the municipal and regional elections.

As already mentioned, the rules regulating the right to vote differ slightly from local to national elections. Those eligible to vote for parliamentary elections are people who 1) are at least 18 years old, *and* 2) have fixed abode in Denmark (or can vote from abroad because of temporary stay) *and* 3) hold Danish citizenship. Eligible to vote at local elections are people who 1) are at least 18 years old, *and* 2) have fixed abode in Denmark (although with no exceptions in this case), *and* 3) either a) hold Danish citizenship *or* b) hold citizenship from another EU country (or Island or Norway) *or* c) have resided in Denmark continuously for the past three years. This opens up two differences in the group of eligible voters: temporarily expatriated Danes (they can vote at national but not at the local elections) and non-Danish citizens who are either citizens from EU/Nordic countries or from elsewhere but residing more permanently in Denmark (they can vote at local but not national elections). The two groups are far from equally sized. At the parliamentary election in 2019, the 4,218,070 eligible voters residing in Denmark were joined by 3,405 expats (the expats were 0.08 per cent of the total). At the local elections in 2017, the then 4,192,817 eligible Danish citizens residing in Denmark were joined by 361,797 foreign citizens (foreign citizens were 7.9 per cent of the total). It is worth mentioning that this relatively large group of foreign citizens who are eligible at the local but not at the national elections tend to vote significantly less than Danish citizens. While the turnout rate among Danish citizens at the 2017 local elections was 74 per cent, it was only 32.1 per cent among non-Danish citizens (Hansen 2018: 18). So, comparing the same group of voters (Danish citizens with the right to vote at both elections), the difference in turnout is not approximately 15 percentage points but closer to 12.

Fluctuations have been seen at two of the more recent elections. At the 2009 municipal elections, turnout dropped from 69.5 to 65.8 per cent, and at the following elections in 2013, it rose to 71.9 per cent. In the public debate, pundits and not least opponents of the 2007 amalgamation reform instantly pointed to the reform and decline-of-community effect of larger polities. However, studies have demonstrated that the reform could explain less than 1.7 percentage points of the decrease (Bhatti et al. 2013). It has also been demonstrated that the modest effect of the amalgamations was just a short-term effect; at the 2017 elections, the effect disappeared (Bhatti and Hansen 2019). As for the significant rise in 2013, the media attention and the focus on the turnout drop in 2009 most likely had a mobilizing effect (Bhatti et al. 2017).

At the individual level, turnout varies quite a lot between different social demographics. While 54.9 per cent of the voters in the 22–29 age bracket voted at the 2017 local elections, no less than 81.1 per cent in their Sixties and 82.1 per cent in their Seventies voted (Hansen 2020, 2018). While more than 80 per cent of voters with a college degree voted, only 61 per cent of voters without a high school diploma did so.

Since the local elections are ninety-eight individual elections, there can also be some variation across municipalities. For instance, at the 2017 elections, turnout varied from 59.6 to 85.7 per cent. The socio-demographic composition of the electorate explains some of this variation as does municipal size (Bhatti and Hansen 2019).

How 'Local' Is the Local Vote?

So, who do the voters vote for? They could go vote for the same parties that they vote for in national elections, or they could choose to deviate from their usual partisan preference. Some might follow their national party choice and simply copy their national vote at the local elections without giving local candidates or issues much consideration. Others might choose to see the local and national elections as two very separate events and vote at the local elections exclusively based on local candidates and their local campaigns even if this means voting for another party than the one preferred at national elections (Kjaer and Steyvers 2017).

Table 24.1 offers a first glimpse into the potential differences in voting patterns by reporting the aggregate results of the local and regional elections on 21 November 2017, along with vote intentions if there had been an election for the *Folketinget* on the same day.

Table 24.1 demonstrates that some voters vote differently at the three kinds of the elections. The Social Democrats (*Socialdemokratiet*), the Liberal Party (*Venstre*), and the Conservative People's Party (*Det Konservative Folkeparti*) had relatively good local elections, while the Liberal Alliance (*Liberal Alliance*), the Red-Green Alliance (*Enhedslisten*), and not least, the Danish People's Party (*Dansk Folkeparti*) fared worse at the local elections compared to vote intentions for parliamentary elections. This pattern has been consistent for several successive elections.

While Table 24.1 demonstrates that some voters vote differently at the three levels, we need individual level data to assess how many split their vote—what has been denoted inter-level split-ticket voting (Elklit and Kjaer 2005). Therefore, in Table 24.2, data from the Danish Local Election Survey have been used to calculate how many voters cast split (or straight) votes based on their reported votes in the municipal and the regional elections and their intended vote in a national election.

According to Table 24.2, no less than 29 per cent of the voters vote for a different party at the municipal elections than they would have voted for at a national election on the same day (the numbers are a little lower for the regional elections), which is consistent with earlier studies (Elklit and Kjaer 2005). However, the number of split-ticket votes

Table 24.1. The Results of the 2017 Local Elections by Political Party Aggregated for All Ninety-Eight Municipalities and Five Regions Compared to Vote Intention in National Election

		Local elections 2017	Regional elections 2017	National election '2017'
A	Social Democrats	32.4	30.4	29.7
B	Social Liberals	4.6	5.1	6.0
C	Conservative People's Party	8.8	6.9	6.1
D	New Right	0.9	1.2	2.2
F	Socialist People's Party	5.7	7.3	5.5
I	Liberal Alliance	2.6	3.1	3.8
O	Danish People's Party	8.8	9.7	12.5
S	The Schleswig Party	0.3	0.2	-
V	Liberal Party	23.1	24.1	21.2
Ø	Red-Green Alliance	6.0	6.3	8.5
Å	Alternative	2.9	2.7	3.5
	Others	3.9	3.0	1.0
Total		100.0	100.0	100.0
N=		3,176,021	3,080,210	4,848

Source: Statistics Denmark 2018, National elections '2017': Danish Local Election Survey, Kjaer and Hansen 2020.

Table 24.2. Inter-Level Split-Ticket Voting at the Municipal and Regional Elections of November 2017 and a Fictive Election for the *Folketinget* on the Same Day

	Per cent
National vote = regional vote = municipal vote	59.9
National vote = regional vote ≠ municipal vote	12.1
National vote ≠ regional vote = municipal vote	9.5
National vote = municipal vote ≠ regional vote	11.2
National vote ≠ regional vote ≠ municipal vote ≠ national vote	7.3
Total	100.0
n=	4,105
Local-national split (row 2 + 3 + 5)	28.9
Local-regional split (row 2 + 4 + 5)	30.6
Regional-national split (row 3 + 4 + 5)	28.0

Source: Calculations based on the Danish Local Election Survey 2017 (Kjaer and Hansen 2020).

does not reveal anything about the motivation behind the vote. It would be possible to cast a split vote without having any local considerations at all by using the local vote as a mid-term vote signalling (dis)satisfaction with the national government party, just as it is possible to cast a straight vote without simply copying the national vote at the local elections but instead making a deliberate choice based on local candidates but still ending up agreeing most with candidates from the same party at both levels. Therefore, in Table 24.3, voters' focus on municipal and national features while voting in the municipal elections is cross-tabulated with whether they cast a split or a straight ticket.

Table 24.3 shows that Danish voters cast a quite local vote at local elections; 30 per cent vote exclusively out of national political considerations but that also means that 70 per cent cast a localized vote. Quite a number of these end up voting for the same party they would have voted for at a national election but not because they automatically copy their national vote at the local elections (instead, their preferred party at the two different elections happens to be identical).

Is the Local Party System a Copy of the National Party System?

From Table 24.1 it appears that local (or non-partisan) lists are a feature of local elections in Denmark. Political parties compete at the local elections. The threshold for running at local elections is extremely low—only 25 signatures from eligible voters (150 in Copenhagen and 50 in the three other large cities) are required for a list to be allowed onto the ballot in a given municipality. A person or a group of people can form a list and nominate candidates—minimum one and no more than the number of seats on the council plus four. The list can either run under the label of a nationwide party or under a self-invented name. All lists will be designated a 'party identification letter' which will be printed on the ballot along with the name of the list. Lists running under the label of one of the nationwide parties who are registered for participation in parliamentary elections will automatically be designated the letter of this party (while other nationwide parties running are not). At the 2017 elections, this was the case for the nine parties represented in the *Folketinget* plus the newly registered party the New Right (*Nye Borgerlige*). The Schleswig Party (*Slesvigsk Parti*) which is the German minority's party is a special case. This party is given the right by law to run in the four municipalities of Southern Jutland bordering Germany and in the regional elections of the Region of Southern Denmark under the letter S. Finally, there are the lists without connection to lists in other municipalities. At the elections in 2017, a total of 1,157 lists were running in the ninety-eight municipalities (averaging 12 lists per municipality). In Table 24.4, they are listed under the four types of lists just described.

Table 24.4 shows that parties from the national parliamentary party system dominate the ballots in the municipal elections but also that there are 182 local lists which

Table 24.3. Inter-Level Split-Ticket Voting at the Municipal Elections of 2017 and a Fictive National Election (Vote Intention) Combined with the Voters' Focus on Local Candidates and Issues or National Politics when Casting the Municipal Vote

	Straight vote	Split vote	Total
Local vote with focus on national politics	25.3	4.5	29.8
Local vote with focus on national as well as local politics	10.1	3.0	13.1
Local vote with focus on local candidates and issues	34.8	22.3	57.1
Total	70.2	29.8	100.0

n=4,142.

Source: Calculations based on the Danish Local Election Survey 2017 (Kjaer and Hansen 2020).

account for 15.7 per cent of all lists running. The nationwide parties are present in most municipalities—even the newcomers the New Right and the Alternative (*Alternativet*) presented candidates in no less than 61 and 83 of the municipalities, respectively. There are also eight nationwide parties without a designated letter that run in some municipalities.

The dominance of the nationwide parties present in the *Folketinget* is even more pronounced when we move from the electoral to the political arena. While the local lists made up 15.7 per cent of the lists running, they are only 6.1 of the elected lists, and their candidates conquered only 3.2 per cent of the 2,432 seats on the ninety-eight councils. So, while it is relatively easy for local lists to run in the local elections, it is harder to be represented. This goes for all four kinds of lists, and that is not least because of the threshold of representation. While there is no formal threshold in local elections, the natural threshold is quite high; with the number of seats on the councils ranging from 9 to 31 (Copenhagen is an outlier and has 55), there is a natural threshold between 3 and 11 per cent (Kjaer and Elklit 2014). Also, the newer nationwide parties the New Right and the Alternative had a hard time getting enough votes to get represented on the councils; the Alternative got 20 candidates elected in 15 different municipalities, while the New Right only had 1 candidate elected. No less than 96 per cent of the councillors elected in 2017 represent one of the nine parties present in the *Folketinget* at the time.

As Table 24.4 illustrates, the difference between the national and the local party system can originate from two sources. First, the nationwide parties can choose to have their local branch in a given municipality run at the local election there. Second, the local lists can play an important role in some municipalities while playing little or no role in others (in 21 municipalities, no local lists were running in 2017, and none were elected in 64 municipalities). The degree to which the local party system resembles the national one has caught some scholarly interest since it is discussed how 'nationalized' the local party system is. More than half a century ago, Norwegian Stein Rokkan (1966: 244) projected that over time the local lists would be squeezed out by the nationwide parties,

Table 24.4. Number of Lists Running and Getting Elected in the Ninety-Eight Local Elections on 21 November 2017

	Number of lists running	Number of lists elected	Number of candidates running	Number of candidates elected
Nationwide parties with designated letter (i.e. allowed to run for the *Folketinget*)				
A. Social Democrats	98	98	1,712	842
B. Social Liberals	91	55	697	80
C. Conservative People's Party	98	79	1,020	225
D. New Right	61	1	240	1
F. Socialist People's Party	96	79	819	126
I. Liberal Alliance	93	24	435	28
O. Danish People's Party	98	91	755	223
V. Liberal Party	98	96	1,719	688
Ø. Red-Green Alliance	87	69	774	102
Å. Alternative	83	15	332	20
Other nationwide parties				
Christian Democrats	39	4	131	9
National Party	9	0	17	0
Taut Course	6	0	8	0
Friends of the Schiller Institute	4	0	8	0
Justice Party	4	0	7	0
Progress Party	2	0	4	0
Danish Unity	2	0	2	0
Lower Taxes	2	0	2	0
Regional parties with designated letter				
S. The Schleswig Party	4	4	59	10
Local lists	182[1]	40[2]	815[1]	78[2]
Total	1,157	655	9,556	2,432

Notes: [1] In 77 different municipalities (a total of 87 municipalities had lists outside the first category running). [2] In 34 different municipalities (a total of 38 municipalities had lists outside the first category elected).

Source: Calculated from Statistics Denmark (2018).

and processes of party politicization have been demonstrated in Norway (Aars and Ringkjøb 2005) as well as Sweden (Bäck 2003).

In Denmark, the local party system has also become somewhat nationalized. In the late 1960s, things were definitely different in the two dimensions listed in comparison to today: the nationwide parties were not running/getting represented in most of the municipalities, and the local lists were heavily present most places. To evaluate the changes in the local party system, an index of local party system nationalization has been suggested, combining the two dimensions, namely how many of the parties from the national party system that run/get represented locally, and how many local lists are participating (Kjaer and Elklit 2010a, 2010b). In Figure 24.1, the two dimensions as well as the index are presented for each of the elections from 1966 to 2017 (for the formulas used, see Kjaer and Elklit 2010a: 433).

The nationalization of the local party systems has been substantial in the past half century. After the 2017 elections, on average 69 per cent of the nine parties represented in the *Folketinget* are also represented on the council (up from 25 per cent in 1966). And among the lists represented on the councils, 8 per cent are not found in the *Folketinget* at the same time (down from 49 per cent in 1966). However, as it has been pointed out, the massive nationalization has not—as originally suggested by Rokkan—been a gradual process (Kjaer and Elklit 2010b). Instead, nationalization has been taking place in the elections of 1970 and 2005—the two elections succeeding the two amalgamation reforms conducted in the same period. At the most recent amalgamation, several municipalities were not amalgamated, and it has been demonstrated that the index did increase much more in amalgamated municipalities on this occasion than in non-amalgamated municipalities (Bækgaard et al. 2017). It has been demonstrated how the degree of nationalization of the local party system increases with the size of the municipality (and with the size of the council), and also, that the local lists are still most present in the Western part of the country where they traditionally have had their stronghold (Kjaer and Elklit 2010a).

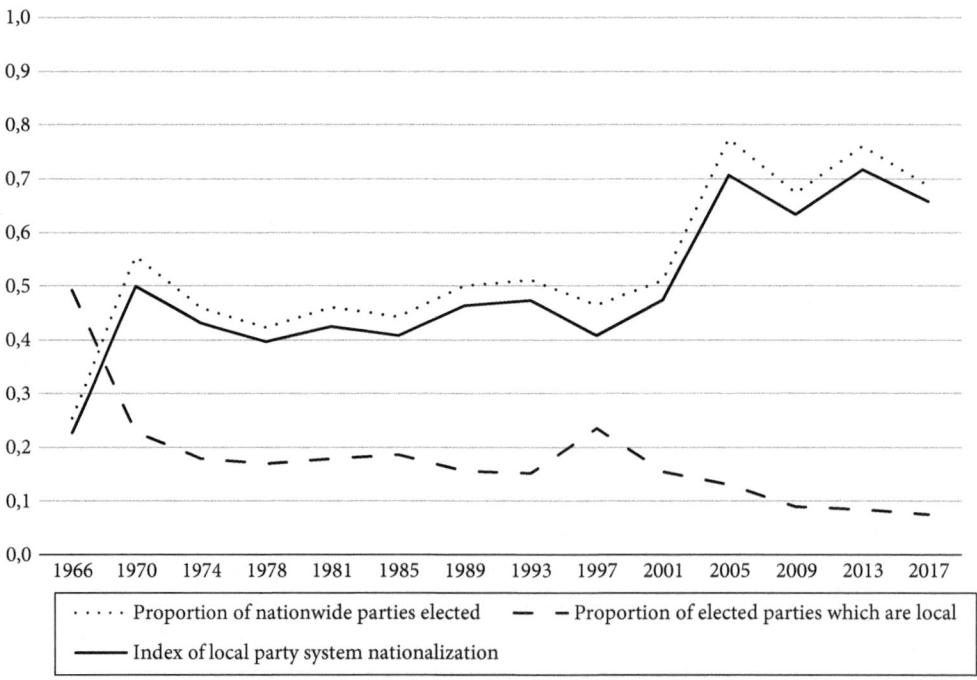

FIGURE 24.1 The nationalization of the party system, 1966–2017 (average for all municipalities).

Note: For calculations, see Kjaer and Elklit 2010a

Source: Statistics Denmark, various publications

STILL MORE MEN THAN WOMEN?

So, who are the 2,432 members of the ninety-eight municipal councils and the 205 members of the regional councils? The answer is in many ways straight forward since those who get elected are pretty much those voted for by the voters. This sounds self-evident and not the least informative, but it is an important point that the seat alloca-tion system used puts the decision of who among a list's candidates should have the seats in the hands of the voters to a large extent. The voters can vote either for one of the lists or cast a preferential vote for one of the list's candidates. When the seats are distri-buted among the lists, all votes are assigned to the list voted for (regardless of whether the voter voted for the list or cast a preferential vote for one of its candidates). But when the seats won by a list are allocated among its candidates, the voters' directions through the preferential votes are considered. The voters end up having an important say because many of them use the option to cast a preferential vote (in 2017, no less than 75.1 per cent did so), and at the same time, the allocation scheme used is favourable to the voters' preferences.

Two allocation schemes are in function since the lists themselves can choose whether an open list or a semi-closed list system should be applied. The open list sys-tem is simple since those among the candidates on the list with the most preferential votes gets the seats assigned to the list. In the semi-closed system, the preferential votes still count, but the non-preferential votes cast on the list are distributed among the candidates according to their ranking on their list so that candidates on the top of the list will be assigned the non-preferential votes if they need that to get the number of votes required. It should be noted, though, that almost three in four lists in 2017 opted for the open-list format and that the number of cases where the semi-closed list format secures a seat for a high-ranking candidate at the expense of a low-ranking candidate is low (less than one in thirteen of the elected candidates on the semi-closed lists [Kjaer and Krook 2019]).

The selection of candidates produces a quite traditional socio-demographic compo-sition of the councillors (e.g. Verhelst et al. 2013). After the 2017 municipal elections, 32.9 per cent of the councillors are women (31.8 per cent of the candidates); 71 per cent of the councillors (61.7 per cent of the candidates) are between 40 and 64 years old (only 5.5 per cent are under the age of 30); 96 per cent of the elected councillors are ethnic Danes (95 per cent among the candidates); 48.7 per cent of the councillors have a college degree (44.3 per cent of the candidates); 95.5 per cent of the councillors are employed (81.3 per cent of the candidates); and 59.4 per cent of these are public employees (47.2 per cent of the candidates) (Statistics Denmark 2018: 3–5).

Each of these socio-demographic dimensions warrants attention, but the gender composition has particularly been in focus in recent years. This is not just because Denmark is lagging behind the other Nordic countries in terms of gender equality—while 32.9 per cent of the councillors are women in Denmark, the percentage is 39 in

Finland, 39 in Norway, 43.3 in Sweden, and 44 in Iceland—but also because two somewhat peculiar patterns have emerged. Both patterns can be seen in Figure 24.2, depicting the gender composition in municipal councils and regional councils as well as in the *Folketinget* for the past half a century.

First, Figure 24.2 demonstrates that at the local elections of 1997, women's representation decreased for the first time in the period covered (first time since 1937), and the 1993 level was not reached again until 2009. This stalemate was somewhat surprising, the traditional expectation being that when women's representation has started to increase it will not stop until equal representation has been reached (Dahlerup 1988). Second, and connected to the first point, Figure 24.2 shows that the level of female representation on the municipal councils is now lower than in the *Folketinget*. This is contrary to the pattern often expected, although the anomaly pattern is actually found in one-third of EU countries (Kjær 2010).

Therefore, when a record high level of female representation was reached with 32.9 per cent at the 2017 municipal elections, it was not really celebrated. The breaking of the 2009 record was somewhat overshadowed by the fact that the level of female representation is not on an ever-increasing trajectory and that women's representation is lower at the municipal level than at the national (and regional) level.

A possible explanation to this pattern is the 'saturation before parity' explanation (Kjaer 1999). According to this, both selectors in the political recruitment process (the nominating parties and the preferential voting voters) are still positive towards having more female candidates and councillors but not so much that they (after reaching a certain level) will override considerations for other preferable candidate characteristics such as geographical affiliation, age, ethnicity, and so on.

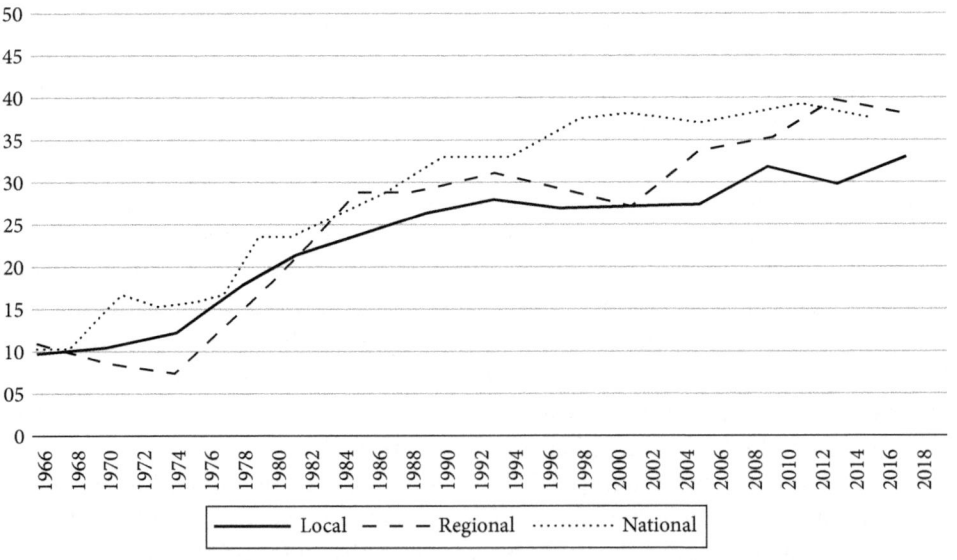

FIGURE 24.2 Female representation at the local, regional, and national level, 1966–2017.
Source: Statistics Denmark, various publications

Table 24.5. Preferential Voting for Male and Female Candidates at the 2017 Danish Local Elections

	Female voters	Male voters	Total
Voted for a list (a non-preferential vote)	25.9	26.0	26.0
Voted for a candidate (a preferential vote)			
voted for a female candidate	27.3	22.3	24.7
voted for a male candidate	46.8	51.7	49.3
Total	100.0	100.0	100.0
n=	2,509	2,483	4,992

Note: The difference between male and female voters is statistically significant (Pearson Chi-Square = 19.262, p=.000).

Source: Data from the Danish Local Elections Survey 2017 (Kjaer and Hansen 2020).

The mechanism can be illustrated by the preferential voting. With 3,037 female candidates (out of 9,556 candidates) and 2,432 seats to be filled, the voters could use their preferential votes to do something serious about the percentage of women. However, as Table 24.5 demonstrates, this is not the case. Among the surveyed voters, 74 per cent cast a preferential vote (75.1 per cent among all voters), but of these only 33.4 per cent voted for a female candidate. Since women were 31.8 per cent of all candidates, the voters seem to have preferred women candidates, but the point is that this positive discrimination towards female candidates is almost inconsequential. An analysis using electoral data and the preferential votes obtained by each candidate returns the same result (Kjaer and Krook 2019). The missing gendered effect is not exclusively due to the male voters— even though female voters tend to cast more preferential votes for female candidates, only a little more than one in four female voters cast a preferential vote for a female candidate.

To further support the argument, in the Danish Local Election Survey voters are surveyed about why they choose to cast a preferential vote for a specific candidate, and among the five descriptives given as potential explanations (gender, age, geographical affiliation, occupational background, and associational affiliation), gender was the lowest scoring, and this goes for both male and female voters.

WHO PERFORMS LOCAL POLITICAL LEADERSHIP?

The local elections are not finished when the votes are counted and the seats distributed. A mayor—along with a deputy mayor and chairmen for the standing committees— must be found by and among the councillors. The indirectly elected mayor is a very important political figure in the municipality (and region). Elected for the full four-year term (and almost irremovable during the term), the mayor takes up a special leadership position. The mayoralty is a full-time position, and the mayor has an office at City Hall and gets a full-time salary, which is not the case for the rest of the councillors who are amateur politicians with another day job and without day-to-day contact with the administrative organization (the four largest municipalities have a slightly different form of government).

With the mayoralty as the great prize, the process of selecting a mayor can be quite messy. As important as the selection process is, it is just as unregulated. The law only stipulates that the council should meet sometime in the first half of December in the year of the election to elect a mayor among them by a simple majority vote. However, the councillors start negotiating as soon as they know the electoral result. It is, of course, possible during these negotiations to discuss only the question of who the mayor should be, but in most cases, more decisions would be included such as who should be the leaders of the committees. The deals cut vary a lot in terms of how specific they are—from deals that only include who should be mayor to deals specifying all appointed posts for the next four years and specific political goals. Most deals are written down and signed, but they are not legally binding. Consequently, there have been cases where already signed agreements have been discarded and new coalitions made in the days before the first meeting of the new council. However, the process is far smoother in most cases. For instance, in those municipalities where one party gets the majority of the seats—after the 2017 elections, this happened in twenty municipalities—the frontrunner of this party will be the mayor. Moreover, in many other municipalities, like-minded parties will form a majority coalition very early on, most often already on the night of the election.

Chaotic coalition formation processes do exist, and they receive a lot of media coverage, and therefore, the prevalence of these coalitions tends to be overestimated. In most election years, including 2017, the number of tumultuary processes tends to be a handful or less. And in general terms, a party will be more likely to win the mayoralty '[...] the larger it is and if it has gained additional seats in the election, occupied the mayor's office in the previous local government, and if it is currently a median party and a very strong party' (Skjæveland and Serritzlew 2010: 202). No matter how tough the negotiations on who should be the mayor, it is a tradition in many municipalities that more parties than necessary are included in the final coalition. A study has demonstrated that after the 2013 elections, as many as 85 per cent of the coalitions were oversized and included more parties than necessary for a majority (Elklit et al. 2017). This is not surprising since Danish local governments are known for having a political culture characterized by compromise and consensus (Berg and Kjaer 2007), and a detailed survey-based study of the Danish case proclaims the norm of consensus as the main explanation for the oversized coalitions (Serritzlew et al. 2008).

As seen in Table 24.6, most mayoralties have traditionally been won by the Social Democrats and the Liberal Party. The local lists have really lost mayoral offices over the decades, and after the 2017 elections, they won only two. Most of the minor parties in the *Folketinget* also have difficulties winning the mayor's office, with the Danish People's Party, the Social Liberals (*Radikale Venstre*), the Alternative, and the Socialist

Table 24.6. Mayoral Parties after the Municipal Elections, 1970–2017, Per cent

	1970	1974	1978	1981	1985	1989	1993	1997	2001	2005	2009	2013	2017
Social Democrats	27	27	29	27	36	44	39	38	31	46	50	34	48
Social Liberals	4	3	3	1	1	1	0	1	1	1	0	1	1
Conservative People's Party	9	9	7	9	10	8	9	11	9	11	12	13	8
Socialist People's Party	0	0	0	0	0	0	0	1	2	1	2	1	1
Danish People's Party	–	–	–	–	–	–	–	0	0	0	0	0	1
Liberal Party	40	45	44	50	43	39	43	42	49	37	32	49	38
Alternative	–	–	–	–	–	–	–	–	–	–	–	–	1
Local lists	20	16	17	13	10	8	9	7	8	4	4	2	2
Total	100	100	100	100	100	100	100	100	100	100	100	100	100
N=	275	275	275	275	275	275	275	275	275	98	98	98	98

Notes: The Progress Party had one mayor after the election in 1997, here included under local lists.

Source: Kjaer and Opstrup 2018.

People's Party (*Socialistisk Folkeparti*) only winning one each. The only party challenging the Liberal Party and the Social Democrats on the list is the Conservative People's Party who have many of their voters concentrated in a few strongholds. The 'party system' among the mayors continues to be a two-party thing with the Social Democrats and the Liberal Party as the main parties (or a two-and-a-half thing if the Conservative People's Party is included).

CONCLUSION

Local elections are important in Denmark. In the Danish case, it is premature to abandon local elections as just part of the plethora of elections held outside the first-order arena (Reif and Schmitt 1980), and the more condescending connotations of the concept does not fit well with the importance many Danes seem to ascribe to local elections. In the UK, Miller (1988) has asked if local elections are 'irrelevant elections'; the answer to that question in Denmark would be a no. With more than 70 per cent of eligible voters turning out on election day to vote for one of the many parties and candidates running locally, it is hard to see local elections as being irrelevant. However, with a turnout at parliamentary elections consistently 15 percentage points higher, there is still some room for improvement. This not least in the larger municipalities since the turnout gap is higher the larger the municipality.

The overall conclusion from the analyses in the chapter is somewhat paradoxical: in Danish local elections, the party system is quite nationalized, while at the same time, the voting is rather localized. The local party system tends to resemble the national party system (and more and more so) with local lists being almost squeezed out by the nationwide parties present in the *Folketinget*. This is also the case in the mayoral offices with the two major parties at the local level the Social Democrats and the Liberal Party victorious most places. However, at the same time, a clear majority of the voters tend to cast their vote in the local elections based on local candidates and local political issues. Seven in ten of the voters include local issues, and almost three in ten end up splitting their vote by voting for another party than the one they would have voted for if there had been a national election on the same day.

We do not know why we find this localized voting within a nationalized party system, but it is probably based on voters as well as the central party organizations 'making room' for the local branches of the political parties and their candidates. Some voters seem not to have a rigid interpretation of what it means for a group of local candidates to run under the label of one of the nationwide parties—if the candidates or the key issues they promote align with the voter's preferences, in many cases that seems to override the preferred party choice of the voter. The same goes for the central party organizations, with party discipline seeming quite loose during both the campaigns and the electoral term. Councillors and even mayors can be out of line with the central party leadership without serious consequences.

At the local elections in 2005 when the Danes were to vote for the first time within a new local political structure with a reduced number of units at the municipal and regional level, there was quite a lot of discussion as to how this would affect local democracy in general, and more specifically, local elections. As demonstrated in Figure 24.1, the reform did influence the local party system, leaving it more nationalized. But the tendency to participate in local elections and not least to cast a localized vote did not change significantly. Some pundits saw the larger municipalities and regions as threatening local democracy since the 'distance between voters and politicians' would increase. However, there might have been an opposite effect. Reif and Schmitt (1980) write that local elections are evaluated negatively because there is 'less at stake', but the amalgamation reform strengthened the municipalities (and weakened the regions) so that there is now 'more at stake' in the municipalities. Despite institutional changes, 'localized voting within a nationalized party system' seems to be an embedded feature of Danish local elections.

REFERENCES

Aars, Jacob, and Hans-Erik Ringkjøb (2005). 'Party politicisation reversed? Non-partisan alternatives in Norwegian local politics', *Scandinavian Political Studies*, 28/2: 161–82.

Bäck, Henry (2003). 'Party politics and the common good in Swedish local government', *Scandinavian Political Studies*, 26/2: 93–123.

Bækgaard, Martin, Jørgen Elklit, and Ulrik Kjaer (2017). 'Den stadig ikke helt fuldendte landspolitisering af de lokale partisystemer', in Jørgen Elklit, Christian Elmelund-Præstekær, and Ulrik Kjaer, eds, *KV13. Analyser af kommunalvalget 2013*. Odense: University Press of Southern Denmark, 265–79.

Berg, Rikke, and Ulrik Kjaer (2007). *Lokalt politisk lederskab*. Odense: University Press of Southern Denmark.

Bhatti, Yosef, Jens O. Dahlgaard, Jørgen Elklit, and Kasper M. Hansen (2017). 'Hvorfor steg valgdeltagelsen?', in Jørgen Elklit, Christian Elmelund-Præstekær, and Ulrik Kjaer, eds, *KV13. Analyser af kommunalvalget 2013*. Odense: University Press of Southern Denmark, 113–32.

Bhatti, Yosef, Jørgen Elklit, and Kasper M. Hansen (2013). 'Hvorfor faldt valgdeltagelsen?', in Jørgen Elklit and Ulrik Kjaer, eds, *KV09. Analyser af kommunalvalget 2009*. Odense: University Press of Southern Denmark, 61–79.

Bhatti, Yosef, and Kasper M. Hansen (2019). 'Voter turnout and municipal amalgamations— Evidence from Denmark', *Local Government Studies*, 45/5: 697–723.

Dahlerup, Drude (1988). 'From a small to a large minority. Women in Scandinavian politics', *Scandinavian Political Studies*, 11: 275–98.

Elklit, Jørgen, Sune W. Hansen, and Robert Klemmensen (2017). 'Kommunale konstitueringskoalitioner: spiller "kernekoalitioner" alligevel den centrale rolle?', in Jørgen Elklit, Christian Elmelund-Præstekær, and Ulrik Kjaer, eds, *KV13. Analyser af kommunalvalget 2013*. Odense: University Press of Southern Denmark, 305–22.

Elklit, Jørgen, and Ulrik Kjaer (2005). 'Are Danes more inclined to ticket splitting than the Swedes and the English?', *Scandinavian Political Studies*, 28/2: 125–39.

Hansen, Kasper M. (2018). 'Valgdeltagelsen ved kommunal- og regionsvalget 2017', *CVAP working paper series* 1/2018. Copenhagen: Department of Political Science, University of Copehagen.

Hansen, Kasper M. (2020). 'Electoral turnout. Strong social norms of voting', in Peter M. Christiansen, Jørgen Elklit, and Peter Nedergard, eds, *The Oxford Handbook of Danish Politics*. Oxford: Oxford University Press, 76–87.

Houlberg, Kurt, and Niels Ejersbo (2020). 'Municipalities and regions. Approaching the limit of decentralization?', in Peter M. Christiansen, Jørgen Elklit, and Peter Nedergard, eds, *The Oxford Handbook of Danish Politics*. Oxford: Oxford University Press, 141–59.

Kjaer, Ulrik (1999). 'Saturation without parity: The stagnating number of female councillors in Denmark', in Erik Beukel, Kurt K. Klausen, and Poul E. Mouritsen, eds, *Elites, Parties and Democracy. Festschrift for Professor Mogens N. Pedersen*. Odense: University Press of Southern Denmark, 149–68.

Kjær, Ulrik (2010). 'Women in politics – The local-national gender gap in comparative perspective', *Politische Vierteljahresschrift Sonderhefte*, 44: 334–51.

Kjaer, Ulrik, and Jørgen Elklit (2010a). 'Local party system nationalisation: Does municipal size matter?', *Local Government Studies*, 36/3: 425–44.

Kjaer, Ulrik, and Jørgen Elklit (2010b). 'Party politicization of local councils: Cultural or institutional explanations for trends in Denmark (1966–2005)', *European Journal of Political Research*, 49: 337–58.

Kjaer, Ulrik, and Jørgen Elklit (2014). 'The impact of assembly size on representativeness', *Journal of Legislative Studies*, 20/2: 156–73.

Kjaer, Ulrik, and Sune W. Hansen (2020). 'Appendiks', in preparation for Ulrik Kjaer, and Sune W. Hansen, eds, *KV17. Analyser af kommunalvalget 2017*. Odense: University Press of Southern Denmark.

Kjaer, Ulrik, and Mona L. Krook (2019). 'The blame game: Analyzing gender bias in Danish local elections', *Politics, Groups, and Identities*, 7/2: 444–55.

Kjaer, Ulrik, and Niels Opstrup (2018). *Danske borgmestre 1970–2018*. Det Samfundsvidenskabelige Fakultet, Syddansk Universitet, Kommunalpolitiske Studier Nr. 33/2018.

Kjaer, Ulrik, and Kristof Steyvers (2017). 'Kommunalvalg i landspolitikkens skygge?', in Jørgen Elklit, Christian Elmelund-Præstekær, and Ulrik Kjaer, eds, *KV13. Analyser af kommunalvalget 2013*. Odense: University Press of Southern Denmark, 21–42.

Kjaer, Ulrik, and Kristof Steyvers (2019). 'Second thoughts on second-order? Towards a second-tier model of local government elections and voting', in Richard Kerley, Joyce Liddle, and Pamela T. Dunning, eds, *The Routledge Handbook of International Local Government*. London: Routledge, 405–17.

Local Election Act [Valgloven for kommuner og regioner] (2018). Lovbekendtgørelse LBK nr. 1030 af 06/07/2018.

Miller, William L. (1988). *Irrelevant Elections? The Quality of Local Democracy in Britain*. Oxford: Oxford University Press.

Oliver, J. Eric (2012). *Local Elections and the Politics of Small-Scale Democracy*. Princeton, NJ: Princeton University Press.

Reif, Karlheinz, and Hermann Schmitt (1980). 'Nine second-order national elections – A conceptual framework for the analysis of European election results', *European Journal of Political Research*, 8/1: 3–44.

Rokkan, Stein (1966). 'Electoral mobilization, party competition and national integration', in Joseph LaPalombara and Myron Weiner, eds, *Political Parties and Political Developments*. Princeton, NJ: Princeton University Press, 241–65.

Serritzlew, Søren, Asbjørn Skjæveland, and Jens Blom-Hansen (2008). 'Explaining oversized coalitions: Empirical evidence from local governments', *The Journal of Legislative Studies*, 14/4: 421–50.

Skjæveland, Asbjørn, and Søren Serritzlew (2010). 'Which party gets the mayoralty? A multivariate statistical investigation of Danish local government formation', *Scandinavian Political Studies*, 33/2: 189–206.

Statistics Denmark (2018). *Valgene til kommunalbestyrelser og regionsråd 21. november 2017*. Copenhagen: Statistics Denmark.

Verhelst, Tom, Herwig Reynaert, and Kristof Steyvers (2013). 'Political recruitment and career development of local councilors in Europe', in Björn Egner, David Sweeting, and Pieter-Jan Klok, eds, *Local councilors in Europe*. Wiesbaden: Springer VS, 27–50.

CHAPTER 25

REFERENDUMS IN DENMARK

Influence on Politics

DEREK BEACH

REFERENDUMS IN DENMARK

REFERENDUMS are a relatively frequently used instrument in Danish politics.[1] While Danish plebiscites on EU matters are best known outside of Denmark's borders,[2] there have also been a range of national and subnational referendums held in Denmark. This chapter first presents the formal rules regarding the use of referendums in Denmark, followed by a brief history of Danish referendums since 1913. Given that almost all academic research on Danish referendums has focused on EU referendums, and that referenda are still a very active part of Danish EU politics, the rest of the chapter focuses on why EU-related referendums have been convened, the effects of campaigns, how voters behave, and the effects of referendum outcomes—in particular, no votes and how they can lead to opt-outs and even exit from the Union, as in the case of Greenland after the 1982 referendum.

THE RULES FOR REFERENDUMS IN DENMARK

There are six ways in which referendums can be convened at the national level in Denmark. The first five are regulated by the Constitution:

1. Amendments to the Constitution (Section 88)
2. Changes to the voting age (Section 29)
3. Transfer of sovereignty (Section 20)

4. Approval of certain legislative acts (Section 42)
5. Approval of international treaty (Section 42, Subsection 6)
6. Voluntary, consultative referendum (no constitutional provisions)

At the national level, there are two situations in which referendums are required without exception in the current (1953) Danish Constitution: changes to the voting age (Section 29) and to ratify amendments to the Constitution (Section 88). The latest amendment to the Constitution was in 2009 to change the rules on royal succession so that male and female children were treated equally. After legislative approval was given before and after an election, the change was approved in a referendum held in conjunction with the 2009 European Parliament election in Denmark.

There are also three other ways in which referendums can be required according to the 1953 Constitution. When Denmark transfers sovereignty to international organizations (e.g. the EU), if the ratifying act is not adopted by a 5/6th majority in Parliament but a parliamentary majority supports it, it can be sent instead to a binding referendum (Section 20). The Danish Ministry of Justice determines whether there is a transfer of sovereignty according to Section 20. Based on the original guidelines set down when Denmark joined the EU, transfers of sovereignty are defined as involving the introduction of new policy competences or the creation of new authorities, whereas changing how decisions are taken in an existing policy area (e.g. from unanimity to majority voting) are not. Both the Treaties of Nice and Lisbon were, therefore, interpreted by the Ministry of Justice as not containing any transfers of sovereignty in the areas applicable to Denmark and were ratified as normal laws.

Another route to referendums is if one-third of the members of Parliament appeal to the chairman of Parliament, they can have the approval of certain types of legislative measures sent to a referendum (Section 42, Subsection 1).[3] The same procedure can be used to adopt a law that states that international treaties should be ratified using a referendum (Section 42, Subsection 6).

Table 25.1 lists all of the national referendums that have been convened in Denmark since the introduction of referendums in 1915 in the Danish Constitution.[4]

The possibility of binding referendums at the municipal level has been introduced in new regulations for the municipal level in 2018. A municipal council can, by a simple majority, decide to send a measure in which they have competence to a binding plebiscite vote.

Finally, while there are no constitutional provisions for it, consultative referendums can be convened both at the national level and subnational level (regions and municipalities). At the national level, this has been used twice: once in connection with the sale of the Danish West Indies (today US Virgin Islands) to the United States in 1916 and again in 1986 for the Single European Act. At the subnational level, consultative referendums have been called by municipalities proposing to merge with other municipalities.

At the national level, only Danish citizens 18 years or older can vote in referendums. According to Section 42, Subsection 5 of the Danish Constitution, for a referendum motion to be rejected, it must have a majority of voters against it who represent at least

Table 25.1. National Referenda in Denmark since 1915

	Date	Required constitutionally?	Turnout	Yes votes	Ratified
Sale of the Danish West Indies	14 December 1916	No (Law no. 294 of 30 September 1916)	37.4%	64.2%	Yes
Constitutional amendment	6 September 1920	Yes (Section 93 of 1915 Constitution)	49.6%	96.9%	Yes
Constitutional amendment	23 May 1939	Yes (Section 94 of 1915 Constitution with changes from 1920)	48.9%	91.9%	No
Constitutional amendment	28 May 1953	Yes (Section 94 of 1915 Constitution with changes from 1920)	59.1%	78.8%	Yes
Voter age from 25 to 23 or 21	28 May 1953	Yes (Law no. 50 dealing with referendum for ratifying 1953 Constitution)	57.1%	54.6%	Yes (for 23)
Voter age from 23 to 21	30 May 1961	Yes (Section 29 of the 1953 Constitution)	37.3%	55.0%	Yes
Land laws (four measures)	25 June 1963	Yes (Section 42(1) of the 1953 Constitution)	73%	38.4%, 38.6%, 39.6% and 42.6%	No
Voter age from 21 to 18	24 June 1969	Yes (Section 29 of the 1953 Constitution)	63.6%	21.4%	No
Voter age from 21 to 20	21 September 1971	Yes (Section 29 of the 1953 Constitution)	86.2%	56.5%	Yes
Accession to EU	2 Oct 1972	Yes (Section 20 of the 1953 Constitution)	90.1%	63.3%	Yes
Voter age from 20 to 18	19 September 1978	Yes (Section 29 of the 1953 Constitution)	63.2%	53.8%	Yes
Single European Act	27 Feb 1986	No (consultative—Law no. 24 of 5 February 1986)	75.4%	56.2%	Yes
Maastricht I	2 June 1992	Yes (Section 20 of the 1953 Constitution)	83.1%	49.3%	No
Maastricht II (Edinburgh Agreement)	18 May 1993	Partially (5/6 majority present and therefore could not use Section 20, but ratifying law mandated approval by referendum following Section 42, Subsection 6 of the 1953 Constitution)	86.5%	56.7%	Yes
Amsterdam	28 May 1998	Yes (Section 20 of the 1953 Constitution)	76.2%	55.1%	Yes

(continued)

Table 25.1. Continued

	Date	Required constitutionally?	Turnout	Yes votes	Ratified
Euro accession (opt-out)	28 Sept 2000	Yes (Section 20 of the 1953 Constitution)	87.6%	46.8%	No
Constitutional change (order of royal succession)	7 June 2009	Yes (Law no. 170 of 27 March 1953)	58.3%	85.3%	Yes
European Patent Court	25 May 2014	Yes (Section 20 of the 1953 Constitution)	55.9%	62.5%	Yes
Justice & Home Affairs opt-out	3 Dec 2015	Yes (Section 20 of the 1953 Constitution)	72.0%	46.9%	No

Note: EU-related referendums are shaded light grey.
Source: Danmarks Statistik (2017: 56).

30 per cent of all eligible voters. Changes to the Constitution (Section 88) have to be approved by a majority who represent at least 40 per cent of all eligible voters. Eligibility to vote in referendums at the municipal level are decided by each municipality, although they have typically allowed voters eligible to vote in normal municipal elections to participate. This means, for instance, that EU citizens who are residents of a municipality can also vote, as well as non-EU citizens who have three or more years of residency.

There are no specific laws regulating referendum campaigns, but the government has to follow normal Danish practice as regards the use of the civil service (e.g. practices codified in parliamentary report no. 1443/2004), which, for instance, means that the administration (civil servants or ministers) cannot release non-truthful material (*sandhedspligt*) to the public. Complaints can be lodged to the Danish Ombudsman or courts. During a campaign, political ads cannot be brought on TV, but commercial radio stations and newspapers can bring political messages. Public service radio and TV have to give equal access to different organized groups, as do publicly funded information material.

WHY ARE (EU) REFERENDUMS CONVENED?

The first key distinction in the academic literature on why EU referendums are convened is whether they are *discretionary or required* (Oppermann 2013). Of the eight EU-related referendums in Denmark since 1972 (Table 25.1), seven have been binding, based on Section 20 of the Constitution. The 1993 referendum on Maastricht II was a peculiar case because there was a clear transfer of sovereignty based on Section 20, but there was also a 5/6th majority present for ratification. For political reasons, it was decided to send the national laws ratifying the Treaty of Maastricht with the Edinburgh clarifications agreed in December 1992 to a binding referendum, based on the rules of Section 42 of the Constitution.

The literature identifies two sets of reasons for why *discretionary* referendums are held. First, referendums can be held for domestic reasons (e.g. due to domestic constraints, as in the case of British PM Cameron promising a referendum in a speech in 2013) or for European reasons (e.g. to boost the negotiating power of a government in a treaty reform because the final outcome has to be ratified in a referendum). Second, referendums can be convened for defensive (e.g. avoiding potential losses) or offensive reasons (e.g. to promote particular objectives). Categorized along these two dimensions, the 1986 ratification of the Single European Act (SEA) can be viewed as a domestic-based decision that was used in an offensive manner by the Schlüter-led, centre-right minority government to sidestep Social Democratic opposition. During the course of the SEA negotiations, there had been efforts by the Schlüter government to keep the Social Democratic Party on board (Petersen 2006: 382–90). However, due to deep disagreements within the party, the Social Democratic leadership decided in January 1986 to recommend voting against the SEA in Parliament (Petersen 2006: 388–90). The 'No' vote left the Schlüter government with three options: either call a parliamentary election, ask the other EU countries to re-negotiate, or convene a consultative referendum. After preliminary inquiries with other EU countries showed significant opposition to re-negotiation, the Schlüter government declared that because the SEA did not involve the transfer of sovereignty, it could convene a consultative referendum (Petersen 2006: 391). After the Social Democrats declared they would respect the outcome of a referendum, the path was paved for the 27 February 1986 referendum and the subsequent ratification after the successful referendum.

DO CAMPAIGNS MATTER?

EU referendums often deal with quite complex topics that do not typically map onto normal national political cleavages, meaning that this is a context in which we might expect that campaigns could matter more than they do in national election contexts (de Vreese 2007; Hobolt 2006). Campaigns can be defined as all of the activities that provide information that inform voters about the proposition under consideration, frame how issues are understood, prime particular aspects of the issue, and potentially persuade voters to change their underlying attitudes.

In situations where the issue is relatively unknown to voters and/or where partisan and ideological conflicts on the issue do not mirror more familiar patterns from regular national elections, voters lack signposts that can help guide them to forming opinions on the issue. In this situation, campaign events and how issues are framed by media and political elites can be very important, shifting public opinion on the issue in the short term in ways that can affect the final outcome. In contrast, at the other extreme, in situations where voters are familiar with EU-related issues, campaigns merely provide information that enable voters to decide based on their underlying, non-malleable issue attitudes, resulting in voter stability.

Research on campaigns has tended to focus on media effects, how priming/framing of issues matters, and the importance of elite cues (e.g. partisan endorsements). Regarding the impact of media coverage per se, de Vreese and Semetko (2004) found in the 2000 Danish euro referendum that voter exposure to specific newspapers and public broadcasting had an impact on how they voted, although the magnitude of the effects found was not very large. Information provided by campaigns can also frame issues in terms of how voters perceive the benefits of the proposition in relation to what happens in the event of a no vote (the reversion point). In the 2000 campaign, the yes side focused their arguments on the economic benefits of joining the euro. However, when this argument was discredited by many experts, the yes side struggled to formulate a convincing alternative argument for why Denmark should join the euro (de Vreese and Semetko 2004). There was a similar dynamic in the 2015 Danish referendum on replacing the Justice and Home Affairs (JHA) opt-out with an opt-in model. The core yes-side argument was that the opt-in model had to be adopted in order for Denmark to remain in Europol after the legal base became community based. However, when the no side and some experts argued that a form of Europol membership was also possible in the event of a no vote because Denmark could negotiate an intergovernmental parallel agreement, this left the yes side without clear arguments in favour of removing the opt-out.

Elite cues can provide voters with heuristic shortcuts that can enable them to make an informed choice 'as if' they had all of the relevant knowledge that would enable them to choose the option that best matches their underlying attitudes (Lupia and McCubbins 1998). Most voters do not possess deep 'expert' understanding of the issues involved in an EU referendum, nor do they have motivations to undertake an exhaustive information search in order to update their information. Instead, research suggests that voters tend to rely on low-cost cognitive shortcuts and different heuristics in order to make sense of the issues in referendums (Hobolt 2006; Lupia and McCubbins 1998). A reliance on cues and endorsements can lead voters to make a decision that reflects the position of the party they normally vote for instead of their own issue attitudes (Hobolt 2006). In the Danish Maastricht referendums in 1992 and 1993, Hobolt (2006) finds that reliance on party endorsements also means that parties can frame the meaning of the choice that voters face—either by making the proposition appear to be more attractive or the reversion point in the event of a no vote less attractive. When comparing the two referendums, she finds evidence that yes parties succeeded in the second vote in 1993 in framing the proposition as more beneficial and the implications of a second no vote as more negative, making supporters of yes parties more prone to support the proposition in comparison to the first referendum.

VOTER BEHAVIOUR: ISSUE VOTING VERSUS SECOND-ORDER ELECTIONS

What factors determine voter choice in EU-related referendums? The core debate in the literature is whether citizens actually decide in relation to their underlying attitudes toward the EU and/or the proposition itself (issue voting), or whether they decide based on other considerations like governmental popularity (second order). This section explores the debate between second-order and issue-voting theories and the evidence for both in the Danish context. First, many scholars claim that voter behaviour in referendums on EU matters is similar to normal elections where voters decide based upon their underlying attitudes towards the issues (Merrill and Grofman 1999; Svensson 1994, 2002; Hobolt 2006, 2009). Early versions of the *issue-voting model* as regards EU referendums argued that voter choice was based upon voters' *general attitudes* towards European integration (Svensson 1994, 2002), whereas more recent formulations focus more explicitly on voter attitudes towards the *specific question* they are posed (e.g. Hobolt 2006, 2009). Hobolt has proposed the most ambitious issue-voting model as regards EU referendums (2006, 2009), where she draws upon a rational choice proximity model where the median voter decides based upon the relative location of his/her ideal point (IP) in relation to the proposition and the reversion point (RP) in the event of a no vote. When the proposition is closer to the median voter's IP than the RP, the voter will vote yes, and vice versa.

In contrast, many scholars and commentators claim that EU referendums are perceived by ordinary citizens as abstract and relatively unimportant affairs, meaning that we should not expect voters to expend the cognitive resources required to evaluate the proposition and the reversion point in relation to their underlying attitudes towards European integration (Franklin 2002; Franklin et al. 1994; Reif and Schmitt 1980; Ivaldi 2006). Instead, voters can be expected to treat an EU referendum as a second order election in which they signal their level of satisfaction with the performance of the government (Franklin 2002; Franklin et al. 1994; Reif and Schmitt 1980; Ivaldi 2006). A popular government will be able to steer a proposition to ratification because a majority of voters will trust that the government will only endorse it if it is good for the country, and vice versa (Franklin et al. 1994: 102). Second-order dynamics should be particularly dominant in low salience referendums (Franklin 2002).

There is some disagreement about the exact causes and mechanisms of the second-order election thesis. At the core is the argument that when voters feel little is at stake, they either abstain from voting (resulting in lower turnout), or if they decide to vote, they merely utilize heuristics drawn from first-order national affairs (Hix and Marsh 2011; Hobolt and Brouard 2011). This could involve using attitudes towards government performance or attitudes to national political issues to punish unpopular incumbents (Hix and Marsh 2011; Hobolt and Brouard 2011). Irrespective of the specific mechanisms, the results of the second-order dynamics are the same: when going to the polls in European referendums, the argument is that voters focus on how they feel about national politics rather than how they feel about European integration.

Is there evidence for issue-voting behaviour, or have Danes treated EU referendums as second-order affairs? In the following, I first discuss cross-case patterns, followed by a more detailed discussion of the 1992/93 switch, and the most recent no vote in 2015.

Based on the post-referendum surveys in six EU referendums (1972, 1986, 1992, 1993, 1998, and 2000), Hobolt (2009: 71–2) finds that Danish voters based their choices on their EU attitudes, with some impact of partisan endorsements also. Svensson (2002) finds little evidence of second-order effects in a comparative analysis of five referendums (1972, 1986, 1992, 1993, and 1998). Given the salience of EU referendums in Denmark—evidenced by the relatively high levels of turnout and amount of public debate—it is perhaps not surprising that issue voting tends to dominate voting behaviour.

The 1992/1993 Referendums

The Danes shocked the EU by voting no to the Treaty of Maastricht by a narrow margin on 2 June 1992 (50.7 per cent no), but then ratified the same treaty with a series of political declarations (Edinburgh Agreement) attached to it on 18 May 1993 (56.7 per cent yes). Both referendums were high turnout, meaning that the difference cannot be explained by higher turnout in the second referendum, as happened in the Irish Nice referendums. What then can explain why some voters switched from voting no to yes? Was the difference due to: the change to a more popular Social Democrat-led government; changes in the proposition itself ('Maastricht without thorns'); and/or whether voters viewed the consequences of voting no in the second referendum as being too high? The analysis first describes the situation leading to the referendums and traces the course of the two campaigns. The analysis then assesses whether post-election surveys can shed light on what factors were most important in accounting for the different outcomes.

If the different outcomes can be explained by second-order factors, we would expect that the unpopular government being replaced by a more popular Social Democrat-led government in early 1993 can explain the difference (Franklin et al. 1994: 120). There is, however, little evidence supporting this explanation. During the 1992 campaign, the Social Democrats were still reeling from the recent bitter leadership battle, leading to a disjointed campaign to convince their voters (Hobolt 2006). However, the two parties in the incumbent Conservative-led government were actually *more popular* in 1992 than in the most recent election. In the 1990 parliamentary election, they had won 31.8 per cent of votes, whereas in spring of 1992, their net support was around 35 per cent (Svensson 2002: 740). In the spring of 1993, the Social Democrats were united behind their new party leader and now prime minister. But if second-order factors could explain the no/yes switch, we would expect that Conservative and Liberal voters would be more likely to vote no in protest against their parties losing power, but as can be seen in Table 25.2 the yes percentage for both parties is basically unchanged in 1993.

Table 25.2. Yes Vote by Party Preference

	1972 Accession	1986 Single European Act	1992 Maastricht I	1993 Maastricht II
Social Democrat	58	23	35	48
Social Liberals (RV)	73	78	68	61
Conservative	89	94	74	80
Socialist Peoples' Party (SF)	16	7	10	19
Liberals (V)	94	94	87	84

Sources: 1972 (Elklit et al. 1979), 1986 (Borre et al. 1986), 1992, and 1993 (Hobolt 2009: 181).

Research has found that there were two differences that mattered: changes in perceptions of the costs and benefits of voting yes and the more united campaign of the Social Democrats (partisan endorsements). Regarding perceptions of the treaty, the yes side was arguably successful in framing the second referendum as pulling out the more polit-ical thorns of unpopular issues from the Treaty of Maastricht (Siune et al. 1994). In both post-election surveys, voters were quite supportive of more 'economic' issues (Internal Market), whereas they were opposed to integration in areas that can be interpreted as being more 'political'. This is illustrated in Table 25.3, where it can be seen that the areas encompassed by the clarifications included in the Edinburgh Agreement are all quite unpopular.

Analysis of the marginal effects of EU attitudes and partisanship has found a large effect of variance in EU attitudes on vote choice, whereas variation in partisanship had smaller marginal effects (Hobolt 2006: 634). In Hobolt's study, there is evidence that suggests that the most important driver of the switch in votes from no to yes was more positive interpretations of the treaty, although the evidence does not enable us to deter-mine whether this is because voters thought the political 'thorns' were removed with the EA, or whether voters were scared of the negative consequences that a second no vote was widely perceived to have. In all, 52 per cent of voters stated that their motivation for voting yes was based upon concerns about the costs of no in 1993, with the most com-mon answers being 'Denmark cannot survive without the EC', 'avoid isolation of Denmark', and 'we cannot continue to vote no' (Siune et al. 2001).

No Votes in Opt-Out Referendums: The 2015 No Vote

Danish voters have rejected removing opt-outs in two referendums: joining the com-mon currency in September 2000 and the Justice and Home Affairs (JHA) opt-out in December 2015. In this section, I focus on the JHA opt-out referendum in December 2015, exploring why a majority of Danes voted no. The original JHA opt-out was part of the Edinburgh clarifications that were later incorporated into the treaties through a protocol to the Treaty of Amsterdam that stated that Denmark would only take part in

Table 25.3. Voter Attitudes towards Different Issue
Areas, 1992 and 1993

	June 1992	May 1993
Internal Market	74	74
Removal of trade barriers	69	65
Economic and Monetary Union	53	42
Reducing economic differences in Europe	49	43
Common foreign policy	38	37
Common currency	34	23
Common defence policy	30	34
United States of Europe	19	21
Union citizenship	13	14

Source: Siune et al. (1994).

JHA cooperation on an intergovernmental basis, which at the time meant that Denmark did not take part in issues like the common asylum and immigration policy, but did take part in police (e.g. Europol) and legal cooperation. When the Treaty of Lisbon moved the rest of JHA cooperation into the supranational first pillar in December 2014, this meant that Denmark would no longer be able to take part in police and legal cooperation , in which a broad majority of pro-EU Danish elites wanted to participate. As a consequence, when the Treaty of Lisbon was being negotiated, the Danish government had negotiated a British-style opt-in protocol that would enable a majority in the Danish Parliament to decide on a case-by-case basis whether to join supranational JHA legal acts or remain outside in order to avoid having the status quo of having to leave these areas of cooperation and then negotiate legally and politically difficult 'parallel agreements' that would enable Denmark to participate in an intergovernmental fashion.

However, moving a policy area from intergovernmental to supranational cooperation involved a clear transfer of sovereignty based on the Ministry of Justice's definition. Therefore, to avoid having to engage in a Section 20 procedure (5/6th majority or a referendum) every time Denmark joined a new supranational JHA act, the new protocol was to be ratified domestically in a manner where the full transfer of sovereignty in all areas of JHA would happen only once—i.e. when the protocol itself was ratified. If the opt-in protocol was ratified, the decision to join a supranational JHA act would then only be based on approval by a parliamentary majority.[5]

An agreement was reached in March 2015 between the then Social Democrat/Social Liberal government and the other major yes parties (Conservatives, Liberals, and Socialist People's Party) that stated that a referendum should be held in the near future to activate the new Lisbon opt-in protocol. At the same time, the parties agreed that Denmark would stay out of existing supranational asylum and immigration legal acts (except the Dublin Regulation and EURODAC) and only join new acts in this area if all of the parties agreed to it. In other areas of JHA, it was decided that Denmark would join twenty-two JHA acts and stay out of the rest and that in the future, they would decide on a case-by-case basis as regards new acts. However, the problem with this agreement was that it was not legally binding on future parliaments, meaning that there was always the risk that a future parliamentary majority decided to opt-in to JHA areas that were opposed by majorities of voters (e.g. the common asylum and immigration policies).

The JHA opt-out issue was highly salient in Denmark because it was related to one of the four Danish opt-outs that were originally agreed in relation to the Treaty of Maastricht. This meant that it was viewed as part of the core of the Danish special relationship with the EU, making it very sensitive for sovereignty-conscious Danish voters. In addition, while the twenty-two legal acts that the yes majority in the Danish Parliament stated that it would join if the proposition was ratified were relatively unimportant, the most salient issue for many voters was one that the yes majority said it would *not* join in the foreseeable future—the common EU asylum and immigration policies. Here, the crucial difference between before and after a potential yes vote was that with the existing opt-out, Denmark could only join the common asylum and immigration policy with either a 5/6th majority or a new referendum, but with the new opt-in, a mere parliamentary majority could decide to join at a later date without convening a Section 20 mandated referendum. This difference proved to be a major strategic mistake from the yes side because it gifted the no side a winning argument: could voters trust the yes majority in Parliament to *not* join the asylum and immigration policy in the future without convening a referendum? Danes were split on the issue of joining the common asylum and immigration policies (44 per cent in favour, 37 per cent opposed, and 19 per cent undecided or 'don't know'), with a majority of left-wing voters in favour and right-wing voters opposed to joining (Beach 2016).

After a narrow victory in the June 2015 parliamentary election, a new Liberal minority government was formed. The new government, with the support of a large majority of pro-EU parties in Parliament, decided to call a referendum on 21 August, with the vote to be held on 3 December 2015. After the campaign had been running over two months, the Danish Prime Minister, on 6 October, tried to counter the no argument about potentially joining the common asylum and immigration policy in the future by promising that his party would not support joining it without convening a consultative referendum. But this promise was purely political and could not be legally binding on future governments or even his own party in the future. Further, the political promise was not perceived as very credible by many voters in a time of dramatically declining levels of trust in politicians in general (in particular amongst voters with Eurosceptic attitudes). The importance of remaining outside of the common asylum and immigration policy became even more salient for voters as the refugee crisis exploded in August and September of 2015.

The core yes-side argument was that the opt-in model had to be adopted in order for Denmark to remain in Europol after the legal base became community based. However, when the no-side and experts argued that a form of Europol membership was also possible in the event of a no vote because Denmark could negotiate an intergovernmental 'parallel agreement' that would allow participation, this left the yes side without clear arguments in favour of removing the opt-out. The referendum campaign was surprisingly low key, with political parties and organizations on both sides deploying relatively few resources. Another strategic mistake by the Danish government was that the campaign was occurring at the same time that they were negotiating their first budgetary law. This meant that top yes-side politicians were unable to dedicate time to the referendum campaign until after the budgetary law was passed in mid-November, leaving only two weeks for active campaigning by high-level politicians. As a result, there was little news coverage and few campaign events held prior to the referendum. Not surprisingly, there were record levels of undecided voters until the final weeks of the campaign. Ten days before the referendum, 35 per cent of voters were either 'very in doubt' or 'somewhat in doubt' (Beach 2016).

In the final vote on 3 December, the yes side was only able to win 46.9 per cent of votes, leading to the measure being rejected. What can explain the no vote? Analysis using a large post-election survey has shown that general EU attitudes, partisan endorsements, and second-order factors were all significantly correlated with the outcome (Beach 2017). Voters with more negative EU attitudes were more likely to vote no, whereas the effect of partisan endorsements was not as pronounced.[6] Second-order factors like approval of the sitting government had little impact on voter choice. The results provide evidence that suggests that voting behaviour in the JHA referendum was dominated by issue-voting, with a secondary impact of partisan endorsements. In other words, a majority of Danes voted no because they did not like the proposition (issue-voting).

THE EFFECTS OF EU REFERENDUMS

This section reviews what we know about the effects that the frequent use of EU referendums have had, focusing first on the internal effects in terms of keeping the EU issue outside of 'normal' Danish politics, followed by a discussion of the external effects in relation to Danish EU policy and Denmark's role in the EU. Finally, the section concludes with a discussion of the impact that the large percentage of no votes in the Faroe Islands and Greenland in the 1972 Accession referendum had on their relationship with Denmark, and the eventual exit of Greenland from the EU after its 1982 referendum.

Internal Effects: Keeping the EU Out of Domestic Politics

The use of referendums to settle major EU matters in Denmark has kept the issue out of domestic political debates. In parliamentary elections, there have been few—if any—sustained debates about EU matters. This has traditionally been very beneficial for the national parliamentary prospects of the Social Democratic Party. Until the mid-1990s, citizens who typically voted Social Democrat in parliamentary elections were split into equally large anti-EU and pro-EU camps (see Table 25.2). In addition, until the two

Maastricht referendums (92/93), Social Democratic politicians themselves have also been split regarding their views towards the EU, especially in relation to the Single European Act. As a result, having major EU matters decided in referendums meant that these disagreements did not spill over into national politics; in particular, they did not result in EU-sceptical voters choosing not to vote for the Social Democrats in national parliamentary elections.

External Effects: Opt-Outs (and Leaving the Union)

The frequent use of referendums in relation to treaty ratification (1986, 1992/93, and 1998) meant that Danish governments negotiating with EU partners always had to be cognizant that the final outcome would have to be approved in a referendum. This was most evident in the mid-1990s during the negotiation of the Treaty of Amsterdam where the most salient issues for the Danish government reflected priorities that could be used to sell the treaty domestically (Petersen 2006: 524–9).

Another effect of referendums was the introduction of opt-outs. During the negotiation of the Treaty of Maastricht in 1990–1, the centre-right Schlüter government pushed for an opt-out of the common currency (EMU) due to pressure from the opposition Social Democrats. A legally binding protocol was adopted that stated that Denmark had the right not to join the third phase of EMU. After the no vote in June 1992, the major yes parties entered into the so-called 'National compromise',[7] which mandated the Danish government to ask for certain clarifications related to the common currency, defence cooperation, justice and home affairs, and citizenship, along with an attempt to push for more 'openness' and subsidiarity. The UK Presidency negotiated directly with the Danish government—assisted by the Council Secretariat Legal Service—leading to the formulation of the four Danish opt-outs that were accepted at the Edinburgh European Council in December 1992 as the Edinburgh Agreement (EA). Denmark declared in the EA that it would utilize its right under the protocol not to join the third phase of EMU, although it could, of course, always reverse this decision later. The EA clarified further that there was nothing in the treaties that forced Denmark to join future supranational cooperation in Justice and Home Affairs (JHA), which, of course, was re-stating legal facts because all JHA cooperation at the time was intergovernmental and any change had to be adopted through an IGC by unanimity. Denmark also clarified that it was not obliged to take part in EU military actions, and therefore, would stay out of any potential future military cooperation. Finally, the EA made clear that the so-called Union citizenship provisions are not intended to replace national citizenship, which was also restating a legal (and political) fact.

The so-called four Danish opt-outs were born. Legally, the Treaty of Maastricht with the clarifications in the EA was not different from the proposition rejected in June 1992. However, the clarifications on JHA would later be turned into a legally binding opt-out protocol in the Treaty of Amsterdam because elements of JHA were made supranational (see above).[8] While Denmark has been able to associate itself with certain JHA measures through parallel intergovernmental agreements (e.g. Schengen), there are many areas in which Denmark cannot participate. Additionally, the EA clarification on military cooperation has kept Denmark outside of the EU's developing security policies.

Therefore, opt-outs have had the effect of keeping Denmark outside of three increasingly important areas of EU cooperation: the Eurozone, common asylum and immigration policies, and EU-led peacekeeping/making missions.

Internal and External Effects: No Votes and Greenlandic Exit from the EU

Referenda votes also had internal and external effects for the relationship between Denmark and the Faroe Islands and Greenland and their membership in the EU. As affiliated parts of Denmark, the 1972 Accession referendum was held in both the Faroe Islands and Greenland. In both territories, there were large percentages of no votes (Petersen 2006: 372). Given that the Faroe Islands already had self-governing status, the Faroe government was able to choose not to follow Denmark into the EU but instead entered into a free trade agreement.

In contrast, Greenland's status as a Danish county (*amt*) meant that Greenland followed Denmark into the EU in 1973, albeit with a 10-year transitional agreement to protect its fishing industry (Petersen 2006: 372–3). However, resistance to joining the EU had the important internal effect of significantly strengthening demands for autonomous status for Greenland, with the result in 1979 that after a referendum, Greenland was granted self-governing status within the realm of Denmark, albeit excluding fisheries policy. After an anti-EU party (*Siumut*) gained a number of seats in the 1979 Greenlandic parliamentary elections (*Landstinget*), pressure grew to hold an in/out referendum on Greenlandic EU membership. This resulted in the unanimous decision by the Greenlandic *Landstinget* in the spring of 1981 to convene a consultative referendum on the issue. During the subsequent referendum campaign, economic issues were very important. On the side of exit, the issue of fisheries played an important role, whereas the large amount of funds that Greenland received in regional support spoke for continued membership (Petersen 2006: 373).

A small majority voted for exit in the referendum on 23 February 1982 (52 per cent leave), after which the *Landstinget* gave the Greenlandic government (*Landstyret*) a mandate to ask the Danish government to leave the EU and instead gain privileged overseas country and territory status (OCT status). The Danish government then took these demands to Brussels. The European Commission, backed by West Germany and its strong fishing interests in Greenlandic waters, was reluctant to create a precedent in which Greenland received a relatively beneficial exit agreement (OCT status without giving fishing access in exchange) because there was a belief that exit should not benefit a country voluntarily asking to leave (Petersen 2006: 375–6). The Danish government countered that Greenland should not benefit but should also not be punished for leaving. Additionally, the Danish government argued that Greenland should also be cut more slack because of the important strategic role it played in the Cold War due to its hosting major US bases (Petersen 2006). The final deal granted Greenland OCT status, coupled with an agreement on fisheries.

Before the Brexit vote in 2016, the 1982 Greenlandic referendum was the only case in which a no vote led to a part of the EU asking to leave, illustrating that referenda can have very strong external effects. However, it is also important not to extrapolate too much from the Greenland (and Faroe Island) cases because of at least four important differences. First, the 'original Grexit' of Greenland could be framed in post-colonial terms, and there were a number of British and French former colonies that already had OCT status. Second, while many regions have different forms of autonomous status within EU countries like Germany (federal states) or Spain (semi-autonomous regions), there are no EU member countries in which it would be possible for a region or state to exit the EU *while* remaining a part of the country. Thirdly, the EU that Greenland left in 1982 was a much weaker association than today. Finally, Greenland's case for exit was represented by an existing member (Denmark), whereas in Brexit, it is the leaver negotiating with EU-27, creating very different power dynamics. Taken together, the 'precedence' created by the 'original Grexit' is therefore very limited.

Conclusion

While referendums have been frequently used in Denmark—in particular in EU matters, they are used much more frequently on all types of issues in countries like Switzerland and Ireland. In this respect, Denmark remains a strong parliamentary democracy but in which referenda are used at the national level for constitutional issues. Several referenda have been held on the voting age, and more minor matters relating to rules of royal succession. The most frequent use of referenda has been to decide EU matters, including accession and transfers of sovereignty in relation to new EU treaties. One of the reasons for the frequent use of referendums in EU affairs were the divisions among voters and elites within the Social Democratic Party, leading party elites to prefer to use referenda to decide major EU matters instead of having to ratify measures in Parliament that could have alienated large segments of the party. In all, eight EU-related referenda have been held.

EU referenda are typically not second-order affairs in Denmark, and there is strong evidence suggesting that direct democracy actually 'works', in that Danish voters tend to answer the questions they are actually asked (i.e. issue voting). Turnout has tended to be relatively high, in particular for the accession vote in 1972 (90.1 per cent) and for the euro in 2000 (87.6 per cent), suggesting that Danes found these issues very important. While issue-voting has dominated, research has also found that how issues are framed by the media and elites does have some impact, in particular when the reversion point in the event of a no vote is successfully framed as much less attractive than the proposition to be approved. Elite cues can also have some impact, although in several unsuccessful referenda (euro in 2000 and JHA in 2015), large majorities of elites recommended voting yes.

A consequence of the use of direct democracy in EU matters has been to create considerable constraints that have resulted in Denmark being on the sidelines of major areas of EU policy. For example, while a large majority of parliamentarians favoured Denmark joining the euro, after the failed 2000 referendum, Denmark has been relegated to the sidelines of the Eurozone. In another rapidly developing policy area, Justice and Home Affairs, the Danish government has also been forced to pursue second-best policies through intergovernmental agreements with the EU to enable Denmark to take part in areas like Schengen cooperation or Europol. These developments make it obvious that one of the consequences of asking the people is that the answer one gets might not be what one wanted to hear.

NOTES

1. Greenland was a county (*amt*) of Denmark at the time of the 1972 referendum.
2. The term EU is used throughout this chapter, although the proper term until 1994 was the European Community (EC).
3. A list of exceptions to the types of legislative measures that can be sent to plebiscites is listed in Section 42, Subsection 6. This includes the national budget and measures relating to taxation.
4. This list does not include the referendum in Southern Jutland in 1920 on the border and referenda in Iceland (1944), the Faroe Islands in 1946, and Greenland in 1978 and 1979 on the status of their relationships with Denmark. The chapter does later discuss the 1982 Greenland EU-exit referendum below.
5. In practice, given the history of minority governments in Denmark, there is an informal tradition that important EU matters are adopted using consensus amongst the major pro-EU parties.
6. A 0.5 standard deviation increase in negative EU attitudes increases the probability of voting no by 50 per cent, whereas the impact of partisan endorsements is slightly weaker (37 per cent).
7. The yes side now included the Socialist People's Party, who chose to change sides in order to gain influence on the terms of the Danish solution but also to pave the way for possible participation in an expected coming Social Democrat-led government.
8. The protocol was revised again with the Treaty of Lisbon when the rest of the EU's JHA policies were made supranational.

REFERENCES

Beach, Derek (2016). 'Undersøgelse om danskernes holdninger til retsforbeholdet.' Survey implemented by Epinion, Fall 2015.

Beach, Derek (2017). 'Denmark: A tale of two referendums – The Contrasts between low and high salience referendums in Denmark', in Fernando Mendez, and Mario Mendez, eds, *Referendums on EU matters*. European Parliament—Constitutional Affairs Committee Study, 174–87.

Borre, Ole, Hans Jørgen Nielsen, Steen Sauerberg, and Torben Worre (1986). *Folkeafstemningen om EF-pakken, 27. februar 1986,* Dansk Data Arkiv. 1 datafil: DDA-1192, version: 1.0.0.

Danmarks Statistik (2017). *Statistisk Årbog 2017.* Danmarks Statistik: Copenhagen, 56.

de Vreese, Claes H. (2007). 'Context, elites, media and public opinion in referendums: Why campaigns really matter', in Claes H. de Vreese, ed., *The Dynamics of Referendum Campaigns in International Perspective.* London: Palgrave, 1–20.

de Vreese, Claes, and Holli Semetko (2004). *Political Campaigning in Referendums: Framing the Referendum Issue.* London: Routledge.

Elklit, Jørgen, Nikolaj Petersen, Ole Tonsgaard, and Peter Hansen (1979). 'EF-undersøgelsen 1972 (før-efter)', Dansk Data Arkiv. 1 datafil: DDA-194, version: 1.0.0.

Franklin, Mark N. (2002). 'Learning from the Danish case: A comment on Palle Svensson's critique on the Franklin Thesis', *European Journal of Political Research,* 41/6: 751–7.

Franklin, Mark. N., Michael Marsh, and Christopher Wlezien (1994). 'Attitude towards Europe and referendum votes: A response to Siune and Svensson', *Electoral Studies,* 13/2: 117–21.

Hix, Simon, and Michael Marsh (2011). 'Second-order effects plus pan-European political swings: An analysis of European Parliament elections across time', *Electoral Studies,* 30/1: 4–15.

Hobolt, Sara B. (2006). 'How parties affect vote choice in European integration referendums', *Party Politics,* 12/5: 623–47.

Hobolt. Sara B. (2009). *Europe in Question: Referendums on European Integration.* Oxford: Oxford University Press.

Hobolt, Sara B., and Sylvain Brouard (2011). 'Contesting the European Union? Why the Dutch and French rejected the European Constitution', *Political Research Quarterly,* 64/2: 309–22.

Ivaldi, Gilles (2006). 'Beyond France's 2005 referendum on the European Constitutional Treaty: Second-Order Model, anti-establishment attitudes and the end of the alternative European utopia', *West European Politics,* 29/1: 47–69.

Lupia, Arthur, and Mathew D. McCubbins (1998). *The Democratic Dilemma. Can Citizens Learn What They Need to Know?* Cambridge: Cambridge University Press.

Merrill, Samuel III, and Bernard Grofman (1999). *A Unified Theory of Voting.* Cambridge: Cambridge University Press.

Oppermann, Kai (2013). 'The politics of discretionary government commitments to European integration referendums', *Journal of European Public Policy,* 20/5: 684–701.

Petersen, Nikolaj (2006). *Dansk Udenrigspolitiks Historie 6—Europæisk og globalt engagement 1973–2006.* Copenhagen: Gyldendal.

Reif, Karl H., and Hermann Schmitt (1980). 'Nine second-order national elections: A conceptual framework for the analysis of European election results', *European Journal of Political Research,* 8/1: 3–44.

Siune, Karen, Palle Svensson, and Ole Tonsgaard (1994). *Fra et nej til et ja.* Aarhus: Politica.

Siune, Karen, Ole Tonsgaard, and Palle Svensson (2001). 'Folkeafstemningen om Edinburghaftalen, 18 May 1993' Data set deposited as DDA-1784. Odense, Dansk Data Arkiv.

Svensson, Palle (1994). 'The Danish Yes to Maastricht and Edinburgh. The EC Referendum of May 1993', *Scandinavia Political Studies,* 17/1: 69–82.

Svensson, Palle (2002). 'Five Danish referendums on the European Community and European Union: A Critical assessment of the Franklin Thesis', *European Journal of Political Research,* 41/6: 733–50.

CHAPTER 26

MEDIA AND POLITICS

The Danish Media System in Transformation?

THOMAS OLESEN

DEMOCRACY AND THE CRISIS OF JOURNALISM

MEDIA and journalism are many things at the same time: businesses that must survive on a market; a profession with its own distinct norms, rules, and educational set-up; and not least, democratic watchdogs. From a political point of view, the watchdog role is prominent. The relationship between journalism and democracy is so deep in fact that Strömbäck (2005: 332) refers to it as a *social contract*: without journalism, there is no democracy, and vice versa.

This self-understanding as democratic watchdogs is pronounced among Danish journalists (Ahva et. al 2017; Willig et al. 2015) and deeply ingrained in the way citizens and politicians conceive of a well-functioning democracy. There are signs, however, that this historical position is being transformed and perhaps even eroded. Recent years have seen a burgeoning scholarly interest in what might be labelled the *crisis of journalism*, characterized by steady declines in readership, advertising revenues, trust, and challenges to professional authority. These developments have been set in motion at least partly by the new media consumption and production patterns in the media ecology of web 2.0 (Nielsen 2016). The crisis should be seen against the backdrop of what is now a well-established analysis: Western democracies have undergone a profound *mediatization* of politics and society over the last decades (Hjarvard 2013; Strömbäck 2008). This co-existence of media crisis and mediatization prompts two questions: is the crisis of journalism reversing the process of mediatization, and does it erode journalism's capacity to perform the role as democratic watchdogs?

The chapter follows a dual strategy. Reflecting the volume's ambition to provide an overview of existing research, the first two sections sketch major debates and findings in the literature on media and politics in Denmark. In the third and concluding sections, the chapter more directly tackles the question of media crisis to assess its impact on Danish democracy.

THE DANISH MEDIA SYSTEM IN A COMPARATIVE PERSPECTIVE

In their path-breaking comparative work on the media, Hallin and Mancini (2004) identify three distinct media models: a North Atlantic or Liberal Model with high degrees of commercialization and limited state intervention (the United States is the most prominent example); a Mediterranean or Polarized Pluralist Model with significant state involvement and limited professionalization (e.g. Spain, Italy, and France); and a Northern/Central European or Democratic Corporatist Model with a historical tradition of political parallelism (links between media and political parties or positions), state involvement through extensive public service sectors and media subsidies, high levels of circulation and readership, and strong degrees of journalistic professionalization. Hallin and Mancini place Denmark and countries such as Sweden, Norway, Finland, and Holland within this latter model. Danish media scholars have largely accepted Hallin and Mancini's overall characterization of the Danish media system (Allern and Blach-Ørsten 2011; Blach-Ørsten and Willig 2016) but also challenge some of their assumptions and observations (see below).

Early Danish newspapers displayed profound degrees of political parallelism. Most newspapers were economically and ideologically tied to the dominant political parties of the latter part of the nineteenth century and early part of the twentieth century (Allern and Blach-Ørsten 2011; Lund 2004). During the twentieth century, and especially from the 1950s onwards, this system began to erode. In a struggle for increased *professional autonomy*, newspapers detached themselves from their bonds to the political parties to become more generalist, independent, and critical in their orientation. Journalism, in parallel, underwent a profound professionalization. Ideals changed towards the journalist as an independent, objective watchdog whose primary job was to scrutinize power and expose wrongdoings (Schultz 2006).

The process of journalistic professionalization culminated in the 1970s with the establishment of the first school of journalism in Denmark (*Danmarks Journalisthøjskole*, known today as the Danish School of Media and Journalism, or DMJX). Despite the dissolution of the party-press system, Danish newspapers retain distinct political profiles, not in the sense of direct ideological or economic attachment to specific parties, but in their general orientation towards either the left or right. This orientation is strongly reflected in reader choices: Danish newspaper readers quite clearly base their newspaper selections on political preference (Hjarvard 2007).

Towards the end of their book, Hallin and Mancini (2004) speculate that the other media models will increasingly converge toward the Liberal Model. Allern and Blach-Ørsten (2011) concede that there are elements pointing in that direction (e.g. commercialization) but also argue strongly against a full convergence thesis. They take their primary evidence from the fact that despite the pressures against it in recent decades, the Danish public service sector (mainly represented by *Danmarks Radio*, or DR) continues to play a strong role in the Danish media market. In 2018, the news programmes of *Danmarks Radio* had a reach of 47 per cent of the Danish population, and DR stands as the most trusted news brand in Denmark (Schrøder et al. 2018: 25).

Equally important, Allern and Blach-Ørsten mention the continued prominence of state media subsidies in Denmark and the other Nordic countries. The most recent specification of media subsidies in Denmark shows that DKK 361,600,000 was channelled into the Danish media system in 2016 (Ministry of Culture 2018). It is a well-known fact that many Danish media organizations depend strongly on subsidies for their economic survival (Schrøder and Blach-Ørsten 2018: 74). The idea behind the state's media subsidies is anchored in the notion of the social contract between democracy and the media (Flensburg 2015; Strömbäck 2005). In the preparatory report for the most recent media subsidies law, the authors thus underline how the purpose of subsidies is to 'support the democratic, critical, and independent function of the media' (Libraries and Media Agency 2011: 4).

The character of the media system has various effects of political relevance. Research including Denmark, for example, shows how political knowledge in countries in the Democratic Corporatist Model (Denmark and Finland) is considerably higher than what is found in the Liberal Model (the United States and the United Kingdom) (Curran et al. 2009). The difference is mainly explained by the presence of strong public service sectors in the former model. Public service ensures a stable supply of high-quality news reporting that is consumed by large and diverse media audiences. An interesting corollary of this observation is that the gap between the politically interested and less interested is smaller in countries within the Democratic Corporatist Model than in the Liberal Model, particularly in the United States (Aalberg and Curran 2012). Again, public service broadcasting is seen as the decisive factor. The broad reach of public service in Denmark and other Northern European countries generate what Aalberg and Curran (2012: 47) refer to as 'inadvertent viewing' where a large proportion of the population receives at least a minimum level of quality news about politics. In the United States, Aalberg and Curran observe, it is much easier to compose a media diet that avoids news.

As these findings suggest, and as pointed out by Hallin and Mancini (2004), there are strong similarities between the Danish media system and those of the other Nordic countries. Ahva et al. (2017) confirm that there is a distinct Nordic conception of the media where journalists strongly emphasize the watchdog role, and importantly, express comparatively low levels of commercializing pressures in their daily work. Ahva et al. link these conceptions to the wider social and political context of the Nordic welfare state. The support for journalism emanating at the state level largely mirrors the distributive, universalist, and interventionist political philosophy of the Nordic welfare state. It shapes journalism in the form of protective laws, subsidies, and an extensive public service sector. This institutional set-up ensures a strong sense of journalistic autonomy where the profession is perceived as relatively insulated from political interference as well as from the brute force of market logics.

There are reasons to at least speculate that some of the democratic advantages of the Nordic model (e.g. high levels of political knowledge and high levels of journalistic autonomy) will decrease in the coming years. In the latest round of political negotiations over the future budget of *Danmarks Radio* in 2018, it was decided by a parliamentary majority of Liberal and Conservative parties to cut the budget by 20 per cent. This pressure on public service is also experienced in other countries with strong public service in Europe and is part of a wider trend of increasing economic challenges for the media sector (Ibarra et al. 2015) (see the section on 'The Crisis of Journalism' below).

The Media-Politics Nexus

Media and politics have always been intertwined. Historically, the balance of this nexus, however, has changed considerably. As discussed above, during the nineteenth and early twentieth centuries, Danish newspapers were largely tied to the logics and requirements of political parties. This balance began to change in the latter half of the twentieth century. Not only did the media increasingly detach themselves from the political system to acquire autonomy, their logics also began to shape the world of politics in new ways. This condition is usually referred to as the *mediatization* of politics (Hjarvard 2013; Strömbäck 2008). It involves an *adaptive* dynamic where politicians and parties develop political ideas, strategies, and events in ways that take into account the requirements, routines, and expectations of the media and their news criteria. These developments are confirmed in one of the few longitudinal studies on Danish MPs and their view of the media. Comparing journalists in 1980 and 2000, Elmelund-Præstekær et al. (2011) find that politicians in 2000 were more frequently present in the media, just as they considered the media to possess greater power and autonomy.

The pressures of mediatization and adaptation are perhaps nowhere clearer than in the emergence of the spin-doctor profession in recent decades. This is a general trend in democratic societies and one firmly established in Denmark. The growth and establishment of the sector is well documented (and also regulated) in a range of politically initiated reports since the late 1990s (for the latest report, see White Paper 1537/2013). While the reports show that the function of spin-doctors is not only limited to press related tasks, their prominence in handling this relationship points to a broader trend, namely the professionalization of political communication. This has reached a level where it is now the primary topic of an extensive range of TV programmes where journalists, former politicians, spin-doctors, and other commentators discuss the strategic reasoning behind political initiatives (Bengtsson 2014).

It is a development that exacerbates a long-standing concern regarding the negative democratic effects of so-called media *game frames* about politics (i.e. portraying politics as a strategic jockeying for power rather than focusing on the substantial content of political initiatives) (Cappella and Jamieson 1997). The power and existence of media game frames is well established for other countries (the United States in particular), but research also confirms its prominence in Danish political coverage. Loftager (2006) has shown, for example, how the majority of media stories about one of the most significant administrative reforms in recent Danish history (a local government and regional government reform; see Christiansen and Klitgaard 2009) focused on strategy and game rather than on the content of the proposal. Game framing potentially affects citizens and their ability and willingness to participate in politics. Pedersen's (2012) study of Danish citizens demonstrates that citizens' sense of internal efficacy (perceptions of one's competence to understand and participate in the political process) is negatively affected by exposure to game frames. The logic behind the finding is that game frames reduce viewers/readers to spectators rather than participants in politics (see also Hansen and Jensen 2007).

The forces of personalization, negativity, and game framing have initiated considerable discussion among Danish journalists over the future of the profession. In 2017, the former head of news at the Danish public broadcaster (*Danmarks Radio*), Ulrik Haagerup, launched an ambitious new journalistic initiative: the Constructive Institute. The problem diagnosis of the Institute is that the media's focus on negativity and conflict leads to political and social cynicism, declining trust in authorities, and frustration/depression (Hansen and Jensen 2007; Skovsgaard and Søberg 2016), just as it demotivates politicians to engage in public debate. The Institute is actively involved in re-educational activities among Danish journalists to develop new ways of covering society and politics that focus more on solutions and successes and less on conflict, drama, and negativity (Constructive Institute 2017).

The political agenda-setting power of the media is perhaps *the* central question in the discussion of media and politics in democratic countries. The mediatization thesis suggests that media wield significant power over politicians when it comes to defining the political agenda. Recent research on Danish politics argues that it is unhelpful to conceive of this dynamic as an either-or. Work by Green-Pedersen and Stubager (2010), for example, demonstrates that the power of the media is not a constant but rather *conditional* on a number of factors. Most notably, they show that media stories are mainly able to shape the political agenda when they fit the strategic rationales and issue ownership patterns of the political parties. This finding importantly indicates that the media may be politically influential but that the political system retains significant control over the political decision-making agenda. Green-Pedersen and Stubager's (2010) conclusions are partly confirmed by comparative studies of agenda setting. In an analysis of political journalism in eight Western European countries, van Dalen and van Aelst (2014) find that less than a quarter of political journalists in Denmark consider the media to wield strong influence over politics. This is considerably below the reported answers for countries such as Sweden, Norway, and Belgium. Much of the time then, the media still primarily serve as arenas (rather than actors) where political agents debate and challenge each other.

This picture is somewhat reversed, however, when politicians are asked the same type of question. In a study of Danish MPs, van Dalen (2016) concludes that Danish politicians generally consider the media highly influential of public opinion. While this may stand in some contradiction to Green-Pedersen and Stubager's (2010) findings, the differences reflect different methodologies. Whereas Green-Pedersen and Stubager searched for correlations between media reports and actual political behaviour, van Dalen asked MPs about their *perception* of media influence. The distinction between actual and perceived media influence is important. If politicians *believe* that the media are powerful, this may have a range of effects. Notably, van Dalen discovers how Danish politicians who perceive the media as influential are also likely to hold rather cynical and negative views of the media as well as of their political colleagues as media puppets (see also Willig et al. 2015).

International and Danish research has demonstrated a so-called 'incumbency bonus' where the government receives more media attention than the opposition (Brants and van Praag 2006; Hopmann et al. 2011). Recent analyses of the Danish media-politics nexus challenge the notion of a linear and uniform incumbency bonus. Green-Pedersen et al. (2017) find that the degree of the incumbency bonus varies so that it is more pronounced in routine periods and less so during elections. During elections, they claim, the media's emphasis on objectivity and balance is the predominant norm guiding the coverage of politics. When the distribution of power is settled, as it is in routine periods, the dominant norm sways towards the watchdog role where those who possess and exercise power (i.e. the government) become of primary interest. This interest, however, can be a double-edged sword. Green-Pedersen et al. (2017) consequently demonstrate that since media coverage of politics is generally negative, more media coverage tends to lead to decreases in electoral support.

Mediatization not only concerns parties and politicians. Research on Danish interest organizations (Binderkrantz 2014, 2016), for example, demonstrates that these actors are equally concerned with media access and media influence. Binderkrantz finds, however, that the access of interest organizations to the media is highly hierarchized, with a small, select group of organizations occupying the bulk of media attention. While the dominant groups are indeed among the largest interest organizations in Denmark, this skewed representation nonetheless presents a democratic challenge to the diversity of standpoints and positions made available in the public sphere. According to Binderkrantz (2016: 206), the pattern she finds is consistent with Bennett's (1990) indexing theory. Journalists and the media, this theory posits, work in a highly routinized fashion where they predominantly (re)use the sources that are most visible, available, and well known. This dynamic, Binderkrantz argues, works strongly in favour of larger, resourceful organizations.

The media's democratic watchdog role is closely linked to the exposure of political scandals. Since the 1960s and 1970s, the revelation of wrongdoing on the part of politicians has been viewed as the pinnacle of professional achievement (Schultz 2006). The nature of the media's coverage of political scandals, however, has changed significantly over this period. Blach-Ørsten's (2011) analysis of Danish political scandals thus demonstrates an important shift from political scandals to so-called norm scandals. Political scandals focus primarily on wrongdoing with clear political content (embezzlement, power abuse, etc.), while norm scandals are oriented towards the private sphere and morality of the politician (sexual behaviour, personal economy, etc.).

These changes have dual roots. On one level, the media's increasing focus on personal and moral issues is indicative of a *tabloidization* of political coverage, which at least partly reflects the pressures of commercialization on the media. On another level, the shift towards norm scandals also speaks to important transformations within the world of politics towards *personalization*. According to Loftager (2006), the personal dimension of politics and politicians becomes increasingly important in a situation where ideological differences between political parties become less pronounced and where voters are less loyal to specific parties. This leads politicians to focus more on personal performance and trustworthiness as ways of distinguishing themselves. Under such conditions, it is inevitable that the media redefine their democratic watchdog role to include the scrutinization of the personal life and behaviour of politicians. The personalization of politics is likely to become even more prominent with the use of social media, and in particular, Facebook, which is a highly individualized performance platform. With almost all Danish MPs being present on Facebook, the opportunities for strategic personal performance are substantial (Sørensen 2016).

Research on Danish politicians' use of social media such as Twitter and Facebook is still nascent. Studies from the two most recent national elections in 2011 and 2015, however, clearly demonstrate that social media use is now deeply integrated in the broader communication strategies of Danish politicians (Blach-Ørsten et al. 2017; Hansen and Kosiara-Pedersen 2014; Jensen et al. 2016; Skovsgaard and Van Dalen 2013; Sørensen 2016). It also shows that in a span of just four years, large-scale changes occurred where social media not only became more prevalent but were also employed in an increasingly professionalized manner in 2015 compared to 2011. This development is likely to accelerate further during the 2019 national election.

In general, however, the prominence of social media has not led to a major shift in balance towards social media and away from newspapers and television. Rather, new media technologies seem to complement and not replace traditional media. In fact, research suggests that social media use in many ways reflects politicians' standing in traditional media. Both Skovsgaard and van Dalen (2013) and Blach-Ørsten et al. (2017) find that social media are predominantly used by younger, less prominent politicians whose access to and newsworthiness for traditional media is lower than it is for high-profile politicians. Social media, consequently, is an addition to the already existing repertoire of communication options (traditional news, face-to-face, etc.) and one that is still embraced very differently by politicians; some are extremely active and interactive on social media, while others use them much less intensively and primarily for one-way communication (Blach-Ørsten et al. 2017; Sørensen 2016).

The Crisis of Journalism

The crisis of journalism has at least three dimensions (Nielsen 2016): falling revenues (in particular for newspapers), a decline in trust, and a challenge for professional independence and status. These changes are obviously negative for the profession, but they are also relevant on a broader, political and democratic, scale. The watchdog role that we take for granted as a crucial element in well-functioning democracies requires a significant degree of *autonomy*. In fact, the historical development of media and journalism has been a long struggle to achieve autonomy from political and clerical authorities (Hallin and Mancini 2004). This status in democracy is now so profoundly secured (Alexander 2016) that the historical pendulum is unlikely to swing all the way back. In Denmark, in particular, autonomy from the political system seems to be very strongly consolidated compared to other European countries (Albæk et al. 2014: 42). Rather, the threats against journalistic autonomy today come from the fundamental changes in the traditional business model of the media and from the media's loss of control and status as the primary curators and gatekeepers of the democratic public sphere.

The economic pressures on the media are important because of the media's rather peculiar position in society. On the one hand, media organizations (with public service media as a partial exception) are businesses that exist and must survive on a market. On the other, their role is imbued with strong public expectations to be something 'more', to not simply strive for profit and economic survival but serve public interest and undergird democracy and the public sphere. The conundrum here is obvious: to be able to fulfil these public and political expectations, the media must possess a certain level of economic resources. Yet the longer and work-intensive formats of hard news and investigative journalism are not sufficient on their own to generate the necessary revenues. In seeking to balance these concerns, the media are forced to work between the tense and sometimes contradictory logics of a commercial and public interest pole (Bourdieu 1996).

While this challenge is a constant in the history of the media, it has been exacerbated in recent decades in many ways. This is evidenced in the dramatic decline in newspaper readership across the Western world (Nielsen 2016). In the period from just 2010 to 2015, Danish newspapers experienced a staggering 26 per cent decline in readership, primarily as a result of increased competition (Blach-Ørsten 2014), digitalization, and changing media consumption habits towards online news (Ministry of Culture 2016). Comparatively speaking, however, Danish newspaper readership remains rather high at around 41.5 per cent of the adult population (Ministry of Culture 2017). This is in line with Hallin and Mancini's (2004) characterization of the Democratic Corporatist Model as one with historically high levels of newspaper readership. In Nielsen's (2016) comparison of the three media models, it is also evident that the media's economic crisis is not as acutely experienced in countries in the Democratic Corporatist Model (Finland and Germany in his case). By far, the steepest declines in newspaper revenue per capita are found in the United States. Nielsen's (2016) numbers cover the period from 2000 to

2009. As the numbers reported above for the period 2010–15 suggest, the downward trend has only accelerated as the impact of digitalization and social media deepens. Importantly, statistics show that the declines in newspaper readership is unevenly distributed in generational terms, and unsurprisingly, most conspicuous among the younger age groups (Ministry of Culture 2016) who increasingly use Facebook as a primary source in their news consumption (Ministry of Culture 2017: 15).

Digitalization involves a reduction in media organizations' control over the news and information flow. All Danish media make significant use of social media and Facebook in particular, with no less than 92 per cent of their news stories shared on social media (Ministry of Culture 2017: 115). This development means that advertising revenues to an increasing extent move away from the individual news organization to information giants such as Facebook and Google (in the United States, 85 per cent of all advertising revenue online now goes to Facebook and Google who have a de facto global duopoly over advertising) (Ministry of Culture 2017: 68). The combination of declining newspaper readership and diminishing advertising revenues undermines the classic business model of the media (Kammer 2018).

This is not simply a problem for the media but has serious short-term and long-term political and democratic consequences. As shown by Lund et al. (2009), newspapers are, despite the importance of television, at the top of the Danish news food chain as it is here that original news content is mainly produced. With the pressures discussed above and no clear solution for new, effective digital business models, this position is severely threatened. Well-researched journalism is time consuming. In a situation of increasing commercial pressure, this type journalism is at risk of being outcompeted by cheaper and faster journalistic outputs. In recent studies of Danish journalists' view of their professional autonomy, scholars have found that they indeed view increasing time and production pressures as the main threat to their autonomy (Albæk et al. 2014; Mollerup et al. 2016; Skovsgaard 2014). This is supported by the fact that journalistic output has grown significantly in recent decades without a corresponding growth in the number of journalists (Blach-Ørsten 2014). These pressures make journalists vulnerable in several democratically problematic ways. With limitations in time and resources, media and journalists become, for example, more susceptible to consider pre-packaged PR or PR-related material from sources (politicians, corporations, interest organizations, authorities, etc.) who have a strategic interest in getting their stories (and angles) into the media circuit (Mollerup et al. 2016; Wedel 2016).

If we add to this already somewhat gloomy picture that journalists are among the least trusted professional groups (Radius 2017), there is much to suggest that Danish newspapers and TV station media will not be able to maintain their historically central position as the primary curators and organizers of the public sphere (comparatively speaking, however, trust in the media in Denmark is relatively high, with Denmark ranking eighth among thirty-six selected countries (Newman et al. 2017: 20)). This negative development is accelerated by social media in various ways. As noted by Chadwick (2017), Western democracies are now *hybrid* media systems where journalists work in an increasingly diverse landscape of both amateur and professional communicators (see Lund 2018 for a related discussion of Denmark).

The blurred lines between communication professionals and amateurs and the difficulty of clearly identifying the rationale behind news and information in the decentralized and non-curated public sphere of web 2.0 has led to various concerns, including over so-called fake news. However, despite the academic and journalistic hype around this phenomenon, relatively few Danes (36 per cent compared to more than 60 per cent in countries such as the United States, France, and Spain) express concern over fake news. In fact, only 9 per cent of Danish media users report having encountered fake news (defined as 'invented' stories) (Schrøder et al. 2018: 33–5). These differences perhaps reflect how Danish media users display high levels of so-called *media literacy* (i.e. the ability to decode the underlying rationales of news production and assess media products in critical ways) compared to other European countries and the United States (ibid.).

Despite this apparent Danish resilience, it is worth noting that concerns over fake news also reflect a real and profound transnationalization of the Danish public sphere with significant implications for democracy and politics. In the media ecology of web 2.0, news can enter the information circuit of Danish citizens and politicians in a much more direct and unmediated manner than previously possible. While Danish media users, as noted, do not yet consider fake news to be a major problem, a recent security assessment report by the Danish Defence Intelligence Service (2017: 20) concluded that Russia systematically initiates campaigns designed to generate mistrust in Western politicians and media and that such efforts are likely to increasingly impact Denmark in the coming years. The prominence of global information platforms such as Facebook and Google in the information consumption of Danish citizens makes the latter highly accessible to misinformation and fake news campaigns initiated by actors and states outside Denmark. Again, it is a dynamic that testifies to how traditional media and journalism have lost and are constantly losing their privileged position as the primary gatekeepers and organizers of the democratic public sphere.

CONCLUSION

Danish media and journalism are part of a distinct Democratic Corporatist Media Model that reflects a number of core traits of the Nordic welfare state tradition. There are signs that the model is moving in the direction of the Liberal Model but also that it displays resilience and the ability to maintain its distinctive characteristics.

Research on the media-politics nexus in Denmark confirms a number of observations made in international research on the mediatization of politics. At the same time, however, several strands of work also suggest that mediatization is in no way total or unidirectional. Media effects are conditional on a wide range of factors, just as evidence clearly indicates that politicians retain a good deal of autonomy vis-à-vis the media.

Journalism in Western democracies is beset by a range of crises that concern their business models, public trust, and professional authority. However, in comparison with other countries, the crisis in Denmark is less profound. There are, nonetheless, grounds for democratic concern because the crisis affects journalistic autonomy, and with that, the ability to perform the role as democratic watchdogs. The overall conclusion then suggests that Danish media are undergoing significant transformations and even crises but that they are not eroded or made irrelevant by them.

When it comes to social media and the new media ecology of web 2.0 in particular, there are also sound reasons not to exaggerate their transformative impact or write them off as predominantly negative for politics and democracy. The uprooting of the media's gatekeeping role and privilege has unleashed a new democratic drive. Most notably, social media such as Facebook and Twitter provide citizens with unprecedented opportunities to engage in the political process and debate without the intervention and mediation of journalists. In a recent study of Danish politicians' use of Facebook, Sørensen (2016) finds that several of them actually use Facebook as a platform for entering into direct debates with Danish citizens. In a broader sense, activists and interest organizations who were strongly dependent on traditional media pre-web 2.0 can now communicate directly with citizens and potential members/supporters and organize events with limited resources (Olesen 2016).

While this decentralization of the public sphere has definite democratic advantages, there are also some potential negative aspects beyond those that have already been mentioned. The crisis of journalism and what Sunstein (2007) calls *general interest intermediaries* (i.e. media organizations offering a broad palette of news and information to diverse audiences) have led to a concern with political *echo chambers and confirmation bias.* The underlying idea has two dimensions: on the one hand, news consumption on social media can now be very precisely tailored to the individual user's preferences, and on the other hand, the digital traces that media users leave behind allow the algorithms of social media such as Facebook to quite precisely 'learn' what kind of news users prefer and serve them more of that (Chadwick 2017; Sunstein 2007). This is in stark contrast to general interest intermediaries where readers and viewers are exposed to a wide range of news that they have not actively sought out and with which they do not necessarily agree (Aalberg and Curran 2012).

This is democratically and politically problematic as the key premise of democracy is the engagement and debate over opposing viewpoints (Loftager 2004; Lund 2004). Without such systematic orchestrations of disagreement, there is an appended risk of increasing polarization among the population. However, concerns over echo chambers and confirmation bias are predominantly based on observations from the United States. In line with the other observations in the chapter, recent results from Danish media users demonstrate that these challenges are perhaps less pronounced in Denmark. For example, 62.3 per cent of Facebook users state that they learn something new when discussing politics and news on Facebook, while about a quarter say that they often or always encounter opinions with which they disagree (DECIDIS 2017). These results should also be seen against the background that only 12 per cent of Danes use social media as their primary news source, as television news is still by far the most important news source with almost 40 per cent stating this as their primary source (Wandsøe-Isaksen et al. 2018).

We can now turn to the two questions posed in the introduction: is the crisis of journalism reversing the process of mediatization, and does it erode journalism's capacity to perform the role as democratic watchdogs? In many ways, mediatization has accelerated with the emergence of web 1.0 and 2.0. We now live in societies with an unprecedented number of communication platforms and where access to the communicative flow is more or less unrestricted and highly multidirectional. 'Amateur' communicators such as bloggers, commentators, influencers, etc. play an ever larger role, just as politicians, social movements, and interest organizations communicate directly with their audiences without the gate-keeping intervention of journalists and the media. We may tentatively conclude then that the crisis of journalism has not reversed the process of mediatization at a general level; quite to the contrary, the crisis is part of a wider trend towards accelerated and hybridized mediatization. It makes sense, however, to label this process a kind of mediatization 2.0 as it is evident that the original conception of mediatization as a process driven by traditional media no longer holds empirically. Research on Danish elections quite clearly confirms this development: since the election in 2007, politicians have become increasingly active on Twitter and Facebook from one election to the next (Jensen 2016).

With those observations, it is also more than suggested that the media's democratic watchdog role is undergoing important changes; however, it is far from being dismantled or made irrelevant. As several of the chapter's observations have noted, Danish newspapers and television retain a strong and still relatively privileged position in the Danish media system and communication landscape despite the crises that have impacted them these years. It is, therefore, more accurate to say that traditional media increasingly *share* the democratic watchdog role with a plurality of other actors who are also engaged in critique and scrutiny of politicians, corporations, and institutions. Rather than viewing the media-politics nexus through an either-or discussion of whether old or new media is the most important, the future of research on media and politics lies in unpacking how traditional media and journalism *interact* with other digitally enabled agents in the communication landscape.

References

Aalberg, Toril, and James Curran (2012). *How Media Inform Democracy: A Comparative Approach*. London: Routledge.

Ahva, Laura, Arjen van Dalen, Jan F. Hovden, Guðbjörg H. Kolbeins, Monica L. Nilsson, Morten Skovsgaard, et al. (2017). 'A welfare state of mind?', *Journalism Studies*, 18/5: 595–613.

Albæk, Erik, Arjen van Dalen, Nael Jebril, and Claes de Vreese (2014). *Political Journalism in Comparative Perspective*. Cambridge: Cambridge University Press.

Alexander, Jeffrey C. (2016). 'Introduction: Journalism, democratic culture, and creative reconstruction', in Jeffrey C. Alexander, Elizabeth B. Breese, and Maria Luengo, eds, *The Crisis of Journalism Reconsidered*. Cambridge: Cambridge University Press, 1–28.

Allern, Sigurd, and Mark Blach-Ørsten (2011). 'The News media as a political institution', *Journalism Studies*, 12/1: 92–105.

Bengtsson, Mette (2014). '*For borgeren, tilskueren eller den indviede? En praksisorienteret retorisk kritik af avisens politiske kommentarer*', PhD dissertation, Copenhagen University.

Bennett, W. Lance (1990). 'Toward a theory of Press-State relations', *Journal of Communication*, 40/2: 103–25.

Binderkrantz, Anne S. (2014). 'Medierne: Kampen om spalteplads', in Anne S. Binderkrantz, Peter M. Christiansen, and Helene H. Pedersen, eds, *Organisationer i politik: Danske interesseorganisationer i forvaltning, folketing og medier*. Copenhagen: Hans Reitzels Forlag, 177–200.

Binderkrantz, Anne S. (2016). 'Interesseorganisationer og medier', in Thomas Olesen, ed., *Medier, politik og samfund*. Copenhagen: Hans Reitzels Forlag, 193–213.

Blach-Ørsten, Mark (2011). 'Politiske skandaler i danske medier 1980–2010', *Tidsskriftet Politik*, 14/3: 7–16.

Blach-Ørsten, Mark (2014). 'The emergence of an increasingly competitive news regime in Denmark', in Raymond Kuhn and Rasmus K. Nielsen, eds, *Political Journalism in Transition: Western Europe in a Comparative Perspective*. London/New York: I.B. Tauris, 93–110.

Blach-Ørsten, Mark, Mads K. Eberholst, and Rasmus Burkal (2017). 'From hybrid media system to hybrid-media politicians: Danish politicians and their cross-media presence in the 2015 national election campaign', *Journal of Information Technology & Politics*, 14/4: 334–47.

Blach-Ørsten, Mark, and Ida Willig (2016). 'Det danske mediesystem', in Thomas Olesen, ed., *Medier, politik og samfund*. Copenhagen: Hans Reitzels Forlag, 13–34.

Bourdieu, Pierre (1996). *On Television*. New York: The New Press.

Brants, Kees, and Phillip van Praag (2006). 'Signs of Media Logic: Half a Century of Political Communication in the Netherlands', *Javnost—The Public*, 13/1: 25–40.

Cappella, Joseph N., and Kathleen H. Jamieson (1997). *Spiral of Cynicism: The Press and the Public Good*. New York: Oxford University Press.

Chadwick, Andrew (2017). *The Hybrid Media System: Politics and Power*, 2nd ed. Oxford: Oxford University Press.

Christiansen, Peter M., and Michael B. Klitgaard (2009). 'Behind the veil of vagueness: Success and failure in institutional reform', *Journal of Public Policy*, 30/2: 183–200.

Constructive Institute (2017). https://constructiveinstitute.org (accessed 30 November 2019).

Curran, James, Shanto Iyengar, Anker B. Lund, and Inka Salovaara-Moring (2009). 'Media system, public knowledge and democracy: A comparative study', *European Journal of Communication*, 24/1, 5–26.

van Dalen, Arjen (2016). 'Medialisering som selvopfyldende profeti. En analyse af, hvordan danske folketingsmedlemmer oplever medieindflydelse, og konsekvenserne heraf', *Økonomi og Politik*, 89/3: 51–67.

van Dalen, Arjen, and Peter van Aelst (2014). 'The media as political agenda-setters: Journalists' perceptions of media power in eight West European countries', *West European Politics*, 37/1: 42–64.

Danish Defence Intelligence Service (2017). 'Efterretningsmæssig risikovurdering 2017: En aktuel vurdering af forhold i udlandet af betydning for Danmarks sikkerhed', https://fe-ddis.dk/SiteCollectionDocuments/FE/EfterretningsmaessigeRisikovurderinger/Risikovurdering2017.pdf (accessed 19 April 2019).

DECIDIS (2017). 'DECIDIS Survey 2017: Insight into Danish information practices', https://blogit.itu.dk/decidis/wp-content/uploads/sites/37/2019/02/DECIDISSurvey2017_report.pdf (accessed 22 April 2019).

Elmelund-Præstekær, Christian, David N. Hopmann, and Asbjørn Nørgaard (2011). 'Does mediatization change MP-Media interaction and MP attitudes towards the media? Evidence from a longitudinal study of Danish MPs', *International Journal of Press/Politics*, 16/3: 382–403.

Flensburg, Sofie (2015). 'Dansk mediestøtte 1960–2014: Fra økonomisk kompensation til publicistisk motivation', *Mediekultur*, 58: 85–103.

Green-Pedersen, Christoffer, Peter B. Mortensen, and Gunnar Thesen (2017). 'The incumbency bonus revisited: Causes and consequences of media dominance', *British Journal of Political Science*, 47/1, 131–48.

Green-Pedersen, Christoffer, and Rune Stubager (2010). 'The political conditionality of mass media influence: When do parties follow mass media attention?', *British Journal of Political Science*, 40/3: 663–77.

Hallin, Daniel C., and Paolo Mancini (2004). *Comparing Media Systems: Three Models of Media and Politics*. Cambridge: Cambridge University Press.

Hansen, Kasper M., and Karina Kosiara-Pedersen (2014). 'Cyber-campaigning in Denmark: Application and effects of candidate campaigning', *Journal of Information Technology & Politics*, 11/2: 206–21.

Hansen, Kathrine A., and Helle N. Jensen (2007). 'Undergraver tv-nyheder den politiske tillid?', *Politica*, 39/1: 14–30.

Hjarvard, Stig (2007). 'Den politiske presse: En analyse af danske avisers politiske orientering', *Journalistica*, 5: 27–53.

Hjarvard, Stig (2013). *The Mediatization of Culture and Society*. London: Routledge.

Hopmann, David, Claes de Vreese, and Erik Albæk (2011). 'Incumbency Bonus in Election News Coverage Explained', *Journal of Communication*, 61/2: 264–82.

Ibarra, Karen A., Eva Nowak, and Raymond Kuhn (2015). *Public Service Media in Europe: A Comparative Approach*. New York: Routledge.

Jensen, Jakob L. (2016). 'Nye medier og offentlighed', in Thomas Olesen, ed., *Medier, politik og samfund*. Copenhagen: Hans Reitzels Forlag, 265–84.

Jensen, Jakob L., Lisbeth Klastrup, and Jens Hoff (2016). *Internettets rolle under Folketingsvalget 2015*. Copenhagen: Danske Medier.

Kammer, Aske (2018). *Digital journalistik*. Frederiksberg: Samfundslitteratur.

Libraries and Media Agency (2011). 'Demokratistøtte: Fremtidens offentlige mediestøtte', https://slks.dk/fileadmin/publikationer/Rapporter/Demokratistoette.pdf (accessed 11 April 2019).

Loftager, Jørn (2004). *Politisk offentlighed og demokrati i Danmark*. Aarhus: Aarhus University Press.

Loftager, Jørn (2006). 'Medierne, kommunalreformen og ideen om et offentligt ræsonnement', *Politica*, 38/2: 135–53.

Lund, Anker B. (2004). *Den redigerende magt: Nyhedsinstitutionens politiske indflydelse*. Aarhus: Aarhus University Press.

Lund, Anker B. (2018). 'Den redigerende magt: centrifugering af dansk politik', *Økonomi & Politik*, 91/1: 75–85.

Lund, Anker B., Ida Willig, and Mark Blach-Ørsten (2009). *Hvor kommer nyhederne fra? Den journalistiske fødekæde i Danmark før og nu*. Aarhus: Ajour.

Ministry of Culture (2016). 'Mediernes udvikling i Danmark 2016', https://mediernesudvikling.slks.dk/2016/avisprint (accessed 18 April 2019).

Ministry of Culture (2017). 'Mediernes udvikling i Danmark 2017: Globaliseringen af den danske mediebranche', https://www.altinget.dk/misc/Mediernes%20udvikling%20i%20Danmark.pdf (accessed 22 April 2019).

Ministry of Culture (2018). 'Medienævnets årsrapport 2017', https://slks.dk/fileadmin/user_upload/o_SLKS/Dokumenter/Medier/Mediestoette/Medienaevnets_aarsrapport_2017._Godkendt__revideret_den_17._august_2018_.pdf (accessed 14 April 2019).

Mollerup, Jacob, Peter Bro, Søren Jørgensen, and Kim Andersen (2016). 'Mediernes tilstandsrapport 2016', *Den Danske Publicistklub & Center for Journalistik*, University Press of Sourthern Denmark.

Newman, Nic, Richard Fletcher, Antonis Kalogeropoulos, David A. L. Levy, and Rasmus K. Nielsen (2017). *Reuters Institute Digital News Report 2017*. Oxford: Reuters Institute for the Study of Journalism, https://reutersinstitute.politics.ox.ac.uk/sites/default/files/Digital%20News%20Report%202017%20web_o.pdf?utm_source=digitalnewsreport.org&utm_medium=referral (accessed 2 April 2019).

Nielsen, Rasmus K. (2016). 'The many crises of Western journalism', in Jeffrey C. Alexander, Elizabeth B. Breese, and Maria Luengo, eds, *The Crisis of Journalism Reconsidered*. Cambridge: Cambridge University Press, 77–97.

Olesen, Thomas (2016). 'Politisk aktivisme', in Thomas Olesen, ed., *Medier, politik og samfund*. Copenhagen: Hans Reitzels Forlag, 215–38.

Pedersen, Rasmus T. (2012). 'The game frame and political efficacy: Beyond the spiral of cynicism', *European Journal of Communication*, 27/1: 225–40.

Radius (2017). 'c', https://www.altinget.dk/misc/Trov%C3%A6rdighedsunders%C3%B8gelsen%202017%20-%20af%20Radius.pdf (accessed 13 March 2019).

Schrøder, Kim C., and Mark Blach-Ørsten (2018). 'Denmark: Country report', in Nic Newman, Richard Fletcher, Antonis Kalogeropoulos, David A. Levy, and Rasmus K. Nielsen, eds, *Reuters Institute Digital News Report 2018*. Oxford: Reuters Institute for the Study of Journalism.

Schrøder, Kim C., Mark Blach-Ørsten, and Mads K. Eberholst (2018). *Danskernes brug af nyhedsmedier 2018*. Roskilde: Roskilde University. https://rucforsk.ruc.dk/ws/portalfiles/portal/62624831/Danskernes_brug_af_nyhedsmedier_2018.pdf (accessed 15 April 2019).

Schultz, Ida (2006). *Bag nyhederne: værdier, idealer og praksis*. Frederiksberg: Forlaget Samfundslitteratur.

Skovsgaard, Morten (2014). 'Watchdogs on a leash? The impact of organisational constraints on journalists' perceived of professional autonomy and their relationship with superiors', *Journalism*, 15/3, 344–63.

Skovsgaard, Morten, and Arjen van Dalen (2013). 'Dodging the Gatekeepers', *Information, Communication & Society*, 16/5: 737–56.

Skovsgaard, Morten, and Pernille F. Søberg (2016). 'Nedtrykt af negative nyheder: Effekten af positive og negative tv-nyheder på seernes humør, hukommelse og lyst til at se nyheder', *Journalistica*, 1: 29–52.

Strömbäck, Jesper (2005). 'In search of a standard: Four models of democracy and their normative implications for journalism', *Journalism Studies*, 6/3: 331–45.

Strömbäck, Jesper (2008). 'Four phases of mediatization: An analysis of the mediatization of politics', *The International Journal of Press/Politics*, 13/3: 228–46.

Sunstein, Cass R. (2007). *Republic.com 2.0*. Princeton, NJ: Princeton University Press.

Sørensen, Mads P. (2016). 'Political conversations on Facebook: The participation of politicians and citizens', *Media, Culture, and Society*, 38/5: 664–85.

Wandsøe-Isaksen, Regitze, Kristine Vasiljeva, and Frederik D. Pedersen (2018). 'Ingen truende medieudvikling – men bekymringspunkter', http://kraka.org/sites/default/files/public/6.1_bagggrundsnotat_medieanalysen.pdf (accessed 28 April 2019).

Wedel, Sanne O. (2016). 'Journalistisk autonomi i relation til PR – en analyse af, hvordan PR-bureauer afsætter stof til danske kvalitetsaviser', *Journalistica*, 53–78.

White Paper (1537/2013). *Betænkning 1536 fra Udvalget om Særlige Rådgivere: Ministrenes Særlige Rådgivere: et serviceeftersyn*. Copenhagen: Ministry of Finance, https://www.fm.dk/~/media/publikationer/imported/2013/betaenkning-1537-saerlige-raadgivere/betaenkning_1537_ministrenes-saerlige-raadgivere_et-serviceeftersyn_web_pdfa.ashx (accessed 11 July 2019).

Willig, Ida, Mark Blach-Ørsten, Jannie M. Hartley, and Sofie Flensburg (2015). *Journalistiske kvaliteter 1999–2014: Specialrapport*. Copenhagen: Agency of Culture.

CHAPTER 27

INTEREST GROUPS

A Democratic Necessity and a Necessary Evil

ANNE SKORKJÆR BINDERKRANTZ

DENMARK is regularly highlighted as a champion of voluntary association. From the mobilization of farmers and workers in the nineteenth century to levels of present-day membership and engagement, voluntary associations have played a central societal role. In addition, there is a strong tradition of involving interest groups in public decision-making, with Denmark being among the most corporatist countries. This chapter discusses the historical development of interest groups in Denmark as well as the present role of interest groups as membership associations and political actors. While the focus is mainly on formally organized groups, it also includes discussions on activities in more loosely structured social movements.

Interest groups are crucial actors in any democracy. From a bottom-up perspective, they help citizens acquire political skills and competencies and provide a channel for citizens to connect to the political system (Torpe 2000: 81). From a top-down perspective, interest groups play a role in public decision-making. Organized interests appear regularly in the news media, they voice their concerns to MPs, and they interact with bureaucrats (Binderkrantz et al. 2015). While interest groups serve democratic functions, their role is contested. Not all groups have the same resources available, and imbalance in the interest group system may lead to policy imbalances (Schlozman et al. 2012). Interest groups are, therefore, a necessity for democracies but also a necessary evil.

A number of questions structure the discussion in this chapter. First, the chapter looks at the historical development of the group system: what are the roots of the Danish interest group systems, and what factors shaped its early development? Second, it focuses on the shift in mobilization occurring in the last half of the twentieth century: what was the role of social movements in Denmark, and what is the effect on the present-day interest group system? Third, the discussion turns to the organizational structure of groups: what resources do groups control, and to what degree are interest groups democratic organizations? Fourth, the focus shifts to the political role of groups:

which arenas are central for political influence, and what groups dominate in politics? Fifth and finally, the chapter discusses the role of new types of political actors: have think tanks and public relations firms changed the contours of interest representation in Denmark?

Interest Groups: Definitions and Distinctions

In line with the Danish literature, interest groups are defined as 'associations of members or supporters who do not run for public office and may potentially seek political influence' (Binderkrantz 2012: 119). Interest groups differ from political parties because they do not seek representation in Parliament. In contrast to parties, interest groups arise from the need for representation of specific groups or causes. Parts of the discussion below include not only formally structured and politically active groups but also more loosely structured and non-political associations.

A central line of division among interest groups is between economic groups and citizen groups. *Economic groups* organize interests related to societal production, and members join based on their vocation or economic role. Important economic groups are trade unions and business groups, and the balance between these have been the centre of much attention. Public sector groups play a large role in Denmark. They include trade unions organizing public sector employees and groups organizing municipalities and regions. In contrast, *citizen groups* represent non-vocation groups or attract members that support common goals. Citizen groups may be divided into those representing sectional groups such as patients or students and public interest groups pursuing causes related to, for example, the environment or human rights (Binderkrantz et al. 2016).

A multitude of forces contributes to shaping the landscape of interest groups. From a *supply perspective*, associations arise from a need for political representation. This is the basic premise in the pluralist perspective where mobilization is assumed to reflect socio-economic structures (Truman 1951). The assumption that such mobilization would happen almost automatically has rightly been criticized, but socio-economic changes as well as shifts in political mobilization clearly affect the interest group system. From a *demand perspective*, the political system contributes to shaping interest group mobilization. This may be intended as is the case for the Danish Consumer Council (*Forbrugerrådet Tænk*) which is heavily subsidized by the state, or unintended as when patient groups proliferate in response to new diagnostics or new treatments (P.M. Christiansen 2012). Finally, political activity may not be the prime motive of group establishment but rather occur as a by-product in associations formed, for example, for recreational purposes.

The Origin and Development of the Interest Group System

The development of Danish interest groups is by no means the result of deliberate planning. Rather, it is the effect of early mobilization in some societal segments and a complex interplay between mobilization and the emerging corporatist traditions (see Christiansen 2020). In the last decades of the nineteenth century, associations became an increasingly important element of local social and political organization. Most of these associations were created bottom-up, and only at later points were national interest groups established (Torpe 2000: 79–88). The associations came to constitute a crucial link between citizens and local as well as national political institutions and contributed to the stable development of democracy in Denmark (Torpe 2000).

Among the most important movements in the nineteenth century were farmers' associations and trade unions. The well-organized farming movement has its roots in the cooperative movement established to organize agricultural production and strengthen the domestic producers in light of competition from overseas. Agricultural production was high politics in the first part of the twentieth century, and farmers' associations became strong partners of the state and assumed a high level of self-regulation. A complex set of interest groups characterized the farmers' movement, but most were part of the umbrella organization now known as the Danish Agriculture and Food Council (*Landbrug og Fødevarer*) which was a result of mergers with other major producer organizations (Daugbjerg 1999; Christiansen 2014).

The mobilization of Danish workers took place in the late nineteenth century. From the 1860s onward, the urban labour class mobilized, and in 1898, a number of Danish trade unions established the organization that became the Danish Confederation of Trade Unions (originally called *De Samvirkende Fagforbund* and later known as *LO*). At that time, the organization had 50,000 members which was a record high level of unionization internationally (Christiansen 2014; Danish Confederation of Trade Unions 2018). After a merger with the main trade union organizing public sector employees in 2019, the organization now has 1.4 million members. Trade union membership is more contested today than at the highpoint of the corporatist system, and traditional trade unions have faced increasing competition from so-called 'yellow' trade unions outside of the highly ordered and functionally differentiated trade union establishment (Schmitter 1974). Still, Danish trade unions remain comparatively strong and display high levels of unionization.

When it comes to business representation, two separate tracks are present. On the one hand, a series of organizations promote the general interests of business. In 1838, companies in Copenhagen established an association with the intent to promote 'industry in the Danish state'. These were the first roots of the present-day organization the Confederation of Danish Industry (*Dansk Industri*, or DI). On the other hand, employers have organized in employers' organizations with the Confederation of Danish Employers (*Dansk Arbejdsgiverforening*, or DA) as a main actor, established in 1896 as a direct reaction to unionization. Today, the DA plays a dominant role in collective wage agreement, but the DI and the Danish Chamber of Commerce (*Dansk Erhverv*, or DE) are very prominent in general lobbyism on behalf of business interests. Both of these groups are members of the DA, testifying to the somewhat complicated organizational structure characterizing Danish business.

While the image of interest group populations in corporatist countries is often associated with Schmitter's (1974) description of hierarchically ordered and functionally differentiated categories, this only partly captures the reality of the Danish interest group system (P.M. Christiansen 2012). Alongside organized labour, farmers' associations, and business groups that correspond relatively well to Schmitter's description, many other types of associations proliferate. This was the case in the formative years of the interest group system where a range of different associations—for example religious groups and the folk school movement—were crucial to the development of the Danish democracy. After the Second World War, the consolidation of the corporatist systems with strong labour market representation co-occurred with a rise in social movements and organized interests representing various citizen groups.

The Rise of New Social Movements and Citizen Groups

From the mid-twentieth century and culminating in the two decades after 1968, a range of social and political movements became crucial forces in Denmark. Social movements are less formally organized than interest groups and emphasize collective action rather than the direct lobbying of decision-makers (Mikkelsen 2002a: 10). In Denmark, an analysis of the number of collective protest actions from 1945–95 finds a general high level of activity from about 1968 to 1987, peaking in 1970. Most protest activities were relatively peaceful gatherings of people demonstrating their dissatisfaction—such as demonstrations, petitions, or public meetings (Mikkelsen 2002b: 53–7). Violent types of activity became more dominant towards the end of the period, where the occupation of buildings as well as physical blockades occurred regularly. For some years around 1982–5, these actions led to arrests in the hundreds (Mikkelsen 2002b: 71–5).

There is a clear connection between the international situation after the Second World War and mobilization in Denmark. Danish movements were, for example, part of the international movement for peace, the fight against nuclear weapons, and the reaction to specific international developments such as apartheid governance in South Africa and the Vietnam War (Mikkelsen 2002b). Conflict also characterized the labour market in the 1970s and the first part of the 1980s. The major trade unions were part of a formalized negotiation system, but more radicalized groups sought to politicize labour market relations through strikes and other types of actions (Mikkelsen 2002b: 63). In addition, protest activity also occurred in other areas such as the environment as well as women's equality (see Fiig and Siim 2020).

While protest activity became less prevalent after the late 1980s, many movements left permanent traces. For example, the environmental group NOAH—Friends of the Earth Denmark—established in 1969 now celebrates its 50th anniversary, and although the group has some level of formal organization, its structure is still relatively decentralized (NOAH 2019). More generally, there is evidence of large-scale changes in the composition of the interest group system. This is the result of a combination of factors related to the supply of members in need of political representation as well as demand factors originating from the political system. From a supply perspective, socio-economic developments affect the interest group system. Most notably, voting and interest group membership increasingly crosscuts traditional social divides. This has led to a growing importance of 'new politics', and citizens increasingly join groups based on new political issues such as immigration, the environment, and law and order (Schmitter 2008: 198; Binderkrantz et al. 2016).

From a demand perspective, the expansion of the welfare state has affected interest group mobilization. The extension of the state into new areas of social regulation and provision has helped citizen groups such as groups representing patients prosper (P.M. Christiansen 2012; Fisker 2013; Binderkrantz et al. 2016). Membership of client organizations has seen dramatic increases. For example, the group DaneAge Association (*Ældre Sagen*) was reported to have about 400,000 elderly members in 1998 (Torpe 2000), and today, it boasts a membership of 900,000. From surveys of citizens, it is also evident that membership of client groups has increased. From 1999 to 2008, the share of the population reporting membership of groups related to health or social affairs rose to 8 per cent and 12 per cent, respectively. It is also notable that more citizens were members of public interest groups related to environmental issues and animal protection as well as the third world and human rights in 2008 compared to the previous decades (Torpe 2011: 227). The most recent membership counts from 2017 indicate stagnation, with some group types experiencing drops in membership, but a continued high level of associational participation overall (Henriksen and Levinsen 2019).

Any estimate of an interest group population is uncertain. While many groups are well-known and long-established political actors, much fluctuation characterizes the group system, with new groups popping up and others vanishing (Fisker 2015). Nevertheless, the Danish population of groups is relatively well-documented due to major research projects mapping the group system around 1975 and 2010 (Buksti 1980; Binderkrantz and Christiansen 2014). Table 27.1 provides an overview of the distribution of groups across different types in these two periods. The table includes all identified associations at the national level even if they do not report to seek political influence.

First, it is evident that the rise in the number of associations is relatively modest compared to the alleged explosion in group numbers, for example, in the United States (Grant et al. 2012). Second, there is a shift in balance towards more representation of citizen interests. In particular, public interest groups were proliferated from 1975 to 2010.

Table 27.1. Overview of Group Types in 1975 and 2010

	1975	2010	Change
Economic groups	*71.1*	*58.3*	*−12.8*
Trade unions	15.9	10.3	−5.6
Business groups	34.3	27.5	−6.8
Institutional groups	4.6	4.4	−0.2
Professional groups	16.3	16.0	−0.3
Citizen groups	*28.8*	*41.7*	*12.8*
Identity groups	10.7	14.3	3.6
Leisure groups	12.9	14.4	1.5
Public interest groups	5.2	13.0	7.8
Total	2,127	2,543	
	100.0	100.0	

Note: (Binderkrantz et al. 2016).

Of the 2,543 groups identified in 2010, it is estimated that about 1,700 were interest groups in the sense that they pursue political influence (Binderkrantz and Christiansen 2014: 94–5). In addition to groups operating at the national level, a multitude of local associations exist (Torpe 2000: 85).

INTEREST GROUPS AS ASSOCIATIONS: MEMBERS, RESOURCES, AND ORGANIZATION

On average, each Danish citizen is a member of at least one group working for political influence, but groups vary greatly in size. Many groups report a membership of less than 100 people, while other groups organize more than 500,000 citizens (Binderkrantz and Christiansen 2014: 96). In addition to groups organizing individual citizens, other groups represent business firms or public authorities and/or institutions. Among the latter, two are particularly important: Danish Regions (*Danske Regioner*) represent the 5 regions, and Local Government Denmark (*Kommunernes Landsforening*) organizes the 98 municipalities. These different membership types render comparison across interest groups difficult, but there is no doubt that the organizations of local government, the trade unions, and the major business groups benefit from a strong membership base.

Other types of resources are more comparable. A key resource for being politically effective is having a professional secretariat. Analyses have found staff dedicated to monitoring political processes and lobbying important for predicting access to political arenas (Binderkrantz et al. 2015). Here, three types of groups stand out as particularly well endowed: trade unions, business groups, and institutional groups. In fact, put together, these groups employed more than three-quarters of all staff working with politics in Danish interest groups in 2011 (Binderkrantz and Christiansen 2014). Even though citizen groups have gained ground in terms of their representation in the interest group systems, economic groups are thus better equipped for achieving political access and influence.

Danish interest groups have professionalized over time. In a survey from 1975, 3 per cent reported secretariats with more than 25 employees, whereas this was the case for 9 per cent of groups in 2011, and 3 per cent had at least 90 staff members (Buksti 1980: 19; INTERARENA 2012). The largest interest groups have secretariats equal in size to many government agencies and political parties. The role as director of these groups is in effect a powerful position. Recent analyses have found that groups often recruit these directors from positions in public administration and among individuals with an academic background in law, economics, or political science (Binderkrantz 2020).

The professionalization of groups raises the question as to what degree groups are democratic organizations or rather run by professional leadership and staff. Interest groups are sometimes described as 'little democracies' where members are schooled in politics, gain experience with the democratic processes of government, and develop an identity as citizens (Torpe 2000; Halpin 2006: 919). Groups are also central in connecting citizens to political institutions (Dahl 1998). For interest groups to perform these democratic functions, a precondition is that members are involved in the political processes in groups. However, while most groups have formal, democratic structures allowing members to participate in decision-making, it is an open question as to the degree to which groups actually function democratically (Binderkrantz 2009).

A number of scholars have pointed out that Robert Michels' 'iron law of oligarchy' seems to have a profound effect on many groups (Grant and Maloney 1997; McLaverty 2002). Public interest groups have been singled out as particularly prone to exhibiting low levels of membership participation. Some of these groups have even been termed 'protest businesses' to indicate a situation where members join to support the group but have little say in group policy-making (Grant and Maloney 1997). A study of Danish interest groups found a lower level of membership activity and influence in public interest groups compared to trade unions, but patient groups and professional associations exhibited lower degrees of membership activity than public interest groups (Binderkrantz 2009). Figure 27.1 displays group information with respect to these dimensions.

It is notable how the answers differ across the questions. For the two general questions about whether members influence the political work of groups and the prevalence of membership meetings, more than 80 per cent of groups respond positively. When it comes to the challenging questions about membership activity in the political work of groups and the existence of contested elections, fewer groups report this to be the case. The 2011 survey also confirms differences between group types. For example, among patient groups and environmental groups, 30 per cent reply that members have little or no influence on the political role of groups (INTERARENA 2012). These numbers confirm that a substantial share of Danish interest groups do not operate as democratic organizations to a degree that is consistent with the notion of groups as 'little democracies'.

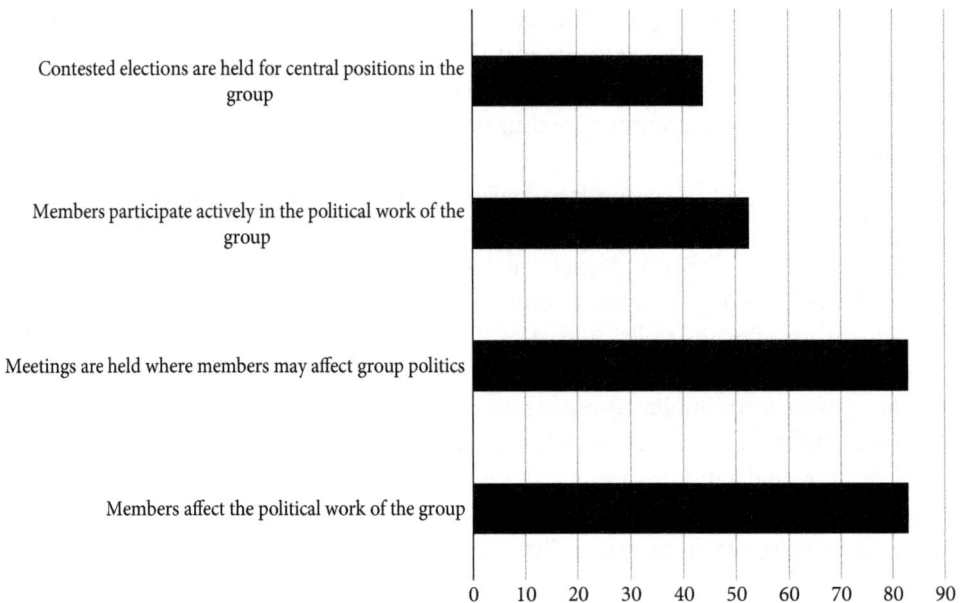

FIGURE 27.1 Membership activity and influence.

Note: Survey of Danish interest groups 2011. Share of groups responding: "to some degree" or "to a large degree" on a question about to what degree the statements fit the group. N (minimum) = 1,056

Conversely, they also give reason to considerable confidence in the role of interest groups. At least according to the groups themselves, the large majority of groups do in fact provide members with options for influencing the political work of the group.

THE POLITICAL ROLE OF INTEREST GROUPS

An important trait in the first half of the twentieth century was the existence of organizational 'pillars' including political parties as well as interest groups. Traditional left-right issues related to economic production and redistribution dominated Danish politics. Thus, voting behaviour as well as interest group membership could largely be predicted by labour market status. The Confederation of Trade Unions (*LO*) had particularly close organizational ties to the Social Democratic Party, and the Liberal Party (*Venstre*) was seen as a prime representative of farmers. The Social Liberals were related to the rural smallholders on their side, while the Conservative party had connections to organizations of urban businesses (Bille 2008).

During the latter part of the twentieth century, an organizational de-integration of political parties and their traditional allies among organized interest groups occurred (F.J. Christiansen 2012). Structural developments led to a shift in the electorate away from class-based voting, new political issues rose in importance, and voting increasingly crosscuts traditional patterns. Political parties no longer represent clear and distinct social groups, and the common ground for parties and organized groups is therefore less solid. As argued by F.J. Christiansen (2012), for parties as well as for interest groups, the costs of mutual tight connections now outweigh the benefits. On their side, parties need to appeal to broad societal groups, and close relations to particular interest groups may harm this. For interest groups, having tight relations to specific parties may affront members that support other parties and limit the ability of the group to lobby across the political spectrum (Binderkrantz 2015).

Interest groups operate in multiple political arenas such as the media, Parliament, and the bureaucracy, and over time, the relative significance of different arenas has changed. In the heydays of corporatism around 1975, interactions between organized interests and bureaucrats were central. Corporatism entailed institutionalized integration of interest groups into decision-making through formal channels such as boards and committees as well as informal contacts between groups, bureaucrats, and ministers. This institutional set-up provided major interest groups such as trade unions and business groups with privileged access to the early stages of decision-making as well as the implementation of decisions. Other channels such as Parliament and the media were deemed less important as most major policy decisions were agreed upon in the corporatist channel (Binderkrantz and Christiansen 2015).

Christiansen (2020) in this volume discusses changes and continuities in the corporatist channel over the last decades, while this section focuses on how Parliament and the media have become more prominent channels of influence for interest groups. In the Scandinavian literature, a dominant position around 1975 was that parliament was little more than a 'rubber stamp' on decisions made in the corporatist channel—or to use Rokkan's famous phrase: 'Votes count, but resources decide' (Rokkan 1966; Dahlerup et al. 1975). Surveys of interest groups as well as members of Parliament confirmed this image with only small shares of groups reporting regular contacts to Parliament. In a 1976 survey, among groups with administrative and political contacts, less than a third described their parliamentary contacts as very important (Christiansen and Nørgaard 2003b: 179).

Over time, interest groups' contacts to Parliament have become central in the political repertoire of groups. This is the result of the less institutionalized integration of groups into administrative decision-making, as well as the so-called 'rise of parliament'. Parliament (*Folketinget*) has thus assumed a more central role in Danish politics as the resources of MPs and political parties have increased (Binderkrantz 2003). Table 27.2 displays the percentage of interest groups reporting contacts to different actors as 'not important', 'somewhat important', or 'very important'. This illustrates that Parliament has assumed a central role in the political work of groups. For example, only 7.5 per cent of groups find contacts to individual MPs insignificant, while 9 per cent choose this response for contacts to ministerial agencies.

It is also evident from Table 27.2 that the two most important types of parliamentary contacts are MPs and parliamentary committees. Almost 90 per cent of groups report that contacts with parliamentary committees are mainly or always initiated by the group, while this is the case for almost 80 per cent of groups with respect to individual MPs (numbers not shown). This reflects that the Danish Parliament—and particularly

Table 27.2. Importance of Contacts to Different Actors

	Not important	Somewhat important	Very important	Don't know
Parliament	15.9	34.0	28.6	21.6
Parliamentary committees	8.6	33.9	42.2	15.3
Party groups	19.5	38.9	19.6	22.0
Individual MPs	7.5	32.8	45.7	14.0
Ministerial departments	10.6	29.9	43.3	16.2
Ministerial agencies	9.0	26.3	50.8	13.9
EU institutions	30.6	30.2	13.0	26.2
Media and reporters	3.6	26.0	62.3	8.1

Note: Survey of Danish interest groups 2011. N (minimum) = 1,053. Question: 'What types of contacts does your group regard as most important?'

parliamentary committees—are relatively open in comparison to other countries. It is possible for any societal actor to approach committees, and there is little tradition of organizing formalized hearings where, for example, parliamentary committees invite experts and relevant interest groups. Compared to other countries, the interaction between the *Folketinget* and external actors is, thus, markedly less structured by Parliament (Pedersen et al. 2015).

The news media has become a highly critical arena for any actor seeking political influence. In a situation where politicians mainly communicate with voters through the media and where decision-makers see news stories as a source of public opinion, it is paramount for groups to get their viewpoints represented in the media (Binderkrantz 2012). Media attention is a means to push issues further up the political agenda and can also be directed towards affecting public opinion or even citizen behaviour, for example, when environmental groups try to make individuals more climate conscious. Furthermore, when interest groups appear in the media, they may target their own membership. Group behaviour can be understood as balancing a logic of influence and a logic of membership, and appearances in the news media are instrumental in demonstrating to members that groups pursue their interests (Binderkrantz 2014).

In Table 27.2, contacts to reporters and news media is the type of contact most emphasized by groups. Less than 4 per cent view such contacts as unimportant, while more than 60 per cent find them very important. Media directed strategies are central in the action repertoire of groups, but it is worth noting that most Danish interest groups refrain from using more unconventional tactics (Binderkrantz 2005). Only 3.5 per cent of groups report engaging in civil disobedience or illegal actions, less than 20 per cent have experience with organizing petitions, and about 30 per cent have at least occasional experience with legal actions, demonstrations, or happenings (INTERARENA 2012).

With respect to the effect of media strategies, media attention is heavily concentrated on a small number of groups. Only twenty-five interest groups received half of all attention in appearances in two newspapers mapped in 2009/2010. In a comparison with

Spain and the UK, media attention in Denmark is concentrated on fewer groups than in the UK, while the Spanish news media display an even higher level of concentration. In all three countries, economic groups appear in the news more often than citizen groups do (Binderkrantz et al. 2017). Over time, increased diversity can, however, be identified in the Danish news media. Two different studies confirm this. First, a study of public radio news finds that public interest groups have increased their share of media attention (Binderkrantz 2012). Second, a comparison of two newspapers from 1975 and 2010 concludes that citizen groups appeared more often in 2010 at the expense of appearances by economic groups and particular trade unions (Binderkrantz et al. 2016).

One thing is to appear in the news media; another thing is the messages groups communicate. In recent years, the framing of political messages has received increasing attention. Policy actors frame by selecting and highlighting some features of a reality (Entman 1993). In the interest group field, particular interest has centred along whether groups justify their policy positions by pointing to their own members, other societal groups, or more general interests (Boräng and Naurin 2015). Figure 27.2 displays a comparison of Danish groups and UK groups with respect to the frames used in the news media. The figure distinguishes between 'economic groups', 'sectional groups', and 'public interest groups'.

It is notable that Danish interest groups appeal to the interests of their own members more than their British counterparts do. Among economic groups and sectional groups, this is even the most frequently occurring type of framing. Two factors are likely at play. First, for all groups, media appearances are partly directed towards their own members, and groups may want to ensure that members feel directly represented by their group. Second, country differences may reflect the legacy of the Danish corporatist tradition. The underlying logic of corporatism is thus the representation and intermediation of different societal interests. In this context, references to membership concerns

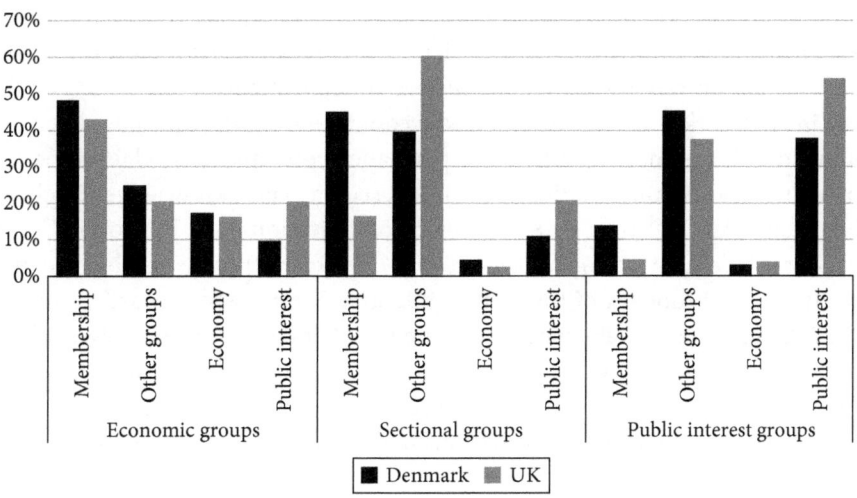

FIGURE 27.2 The use of different frames in Denmark and the UK, percentages.
Note: N (UK) = 1,958; N (DK) = 3,284. (Binderkrantz 2019)

may seem more legitimate than in the more pluralist and competitive British system (Binderkrantz 2019).

Does it make a difference? Ultimately, the political activity of groups must be evaluated based on whether groups gain access to political arenas and affect political decisions. Table 27.3 provides an overview of group access to the administration—seats in public boards and committees—and appearances in the news media in 1975 and 2010.

The numbers testify to a shift in access in favour of citizen groups, particularly in the news media. Trade unions stand out as having lost the most terrain, whereas public interest groups have gained the most. Still, it is notable that economic groups occupied 84 per cent of all seats in public committees in 2010, whereas 67 per cent of media appearances were made by an economic group. Even though citizen groups have gained ground, this is from a situation of a marked stronghold of economic groups. Among the individual interest groups that access arenas most often, economic groups also dominate. Only nine specific groups control more than one-third of all the access points mapped across the media, Parliament, and the administration, and among these nine, the Danish Consumer Council stands out as the only non-economic group (Binderkrantz et al. 2014).

New Actors: Think Tanks and Public Affairs Bureaus

This chapter has focused on organized interests. These are major actors in Danish politics and have a long history of connecting citizens to public decision-making. Over the last decade, interest groups have seen increasing competition from other types of actors, including think tanks and communication agencies. Compared to the large number of interest groups with professional secretariats, these are still a less important factor than in many other countries, but they, nevertheless, warrant attention.

First, in Denmark—and the other Nordic countries—think tanks have been a rising phenomenon. These may be defined as permanent organizations claiming a level of independence and seeking political influence based on expert knowledge (Blach-Ørsten and Nørgaard 2016; Kelstrup 2018). One such organization—the Economic Council of the Labour Movement (*Arbejderbevægelsens Erhvervsråd*)—was established in 1936, before anyone had thought of the term think tank. From 2000 onwards, a number of other think tanks were established, including the liberal CEPOS and Cevea which was established in opposition to CEPOS. In addition, more policy-focused think tanks operate within areas such as environmental issues, macro-economics, and law and order (Kelstrup 2018: 84). They have managed to attract considerable media attention in a relatively short time span (Kelstrup 2018: 94).

Second, agencies working with public affairs have become more important. In a survey among large Danish corporations in 2001, only 5 per cent regularly (at least once a month)

Table 27.3. Access to the Administration and the News Media, 1975 and 2010

	Administration			Media		
	1975	2010	Change	1975	2010	Change
Economic groups	*88.8*	*84.1*	*−4.7*	*80.7*	*67.0*	*−13.7*
Trade unions	30.3	25.2	−5.1	41.7	27.3	−14.4
Business groups	39.1	40.9	1.8	26.8	17.6	-9.2
Institutional groups	16.5	13.7	−2.8	10.6	18.8	8.2
Professional groups	2.9	4.2	1.3	1.7	3.4	1.7
Citizen groups	*11.2*	*15.9*	*4.7*	*19.3*	*33.0*	*13.7*
Identity groups	6.7	4.3	−2.4	7.7	12.9	5.2
Leisure groups	1.8	3.0	1.2	3.1	1.9	−1.2
Public interest groups	2.7	8.6	5.9	8.4	18.3	9.9
Total	1,748	1,964		545	800	
	100.0	100.0		100.0	100.0	

Note: (Binderkrantz et al. 2016).

enlisted the assistance of a communication agency, while more than 40 per cent conducted their own lobbyism or was in contact with a relevant business group (Christiansen and Nørgaard 2003a). No similar survey has been done since, but it is evident that the number of firms using lobbyists has risen. Establishing precise estimates of the number of people engaged with lobbying in such agencies or insight into their activities is difficult. In contrast to traditional interest groups, they are not particularly open about their work.

A notable feature is that many of these agencies employ staff with a previous career in politics. The term 'policy professional' has been coined to describe the rise of a new type of political career where individuals take up positions in parties, interest groups, and lobby firms based on expertise in political processes and networks connecting them to central political actors. For former MPs, their parliamentary experience has been a valuable asset, and a mapping of the careers of previous MPs demonstrate that it is not uncommon for them to take up jobs in lobby firms or interest groups, although most MPs pursue other types of careers (Blach-Ørsten et al. 2017).

Conclusion

Any discussion of political phenomena easily becomes a discussion of change. As is evident from the above discussion, a number of large-scale changes have indeed characterized the role of interest groups in Denmark. Political mobilization has gradually moved towards more emphasis on citizen groups where members join based on shared traits or opinions. Parliament has assumed a more central role in the political work of groups, and the news media are now an unsurmountable part of any lobbying campaign.

In addition, new actors have entered the scene, challenging the conventional wisdom of a well-organized Danish interest group system. In many ways, this can be seen as increased convergence to other European countries as well as the United States.

From a bird's-eye perspective it is, however, necessary to stress the large elements of continuity in interest group politics. Danish voluntary associations attract large memberships, and although some groups lose members, others gain ground. The Danish trade unions are still strong, with comparatively high unionization rates, and business groups as well as organizations of municipalities and other public organizations remain strong factors in Danish politics. Despite the changes described in the political role of groups, close contacts to the administration and early involvement in decision-making are still crucial. Finally, even though political access is more diverse than it was thirty years ago, there is still heavy concentration on a small number of groups—many of these the exact same ones as 3–4 decades ago.

Many aspects of the role of Danish interest groups have been thoroughly researched. For example, associational membership is routinely included in population surveys (Henriksen and Levinsen 2019). Large research projects from the 1970s onward have established accounts of group populations, group representation in boards and committees, and group surveys (Buksti 1980; Christiansen and Nørgaard 2003b; Binderkrantz et al. 2014). Still, less is known about interest groups as organizations, and the rise of new political actors also merits increasing scholarly attention. Directing more attention to these issues as well as updating existing data is a crucial task for future work.

References

Bille, Lars (2008). 'Partier og interesseorganisationer', in Karstin Ronit, ed., *Interesseorganisationer i dansk politik*. Copenhagen: Jurist- og Økonomforbundets Forlag, 85–117.

Binderkrantz, Anne S. (2003). 'Strategies of influence: How interest organizations react to changes in parliamentary influence and activity', *Scandinavian Political Studies*, 26/4: 287–306.

Binderkrantz, Anne S. (2005). 'Interest group strategies: Navigating between privileged access and strategies of pressure', *Political Studies*, 53/4: 694–715.

Binderkrantz, Anne S. (2009). 'Membership recruitment and internal democracy in interest groups: Do group-member relations vary between group types?', *West European Politics*, 32/3: 657–78.

Binderkrantz, Anne S. (2012). 'Interest groups in the media. Bias and diversity over time', *European Journal of Political Research*, 51/1: 117–39.

Binderkrantz, Anne S. (2014). 'Medierne: Kampen om spalteplads', in Anne S. Binderkrantz, Peter M. Christiansen, and Helene H. Pedersen, eds, *Organisationer i politik. Danske interesseorganisationer i forvaltning, Folketing og medier*. Copenhagen: Hans Reitzels Forlag, 177–200.

Binderkrantz, Anne S. (2015). 'Balancing gains and hazards: Interest groups in electoral politics', *Interest Groups & Advocacy*, 4/2: 120–40.

Binderkrantz, Anne S. (2019). 'Interest group framing in Denmark and the UK: Membership representation or public appeal?', *Journal of European Public Policy*, doi:10.1080/13501763.20 19.1599041

Binderkrantz, Anne S. (2020). 'Ildsjæle eller professionelle lobbyister? Karriereveje blandt topchefer i interesseorganisationer', *Politica*, 52/1: 41–58.

Binderkrantz, Anne S., Laura C. Bonafont, and Darren R. Halpin (2017). 'Diversity in the news? A study of interest groups in the media in the UK, Spain and Denmark', *British Journal of Political Science*, 47/2: 313–28.

Binderkrantz, Anne S., and Peter M. Christiansen (2014). 'Præsentation af de danske interesseorganisationer', in Anne S. Binderkrantz, Peter M. Christiansen, and Helene H. Pedersen, eds, *Organisationer i politik. Danske interesseorganisationer i forvaltning, Folketing og medier*. Copenhagen: Hans Reitzels Forlag, 91–115.

Binderkrantz, Anne S., and Peter M. Christiansen (2015). 'Decades of change? Interest group representation in Danish public committees in 1975 and 2010', *Journal of European Public Policy*, 22/7: 1022–39.

Binderkrantz, Anne S., Peter M. Christiansen, and Helene H. Pedersen (2014). 'På tværs af politiske arenaer', in Anne S. Binderkrantz, Peter M. Christiansen, and Helene H. Pedersen, eds, *Organisationer i politik. Danske interesseorganisationer i forvaltning, Folketing og medier*. Copenhagen: Hans Reitzels Forlag, 201–23.

Binderkrantz, Anne S., Peter M. Christiansen, and Helene H. Pedersen (2015). 'Interest group access to the administration, parliament and media', *Governance: An International Journal of Policy, Administration, and Institutions*, 28/1: 95–112.

Binderkrantz, Anne S., Helene M. Fisker, and Helene H. Pedersen (2016). 'The rise of citizen groups? From mobilization to representation', *Scandinavian Political Studies*, 39/4: 291–311.

Blach-Ørsten, Mark K., and Nete Nørgaard (2016). 'Introduktion: Tænketanke i de nordiske lande', *Politik*, 19/1.

Blach-Ørsten, Mark W., Ida Willig, and Leif H. Pedersen (2017). 'Fra politiker til policy professionel – En analyse af danske politikeres karriereveje efter Folketinget fra 1981 til 2015', *Økonomi og politik* 3: 15–26.

Boräng, Frida, and Daniel Naurin (2015). ' "Try to see it my way!" Frame congruence between lobbyists and European Commission officials', *Journal of European Public Policy*, 22/4: 499–515.

Buksti, Jakob A. (1980). 'Organisationerne, den politiske proces og samspillet med samfundsudviklingen' in Jakob A. Buksti, ed., *Organisationer under forandring*. Aarhus: Politica, 9–33.

Christiansen, Flemming J. (2012). 'Organizational de-integration of political parties and interest groups in Denmark', *Party Politics*, 18/1: 27–43.

Christiansen, Peter M. (2012). 'The usual suspects: Interest group dynamics and representation in Denmark', in Darren Halpin and Grant Jordan, eds, *The Scale of Interest Organization in Democratic Politics. Data and Research Methods*. New York: Palgrave Macmillan, 161–79.

Christiansen, Peter M. (2014). 'Organisationernes politiske rolle efter 1975', in Anne S. Binderkrantz, Peter M. Christiansen, and Helene H. Pedersen, eds, *Organisationer i politik. Danske interesseorganisationer i forvaltning, Folketing og medier*. Copenhagen: Hans Reitzel Forlag, 55–90.

Christiansen, Peter M. (2020). 'Corporatism. Exaggerated death rumours', in Peter M. Christiansen, Jørgen Elklit, and Peter Nedergaard, eds, *The Oxford Handbook of Danish Politics*. Oxford: Oxford University Press, 160–76.

Christiansen, Peter M., and Asbjørn S. Nørgaard (2003a). *De som meget har...Store danske virksomheder som politiske aktører*. Aarhus: Magtudredningen.

Christiansen, Peter M., and Asbjørn S. Nørgaard (2003b). *Faste forhold—flygtige forbindelser. Stat og interesseorganisationer i Danmark i det 20. århundrede.* Aarhus: Aarhus University Press.

Dahl, Robert A. (1998). *On Democracy.* New Haven, CT: Yale University Press.

Dahlerup, Drude, Lars N. Kristiansen, and Ole P. Kristensen (1975). 'Korporatismebegrebet og studiet af samspillet mellem politiske institutioner', *Økonomi og politik*, 4: 328.

Danish Confederation of Trade Unions (2018). 'LO's Historie – store begivenheder', https://fho.dk/wp-content/uploads/2018/12/loshistoriestorebegivenheder.pdf (accessed 5 April 2019).

Daugbjerg, Carsten (1999). 'Landbrugspolitik: Stabilitet eller forandring?', in Jens Blom-Hansen and Carsten Daugbjerg, eds, *Magtens organisering. Stat og interesseorganisationer i Danmark.* Aarhus: Forlaget Systime, 107–26.

Entman, Robert M. (1993). 'Framing: Toward clarification of a fractured paradigm', *Journal of Communication*, 43/4: 51–8.

Fiig, Christina, and Birte Siim (2020). 'Gender and politics. The limits of equality politics', in Peter M. Christiansen, Jørgen Elklit, and Peter Nedergaard, eds, *The Oxford Handbook of Danish Politics.* Oxford: Oxford University Press, 365–81.

Fisker, Helene M. (2013). 'Density dependence in corporatist systems: Development of the population of Danish patient groups (1901–2011)', *Interest Groups & Advocacy*, 2/2: 119–38.

Fisker, Helene M. (2015). 'Dead or alive? Explaining the long-term survival chances of interest groups', *West European Politics*, 38/3: 709–29.

Grant, Jordan, Frank R. Baumgartner, John D. McCarthy, Shaun Bevan, and Jamie Greenan (2012). 'Tracking interest group populations in the US and the UK', in Darren Halpin and Grant Jordan, eds, *The Scale of Interest Organization in Democratic Politics. Data and Research Methods.* Chippenham and Eastbourne: Palgrave Macmillan, 141–16.

Grant, Jordan, and William Maloney (1997). *The Protest Business? Mobilizing Campaign Groups.* Manchester: Manchester University Press.

Halpin, Darren (2006). 'The participatory and democratic potential and practice of interest groups: Between solidarity and representation', *Public Administration*, 84/4: 919–40.

Henriksen, Lars S., and Klaus Levinsen (2019). 'Forandringer i foreningsmedlemskab og frivilligt arbejde', in Morten Frederiksen, ed., *Usikker modernitet.* Copenhagen: Hans Reitzels Forlag, 193–230.

INTERARENA (2012). 'Spørgeskema til danske interesseorganisationer – svarfordeling', http://interarena.dk/ (accessed 5 April 2019).

Kelstrup, Jesper D. (2018). *Tænketanke—nye aktører i dansk politik.* Copenhagen: Jurist- og Økonomforbundets Forlag.

McLaverty, Peter (2002). 'Civil society and democracy', *Contemporary Politics*, 8/4: 303–18.

Mikkelsen, Flemming (2002a). 'Indledning', in Flemming Mikkelsen, ed., *Bevægelser i demokrati. Foreninger og kollektive aktioner i Danmark.* Aarhus: Aarhus University Press, 9–44.

Mikkelsen, Flemming (2002b). 'Kollektive aktioner og politiske bevægelser i Danmark efter anden verdenskrig', in Flemming Mikkelsen, ed., *Bevægelser i demokrati. Foreninger og kollektive aktioner i Danmark.* Aarhus: Aarhus University Press, 45–80.

NOAH (2019). https://noah.dk/om-noah/organisation (accessed 5 April 2019).

Pedersen, Helene H., Darren R. Halpin, and Anne Rasmussen (2015). 'Who give evidence to parliamentary committees? A comparative investigation of parliamentary committees and their constituencies', *Journal of Legislative Studies*, 21/3: 408–27.

Rokkan, Stein (1966). 'Norway: Numerical democracy and corporate pluralism', in Robert A. Dahl, ed., *Political Oppositions in Western Democracies*. New Haven, CT: Yale University Press, 70–117.

Schlozman, Kay L., Sidney Verba, and Henry E. Brady (2012). *The Unheavenly Chorus. Unequal Political Voice and the Broken Promise of American Democracy*. Princeton, NJ: Princeton University Press.

Schmitter, Philippe C. (1974). 'Still the century of corporatism?', *Review of Politics*, 36/1: 85–131.

Schmitter, Philippe C. (2008). 'The changing politics of organised interests', *West European Politics*, 31/1–2: 195–210.

Torpe, Lars (2000). 'Foreninger og demokrati', in Jørgen G. Andersen, Lars Torpe, and Johannes Andersen, eds, *Hvad folket magter. Demokrati, magt og afmagt*. Copenhagen: Jurist- og Økonomforbundets Forlag, 79–122.

Torpe, Lars (2011). 'Foreningsdanmark. Små og store forandringer', in Peter Gundelach, ed., *Danskernes værdier siden 1981*. Copenhagen: Hans Reitzels Forlag, 221–39.

Truman, David B. (1951). *The Governmental Process. Political Interests and Public Opinion*. New York: Alfred A. Knopf.

PART III

POLICIES

SECTION EDITOR: PETER NEDERGAARD

CHAPTER 28

IN WAR AND PEACE

Security and Defence Policy in a Small State

ANDERS WIVEL

THE WILLING BUT PRAGMATIC ACTIVIST

DANISH security and defence policies are activist and offensive (see Larsen 2020 for an analysis of Danish foreign policy).[1] They are activist in the sense that they reflect the deliberate choice to engage Denmark in military affairs even when it has political and economic costs and puts the lives of Danish troops in danger (cf. Pedersen and Ringsmose 2017: 344–6). They are offensive in the sense that they engage Denmark militarily in international conflicts beyond traditional peacekeeping on behalf of international society, i.e. in peacemaking and protection of civilians even when this means taking sides between the great powers (Mortensen and Wivel 2019). This policy contrasts with previous defence and security policies characterized by a strong commitment to non-partisan, peaceful conflict resolution (Rynning 2003) or even latent or active neutrality (Holbraad 1991). Change, however, is tempered by strong traits of continuity. With few exceptions, Danish security and defence policy remains pragmatic and with a keen eye on the interests and actions of the great powers.

This chapter identifies the most important characteristics of Danish security and defence policy. It explains the historical context of current security and defence policies and discusses how and why they have developed into their present form and content. The chapter's main argument is that the development of Denmark's activist and offensive security and defence policy reflects the combination of increased international demand for military engagement since the end of the Cold War and the ability and willingness of Danish decision-makers to meet this demand.

The chapter is structured into three main sections and a conclusion. The first section shows how the Danish defeat to Prussia and Austria in 1864 was the starting point for two rival views on what would be the ideal security and defence policy for the newly created small state: one focused on armament and the other on disarmament. The second section focuses on Denmark in the Cold War. It argues that the failure of Danish security and defence policy in the Second World War resulted in a Danish compromise between the proponents of armament and disarmament, leading to a division between national interest defence policy (embedded in NATO) and value-promoting peace policy (embedded in the United Nations and typically conducted in cooperation with other Nordic states). The third section shows how the end of the Cold War ended this division of labour, creating a bigger action space for Danish security and defence policy and also increased international demand for military activism.

THE SHADOW OF 1864: TWO DANISH TRADITIONS ON WAR AND PEACE

Historians have depicted '1864' as a *Stunde Null* or 'zero hour' in Danish politics (Glenthøj 2018). In a war with Prussia and Austria, Denmark lost the duchies of Schleswig, Holstein, and Lauenborg, i.e. a third of the kingdom's territory. The defeat was the conclusion of a gradual shrinking of the Kingdom of Denmark since the early fourteenth century when Queen Margaret I had ruled a Baltic Sea empire (Petersen 2005). From the seventeenth century, Denmark was no longer the strongest military power in Scandinavia, and from the early nineteenth century, Denmark was no longer an important Nordic or European naval power. The British Navy destroyed a large part of the Danish-Norwegian fleet in an attack on the Copenhagen Red in 1801, and what remained effectively became British war booty after the bombardment of Copenhagen in 1807. Denmark subsequently lost Norway to Sweden as part of the peace settlement after the Napoleonic Wars in 1815. After the 1864 defeat, Denmark was no longer a military-based state organization with a strong international military commitment, but a nation-state with a focus on defending the population's sovereignty and territorial integrity (Heurlin 2007: 19).

The defeat in 1864 resulted in a major review of Danish foreign policy, starting from the assumption that Denmark was now a small state and had to organize its foreign policy in accordance with this (Branner 2013: 140). Foreign policy was to be organized defensively and pragmatically, taking into account the great powers, not least Germany after the unification in 1871, and as a small state, Denmark needed to pursue diplomatic rather than military solutions to international conflicts (Knudsen 2006: 128). Only by observing these principles would Denmark be able to safeguard the security of the population and the territorial integrity of the state, a task failed by the political elite in 1864 according to the dominant interpretation of the war.

Leading Danish politicians disagreed on whether this was a temporary condition, a necessary evil to be tolerated until Denmark had recovered from its defeat, or if this was a permanent condition, a new normal serving as the basis for Denmark's future security and defence policy (Olesen 2013: 256–60). Proponents of the so-called 'defence cause' argued that Danish security and defence policy should be aimed at rearmament. Only by rebuilding the military forces would Denmark be able to deter Germany and actively re-enter European politics as an actor to be reckoned with in the future. In contrast, proponents of the so-called 'peace cause' argued that rearmament would be counterproductive. A small state like Denmark could never deter, let alone defend itself militarily, against a neighbouring great power like Germany. The 'peace cause' proponents' position on armament was summed up in social-liberal Viggo Hørup's rhetorical question in the Danish Parliament's negotiations on the defence appropriations in March 1883: 'What is the use of it?' For a small state, a strong military was, at best, a useless waste of money, and at worst, a morally corrupt route to endangering the security of the nation and international society. Consequently, to 'peace cause' proponents, pragmatic diplomacy would serve Denmark better than military strength in its pursuit of national security, and furthermore, allow Denmark to live up to a moral commitment to contribute to a more peaceful world (Gram-Skjoldager 2012).

The peace cause came to dominate Danish thinking on security and defence policy between the late nineteenth century and the Second World War (Rasmussen 2005). This had three important consequences for Danish security and defence policy. First and most fundamentally, the peace cause approach to national security was based on a separation of short-term pragmatic security policy and long-term idealistic peace policy. Accepting the geopolitical realities as the baseline for pragmatic adaptation to the interests of nearby great powers, influential policymakers such as long-term foreign minister and prominent academic P. Munch viewed Denmark's national interest as a small state as a function of Germany's acceptance of Denmark's continued independence. While smallness was viewed as a liability in the military affairs of short-term security policy, politicians such as P. Munch saw it as an asset in long-term peace policy aimed at strengthening international society. A strong international society with common norms and rules would help 'level the playing field' in international affairs to the benefit of the weaker states. In addition to this obvious self-interest in a more rule-governed international realm, small states had both the practical opportunity and the moral obligation to contribute to international affairs because they were excluded from great power politics. Consequently, Denmark and the other Nordic countries worked actively (but with little success) in the League of Nations, promoting disarmament among the great powers (Lidegaard 2003).

Second, like other European small states of the time, Denmark pursued a policy of neutrality, aiming to stay out of trouble by staying out of sight. The defence posture corresponded well with the division of security and peace policies, allowing for pragmatic adaptation to the interests of the strong in questions of national security while maintaining independence when it came to influencing international society in the long-term. By hiding behind its status as a neutral, non-aligned country seeking to maximize its political autonomy, Danish policymakers aimed to avoid the many challenges of international relations, particularly power struggles among the great powers. In the First World War, this policy translated into armed neutrality with Denmark pursuing a non-provocative policy towards Germany and simultaneously tightening its relations with the United States, an important supplier of munitions to Denmark.

Finally, a 'peace cause' approach to international security was concomitant with scepticism towards defence expenditure. Liberal governments in the 1920s and Social Democratic governments in the 1930s spent only reluctantly on defence, leaving the country unable to defend itself in the case of an armed attack. Thus, the political decision of the Danish government in April 1940 to accept a German occupation of the country was as much a consequence of the defence policies of the previous decades as it was a decision made at the time of the invasion.

THE SHAME OF 1945: FROM DE-MILITARIZED NEUTRAL TO ALLIED WITH RESERVATIONS

Denmark entered the post-war era as a state on the margins of international society with virtually no military capabilities (Heurlin 2017: 10). If the dominant political lesson of the 1864 defeat was that Denmark could no longer base its security and defence policies on middle power activism, then the dominant political lesson of the Second World War was close to the opposite: Denmark could not base its security and defence policies on modestly armed small state neutrality (Olesen 2018). This left the political decision-makers bewildered on what defence should and could do after the war (Petersen 2011: 276). The defence laws in 1950 and 1951 reorganized Danish defence. They established a unified Ministry of Defence and an air force service in addition to the existing services, the fleet and the army. The Royal Danish Defence College was established in 1951 in order to strengthen the education of officers and allow officers from all three services to meet in the process in order to create a stronger point of departure for cross-service cooperation. The primary aim of the defence forces was the defence of the territorial integrity of the Kingdom of Denmark based on the combination of a corps of professional military officers and a large mobilization force of former conscripts (Heurlin 2007; Petersen 2011).

This policy was the product of reconciliation between the peace cause proponents (Social Liberals and large segments of the Social Democrats) and defence cause proponents (Conservatives and large segments of the Liberals). On the one hand, peace cause proponents accepted a considerable rise in defence expenditure and modernization of the armed forces. On the other hand, defence cause proponents accepted that Danish defence expenditures remained comparatively low, drawing regular criticism from NATO, and that Denmark sometimes deviated from official NATO policy in favour of a more 'Nordic' position promoting détente rather than deterrence. However, this Nordic peace policy was mostly insulated from security and defence policy. It continued the diplomatic détente and disarmament efforts of the Nordic countries from the interwar period, now under a more explicit Swedish lead and with an accentuation of welfare state values such as equality and peacefulness (Wivel 2017: 490).

It also involved a militarization of peace policy in the form of deployment of soldiers in United Nations (UN) peace operations. Denmark's eagerness to meet the UN demand for troops meant that Denmark participated in all but three UN missions during the Cold War, and Danish troops alone amounted to 7 per cent of all UN troops in the 1948–89 period (Jakobsen and Kjærsgaard 2017: 386). UN missions had their own budget, and the personnel was almost exclusively voluntary, and therefore, had no negative impact on national defence and NATO obligations, thereby also signalling the continued separation of pragmatic security and defence policy and value-based peace policy.

The Social Democrats, the Liberals, and the Conservatives were the main parties behind the rebuilding and reorganization of the Danish defence forces in the post-war years. All three parties continuously supported Danish NATO membership since 1949, and they were united in their intention to provide Denmark with a 'credible' defence (Petersen 2011: 276). The Social Liberals advocated Danish neutrality in the early Cold War and argued against Danish NATO membership in 1949 but changed their position when junior partner in coalition governments under Social Democrat leadership during 1957–64. From that point, the four parties—despite occasional disagreements—served as the parliamentary basis for Danish security and defence policy and continue to do so today.

The pragmatic approach of the Danish government during the German occupation had neither placed Denmark on the side of Nazi Germany nor as part of the allied winners of the war. However, during the war, the Danish resistance movement had had its political headquarters in London, and even before the end of the war, it had negotiated a Danish military engagement under British command in the occupation of Germany after the war. Consequently, from 1947 to 1958, a total of 45,000 Danish troops contributed to the military occupation of Germany, the first of thirteen international military engagements by Denmark in the Cold War and the only one not under the auspices of the UN (Mortensen and Wivel 2019). The British government also played an active role in Denmark's formal re-admittance into international society by working actively for Danish UN membership, and in the following years, Denmark pursued close political, economic, and military relations with the United Kingdom, with the Danish government expressing its desire to support British leadership in Europe (Mariager 2012).

This support did not immediately translate into alliance politics. Initially, the Danish government pursued a Scandinavian Defence Union as its preferred solution to Denmark's national security problem. However, when the United States refused to back a Scandinavian Defence Union, and Norway rejected a British proposal of overlapping Swedish, Danish, and Norwegian defence commitments, Denmark became a founding member of NATO in 1949 (Forsberg 2013: 1165–6). Inside the alliance, in 1953, Denmark declared its refusal to allow foreign bases and troops on its territory in peacetime with the notable exception of Greenland which was used as a bargaining chip in Denmark's relationship with the United States. From 1957, it was official Danish policy not to accept nuclear weapons on Danish territory, including in Danish waters. In general, Danish NATO policies shadowed Norwegian alliance policies, although Danish policies were

FIGURE 28.1 Danish defence expenditure 1950–1989 as percentage of Gross Domestic Product (GDP).

Source: SIPRI (2018)

'slightly more characterized by less deterrence, more reassurance, less integration, and more screening' (Petersson and Saxi 2013: 765–6). For most of the Cold War, Danish defence expenditures fluctuated between 2 and 3 per cent of GDP, although with a downward trend never rising above 2.5 per cent from 1969 and onwards (Figure 28.1).

Denmark's low defence expenditures were the subject of sustained criticism from NATO, but Denmark's geopolitical location was of vital importance for the alliance during the Cold War. First, Denmark was a frontline state, and command over its straits was decisive for controlling access from the Baltic Sea to the North Sea and beyond. Second, the United States considered Greenland to be a vital asset in (and even possibly the location of) a future Third World War between the United States and the Soviet Union. Greenland had caught the attention of US decision-makers during the Second World War because of its strategic location between North America and the war in Europe. During the Cold War, the Thule Air Base became the largest American air base outside US territory, and Greenland served as a point of departure for both defence and reconnaissance and a hub for a range of scientific activities related to military interests.

The combination of low defence expenditures and self-imposed limitations on NATO commitments earned Denmark a reputation as an 'ally with reservations' (Villaume 1995) or even 'quasi-neutral' (Holbraad 1991). Danish NATO-scepticism culminated in the late Cold War from 1982 to 1988 when a majority in the Danish Parliament explicitly expressed the Danish dissatisfaction with NATO's nuclear policy and the hardened US rhetoric towards the Soviet Union by forcing the centre-right Danish minority government to footnote a series of NATO communiqués. Despite occasional scepticism and 'footnoting', NATO remained the cornerstone in Denmark's security and defence policy.

Denmark was consistently reluctant towards any role in security and defence policy for the EU, and Denmark delivered when the United States and NATO insisted, for example by acquiescing to German rearmament from 1955 and the presence of US nuclear weapons in Greenland from 1957 (Mouritzen and Olesen 2010; Danish Institute of International Studies 1997).

THE SOLUTION OF 1989: DENMARK'S MILITARY ACTIVISM

The end of the Cold War was simultaneously a triumph and a challenge for Danish security and defence policy. It was a triumph in the sense that Denmark was a member of the winning alliance—a contrast to 1864 and 1945. It was also a triumph for values such as democracy and human rights which had been fundamental to Nordic peace policy during the Cold War. Moreover, the first few years after the end of the Cold War saw a 'Nordification' of the European political space, including a focus on the non-military aspects of security and various overlapping networks with strong civil society involvement. The collapse of the Soviet Union in 1991 left Denmark surrounded by friendly states and more secure than it had been the previous 1300 years (Petersen 2006: 427). A 1992 report by a committee of leading defence officials, including the Chief of Defence and chaired by the Permanent Secretary for Defence, concluded that a territorial military threat against Denmark had been replaced by political and economic instability with arms proliferation, Islamic fundamentalism, poverty, and migration as potential long-term challenges (Ministry of Defence 1992).

Despite these developments, the end of the Cold War left Denmark and the other Nordic countries with a sense of 'Nordic nostalgia' (Wæver 1992). Nordic 'humane internationalism' in the form of peaceful conflict resolution, global equality, and support for international society had served as an important focal point during the Cold War. Humane internationalism gave the Nordic countries a distinct voice in international relations as a 'third way' between East and West. It allowed the Nordic countries to cultivate a strong international brand, building both on the strong UN engagement of the Nordic countries and the (somewhat imagined and exaggerated) perception that the societal model of the Nordic countries represented a distinct alternative to both capitalism and communism (Browning 2007). However, with the win of the West and the collapse of the East, the Nordic model had lost its rationale as a foreign policy instrument, and consequently, as a platform for Danish peace policy.

It was not only the Nordic platform for long-term peace policy that was called into question by the end of the Cold War. NATO, the Cold War cornerstone for Danish security and defence policy, was now viewed by decision-makers and observers as 'an alliance in search of a role' (Villaume 1999: 49), and it was by no means self-evident that NATO would become the principal institutional framework for Danish military activism less than a decade later (Ringsmose and Rynning 2017: 406). In contrast, Danish decision-makers initially looked to other forums less steeped in the confrontational Cold War superpower logic than the Atlantic Alliance. Compared to other Nordic countries, Denmark used these forums more pragmatically, with the UN losing its monopoly as a framework for Danish military engagement and Danish security and defence policy becoming closer coupled to the interests of the United States and less focused on territorial defence (Wivel 2014a).

To Danish foreign policy elites, Europe's new security order was 'a unique window of opportunity', allowing a new foreign and security policy based on so-called 'active internationalism' (Holm 2002: 21–3). The result was a military activist security and defence policy that collapsed the previous distinction between pragmatic short-term security and defence policy aimed at protecting territorial integrity and sovereignty of the Kingdom of Denmark and a long-term, value-based peace policy aimed at changing the norms and rules of the international order (Wivel 2013). The lack of a conventional military threat to Danish territory combined with a (relatively) liberal world order under US leadership created an action space for policies that were both short term and long term and where Danish policymakers viewed the protection of interests and the promotion of values as two sides of the same coin (Mariager and Wivel 2019: 361–2). In short, in the eyes of the decision-makers, the solution to the challenges of the new security order was providing a positive Danish response to the increased international demand for military engagement. From 1990 to 2018, Danish foreign policy makers committed Danish troops to 76 military operations abroad (see Figure 28.2).

In this context, Danish policymakers viewed the UN as an ideal organization for meeting the challenges of the post-Cold War security order just as they had regarded the

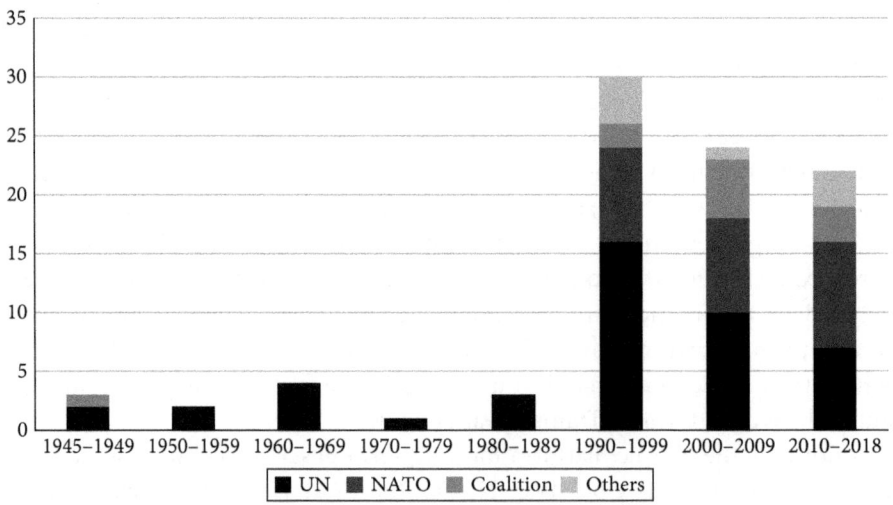

FIGURE 28.2 Denmark's military contributions to international operations.

Source: Mortensen and Wivel (2019). Numbers indicate parliamentary decisions authorizing \Denmark's military engagement

UN an ideal organization for collective security in the early post-war years (Villaume 1999: 48). It allowed Denmark to continue elements of humane internationalism although the tasks of UN troops were rapidly changing from peacekeeping to peacemaking and the protection of civilians, reflecting a new, less stable and more fluid security order. From 1990 to 2018, the Danish Parliament authorized Danish troop contributions to 33 UN operations. While this compares favourably to the 12 operations during the 1945–89 period, it was primarily a function of increased demand from the international society reflecting post-Cold War instability (Jakobsen 2015), and since the 1990s, the importance of the UN for Danish security and defence policy has waned. While Parliament authorized Danish military engagement in 16 UN operations in the 1990–99 period, they only authorized 10 in the 2000–9 period and 7 in the 2010–18 period (see Figure 28.2). Thus, in parallel to the Cold War, the UN did not live up to the hopes of Danish decision-makers, and just like in the Cold War, the reason was the inability of the UN to effectively meet the security challenges of the day. The UN did not have the necessary competencies to fulfil the aims of operations that included peacemaking, and too often the soldiers did not have the necessary mandate to defend themselves or protect civilians (Jakobsen and Kjærsgaard 2017). In the words of a former Danish ambassador to the UN, the organization was willing but not able (Staur 2011: 106–7).

The UN had served as a cornerstone for Danish value promotion during the Cold War, but Denmark's first military engagement after the fall of the Berlin Wall had no institutional framework although authorized by the UN. In 1990, the Danish Parliament decided to dispatch a corvette to the Persian Gulf to contribute to the enforcement of UN sanctions in a coalition under US leadership. This was Denmark's first contribution to an ad hoc military coalition since Denmark's contribution to the British occupation zone in Germany 1947–58. From 1990 to 2018, Denmark contributed to ten international military coalitions. The UN Security Council authorized eight out of ten, with the coalition acting de facto on behalf of international society. One of the operations, Operation Inherent Resolve (2014–), was launched without direct UN authorization but at the request of an invitation from the Iraqi regime, while Operation Iraqi Freedom, initially without a direct UN mandate, caused considerable controversy in Denmark as well as in other countries. In contrast to questions related to Danish defence and security in general and to Denmark's military engagement in particular, a very narrow majority in Parliament consisting of the Liberal-Conservative government and the Danish People's Party decided that Denmark should be part of the coalition invading Iraq in 2003.

Regarding European security, Danish policymakers viewed the EC (from 1993, the EU) and the CSCE (from 1995, the OSCE) as more appropriate forums for meeting all-European challenges than NATO in the immediate aftermath of the Cold War. Denmark had been a strong supporter of the CSCE since its establishment in 1973 as a multilateral forum for East-West dialogue. Its non-military nature and focus on political, economic, environmental, and human rights issues resonated well with Denmark's long-term peace policy. In the first years after the Cold War, Denmark worked actively to make it one of the core organizations for peace and security in Europe, because of its comprehensive membership. The inclusion of East and West bloc European states as well as Russia, the United States, and Canada was an ideal starting point for confidence and bridge-building across the old East-West division (Ministry of Foreign Affairs 1993: 50). However, wide membership and a very broad agenda soon limited decision-making capacity and made the organization less operational than hoped for by Danish decision-makers. Consequently, the OSCE has played only a marginal role in Danish security and defence policy since the 1990s.

In the negotiations leading up to Danish EEC membership in 1973, Denmark had insisted that Danish security and defence policy was not to be discussed in the context of European Political Cooperation since security and defence issues were exclusively embedded in NATO (Rüdiger 1995: 166–7). From early 1990, a few months after the fall of the Berlin Wall, an emerging consensus between the Danish centre-right (Conservatives and Liberals) and centre-left (Social Democrats and Social Liberals) pointed to an increased role for the EU in Europe and in Danish foreign policy. A government white paper from October 1990 saw a bigger role for the EU in international diplomacy but rejected Franco-German ideas on developing the EU's role in defence policy (Ministry of Foreign Affairs 1990). In effect, the white paper was negotiated between the three parties in government, the Conservatives, the Liberals, and the Social Liberals, and the main party of the opposition, the Social Democratic Party (Pedersen 2010: 55). It subsequently served as the basis for Danish negotiations on the Treaty of the European Union, but Denmark was ultimately unsuccessful in keeping defence out of the Treaty. The four parties accepted that the Treaty stipulated the long-term aim of a common defence policy which could also lead to a common defence. They argued it would have little practical implications for Danish security and defence policy (Petersen 2006: 506). However, in a 1992 referendum, Danish voters rejected accession to the Treaty with a 50.7 per cent majority. The subsequent renegotiation between Denmark and the EU resulted in the Edinburgh Agreement, which passed a referendum in 1993 with a majority of 56.7 per cent but included an opt-out on defence policy (see also Beach 2020 and Jensen and Nedergaard 2020).

The Edinburgh Agreement effectively precluded formal Danish influence on future developments of the EU as an actor in defence policy and the participation of Danish troops in EU military missions. Even so, the EU continues to be of importance for Danish security and defence policy. Danish policymakers act from a 'permissive' understanding of the defence opt-out, allowing them to participate in discussions 'in the Council of Ministers with possible implications for defence and allowing (and expecting) civil servants to engage actively in EU security and defence discussions on all issues except those with direct consequences for the operational level' (Wivel 2014b: 93). In the Ministry of Foreign Affairs and the Ministry of Defence, a number of civil servants work on ESDP-related issues. Over the past decades, Danish civil servants have been actively involved in numerous EU working groups on security and defence-related topics, including all groups on defence issues except the group on the European Defence Agency (Olsen 2011: 21). Moreover, despite the opt-out, Danish security policy and conflict management are Europeanized by Denmark's participation in a number of military operations where Danish troops are either in direct contact with troops under the auspices of the EU and/or work on the auspices of an organization cooperating with the EU such as NATO or the UN. In these operations, the EU plays a role in shaping both the values serving as a point of departure for actions and the instruments used in day-to-day attempts at meeting the challenges on the ground (Nissen 2018). Finally, facing a more assertive Russia, in particular since the Russian annexation of Crimea in 2014, Danish positions and sanctions on Russia have been sheltered by the EU, with Denmark promoting sanctions against and criticisms of Russia within the EU but speaking as part of the EU collective against Russia. However, Danish reactions to Russian assertiveness also illustrate that Danish military defence is exclusively embedded in NATO. Since 2018, Denmark has deployed 200 troops plus support staff to NATO's Operation Enhanced Forward Presence in Estonia (Mortensen and Wivel 2019: 616).

As early as 1993, a government white paper stressed that NATO remained irreplaceable as the main guarantor of Danish territorial integrity. To Danish decision-makers, NATO secured continued US engagement in European security, a necessary condition for preventing renationalization of national defence policies in the region, and therefore, remained the core defence organization in Europe (Ministry of Foreign Affairs 1993). NATO was now more than a defensive alliance, having transformed its strategic concept in 1991 to focus on meeting instability caused by a range of political, economic, and social challenges. Denmark became part of the alliance 'mainstream', supporting the alliance's increased focus on conflict prevention, crisis management, and membership expansion (Petersen 2006: 651). In contrast to the Cold War, the centre-left/centre-right coalition of 'NATO friendly' political parties now agreed that Denmark should take the lead on a number of issues. These most notably included support and coordination of the construction of a Baltic battalion from 1994, advocacy of full Baltic NATO membership from 1996 (in the beginning as the only NATO country and in the face of Russian opposition), and military advice for Central Asian countries under the auspices of the Partnership for Peace programme from 1998 (Villaume 1999: 51).

From the mid-1990s, NATO gradually overtook the UN's role as the primary organizational framework for Denmark's military engagement. Denmark's diplomatic activism in NATO was now increasingly partnered with (and gradually overtaken by) military activism which involved all three services: army, navy, and air force. The post-Cold War security environment and the ensuing reform of NATO's rationale and strategic concept had resulted in a military activism collapsing the previous distinction between pragmatic short-term security and defence policy aimed at protecting territorial integrity and a long-term value-based peace policy aimed at changing the norms and rules of the international order. To Danish policymakers, it no longer made sense to make a clear distinction between security and defence policy on the one hand and peace policy on the other. From 1990 to 2018, the Danish Parliament authorized troop deployments to 25 NATO operations (See Figure 28.2). The objective of these operations is typically either to protect the territorial integrity of NATO member states, such as monitoring Baltic and Icelandic airspace and the Danish contribution to the Enhanced Forward Presence in Estonia, or to uphold and protect the interests of international society under UN authorization. The latter was the case in the two longest running Danish military engagements after the Cold War which were also the two engagements with the most

Danish troops involved (more than 10,000 troops in each case), namely the wars follow-ing from the break-up of Yugoslavia[2] and the war in Afghanistan.

In addition, Danish troops have contributed to operations based on NATO's Article 5, activated as a response to the terrorist attacks on New York and Washington D.C. on 11 September 2001. Finally, in 1999, Denmark participated in Operation Allied Force in the Kosovo War, bombing Serbian positions outside the NATO area without UN authorization or basis in Article 5. This was the first time Danish troops attacked another country since 1710 when the Danish King unsuccessfully attempted to regain Scania lands lost from Sweden five decades earlier. Parliament's decision to authorize fighter jets to attack Serbian positions constituted a notable break with fifty years of Danish UN policy as it was the first time that Danish troops fought without UN authorization since the establishment of the UN in 1948. Like all other decisions by the Danish Parliament to contribute to post-Cold War NATO operations, this decision was supported by a broad centre-left/centre-right coalition, thus continuing Denmark's consensus-based military engagement which has also been the case for Denmark's military engagement under the auspices of the UN since 1948. However, in contrast to the Cold War, Denmark was now an 'impeccable ally' in NATO (Ringsmose and Rynning 2008) or even a 'super-Atlanticist' (Mouritzen 2007; Wivel and Crandall 2019).

While Denmark was an 'impeccable ally' when measured on output, input continued to fall short of NATO expectations. In the 1990s, Denmark embarked on defence reforms calibrating the armed forces to a new security order. The parliamentary decision in 1993 to create a Danish International Brigade was an important political signal although it had little operational significance. The defence budget agreements in 1995 and 1999 increased the share of budget designated for international military operations.[3] However, only the 2004 defence budget agreement initiated a fundamental restructuring, effectively giving up territorial defence in favour of a smaller and more flexible force ideal for deployment in 'out of area' operations (Rahbek-Clemmensen 2017: 26; Ministry of Defence 2004). The subsequent defence budget agreements in 2009 and 2012 build on this decision. Financed by a lower 'peace dividend' than most NATO member states and by cuts in territorial defence, this development served as the basis for Danish military activism. However, it also created a growing strain between political ambitions and operational capacity as the first decades after the Cold War saw Denmark increasing its military activism considerably while reducing the defence budget from 2–3 per cent of GDP to 1–2 per cent of GDP. As shown in Figure 28.3, the Danish Parliament did not reverse this development until the defence budget agreement in 2018 and the subsequent supplementary increase in the defence budget in 2019 (Ministry of Defence 2018, 2019).[4]

Conclusion

Small allies of the United States face a choice between a niche approach and a lead nation approach in their security and defence policies (Rickli 2008). The niche approach entails meeting demand for highly specialized forces and capacities, while the lead nation approach

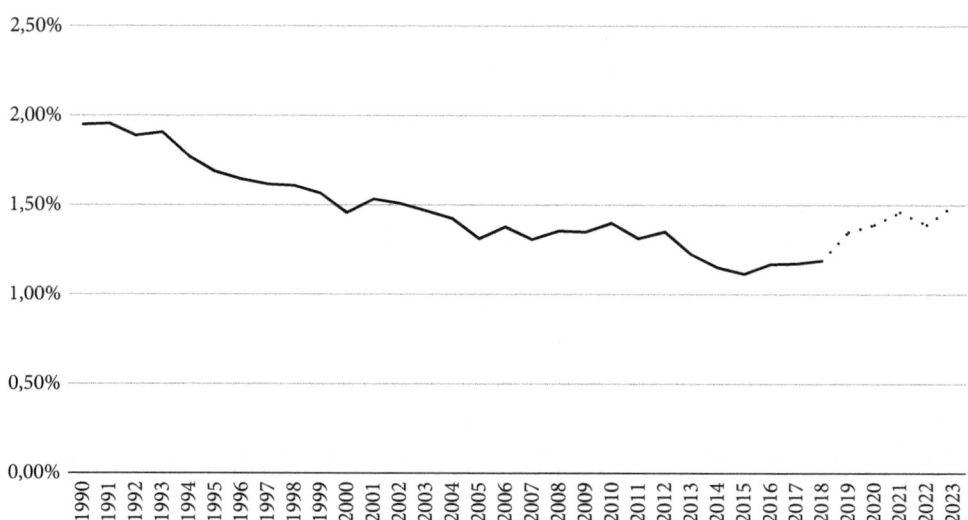

FIGURE 28.3 Danish defence expenditure 1990–2023 as percentage of Gross Domestic Product (2019–2023 projected).

Source: Expenditures 1990–2017 are from SIPRI (2018). Expenditures for 2018 are based on data from the Danish Ministry of Finance (2017), SIPRI (2018), and Statistics Denmark (2017). Expenditures from 2019–2023 are from the Danish Ministry of Defence (2019)

entails supplying command or support structures for military operations. In the choice between the two approaches, Denmark has opted for both, for instance, with special forces in Afghanistan and by taking leadership in Baltic Air Policing. Denmark's military activism provides a marked contrast to Danish security and defence policy during the Cold War when Denmark was a reserved and reluctant ally. In the eyes of the political decision-makers, the post-Cold War security environment collapsed the distinction between short-term security and defence policy and long-term peace policy. Military activism was demand driven by international society represented by the UN and the world's only super-power the United States. Building on and gradually merging 'peace cause' and 'defence cause' arguments, Denmark was willing to meet this demand, seeing military activism as a way of strengthening international society as well as protecting Danish security interests.

However, there are strong traits of continuity as well. Since 1864, Denmark has been a small state, pragmatically adapting its defence and security policy to the interests of the great powers. From 1864 to 1945, Danish policymakers pursued non-provocative security and defence policies towards Germany, and from 1945 to 1989, non-provocation was directed at the Soviet Union and the United States, seeking security shelter from the latter while attempting not to get into trouble with the former. After the Cold War, major Danish decisions on military engagement were made in anticipation of US reactions but with little systematic consideration of costs and benefits (Mariager and Wivel 2019). While the defence forces were reformed to facilitate out of area deployments, the defence budget as share of GDP was reduced until 2018.

The future of Danish security and defence policy is likely to look different than the previous decades. A more assertive Russia and a less reliable United States creates incentives for a more independent European, if not necessarily EU, approach to security and defence in the region with impact on Danish security and defence policy. In 2018, the Danish government commissioned an independent inquiry into the consequences of the Danish defence opt-out. Danish policymakers have shifted their focus to Denmark's geopolitical vicinity in the Baltic Sea and the Arctic (Taksøe-Jensen 2016; Ministry of Defence 2018). Territorial defence in the traditional sense is not on the agenda, but forward defence with troops in the Baltic countries is. To be sure, the United States and NATO continue to play a decisive role in Danish security and defence policy. The 2016 decision to buy twenty-nine F35 fighter jets was—like the 1975 decision to buy F16 fighter jets—heavily influenced by allies' decisions on new procurements. The increase in Danish defence spending reflects US demands rather than a Russian threat, and the Danish government's Foreign and Security Policy Strategy 2019–20 stresses that NATO and a strong relationship between Denmark and the United States continue to be decisive for Denmark's national security (Danish Government 2018).

This creates new challenges for Danish security and defence policy as well as for how we conceptualize and analyse this policy. Our understanding of the current threats and opportunities would benefit from comparative case studies with other small NATO member states and the Nordic countries, as well as a stronger engagement with political and administrative decision-making processes. Most fundamentally, we need a better understanding of the changing content and consequences of military activism and the relationship between military activism and foreign policy activism in other issue areas. A more restrained military activism may free human and economic resources for diplomatic activism and a rethinking on how most effectively to combine military and diplomatic means to further the national interests of the Danish small state.

NOTES

1. I would like to thank Kristin Haugevik for useful comments on an earlier draft and Clara Lyngholm Mortensen for research assistance.
2. With the notable exception of Operation Allied Force.
3. The Danish defence budget is typically based on a five-year agreement between a large majority of centre-right and centre-left parties in the Danish Parliament.
4. The 2019 increase was a combination of additional funds and a revised method for calculating the budget, including budgetary posts not previously included.

REFERENCES

Beach, Derek (2020). 'Referendums in Denmark. Influence on politics', in Peter M. Christiansen, Jørgen Elklit, and Peter Nedergaard, eds, *The Oxford Handbook of Danish Politics*. Oxford: Oxford University Press, 400–416.

Branner, Hans (2013). 'Denmark between Venus and Mars: How great a change in Danish foreign policy?', in Nanna Hvidt and Hans Mouritzen, eds, *Danish Foreign Policy Yearbook 2013*. Copenhagen: Danish Institute for International Studies, 134–66.

Browning, Christopher S. (2007). 'Branding nordicity: Models, identity and the decline of exceptionalism', *Cooperation and Conflict*, 42/1: 27–51.

Danish Government (2018). *Udenrigs- og sikkerhedspolitisk strategi 2019–2020*. Copenhagen: Danish Ministry of Foreign Affairs, http://um.dk/da/udenrigspolitik/aktuelle-emner/udenrigs-og-sikkerhedspolitisk-strategi-2019–20/ (accessed 14 March 2019).

Danish Institute for International Studies (1997). *Grønland under den kolde krig. Dansk og amerikansk sikkerhedspolitik 1945–68*. Copenhagen: Danish Institute for International Studies.

Forsberg, Tuomas (2013). 'The rise of Nordic defence cooperation: a return to regionalism?', *International affairs*, 89/5: 1161–81.

Glenthøj, Rasmus (2018). '1864 før, nu og i fremtiden. Fortællinger i nyere og ældre dansk 1864-historiografi', *Historisk Tidsskrift*, 117/2: 566–98.

Gram-Skjoldager, Karen (2012). *Fred og folkeret. Dansk internationalistisk udenrigspolitik 1899–1939*. Copenhagen: Museum Tusculanum.

Heurlin, Bertel (2007). 'Forsvar og sikkerhed i Norden: Ligheder og forskelle hos de nordiske lande', in Bertel Heurlin, ed., *Nationen eller Verden? De nordiske landes forsvar i dag*. Copenhagen: Jurist- og Økonomforbundets Forlag, 15–70.

Heurlin, Bertel (2017). 'Danmark: Et land under indflydelse', *Udenrigs*, 2017/3: 4–15.

Holbraad, Carsten (1991). *Danish Neutrality: A Study in the Foreign Policy of a Small State*. Oxford: Oxford University Press.

Holm, Hans-Henrik (2002). 'Danish foreign policy activism: The rise and decline', in Bertel Heurlin and Hans Mouritzen, eds, *Danish Foreign Policy Yearbook 2002*. Copenhagen: Danish Institute for International Studies, 19–45.

Jakobsen, Peter V. (2015). 'Danmarks militære aktivisme fortsætter med eller uden USA', *Politik*, 18/4: 5–13.

Jakobsen, Peter V., and Kristine Kjærsgaard (2017). 'Den danske FN-aktivismes storhed og fald 1945–2016', *Politica*, 49/4: 377–400.

Jensen, Mads D., and Peter Nedergaard (2020). 'Danish European Union policies. Sailing between economic benefits and political sovereignty', in Peter M. Christiansen, Jørgen Elklit, and Peter Nedergaard, eds, *The Danish Handbook of Danish Politics*. Oxford: Oxford University Press, 487–501.

Knudsen, Tim (2006). *Fra enevælde til folkestyre*. Copenhagen: Akademisk Forlag.

Larsen, Henrik (2020). 'Foreign policy. New direction in a changing world order?', in Peter M. Christiansen, Jørgen Elklit, and Peter Nedergaard, eds, *The Oxford Handbook of Danish Politics*. Oxford: Oxford University Press, 470–486.

Lidegaard, Bo (2003). *Overleveren 1914–1945*. Copenhagen: Gyldendal.

Mariager, Rasmus (2012). ' "British Leadership is Experienced, Cool-Headed and Predictable": Anglo-Danish relations and the United States from the end of the Second World War to the Cold War', *Scandinavian Journal of History*, 37/2: 246–60.

Mariager, Rasmus, and Anders Wivel (2019). *Hvorfor gik Danmark i krig? Uvildig udredning af baggrunden for Danmarks militære engagement i Kosovo, Afghanistan og Irak*. Copenhagen: Rosendahls.

Ministry of Defence (1992). 'Rapport om forsvarets fremtidige struktur og størrelse. Rapport fra det af Forsvarsministeren den 11. april 1991 nedsatte Udvalg vedrørende forsvarets udvikling mv'. Copenhagen: Ministry of Defence.

Ministry of Defence (2004, 10 June). 'Forligstekst forsvarsforlig 2005–2009', http://www.fmn.dk/videnom/Documents/forlig04_forligstekst.pdf (accessed 14 March 2019).

Ministry of Defence (2018, 28 January). 'Aftale på forsvarsområdet 2018–2023', http://www.fmn.dk/temaer/forsvarsforlig/Documents/Forsvarsforlig-2018–2023.pdf (accessed 14 March 2019).

Ministry of Defence (2019, 29 January). 'Tillæg til aftale på forsvarsområdet 2018–2023', https://fmn.dk/nyheder/Documents/Tillaegsaftalen-2019.pdf, https://fmn.dk/nyheder/Documents/Tillaegsaftalen-2019-bilag.pdf (both accessed 14 March 2019).

Ministry of Finance (2017, August). 'Opdateret 2025-forløb', https://www.fm.dk/publikationer/2017/opdateret-2025-forloeb (accessed 16 January 2019).

Ministry of Foreign Affairs (1990). *Det danske regeringsmemorandum af 4. oktober 1990.* Copenhagen: Danish Ministry of Foreign Affairs.

Ministry of Foreign Affairs (1993). *Principper og perspektiver i dansk udenrigspolitik.* Copenhagen: Danish Ministry of Foreign Affairs.

Mortensen, Clara L., and Anders Wivel (2019). 'Mønstre og udviklingslinjer i Danmarks militære engagement 1945–2018', in Rasmus Mariager and Anders Wivel, eds, *Hvorfor gik Danmark i krig? Irak og tværgående analyser.* Copenhagen: Rosendahls, 541–638.

Mouritzen, Hans (2007). 'Denmark's super Atlanticism', *Journal of Transatlantic Studies*, 5/2: 155–67.

Mouritzen, Hans, and Mikkel R. Olesen (2010). 'The interplay of geopolitics and historical lessons in foreign policy: Denmark facing German post-war rearmament', *Cooperation and Conflict*, 45/4: 406–27.

Nissen, Christine (2018). 'Choosing the EU with an opt-out', PhD Dissertation, Roskilde University.

Olesen, Mikkel R. (2013). 'In the eye of the decision-maker', PhD Dissertation, University of Copenhagen.

Olesen, Mikkel R. (2018). 'To balance or not to balance: How Denmark almost stayed out of NATO, 1948–1949', *Journal of Cold War Studies*, 20/2: 63–98.

Olsen, Gorm R. (2011). 'How strong is Europeanisation, really? The Danish defence administration and the opt-out from the European security and defence policy', *Perspectives on European Politics and Society*, 12/1: 13–28.

Pedersen, Rasmus B. (2010). 'Regeringsautonomi og delegeringstab i dansk EU-politik: Et principal-agent teoretisk perspektiv', *Politik*, 13/3: 49–58.

Pedersen, Rasmus B., and Jens Ringsmose (2017). 'Aktivisme i dansk udenrigspolitik: Norden, FN, NATO og EU', *Politica*, 49/4: 339–57.

Petersen, Nikolaj (2005). 'Danmark som international aktør 705–2005', *Politica*, 37/1: 44–59.

Petersen, Nikolaj (2006). *Europæisk og globalt engagement, 1973–2003.* 2nd ed. Copenhagen: Gyldendal.

Petersen, Nikolaj (2011). 'Forsvarspolitik', in John T. Lauridsen, Rasmus Mariager, Thorsten B. Olesen, and Poul Villaume, eds, *Den Kolde Krig og Danmark.* Copenhagen: Gad, 276–80.

Petersson, Magnus, and Håkon L. Saxi (2013). 'Shifted roles: Explaining Danish and Norwegian alliance strategy 1949–2009', *Journal of Strategic Studies*, 36/6: 761–88.

Rahbek-Clemmensen, Jon (2017). 'Efter Taksøe–Dansk militær aktivisme som interessepolitik', *Økonomi & Politik*, 90/1: 24–33.

Rasmussen, Mikkel V. (2005). ''What's the use of it?' Danish strategic culture and the utility of armed force', *Cooperation and Conflict*, 40/1: 67–89.

Rickli, Jean-Marc (2008). 'European small states' military policies after the Cold War: From territorial to niche strategies', *Cambridge Review of International Affairs*, 21/3: 307–25.

Ringsmose, Jens, and Sten Rynning (2008). 'The impeccable ally? Denmark, NATO, and the uncertain future of top tier membership', in Nanna Hvidt, and Hand Mouritzen, eds, *Danish Foreign Policy Yearbook 2008*. Copenhagen: Danish Institute for International Studies, 55–84.

Ringsmose, Jens and Sten Rynning (2017). 'Rutsjebane: udsving og udfordringer i Danmarks NATO-aktivisme', *Politica*, 49/4: 401–25.

Rüdiger, Mogens (1995). 'Denmark and the European Community 1967–1985', in Carsten Due-Nielsen and Nikolaj Petersen, eds, *Adaptation and Activism*. Copenhagen: Jurist- og Økonomforbundets Forlag, 163–88.

Rynning, Sten (2003). 'Denmark as a strategic actor? Danish security policy after 11 September', in Per Carlsen and Hans Mouritzen, eds, *Danish Foreign Policy Yearbook 2003*. Copenhagen: Danish Institute for International Studies, 23–46.

SIPRI (2018). 'SIPRI Military Expenditure Database: Data for all countries 1949–2017 (excel spreadsheet)'. https://www.sipri.org/databases/milex (accessed 16 January 2019).

Statistics Denmark (2017, June). 'Nationalregnskab 2017. Juniversion', https://www.dst.dk/da/Statistik/emner/nationalregnskab-og-offentlige-finanser/aarligt-nationalregnskab (accessed 16 January 2019).

Staur, Carsten (2011). *Den globale udfordring. FN mellem relevans, legitimitet og handlekraft*. Copenhagen: Jurist- og Økonomforbundets Forlag.

Taksøe-Jensen, Peter (2016). *Dansk diplomati og forsvar i en brydningstid*. Copenhagen: Ministry of Foreign Affairs http://um.dk/da/Udenrigspolitik/aktuelle-emner/dansk-diplomati-og-forsvar-i-en-brydningstid/ (accessed 5 December 2019).

Villaume, Poul (1995). *Allieret med forbehold. Danmark, NATO og den kolde krig. En studie i dansk sikkerhedspolitik 1949–1961*. Copenhagen: Eirene.

Villaume, Poul (1999). 'Denmark and NATO through 50 years', in Bertel Heurlin and Hans Mouritzen, eds, *Danish Foreign Policy Yearbook 1999*. Copenhagen: Danish Institute for International Studies, 29–61.

Wæver, Ole (1992). 'Nordic nostalgia: Northern Europe after the Cold War', *International Affairs*, 68/1: 77–102.

Wivel, Anders (2013). 'From peacemaker to warmonger? Explaining Denmark's Great Power politics', *Swiss Political Science Review*, 19/3: 298–321.

Wivel, Anders (2014a). 'Birds of a feather flying apart? Explaining Nordic dissonance in the (post)unipolar world', in Ann-Sofie Dahl and Pauli Järvenpää, eds, *Northern Security and Global Politics: Nordic-Baltic Strategic Influence in a Post-Unipolar World*. London: Routledge, 79–92.

Wivel, Anders (2014b). 'A pace-setter out of sync? Danish foreign, security and defence policy and the European Union', in Lee Miles and Anders Wivel, eds, *Denmark and the European Union*. London: Routledge, 80–94.

Wivel, Anders (2017). 'What happened to the Nordic Model for international peace and security?', *Peace Review*, 29/4: 489–96.

Wivel, Anders, and Matthew Crandall (2019). 'Punching above their weight, but why? Explaining Denmark and Estonia in the transatlantic relationship', *The Journal of Transatlantic Studies*, 17: 392–419.

....

CHAPTER 29

FOREIGN POLICY

New Directions in a Changing World Order?

....

HENRIK LARSEN

A VARIETY OF APPROACHES TO STUDYING DANISH FOREIGN POLICY

RESEARCH on Danish foreign policy after the end of the Cold War has seen an expansion from the use of one dominant approach during the Cold War to the use of many different approaches in the analysis of Danish foreign policy. Danish foreign policy after the Cold War can be and has been studied from many theoretical perspectives: adaptation theory, constellation theory, smart-state theory, lessons and traditions, discourse analysis, Denmark as a semi-integrated foreign policy actor within the European Union (EU), and Denmark as a 'competition state' (Larsen 2017, 2018). These different theoretical lenses not only influence our interpretations of important trends and events in Danish foreign policy but also what is identified as significant current trends and events in Danish foreign policy. The broad approach taken in this chapter is a discourse analytical approach where the focus is on Danish foreign policy discourses and the way they frame and enable Danish foreign policy. The international surroundings of Denmark are not neglected, but they primarily enter through the way they are read and constructed in dominant discourses. The focus will be on the balance between and the roles of the different organizations (the EU, NATO, the UN, the WTO,[1] and the OSCE[2]) and partners in Danish foreign policy and the variations between foreign policy issue areas (for the military aspects of security, see Wivel 2020). What are the important organizations in Danish foreign policy at the beginning of the twenty-first century? And what are considered central problems and goals?

The chapter will first outline the use and understanding of discourse analysis in this text. After briefly sketching out the dominant discursive structures in Danish foreign policy during the Cold War, it then presents the break with the coming of the post-Cold

War period. The main part of the chapter outlines the developments during the post-Cold War period followed by an analysis of activism. In the final section, some currents trends and tensions in Danish foreign policy are laid out.

Discourse Analysis and Danish Foreign Policy

The article takes its point of departure in discourse analysis. Basic frameworks of representation in Danish foreign policy are conceptualized as discourses. The key assumption is that people's way of speaking are organized in discourses that do not mirror our surroundings, identities, and social relations in a neutral way but play an active role in shaping and changing them. Discourses are used as resources to form representations of the world. They are never just representations of an already existing reality, but they contribute to creating the social world, including foreign policy. In this sense, discourse is a constitutive force in the construction of foreign policy (Larsen 1997, 2005).

We can, therefore, study discourse to provide an understanding of the framework for national foreign policy. Discourse is understood in the broad societal sense of Laclau and Mouffe (1985: ch.3) and Foucault (1972/1989). Along the lines of Foucault, discourse is understood as a limited range of statements promoting a limited range of meanings. Discourse creates the social world by constituting certain forms of knowledge, identities, and social relations which are socially and culturally specific, and therefore, contingent (Foucault 1972/1989).

In work within foreign policy analysis, discourse analysis has been used to analyse foreign policy, particularly in the European setting (e.g. see Larsen 1997, 2005; Wæver 2002). This work has focused on how discourses on Europe, states, and nations have framed and shaped national foreign policy. The aim in this article is to present the discursive framework that has framed and shaped Danish foreign policy in the post-Cold War era. It focuses on the dominant political discourse—that is, the discourse that has primarily shaped Danish foreign policy through its dominance within the government and the Danish Parliament—although, as we shall see, Danish foreign policy has not been shaped by only one discourse (see Pedersen 2020).

Discourses and Foreign Policy after the Cold War

According to the dominant discourse of Danish foreign policy during the Cold War, Danish foreign policy was based on four functionally separate cornerstones: the European Community (EC; now EU), NATO, the UN, and Nordic Cooperation. The EC was about 'market policy', NATO about security, and the UN about promoting universal values and development. Nordic cooperation was a strong identity base for Denmark where values and global foreign policy issues were discussed. The Conference on Security and Co-operation in Europe (CSCE; now OSCE[3]), which also included the Eastern European countries, was later added to the original four cornerstones formulated by Foreign Minister Per Hækkerup in 1965. The point was that each cornerstone fulfilled particular functions that could not and should not be merged with each other (Due-Nielsen and Petersen 1995; Larsen 2011: 94; Hækkerup 1965). Foreign policy debates did not question the four cornerstone understanding; critical debates discussed the issue of whether concrete policies respected this understanding, not the cornerstone discourse in itself. The dominance of this discourse led to a compartmentalization of Danish foreign policy between distinct fora and institutions, the boundaries of which could not easily be crossed.

The EU as the Key Platform for Danish Foreign Policy

After the end of the Cold War, the importance of the EU cornerstone in Danish foreign policy has grown significantly. In the post-Cold War period, the functions of the four cornerstones have been understood as coming together in the EU (Larsen 2005). After the Cold War, the EU could and should deal with economics, politics, security (if not at the expense of NATO), and the promotion and protection of values. Danish participation in the EU was in the dominant discourse, adhered to by the majority of the parliamentary parties and the political elite, articulated as the key forum for Danish foreign policy. The involvement in the making of EU foreign policy was crucial. However, this does not mean that the language of the dominant discourse used in relation to the EU has been one which presents the EU in cultural and mythical terms—as is often the case in France and Germany. The essential cooperation discourse is an instrumental discourse, and it has been and still is dominant in Danish foreign policy today. Proponents of the dominant discourse have also articulated the EU as a 'project of peace', and thus, it approached a cultural and mythical conception of Europe at times (Larsen 2000). For example, the Danish Prime Minister in the period 2001–9 Anders Fogh Rasmussen called the EU 'the greatest peacekeeping project in history' (Rasmussen 2007). Even so, the main weight in arguments within this discourse is on the instrumental value of the EU for Denmark and the other member states.

The dominance of this essential cooperation discourse as a framework for government policy towards the EU has kept in check the role of four Danish EU opt-outs from 1993 (see Jensen and Nedergaard 2020). The four opt-outs were based on an interstate cooperation logic, according to which the EU should take the form of normal interstate cooperation with no substantial abrogation of sovereignty. This discourse is adhered to by the left-wing Red-Green Alliance, the Danish People's Party, and the People's Movement against the EU, as well as significant parts of the public. However, Danish governments have acted on the basis of the essential cooperation discourse in spite of the opt-outs introduced after the Maastricht Treaty in 1992. According to this discourse, Denmark has to be as close as possible to the policy stances of the core countries (the countries that take full part in all the EU's policy areas) to compensate for the opt-outs (Larsen et al. 2018: 126–7).

As a result, Denmark has been deeply involved in EU foreign policy in the post-Cold War period (Larsen 2005) despite the Danish defence opt-out, which is sometimes said to prevent full Danish participation in the EU's foreign policy. The defence exemption has been interpreted by all governments to mean that Denmark cannot take part in the concrete implementation of EU military actions and the planning and political discussions associated with them, including the Permanent Structured Cooperation (PESCO) introduced in 2017. At the same time, Denmark has clearly supported the EU as an actor in military operations (even if it has repeatedly made clear that they should not compete with NATO). There is a bifurcated line between what Denmark does (and does not) participate in within the EU and what it supports in general political terms (Larsen 2011: 96–7). Nevertheless, Denmark is involved in shaping all other aspects of EU foreign policy, including the civilian dimensions of the Common Security and Defence Policy (CSDP) and foreign economic policy (see Jensen and Nedergaard 2020).

A study of Danish foreign policy across issue areas concluded that the EU is the most operational multilateral forum in most Danish foreign policy and foreign economic areas even if it is not always the only one (Larsen 2005). Where the EU has exclusive competence to negotiate trade agreements on behalf of the member states such as in the WTO, there are no other fora. The EU is also the main setting for foreign policy coordination in many international fora, most importantly in the UN General Assembly. The two important exceptions to this are specific development issues where the UN is the key framework, and defence and military issues where NATO and sometimes the UN were the central fora. The contexts in which the bilateral perspective trumped that of the EU are few: practical development policy towards the countries which receive high levels of Danish development aid and the relationship with the United States on certain security issues, including Greenland (Larsen 2005, 2011: 108–9).

THE TRANSATLANTIC LINK

Within the dominant foreign policy discourse, the transatlantic link to the United States is also constructed as crucial. Defence Minister Claus Hjort Frederiksen has written that 'NATO remains the cornerstone of Danish security policy and the Danish Government is committed to maintaining Denmark's status as a core member of the Alliance' (Frederiksen 2018: 34). The way in which the dominant discourse reads, the stronger post-Cold War role for the EU *and* the continued importance of the United States are interlinked parts of an all-embracing Euro-Atlantic structure. However, the dominant discourse does not give equal weight to the Atlantic and the European components of this structure. While the crucial role of the Atlantic structures is stressed in relation to hard security in order to protect common values, the EU is described as 'the cornerstone of Danish foreign policy' (see e.g. Knudsen 2014: 18). In spite of the strong Atlantic emphasis, the role of the EU is presented in terms that suggest that the EU is the primary framework for Danish foreign policy. This is a considerable change from the four cornerstone understanding during the Cold War where the EU (or the EC as it was then) was only one of the four cornerstones, with the Nordic setting, the UN, and NATO being equally important.

In fact, general support for the role of NATO in Danish foreign and security policy went up immediately after the end of the Cold War, both in terms of the positive role that NATO was ascribed within the dominant discourse and in opinion polls. Since the coming to power of the Liberal-Conservative government in November 2001, the role of the United States in Danish foreign and security policy has been stressed as even more important (Petersen 2004, 2006). Even if the relationship between Denmark and the United States peaked during the time of the cordial relationship between then Prime Minister Anders Fogh Rasmussen and then President George W. Bush, the articulation of a strong role of the United States in Danish foreign policy has continued after the changes of government in 2009, 2011, 2015, 2016, and 2019. This has constituted the background for the Danish military contributions to the wars in Iraq (2003–) and Afghanistan (2001–); the offer to contribute to removing Syria's chemical weapons (2013); and the campaign against the Islamic State in Northern Iraq and in Syria (2014–). Yet at the same time, the dominant discourse in official documents has continued to attribute a central role to the EU in Danish foreign policy in formulations such as 'the EU is the key to Denmark's ability to influence the world around us' (Danish Government 2003; Knudsen 2014: 18). Thus, although the role of the United States has clearly increased after 2001, the EU continues to be understood as 'the key to influenc[ing] the world around us' in official documents. The 2006 Cartoon Crisis, for example, did not fundamentally alter the way the balance between the EU and the United States was articulated in Danish foreign policy discourse although there were indications that both the EU and the United States had played important roles in diffusing the crisis (Larsen 2007).

So far we have mainly dealt with the EU and the United States/NATO to a lesser extent. But what about other organizations? In the dominant Danish discourse during the Cold War, the UN was the centrepiece of a rule-based international order. This discourse carried through into the first decade of the post-Cold War era where the UN was finally seen as coming to the fore and being able to fulfil its potential (Jakobsen and Kjærsgaard 2017). It is within this broadly shared Danish discourse that we can understand the upturn in Danish contributions to UN military operations and Denmark's active role (including financial contributions) in the development and shaping of the UN structures under the heading of 'active multilateralism' in the first decade after the fall of the Berlin Wall. The UN became a central scene for the Danish doctrine of 'active internationalism', a phrase articulated in a speech by Foreign Minister Uffe Elleman-Jensen in 1989. From 1995, however, there was a downturn in Danish contributions to UN peace operations as the majority of the operations took place under the aegis of NATO such as in Afghanistan or Kosovo or in a coalition of the willing as in the wars in Iraq and Syria. The tendency has also been a diminishing Danish emphasis on the economic and diplomatic capacity of the UN (Jakobsen and Kjærsgaard 2017). While the official Danish government line was that the operations in Iraq, Kosovo, and Syria took place under a broad UN mandate (even if the mandate was not explicit), the international controversy about this position signalled a Danish departure from the mainstream of the UN members. Denmark has also been less concerned with UN legitimation than the other Nordic countries. According to Wivel (2018: 9), Denmark emphasized the 'unipolar' in the unipolar international order, whereas the other Nordic states emphasized the 'order' element. At the same time in the Danish foreign policy discourse, the UN continued to be the important umbrella for international order and for the development of norms and principles.

The Nordic cornerstone, one of the four cornerstones in Danish foreign policy discourse during the Cold War, can no longer be found in a strong form in official general accounts of Danish foreign policy. The Atlantic/NATO context and the EU in particular have crowded out the Nordic context in Danish foreign policy identity. This movement was already identifiable shortly after the end of the Cold War (Wæver 1992). There are references to the Nordic context in general Danish foreign policy documents, but the presentation of Nordic cooperation as a cornerstone in Danish foreign policy is no longer there. In the 2019–20 Foreign Policy and Security Strategy, 'Norden' (the Nordic countries) is only mentioned once, namely within a section on the EU where the EU member states and the Nordic countries are placed at the same level as the tightest communities of values for Denmark (Danish Government 2018: 15). 'Norden' is not mentioned in the 2017–18 Strategy, whereas close security cooperation between the countries around the Baltic Sea is (Danish Government 2017: 16). This has been reflected in a decline in activities within the Nordic context. Compared with the other Nordic countries, there is a 'Nordic-sceptic' strand in the Danish outlook in certain areas, and Danish citizens are the most sceptical towards the Nordic institutions. Bailes (2016: 32–4) has argued that for Denmark after the Cold War, the group of five Nordic states is both too large (because the Nordic countries are too different) and too small (because Danish needs can only be met in the larger European-Atlantic context) to meet significant Danish concerns. However, the importance of the Nordic dimension in Danish foreign policy very much depends on the issue area (Olesen 2017). Nordic cooperation today is most prominent in the field of practical/economic aid policy where there is substantial informal cooperation (which peaked in the 1980s to 1990s). To a lesser extent, there is diplomatic cooperation—in particular between embassies in third countries. Nevertheless, this is constrained by the Nordic differences regarding membership of NATO and the EU. Even so, there are recent tendencies towards more cooperation in the military field, not least linked to Russia's more assertive policy line (Olesen 2017). A proposal from the Nordic-Baltic Eight (NB8), which was under Danish presidency, for the establishment of an EU unit against Russian propaganda in 2015 played a significant role in setting up the EU's East StratCom Task Force.[4]

During the Cold War, the Conference on Security and Co-operation in Europe (the CSCE; now OSCE) was a candidate for a fifth cornerstone in Danish foreign policy, an all-European one (the CSCE was created after Foreign Minister Per Hækkerup's original conception of the four cornerstones in 1965). One of Denmark's central aims in the post-Cold War period was the political unification of Europe. The OSCE was seen as an important instrument for that along with a comprehensive EU enlargement. Together with the other Nordic EU members, Denmark was a champion of a 'big bang' EU enlargement. With the enlargement with twelve new member states in 2004–7, Denmark's all European vision had largely been fulfilled. For Denmark (and most other EU member states), the OSCE was now mainly a forum for all-European cooperation with the EU's neighbours to the East and Russia. The Council of Europe had the same function, but within the last ten years, the Council of Europe has declined as a forum for Danish foreign policy as Denmark has attempted to reduce the role of the human rights court on national policies following some cases where Danish courts had to overturn their verdicts (Denmark's policy in the OSCE and the Council of Europe is, to a large extent, coordinated with the EU partners).

Activism

The term 'activism' or activist foreign policy has been one of the main themes, if not the main theme, in the study of Danish foreign policy after the Cold War (Pedersen and Ringsmose 2017). Sometimes it is simply assumed that Danish policy has been active without specifying the meaning of activism. At other times, definitions are presented which show that Danish foreign policy has been active, sometimes varying in degree and kind, between the different time periods after the Cold War (see e.g. Pedersen 2015)[5]. A common background for much of the discussion is that there is an essential quality to activism: that it can be determined whether Danish policy behaviour has been activist or not according to certain criteria. This, of course, raises the question of which criteria are relevant (including which criteria are relevant for a country the size of Denmark given its geographical position, organizational links, and political surroundings).

From the discourse analytical perspective taken in this chapter, it is less relevant to examine whether Danish foreign policy behaviour has been active according to a particular yardstick. Rather, what is interesting is how 'activism' (or whichever term may be used in its place) has been articulated by Danish political actors. 'Activism' is in discourse analytical terms an empty signifier: a term that is nearly void of meaning in itself but becomes the centre of chains of equivalence—discourses—through the articulations of political actors (Laclau and Mouffe 1985: ch.3; Larsen 2017: 186). Danish foreign policy activism (or other terms used in its place) has been a signifier with positive connotations for all parts of the political spectrum in Denmark since the end of the Cold War, and Denmark's foreign policy was and should continue to be active. The empty signifier activism is filled out by every government, usually with reference to how it is different from the previous government's activism. Since 'active internationalism' was first articulated in a speech by Foreign Minister Uffe Elleman-Jensen in 1989, successive Danish governments have formulated their foreign policy projects with reference to how these were active in a different way than their predecessors' foreign policy projects. After the 'active internationalism' of the Poul Schlüter government in the period 1989–93, the project of the Poul Nyrup Rasmussen government became 'engaged internationalism', only to become 'international activism' or 'an offensive foreign policy' in 2001 under the Anders Fogh Rasmussen government. It is these projects, the differences between them and the way they frame or shape Danish foreign policy that is the discourse analytical point of interest (Larsen 2017: 186–7).

In this context, a significant break was constituted by the change of discourse from active internationalism/engaged internationalism to international activism/an offensive foreign policy with the Anders Fogh Rasmussen government in 2001. An offensive foreign policy should take clear stances and engage directly in the defining questions of international politics and security. As Rynning (2003) has pointed out, Denmark was now articulated as a strategic actor who should take a clear and active side in the defining conflicts in world politics. This was different from the previous activism which was aimed at mitigating or stopping these conflicts without taking sides (Rynning 2003). The Anders Fogh Rasmussen government presented the previous Danish governments' stances as unclear and as having avoided hard and principled choice; they had not broken with the historical Danish 'adaptation policy' and the spirit of 1864 (Larsen 2009). In an article in *Berlingske Tidende* in 2003, Anders Fogh Rasmussen wrote about '[…] the small state complexes and the passive adaptation theory that have dominated thinking about Danish foreign and security policy for generations', going on to state, 'There is an unspoken expectation of sorts that Denmark should adapt humbly, willingly, and passively to what the dominant European great powers say' (Rasmussen 2003a).

Taking part directly in the central strategic issues in international politics was seen as giving unequivocal support to the leading power in the struggles, the ones whose views Denmark sided with fundamentally. Military support was a clear expression of commitment and of taking responsibility in international affairs (Rynning 2003). There was, therefore, a link between the understanding of international activism and political and military support for the US, including on issues where the need for military support was invoked by the US. However, international activism was also invoked with regard to the EU. Here, the argument was that Denmark should be active in spite of its size (Rasmussen 2003b; Larsen 2009).

International activism was also linked to the domestic project of the Danish government after 2001 (Petersen 2006). Although the Conservative-Liberal government stated that it defended the Danish welfare state, it criticized the historical record of centre-left political forces that were prominent in shaping the welfare state. For these political forces, the idea had been to create a political-economic 'Third Way' between the East and the West. By stressing the need for clear strategic choices in foreign policy, and by criticizing the lack of clear foreign policy choices in the past, the emphasis on strong support of the United States and its values could also be seen as an attack on the legitimacy of the centre/

left as defenders of the welfare state (Larsen 2009: 220). The understanding of activism as a willingness to take part in the central strategic struggles in the world with the United States was, to a large extent, taken over by the governments after Anders Fogh Rasmussen as far as military operations with the United States was concerned.

There has been a tendency in the literature on Danish post-Cold War activism to focus on Danish military activities, which has often (or only) been seen as the defining trait of Danish foreign policy activism. The question of Danish foreign policy activism should, of course, be considered across the different areas and institutional arenas in which Denmark is engaged (Pedersen and Ringsmose 2017). Policies that could be seen as flowing from the Danish understanding of activism before Anders Fogh Rasmussen was participation in UN operations in the former Yugoslavia. However, NATO was the forum that most clearly saw Danish independent initiatives (Ringsmose and Rynning 2017). In addition, there was also the active diplomacy vis-à-vis the independence and empowerment of the Baltic states and the 'active multilateralism' in international organizations. The increased Danish contributions to peace, stability, and the environment (the so-called MIFRESTA[6]) could also be seen as an expression of activism, along with the increase in Danish development aid to 1 per cent of GDP in 1992, which was maintained throughout the 1990s. Within the EU, Denmark was strongly promoting a comprehensive enlargement of the EU and was actively pursuing policies within the EU's Common Foreign and Security Policy (CFSP) (Larsen 2000).

After 2001, many of these policies, such as the strong support for EU enlargement (which culminated successfully with the EU enlargement in 2004), have continued. However, as mentioned earlier, contributions to UN military operations have decreased further, and there have been tendencies towards a less active line in the UN in other fields as well (Jakobsen and Kjærsgaard 2017). The contributions to the Iraq War and its aftermath, the war in Afghanistan and the operations in Iraq and Syria (2013/2014–) could be seen as enabled by the new understanding of activism where acting as a strategic actor became a central part. The participation in the military operation in Libya (2011) fitted less obviously into a strategic narrative, but it was (initially) widely supported in the Danish Parliament for humanitarian reasons, which was more in line with the version of activism that was dominant before 2001. The Danish-Arab Partnership Programme was launched in 2003 to contribute to democratization in North Africa and the Middle East. At the same time, Danish development aid was lowered to 0.7 per cent, and the MIFRESTA initiative was abolished (see Kjær 2020).

DANISH FOREIGN POLICY IN A CHANGING WORLD

The dominant discursive pattern in Danish foreign policy presented above has been the general pattern after the Cold War. In fact, the discourse about seeking to follow the

United States as closely as possible in terms of military engagements while the membership of the EU remains the essential point of departure for Danish foreign policy has been consolidated across the changes of government for the last decade. In the remainder of the chapter, we will look at whether these basic understandings are under pressure as a result of international, regional, and national developments. At a very general international level, it is a question of the impact of the (long-term) move towards more powers and centres in world politics away from the dominance of the West. But in more specific terms, it looks at how the basic discourses in Danish foreign policy read or incorporate recent changes such as Korteweg's (2015) 'four horsemen of the apocalypse': the economic crisis; threats from a more assertive Russian foreign policy; Euroscepticism/Brexit; and migration towards Europe. We will also include a fifth horseman: the election of Donald Trump as president of the Unites States in 2016.

First, we have seen articulations of fundamental concern about the role of the United States in Danish foreign policy discourse following the election of Trump as the US president. Denmark was initially amongst the least critical of the European countries in its official reactions following the change of president in the United States. It was stressed that the Danish-American relationship went deeper than the person occupying the White House (Jørgensen 2016). Nevertheless, the policies of the Trump administration have put pressure on the basic discourse on the central role of the United States in Danish security. The uncertainty about US commitment to NATO's Article 5 and the pressure for a 2 per cent (the figure 4 per cent has also been mentioned) increase in defence expenditure for NATO member states (without the level of Danish contributions to international operations seemingly being able to compensate for this demand); the White House's report about the living standard being lower in the Nordic countries; lack of consultations with coalition partners before the announcement of a possible US military withdrawal from Afghanistan; and US withdrawal from the climate negotiations (which are seen as crucial in Denmark) have all led to hitherto unseen direct Danish criticism of the United States (e.g. see Danish Government 2017: 7, 2018: 8). However, the official Danish discourse continues to stress the role of the Atlantic structures. The 2019–20 Foreign and Security Strategy states:

> The US is Denmark's most important security policy ally, and the guarantor of our security through NATO. The transatlantic ties form the cornerstone of efforts to protect Danish security interests, and it is essential to maintain the American engagement in Europe through NATO. This requires that Europeans invest more in their own security [...] The ambitious Defence Agreement increases defence spending by 20%.
>
> (Danish Government 2018: 11)

Denmark has responded to the US request for higher defence expenses in the 2018 Defence Agreement, although only amounting to 1.5 per cent of GDP at the time of writing. The 2019–20 Strategy also states that 'American global leadership is in Denmark's national interest and crucial to rules-based international cooperation. We must therefore intensify our commitment to maintaining US global leadership' (Danish Government 2018: 5).

Other parts of the strategy, however, articulate the United States as less of a permanent pillar: 'Now and in the years to come, Denmark will have to navigate in an increasingly challenging foreign and security policy environment [...] The United States of America (US) is putting 'America First', raising doubts about its global leadership and its willingness to defend the world order' (Danish Government 2018: 6). It is also stated in the strategy that 'The US is increasingly questioning the value of the international organisations and agreements that it has been instrumental in establishing since World War II' (Danish Goverment 2018: 8). So even if the articulation regarding the Transatlantic ties as the cornerstone in the safeguarding of Danish security remains, there are also articulations to the effect that this situation cannot be taken for granted due to developments in the United States. This change of emphasis can be seen across Europe; what is interesting is that it can also be found in the profoundly pro-Atlantic Denmark.

Second, Brexit has been followed by an increased stressing of the key role of the EU in Danish foreign policy, with official policy articulations firmly within the essential cooperation discourse presented above. This has been particularly clear since spring 2018 when Prime Minister Lars Løkke Rasmussen stated that politicians tended to talk down about the EU (Albrechtsen 2018). This has been followed by the aim of opening up a discussion about the Danish defence opt-out (Danish Government 2018). The 2019–20 Strategy states:

> EU membership remains the best opportunity for Denmark to pursue Danish interests internationally – not least in a time when the global order is changing. Therefore, Denmark has a clear self-interest in actively contributing to ensuring a dynamic EU [...] we must take the lead as a united EU to protect and advance liberal values in a time of uncertainty about global leadership.   (Danish Government 2018: 15)

The articulation of the EU as the key platform for the protection of Danish interests internationally can be found within the dominant Danish discourse on the EU since the end of the Cold War. But the last part of the quote can be read as an articulation of the prominent role of the EU in Danish foreign policy at a time when the United States (among others) is challenging elements of the post-Cold War order. It is a sign of Denmark's navigation towards the EU in a world order where the United States is less engaged and less benevolent towards Denmark.

The suggestion that the defence opt-out may be abolished can also be seen as part of a political rapprochement towards France and Germany (and their PESCO initiative) at a time where Britain's political role in the EU is most likely a thing of the past. This movement has been underway for some time as the United Kingdom has increasingly distanced itself from the European mainstream. The position of France and Germany in Danish foreign policy is bound to become more important in the years to come, just like the attempts to establish new partnerships within the EU to compensate for the absence of Britain (Larsen et al. 2018: 131).

Paradoxically, the signs of a more prominent role for the EU in Danish foreign policy are occurring at the same time as the Danish Social Democrats (in government from 2019) are moving into a (opposite) position where they do not want the opts-outs to go. For the first time since the introduction of the Danish opt-outs in 1993, there is difference amongst the parties that adheres to the dominant discourse as far as the Danish defence exemptions are concerned (see Jensen and Nedergaard 2020). Like in most other EU countries, there has also been an increase in public support for the EU after Brexit. However, a clear majority is still in favour of maintaining the Danish opt-outs (Holstein 2019).

Third, the 2019–20 Strategy has an increasing focus on multilateralism and international rules. Multilateralism and rules are permanent features in Danish foreign policy discourse, but within the last 15–20 years, they have not always had a prime position in official documents. In the 2017–18 Strategy, 'international rules' are only mentioned in one sentence (Danish Government 2017: 12), whereas in the 2018–19 Strategy, 'Rule-based international cooperation' is made the first priority out of six, with the other five priorities (security, Europe, migration, globalization, and the Arctic) being virtually the same as in the 2017–18 Strategy. According to the strategy, 'We must strengthen the international rules that protect our country [...] Therefore, we will engage even more in binding international cooperation and work to reform the international institutions to bolster their strength and legitimacy' (Danish Government 2018: 6). This may indicate a new Danish focus on multilateralism and international rules, bearing a resemblance to the traditional UN/universalism cornerstone during the Cold War and the focus during the first 5–10 years after the fall of the Berlin Wall. However, the tenor of the new emphasis is defence of an international order under threat as well as a new project as 'The international order that has shaped the world in recent decades can no longer be taken for granted' (Danish Government 2018: 6).

Fourth, since the Russian annexation of Crimea in 2014, military threats against Danish territory have reappeared as an element in Danish foreign policy after nearly 30 years during which territorial defence had left the political agenda and participation in international operations had taken its place. This, together with terrorism, is one of the priorities in the 2017–18 and 2019–20 strategies. While these threats are articulated within the dominant discourse as expressed in the strategies, it is important to note that there are also opposing Danish discourses. For the Danish People's Party, Russia is not a territorial threat to Denmark but rather an ally in the war against militant Islam (Sand 2018).

Fifth, there is an increasing focus on the prevention of unwanted immigration to Denmark as a foreign policy and security issue (it has been discussed with increasing intensity as a domestic issue since the late 1990s). It is mentioned as a priority in both strategies (Danish Government 2017, 2018).

Sixth, the Arctic is attributed a bigger role, not least in the light of the possibilities created by the rising temperatures in the area and the technological development. An Arctic strategy was formulated (for the first time) for the Kingdom of Denmark in 2011 with the overall aim of 'creating a peaceful, prosperous, and sustainable future for the Arctic in close cooperation within the Kingdom and with our international partners' (Ministry of Foreign Affairs 2011: 7) (see Gad 2020 on Greenland's status within the Kingdom of Denmark). A stronger prioritization of resources towards the Arctic in Danish foreign policy is also one of the recommendations in the semi-official so-called

'Taksøe Report' about future priorities in Danish foreign policy (Taksøe-Jensen 2016). The Arctic is one of the five priorities in the Foreign and Security Strategies for 2017–18 and one of the six priorities in 2019–20 (Danish Government 2017, 2018).

Finally, the role of trade promotion in Danish foreign policy has increased gradually after the end of the Cold War. This trend has become more significant after the change of government in 2015, and it seems likely to continue as 'economic diplomacy' is also one of the five priorities in the recent strategies (Danish Government 2017, 2018). Providing services to Danish businesses has become an important reason for the existence of Danish embassies, as well as for closing them down when the economic potential for business is no longer present in the country. Economic rather than diplomatic/political concerns are increasingly given weight in Denmark's diplomatic endeavours (Larsen 2017: 237). A study has shown that Denmark's foreign policy identity after 2016 is also (if not only) articulated as that of a competition state. The study demonstrates that the articulation of Denmark as a competition state has influenced decisions in the Danish Foreign Service such as the (re)location of Danish embassies towards potential markets for Denmark (Bækbo 2018). The decision to appoint a Danish ambassador for technology in 2017 can be understood along the same lines. The Tech Ambassador is meant to influence the global rules for non-state actors and attract foreign IT companies to establish themselves in Denmark. There are indications that a competition state discourse has played a more prominent role in Danish diplomacy than in the other Nordic countries and that resources for traditional diplomacy have steadily been reduced to a lower level than in the other Nordic countries (Marcussen 2017).

CONCLUSION

This chapter has taken its point of departure in discourse analysis where basic frameworks of representation in Danish foreign policy are conceptualized as discourses. The chapter has presented the dominant discourses in Danish foreign policy and policies that are enabled by these discourses. The dominant discourse articulates the EU as essential and the key platform for Danish foreign policy, while NATO and the United States are also articulated as crucial if mainly in the field of security. This is the background for the deep Danish involvement in EU foreign policy and the strong engagement with NATO and the United States in the post-Cold War era. The UN and in particular Nordic cooperation are not attributed the same value as the EU and NATO/the United States. During the Cold War, these two fora were equal parts of the four cornerstones which defined Danish foreign policy. In Danish foreign policy discourse, the UN continues to be an important umbrella for international order and the development of norms and principles, but it is not attributed as much weight as it was in the first decade after the Cold War. References to Nordic cooperation can no longer be found in a strong form in official general accounts of Danish foreign policy. The Atlantic/NATO context and the EU in particular have crowded out the Nordic context in Danish foreign policy identity.

Since 1989, successive Danish governments have formulated their foreign policy projects with reference to how they were 'active' in a different way from their predecessors. The articulation of an activism that breaks with what is constructed as the strategic passivity in the past is the background for Denmark's support in the recent conflicts in Syria and Iraq. The chapter has pointed to some tendencies in Danish foreign policy which may challenge or reinforce the main pattern laid out in the chapter.

First, there have been articulations of fundamental concern about the role of the United States in Danish foreign policy after the election of Donald Trump as president of the United States. Second, the Brexit process has been followed by an increased stressing of the key of the EU in Danish foreign policy with articulations firmly within the essential cooperation discourse. Third, the 2019–2020 Strategy has a stronger focus on multilateralism and international rules than in the previous strategy. Fourth, since the Russian annexation of Crimea in 2014, military threats against Danish territory have reappeared in Danish foreign policy after nearly 30 years. Fifth, there is an increasing focus on the prevention of unwanted immigration to Denmark as a foreign policy and security issue. Sixth, the Arctic is attributed a stronger role in the light of the rising temperatures in the area and technological developments. Finally, the role of trade promotion in Danish foreign policy has become more significant after the change of government in 2015, increasing gradually after the end of the Cold War.

Future research should engage with the question of whether these tendencies will challenge or reinforce the basic discursive structures in Danish foreign policy in the years to come, including the central roles attributed to the EU and NATO. Some of the tendencies appear to run counter to each other, and time will tell whether any of them will dominate.

Notes

1. The World Trade Organization.
2. The Organization for Security and Co-operation in Europe.
3. The original Conference for Security and Co-operation in Europe became the Organization for Security and Co-operation in Europe (the OSCE) in 1990.
4. A task force set up under the EU External Action Service in order to counter misinformation about the EU.
5. For an overview of the historical literature on Danish international activism, see Pedersen and Gram-Skjoldager (2015).
6. An environmental aid programme which existed from 1993–2002.

References

Albrechtsen, Rikke (2018). 'Løkke vil tone rent EU-flag', Altinget, https://www.altinget.dk/eu/artikel/loekke-vil-tone-rent-eu-flag (accessed 1 February 2019).

Bækbo, Amalie (2018). 'En konkurrencestats udenrigspolitik: en poststrukturalistisk analyse af dansk udenrigspolitisk identitet efter Taxøe-rapporten', Master thesis, Department of Political Science, University of Copenhagen.

Bailes, Alyson (2016). 'Denmark in Nordic cooperation: Leader, player, sceptic?', in Nanna Hvidt and Hans Mouritzen, eds, *Danish Foreign Policy Yearbook*. Copenhagen: Danish Institute of Political Studies, 31–50.

Danish Government (2003). 'En verden i forandring – regeringens bud på nye prioriteter i dansk udenrigspolitik', http://www.stm.dk/multimedia/En_verden_i_forandring_-_Regeringens_bud_p__nye_prioriteter_i_Danmarks_udenrigspolitik.pdf (accessed 5 December 2019).

Danish Government (2017). 'Foreign and Security Policy Strategy 2017–18', http://um.dk/en/news/newsdisplaypage/?newsid=030b755e-643a-44db-989a-528847f6671b (accessed 22 August 2019).

Danish Government (2018). 'Foreign and Security Policy Strategy 2019–2020', https://www.dsn.gob.es/sites/dsn/files/2018_Denmark%20Foreign%20and%20security%20policy%20strategy%202019-2020.pdf (accessed 7 May 2019).

Due-Nielsen, Carsten, and Nikolaj Petersen (1995). *Adaptation & Activism. The Foreign Policy of Denmark 1967–1993*. Copenhagen: Jurist- og Økononomforbundets forlag.

Foucault, Michel (1972/1989). *The Archaeology of Knowledge* [*Archéologie du Savoir*]. London: Routledge.

Frederiksen, Claus H. (2018). 'The role of Denmark in a more complex security environment', in Kristian Fischer and Hans Mouritzen, eds, *Danish Foreign Policy Review 2018*. Copenhagen: Danish Institute for International Studies, 32–44.

Gad, Ulrik P. (2020). 'Greenland, the Faroe Islands, and Denmark. Unity or community?', in Peter M. Christiansen, Jørgen Elklit, and Peter Nedergaard, eds, *The Oxford Handbook of Danish Politics*. Oxford: Oxford University Press, 28–45.

Hækkerup, Per (1965). *Danmarks udenrigspolitik*. Copenhagen: Fremad.

Holstein, Erik (2019). 'Ny måling: vælgerne vil blive i EU, men de vil ikke af med forbeholdet', Altinget, https://www.altinget.dk/artikel/178869-danskerne-rykker-mod-midten-i-eu-politikken (accessed 1 February 2019).

Jakobsen, Peter V., and Kristine Kjærsgaard (2017). 'Den danske FN-aktivismes storhed og fald 1945–2016', *Politica*, 49/4: 377–400.

Jensen, Mads D., and Peter Nedergaard (2020). 'Danish European Union policies. Sailing between economic benefits and political sovereignty', in Peter M. Christiansen, Jørgen Elklit, and Peter Nedergaard, eds, *The Oxford Handbook of Danish Politics*. Oxford: Oxford University Press, 487–501.

Jørgensen, Steen (2016). 'Overblik: Sådan reagerer de danske partier på Trumps valgsejr', *Jyllands-Posten*, https://jyllands-posten.dk/politik/ECE9136792/overblik-saadan-reagerer-de-danske-partier-paa-trumps-valgsejr/ (accessed 1 February 2019).

Kjær, Mette (2020). 'Development policy. From consensus to contention?', in Peter M. Christiansen, Jørgen Elklit, and Peter Nedergaard, eds, *The Oxford Handbook of Danish Politics*. Oxford: Oxford University Press, 502–20.

Knudsen, Ulrik (2014). 'The international situation and Danish foreign policy 2013', in Nanna Hvidt and Hans Mouritzen, eds, *Danish Foreign Policy Yearbook 2014*. Copenhagen: Danish Institute of International Studies, 11–23.

Korteweg, Rem (2015). 'Beware of the four horsemen circling Europe: Greece, Russia, migrants and the Brexit', https://www.independent.co.uk/voices/comment/beware-the-four-horsemen-circling-europe-greece-russia-migrants-and-the-brexit-10343447.html (accessed 29 March 2019).

Laclau, Ernesto, and Chantal Mouffe (1985). *Hegemony and Socialist Strategy*. London: Verso.

Larsen, Henrik (1997). *Discourse Analysis and Foreign Policy: France, Britain and Europe.* London: Routledge.

Larsen, Henrik (2000). 'Danish CFSP policy in the post-Cold War period: Continuity or change?', *Cooperation and Conflict*, 35/4: 37–63.

Larsen, Henrik (2005). *Analysing Small State Foreign Policy in the EU: The Case of Denmark.* Basingstoke: Palgrave Macmillan.

Larsen, Henrik (2007). 'The cartoon crisis in Danish foreign policy: A new balance between the EU and the US?', in Nanna Hvidt and Hans Mouritzen, eds, *Danish Foreign Policy Yearbook 2007*. Copenhagen: Danish Institute for international Studies, 51–85.

Larsen, Henrik (2009). 'Danish foreign policy and the balance between the Brussels and Washington after 2001', *Cooperation and Conflict*, 44/2: 209–30.

Larsen, Henrik (2011). 'Denmark: a committed member with opt-outs', in Christopher Hill and Reuben Wong, eds, *National and European Foreign Policies: Towards Europeanization?* London: Routledge, 93–109.

Larsen, Henrik (2017). *Teorier om dansk udenrigspolitik efter den kolde krig.* Copenhagen: Hans Reitzel.

Larsen, Henrik (2018). 'Theorising post-Cold War Danish foreign policy: The expansion from one dominant to seven distinct approaches', in Kristian Fischer and Hans Mouritzen, eds, *Danish Foreign Policy Review 2018*. Copenhagen: Danish Institute of International Studies, 77–114.

Larsen, Henrik, Juha Jokela, and Göran von Sydow (2018). 'Nordic member states: Denmark, Finland and Sweden', in Tim Oliver, ed., *Europe's Brexit: EU Perspectives on Britain's Vote to Leave*. London: Agenda, 126–45.

Marcussen, Martin (2017). *Diplomati på bar bund: hverdagens diplomati på de danske ambassader.* Copenhagen: Jurist- og Økonomforbundets forlag.

Ministry of Foreign Affairs (2011). 'Danmark, Grønland of Færøerne: Kongeriget Danmarks arktiske strategi', https://mst.dk/media/89974/arktiskstrategi.pdf (accessed 31 January 2019).

Olesen, Mikkel Runge (2017). 'Aktivismen med de nordiske brødre: forsigtig spiren efter lang tids tørke?', *Politica*, 49/4: 358–76.

Pedersen, Helene H. (2020). 'The Parliament *(Folketinget)*', in Peter M. Christiansen, Jørgen Elklit, and Peter Nedergaard, eds, *The Oxford Handbook of Danish Politics*. Oxford: Oxford University Press, 88–106.

Pedersen, Rasmus B. (2015). 'Tilkoblings- og afkoblingsstrategier i dansk udenrigs udenrigspolitik', *Politik*, 18/4: 37–45.

Pedersen, Rasmus B., and Karen Gram-Skjoldager (2015). 'International aktivisme i dansk udenrigspolitik 2001–2009 – en tværfaglig forskningsstatus', *Historisk Tidsskrift*, 115/1: 163–88.

Pedersen, Rasmus B., and Jens Ringsmose (2017). 'Aktivisme i dansk udenrigspolitik: Norden, FN, NATO og EU', *Politica*, 49/4: 339–57.

Petersen, Nikolaj (2004). *Europæisk og globalt engagement. Dansk udenrigspolitisk historie,* vol.6. Copenhagen: Gyldendal.

Petersen, Nikolaj (2006). 'Efter Muhammed: handlerummet for den borgerlige udenrigspolitik', *Militært Tidsskrift*, 44/2: 135–85.

Rasmussen, Anders F. (2003a). 'Hvad kan det nytte?', Article in *Berlingske Tidende* 26 March 2003.

Rasmussen, Anders F. (2003b). Feature article in *Politiken* by the Danish Prime Minister 15 May 2003.

Rasmussen, Anders F. (2007). 'A look into Europe's Chrystal ball', http://www.stm.dk/_p_5373.html (accessed 1 February 2019).

Ringsmose, Jens, and Sten Rynning (2017). 'Rutsjebane: udsving og udfordringer i Danmarks NATO aktivisme', *Politica*, 49/4: 401–25.

Rynning, Sten (2003). 'Denmark as a strategic actor: Danish security after 11 September 2001', in Per Carlsen and Hans Mouritzen, eds, *Danish Foreign Policy Yearbook 2003*. Copenhagen: Danish Institute of International Affairs, 23–46.

Sand, Christian (2018). 'Hvilken militær aktør er Danmark? En diskursanalyse af de danske militære bidrag til den amerikanskledede koalition mod ISIL 2014-2018', Master thesis, Department of Political Science, University of Copenhagen.

Taksøe-Jensen, Peter (2016). 'Dansk diplomati i en brydningstid. Vejen frem for Danmarks værdier og interesser mod 2030. Udredning og dansk udenrigs- og sikkerhedspolitik', https://udenrigs.dk/wp-content/uploads/2017/01/TakspercentC3percentB8erapporten.pdf (accessed 31 January 2019).

Wæver, Ole (1992). 'Nordic nostalgia: Northern Europe after the Cold War', *International Affairs*, 68/1: 77–102.

Wæver, Ole (2002). 'Identity, community and foreign policy', in Lene Hansen and Ole Wæver, eds, *European Integration and National identity: the Challenge of the Nordic States*. London: Routledge, 20–49.

Wivel, Anders (2018). 'Forerunner, follower, exceptionalist or bridge builder? Mapping Nordicness in Danish foreign policy', *Global Affairs*, 4/4–5: 419–34.

Wivel, Anders (2020). 'In war and peace. Security and defence policy in a small state', in Peter M. Christiansen, Jørgen Elklit, and Peter Nedergaard, eds, *The Oxford Handbook of Danish Politics*. Oxford: Oxford University Press, 453–469.

CHAPTER 30

DANISH EUROPEAN UNION POLICIES

*Sailing Between Economic Benefits
and Political Sovereignty*

MADS DAGNIS JENSEN AND PETER NEDERGAARD

VARIETIES OF EU POLICIES

HANDLING European Union (EU) policy issues is an integral part of being a member state of the EU, which Denmark has been since 1973. This chapter analyses the developments of the Danish government's positions since 1973 regarding the following EU policies:

1) External trade policy (the Common Commercial Policy);
2) the Common Agricultural Policy (CAP);
3) the Internal Market (and its predecessor the Common Market); and
4) the Danish opt-outs from the EU in relation to security and defence, police and justice, and the adoption of the euro.

The four policy areas have been selected because they are of key importance to Denmark but differ significantly with regard to the level of national sovereignty involved. The external trade policy is largely decided by the EU institutions, especially by the European Commission because the Customs Union is an EU matter where national sovereignty has been transferred to the European level. The CAP is also a common EU policy with a great degree of EU involvement; however, in this case, the national room for manoeuvre is larger than in the case of trade policy and has increased over time since 1973. When it comes to the Internal Market, the EU institutions decide the framework. However, it is filled out by the member states through an implementation processes and via elements that are left to the member states themselves to decide. As for the opt-outs, they are

Table 30.1. Comparison of EU Policies

	Trade policy	Agricultural policy	Internal market	Opt-outs
Transfer of sovereignty	Very high	High	Moderate	Low (indirect)
Politicization				
Position				

formally a purely national matter, yet this does not mean that they are not influenced by policies decided by the other member states without opt-outs.

The EU policies are analysed sequentially, which entails that the degree of national sovereignty involved increases. For each policy area, the chapter traces the national position over time and the extent to which it has been politicized. Table 30.1 is used to structure the analysis and allow for comparison between the areas. At the end of the chapter, the cross-cutting pattern is identified by comparing the four policy areas, and Table 30.1 will be completed. By and large, the analysis shows that Denmark seems to follow an interest-based approach to European integration in the four areas, where the support for transfer of sovereignty can be calculated based on the economic benefits it brings to the country. More specifically, support for European integration is strongly positively correlated with the economic benefits it brings Denmark: transfer of national sovereignty to the EU is traded in return for economic benefits. This also reveals that the transfer of sovereignty is seen as a zero-sum game rather than a positive-sum game where the country loses rather than gains influence.

TRADE POLICY

For many years, trade policy was considered an uninteresting policy for both politicians and political science researchers within European studies. Trade liberalizations were progressing more or less automatically after some initially decisive political decisions. However, new developments have changed that perception. The crisis of the Doha Development Round in the multilateral trading system, the rise of China as the world's factory out-competing other exporters of industrial goods, the increasing number of bilateral trade arrangements, the US president's explicit exploitation of trade policy instruments to serve American interests, and the referendum of the United Kingdom (UK) on whether to leave the EU (Brexit): all these developments have put trade policy at the forefront of decision-makers' minds in government and companies as well as among political science researchers (Odermatt 2018).

As far as the EU's trade policy or Common Commercial Policy is concerned, the Danish position has been firmly on the trade liberal side since the beginning of Danish membership (except for agriculture in the beginning of Danish membership to the European Community [EC]). In the latest published trade policy strategy, the Danish government put forward its firm liberal trade policy position. In this strategy, the government situates itself accordingly concerning its trade policy:

> Trade liberalization is also fundamentally in Denmark's interest because our wealth and welfare are deeply dependent on Denmark's companies being capable of selling their goods and services abroad. Moreover, imports from other countries enable us to focus on what we are best at doing. In a time of increased international competition, it is extremely important that we as a nation make it clear that there is a connection between global free trade, the Danish prosperity and thus the Danish welfare society.   (Ministry of Foreign Affairs 2013: 8)

This approach is largely independent of the colour of the government, which is illustrated by the fact that it was a centre-left government consisting of the Social Democratic Party (Olesen and Mariager 2020), the centric Social-Liberal Party as well as the leftist Socialist People's Party that adopted this strategy. Hence, there is a broad political consensus that the more trade liberal the EU is, the better off Denmark is. At the same time, the government recognizes the EU as decisive for Denmark's trade policy:

> Exercising the trade policy interest of the government primarily takes place through the EU. The Commission thus represents the Member States externally in the trade policy negotiations on the basis of consultations of all EU Member States. On the one hand, it gives Denmark a potentially great influence, as Danish interests in international trade negotiations are being treated as part of the world's largest economy. But on the other hand, it also means that it is important to be able to exert great influence on the EU's negotiating line. This is the central starting point and framework for the government's trade policy strategy.
> (Ministry of Foreign Affairs 2013: 10)

Even though the government has shifted since 2013, the trade policy strategy presented above remains the same. According to the original Treaty establishing the European Economic Community (EEC Treaty), the EU is committed to work for the development of world trade, the abolition of restrictions on international trade, and the lowering of customs barriers. In 1968, the EU's Customs Union—the bedrock of the EU's trade policy—was in place. Nevertheless, it has always been an open question as to how the commitments of the EEC Treaty should be interpreted in practice. On that question, Denmark has constantly been in the same camp as the UK, the Netherlands, Sweden, Finland, and (sometimes) Germany *vis-à-vis* France and the Southern EU member states like Italy, Greece, Spain, and Portugal, as well as some Eastern European member states depending on the trade area (Nedergaard 2008; Young and Peterson 2015). Hence, Brexit is a big loss when it comes to securing support for what is in Denmark's interest regarding trade policy (Odermatt 2018).

COMMON AGRICULTURAL POLICY

During the negotiations on the creation of the Common Market in the mid-1950s, agriculture was included for various reasons. France feared that a common market without agriculture would mostly benefit Germany. It would also have left a then great proportion of the populations outside of the European integration processes in the six founding member states. The result was that agriculture became regulated in the Treaty on the European Economic Community. The regulation was based on minimum prices for most agricultural products and with a common EC financing of the fund for intervening in the agricultural markets (Nedergaard 2006a).

Until the beginning of the 1960s, Danish agricultural production accounted for nearly half of the total export, and the UK was the most important market whereas Germany was number two. The Danish government, therefore, decided to follow the UK both when the European Free Trade Area (EFTA) was created and when the UK applied for membership of the EC. When France in 1963 and again in 1967 vetoed the admission of the UK into the EC, Denmark also withdrew its application. However, just following the UK was not perceived to be a long-term solution to Danish economic interests (Nedergaard 1992).

From the beginning, the perception among key decision-makers in Denmark was that the construction of the CAP would hit Danish agricultural exports hard. Time showed that they were right. At the beginning of the 1960s, Denmark pressed for long-term guarantees for its agricultural exports to Germany; however, they did not get any promises. Gradually, the erection of the Customs Union around the EC member states began to take its toll on Denmark's agricultural exports (Nedergaard 2014: 33).

Finally, in 1969, France lifted its veto against the UK, and the negotiations between Denmark and the EC representatives began. Denmark wanted a short transition period because it wanted its agriculture to get out of the so-called 'waiting room' as quickly as possible (Nedergaard 1992). The CAP was the main reason for the yes vote in the Danish referendum on membership in 1972. Giving up sovereignty was not at all considered a problem due to the exorbitant economic benefits from the CAP. Danish agricultural exports would suffer in case the UK became a member whereas Denmark was left out.

For the first decades of Danish membership, the Danish government's position on the CAP was that the traditional high-price system with guaranteed prices for farmers should be kept as intact as possible. Hence, Denmark often supported France on its insistence that the CAP should not be reformed. For Denmark as a whole, the economic benefits embedded in the CAP for decades meant that Denmark had a net surplus as far as the EC/EU budget was concerned (the payments to Danish farmers were much bigger than the payments by the Danish state to the EU budget).

However, the Danish government's position on the CAP gradually changed in the late 1990s when it became clear that many Central and Eastern European countries would join the EU sooner or later which would erode the Danish surplus. From then on, shifting Danish governments became supportive of a reform of the CAP. In consequence, Denmark got much in line with the UK government and its insistence on a reform of the CAP. Since then, Denmark has fully supported all reform initiatives as far as the CAP is concerned and has even insisted on the need for more reforms with less EU support for farmers. One interpretation of the shift of the position of the Danish government on CAP reforms is that that it coincides with the time where Denmark changed from being a net receiver from the EU budget to the present role as net contributor to the EU budget (Nedergaard 2014).

An important reason for the negative budgetary position was the so-called MacSharry reform (named after the Irish EU Commissioner for Agriculture) of the CAP in 1993–4, with less of the budget spent on upholding price support and more on direct payment to farmers, no matter the future production levels. The pressure from the United States during the international trade negotiations in the so-called Uruguay Round was the main explanation for this reform. Leaving aside that the reform meant a reallocation of the CAP budget from efficient farmers (like Danish farmers) to less efficient farmers, with the so-called Fischler reform (the then EU Commissioner for Agriculture) of the CAP in 2003, the shift in the set-up of the CAP was accelerated as even more of the CAP funding went to rural development from which Denmark does not benefit much economically (Nedergaard 2006b).

According to the interpretation above, Denmark has had a rational interest in reforming the CAP from around 2000 since it would potentially decrease the Danish net contribution to the EU budget. There was also increasing awareness from NGOs of the damages on developing countries (because of CAP protectionism) and the environment (because of the intensive and industrialized farming) that came from an un-reformed CAP which were important factors for the Danish government's U-turn (Nedergaard 2014: 34–5).

However, it was only after the change in government in 2001 when a centre-right Liberal-Conservative government took over office from a centre-left Social Democratic-led government that the Danish governmental position towards the CAP changed profoundly. The year 2003 seems to have been the turning point for this new governmental stance on the CAP. In a parliamentary report from that year, it is noted that a majority of the Agricultural Committee (including representatives from the Danish People's Party that otherwise normally supported the government) were in favour of a Danish 'no' to the introduction of new export subsidies for pork. This was interpreted as a general recommendation from a majority of the Parliament. In consequence, Danish officials of the Commission's Agricultural Committees, which oversee the implementation of the CAP, afterwards always opposed the introduction of new export subsidies for agricultural exports out of the EU (Nedergaard 2014: 36–7).

In 2007, the opposition parties including the Danish People's Party (see Kosiara-Pedersen 2020) further strengthened their opposition *vis-á-vis* the existing CAP. The Parliament adopted a resolution that gave the government the task of preparing a strategy on ways of actively phasing out the EU's agricultural support. This resolution has since acted as 'the Bible' for all Danish decision-makers (politicians and civil servants alike) vis-á-vis the CAP. In accordance with the majority of the Danish Parliament, some years later in 2010, the government put forward a policy paper titled 'Towards a New Common Agricultural Policy'. Following this paper, the CAP should be 'focusing on research, development and innovation in the agricultural sector' (Nedergaard 2014: 37).

However, the new direction of the CAP that shifting Danish governments has wished for has never materialized. Denmark remains an outlier when it comes to phasing out the CAP subsidies. Only Sweden (and partly the Netherlands) support the Danish position of phasing out the support. The majority of member states more or less want to uphold the status quo as much as possible with a CAP, focusing on rural development in the Eastern, Central, and Southern EU member states. This is even more the case after the European Parliament gained co-decision power in 2009 as far as the CAP is concerned with the Lisbon Treaty. Hence, there is no resonance for the Danish call for a radical CAP reform.

THE INTERNAL MARKET

At the beginning of the European integration process, the membership of the EC was considered much more a doubled-edged sword for the Danish manufacturing sector than for Danish agriculture as it would both increase export possibilities and also strongly increase competition in the Danish market for industrial goods. The export of industrial goods and services was never the reason for Denmark's first application for membership to the EC in 1961. On the contrary, the Danish industry was perceived to be much less competitive than that of the industries of the EC member states. In 1958, the government published a report with a scenario where Danish industry at that time would face a drastic and quick reduction in the existing tariffs in case of an inclusion into the Customs Union of the EC. The conclusion of the report was that 40 per cent of Danish industry would, as a result, be exposed to hard and severe competition in its home market. This report was named the 'shock report', and it had an enormous impact on both decision-makers and the broader public (Nedergaard 2014: 38).

Later reports were less pessimistic about the economic impact of an integration of Danish industry into the EC Customs Union as they emphasized the potential of driving industrial development through competitive pressure. However, compared to agriculture, the situation for the industry was always seen as a challenge (Ministry of Foreign Affairs 1968). Hence, in the negotiations between the government and the EC officials from 1970 through 1972, Denmark still sought to obtain exemptions for sectors of industry or (at least) longer periods of transition in contrast to the export of agricultural goods where a short period of transition and no exemptions was preferred. The EC officials, on the other hand, referred to the principle of *aquis communautaire* that all member states of the EC should accept after a membership.

In the years after Danish membership to the EC's Common Market in 1973 (the name of the EU's Internal Market until 1985), the Western world suffered from a global economic crisis triggered by a drastic rise in the prices of crude oil. This led to low economic growth, high unemployment, and high inflation in most EC member states. In this situation, many member states adopted beggar-thy-neighbour types of national solutions to the crisis. For example, they introduced the following initiatives: 1) the favouring of national companies in public procurement procedures; 2) the implementation of specific national standards and prescriptions; 3) high taxation on foreign products and low on those nationally produced; and 4) devaluations that improved the competitiveness of national firms but impaired that of companies from other member states (Nedergaard 1990: 86–90).

In addition to all these unfortunate circumstances came a constant claim on part of the UK for a reform of the EC budget in order to decrease the British contribution. In particular, this demand increased after Margaret Thatcher took over power in 1979 ('I want my money back!'), and it paralyzed top EC decision-making until a solution was found at the EC summit in Fontainebleu in 1984 (Nedergaard 1990: 67–78).

After this, the situation began to change as far as the Internal Market was concerned. A new President of the European Commission in form of Jacques Delors took seat in Brussels in 1985, and he presented a comprehensive plan with the Commission's White Paper of 14 June 1985 on the completion of the Internal Market (Commission of the European Communities 1985). This plan included nearly 300 proposals as to how the Internal Market should become a reality without physical, technical, and fiscal barriers to trade (Nedergaard 1990: 127–68).

In Denmark, the centre-right government was strongly in favour of the Commission's White Paper. However, the opposition parties in the Parliament continued to resist the integration of the Internal Market into the new EC Treaty (in form of the so-called Single European Act). Hence, the government called for a referendum on the issue in 1986. The government won the referendum on the so-called 'EC Package' (*EF-pakken*) with an overwhelming majority. In the years that followed, the most important opposition parties (and not least the Social Democratic Party) accepted the Internal Market in principle, but they have often had some strong reservations concerning specific elements of the programme (Nedergaard 2014: 39). The last point did concern and still concerns not least the Internal Market's impact on the Danish labour market. Another concern of the Social Democratic Party was that the Danish rules on health and safety at work and the environment could come under pressure from lower standards in other member states and at the EU level. Consequently, due to pressure from Denmark, a so-called environmental guarantee was introduced in the Treaty as Article 100a (Section 4), and it was recognized in Article 130 that the EU's new cooperation on the environment should be based upon minimum rules.

Generally, Danish trade unions have a much more ambivalent position on the Internal Market than the Danish industry on the employers' side. Nevertheless, there were considerable reservations from trade unions until the end of the 1980s that were also seen among many centre-left politicians; however, they changed their attitude afterwards. In general, they are now all positive as far as the trade in goods is concerned. To a certain extent, they are also positive when it comes to free trade in services and the free flow of capital; however, they do still have reservations concerning the free movement of labour. The reason for this last reservation is that the Danish labour market is organized without minimum wages. The setting of wages is all in the hands of the organizations of the employees and employers, cf. the so-called Danish labour market model presented by Høgedahl (2020).

Danish centre-right governments normally lean towards the employers' organizations, whereas centre-left governments lean towards trade unions when it comes to the positioning vis-á-vis the Internal Market. This, however, does not mean that no Danish centre-right resistance exists as to certain aspects of the Internal Market as was seen concerning the Services Directive (Nedergaard 2014: 41; Jensen and Nedergaard 2012). Even though there is general broad support of the Internal Market from the major political parties such as The Liberal Party (see Christiansen 2020), the Conservative People's Party, the Social Liberal Party, the Danish People's Party, the Social Democratic Party, and the Liberal Alliance, there is certainly criticism of individual directives. This is sometimes pronounced as a 'realistic' support for the Internal Market initiatives from the abovementioned parties, i.e. support that takes into consideration Danish economic interests. The Services Directive is an illustrative case in this regard (Nedergaard 2014: 41; Jensen and Nedergaard 2012).

Initially, the centre-right government was positive and enthusiastic in its support for the Commission's original proposal for a Services Directive, including the so-called 'country of origin' principle. Then a consensus arose among top officials dealing with the issue that the country of origin principle meant that everybody covered by the Directive could come to Denmark and offer their services according to the rules and regulations in their home country. After some time, they found that there were, in fact, several exemptions from the general principle of country of origin. However, there was still anxiety that the Services Directive would potentially undermine the Danish labour market model (Nedergaard 2014: 41). Trade unions were particularly afraid that this would happen, whereas the employers' association was eager to see cheaper suppliers of services in the Danish market even though they also are strong supporters of the Danish labour market model.

The new, broader, 'realistic' view on Internal Market directives among Danish decision-makers also includes the wish for a deeper and earlier scrutiny of the proposals for Internal Market directives in the Danish Parliament's European Affairs Committee, based on the so-called 'basic memorandum' (*grundnotat*), among other things. Yet the 'realistic' support has been amplified in the wake of the Brexit referendum in the UK which has served to underscore the value of the internal market to Denmark and the potential costs of leaving it.

OPT-OUTS: THE EURO, JUSTICE AND HOME AFFAIRS, AND DEFENCE POLICY

The Danish opt-outs were part of the Edinburgh Agreement concluded by the Heads of State or Government of the EU in December 1992. The Danish opt-outs from the EU concerned key areas of the new Treaty such as the adoption of the euro, justice and home affairs, security and defence, and the EU citizenship (this last opt-out is no longer relevant). At the Danish referendum on the Maastricht Treaty in 1992, a majority (50.7 per cent) of the voters had voted no. The basis for a new referendum in 1993 (which gave a yes with 56.7 per cent of the vote) was the memorandum 'Denmark in Europe'—the so-called national compromise—signed by all political parties in Parliament except the anti-taxation party the Progress Party. The memorandum singled out the areas of the Maastricht Treaty from which Denmark should be exempted. The Danish opt-outs are Denmark's contribution to a 'differentiated' EU.

Below, follows an analysis of the Danish opt-outs concerning the euro, justice and home affairs, and defence, in that order, which also signalizes their degree of importance for Danish society. It might seem a paradox why Denmark is not a full member of the European and Monetary Union (EMU) with the euro. Technically, it would be unproblematic for Denmark to meet the EMU conditions. Still, it remains problematic for Denmark to join the euro due to the lack of popular support—basically because the population seems to prefer what they perceive to be full political sovereignty on monetary matters (Marcussen 2014: 48).

The consensus on the no side during campaign before the referendum on the Maastricht Treaty in June 1992 was that a Danish 'no' would not lead to a renegotiation of the entire Treaty. Instead, a no should allow for the possibility that the Danish government could make a list of areas of the Treaty that should not have legal effect in Denmark (Marcussen 2014: 48). Various lists were circulated among the actors on the no side, and they all contained a wish to be exempted from the new European currency (third stage) of the planned EMU.

In October 1992, partly based on these circulated lists, the Social Democratic Party, the Socialist People's Party, and the Social-Liberal Party agreed on the memorandum 'Denmark in Europe'. In the memorandum, it was also emphasized that the no to the EMU should not prevent closer European cooperation between the other member states on the matter.

After intense diplomatic negotiations, at the summit in Edinburgh on 12 December 1992, the Heads of State or Government of the EU Member States adopted the Edinburgh Agreement (*Edinburgh-aftalen*) which would come into force at the same time as the Maastricht Treaty and was binding under international law and designed to meet Danish concerns. The decision included a notification from Denmark that it would not participate in the third stage of the EMU. On 18 May 1993, a new Danish referendum was held and resulted in a clear yes to the Maastricht Treaty, minus the exceptions secured in the Edinburgh decision (Marcussen 2014: 49). During the campaign, it was of particular importance that the former no party, the Socialist People's Party, now recommended a yes. This meant that not only did many of this party's voters change their minds, but the same also happened for many former Social Democratic no voters on the party's left wing.

After the referendum in 1993, the political situation concerning the Danish opt-outs was relatively unaltered until 1998–9 when the EMU project came into practical reality with the introduction of the euro. In the beginning of 2000, opinion polls indicated that Danes were now in favour of Denmark joining the EMU's third stage in the euro area which had started by 1 January 1999. It was on this backdrop that the Social Democratic then Prime Minister Poul Nyrup Rasmussen decided to call for another referendum on the euro in 2000 (Marcussen 2014: 49).

As during the campaign in 1992, most politicians recommended a yes to the euro. This was often backed by pointing out the gloomy situation concerning job creation for the Danish economy in case of a no. The independent Economic Council[1] as well as the Central Bank Director, however, declared that participation in the third stage of the EMU would only have small and uncertain economic advantages or disadvantages for the Danish economy (Marcussen 2014: 50). In addition, the campaign before the referendum took place at the same time as an (according to many Danes, unsympathetic) European campaign and boycott unfolded against the newly elected right-wing government in Austria. Also, the fact that the euro was weakened vis-á-vis the US dollar and the British pound seems to have made an impression of the euro being a weak currency. As a result, the opinion polls turned negative and stayed that way until the final no vote (53.2 per cent) was a reality. This meant that Denmark remained in the so-called Exchange Rate Mechanism (ERM) II, where the Danish krone is pegged against the euro around a fluctuation band of plus/minus 2.25 per cent.

Since the referendum in 2000, not much has changed as far as the decision-makers' appetites on another referendum on full Danish membership of the EMU is concerned. On the contrary, the euro crisis from 2008 onwards in Greece and other Southern European euro countries seems to have created the impression that the euro area is no longer only associated with strong German (and Danish) values of stability and responsible public finances.

Generally, the major political parties such as the Social Democratic Party and the Liberal Party are still in favour of abolishing the Danish euro opt-out whereas the also large Danish People's Party is against it. However, lately, the Social Democratic Party chairman, Mette Frederiksen, has announced that she sees no good reason for not keeping all three Danish opt-outs as they are (Ritzau 2018).

Nevertheless, the fact that Denmark is a member of the ERM II did affect the way Denmark handled the financial and economic crisis from 2008 and onwards. Because of the fixed exchange rate within the ERM II (i.e. +/- 2.25 per cent vis-á-vis the euro), Denmark was not allowed, like Sweden, to let the krone decline to a lower level in order to gain more competitiveness for its exports. Hence, Denmark had to rely on fiscal expansion during the financial crisis. For many Danes, however, this is a price worth paying for upholding a stable currency regime.

In 2016, part of the Danish opt-out concerning the EU's cooperation in the field of justice and home affairs was up for a referendum where the Danish government proposed to substitute the opt-out with an opt-in arrangement similar to one the UK and Ireland had. But again, a majority of 53.1 per cent of the participating electorate voted no. However, the wish to keep the opt-outs has not meant that Danish support for EU membership (with the opt-outs) has decreased. At the height of the financial crisis, the Economic Council concluded in 2009 that considerations regarding Denmark's relationship to the euro area is still primarily a political issue. The economic benefit from giving up the opt-out in this area is moderate (Marcussen 2014: 53). The political benefit of membership is that Denmark would then become part of the EMU's inner circle in decision-making, including the so-called Euro Group of ministers of finance from the euro area.

Since 11 September 2001, the EU's cooperation in the field of justice and home affairs (JHA) has been a rapidly growing area. It covers everything from the free movement of persons, immigration, visa, and asylum policy, and external border policy, as well as judicial cooperation in police, criminal, and civil law matters. As mentioned above, Denmark has had an opt-out from all supranational cooperation in the field of JHA since 1993, leaving Denmark free to participate as long as cooperation remains intergovernmental (Adler-Nissen 2014: 66–7).[2]

Therefore, when the Danish opt-out in the field of JHA was introduced, it was without practical significance because it was all intergovernmental. Hence, Denmark participated fully in all aspects of the JHA cooperation. However, with the Amsterdam Treaty in 1999, areas such as asylum, border control, and civil law policies shifted to the supranational sphere of EU cooperation. This triggered the Danish opt-out in these areas of cooperation. Only criminal law and police cooperation remained intergovernmental, and Denmark could continue to participate in these policy areas (Adler-Nissen 2014: 68).

With the Lisbon Treaty coming into force in 2009, the JHA policy areas (now labelled 'Freedom, Security and Justice') took yet another step towards supranationalism. In consequence, all JHA legislation adopted after this point in time is now covered by the Danish opt-out, and Denmark has since gradually been excluded from cooperation on police and criminal matters. In spite of the opt-outs, shifting Danish governments have sought to keep Danish legislation consistent with EU legislation in most aspects of JHA. In other words, Denmark engages in systematic mimicking and copying of the EU's JHA legislation in areas covered by the opt-outs (Adler-Nissen 2014: 69).

However, the copying of JHA legislation takes various forms. As far as the Schengen framework is concerned, Denmark is entitled to conclude an agreement with the EU under international law on all Schengen measures and has transposed all initiatives into national law in this manner so far. Outside the Schengen area, Denmark can only ask for an agreement with the EU. If an EU measure is based upon reciprocity, Denmark cannot just copy EU legislation. An example is the Dublin system of asylum-seekers. This system is founded on a reciprocity principle that commits all member states to receive asylum-seekers from other member states. Denmark could easily copy the EU legislation and decide to receive asylum-seekers from other member states, but it has no way of ensuring that other member states will accept asylum-seekers from Denmark. This is all the more challenging as these reciprocity mechanisms are applied to an increasing number of JHA regulations from recognition of divorces to court rulings regarding terrorism. In these areas, Denmark may try to conclude an agreement under international law with the other EU member states, creating an obligation between the parties (Adler-Nissen 2014: 70).

According to the Commission, such agreements should be of an exceptional nature, and they should be in the interest of the rest of the EU (Adler-Nissen 2014: 71). In consequence, very few such agreements have been asked for, and the Commission has granted even fewer. They are all in the JHA areas of asylum and civil law.

The JHA opt-outs have made Denmark a rule-taker. This does not imply that Denmark has not—through its JHA opt-out—kept a larger degree of political sovereignty than it would otherwise have had. If Denmark were to abolish its JHA opt-out right away, this would imply substantial changes to Danish asylum and immigration legislation (*Udlændingeloven*). In that case, Denmark would have to change its 24-year rule, the association requirement, the housing requirement, and other special requirements for obtaining family reunification (Adler-Nissen 2014: 73).

This is also why the area of immigration and asylum was exempted from the referendum on the Danish JHA opt-out in 2016. The government's justification for the referendum was primarily the wish to continue Denmark's participation in the new supranational Europol. In spite of the fact that only a partial lifting of the JHA opt-out was at stake, the Danish voters voted no with a small majority. Subsequently, the Danish government managed to secure a special arrangement for the Danish police concerning some of the important JHA police and criminal law measures despite their transfer to supranational mode.

The third Danish opt-out excludes Denmark from participation in the implementation of EU decisions and actions with defence implications (Wivel 2014: 81). For this reason, Danish military foreign policy activism has since taken place under the auspices of NATO and the UN, and Denmark's influence within the EU's European Security and Defence Policy (ESDP) has been limited.

Generally, the defence opt-out has limited Denmark's participation in the development of the EU as a military actor. However, as mentioned by Anders Wivel:

> The effects of this development have been cushioned by the permissive interpretation of the Danish defence op-out by Danish foreign policy-makers. This interpretation has allowed them to engage in debates in the Council of Ministers with possible implications for defence, allowing (and expecting) civil servants to engage actively in EU security and defence discussions on all issues except those with direct consequences for the operational level.   (Wivel 2014: 93)

At the same time, the Danish defence policy has also been 'Americanized' at the operational level because of the Danish defence opt-out, and the Danish defence has—contrary to major EU member states—actively taken part in the American-led interventions in, for example, Iraq.

Lately, both the German and French government have proposed a strengthening of the ESDP in order to give it a much clearer military dimension. There have also been proposals to strengthen the European production of military material (Rasmussen 2018). This will—as in the JHA area—make the Danish defence opt-out more important. As a result, the minister of defence from the Liberal Party (see Christiansen 2020) has advocated for a referendum to get rid of the Danish defence opt-out. In contrast, the leading opposition party the Social Democratic Party (see Olesen and Mariager 2020) is against such a referendum. In fact, as mentioned above, the Social Democratic Party wants to keep all the Danish opt-outs intact.

CONCLUSION

This chapter has examined four important EU policy areas as seen from a Danish perspective, which vary in terms of transferred sovereignty and the degree to which they have been politicized. The results are summarized in Table 30.2. Trade policy is an area that has become increasingly salient over time but where Denmark's position in favour of free trade has remained constant. By contrast, agricultural policy is an area that has always had political attention in Denmark but where there has been a major change from supporting the high spending on the Common Agricultural Policy to wanting to decrease spending following its downgrading from EU high politics to a marginalized policy area.

The Internal Market is an example of a policy that has been politicized over the years where the centre-right has been supportive while the centre-left has been more sceptical. Yet a consensus has emerged where the mainstream parties nowadays support most principles of the internal market, though with some reservations regarding those which constitute a potential threat to the Danish labour market and welfare model due

Table 30.2. Characteristics of the Analysed EU Policies

	Trade policy	Agricultural policy	Internal market	Opt-outs
Transfer of sovereignty	Very high	High	Moderate	Low (indirect)
Politicization	Low degree of domestic politicization	Moderate degree of domestic politicization	Moderate degree of domestic politicization	High degree of domestic politicization
Position	As a small open market economy, free trade in the EU and the world is in Denmark's interest.	Denmark supported high funding for farmers through the Common Agricultural Policy until Denmark became a net contributor to the EU's budget. Since then, Denmark has worked to minimize the support.	High support for the Internal Market from the centre-right. Increasing support from the centre-left over time. Lack of support for initiatives that threaten the Danish welfare and labour market models.	While the centre parties are working to abolish the opt-outs, their wish to do so has diminished over time.

to a clash between the rule-based EU model and the Nordic model of collective agreement. The opt-outs comprise very different polices in terms of the euro, justice and home affairs, and defence policy which are all highly politicized and which have remained intact despite attempts to remove two of them.

Looking across the different policy sectors covered in this chapter, it demonstrates that Denmark supports areas that are associated with economic benefits for the country, whereas it is hesitant when it comes to areas that do not provide such economic benefits and involve the transfer of sovereignty at the same time.

Acknowledgements

We acknowledge the highly qualified comments we have received from experts in the MFA, the Ministry of Business, the Ministry of Food and Agriculture, and the EU-secretariat of the Danish Parliament (Morten Knudsen and Iben Tybjærg Schacke-Barfoed).

Notes

1. 'The Danish Economic Councils is an independent economic advisory body. The primary objective of the institution is to provide independent analysis and policy advice to Danish policy makers. The Chairmanship consists of four university professors in economics and is publicly often referred to as the "wise men". The Chairmanship is independent and responsible for the analyses and conclusions provided in the three main reports presented to the councils. [...] The Economic Council was established by law in 1962. The Council has 25 members representing unions, employers, the Danish Central Bank and the Danish Government. The members of the Economic Council meet twice a year to discuss a report prepared by the Chairmanship' (Danish Economic Councils n.d.).
2. Supranational cooperation implies, among other things, that EU legislation has direct effect in member states for citizens. In contrast, intergovernmental cooperation has to be transposed into national law via national parliaments.

References

Adler-Nissen, Rebecca (2014). 'Justice and home affairs', in Lee Miles and Anders Wivel, eds, *Denmark and the European Union*. Abingdon: Routledge, 65–79.

Christiansen, Flemming J. (2020). 'The Liberal Party. From agrarian and liberal to centre-right catch-all', in Peter M. Christiansen, Jørgen Elklit, and Peter Nedergaard, eds, *The Oxford Handbook of Danish Politics*. Oxford: Oxford University Press, 296–12.

Commission of the European Communities (1985). *Completing the Internal Market. White Paper from the Commission to the European Council (Milan, 28–29 June 1985)*. COM (85) 310 final, 14 June 1985, http://aei.pitt.edu/1113/1/internal_market_wp_COM_85_310.pdf (accessed 5 December 2019).

Danish Economic Councils (n.d.). 'Danish Economic Councils', https://dors.dk/english (accessed 24 May 2019).

Høgedahl, Laust (2020). 'The Danish labour market model. Is the bumblebee still flying?', in Peter M. Christiansen, Jørgen Elklit, and Peter Nedergaard, eds, *The Oxford Handbook of Danish Politics*. Oxford: Oxford University Press, 559–76.

Jensen, Mads D., and Peter Nedergaard (2012). 'From "Frankenstein" to "toothless vampire"? Explaining the watering down of the Services Directive', *Journal of European Public Policy*, 19/6: 844–62.

Kosiara-Pedersen, Karina (2020). 'The Danish Peoples Party. Centre-oriented populists?', in Peter M. Christiansen, Jørgen Elklit, and Peter Nedergaard, eds, *The Oxford Handbook of Danish Politics*. Oxford: Oxford University Press, 313–28.

Marcussen, Martin (2014). 'Denmark and the euro-opt out', in Lee Miles and Anders Wivel, eds, *Denmark and the European Union*. Abingdon: Routledge, 47–64.

Ministry of Foreign Affairs (1968). *Danmark og de europæiske fællesskaber*. Copenhagen.

Ministry of Foreign Affairs (2013). *Ny handelspolitisk strategi*. Copenhagen.

Nedergaard, Peter (1990). *EF's markedsintegration. En politisk økonomisk analyse*. Copenhagen: Jurist- og Økonomforbundets Forlag.

Nedergaard, Peter (1992). 'Agricultural policy', in Lise Lyck ed., *Denmark and the EC Membership Evaluated*. London: Pinter Publishers, 109–13.

Nedergaard, Peter (2006a). 'Market failures and government failures: A theoretical model of the Common Agricultural Policy', *Public Choice*, 127/3–4: 385–405.

Nedergaard, Peter (2006b). 'The 2003 reform of the Common Agricultural Policy: Against all odds or rational explanations?', *Journal of European Integration*, 28/3: 203–23.

Nedergaard, Peter (2008). *Business and Politics in the European Union: Cases in Service, Agriculture and Textiles*. Copenhagen: Jurist- og Økonomforbundets Forlag.

Nedergaard, Peter (2014). 'The Internal Market Policy and the Common Market Policy. The normalization of EU policy-making in Denmark', in Lee Miles and Anders Wivel, eds, *Denmark and the European Union*. Abingdon: Routledge, 30–46.

Odermatt, Jed (2018). 'Brexit and British trade policy', in Patrick Diamond, Peter Nedergaard, and Ben Rosamond, eds, *Routledge Handbook of the Politics of Brexit*. Abingdon: Routledge, 80–91.

Olesen, Niels W., and Rasmus M. Mariager (2020). 'The Social Democratic Party. From exponent of societal change to pragmatic conservatism', in Peter M. Christiansen, Jørgen Elklit, and Peter Nedergaard, eds, *The Oxford Handbook of Danish Politics*. Oxford: Oxford University Press, 278–95.

Rasmussen, Mikkel V. (2018). 'Brexit and European defence: Why more defence does not equal more integration', in Patrick Diamond, Peter Nedergaard, and Ben Rosamond, eds, *Routledge Handbook of the Politics of Brexit*. Abingdon: Routledge, 233–44.

Ritzau (2018). 'S-formand: Vi vil ikke afskaffe de danske EU-forbehold', https://www. dr.dk/nyheder/politik/s-formand-vi-vil-ikke-afskaffe-de-danske-eu-forbehold (accessed 18 March 2019).

Wivel, Anders (2014). 'A pace-setter out of sync? Danish foreign, security and defence policy in the European Union', in Lee Miles and Anders Wivel, eds, *Denmark and the European Union*. Abingdon: Routledge, 80–94.

Young, Alasdair R., and John Peterson (2015). 'Trade', in Knud E. Jørgensen, Asne K. Aastad, Edith Drieskens, Katie Laatikainen, and Ben Tonra, eds, *The Sage Handbook of European Foreign Policy*. London: Sage, 837–52.

CHAPTER 31

DEVELOPMENT POLICY

From Consensus to Contention?

ANNE METTE KJÆR

POLICY CHANGES IN THE NEW MILLENNIUM

FOR decades, Danish development policy was generally a consensual affair. A broad majority across the centre in the Danish Parliament was supportive of a generous aid budget. So were Danish stakeholders such as the business sector, trade unions, and development nongovernmental organizations (NGOs). A large proportion of the Danish population shared the wish to help reduce poverty and promote economic development in low-income countries. However, this state of affairs gradually changed after the turn of the millennium. Development aid has become a subject to debate, especially around election time. The continuous and gradual increase in aid allocations has been reversed, the composition of aid has changed, and the focus has moved away from poverty reduction. This chapter examines these changes and seeks to identify the main drivers behind them.

Multiple purposes lie behind development policy and foreign aid giving. They can be diplomatic, developmental, humanitarian, or commercial. In her study of the purposes of foreign aid, Carol Lancaster (2007: 13) emphasizes that the purposes are always mixed. The particular mix will, according to Lancaster, depend on a range of country-specific domestic factors. In the following sections, I first sketch the most important changes in Danish development policy, and then drawing on Lancaster's framework, I discuss the main driving forces behind them.

CHANGES IN DANISH DEVELOPMENT POLICY

Danish development policy was established relatively late. Denmark got its first Law of International Development Cooperation (*Lov om internationalt udviklingssamarbejde*) in 1962 when Denmark decided to contribute to the United Nations (UN) (Bach et al. 2008; Brunbech and Olesen 2013). In those years, Denmark only spent about 0.13 per cent of Gross National Income (GNI) on foreign aid (Lancaster 2007: 198). However, during the 1970s, Denmark became a generous donor and established an aid structure consisting of an international aid agency within the Ministry of Foreign Affairs (MFA), popularly labelled Danida (n.d.), an advisory board to the minister of development with a broad representation of stakeholders and popular support for aid. The broad support in Parliament and among stakeholders was behind a remarkable continuity in development policy during the 1980s and 1990s that can best be described by continuously increasing aid budgets, a constant balance between multilateral and bilateral aid, and a continuous but strengthened focus on poverty reduction (Brunbech and Olesen 2013; Lancaster 2007). In the new millennium, this has changed. In this chapter, I focus on changes in the size and composition of aid, as well as in the thematic focus of aid as described in the Development Strategies passed in Parliament.[1]

Size and Composition of the Aid Budget

The Danish tradition for generous aid spending was established in the early 1970s. The chairman of the Organization for Economic Cooperation and Development's Development Assistance Committee (OECD-DAC) had expressed criticism of Denmark's low allocations, and after this, the government decided to increase development aid towards a target of 0.7 per cent of GNI. This was reached in 1978. Subsequently, the aid budget increased to 1 per cent in the early 1990s (Paldam 1997: 139). Internationally, the 1990s witnessed a generally declining trend in Overseas Development Assistance (ODA), but Denmark went against this current and increased aid throughout this decade. The 1980s and 1990s have thus been termed 'the heyday of Danish development Aid' (Engberg-Pedersen and Fejerskov 2018: 145; Marcussen 2018).

After 2001, aid allocations declined. Figure 31.1 shows Danish ODA as compared to that of Sweden, Norway, and the OECD-DAC average. As can be seen, Danish aid has remained generous, but it has gone down from a high of 1.06 per cent of GNI in 2000 to 0.7 per cent, the UN target. Moreover, this was in a time in the 2000s where international aid allocations, and particularly those of Norway and Sweden, did not decline. So, with regard to aid allocations, Denmark has been 'out of sync' with international trends (Bach et al. 2008: 515).

In the very early days of Danish development aid, most of it was allocated as multilateral aid. However, since around 1966, the relative share of bilateral and multilateral aid remained at about 50–50 according to the '50–50 principle' which was seen 'as one of the great constants in Danish development policy' (Bach et al. 2008: 131). The 50-50 balance was maintained throughout the 1990s, but in the new millennium, as can be seen in Figure 31.2, bilateral allocations began to take a larger share.

In addition to the balance between bilateral and multilateral aid, the composition of aid is about recipient countries. From the early days of Danish development aid,

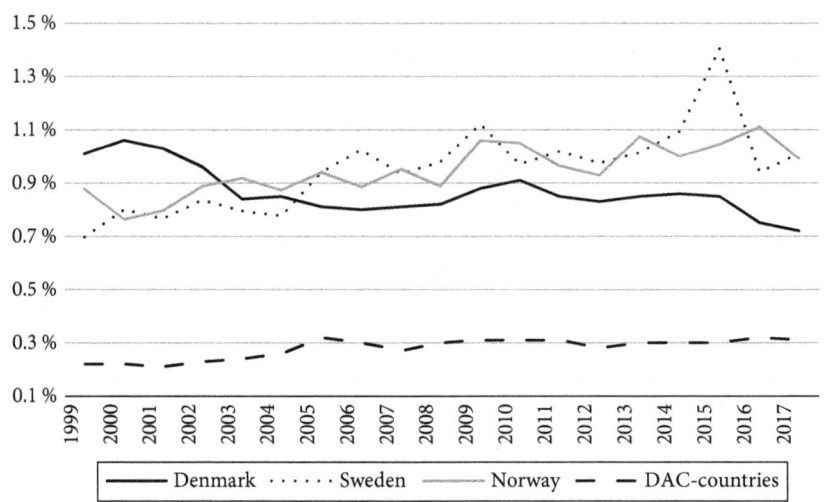

FIGURE 31.1 Overseas development assistance as proportion of GNI, selected countries.
Source: OECD data, 2018

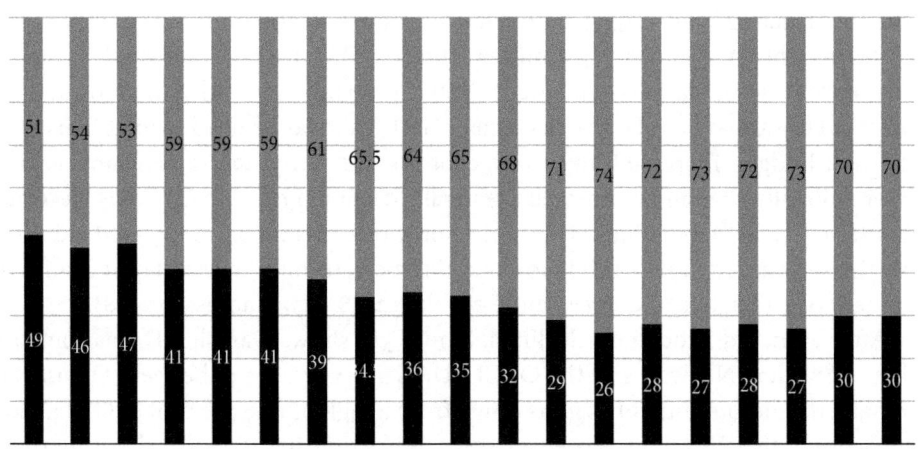

FIGURE 31.2 Composition of multilateral (black) and bilateral (striped) aid of Danish ODA.
Source: Danida (n.d.) annual reports, 1999–2018

allocating to the poorest countries was a priority. Tanzania and Bangladesh were some of the early recipients of Danish aid. From the mid-1970s and up until 1989, the main recipients were Kenya, Tanzania, Bangladesh, and India (Bach et al. 2008: 360), but Denmark additionally financed projects in sixty-six countries (Bach et al. 2008: 429). In 1988, the government decided to focus on fewer countries, to cut aid for countries in which Denmark only had very few projects, and to decide on about twenty partner countries.

There were two main requirements to qualify as partner country: it had to be a poor country, and there had to be good enough governance to make use of the aid allocations. This meant that African countries received the largest share of bilateral aid. However, in the new millennium, and especially since 2011, African countries have received a smaller share of (the declining) bilateral aid. In 2013, Africa received about 25 per cent of bilateral aid, whereas in 2017, the share was 17 per cent (Heldgaard 2018). In addition, the region around Syria surpassed Afghanistan in being the largest recipient of Danish bilateral aid.

The Danish Development Strategy Papers and Their Thematic Focus

Through the 1990s, Denmark increasingly emphasized criteria developed in international forums for good and effective aid. The United Nations' Millennium Development Goals established at the Millennium Summit in 2000 had 'global partnerships for development' as the eighth goal. More and better aid was emphasized in the Monterrey Consensus (the outcome of a UN conference on financing development) in 2002, and in 2005, OECD-DAC countries outlined the principles for aid effectiveness in the Paris Declaration: alignment, coordination, harmonization, ownership, and partnerships. Two strategies, 'Strategy 2000' from 1994 and 'Partnership 2000', thus emphasized 'better aid' focusing on fewer countries and with a priority of partnerships and alignment with recipient country priorities. As Table 31.1 indicates, Denmark focused on poverty reduction, partnerships with the governments of poor countries, the promotion of human rights, good governance, and sector wide approaches in the late 1990s and early 2000s.

By the time of the Paris Declaration, Denmark was already implementing these principles to a large extent. The rule of thumb in any poor country where Denmark was present was, therefore, to first ask about the country's own national poverty reduction strategy in order to best align with it; then ask what other donors were supporting this strategy in order to coordinate with them; and finally, focus on the sectors Denmark would be best at supporting, such as the health sector or the water sector. In the OECD-DAC peer review from 2003, it was noted how Denmark was recognized among DAC members:

> [F]or the generosity of its aid and for its innovations in such leading development co-operation policy and management areas as partnership, poverty reduction, sector approaches and evaluation. Its operational focus on a small number of priority countries and a substantive concentration on a maximum of four sectors per country make Denmark's bilateral programmes among the more strategically framed in the DAC. This is matched on the multilateral side by an active engagement with a small number of priority institutions. Despite its relatively small economic size, it was the ninth largest DAC donor in 2001.   (OECD 2003: 11)

Table 31.1 Danish Development Strategies Since 2000

Name	Support	Focus	Changes from Last Strategy
'A Developing World: Strategy for Danish Development Policy Towards the Year 2000'. (Ministry of Foreign Affairs 1994)	Centre-left government passes the strategy with support from the entire Parliament except the Danish Progress Party.	- Poverty reduction - Partnerships with recipient governments - Democracy and human rights	- Fewer countries - Fewer sectors - Sector-support&sr;General budget support and earmarked sector support - Active multilateralism
'Denmark's Development Policy Strategy. Partnership 2000'. (Ministry of Foreign Affairs 2000)	Centre-left government passes the strategy with support from the entire Parliament except the Danish People's Party and the Red-Green Alliance.	- Poverty reduction - Partnerships with recipient governments - Democracy, sustainability, human rights, and gender equality	- Even stronger focus on poverty reduction and partnerships - Incorporation of MDGs and focus on alignment, harmonization, and ownership
'Freedom from Poverty—Freedom to Change: Strategy for Denmark's Development Cooperation'. (Ministry of Foreign Affairs 2010)	Centre-right government passes the strategy with support from the Danish People's Party but not from the opposition parties (who protested aid cuts not contents).	- Human rights, civil liberties, and freedom - Poverty reduction - Partnerships (not only with recipient governments)	- Stronger focus on fragile states, terrorism, and migration - Areas of origin - More cooperation with Danish Ministry of Defence - Introduced Danish interests as criterion for selecting partner countries

'The Right to a Better Life. Strategy for Denmark's Development Cooperation', (Ministry of Foreign Affairs 2012)	Centre-left government passes the strategy with support from the entire Parliament.	- Human rights (universal and inseparable) - Complex partnerships - Poverty reduction - Fragile states and regions of origin - Policy coherence	- More explicit rights-based approach - More focus on green growth
'The World 2030. Denmark's Strategy for Development Cooperation and Humanitarian Action', (Ministry of Foreign Affairs 2017)	Decided as broad political agreement between the centre-right government and all parties in Parliament except the Red-Green Alliance.	- SDGs (of which poverty reduction is one) - Danish foreign policy, security, and economic interests - Regions of origin and migration - Private sector partnerships - Policy coherence	- Stronger emphasis on Danish interests - Abandonment of sector-budget support - Use of SDGs to move away from a focus on low-income countries - Focus on combining humanitarian and development aid

The 1990s were characterized by a so-called 'active multilateralism' in which Denmark used the relatively large multilateral allocations to influence UN decisions such as the placement of a number of UN offices in Copenhagen (Bach et al. 2008: 507–11). A strong UN was an explicit foreign policy aim. For Denmark, taking part in military operations would be fine as long as it was backed by a UN resolution (see also Wivel 2020).

The year 2001 is a significant year for Danish aid policy because the 9/11 terror attacks on the World Trade Centre coincided with a shift in government in Denmark to a centre-right government under Anders Fogh Rasmussen (Olesen 2015). Danish security interests and migration had already begun receiving attention in the 1990s with a focus on the UN. Now, they were combined with combatting terror, and they became a more central concern in the strategy documents. As the strategy Partnership 2000 had been approved by the entire Parliament (except the Danish People's Party), the new government did not have to decide on a new development strategy. But in a 2003 priority paper, two new areas were introduced: the use of aid to combat terrorism and its use in regions of origin of refugees. In spite of the fact that aid funds had been used for the reception of Yugoslavian refugees in the 1990s and support for regions of origin had also taken place before, it was the first time that the issues were explicitly prioritized in a policy paper. The war in Afghanistan made Denmark increase development aid to that country. This shift of aid focus reflected a foreign policy shift away from the UN and towards an emphasis on being an ally to the United States (Brunbech and Olesen 2013). During the 2000s, Afghanistan became the country receiving the largest share of Danish ODA. This shift ran counter to an important criteria for selecting a partner country, namely that of good governance. Afghanistan was chosen as recipient of development aid to complement Danish military involvement there, while its ability to, for instance, live up to requirements for sector-programme support was not equally considered. Finally, the term 'value for aid money' was explicitly used, reflecting a new scepticism as to whether aid had the intended effects (Bach et al. 2008; Ministry of Foreign Affairs 2003).

Since the late 2000s, general and sector budget support were gradually abandoned. Partnerships remained in focus but from a matter of partnership primarily between Denmark and recipient governments, creating so-called innovative partnerships between the private and public sector, with civil society actors and other stakeholders now being emphasized. Also, the focus on fragile states and on integrating the areas of security, foreign policy, and development policy has become stronger. In 2010, new Liberal Party Development Minister Søren Pind codified many of these issues in a white paper entitled 'Freedom from Poverty' (Ministry of Foreign Affairs 2010). This White Paper was passed by a narrow majority of the government backed by the Danish People's Party (see Kosiara-Pedersen 2020). In withholding their support, the opposition parties were not expressing disagreement with the contents of the strategy but rather with a large, simultaneous aid cut (as seen in Figure 31.2 from 2010 to 2011).

In 2011, Helle Thorning-Schmidt, the new head of the new centre-left government, appointed a new minister of development, Christian Friis-Bach. He had previously been employed by a large NGO and was in favour of a human rights-based approach to development. The 2012 strategy reflected his concerns and focused on human rights and green growth. Nevertheless, other than a new human rights language, the trend towards focusing more on areas of origin, fragile states, and on policy coherence continued.

The latest development strategy 'The World 2030' is grounded in the Sustainable Development Goals (SDGs) (Ministry of Foreign Affairs 2017). As made clear by Development Minister Ulla Tørnæs (2017), it is a joint strategy for humanitarian and development aid, and as such, in line with the SDGs. The World 2030 is very explicit in its emphasis on Danish interests. While the strategy takes its point of departure in the SDGs, these are systematically related to the ways in which Danish trade or other concerns can be considered. Supporting sustainable development, poverty reduction, etc. are not so much seen as ends in themselves but rather as a way to 'ameliorate threats against our own security and lifestyle, and to promote our own economic and trade interests' (Ministry of Foreign Affairs 2017: 1). In fact, the word 'poverty' is mentioned 23 times, and the word 'interest' appears 25 times in a 42-page document but only once in connection with the interests of poor countries (Ministry of Foreign Affairs 2017: 30).

In contrast, the older strategy Partnership 2000 uses 'poverty' 59 times. It only mentions the word 'interest' in connection with the 'interests of developing countries' (Ministry of Foreign Affairs 2000: 39) or Denmark wanting to 'promote the interests of the poor' (Ministry of Foreign Affairs 2000: 32). Out of the ten times the word 'interest' is mentioned in the 53-page document Partnership 2000, only once is it in connection with Danish interests (Ministry of Foreign Affairs 2000: 15), and this occurrence is framed as a Danish interest 'in long-term cooperation with the partner countries'. In 2017, Development Minister Tørnæs (2017) argued in an op-ed that aid should be seen as a type of 'venture capital' catalysing other investments from other sources such as Danish pension funds or the IFU (the Investment Fund for Developing Countries), i.e. an investment unit partly funded by the aid budget.

Over the years, the criteria for selecting partner countries have shifted away from being mainly based on poverty reduction. While attention was still fully on the least developed countries at the beginning of the 2000s, the Danish government now sees cooperation with lower middle or middle income countries as an opportunity for Danish companies (Ministry of Foreign Affairs 2017: 12). The strategy divides countries into three so-called 'spheres of interest': the poor and fragile countries, the poor but stable ones, and the transition and growth countries (Ministry of Foreign Affairs 2017: 7). It is emphasized that 'we will focus particularly on the fragile countries, on regions characterized by fragility where poverty and vulnerability are extensive, and where there may be a direct impact on Danish interests' (Ministry of Foreign Affairs 2017: 8).

Generally, the Development Strategy Papers in the new millennium have put less emphasis on poverty reduction. They phrased Danish interests less in connection with a strong UN or the mutual benefit of development in the South, and more in connection with countering the threat of terror or preventing migration.

FACTORS BEHIND THE CHANGING
DEVELOPMENT POLICY

As is the case with most governments' development policies, Denmark's foreign aid has multiple purposes, and therefore, explanations of changes in development policy cannot be unidimensional. Denmark has reacted to a changing international environment to promote foreign policy, security, and commercial aims. At the same time, domestic politics is important. Carol Lancaster (2007: 18–19) thus points to the domestic political scene in explaining aid levels and composition of aid. She points to ideational, institutional, interest-based, and organizational factors as possible explanatory categories. In the following, I address how Denmark reacted to changes in the international system, and then I discuss the domestic explanatory factors.

Denmark Reacted to International Trends

The post-9/11 wars against terror in Afghanistan and Iraq, and subsequently, the aftermath of the Arab Spring have increased concerns about security, terror, and migration globally. Many donors focus more on humanitarian aid in regions of origin than on long-term development aid in the poorest countries. Denmark's military presence in Afghanistan and Iraq served to not only think of development aid in connection with military intervention but also increased the threat of terror at home. Denmark developed new guidelines for development aid in which support to enable so-called 'third-party countries' to live up to international obligations to combat terror were emphasized (Ministry of Foreign Affairs 2003; Aning 2010).

Denmark is also following international trends in thinking about development in broader terms. The Millennium Development Goals (MDGs) were focused on how to create development in low-income countries, but the SDGs address development globally, and they look to financing such development through diverse channels such as the private sector and improving domestic tax collection and not merely through traditional aid (Gavas et al. 2015). Over the years, international development aid has become less important to many developing countries. Their GDP has grown, meaning that even if ODA has increased, it makes up a smaller proportion of these countries' GDP.

The SDGs express that aid is of declining importance. At the same time, the SDGs are so broad that it is possible to be in line with the SDGs while spending development aid promoting national interest. As Olesen observes, 'Danish development policy is no longer aimed at supporting UN-based internationalism but rather at being an element in an international security policy centred on being an ally to the US while still referring to the same norm-based buzzwords' (Olesen 2015: 32, own translation).

Another international trend is a gradual move away from the Paris Declarations' principles of alignment and general budget support. Budget support is still acknowledged as the best way to ensure that there is enough predictability in aid transfers to enable poor countries' governments to make realistic budgets and development plans. Nonetheless, many aid donors are concerned that aid money will be misspent, and they want to be better able to show value for money. For that purpose, aid for specific projects is more useful. The trend away from sector support can, therefore, be seen in many OECD-DAC member countries after the latter half of the 2000s, and Denmark has been one of them (Koch et al. 2017).

An additional general feature among OECD-DAC members has been a widespread questioning of the effects of aid. The 'does-aid-work' debate may have affected some governments' decisions to cut aid budgets. For example, some scholars have argued that aid may undermine the state-society fiscal contract by making the state more accountable to foreign donors rather than to its citizens (Moore 1998; Deaton 2013). In contrast, others have raised the point that aid may not have the same effect as oil, for example, because donors are supportive of tax reforms (Therkildsen 2002). Clist and Morrissey (2011) have tested this empirically and have found that aid does not have a negative effect on domestic revenue collection (Therkildsen 2002). Likewise, contributions to the so-called macro-debate on the effect of foreign aid on economic growth have come up with different results, some showing a negative effect of aid on savings and investments (Boone 1996) and others pointing to an interaction-effect with the recipient countries' policy environment (Burnside and Dollar 2000). Recently, most contributions seem to find a positive yet moderate effect of aid (Doucouliagos and Paldam 2015; Galiani et al. 2017).

This debate has had varying impact on domestic political decisions on aid in different OECD countries. In the UK, for example, a cross-party policy consensus on increasing the aid budget had developed and became stronger under Prime Minister Cameron (Heppell et al. 2017). In Denmark, however, the academic contributions highlighting the negative effects of aid have found more uptake among centre-right-wing politicians. Neither Norway nor Sweden have cut aid to the same extent as Denmark, and they remain more focused on the poorest countries. Hence, both Swedish and Norwegian ODA continued to increase in the new millennium, and in 2017, it was at 1 per cent of GNI (OECD 2018). Similarly, the Swedish policy framework paper for development cooperation and humanitarian assistance has a much stronger focus on poverty reduction than the World 2030 (Government of Sweden 2016).

Whereas Denmark has indeed followed an international trend in turning its gaze more on the refugee situation, countries with which Denmark is normally compared such as Sweden and Norway spend a smaller proportion of aid money on refugees. The OECD-DAC operates with guidelines as to which so-called in-donor expenses on refugees can be covered by the aid budget. For example, the guidelines permit the inclusion of sustenance costs of refugees in a donor country for the first twelve months. However, the guidelines are broad and allow room for interpretation by individual OECD-DAC members. In their enactment of the National Budget for 2017, the centre-right government stressed that the scope for reporting in-donor refugee costs should be fully utilized (Oxfam IBIS 2016). In the 2017 budget, Denmark had allocated DKK 2.77 billion

(18.4 per cent of the aid budget) for receiving an estimated 5,829 persons, whereas Sweden had set aside SEK 8.1 billion (17.6 per cent of aid) for receiving 24,719 asylum seekers, and Norway was expected to spend NOK 3.7 billion (11 per cent) from its aid budget on receiving 17,169 asylum seekers (Oxfam IBIS 2016). In 2016, Denmark thus spent a larger share of ODA on receiving refugees and asylum seekers in Denmark than any other European country with the exception of Holland in 2015 (Frandsen 2016; Quinn 2016). In that year, Denmark became the single largest recipient of Danish development aid because of the increased allocation for refugees and asylum seekers (Heldgaard 2016; Engberg-Pedersen and Fejerskov 2018). In brief, while Denmark certainly did follow international trends in aid, these interact with domestic political factors.

Domestic Factors Before 2001

In explaining the remarkable continuity and consensus around a generous aid budget, a 50-50 share of multilateral and bilateral aid, and a focus on the poorest countries prior to 2001, Lancaster (2007: 203–10) emphasizes institutional, organizational, interest group-based, and value-based explanations. With regard to *institutions*, she points to Denmark's electoral system of proportional representation. The multi-party system has often allowed small parties in favour of generous aid to be decisive in forming coalitions. In 1984, a parliamentary majority even voted for increasing the aid budget to 1 per cent against the views of Poul Schlüter's minority centre-right government.

Lancaster places less emphasis on the corporatist *interest* representation in Danish development policy's decision-making structure. However, most observers stress the importance of this arrangement, bringing together Lancaster's two dimensions of *interests* and *organization* (Holm 1982; Olsen 1995, 2001; Bach et al. 2008; see P.M. Christiansen 2020 on corporatism). At its core was Danida's board advising the Minister for Development on all significant aid allocations, country strategies, and programmes. Only the overall development strategies were debated in Parliament. The Federation of Danish Industries, the Danish Trade Union Confederation, the Danish Agriculture and Food Council, the largest NGOs, and representatives from research institutions were all represented on the board.

This set-up can, on the one hand, be seen as more open and inclusive than other foreign policy areas since the main interest groups and stakeholders were able to influence the decision-making process. On the other hand, observers have argued that the inclusion served to remove the debate from an open democratic forum in the Parliament and into a relatively closed policy-community. For instance, one reader of annual parliamentary debates on ODA concludes that the debates were rather remote and uninformed about actual decisions regarding Danish development aid (Paldam 1997: 175–6). Others notice that the debates in Parliament were only about rather lofty and broad principles on which political parties were generally able to agree, allowing the aid administration considerable policy autonomy (Olsen 2001). The aid bureaucracy interacted closely with

NGOs and the business community and saw to it that there would be agreement on important issues, a coming together of interests in an organized way, which Olsen (1995) has termed a 'policy community'. The policy community served to ensure consensus and continuity.

The corporate sector got contracts, jobs were created in Denmark, the farmers got contracts for food aid, the NGOs got allocations that enabled them to expand activities in the developing world, and the research institutions got allocations for projects in the field of development research (Bach et al. 2008: 129, 146; Paldam 1997). This corporatist interest representation explained why Denmark was 'lukewarm' when it came to the untying of aid (Brunbech and Olesen 2013: 99). Tied aid was a part of the balanced considerations in the 50-50 system: 'The multilateral component underlined the foreign policy priority of supporting the UN [...] a position strongly supported by Parliament [...]', and the tied loans were part of the bilateral allocations and were favoured by 'Danish industry and the bourgeois parties, while NGOs liked project aid' (Brunbech and Olesen 2013: 102). The centre-right parties thus continued to be supportive of aid through the 1990s.

The combination of a parliament largely in favour of aid along with a corporatist interest-representation served to minimize criticism of aid and helped create support for aid among the Danish population (Lancaster 2007: 205). Generous development aid was seen to be in line with the *values* of redistribution from rich to poor as embedded in the Scandinavian welfare model, the last of Lancaster's four explanatory categories (Lancaster 2007; Brunbech and Olesen 2013). Indeed, opinion surveys showed widespread support for generous aid. In 1998, for example, 84 per cent of Danes thought that aid to developing countries was important (Lancaster 2007: 205).

Domestic Factors after 2001

The *institutional* features changed during the years after 2001. The composition of Parliament changed with the 2001 elections, as Figure 31.3 indicates. When Anders Fogh Rasmussen formed a centre-right coalition government after the elections, ODA took up over 1 per cent of GNI, whereas this had declined to 0.82 per cent in 2003. The year 2001 marked a critical juncture because development policy had been decided by broad consensus across the centre in Parliament up until then, with the small parties in the middle favouring aid playing an important role. However, the centre-right government of 2001 was able to form a majority *without* these small parties at the centre and with support from the Danish People's Party instead. This enabled them to make significant aid cuts (Olesen 2015). In 2015, ODA took up 0.85 per cent of GNI, and the new Løkke Rasmussen government reduced this share to slightly over 0.7 per cent.

Interestingly, the centre-left government under Helle Thorning-Schmidt (2011–2015) did not increase aid back to the high of 2000, despite the fact that the Social Democratic Party had announced their intention to work towards a 1 per cent target. During the 2015

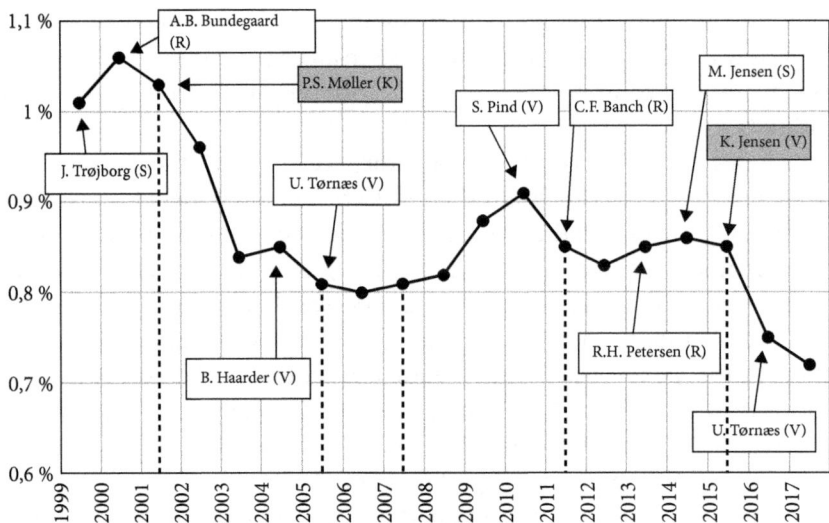

FIGURE 31.3 Danish ODA 2000–2017 with shifts in governments.

Note: New right-wing government: blue-dotted line; New Social-Liberal government: red dotted line; Grey box: Minister of Foreign Affairs also in charge of development policy; White box: Minister of Development

Source: OECD data 2018

election campaigns, Thorning-Schmidt announced that her party did not intend to increase aid if re-elected (Vangkilde et al. 2015).

Regarding the *organizational and interest-based categories,* the corporatist aid architecture underwent changes in the 2000s. This was partly because the centre-right government made it an explicit goal to reduce the involvement of lobbyist groups in general (Brunbech and Olesen 2013) and partly because the technical advice of the board had become less in demand. In line with OECD-DAC guidelines, Denmark had shifted to sector-wide programmes, which implied building capacity in sector ministries in recipient countries. Denmark had also decentralized aid management to embassies and country offices (OECD 2011). Now, most allocations were channelled through ministries of finance in recipient countries and subject to the country's sector priorities. The inputs of the board were less needed for sector programmes than for projects (Bach et al. 2008: 457).

Moreover, sector budget support meant that the soft loans for projects that enabled Danish companies to win contracts were phased out. Furthermore, Danish food aid, which was managed by the Ministry of Agriculture and mainly consisted of canned meat and cream cheese, was phased out and organizationally moved to the Ministry of Foreign Affairs. During the 1990s and early 2000s, aid thus became increasingly untied, and in 2004, the EU regulations on international tenders brought the tying of aid to a complete halt (Bach et al. 2008: 494). The untying of Danish aid had the implication that the business and agricultural interests in maintaining a strong board probably waned. During the centre-left government of 2011–15, a new Law of International Development Cooperation was passed, and the board was abolished. However, the centre-right government has re-instated a similar body, now labelled the Council for Development Policy. It has the same mandate as the previous board—to advise the minister—but it is less powerful than in the heydays of development aid.

Brunbech and Olesen (2013: 109) argue that corporate interests are still being satisfied through increased bilateral allocations and that this explains that there is no longer interest in upholding the 50-50 principle. However, the centre-right government has also allocated more aid money to the IFU, the investment fund for developing countries. The IFU is a state-owned fund which, among others, invests in Danish companies in developing countries. The IFU also manages investments in these countries on behalf of other large funds. This has raised concerns that aid money is being used to support Danish businesses rather than development for the poorest (Laursen 2018, Afrika Kontakt 2018). The latest OECD-DAC review thus expresses concern that Denmark may not be able to keep its track record of not tying aid, and it encourages Denmark to seek 'ways to promote private sector engagement that do not increase the share of tied aid' (ibid.: 19).

Summarizing the organizational and interest-based categories, the declining significance of the corporatist structure combined with a new government with a new majority in Parliament implied that the longstanding 50-50 system was abandoned, that the foci of the Development Strategy Papers changed, and that aid was cut.

Regarding Lancaster's fourth category *values and attitudes*, the 2001 campaigns had debated aid in a new way with more focus on the effectiveness of aid. In addition, an increasingly professionalized aid bureaucracy might also have served to disembed development aid from Danish civil society. In any case, Denmark has seen a declining trend in the popular support for aid. In 2010, 76 per cent of the population believed that Denmark should give development aid to poor countries according to opinion surveys carried out by Danida for the Ministry of Foreign Affairs (2013: 6). In 2017, this figure had dropped to 61 per cent (Ministry of Foreign Affairs 2017: 5). In 1998, when asked whether Denmark spends too much on aid—at a point in time when Danish ODA had almost reached its peak at over 1 per cent of GNI—49 per cent of Danes thought too much was spent on aid. This proportion declined as the centre-right government carried out cuts, and only 22 per cent thought Denmark spent too much in 2004. Since then, however, the number of Danes thinking too much money is spent on aid has increased to 44 per cent in 2015 (Stubager et al. 2016: 29). This is perhaps part of the explanation as to why the Social Democratic Party (see Mariager and Olesen 2020) has expressed no desire to increase aid allocations.

Finally, during the 1980s and 1990s, the generous aid allocations had been seen as a value independent of the economic situation at home. What the centre-right governing parties did very effectively prior to the 2001 elections was to reframe development aid as something that could be traded with better public services in Denmark. An article count in the seventeen countrywide dailies shows that the number of articles about development aid increases around the elections, as shown in Figure 31.4. Over the period from 1999 to 2017, there is no general increase in the number of articles about development aid, but when the number of articles in the three weeks leading up to the elections is

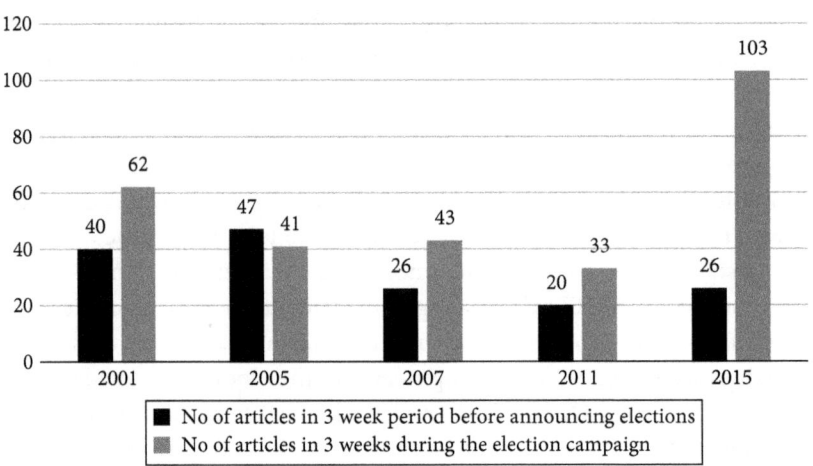

FIGURE 31.4 Articles debating aid before and during election campaigns.

compared to a three-week period around the time when the elections were announced, aid has, except for 2005, been debated more around elections, especially in 2001 and most markedly in 2015, indicating increased politicization of foreign aid.

The year 2001 marked the first elections in Denmark in which development aid became a campaign issue. The overriding theme in the articles (a count says 60 per cent of the articles that mention development aid) was aid cuts to raise money for hospitals in Denmark. The post-election national budget was passed with support from the Danish People's Party and moved DKK 1.5 billion directly from the aid budget to the health sector (Jakobsen 2015). In 2015, development aid was a hot issue once again. Just as in 2001, around 60 per cent of the articles mention the size of the aid budget and health expenses at home. This time, the Liberal Party (see F.J. Christiansen 2020) had announced their intention to cut aid by DKK 2.5 billion, an announcement that set the agenda for the debate. Most articles thus argue either against or in favour of this cut. The subsequent budget proposal did as promised and financed increases in the health budget largely with cuts in development aid (Ministry of Finance 2015). In all then, development and aid policies have been politicized more in the new millennium than in the four decades between 1960 and 2000.

CONCLUSION

This chapter has identified the most important changes in Danish development policy, with a focus on the 2000s and 2010s, as representing a move away from an overriding emphasis on poverty reduction to one in which not only the poorest countries but also middle income countries and areas of origin can be beneficiaries of Danish development aid. The 50-50 system which lasted through the 1980s and 1990s was abandoned, and the aid budget was cut, most notably after the 2001 and the 2015 elections where development policy was an issue debated during the campaigns. Danish economic interests were always a factor in Danish development aid, but in the most recent Development Strategy Paper, the emphasis on Danish economic interest is more explicit than it has been before.

A complex combination of international and domestic factors explain these changes. Particularly 9/11 and the subsequent wars in Afghanistan and Iraq changed the way Denmark framed its foreign policy, with less focus on the UN and more focus on being an ally to the United States. In 2001, the new centre-right government with support from the Danish People's Party was able to disregard the smaller parties favouring aid and carry though aid cuts. The decision-making structure transformed from a policy community creating consensus and continuity to a looser decision-making structure in which development policy was more politicized. More research into how the decision-making structure of development policymaking evolves and what the implications for policy are would not only help with better understanding the sector but also increase the knowledge of policy determinants in general.

The implications of the described policy changes have yet to be seen. Denmark has been a model donor for decades, known for patient commitment for support for sectors such as rural infrastructure or rural water programmes. Evaluations of aid show that it is the kind of long-term commitment to build the capacity of institutions in recipient countries that ensures results (see e.g. Ministry of Foreign Affairs 2019). However, the increased politicization of aid in Denmark may make such commitments less predictable. In its latest review, the OECD (2016: 17) thus expresses concern that 'the significant change of ODA allocation presents significant challenges for the predictability and quality of Danish development cooperation overseas'.

As mentioned, a new consensus on a lower aid level may have emerged. Development aid did not become an issue in the 2019 election campaigns. The Social Democrats have not expressed a wish to increase aid allocations, and they have recently emphasized their wish to target aid funds for areas of origin (Social Democratic Party 2018). This means that the move away from long-term development aid for the poorest countries is likely to continue under a different government. Using development aid to pay for in-country reception of refugees is less likely to be permanent because it will depend on the influx of asylum-seekers, a number that is likely to fluctuate. However, the tendency to channel aid money to investment funds which then support Danish businesses is more likely to continue. While this may spur economic activity for the company in question, the extent to which it will contribute to economic development in the poorest countries is questionable.

NOTE

1. Development policy has sometimes been defined as the policies to do with aid to poor countries, and sometimes it has been referred to more broadly as all policies affecting poor countries, including trade policies, foreign policies, and industrial policy (Holm 1982:

14–15). In this chapter, I use development policy in the broader sense, and I use the terms 'development policy' and 'aid policy' interchangeably. I focus mainly on Danish development strategies as they have been passed in Parliament (not all other policy papers to do with foreign policy and/or trade policy).

REFERENCES

Afrika Kontakt (2018). *Big business på bistand. Rapport om Investeringsfonden for udviklingslande (IFU) og dens investeringer i store danske virksomheder*. Copenhagen: Afrika Kontakt.

Aning, Kwesi (2010). 'Security, the War on Terror, and official development assistance', *Critical Studies on Terrorism*, 3/1: 7–26.

Bach, Christian F., Thorsten B. Olesen, Sune Kaur-Pedersen, and Jan Pedersen (2008). *Idealer og Realiteter. Dansk Udviklingspolitiks historie 1945–2005*. Copenhagen: Gyldendal.

Boone, Peter (1996). 'Politics and the effectiveness of aid', *European Economic Review*, 40/2: 289–329.

Brunbech, Peter Y., and Thorsten B. Olesen (2013). 'The late front-runner: Denmark and the ODA percentage question, 1960–2008', in Thorsten B. Olesen, Helge Ø. Pharo, and Kristian Paaskesen, eds, *Saints and Sinners. Official Development Aid and its Dynamics in a Historical and Comparative Perspective*. Oslo: Akademika Publishing, 89–121.

Burnside, Craig, and David Dollar (2000). 'Aid, policies, and growth', *The American Economic Review*, 90/4: 847–68.

Christiansen, Flemming J. (2020). 'The Liberal Party. From agrarian and liberal to centre-right catch-all', in Peter M. Christiansen, Jørgen Elklit, and Peter Nedergaard, eds, *The Oxford Handbook of Danish Politics*. Oxford: Oxford University Press, 296–312.

Christiansen, Peter M. (2020). 'Corporatism. Exaggerated death rumours?', in Peter M. Christiansen, Jørgen Elklit, and Peter Nedergaard, eds, *The Oxford Handbook of Danish Politics*. Oxford: Oxford University Press, 160–76.

Clist, Paul, and Oliver Morrissey (2011). 'Aid and tax revenue: Signs of a positive effect since the 1980s', *Journal of International Development*, 23/2: 165–80.

Danida (n.d.). Annual Reports, 1999–2018, Ministry of Foreign Affairs (since 2013 on openaid.dk).

Deaton, Angus (2013). *The Great Escape. Health, Wealth and the Origins of Inequality*. Princeton, NJ: Princeton University Press.

Doucouliagos, Hristos, and Martin Paldam (2015). 'Finally a breakthrough? The recent rise in the size of the estimates of aid effectiveness', in Mak Arvin and Byron Lew, eds, *Handbook on the Economics of Foreign Aid*. Cheltenham: Edward Elgar, 325–49.

Engberg-Pedersen, Lars, and Adam M. Fejerskov (2018). 'The transformation of Danish foreign aid', in Kristian Fischer and Hans Mouritzen, eds, *Danish Foreign Policy Review 2018*. Copenhagen: DIIS, Danish Institute for International Studies, 138–59.

Frandsen, Kasper (2016, 28 Apr.). 'Danmark i front med at udhule ulandsbistanden', Altinget, https://www.altinget.dk/artikel/147809- (accessed 6 December 2019).

Galiani, Sebastian, Stephen Knack, Lixin C. Xu, and Ben Zou (2017). 'The effect of aid on growth: evidence from a Quasi-experiment', *Journal of Economic Growth*, 22/1: 1–33.

Gavas, Mikaela, Nilima Gulrajani, and Tom Hart (2015). *Designing the Development Agency of the Future*. London: ODI.

Government of Sweden (2016). 'Policy framework for Swedish development cooperation and humanitarian assistance', Stockholm: Government Communication.

Heldgaard, Jesper (2016). *Engang Verdens Bedste. En uafhængig analyse af dansk udviklingsbistand, 2014–2016.* Timbuktu Fonden.

Heldgaard, Jesper (2018). *På kanten. En analyse af det internationale udviklingssamarbejde i finansloven, 2019.* Timbuktu Fonden.

Heppell, Timothy, Andrew Crines, and David Jeffery (2017). 'The UK Government and the 0.7% international aid target: Opinion among Conservative parliamentarians', *British Journal of Politics and International Relations*, 19/4: 895–909.

Holm, Hans-Henrik (1982). *Hvad Danmark Gør. En analyse af dansk u-landspolitik.* Aarhus: Politica.

Jakobsen, Joakim (2015, 19 Jun.). 'Sjælelige gevinster', *Weekendavisen.*

Koch, Svea, Stefan Leiderer, Jörg Faust, and Nadia Molenaers (2017). 'The rise and demise of European budget support: Political economy of collective European Union donor action', *Development Policy Review*, 35/4: 455–73.

Kosiara-Pedersen, Karina (2020). 'The Danish People's Party. Centre-oriented populists?', in Peter M. Christiansen, Jørgen Elklit, and Peter Nedergaard, eds, *The Oxford Handbook of Danish Politics.* Oxford: Oxford University Press, 313–28.

Lancaster, Carol (2007). *Foreign Aid: Diplomacy, Development, Domestic Politics.* Chicago, IL: University of Chicago Press.

Laursen, Jytte B. (2018, 4 Nov.). 'IFU- får vi udvikling for pengene?', Globalnyt.

Marcussen, Martin (2018, 27 Aug.). 'Dag-til-dag indsatser fjerner fokus fra den udviklingspolitiske strategi', Altinget, https://www.altinget.dk/udvikling/artikel/professor-dag-til-dag-indsatser-fjerner-fokus-fra-den-udviklingspolitiske-strategi (accessed 6 December 2019).

Mariager, Rasmus, and Niels W. Olesen (2020). 'The Social Democratic Party. From exponent of societal change to pragmatic conservatism', in Peter M. Christiansen, Jørgen Elklit, and Peter Nedergaard, eds, *The Oxford Handbook of Danish Politics.* Oxford: Oxford University Press, 278–95.

Ministry of Finance (2015). *Stramme rammer –klare prioriteter, Finanslovsforslaget 2016.* Copenhagen: Ministry of Finance.

Ministry of Foreign Affairs (1994). *A Developing World: Strategy for Danish Development Policy Towards the Year 2000.* (In Danish) Copenhagen: Ministry of Foreign Affairs.

Ministry of Foreign Affairs (2000). *Partnership 2000. Denmark's Development Policy.* Copenhagen: Ministry of Foreign Affairs.

Ministry of Foreign Affairs (2003). *A World of Difference. The Governments' Take on New Priorities for Danish Development Aid 2004–2008.* Copenhagen: Ministry of Foreign Affairs.

Ministry of Foreign Affairs (2010). *Freedom from Poverty – Freedom to Change: Strategy for Denmark's Development Cooperation.* Copenhagen: Ministry of Foreign Affairs.

Ministry of Foreign Affairs (2012). *The Right to a Better Life: Strategy for Denmark's Development Cooperation.* Copenhagen: Ministry of Foreign Affairs.

Ministry of Foreign Affairs (2013). *Danskernes holdninger og kendskab til udviklingsbistand 2012.* Copenhagen: Danida.

Ministry of Foreign Affairs (2017). *The World 2030. Denmark's Strategy for Development Cooperation and Humanitarian Action.* Copenhagen: Danida.

Ministry of Foreign Affairs (2019). *Evaluation of Water, Sanitation, and Environment Programmes in Uganda, 1990–2017.* Copenhagen: Danida.

Moore, Mick (1998). 'Death without taxes: Democracy, state capacity and aid dependence in the Fourth World', in Gordon White, and Mark Robinson, eds, *Towards a Democratic Developmental State.* Oxford: Oxford University Press.

OECD (2003). *Denmark. Development Assistance Committee (DAC). Peer Review*. Paris: OECD.

OECD (2011). *Denmark. Development Assistance Committee (DAC). Peer Review*. Paris: OECD.

OECD (2016). *Denmark. Development Assistance Committee (DAC). Peer Review*. Paris: OECD.

OECD (2018). OECD DACs online data base. https://www.oecd.org/dac/stats/idsonline.htm (accessed 6 December 2019).

Olesen, Thorsten B. (2015). 'Prioritering, profilering og politisk orientering. Engagement og aktivisme i dansk udviklings- og bistandspolitik, 1962–2015', *Tidsskriftet Politik*, 18/4: 25–36.

Olsen, Gorm R. (1995). 'Dansk Udviklingspolitik. Kompromisets kunst', *Politica*, 27/2: 195–212.

Olsen, Gorm R. (2001). 'European public opinion: Aid to Africa', *Journal of Modern African Studies*, 39/4: 645–74.

Oxfam IBIS (2016, Dec.). 'Oxfam IBIS analysis of Denmark's financing of in-donor refugee costs', Oxfam IBIS.

Paldam, Martin (1997). *Dansk U-landshjælp. Altruismens politiske økonomi*. Aarhus: Rockwool Fonden, Aarhus University Press.

Quinn, Ben (2016, 26 Oct.). 'NGOs censure EU countries for spending foreign aid on Asylum costs', *The Guardian*, https://www.theguardian.com/global-development/2016/oct/26/watchdog-censures-eu-countries-spending-foreign-aid-on-asylum-costs-concord-aidwatch-report (accessed 6 December 2019).

Social Democratic Party (2018). *Retfærdig og Realistisk. En udlændingepolitik der samler Danmark*, https://www.socialdemokratiet.dk/media/7011/en-udlaendingepolitik-der-samler-danmark.pdf (accessed 6 May 2019).

Stubager, Rune, Kasper M. Hansen, Kristoffer Callesen, Andreas Leed, and Christine Enevoldsen (2016). 'Danske vælgere 1971–2015. En oversigt over udviklingen i vælgernes holdninger mv.' Det Danske Valgprojekt.

Therkildsen, Ole (2002). 'Keeping the state accountable: Is aid no better than oil?', *IDS Bulletin*, 33/3: 1–17.

Tørnæs, Ulla (2017, 30 Jun.). 'Tørnæs: De store perspektiver drukner i kritik'. *Altinget*, https://www.altinget.dk/udvikling/artikel/toernaes-de-store-perspektiver-drukner-i-kritik (accessed 6 December 2019).

Vangkilde, Jesper, Kristian Klarskov, and Morten Skærbæk (2015, 30 May). 'Kursskifte: Hård kritik af Thornings nulvækst i ulandshjælp', *Politiken*.

Wivel, Anders (2020). 'In war and peace. Security and defence policy in a small state', in Peter M. Christiansen, Jørgen Elklit, and Peter Nedergaard, eds, *The Oxford Handbook of Danish Politics*. Oxford: Oxford University Press, 453–69.

CHAPTER 32

ECONOMIC POLICY

From Disequilibrium to Flexicurity

TORBEN M. ANDERSEN

A SMALL OPEN ECONOMY WITH AN EXTENDED WELFARE STATE

DENMARK is routinely classified as a small open economy, referring to its size and tight global integration. Other hallmarks are an extended welfare state resulting in a large public sector (and a high tax share) as well as a rather liberal private sector. Measured by expenditures, the public sector has constituted about 50 per cent of Gross Domestic Product (GDP) for several decades. Denmark ranks[1] 6 out of 207 countries on the KOF Index of Globalization for 2018 and as number 3 out of 190 countries on the World Bank Index[2] of 'ease of doing business'.

The importance for a small open economy to stay competitive to sustain a high standard of living has always taken centre stage in economic policy discussions. Ensuring a high employment level and decent wages are primary objectives, not only for social and distributional reasons but also to ensure the financial viability of the welfare state. A pertinent question in economic policy discussions is how to balance concerns for social and distributional issues with a competitive economy supporting high income and employment levels.

Governments in Denmark have mainly been minority governments. However, a strong consensus tradition has evolved over the years, particularly in economic policy issues. There is a long-standing tradition of tripartite agreements on labour market issues (see Høgedahl 2020). Thus, economic policy initiatives and reforms have usually had rather broad support and have, therefore, been consistent across elections.

In a comparative perspective, Denmark stands out by having achieved both a high level of income and an equal distribution of income. In recent years, Denmark has become a 'model example' of how to strike a balance between economic and social concerns—occasionally heralded as the flexicurity model. Assessed in terms of all standard macroeconomic indicators, the Danish economy is presently in a rather favourable position. This has not always been the case; imbalances were growing during the 1970s and into the early 1980s, and the Danish economy was in a severe disequilibrium. Thus, the situation of the Danish economy has changed radically between the late 1970s/early 1980s and up to the present. Over this period, there has been much economic policy activism, including notable changes in the views on economic policy. This chapter lays out both the general developments since 1970 and crucial economic policy initiatives over the period. The chapter starts by providing a brief overview of economic developments over the last 50 years as the foundation for laying out developments and economic policy initiatives in specific periods.

Economic Developments

Economic developments since the mid-1960s can be summarized by considering both the trend and the cyclical development in GDP (see Figure 32.1). Economic activity has been on a clear upward trend (left panel), and today, it is about 2.8 times larger than in 1966, and measured on per capita basis, 2.4 times larger. Material well-being has thus increased significantly. However, the annual changes (growth rates) in activity (right panel) have been rather volatile and economic development far from smooth. While the average annual growth rate over the period has been about 2 per cent, it has varied between 6.5 per cent in 1969 and minus 5.1 per cent in 2009.

Considering developments by GDP in fixed prices gives an activity measure but does not fully capture the developments in income. In particular, changes in relative prices between exports and imports (terms-of-trade changes) can be important, and in recent years, terms-of-trade developments have been favourable for Denmark. A better metric for international comparisons of living standards is GDP measured in current prices and in terms of purchasing power. Using this measure, Danish per capita income in 2017 was the ninth largest in the OECD area. Relative to the US—an often-used benchmark—there is a gap of about 15 per cent over the entire period. Measured by this metric, Denmark has neither been catching-up nor lagging behind development in the United States. However, income is much more equally distributed, and Denmark has the sixth lowest level of income inequality among OECD countries (in 2015) measured by the Gini coefficient.

Unemployment rates have followed a rollercoaster pattern. The late 1960s and early 1970s had unemployment rates below 2 per cent, and thus full employment, but unemployment rose during the 1970s and 1980s, reaching a peak of 12 per cent in the early 1990s (see Figure 32.2). From this peak, unemployment rates have been falling and have reached a low level. In a comparative perspective, unemployment was higher than the OECD average until the early 1990s and below afterwards, including during the financial crisis even though Denmark was more adversely hit than the average OECD

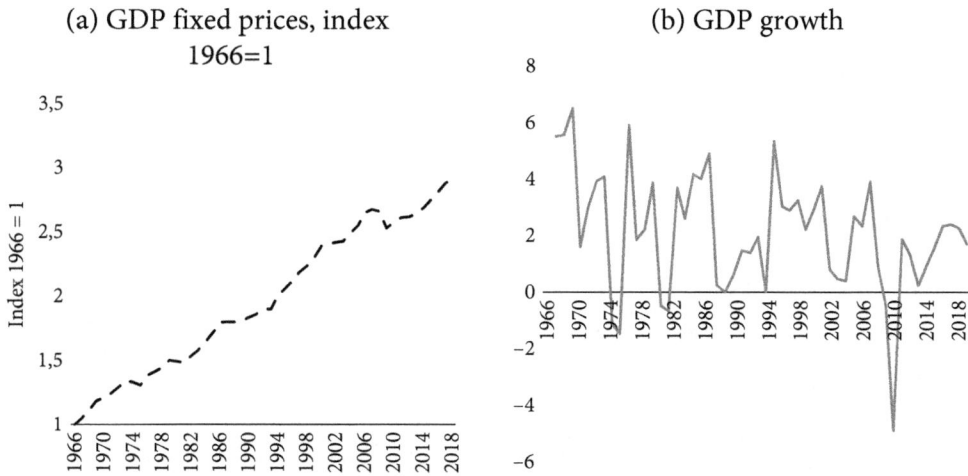

FIGURE 32.1 Real Gross Domestic Product (GDP): Level and growth rates, 1966–2018.

Note: ADAM data bank (data for the period 1966 to 2017) and updates from the Ministry for Economic Affairs and the Interior (2018). Gross Domestic Product, fixed prices

FIGURE 32.2 The employment and unemployment rate, 1966–2018.

Note: The employment rate is defined as total employment relative to the population between the ages 16 and 64. The unemployment rate is defined as the ratio of the unemployed to the labour force

Data: Statistics Denmark, ADAM data bank

country when measured by GDP developments. The Danish labour market is also characterized by high employment rates for both men and women.

Both price and wage inflation rose during the 1970s and peaked at double-digit levels in the early 1980s (cf. Figure 32.3). Inflation rates have since converged to rather low levels as in most other OECD countries. Developments in the nominal interest rate

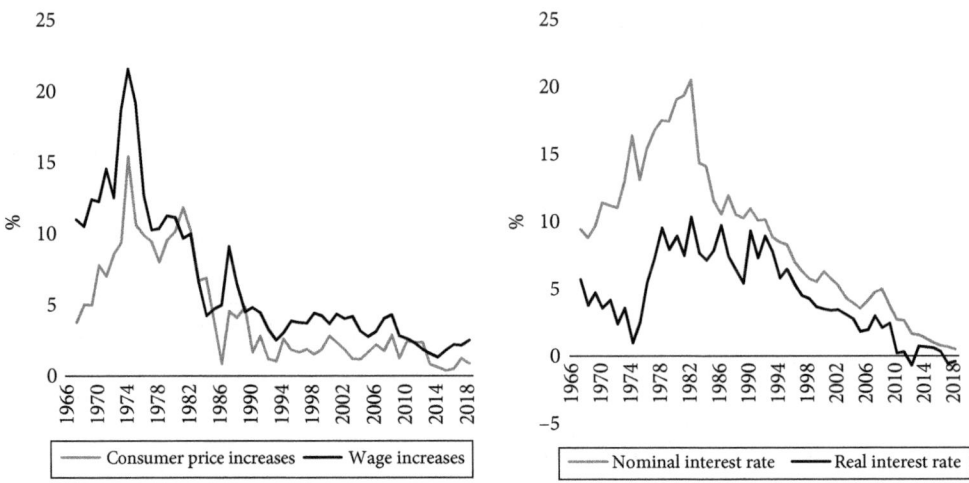

FIGURE 32.3 Price and wage inflation and interest rates, 1966–2018.

Note: The interest rate is measured by the effective returns on ten-year bonds, and the real interest rate is defined as the nominal interest rate corrected for consumer price increases. Price increases are measured by increases in the implicit private consumption deflator, and wage increases are increases in the wage for manufacturing workers

Source: Statistics Denmark, ADAM data bank

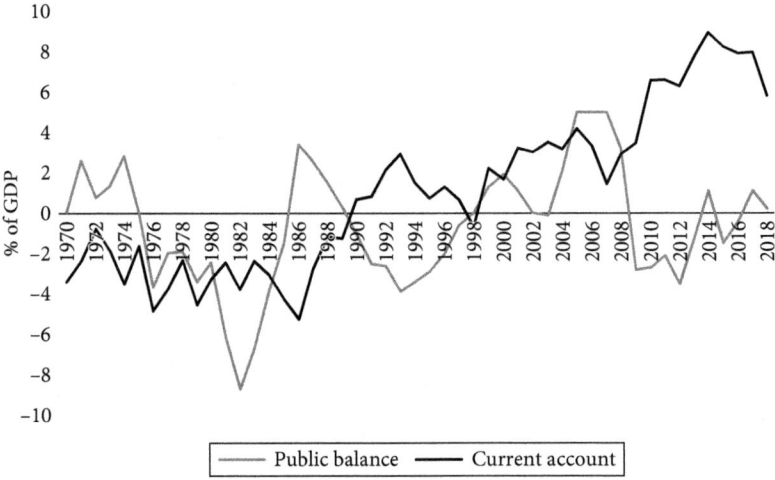

FIGURE 32.4 Current account and public sector balance, 1966–2018, per cent of GDP.

Note: The series for the public budget has a break in 2000. Data from 2000 and onwards is the EMU budget balance, and before, the DAU balance

Source: Statistics Denmark, ADAM data bank, and www.statistikbanken.dk/EDP3

mirror the developments in inflation. The real interest rate has followed a hump-shaped path and is currently at a low level, reflecting a global low-rate-of-return environment.

The current account displayed systematic deficits until the mid-1980s and epitomized the economic imbalances (cf. Figure 32.4). Consequently, foreign debt increased, reaching a peak of about 40 per cent of GDP in the 1980s. Since then, the current account has displayed systematic surpluses, and consequently, the foreign net debt position has changed to a net foreign asset position amounting to close to 60 per cent of GDP. Public finances are very sensitive to the developments in economic activity improving (deteriorating) when the economy is expanding (contracting). During the 1970s/1980s and 1990s, there were prolonged periods with systematic deficits leading to debt accumulation, but consolidation in the 2000s resulted in a significant debt reduction. By the end of 2018, public (gross) debt was close to 35 per cent of GDP—one of the lowest levels among EU countries and well below the EU Economic and Monetary Union (EMU) limit.

THE 1970S: DISEQUILIBRIA BUILD UP

The 1960s and early 1970s are often referred to as the 'golden sixties'. Growth rates were high, and there was full employment with an unemployment rate about 2 per cent. Most families experienced significant improvements in living standards, and welfare state arrangements expanded over this period.

The oil crises (1973/4–1982/3) marked a significant change in the economic situation. Denmark suffered particularly from the supply-side shock caused by higher oil prices due to a strong reliance on imported energy. The steep increase in oil prices and the associated global downturn caused low growth and high unemployment at the same time as inflation surged; the economy was stuck in stagflation (see e.g. Pedersen et al. 1987).

On impact, the crisis was considered temporary. An expansionary fiscal policy including a temporary VAT reduction was part of a so-called bridging strategy to support economic activity until foreign demand and the private sector would pick up again. However, as it became apparent that the crisis was more lasting, the key policy question became how to ensure both internal (low unemployment) and external (avoiding current account deficits) balance. These twin problems were perceived solvable by a so-called twist strategy. The logic was to twist aggregate demand away from foreign produced goods towards domestically produced goods by means of a demand management policy. This would improve the trade balance and expand domestic production and employment. Accordingly, taxes were increased to reduce private demand since it has a high import content, and public expenditures were increased to boost demand with a low import content. This policy was supported by attempts to improve competitiveness via income policies and devaluations. The fiscal policy changes associated with the twist strategy did not take place simultaneously, but often in a stop-go fashion where public expenditures were increased when unemployment was in focus. These changes were later followed by tax increases to curb private demand and improve the trade balance. This was a period characterized by a strong crisis sentiment and frequent economic policy interventions and changes of government.

This policy approach was not successful. Unemployment remained high, the current account displayed systematic deficits and double-digit inflation rates, and public budget deficits were added to the list of economic problems.

THE 1980S: THE BIG UPTURN AND THE SEVEN MEAGRE YEARS

The economic situation in the early 1980s was rather dismal. Knud Heinesen, the then finance minister, summarized this by saying 'Denmark is heading for the abyss', and in the public debate it was added: 'Yes, but on first class', referring to high living standards in combination with large deficits on the current account, as well as on public finances. At the time, unemployment had reached a level of about 10 per cent, the economy was clearly in disequilibrium, and views on the adequacy of the traditional economic policy approach were rather pessimistic.

After a change in government in 1982, a centre-right government (led by Poul Schlüter) launched a policy package to reduce inflation and eliminate the current account deficit. The main ingredients were a firm commitment to a fixed exchange rate, suspension of automatic wage indexation, wage guidelines, a tight fiscal policy, and capital market deregulations. This policy change was to some extent inspired by Thatcher's policies in the United Kingdom during the same period.

This was a disinflationary programme, and according to conventional wisdom, it should have resulted in increasing unemployment, at least for a significant transition period, until low inflation was anchored in expectations. The outcome turned out differently. Inflation and nominal interest rates declined rapidly, economic growth picked up, and unemployment decreased. Several factors contributed to these developments.

Capital markets were liberalized over this period, including both capital mobility across borders and housing financing. The sharp reduction in interest rates led to a booming housing market and a steep increase in private consumption and thus domestic demand. This contributed to economic growth but also to high wage increases and a deteriorating current account. As a result, economic policy was tightened in 1987 to reduce loan-financed private consumption. The fact that wage increases remained relatively high despite an unemployment rate close to 10 per cent was taken as a sign that unemployment had become a structural problem.

The late 1980s and early 1990s—'the seven bad years'—had low growth rates and persistently high unemployment. There were few economic policy initiatives during the period, and a sense of pessimism developed, especially in relation to bringing unemployment down. However, during this period, the current account improved because domestic demand declined and low wage increases contributed to improving competitiveness. Moreover, Denmark shifted from being strongly dependent on the import of energy in the 1970s to becoming a net exporter of energy (North Sea oil and gas).

Some notable policy changes in the 1980s have been lasting and thus crucial for later economic developments.

The Exchange Rate Peg

Although Denmark pursued a fixed exchange policy in the 1970s and early 1980s, it was a soft peg with frequent devaluations. From the inauguration of the European Monetary System in March 1979 to the autumn of 1982, the Danish krone was devalued no less than four times. The credibility of the announced exchange rate peg was thus low, which was reflected in a high 'devaluation' premium in interest rates, among other things.

Hence, the announcement by the Schlüter government that the exchange rate was fixed was, in itself, insufficient for this policy to gain credibility. The other policy changes, in particular the suspension of wage indexation, were important since they contributed to an improvement in wage competitiveness (helped by the 'last' devaluation made in the spring of 1982). Moreover, the 'new' exchange rate policy was tested in late 1982 when turmoil in the European Monetary System (EMS) caused a number of countries to undertake discrete devaluations. The Danish government abstained, and the fixed exchange rate policy gained credibility, which in combination with the lower inflation led to a sharp drop in nominal interest rates (cf. Figure 32.3). Consequently, the interest rate spread to Germany (D-Mark) and fell sharply—a clear sign that the fixed exchange rate policy had gained credibility in financial markets (Andersen and Risager 1988).

The fixed exchange rate policy has important implications for macroeconomic policies. Given the peg of the exchange rate to the D-Mark (later the euro), the Danish Central Bank's main task is to support the fixed exchange rate, while monetary policy (interest rates) follows interest rates in Germany (the euro area) (see e.g. Abildgren et al. 2010). This also implies an implicit inflation target. Currently, Denmark implicitly has the same inflation target as the euro area (inflation not to exceed 2 per cent). If Danish inflation exceeds this target, competitiveness deteriorates, and the viability of the fixed exchange rate will be at stake. This policy assignment leaves fiscal policy as the primary instrument to make wage and price development consistent with the exchange rate peg. Fiscal policy recognizes this constraint, as was perhaps most clearly seen in 1997 where the anticipation of inflation becoming too high to be consistent with the exchange rate peg prompted a fiscal tightening (Andersen and Chiriaeva 2007).

In the early 1980s, the exchange rate was thus effectively pegged to the D-Mark, and since 1999, to the euro. Denmark has adopted a narrow band for variations of the Danish krone relative to the euro of +/− 2.25 per cent within the ERM II, and this policy has attained strong credibility. The interest rate spread to the euro area (D-Mark) has been very small, and occasionally, even negative. There is a strong political consensus on the fixed exchange rate policy. Although pegged to the euro, Denmark has opted not to join the EMU. The issue of EMU membership is highly sensitive and has become taboo in policy debates. In Parliament, there is a clear majority for membership, but there is a political commitment that the issue should be decided in a referendum. A referendum has been held twice without obtaining support for membership, and the political risk of calling a new referendum is therefore high (see also Beach 2020). In recent polls, the no side has a majority. There is hardly any public debate on the issue, and the positions are at a stalemate. The proponents argue that since the fixed exchange rate policy is politically uncontested, we might as well join the EMU to have a voice on important decisions, while the opponents argue that staying out has not been a problem so why join.

Current Account Problems and Savings Shortage

The persistent current account deficit (savings minus investments) led to the view that savings were too low (see Figure 32.4). National account identities imply that the current account is equal to the difference between total savings and total real investments in the economy. Thus, a persistent current account deficit suggests that savings are too low. If savings could be increased, reducing domestic demand, imports would decline and exports would increase, all contributing to improving the current account. A prelude to the 'savings' discussion was a debate in the 1970s and 1980s about 'wage earner funds' to enhance worker ownership and influence companies, but it did not gain political support. The compromise became the build-up of the labour market pension system as marked by the tripartite agreement—*Fælleserklæringen*—from 1987, which was pivotal both in relation to wage moderation and the build-up of labour market pensions. At the time, some groups—primarily public employee and high-income groups—already had work-related pension arrangements, but the agreement extended coverage to all workers covered by collective agreements. The contribution rate is determined in collective agreements and is voluntarily determined in that sense, but contributions are mandatory for the wage earners. The contribution rates increased in steps over the years and are now at 12 per cent or higher. Although this move had multiple motivations, the outcome was the foundation for what is considered today a robust pension system with a mixture of tax-financed pensions (base pension and means-tested supplements) and funded labour market pensions. Thus, this system ensures both a minimum income for all pensioners and high replacement rates (pensions relative to income when working) (Pension Commission 2015).

Regulation of labour market issues has traditionally relied on voluntarily negotiated arrangements between the social partners. Collective agreements rather than formal legal regulations constitute the core of the so-called 'Danish labour market model'. Political interventions have occurred when collective bargaining has failed, but intervention has usually been based on the (implicit) compromise advanced by the official Conciliation Board (*Forligsmandsinstitutionen*). However, since labour market developments also depend on social and labour market policies, and the threat of political intervention may have deterred social partners, it is difficult to disentangle the role of collectively bargained arrangements from implicit political influence.

The Danish labour market is well organized. Although union membership has been declining (in 2016, 67 per cent were members of a union), about 85 per cent of all workers are working under conditions decided by collective agreements (100 per cent in the public sector). The Danish labour market has traditionally been highly centralized, but it has moved towards a model of so-called centralized decentralization. With centralized decentralization, collective arrangements retain their role as regulators of labour market conditions although parts of the decision-making process have become more decentralized. The pivotal change came in 1989 with sector-specific negotiations between Danish Industries (DI) (organising firms in the manufacturing sector) and CO-Metal (a bargaining conglomerate representing unions organizing workers employed in DI firms). Subsequently, decentralization has been expanded to other areas.

The decentralization process has involved changes in both the horizontal and the vertical dimension. In the horizontal dimension, general negotiations for the larger part of the labour market have been replaced by sector-specific bargaining. In the vertical dimension, collective agreements increasingly stipulate general conditions only (working hours, rules for flexible working hours, minimum wages, etc.), leaving wage settlement to local negotiations. About 80 per cent of all collective arrangements currently allow for decentralized wage formation. This is a source of more flexible wage adjustment but also increasing wage dispersion (see e.g. Dahl et al. 2013).

Tax Reforms

A tax reform in 1987 is the first in a long string of tax reforms with an agenda of broadening tax bases and reducing marginal tax rates. In the mid-1980s, top marginal tax rates were as high as 75 per cent, and in 2019, about 56 per cent. Moreover, the possibility of deducting interest rate expenditures implied a negative after-tax real cost of borrowing (the after-tax rate of return minus inflation). A sequence of tax reforms have reduced the taxation value of interest rate deductions. In this process, the marginal tax rates, and thus the degree of progressivity in the tax system, have been reduced. More recently, tax reforms have focused on the so-called participation tax (effective taxation when going from no work to work) and the work incentives for recipients of income transfers. In the same vein, an earned income tax credit was introduced in 2004 and has since been expanded.

THE 1990S: FOUNDING THE FLEXICURITY MODEL

In the early 1990s, the economic mood was on the pessimistic side, with low growth and no signs that unemployment would fall. It became a widespread view that 'we have to learn to live with unemployment'.

A centre-left government took office in 1993 (led by Poul Nyrup Rasmussen) and launched, in the spirit of this pessimistic viewpoint, a paid leave scheme to reduce registered unemployment and to share available jobs more evenly. However, policies soon changed direction.

Fiscal policy was changed in an expansionary direction. Rules for mortgages with property as collateral were liberalized, and taxes were lowered (partly the result of a phasing in of a tax reform lowering marginal tax rates) to 'kick-start' the economy. The economic situation changed markedly. Growth picked up and employment increased (see Figures 32.1 and 32.2), causing a turning point in the rate of unemployment. In the wake of these changes, labour market policies changed from a passive orientation focusing on income support towards a more active one stressing job search and activation requirements for the non-employed. This change took place in a sequence of reforms, and the fact that employment increased and unemployment decreased was clearly crucial in getting support for these policies. The period 1994–2000 was unique in many respects: growth was high and unemployment falling, without the usual problems of wage increases and deteriorating competitiveness showing up. Moreover, both the current account and public finances improved.

Flexicurity Reforms

The labour market reforms in the second half of the 1990s were crucial for laying the foundation for the favourable labour market performance associated with the so-called Danish flexicurity model.

The short version of the flexicurity model is as follows: hiring and firing rules are rather flexible, and the unemployment insurance scheme is generous by international standards. However, this was also the case from the mid-1970s to the early part of the 1990s where Denmark was routinely listed as a crisis country with problems by almost any macroeconomic indicator, including high and persistent unemployment (e.g. Andersen and Svarer 2007). Therefore, the *flex* and the *security* parts of the Danish policy package cannot in isolation account for the performance of the Danish labour market. This is not denying the importance of these elements, but experience points out that they in themselves are no guarantee for a low and stable unemployment rate. To account for the Danish experience, a series of reforms during the last half of the 1990s are important.

The main thrust of these reforms was a shift from a passive focus on income protection to a more active focus on job search and employment. The policy restricted eligibility for unemployment benefits and shortened their duration to four years, as well as introduced workfare (activation) elements into unemployment insurance and social policies in general.

The latter resulted in rather elaborate and rigid rules that when unemployed (either on unemployment benefits or on social assistance), one should participate in activation programmes. These programmes could be job training, subsidized work, or education and the like. In short, the programmes had the two-fold purpose of enhancing the qualifications and employability of the unemployed as well as testing whether they were actually willing to work. The specific rules and requirements have changed over the years, in part due to evidence on the effects of these policies. Denmark is the OECD country spending most on active labour market programmes as a share of GDP among OECD countries.

2000–2018: Overheating and the Financial Crisis

A centre-right government (led by Anders Fogh Rasmussen) took power in 2001, and economic developments were soon affected by two international events, namely the stock market crash following the burst of the so-called IT bubble and the terror attack on the World Trade Centre in New York on 11 September 2001. The global growth decline caused lower growth and increasing unemployment in Denmark. The setback turned out to be short-lived; growth soon picked up and unemployment decreased to very low levels (cf. Figure 32.2). Inflation remained low and the current account was in surplus as were public finances (see Figures 32.3 and 32.4). In short, the usual balance problems seemed to have been overcome, and the problems associated with the disequilibrium period of the 1970s had been solved. The early 2000s saw few major economic reforms, but there was some fine-tuning of policies, including the active labour market policies.

During the 2000s, domestic demand picked up, partly due to further liberalization of house financing. Unemployment reached the lowest level for decades, wages rose, and competitiveness deteriorated. In short, the economy was overheating. The housing market in particular displayed an unsustainable path with very high price increases at the same time as growth in public expenses exceeded the stipulated targets.

The Danish economy went through a boom-bust pattern. On the eve of the Great Recession, there were already signs that economic activity was fading. The Great Recession accelerated this development and caused a steep decrease in GDP (see Figure 32.1b) and employment (Figure 32.2). Unemployment increased by 2.5 percentage points between 2008 and 2009, and 4 percentage points between 2008 and 2010, almost twice the average increase across OECD countries, although the level of unemployment remained below the OECD average.

The recession thus had both foreign and domestic causes. The financial sector was severely affected by the crisis, and 'bank packages' were launched. Importantly, they relied on bail-in mechanisms, and there were no public bailouts of the financial sector. It is also noteworthy that despite the large turnaround, not least in the housing market, there was no significant increase in household bankruptcies. The boom-bust pattern was in some respects similar to the one experienced in some Southern European countries (e.g. Portugal and Spain), but with the important difference that the Danish financial sector was more resilient and public finances were in a much better position to absorb the consequences of the downturn in economic activity.

A centre-left government took over in 2011 with Helle Thorning-Schmidt as prime minister. A particularly controversial policy element was the shortening of the maximal unemployment benefit period from four to two years, and a tightening of the employment history required to regain unemployment benefits from 26 weeks to 52 weeks of employment within the preceding three years. This was part of a political agreement made by the previous government, but the Thorning government adopted and implemented it nonetheless. When the reform was agreed, the business cycle was expected to improve. The recovery, however, turned out to be slower than expected, raising concerns that many unemployed people would lose their right to unemployment benefits and become dependent on the lower means-tested social benefits (which could be zero if one's partner had a sufficiently high income). To avoid this, several ad hoc measures were implemented to prevent the decline in compensation after a two-year unemployment spell (Danish Economic Councils 2014), but these reform elements remained a controversial political issue.

Although Denmark, assessed in terms of standard macroeconomic indicators, is among the European countries with the least problems, the crisis proved very persistent. Aggregate demand remained subdued, due to domestic private consumption and investment in particular, while net export has been growing. The protracted reduction in private domestic demand is partly explained by debt consolidation, precautionary savings, and pessimistic expectations driven by the boom-bust pattern. Subsequently, growth has been picking up, driven by increasing foreign demand and some improvements in domestic demand. As a result, employment increased. In 2017–18, the business cycle situation was normalized, and the debate has turned to the risk of 'shortage' of labour.

Fiscal Policy

The boom-bust pattern in the mid-2000s can in part be attributed to a too pro-cyclical fiscal policy. The economy was booming with high growth in private consumption and investments (housing), and at the same time, fiscal policy was expansionary. However, policymakers were reluctant to tighten fiscal policy. The then Prime Minister Anders Fogh Rasmussen was confronted with calls from several economists to tighten fiscal policy. He stated, however, that the textbooks had to be rewritten since 'this time is different'. Later developments confirmed that the textbooks were closer to the mark than the prime minister was.

The destabilizing effects originating from fiscal policy had two main sources: a tax freeze and high public expenditure growth. The centre-right government introduced a so-called tax-freeze with the intention of curbing public sector expenditures. The tax freeze meant that tax rates were not to increase, but for property taxes and some excise taxes, the freeze was effectively defined in terms of nominal tax payments. In a situation with rapidly increasing house prices, this reduced effective tax rates, which in turn contributed to further house price increases. At the same time, public consumption growth was high. The average annual growth rate for public expenditures was about 2 per cent in the period prior to the Great Recession (primarily driven by increasing health expenditures), while the target was about 1 per cent (see Larsen 2020). Thus, fiscal policy was clearly pro-cyclical during this period.

After the onset of the Great Recession, fiscal policy has been expansionary. Denmark is among the countries that have pursued the most expansionary fiscal policy over the period 2009–10. There was fiscal space to pursue such a policy because public finances were consolidated in the years prior to the crisis. There were systematic budget surpluses (although they could have been higher given the unusually high level of activity), and debt was reduced in the years prior to the crisis. This left fiscal space to pursue a counter-cyclical fiscal policy when the crisis set in. Moreover, countercyclical fiscal policies had two components. Discretionary changes in fiscal policy contributed to support economic activity, and measured by the so-called fiscal effect, the GDP effect of the fiscal policy changes was close to 1 per cent of GDP in both 2009 and 2010. Quantitatively, the automatic stabilizers were even more important. With an extended welfare state offering income support to people out of work and financing it via taxes on incomes, it follows that expenditures and revenues automatically change when economic activity changes. These automatic budget effects tend to stabilize the economy, hence the label 'automatic stabilizers'. When the economy is booming with increasing employment and incomes, tax revenue increases and spending decreases. This reduces aggregate demand in the economy and vice versa when economic activity is declining. The presence of fiscal space allowed automatic stabilizers to work (the strongest within the OECD area) and left room for discretionary policies. The budget balance changed from a surplus of about 5 per cent in 2007 to a deficit close to 3 per cent of GDP in 2009 and 2010, but still debt levels were moderate in a comparative perspective.

Although Denmark is not a euro member, EU rules on fiscal policy apply. They set limits for budget surpluses and public debt (see also Jensen and Nedergaard 2020). Moreover, a budget law introduced in 2012 further strengthens the fiscal framework (Danish Economic Councils 2015; Danish Ministry of Finance 2014). A prime reason for the law was public expenditure growth tending to exceed planned levels (cf. above). The budget law stipulates that (1) the structural total budget balance cannot have a deficit in excess of 0.5 per cent of GDP, and (2) public expenditures are managed according to four-year expenditure ceilings for (a) current expenses for the state, (b) state expenditures for non-unemployment related income transfers, (c) a municipal expenditure ceiling for net-running expenditures, (d) a regional expenditure ceiling for health expenditures, and (e) a regional expenditure ceiling for expenditures on regional development projects. Note that the expenditure ceiling does not comprise expenditures on unemployment related income, transfers, and expenditures on activation measures (key elements of the automatic stabilizers) as well as public investments, debt servicing, and expenditures for Parliament and the royal family. For municipalities and regions, violation of the expenditure ceilings is sanctioned by reductions in block grants from the state. Finally, the Economic Council has been given the role of fiscal watchdog to oversee adherence to the fiscal rules.

Testing the Flexicurity Model

Since Denmark took a severe beating during the Great Recession, the flexicurity model was seriously put to the test. The model as such cannot prevent business cycles, and the interesting question is whether the model can weather a significant downturn. Lax firing rules make it likely that employment will fall drastically when aggregate demand drops, and although the social safety net cushions incomes for the unemployed, the financial viability of the model is at risk, if employment persistently declines. A prolonged decline in employment will reduce tax revenues and increase social expenditures, putting public finances under strain.

A hallmark of the flexicurity model is a high level of job turnover, implying that the unemployed (also the young entering the labour market) can easily find a job and that most unemployment spells are short. This feature was intact during the Great Recession despite the large drop in employment. Although outflows from jobs increased and inflows into jobs declined because of the crisis, the turnover levels soon recovered to the levels seen prior to the boom period, despite the overall level of activity still being gloomy. Even though unemployment increased during the crisis, most unemployment spells were short (close to 50 per cent of total unemployment is made up of spells less than three months). Therefore, both youth unemployment and long-term unemployment are low by international comparison, including during the crisis years. High turnover rates thus effectively work as an implicit work-sharing mechanism. Equal burden sharing is important from a distributional perspective, but it is also of structural importance. The alternative would be longer unemployment spells concentrated on a smaller group of individuals, more people unemployed long-term, and a corresponding depreciation of human and social capital. In short, the high turnover rates reduce the negative structural implications of high unemployment.

Ageing, Fiscal Sustainability, and Reforms Directed at Labour Supply

The debate on ageing intensified in the early 2000s, and focus shifted towards long-term developments of public finances and the pertinent question as to whether fiscal policies would be sustainable in the wake of an ageing population. In short, would expenditures outpace revenues, causing a non-viable financial situation? The public budget need not balance period-by-period, but systematic imbalances are not possible. The present value of revenues must be able to cover the present value of expenditures plus initial debt.

A so-called fiscal sustainability analysis has the purpose of analysing whether this is the case. If sustainability is not ensured, it provides the order of magnitude of needed policy changes. The results of such analyses showed that public finances would display systematic deficits, in particular due to increasing longevity. Consequently, fiscal policies were not sustainable (Welfare Commission 2006). Long-term programmes and projections have, for some years, been standard in the economic policy process. Fiscal policies are planned under a long horizon, and ensuring fiscal sustainability is a constraint on the process. The reforms outlined below ensure that the conditions for fiscal sustainability are now satisfied (Danish Ministry of Finance 2018; Danish Economic Councils (2017).

Since neither tax increases nor retrenchment of welfare arrangements were politically acceptable solutions to the sustainability problem, attention turned to reforms to increase labour supply and employment. Since the welfare state has been expanded, public finances are highly sensitive to the employment level. An increase in the structural employment level significantly affects public finances, contributing to solving the fiscal sustainability problem (see also Petersen 2020).

To address the sustainability problem, major steps were undertaken by *velfærdsreformen* (the welfare reform) in 2006 and *tilbagetrækningsreformen* (the retirement reform) in 2011, increasing the statutory eligibility ages for early retirement and public pensions, and reducing the early retirement period. First, statutory ages for early retirement and pensions are increased in stages over the period 2014–2022 (from 60 to 62 years and 65 to 67 years, respectively), and the early retirement period is shortened from five to three years (2018–23). Second, after these changes have been phased in, the early retirement age and pension age will be indexed to the development in life expectancy at the age of 60 to target an expected pension period of 14.5 years (17.5 years including early retirement) in the long run (currently about 18.5/23.5 years).

These reforms came as a response to increasing longevity being the main driver behind the ageing problem. Increases in retirement ages alongside increases in longevity were motivated as a way to rebalance the number of years that an average person contributes to and benefits from welfare arrangements. Since longevity increases are associated with healthy ageing, higher retirement ages were seen as the straightforward way to ensure the financial viability of welfare arrangements. These reforms mainly affected core workers, those already in employment, who were now asked to postpone their retirement. Hence, an increase in the retirement age would have a relatively certain effect on labour supply and employment. However, it is increasingly questioned whether the current system adequately copes with people with deteriorating work capabilities, for instance due to life-long, hard physical work, especially given the tightening of the disability scheme and the early retirement scheme.

Subsequently, economic policy debates increasingly focused on the number of people of working age being on various forms of public transfer (cf. Figure 32.5), and there was widespread agreement that too many people of working age were living on transfers. Accordingly, all major elements in the social safety net have been reformed in recent years, with a focus on strengthening labour supply and employment (e.g. Danish Economic Councils 2017). Such reforms are more challenging since they target groups

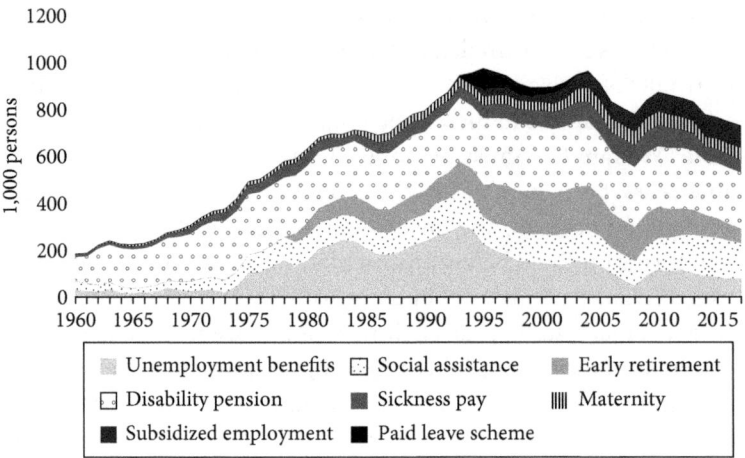

FIGURE 32.5 Recipients of social transfers, 1960–2017.

Note: Recipients between 16 and 64 years, exclusive study grants

Source: Statistics Denmark

that, for various reasons, are marginalized in the labour market, and various barriers need to be overcome to make work possible. In sum, labour market reforms over the last decade have been aimed at making the young enter the workforce early with appropriate education/skills and ensuring that the elderly stay longer on the labour market, while increasing employment rates for everyone in between.

The ultimate floor of the social safety net is social assistance (*kontanthjælp*). All individuals are entitled to support if they have become unable to support themselves and their family (cf. *Lov om aktiv socialhjælp*). The purpose of the support is to enable the recipient to become self-supporting, and therefore, the recipient has an obligation to use and develop his/her individual work capabilities and to participate in activation programmes. Social assistance is means-tested on a family basis and can be supplemented by housing support, child allowances, and support for special needs (see e.g. Hansen and Schultz-Nielsen 2015).

The social assistance scheme has been reformed numerous times, and it is beyond the scope of this chapter to detail all the changes. The following highlights some major elements or conditionalities built into the system with the purpose of targeting support and strengthening work incentives. Important new elements are the residence and employment requirements, which break with universalism by granting entitlements dependent on past behaviour. The residence requirement stipulates that eligibility for social assistance for non-EU/EEA citizens is contingent on residency in Denmark for 7 of the last 8 years (as of 2019, for 9 of the last 10 years). If this condition is not met, 'integration benefits' are available, which constitute about 50–80 per cent of social assistance, depending on the family's situation (introduced in 2002, abolished in 2012, and reintroduced in 2015). The employment criterion makes eligibility dependent on at least 225 hours of (non-subsidized) work within the last 12 months, otherwise benefits are reduced or lost (introduced in 2006, removed in 2012, and reintroduced in 2015). In addition, (from 2019) 2.5 years of employment within the last 10 years are also required. Moreover, there is a cap on the total amount of benefits a family/person can receive, be it social assistance/education cash benefits, housing supplements, or special allowances (introduced in 2014). While these rules are general, they do affect immigrants from low-income countries in particular, among whom many are non-employed.

The major aim of the social safety net reforms is to 'make work pay', both along the intensive (working hours) and extensive (labour market participation) margin. The higher the net replacement rate for unemployment benefits for instance, the more the social safety net protects against income loss in case of unemployment or other events precluding work, but it also reduces the incentives to return to work. Thus, there is a clear trade-off between incentives and insurance in the design of the social safety net, and recent reforms have stressed the incentive side. The employment consequences of social benefits depend critically on the reason for non-employment. Employment can be constrained from the supply side due to insufficient economic work incentives, or from the demand side due to lack of demand or if the individual does not possess relevant qualifications or is unable to provide the required effort for firms to hire at the going wage level (minimum wage). The policy dilemma is that lower benefit levels or tighter eligibility conditions may work to bring some people into employment if the incentive constraint is binding, but not if the other reasons are the cause of non-employment. The latter group would experience a worsening in their economic situation, leading to an increase in inequality and poverty—issues that are heatedly discussed.

Conclusion

The comparatively favourable performance of the Danish economy is not the result of a quick fix, but the outcome of a long string of reforms addressing structural problems and very explicitly taking into account the constraints faced by a small open economy. The latter is immediately clear from the fixed exchange rate policy and the need to ensure its credibility. This policy has passed the market test, since the interest spread vis-à-vis the euro area has been very small for years and even negative in some periods. The Danish case also shows that policy choices are possible even in an era of globalization. The public sector plays a larger role than in most other countries. The interesting lesson is how the welfare state has been designed to balance concerns for economic performance on the one hand and public provision of welfare services and the pursuit of egalitarian outcomes on the other. Two points are particularly important. First, while the public sector is large, the private sector is regulated in a market-conform way. The Danish model is thus not 'politics against markets'. Second, the welfare arrangements have a strong, active focus on supporting labour market participation and human capital acquisition. Since the financial viability of the welfare model ultimately depends on maintaining a high employment level in the private sector, the conflict between welfare objectives and economic performance is not as stark as it may first appear.

The policies applied in Denmark are not unique; their packing may differ, but the ingredients are familiar. The recent favourable economic performance is the result of economic reforms, initially directed at overcoming crises and subsequently becoming forward-looking and more pro-active. The reform capacity has been high in recent years as exemplified by the labour market and retirement reforms. The noteworthy aspect of this development is the political economy process of establishing consensus across a broad political spectrum. This is essential for the support for reforms but also for continuity and consistency in economic policy. This is so, despite the fact that most governments have been minority governments (and usually coalitions among several parties) and that there have been frequent changes in government.

The cornerstones of the framework for economic policy are the fixed exchange rate policy, labour market policies, and the fiscal framework. The latter includes the short-term budget process focusing on expenditure control and budget targets (deficit targets), and the long-term requirements of ensuring fiscal sustainability. This framework has contributed to stability and credibility on economic policy despite changing governments. This economic policy framework does not preclude political prioritization. A key issue in recent years has been taxation versus welfare, spanning from arguments that taxes (and thus expenditures) should be reduced to support competitiveness and employment, to arguments that welfare arrangements have to cope with not only the ageing population but also the need for standard improvements, not least in health services. Immigration is a particularly contested issue having affected both emigration rules (for non-EU citizens) and the design of the social safety net. More recently, climate and environmental policies have gained importance in policy debates.

NOTES

1. See http://globalization.kof.ethz.ch/. 2017.
2. See http://www.doingbusiness.org.

REFERENCES

Abildgren, Kim, Bodil Nyboe, and Jens Thomsen (2010). *Dansk pengehistorie 1990–2005, Bind 6.* Copenhagen: Danmarks Nationalbank.

Andersen, Torben M., and Julia Chiriaeva (2007). 'Exchange rate pegs, fiscal policy and credibility', *Open Economies Review*, 18/1: 53–76.

Andersen, Torben M., and Ole Risager (1988). 'Stabilization policies, credibility and interest determination in a small open economy', *European Economic Review*, 32: 669–79.

Andersen, Torben M., and Michael Svarer (2007). 'Flexicurity—Labour Market Performance in Denmark', *CESifo Economic Studies*, 53/3: 389–429.

Beach, Derek (2020). 'Referenda in Denmark. Influence on politics', in Peter M. Christiansen, Jørgen Elklit, and Peter Nedergaard, eds, *The Oxford Handbook of Danish Politics*. Oxford: Oxford University Press, 400–16.

Dahl, Christian, Daniel Le Maire, and Jakob R. Munch (2013). 'Wage dispersion and decentralization of wage bargaining', *Journal of Labor Economics*, 31/3: 501–33.

Danish Economic Councils (2014). *Dansk Økonomi—Efteråret 2014*. Copenhagen: Danish Economic Councils.

Danish Economic Councils (2015). *Dansk Økonomi -Forår 2015*. Copenhagen: Danish Economic Councils.

Danish Economic Councils (2017). *Dansk Økonomi -Efterår 2017*. Copenhagen: Danish Economic Councils.

Danish Ministry of Finance (2014). *Finansredegørelse*. Copenhagen: Danish Ministry of Finance.

Danish Ministry of Finance (2018). *Danish Convergence Programme*. Copenhagen: Danish Ministry of Finance.

Hansen, Hans, and Marie Louise Schultz-Nielsen (2015). *Kontanthjælpen gennem 25 år: modtagere, regler, incitamenter og levevilkår fra 1987 til 2012*. Copenhagen: Gyldendal.

Høgedahl, Laust (2020). 'The Danish Labour Market Model. Is the bumblebee still flying?', in Peter M. Christiansen, Jørgen Elklit, and Peter Nedergaard, eds, *The Oxford Handbook of Danish Politics*. Oxford: Oxford University Press, 559–76.

Jensen, Mads D., and Peter Nedergaard (2020). 'Danish European Union policies. Sailing between economic benefits and political sovereignty', in Peter M. Christiansen, Jørgen Elklit, and Peter Nedergaard, eds, *The Oxford Handbook of Danish Politics*. Oxford: Oxford University Press, 487–501.

Larsen, Lars T. (2020). 'Health policy. The submerged politics of free and equal access', in Peter M. Christiansen, Jørgen Elklit, and Peter Nedergaard, eds, *The Oxford Handbook of Danish Politics*. Oxford: Oxford University Press, 592–608.

Ministry for Economic Affairs and the Interior (2018). *Økonomisk Redegørelse, December 2018*. Copenhagen: Ministry for Economic Affairs and the Interior.

Pedersen, Peder J., Christen Sørensen, and Claus Vastrup (1987). 'Træk af udviklingen i dansk økonomi efter 1960', in Det Økonomiske Råd ed., *Råd og realiteter 1962–1987*. Copenhagen: Det Økonomiske Råd, 7–34.

Pension Commission (2015). *Det danske pensionssystem—international anderkendt, men ikke problemfrit*. Copenhagen: Pension Commission.

Petersen, Klaus (2020). 'Welfare State policies. From the beginning towards an end?', in Peter M. Christiansen, Jørgen Elklit, and Peter Nedergaard, eds, *The Oxford Handbook of Danish Politics*. Oxford: Oxford University Press, 540–58.

Welfare Commission (2006). *Fremtidens velfærd—vores valg*. Copenhagen: Welfare Commission.

CHAPTER 33

WELFARE STATE POLICIES

From the Beginning Towards an End?

KLAUS PETERSEN

CHARACTERISTICS OF THE DANISH WELFARE MODEL

THE term 'welfare state' slipped into the Danish language in the mid-1950s (Petersen and Petersen 2019).[1] However, it also created some conceptual confusion. Social Democratic Minister Jens Otto Krag asked his officials for a memorandum explaining what this 'welfare state' was all about. Today, the concept of the 'welfare state' is an established term in Danish. The entire Danish political landscape embraces the welfare state, and the few who do not love it, love to hate it. For most Danes, as well as international commentators, the welfare state is simply the very equivalent of Danish society. However, the welfare state is not just an idea. It is also a collective term subsuming policies and institutions aimed at solving social problems and supporting citizens who must deal with a range of difficult social and economic events in their lives. The abovementioned Jens Otto Krag ended up defining the welfare state as 'the sum of our social policy legislation', but what characterizes Danish social policy legislation and the Danish welfare state?

Comparative welfare research typically portrays the Danish welfare state as a variant of the Nordic welfare model, referring to the typology established by Esping-Andersen's (1990) seminal work on *Three Worlds of Welfare Capitalism*.[2] The Nordic welfare model is based on a regulated market economy with dual-earner families and characterized by comprehensive (universal) social security and social services, tax financing, and regulated labour markets. Furthermore, the Nordic model of welfare has been very successful with respect to poverty reduction and has significant redistributional effects.

However, we need to remember that the idea of a distinct Nordic model is an ideal type painted with a broad brush. The listed key features certainly offer important insights into the major characteristics of the national welfare policies within the Nordic family of nations.

Still, even though, the Nordic region offers a case of very intensive internal diffusion and cooperation (Petersen 2006), welfare policies are national legislation based on national historical trajectories. What might look very similar from afar—compared to other types of welfare states—has more nuances when inspected up close. We find variation in policy design between the Nordic welfare states as well as across policy programmes within them. Consequently, we should talk about 'one model with five exceptions' (Christiansen et al 2006). As any systematic account of similarities and differences between Nordic welfare models and policies falls well outside the scope of this chapter (but see Kautto et al. 1999; Christiansen et al. 2006; Kautto 2010), in the following, we will briefly look at key features of the Danish welfare policies: universalism, tax financing, comprehensive social security and social services, redistribution, and consistency over time.

First, the Danish welfare state is universalistic in the sense that social rights are linked to citizenship, bringing together all citizens in a single risk group. This applies, for example, to old age pensions where a single system for all citizens has existed since 1891. However, the fact that coverage is universal does not mean that everyone has the actual right to all benefits. All social legislation contains filtering in the form of means testing, income testing, and conditionality. In order to receive an old age pension, for example, one must have reached a certain age (historically fluctuating between 60 and 68 years). Similarly, daycare institutions serve children in a particular age group, and in their early days, they prioritized working single mothers. Most cash benefits depend on the individual's income and assets, but it can also be tied to one's family situation (whether or not one has dependents), prior income, or employment history.

Second, most welfare services are tax funded. This applies to core services such as retirement pensions, social care, family benefits, and services including health and education. However, there are exceptions such as occupational accident insurance (compulsory insurance for the employer), and in the early decades of the twentieth century, childcare was carried out mainly by charitable or philanthropic organizations. There are also schemes with a degree of user payment, and the so-called 'help-to-self-help' principle, where the state supports social schemes based on membership contributions, has played a central role with respect to health insurance and unemployment insurance (see below).

Third, compared to most other countries, the Danish welfare state is extensive, both in terms of size (e.g. social expenditures and number of persons receiving benefits or number of employees working in the welfare sector) and in terms of the types of benefits offered. Of course, the nature of these benefits have changed over time, but the Danish welfare state continues to provide a comprehensive catalogue of both transfer payments and social services that ameliorate social risks and challenges throughout the individual's entire life cycle. Compared to most other countries, the proportion of social spending directed to social services (rather than cash transfers) is very high (Jensen 2011: 407–8).

Fourth, the public sector (state and municipalities) plays a central role both as the organizer (through national law) and as a provider of welfare services. However, there is a general tendency to overestimate the statist character of the Danish welfare model. The fact that welfare rights are regulated by national legislation does not necessarily mean it is provided by the public sector. For example, as mentioned, philanthropic associations have historically played an important role in providing childcare and in relation to marginalized groups, and the trade union movement has played a role in the implementation of unemployment insurance. In the primary health sector, physicians in private practice are responsible. Similarly, private companies provide a portion of eldercare and other services. Nevertheless, for the most part, the privately provided welfare services are both funded and organized by the state or municipality.

Fifth, great emphasis is placed on redistribution. Measured by the Gini co-efficient, Denmark is one of the most egalitarian societies in the world, and the redistribution perspective has remained a central welfare policy objective. This is primarily a matter of economic redistribution. It is reflected in a progressive tax system and by a degree of targeting within social services (Friis 1969). Beginning in the 1970s, the discussion of equality also included gender equality which has been particularly reflected in family policy and women's employment. In general, however, pursuit of gender equality has had less political attention in Denmark than in the other Nordic countries (see also Fiig and Siim 2020).

One can add an additional feature to these more institutional characteristics. The Danish welfare policies feature a very high degree of consistency over time. Arguably, path dependency is a feature of public policies in most countries. However, in the Danish case, this is more pronounced (also compared to other Nordic countries). The history of the Danish welfare state is all about numerous minor innovations of the existing system rather than dramatic changes and paradigm shifts. The idea of building on the existing legislation has been a kind of social-political mantra, and most reforms have been adopted as broad political compromises across the political centre, ensuring a high level of continuity of legislation.

Some have pointed to a special interaction between state, society, and the individual, where a strong state with a welfare system based on social solidarity supports individual autonomy. This 'statist individualism' (cf. Trägårdh 1997) is reflected in a welfare policy targeted at individuals rather than families. Other have pointed to the connections between social capital and a universal welfare society (Svendsen and Svendsen 2015).

HISTORICAL DEVELOPMENTS
UP TO THE 1980S

The Danish welfare state has a much longer history than is often thought. Some researchers have found historical roots in Christian philanthropy, in the Poor Laws, in

Lutheranism, in the Danish state building from the seventeenth century, or even as far back as the Viking Age (Petersen 1998). Without entirely rejecting the importance of such deep and long historical roots, it is reasonable to see the development that started in the late 1800s as something new. In the following, we divide this story into five phases (see also Christiansen and Petersen 2001).[3]

The first phase is the emergence of the modern welfare state in the late 1800s. In the wake of industrialization, urbanization, and democratization, Denmark, like other European countries, experienced a debate about 'the social question'. With inspiration particularly from Germany, the 1890s saw the introduction of national social policy legislation in Denmark. Hence, in 1891, the Danish Parliament adopted a needs-based and tax-financed old age pension for citizens over the age of 60. In 1892, a health insurance scheme based on membership in independent illness insurance funds with state subsidies followed. The law thus represented a 'help-to-self-help' principle whereby the state supported those who paid their dues into a sickness insurance fund.

The same principle characterizes the unemployment insurance legislation from 1907, following the so-called 'Ghent system' where unemployment funds were managed by the trade unions with membership contributions and state aid giving access to benefits in the event of unemployment. A law on compulsory occupational injury insurance was enacted in 1898, and after long deliberations in 1905, a law on child welfare was enacted where the state played a coordinating role, though they left most of the care tasks to philanthropic organizations. In this way, specific groups were extracted from the poverty legislation with the possibility to receive assistance without the stigma of the Poor Law. This early wave of legislation blended several social policy principles: tax-funded services, compulsory insurance, help-to-self-help, and charity/philanthropy. The basic characteristics of the Danish model evolved only gradually over more than a century. Over time, increased public tax funding came into being, coverage expanded, allocation criteria liberalized, new social needs were included, and the social services became more generous.

The second phase is the inter-war period, characterized by the institutionalization of social policy. This period saw the establishment of the Ministry of Social Affairs in the wake of the First World War (1920) and the more dominant political role of the Social Democratic Party (see Mariager and Olesen 2020). As a result, new welfare reforms and rights-based thinking entered the agenda. Where the focus in the first phase was on cash benefits in the event of the loss of wages, the focus from the 1930s also included prophylactic social policies and the development of the service sector. This occurred especially in the area of family policy. Another feature was the rights-based approach. In the early phase, benefits were based on local assessments. This resulted in local variations in benefit levels and access to benefits. Opposite to this was the idea of social rights where the legislation defined the rights of the individual citizen in a specific situation. The first legislation based on the social rights principle was the widow's pension in 1917, but the principle became increasingly dominant with the 1933 Social Reform which coordinated existing welfare legislation based on a rights-based approach to welfare and the central role of the state.

The Danish welfare state did not develop according to some grand master plan. Rather, it took the form of incrementalistic changes and extensions. There were ideological battles where especially the Social Democratic Party, the Social-Liberal Party, and various groups of policy experts[4] pushed for expanding social rights, while the centre-right parties were far more hesitant. In practice, however, most welfare reforms were a product of broad political compromise.

It is important not only to explain this in terms of domestic factors alone. Both the First World War and the economic crisis of the 1930s paved the way for growing state intervention and cemented the idea of state responsibility for social cohesion and social welfare (Petersen and Sørensen 2018). Furthermore, national social policy-making built on the transnational exchange of ideas. Around the turn of the century, Germany was the epicentre of social policy debate in Europe, but since the beginning of the inter-war period, Nordic social policy co-operation came to play an increasingly important role with the establishment of social policy treaties between the Nordic countries and a very intense exchange of ideas (Petersen 2006).

The third historical phase, the decades from 1945 until the 1970s, was the golden age of the welfare state, resulting in a major expansion of the welfare sector. With the introduction of the universal Old Age Pension Act (*Lov om folkepensionen*) in 1956, the idea of the welfare state saw its breakthrough—something clearly reflected in the political semantics of the time (Petersen and Petersen 2019). Now there was no turning back the clock. Political parties (though some only reluctantly) had to accept the facts on the ground: the welfare state was on the agenda, and the voters liked it a lot. During the following decades, the welfare state expanded, carried forward by strong economic growth, changing family patterns, and a political alliance between the centre-left and the social policy experts. As pointed out by more critical observers (such as Kristensen 1987), this was based on a structural asymmetry where benefits or groups of recipients were concentrated on specific groups of recipients, whereas the financing of the expansion of public policies was spread out among all taxpayers. Consequently, there was a structural pressure leading to growing public spending and welfare state expansion.[5] In 1960, Danish public spending (26.7 per cent of GDP) was among the lowest in the OECD, and only ten years later in 1960, Denmark was competing to be the top spender (49.2 per cent of GDP, rising to 56 per cent in 1980) (OECD 1982: 161). The result was that the list of items on the welfare state's 'menu' became much longer, the portions larger, more people could sit at the 'welfare table', and the bill was already paid via taxes.

As mentioned, among the major welfare reforms during the period was the universal old age pension (1956) which gave all citizens the right to a tax-funded basic pension (although also maintaining the needs-assessed supplementary benefit). The Social Assistance Act (*Forsorgsloven*) of 1961 eliminated the last remnants of stigmatizing effects on the recipients (loss of civil rights) and introduced a number of new initiatives. Reforms in unemployment insurance in the late 1960s meant that both benefits and the state's financial responsibility became markedly greater. The individual membership-based sickness funds (*sygekasser*) were eliminated in 1970 in favour of a tax-funded healthcare system. Women's increased participation in the labour market and changing family roles stimulated improvements in maternity leave and increased family cash benefits. The Children and Youth Act (*Lov om børne- og ungeforsorg*) from 1964 signalled that daycare institutions not only had a social care objective but also pedagogical goals, thus paving the way for a huge expansion of the daycare sector in the decades that followed.

This golden age of the Danish welfare state closed with the adoption of a new social reform, which on the ideational level qualifies as one of the most ambitious in world history. The combination of historically high growth rates, full employment, and planning optimism led to a reformulation of social policy with emphasis on prevention and individual compensation. The underlying logic was that social benefits should replace the previous income rather than offer a basic social security. However, the law took effect just as the economic growth turned into a recession in 1973, which meant that the law's ambitions were never fully implemented. The Social Reform Act (*Bistandsloven*) of the late 1960s thus marked the end of a major expansion phase more than the beginning of a new era.

The fourth historical phase, from the 1970s until today, is characterized by the crisis of the welfare state and the restructuring that has followed. The international recession of the early 1970s was a hard blow to Denmark. Growing unemployment, inflation, and government debt created financial challenges for the welfare state. It also led to an ideological crisis, questioning the positive relationship between growth and welfare that had characterized the 1960s.

Even though there is overall agreement on the details of policy formation (see below), there is less agreement on its causes. Structurally oriented explanations can hardly explain the specific characteristics of the Danish welfare state, and most actor-oriented explanations have pointed to the importance of the Danish Social Democratic Party for the expansion of social rights in the twentieth century (Esping-Andersen 1985; Petersen 1998). However, we cannot reduce the growth of the welfare state to the outcome of the actions of a single actor. The first social reforms in the 1890s took place before the Social Democratic Party gained political influence. In fact, most of the major welfare reforms were based on broad political agreements, allowing centre-right parties to play a role (Baldwin 1990; Christensen 1998) alongside religious philanthropy (Lützen 2002), the social partners (Martin 2008; Nørgaard 1997) and policy experts (Petersen 1998; Lundqvist and Petersen 2010). The development of the Danish welfare state was the result of a complicated interaction between structural conditions, various key actors, and the construction of social policy institutions.

NEW CHALLENGES TO THE DANISH WELFARE STATE

From the 1970s, the view of the welfare state changed, increasingly seeing the welfare state itself as a political and economic problem. The brutal combination of economic and legitimacy crisis led to a widespread perception of the welfare state in crisis (Petersen 1998: 257–308). On the left, the crisis of the welfare state was articulated as the crisis of capitalism, the solution to which was socialism. On the right, the Progress Party (see Green-Pedersen and Kosiara-Pedersen 2020) launched a severe attack on the public sector, and the party's views on taxes left no possibility of financing a large welfare state. Between these two extremes were the established political parties that had stood behind the welfare reforms of the 1950s and 1960s. They had to deal with acute challenges, among them increasing unemployment and government budget deficits. Over the longer term, they also had to manage an entirely new set of challenges and secure the welfare state for the future.

The Social Democratic Party considered themselves the party of the welfare state. In the 1970s, Social Democratic policy became the defence of the existing order, which in some cases entailed unpopular reductions in benefits such as reducing payments to unemployed youth. The only significant expansive reform in the 1970s was the early retirement benefit scheme (*efterløn*) in 1979 which allowed for early retirement with a pension from the labour market (Petersen 2011). The early retirement benefit scheme emerged as a response to high youth unemployment and achieved great popularity—much more than expected—in terms of the number of recipients. At the same time, however, early retirement became the target of experts, economists, and conservative politicians who, anxious over the demographic ageing of society, desired that workers should withdraw later from the labour market.

Generally, centre-right parties were subject to ideological inspiration from the neoliberal ideas that had gained ground in Denmark, for example, with the Progress Party's successful tax protest but also from a rather successful Margaret Thatcher who took over the power in the United Kingdom on a neoliberal political platform. This caused the centre-right parties, at the ideological level at least, to distance themselves from the welfare state in the 1980s. This tendency can be illustrated by the ambitious 'modernization plans' launched by the centre-right governments after 1982. They brought issues such as privatization, outsourcing, freedom of choice, and budgetary management of the public sector to the agenda, and they argued for a new balance between state and market. Nevertheless, for the centre-right governments, a genuine change of course turned out to be difficult.

The welfare state, despite all its problems and challenges, was extremely popular and hard to reform. Study after study has documented high and stable support among voters for the welfare policy schemes. Voters' readiness for major changes was limited, and this has ensured a high degree of inertia as politicians were confronted with the risk of alienating voters. Nevertheless, in the 1980s, the centre-right governments succeeded in setting a new agenda for the welfare state's economic sustainability, which led to a number of changes in welfare policy in the following decades.

There was a widespread understanding that the Danish welfare state faced major challenges. Various actors produced a high number of analyses of the welfare state's societal challenges in the form of debate books, political proposals, and official reports. Arguably, the Welfare Commission (2003–6) produced one of the most comprehensive assessments of the challenges to the Danish welfare model.[6] The Commission's reports identified four main challenges:

- Increased globalization: the Commission pointed out that it will be difficult to maintain a welfare model that rests so heavily on income taxation in a globalized reality. It can also adversely affect competitiveness and thus long-term financing of welfare.
- Demographic shifts: demographic projections show that there will be more old Danes in the coming decades, and the elderly will be living longer. This would not only mean increasing spending on pensions, eldercare, and health, but also increased 'financing pressures' on those in the workforce.
- Changed norms and increased individualization: the weak link between rights and duties, between contribution and services, which characterizes the Danish welfare model, can lead to individual utility maximization and free-rider behaviour that threatens the underlying social contract.
- Increased demand for welfare services from the public sector and increased leisure time: the historical development with higher prosperity had led to shorter working hours, and people expect more services of higher quality. This places pressure on the welfare model in that it simultaneously creates pressure on expenditures and reduces contribution.

The public and political debates on welfare reforms did not pay much attention to the issue of individualization. They have mainly focused on the changing demographics and the size of the active work force (future labour supply). The combination of lower working hours and a growing number of elderly threatened the financial sustainability of the Danish welfare model by changing the balance been taxpayers and welfare recipients. Globalization has lurked in the background of debates but has been discussed mainly in terms of what arguably could be listed as a fifth challenge:

- Immigration and integration: this was mentioned in the report of the Welfare Commission, pointing out the need for improving labour market integration of immigrants. However, in the public debate, this has been arguably the most salient topic since the late 1990s, including both worries about the cost of unsuccessful integration and the need for a stricter control of immigration, as well as intense debates on culture and religion in relation to immigrant groups.

This means that issues such as raising the retirement age, incentives for employment, and the regulation of immigration have dominated public debate, along with a general focus on managing public spending and making the public sector more efficient. Overall, these issues have occupied a greater place in the debate and the direction of reforms than, for example, the quality of services and social rights.

RESTRUCTURING AND REFORMING THE DANISH WELFARE STATE FROM THE 1980S

Since the 1980s, the welfare debate has been about whether welfare policy works as intended and about the welfare state's economic sustainability. The above-mentioned challenges, in combination with the political actors' more ideological goals, dictated the agenda. On the ideological side, domestic and international neo-liberal ideas have had an impact. As mentioned above, in the early 1980s, the newly elected centre-right government announced their plans for privatization, outsourcing, and a rollback of the public sector. This was met with resistance from the centre-left opposition defending the classic Danish welfare model.

However, the neoliberal agenda mainly affected public sector organization, affecting the core welfare policies less. The important exception was an emerging focus on individual incentives and responsibility which gradually developed into so-called workfare policies affecting mainly working-aged welfare recipients. Social Democratic governments in the 1990s embraced parts of this reform agenda (Klitgaard 2007), added a stronger emphasis on employment, and continued reforming the public sector. As the centre-right developed a more positive attitude towards the welfare state from the late 1990s, the outcome was a kind of convergence or a new welfare consensus. What once was differences in kind had become differences in degree. Three factors drove this process of convergence. First, the existing consensus around the main challenges for the Danish welfare model. Second, the widespread popularity of the Danish welfare model among the voters. In order to win broad support, parties have to offer a convincing strategy for protecting key welfare policies. Third, the emergence of a new more market-aligned welfare model made it possible for the centre-right to embrace the welfare state—or using their preferred terminology, 'the welfare society'.

The period from the 1980s is not easy to label. It involves numerous minor changes, large-scale reforms that have the character of reform packages with measures going in different directions and across policy areas, and organizational reforms. Any detailed description is thus impossible within the framework of a single chapter (see instead Petersen et al. 2013, 2014; Kvist and Greve 2011; Andersen 2011a, 2011b). Some changes qualify as retrenchment, but there have also been changes in priorities, new ways of organizing welfare institutions, adjustments in benefit levels and conditionality, and extensions of social rights and the quality of public service. On the one hand, the extensive Danish welfare model seems to have survived both neo-liberalism and economic hard times. The broad popularity of the welfare state made the reduction of programmes a very delicate and unpopular task, and politicians only moved in that direction to a limited degree. As mentioned above, this is also due to the welfare benefits being concentrated and the financing being diffused. We see a continued growth in social expenditure; the key programmes still exist and comparative studies still rank Danish welfare at the top.[7] At the same time, many things have changed, undergone reform, and been adapted to a changing economic, political, and social context. The major trends are summarized in the following.

Welfare Cutbacks and Expansions

Cutbacks were most noticeable in the 1970s and the early 1980s marked by recession, budget deficits, and growing debt. In 1979, Social Democratic Minister of Finance Knud Heinesen declared bombastically that Denmark was 'looking into the abyss' (*se ned i afgrunden*). This led to cuts in public services, particularly in the new Public Assistance Act (*Bistandsloven*, see above), especially for unemployed youth, witnessing the lowering of benefits. The centre-right governments of the early 1980s maintained this line of welfare retrenchment with changes in the indexing of services and budget cuts for public institutions. In the following decades, there was a continued caution for the growth of public expenditure. Changing governments, for example, have introduced strict regulation of municipal budgets and reduced municipal budgets, compelling municipalities not to expand their service level. In 2015, the government introduced a fixed budget reduction for public institutions (with the exception of the health sector) of 2 per cent annually. Furthermore, we also find examples of retrenchment motivated by anti-immigration rather than budget concerns. A controversial example in this respect is the so-called 'introduction benefit' (*startydelse*) introduced by a centre-right government in 2002, abolished by a Social Democratic government in 2012, and reintroduced after a new change of government in 2015. This reform meant that the level of benefits was nearly halved for new recipients who had resided outside the EU for more than one out of the preceding eight years.

However, the same period has also seen an expansion of social rights in certain areas. For example, in the mid-1980s, there were significant improvements in the state educational scholarships and in cash family benefits offering higher benefits to more people. New benefits have been introduced such as a flexible job scheme (*flexjob*) in 1998 offering people outside the normal labour market access to work on special terms, childcare leave 1993–2001, and special cash benefits for the elderly (*ældrecheck*) in the 2000s. There has been a massive expansion in the health sector and the daycare sector. In 2004, after decades of not having enough daycare institutions, despite growth in the coverage ratio, the government introduced a so-called 'daycare guarantee' that obliged the municipalities to provide daycare following the end of maternity leave. The result being that Denmark is the country with the highest proportion of children being cared for outside the home.

A Strong Focus on Getting More People into the Workforce

The late 1970s witnessed a shift in the view of unemployment from being cyclically to structurally determined, which triggered a stronger emphasis on individual incentives and work skills. The stated goal was to increase the work force and to have fewer people on public assistance. The policy implications were the tightening of access to cash transfers and the introduction of 'activation programmes' to bring the unemployed back into employment.

The combination of social security, workfare programmes (with sticks and carrots), and a highly flexible labour market where it is easy to hire and fire has attracted international attention as the so-called 'flexicurity' model (see also Høgedahl 2020). The model has been comparatively successful in combining economic growth, low unemployment, and social stability. However, over the last decades, the balance within the model has gradually shifted the model from security towards flexibility and employment (Andersen 2011a).

A major labour market reform in 1993 marked the shift from so-called passive to active labour market policy and was pushed further with the Active Social Policy Act (*Lov om Aktiv Socialpolitik*) of 1997. Participation in municipal activation programmes became a requirement for receiving social benefits. This incentive-based thinking in relation to the individual recipient expanded in the 2000s with a comprehensive activation programme and a reduction of cash benefits in order to increase recipients' incentive to take jobs. The mantra at the time was 'it should pay to work' (*det skal kunne betale sig at arbejde*). In 2010, the period in which one can receive unemployment benefits was reduced from a maximum of four years to two years, and in 2012, a mandatory training scheme for unemployed persons was introduced. A broad political agreement in 2013 led to the abolition on the time limit as to how long one could receive sickness benefits. Citizens' right to these benefits was now subject to periodic reassessment.

The 'activation' trend put its mark on permanent benefit types such as disability pensions (see also about old age pensions below). In 2003, there was a comprehensive reform of the disability pension with a focus on activation. Loss of work capacity was replaced as access criteria by the continuing testing and assessment of work abilities. A continued growing number of disability pensioners meant that the scheme was again revised in 2012, especially to prevent young people under the age of 40 from being entitled to lifetime benefits as 'permanently disabled'. Resource assessment processes, essentially a testing of potential work skills, were introduced in which the individual recipient's work skills were continuously tested in the hope that they could be able to resume work. The municipalities' concrete handling of the resource assessments has subsequently been strongly debated in the media, sparked by sensational cases where severely disabled persons were subjected to continual testing to see if their condition had improved.

The Challenge of an Ageing Population

The discussion about the ageing population has a clear impact on pension policy where there has been broad political support for increasing the age of retirement. The core pillar of the Danish pension system remains the universal tax-funded old age pension.

However, the pension system has gradually changed since the 1980s, becoming less dependent on the government pension and turning into more of a three-pillar pension system (public, labour market/employer, and private) (Andersen 2011b). Higher civil servants and functionaries hold a long history of special pension agreements, but now an increasing number of professional groups have established their own job-based, income-related pension plans. The breakthrough was in the late 1980s when occupational pensions grew out of tripartite negotiations and became part of the collective agreements on the labour market. Since then, these so-called 'labour market pensions' have gradually grown in importance, and for a large proportion of the elderly population, these will comprise the most important part of their pension portfolio (Ministry of Finance 2017).

However, the reforms were not just about the balance of the Danish pension system. The demographic projections showed an increasing number of older citizens in the near future. This led to linguistic innovations such as the 'pension bomb' and the 'elderly burden'. From a political perspective, it was a double-sided pressure caused by increased expenditures on pensions and elderly services on the one hand, and a shrinking labour force on the other. The universal cure was to delay workers' withdrawal from the labour market: the age of retirement had to be increased.

This formed the background for several reforms in the 1990s and 2000s. The most significant 'victim' of the desire for delayed retirement was the early retirement benefit scheme (see above). Economic experts—and a majority of the political parties—perceived the scheme as a main driver behind otherwise able-bodied workers choosing to retire early. Over time, the social policy argument, by which early retirement was a response to wear and tear, lost out to the economic argument about financial sustainability. Through three reforms in 1998, 2006, and 2011, the minimum age of taking early retirement thus increased (parallel to the ordinary old age pension system). The reforms also introduced an individual contribution as a prerequisite for access to the early retirement benefit scheme, increased the mandatory reduction in allowance in case of other pension schemes, and increased the requirement for number of years of prior employment. After the 2011 reform, many workers chose to have their personal contributions paid out and thus exited the scheme, which is currently being phased out entirely.

For the public old age pension, developments were slightly less dramatic. The popularity of the national old age pension made it difficult to tamper with the payments themselves. In 2011, the indexing of benefits was reduced, but at the same time, there have been individual improvements such as the special cash benefits (*ældrecheck*) initiated by the Danish People's Party (see Kosiara-Pedersen 2020) targeted toward those pensioners who do not have supplementary pensions. Political attention has mainly been directed towards increasing the age of retirement. The retirement age was lowered in 1999 from 67 to 65 years, but this was rolled back in 2006 when an indexing mechanism was also introduced so that the retirement age would automatically increase in tandem with life expectancy projections. This means that based on 2018 projections, the retirement age in 2040 will have risen from the present 65 years to 70 years (for people born in 1971 or later).

Immigration and Integration of Immigrants as a New and Highly Politicized Policy Area

Like other Western countries in the 1960s, Denmark opened for labour immigration for a short period. By the early 1970s, the immigration law had become strict again. In the following years, a combination of family reunification laws as well as an increasing number of refugees in the wake of a liberal refugee law in 1984 meant that immigration policies[8] were high on the political agenda (Jønsson 2018). Integration policies were, until the adoption of a comprehensive national integration law in 1997, mainly based on local municipal initiatives. After the change of government in 2001, when the Danish People's Party (see Kosiara-Pedersen 2020) became part of the centre-right government's parliamentary support, immigration policy has gradually become more and more strict. In recent years, for economic and other reasons, the Social Democratic Party also embraced this new immigration policy regime, so today there is broad support for restrictive immigration policies (Social Democratic Party 2018; see also Mariager and Olesen 2020; Nedergaard 2018).

Public Sector Reforms and Strict Control of Expenditure Levels

The public (national and municipal) production of welfare services in Denmark is extensive. Most schools, hospitals, elderly care, daycare centres, etc. are operated and funded by the government and municipalities. The centre-right government of the 1980s launched a comprehensive programme for the modernization of the public sector (cf. above). This process continued in the following decades, driven both by Social Democratic-led and centre-right governments. In the eldercare area, for example, this has meant that the municipalities have allowed certain tasks to be contracted out to private eldercare providers (Rostgaard 2006). It opened for private hospitals, private cleaning firms in hospitals, and the contracting out of activation and training of unemployed persons. In some areas such as daycare centres, developments proceeded more slowly. However, figures from 2019 show that almost 30 per cent of Danish children below the age of six attend private daycare centres or kindergartens (Mandag Morgen 2019). Key instruments in facilitating this outsourcing process were increased freedom of choice for citizens and increased use of budgetary control. The goal was to streamline the public sector to increase productivity, lower the costs, and (at least ideologically) to make the sector more responsive. This development where the public sector purchases services rather than providing them has changed not only everyday life in the public sector, which has become more cost-effective, but also the relationship between state and municipality.

Although Denmark is termed a welfare state, it is on the local level, in the municipalities, that citizens meet the welfare policies head on. Most transfer payments are centrally determined, but there is variation with regard to the services such that the individual municipality has some flexibility in terms of priorities and adaptation to local conditions. The balance between national rules and local flexibility has always been disputed. The centre-right governments of the 1980s opened up for increased municipal flexibility, allowing for privatization and outsourcing, whereas the municipalities have chosen diverse strategies. On the other hand, new economic governance mechanisms mean that the municipalities' flexibility has been financially constrained. Via the annual negotiations on state grants (*bloktilskud*) to the municipalities and the introduction of a new strict spending regime (*Budgetloven*) from 2012, municipalities have been subjected to increasingly tighter management of their finances (Suenson et al. 2016). This is not because the municipalities have obtained fewer tasks. A growing elderly population and growing numbers of children entail rising service costs, and expectations have not diminished. In recent years, this has led to a renewed discussion about the quality of public services (e.g. in the primary schools or concerning the quality of eldercare) that have partially taken the form of a blame game where responsibility for welfare provision and blame for relative cuts in services has been pushed around between national and local level politicians.

Conclusion

Do we still have the classic Danish welfare state, or should we speak of a paradigm shift? This depends on how one views the processes that have taken place before and how to evaluate the developments in recent decades. Neither the construction phase (1900 to the 1970s) nor the reforms in the subsequent decades followed a clear plan. In addition, from a historical perspective, the welfare state has always been changing.

On the one hand, Danish welfare policy remains universalistic, predominantly tax financed, and comprehensive with a very large element of public welfare provision, and despite tendencies toward increasing inequality, Denmark remains one of the most egalitarian countries in the world, and poverty rates are comparatively low. If one examines the amount of total social or public expenditures, these have also been increasing (Ministry of Finance 2018; Kvist and Greve 2011).

At the same time, however, there are significant signs of change. In the wake of the crisis of the 1970s and the entry of neoliberalism, the view of the welfare state has changed, leading to a number of reforms from the 1980s onwards. One can argue that these reforms point towards what has been termed a 'competition state' (Pedersen 2011) or express a marked change in the link between rights and duties (Petersen 2013). In some cases, the practice of work testing in relation to the activation ideology has been criticized for going too far and being in conflict with the basic idea that the welfare state is about protecting the most vulnerable citizens (Müller 2018). The tough immigration policy has problematized universalism. Strict management of public expenditures combined with ideological trends have allowed for the entry of private actors so that private old age insurance, labour market pensions, private health insurance, private schools, etc. have grown in importance. Although total social expenditures have continued to increase, things look different if one looks at the expenditures per pupil in schools, per elderly in care, per patient in the health system, per child in kindergartens, and so on. In recent years, this has led to an intensified discussion about the quality of public sector services and the relative importance of better welfare services versus tax cuts.

Consequently, the answer is probably still, to use Bob Dylan's phrase, 'blowing in the wind'. Something has happened in the past decades, but we still do not know exactly what that is (for a discussion, see also Kvist and Greve 2011; Andersen 2008). Is it a renewal, retrenchment, or a defence of the institutions of the classic welfare state? Is it continuity or dramatic change? This will be a key concern for researchers as well in the coming years. Recent political developments might even point to new avenues of research. First, the spatial dimensions of inequality in access to welfare services as well as in welfare outcomes is receiving political attention. For welfare scholars, this raises very interesting questions—also in a more historical perspective. We know that welfare development in spatial terms was highly asymmetrical. The expansion of welfare services typically favoured major cities, and sometimes the development in rural areas lagged 20–30 years behind. But what was the political and social dynamics of this asymmetry? Second, so far, a growing research interest in wellbeing has not been paralleled by studies on how the welfare state expansion and more recent reforms have been experienced by the population. We need more qualitative studies on the relationship between welfare state development and the human experiences of this both on an individual and group level.

The welfare state is still very popular with the citizens, but we face challenges such as an ageing population, immigration, individualization, and the like that require policy responses in the near future. At the same time, the Danish welfare state has historically shown itself to be both dynamic and institutionally sluggish. Whether this means that we will also have a welfare state 100 years from now is difficult to predict, but a good bet is that the Danish model is well equipped to survive the coming decades. However, it will hardly do so in the precise form that we know today.

Notes

1. This essay is to a large degree based on a comprehensive, six-volume long *History of the Danish Welfare State* (*Dansk Velfærdshistorie*), which was published in Danish between 2010 and 2015. See Petersen et al. 2010, 2011, 2012a, 2012b, 2013, 2014.
2. There is a comprehensive literature elaborating the specific characteristics of the Nordic welfare model. For example, Hernes (1987) has labelled it as 'women friendly', Esping-Andersen (1985, 1990) as social democratic, Markkola (2011) as Lutheran, Trägårdh (1997) as 'statist individualist', and Svendsen and Svendsen (2015) have pointed to the connection between social capital and universal welfare states. Each of these perspectives has facilitated continued discussion based on both empirical findings and more normative analysis.
3. The concept of the 'welfare state' is used here anachronistically. The term was first used in the 1950s, and in earlier phases welfare discussions used terms such as 'social policy' (*socialpolitik*) or 'the social state'.

4. The broad term 'policy experts' refers to a number of experts or 'social engineers' typically active within specific policy fields and networks such as the Social Policy Association (*Socialpolitisk Forening*) which served as an arena for intense exchange between politicians and experts from the 1940s to the 1960s. For a discussion on the role of experts more generally, see Lundqvist and Petersen (2010).

5. It is important to note that this theoretical perspective has difficulties explaining why some policy fields grew more than others and that this logic also applies to other types of public spending than welfare policies. As early as 1958, the Danish economist Jørgen Dich (1965) pointed out that public subsidies to a farmer were more than twenty times higher than subsidies to a worker. However, subsidies to agriculture are typically not considered 'social policy'. This can be illustrated by internal discussion among Liberal-Agrarian (*Venstre*) parliamentarians as the subsidies to agriculture multiplied greatly in 1960–1. One of the major concerns was that the dramatic expansion of subsidies should not be labelled as 'social policy' (see Petersen 1998: 168).

6. See: https://www.fm.dk/publikationer/velfaerdskommissionen/2008/rapporter-fra-velfaerdskommissionen/analyserapport.

7. For example, *Social Progress Imperative* is currently (2019) ranking Denmark number 4. See: https://www.socialprogress.org/. The *OECD Better Life Index* (2017) is ranking Denmark number 2. See: http://www.oecdbetterlifeindex.org.

8. The term 'immigration policies' includes both immigration policy (regulation of access), refugee policies (typically regulated by international conventions), and integration policies (facilitating the integration of new residents into Danish society). In the Danish debates, these policy areas are often lumped together in debates and policy initiatives.

References

Andersen, Jørgen G. (2008). 'Welfare state transformation in an affluent Scandinavian state: The case of Denmark', in Martin Seeleib-Kaiser, ed., *Welfare State Transformations*. London: Palgrave Macmillan, 33–55.

Andersen, Jørgen G. (2011a). 'Denmark: Ambiguous modernization of an inclusive unemployment protection system', in Jochen Clasen and Daniel Clegg, eds, *Regulating the Risk of Unemployment: National Adaptions to Post-Industrial Labour markets*. Oxford: Oxford University Press, 187–206.

Andersen, Jørgen G. (2011b). 'Denmark: The silent revolution towards a multipillar pension system', in Bernhard Ebbinghaus, ed., *The Varieties of Pension Governance: Pension Privatization in Europe*. Oxford: Oxford University Press, 183–209.

Baldwin, Peter (1990). *The Politics of Social Solidarity. Class Bases of the European Welfare State 1875–1975*. Cambridge: Cambridge University Press.

Christensen, Jacob (1998). *Socialpolitiske strategier 1945–1972*. Odense: University Press of Southern Denmark.

Christiansen, Niels Finn, Nils Edling, Per Haave, and Klaus Petersen (2006). *The Nordic Welfare State. A Historical Re-appraissal*. Copenhagen: Museum Tusculanum Press.

Christiansen, Niels Finn, and Klaus Petersen (2001). 'The dynamics of social solidarity. The Danish welfare state 1900–2000', *Scandinavian Journal of History*, 26/3: 177–96.

Dich, Jørgen S. (1965). 'Udviklingen af skatte-og tilskudspolitikken siden 1939. Et bidrag til forklaringen af de politiske kræfter i Danmark', *Økonomi og Politik*, 39/3: 227–60.

Esping-Andersen, Gøsta (1985). *Politics against Markets. The Social Democratic Road to Power*. Princeton, NJ: Princeton University Press.

Esping-Andersen, Gøsta (1990). *Three Worlds of Welfare Capitalism*. Princeton, NJ: Princeton University Press.

Fiig, Christina, and Birte Siim (2020). 'Gender and politics. The limits of equality politics', in Peter M. Christiansen, Jørgen Elklit, and Peter Nedergaard, eds, *The Oxford Handbook of Danish Politics*. Oxford: Oxford University Press, 365–381.

Friis, Henning (1969). 'Issues in social security policies in Denmark', in Shirley Jenkins, ed., *Social Security in International Perspective*. New York: Columbia University Press, 129–150.

Green-Pedersen, Christoffer, and Karina Kosiara-Pedersen (2020). 'Party system. Open yet stable', in Peter M. Christiansen, Jørgen Elklit, and Peter Nedergaard, eds, *The Oxford Handbook of Danish Politics*. Oxford: Oxford University Press, 213–229.

Hernes, Helga Maria (1987). *Welfare States and Women Power. Essays in State Feminism*. Oslo: Norwegian University Press.

Høgedahl, Laust (2020). 'The Danish Labour Market Model. Is the bumblebee still flying?', in Peter M. Christiansen, Jørgen Elklit, and Peter Nedergaard, eds, *The Oxford Handbook of Danish Politics*. Oxford: Oxford University Press, 559–576.

Jensen, Carsten (2011). 'The forgotten half: Analysing the politics of welfare services', *International Journal of Social Welfare*, 20/4: 404–12.

Jønsson, Heidi V. (2018). *Fra lige muligheder til ret og pligt: Socialdemokratiets integrationspolitik i den moderne velfærdsstats tidsalder*. Odense: University Press of Southern Denmark.

Kautto, Mikko (2010). 'The Nordic countries', in Francis G. Castles, Stefan Liebfried, Jane Lewis, Herbert Obinger, and Christopher Pierson, eds, *The Oxford Handbook of the Welfare State*. Oxford: Oxford University Press, 586–600.

Kautto, Mikko, Matti Heikkilä, Bjørn Hvinden, Staffan Marklund, and Niels Ploug (1999). *Nordic Social Policy. Changing Welfare States*. London: Routledge.

Klitgaard, Michael B. (2007). 'Why are they doing it? Social democracy and market oriented welfare reforms', *West European Politics*, 30/1: 172–94.

Kosiara-Pedersen, Karina (2020). 'The Danish People's Party. Centre-oriented populists?', in Peter M. Christiansen, Jørgen Elklit, and Peter Nedergaard, eds, *The Oxford Handbook of Danish Politics*. Oxford: Oxford University Press, 312–28.

Kristensen, Ole P. (1987). *Væksten i den offentlige sektor: Institutioner og politik*. Copenhagen: Jurist- og Økonomforbundets Forlag.

Kvist, Jon, and Bent Greve (2011). 'Has the Nordic welfare model been transformed?', *Social Policy and Administration*, 45/2: 146–60.

Lundqvist, Åsa, and Klaus Petersen (2010) (eds). *In Experts We Trust. Knowledge, Politics and Bureaucracy in Nordic Welfare States*. Odense: University Press of Southern Denmark.

Lützen, Karin (2002). 'The roots of the Danish welfare state. Benevolent societies and homes in 19th century Copenhagen', in Henrik Jensen, ed., *The Welfare State: Past, Present, Future*. Pisa: Pisa University Press, 201–11.

Mandag Morgen (2019, 8 Apr.). 'Den stille privatisering: Dansk velfærd træder ind i en ny periode'. *Mandag Morgen*.

Mariager, Rasmus, and Niels W. Olesen (2020). 'The Social Democratic Party. From exponent of societal change to pragmatic conservatism', in Peter M. Christiansen, Jørgen Elklit, and Peter Nedergaard, eds, *The Oxford Handbook of Danish Politics*. Oxford: Oxford University Press, 278–95.

Markkola, Pirjo (2011). 'The Lutheran Nordic welfare states', in Pauli Kettunen and Klaus Petersen, eds, *Beyond Welfare State Models. Transnational Historical Perspectives on Social Policy*. Cheltenham: Edward Elgar, 102–18.

Martin, Cathie Jo (2008). 'Party competition and the origins of collective capitalism in Denmark', in Peter Nedergaard and John L. Campbell, eds, *Institutions and Politics—Festschrift in honour of Ove K. Pedersen*. Copenhagen: Jurist- og Økonomforbundets Forlag, 316–40.

Ministry of Finance (2017). *Det danske pensionssystem nu og i fremtiden*. Copenhagen: Ministry of Finance.

Ministry of Finance (2018). *Økonomisk analyse: Udviklingen i de offentlige udgifter 2000–2017*. Copenhagen: Ministry of Finance.

Müller, Tue F. (2018, 5 Mar.). 'Stop nu med at trække syge mennesker gennem udsigtsløse arbejdsprøvninger', *Ugeskrift for læger*, 5, 40.

Nedergaard, Peter (2018). 'Back to its roots: Why do the Danish Social Democrats want a more restrictive immigration policy?', Budapest: Friedrich Ebert Stiftung.

Nørgaard, Asbjørn S. (1997). *The Politics of Institutional Control: Corporatism in Danish Occupational Safety and Health Regulation and Unemployment Insurance*. Aarhus: Politica.

OECD (1982). *Economic Outlook*, No. 32. Paris: OECD.

Pedersen, Ove Kaj (2011). *Konkurrencestaten*. Copenhagen: Hans Reitzels Forlag.

Petersen, Jørn Henrik (2013). *Ret og pligt. Pligt og Ret. Refleksioner over den socialdemokratiske idéarv*. Odense: University Press of Southern Denmark.

Petersen, Jørn Henrik, and Klaus Petersen (2019). 'The concept of "welfare state" in Danish public and political debates', in Nils Edling, ed., *The Changing Meaning of the Welfare State. Histories of a Key Concept in the Nordic Countries*. New York: Berghahn Press, 137–78.

Petersen, Jørn Henrik, Klaus Petersen, and Niels Finn Christiansen (2010) (eds). *Dansk velfærdshistorie, Vol. 1: Perioden 1536–1898. Frem mod socialhjælpsstaten*. Odense: University Press of Southern Denmark.

Petersen, Jørn Henrik, Klaus Petersen, and Niels Finn Christiansen (2011) (eds). *Dansk velfærdshistorie, Vol. 2: Perioden 1899–1933. Socialhjælpsstaten*. Odense: University Press of Southern Denmark.

Petersen, Jørn Henrik, Klaus Petersen, and Niels Finn Christiansen (2012a) (eds). *Dansk velfærdshistorie, Vol. 3: Perioden 1933–1956. Velfærdsstaten i støbeskeen*. Odense: University Press of Southern Denmark.

Petersen, Jørn Henrik, Klaus Petersen, and Niels Finn Christiansen (2012b) (eds). *Dansk velfærdshistorie, Vol. 4: Perioden 1956–1973. Velfærdsstatens storhedstid*. Odense: University Press of Southern Denmark.

Petersen, Jørn Henrik, Klaus Petersen, and Niels Finn Christiansen (2013) (eds). *Dansk velfærdshistorie, Vol. 5: Perioden 1973–1993. Velfærdsstaten i tidehverv*. Odense: University Press of Southern Denmark.

Petersen, Jørn Henrik, Klaus Petersen, and Niels Finn Christiansen (2014) (eds). *Dansk velfærdshistorie, Vol. 6, Perioden 1993–2014. Hvor glider vi hen?* Odense: University Press of Southern Denmark.

Petersen, Klaus (1998). *Legitimität und Krise. Die politische Geschichte des dänischen Wohlfahrtsstaates 1945–1973*. Nordeuropäische Studien, Vol. 13. Berlin: Berlin Verlag.

Petersen, Klaus (2006). 'Constructing Nordic welfare? Nordic social policy cooperation 1919–1955', in Niels Finn Christiansen, Klaus Petersen, Nils Edling, and Per Haave, eds, *The Nordic Model of Welfare. A Historical Reappraissal*. Copenhagen: Museum Tusculanum, 67–98.

Petersen, Klaus (2011). *Efterløn. Tilblivelsen 1975–1979*. Odense: University Press of Southern Denmark.

Petersen, Klaus, and Nils Arne Sørensen (2018). 'From military state to welfare state: The warfare-welfare nexus in Denmark, 1848–1950s', in Herbert Obinger, Klaus Petersen, and Peter Starke, eds, *Warfare and Welfare. Military Conflict and Welfare State Development in Western Countries*. Oxford: Oxford University Press, 290–319.

Rostgaard, Tine (2006). 'Constructing the care consumer: Free choice of home care for elderly in Denmark', *European Societies*, 8/3: 443–63.

Social Democratic Party (2018). *Retfærdig og realistisk. En udlændingepolitik der samler Danmark*. Copenhagen: Social Democratic Party.

Suenson, Emil L., Peter Nedergaard, and Peter M. Christiansen (2016). 'Why lash yourself to the mast? The case of the Danish "Budget Law"', *Public Budgeting and Finance*, 36/1: 3–21.

Svendsen, Gert T., and Gunnar L. H. Svendsen (2015). 'Social capital and the welfare state', in Michael Böss, ed., *The Nation State in Transformation: Economic Globalisation, Institutional Mediation and Political Values*. Aarhus: Aarhus University Press, 315–39.

Trägårdh, Lars (1997). 'Statist individualism: On the culturality of the Nordic welfare state', in Øystein Sørensen and Bo Stråht, eds, *The Cultural Construction of Norden*. Oslo: Scandinavian University Press, 253–85.

....

CHAPTER 34

THE DANISH LABOUR
MARKET MODEL
Is the Bumblebee Still Flying?

....

LAUST HØGEDAHL

THE DANISH LABOUR MARKET MODEL
AND LABOUR MARKET POLICIES

THE Danish—and Nordic—labour market system has gained international recognition for combining good economic performances with social security for workers. The *Economist* recently proclaimed the Nordic countries as the world's next 'supermodel' due to the emphasis on market dynamics and income security rather than job tenure—a useful blueprint for labour market policy configured for the rapid technological changes foreshadowed in the twenty-first century (Wooldridge 2013).

The Danish labour market model is, in fact, a mix of different models, institutions, and systems, creating strong cooperative adaptation to changes in international markets. The Danish labour market model is based on a small open economy dependent on international trade. The labour market policy (LMP) draws on different institutions and systems that in combination make up the Danish model of labour market regulation. The labour market regulation is based on a pattern of policy (national and European law) and collective agreements. In theory, the labour market model consists of three different models bound together by different arenas of negotiations, governance, and corporations. First, the Danish welfare model or regime is characterized by universalism based on a high degree of decommodification where welfare services are provided mainly by the state (Esping-Andersen 1993: 26–9). Second, the Danish flexicurity model is widely known for combining a high degree of flexibility for employers in terms of hiring and firing and security for workers in terms of a compensation provided primarily by unemployment insurance funds in case of unemployment (Madsen 2002, 2003).

Third, the Danish model of industrial relations is characterized by the important role of collective agreements conducted voluntarily by the labour market parties in both the private and the public sector (Due and Jensen 1993). Hence, key elements of the labour market regulation such as wages, working hours, and other working conditions are agreed upon by the labour market parties and not by national policymakers (Høgedahl and Jørgensen 2017). In comparison to most other countries, no minimum wage defined by national law exists in Denmark. Social pacts between the central government and labour market parties have also played an important role in reforming the labour market regulation throughout modern Danish history.

However, the Danish model of labour market regulation is not a product of an intentional policy design but rather of unintended consequences of a wide range of compromises and power struggles among the labour market parties and policymakers, creating the stable institutions of the model, many of which date back to the early 1900s (Jørgensen and Madsen 2007). The practice of collective agreements is based on a longstanding tradition dating back to the early 1900s, characterising Danish LMP with a strong path dependency (Ibsen and Jørgensen 1979). Seen in a historical-institutional perspective, the Danish industrial relations system can be regarded as an important foundation for the development of the Danish welfare state, where the introduction of active labour market policy (ALMP) in the 1990s provided the final component of the Danish flexicurity model.

In this chapter, I first outline in detail the development of the Danish industrial relations system, the unemployment system, and the creation of Danish ALMP. I then turn to a more exhaustive description of the Danish flexicurity model before outlining recent policy changes associated to the labour market model and in Danish LMP. In the final section, I discuss some of the future prospects and challenges for the Danish labour market model by pointing to new balances between flexibility and security.

The Creation of the Stable Institutions of the Danish Labour Market Model of Regulation

After more than a hundred days of labour dispute in 1899, involving both strikes and lockouts for the majority of the Danish labour market, the Danish labour market parties settled the so-called September Compromise of 1899. The September Compromise was the world's first general agreement adopting the fundamental principles of the regulation of the labour market and the relations between the labour market parties. Workers accepted the managerial right of employers to hire and fire, as well as not striking when a collective agreement has been concluded (the no-strike agreement). On the other hand, employers acknowledged trade unions as legitimate negotiating partners and accepted collective agreements as the basis for labour market regulations. Policymakers from the

Danish Parliament (*Folketinget*) accepted the September Compromise, marking the beginning of a longstanding tradition of collective bargaining based on the independence of the labour market parties and involving important aspects such as wages and working hours (Due and Jensen 1993).

The state has traditionally entrusted the labour market partners to do their own negotiations and solve their own industrial conflicts and disputes. In 1910, the state supported the system by establishing the legal framework for the Danish Conciliation Board (*Forligsinstitutionen*) and the Danish Labour Court (*Arbejdsretten*). The function of the Danish Conciliation Board is to conciliate the labour market parties while conducting collective bargaining, thereby minimizing the possibility of industrial conflicts. The Labour Court deals with disputes in terms of alleged violation and non-compliance of collective agreements in force. Both the Conciliation Board and the Labour Court are very much a product of a common understanding and vision of the labour market parties. The Danish Parliament might have prepared, decided, and implemented the regulation in the form of legislation, but the system is based on the organizations—both in terms of origin and implementation (Jørgensen 2002). Both employers and workers have a seat in the Labour Court within this independent system, and only they are entitled to bring cases before the court. Only the organizations are allowed to conduct cases, and individual workers and employers are, therefore, not allowed to have their rights tested in the court. This collective-based legal system distinguishes the Danish—and other Nordic countries—from that of other countries, and thus, from legal proceedings in the EU which are, in general, based on individual rights, not collective ones (Dølvik et al. 2018). Apart from only minor revisions, the two institutions—the Conciliation Board and the Labour Court—remain largely unaltered since their establishment in 1910 (Høgedahl 2019).

Although the policymakers from the Danish Parliament have great respect for the autonomy of collective bargaining in general, state intervention does occur, especially as a means to end long-lasting labour disputes. Former Minister and Member of the Danish Parliament Viggo Hørup once stated at a public rally: 'No one is above or equal to the Folketinget [the Danish Parliament]'. The phrase has since been associated with state intervention in industrial conflict by implying that collective bargaining is second to national law. There is (or should be) no greater political power than the *Folketinget*.

The first important state intervention in the labour market occurred in 1933. When a state intervenes in a labour dispute, a law is passed in Parliament as a substitute for the collective agreement that the labour market parties were unable to reach. In that sense, state interventions work as a *de facto* industrial arbitration (Høgedahl and Ibsen 2017). Since the first state intervention in 1933, more than 50 have occurred, the most recent of which ended in a 25-day lockout of Danish teachers in the public sector in 2013.

The September Compromise was due to an industrial conflict among the labour market parties in the private sector and had no immediate impact on the public sector since all public employees at that time were civil servants or roustabouts (Hoffmann 1999). Wages and working conditions for civil servants are based on law and not collective agreements. Although civil servants have gained the right to negotiate collectively through two reforms in 1919 and 1969, they are not allowed to strike to this day. In return for renouncing the right to strike, civil servants enjoy good employment protections and pensions. However, during the establishment of the Danish welfare system in the 1950s and 1960s, a number of new public-sector professions like healthcare workers and pedagogues were employed on collective agreements and not as civil servants. In this process, trade unions and public employers (state, regions, and municipalities) adopted the principles of the September Compromise into their own general agreements, and by 1973, the Danish Conciliation Board and Danish Labour Court were given the competence to include the public sector (Høgedahl 2019).

Today, public sector employment based on collective agreement terms have largely supressed the civil servant employment. However, there are pivotal structural and organizational differences between the private and the public sectors that, in recent years, have led to the discussion whether the Danish model of industrial relations are suited for the public sector (Scheuer et al. 2016). The discussion was sparked after a number of industrial conflicts in the public sector, and most recently, in connection with the public employer lockout of teachers in 2013. The combination of an offensive lockout and a state intervention made many question the dual roles of public (state) employers as not only employers but also legislators. During the teacher lockout in 2013, it also became clear that industrial conflict in the public sector differs notably from the private sector in the sense that public employers save money on wages in many cases, while the trade unions are forced to empty their war chests (Høgedahl and Ibsen 2017).

Although the September Compromise is more than 100 years old, its principles are still present and relevant today in both the private and the public sector, which is why the Compromise is also referred to as the 'constitution of the labour market' (Ibsen and Jørgensen 1979: 25). Wages and working conditions are still being regulated through collective agreements voluntarily negotiated by the labour market parties. However, today, there are some areas regulated and complemented by law in the Danish labour market such as working environment, the Holiday Act (*Ferieloven*), and employment protection and working conditions for a few specific professions, including the Danish Salaried Employees Act (*Funktionærloven*) aimed at white-collar workers and the Seamen's Act (*Sømandsloven*) (Scheuer 2012). Today, EU law also plays a significant role in the Danish labour market (Kristiansen 2013).

THE ESTABLISHMENT OF THE DANISH GHENT SYSTEM

In 1907, the Danish unemployment insurance system was created. The system, also referred to as the Ghent system, is based on voluntary membership of unemployment insurance funds run by the labour movement yet subsidised and regulated by the state. The system takes its name from the town of Ghent, Belgium where the system was first developed and implemented in 1901.

The Danish Ghent system has long played a crucial role as an important recruiting mechanism for trade unions, securing a high trade union density since many workers tend to join a trade union while joining an unemployment insurance fund (Rothstein 1992; Lind 2009; Høgedahl 2014). Besides Denmark, the Ghent system is found in Sweden, Finland, Iceland, and partially in Belgium (Vandaele 2006). As a result, these countries possess the highest trade union densities in the world (Høgedahl and Kongshøj 2017). Norway is the only Nordic country not operating a Ghent model but a state-run and compulsory unemployment system, with a lower trade union density as a result (Nergaard and Stokke 2007).

The main argument for implementing the Ghent system in Denmark in 1907 lay mainly in the fact that it was the cheapest solution for the state as it originally put the highest economic burden on the insured persons (Lind 2009). However, from the very beginning, the Danish version of the Ghent system differed from the Belgian model. Workers were not forced to join an unemployment insurance fund controlled by the labour movement in the original Belgian model, but they had the opportunity to enrol in a publicly controlled unemployment insurance fund managed by the local city council (Vandaele 2006). In addition, unemployed insurance funds controlled by the trade unions in the Belgian model were, in fact, interdisciplinary from the beginning, which meant that they were able to enrol members across education levels, sectors, and from different trades. In the Danish version of the Ghent system, however, no public alternative to the union-controlled unemployment insurance funds existed. From their introduction in 1907, Danish unemployment insurance funds were organized according to their trade, only allowing workers to join an unemployment insurance fund that was associated with their specific line of work (Nørgaard 1997). That meant that if you were a Danish metalworker and wanted to insure yourself financially against unemployment, your only option was the unemployment fund for metalworkers. Obviously, this gave the labour movement a strong monopoly. The Danish Ghent system has since been an important component in the Danish labour market model in terms of delivering security for workers and as an important recruiting mechanism for their associated trade unions.

THE DEVELOPMENT OF ACTIVE LABOUR MARKET POLICY

Since the labour market partners regulate important components of the labour market through their own collective agreements, Danish labour market policies were originally social policies aimed at cushioning the social consequences of unemployment (Larsen 2004). The second industrial revolution of the 1950s and 1960s demanded a flexible and mobile labour market, and during the economic boom in the 1960s, the need for a more active and intervening LMP became clear in order to accommodate a growing demand for labour. LMP went from being just a social issue to becoming a tool to cope with imperfections in the labour market. LMP became an area of responsibility under the Ministry of Labour (Ministry of Employment from 2001) established in 1942 and has, traditionally, been designed to target a wide variety of issues related to the labour market. The 1960s became the formative period for Danish LMP with the creation of the public employment service 'AF' (*Arbejdsformidlingen*) in 1969 after many years of preparation in commissions. The new and main idea was that during an economic boom, there is a special need to promote mobility in order to prevent large wage increases and inflation while supporting employers in need of labour. It was also recognized that a flexible labour market demanded a state guarantee to support workers who are temporarily unemployed; hence, the state gradually took over the main financing of the Ghent system during the late 1960s (Rasmussen 2013).

During the 1970s and 1980s, additional active elements were applied to the existing LMP. In 1989, the centre-right government and the labour market parties conducted one of the most renowned social pacts in Danish history known as 'The Declaration of Solidarity' in which workers accepted wage restraints in return for new private labour market pensions regulated through collective agreements. Today, labour market pensions have grown to be the most applied and important in the three-stringed Danish pension system besides the minimum public pension and purely private individual arrangements. The implementation of labour market pensions in collective agreements marked a new path in which additional social elements progressively found its way to the collective agreements, for instance, maternity funds. Nowadays, Danish collective agreements include not only wages and working conditions but also a large number of social or welfare elements compared to the other Nordic countries (Høgedahl 2019).

New employment policies and social pacts during the 1980s, however, were not able to combat the growing unemployment rate, which ultimately peaked in 1993 when 12.4 per cent of the Danish workforce was out of a job. Denmark (together with Germany) was considered the sick man of Europe due to high unemployment rates. Something drastic and different was needed. Hence, in 1992, a commission comprised of the labour market parties and experts called the Zeuthen Commission was given the task of developing new policy strategies aimed at combatting the structural problems linked to unemployment. The commission took its name from the commission chair J.H. Zeuthen, Permanent Secretary at the Ministry of Internal Affairs. Next, the newly elected centre-left Poul Nyrup Rasmussen government adopted the recommendations put forward by the Zeuthen Commission in 1993. This marked the beginning of Danish active labour market policy (ALMP) which since became well-known internationally serving as best-practice for mutual learning among the European members states (Nedergaard 2006). The rights and responsibilities of the unemployed were redefined in the new Act on ALMP in 1993 by composing new rules that prevented renewed earnings-related benefit eligibility through participation in activation measures, as had been the case prior to the reform. Activation measures with training and educational elements were to become the main focus of the new system, and a great deal of policy innovation took place in designing the administration, implementation, and underlying principles and functions of the ALMP. For more than two decades, ALMP had been part of Danish labour market regulation prior to the 1993 reform, but the new supply and demand side logic changed its functions in some fundamental ways, especially by implying new and strong elements of Lifelong Learning. ALMP was now meant to focus on getting people back to work with new and updated skills rather than just redistributing resources among the population. The transformation to a more active approach in LMP has been described as a silent change in policy (Torfing 2004).

Since the Danish labour market parties played an important role in terms of regulating wages and working conditions, they have had a significant influence on the creation and implementation of Danish ALMP until the early 2000s (Larsen 2004). Policymaking on labour market issues have been based on a strong element of corporatism in the past, and in contrast to other policy-areas, LMP have traditionally been labelled the 'policies of the labour market parties' (Jørgensen 2002: 173). New local agencies or boards (*Regionale Arbejdsmarkedsråd*, RAR) were established with the 1993 ALMP reform (Christiansen et al. 2000). The boards were responsible for ALMP measures for insured job seekers. Through social policies, the municipalities were responsible for uninsured people and people on sick pay.

The Components of the Danish Labour Market Model

With the implementation of ALMP in the 1990s, and in combination with the high degree of flexibility for employers in terms of hiring and firing cemented by the September Compromise, as well as the security provided by the Ghent system, the Danish flexicurity model was taking a final form. The Danish flexicurity model has been a significant beacon for the overall European Employment Strategy (EES) during the 2000s, setting guiding principles or pathways for employment policies for the European member states (Mailand 2010; Nedergaard 2006).

The flexibility component of the flexicurity model makes the Danish labour market highly flexible in terms of adapting to changes in the overall economy and shifting demand in export markets—an important ability for a small open economy like Denmark (Kristensen et al. 2011). Cooperative adaptation is taking place with help from both labour market parties and policymakers (Jørgensen 2002).

The security component of the model is meant to cushion the economic and potentially social consequences of unemployment for the individual worker. However, a high degree of social security is also conducive in terms of a high degree of external flexibility since Danish workers do not fear unemployment compared to workers in other European countries even though the job turnover is high in the Danish labour market (Madsen 2014). The perception of economic security makes adaptation more acceptable for workers.

The last component in ALMP can be seen as the grease that makes the model run by helping workers find new jobs and by supplying companies with labour (Svarer et al. 2015). Lifelong learning programs were a very important element in terms of enhancing the qualifications of the labour supply in order to match the demand of the labour market by letting workers re-enter the labour market with updated qualifications. However, since the early 2000s, the lifelong learning elements have been reduced for various reasons.

The Danish flexicurity model (see Figure 34.1) had its heyday, politically and in academia, during the early and mid-2000s. The combination between flexibility and security supplemented by ALMP was described as the missing link in order to understand how the Nordic countries, and Denmark in particular, were able to achieve high minimum wages, relatively generous social benefits, and full employment without the loss of economic growth and growth in labour productivity—a socio-economic success (Andersen 2007). Flexicurity was seen as the formula that made the bumblebee fly even though it should not be possible according to mainstream economics (Madsen 2002; Halvorsen et al. 2016). In more contemporary political economy theory surrounding the varieties of capitalism (VoC) literature, the miracle of flexicurity has been explained through the concept of institutional complementarities (Klindt 2008; Campbell and Pedersen 2007). One set of institutions is said to be complementary to another when its presence raises the returns available from the other (Hall and Gingerich 2009). Denmark shares traits from both the liberal market economies (LME), in terms of liberal employment protections and strong supporting political institutions like the Ghent system, and ALMP affiliated with the coordinated market economies (CME). It is claimed that the best of both worlds is seen in the Danish 'hybrid' model, creating novel institutional complementarities.

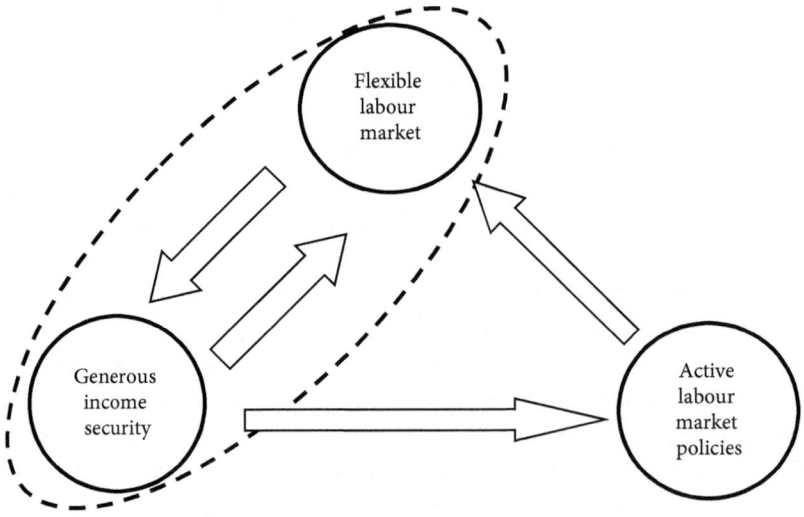

FIGURE 34.1 The Danish flexicurity model.
Source: Madsen (2006)

New Employment Policies and Reforms of the Ghent System in the New Millennium

A number of policy changes since the turn of the millennium have altered the components of the Danish labour market system in different ways (Jørgensen and Klindt 2018; Klitgaard and Nørgaard 2014). The policy changes can be traced to both the reduction and deterioration of the unemployment benefit system, while employers' flexibility seems somewhat intact—although demands on more employment protections have surfaced in the recent collective bargaining rounds (Jørgensen and Klindt 2018). During the 2000s, the labour market parties have also lost more control on the development and implementation of ALMP since the governance of the system was handed over to the municipalities from 2009. Already back in 2007, de-corporatisation took place as the regional labour market boards were abolished as part of the dismantling of the AF system.

A pivotal policy change came in 2002 when the newly elected centre-right government adopted The Liberation Package for the Labour Market Act (*Frihedspakken*). The policy proposal was one of the very first initiatives the government took after taking office in November 2001. Part of the original policy framing was the prevention of 'forced membership' in trade unions. One potential solution was the establishment of a state-run unemployment insurance fund as an alternative to the existing Ghent system described above. However, the government could not find majority support for this proposed legislation in the Danish Parliament (Høgedahl 2014). The negotiated compromise was, therefore, a somewhat less drastic yet major change for the labour movement in particular and the Danish labour market model in the long term.

The old delineation of the unemployment insurance funds, organized along trade-related and professional lines and a central element in the Danish Ghent system since its establishment in 1907, was abolished. Since 2002, all unemployment insurance funds have been able to become *interdisciplinary* and recruit members from outside of their own traditional trade or profession-oriented territory (Lind 2009; Høgedahl et al. 2013). This broke with the de facto monopoly of the traditional labour movement by opening the market for the new interdisciplinary unemployment insurance funds and their associated alternative unions (Høgedahl and Kongshøj 2017).

This institutional change is fundamental to the success of the so-called alternative unions since it transformed the nature of the Ghent system (Høgedahl 2014). The alternative unions are also interdisciplinary, organizing members across the board, i.e. across different trades and professions in both the public and the private sectors. The main feature that distinguishes the alternative unions from the traditional unions, however, is their lack of use of collective action. The alternative unions do not engage in collective bargaining activities with employer organizations, nor are they in favour of the use of

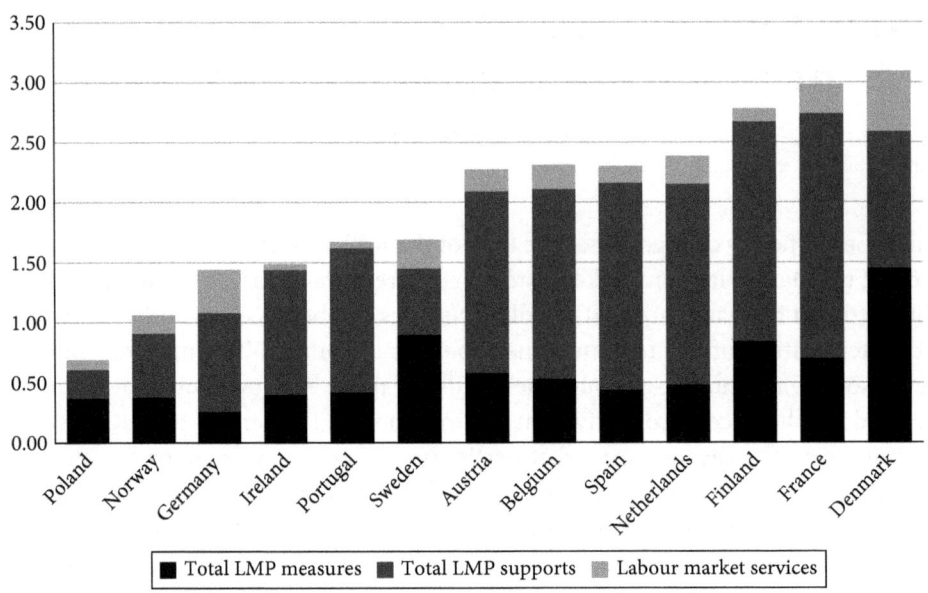

FIGURE 34.2 Public expenditure in labour market policy interventions by broad type in GDP for selected EU member states—in per cent.

Source: Eurostat

strikes or any other collective actions; in fact, the statute book of the Christian Union, the biggest alternative trade union, explicitly bans its members from striking (Høgedahl 2014). The alternative trade unions have around 280,000 members (for more on the rise of alternative unionism in Denmark, see Høgedahl et al. 2013; Høgedahl 2014).

The centre-right government also reformed the labour market policies—now labelled 'employment policies'—according to a stronger work-first approach with an emphasis on work-orientated activation, firm control of unemployed people, and reduced opportunities for education and vocational training. Denmark is still investing in ALMP as Figure 34.2 shows, yet the context has shifted. This change in policy must partly be seen in the light of the economic situation during the 2000s where the Danish economy experienced a strong upturn, creating a growing demand for labour. However, a new liberal ideology can also be identified by putting more emphasis on individual motivation for taking work rather than skills in terms of education and vocational training (Larsen 2013). The role of municipalities as central actors has been strengthened since more social policy groups have been included in the employment policy. In combination with a stronger emphasis on performance management governance, the context of the policy has shifted (Jørgensen and Larsen 2013). The change in policy has been characterized as a shift from 'train first' to 'work first' (Bredgaard and Larsen 2008).

In 2010 and after the economic crisis, a new reform was implemented, deteriorating the unemployment benefits by doubling the requalification requirement for unemployment benefits to 52 weeks (from 2012). The 2010 reform also shortened benefit duration from four to two years. Three labour market reforms from 1993–8 had already shortened the maximum duration from nine to four years. However, the reforms of the 1990s happened in a context of declining unemployment, whereas the 2010 reform was implemented in the wake of the financial crisis from 2008 with rising unemployment levels (Andersen 2011).

In 2015, another reform of the Ghent system was passed (the Unemployment Benefit Reform), bringing rather comprehensive changes to the system in terms of (again) entailing stricter eligibility criteria and shorter benefit duration. The reform also introduced new principles for benefit calculations where incitements for taking on short-term jobs while being unemployed was enhanced. The deterioration of unemployment benefits have created a growing market for supplemental unemployment benefits supplied by private insurance companies and as collective insurances schemes obtainable by a trade union membership. Both the private and collective schemes have rather strict eligibility criteria of around 12 months of employment.

Are the Stable Institutions of the Danish Labour Market Model Eroding?

The functionality of the Danish labour market model is highly based on strong labour market parties (Dølvik et al. 2015). This means high membership densities for both trade unions and employer associations. If one or both of the labour market parties experience a strong drop in membership, they will potentially lose resources, legitimacy, and representativity to participate in collective agreements and as relevant stakeholders in the policy-making process (Ibsen et al. 2011). A high degree of collective bargaining coverage is also crucial for the functionality of the Danish labour market system. Hence, if the collective bargaining coverage is dropping in parts of the labour market, the effectiveness of collective agreements as a regulating mechanism will be diminished.

Danish Employer organizations are not affected by a loss of membership. On the contrary, the employer membership density increased from 60 per cent in 2004 to 68 per cent in 2015 (Dølvik et. al. 2018: 331). However, since it takes two to tango, employers are also dependent on a high density for their trade union counterpart. The Danish trade union density peaked in 1995 but has since been decreasing (Høgedahl 2014). However, not all trade unions have experienced a decrease in membership as shown in Table 34.1.

Traditionally, the Danish labour movement has been characterized by trade unions and professional organizations and defined by trade (i.e. by type of training or education or by field of employment) with relatively clear demarcation lines between them such as school teachers in the Danish Union of Teachers, electricians in the Danish Union of Electricians, etc. (Ibsen et al. 2011). Thus, the external structure of the Danish labour

Table 34.1. Trade Union Membership from 2000–2018 (in Thousands, 'Share of' in per cent)

Union Confederation	Year					Share of	
	2000	2005	2010	2014	2018	2000	2018
LO	1.167	1.142	955	867	788	62 per cent	43 per cent
FTF	350	361	358	346	346	19 per cent	19 per cent
Academics (AC)	150	163	137	203	236	8 per cent	13 per cent
Association of Managers (LH)	80	76	83	97	102	4 per cent	6 per cent
Not member of Union Confederation	123	151	271	290	349	7 per cent	19 per cent
Total membership	1.870	1.893	1.804	1.803	1.821	100 per cent	100 per cent
Total workforce	2.771	2.743	2.693	2.647	2.842		
Trade union density	**67,5 per cent**	**69,0 per cent**	**67,0 per cent**	**68,1 per cent**	**64,1 per cent**		

Note: From 1 January 2019, LO and FTF have merged into *Fagbevægelsens Hovedorganisation* (FH).

Source: Statistic Denmark.

movement can be described as craft, and to some degree, general unionism (Clegg 1976). These trade unions and professional organizations are, for the most part, members of one of the three peak organizations:

- LO (the Danish Confederation of Trade Unions): seventeen member organizations representing around 788,000 workers. Organizing trade unions for skilled and unskilled workers, both blue collar and white collar, employed in both the public and private sector.
- FTF (the Confederation of Professionals in Denmark): seventy member organizations representing around 346,000 wage earners. Mainly public sector trade unions and professional organizations.
- AC (the Danish Confederation of Professional Associations): twenty-eight member organizations representing around 236,000 wage earners. Academic associations organizing members in both the private and public sector.

The overall trade union density in Denmark has dropped from 68 per cent in 2000 to 64 per cent in 2018, which can be described as a modest decrease in an international comparison. However, since the alternative unions do not support collective bargaining and are not part of the labour market regulation as a result, it is appropriate to excluded them from the trade union density (Due et al. 2010). If the alternative unions are

Table 34.2. Private Sector Collective Agreement Coverage from 1998–2015

Employer association	1998		2015	
	Number of workers (in thousands)	Share covered by a collective agreement (per cent)	Number of workers (in thousands)	Share covered by a collective agreement (per cent)
Confederation of Danish Employers (DA)	615	89	676	87
The Danish Employers' Association for the Financial Sector (FA)	57	96	61	89
Danish Confederation of Employers' Associations in Agriculture (SALA)	59	95	-	-
Others unorganized	654	60	656	59
Total private sector	1.385	76	1.393	74

Note: From 2012, SALA became part of Confederation of Danish Employers.
Source: Confederation of Danish Employers (1998, 2014).

excluded, the trade union density drops to 53 per cent in 2018, which leaves almost half of the Danish workforce outside the labour movement constituted of the Danish model of industrial relations and regulations (Høgedahl 2019). The shifts and new patterns in unionization in Denmark can very well be regarded as the most severe threat against the Danish labour market model based on collective agreements and corporation.

Looking at the collective bargaining, the overall coverage has been rather stable (cf. Table 34.2). There is a 100 per cent collective bargaining coverage for the public sector, while the private sector has more or less seen a stability of 76 per cent in 1998 to 74 per cent in 2015.

However, it is possible to identify great variation between sectors (Høgedahl and Jørgensen 2017). Agriculture, hotel, restaurant, and the cleaning sectors have all seen decreasing collective bargaining coverage, leaving many workers without the rights provided by the collective agreements. It is important to stress that no *erga omnes* principles exist in Denmark, which means that there is no extension of the collective agreements by law.

Conclusion

In this chapter, I have presented the key features of the Danish labour market system and the shifts in LMP and employment policies. The stable institutions of the system were created in the early 1900s, in which the September Compromise and the creation of the Danish Ghent system constitute the main features by providing the institutional set-up for a highly flexible labour market in terms of hiring and firing for employers and security for workers in terms of compensation in case of unemployment. Since the labour market parties regulate important elements such as wages and working conditions, Danish LMP have traditionally been designed to help solve imperfections in the labour market and provide workers with new skills. Central and regional corporatism during the 1990s supported the introduction and implementation of ALMP.

The class compromise between trade unions and employer organizations supported by policymakers have created novel institutional complementarities which have been an important success of the Danish open economy that is highly dependent on free trade. The flexicurity model has gained great recognition abroad during the 2000s and even served as an important 'model for learning' in the overall European Employment Strategy.

Recent policy changes have challenged the nexus of security and flexibility in different ways. Unemployment insurance funds have been liberalized, opening up new alternative funds and associated alternative trade unions, challenging the density of the labour movement involved in collective bargaining. A number of reforms, and in particular the reform passed in 2010, have also deteriorated unemployment benefits in terms of shortening the overall length of unemployment benefits and by tightening the eligibility criteria. APLM have also changed into employment policy, reformulating purpose and content by putting more emphasis on work-first elements and by downplaying vocational training and education to a minimum (Bredgaard and Madsen 2018). From 2009, municipalities have been the main actor in implementing employment policy.

The main institutional complementarities in the Danish system have not been abolished even though there is a much stronger emphasis on quick labour market reintegration nowadays and less security to be recorded. However, a stronger dualism in the Danish labour market can be traced where people on the margins or outside the labour market are not covered by the security-mobility nexus (Jørgensen and Klindt 2018).

The most important stress test of the Danish labour market system does not seem to originate directly from policy changes—although the reformation of the Ghent system has enabled Danish workers easier access to alternative unionism. The declining trade union density, especially for trade unions based in the private sector, are concerning in terms of the future functionality of the Danish labour market model of regulation. Employers have been able to maintain and even increase their collective organization; however, the model implies two representatives, and if the trade union density keeps decreasing, this trend will bring additional fundamental changes to the Danish labour market system. Until now, trade unions have been able to muster the strength to keep the collective bargaining at a high level. However, we do find a correlation between a low trade union density and decreasing collective agreement coverage in certain sectors such as agriculture and cleaning. If this trend continuous, a further parallelization of the Danish labour market will occur where insiders are still a part of a classic flexicurity model, while outsiders are subjected to high degrees of flexibility but without the compensation of strong security elements. This trend can lead to precarization of more groups in the labour market, notably unskilled workers in the private sector. If trade unions, along with their employer counterparts, are unable to reinstall security for these groups, it will unavoidably call upon policymakers to regulate the situation through law, which might hamper the flexibility of a model based on collective agreements in the end. For now, though, the bumblebee is still flying.

References

Andersen, Jørgen G. (2007). 'The Danish welfare state as "politics for markets": Combining equality and competitiveness in a global economy', *New Political Economy*, 12/1: 71–8.

Andersen, Jørgen G. (2011). 'Denmark-ambiguous modernisation of an inclusive unemployment protection system', in Jochen Clasen and Daniel Clegg, eds, *Regulating the Risk of Unemployment. National Adaptations to Post-Industrial Labour Markets in Europe*. Oxford: Oxford University Press, 187–207.

Bredgaard, Thomas, and Flemming Larsen (2008). 'Lokale beskæftigelsesråd i krydsfeltet mellem stat og kommune', *Tidsskrift for Arbejdsliv*, 10/3: 57–73.

Bredgaard, Thomas, and Per K. Madsen (2018). 'Farewell flexicurity? Danish flexicurity and the crisis', *Transfer: European Review of Labour and Research*, 24/4: 375–86.

Campbell, John L., and Ove K. Pedersen (2007). 'The varieties of capitalism and hybrid success: Denmark in the global economy', *Comparative Political Studies*, 40/3: 307–32.

Christiansen, Peter M., Asbjørn Nørgaard, and Niels C. Sidenius (2000). *Organisationer og korporatisme på dansk: et historisk perspektiv*. Aalborg: Aalborg University.

Clegg, Hugh A. (1976). *Trade Unionism under Collective Bargaining: A Theory based on Comparisons of Six Countries*. Oxford: Basil Blackwell.

Confederation of Danish Employers (1998). *Arbejdsmarkedsrapport 1998*. Copenhagen: DA Forlag.

Confederation of Danish Employers (2014). *Arbejdsmarkedsrapport 2014*. Copenhagen: DA Forlag.

Dølvik, Jon E., Jørgen G. Andersen, and Juhana Vartiainen (2015). 'The Nordic social models in turbulent times', in Jon E. Dølvik and Andrew Martin, eds, *European Social Models from Crisis: Employment and Inequality in the Era of Monetary Integration*. Oxford: Oxford University Press, 246–86.

Dølvik, Jon E., Paul Marginson, Kristin Alsos, Jens Arnholtz, Guglielmo Meardi, Torsten Müller, and Sissel Trygstad (2018). 'Collective wage regulation in northern Europe under strain: Multiple drivers of change and differing responses', *European Journal of Industrial Relations*, 24/4: 321–39.

Due, Jesper, and Carsten S. Jensen (1993). *Den danske model: en historisk sociologisk analyse af det kollektive aftalesystem*. Copenhagen: Jurist- og Økonomforbundets Forlag.

Due, Jesper, Jørgen S. Madsen, and Mie D. Pihl (2010). *Udviklingen i den faglige organisering: årsager og konsekvenser for den danske model*. Copenhagen: Landsorganisationen i Danmark.

Esping-Andersen, Gøsta (1993). *The Three Worlds of Welfare Capitalism*. Princeton, NJ: Princeton University Press.

Hall, Peter A., and Daniel W. Gingerich (2009). 'Varieties of capitalism and institutional complementarities in the political economy: An empirical analysis', *British Journal of Political Science*, 39/3: 449–82.

Halvorsen, Rune, Bjørn Hvinden, and Mi Ah Schoyen (2016). 'The Nordic welfare model in the twenty-first century: The bumblebee still flies!', *Social Policy and Society*, 15/1: 57–73.

Hoffmann, Finn (1999). 'Den danske model og den offentlige sektor' in Finansministeriet, ed., *100-året for Septemberforliget—Et festskrift*. Copenhagen: Schultz Information, 75–106.

Høgedahl, Laust (2014). 'The Ghent effect for whom? Mapping the variations of the Ghent effect across different trade unions in Denmark', *Industrial Relations Journal*, 45/6: 469–85.

Høgedahl, Laust (2019). *Den danske model i den offentlige sektor. Danmark i et Nordisk perspektiv*. Copenhagen: Jurist- og Økonomforbundets forlag.

Høgedahl, Laust, and Flemming Ibsen (2017). 'New terms for collective action in the public sector in Denmark: Lessons learned from the teacher lock-out in 2013', *Journal of Industrial Relations*, 59/5: 593–610.

Høgedahl, Laust, and Henning Jørgensen (2017). 'Development in the regulation of wages and working conditions: The employee perspective', *Nordic Journal of Working Life Studies*, 7/1: 3–17.

Høgedahl, Laust, Flemming Ibsen, and Steen Scheuer (2013). 'Free riders: The rise of alternative unionism in Denmark', *Industrial Relations Journal*, 44/5-6: 444–61.

Høgedahl, Laust, and Kristian Kongshøj (2017). 'New trajectories of unionization in the Nordic Ghent countries: Changing labour market and welfare institutions', *European Journal of Industrial Relations*, 23/4: 365–80.

Ibsen, Flemming, Laust Høgedahl, and Steen Scheuer (2011). *Kollektiv handling*. Copenhagen: Nyt fra Samfundsvidenskaberne.

Ibsen, Flemming and Henning Jørgensen (1979). *Fagbevægelse og stat: Den faglige kamp, statsindgreb og indkomstpolitik 1930*. Copenhagen: Gyldendal.

Jørgensen, Henning (2002). *Consensus, Cooperation and Conflict—The Policy Making Process in Denmark*. Cheltenham: Edward Elgar.

Jørgensen, Henning, and Mads P. Klindt (2018). 'Revisiting Danish flexicurity after a decade of reform: Does the labour market still work for everyone?', in Mark Fabian and Robert Breunig, eds, *Hybrid Public Policy Innovations: Contemporary Policy Beyond Ideology*. London: Routledge, 134–51.

Jørgensen, Henning, and Flemming Larsen (2013). 'Fagbevægelsens institutionelle magttab og korporatismens krise', *Okonomi and Politik*, 86/1: 58–70.

Jørgensen, Henning, and Per K. Madsen (2007). *Flexicurity and Beyond: Finding a New Agenda for the European Social Model*. Copenhagen: Jurist- og Økonomforbundets Forlag.

Klindt, Mads P. (2008). 'Arbejdsmarkedspolitik og institutionel komplementaritet', *Samfundsøkonomen*, 6: 26–31.

Klitgaard, Michael B., and Asbjørn S. Nørgaard (2014). 'Structural stress or deliberate decision? Government partisanship and the disempowerment of unions in Denmark', *European Journal of Political Research*, 53/2: 404–21.

Kristensen, Peer H., Maja Lotz, and Robson Rocha (2011). 'Denmark: Tailoring flexicurity for changing roles in global games', in Peer H. Kristensen and Kari Lilja, eds, *Nordic Capitalism and Globalization: New Forms of Economic Organization and Welfare Institutions*. Oxford: Oxford University Press, 86–140.

Kristiansen, Jens (2013). *Aftalemodellen og dens europæiske udfordringer*. Copenhagen: Jurist- og Økonomforbundets Forlag.

Larsen, Flemming (2004). 'The importance of institutional regimes for active labour market policies—The case of Denmark', *European Journal of Social Security*, 6/2: 137–54.

Larsen, Flemming (2013). 'Active labour market reform in Denmark: The role of governance in policy change', in Evelyn Z. Brodkin and Gregory Marston, eds, *Work and the Welfare State: The Politics and Management of Policy Chance*. Washington, DC: Georgetown University Press, 103–24.

Lind, Jens (2009). 'The end of the Ghent system as trade union recruitment machinery?', *Industrial Relations Journal*, 40/6: 510–23.

Madsen, Per K. (2002). 'The Danish model of flexicurity: A paradise with some snakes', in Hedva Sarfati and Giuliano Bonoli, eds, *Labour Market and Social Protections Reforms in International Perspective: Parallel or Converging Tracks?* Farnham: Ashgate, 243–65.

Madsen, Per K. (2003). '"Flexicurity" through labour market policies and institutions in Denmark', in Peter Auer and Sandrine Cazes, eds, *Employment Stability in a Age of Flexibility*. Geneva: International Labour Organization, 59–105.

Madsen, Per K. (2014). 'The Danish road to "flexicurity": Where are we compared to others? And how did we get there?', in Ruud Muffels ed., *Flexibility and Employment Security in Europe*. Cheltenham: Edward Elgar, 341–62.

Mailand, Mikkel (2010). 'The common European flexicurity principles: How a fragile consensus was reached', *European Journal of Industrial Relations*, 16/3: 241–57.

Nedergaard, Peter (2006). 'Which countries learn from which? A comparative analysis of the direction of mutual learning processes within the open method of coordination committees of the European Union and among the Nordic countries', *Cooperation and Conflict*, 41/4: 422–42.

Nørgaard, Asbjørn S. (1997). 'The politics of institutional control: Corporatism in Danish occupation safety and health regulation and employment insurance, 1870–1995', PhD dissertation, Aarhus University.

Nergaard, Kristine, and Torgeir A. Stokke (2007). 'The puzzles of union density in Norway', *Transfer: European Review of Labour and Research*, 13/4: 653–70.

Rasmussen, Stine (2013). 'Arbejdsløshedskasserne under udvikling eller afvikling? Et studie af forandringsprocesser i den danske arbejdsmarkedsmodel', PhD dissertation, Aalborg University.

Rothstein, Bo (1992). 'Labor-market institutions and working-class strength', in Sven Steinmo, Kathleen Thelen and Frank Longstreth, eds, *Structuring politics: Historical Institutionalism in Comparative Analysis*. Cambridge: Cambridge University Press, 33–56.

Scheuer, Steen (2012). 'De usynlige: Inklusion og eksklusion på det danske arbejdsmarked', *Tidsskrift for Arbejdsliv*, 14/2: 49–67.

Scheuer, Steen, Flemming Ibsen, and Laust Høgedahl (2016). 'Strikes in the public sector in Denmark—Assessing the economic gains and losses of collective action', *Transfer*, 22/3: 367–82.

Statistic Denmark. http://www.dst.dk (accessed 6 December 2019).

Svarer, Michael, Torben M. Andersen, and Michael Rosholm (2015). 'Flexicurity, dansk økonomi og den økonomiske krise' in Thomas Bredgaard and Per K. Madsen, eds., *Dansk Flexicurity: Fleksibilitet og sikkerhed på arbejdsmarkedet*. Copenhagen: Hans Reitzels Forlag, 245–64.

Torfing, Jacob (2004). *Det stille sporskifte i velfærdsstaten: en diskursteoretisk beslutningsprocesanalyse*. Aarhus: Aarhus University Press.

Vandaele, Kurt (2006). 'A report from the homeland of the Ghent system: Unemployment and union membership in Belgium', *Transfer*, 13/4: 647–57.

Wooldridge, Adrian (2013). 'Northern lights: Special report on the Nordic countries', *The Economist*, 2/2.

CHAPTER 35

....

EDUCATION POLICY

Power, Conflict, and Cooperation

....

SUSANNE WIBORG

THE REGRETTABLE STATUS OF RESEARCH ON DANISH EDUCATION POLITICS

GIVEN the fact that education has become increasingly salient in Danish politics, there ought to be a lively, well-developed body of political science on the topic investigating the politics of education. However, political scientists in Denmark have never paid much attention to this topic. This situation is not peculiar to Denmark as the field of education politics has also been neglected internationally. As the political scientists Gift and Wibbels (2014: 292) stated in relation to this field of research in Europe and the United States:

> One could argue that no single policy domain lies more clearly at the heart of key social, political, and economic dynamics of our age [...] In academia, the salience of education is reflected in booming research programs in economics and sociology [...] Political science, however, is oddly underrepresented among social science disciplines in the study of education. It is hard to identify a community of political scientists who are dedicated to the comparative study of education.
>
> (Gift and Wibbels 2014: 292)

The vast literature on comparative politics has been animated by grander issues such as the rise of the welfare state, the onset of retrenchment and austerity, party politics and their right-left dynamics in public policy, and elections and voting behaviour. Education as a specific sub-field of comparative politics has never been developed and given a short shrift at best (Moe and Wiborg 2017: 9–13). To the extent that the politics of education has been central to the comparative politics literature, the focus has been on vocational training and skill formation in shaping the 'varieties of capitalism' and higher education (e.g. Dobbins and Busemeyer 2015; Iversen and Stephens 2008; Thelen 2004). This is rather peculiar given how far more fundamental a function primary and secondary education is of governments and is of far greater salience to public policy and politics—perhaps even more so in modern times—with the performance-based pressures of globalization and the OECD's Programme for International Student Assessment (PISA) tests (Moe and Wiborg 2017: 9–13).

Not only have political scientists ignored the field of education politics, so have education researchers. For instance, the Danish School of Education, Aarhus University, with its 155 scholars, is one of the largest education research institutions in Europe, yet the politics of education is rarely studied and taught in its post-graduate programmes. Instead, the research draws on the disciplines of educational philosophy, psychology, sociology, and anthropology in dealing with subjects such as knowledge, learning, socialization, and so on. Whilst this has generated a voluminous body of educational research, very little of it in general deals with policy analysis. In fact, the research deems the larger political system so far remote from these topics that the role of politics and power in shaping Danish education has not been subjected to serious empirical investigation. Consequently, policy-making processes, partisan politics, organized interests, and other matters that explain how politics shape education are, for the most part, excluded in the research. When the research does deal with politics, it is often a mixture of theoretical, normative, and aspirational aspects, addressing issues of inequity, welfare, citizenship, social justice, and so on in Danish education (see 'profile' at edu.au.dk [Ministry of Education n.d.]).

Education politics has neither been an integral part of the comparative politics mainstream nor the education research discipline and has essentially been pushed to the periphery. However, a small but burgeoning literature is dealing head-on with the politics of education. This research primarily involves Europe, Latin America, and the United States but only occasionally includes one or more of the Nordic countries as case studies in the comparisons (Busemeyer and Trampusch 2011; Gift and Wibbels 2014; Moe and Wiborg 2017: 12). In the following, a brief account of the history of the Danish school system focusing primarily on the post-war period will be offered, informed by some of this recent comparative politics of education research. This chapter thus presents some of the most important insights from this research but also point to major gaps. The final part of the chapter suggests future directions for research.

The Restructuring of the Danish School System along Egalitarian Lines, 1903–1958

The history of Danish school reforms has primarily been conducted as single country research studies (e.g. Skovgaard-Petersen 1967; Markussen 1988; Bregnsbo 1971; de

Coninck-Smith and Appel 2015). These studies 'drill down' into the rich context of usually one school reform during a relatively short time period. They have provided thick contextual descriptions, yet their important insights have rarely led to new research puzzles or generated hypotheses to confirm and reject existing theories or illuminate deviant countries. There is thus little engagement with comparative analysis among Danish scholars with the explicit purpose of eliminating rival explanations about particular events, actors, structures, and so on in an effort to build more general theories about education development. One recent study which makes such an attempt is Wiborg (2009) who includes Denmark as a unit of analysis in a comparative study on school structures in Europe, 1860–2000. Specifically, she sought to explain the complex interactions of politics that led to various forms of integrating school structures into comprehensive education systems. This was one of the most important reform movements (*enhedsskolebevægelsen*) in Europe; it aimed to link the various, often isolated, school types into coherent systems which most students would attend and progress through with no or little selection and academic tracking. The school structure was designed to minimize social class differences and promote educational equality as well as labour market opportunities.

In striking contrast to Europe and the UK, Denmark as well as the other Nordic countries went furthest in the development of integrating school structures. They integrated the elementary and lower secondary school stages into a nine-year non-selective school with mixed ability classes in all the grades (*Enhedsskole*). In Scandinavia, this development was initiated in the mid-nineteenth century—much later in Finland in the 1960s and 1970s—and was consolidated in the early 1990s. Despite subsequent policies that allow some academic ability grouping, parental choice within the public school sector, and a growing semi-private school sector, the Danish comprehensive education system has been remained almost unchanged until present day. In Germany, for instance, the re-organization attempts in the 1960s and 1970s failed completely, resulting in the survival of the tripartite system (*Gymnasium, Realschule,* and *Hauptschule*) although some integration of the system has happened in a few *Länder* in very recent years (Nikolai et al. 2017; Wiborg 2010). Furthermore, the tripartite system in England (*Grammar, Secondary Modern,* and *Technical Schools*) was largely integrated into a comprehensive system, but since 1979, it has been dismantled in favour of delivering various types of semi-independent schools (McCulloch 2016; Whitty and Power 2000). Denmark thus presents an interesting puzzle: the continuation of the comprehensive school system (*Enhedsskole*).

One of the most important events in the integration of school systems along egalitarian lines in Scandinavia was the abolishment of the parallel system of education at the turn of the nineteenth century. The primary schools and the secondary schools (with their own usually private primary feeder schools, *private grundskoler*) existed largely independently of one another, with each differing in the relative level of academic and social prestige, courses of study, administration, and significantly, associated alignments of political interests (see Wiborg 2017: 145–50). The parallel system was thoroughly transformed by the introduction of a new school type, the middle school, which was designed to bridge between the elementary and the secondary school. In order for this new structure to be implemented, the bottom part of the nine-year secondary school was abolished. This re-organization thus created a ladder system of education, which, in theory, allowed children from different social class backgrounds to progress through according to ability and aptitude. This is quite striking seen in contrast to Europe where little or no effort was made at the time to bring various school types together in more coherent systems (Archer 1978/2014; Green 1990/2013).

Common to the Scandinavian countries was that Liberal governments introduced the middle schools but did so at different times: in Norway already in 1869, Denmark in 1903, and Sweden in 1905 (Wiborg 2009: 76–125). It is perhaps peculiar that the Liberals were successful in the early restructuring of the school system considering the fact that political liberalism wasn't a particularly powerful force in Scandinavia. The Liberals came rather late to power and only held it for a relatively short period, as the nascent Social Democrats were quick to bypass them (Esping-Andersen 1985/2017). However, they differed strongly from Liberal parties in Europe and Britain in having their mass support amongst the agrarian class of farmers, comprising the overwhelming majority of the population, and became influential parties at the expense of the Conservatives (Luebbert 1991; Rokkan 1989; see Christiansen 2020). Their stance on education was to use schools as a vehicle of enhancing education for the rural population, thereby creating social 'circulation' or mixing, and introducing a curriculum consisting of modern subjects by phasing out classical languages (Skovgaard-Petersen 1967; Myhre 1992).

The time difference in introducing the middle school is significant. The rural-urban conflict that dominated liberalism in Scandinavia was also expressed in education politics and largely determined the policy outcomes (Lipset and Rokkan 1967). National differences aside, liberalism in Sweden and Denmark was embroiled in these conflicts, causing a 'delay' in the introduction of the middle school, whereas it was enacted in Norway well before these conflicts started to seriously impact education politics (Wiborg 2009: 76–125). In Denmark, the middle school might already have been introduced in 1876 when the Liberal Party (*Venstre*) had sufficient electoral power to do so, but the school initiative became caught up in the urban-rural conflict. The rural contingency, which was much more influenced than its Norwegian and Swedish counterparts by the national romantic ideology (Grundtvigianism), wanted the entire education system to be imbued with Danish culture, mother tongue instruction, and the teachings of national history. Only when the secondary school had removed the 'Roman yoke' or 'dead classical languages' would they endorse a middle school linking elementary and secondary education together into one system. The entire issue was resolved with the School Act of 1903 when the fraction of national romantics lost ground to the more socially inclined rural members and urban radicals (Skovgaard-Petersen 1967). Grundviganism is commonly viewed by scholars as having a progressive influence on the Danish school system, but this can be questioned in regard to this particular act as the ideology clearly constituted an obstacle in creating social mobility through the middle school (see Korsgaard and Wiborg 2006).

Fifty years later, the middle school was abolished. This may seem surprising given the fact that an increasing number of children from lower social background enrolled in the middle school after having successfully passed an entrance exam that required knowledge of Latin. However, it was expressed as a concern that children who failed this exam instead had to complete their schooling in two extra top classes in the elementary school (5+2 years). The issue of selection at the age of 10/11, affecting primarily children from rural areas, became the focal point in education politics. Centre-left governments in Norway and Sweden abolished the middle school in 1920 and 1927/36, respectively, to create a seven-year integrated comprehensive school, but in Denmark, this happened as late as in 1958 (Wiborg 2009: 147–50). Due to stronger rural liberalism in Danish politics, the middle school was, in fact, strengthened during the interwar period. The Social-Liberal Minister for Education, Jørgen Jørgensen in the centre-left government introduced a new type of middle school in 1937 in parallel with the existing middle school. Profoundly concerned with rural education, he argued successfully against comprehensive school supporters in his party that the new middle school in providing a practical-oriented curriculum and requiring no final exam would facilitate rural youngsters more than abolishing selection to the academic-oriented middle school (Markussen 1978; Wiborg 2009: 147–50).

Comprehensive Education Consolidated, 1958–1975

The proposal to introduce a seven-year comprehensive school was launched again in 1949, but only in 1958 was the centre-left government able to reach a compromise. Not only did shifting governments cause the long delay but also an important change in the policy-making process in education. Organized educational interests, particularly the two main teachers' unions DL (*Danmarks Lærerforening*, for primary and lower secondary school teachers) and GL (*Gymnasieskolernes Lærerforening*, for upper secondary school teachers) became included in the process and started to gain political influence. From the very beginning, both teachers' unions were unanimously against the comprehensive school proposal as it was seen a threat to their vested interests. They argued that it was not the system that needed reform but the individual schools within the existing system. During the formal consultation period, the teachers' unions offered various proposals that provided minimum concessions in order to protect their 'own' schools and cause the least disruption to the existing school system. However, the teachers' union for elementary teachers, DL, started to lend support to the seven-year comprehensive school late in the negotiations as two class years from the middle school would be attached to the elementary school (i.e. more jobs for teachers), but they maintained their opposition to the government proposal of abolishing academic tracking in grades

6 and 7. The teachers' union for secondary school teachers, GL, argued fiercely against the seven-year comprehensive school to safeguard a separate secondary education stage (five or six years) taught by university-educated teachers. This union suffered a major defeat as a result of the political compromise in 1958. The new seven-year comprehensive school with academic tracking at grades 6 and 7 (unless parents preferred the two grades to be organized as mixed ability classes) resulted in a sharp decrease of their teaching jurisdiction (Bregnsbo 1971; Wiborg 2009: 169–72).

Subsequently, centre-left governments in all of Scandinavia initiated major reforms to expand and integrate the comprehensive school system even further. The seven-year comprehensive school, which was followed by two extra classes (grades 8 and 9), were now integrated into nine-year comprehensive schools. This occurred at different times: first in Sweden in 1962 and in Norway in 1969, and latest in Denmark in 1975. In Denmark, the centre-right parties would not agree to the Social Democratic Party's radical ideas of abolishing academic tracking, grades, and even exams. Galvanized by sociological studies showing that social economic background impacts educational attainment, the Social Democrats wanted to eliminate these 'obstacles' to increase social mobility. During the political negotiations, interest groups played an even stronger role as they became an integrated part of the political system. Large and long-serving commissions were established, comprising various education interests, most notably the two teachers' unions. The newly empowered teachers' union for the elementary school teachers pushed for a nine-year school as this would allow them to advance even further into the secondary school stage. The weakened union for upper secondary school that had already witnessed elementary school teachers with merely three years of college training moving into the lower secondary level, grades 6–9/10, fought a futile battle against this. The political compromise achieved with the School Act of 1975 entailed a nine-year comprehensive school with academic tracking and grades in grades 8 and 9 and a final exam. However, the Minister for Education Ritt Bjerregaard was able to negotiate that academic tracking could be abolished after approval of the local school authorities (Wiborg 2009: 184–90; Wiborg 2017: 152–4).

It is striking that the lower secondary stage of education became fully integrated with elementary education and not secondary education, creating an all-through system of education for nine/ten years with mixed ability classes. The opposite was the case in most other European countries, as well as maintaining tracking at the lower secondary stage (in England, even at the primary level). As a result, university-educated teachers in Denmark saw their jurisdiction restricted to the three-year upper secondary schools (age group 15–18). Having secured a near monopoly of non-academic teachers in the comprehensive schools, the teachers' union for primary and lower secondary school teachers, DL, became heavily involved in reforming teacher training. The reform of teacher training, which also took place in government commissions, allowed the union strong influence in developing a type of training that would demarcate the teaching corps strongly from upper secondary school teachers. According to Christensen (1978: 100): 'The teacher training reform […] is a product of the teacher unions' exploitation of their peculiar position as advisor within in the state apparatus. This position has until now—in spite of attacks from different administrative and political sides—been defended with incredible success.' A four-year integrated training programme was introduced that was designed to prepare primary school teachers to teach all subjects at all grades, including the newly acquired secondary grades 7–9/10, guided by progressive, child-oriented educational principles. It is striking that teachers in Finland at this time would have received five years of specialized university education to teach in the academic-oriented comprehensive schools (Wiborg 2017: 153–8).

Teacher training has since been reformed to increase academic standards (subject and age group specialization), but only a single route into initial teacher training is still provided. This is highly unusual as most other European countries offer at least two options (e.g. school-based, tertiary-college, and university routes) to become a teacher. More recently, the teachers' union has been lobbying for university-based training, but in fact for many years, the union has tried to erect barriers for people with university degrees or from different professions entering the teaching profession. The teacher training reform and the role of the teachers' union in shaping it as well as how this may impact student achievement remain one of the most under-investigated topics in Danish educational research.

MARKET-LED REFORMS OF DANISH EDUCATION, 1982–2014

More attention has been paid to market-led school reforms introduced over the past 40 years. Even though mostly historians have studied these reforms, a few political scientists have joined in, bringing in fresh perspectives. There are puzzling differences across the Nordic states as to the extent to which market-led reforms have been implemented. For instance, Sweden, the epitome of social democracy, has pursued these reforms to a much further degree than Denmark, which has had many years of centre-right governments. Norway and Finland have been the most reluctant countries in creating quasi-markets of educational provision. The comparative explanations of these differences have primarily focused on partisan politics, particularly the right-turn by social democrats, but also the role of teachers' unions in curbing market-led policies (Green-Pedersen 2002; Klitgaard 2007; Wiborg 2017: 158–82).

The Danish case is indeed remarkable in that the country was ruled by long-serving centre-right governments (1968–71; 1973–5; 1982–93; 2001–11; 2015–19) for a total of 26 years out of the last 50 years, yet it only implemented market-oriented reforms to a relatively limited degree. To be sure, the long-serving Minister for Education Bertel Haarder (1982–93) vigorously sought to reform the school system along market lines, advocating a policy of devolution that would give schools managerial autonomy, introduce greater parental influence on the school boards (of the individual schools), enhance school choice, and foster in quasi-market regulation of resource allocation to the schools.

However, his power to enforce these policies was heavily restricted because the governments of the 1980s were coalitions without majority support in Parliament. Moreover, opposition parties and organized interests would form shifting alliances against Haarder's initiatives. For instance, the teachers' union and the Local Government Denmark, LGDK, created a bulwark against his proposal to devolve decision-making powers to the school boards. This resulted in a diluted compromise coined the Little School Act of 1989 (Christensen 2000). In fact, this was the only policy achievement during this period as most other initiatives were blocked or watered down by organized interests. When a centre-left government returned in 1993, comprehensive education was even further strengthened. The School Act of 1993 abolished academic tracking in grades 8 and 9 (pupils were divided in two ability bands in core subjects) and introduced mixed ability classes throughout the nine/ten years of schooling. This implied that pupils were now taught together in the same class despite their differences in academic capabilities and social needs.

During the centre-right government of 2001–11, in which Bertel Haarder again acted as minister for education (five years), the marketization of education was pursued more strongly, and this time, the government was more successful in backing its policies with legislation. This was partly due to a decline in corporate policy-making whereby a range of commissions representing educational interests were abolished. The teachers' union was now circumvented and unable to block or shape national policies as previously; it had now been relegated to a position, along with other education interests, whereby it was primarily consulted during a hearing process. Moreover, the tradition of broad consensus-oriented policy agreements in which the opposition was usually included diminished in favour of narrow majority agreements.

School Choice and Private Schools

School choice was introduced in 2005 which gave parents the right to choose a different public school than the one allocated to them by the municipality—even across municipality boundaries. Until then, choice could only be exercised in the relatively large private sector. The centre-right government (2001–11) mustered a broader political consensus as the Social Democrats, perhaps surprisingly, supported the choice reform. The Danish Social Democratic Party, like many of their European counterparts, had started to move to the right on the left-right axis in the 1990s and 2000s (Green-Pedersen 2002; Klitgaard 2007). This right move by the Danish Social Democratic Party was essential for the government in pushing through the School Choice Act, something the party would have refused to do a decade earlier. The other opposition parties and the teachers' union, who remained fiercely against school choice, refused to support the legislation, claiming it would lead to increased educational segregation in Danish society. The teachers' union was bypassed in the negotiations, thus enabling the government to push through the act with sufficient majority consensus.

Even more than a decade after the introduction of school choice, surprisingly few parents—12 per cent—choose a school for their children (Rangvid 2008; Wiborg and

Larsen 2017). A major reason behind this low number can be found in the municipalities' persistent use of pupil assignment schemes, which are supported by teachers' union branches at the local level. A peculiarity of the Act is that, on the one hand, it attempts to establish an education market where parents can freely choose, but on the other hand, it only enables free choice when there are surplus places in the schools. The Act thus gave the municipalities the authority to decide the capacity limit of the schools, which can be fewer than the maximum of 28 pupils in one class. Municipalities often lower the number of pupils in the schools, resulting in restrictions on parental choice and the rejection of children. Moreover, when schools receive more applications than there are available places, the municipalities are legally required to issue admissions rules. The consequence is that the municipality, just as prior to the School Choice Act, assigns children residing within a precisely defined geographical district to each school. The teachers' unions, having lost clout at the national level, have now gained power through corporatist-like practices at the municipality level. The teachers' union is strongly against school choice as it leads to competition between schools, resulting in mergers and closures of schools as well as the loss of pupils to private schools, and ultimately, loss of jobs for teachers. The municipalities who seek to maintain a children allocation scheme do this primarily to distribute children from immigrant backgrounds more evenly, and the teachers' union lends them support to do this primarily to save teachers' jobs (Wiborg and Larsen 2017). The teachers' union still plays an important role in Danish politics as it continues to stymie government reform through opportunity structures available to them at the local level.

The private school sector has grown significantly in recent years. In the 1990s, about 12 per cent of children went to private schools, and in 2014, the figure had increased to 15.6 per cent (Holm-Larsen 2015: 129). In comparison to Norway and Sweden, the private school sector in Denmark has traditionally been considerably larger as much political effort in both Norway and Sweden was directed at limiting private school provision at least until the early 1990s. For example, less than 1 per cent would attend a private school in the late 1980s. In Denmark, a much more tolerant attitude was shown by government toward private education for historical reasons (see Wiborg and Larsen 2017). Private schools remain popular among parents who choose these for their perceived attractiveness, for example, their smaller size and pedagogical orientation or if a public school in their area is closed and then re-opens as a private school (for instance, 98 schools were reduced to 30 schools in 2015—a decline of 4.6 per cent of public schools in order to make savings on public spending). Another typical reason for choosing a private alternative is if a public school has a high concentration of children with immigrant backgrounds—also known as the white flight (Rangvid 2008).

PISA Shock

One could argue that the shift in the national policy-making style was propitious for implementing major reforms following the 2000 OECD Programme for International Student Assessment (PISA) results. The PISA results showed high spending per student in Denmark but only produced middle-range results in regard to the quality and equity in educational outcomes. The results caused a 'PISA shock' among the Danish educational profession who seemed to believe they had created 'the best school system in the world' (see Wiborg 2013). The PISA results demonstrated the contrary, sparking an intense public debate, and substantial policy change aimed at enhancing academic standards in the school system ensued.

Thus, in 2001, a national curriculum was introduced. However, it was already replaced in 2003 with one that contained even more detailed descriptions of skills and subjects to similar standards in the curriculum. In 2009, the curriculum was tightened even further. The government also required teachers to develop study plans for their students in order to evaluate their academic progress. In 2006, the government introduced national tests, which came into force in 2010. National testing on different subjects took place in grades 2, 3, 4, 6, 7, and 8. Students also sit a mandatory school leaving test in grade 9 (Wiborg 2013). In 2010, a mandatory assessment of language development for all three-year-olds to diagnose possible language issues prior to when children start school was also introduced. In 2011, the government set specific targets to be achieved by 2020, including, for instance, upper secondary completion rates of 95 per cent.

It appears that this major policy change on raising standards has led to enhanced PISA results. The 2015 PISA test showed that the Danish students' results in mathematics, reading, and science were above the OECD average for the first time, placing their performance overall in a 21 place ranking out of 72 countries (Education GPS).

The Teachers' Union Reacts: Lock-Out

The successful introduction of these major reforms, significantly increasing standards as measured in the OECD PISA, is partly caused by the curbed teachers' union, DL, who could not as in the past muster a serious bulwark against government policies or be directly involved in making these. To be sure, the union, having had expressed that these reforms would undermine teachers' autonomy and lead to increased and heavier control of their activities, could still frustrate government reforms. An industrial dispute broke out between the LGDK and the teachers' union DL. The teachers' union had refused to sign on to a new collective agreement that was put forward by the LGDK and fully backed by the government. The agreement sought to change the conditions of the teachers' working week, specifically the amount of time teachers have to prepare their lessons. Prior to the dispute, teachers taught a maximum of 25 hours per week, and the rest of the 37-hour week was allocated to preparation and other work-related duties.

The proposal of the LGDK was to increase the authority of the school principals whereby they could decide on preparation and classroom time for individual teachers depending on the specific needs of the school and class. At this time, teachers' union representatives in schools still held much influence over the use of teachers' time, whereas the influence of school principals was limited. Furthermore, the LGDK wanted to extend teaching hours per day (two and three hours depending on age group) so that children who would normally finish school at 1 pm would receive further classes rather than be allowed playtime in school clubs. The teachers' union was furiously against this and demanded the right to have national regulation of classroom teaching and preparation (a cap of 25 hours a week spent on teaching so that it is clear what counts as overtime), and under no circumstances was this to be left to the authority of local school principals.

This dispute led the LGDK to bar teachers from their places of work without pay for a few weeks. More than 90,000 teachers were part of this lock-out, which was finally brought to an end by government intervention. The centre-left coalition government hastily passed an act that stipulated the terms and conditions of teachers' working conditions without consulting the teachers' union. The government had *de facto* changed the collective agreement for teachers by passing on the responsibility of school principals to decide individual work and preparation time. Importantly, this is extremely rare that a collective bargaining collapse should result in government intervention and legislation. The tradition of collective bargaining in Denmark is characterized by the absence of government legislation. The outcome of this dispute was that the teachers' union lost further power at municipality level, with more power passed on to principals, resulting in less influence for the union representatives in schools. The newly formed union for the principals, which had tried to steer away from the two bodies in the dispute, was clearly the 'winner' of the battle (Holm-Larsen 2015: 131–43).

Enhancing Academic Standards Further: The 2014 School Act

In the immediate aftermath of the dispute, a centre-right government introduced a new school act in 2014. The reform was designed to further enhance academic standards by, for instance, extending the school day (30 hours for grades 1–3; 33 hours for grades 4–6; and 35 hours for grades 7–9), increasing the number of classes taught and reducing preparation time for teachers, introducing compulsory homework in schools, and providing further professional training for teachers and school leaders. Moreover, a major reform of teacher education was introduced the same year to develop a bachelor's programme based on modular teaching, with greater autonomy bestowed to the teacher training colleges in the delivery of the programme.

The school reform was soon made subject to intense criticism from organized interests. It was especially the introduction of homework at schools and the extension of the school day that caused a furore. The reform stipulated that homework could be provided by both social workers (early years educators with specialist knowledge in child psychology) and teachers. The teachers' union opposed this decision and claimed that only teachers should be allowed to provide homework. According to the vice-president of the union, Dorte Lange, 'This is the only way in which we can provide proper and qualified support to them [the pupils] so that they don't waste their time' (Holm-Larsen 2015: 117, own translation). In regard to the longer school day, the national organization for parents, School and Parents, stated that more than a third of parents were opposed to this (Holm-Larsen 2015: 116). A survey conducted by the newspaper *Berlingske* stated that half of parents and 41 per cent of school leaders felt that the school days were too long. So intense was the opposition to the extended school day that a new cross-political parental group School Parents (*Folkeskoleforældre*) was established in parallel to the existing parental organization. In 2016, pupils organized a large demonstration against the long school days.

The teachers' union was also outspoken against the extended day but mainly because of the workload. The new work regulations for teachers had increased teaching hours and reduced the preparation time for the classes. The school reform had stipulated that teachers must be present at the school during day-time and required that their teaching responsibilities, including preparation for classes and marking, should be achieved during a normal work day at the school (until 4 pm).

In the wake of the reform, the teachers' magazine *Folkeskolen* conducted a survey that showed that 79 per cent of teachers felt they were unable to complete all their tasks within a school day, and 82 per cent of teachers stated that they felt ill-prepared for teaching their classes. Teacher absence increased rapidly during 2014, resulting in a significant use of supply teachers (Holm-Larsen 2018: 140). The reform intended to increase the number of taught classes for the pupils in order to increase academic performance. However, only half of the schools in the country had actually increased the number of taught classes per week to the minimum requirements. In the schools that followed the school act's (Act 409) requirement of teachers remaining on school grounds during office hours (some schools were using clocking-in machines), it resulted in early retirement of teachers or teachers moving to private schools or to schools that had adopted a more flexible approach to the law's stipulations. Furthermore, the provision of homework at the schools was patchy and varied across schools and sometimes resembled either traditional classroom teaching or play on school grounds.

In 2015, the national curriculum was revised again. To this end, the Ministry of Education launched guidelines that increased the number of common goals of the learning process for a class (rather than the individual pupil) throughout the school year. Around 3,000 goals were formulated in the guidelines, but this was seen as overregulation of the curriculum, and hence, in 2017, the government proposed a reduction and simplification of these. The overall goals in regard to competence, skills, and knowledge development should continue to be compulsory, but the municipalities could decide if they wanted to make all 3,000 goals compulsory or voluntary. The overall common goals were also linked to the national tests in literacy and numeracy in terms of testing criteria and academic levels. Moreover, the national testing regime was expanded in 2014 (with effect from 2017) to include testing of English language skills in grade 4 and further testing in numeracy so that all pupils are tested in grades 3, 5, and 7 (rather than just grades 3 and 6) (Holm-Larsen 2016, 2017, 2018).

In 2016, it was decided that the mandatory school leaving test in grade 9 (not to be confused with national testing) should be replaced with a regular exam (to take effect in 2019). The new exit exam was a result of the new entry requirements to upper secondary education which require that pupils pass primary/lower secondary education (the old leaving test didn't require pupils to exit with a pass). Also, a new grade system is currently being reviewed to combat problems with grade inflation.

Over the past few decades, shifting governments have sought vigorously to create a market-based school system and increase academic standards though effective learning strategies. The government has been able to implement many of its policies to this effect largely because interest groups, especially the teachers' union, no longer take formal part in formulating these. However, the groups still play an important role in the implementation stages at the local level and are able to frustrate polices. Consequently, the outcome of the policies can be considerably different to what the reformers intended. This problem was highlighted in a report by Cevea in 2017 that argued that too many social partners have and will have influence on the Danish public schools (Holm-Larsen 2018). The report recommended that the government experiments with autonomous schools under direct central control such as in the UK and elsewhere in Europe.

Conclusion

Education is an institutional arena of great potential as a booster of human capital and economic growth as well as fostering a common culture through a national curriculum, socializing citizens to democratic values, and advancing social equity and mobility. Precisely because this is so, governments have strong incentives to put this potential to use by getting actively involved in the design, control, and operation of education systems for their societies. As a result, these systems cannot help but be profoundly influenced by the political processes through which governmental decisions get made. It is, therefore, surprising that so little research has been conducted on the *politics* of school reforms in Denmark although the few studies available have made important strides. Much more work needs to be done to unravel further causes and the historical contexts of the reforms described above, the effects of which are still unfolding. Any serious effort to understand the Danish school system or any given system needs to study how power is structured within the politics of education: who wields political power; how they wield it; what their interests are; what the relevant coalitions are; how their power and interests connect with the political party system and the larger apparatus of government; and more generally, how the type of political system and its institutions shape the way power and interests find expression in the political process. Given the profound importance of education to nations and their citizens, and given the inevitable role of politics in shaping education systems in all their aspects, more scholars will hopefully join the effort of providing new insights into education politics in Denmark from a comparative perspective.

References

Archer, Margaret S. (1978/2014). *Social Origins of Educational Systems*. London: Routledge.

Bregnsbo, Henning (1971). *Kampen om skolelovene af 1958: En studie i interesseorganisationers politiske aktiviteter*. Odense: University Press of Southern Denmark.

Busemeyer, Marius, and Christine Trampusch (2011). 'Review article: Comparative political science and the study of education', *British Journal of Political Science*, 41/2: 413–43.

Christensen, Christian D. (1978). 'Lærerinteresser i læreruddannelsen', *Aarbog for dansk skolehistorie*. Copenhagen: Selskabet for Skole-og Uddannelseshistorie.

Christensen, Jørgen G. (2000). 'Governance and devolution in the Danish school system', in Margaret. A. Arnott and Charles D. Raab, eds, *The Governance of Schooling: Comparative Studies of Devolved Management*. London: Routlegde, 198–216.

Christiansen, Flemming J. (2020). 'The Liberal Party. From agrarian and liberal to centre-right catch-all', in Peter M. Christiansen, Jørgen Elklit, and Peter Nedergaard, eds, *The Oxford Handbook of Danish Politics*. Oxford: Oxford University Press, 296–312.

de Coninck-Smith, Ning, and Charlotte Appel (2015) (eds). *Dansk Skolehistorie 1–5*. Aarhus: Aarhus University Press.

Denmark Student Performance (PISA 2015). http://www.oecd.org/denmark/pisa-2015-denmark. htm (accessed 11 December 2019).

Dobbins, Michael, and Marius R. Busemeyer (2015). 'Socio-economic, organized interests and partisan politics: The development of vocational education in Denmark and Sweden', *Socio-Economic Review*, 13/2: 259–84.

Education GPS. http://www.oecd.org/denmark/pisa-2015-denmark.htm (accessed 11 December 2019).

Esping-Andersen, Gösta (1985/2017). *Politics against Markets: The Social Democratic Road to Power*. Princeton, NJ: Princeton University Press.

Gift, Thomas, and Erik Wibbels (2014). 'Reading, writing, and the regrettable status of education research in comparative politics', *Annual Review of Political Science*, 17: 291–312.

Green, Andy (1990/2013). *Education and State Formation: Europe, East Asia and the USA*. London: Palgrave McMillan.

Green-Pedersen, Christoffer (2002). 'New management reforms of the Danish and Swedish welfare states: The role of different social democratic responses', *Governance: An International Journal of Policy, Administration, and Institutions*, 15/2: 271–94.

Holm-Larsen, Signe (2015). 'Reformer og praksis – Uddannelserne if folketingsaret 2014–2015', *Uddannelseshistorie*. Copenhagen: Selskabet for Skole-og Uddannelseshistorie.

Holm-Larsen, Signe (2016). 'Flygtningeborn, gymnasieforlig og kornfed fremdrift. Uddannelserne i folketingsaret 2015–2016', *Uddannelseshistorie*. Copenhagen: Selskabet for Skole-og Uddannelseshistorie.

Holm-Larsen, Signe (2017). 'Her star vi – kan vi andet? Uddannelser i folketingsaret 2016–2017', *Uddannelseshistorie*. Copenhagen: Selskabet for Skole-og Uddannelseshistorie.

Holm-Larsen, Signe (2018). 'Udflytninger, centralisering og liberalisme – uddannelser i folketingsaaret 2017–2018', *Uddannelseshistorie*. Copenhagen: Selskabet for Skole-og Uddannelseshistorie.

Iversen, Torben, and John D. Stephens (2008). 'Partisan politics, the welfare state, and three worlds of human capital formation', *Comparative Political Studies*, 41/4–5: 600–37.

Klitgaard, Michael B. (2007). 'Do welfare state regimes determine public sector reforms? Choice reforms in American, Swedish and German schools', *Scandinavian Political Studies*, 30/4: 444–68.

Korsgaard, Ove, and Susanne Wiborg (2006). 'Grundtvig – the key to Danish education?', *Scandinavian Journal of Educational Research*, 20/3: 361–82.

Lipset, Seymour M., and Stein Rokkan (1967). 'Cleavage structures, party systems, and voter alignments: An introduction', in Seymour M. Lipset and Stein Rokkan, eds, *Party Systems and Voter Alignmnets: Cross-National Perspectives*. New York: Free Press, 1–64.

Luebbert, Gregory (1991). *Liberalism, Fascism, or Social Democracy: Social Classes and the Political Origins of Regimes in Interwar Europe*. New York: Oxford University Press.

Markussen, Ingrid (1978). 'Kampen om den udelte skole', in Ingrid Markussen, ed., *Danske skoleproblemer—før og nu*. Copenhagen: Gjellerup.

Markussen, Ingrid (1988). *Visdommens Lænker. Studier i enevældens skolereformer*. Copenhagen: Landbohistorisk Selskab.

McCulloch, Gary (2016). 'British Labour Party education policy and comprehensive education reform: From learning to live to Circular 10/65', *History of Education*, 45/2: 225–45.

Ministry of Education (n.d.). www.edu.au.uk

Moe, Terry M., and Susanne Wiborg (2017) (eds). *The Comparative Politics of Education. Teacher Unions and Education Systems Around the World*. Cambridge: Cambridge University Press.

Myhre, Jan Eivind (1992). *Den norske almueskole*. Oslo: Gyldendal.

Nikolai, Rita, Kendra Briken, and Dennis Niemann (2017). 'Teacher unionism in Germany: Fragmented competitors', in Terry M. Moe and Susanne Wiborg, eds, *The Comparative Politics of Education. Teacher Unions and Education Systems Around the World*. Cambridge: Cambridge University Press: 114–43.

Rangvid, Beatrice (2008). 'Private school diversity in Denmark's national voucher system', *Scandinavian Journal of Educational Research*, 52/4: 331–54.

Rokkan, Stein (1989). *Stat, national, klasse. Essays i politisk sociologi*. Oslo: Universitetsforlaget.

Skovgaard-Petersen, Vagn (1967). 'Den politiske drøftelse af forbindelsen mellem almueskolen og den lærde skole', *Årbog for dansk skolehistorie*. Copenhagen: Selskabet for Skole- og Uddannelseshistorie.

Thelen, Kathleen (2004). *The Political Economy of Skills in Germany, Britain, the United States and Japan*. New York: Cambridge University Press.

Whitty, Geoff, and Sally Power (2000). 'Marketization and privatization in mass education systems', *International Journal of Educational Development*, 20/2: 93–107.

Wiborg, Susanne (2009). *Education and Social Integration. The Development of Comprehensive Schooling in Europe*. New York: Palgrave MacMillan.

Wiborg, Susanne (2010). 'Why is there no comprehensive education in Germany? An historical explanation', *History of Education*, 39/4: 539–56.

Wiborg, Susanne (2013). 'Neo-liberalism and universal state education: The cases of Denmark, Norway and Sweden 1980–2011', *Comparative Education*, 48/2: 407–23.

Wiborg, Susanne (2017). 'Teacher unions in the Nordic countries: Solidarity and the politics of self-interest', in Terry M. Moe, and Susanne Wiborg, eds, *The Comparative Politics of Education. Teacher Unions and Education Systems Around the World*. Cambridge: Cambridge University Press, 144–91.

Wiborg, Susanne, and Kristina R. Larsen (2017). 'Why school choice reforms in Denmark fail: The blocking power of the teacher union', *European Journal of Education*, 52/1: 92–103.

CHAPTER 36

HEALTH POLICY

The Submerged Politics of Free and Equal Access

LARS THORUP LARSEN

CONSENSUS ABOUT UNIVERSAL HEALTHCARE

No part of the Danish welfare state is supported as strongly by voters and political elites as the healthcare system (see Petersen 2020). There may be disagreements about how specific aspects of healthcare should be organized or regulated, or how much autonomy should be granted to health professionals in specific institutions, but few politicians, if any, would dare to show anything but unequivocal support for the universal national health insurance. The broad consensus about universal health insurance stands out as particularly significant because most other forms of social citizenship in the Danish welfare state such as unemployment insurance and pensions have been reformed with elements of means-testing, work requirements, or qualification periods during the past few decades. These areas are also often the topic of contentious political debates about the deservingness of recipients. In healthcare, however, universalism seems to be intact and immune to political contestation. All legal residents in Denmark have so-called 'free and equal access' to healthcare services from both general practitioners (GPs) and hospitals. Just as there are relatively few barriers to get free access to healthcare, it is also rare—but not totally unprecedented—for health policy debates to degrade into 'targeted' (Schneider and Ingram 1997) moral accusations against recipients' use of public resources.

Given the broad political and popular consensus about universal health access, it would be easy to brush off healthcare as entirely depoliticized and irrelevant to politics and party competition. This, however, would be a mistake because the area is in fact characterized by significant party competition between the government and opposition parties. A testament to this status is the fact that the major political parties often put healthcare plans up front when they run for office. Political parties often flash their willingness to increase healthcare spending or at least hide their efforts to cut spending. Despite consensus about the core beliefs in universal health insurance, there are disagreements among the political parties, especially regarding the use of private health providers and patients' right to choose between providers. The objective of this chapter is to demonstrate that Danish health policy is far from being depoliticized because there is a 'submerged' (Mettler 2011) political dynamic hidden underneath the broad consensus around the universal healthcare system. In other words, the political conflict about healthcare is very uneven in Denmark because there is a strong consensus about citizens' universal access to tax-financed health services but a higher degree of political conflict on the administrative level, especially regarding the use of private providers in healthcare delivery. Danish health politics was not always like this; the area received less attention prior to the 1990s where it gained salience and where popular demands for increased resources for the public healthcare sector became a permanent feature of Danish politics.

THREE DIMENSIONS OF THE DANISH HEALTHCARE SYSTEM

A key ambition in the following is to analyse and understand the intersection between health politics and policy. This involves discussions about which factors contribute to the broad consensus on universal health access but also some considerations about the likely consequences of this political dynamic. In order to substantiate the main argument, however, it is also necessary to give a somewhat detailed account of how the Danish healthcare sector is organized and describe the principal characteristics of Danish health policy more broadly. It is also necessary to describe some of the historical developments behind the present state, although it is not the ambition to analyse the history of healthcare institutions in its own right (Jacobsen and Larsen 2017). The current healthcare system in Denmark is a rare combination of old and stable institutional structures on one hand and an ongoing modernization of regulatory mechanisms on the other hand. For example, the central agency for medical governance the Danish Health Authority (*Sundhedsstyrelsen*) is built on the remains of the original Royal Health College established in 1803, and the fundamental principle of 'equal' treatment regardless of income was formulated as far back as 1806 (Petersen and Blomquist 1996). These two features, centralized medical governance and the principle of equal treatment for all citizens, have been substantiated by a variety of different institutional underpinnings since the early nineteenth century. Therefore, it is important to understand the dynamic between stable and changing elements in Danish health policy, also in regard to health policy in the present.

The chapter begins with three largely descriptive sections covering the main features of health policy in Denmark: financing, regulation, and delivery. It is customary in health policy scholarship to distinguish between these three dimensions (Freeman and Rothgang 2010; Blank et al. 2018), although they can be difficult to separate in a Danish context because the state plays such a central role in all three. Section two below gives a brief overview of healthcare financing in Denmark, whereas section three describes what is often termed medical governance, i.e. the regulation of medical practice, treatment technology, and pharmaceuticals. Section four describes the key organizations responsible for healthcare delivery in Denmark, including some of the major reforms of this large field in recent decades.

Based on the three descriptive dimensions of Danish health policy, section five brings back the issue of politics and aims to analyse—albeit in relatively short form—how the political dynamic over healthcare has developed from the late 1980s to the present day. Finally, section six ties the various ends together and offers a conclusion to how Danish health policy and politics are connected in a 'submerged' political conflict between centre-left and centre-right. The conclusion also discusses the implications of the submerged political conflict for the development of healthcare costs in comparison with both earlier periods and other healthcare systems. Public spending on healthcare has increased significantly in recent decades in Denmark, about 43 per cent since the year 2000 and much more than all other welfare sectors (Ministry of Finance 2018), and yet many voters and observers in public debate argue that the area is constantly starved by dramatic cutbacks and rationalization. Some of the reasons for this discrepancy are, of course, generic to the public perception of government, and some reasons behind the cost increases are generic to healthcare, such as price hikes on pharmaceuticals and treatment technology. Nevertheless, my argument is that structural and apolitical explanations such as these tend to drastically underestimate the role of politics in health policy expansion.

FINANCING: EXPANSION OF ACCESS AND TAX-FINANCED HEALTH INSURANCE

As in most countries, the Danish development of healthcare financing is closely tied to the gradual expansion of popular access to health services. This section begins with the gradual development of national health insurance and then goes on to describe how Danish healthcare is financed today.

Hacker (1998) demonstrates in a comparative perspective how the historical timing and sequence of national health insurance schemes are very important for the expansion of health services to the general population. What is essential is whether a country effectively expands health coverage to most if not all social classes before the great take-off in health costs and especially increases in hospital services during the middle of the twentieth century. The longer expanded access is delayed, the more difficult it is to pass national health insurance laws. The Danish system may seem at odds with this comparative theory since a unified national health insurance was introduced relatively late in 1971 but still without significant resistance from stakeholders in the previous system of sickness funds.

Doctors were initially publicly employed around 1800 but also limited to the Copenhagen area. With the spread of industrialism in the latter part of the nineteenth century, doctors set up private practices across the entire country and laid the groundwork for private ownership in general practice existing to this day (Jacobsen and Larsen 2017: 237). The principle of equal treatment of the rich and poor had been established as early as 1806 (Petersen and Blomquist 1996: 185), but without a system of health delivery and finance, this was largely an empty promise. The act on health sickness funds from 1892 provided such a system by establishing both a framework of membership-based sickness funds and a combination of public subsidies for the indigent. Politically, the act was the result of mobilization from the Social Democrats as well as an effort by the centre-right Liberal Party (see Mariager and Olesen 2020 and Christiansen 2020) to 'absorb the waves' of socialism through the expansion of welfare services (Jacobsen and Larsen 2017: 242).

The public subsidies to the sickness funds were not universal but means-tested. Nevertheless, the system of sickness funds expanded access to health services to the whole population during the first decades of the twentieth century. Denmark thus fits the broad pattern identified in comparative health systems research where almost all countries expanded health coverage to almost all their citizens during the course of the twentieth century (Freeman 2000: 6). The Danish system offered treatment to different social classes in the same healthcare facilities, mainly through general practitioners at first, but from the mid-twentieth century, also through a broad expansion of hospital services to all parts of the country. An indirect but significant effect of the large growth in public hospitals was to increase the level of state financing in healthcare.

The largest reform of the system by far was passed in 1971 following the previous year's reform of the municipal structures in which fifteen counties were created with healthcare as a core function. The 1971 reform disbanded all the sickness funds and replaced them with universal health insurance for all residents in Denmark financed through general taxes. Similar to their initial introduction, sickness funds were also abolished by a large political majority and replaced with a unified system. Jacobsen and Larsen (2017: 455) argue that this large reform in healthcare financing was eased by the fact that around 90 per cent of the population were already members of a sickness fund, and a system of public funding was in place for poor non-members. That is certainly possible but also somewhat contrary to some of the comparative literature where path dependency works in favour of the existing institutions and providers of health insurance with much to lose in a national system (Hacker 1998; Pierson 2000; Steinmo and Watts 1995). It is possible that due to the long-standing values of free and equal treatment, the Danish sickness funds were simply less stratified in terms of membership and financing compared with private health insurance plans in liberal welfare regimes.

The 1971 reform not only replaced sickness funds with national health insurance, but also changed the system of payment. Instead of the previous system with subsidies and reimbursement, both general practitioners and specialists—while still mostly operating under private ownership—were now paid directly by the counties and the state. Overall, this is still the system of healthcare financing and coverage that exists in Denmark today, although a 2007 reform replaced the fifteen counties with five regions with no right to levy taxes directly. There has been some variation over time in the composition of public financing of health between central government, counties/regions, and municipalities. For example, from 2007 through 2018, there was a so-called 'health contribution' (*Sundhedsbidrag*) on all citizens' tax returns, which initially replaced the county taxes and was ultimately replaced by general taxes. It is, nonetheless, misleading to think of this tax as an earmarked health contribution similar to the social contributions and pay-roll taxes used in other systems like the German or the French health system. The health contribution may have been introduced to make health costs more visible to citizens, but it does not change the fact that the healthcare system was financed by general taxes both before, during, and after this contribution.

Denmark is, thus, still largely a single-payer healthcare system. In this respect, the Danish system is quite similar to the British health system although the two countries are usually identified with two separate welfare regimes (Esping-Andersen 1990). As measured in OECD health data, around 85 per cent of total health consumption in Denmark is financed by public funds in the form of general taxes. The remaining part consists mainly of out-of-pocket private payments for dental care, pharmaceuticals, and other services from private clinics or types of health providers not covered by national health insurance. Part of the private cost comes from employer-financed sup-plementary private health insurance, a market that has grown significantly since 2001 when a tax exemption made these supplementary plans very popular among employ-ees in the private sector (Olesen 2009). The private plans still occupy a relatively small proportion of overall health costs because the plans are supplementary and only come into use when members use them to skip the line for planned surgery in the public system. The use of private providers is discussed further below in relation to health-care provision.

As the final element in healthcare financing, the level of total healthcare costs is also important. The Danish system was characterized by significant stability during the 1980s and 1990s with total health costs hovering around 8 per cent of GDP. This period of stability is remarkable compared to both other health systems and the rise in other areas of welfare expenditure in Denmark during the same period (Andersen and Christiansen 1991), but it also generated a debate about underfunding because of long waiting times for treatment in the public system (Vrangbæk 2004; Pallesen and Pedersen 2008). Since 2000, total health costs have risen dramatically in Denmark, both in response to increased demand and because of strengthened patient rights as explained in the following. A report from the Danish Ministry of Finance (2018) shows a 43 per cent increase in public health funding controlled for inflation between 2000 and 2017, and more than half of the total increase in public expenditure in this period comes from the healthcare sector. At the aggregate level, total Danish health spending (both public and private) now comprises between 10–11 per cent of GDP.

REGULATION AND MEDICAL
GOVERNANCE

The regulation of medical practice has a long history in Denmark, given that it precedes the establishment of the healthcare system. The Royal Health College (*Det Kgl. Sundhedskollegium*) was formed in Copenhagen in 1803 with the principal task of regulating medical practice (Petersen and Blomquist 1996). Similar to the Prussian tradition (Foucault 2001), the regulation and standardization of medical practice was a high priority of early modern state administrations, especially considering that the number of doctors was quite small. The Royal Health College was abolished in 1907 and replaced in 1909 with the Danish Health Authority (*Sundhedsstyrelsen* DHA) which remains the main institution of medical governance to this day. The DHA is now a subsidiary agency under the Ministry of Health, which was formed relatively late in 1987. The core functions of the DHA is to advise the Ministry on all matters related to medical expertise, medical practice, and treatment technology as well as prevention and health promotion. A 2015 reform split the regulation of pharmaceuticals, patient safety, and health professionals into separate agencies, but the DHA remains the highest authority on medical expertise and governance.

Comparatively speaking, medical governance in Denmark is still mostly characterized by formal hierarchy with a command and control system even though some tasks are delegated to decentralized institutions, for instance, the regional health authorities who run public hospitals. It is interesting to compare Denmark with the UK again because whereas the two countries finance healthcare in much of the same way, medical governance is based much more on professional self-regulation in the UK (Burau et al. 2009: 273). The core institutions of medical governance in Denmark, not least the DHA, may originally have been controlled by medical doctors, but they were, nevertheless, centralized state institutions. When these institutions were later largely staffed with generalists rather than doctors, they became strong, external controls on the medical profession. For example, the authorization of health personnel—not least doctors and nurses—is governed by national legislation and administered by central government, not through professional self-regulation to the extent that is seen in countries with stronger and more autonomous medical professions (Starr 2017; Larsen 2016). Professional associations such as the Danish Medical Association or the various scientific societies of medical specialists are still quite powerful organizations with significant influence, particularly in areas such as medical education, medical pricing and collective agreements on salary, working time, etc.

Although the formal hierarchy of medical governance is relatively clear, the main line of conflict in the public debate about the Danish healthcare sector concerns the balance of power between health professionals and managers with a non-medical background. This conflict is often labelled *djøficering*, named after DJØF (the trade union for lawyers, economists, and social scientists), and it basically concerns whether the healthcare sector—both centrally at hospitals and in individual hospital wards—is managed by medical specialists (head doctors or nurses) or by generalists. For example, high-profile doctors routinely make the headlines with harsh critiques of managerialism and new public management in the healthcare sector, calling either for a return to professional self-regulation or simply quitting their posts in the public system in protest (Højgaard 2017). These critical debates often concern funding because even though total health costs rise, individual hospital wards routinely go through series of cutbacks or productivity reforms in order to meet a rising demand for health services with fewer or a stable level of resources. At its heart, however, the conflict about *djøficering* in the healthcare sector is not simply a struggle about resources but rather a generic conflict between managerialism and professional self-regulation as found in many countries and in other policy sectors (Kuhlmann et al. 2013).

In contrast to the stable institutional framework, the instruments used in medical governance change significantly over time, which also contributes to the medical professionals' reactions against what may seem like a constant state of reform. A fair amount of policy instruments applied in the healthcare sector since the late 1970s can reasonably be labelled as New Public Management (Mattei et al. 2013). This includes measures like the decentralization of budget responsibility, the separation of purchase and delivery of health service, and not least a series of efforts to measure the goal achievement of health services. All of these measures require detailed documentation of professional work tasks and patient outcomes, which in itself has generated a fair amount of professional resistance. Between 2009–16, a comprehensive quality accreditation system DDKM (*Den danske kvalitetsmodel*) was rolled out across all Danish public hospitals and all private clinics and hospitals delivering services to the public system (Pedersen 2018: 18). Similar to accreditation systems in education and other policy sectors, the DDKM involved large amounts of documentation and standardized indicators at every level of public service delivery (Örnerheim and Triantafillou 2016). The model was a continuous target of criticism from medical professionals who saw little, if any, benefit to clinical practice from all the involved documentation work. The DDKM was finally abandoned in 2016 after only having been fully implemented for relatively few years. This turbulent process demonstrates that no matter how many times both New Public Management and medical autonomy have been proclaimed dead in public debates, the fault line between managerialism and professionalism continues to be at the centre of medical governance in Denmark.

An area of medical governance that has gathered increased attention over the last decade is the use of expensive drugs in hospitals, and more generally, the use of health economic prioritization and medical pricing in the whole sector. Access to expensive drugs is almost by definition hard to regulate because of the asymmetry between deserving patient groups and strong pharmaceutical industrial interests on the one hand, and on the other hand, pressure on politicians if they say no even when evidence of better treatment effects is weak. This situation has probably been intensified in all health systems over the past decades due not only to broader media attention given to patients seeking access but also to occasional dramatic increases in prices for highly specialized medication with perhaps only marginal or questionable benefits. However, the difficulties of regulating drug prices are not only driven by market supply but also by the institutions that control the demand or intake of new medication. For example, it has been shown that prices have actually fallen significantly for over-the-counter drugs paid by consumers in pharmacies due to increased competition and rules forcing pharmacists to choose the cheapest available medication. However, the costs of hospital drugs, which are given to patients without any charge, have risen dramatically over the past two decades (Søgaard 2018).

Several attempts have been made to introduce some form of economic prioritization of new drugs, primarily driven by the organization of Danish Regions who runs public hospitals and whose budgets have to cover the drugs. The organization first set up a council on expensive drugs in 2009, added a second advisory council in 2012, and established the more ambitious Medicine Council (*Medicinrådet*) in 2017. The Medicine Council evaluates whether new drugs offer significant 'added value' compared with the extra cost, and the institution is inspired by its Norwegian and British equivalents. Unlike them, however, the Danish institution does not operate with a fixed value of how much an added QALY (Quality Adjusted Life Years) can cost, and until now, the Danish council also seems to say no more rarely than its overseas counterparts (Højgaard et al. 2016, 2017). The Medicine Council can only offer recommendations to the regions, and each doctor still has the 'free right to prescribe medicine' (Højgaard et al. 2017: 44). It is, therefore, questionable whether this council will be able to curb cost increases on hospital drugs in the following years. It has proven difficult to recruit the most qualified medical specialists to sit on the council because this would require them to cut all financial ties to the pharmaceutical industry. The council is also to some extent buried in the same entrenched conflict between professional specialists and generalist principals (the regions) as the rest of the healthcare system, but it is still somewhat surprising that the Danish system has not yet been able to go as far in terms of prioritization as the British, given that the latter is known for its highly autonomous medical profession.

DELIVERY: PUBLIC AND PRIVATE PROVISION OF SERVICES IN THE DANISH HEALTHCARE SYSTEM

If asked about it, most Danes would probably say that the health services they receive are almost exclusively delivered by public providers. This perception likely reflects that Denmark does not have a long tradition of a private hospital sector—neither non-profit nor for-profit—compared to other countries like France or Germany. Most of the hospital sector was built during a period of welfare state expansion between 1960 and the mid-1970s (Petersen and Pedersen 1979) with no sharp distinction between public financing, ownership, and delivery of services. As a consequence, Danes are not used to thinking of healthcare financing and delivery as being separate because even visits to their general practitioner are understood as welfare services delivered to them with no requirements for out-of-pocket payment or cost-sharing. In reality, almost all practices of primary care general practitioners are privately owned by one doctor or several doctors together. Corporate ownership is not common in the primary sector. General practitioners, specialists, and other health clinics who wish to be remunerated through the public healthcare system need to acquire an identification code (*ydernummer*) from the national health insurance which allows them to be paid on a fee-for-service basis.

Anyone with legal residence in the country can get access to free healthcare services through the general practitioner, and with a few exceptions, each individual is assigned to a specific general practitioner who receives a lump sum for each patient in addition to standardized rates for all services.[1] The patient's designated general practitioner functions as the gatekeeper to almost all services in the healthcare system including referrals to treatment in specialist clinics and hospitals (Pallesen and Pedersen 2008: 231). Although patient rights have generally been strengthened in various reforms, the gatekeeping role of general practitioners remains a core institutional feature of the Danish healthcare system. With the increased centralization and specialization of hospitals, patients are increasingly redirected to their general practitioners, for example, instead of a visit to the emergency room.

It is sometimes debated whether patients should be charged a small co-payment to visit their general practitioner or medical specialists or for hospital stays. This is common in most neighbouring countries, including Norway, Sweden, Finland, and Germany, but Denmark and the UK are again the most similar in having almost no co-payments in healthcare. Dental care and pharmacy drugs do involve significant co-payments, however, which is sometimes highlighted as an argument for spreading co-payments more evenly across the different sectors. Political interest in the issue is relatively low, and only a few centre-right parties are in support of co-payments—at least openly. For instance, the 2005 proposal from the Welfare Commission to introduce co-payments similar to the Swedish or Norwegian models was quickly buried by the major political parties (Welfare Commission 2005: 344–56). The differences in patient co-payments among the Nordic countries are most likely the effect of path dependency, given that Norway and Sweden have always had co-payments for visits to the doctor, whereas Denmark did not. Few politicians are interested in taking away well-established welfare rights. Among the various proposals offered by health economists, it is also difficult to find a solution without regressive distributional effects unless the maximum co-payment is set so low that the co-payment has no real effect on patient demand or does not even generate significant revenue compared to the administrative costs of the payment system.

Hospitals in Denmark are primarily owned and operated by the five regions, each governed by a democratically elected regional council. The number of hospitals has decreased significantly over the past few decades due mainly to centralization into larger units with higher degrees of specialization. At the moment, all regions outside Copenhagen are in the process of building a series of new 'super hospitals', usually placed near key infrastructure at the outskirts of the major cities, while several old hospital buildings in inner cities are being closed. All of these highly specialized super hospitals are—or will be—associated with the country's four medical schools. Although the regions generally run the hospitals and functions as the largest employer of health professionals by far in Denmark, it is essential to notice that their autonomy is highly regulated by centralized political regulation and agreements between the association of regions and central government.

The role of private hospitals in Denmark is relatively recent, because aside from smaller specialist clinics, the first private hospitals did not open until the mid-1980s. At that time, private hospitals suffered a bad reputation for trying to profit from healthcare, even in the medical community and among right-wing columnists (Olesen 2010: 74–5). Until around 2000, private hospitals struggled to stay in business because the public system rarely purchased services from the private sector, and because private health insurance was a marginal phenomenon, patients had no direct access to private providers except paying for treatment that they could get for free in the public system, albeit with a wait.

After the shift to a centre-right government in 2001, a series of reforms were introduced with the dual aim of strengthening patient rights and breaking the *de facto* producer monopoly of public hospitals (Larsen and Stone 2015). It is essential to underline that none of these reforms challenged the consensus around universal health access and tax-based financing; rather, they offered patients more publicly funded healthcare largely delivered by private providers. The first reform was a tax deduction that indirectly subsidized the spread of supplementary private health insurance (Olesen 2009), which continued to rise even after the deduction was removed in 2012 although mainly employees in the private sector are covered. Second, a 2002 reform introduced a waiting time guarantee, officially labelled 'The Extended Free Choice of Hospitals' (*Udvidet Frit Sygehusvalg*). The reform gave patients the right to receive treatment in private hospitals if the regional public provider could not deliver treatment within two months. This was shortened to 30 days in 2007 and later altered into a diagnosis guarantee. Third, public hospitals were incentivized and partly forced to make more use of private providers, while the private providers were given very favourable rates to grow the private market. The latter was highly criticized by the centralized National Audit Office (Auditor General's Office 2009) as being systematic overcompensation of the private sector.

It has been debated whether the growth of private healthcare providers since 2001 constitutes a privatization, marketization, or 'neoliberalization' of the Danish healthcare sector (Larsen and Stone 2015; Jensen 2011; Jost 2007). The reforms were introduced by the cabinet of Anders Fogh Rasmussen (Liberal Party, Prime Minister 2001–9) whose 1982 visit to Milton Friedman at the University of Chicago had inspired him to use free choice 'vouchers' or 'exit rights' to reform welfare services in Denmark (Pedersen 2018: 98; Larsen 2000; Hirschman 1970). During the reforms of the early 2000s, this principle was labelled as an ideal to 'let the money follow the patient' but also identified as a governing mechanism designed to make public hospitals increase production and thereby shorten waiting time. It is indisputable that the voucherization of healthcare has put public hospitals under more pressure, especially concerning waiting time, because the instruments directly penalize public hospitals when patients take their vouchers to a private hospital (Larsen and Stone 2015). It is also likely that these reforms contributed to a significant drop in waiting time, although in some areas the drop essentially preceded the reform. Finally, it is important to stress that vouchers and marketization did not result in a smaller public sector nor did it lessen the tax burden of healthcare. Contrary to neoliberal reforms in other policy sectors and perhaps counterintuitively, the use of marketization has not compromised universalism in the Danish healthcare system but rather strengthened patient rights. Winblad et al. (2010) find that waiting-time guarantees have generally empowered patients in all Scandinavian countries, albeit less in Sweden due to a softer implementation of rights.

The effects of marketization on overall health costs is also significant. With a few exceptions, and sometimes indirectly through tax breaks, the growth of the private market of healthcare providers and insurers has been financed through general taxes. Most likely, this has contributed to higher demand for health services and significantly higher overall costs of the healthcare system. In order to analyse how and why this shift took place, the final section brings back the issues of politics and party competition.

Health Politics: Party Politics and Competition for Issue Ownership

The political salience of healthcare is generally very high, but the topic of party political conflict varies substantially between the three dimensions of health policy analysed above: healthcare financing, regulation, and delivery. In contrast to the major political conflict over healthcare in American politics (Jacobs and Skocpol 2015), there is no major political conflict between left and right about national health insurance in Denmark. The quintessential role of the government in financing healthcare through general taxes is a frozen battle so to speak. Healthcare is, nevertheless, on the macro-political agenda, but this is mainly a competition about healthcare delivery. The major political parties compete about whether centre-left or centre-right parties are seen as better able to deliver high-quality health services quickly. Indirectly, this means that the party political conflict also concerns the use of private providers in the public healthcare system. In most cases, governments and regions led by the Social Democratic Party (see Mariager and Olesen 2020) have tried to limit the use of private hospitals without taking voucher rights away from voters. Governments and regions led by centre-right parties such as the Liberal Party (see Christiansen 2020) have mostly attempted to pressure public hospitals into purchasing much more from private hospitals. One study demonstrates high fluctuations in the proportion of patients treated in private hospitals, not just between medical specialities but from year to year as well. The fluctuations between 2007 through 2015 mostly reflected the regions' efforts to keep up with demand within the short waiting-time guarantee and not directly the colour of the Cabinet (Toft 2016).

If we go back a few decades to the 1980s, health policy was less salient and mostly concerned efforts by central government to control costs in public hospitals and the primary sector (Pallesen and Pedersen 2008). Cost control was perhaps too effective in the sense that public perception began to see the healthcare system as systematically underfunded, a perception that was mostly focused on the accumulation of waiting time (Vrangbæk 2004). The area definitely gained salience during the 1990s, and although funding went up and waiting time mostly went down under the Social Democratic-led government (1993–2001), the broad perception of an underfunded and perhaps also inefficient public system persisted. This challenged the issue ownership of the Social Democrats on healthcare, epitomized in the Liberal Party's promise to increase public funding for (mostly privately delivered) healthcare at the 2001 election (Hjort 2017: 194). The belief in centre-right governments' ability to deliver better healthcare was higher in 2001 than ever before, but it did not permanently challenge the centre-left's issue ownership in the area. Health policy continues to be high on the political agenda, most likely because the political parties seek to respond to voters who want more resources for healthcare.

The Danish election study demonstrates that Danish voters generally have strong preferences for more public funding to the healthcare sector. Figure 36.1 illustrates a stable majority of voters in favour of increased health funding, larger than any other policy area in the study. It has similarly been shown that preferences for higher public funding is high among voters from all political parties, although to a lesser extent among voters from smaller parties in the centre (Arndt and Jensen 2017: 253). It is interesting, however, that even voters from the libertarian party the Liberal Alliance—whose party platform centres on reducing the size of the welfare state and significantly lowering taxes—also favour more public funding for the healthcare sector.

It is not clear from this study what exactly explains voters' preference for higher healthcare spending. Are these perceptions, for instance, driven by the real development in healthcare spending? This does not seem to be the case since, for instance, 75 per cent favoured increased spending in 2007 after health costs had already risen at very high rates since 2000 (Ministry of Finance 2018). Jensen (2011) argues that increased party competition over healthcare leads to a shift in centre-right health policies to accommodate voter preferences for flexibility and exit rights instead of lower taxes. Other studies point to the impact of political agendas and attention because increased attention to a policy area in Parliament leads to higher growth in both costs and the number of rules in an area such as healthcare (Mortensen 2006; Jakobsen and Mortensen 2015). These explanations are not necessarily mutually exclusive because both underline how there is a significant amount of 'Downsian' party competition in an area such as health policy even though—or perhaps also because—the differences between parties' positions on health policy are so small.

Another interesting feature of Danish voters' strong commitment to the universal healthcare system is that the public simultaneously tends to be quite critical of public health interventions that intervene in individual lifestyle behaviour such as smoking,

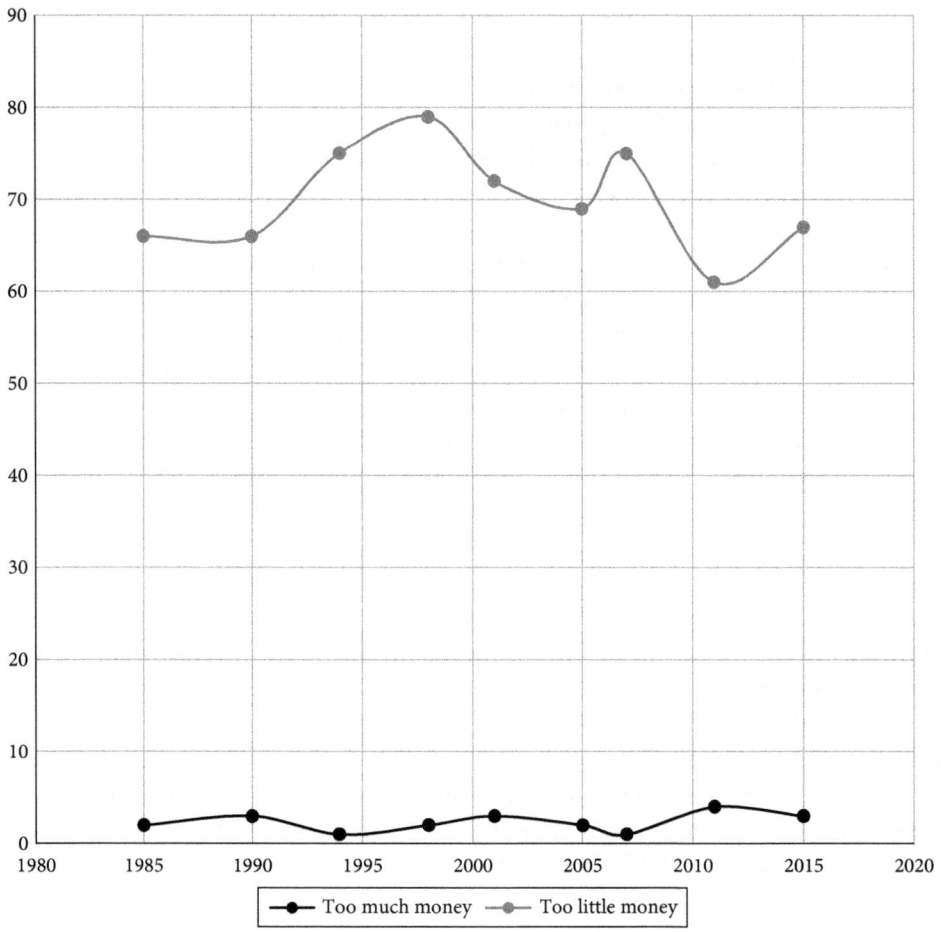

FIGURE 36.1 Voters' attitudes to whether government spends too much or too little money on the healthcare sector.

Source: Stubager et al. (2016: 25)

diet, or alcohol consumption (Larsen 2019). Unlike the Swedish welfare state where public health interventions in individual health behaviour are both accepted and typically of a more structural nature, Danes are generally much less willing to accept government interventions in individual lifestyle behaviour (Valgårda 2003). For the same reason, Danish public health policies still rely more on milder policy instruments such as information campaigns than in other countries (Larsen 2012), most likely because politicians fear a backlash from voters. In other words, the 'politics' of health policy is generally limited to the types of health policy changes favoured by voters, such as quick and easy access to specialized medical treatment. On the contrary, the major political parties are much more hesitant to propose public health interventions on unpopular issues such as higher tobacco and alcohol prices.

CONCLUSION

This chapter has attempted to demonstrate how Danish health policy is double-faced in several respects. On the one hand, the area is characterized by highly stable institutional structures and a rock solid consensus about the value of a strong, publicly based healthcare system. Even when the public has doubts about the quality of the healthcare services, this does not seem to undermine their belief in the role of government in healthcare or call for a replacement of the system with more market-based alternatives. It mainly seems to lead voters to call for more resources as well as quick and easy access. On the other hand, the broad popular consensus about the public healthcare system has not led to any sort of truce among the political parties. It is no surprise, of course, that political parties generally respond to voter preferences for higher spending in popular policy areas.

What can be difficult to grasp is how it is possible for parties to continuously maintain high political attention and competition in this area, given that the differences between the political positions of right-wing and left-wing parties on health policy are relatively small. There are differences between left and right but mainly differences of a relatively technical or administrative nature, i.e. something that is likely more important to policymakers and researchers than it is to citizens. These differences concern the extent to which private providers should be used more or less in the public healthcare system. On occasion, minor political debates also emerge about whether visits to general practitioners should require co-payment from patients as in Norway and Sweden. Usually, however, the major political parties shut down these types of debates, most likely due to blame avoidance in a policy area with preferences for higher—not lower—spending.

Despite the fact that overall increases in public consumption since 2000 are 'primarily due to the health care sector' (Ministry of Finance 2018), perception in both the public and among healthcare professionals is that the sector sees nothing but cutbacks. This perception is not necessarily wrong given that total health costs also rise due to other factors. There is generally an increased demand for health services due to demographic changes caused by a growing number of elderly citizens and other systemic changes to health costs such as higher drug costs. Some would probably argue that cost increases are endemic to an area such as health policy. This may be true, but in order to understand the substantial comparative differences between countries or even within Denmark over time, it is necessary to consider the impact of health politics on the development of health policy.

The key conclusion, therefore, is that a combination of strong consensus and intense party competition to accommodate voter preferences contributes to the significant growth in health spending and to other policy changes that increase public commitment to the healthcare sector. The political conflict about health policy is partly 'submerged', and this is not only due to the path dependency that characterizes most, if not even all, health systems in a comparative perspective. Moreover, although the political conflict is submerged, it is not necessarily small or insignificant. It is submerged because when the political parties face the voters, their ideological differences on health policy often implode since showing anything less than full commitment to the core values of universal health insurance is politically risky. The political conflict comes to the front on issues related to the delivery and organization of healthcare, but even here, the strong consensus about free and equal treatment keeps the conflict from being more than a dispute over the choice of policy instruments. As such, there is no clear sign ahead that this political dynamic will change in the near future, although demographic changes will almost certainly put further pressure on a system that is already pressured between political demand and a scarce supply of resources and doctors.

NOTE

1. Technically, it is possible to register in 'Group 2' under the national health insurance. This group, which is rarely used, is a remnant of the old sickness funds and gives direct access to specialists without having to go through a general practitioner. Patients in this group pay up front out of pocket and are reimbursed later. This option is of limited use and relevance for the broader system, and therefore it is not discussed further here.

REFERENCES

Andersen, Jørgen G., and Peter M. Christiansen (1991). *Skatter uden velfærd*. Copenhagen: Jurist- og Økonomforbundets Forlag.

Arndt, Cristoph, and Carsten Jensen (2017). 'Partivalg og holdninger til velfærdsstaten', in Kasper M. Hansen and Rune Stubager, eds, *Oprør fra udkanten. Folketingsvalget 2015*. Copenhagen: Jurist- og Økonomforbundets Forlag, 245–63.

Auditor General's Office (2009). *Beretning til Statsrevisorerne om pris, kvalitet og adgang til behandling på private sygehuse*. Copenhagen: Auditor General's Office.

Blank, Robert H., Viola Burau, and Ellen Kuhlmann (2018). *Comparative Health Policy*. London: Palgrave Macmillan.

Burau, Viola, David Wilsford, and George France (2009). 'Reforming medical governance in Europe. What is it about institutions?', *Health Economics, Policy and Law*, 4/3: 265–81.

Christiansen, Flemming J. (2020). 'The Liberal Party. From agrarian and liberal to centre-right catch-all', in Peter M. Christiansen, Jørgen Elklit, and Peter Nedergaard, eds, *The Oxford Handbook of Danish Politics*. Oxford: Oxford University Press, 296–312.

Esping-Andersen, G. (1990). *The Three Worlds of Welfare Capitalism*. Princeton, NJ: Princeton University Press.

Foucault, Michel (2001). 'Socialmedicinens fødsel', *Distinktion*, 3: 11–23.

Freeman, Richard (2000). *The Politics of Health in Europe*. Manchester: Manchester University Press.

Freeman, Richard, and Heinz Rothgang (2010). 'Health', in Francis G. Castles, Stephan Leibfried, Jane Lewis, Herbert Obinger, and Christopher Pierson, eds, *The Oxford Handbook of the Welfare State*. Oxford: Oxford University Press, 367–77.

Hacker, Jacob S. (1998). 'The historical logic of National Health Insurance: Structure and sequence in the development of British, Canadian, and U.S. Medical Policy', *Studies in American Political Development*, 12/1: 57–130.

Hirschman, Albert O. (1970). *Exit, Voice, and Loyalty. Responses to Decline in Firms, Organizations, and States*. Cambridge, MA: Harvard University Press.

Hjort, Frederik (2017). 'Emneejerskab - hvilke partier ejer hvilke emner?', in Kasper M. Hansen and Rune Stubager, eds, *Oprør fra udkanten. Folketingsvalget 2015*. Copenhagen: Jurist- og Økonomforbundets Forlag, 193–205.

Højgaard, Betina, Sarah Wadmann, Marie Jakobsen, Susanne R. Rasmussen, Niels J. M. Pedersen, and Jakob Kjellberg (2016). *Regulering af sygehusmedicin med udgangspunkt i omkostning og effekt. Erfaringer fra Tyskland, Holland, Schweiz, England, Norge og Sverige*. Copenhagen: KORA.

Højgaard, Betina, Sarah Wadmann, Susanne R. Rasmussen, and Jakob Kjellberg (2017). *Kortlægning af lægemiddelområdet i de nordiske lande. Danmark, Finland, Grønland, Island, Norge og Sverige*. Copenhagen: KORA.

Højgaard, Liselotte (2017). *Hvordan får vi verdens bedste sundhed?* Copenhagen: Informations Forlag.

Jacobs, Lawrence R., and Theda Skocpol (2015). *Health Care Reform and American Politics: What Everyone Needs to Know*, 3rd ed. Oxford: Oxford University Press.

Jacobsen, Kurt, and Klaus Larsen (2017). *Ve og Velfærd. Læger, sundhed og samfund gennem 200 år*. Copenhagen: FADL's Forlag.

Jakobsen, Mads L. F., and Peter B. Mortensen (2015). 'How politics shapes the growth of rules', *Governance: An International Journal of Policy, Administration, and Institutions*, 28/4: 497–515.

Jensen, Carsten (2011). 'Marketization via compensation: Health care and the politics of the right in advanced industrialized nations', *British Journal of Political Science*, 41/4: 907–26.

Jost, Timothy S. (2007). *Health Care at Risk: A Critique of the Consumer-Driven Movement*. Durham, NC: Duke University Press.

Kuhlmann, Ellen, Viola Burau, Tiago Correia, Roman Lewandowski, Christos Lionis, Mirko Noordegraaf, and Jose Repullo (2013). '"A manager in the minds of doctors": A comparison of new modes of control in European hospitals', *BMC Health Services Research*, 13/1: 246.

Larsen, Lars T. (2012). 'The leap of faith from disease treatment to lifestyle prevention: The genealogy of a policy idea', *Journal of Health Politics, Policy and Law*, 37/2: 227–52.

Larsen, Lars T. (2016). 'No third parties. The medical profession reclaims authority in doctor-patient relationships', *Professions and Professionalism*, 6/2.

Larsen, Lars T. (2019). *Sundhed*. Aarhus: Aarhus University Press.

Larsen, Lars T., and Deborah Stone (2015). 'Governing health care through free choice: Neoliberal reforms in Denmark and the United States', *Journal of Health Politics, Policy and Law*, 40/5: 941–70.

Larsen, Thomas (2000). *I godt vejr og storm. Samtaler med Anders Fogh Rasmussen*. Copenhagen: Gyldendal.

Mariager, Rasmus, and Niels W. Olesen (2020). 'The Social Democratic Party. From exponent of societal change to pragmatic conservatism', in Peter M. Christiansen, Jørgen Elklit, and Peter Nedergaard, eds, *The Oxford Handbook of Danish Politics*. Oxford: Oxford University Press, 278–295.

Mattei, Paola, Mahima Mitra, Karsten Vrangbæk, Simon Neby, and Haldor Byrkjeflot (2013). 'Reshaping public accountability: Hospital reforms in Germany, Norway and Denmark', *International Review of Administrative Sciences*, 79/2: 249–70.

Mettler, Suzanne (2011). *The Submerged State. How Invisible Government Policies Undermine American Democracy*. Chicago, IL: University of Chicago Press.

Ministry of Finance (2018). *Økonomisk Analyse: Udviklingen i de offentlige udgifter fra 2000 til 2017*. Copenhagen: Ministry of Finance.

Mortensen, Peter B. (2006). *The Impact of Public Opinion on Public Policy: A Study of Why, When, and How Agenda Setting Matters*. Aarhus: Politica.

Olesen, Jeppe D. (2009). 'Policymaking without policy choice: The rise of private health insurance in Denmark', *Journal of Public Policy*, 29/3: 263–85.

Olesen, Jeppe D. (2010). 'Adapting the welfare state. Privatisation in health care in Denmark, England and Sweden', PhD dissertation, European University Institute, Florence.

Örnerheim, Mattias, and Peter Triantafillou (2016). 'Explaining quality management in the Danish and Swedish public health sectors: Unintended learning and deliberate co-optation', *International Journal of Public Administration*, 39/12: 963–97.

Pallesen, Thomas, and Lars D. Pedersen (2008). 'Health care in Denmark: Adapting to cost containment in the 1980s and expenditure expansion in the 1990s', in Erik Albæk, Leslie C. Eliason, Asbjørn S. Nørgaard, and Hermann M. Schwartz, eds, *Crisis, Miracles, and Beyond. Negotiated Adaptation of the Danish Welfare State*. Aarhus: Aarhus University Press, 227–50.

Pedersen, Kjeld M. (2018). *Dansk Sundhedspolitik*. Copenhagen: Munksgaard.

Petersen, Jørn-Henrik, and Kjeld M. Pedersen (1979). *Hvorfor kan den offentlige sektor ikke styres?* Copenhagen: Berlingske.

Petersen, Klaus (2020). 'Welfare state policies. From the beginning towards an end?', in Peter M. Christiansen, Jørgen Elklit, and Peter Nedergaard, eds, *The Oxford Handbook of Danish Politics*. Oxford: Oxford University Press, 540–558.

Petersen, Niels, and Helle Blomquist (1996). *Sundhed. Byrokrati. Politik*. Copenhagen: Jurist- og Økonomforbundets Forlag.

Pierson, Paul (2000). 'Increasing returns, path dependence, and the study of politics', *American Political Science Review*, 94/2: 251–67.

Schneider, Anne, and Helen Ingram (1997). *Policy Design for Democracy*. Lawrence, KY: University Press of Kansas.

Søgaard, Jes (2018, 29 Nov.). 'Stigende medicinudgifter presser sundhedsbudgetterne', *Altinget* (accessed 19 June 2019).

Starr, Paul (2017). *The Social Transformation of American Medicine. The Rise of a Sovereign Profession and the Making of a Vast Industry*, 2nd ed. New York: Basic Books.

Steinmo, Sven, and Jon Watts (1995). 'It's the institutions, stupid! Why comprehensive national health insurance always fails in America', *Journal Health Politics, Policy and Law*, 20/2: 329–72.

Stubager, Rune, Kasper M. Hansen, Kristoffer Callesen, Andreas Leed, and Christine Enevoldsen (2016). *Danske vælgere 1971–2015. En oversigt over udviklingen i vælgernes holdninger mv.* Aarhus: Det Danske Valgprojekt.

Toft, Ole N. M. (2016, 13 Jul.). 'Historisk mange patienter på privathospital', *Altinget* (accessed 19 June 2019).

Valgårda, Signild (2003). *Folkesundhed som politik*. Aarhus: Magtudredningen.

Vrangbæk, Karsten (2004). *Ingeniørarbejde, hundeslagsmål eller hovedløs høne? Ventetidsgaranti til sygehusbehandling*. Aarhus: Magtudredningen.

Welfare Commission (2005). *Analyserapport—Fremtidens velfærd—sådan gør andre lande*. Copenhagen: Welfare Commission.

Winblad, Ulrika, Karsten Vrangbæk, and Katarina Östergren (2010). 'Do the waiting-time guarantees in the Scandinavian countries empower patients?', *International Journal of Public Sector Management*, 23/4: 353–63.

CHAPTER 37

IMMIGRATION AND IMMIGRANT INTEGRATION POLICY

Public Opinion or Party Politics?

KRISTINA BAKKÆR SIMONSEN

THE SHATTERED IMAGE OF DENMARK

DENMARK is known as a generous and tolerant nation, a description that also used to characterize the image of the country in relation to immigration issues at home as well as internationally. Denmark was the first country to ratify the 1951 UN Refugee Convention (UNHCR 2011); its liberal asylum and immigration act of 1983, named the most 'people-friendly' law in the world (Arvin 2012), was repeatedly emphasized by the UN as an example for other countries to follow (Skaksen and Jensen 2016: 34); and relative to its size, Denmark took many refugees fleeing from war and ethnic conflict during the 1980s and 1990s.

However, in recent years, the rosy picture has waned, if not disappeared altogether. Big international media outlets such as *The New York Times*, *The Atlantic*, *Time*, and *The Guardian* have reported to the world about the 'harsh politics' and 'tough approach' of Danish governments in relation to immigration and immigrant integration. Rather than being celebrated as a positive pioneering country, Denmark is presented as having 'some of the most aggressive anti-immigrant policies in Europe' (Abend 2019 in *Time*), leading 'a race to the bottom in Europe when it comes to deterring refugees' (Gammeltoft-Hansen and Malmvig 2016 in *Huffington Post*). While using a less inflamed rhetoric, researchers agree to place the current Danish policy regime among the most restrictive in Western Europe (Goodman 2014: 50–60; Jensen 2016: 11).

The seemingly obvious analysis many commentators have offered is that Danes have become particularly opposed to immigrants (e.g. Orange 2018 in *The Observer*) and that public opinion in Denmark has, therefore, necessitated the move toward more restrictive policies over time. In this chapter, I will evaluate that claim. First, I give an overview of Danish immigration history and policy developments since the 1960s. I then discuss the evidence for the 'public opinion thesis'—that is, the notion that Danish policies are restrictive because the population is so. I will argue that while Danes can be said to be aversive of ethnic difference in some respects, they are not more anti-immigrant than they used to be, nor are they more anti-immigrant than many other Western European populations. This leads me to discuss research evidencing the political opportunity structures that led Danish politicians to politicize immigration and immigrant integration issues. I will close the chapter by moving from policy inputs to outcomes, namely the potential effects on minority-majority relationships and immigrant integration.

DANISH IMMIGRATION HISTORY AND POLICY DEVELOPMENT

While the two policy areas are obviously connected, not least in contemporary political rhetoric, it is relevant to note the distinction between immigration policy and immigrant integration policy. The former concerns the regulation of the external boundaries of the nation: who is allowed to enter national territory and take residence? The latter covers a variety of measures focused on the nation's internal boundaries: who belongs to the national community, and how can former foreigners become one of 'us'? Denmark was rather late to the game (compared to other Western European countries) in terms of developing an immigration policy, and the country was even slower to formulate immigrant integration policies. This is a reflection of the trends displayed in Figure 37.1 and Table 37.1 and elaborated below. Immigration to Denmark was very modest until the

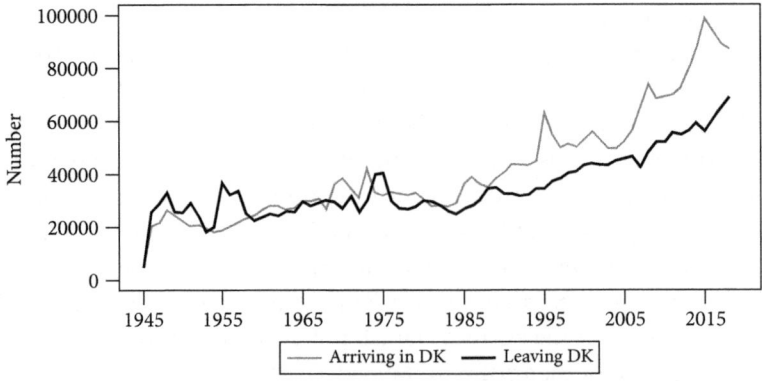

FIGURE 37.1 Immigration to and emigration from Denmark, 1946–2018.
Source: Statistics Denmark, HISB3

mid-1960s, and even when more people began to arrive in the late 1960s and throughout the 1970s, they were considered 'guests' or temporary refugees, that is, expected to leave again within a relatively short period of time.

Prior to this, Denmark had received various smaller groups of migrants and refugees. Workers from Sweden came at the end of the 1800s, Jews fleeing from Russia in the early 1900s, along with the so-called 'sugar beet Poles' who came for the harvesting season. The Russian revolution in 1917 set in motion a new Russian refugee wave, and Denmark received refugees from Nazi Germany during the 1930s (Pedersen 1999: 233). However, until the 1960s, emigration rates exceeded immigration rates, with the period from 1870 to 1920 characterized as one of 'mass emigration' as almost 300,000 Danes moved to the United States where they were lured by the prospect of a better quality of life (Skaksen and Jensen 2016: 26).

In the 1960s, tides turned, and—as in most of North-Western Europe—the economic boom attracted many so-called 'guest workers' to Denmark to keep the economic wheels turning at a high pace. These workers came mostly spontaneously (i.e. without prior invitation from Danish companies or the Danish state) and primarily from Yugoslavia, Turkey, and Pakistan (Skaksen and Jensen 2016: 28). While Danish employer organizations welcomed the new workers, workers' unions and centre-left politicians were more sceptical and expressed concern over potential wage dumping. Following the oil crisis and sudden slowdown of the economy in 1973, the first political immigration-stop was introduced by the Social Democratic Minister of Labour, making it very difficult for prospective workers from outside the Nordic countries and the European Community (EC; which Denmark joined in 1973) to obtain a work permit. However, as the law did not enforce repatriation, many of the former 'guests' not only stayed but also brought their families to Denmark to establish a more permanent life. By 1980, immigrants made up 2.6 per cent of the Danish population (cf. Table 37.1).

With an overwhelming majority (where only the anti-immigrant Progress Party voted against), Denmark introduced a very liberal asylum and immigration act in 1983, pronounced the world's most 'people-friendly' law by the Danish Refugee Council

Table 37.1. Percentage of Danish Population with Danish and Immigrant Origin, 1980–2018

	1980	1990	2000	2010	2018
Danish origin	97.0	95.8	92.9	90.2	86.7
First-generation immigrants	2.6	3.5	5.6	7.5	10.2
Second-generation immigrants	0.4	0.7	1.5	2.3	3.1
Total	100	100	100	100	100

Note: Second-generation immigrants are born in Denmark of (first-generation) immigrant parents.

Source: Statistics Denmark, FOLK2.

(Arvin 2012). While the original bill proposed by the Minister of Justice Erik Ninn-Hansen of the Conservative Party was less extensive, the final, adopted policy—pushed by the left-wing opposition—strengthened the legal status of asylum seekers by easing eligibility to apply for and obtain asylum. In addition, the law guaranteed immigrants the right to family reunification with their partner, children under 18, and parents above 60 (if the parents did not have other children in the home country). The act of 1983 coincided with several conflicts around the world, and during the 1980s, Denmark received substantial numbers of refugees from Iraq, Iran, stateless Palestinians, and Tamils from Sri Lanka. In the 1990s, refugees came from Bosnia, Iraq, and Somalia, as well as more stateless Palestinians.

The combination of the 1973 stop for work-related immigration and the 1983 strengthening of refugees' access to asylum and family reunification changed the composition of the immigrant population in Denmark. Many immigrants were not incorporated into the labour market; instead, they were dependent on welfare payments. This led to political discussions on the burden that immigration presented to the Danish welfare state, and in the late 1990s, the centre-left government (consisting of the parties that had pushed for the liberal 1983 law) first drew back immigrants' right to reunification with their parents and later introduced the 'attachment requirement' (*tilknytningskrav*). This requirement stated that in order to be reunified in Denmark with a partner from the home country, the total attachment of the couple to Denmark needed to be at least as great as that to their home country. While previous policies mainly focused on regulating immigration, i.e. the external boundaries of the nation, the first immigrant integration law was passed in 1998, focusing on immigrants' labour market incorporation by cutting the level of welfare payments. However, the law was against EU regulations as it discriminated between nationals and non-nationals, and therefore, the government abolished the policy measure in 2000 (Skaksen and Jensen 2016: 36).

While the initiatives of the centre-left government in the late 1990s did signal somewhat of a withdrawal from Denmark's previously very liberal position, it was not until the turnover of government in 2001 that a real break with the line of policy happened. Election campaigns centred on immigration and immigrant integration issues and the election result signified a substantial change in Danish politics: the former government party, the Social Democratic Party (see Mariager and Olesen 2020), lost eleven mandates, while the Liberal Party (*Venstre*) (see Christiansen 2020) gained fourteen mandates, and the Danish People's Party (see Kosiara-Pedersen 2020) gained nine mandates. The new Liberal-Conservative government (composed of the Liberal Party and the Conservatives with the Danish People's Party as a support party) tightened immigration and immigrant integration policies over the years. This included restricting the right to permanent residence in connection to family reunification and asylum while making it easier to come to Denmark to work, particularly in specialized fields. The Liberal-Conservative government also made substantial cuts in welfare benefits by introducing a new scheme (*starthjælpen*) for non-EU and non-Nordic refugees and immigrants. As formulated by several ministers, this was a 'quid pro quo' policy intended to strengthen immigrants' economic incentives to seek work by making it relatively less 'attractive' to be on welfare benefits (Jønsson 2018: 84–6). As such, the policy broke with the classic principle of unconditional welfare benefits that is characteristic of the universal welfare state (see Petersen 2020). The economic integration measure was abolished by the centre-left government that held power from October 2011 to February 2014 but reintroduced by the new Liberal-Conservative government in 2015 (under the name *integrationsydelse*). To respect EU regulations, the cuts in welfare payments apply to individuals, including Danish nationals, who have lived for more than one year out of the past eight years outside of the Kingdom of Denmark (see Gad 2020).

By 2019, Denmark has moved toward one of the most restrictive policy positions in Western Europe. Not least in response to the 2015/2016 'refugee crisis' across Europe, access to asylum has been further restricted. In fact, a set of policies that the Danish People's Party succeeded in coining 'the paradigm shift' stresses that refugees should not be integrated into Danish society: the clear goal is that they return home as soon as possible (Korsgaard 2018). In this connection, the reduced welfare benefits available to immigrants and refugees have been renamed from 'integration benefit' to 'repatriation benefit' (*hjemsendelsesydelse*).

For those who do stay, becoming a Danish citizen is also increasingly difficult and deliberately so, as repeatedly underlined by the former Minister of Integration Inger Støjberg of the Liberal Party (Ritzau 2018). To get a sense of the Danish policy development in a comparative perspective, Table 37.2 (updated from Jensen 2016: 25) displays the citizenship regimes of Denmark and neighbouring Sweden and Norway since 1995. As can be seen, while Sweden has maintained a very liberal position, both Norway and Denmark have introduced a number of restrictions, the most extensive of which are in Denmark. Citizenship is (still) seen in Sweden as a catalyst or starting point for immigrants' integration, whereas in Denmark, it is now considered a prize or reward that immigrants should only receive once having demonstrated their complete integration (Ersbøll 2010: 137–9; Mortensen 2018).

The most recent addition to the list of criteria for naturalization is participation in a constitutional ceremony where the applicant is officially granted Danish citizenship by signing a loyalty declaration and shaking hands with the mayor in his/her municipality. The heavily debated 'handshake requirement'—explicitly pitted against 'Muslims who do not wish to shake hands with the opposite gender' (former Minister of Integration Inger Støjberg in an interview with Olsen [2018])—exemplifies the development of the policy field. The earlier focus on integration through work has been supplemented with strong demands on immigrants to not only learn about but also actively demonstrate their commitment to Danish norms and values (Jønsson 2018: 86–7). While these norms are founded in liberal-democratic principles (gender equality, freedom rights, etc.), they are presented by Danish politicians as part of a deep, national culture (Mouritsen and Olsen 2013). Therefore, integration is considered to require a long process of socialization on the part of immigrants, with the Danish national community being historically fixed and not open for dynamic redevelopment (Jensen 2014). In this connection, it is worth noting the strong focus in public and political discourse on 'descendants' (*efterkommere*), i.e. children born in Denmark of immigrant parents. Politicians highlight

Table 37.2. Requirements for Citizenship in the Scandinavian Countries, 1995–2019

	Language requirements[a]			Citizenship test			Social benefits			Dual citizenship allowed			Years of residence[d]		
	DK	NO	SE	DK	NO	SE	DK	NO	SE	DK	NO	SE	DK	NO	SE
1995	Informal	-	-	-	-	-	-	-	-	-	-	-	7/6	7	5/4
2005	B1	-	-	-	-	-	-	-	-	-	-	Yes	9/8	7	5/4
2015	B2	-	-	Yes	-	-	Yes[b]	-	-	Yes	-	Yes	9/8	7	5/4
2019	B2	A2	-	Yes	Yes	-	Yes[b]	-	-	Yes	-[c]	Yes	9/8	7	5/4

a. Language requirements are translated into the Common European Framework for Reference for Language. A1 is beginner, and C2 is proficient user.
b. The applicant must not have received unemployment benefits for more than four months within the past five years and not at all during the past two years.
c. On 8 December 2018, the Norwegian Parliament passed a law to allow dual citizenship. It will take at least one year until the new rules are introduced.
d. Number before/after the slash: the number of years required for immigrants/refugees.

continued integration challenges for this group (and even for their children, 'the third generation', cf. Ministry of Immigration and Integration and Ministry of Education [2018]), citing higher levels of crime and lower levels of employment, among other things (Danish Government 2018). Not counted as part of the 'ethnically Danish' population in official statistics, this group makes up 3 per cent of the Danish population overall (cf. Table 37.1) and 10 per cent of the population under age 25 (Statistics Denmark, FOLK1C, my calculations).

ANTI-IMMIGRANT DANES?

What explains the substantial shift from liberal to restrictive policies within the past few decades? As suggested in much of the international journalistic reporting, one potential driver of policy developments is public opinion (Orange 2018). This explanation is based on a cornerstone principle of representative democracy by which elected politicians govern their country according to the will of (the majority of) the people. Consequently, cross-national policy differences should reflect cross-national differences in the populations' convictions on immigration issues, as well as Danish public opinion having moved in a more restrictive direction over time.

Assessing the longitudinal perspective requires data tracing public opinion to before some of the substantial changes in policy. The first piece of evidence that offers such a long time span addresses opinions about immigrants' access to citizenship, in particular whether conforming to Danish behavioural norms should be a condition for naturalization. Of course, what it means to 'behave like Danes' is open to interpretation, but the focus on a particular type of (Danish) behaviour taps into the prioritization of civic values that was characteristic of the citizenship policy changes introduced by the Liberal-Conservative government and the Danish People's Party in December 2005 (coming into effect in 2007; Goodman 2014: 112; see also Table 37.2). In particular, the higher demand on language proficiency and on testing immigrants' knowledge of Danish history, society, and culture was motivated—in the words of the then Minister for Integration Rikke Hvilshøj—by a wish to make sure immigrants know 'how to get along in Danish society' (Ersbøll 2010: 138). Table 37.3 displays the percentage of respondents in nationally representative samples who would *not* make 'behaving like Danes' a requirement for obtaining citizenship. While the question is not asked regularly and not in recent years, the story suggested in Table 37.3 is one of stability, with a small relaxation in 1993 and 2003 of behavioural demands on prospective citizens. In other words, there is no evidence for Danish public opinion pushing for the citizenship test and the heightened language requirements that were passed in December 2005. If anything, there seems to have been a stronger push in 1970 than in the years leading up to the passing of the law.

Survey data has also been collected over an extended period on the extent to which Danes view immigration as a threat to maintaining 'our distinct national character' and on their support for immigrants' equal access to social benefits. The first question concerns the need for protecting the external boundaries of the nation, while the latter concerns hierarchies of deservingness in relation to the internal boundaries of the nation. What stands out again is the relative stability over time in Danes' opinions of immigrants, cf. Figures 37.2 and 37.3. There is some fluctuation, but the movements in public opinion have not been as dramatic as policy developments would suggest, and on both measures, the balance of public opinion in 1987/94 is very similar to that in 2015. In addition, 2001, the year of the government turnover from centre-left to centre-right seen to mark an important break with the previous line of policy, seems to be a modal year on both questions. To underline this finding, a comprehensive analysis of survey data collected over the period 1993–2003 concluded that Danes' attitudes on more than twenty-five questions related to immigration and immigrant integration were surprisingly

Table 37.3. 'Danish Behaviour' as a Condition for Danish Citizenship

Year	Per cent refusing the statement that 'foreigners should only be able to obtain Danish citizenship when they have learnt to behave like Danes'
1970	43
1993	55
2003	48
2006	45

Source: Table 4.1 in Togeby (2004: 60), updated with my own analyses for 2006.

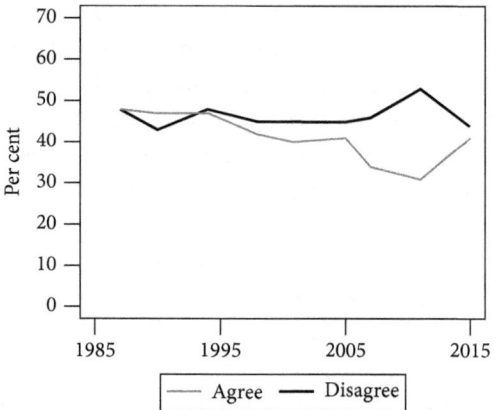

FIGURE 37.2 External boundary: Immigration as a serious threat to 'our distinct national character', 1967/88–2015.

Notes: Percent indicating agreement/disagreement with the statement 'Immigration constitutes a serious threat to our distinct national character'. N = 17066

Source: Danish Election Studies

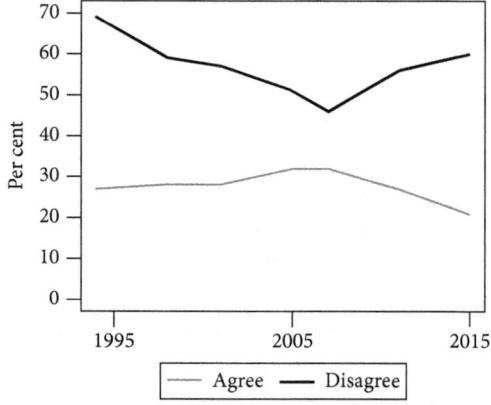

FIGURE 37.3 Internal boundary: Immigrants' equal access to social benefits, 1994–2015.

Notes: Percent indicating agreement/disagreement with the statement 'Refugees and immigrants should have the same right to social benefits as Danes, even if they are not Danish citizens'. N = 15905

Source: Danish Election Studies

stable (Togeby 2004: 50–77; see also Larsen 2016: 91–5). In addition, the fluctuations that could be detected during that period coincided with intense media coverage of immigration and refugee stories. Once media attention withdrew, public opinion returned to previous levels.

The public opinion thesis fares no better when turning to cross-national comparisons. Table 37.4 compares Danish public opinion to that of the country's neighbours (Germany, Sweden, and Norway) and to big immigrant receiving countries in Western Europe (France, the UK, and the Netherlands). In this comparison, Danes stand out as

Table 37.4. Public Opinion in Selected Western European Countries, Percentage Restrictive/Anti-Immigrant Responses, 2014

	DK	D	F	UK	NL	N	S
It is generally bad for [country's] economy that people come to live here from other countries[a]	36	*24*	**41**	39	36	*24*	*24*
[Country's] cultural life is undermined by immigrants[a]	27	21	33	**40**	20	26	*10*
Immigrants make [country] a worse place to live[a]	23	29	33	**41**	27	25	*12*
Immigrants make [country's] crime problems worse[a]	59	64	*46*	53	69	**76**	56
Immigrants take out more than they put in (taxes and services)[a]	42	31	42	43	**47**	34	*26*
Government should be generous judging applications for refugee status (strongly disagree + disagree)	29	34	17	28	**46**	18	*10*
Allow many or few Muslims to come and live in [country] (few + none)	**46**	31	35	**46**	**46**	34	*19*

Note: Bold indicates most restrictive/anti-immigrant public opinion in the seven-country comparison; italics indicate most liberal/pro-immigrant public opinion in the seven-country comparison.
a: Scores 0–4 on 0 (bad/undermined/worse/take out more) to 10 (good/enriched/better/put in more) scale.
Source: My analyses of ESS7 (2014) data.

the most restrictive population only on one question: whether to allow many or few Muslims to come and live in the country. What is more, Danes share their restrictive position with the British and the Dutch on this issue (in all three countries, 46 per cent of the population think that none or only a few Muslims should be allowed to come and live in the country). In addition, only on the question of immigrants' potentially negative impact on the country's crime problems does a majority of Danish respondents subscribe to negative judgement. Again, this is not exceptional in comparison with other Western European populations.

It even appears that the Danes have become slightly more liberal/pro-immigrant over the years, while other populations have become slightly more restrictive/anti-immigrant. Based on 2002 data from the same survey programme looking at the same countries (except Norway which is added here) and some of the same issues, Sniderman et al. (2014: 15) concluded that 'Denmark tends to score toward the higher end of opposition to immigrants, but not markedly or distinctively more so than comparable countries'. What stood out in 2002 and what stands out in the most recent (2014) data reported here is the liberal/pro-immigrant attitudes of Swedes compared to the other populations. In that sense, Sweden—not Denmark—is the exceptional case.

To further boost the conclusion from this cross-national comparison, two findings are worth highlighting. Analysing survey data from 2003 and 2013 on the criteria that non-immigrant majority populations require immigrants to meet in order to be considered part of the nation, Simonsen (2016a) finds that Danes fall in a middle field compared to populations in other Western democracies. In particular, Danes value attainable criteria such as citizenship and language skills to a very high degree and ascriptive criteria such as religion and being born in the country to a relatively high degree. This finding is echoed in an analysis of inclusive/exclusive attitudes toward immigrants across Western European countries in the period from 2002–12. Danes are generally slightly more inclusive than exclusive, a balance of opinion that leads Denmark to be placed in a middle field when ranking national populations from the most exclusive to most inclusive (Simonsen 2016b). Finally, the analyses demonstrate a high degree of stability in these attitudes over time, not only in Denmark but across the countries included in the two studies.

To conclude, Danes may be said to be restrictive/anti-immigrant on some issues (especially in relation to anti-Muslim sentiment, their view of immigrants as welfare exploiters and criminals, and valuing ascriptive criteria of national belonging). However, on many issues, public opinion is quite divided, with at least as many Danes exhibiting relatively liberal and pro-immigrant attitudes as the opposite. In addition, Danes are no more restrictive than other Western European populations, and public opinion has neither changed significantly nor unequivocally in a more restrictive direction, in particular not to a degree comparable to the policy changes in the field.

POLITICAL DYNAMICS AND POLITICIZATION

While a certain level of restrictive/anti-immigrant sentiment in the population may be a necessary condition for making substantial policy changes in the field, it does not appear to be sufficient for explaining Danish immigration and immigrant integration policy developments. Instead, a handful of studies point to autonomous (party) political dynamics. The central argument is that substantial policy shifts only occurred when it became advantageous for mainstream political parties to change policy strategies and make immigration issues an arena for party competition, in effect politicizing the issue.

To appreciate this argument, one needs to consider the political conditions of the 1970s and 1980s, which—despite potential popular support for a more restrictive line of policy as evidenced above—led all mainstream parties to support a rather liberal/moderate policy position, thus ensuring minimal political competition over immigration issues. Except for shorter flashes of public debate in connection to specific media stories, the 1970s and 1980s were not characterized by extensive party-political attention to immigration and immigrant integration issues. The 1980s did present politicization opportunities (e.g. in the form of media stories about problems at asylum centres), but the Liberal-Conservative minority government were dependent on parliamentary support from the Social Liberals (*Radikale Venstre*) who subscribed to a multicultural and liberal view on immigration issues (Green-Pedersen 2009: 69). The government already had problems with the so-called 'alternative majority' deciding on the country's foreign policy (and in some cases environmental and justice policy) and could not afford to lose face on other issues. In fact, this is part of the explanation for the broad support across the political spectrum for the very liberal 1983 asylum act (see above). The Liberal-Conservative minority government ended up supporting a more liberal law than the one it had initially proposed because a majority (interested in making the government look weak) had already formed. By supporting the more liberal version of the law, the new government (of 1982) saved face by avoiding being immediately overruled by the left-wing opposition (Brøcker 1990: 337–8).

However, when the Social Liberals entered into government with the Social Democratic Party in 1993, it was obvious to the Liberals that they, together with the Conservative Party, had to find support from other parties if they were to build up a new majority to take over government. In this situation, it became advantageous to politicize immigration issues and form a partnership with the Danish People's Party. The fact that the Danish People's Party arrived at the scene as a more 'moderate' party than the extreme right-wing Progress Party (from which the founders of the Danish People's Party broke out in 1995) made it easier for the Liberal-Conservative opposition to cooperate with an anti-immigrant party (Green-Pedersen 2009). Thus, the 1990s were characterized by strong politicization of immigration issues, which also contributed to exposing disagreement within the centre-left government. In a comparative study of Denmark and Sweden, Green-Pedersen and Krogstrup (2008: 628) convincingly demonstrate how 'the difference in politicization between Denmark and Sweden in the 1990s can thus be explained by whether or not the mainstream right-wing parties have been forced to seek government power with the support of Social Liberals or centre par-ties'. This was the case in Sweden but not an option in Denmark, in turn making room for the Danish People's Party to influence the Liberal-Conservative opposition. In fact, Green-Pedersen and Otjes (2017: 8) argue that 'the change of strategy of the Liberals after having given away power in 1993 seems the decisive moment in terms of turning immigration into a central issue of Danish party competition'.

The question remains as to why the Social Democratic Party also moved considerably from moderate scepticism concerning work-related migration in the 1970s combined with advocacy for a very liberal asylum regime to recent years' support for the Liberal-Conservative government's restrictive measures (not least in relation to refugees' rights). Most recently, the Social Democrats have even proposed policies that compete with those of the Liberal-Conservative government in restrictiveness. As discussed, strategic concerns led the Social Democratic Party together with the Social-Liberal Party to exert liberalizing pressures on the Liberal-Conservative government in the 1980s. However, the combination of increased politicization in the 1990s and internal divisions within the party (and thus, within the government), led the Social Democrats to pursue a strat-egy of diffusion (Bale et al. 2010). The internal divisions were mainly a matter of national versus local politics: as far back as the 1980s, Social Democratic mayors from munici-palities around Copenhagen with many immigrants voiced their concerns over problems with immigrant integration, while national level politicians maintained a liberal position (Bale et al. 2010: 415; Jønsson 2018: 59–62). Some scholars even suggest that Social Democratic parliamentarians did not have strong ideological commitments but were rather 'ideologically blind' (Jensen 2016: 70) and failed to formulate 'any notion of nationhood that speaks to the relationship between a multicultural society and the universal welfare state' (ibid.: 70). This made the party 'unable, or unwilling, to present strong alternative frames, or counter-frames, of how to define social problems in contemporary Denmark' that could compete with the Liberal-Conservative government's increasingly restrictive frame (Rydgren 2004: 491).

After the defeat in 2001, the Social Democratic Party switched to a strategy of adopting the right-wing position on immigration and immigrant integration. Bale et al. (2010) suggest that this strategy was not only a response to the challenge presented by the Danish People's Party capturing working-class voters from the Social Democratic Party; it was also a necessity given the strategy of other mainstream parties (in particular the centre-right). If the centre-right had not politicized the area, diffusion would have been an effective strategy. However, in light of the continued politicization, the Social Democratic Party was pushed to take a clearer stance (Bale et al. 2010: 415). Combined with the alleged lack of ideological commitment within the party, this made room for the Danish Social Democrats to move toward a much more restrictive position on immigration and immigrant integration issues than Social Democratic parties have done in other countries (Jensen 2016: 70–1; Nedergaard 2018: 5). While the scholarly literature considers such a substantial shift in policy position (a shift that mimics the opponent) to be in risk of damaging a party's credibility, leading members of the Social Democratic Party have sought to underline the historical foundation of the restrictive policy position. For instance, in a recent book, the party's then spokesman on foreigners (and now minister of integration) argues that the Social Democratic Party has rediscovered its working-class roots by finally respecting the cry from the Copenhagen mayors and workers' unions (Tesfaye 2017). This framing is echoed in the party's largescale immigration policy proposal of 2018, which—in acknowledging that the Social Democrats have made a restrictive turn—presents the new(/old) policy position as necessary, given the financial burden that immigrants present to 'our' (i.e. the Social-Democratic) welfare state (Social Democratic Party 2018).

In sum, the present analysis suggests that while public opinion cannot stand alone as an explanation for the developments in Danish immigration and immigrant integration policy, (party) political dynamics in Denmark have made immigration issues particularly salient to Danish voters, long before it received the same kind of popular attention in other countries. Public concern over immigration did not increase in the period studied, but Danish politicians made existing concerns more salient among voters and thus increased the political relevance of these concerns. To illustrate, while 4–6 per cent of Norwegian voters mentioned immigration as important for their vote in 1993, 1997, and 2001, and 12–13 per cent of Swedish voters mentioned immigration as important for politicians to deal with during the period 1993–2003, 51 per cent of Danish voters said the same in 2001 (Togeby 2004: 50). One consequence of the politicized climate in Denmark is that Danish voters are more ideologically motivated when forming opinions about immigration policy. A comparative study of Denmark and Sweden spanning the period 1990–2008 shows that the individual-level association between self-reported ideology and ethnic exclusionism (measured in terms of respondents' support for reducing the number of refugees accepted to the country) is much stronger in Denmark than in Sweden (Jensen and Thomsen 2011). In other words, one effect of the intense politicization driven by Danish politicians has been to create a feedback mechanism by which immigration has become more ideologically divisive and electorally relevant for voters.

POLICY AND POLITICIZATION EFFECTS

Given how politicians motivate policy changes, a relevant topic of study are the potential effects of these policies for majority-minority relations and immigrant integration. It is important to note that policy effects are complicated to assess because of the difficulty in isolating causes. In addition, I will argue that it is impossible to assess potential policy effects for several outcomes without considering the interacting and/or independent effects of politicization.

As already discussed, one consequence of politicization is the tendency for Danish voters to be more ideologically polarized on immigration issues than voters in countries such as Sweden where the issue has been less politicized. However, evidence also suggests that politicization can have a surprising positive effect on majority-minority relations. A common finding within the 'contact literature' is that majority members' contact with minority individuals can serve to break down prejudice and negative attitudes. This mechanism has been found to be stronger in contexts such as the Danish where intergroup relations are politicized (Sønderskov and Thomsen 2015). The authors suggest that because politicization heightens the salience of us-them categorizations in everyday interactions, majority members are more aware of immigrants' out-group status in these encounters. Positive contact experiences with individual immigrants are more likely to be 'generalized' to immigrants as a group as a result (Sønderskov and Thomsen 2015).

Simonsen's work contributes further to underlining the independent effect of politicization on immigrant integration outcomes. In particular, while she does not find any evidence that citizenship *policies* affect first and second-generation immigrants' sense of belonging to the nation (Simonsen 2016a), she demonstrates—on the basis of a Danish case study and statistical analyses of cross-national survey and manifesto data from eighteen Western European countries over a 12-year period—that anti-immigrant political *rhetoric* has a negative effect on immigrants' political trust and faith in democracy (Simonsen in press). As the Danish case is characterized by extreme levels of anti-immigrant political rhetoric compared to other Western European countries (as measured in party manifestos) (Simonsen in press; Sønderskov and Thomsen 2015), this finding gives reason for concern over the future political incorporation of immigrant minorities in Denmark. One may speculate that this is part of the explanation for first and second-generation immigrants' low turnout at Danish elections. While access to participation in local Danish elections is comparatively easy (anyone, including non-citizens, who has resided in Denmark for four years is allowed to vote), the turnout gap between majority Danes and first and second-generation immigrants is more than 30 per cent. This gap cannot be explained by the literature's standard resource-related explanations (Bhatti and Hansen 2017), suggesting that other factors such as political alienation may be at play. Investigating this hypothesis is an important task for future research.

A final set of findings concerning policy effects focuses on naturalization. One may argue that to assess the restrictiveness of Danish citizenship policy, one should not only compare policy regimes 'on paper' but also examine whether immigrants are really prevented from obtaining citizen status in countries with high requirements. In a study of refugees granted asylum in Denmark between 2007 and 2009, Bech et al. (2017) show that only 23 per cent live up to the requirements for citizenship in 2017. A substantial number of refugees fall for the high language requirement. If the language requirement was relaxed, 52 per cent of the refugees included in the study would have been able to naturalize (ibid.). The stricter rules for obtaining citizenship can also be read in official statistics. In the beginning of the 2000s, 15,000-20,000 immigrants naturalized each year, but this fell markedly after 2005 to a level below 5,000 a year (Statistics Denmark 2018) at the same time as immigration rates increased (cf. Figure 37.1). In recent rounds of the citizenship test, pass rates have been just above 50 per cent, suggesting that the test is not merely symbolic but excludes people who otherwise live up to the citizenship demands from becoming Danish citizens. In 2018, 25 per cent of immigrants in Denmark were Danish citizens (Statistics Denmark, FOLK2, my calculations), compared to 57 per cent of immigrants in Sweden being Swedish citizens (Statistics Sweden 2019). A hypothesis for future study is that an additional factor hindering immigrants from naturalizing is the discouraging effects of policy and politicization that may deter some from even starting the application process.

CONCLUSION

Substantial shifts in Danish immigration and immigrant integration policies have made international headlines in recent years as well as occupied academic research. This chapter demonstrates that the restrictive policy turn is explained neither easily nor straightforwardly by Danes being exceptionally anti-immigrant. Instead, what appears consequential is the strategically driven politicization which resonated with public concerns and made the immigration issue salient to Danish voters. This also made the Danish People's Party a key player in Danish politics, driving first the centre-right to seek support from the party, and later to Social Democratic flirtations; in 2018, Social Democratic parliamentarians voiced the possibility of entering into government with the Danish People's Party in a few years (Larsen and Henriksen 2018)—a scenario that was completely unimaginable just a few years ago.

However, the parliamentary election results of June 2019 suggest that the Danish People's Party may have been undermined by its own (policy) success. In particular, the party lost more than half of its seats (vote share 2019: 8.7; vote share 2015: 21.1), while the Social Democratic Party maintained its size (vote share 2019: 25.9; vote share 2015: 26.3), and as the biggest party in Parliament, succeeded in taking over government power. This result is seen by many commentators as evidence of the effectiveness of the Social Democratic Party's restrictive turn, including the framing of this turn as based on concerns for the survival of the Social Democratic welfare state. The significance of this result becomes even more evident in comparison to the struggle of many contemporary European Social Democratic parties to hold on to their voter bases.

Does the decline of the Danish People's Party and the overall agreement on the restrictive line of policy between the two biggest parties in Parliament, the Liberals and the Social Democrats, signal a new era in Danish politics with decreased politicization of immigration? That clearly was the goal of the Social Democratic leader and now Prime Minister Mette Frederiksen who during the election campaign repeatedly underscored her commitment to maintaining the 'tight immigration policy that a large majority both in the population and in parliament support' (Ingvorsen 2019). However, the June 2019 election did not see immigration disappear from the political agenda. Quite the opposite, as the left-wing parties—especially the centre-left Social Liberals—that now support the Social Democratic government campaigned on platforms to draw back some of the restrictive policies of the former government. In effect, while traditional welfare issues and the environment did take up some space, immigration was again centre stage in election debates.

It is never wise to make predictions about future policy developments, especially not with highly politicized issues. However, it does appear that the restrictive move on immigration and immigrant integration policy may have plateaued out, for now at least. In particular, while the Social Democratic Party is committed to many of the former government's policies, the Social Liberals have pushed for changes that, albeit somewhat small in substantive terms, carry symbolic weight. For instance, Denmark is to receive UN refugees again (after refusing such refugees since 2016), and the stated goal of policy is integration, not (only) repatriation.

Considering the potential outcomes of current policies, existing research demonstrates the mixed and sometimes ambiguous effects of the restrictive turn and strong politicization. For instance, while immigration issues are more ideologically divisive for Danish voters, the politicization of group identities also appears to make the majority of Danes more responsive to positive contact experiences with immigrants. In addition, while there is no evidence for restrictive citizenship policies affecting immigrants' belonging in a negative direction, the Danish citizenship regime limits immigrants and refugees' access to becoming Danish citizens, and the tone of political debate risks damaging immigrants' sense of political inclusion. Future research should examine how politicization interacts with policy changes and public opinion to affect immigrant integration outcomes such as political engagement and social incorporation more broadly. These outcomes may in turn have their own impact on future policy developments.

REFERENCES

Abend, Lisa (2019, 16 January). 'An island for "unwanted" migrants is Denmark's latest agres-sive anti-immigrant policy', *time.com*.

Arvin, Sanne (2012). 'Kampen om indvandringen', https://www.dr.dk/presse/kampen-om-indvandringen (accessed 7 December 2019).

Bale, Tim, Christoffer Green-Pedersen, André Krouwel, Kurt R. Luther, and Nick Sitter (2010). 'If you can't beat them, join them? Explaining social democratic responses to the challenge from the populist radical right in Western Europe', *Political Studies*, 58/3: 410–26.

Bech, Emily C., Kristian K. Jensen, Per Mouritsen, and Tore V. Olsen (2017). 'Hvem er folket? Flygtninge og adgangen til dansk statsborgerskab', *Politica*, 49/3: 227–48.

Bhatti, Yosef, and Kasper M. Hansen (2017). 'Valgdeltagelsen blandt ikke-vestlige indvandrere og efterkommere', *Politica*, 49/3: 249–72.

Brøcker, Anne (1990). 'Udlændingelovgivning i Danmark 1983–86: Faktorer i den politiske beslutningsproces', *Politica*, 22/2: 332–435.

Christiansen, Flemming J. (2020). 'The Liberal Party. From agrarian and liberal to centre-right catch-all', in Peter M. Christiansen, Jørgen Elklit, and Peter Nedergaard, eds, *The Oxford Handbook of Danish Politics*. Oxford: Oxford University Press, 296–312.

Danish Government (2018). *Ét Danmark uden parallelsamfund—Ingen ghettoer i 2030*. Copenhagen: Danish Government.

Ersbøll, Eva (2010). 'On trial in Denmark', in Ricky van Oers, Eva Ersbøll, and Dora Kostakopoulou, eds, *A Re-definition of Belonging? Languag and Integration Tests in Europe*. The Hague: Brill-Nijhoff, 107–52.

Gad, Ulrik P. (2020). 'Greenland, the Faroe Islands, and Denmark. Unity or community?', in Peter M. Christiansen, Jørgen Elklit, and Peter Nedergaard, eds, *The Oxford Handbook of Danish Politics*. Oxford: Oxford University Press, 28–45.

Gammeltoft-Hansen, Thomas, and Helle Malmvig (2016, 4 May). 'The ugly duckling: Denmark's anti-refugee policies and Europe's race to the bottom', *The Huffington Post*.

Goodman, Sara W. (2014). *Immigration and Membership Politics in Western Europe*. Cambridge: Cambridge University Press.

Green-Pedersen, Christoffer (2009). 'Hvordan kom flygtninge- og indvandrerspørgsmålet på den politiske dagsorden?', in Jens Blom-Hansen and Jørgen Elklit, eds, *Perspektiver på politik. Bidrag til samfundsdebatten*. Aarhus: Academica, 67–72.

Green-Pedersen, Christoffer, and Jesper Krogstrup (2008). 'Immigration as a political issue in Denmark and Sweden', *European Journal of Political Research*, 47/5: 610–34.

Green-Pedersen, Christoffer, and Simon Otjes (2017). 'A hot topic? Immigration on the agenda in Western Europe', *Party Politics*, Online first: 1–11.

Ingvorsen, Emil Søndergård (2019, 11 June). 'Mette Fredriksen står fast på stram udlænding-epolitik – nu skal der forhandles', *dr.dk*.

Jensen, Carsten, and Jens Peter F. Thomsen (2011). 'Can party competition amplify mass ideo-logical polarization over public policy? The case of ethnic exclusionism in Denmark and Sweden', *Party Politics*, 19/5: 821–40.

Jensen, Kristian K. (2014). 'What can and cannot be willed: How politicians talk about national identity and immigrants', *Nations and Nationalism*, 20/3: 563–83.

Jensen, Kristian K. (2016). *Scandinavian Immigrant Integration Policies: Varieties of the Civic Turn*. Aarhus: Politicas ph.d.-serie.

Jønsson, Heidi V. (2018). *Indvandring i velfærdsstaten*. Aarhus: Aarhus Universitetsforlag.

Korsgaard, Kristine (2018, 30 November). 'Sådan endte DF's paradigmeskifte: "Jeg kan ikke give garanti for et tal, men jeg kan give garanti for, at det virker"', *Altinget*.

Kosiara-Pedersen, Karina (2020). 'The Danish People's Party. Centre-oriented populists?', in Peter M. Christiansen, Jørgen Elklit, and Peter Nedergaard, eds, *The Oxford Handbook of Danish Politics*. Oxford: Oxford University Press, 313–328.

Larsen, Christian A. (2016). *Den danske republik. Forandringer i danskernes nationale forestillinger*. Copenhagen: Hans Reitzels Forlag.

Larsen, Johan B., and Morten Henriksen (2018, 22 November). 'Socialdemokratiske folketingsmedlemmer åbner for regering med DF om nogle år', *dr.dk*.

Mariager, Rasmus M., and Niels W. Olesen (2020). 'The Social Democratic Party. From exponent of societal change to pragmatic conservatism', in Peter M. Christiansen, Jørgen Elklit, and Peter Nedergaard, eds, *The Oxford Handbook of Danish Politics*. Oxford: Oxford University Press, 278–295.

Ministry of Immigration and Integration, and Ministry of Education (2018). *Analyse af børn af efterkommere med ikke-vestlig oprindelse*. Copenhagen: Ministry of Immigration and Integration, and Ministry of Education.

Mortensen, Mikkel W. (2018, 15 May). 'Der er kæmpe stor forskel på at være født som dansk statsborger og at ønske at blive dansk statsborger', *Berlingske Tidende*.

Mouritsen, Per, and Tore V. Olsen (2013). 'Denmark between Liberalism and Nationalism', *Ethnic and Racial Studies*, 36/4: 691–710.

Nedergaard, Peter (2018). 'Back to its roots: Why do the Danish Social Democrats want a more restrictive immigration policy?', *Friedrich Ebert Stiftung*, 1–7, http://library.fes.de/pdf-files/bueros/budapest/14498.pdf (accessed 10 December 2019).

Olsen, Theis L. (2018, 3 November). 'Inger Støjberg efter V-kritik af håndtryk: 'Ingen er tvunget til at blive dansker', *dr.dk*.

Orange, Richard (2018, 10 June). 'Denmark swings right on immigration – and Muslims feel besieged', *The Guardian*, sec. *The Observer*.

Pedersen, Søren (1999). 'Vandringen til og fra Danmark i perioden 1960-1997', in David Coleman and Eskil Wadensjö, eds, *Indvandringen til Danmark. Internationale og nationale perspektiver*. Copenhagen: Rockwool Fonden, 233–84.

Petersen, Klaus (2020). 'Welfare state policies. From the beginning towards an end?', in Peter M. Christiansen, Jørgen Elklit, and Peter Nedergaard, eds, *The Oxford Handbook of Danish Politics*. Oxford: Oxford University Press, 540–558.

Ritzau (2018, 15 May). 'Støjberg: Det er ganske særligt at blive dansk statsborger', *Jyllands-Posten*.

Rydgren, Jens (2004). 'Explaining the emergence of radical right-wing populist parties: The case of Denmark', *West European Politics*, 27/3: 474–502.

Simonsen, Kristina B. (2016a). 'How the host nation's boundary drawing affects immigrants' belonging', *Journal of Ethnic and Migration Studies*, 42/7: 1153–76.

Simonsen, Kristina B. (2016b). 'Ripple effects: An exclusive host national context produces more perceived discrimination among immigrants', *European Journal of Political Research*, 55/2: 374–90.

Simonsen, Kristina B. (in press). 'The democratic consequences of anti-immigrant political rhetoric: A mixed methods study of immigrants' political belonging', *Political Behavior*.

Skaksen, Jan R., and Bent Jensen (2016). *Hvad ved vi om indvandring og integration? Indvandringen til Danmark og forløbet af integrationen fra 1960'erne til i dag*. Copenhagen: Gyldendal.

Sniderman, Paul M., Michael B. Petersen, Rune Slothuus, and Rune Stubager (2014). *Paradoxes of Liberal Democracy: Islam, Western Europe and the Danish Cartoon Crisis*. Princeton, NJ: Princeton University Press.

Social Democratic Party (2018). 'Retfærdig og realistisk. En udlændingepolitik der samler Danmark'.

Statistics Denmark (2018). 'Skift til dansk statsborgerskab', https://www.dst.dk/da/Statistik/emner/befolkning-og-valg/indvandrere-og-efterkommere/skift-til-dansk-statsborgerskab (accessed 21 January 2019).

Statistics Sweden (2019). 'Summary of population statistics, 1960–2018', https://www.scb.se/en/finding-statistics/statistics-by-subject-area/population/population-composition/population-statistics/pong/tables-and-graphs/yearly-statistics—the-whole-country/summary-of-population-statistics/ (accessed 1 July 2019).

Sønderskov, Kim M., and Jens Peter F. Thomsen (2015). 'Contextualizing intergroup contact: Do political party cues enhance contact effects?', *Social Psychology Quarterly*, 78/1: 49–76.

Tesfaye, Mathias (2017). *Velkommen Mustafa. 50 års socialdemokratisk udlændingepolitik* Copenhagen: Gyldendal.

Togeby, Lise (2004). *Man har et standpunkt... Om forandring og stabilitet i befolkningens holdninger*. Aarhus: Aarhus Universitetsforlag.

UNHCR, The UN Refugee Agency (2011). 'UNHCR marks 60th anniversary of Refugee Convention', http://www.unhcr.org/4e3106fa6.html (accessed 23 October 2018).

CHAPTER 38

AGRICULTURAL AND FISHERIES POLICY

Towards Market Liberalism

CARSTEN DAUGBJERG, PEDER ANDERSEN, HENNING
OTTE HANSEN, AND BRIAN H. JACOBSEN

MARKET ORIENTATION OF AGRICULTURAL AND FISHERIES POLICIES

DANISH agricultural policy has a strong focus on facilitating and assisting farmers in improving their market returns, enabling them to compensate for the declining terms of trade. For decades, Danish agricultural policy has been aimed at providing conditions that enable efficient farmers to remain competitive in international markets, primarily within the EU (Daugbjerg 1998). Recent policy developments resemble this strategy. At the same time, the environmental impact of intensive farming methods practiced in the Danish farming sector continues to cause concern and necessitate agri-environmental policy measures. Successive governments have accepted that environmental regulation inflicts costs on farmers, but recently, the government has attempted to reduce the regulatory burden by introducing a more targeted regulatory approach believed to reduce the regulatory costs. Furthermore, measures are to a larger extent financed by the state or through the EU Rural Development Programme than was previously the case.

Danish policy strategy in the agricultural sector can be characterized as a move towards market liberalism, based on the realization that incomes in relative terms must increasingly be derived from the market. The policy strategy is aimed at providing enabling conditions for farmers to survive in a situation in which farm support will gradually lose relative importance, and markets will become more global. To reduce regulatory burdens, the government has set out to remove or reform regulations that hamper adjustment to these envisaged conditions for farming while ensuring that the negative externalities are addressed. Over the last ten years, Danish fisheries policy has moved—within the Common Fisheries Policy (CFP) framework—towards a very market-oriented system by implementing an ITQ system (Individually Transferable Quotas) for most of the fishery (European Union 2013). This has resulted in a significant increase in productivity and profitability. As a result, market interventions and subsidies are of less importance today.

In this chapter, we select three national agricultural policies to illustrate that market liberalism has gained a stronger foothold in the agricultural sector. Policies aimed at reducing nutrient run-offs are shifting from reliance on universal measures to more emphasis on site-specific regulation. Restrictions on farm ownership have been considerably lessened. Danish organic farming and food policy is distinct as it is actively pursuing market-driven development. Danish fisheries policy has evolved into a property rights-based and market-based management system for most fisheries.

Market Liberalism

Since the early 1990s, Denmark has belonged to the liberal group of member states in EU agricultural policy-making which has been attempting to pull the Common Agricultural Policy (CAP) in a more market liberal direction (see Jensen and Nedergaard 2020). In fisheries policy, Denmark has also pursued a more market liberal policy strategy by implementing national regulatory measures based on individually transferable fishing rights. A market liberal policy paradigm prescribes a limited role for the state in the two sectors as 'market allocation takes precedence over state intervention, and efficiency over equity' (Coleman et al. 1996: 275–6).

Despite its more market liberal stance than most other European countries, there has been very little research aimed at identifying the liberalization trends in the developments of Danish agricultural and fisheries policy. The few publications on Danish agricultural policy attempting to provide a broader overview date back to the 1980s and 1990s (e.g. Buksti 1983; Daugbjerg 1999). However, agri-environmental policies have attracted continuous scholarly interest over the last three decades as limiting pollution from the agricultural sector has been a major political and policy design challenge. With few exceptions, social science research in this field can be characterized as applied economic policy analysis and has very much been driven by a demand for such analysis to inform policy-making (e.g. Jacobsen et al. 2004). Organic food policy has also attracted some scholarly interest (e.g. Michelsen 2001; Daugbjerg and Halpin 2010), but this research did not situate the organic food and farming policy in the broader Danish agricultural policy context. As for fisheries policy, the literature is composed of empirical studies of the economic consequences of applying rights-based management measures compared to classic input restrictions such as vessel size and extent of fishing (e.g. Frost et al. 2011; Andersen et al. 2010).

WATER, CARBON EMISSIONS, AND ENVIRONMENTAL POLICIES: COST-EFFECTIVE REGULATION

Since 1984, water pollution caused by farming has been a contested issue in Danish agricultural politics, particularly in the late 1980s and early 1990s (Daugbjerg 1998; Danish Academy of Technical Sciences 1990). However, in recent years, the discussions have gained momentum with analyses and the implementation of measures being challenged by the farming sector (Jacobsen et al. 2017). The first water plans were based on general top-down regulation with control, but the approach is now moving further towards more local participation and targeted regulation in order to achieve higher flexibility and cost-effectiveness (Dalgaard et al. 2014; Ministry of Food 2015; Graversgaard et al. 2017).

In the mid-1980s, a number of events focused on the death of fish due to oxygen depletion, and this started a discussion on responsibility, targets, and measures (Danish Academy of Technical Sciences 1990). Since then, several action plans have been implemented in Denmark to reduce nitrate leaching from agriculture. The aim of the first Aquatic Action Plan (*Vandmiljøplan 1*) from 1987 was a 50 per cent reduction in nitrogen losses and an 80 per cent reduction regarding phosphorus, but this was not directly linked to a target for the desired water quality (Danish Academy of Technical Sciences 1990). The farm unions opposed the need for policies and rejected the role of the Danish agricultural sector as a polluter (Danish Academy of Technical Sciences 1990). The first action plan also included a number of measures targeting point source pollution from industry and sewage works, which reduced losses significantly and fairly quickly (Jensen et al. 2018; see also Sørensen 2020).

Over time, the farming measures aimed at reducing nitrogen from agriculture were based on some key policies (Dalgaard et al. 2014; Jacobsen et al. 2004). First, they were aimed at increasing the utilization of nitrogen in animal manure, and second, compulsory fertilizer accounting was introduced in 1987. The third leg was the use of catch crops to keep the nitrogen from leaching in the autumn, and finally, the use of wetlands and later mini-wetlands to reduce nitrogen losses to the sea, both of which have been widely used.

In later years, there has been an increased focus on the targeting of measures, including a more flexible implementation at the farm level in order to reduce costs and ensure that measures are applied where the effect is the greatest (Jacobsen and Hansen 2016). However, this increases the need for detailed data as well as the risk that the data might have a high degree of uncertainty.

The implemented measures have reduced nitrogen (N) leaching from the root-zone and the use of nitrogen from mineral fertilizer by around 50 per cent from the mid-1980s to 2013–15 (Danish Agricultural Agency 2018), just as it has reduced N losses to the sea by almost 50 per cent (Jensen et al. 2018). In other words, the aims from the mid-1980s have been reached, just at a slower pace than anticipated. However, since 2004, there has not been any significant reduction in N lost to the sea (Jensen et al. 2018), and further reductions are required to reach the targets set in the EU's Water Framework Directive.

Various models of nitrogen taxation have been suggested over time, but these were dismissed outright by the farm unions and politicians. The command and control approach regulating fertilizer use through, for example, norms for N application per crop, were adopted as the Ministry of Food, Agriculture and Fisheries and the farm unions were eager not to punish farmers who did apply the right nitrogen levels at the right time. Another aspect has been the required balance between livestock production and arable area at the farm level ('the harmony rule') supporting a sustainability approach (Jacobsen 2004). In hindsight, this has ensured that the phosphorus surplus in Denmark has been limited.

The measures implemented in the second Aquatic Action Plan (*Vandmiljøplan 2*) were financed by both the farming sector and the state, whereas the Food and Agricultural package from 2015 aimed at reaching the targets without costs for the agricultural sector (Jacobsen 2004; Brink et al. 2011).

The voluntary measures such as the creation of wetlands and organic farming were funded by the Danish state and the EU (the Rural Development Programme; *Landdistriktsprogrammet*). In many cases, the uptake of these voluntary measures was lower than expected. From the beginning, the creation of wetlands was a cheap way of reducing nitrogen losses. This led to too large an area being included in the second aquatic plan (Jacobsen 2004). In several cases over the years, the political ambitions regarding new voluntary measures have been too optimistic. This also includes the pesticide policies which have also relied on voluntary measures combined with taxation, where the taxes paid are fully reimbursed to the agricultural sector through lower land taxes. Critics argue that the voluntary approach has not helped to reduce pesticide use significantly. Others find that the increased advisory effort has ensured that pesticide use in agriculture is lower than in many other countries. The most recent pesticide taxes are directly linked to the environmental load and not just the consumption as before.

Within the farming community, it is believed that the intensive regulation has made it more difficult to farm. The most important farmers' union, the Danish Agriculture and Food Council (*Landbrug og Fødevarer*), fears loss of international competitiveness, and a number of farmers have, partly due to the regulatory demands, started farming in other countries, primarily in former Eastern Europe. It has also led to increased protests against the established 'old' Danish Agriculture and Food Council, materializing in 2010 in a new, more radical union called Sustainable Farming (*Bæredygtigt Landbrug*). This new farmers' union focuses on increasing farmers' incomes through reducing the environmental regulations, contradictory to what one would expect from the name. The more conflict-oriented approach pursued by Sustainable Farming (in order to be heard) has led to their use of court cases regarding several issues, most noticeably the retraction of the 10 meter riparian zones along all streams, which was seen as an infringement of the right to farm. The case also showed how an idea previously supported by the Danish Agriculture and Food Council and the Liberal Party (which has traditionally represented farming interests, cf. Christiansen 2020) was redrawn when the farming opposition gained momentum (Jacobsen et al. 2017; Thorsøe et al. 2017).

Having lost support in rural areas, the Liberal Party had to promise improvements for the farming community, and this was done through the Food and Agricultural Package from 2015. The N norms were increased to economic optimum, and the farmers were now paid for the measures using the EU's Rural Development Programme. The environmental impact of the higher N norms in the Food and Agricultural Package was widely discussed among politicians and researchers, and it can be a challenge to ensure significant reductions in nitrogen losses to the sea, as there has been no decrease for a number of years. The two political sides in Parliament do not agree, with the centre-right wing parties seen to be neglecting the environmental targets and having lower ambitions, whereas the centre-left wing parties want immediate action in order to achieve ambitious targets, which the right-wing parties claim will be too expensive.

Based on the Danish National Inventory Report 2018, the agricultural sector contributes around 20 per cent of the total Danish carbon dioxide (CO_2) emissions. The agricultural sector has reduced the emissions by 17 per cent from 1990 to 2016, partly through more efficient production and partly as a side effect of the aquatic plans mentioned above (Dubgaard and Ståhl 2018; see also Sørensen 2020). The changes have led to a reduction in the number of cows over time while simultaneously maintaining the level of milk production, just as the use of mineral fertilizer has been reduced without a reduction in yields.

Further measures are not straightforward, but analyses have suggested taking organogenic soils out of production and increasing biogas production; however, it is a challenge to differentiate and promote CO_2-friendly production at the farm level (Dubgaard and Ståhl 2018). Levies and CO_2 accounting at the farm level have been discussed as possible measures. Another aspect often discussed is the issue of leakage as there is a risk that CO_2-efficient agricultural production in Denmark is being replaced by less CO_2-efficient production in another country, leading to higher total emissions. It is not clear how some of the measures aimed at increasing carbon in soils (carbon sinks) can be implemented in practice and how cost efficient these measures will be (Dubgaard and Ståhl 2018). Towards 2030, a further reduction of 39 per cent compared to the 2005 level has to be achieved in the non-quota restricted sectors. Analyses indicate that the mitigation costs in the agricultural sector will be lower than the reduction costs for the transport sector. However, since 1990, the emissions in the transport sector have increased, whereas they have been reduced in the agricultural sector. Therefore, politically, it may be difficult to push for further reduction in the agricultural sector until emissions have been reduced in the transport sector. It is not clear how large a reduction will be achieved in the agricultural sector in the short run, but the ambitions among dairy and pork producers are clear as they want to be seen to promote substantial emission reductions towards 2050 (Arla 2019).

STRUCTURAL DEVELOPMENT POLICY: FROM RESTRICTIONS TO MARKET LIBERALISM

During the previous three to four decades, the Agricultural Act (*Landbrugsloven*) has been significantly liberalized. Restrictions on acquisitions, mergers, financing, ownership, and size in agriculture have been reduced. With the structural development in the farming industry driven by economies of scale and with increasing international competition, it has been necessary to ensure the farming industry more economically favourable framework conditions free of political attempts to govern structural development. Thus, the importance of the Agricultural Act for structural development has been reduced, and control and regulations have been liberalized.

For many years, the Agricultural Act has provided the legal framework for the structural development of agriculture as wanted by society. The regulatory framework had two dimensions. On the one hand, the purpose of regulation was to support the competitive farms and ensure access to the necessary resources such as capital, labour, extension services, etc. Special support schemes offered favourable loans and supported advisory services to farmers. Increasing productivity has also been an important objective of the Agricultural Act. Through research, development, and knowledge dissemination, the government has sought to strengthen the competitiveness of the primary farm industry and the food processing industry. Agricultural land should be reserved for agricultural purposes, and there were requirements set for the education of farmers.

On the other hand, there was a desire to influence and control the structural development to meet a number of political preferences for agricultural development. For a long period until the 1970s, governments wanted to support smallholder farmers. The Act also set upper limits for how large the farms could grow through acquisitions. These limits on size have continually increased in line with structural developments and in order to enable the utilization of the benefits from economies of scale. An important and longstanding motivation behind the restriction on farm size was to protect the dominant family farming model in Denmark in which the farmers own the farms. Over time, business and investor ownership of farmland has, therefore, been either prohibited or very limited. From the late 1980s, the Act included a requirement for maintaining a harmonious relationship between livestock and agricultural land as a measure to limit nitrogen leaching from the application of animal manure on the fields following the Nitrate Directive's requirements.

Changes to the Agricultural Act have repeatedly been adopted on the basis of reports and studies on agricultural development. During the 1970s, the Agricultural Act was further regulated and tightened in a number of areas in order to ensure (politically) appropriate structural development. An important goal was to give preference to the purchase of agricultural properties for people who had farming as their primary occupation. At the same time, it was also an objective to ensure that young people with an agricultural education were given a reasonable opportunity to establish themselves as farmers. Thus, a requirement on education to allow purchase of an agricultural property was introduced. Furthermore, a requirement that farming was the main occupation of the landowner and a requirement for residence on the farm were introduced. As an indirect effect, these restrictions slowed down price increases on agricultural properties, easing young people's chances of establishing themselves as farmers.

At the end of the 1980s, a committee prepared a report on the structure, financing, and ownership of agriculture (Ministry of Agriculture 1988). The government's objective was that Danish agriculture should be able to manage without public support and that efficient farms within the framework of the EU's Common Agricultural Policy should be able to provide earnings and working conditions that were comparable with other industries while also allowing for increasing equity on the individual farm (see also Jensen and Nedergaard 2020). Based on this, the task of the committee was to present proposals for measures that would contribute to making agriculture economically sustainable over a period of time.

The findings of the committee formed the basis for a reform of the Agricultural Act, resulting in considerable liberalization of the Act with the aim of ensuring the existence and expansion of profitable businesses. The main purpose was to ensure that the farming industry was able to adapt to the current business conditions. The regulatory changes made it easier to obtain exemptions from restrictions on farm co-operation and on mergers, and rules on the acquisition of farms were liberalized.

The next major revision of the Act came as a result of the so-called Growth Plan for the Food Industry (*Vækstplan for Fødevarer*) (Ministry for Industry, Business and Financial Affairs 2013). This business growth plan included several elements, but the recurrent initiatives mentioned related to competitiveness, sustainability, and growth. Thus, it was a relatively offensive approach where increased production and exports were implicitly or explicitly objectives. Improving access to capital was also a tool for achieving the desired outcomes.

There was a common understanding that access to new types of finance and new forms of ownership were necessary in order to utilize the potential of the industry. With the structural development continuing, the anticipated cessation of dairy quotas (which was a supply management tool to limit milk production within the EU), the continued need to exploit new economies of scale, and improved access to capital would be crucial. Furthermore, previous notions of agriculture as an exceptional industry requiring special conditions diminished in importance, and the independent status of the Ministry of Agriculture and Food ended as it was merged with the Ministry of the Environment. Finally, market regulation in the EU's Common Agricultural Policy had been reduced as a result of a succession of reforms transforming substantial parts of the price support to decoupled direct support (see Jensen and Nedergaard 2020). Agriculture was, therefore, increasingly expected to be able to compete on an equal footing with other industries under the same conditions and without significant positive or negative support schemes.

In the latest revision of the Agricultural Act from 2016, four objectives are stated:

- To ensure proper use of agricultural properties, taking into account agricultural production, nature, the environment, and landscape values.
- To ensure the sustainable development of the agricultural industry and improve its competitiveness.
- To facilitate settlement and development in rural areas.
- To maintain the family-owned farms as the overall ownership and operating form as well as to ensure the necessary production base for the agricultural industries.

With this Agricultural Act, significant deregulation and liberalization have taken place. There is no longer an upper limit on how much land a farmer can own, no education requirement, and no longer the requirement for the owner to run the property themselves. Moreover, the requirement that the owner must live on the property has been dismantled.

Access for companies to own agricultural property has been improved. Investors—Danish or foreign—can form a company that can acquire an agricultural property. It is required that the person who fulfils the conditions for personal acquisition of the agricultural property must have a controlling influence in the company.

The liberalization of the Agricultural Act was particularly driven by a growing demand for capital. With ever-increasing farms, the family-owned farm model was challenged in several ways, and new forms of ownership—including company ownership in particular—appeared on the agenda and increasingly became an opportunity for farmers. As more and more economies of scale are exploited, and with a persistent structural pressure, restrictions on the size of farms have also been eased.

ORGANIC FOOD POLICY: ACTIVELY DEVELOPING MARKETS

From a global perspective, Denmark is a forerunner in developing the organic food sector (cf. below). Banning the use of mineral fertilizers and synthetic pesticides, organic farming is considered an environmentally friendly agricultural production mode. This has been the driving force behind organic policies in most countries actively intervening in the farming sector to facilitate growth of the organic sector. While this has also been an increasingly important concern in Denmark, the organic farming sector was originally, and is still, based on a more market liberal approach than in other countries. A mantra running thorough the policy formation over the years is that growth of the farming sector has to be 'market-driven' (*markedsdrevet*), meaning that market allocation should play a significant role.

In practice, this resulted in a policy model resting on both push policy (or supply-side) instruments aimed at creating conditions for farmers to convert to organic farming, and pull policy (or demand-side) instruments designed to increase the sale of organic food. Such an organic policy model has been coined *active market development policy* (Halpin et al. 2011; Daugbjerg and Sønderskov 2012). The simultaneous use of demand-side and supply-side policy instruments means that Danish organic food policy has developed very differently from those of other countries and has resulted in a comparatively high level of organic consumption (see Daugbjerg and Sønderskov 2012; Schvartzman 2012 for an analysis of the implementation of demand-side measures). In terms of organic retail sales, Denmark belongs to a group of five front-running countries including Austria, Luxembourg, Switzerland, and Sweden. In these countries, the organic share of food retail sales amounts to more than 8 per cent, with Denmark topping the list with 9.7 per cent and Luxembourg coming second with 8.6 per cent (Willer and Lernoud 2018: 70). Including online shopping, the organic share of the total food sales in Denmark exceeded 13 per cent in 2017 (Ministry of Environment and Food 2018). In the current Danish agricultural policy context, organic farming is seen as serving two purposes: a mode of farming that contributes to reduction of the total nutrients leaching from the farming industry, and a response to a more differentiated food market in which consumers demand food produced with particular process attributes such as environmental protection and animal welfare.

The Danish state's engagement with the organic sector began with the Act on Organic Farming (*Økologiloven*) from 1987.[1] As mentioned above, Danish organic food policy was based on the two pillars: supply-side instruments and demand-side instruments. Firstly, subsidies were provided to ease both farm conversion and fund initiatives related to the processing, marketing, and distribution of organic food. Secondly, state engagement in the Danish organic sector in the late 1980s entailed a shift from certification by non-state bodies to a fully state-operated certification and labelling system (the so-called Ø label). By strongly engaging in the organic sector, the Danish government pursued an active market development policy strategy. While there had been increasing spending on organic policy under the Social Democratic coalition governments of the 1990s, the Liberal-Conservative government formed in 2001 initially lowered organic subsidies, but the two-pillared policy strategy was left intact. As a result of several years of considerable overproduction of organic milk and cereals, it was decided to abolish support schemes directed at selective commodity groups. It was believed that the market, rather than selective support schemes, was a better mechanism to determine the level and type of organic production. In 2004, a flat-rate conversion and permanent organic payments replaced the complicated and commodity differentiated subsidy system. Spending on demand-side policy measures was scaled down five-fold between 2002 and 2005 as a result of the change of government from centre-left to centre-right, but this did not halt efforts devoted to increasing the demand for organic produce. After 2002, demand creation initiatives were still implemented, but the sources of funding were to an increasing extent the Land Tax Foundation (*Promilleafgiftfonden*) and the Foundation for Organic Agriculture (*Økologifonden*). Increased demand for organic food domestically and internationally in 2006 and 2007 persuaded the government to increase funding again for marketing activities to levels just short of the highs of 2005.

In 2009, a government organic cuisine label for public and private food services was introduced. Later that year, the government's Green Growth Agreement (*Aftale om Grøn Vækst*) stated that the area farmed organically should increase from 6 per cent of the utilized agricultural area in 2007 to 15 per cent in 2020. It was emphasized that the increase should be market based. Organic farm subsidies and extension services would be increased. Aligned with the previous policy trajectory, the growth in the organically farmed area would continue to be based on the two-pillared policy model by also emphasizing market promotion, particularly export promotion (Environmental Committee 2009: 5, 14).

In the 2010s, there has been continued emphasis on facilitating growth in the demand for organic food and creating conditions for more farmers to convert production. The Organic Action Plan 2020 (*Økologisk Handlingsplan 2020*) launched in 2012 by the Minister of Food and Agriculture had as its flagship policy measure a scheme that supported the conversion of food services in the public sector. It was realized that if 60 per cent of the meals served in the public sector were organic, this would require an additional 20,000–30,000 hectares of land farmed organically. To be eligible for government subsidized training of kitchen staff and various advisory services, individual kitchens in state, regional, and local institutions were required to work towards using 60 per cent organic food products. Though not mandatory, the kitchens were urged to obtain certification under the organic cuisine label (Ministry of Food, Agriculture and Fisheries 2012). The scheme turned out to be successful. At the time of writing, 2,755 kitchens are certified, the majority of which are in the public sector.[2] The policy directions and priorities set out in the Action Plan were reaffirmed in the subsequent Organic Plan Denmark (*Økologiplan Danmark*) (Ministry of Food, Agriculture and Fisheries 2015).

In 2018, the Growth Plan for Organics was adopted. Similar to the preceding action plans, it maintained the mantra of 'market-driven' development of the organic industry and the two-pillar policy strategy. Funding for organic farm conversion was granted as part of the Agricultural Plan which saw organic farming as a measure to reduce nutrient leaching. In addition, the government provided DKK 130 million for the Foundation for Organic Agriculture to support innovation, marketing, research and development, education, advisory services, etc. (Ministry of Environment and Food 2018: 9).

FISHERIES POLICY: FROM ALMOST OPEN ACCESS TO PROPERTY RIGHTS AND MARKET-BASED MANAGEMENT

Across the world, fisheries policies have changed significantly during the last three to four decades. The regulatory framework has changed in many regions and countries from being almost open access regimes to complicated 'demand and control' regimes. Furthermore, many fisheries now function within market liberal regimes based on well-defined property rights. This development has also influenced the European fisheries policy (Frost and Andersen 2006). Since 1983, the Common Fisheries Policy (CFP) has played a key role in the development of national fishery policies and for agreements between EU and non-EU countries. What will happen to the Common Fisheries Policy as a consequence of Brexit is unclear (see Andersen et al 2017).

The most important feature of the CFP is the relative stability principle. This principle constitutes a rights-based management (RBM) system on the country level. This system works like an individual non-transferable quota system where the 'individual' is the country. The present version of the quota system does not allow for transferability between countries but allows for bilateral trading of quotas in the beginning of the year as well as during the year. The way in which the individual countries allocate quotas between segments of the fleet and between vessels as well as the degree of flexibility of quota trading among vessels relies on national regulation. This gives each country the right to decide the degree of market liberalism in the sector.

As for fisheries policy, Denmark is the most market liberal country among EU countries, and it has followed the development in countries such as Iceland, Australia, and New Zealand (Marchal et al. 2016). To understand this significant change in the principles of fish resources management and why Denmark now has an economically healthy fishery sector, it is important to remember that a lack of property rights results in the so-called 'race for fish' and the 'tragedy of the commons' phenomena. The outcome is economically overfishing, and most likely, a fishing fleet of high-efficiency vessels, and therefore, biologically overfished stocks. This will result in low catches in the longer run. The tragedy is that the supply of fish is significantly below the optimal and that the economic surplus of the fishery, the profit, and the resource rent will be very low or disappear completely (see e.g. Clark 1990). To reduce the race for fish, it is important to control effort and catches, but to gain resource rent, regulations need to give the right economic incentives to avoid too high fishing capacity and to make the fishing fleet cost efficient.

A system based on Individual Transferable Quotas (ITQ) is an effective and commonly used method that has the right economic incentives. By giving fishermen fishing rights and the right to trade quotas, quotas will be allocated to the most economically efficient fishermen. The value of the quotas will be like a tax revenue if the quotas are sold by the state. If the state allocates the quota to the fishery sector for free (the grandfathering method), the owners of the quotas gain the resource rent (Clark 1990).

Often applied methods such as closed areas, days in harbour, total allowable catches (TAC), mesh size, fleet, and horsepower restrictions will reduce the pressure on the stock as the fishing effort will be less efficient, but it also means that the cost of fishing a certain amount of fish goes up. Therefore, the resource rent will dissipate. In complicated fisheries (multispecies fisheries, different fishing areas, different fishing methods, and various types of fishing vessels), the right economic incentives have to be combined with other regulations to balance different goals and reduce conflicts. It is important to notice that the use of only biologically oriented regulations will not take into account fishermen's behaviour in a sufficient way and therefore lead to vast resource rent due to high fishing costs.

The fisheries sector plays a minor macroeconomic role in Denmark. The share of GDP is less than 0.5 per cent, and the export of fish and fish products is about 4 per cent of the total Danish exports, but the fishery sector is an important industry in some Danish regions. In spite of the minor macroeconomic importance of the fishery sector, the overall picture is that there has been a clear awareness of the development in the fishery sector regarding economic efficiency and how national policies have a role to play within that CFP framework. This means that the Danish fisheries management is restricted by TAC allocations, EU measures such as effort regulation, technical conservation measures, management/recovery plans, and stock enhancement operations (e.g. OECD 2013), but that the CFP at the same time opens up for various national policy initiatives to meet national targets.

The first Danish initiatives to introduce an almost full-scale individual transferable quota system (ITQ system) were launched in 1991, but due to lack of political support, the system was not implemented until 2003 when the first group of vessels entered into an ITQ system. Danish pelagic herring fishery transferred to the new regulatory framework on an experimental basis in order to overcome the classic problems and to meet the need for modernization of the pelagic fishing fleet. In 2007, the ITQ system was made permanent and extended to cover other pelagic species such as mackerel, sandeel blue whiting, and horse mackerel, and all demersal quota-regulated species. At the same time, a minor share of the TACs was reserved for a segment of small-scale vessels. These vessels are not part of the ITQ system but are regulated by effort restrictions. However, the EU regulations regarding capacity control continued, along with some technical measures and closed areas (Semrau and Gras 2013).

The results of the significant policy change in Danish fishery policy from a demand and control based system to an economic incentive-based regulatory system with ITQs are very clear. The economic surplus (profit and resource rent) increased over twenty years (1996–2016) by more than 50 per cent in real terms, and on average, significantly more per fishing company (Statistics Denmark 2016). The significant improvements started with the implementation of the ITQ system. Over the years, fishing capacity has been reduced. The number of fishing vessels declined by around 65 per cent for larger vessels and by around 50 per cent for smaller vessels, and the capacity measures by tonnage declined by 29 per cent for larger vessels and around 60 per cent for smaller vessels. During the transition of the Danish fleet, vessel sizes increased. This development is the result of technical changes as well as changes in the regulatory system. Finally, Danish fishery is now an almost non-subsidized sector.

The development in Danish fishery is the outcome of changes in the CFP and the implementation of national fishery policies based on the idea that well-defined fishing rights improve efficiency through structural changes. The trade-off between economic efficiency and social transformation costs has become very clear as economically inefficient vessels are leaving the fleet and a concentration of fishing rights has occurred. Political concerns relating to an unequal development of the distribution of fishing activities across fleet segments and regions demanding restrictions on the transferability of fishing rights will happen at the cost of economic efficiency and loss of resource rent. This is part of the political debate about a balanced fishery policy in Denmark. The Danish ITQ system is based on the grandfathering method, and quota owners get their quotas for free for a period of sixteen years. Therefore, most of the resource rent has stayed within the fishery sector.

CONCLUSION

Farming and fisheries have been highly regulated and subsidized industries for decades. The justification for intensive regulation and government support was that these two sectors were considered exceptional and allowing market forces to operate in an unrestricted manner would result in suboptimal outcomes. In contrast to many other countries, the Danish farming and fisheries industries are strongly export-oriented, and government policies have had a strong focus on maintaining international competitiveness. At the same time, various Danish governments have pursued a number of non-economic objectives such environmental protection, climate mitigation, rural livelihood, food quality, bio-security, and animal welfare in the farm sector at the national level as well as the EU level. In the fisheries sector, governments have adopted policies preserving fish stocks and pursued goals related to regional employment and livelihood to varying extents.

In both policy sectors, this chapter has identified a movement towards market liberalism. Maintaining a balance between international competitiveness and the more value-based objectives listed above has been a challenging exercise as the two types of concerns do not necessarily go hand in hand. Based on a realization that farm and fisheries incomes must increasingly be derived from the market, the Danish government has liberalized policies to better enable farmers and fishermen to realize economies of scale. The policy changes in the fisheries sector have amounted to an almost complete transformation to market liberal conditions. Over the last twenty years, reforms of the fisheries policy have enabled a shift from a sector with low profitability and overcapacity to a sector with relatively high profitability and a fishing capacity that balances the fishing opportunities set as a part of the EU's Common Fisheries Policy. This change has been a result of the introduction of transferable fishing rights as a main component of the Danish fisheries policy.

Similarly, in terms of land ownership, the policy changes have resulted in an almost full-scale transformation to market liberalism. The family farm has traditionally been the bedrock of the Danish farm sector. To maintain its viability, government regulations on ownership restricted who could own farms and how many farms could be owned. Driven by growing demand for capital, the Agricultural Act has been liberalized recently. As farm businesses grew in size, the family farm was challenged, and new forms of ownership—company ownership in particular—became a relevant option for farmers, and consequently, restrictions affecting the size of farms have been relaxed.

In the organic farming sector, government intervention has been aimed at creating the conditions for a growing organic food market by facilitating farm conversion, and importantly, supporting various types of initiatives aimed at increasing the demand for organic food. While development in the sector has not been left to market forces alone, the government has actively engaged in developing markets for organic food. In comparison with other countries, the Danish organic food policy is distinct as it has relied more on market forces to grow the sector.

Recent changes to policies aimed at limiting water pollution caused by farming have aimed at lowering the regulatory costs for the agricultural sector, a step towards market liberalism. Until 2005, significant reductions in nitrogen leaching were obtained through universal measures that significantly increased the utilization of nitrogen in animal manure and reduced the use of mineral fertilizers. In later years, it has been more difficult to ensure further reductions of the nitrogen loading, but there is a clear move from national regulation towards site-specific regulation, which is assumed to be more cost efficient. At the same time, we have seen a move from the polluter pays principle towards a policy reducing the additional costs on the sector in order to maintain international competitiveness.

This chapter has explained how Danish agricultural and fisheries policies have changed over time. While this is a contribution to the relatively limited policy-focused literature on these two sectors, the future research agenda should devote attention to understanding the political and institutional dynamics driving the liberalization process, of which we know relatively little.

Notes

1. This paragraph is based on Halpin et al. (2011).
2. See Organic Cuisine Label (2019).

References

Andersen, Peder, Jesper L. Andersen, and Hans Frost (2010). 'ITQs in Denmark and resource rent gains', *Marine Resource Economics*, 25/1: 11–22.

Andersen, Peder, Jesper L. Andersen, Ayoe Hoff, and Lisa Ståhl (2017). 'The economic consequences for the Danish fishery following the United Kingdom's decision to leave the European Union', IFRO Report 263, Department of Food and Resource Economics, University of Copenhagen.

Arla (2019). 'Fremtidens mejeriprodukter skal være Klima-neutrale', Arla, https://www.arla.dk/om-arla/nyheder/2019/pressrelease/fremtidens-mejeriprodukter-skal-vaere-klima-neutrale-2845584/ (accessed 10 April 2019).

Brink, Corjan, Hans van Grinsven, Brian H. Jacobsen, Ari Rabl, Ing-Marie Gren, Mike Holland, et al. (2011). 'Costs and benefits of nitrogen in the environment', in Mark A. Sutton, ed., *The European Nitrogen Assessment: Sources, Effects, and Policy Perspectives*. Cambridge, New York: Cambridge University Press, 513–30.

Buksti, Jacob A. (1983). 'Organisationer og offentlig politik: Interesseorganisationernes deltagelse i den politiske beslutningsproces i Danmark og den samfundsmæssige udvikling på området', *Nordisk Administrativt Tidsskrift*, 64/2: 191–212.

Christiansen, Flemming J. (2020). 'The Liberal Party. From agrarian and liberal to centre-right catch-all', in Peter M. Christiansen, Jørgen Elklit, and Peter Nedergaard, eds, *The Oxford Handbook of Danish Politics*. Oxford: Oxford University Press, 296–312.

Clark, Colin W. (1990). *Mathematical Bioeconomics: The Optimal Management of Renewable Resources*. 2 ed. New York: Wiley-Interscience.

Coleman, William. D., Grace D. Skogstad, and Michael M. Atkinson (1996). 'Paradigm shifts and policy networks: Cumulative change in agriculture', *Journal of Public Policy*, 16/3: 273–301.

Dalgaard, Tommy, Birgitte Hansen, Berit Hasler, Ole Hertel, Nicholas J. Hutchings, Brian H. Jacobsen, et al. (2014). 'Policies for agricultural nitrogen management – Trends, challenges and prospects for improved efficiency in Denmark', *Environmental Research Letters*, 9/11: 115002.

Danish Academy of Technical Sciences (1990). *Vandmiljøplanens tilblivelse og iværksættelse*. Lyngby: Danish Academy of Technical Sciences.

Danish Agricultural Agency (2018). *Salg af handelsgødning i Danmark*. Copenhagen: The Danish Agricultural Agency (BLST).

Daugbjerg, Carsten (1998). *Policy Networks under Pressure: Pollution Control, Policy Reform, and the Power of Farmers*. Aldershot: Ashgate.

Daugbjerg, Carsten (1999). 'Landbrugspolitik: Stabilitet eller forandring?', in Jens Blom-Hansen and Carsten Daugbjerg, eds, *Magtens organisering: Stat og interesseorganisationer i Danmark*. Aarhus: Systime, 106–27.

Daugbjerg, Carsten, and Darren Halpin (2010). 'Generating policy capacity in emerging green industries: The development of organic farming in Denmark and Australia', *Journal of Environmental Policy and Planning*, 12/2: 141–57.

Daugbjerg, Carsten, and Kim M. Sønderskov (2012). 'Environmental policy performance revisited: Designing effective policies for green markets', *Political Studies*, 60/2: 399–418.

Dubgaard, Alex, and Lisa Ståhl (2018). '*Omkostninger ved virkemidler til reduktion af landbrugets drivhusgasemissioner: Opgjort i relation til EU's 2030-målsætning for det ikke-kvotebelagte område*', IFRO Report no. 271, Department of Food and Resource Economics, University of Copenhagen.

Environmental Committee (2009). 'Aftale om Grøn Vækst', Environmental Committee, https://www.ft.dk/samling/20111/almdel/miu/bilag/21/1030569.pdf (accessed 21 January 2019).

European Union (2013). No 1380/2013 of the European Parliament and of the Council of 11 December 2013 on the Common Fisheries Policy.

Frost, Hans, and Peder Andersen (2006). 'The Common Fisheries policy of the European Union and fisheries economics', *Marine Policy*, 30/6: 737–46.

Frost, Hans, Peder Andersen, and Ayoe Hoff (2011). 'An application of fisheries economics theory: 100 years after Warming's paper: "Rent of fishing grounds"', *Nationaløkonomisk Tidsskrift*, 149/1–3: 55–84.

Graversgaard, Morten, Brian H. Jacobsen, Chris Kjeldsen, and Tommy Dalgaard (2017). 'Stakeholder engagement and knowledge co-creation in water planning: Can public participation increase cost-effectiveness?', *Water*, 9/3: 191.

Halpin, Darren, Carsten Daugbjerg, and Yonatan Schvartzman (2011). 'Interest group capacities and infant industry development: State-sponsored growth in organic farming', *International Political Science Review*, 32/2: 147–66.

Jacobsen, Brian H. (2004). *Økonomisk slutevaluering af Vandmiljøplan II*. Report no. 169, Institute of Food Economics, Copenhagen, Denmark.

Jacobsen, Brian H., and Anne L. Hansen (2016). 'Economic gains from targeted measures in agriculture based on detailed nitrate reduction maps', *Science of the Total Environment*, 556: 264–75.

Jacobsen, Brian. H., Jens Abildtrup, Martin Andersen, Tove Christensen, Berit Hasler, Zubair B. Hussain, et al. (2004). *Omkostninger ved reduktion af landbrugets næringsstoftab til vandmiljøet*. Report no. 167, Institute of Food Economics, Copenhagen, Denmark.

Jacobsen, Brian H., Helle Tegner, and Lasse Baaner (2017).'Implementing the water framework directive in Denmark – Lessons on agricultural measures from a legal and regulatory perspective', *Land Use Policy*, 67: 98–106.

Jensen, Mads D., and Peter Nedergaard (2020). 'Danish European Union policies. Sailing between economic benefits and political sovereignty', in Peter M. Christiansen, Jørgen Elklit, and Peter Nedergaard, eds, *The Oxford Handbook of Danish Politics*. Oxford: Oxford University Press, 487–501.

Jensen, Poul N., Susanne Boutrup, Jesper R. Fredshavn, Vibeke V. Nielsen, Lars M. Svendsen, Gitte Blicher-Mathiesen, et al. (2018). *Vandmiljø og Natur 2016. NOVANA. Tilstand og udvikling—faglig sammenfatning*. Aarhus Universitet, DCE—Nationalt Center for Miljø og Energi, 58—Videnskabelig rapport fra DCE—Nationalt Center for Miljø og Energi nr. 274. http://dce2.au.dk/pub/SR274.pdf (accessed 29 March 2019).

Marchal, Paul, Jesper L. Andersen, Martin Aranda, Mike Fitzpatrick, Leyre Goti, Olivier Guyader, et al. (2016). 'A comparative review of fisheries management experiences in the European Union and in other countries worldwide: Island, Australia, and New Zealand', *Fish and Fisheries*, 17/3: 1–22.

Michelsen, Johannes (2001). 'Organic farming in a regulative perspective: The Danish case', *Sociologia Ruralis*, 41/1: 62–84.

Ministry of Food, Agriculture and Fisheries (2012). 'Økologisk Handlingsplan 2020', Ministry for Food, Agriculture and Fisheries, https://mfvm.dk/fileadmin/user_upload/FVM.dk/Dokumenter/Landbrug/Indsatser/Oekologi/Oekologisk_Handlingsplan_2020.pdf (accessed 21 January 2019).

Ministry of Food, Agriculture and Fisheries (2015). 'Økologiplan Danmark: Sammen om mere Økologi', Ministry of Food, Agriculture and Fisheries, https://mfvm.dk/fileadmin/user_upload/FVM.dk/Dokumenter/Landbrug/Indsatser/Oekologi/OekologiplanDanmark.pdf (accessed 21 January 2019).

Ministry for Industry, Business and Financial Affairs (2013). 'Danmark i arbejde - Vækstplan for Fødevarer', Ministry for Industry, Business and Financial Affairs, https://www.regeringen.dk/tidligere-publikationer/danmark-i-arbejde-vaekstplan-for-foedevarer/ (accessed 8 December 2019).

Ministry of Agriculture (1988). 'Struktur og ejerformer', Ministry of Agriculture, http://kb-prod-dab-01.kb.dk:8080/wayback/20150917114133/http://www.statensnet.dk/betaenkninger/1001-1200/1152-1988/1152-1988_pdf/searchable_1152-1988.pdf (accessed 9 August 2019).

Ministry of Environment and Food (2015).'Aftale om Fødevare- og landbrugspakken', Ministry of Environment and Food, https://mfvm.dk/landbrug/vaekst-eksport-og-arbejdspladser/foedevare-og-landbrugspakke/ (accessed 29 March 2019).

Ministry of Environment and Food (2018). 'Vækstplan for dansk økologi', Ministry of Environment and Food, https://mfvm.dk/fileadmin/user_upload/MFVM/Vaekstplan_for_dansk_oekologi.pdf (accessed 21 January 2019).

OECD (2013). *OECD Review of Fisheries: Policies and Summary Statistics 2013*. OECD, http://dx.doi.org/10.1787/rev_fish-2013-en (accessed 8 December 2019).

Organic Cuisine Label (2019). 'Om Det Økologiske Spisemærke', https://www.oekologisk-spisemaerke.dk/om-spisemaerket/ (accessed 24 April 2019).

Schvartzman, Yonatan (2012). *Metastyring af markedsudvikling: Policystrategier og netværks-skoordinering i udvikling af nye markeder: Et komparativt studie af udviklingen af det danske og det svenske økologimarked*. Aarhus: Politica.

Semrau, Jakub, and Juan J. O. Gras (2013). *Fisheries in Denmark*. Policy Department B: Structural and Cohesion Policies. European Parliament: Brussels.

Statistics Denmark (2016). 'Regnskabsstatistik for Fiskeri og Akvakultur 2017', Statistics Denmark, www.dst.dk/publ/RegnFiskAkva (accessed 25 March 2019).

Sørensen, Peter B. (2020). 'Environmental, energy, and climate policy. From energy supply to climate gases', in Peter M. Christiansen, Jørgen Elklit, and Peter Nedergaard, eds, *The Oxford Handbook of Danish Politics*. Oxford: Oxford University Press, 644–663.

Thorsøe, Martin H., Morten Graversgaard, and Egon Noe (2017). 'The challenge of legitimizing spatially differentiated regulation: Experiences from the implementation of the Danish Buffer zone Act', *Land Use Policy*, 62: 202–12.

Willer, Helga, and Julia Lernoud (2018). 'Current statistic on organic agriculture worldwide: Areas operators and markets', in Helga Willer and Julia Lernoud, eds, *The World of Organic Agriculture: Statistics and Emerging Trends*. Frick and Bonn: Research Institute of Organic Agriculture (FiBL) and IFOAM—Organics International, 34–125.

CHAPTER 39

ENVIRONMENT, ENERGY, AND CLIMATE POLICY

From Energy Supply to Climate Gases

PETER BIRCH SØRENSEN

DENMARK: A GREEN FRONTRUNNER NATION?

WHILE environmental and climate policy has sometimes been an ideological and political battlefield between the left and the right, promoting Denmark as a green frontrunner country has often been a vote-winning strategy in Danish politics. Historically, Denmark has indeed been one of the frontrunners in this policy area, and the 2018 Environmental Performance Index ranked Denmark as number 3 out of 180 countries, based on 24 indicators of environmental quality (Wendling et al. 2018). However, as this chapter will show, the country must overcome significant future hurdles if it wishes to maintain its status as a green paragon.

The chapter traces the evolution of Danish environmental and climate policy since the early 1970s, which saw the birth of the Ministry of Environment and the creation of energy policy in the wake of the first OPEC oil price shock. The first part of the chapter focuses on environmental policy, describing the most important Danish environmental problems and policy responses and the resulting evolution of environmental quality. The second part of the chapter provides a similar overview of energy and climate policy. Following the description of historical developments, both parts of the chapter will end by reviewing the main current policy issues.

ENVIRONMENTAL POLICY

Environmental Problems in Denmark: The Special Role of Agriculture

The main challenges for environmental policy are to protect the air, water, and land from pollution and to preserve key areas of unspoiled nature and wildlife habitats. To meet the challenges, Danish environmental policies have relied on direct control, green taxes, land use regulation, and spatial planning.

The protection of water quality and biodiversity in particular has required a special effort for many years. While only 13 per cent of Danish land is covered by forest, agricultural crops cover almost two thirds of the land area (Statistics Denmark 2018: 172). This is more than twice the EU average cropland cover. Moreover, Danish agricultural production is very intensive in terms of animal husbandry per hectare. These factors cause large emissions of nitrogen, phosphorus, methane, and ammonia while leaving little space for unfettered wildlife. At the same time, the Danish countryside contains many small watercourses and numerous lakes, and Denmark has a relatively long coastline. The quality of the maritime environment has turned out to be quite sensitive to nitrate leaching from agricultural land. For these reasons, the regulation of agriculture has played a prominent role in environmental policy in recent decades.

The Organization of Environmental Administration

An important aspect of Danish environmental administration is its relatively high degree of decentralization. While the Environmental Protection Agency supervises and advises Danish municipalities, the latter act as environmental authorities to essentially all enterprises in industry, agriculture, and other sectors that may give rise to environmental problems. The municipalities are responsible for issuing environmental consents to firms and monitoring whether firms comply with environmental laws and statutory orders issued by the Minister for Environment.

According to Moe (1995: 57), the motives for the decentralization of pollution control were to allow for the exploitation of first-hand knowledge of local conditions and to commit local politicians to the goals of environmental policy. Previously, the regulation of large enterprises with complex environmental impacts was delegated to the Danish counties, which also played a coordinating and supervisory role in relation to the municipalities. However, as part of the major reform of local government in 2007, much pollution control was transferred from the counties to the new, larger municipalities.

Key Principles and Instruments in Danish Environmental Policy

The Environmental Protection Act of 1973 established some important principles of environmental policy which are still adhered to—although sometimes in modified form. With inspiration from Sweden, the approach to regulating industry has been to draw up a list of the most polluting branches and then imposing individualized environmental requirements such as a maximum acceptable level of emissions of various pollutants, a maximum noise level, and so on.

Like other OECD countries, Denmark adheres to the Polluter Pays Principle (PPP), which implies that polluting enterprises must bear the cost of meeting the environmental requirements. The limit values for emissions have typically been set based on what can be achieved by using the Best Available Technology (BAT), but firms have not been required to use a particular abatement technology as long as they are able to stay within the limit values.

Apart from acts passed by the Parliament, environmental regulation also relies on statutory orders, guidelines, and individual rulings. Statutory orders are issued by the Minister for Environment to specify the detailed rules to be followed in the implementation of the various sections of framework acts like the Environmental Protection Act. Guidelines contain advice from the issuing body, such as the Environmental Protection Agency, on how to interpret and administer environmental laws and statutory orders. Although they are not binding, guidelines have considerable influence on administrative practice, including the individual rulings by municipalities directed at individual

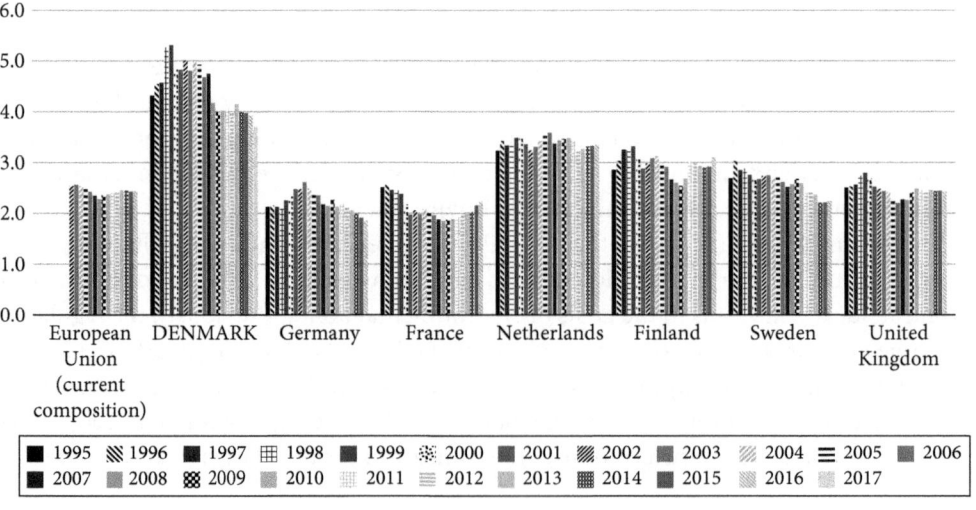

FIGURE 39.1 Environmental taxes—per cent of GDP.
Source: Eurostat

polluters, granting a polluting firm permission for some activity or requiring it to undertake some action to protect the environment.

As a supplement to the above regulatory instruments of the so-called command-and-control type, Denmark has made extensive use of environmental charges and levies related to water supply, waste and wastewater, emissions of CO_2 and SO_2, use of pesticides, CFCs, petrol, vehicles, and so on. Such economic instruments are well suited for curbing pollution stemming from a large number of polluters, and Denmark relies more on green taxes than other advanced economies as illustrated in Figure 39.1 (although this lead position in green taxation is partly due to the very high Danish registration duty on cars which is counted as an environmentally related tax).

When evaluating Danish environmental policy, it is important to keep in mind that it must respect the rules set by EU regulations and directives. While member states may implement rules stricter than those stipulated by directives, the EU sets the ground rules, and the main role of member states is to make sure that the rules are adhered to in practice.

The Build-Up Phase of Environmental Regulation, 1971–1987

According to Moe (2018), the period from 1971 to 1987 may be seen as a build-up phase in Danish environmental policy. During the 1960s, the degradation of environmental quality due to the combination of rapid economic growth and insufficient environmental regulations became increasingly visible. Discharge of untreated wastewater resulted in the serious pollution of many streams, lakes, and coastal waters, and air pollution from industry and transport reduced air quality in the cities and caused damage to the vegetation and life in the lakes.

Reacting to growing public concerns, the Social Democratic government responded by establishing a separate Ministry for Pollution Control in 1971. In 1973, this was replaced by the larger Ministry of the Environment with responsibilities in the areas of environmental protection, conservation of nature, and land use planning. The Ministry became responsible for the administration of the Environmental Protection Act of 1973, which was supported by the Social Democrats and the Conservative People's Party and had gained prior acceptance from the Confederation of Danish Industry.

By international standards, the Environmental Protection Act was quite ambitious, establishing most of the policy principles mentioned above, but their implementation turned out to be difficult. Some of the efforts at environmental protection during the 1970s took the form of diverting the emission of pollutants away from local areas via higher chimneys and longer sewers ending further away from the coastline. Many municipalities lacked the administrative capacity (and apparently, sometimes the political will) to ensure effective enforcement of the new stricter environmental standards.

In the early years, compliance with environmental requirements was usually not controlled by local authorities in a systematic manner. It was not until 1986 that systematic on-site supervision of compliance was made mandatory through an act of Parliament.

Nevertheless, the 1970s and early 1980s did see progress in important areas of environmental protection. Stricter limits on the amount of sulphur in mineral oils and the amount of lead in petrol were imposed, and Denmark signed the Geneva Convention on cross-border air pollution in 1979, leading to tighter control of emissions of SO_2 and particles. Moreover, an increasing number of municipalities built biological wastewater treatment plants to remove organic matter from sewage, and a few even established sophisticated plants that could also remove nitrogen and phosphorous. The technology underlying these advanced treatment plants was exported to several countries in the following decades (Sørensen 2019: 8).

However, by the early 1980s, it was increasingly clear that diffuse emissions of nitrogen (N) and phosphorous (P) from agriculture was a major cause of water pollution, in addition to the discharges from industry and municipal sewage treatment plants. This was documented in a 1984 report from the Environmental Protection Agency (EPA). A couple of years later, some serious incidents of eutrophication of Danish marine waters causing oxygen depletion and large numbers of dead fish in the summer of 1986 created strong public pressure for political action and marked the beginning of a new 'heyday' phase of environmental policy (Moe 2018).

The Heyday of Environmental Policy, 1987–2002

The growing problems with eutrophication combined with the new insights from the 1984 EPA report provided the impetus for the first Action Plan for the Aquatic Environment I adopted by Parliament in 1987. The plan aimed to reduce N loading of the aquatic environment by 50 per cent and P loading by 80 per cent and required all major sewage treatment plants to treat the sewage for nitrogen and phosphorous as well as for organic matter. Industrial enterprises with individual discharges of wastewater were required to undertake treatment corresponding to the Best Available Technology, and the agricultural sector was required to reduce its total discharges from 260,000 tonnes to 133,000 tonnes. For this purpose, the action plan tightened some requirements regarding the handling of slurry and manure and the use of fertilizers that had already been introduced in 1985–6 in reaction to the 1984 EPA report. The plan also introduced requirements on wintergreen fields.

The action plan did lead to a rapid and significant improvement of wastewater treatment, and its success in this area inspired the 1991 EU directives on wastewater treatment and nitrates, which introduced similar standards at the EU level (Sørensen 2019: 13). However, by 1990, it was clear that the plan had not significantly reduced the N leaching from agriculture. This led to the adoption of the Action Plan for Sustainable Development in Agriculture in 1991 which tightened some regulatory measures in the first plan, particularly those relating to fertilization strategy. The new plan maintained the target of a 50 per cent reduction in N leaching but extended the time horizon for the target until 2000. Despite the new plan, the reduction in leaching still failed to live up to expectations, so in 1998, Parliament adopted the second Action Plan on the Aquatic Environment II. This plan introduced further constraints on the use of fertilizer plus requirements to use less N-intensive animal fodder, among other things. By 2010, it finally seemed that the target of a 50 per cent reduction of N leaching from agriculture had been met.

Another important trend starting in the late 1980s was the increasing use of environmental charges and taxes, partly motivated by the need to finance higher expenditure on environmental protection. An important example was the CO_2 tax introduced in 1991 that helped finance new expenses on the extension of district heating, subsidies to bioenergy, and various energy savings measures.

The Increasing Role of the EU since 2002

At the end of 2001, a new government with a less ambitious environmental policy platform took office. At the same time, EU regulation of environmental affairs was becoming increasingly comprehensive and gradually catching up with Danish policy goals and standards in many areas. Moe (2018), therefore, sees the period since 2002 as a phase during which Danish environmental policy has become increasingly dominated by the requirements of EU directives. For example, in recent years, the Danish authorities have realized that additional efforts may be needed to live up to the Birds and Habitats Directives for the protection of species and wildlife.

Meeting the targets implied by the Water Framework Directive of 2000 will also be a considerable challenge for Denmark. The directive requires that surface waters have a 'good ecological status', which only allows a slight departure from the biological quality that would be expected in conditions of minimal anthropogenic impact. While the Danish Action Plans for the Aquatic Environment have focused on reducing emissions to the aquatic environment to a certain level, the Water Framework Directive focuses on achieving an acceptable quality of the environment.

The Evolution of Environmental Quality: Has Environmental Policy Worked?

Environmental quality has an overwhelming number of dimensions, so evaluating its evolution is a complex task. However, there is no doubt that air quality in Denmark is now much higher than before the onset of systematic regulation around 1970 (Palmgren et al. 2018). For example, Figure 39.2a shows that Danish emissions of SO_2 have fallen dramatically and somewhat more than emissions in the rest of Europe (indicated by an index number in the figure). Figure 39.2b illustrates that emissions (the solid graphs) and concentrations of NO_2 (the dotted graphs) have also fallen since the late 1980s,

(a)

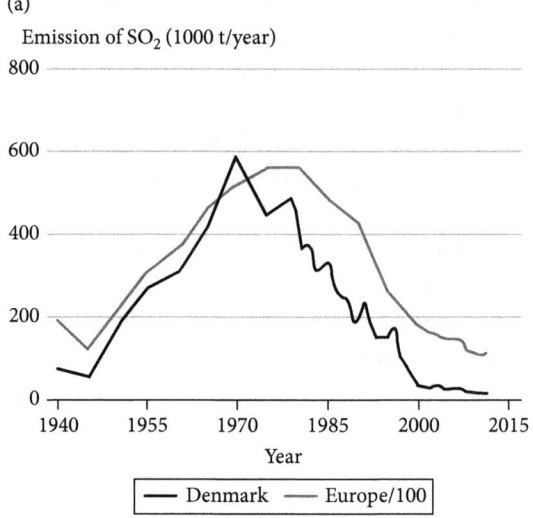

(b)

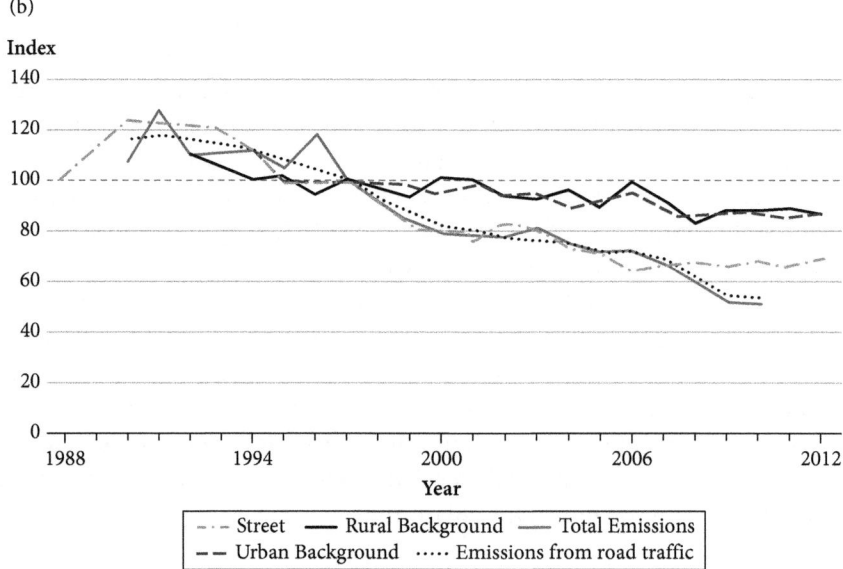

FIGURE 39.2A Evolution of SO₂ emissions.

Source: Danish Centre for Environment and Energy, Aarhus University

FIGURE 39.2B Evolution of NO$_X$ emissions.

although not by much in recent years. Emissions and concentrations of most other air pollutants have likewise declined significantly since the 1970s due to Danish regulation and enhanced international cooperation in the fight against cross-border air pollution. However, due to increased traffic volumes and a growing number of diesel vehicles, the concentration of NO₂ in some streets in major Danish cities still occasionally exceeds the permitted limit values. Emissions of particles from older wood-burning stoves is also a problem in some densely populated areas (Environmental Economic Council 2016).

When evaluating the evolution of water quality, it is necessary to distinguish between groundwater, marine surface waters, and streams and lakes.

The reduction in N loading especially from agriculture has reduced the content of nitrate in the groundwater, and in recent years, the N content has hovered around the permitted limit value of 50 mg/l; however, with higher values in 20 per cent of the samples taken in the 2016 groundwater-monitoring programme. One or more pesticides or metabolites were found in 34 per cent of the sample checks (Danish Centre for Environment and Energy 2018).

The extent of eelgrass and macroalgae are often used as indicators of the quality of marine coastal waters. Despite the reduction in N and P loading achieved through the Action Plans for the Aquatic Environment, it has taken a long time before these indicators have started to signal a recovery of marine water quality. This is illustrated in Figure 39.3, where the vertical lines indicate 95 per cent confidence intervals for the estimates. Indeed, the volume of eelgrass has only recently returned to the level prevailing in the early 1990s.

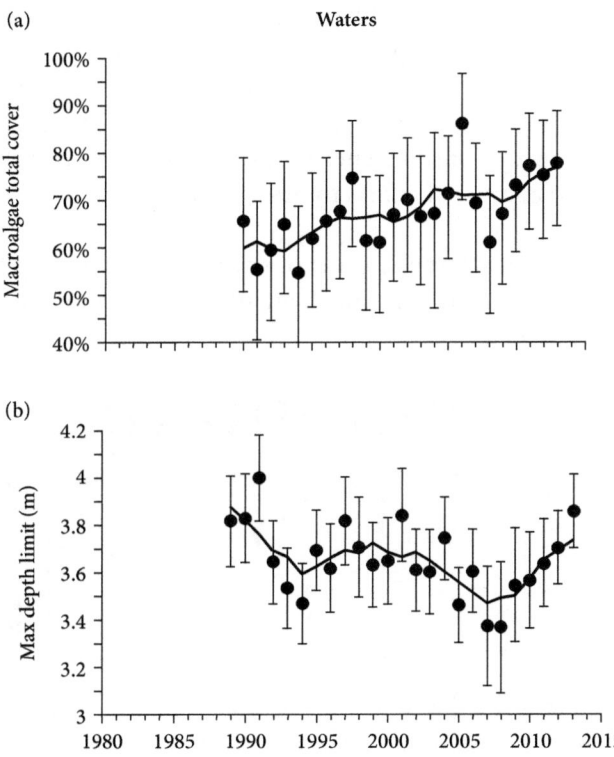

FIGURE 39.3 Macroalgae (total cover) and eelgrass (maximum depth limit) in marine waters.
Source: Riemann (2018, Figure 5)

The most serious environmental problem in Danish lakes is the large volume of algae in the water that tends to crowd out many other forms of life in the lakes. Despite reductions in the emissions of organic matter and phosphorous to the lakes, the total amount of algae has not shown any systematic downward trend in recent decades (Danish Centre for Environment and Energy 2018), suggesting that significant improvements will require further reductions of emissions of phosphorus from agriculture and dispersed settlements.

The presence of small animals (invertebrates) is used as a main indicator of the quality of Danish watercourses. A distinction between seven fauna classes ranging from FK1 to FK7 is made, with a higher number signifying higher water quality. A fauna class of at least 5 is deemed to indicate a satisfactory water quality. Measured in this way, Figure 39.4 shows that the proportion of watercourses in at least good status has increased from around 20 per cent in 1994 to about 50 per cent in 2016. However, the EU Water Framework Directive also specifies a number of other indicators of water quality, including the presence of plants and fish, all of which must satisfy some minimum standards for the watercourse to be considered in 'good ecological condition'. When these indicators are included, the proportion of watercourses in a satisfactory state is much lower than 50 per cent (Andersen and Jensen 2019).

The total production of waste has increased dramatically from 3.0 million tonnes in 1970 to 11.7 million tonnes in 2016 (Veltze et al. 2019), but the proportion of deposited waste fell from 59 per cent to 4 per cent over the same period, aided by frequent increases in the excise tax on deposited waste introduced in 1987. Although the fraction of recycled waste has increased significantly, the recycling of 48 per cent of household and municipal waste in 2016 only matched the average degree of recycling in the EU, so Denmark must make additional efforts to meet the EU target of a 65 per cent rate of recycling by 2035.

Among the many other relevant aspects of environmental quality, biodiversity and conservation of nature has attracted much attention in recent decades. I discuss the status on this front below.

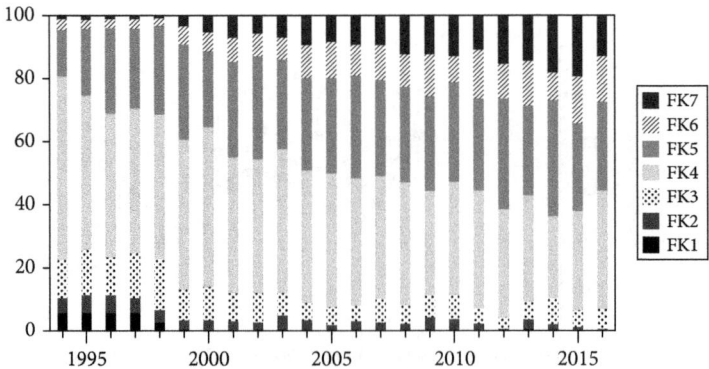

FIGURE 39.4 Share of fauna classes in water courses (per cent).

Source: Danish Centre for Environment and Energy, Aarhus University

Recent Bones of Contention in Environmental Policy

In 2001, a report from a government expert committee concluded that Danish nature and biodiversity was under serious pressure from economic development in general and from intensive farming practices in particular. The committee recommended several policy measures designed to improve nature conservation and protect biodiversity (Wilhjelmudvalget 2001).

These themes were followed up in a report from the Commission on Nature and Agriculture (2013) recommending numerous specific actions aimed at increasing the quantity and quality of nature areas and forests, reducing the use of pesticides, protecting the groundwater, strengthening sustainable use of biomass, promoting the development of environmentally friendly agricultural techniques, reducing agricultural greenhouse gas emissions, etc. An important recommendation was to replace the uniform regulation of emissions of nitrate and phosphorous (requiring all farmers to reduce their use of fertilizer by the same percentage) with a more flexible regulation that would concentrate emissions reduction in the areas and on the types of land where the environment was most vulnerable.

In 2015, this idea was picked up by the Liberal Party government, although probably not in the way envisioned by the Commission on Nature and Agriculture. In December 2015, a majority in Parliament agreed on an 'Agricultural Package' with the main purpose of strengthening growth and employment. The package allowed farmers to increase their use of fertilizer by 20 per cent already from 2016 and eliminated the previous riparian buffer strips that prevented the cultivation of land very close to streams and lakes. The potential negative impacts on water quality was supposed to be more than offset by the transition to a new flexible regulatory system along the lines proposed by the Commission on Nature and Agriculture. The Minister for Food and Agriculture claimed that the package would reduce the emission of nitrates already from 2016 and onwards, but the credibility of this claim was soon undermined by criticism from independent experts. The criticism led to the resignation of the Minister and to the adoption of a compensatory 'Nature Package' which was also aimed at cushioning warnings from the European Commission that the package might violate the Water Framework Directive, the Nitrate Directive, and the Habitat Directive. The Nature Package included, among other things, initiatives for afforestation to support biodiversity and additional subsidies to wintergreen fields to reduce nitrate leaching. Nevertheless, by early 2019, it became clear that nitrate emissions actually increased a bit from 2016 to 2017, whereas they ought to have fallen according to government plans.

As another indication of the growing challenges for environmental policy, a recent joint report from the Danish Society for Nature Conservation and the World Wildlife Fund (2017) concluded that Denmark will most likely fail to live up to most of the 20 biodiversity targets for 2020 specified in the Aichi Convention on Biological Diversity.

These examples illustrate the strategic and controversial role of land use and agriculture in Danish environmental policy. However, in a rare display of unity in February 2019, the Danish Society for Nature Conservation and the Danish Agriculture and Food

Council (the main agricultural lobby) proposed a plan for shifting large tracts of low-lying organogenic agricultural land from intensive to extensive use. Implementing the plan would require government compensation or subsidies to farmers. The plan was presented not only as a means of protecting the aquatic environment, biodiversity, and nature but also as a necessary step towards reducing greenhouse gas emissions from agriculture. This takes us to the issue of climate policy.

ENERGY AND CLIMATE POLICY

The bulk of greenhouse gas emissions takes the form of CO_2 stemming from the use of fossil fuels in energy consumption, including energy for transport. Hence, energy and climate policies are inextricably linked, so my review will cover both policy areas. I will track the evolution of energy policy since the early 1970s when the foundations for important ingredients in current climate policy were laid even though global warming was not yet a concern.

The Danish heat and electricity sector has undergone a remarkable transition from a centralized system heavily dependent on imported oil in the early 1970s to a highly decentralized and more energy-efficient system with a high share of renewable energy today. The transition was implemented via heavy-handed direct regulation coupled with high energy taxes and subsidies to renewable energy. Below, I outline three distinct phases of this transition.

1974–1989: Energy Security as the Overriding Concern

When the first OPEC oil price shock hit the world economy in the fall of 1973, Denmark relied on imported oil for more than 90 per cent of the nation's primary energy supply. Hence, the Danish economy was hit particularly hard by the first oil price shock. This experience initiated an era of energy planning aimed at increasing energy security. The commitment to energy security was strengthened by the second OPEC oil price shock in 1979–80 and remained the overriding goal for energy policy until the end of the 1980s.

The energy plan Danish Energy Policy 1976 outlined many of the policies that have been followed since then (Tornbjerg 2015). The plan was aimed at diversifying energy supply and improving energy efficiency. This was to be achieved by switching from oil to coal, natural gas, nuclear energy, and (a bit of) wind power, and by introducing regional and municipal planning of collective heat supply as well as energy savings measures in industry and households. The plan was followed up by the establishment of the Danish Energy Agency, which has supervised and regulated the Danish energy system since 1976. The Agency became part of the new Ministry of Energy established in 1979.

The plan to introduce nuclear energy turned out to be politically divisive and was postponed. Instead, oil was replaced by coal at an impressive pace. Within a mere nine years, Danish production of electricity and district heating changed from being 81 per cent oil-based in 1972 to being 69 per cent coal-based in 1981 according to statistics from the Danish Energy Agency.

The objective of energy savings was supported by the introduction of excise taxes on oil and electricity in 1977, and the 1979 Heat Supply Act provided the basis for the development of the comprehensive Danish system of district heating and decentralized power supply through the expansion of Combined Heat and Power (CHP) plants. The joint production of heat and power greatly helped to improve energy efficiency and gradually made Denmark an international leader in the use of CHP (Sovacool 2013).

As the second OPEC oil price shock hit Denmark in 1979–80, policymakers increased energy taxes in two successive rounds as part of an effort to reduce ballooning deficits in foreign trade and public finances. Efforts to establish a network for the distribution of natural gas from the Danish part of the North Sea were intensified, and in 1984, the state-owned network was ready for use. To support the natural gas project, Danish power stations were obliged to buy the natural gas supply exceeding the demand from households and industry, and decentralized CHP plants in districts covered by the gas distribution network were obliged to use natural gas as a fuel. In a further move towards a diversified supply system, many decentralized CHPs in other parts of the country began to use waste and straw as fuel (Danish Energy Agency 2016). The trend towards more use of natural gas, straw, and waste for production of district heating continued into the 1990s.

To protect investments in renewable energy plants such as wind turbines and to maintain incentives for energy savings, policymakers reacted to the collapse in oil prices in the mid-1980s by increasing taxes on fossil fuels to keep consumer prices of energy roughly unchanged. In 1986, electricity utilities—mostly owned by municipalities or local cooperatives—were also made responsible for an intensified effort to help their customers save on electricity use, and in 1988, it was even forbidden to use electricity for individual heating in areas with district heating or a natural gas network.

Energy labelling for buildings and appliances became another popular instrument to promote energy savings during the 1980s, starting with the introduction of a labelling regime for the energy efficiency of buildings in 1979.

Following years of debate, the 'green' majority in Parliament decided in 1985 to rule out nuclear energy as a part of Denmark's future energy supply. This far-reaching decision has not been seriously challenged since then.

1990–2001: Climate Policy Takes Precedence

By the end of the 1980s, awareness of the problem of global warming was growing, and in 1990, the Minister for Energy Jens Bilgrav-Nielsen presented the world's first national action plan for the reduction of CO_2 emissions, 'Energy 2000'. The plan aimed at a 20 per cent reduction of CO_2 emissions by 2005 to be achieved partly by the introduction of a carbon tax and higher energy taxes and partly by support for wind energy and various measures to improve energy efficiency, including further establishment of decentralized CHP plants fuelled by natural gas or biomass.

In 1991, Parliament enacted a carbon tax, and in the Biomass Agreement of 1993, Parliament obliged electricity utilities to increase their use of straw and woodchips. In 1995, the taxes on emissions of CO_2 and SO_2 by business firms were increased, and in 1996, electricity utilities were ordered to increase their wind power capacity. That year also saw a new, ambitious energy plan 'Energy 21' presented by Minister for Environment and Energy Svend Auken who was anxious to secure public service obligations relating to environment and climate in a future liberalized market for electricity as Denmark headed towards the liberalization mandated by an EU directive of 1996.

The electricity market reform of 1999 initiated a gradual liberalization of the Danish electricity market. In principle, all potential suppliers of power (including suppliers from neighbouring countries interconnected with Denmark) got access to the Danish distribution network on equal terms and at prices subject to free competition. This was, however, with one important exception; power produced by wind, biomass, and CHP plants fuelled by natural gas was guaranteed priority network access at regulated prices covering the estimated additional production costs of such power. In practice, climate policy objectives thus overruled the goal of full liberalization (Olsen 2006).

As envisioned by the energy action plan of 1990, the 1990s saw an accelerated expansion of decentralized CHP plants. From 1990 to 1997, more than three quarters of all new capacity added to the Danish power grid consisted of small CHP plants for district heating or industrial use fuelled by natural gas or straw (Lehtonen and Nye 2009). Another remarkable development was the fast expansion of wind power in the second half of the 1990s, strongly supported by regulatory polices (see below).

Since 2002: Stop-Go Policy

Just as the advent of a Liberal-Conservative government in late 2001 led to a shift in environmental policy, it also marked a reversal of energy and climate policy. The large Ministry for Environment and Energy was split up, the department for energy was transferred to the Ministry of Economics and Business, total staff was reduced, and the new Centre for Environmental Assessment headed by the climate-sceptic Bjørn Lomborg was established. The new government declared that the interventionist policies pursued by the previous government had unduly increased the cost of energy to the detriment of Danish industry (Petersen 2018: 192), and in 2002, a new support scheme for wind turbines reduced the subsidy to wind power. Consequently, the expansion of wind power capacity was brought to a complete halt in the period 2003–8.

However, by 2006, Danish Prime Minister Anders Fogh Rasmussen had apparently become convinced that climate change was a serious problem and that dependence on fossil fuels had problematic geopolitical implications. Hence, in a remarkable policy shift, the government announced in 2007 that Denmark should move towards complete independence of fossil fuels in the long term. Therefore, the government's new energy plan of 2007 was aimed at reducing fossil fuel use, increasing the efforts at energy saving, and increasing the share of renewable energy in energy production and the use of biofuels in the transport sector. The plan laid the foundation for the Parliament's broad Energy Agreement in early 2008, which included more support for wind power and for the use of biomass and waste in CHP plants and a rise in the CO_2 tax, as well as a new excise tax on NO_x emissions. A major goal of the plan was to increase the share of renewable energy in total gross energy consumption to 20 per cent by 2011.

Inspired by the report from the Danish Commission on Climate Change Policy (2010) which provided a blueprint for a fossil fuel free Denmark by 2050, the Energy Agreement of 2008 was followed up by the even more ambitious Energy Agreement of March 2012 under a new centre-left government. The agreement aimed at a 12 per cent reduction of energy consumption by 2020 relative to 2006, a 35 per cent share of renewable energy in total energy consumption, and a 50 per cent share of wind power in total electricity consumption, likewise to be achieved by 2020. Energy companies were to intensify their support for energy savings in households and businesses, a large volume of offshore and onshore wind power capacity was to be added to the electricity supply, and the use of biomass and biogas in the production of heat and electricity was promoted in various ways. The large investments in energy savings and renewable energy were to be financed by energy consumers via user charges, including the PSO (Public Service Obligation) tariff on electricity. Although the Liberal Party expressed great scepticism during the political negotiations, it ended up supporting the energy agreement following pressure from the business community which stressed the need for a stable framework for energy policy.

In 2014, a parliamentary majority consisting of the centre-left parties and the Conservative People's Party passed the Climate Act of 2014, which established a Council on Climate Change of independent experts to monitor progress towards the targets for climate policy and to propose cost-effective ways of meeting the targets. The comments following the text of the bill mentioned a national target of reducing total Danish greenhouse gas emissions by 40 per cent by 2020 relative to 1990. The Liberal Party did not support this target and voted against the Climate Act.

In 2015, a new Liberal Party minority government announced that its climate policy would be based on 'green realism', signalling a desire to reduce the pace of the transition to renewable energy. Echoing the motivation for the policy reversal back in 2002, the government expressed concern that the ambitious climate policy drove up the cost of energy, mainly via the increase in the PSO tariff needed to finance the Energy Agreement of 2012. The government also claimed that EU law required an abolition of the PSO tariff, implying that subsidies to green energy would have to be financed via the general government budget. The Council on Climate Change pointed out that there were other ways of financing the subsidies via cost-based user charges compatible with EU law. The Council added that a lower consumer price of energy would not in itself increase the supply of renewable energy, but a broad majority in Parliament supported the government's proposal for a gradual phase-out of the PSO tariff—to the delight of the business community.

In late 2016, two more political parties were invited to join the government, including the Conservative People's Party which did not subscribe to the Liberal Party's version of 'green realism'. The new government programme included a target for the share of renewable energy in total energy consumption of 50 per cent by 2030 and signalled a return to a more ambitious climate policy. In the new Energy Agreement of 2018 backed by all parties in Parliament, the target for the 2030 share of renewables was raised to 55 per cent as recommended by the Council on Climate change, and a target of zero net emissions by 2050 was set. The agreement gives priority to the expansion of offshore wind farms rather than onshore wind turbines and anticipates that continued subsidization of new offshore wind turbines will soon become redundant due to further technological progress. According to the agreement, future onshore wind and solar power plants must compete for subsidies in a technology-neutral bidding process. The development of technologies for the production of 'green' gases will receive continued support, and the electrification of heat production will be supported via a cut in the excise tax on electricity for heating purposes.

The Outcome: Energy Production and Consumption Since the Early 1970s

The transformation of the Danish energy system resulting from the development of technologies, world market prices, and the policies outlined above is illustrated below. As shown in Figure 39.5, gross energy consumption has stayed roughly

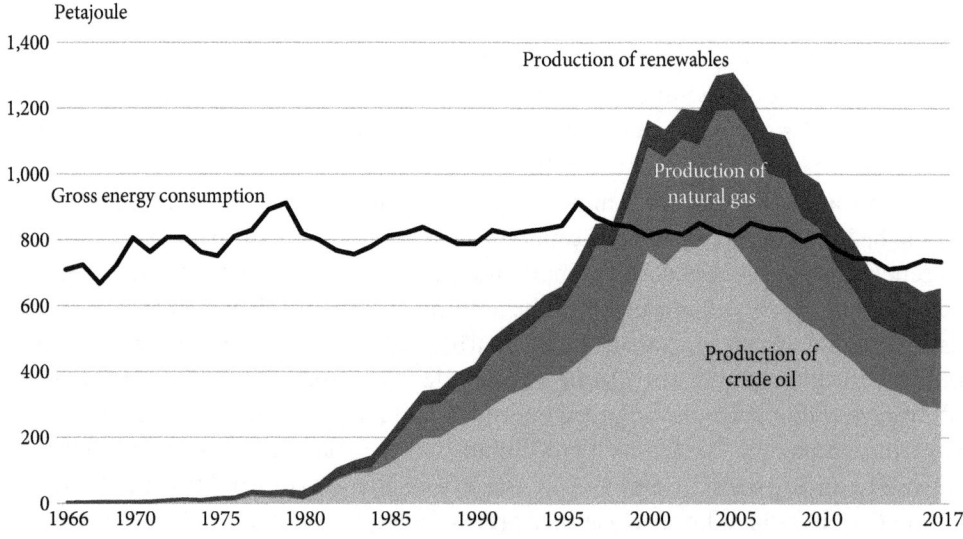

FIGURE 39.5 Denmark's gross energy consumption and production of primary energy.
Source: Statistics Denmark

constant since the mid-1960s, despite an almost three-fold increase in real GDP from 1966 to 2017. During the same period, Danish production of oil and natural gas in the North Sea rose from zero to exceeding domestic energy consumption by almost a third in the mid-2000s, followed by a decline in recent years as the most easily accessible reserves were gradually exhausted. Despite the increase in domestic production of renewable energy during the last two decades, the fall in fossil fuel production means that Denmark is once again a net importer of energy, although much less so than around 1970.

The Evolution of Renewable Energy

The evolution of Danish production of renewable energy is recorded in Figure 39.6. While the expansion of wind power has caught most of the public attention, straw and other forms of biomass actually make up a larger share of domestic renewable energy production.

The evolution of the Danish wind industry is an interesting example of a fruitful interaction between private entrepreneurship and government regulation. In the pioneering days of the 1970s and 1980s, the development of wind power technology was very much driven by the 'animal spirits' of dedicated entrepreneurs experimenting with new technologies on a learning-by-doing basis, and the investment in and operation of the new wind turbines was mostly carried out by individual farmers and by local cooperatives (Petersen 2018). From 1979, the state offered a 30 per cent investment subsidy to the installation of wind and solar energy plants and biogas digesters. The subsidy was granted on the conditions that ownership (individual or cooperative) had to be local and that local residents had the option of joining the cooperatives which financed and owned the plants. This policy helped to secure broad public support for wind power.

In 1981, a feed-in tariff was introduced, requiring utilities to buy all power from renewable energy technologies at a certain rate above the wholesale price of electricity. In 1985, an agreement was reached between the government and the electricity utilities, committing the latter to install 100 MW of wind capacity over a five-year period. That same year, the government established the Wind Turbine Guarantee, providing long-term financing of large wind projects that used Danish-made wind turbines, and the Danish Energy Agency mandated open and guaranteed access for wind power to the electricity grid, with grid connection costs to be shared between the owner of the wind turbine and the electricity utility. In addition to this regulatory support for wind energy, the industry also benefited from extensive cooperation with research institutions.

While many observers saw the expansion of the Danish wind industry as a success story, a report from the Danish Economic Councils (2002) estimated that—despite environmental gains and cost savings achieved through 'learning-by-doing' effects— the investments in wind energy during the 1990s had actually generated a net social loss

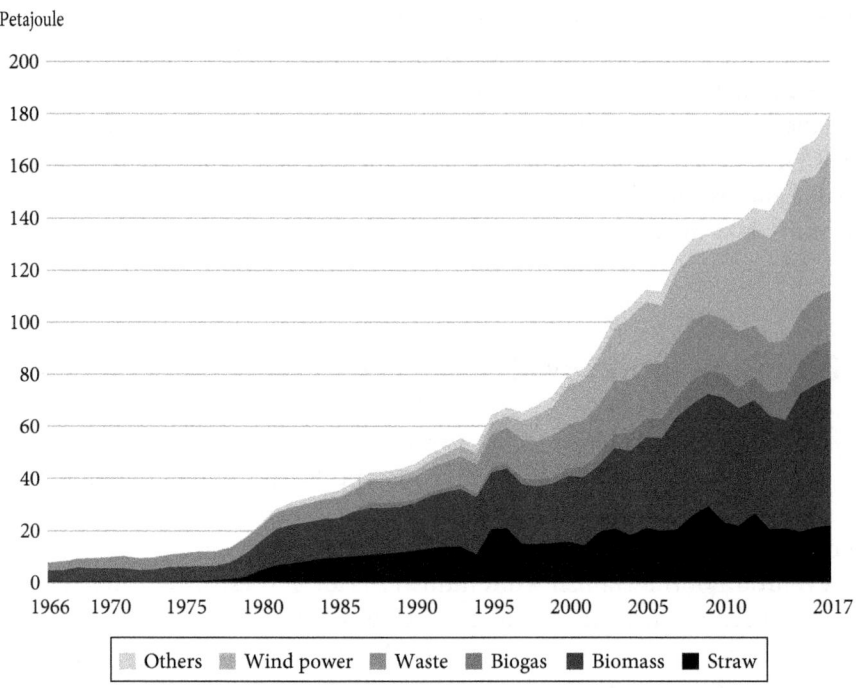

FIGURE 39.6 Denmark's production of renewable energy.
Source: Statistics Denmark

of DKK 3 billion, mainly due to an initial excess production capacity in the electricity sector. However, the report also anticipated that future investments in wind energy would in fact be socially profitable due to continued technical progress in the wind industry.

In recent decades, technological and commercial developments have transformed the wind industry. The optimal size of wind turbines has grown dramatically, and 'not-in-my-backyard' local resistance to gigantic turbines has provided incentives to shift the expansion of wind power from onshore to offshore locations, requiring large-scale investments and intensive R&D that has favoured a concentration of the wind industry. In this competitive race, large companies like Vestas (producer of wind turbines) and Ørsted (builder and operator of offshore wind farms) have established themselves as domestic and international market leaders.

Despite the growing share of fluctuating wind power in electricity consumption (approaching 50 per cent at the time of writing), Denmark has maintained an almost 100 per cent security of electricity supply thanks to intelligent management and development of the grid by utilities and the Danish TSO (*Energinet*), including investments in interconnectors with neighbouring countries. For this reason, and because of the achievements in energy efficiency mentioned earlier, Denmark's energy system often comes out on top in international rankings.

Conclusion

By the end of the 2010s, Denmark is facing a new and more difficult phase in the transition to a society with zero net emissions. First, as the share of fluctuating wind power increases, it is increasingly difficult to utilize power efficiently in periods with strong winds where the marginal power supply sometimes has to be exported at very low or even negative prices. Experts agree that a combination of extensive electrification of the heat and transport sectors, development of technologies for energy storage, establishment of new interconnectors with neighbouring countries, and promotion of a more flexible demand for electricity is needed to pave the way for further expansion of wind and solar energy. This will require new funds for investment and a reform of energy taxes and taxes on motor vehicles that may cause a loss of government revenue.

Second, the energy system is becoming heavily dependent on imported wood-based biomass, mainly because biomass is exempt from the energy tax. Experts have pointed out that heat can typically be produced at a lower social cost by using power-driven heat pumps rather than biomass, and the Energy Agreement of 2018 did indeed include a cut in the energy tax on electricity for heating to promote heat pumps. However, because large investments in CHPs fuelled by wood-based biomass have already been undertaken, an important part of the Danish energy system will be locked into this technology for a decade or two. Furthermore, many observers have challenged the dubious assumption that the use of woodchips and wood pellets is 'carbon neutral' and have called for a tighter regulation to ensure that the biomass is sourced from locations where forests are managed in a climate-friendly way.

Third, as agriculture is responsible for more than one fifth of Danish greenhouse gas emissions, it must be subjected to systematic regulation of emissions if Denmark is to meet the target of zero net emissions by 2050. The lobby for conventional farming has resisted any regulation that would increase the cost of production so far, arguing that this would only cause carbon leakage by shifting agricultural production abroad. In any case, a cost-effective regulation via taxes or subsidies will have to rely on measurement of emissions from individual farm units, and inspired by a proposal from the Council on Climate Change (Danish Council on Climate Change 2016), policymakers are currently considering how this might be done.

Fourth, there is a debate on the best way to meet Denmark's EU-mandated target for the reduction of GHG emissions from transport, agriculture, buildings, and other sectors not covered by the European Emissions Trading System (ETS). The government wishes to use Denmark's option of meeting a large part of the target by cancelling the auctioning of 8 million tons of CO_2 emission permits to firms within the ETS. The Council on Climate Change has warned that such a reduction of permit supply will not succeed in reducing actual emissions very much before 2030 because of the huge surplus of permits within the ETS and that annulling emission allowances rather than cutting domestic emissions will only postpone the necessary reduction of non-ETS emissions (Danish Council on Climate Change 2018).

The resolution of these issues in the coming years will determine whether Denmark will remain a green frontrunner country.

ACKNOWLEDGEMENTS

Without implicating them in any remaining shortcomings, I wish to thank Jørgen Henningsen, Mogens Moe, Peter Nedergaard, and Ole Gravgård Pedersen for valuable comments on earlier drafts of this chapter.

REFERENCES

Andersen, Jens M., and Poul N. Jensen (2019 Jan.). 'Danske vandløb ca. 1970–2018: Miljøets fodspor nr. 4', Environmental Protection Agency, https://miljoetsfodspor.mst.dk/media/204406/miljoeets-fodspor-nr-4-vandloebsartikel.pdf

Commission on Nature and Agriculture (2013, Apr.). 'Natur og Landbrug – en ny start', Commission on Nature and Agriculture, https://openarchive.cbs.dk/bitstream/handle/10398/8851/Oestrup_2.pdf?sequence=1 (accessed 8 December 2019).

Danish Centre for Environment and Energy (2018). 'Vandmiljø og Natur 2016. NOVANA. Tilstand og udvikling – faglig sammenfatning', *Danish Centre for Environment and Energy*, Report no. 274.

Danish Commission on Climate Change Policy (2010). 'Green energy - the road to a Danish energy system without fossil fuels', Danish Commission on Climate Change Policy, https://ens.dk/sites/ens.dk/files/Globalcooperation/green_energy_eng_publication.pdf (accessed 8 December 2019).

Danish Council on Climate Change (2016). 'Effektive veje til drivhusgasreduktion i landbruget', Danish Council on Climate Change, https://www.klimaraadet.dk/da/analyser/effektive-veje-til-drivhusgasreduktion-i-landbruget (accessed 8 December 2019).

Danish Council on Climate Change (2018). 'Status for Danmarks klimamålsætninger og – forpligtelser 2018', Danish Council on Climate Change, https://www.klimaraadet.dk/da/analyser/analyse-status-danmarks-klimamaalsaetninger-og-forpligtelser-2018

Danish Economic Councils (2002). 'Dansk økonomi, forår 2002', Danish Economic Councils, https://dors.dk/vismandsrapporter/dansk-okonomi-forar-2002 (accessed 8 December 2019).

Danish Energy Agency (2016 Apr.). 'Danmarks energifortider – Hovedbegivenheder på energiområdet', Danish Energy Agency, https://ens.dk/sites/ens.dk/files/EnergiKlimapolitik/danmarks_energifortider_samlet.pdf (accessed 8 December 2019).

Danish Society for Nature Conservation and the World Wildlife Fund (2017, Dec.). 'Biodiversitetsbarometer 2017: Vurdering af Danmarks indsats for biodiversitet', https://www.dn.dk/vi-arbejder-for/biodiversitet/biodiversitetsbarometer-vurdering-af-danmarks-indsats-for-biodiversitet/ (accessed 8 December 2019).

Environmental Economic Council (2016). 'Economy and Environment 2016'.

Lehtonen, Markku, and Sheridan Nye (2009). 'History of electricity network control and distributed generation in the UK and Western Denmark', *Energy Policy*, 37/6: 2338–45.

Moe, Mogens (1995). *Environmental Administration in Denmark*. Copenhagen: Ministry of Environment and Energy.

Moe, Mogens (2018). *Miljørettens udvikling siden 1971*. Noter til afskedsforelæsning for Danske Miljøadvokater, 18 January 2018, unpublished.

Olsen, Ole J. (2006). *Konkurrence på det danske elmarked efter reformen i 1999*. AKF.

Palmgren, Finn, Thomas Ellermann, and Ole Hertel (2018 Dec.). 'Luftkvaliteten: Miljøets fodspor nr. 2', Environmental Protection Agency, https://miljoetsfodspor.mst.dk/media/191314/miljoeets-fodspor-nr-2-luftkvaliteten.pdf (accessed 8 December 2019).

Petersen, Flemming (2018). *Da Danmark fik vinger: vindmøllehistorien 1978–2018*. Aarhus: Danmarks Vindmølleforening.

Riemann, Bo (2018 Dec.). 'Miljøforholdene i havet: Miljøets fodspor nr. 1', Environmental Protection Agency, https://miljoetsfodspor.mst.dk/media/204391/miljoeets-fodspor-nr-1-miljoeforholdene-i-havet1.pdf

Sovacool, Benjamin K. (2013). 'Energy policymaking in Denmark: Implications for global energy security and sustainability', *Energy Policy*, 61: 829–39.

Statistics Denmark (2018). *Green National Accounts for Denmark 2015–2016*. Copenhagen.

Sørensen, Poul E. (2019 Jan.). 'Spildevand: Miljøets fodspor nr. 3', Environmental Protection Agency, https://miljoetsfodspor.mst.dk/media/204405/miljoeets-fodspor-nr-3-spildevand.pdf

Tornbjerg, Jesper (2015). *Green Energy for All*. Hillerød: Tornmountain.

Veltze, Suzanne A., Christian Fischer, and Stig Hirsbak (2019 Feb.). 'Affald og genanvendelse: Miljøets fodspor nr. 5', Environmental Protection Agency, https://miljoetsfodspor.mst.dk/media/204433/miljoeets-fodspor-nr-5-affald-og-genanvendelse.pdf (accessed 8 December 2019).

Wendling, Zachary A., Jay Emerson, Daniel Esty, Marc A. Levy, and Alex de Sherbinin (2018). *2018 Environmental Performance Index*. New Haven, CT: Yale Center for Environmental Law and Policy.

Wilhjelmudvalget (2001, Nov.). *En rig natur i et rigt samfund*. Copenhagen: Wilhjelmudvalget.

CHAPTER 40

RESEARCH POLICY
Transformations and Tensions

KAARE AAGAARD AND NIELS MEJLGAARD

THE SOCIAL CONTRACT OF SCIENCE

UP until the turn of the millennium, Denmark was characterized as a slow and pragmatic adopter of international research policy ideas (Hansen 2002; Mejlgaard and Aagaard 2009). However, much has happened since then. During the latest decade, Denmark has repeatedly been singled out as 'one of the most reform intensive European countries' (e.g. Aagaard and de Boer 2017: 143) and as a trailblazer among the Nordic countries (Kallerud 2006; Antikainen 2016: 239). While such claims certainly find support in the sheer number and in the comprehensiveness of the implemented reforms over the last fifteen years, there are important nuances to the story. Rather than seeing international research policy development as the manifestation of a single, coherent reform agenda, it is more accurate to view it as consisting of several partly integrated and partly competing reform dimensions. As we will show in this chapter, Denmark's reform pace has only been high along some of these dimensions, while others have mostly received symbolic attention or have even been deliberately downplayed.

A useful theoretical starting-point in order to capture these nuances is the classical accounts of the developing relationship between science and the state. This relationship has often been characterized using the metaphor of a changing 'social contract' (Guston and Keniston 1994). The metaphor captures the historical transformation process from a traditional, trust-based social contract of science towards a new one, explicitly emphasizing accountability, societal impact, and academic excellence. However, while the notion of a changing social contract has proved to be useful as an analytical lens in the examination of long-term changes in national research policies, it needs to be further developed when focus is shifted towards more contemporary research policy developments. Hence, in addition to presenting an empirical analysis of central Danish research policy trends, this chapter also offers a theoretical refinement to the body of literature concerned with the Social Contract of Science.

From this outset, we argue that there are inherent tensions within the emerging 'social contract' and that understanding this provides a platform for examining recent changes in research policy. Particularly, we will show how tensions between output-oriented and process-oriented conceptions of research quality and societal impact shape contemporary research policies. Hence, with a particular emphasis on the period from 2000 and onwards, this chapter examines the way in which broad and abstract ideas underpinning the emerging 'social contract of science' have been translated into practical policies in a Danish research policy context.

The chapter proceeds as follows. First, we present an analytical framework highlighting inherent tensions in the emerging 'social contract of science'. We continue by providing a brief account and a timeline of major long-term developments in Danish research policy. Subsequently, we examine in more detail two important sets of recent Danish research policy reforms, specifically 1) the transformation of the public research funding system and 2) initiatives targeting knowledge dissemination in its various forms. Finally, we discuss the implications of the findings and highlight how different accentuations of research quality and societal impact may lead to either polarization or integration in actual research practices. We conclude by relating the current Danish developments to dominating international discussions.

COMPETING CONCEPTIONS OF RESEARCH QUALITY AND SOCIETAL IMPACT

In the aftermath of the Second World War, increased recognition of the military, economic, and social consequences of science triggered early policy narratives around science's role in society and sparked academic interest in studying the norms and dynamics of science as a social system. Influential policy prescriptions such as Vannevar Bush's *Science: The Endless Frontier* (1945/1990), alongside seminal work in the emerging Sociology of Science, and particularly Merton's (1942/1973) essay *The Normative Structure of Science* provided the contours of what has come to be considered the 'traditional' social contract. It involves extensive reliance on science's internal mechanisms for quality assurance, significant individual and organizational discretion, and high but largely unspecified expectations that academic advancements and discoveries will eventually create societal value, new products, and technologies (Mejlgaard and Aagaard 2017; Guston and Keniston 1994).

Since then, different developments have put the traditional contract under strain. Growing confidence in science as a core engine of national competitiveness has led to increased public funding, flanked by growing attention to tangible returns on investment. Improved understanding of the complex dynamics by which technological development and innovation occurs has challenged the linear 'science push' model and accentuated the need to consider 'societal pull' as well as various feedback mechanisms and interdependencies. Public discontent and scepticism related to the adverse environmental, ethical, and social effects of controversial information, energy, and biotechnologies has invoked a stronger desire for giving science direction and for developing mechanisms for assessing the 'societal robustness' of science and technology (Gibbons 1999; Nowotny et al. 2001).

In combination, such developments have stressed the relevance of renegotiating science's traditional social contract. In very broad terms, research policy has tried to tackle this challenge over the latest decades. As knowledge production has become increasingly global but also increasingly competitive, research policy has emerged as a central policy area in most countries. And while there is variation, attempts to flesh out a 'new contract' for science tend to revolve around the exchange of public funding for research, which is not only scientifically sound but also societally relevant, through mechanisms ensuring higher degrees of transparency and accountability (Martin 2003). What is emerging, then, is a social contract in which interdependency features prominently. It is also one in which distinct, sometimes contradictory, concerns and objectives co-exist, and where practical research policy becomes a matter of striking the right balance.

A major anchor point for such research policy formulations has been the notion of a global transition towards a 'knowledge economy' in which innovation capacity and intellectual capital are crucial for competitiveness and in which commercialization, university-industry collaboration, and entrepreneurial skills become markers of success in research. Another co-existing and related anchor point is that of scientific 'excellence' which is increasingly considered a precondition for achieving the breakthroughs that can be game-changers in global competition. According to these dominant ideas behind recent research policy developments, research quality and societal impact are not, necessarily, at odds.

While notions of excellence and innovation provide strong impetus concerning the goals for research policy, they are less helpful in prescribing relevant means to achieve these goals. Hence, as in other policy areas, research policymakers have looked to generic approaches such as New Public Management when designing governance arrangements for science. Therefore, current conceptualizations and performance indicators concerning both research quality and societal impact tend to be rather narrowly concerned with outputs. Research quality is often reduced to crude counting of publications and citations, and societal impact is often reduced to varieties of technology transfer measures. While the dominant storylines around innovation and excellence could potentially be conceptually integrated, their actual manifestations in policy and performance measurement are distinctly different.

However, since around 2000, but more strongly in the last five to ten years, a residual, broader conceptualization of research quality and societal impact has emerged. Here, the notion of a 'knowledge society' in which rights and duties in relation to science are more widely and equally distributed is key. Citizens and societal stakeholders are considered legitimate participants in societal decision-making around science, and importantly, they are relevant co-creators of knowledge. Part of this emerging narrative addresses what is now sometimes referred to as 'crises of trust and truth in science' (Saltelli and Funtowicz 2017; Bouter et al. 2016). Increased public and political

Table 40.1. Competing Conceptions of Research Quality and Societal Impact

	Narrow; Output-oriented	Broad; Process-oriented
Research quality	Publications Citations	Open Science/Open data Citizen science Responsible metrics Research integrity/Research ethics
Societal impact	Patents Spin-outs Science popularization Policy advice	Responsible Research and Innovation Public engagement 'Productive interactions' Stakeholder involvement

contestation of science-based knowledge alongside symptoms of difficulties maintaining quality assurance mechanisms and professional norms in a context of accelerated knowledge production are core elements of the crises.

These emerging anchors for research policy command a focus on processes or practices rather than outputs. In terms of research quality, the process-oriented perspective is concerned with practices that support transparency, inclusivity, and integrity as mechanisms for enhancing the epistemic quality of scientific knowledge claims. The open science and open data movements are examples. In terms of societal impact, corresponding mechanisms to determine desirable social ends for scientific and technological development become relevant. Engagement with diverse stakeholders, or what Molas-Gallart et al. (2015) refer to as 'productive interactions', is part of the process requirement for optimizing the (right) societal impact of research. Table 40.1 above summarizes the dominant (output-oriented) and the residual (process-oriented) conceptions of research quality and societal impact.

While both the output-oriented and the process-oriented approaches are concerned with research quality and societal impact, they accentuate and value different attributes of these concepts. Likewise, the two approaches understand the level of integration and interdependency between the two concepts differently. As we will show in the following sections, this distinction between output-oriented and process-oriented approaches provides a useful lens to analyse central tensions in the implementation of recent Danish research policy.

BROAD TRENDS IN DANISH
RESEARCH POLICY

It is generally acknowledged that the institutionalization of a distinct Danish research policy was quite late compared to other Western countries (Aagaard 2017). In the first decades after the Second World War, research and development investments were modest, there was almost no formal central organization, and up until the late 1970s, the funding of public research was almost fully dominated by floor funding with very few strings attached. Likewise, the research council system, which was slowly institutional-ized during this period, was very academically oriented in general and closely linked to the universities (Aagaard 2011).

However, during the 1980s, it was increasingly argued that major reforms were needed in order to increase cooperation with the outside world in general and with the private sector in particular (Grønbæk 2001). In addition, university research was seen to suffer from lack of competition, from environments of sub-critical mass and from lack of mobility. This was perceived as serious systemic dysfunctions in light of the emerging policy belief that renewed industrial growth should be based on key research based technologies such as IT, biotech, and materials science (Aagaard 2017; Grønbæk 2001). As a result, large-scale programme funding of strategic research took off during the fol-lowing years.

By the early 1990s, it became increasingly clear that the strong growth of earmarked research funding was dragging new problems along in terms of other types of imbal-ances and fragmentation. Further displacement towards strategic programme fund-ing accordingly came to be perceived as harmful to the overall balances of the system and as a threat to the diversity, risk-taking, and the long-term viability of public research activities. As a result, it was agreed to maintain the existing balance between floor funding and external funding at a stable level in the years to come (Aagaard 2017). In addition, an overhead system was established in 1995, further reducing the pressure on the floor funding. Moreover, the so-called Danish National Research Foundation was created with effect from 1993 to supply long-term support to new 'centres of excel-lence' solely based on academic quality criteria. These initiatives were all part of a gen-eral academic reorientation after a decade dominated by a growing emphasis on strategic research.

While the period up until 2000 was characterized by somewhat shifting research pol-icy agendas, the basic institutional configuration of the system was rather stable. However, in late 2001, a new Danish government took office and started a sweeping reform-process. A new Ministry of Science, Technology, and Innovation assumed the overall responsibility with a clear vision of subsuming the public research activities much more directly under an overall innovation policy umbrella. This ambition proved to be crucial for the coming reforms which aimed at transforming the universities into key players in the global knowledge economy rather than strengthening the traditional 'Republic of Science' elements of Danish research policy (Aagaard and Mejlgaard 2012). Consequently, new and explicit policy demands for increased accountability, strategic capacity, responsiveness, and social responsibility were launched at a rapid pace.

In particular, it was (again) argued that the research funding system needed an over-haul. In response to this, a number of new strategic/mission-oriented research funding councils were established, a performance-based research funding system was later added to the system, and the overall share of funding allocated under competition was increased. While some of these changes in the funding systems were initiated in the early 2000s, they were all considerably strengthened because of the comprehensive Danish 2006 Globalisation Strategy aiming to make Denmark a leading growth, knowledge, and entrepreneurial society (Danish Government 2006). A central objective herein was also to increase the public Danish R&D investments to 1 per cent of GDP by 2010.

Alongside these changes in the funding system, a new university act from 2003 introduced boards with a majority of external members as the superior authority of universities, and furthermore, it abolished the *primus inter pares* model by requiring appointed university leaders at all levels of the institutions instead of elected ones. The objective was to accentuate the profiles of the individual institutions, to professionalize and empower managerial structures, and to increase collaboration between research and innovation activities (Degn and Sørensen 2015).

Finally, in 2007, the government also implemented a far-reaching merger process, which reduced the number of universities from 12 to 8. In the process, 12 out of 15 Government Research Institutes (GRIs) were transferred to one of the 8 remaining universities—in reality, closing down the GRI sector. The result was a large concentration of resources within a few select institutions and a clear break with the former division of labour between academic researchers and the more applied or sector-oriented GRI research (Aagaard et al. 2016).

Figure 40.1 below provides an overview of major policy reforms in Denmark from the 1980s onwards. It gives a visual impression of the density of reforms in the 2000s, a remarkable period for Danish research policy in which no stone was left unturned in the pursuit of a governance arrangement conducive to optimizing academic excellence and societal impact. The veritable wave of reforms depended in large part on the fact that there was a widespread, shared demand for change among societal constituencies, including trade unions, employers' organizations, think tanks such as the Danish Academy of Technical Sciences, and an independent, appointed Research Commission with a mandate to offer recommendations for future trajectories (Aagaard 2012). However, it also significantly depended on a consensual, collaborative political tradition for this policy area in Denmark, with very minor differences across the dominant political parties (Hansen 2002; Aagaard and Mejlgaard 2012). This reform-fertile context was

Major policy changes

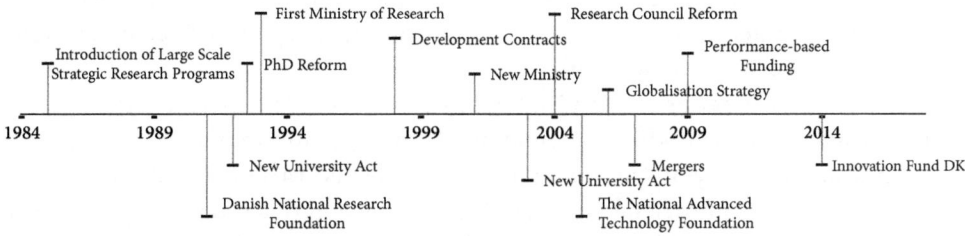

FIGURE 40.1 Major Danish research policy reforms.

further augmented by the personal dedication of incoming Prime Minister Fogh Rasmussen (in 2001) who was unusually interested in and ambitious about research and innovation policy. Hence, when Helge Sander was appointed Minister for Science, Technology, and Innovation in the Fogh Rasmussen government, he had optimal working conditions for rolling out an intensive reform programme, executed with powerful slogans such as 'from science to invoice'.

However, as we will show in the following sections, most of these fairly recent elements in the Danish research policy trajectory have inbuilt tensions. The way in which the reforms have been implemented reflects underlying perceptions of research quality and societal impact and shows how balances have been found between different conceptualizations. In the following, we zoom in on two selected sets of reforms in order to highlight how the balancing of such tensions have played out in more detail.

TRANSFORMATION OF THE RESEARCH FUNDING SYSTEM AND NEW CONCEPTIONS OF THE UNIVERSITIES' THIRD MISSION

As outlined above, the tension between the competing conceptions of research quality and societal impact can be seen as a persistent underlying theme in relation to the majority of Danish research policy reforms since 2000. The following subsections analyse two research policy areas which have both been central in the overall research policy transformation.

Transformation of the Public Research Funding System

The research funding system works as the single most important element in defining the scope, content, and direction of public research and is seen as one of the main channels by which authority is exercised over research (Edquist 2003; Whitley et al. 2010). Funding, in other words, mirrors salient features of policy and reveals, in empirical terms, the ambitions that governments have with higher education and research (Sörlin 2007). Hence, when a new Danish government took office in 2001, an overhaul of the funding system stood out as the most obvious first step towards an overall reformation of the public research system.

Up until the early 2000s, the Danish funding system could be characterized as pluralistic, consisting of many different funding channels, many individual funding programmes, and a variety of specific funding mechanisms. This organization reflected a need to serve different societal purposes, the involvement of a broad array of sectorial interests, and an aim to underpin a variety of different outcomes. However, the system as a whole was seen as inefficient, messy, unfocused, and as lacking clear incentives. Most importantly, it was argued by the government that there was too little competition for research funding, that the money was spread too thin, and that stronger support for market orientation and public-private partnerships was needed. Initiating a transition to a more competitive and more strategic research funding system was, therefore, one of the very first priorities for the new Liberal Minister Helge Sander when he took office in late 2001.

To address the perceived shortcomings of the existing system, the ministry took two interconnected steps. Most importantly, a development was started towards turning the existing 65/35 balance between floor funding and external funding into an approximately equal 50/50 balance (Danish Government 2006). Secondly, a large part of this increasing share of competitive funding was to be channelled into three newly established strategic or innovation-oriented research funding organizations which were institutionalized alongside the traditional research council system and the Danish National Research Foundation. The new funding organizations included the Council for Technology and Innovation (established in 2002); the Council for Strategic Research (established in 2004); and the Advanced Technology Foundation (established in 2005). Recently, these three research-funding organizations have been merged into one, namely the Innovation Fund Denmark (established in 2014). The merger of the three strategic funding organizations has further strengthened the market orientation of the part of the funding system concerned with strategic and mission-oriented research.

Hence, in the overall research funding landscape, the Innovation Fund Denmark now stands opposite the Independent Research Fund Denmark (which is the umbrella organization consisting of the traditional, academically oriented research councils) and the Danish National Research Foundation with its focus on Centres of Excellence. These structural changes have accordingly led to a more separated and sharply divided research funding system with more clearly defined, but also narrower, incentives for researchers. At the same time, increased pressure on the universities' internal floor funding has amplified the weight of the incentives in the external research funding channels. As internal funding has become scarcer, external priorities have to a higher and higher degree also come to shape the internal priorities and the direction of the research activities funded by the universities themselves (Aagaard 2017).

As outlined above, this present situation—to some extent—stands in contrast to former Danish research funding configurations, which, as a general rule, aimed to target the whole value chain of research and operated with a substantially higher share of floor funding. While the purely academic orientation of the funding system has been strong at least since the early 1990s, there has also historically been support for research oriented towards sectorial interests. This part has not least been institutionalized in the GRI sector. What has historically been less consistently prioritized, however, have been the more innovation-oriented or market-directed research activities. As outlined above, big strategic research programmes have been launched from time to time, but they have often been temporary in nature and primarily organized in ad hoc fashion in non-permanent committees.

Over the latest decade, it has, however, become increasingly difficult to obtain funding for areas in between the pure curiosity driven research on the one end of the spectrum and the now highly prioritized innovation or market-oriented research on the other. What is rewarded to a higher and higher degree in the current research funding system is thus either promises of excellence in a narrow academic sense or research proposals with an explicit market orientation. In terms of our analytical distinction, this 'product' or output orientation is often measured in the form of publications in high-impact journals on the one side and patents, spin offs, and university-industry collaborations on the other.

A similar focus on such products or outputs is also highly visible in the current Danish performance-based research funding model which was established with effect from 2010 to reallocate (a marginal but growing) part of the floor funding of the universities. In reality, what was introduced was not an entirely new model but rather a modification of a previous model. Where the previous model had three indicators with different weights: education (50 per cent), external research funding (40 per cent), and PhD production (10 per cent); the new model had four: education (45 per cent), external research funding (20 per cent), PhD production (10 per cent), and the so-called BFI ('Bibliometric Research Indicator') as a new element (25 per cent). The BFI, which is highly inspired by the Norwegian performance-based model, reallocates funding based on differentiated publication activity, with two levels determined by a large number of field-specific expert groups. Unlike the Norwegian model, the BFI, however, also includes patents (Aagaard 2019).

When assessing these changes, it should be highlighted that there are strong and obvious reasons to prioritize both academic excellence and direct socio-economic impact and that the former Danish research funding configurations were most likely lacking sufficiently clear incentives to underpin such objectives, in particular concerning the innovation-oriented public research. Hence, at the time of the change of government in 2001, there were compelling reasons to consider whether the design of the research funding system as a whole was appropriate.

However, there are equally important reasons to also pay attention to the interaction between these central research policy objectives and the way in which they are both dependent of a coherent, healthy, and dynamic overall science ecosystem. As the funding system strongly influences the general reward and assessment system of science, and thus, the activities of individual researchers, it is crucial to incentivize behaviour that underpins a well-functioning system as a whole where different policy objectives—such as the aims to strengthen academic quality and societal impact, respectively—are not seen as independent but rather as interdependent. But by mainly rewarding the activities and products that fit into one of the two poles of the broad spectrum of public research activities, the incentives to explore questions and solve tasks that fall outside of either the academic excellence sphere on the one end of the funding spectrum or the innovation and market-oriented sphere on the other will be weak.

What may suffer in such a divided and narrowly defined funding configuration is the more process-oriented conceptions of research quality and societal impact coined under headings such as RRI, public engagement, 'productive interactions', stakeholder involvement, transparency, openness, etc. Along the same lines, the clear separation and division in the organization of the funding system may also hinder rather than promote the ability of researchers to move back and forth between different modes of research.

While these changing funding configurations have implications for the research activities carried out in the public system, they also strongly influence the way in which the universities carry out their 'third mission' obligations. The next sub-section examines the changes within this area.

New University Third Mission Demands

As described earlier, the 2003 University Act significantly altered university management by changing the composition of university boards and by introducing appointed— rather than elected—leaders at all levels. Nevertheless, the Act was not exclusively a management reform. It was also the first formalization of the 'third mission', i.e. universities' legal obligation to 'exchange knowledge and competencies with society and encourage its employees to take part in the public debate' (Act no. 403 of 28/05/2003 [translated in Mejlgaard and Ryan 2017]).

The third mission can be understood as a collection of activities 'concerned with the generation, use, application, and exploitation of knowledge and other university capabilities outside academic environments' (Molas-Gallart et al. 2002: 2). In the Danish context since 2003, policies addressing such university activities with an explicit societal and interactional orientation have fallen into three clusters reflecting universities' core constituencies: policies concerning universities' collaboration with industry, reform of the institutional architecture of science-based policy advice, and initiatives targeting scientists' engagement with citizens.

Among these, university-industry interaction has clearly been the dominant policy concern. The 2003 action plan 'New Ways of Interaction between Universities and Industry—Turning Science into Businesses' captures the essence of the then centre-right government's ambitions for universities. It pointed to unexploited potential for collaboration between the business and industrial sectors and knowledge institutions, and fleshed out avenues for integration. During the following years, a range of targeted policy measures ensued. The establishment of the Council for Strategic Research and the Danish National Advanced Technology Foundation (in 2003 and 2005, respectively; later to be merged with the Danish Council for Technology and Innovation into Innovation Fund Denmark as described above) provided platforms for administering new funding schemes aimed at collaboration (Bloch and Aagaard 2012).

The crucial role of university-industry collaboration for national competitiveness was a core element of the comprehensive 2006 Globalisation Strategy (Danish Government 2006) and has repeatedly been highlighted by changing governments since. Notably, the first official Danish innovation strategy 'Denmark – A Nation of Solutions' (Danish Government 2012) produced under the Social Democratic-led government, and its successor 'Denmark – Ready to Seize Future Opportunities' (Danish Government 2017) presented by the current government have signalled a sustained political commitment to activities facilitating a stronger position for universities in the national innovation system.

When it comes to universities' responsibilities towards the political system and decision-makers in the public sector, the process of organizational mergers in 2007 was highly important. The structural reform reduced the number of universities from 12 to 8, and merged universities with what had until then been 12 independent GRIs dedicated to providing an informed knowledge base for decisions across their respective policy areas. Arguments favouring the mergers included 'big is better' and expected benefits from connecting policy advice and teaching, but on the whole, the structural reform seemed to be a solution to an underspecified problem (Hansen 2012).

For the universities, the embedding of the policy advising units was not an unproblematic process. The missions, professional norms, publication patterns, and incentive structures at the former GRIs did not always align well with those of academia. A series of organizational re-calibrations pursued, but the integration of disparate research environments continues to be a challenge at the eight new universities. For the interaction of science and policy, anchoring the former in-house agencies in the university sector could potentially contribute to extending and deepening the research and evidence base for decision-making. In reality, though, the marked change has been a considerable increase in concerns about academic values clashing with policy needs (Andersen 2017). A number of spectacular examples of selective, sometimes even manipulative, political use of science-based advice have emerged, and a recent study demonstrated that a significant share of university employees, particularly those who were formerly part of the governmental research agencies, have felt pressured to change, temporarily retain, or fully refrain from publishing research results (Ejersbo et al. 2018; Politiken 2018). In effect then, a decade after the mergers, the universities are still adapting to the new responsibilities towards decision-makers, and there is no clear indication that the overall quality of advice has improved.

Finally, policies addressing the interaction of science and citizens have seen a distinct trajectory in Denmark as compared to other European countries. During the 1980s and 1990s, as a response to massive 'no nukes' mobilization, the Danish Board of Technology championed a new approach to science communication, one that emphasized dialogue, active citizen participation, collective agenda setting, and two-way knowledge sharing. This 'Danish model' (Goven 2003; Davies and Horst 2016) later became highly influential across Europe, specifically in the wake of major controversies related to regenerative medicine and agricultural biotechnologies.

However, while the international trend since around 2000 has seen a move from one-way science popularization or 'selling science' (Nelkin 1995) approaches towards the 'Danish model' of science democratization, Danish policies have invoked the opposite development. Following recommendations arising from a 2003 think tank appointed by the Minister of Science, Technology, and Development with the mandate of rethinking science communication approaches in order to ensure sustained public support for science, political initiatives in this area have changed. Actions such as awards for science communication, university open days, expeditions covered by traditional media, establishment of a national dissemination platform (Videnskab.dk), and development of professional communication offices at universities have been given priority, whereas critical, dialogical formats have been significantly less prominent (Kjærgaard 2006; Mejlgaard 2012a). In fact, the internationally celebrated Danish Board of Technology suffered significant cuts in the early 2000s (Horst 2012) and was removed from the national budget in 2012 (Mejlgaard 2012b).

Quite a lot has happened then within each of these three clusters of policies concerning the third mission of universities. Industrial collaboration has been heavily promoted and incentivized through new funding organizations and schemes. A structural reform merging former in-house governmental agencies into universities significantly elevated universities' role in policy advice. In addition, the volume of science dissemination activities aimed at the broader public has increased. Collectively, these changes resonate well with the general trend of growing demand on science to provide tangible outputs that are relevant to societal stakeholders. However, it is striking that these clusters are treated as entirely compartmental in Danish research policy, as independent rather than interdependent.

The Two Cases in a Comparative Perspective

The two specific analyses presented above highlight some of the inherent tensions of research policy under a new social contract and point to some differences between the Danish and broader European state of play.

In both areas, namely funding and third mission, the implemented policies have invoked dynamics of segregation or even polarization rather than integration. The restructuring of the funding system has led to a concentration of efforts either narrowly pursuing academic excellence or market impact, while the middle ground has been evaded. Similarly, third mission policies have tended to compartmentalize activities. The economic impact agenda has been given strong priority through schemes supporting university-industry collaboration, while policy advice functions previously entertained by 'hybrid' institutes on the midfield between policy-making and science have been embedded in the sites for academic excellence. Policies have also tended to focus on products over processes in both areas. This is evident in the unprecedented focus on articles in high-impact journals in combination with the growing prominence of measures of market relevance like patents and spinouts. It is also detectable in the re-orientation of Danish science communication from dialogue and transaction towards the one-way transmission of research results.

In comparison to Denmark, what has emerged in Europe during the 2010s are policy prescriptions and priorities that are substantially more integrative and process-oriented. An example is the European Commission's notion of 'Responsible Research and Innovation' (RRI), which developed in the course of the Seventh Framework Programme and became a crosscutting priority area in 'Horizon 2020' (Zwart et al. 2014; de Saille 2015). The intention of RRI is to promote governance arrangements that are helpful in aligning research and innovation to the values, needs, and expectations of society at large (von Schomberg 2011, 2013). However, importantly, it advances a much more inclusive and integrative understanding of societal actors which covers industry, businesses, policymakers, civil society organizations, interest groups, media, and individual citizens, and aims to understand the patterns, connections, and conflicting concerns in the totality of claims on science. Moreover, RRI advocates attention not primarily to the knowledge outputs and products provided by research and innovation, but rather to the processes by which these materialize. Effectively, this approach implies that the central mechanisms for ensuring appropriate, socially robust research and innovation outputs are stakeholder involvement in priority setting and knowledge production, *ex ante* or 'upstream' ethical assessment, open access to data and results, inclusive and value-sensitive design processes, and sensitivity to issues of gender and marginalization in research contents and technology development (European Union 2012).

Another example is the recent vision for European research to become characterized by being 'Open innovation, open science, and open to the world' (European Commission 2016). Championed by President Juncker and Commissioner Moedas, the vision calls for significantly increased levels of collaboration and inclusion of a broad range of societal stakeholders throughout knowledge production cycles. Within this broad framework, a range of concrete activities is rolled out. Elements include the implementation of a European Science Cloud and open access to scientific data. In parallel, a coalition of influential research funding agencies, academies, and umbrella organizations for research organizations are spearheading the so-called 'Plan S' which insists that publicly funded research should be publicly available, hence requiring a re-thinking of current structures for academic publishing.

Common for these recent trends is that focus is shifted towards the properties of the research *process*, the *interdependency* between different parts of the research ecosystem, and the need for *integration* of diverse actors in agenda setting and knowledge production. The European Union has been a strong advocate for a new approach to research policy, but the emerging paradigm is also clearly trickling down to national research policies, prominently in countries like the Netherlands and Norway. However, so far, Denmark has been less inclined to adopt these emerging elements in the new social contract of science. Hence, while Denmark clearly has been a frontrunner in adopting and implementing the product or output-oriented elements in the emerging social contract of science, the Danish policy system has emphasized the more process-oriented accentuations to a much lower degree.

CONCLUSION

As outlined, Denmark became a strong adopter of research policy ideas promoted by the OECD and the EU in the early 2000s. This was followed up with large and long-term growth in funding and increased political attention to the role of the universities towards competitiveness, welfare, and prosperity. In this process, Danish research policies have forcefully contributed to keeping a high pace in knowledge production and to steer research activities in the direction of both excellence and impact, although the conceptions of those end objectives have been rather narrow. Excellence has tended to be interpreted in strictly academic terms, and notions of market relevance and the economic benefits of science have significantly dominated the impact agenda. Moreover, developments in Danish research policies have been highly oriented towards tangible products: academic production as measured by the volume of outputs and citations, and societal impact captured by the number of patents, spinouts, and formalized collaborations between universities and industry.

In an international comparative perspective, the Danish research and innovation policy developments are often viewed as highly successful based on the measurement of such traditional research policy indicators. On the academic side, Danish research performs extremely well when measured in terms of bibliometric indicators. Alongside other high-performing countries such as Switzerland and the Netherlands, Denmark consistently comes out on top in international rankings of research performance (see e.g. Aagaard and Schneider 2015). Similarly, Denmark is also consistently placed among the highest performing nations when it comes to comparative assessments of innovation performance. In the European Innovation Scoreboard from 2018, for instance, Denmark was placed second—only surpassed by Sweden.

But as the two core developments during the 2000s—the transformation of the research funding system and the reforms addressing universities' third mission—illustrate, there are important tensions in the broader trajectory of Danish research policy. While the Danish reform intensity and the strong embracement of the excellence and impact agendas have resulted in Denmark changing position from laggard to frontrunner to some degree, new layers have been added to the international research policy agenda, or rather, other elements in the emerging social contract have been more strongly accentuated recently. A re-orientation towards broad, integrative rather than narrow, distinct conceptions of excellence and impact alongside an emphasis on the processes and practices of research rather than products has been promoted by the European Commission but also emerged strongly in research policies in countries like the Netherlands and Norway. But so far, Danish research policy has not picked up these trends.

So while the Danish research policy strategy as indicated above can be seen as highly successful measured by traditional output-oriented indicators, the question is whether this high performance comes at a cost. Will the strong segregation of tasks and aims and the narrow incentives for researchers have negative long-term effects on the viability of the Danish research system and its ability to deliver to emerging policy agendas? This question in particular is relevant perceived in light of some of the grand challenges ahead which appear to require much more integrated as well as open and process-oriented approaches to the organization of public research activities than today. A key part of this question is also whether it is possible to embrace a more process-oriented approach while maintaining the current position of strength related to the more narrow output-based measures.

Another open question is how this specific Danish research policy trajectory might be explained. As outlined above, the Danish research policy development has been characterized by a high degree of political consensus and has been backed by all the major political parties throughout the period under examination. Nonetheless, a number of distinctive paths were laid out in the wake of the change of government in 2001, which have since been defining for the overall policy direction. While the general lines of this development were in accordance with broad international trends, the Danish Prime Minister Anders Fogh Rasmussen and the Minister of Science, Technology, and Innovation Helge Sander who were in charge of this area for almost a decade clearly championed and accentuated a rather narrow output-based vision and backed it with massive increases in resources. This combination of long-term commitment to a strong research policy vision and a corresponding willingness to invest in it appears to have been so powerful that other alternative, more process-oriented visions have had difficulties in gaining ground—even as new governments and new ministers took office and the strong growth in funding levelled off. From both a political science and a practical research policy perspective, an interesting question is, therefore, how sticky this path dependency will be in the coming years. Is Denmark in the process of returning to the role as a laggard when it comes to adopting new international policy visions?

References

Aagaard, Kaare (2011). 'Kampen om basismidlerne', PhD dissertation, Aarhus University.

Aagaard, Kaare (2012). 'Reformbølgen tager form' in Kaare Aagaard and Niels Mejlgaard, eds, *Dansk forskningspolitik efter årtusindskiftet*. Aarhus: Aarhus University Press, 37–57.

Aagaard, Kaare (2017). 'The evolution of a national research funding system: Transformative change through layering and displacement', *Minerva*, 55/3: 279–97.

Aagaard, Kaare (2019). 'Performance-based research funding in Denmark: The adoption and translation of the Norwegian model', *Journal of Data and Information Science*, 3/4: 20–30.

Aagaard, Kaare, and Harry de Boer (2017). 'The Danish UNIK initiative: An NPM-inspired mechanism to steer higher education', in Harry de Boer, Jon File, Jeroen Huisman, Marco Seeber, Martina Vukasovic, and Don F. Westerheijden, eds, *Policy Analysis of Structural Reforms in Higher Education*. Cham: Palgrave Macmillan, 141–59.

Aagaard, Kaare, Hanne F. Hansen, and Jørgen G. Rasmussen (2016). 'Mergers in Danish higher education: An overview over the changing landscape', in Romulo Pinheiro, Lars Geschwind, and Timo Aarrevaara, eds, *Mergers in Higher Education: The Experience from Northern Europe*. Heidelberg: Springer, 73–88.

Aagaard, Kaare, and Jesper W. Schneider (2015). 'Research funding and national academic performance: Examination of a Danish success story', *Science and Public Policy*, 43/4, 518–31.

Aagaard, Kaare, and Niels Mejlgaard (2012). *Dansk forskningspolitik efter årtusindskiftet*. Aarhus: Aarhus University Press.

Andersen, Heine (2017). *Forskningsfrihed: Ideal og virkelighed*. Copenhagen: Hans Reitzels Forlag.

Antikainen, Ari (2016). 'The Nordic model of higher education', in James E. Côté and Andy Furlong, eds, *Routledge Handbook of the Sociology of Higher Education*. London: Routledge, 234–40.

Bloch, Carter, and Kaare Aagaard (2012). 'Fra tanke til faktura', in Kaare Aagaard and Niels Mejlgaard, eds, *Dansk forskningspolitik efter årtusindskiftet*. Aarhus: Aarhus University Press, 95–131.

Bouter, Lex M., Joeri Tijdink, Nils Axelsen, Brian C. Martinson, and Gerben ter Riet (2016). 'Ranking major and minor research misbehaviors: Results from a survey among participants of four World Conferences on Research Integrity', *Research Integrity and Peer Review*, 1/17: 1–8.

Bush, Vannevar (1945/1990). *Science: The Endless Frontier*. Washington, D.C.: National Science Foundation.

Danish Government (2006). *Progress, Innovation and Cohesion: Strategy for Denmark in the Global Economy*. Copenhagen: The Danish Government.

Danish Government (2012). *Denmark—A Nation of Solutions*. Copenhagen: The Danish Government.

Danish Government (2017). *Denmark—Ready to Seize Future Opportunities*. Copenhagen: The Danish Government.

Davies, Sarah, and Maja Horst (2016). *Science Communication: Culture, Identity and Citizenship*. London, New York and Shanghai: Palgrave Macmillan.

de Saille, Stevienna (2015). 'Innovating innovation policy: The emergence of 'responsible research and innovation', *Journal of Responsible Innovation*, 2/2: 152–68.

Degn, Lise, and Mads P. Sørensen (2015). 'From collegial governance to conduct of conduct: Danish universities set free in the service of the state', *Higher Education*, 69/6: 931–46.

Edquist, Olle (2003). 'Layered science and science policies', *Minerva*, 41/3: 207–21.

Ejersbo, Niels, Kira S. Larsen, Niels M. Søndergaard, Rasmus H. Jacobsen, Emil Thranholm, and Tobias S. Jørgensen (2018). *Undersøgelse af forskningsfrihed i forhold til offentliggørelse på Aarhus Universitet*. Copenhagen: Det Nationale Forsknings- og Analysecenter for Velfærd.

European Commission (2016). *Open Innovation, Open Science, Open to the World—A Vision for Europe*. Brussels: European Commission.

European Union (2012). *Responsible Research and Innovation: Europe's Ability to Respond to Societal Challenges*, https://ec.europa.eu/research/swafs/pdf/pub_public_engagement/ responsible-research-and-innovation-leaflet_en.pdf (accessed 10 January 2019).

Gibbons, Michael (1999). 'Science's new social contract with society', *Nature*, 402/6761 suppl: C81–4.

Goven, Joanna (2003). 'Deploying the consensus conference in New Zealand: Democracy and de-problematization', *Public Understanding of Science*, 12/4: 423–40.

Grønbæk, David (2001). 'Mellem politik og videnskab', PhD dissertation, Copenhagen University.

Guston, David H., and Kenneth Keniston (1994). *The Fragile Contract: University Science and the Federal Government*. Cambridge, MA: MIT Press.

Hansen, Hanne F. (2002). 'Hvilken slags politik er forskningspolitik?', *Økonomi & Politik*, 75/3: 41–56.

Hansen, Hanne F. (2012). 'Fusionsprocesserne: Frivillighed under tvang', in Kaare Aagaard and Niels Mejlgaard, eds, *Dansk forskningspolitik efter årtusindskiftet*. Aarhus: Aarhus University Press, 195–227.

Horst, Maja (2012). 'Deliberation, dialogue or dissemination: Changing objectives in the communication of science and technology in Denmark', in Bernard Schiele, Michel Claessens, and Shi Shunke, eds, *Science Communication in the World: Practices, Theories and Trends*. London: Springer, 95–108.

Kallerud, Egil (2006). 'Den nordiske modellen – redefinert og ettertraktet', *Forskningspolitikk*, 29/4: 8–9.

Kjærgaard, Rikke S. (2006). *Elfenbenstårnet: Universiteter mellem forskning og formidling*. Aarhus: Aarhus University Press.

Martin, Ben R. (2003). 'The changing social contract for science and the evolution of the university', in Aldo Geuna, Ammon J. Salter, and W. Edward Steinmueller, eds, *Science and Innovation: Rethinking the Rationales for Funding and Governance*. Cheltenham: Edward Elgar, 7–29.

Mejlgaard, Niels (2012a). 'Forskningskommunikation: Det tredje bens andet ben!', in Kaare Aagaard and Niels Mejlgaard, eds, *Dansk forskningspolitik efter årtusindskiftet*. Aarhus: Aarhus University Press, 133–58.

Mejlgaard, Niels (2012b). 'Teknologirådet nedlagt og genrejst som Fonden Teknologirådet: Interview med direktør Lars Klüver', *Forskningspolitikk*, 35/3: 6–9.

Mejlgaard, Niels, and Kaare Aagaard (2009). 'Hvilken slags politik er forskningspolitik – nu?', *Økonomi and Politik*, 82/2: 50–66.

Mejlgaard, Niels, and Kaare Aagaard (2017). 'The social contract of science', in Jung Shin and Pedro Teixeira, eds, *Encyclopedia of International Higher Education Systems and Institutions*. Dordrecht: Springer, 1–4.

Mejlgaard, Niels, and Thomas K. Ryan (2017). 'Patterns of third mission engagement among scientists and engineers', *Research Evaluation*, 26/4: 326–36.

Merton, Robert K. (1942/1973). 'The normative structure of science', in Robert K. Merton, ed., *The Sociology of Science: Theoretical and Empirical Investigations*. Chicago, IL: University of Chicago Press, 267–80.

Molas-Gallart, Jordi, Ammon Salter, Pari Patel, Alister Scott, and Xavier Duran (2002). *Measuring Third Stream Activities: Final Report to the Russell Group of Universities*. Brighton: SPRU.

Molas-Gallart, Jordi, Pablo D'Este, Oscar Llopis, and Ismael Rafols (2015). 'Towards an alternative framework for the evaluation of translational research initiatives', *Research Evaluation*, 25/3: 235–43.

Nelkin, Dorothy (1995). *Selling science: How the Press Covers Science and Technology*. New York: W.H. Freeman and Co.

Nowotny, Helga, Peter B. Scott, and Michael Gibbons (2001). *Re-thinking Science: Knowledge and the Public in an Age of Uncertainty*. Cambridge: Polity.

Politiken (2018). 'Forskere svarer igen: Vi er udsat for politisk pres', https://politiken.dk/indland/politik/art6321797/Forskere-svarer-Vi-er-udsat-for-politisk-pres (accessed 10 January 2019).

Saltelli, Andrea, and Silvio Funtowicz (2017). 'What is science's crisis really about?', *Futures*, 91: 5–11.

Sörlin, Sverker (2007). 'Funding diversity: Performance based funding regimes as drivers of differentiation in Higher Education systems', *Higher Education Policy*, 20/4: 413–40.

von Schomberg, Rene (2011). *Research and Innovation in the Information and Communication Technologies and Security Technologies Fields: A Report from the European Commission Services*. Luxembourg: Publications Office of the European Union.

von Schomberg, Rene (2013). 'A vision of responsible research and innovation', in Richard Owen, John R. Bessant, and Maggy Heintz, eds, *Responsible Innovation: Managing the Responsible Emergence of Science and Innovation in Society*. London: John Wiley and Sons, 51–74.

Whitley, Richard, Jochen Gläser, and Lars Engwall (2010). *Reconfiguring Knowledge Production: Changing Authority Relationships on the Sciences and Their Consequences for Intellectual Innovation*. Oxford: Oxford University Press.

Zwart, Hub, Laurens Landeweerd, and Arjan van Rooij (2014). 'Adapt or perish? Assessing the recent shift in the European research funding arena from "ELSA" to "RRI"', *Life Sciences, Society and Policy*, 10/1: 11.

PART IV

POSTSCRIPT

CHAPTER 41

POLITY, POLITICS, AND POLICIES

A Reconsideration

PETER MUNK CHRISTIANSEN, JØRGEN ELKLIT,
AND PETER NEDERGAARD

The aim of this book has been to take stock of what we in the social science community know about how Danish politics has developed during recent decades. Danish political institutions, processes, and policies have many similarities with political institutions, processes, and policies in countries to which Denmark is normally compared. In some respects, however, Danish politics also deviates from what we know from other countries. In this final chapter, we wrap up some of the conclusions from Chapters 2–40 and provide them with some critical afterthoughts. For suggestions for further study in the various fields of Danish politics, we refer to the conclusions in the individual chapters.

POLITY

Basic State Institutions: Aged but Still Functioning Quite Well

Danish democracy and political institutions are based on the Constitution, which is the topic of the first substantial chapter (Chapter 2). It is noteworthy that words such as 'democracy' or 'political parties' do not appear in the Constitutional Act. The explanation is that the current Constitutional Act (from 1953) in its relatively brief form reflects in a number of ways the very first Constitutional Act from 1849 where there was no space for such words. Amendments have usually taken the form of elaborations on existing wording reflecting necessary political compromises, thus also reflecting the strata in the constitutional development. The conditions for amending the Constitution reflect a particular complicated situation in 1915 which now makes it almost impossible to amend the Constitution. However, even though this makes the Constitution a stable frame around political life, it also allows for a certain flexibility, which, for instance, has been instrumental in relation to issues related to the European Union. The current Constitutional Act has now lasted for two generations and there is no expectation that it might be changed anytime soon, as even the slightest amendments must be made following the very demanding amendment procedures. Therefore, the current generation of Danes will not see a new constitutional act either.

The so-called Community of the Realm has three constituents, which are quite unequal polities, so it is sometimes categorized as a so-called federacy including Denmark, the Faroe Islands, and Greenland. The polities share the ideal of a world of nations, each homogeneous in ethnic terms and each in command of their own state. As described in Chapter 3, the reality is somewhat different, however, as the three parts are different, have command of their own states to quite different degrees, have different negotiating power, different short-term and long-term objectives for the development of the realm, etc. Social problems are much more serious in Greenland than in the two other parts of the Realm, making Greenland reminiscent of the social problems of other indigenous peoples. The constitution issue is telling as the drafting of constitutions for the North Atlantic polities could only start after approval from Denmark. It is an open question if and when Greenland and the Faroese Islands will secede, but some see it as inevitable, at least in the long run. If independence occurs, the two polities will probably associate from outside, but what then? And how will an independent Greenland handle issues related to security politics when the United States starts to put pressure on it if security problems in the Arctic start to escalate in earnest?

The monarchy is sometimes considered an anachronistic institution in a modern democracy, but things are more complicated, as discussed in Chapter 4. Queen Margrethe II has no formal political authority, but she is still head of state, a symbol of the nation, and attracts attention and respect from most Danes. The institution is quite costly, but that does not really matter politically as the institution—and the Queen—is popular. Danish monarchs have gradually adapted to society's increasing equality during the twentieth century, recently also by reaching out to the general public through the use of media, including social media. Monarchy as an institution depends on public affection for the reigning monarch, but there is a risk that missteps might entail a serious loss of popularity. In that case, a Danish republic might be the consequence, even though it is not very likely.

Basic Political Institutions: Generally Well-Functioning and Supported by Trust and Civic Norms

Political institutions shape the rules of the game. One key political institution is the electoral system which translates votes cast in elections into seats won by parties and candidates. It is, therefore, of considerable importance what kind of electoral system a country has as it will have an impact on what kind of party system will develop. Political and social developments around the previous turn of century meant that a multi-party system developed despite the electoral system being an ordinary First Past the Post system. Consequently, proportional representation was included when the Constitution was amended in 1915. Chapter 5 demonstrates how the current electoral system reflects the strongly revised proportional representation (PR) system which was introduced in 1920 with its strong emphasis on geographical representation and mathematical fairness in the distribution of seats in the Danish Parliament, *Folketinget*. The conventional critique of PR electoral systems—that they will produce weak minority governments most of the time (maybe even coalitions)—are seen by some as contributing to the development of the costly welfare state. It is, however, far from certain that a different electoral system would have implied better quality legislation or representation. Elections are conducted without problems, so the legitimacy and integrity of the entire electoral system remain unchallenged, which, of course, does not exclude negative externalities.

The turnout level in elections to the *Folketinget* is oscillating around 86 per cent, which is not only indicative of the electorate's general acceptance of representative democracy as an abstract concept but also of its actual way of functioning. It also reflects that the norm of voting as a civic duty is broadly shared. The constant high turnout level thus adds not only to the legitimacy of the political system as such but also to that of Parliament. The turnout level in local elections and elections to the European Parliament is certainly lower but still high compared to most other countries. Chapter 6 relies to a considerable degree on an impressive study of turnout, which is based on access to a number of population registers, including the voter register which in Denmark automatically ensures that all eligible voters are registered. Two findings are particularly interesting. The first is that the very young voters (18 years old) vote in considerably larger numbers than their slightly older compatriots. This is primarily explained by social ties being only disrupted when young people eventually leave home. The other important finding is that major inequalities in turnout are also found in Denmark between the educated, middle-aged, and reasonably well-off middle-class voters on the one hand, and on the other hand, the younger, less educated voters with complicated relations to the labour market (and even more so if some kind of immigrant background is added to the equation). Attempts to establish convincing explanations of the high turnout level in Denmark are scarce, but both individual and collective mobilization contribute to the high turnout, which also must be seen in relation to the entire voting age population because voter registration is automatic.

The *Folketinget*, the Danish Parliament, is generally seen as powerful, professional, and trusted as analysed in Chapter 7. Recent figures even show an increasing trust in the *Folketinget* among Danish citizens after some years with declining trust. Despite the relatively high number of parties, and no majority party, Parliament has been able to produce governments able to govern, even though governments have sometimes been helped by the Constitution's rules about negative parliamentarianism and that the prime minister can always call a snap election. The *Folketinget* has, on occasion, also demonstrated an ability to solve collective problems as was the case in 1992 when voters rejected the Maastricht Treaty in a referendum, which left Denmark in a kind of vacuum. A solid majority in Parliament managed to agree on four opt-outs, which were then accepted in Edinburgh and approved in a subsequent referendum. It is a problem that Parliament has difficulties in matching the government when it comes to resources, organization, and internal coherence as the government always has a heavy hand in controlling MPs from its own party as well as MPs from coalition partners and supporting parties to a considerable degree. This makes the 'separation of powers' a nice and powerful concept, but it is not a true reflection of reality.

As analysed in Chapter 8, one consequence of the lack of a majority party in Parliament since 1909 is that Danish parliamentarians have been well trained in the formation of both legislative and governmental coalitions and in living with minority governments, whether coalitions or single-party. The 2019 government formation situation is a good illustration of this as the leader of the Social Democratic Party had said clearly during the election campaign that she aimed for a Social Democratic minority government. The issue then became how to satisfy her three centre-left, in-waiting support parties from the so-called 'red bloc'. The result was a publicized 'paper of understanding', which makes relatively clear what the government and the support parties are in agreement on and thus demonstrates the active role of potential support parties during the government formation phase.

Administrative Institutions

The claim of Chapter 9 is that the public sector in Denmark is generally functioning well, not least central government. The key word is institutional flexibility where relatively weak organizations allow for a certain level of organizational autonomy in which general trust plays a role replacing strong control mechanisms, thereby reducing transactions costs and increasing efficiency and flexibility. Trust in government and civil servants has been decreasing in recent years but is now on the increase again. There is no obvious explanation of this change available yet, and it also remains to be seen whether it is permanent. But it raises the issue of how to ensure the survival of the strong informal norms needed to support the relatively weak formal institutions on which central government rests. There appears to be a risk that things may change. A couple of scandals in the public sector have contributed to that, and the work relationship between politicians and civil servants is a recurring theme. This might blur the picture of the organization of central government even further.

The local government system discussed in Chapter 10 is one of the most decentralized local government systems in the Western democracies, but things are changing as the state has been introducing a tougher national spending regime. In 2007, a local government reform was implemented which reduced the number of municipalities to 98 and the number of regions to 5, simultaneously changing the division of tasks between the local, the regional, and the national level. Municipalities still enjoy considerable flexibility and decentralization of tasks at the same time as the autonomy to locally decide on local taxes, and expenditure is significantly reduced due to increased central regulation. The chapter thus demonstrates that the current variations between municipalities is increasingly a reflection of historical differences rather than a reflection of current choices and preferences. The system is still highly decentralized, but it might be in a process where it gradually becomes more of an implementing state agency, and the municipalities might suffer from not being able to handle still more complex tasks and secure coordination of the economic activities at the local government level with national policies and increasing politicization of the equalization scheme, which is equally important for both well-off and poor municipalities. However, the local government system still—despite many challenges—demonstrates viability and adaptation capability. The regional political institutions are politically contested and might disappear in a future reform.

Corporatism is not dead, as some have occasionally claimed, but it manifests itself in different ways. Corporatist structures and actors were instrumental in the development of the Danish welfare state as argued in Chapter 11, but present-day corporatism has taken on new forms and shows itself in different ways, even though more traditional corporatist processes are also present in certain venues. When economic crises, fiscal austerity, and reforms demanded harsh concessions from corporatist actors, things changed. The state started to organize policy-making differently in order to pursue policy reforms. The means were stricter control with policy preparation, including information control and sometimes even the exclusion of interest groups that used to be among the usual suspects. But interest groups that can and will contribute and deliver are still interesting for policymakers; as such, the forms may have changed, but corporatism is still an important feature of Danish politics and policy-making.

At various instances in the book, references are made to Denmark's high level of social trust, which is the topic of Chapter 12. The argument is that the high level of trust can be traced back to a set of bureaucratic reforms and anti-corruption measures implemented no later than the mid-nineteenth century, which had a marked impact on the state-building process and even the development of the modern welfare state later on. Presently, international comparisons also demonstrate an inverse relationship between levels of corruption and levels of social trust. The Danish case makes it relative clear what comes first, namely a low level of corruption. Denmark has a strong, competent, and nearly uncorrupt bureaucracy, which is one of the most important backbones of Danish society. However, trust in Parliament and government is lower than it used to be, but it has been on the increase again over the last couple of years and is, therefore, not really a cause for concern. Denmark is also still among the highest trust levels among the European Union member states.

The last chapter in the Polity section (Chapter 13) examines the Danish system for co-ordination with and for the European Union, which has been around even longer than the time Denmark has been a member state of the EC/EU. This explains the evolution of the system, which is a unicentric system with central coordination under the auspices of the Ministry of Foreign Affairs. The ambition has been to develop a durable and tenable position on all upcoming cases, which is attempted by involving actors from the entire spectrum, namely Parliament, interest organizations, ministries with an interest in the various topics, and so on. The system has been highly effective and has been able to deliver clear and consistent positions on time. The central role of Parliament's Committee on European Affairs—and the system as such—has been noticed in other countries and has even served as inspiration in countries such as Sweden and Finland, even though the ability to fully control EU coordination processes is questionable.

POLITICS

Party System, Minority Governments, Classes, and Long-Term Voting

The 1973 earthquake elections seriously challenged the Danish party system. The number of parties doubled and new protest parties entered the *Folketinget*. Particularly well-known is the anti-establishment and anarchistic Progress Party. The election foreshadowed a decade of weak governments and concomitant economic crises. Now, almost 50 years later, as shown in Chapter 14, the Danish party system is in no way in any kind of crisis, as we have recently seen in a number of other countries. At the general election in 2019, the four old parties—the Social Democratic Party, the Social-Liberal Party, the Liberal Party, and the Conservative Party—received two out of every three votes, and the anti-immigrant party—the Danish People's Party—suffered a significant loss. The election confirmed the bloc nature of Danish politics: governments have been formed on a centre-right or a centre-left basis for almost a century. However, in spite of the support for the old political parties, with ten parties in Parliament, fragmentation of the party system may be a future challenge. The Danish party system has shown continuity with the strong positions of the old parties, as well as changes by incorporating new parties, some of which appear to have become permanent parts of the system while others vanish after a shorter or longer period.

Chapter 15 analyses the many Danish minority governments in more detail. During the last 60 years, Denmark has only held majority governments during two periods: 1968–71 and 1993–4. While weak minority governments may have been accomplices in bad economic outcomes during the 1970s, minority governments have not prevented the Danish economy from being generally strong and changing governments from carrying through complicated and controversial reforms after the 1970s. A couple of institutions support the correlation between minority governments and the proficient policies pursued: negative parliamentarianism, where the only requirement for a government is not to be opposed by a majority, makes it easier to form governments compared to countries where a positive vote for the government is required. A very important institution is legislative agreements (*forlig*) where a minority government enters an agreement on a specific issue with one or more parties not in government.

Such agreements are entered with different party constellations, and they last until they are explicitly denounced by one of the signing parties. However, agreements also blur the line between government and opposition, making it difficult to know who voters should hold accountable for specific decisions.

To a large extent, the Danish party system was created on the basis of well-organized class parties. The Social Democratic Party attracted votes from the urban working class, the Liberal Party from the peasants, the Conservative Party from the urban bourgeois professions, and the Social Liberals from the rural smallholders and the urban intellectuals. However, as shown in Chapter 16, this is indeed a picture of the past, but the concept of classes has not become obsolete. Class relations have changed, but they have not disappeared. Danes still find it meaningful to articulate societal structures in class terms. However, occupation-based class identity has changed dramatically for some groups. The traditional working class—the backbone of the labour union movement and the Social Democratic Party—are much less inclined to vote centre-left than it used to be, although the Social Democrats won back some working class voters at the 2019 elections by applying a restrictive immigrant policy agenda close to that of the Danish People's Party. While occupational class relations have diminished, those related to culture and education are still—or even increasingly—relevant. An example is that despite tax-financed education and generous student stipends, Denmark is performing quite badly when it comes to lifting the educational level of children of poorly educated parents.

During the last couple of decades Denmark has been in the international news media on several occasions because of what is reported as xenophobic policies. What does this reflect? Strong anti-immigrant sentiments among the Danish voters or something else? Chapter 17 studies Danes' public opinion over four decades. The analysis shows a high degree of stability in voters' attitudes towards immigration since the late 1970s. However, Danes are also highly divided on the issue. This may explain policy shifts: elections where immigration has been high on the agenda have repeatedly resulted in centre-right governments with the anti-immigrant Danish People's Party as a support party. The chapter also scrutinizes voter attitudes towards economic redistribution, the environment, and the EU: Danes continuously support a more equal distribution of incomes, they strongly favour a restrictive environmental policy, and they are generally positive towards the EU, but Danes do not prefer a deepened European Union. While the overall opinions are remarkably stable, an increased partisan polarization has taken place in relation to the immigration issue and partly also towards the EU.

Four Political Parties and the Anchors of Voting Behaviour: The Social Democratic Party, the Liberal Party, the Danish People's Party, and the Red-Green Alliance

We have chosen to give four political parties a chapter each. The Social Democratic Party and the Liberal Party were chosen because they are the oldest and biggest parties with a history going back 150 years. The Danish People's Party was chosen because it is the Danish version of an anti-immigrant party that has had great political influence since the turn of the century. The Red-Green Alliance was chosen because it is an example of an originally small and revolutionary party that has developed into a left-wing and medium-sized party working on the foundation of representative democracy.

From the end of the First World War, the Social Democratic Party—dealt with in Chapter 18—became the clearly most powerful party for the remaining part of the twentieth century. It was never as powerful as its Scandinavian sister parties, but the party certainly has had a great influence on the development of the Danish welfare state, not least in the decades after the Second World War. Integration in NATO and later the EEC/EU also had high priority. Failure to accommodate the changing winds of deindustrialization during the 1970s and too many conflicts in relation to the trade unions made the Social Democratic Party unable to govern and brought the economy under the party's leadership to the 'brink of the abyss' as expressed by a former Social Democratic minister of finance. These years were expensive lessons for the party, and it has played a less prominent role since the early 1980s, only being in power for 16 years in the period 1980–2020. The 2019 election resulted in a Social Democratic, one-party minority government. The unusually big centre-left share of seats after the 2019 election (96 out of 175 seats [exclusive of the four North Atlantic seats]) may entail a more benign future for the party.

Chapter 19 analyses the largest party of the centre-right bloc, the Liberal Party. The party was the driving force when parliamentarianism was introduced in Denmark in 1901. It was also the largest parliamentary party until the 1924 election when this position was taken over by the Social Democratic Party, who kept it until 2001 when the Liberal Party got it back, only to return it again in 2015. Contrary to most other European agrarian parties, the Danish Liberal Party has succeeded in transforming itself into a catch-all party with a solid hold of large groups of urban voters. The party's ideology developed in two steps. A neo-liberal ideology dominated before the turn of the twenty-first century but proved not to be broadly marketable to the voters. With the 2001 Liberal-Conservative government, the ideology turned much more towards pro-welfare state positions, helping the party not only to gain power but also to become the largest party. Pro-welfare positions as well as tough immigration and law and order positions challenge the liberal principles of segments of the party from time to time.

The Danish People's Party—the object of Chapter 20—evolved in 1995 as a split from the Progress Party. Only two years after Social Democratic PM Poul Nyrup Rasmussen in 1999 had declared, 'Therefore, I say to the Danish People's Party that no matter how much effort is made, in my eyes, you will never be housebroken', the party became the third largest party in Parliament and support party for the Liberal-Conservative governments in 2001–11 (and again in 2015–19). The party's primary platform has continuously been anti-immigrant, supplemented by a law and order platform. During the 2000s, the party went left on economic redistribution. Consequently, the party is only far right on immigration and law and order, and centrist, even left leaning, when it comes to economic redistribution. The party's success during the 2000s and the 2010s culminated in 2015 with the status as second largest party. Probably because of its reluctance to accept responsibility in government—and because of the advent of two new parties with even tougher anti-immigrant platforms, New Right and Taut Course—the party suffered a severe defeat at the 2019 elections.

The Red-Green Alliance was formed in 1989—alongside the fall of the Berlin Wall—as a merger of three extreme left parties that had all lost parliamentary representation during preceding elections. The Alliance was first represented in the *Folketinget* in 1994, and it stayed at a level of around 3 per cent until the 2011 elections when it jumped to 6.7 per cent—almost the same as its 2019 election result (6.9 per cent). With its electoral success, the party has left behind ideas of revolution and non-democratic takeover of power. Chapter 21 asks whether the Red-Green Alliance is most red or most green. Like the chameleon, the party chooses colour to fit the present situation, but overall, the party is more red than green. The party's platform is more on labour issues than on environmental issues, and it also runs an EU-sceptical platform. The party ran for the European Parliament elections for the first time in 2019 and did so successfully as it gained an MEP seat. With the formation of the Social Democratic government in 2019, the Red-Green Alliance—in full accordance with the Danish tradition for bloc politics—became part of the majority behind the government. From this position, the party may pursue a red as well as a green platform.

What are the drivers of the Danes' votes? Although voter volatility has been high during recent elections and although many voters decide quite late whom and what to vote for, voter volatility between the two blocs is modest as shown in Chapter 22. Some voter volatility is caused by the advent of a two-dimensional political space: economic redistribution and cultural values. The party system does indeed structure the votes, and to some extent, the party system also accommodates the voters' preferences, particularly in relation to the move of the traditional working class to the right on the immigration policy issue. The voters' changing votes is thus not the result of a destructuration of voting behaviour but rather voters searching for preferred parties in a more complex political space where parties are also on the move. With the decline of class voting, education, gender, and geographical location have come to play a more prominent role.

While the Danish party system is well functioning in terms of delivering workable minority governments and in structuring choices for the voters, party finances and party membership are fragile elements of the Danish political system. Parties are increasingly financed by the tax-payers, and the money tends to stay at the upper levels of the parties. At the same time, only a modest number of Danes are party members. The lack of bottom-up legitimacy and a tiny member throng are fragile characteristics of Danish political parties.

Gender, Local Elections, Referendums, Media, and Interest Groups

Chapter 23 is devoted to the role of gender in Danish politics. In many respects, Denmark has pursued a path that paves the way for equality between the sexes. During the 1970s, female workforce participation grew significantly and approached that of men, and it was supported by subsidized daycare for children aged 1 to 5, generous maternity rules, and a universal welfare state that also paved the way for female participation in other aspects of societal life. However, things did not continue quite that way. Women have been successful in entering political positions although it seems difficult to pass 40 per cent representation in Parliament. While some progress has taken place in women's part of the public sector top jobs, the glass ceiling is evident in the private sector where very few women have top jobs. Contrary to Norway and Sweden, gender equality has not been at the forefront of the political agenda, and some of the instruments used in other countries—such as mandatory paternity leave and quotas—do not have broad political support in Denmark. Denmark, on the other hand, has not experienced broad political resistance towards abortion, sexual rights, or gender equality.

Denmark runs one of the worlds' biggest local and regional government sectors. They run the lion's share of the large Danish welfare state: daycare, primary schools, hospitals and other healthcare services, eldercare, libraries, etc. Chapter 24 shows that local and regional elections every fourth year are by no means second-order elections, and they have substantial influence on Danish society. It is noticeable that the local election system is quite nationalized in terms of replicating the national party system, while at the same time, voting is localized, i.e. related to local issues and candidates. This tendency was reinforced with the 2007 amalgamation reform. Turnout was 70.8 per cent at the 2017 election which is 14 per cent lower than the national election in 2019, namely the picture is the same as in other countries that do not have simultaneous national and local elections, but it still leaves space for improvement in terms of local and regional election turnout.

In Denmark, referendums are used particularly for constitutional issues, including the most frequent reason for a referendum: transfer of sovereignty to the EU (cf. Chapter 25). The only other themes for referendums since 1970 have been the voting age and female royal succession. With the first referendum on the EC in 1972, Denmark has held eight EU-related referendums. Five ended with a 'yes' and three with a 'no'. While this, on the one hand, has put severe restrictions on Danish EU policies—and still does today with the Danish opt-outs—it has also helped EU-sceptical Danes to generally accept the EU they know by now. Referendums have thus created a level of EU legitimacy that would have been difficult to obtain in other ways. To go further down the road of integration is probably not feasible in the foreseeable future taking the 'no' to the Euro (2000) and the 'no' to the justice and home affairs opt-out (2015) into consideration.

Together with some other North Western countries, the Danish media system belongs—as shown in Chapter 26—to a corporatist media model that reflects some of the traits of the Nordic welfare state tradition. This implies a historical tradition of political parallelism, state involvement through public media service and media subsidies, and high levels of readership and journalistic professionalization. It is a model that also tends to correlate with high levels of political trust. Much hints that this model is relatively resistant towards global media traits such as falling revenues, distrust, and challenged professionalism. Nevertheless, Danish politics is also affected by these trends and thus increasingly mediatized. The Danes' trust in democracy is still high, while trust in the politicians elected have fallen almost dramatically during the later years but may be on an upwards turn again. One cannot rule out that increased mediatization is related to falling trust in politicians.

Denmark has an old and relatively strong corporatist tradition as shown in Chapter 11. Corporatism primarily favours interest groups with relation to the labour market, different industries, and the public service sector. Chapter 27 shows that corporatism still affects the Danish interest group system: a high level of unionization keeps unions relatively strong, and strong industrial organizations and organizations for public institutions are still powerful. There are, however, also signs of changes that challenge the conventional wisdom of the Danish system as new groups of civil society organizations increase in number and access to political decision-makers. However, interest group access to the central administration, to politicians, and to the media is still biased and skewed, leaving top access to political arenas to almost the same groups as three to four decades ago.

POLICY

Looking to the Outside World: Security and Defence, New World Order, the EU, and Development Policy

As outlined in Chapter 28, Denmark's security and defence policy has changed dramatically since the end of the Cold War in 1989. This is, in particular, the case when seen against a broader historical backdrop. Until 1989, Denmark's main concern was not to get into trouble with potential enemies. Since 1864, Denmark has been a small state. From 1864 to 1945, Denmark pursued a non-provocative security and defence policy towards Germany. From 1945 to 1989, non-provocation was directed towards the Soviet Union and the United States. Denmark was attempting not to get into trouble with the former while seeking shelter from the latter. After 1989, Denmark opted for military activism driven by the international society represented by the UN and the United States. This activism was played out in Afghanistan, in Iraq, and in the Baltic states. However, in the future, a more unreliable United States and a more assertive Russia will probably lead to a more restrained military activism and a stronger reliance on diplomacy. As always since 1864, Denmark sees itself as a small animal in an international jungle with predators.

Chapter 29 deals with the same issue as Chapter 28 but in a broader contemporary foreign policy perspective. The chapter presents the dominant discourses on Danish foreign policy. They seem to be that the EU is the key platform of Danish foreign policy—the only show in town—while NATO and the United States are articulated as being crucial but mainly in the field of security. At the same time, the UN and Nordic cooperation in particular are not attributed the same value as the EU and NATO/the

United States. During the Cold War, all four parts were equal cornerstones which defined Danish foreign policy. As also stressed in Chapter 28, another change in the Danish foreign policy project—as formulated by successive governments since 1989—is that they are 'active' in a different way from their predecessors, which is the background for Denmark's support in recent conflicts in the Greater Middle East. Future tendencies will probably involve a stronger focus on multilateralism, on Russia, on unwanted immigration to Denmark, and on the Arctic.

The EU is the sole object of Chapter 30, which examines four important EU policy areas. Trade policy is an area that has become increasingly politicized in a global context, but Denmark has remained constantly in favour of free trade. By contrast, as far as the EU's Common Agricultural Policy is concerned, Denmark has moved from supporting high spending towards less subsidized agricultural markets. The Internal Market policy was a highly politicized policy issue in a Danish context when it was introduced, but now there is a broad consensus on supporting this policy except in areas where it potentially clashes with the Danish labour market model (cf. Chapter 33). Lastly, the opt-outs comprise very different policies in terms of the euro, justice and home affairs, and defence policy, which are all highly politicized and which have remained intact despite attempts to remove them. Looking across the various policy areas, they demonstrate that Denmark supports areas associated with economic benefits for the country, whereas it is hesitant when it involves the transfer of sovereignty.

Another policy area that has undergone changes in recent decades is development policy, which is analysed in Chapter 31. Since 2000, Danish development policy has seen a move away from an overriding emphasis on poverty reduction to one in which not only the poorest countries but also middle-income countries can receive Danish development aid. In addition, Danish economic interests were always a factor in development aid, but the emphasis on this subject is now more explicit than previously. Several factors explain these changes. The centre-right government from 2001 onwards politicized the area. Development aid to Afghanistan and Iraq became a priority after 9/11 and the Danish military support for the US invasion. Further, there was a general wish for more business-oriented development policy. In spite of a change of government in 2019, there are many indications that the new line will remain as it is.

The Welfare State Machinery: Economic Policy, the Welfare State, the Labour Market, Education, Health, and Immigration

Chapter 32 covers Danish economic policy. For the last 40 years, economic policy has undergone a long string of reforms in order to ensure its competitiveness and credibility. The interesting lesson from this is how the welfare state has been designed to balance consensus for economic performance on the one hand and provision of welfare services and the pursuit of egalitarian outcomes on the other. In this regard, two points are particularly important in explaining how this is possible. First, the private sector is regulated in a market-conform way; the Danish economic model is not 'politics against markets'. Second, welfare arrangements have a strong focus on supporting labour market participation because the Danish welfare model depends on a high employment level in the private sector. The big question in the future is whether it will be possible for the political decision-makers to keep on reforming the Danish economic policy as some 'reform fatigue' seems to have hit the voters.

Precisely the development of the Danish welfare model is the issue of the next chapter, Chapter 33. Danish welfare politics remain universalistic, predominantly tax financed, and comprehensive, and despite tendencies toward increasing inequality, Denmark remains one of the most egalitarian countries in the world. There has been a large number of reforms of the welfare state since the beginning of the 1980s which have intensified discussions about the quality of public sector services and the relative importance of better welfare services versus tax cuts. In addition, welfare development in spatial terms is highly asymmetrical. Typically, the expansion of welfare services favour major cities. Nevertheless, the welfare state is still very popular among citizens. This is also because they get tangible services that are promoted by interest organizations and financed broadly by taxpayers without any interest organizational backup. In addition, the Danish welfare state faces challenges such as an ageing population, immigration, individualization, and fiscal austerity.

Closely connected to economic policy and the welfare state is the Danish labour market policy analysed in Chapter 34. The labour market model is old. Its institution dates back to the early 1900s with a highly flexible labour market in terms of hiring and firing for employers, and security for workers in terms of compensation in case of unemployment. Labour market parties regulate important elements such as wages and working conditions themselves. Later on, regional and central corporatism supported the introduction and implementation of an active labour market policy. The Flexicurity Model has gained international recognition during the 2000s. It is not, however, without problems. The declining union density—especially for trade unions in the private sector—is a potential danger for its future functionality. The decline of coverage in case of unemployment lessens the value of unemployment benefits for large groups of employees. In addition, it has proved itself very difficult to 'export' the Danish model to other countries because of its deep historical roots.

Education policy is the subject of Chapter 35. This policy area has played an important role for building the welfare state; however, the analysis also shows how educational policy in Denmark is shaped through the corporatist involvement of the teachers' unions. This also explains why the teachers' occupation remains a territory from which university-educated candidates are largely excluded, contrary to the situation in many other European countries. In the last two decades, however, the influence of the teachers' unions has diminished, and the centre-right governments have emphasized free school choice and better private school opportunities for parents. In addition, low scores in the PISA tests have also led to strengthened control of academic standards in the primary schools. However, the 2015 international PISA tests showed for the first time that Danish students' results in mathematics, reading, and science were above the OECD average.

Chapter 36 on health policy demonstrates how Danish health policy is double-faced in several respects. On the one hand, the area is characterized by highly stable institutional structures and consensus about the value of a publicly based healthcare system. On the other hand, the broad popular consensus has not led to any sort of truce among political parties. In addition, the Danish healthcare system is under pressure because of increasing demand for health services due to demographic changes. The bottom line is that there is political competition to accommodate voter preferences as far as health services are concerned. This will probably contribute significantly to continued growth in the output of healthcare services.

As analysed in Chapter 37, immigration policy was politicized by the Danish People's Party during the mid-1990s which resonated with public concerns and made the immigration issue salient to Danish voters. This politicization pushed first centre-right parties and later the Social Democratic Party in the direction of a more restrictive immigration policy, although Social Democrats would claim that this policy change is a change back to the roots of the party's ideology. The results of the strong politicization of immigration policy are ambiguous. On the one hand, the immigration issues are more ideologically divisive for Danish voters; on the other hand, the politicization of group identities also appears to make majority Danes more responsive to positive contact experiences with immigrants.

Natural Resources and Know-How: Agriculture and Fisheries, Environment and Climate Policy, and Research Policy

Agriculture and fisheries are traditional businesses which have remained relatively more important in Denmark than in many other developed countries. Chapter 38 provides an analysis of these sectors. The farming and fisheries industries in Denmark are strongly export oriented, and government policies have a strong focus on maintaining international competitiveness. At the same time, various Danish governments have pursued a number of non-economic objectives like, for example, environmental protection and rural livelihood (see also the presentations of the conclusions of Chapter 39 below). In addition, there has been a move towards market liberalism in both sectors, with regulation underpinning market forces, not undermining them. This is in accordance with the same development in the EU.

Environment and climate policy is an issue dealt with in Chapter 39. The focus in Denmark has been marked by a shift in focus from environment to climate policy in recent years. By the end of the 2010s, Denmark is facing a new and more difficult phase of transition to a society with zero emissions. First, as the share of fluctuating wind power increases, it becomes still more difficult to utilize power efficiently in periods with strong winds. Second, the energy system is becoming heavily dependent on imported wood-based biomass, which is problematic because it is far from being 'carbon neutral'. Third, as agriculture is responsible for more than one fifth of Denmark's greenhouse emissions, there is a need for stricter regulation if Denmark is to meet the target of zero emissions by 2050.

Danish research policy is analysed in Chapter 40. Denmark became a strong adopter of research policy ideas promoted by the OECD and the EU from 2001 after the centre-right government took power. As a result, Denmark moved from laggard to front-runner, and Danish research policies became highly influenced toward tangible products, namely academic production as measured by volume and citations as well as formalized collaboration between universities and industry. Denmark consistently comes out on top in international rankings of research performance. However, the former expansion of research funding is levelling out, and the question therefore is whether Danish research is in the process of returning to the role as laggard as far as research policy is concerned.

STILL WORTH GETTING TO DENMARK?

'Getting to Denmark' has become a phrase in the literature when one refers to a developed country with well-functioning state institutions (Woolmark and Pritchett 2002), and the phrase has been used several times by Francis Fukuyama (e.g. 2011), cf. also Jensen and Svendsen (2020).

Is it still worth going to Denmark? In many respects the answer is 'yes'. Denmark has comparatively well-functioning political institutions. High voter turnout produces a parliament with many parties, of which the majority has been around for many years, and there is certainly no party system crisis. Voters are enthusiastic about democracy and democratic principles; however, they are less satisfied with the politicians elected—even if trust in Parliament and parties is on the rise again. Trust towards other citizens is high. A nearly uncorrupt bureaucracy has been the backbone of the state apparatus for centuries. Minority governments do remarkably well in terms of economic and other policies. They have carried through reforms of a type that many other countries still struggle with such as more or less overcoming the double payment problem in pension systems and turning a non-funded pension system into an almost fully funded system. Large-scale public sector reforms, such as a local government amalgamation reform, is another example. Easy hire and easy fire combined with (what used to be) generous unemployment benefits have created a very flexible labour market known as flexicurity. Many controversial reforms have been passed, not without resistance but with a relatively high level of efficiency and legitimacy at the end of the day.

A nice and ideal society in a changing and messy world? Not only so. Denmark does still have well-functioning state institutions, but Denmark has also experienced some of the setbacks produced by dysfunctions of its own institutions as well as by international developments. Running a universal welfare state is extremely popular, but it is also expensive and far from always efficient. It creates strong vested interests and strong client groups. People tend to want more of all the expensive stuff only to reduce spending on the cheap stuff. This has brought Denmark to a situation of more or less permanent fiscal austerity in combination with the popular feeling that public spending is characterized by cuts and retrenchment. While it is relatively easy to establish programmes where all involved benefit—although not to the same degree—it is much more difficult to change programmes in disfavour of organized interests. In several cases, this has implied less consensual political processes, even brutal ones in some cases. Danish politics is not always consensual and peaceful.

While income distribution in Denmark is still among the most equal in the world, it has become less equal during the later decades, partly as a consequence of tougher global competition but mainly as a consequence of deliberate political decisions, some of which have been targeted towards immigrants on social welfare. Increasing correlation between ethnicity and poverty may deem future integration efforts even more difficult. The immigration issue has also increased political polarization, and the debate on the issue has been rather tough from time to time, even though there is now an almost general consensus on a relatively restrictive immigration policy line.

Other less flattering aspects of Danish politics could be mentioned. If the standard of measurement is an ideal, unflawed state, much is wrong. If the standard of measurement is the world's existing countries, it is still worth getting to Denmark.

References

Fukuyama, Francis (2011). *The Origins of Political Order: From Prehuman Times to the French Revolution*. London: Profile Books.

Jensen, Mette F., and Gert T. Svendsen (2020). 'Corruption and bureaucratic reforms. "Getting to Denmark"?', in Peter M. Christiansen, Jørgen Elklit, and Peter Nedergaard, eds, *The Oxford Handbook of Danish Politics*. Oxford: Oxford University Press, 177–92.

Woolmark, Michael, and Lant Pritchett (2002). *Solutions When the Solution Is the Problem: Arraying the Disarray in Development*. Washington, D.C.: Center for Global Development.

Index